PART 7 ■ Making Choices about Style 721

PART 8 ■ Understanding and Revising Sentences 795

PART 9 ■ Punctuating with Purpose 911

PART 10 ■ Understanding Mechanics 969

PART 11 ■ Grammar for Multilingual Writers 1005

Writing: A Manual for the Digital Age

Writing: A Manual for the Digital Age

David Blakesley
Purdue University

Jeffrey L. Hoogeveen
Lincoln University

Australia • Brazil • Japan • Korea • Mexico • Singapore • Spain • United Kingdom • United States

Writing: A Manual for the Digital Age
David Blakesley/Jeffrey L. Hoogeveen

Editor in Chief: PJ Boardman

Publisher: Lyn Uhl

Acquisitions Editor: Star MacKenzie Burruto

Development Editor: Leslie Taggart

Managing Development Editor: Karen Judd

Assistant Editor: Cheryl Forman

Senior Technology Project Manager: Joe Gallagher

Managing Marketing Manager: Mandee Eckersley

Senior Marketing Communications Manager: Stacey Purviance

Signing Representative: Ron Shelly

Senior Project Manager, Editorial Production: Samantha Ross, Lianne Ames

Senior Art Director: Cate Rickard Barr

Senior Print Buyer: Mary Beth Hennebury

Permissions Manager: Ron Montgomery

Text Permissions Researcher: Marcy Lunetta

Production Service: Lifland et al., Bookmakers

Text Designer: Linda Beaupré, Stone House Art

Photo Manager: Sheri Blaney

Photo Researcher: Francelle Carapetyan

Cover Designer: Bill Reuter, Reuter Design

Cover Printer: Phoenix Color

Compositor: Graphic World

Library of Congress Control Number: 2006937514
ISBN-13: 978-1-4282-9029-7 (casebound)
ISBN-10: 1-4282-9029-X (casebound)
ISBN-13: 978-1-4282-9030-3 (paperbound)
ISBN-10: 1-4282-9030-3 (paperbound)

Wadsworth
20 Channel Center Street
Boston, MA 02210
USA

Cengage Learning is a leading provider of customized learning solutions with office locations around the globe, including Singapore, the United Kingdom, Australia, Mexico, Brazil, and Japan. Locate your local office at:
international.cengage.com/region

Cengage Learning products are represented in Canada by Nelson Education, Ltd.

For your course and learning solutions, visit **academic.cengage.com**

Purchase any of our products at your local college store or at our preferred online store **www.ichapters.com**

Credits appear on pages C1–C6, which constitute a continuation of the copyright page.

Printed in the United States of America
1 2 3 4 5 6 7 12 11 10 09

Contents

PART 2 Reading and Writing Critically 121

PART 3 Conducting Research 245

PART 4 Citing Sources 375

PART 5 Designing and Presenting Information 555

PART 6 Writing in Digital Spaces 601

CHAPTER 27

Reading and Writing Email Purposefully 603

CHAPTER 28

Networking with Others on the Web 621

CHAPTER 29

Writing and Rhetoric on the Web 641

CHAPTER 30

Designing Simple Web Pages 659

CHAPTER 31

Designing Complex Websites 681

CHAPTER 32

Multimedia Composing 705

PART 7 Making Choices about Style 721

CHAPTER 33

Sentences in Context 723

CHAPTER 34

Parallelism 730

CHAPTER 35

Coordination and Subordination 736

CHAPTER 36

Concise Sentences 746

CHAPTER 37

Variety and Emphasis 757

CHAPTER 38

Effective Word Use 769

CHAPTER 39

Language and Diverse Audiences 782

PART 8 Understanding and Revising Sentences 795

Writing Projects

What kind of writing project are you working on—an informative essay, a proposal argument, a critical review, an email letter to the editor, a research paper, a website?

Some writing projects are discussed within a single chapter. Other projects thread through several chapters. **Writing project threads** of this type are distinguished by images that also appear on the page.

If your project is not listed here, consult the list of Project Checklists on page xxiii. Project Checklists appear throughout the handbook as an aid for any writing project.

Blogs (Weblogs)

Brochures

Case Analyses

Cover Letters to Accompany Resumes

See Job Search Process and Documents.

Writing Projects

Critical Reviews (Evaluations)

Discussion Board Postings

Email Letters to the Editor

Essay Exams

Flyers

Writing Projects

Informative Essays

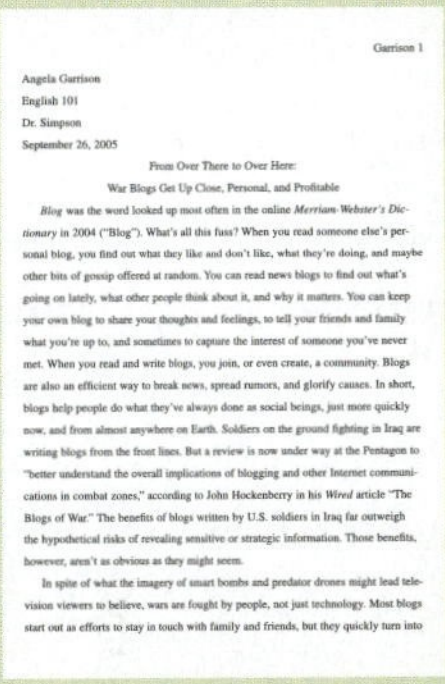
Garrison 1

Angela Garrison

English 101

Dr. Simpson

September 26, 2005

From Over There to Over Here:

War Blogs Get Up Close, Personal, and Profitable

Blog was the word looked up most often in the online *Merriam-Webster's Dictionary* in 2004 ("Blog"). What's all this fuss? When you read someone else's personal blog, you find out what they like and don't like, what they're doing, and maybe other bits of gossip offered at random. You can read news blogs to find out what's going on lately, what other people think about it, and why it matters. You can keep your own blog to share your thoughts and feelings, to tell your friends and family what you're up to, and sometimes to capture the interest of someone you've never met. When you read and write blogs, you join, or even create, a community. Blogs are also an efficient way to break news, spread rumors, and glorify causes. In short, blogs help people do what they've always done as social beings, just more quickly now, and from almost anywhere on Earth. Soldiers on the ground fighting in Iraq are writing blogs from the front lines. But a review is now under way at the Pentagon to "better understand the overall implications of blogging and other Internet communications in combat zones," according to John Hockenberry in his *Wired* article "The Blogs of War." The benefits of blogs written by U.S. soldiers in Iraq far outweigh the hypothetical risks of revealing sensitive or strategic information. Those benefits, however, aren't as obvious as they might seem.

In spite of what the imagery of smart bombs and predator drones might lead television viewers to believe, wars are fought by people, not just technology. Most blogs start out as efforts to stay in touch with family and friends, but they quickly turn into

Job Search Process and Documents

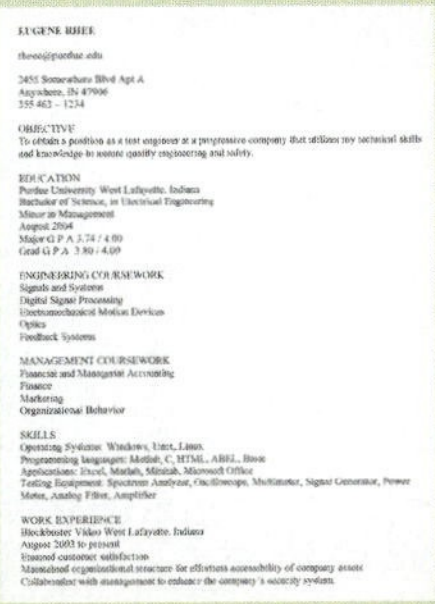
OBJECTIVE

EDUCATION

Purdue University West Lafayette, Indiana

Minor in Management

August 2004

ENGINEERING COURSEWORK

Signals and Systems

Digital Signal Processing

Optics

Feedback Systems

MANAGEMENT COURSEWORK

Financial and Managerial Accounting

Finance

Marketing

Organizational Behavior

SKILLS

WORK EXPERIENCE

Blockbuster Video West Lafayette, Indiana

August 2003 to present

Literary Interpretations

Writing Projects

Photographic Essays

Position Arguments (Taking a Position)

Posters

Poster Display Boards

Proposal Arguments (Proposing a Solution)

Harrington 1

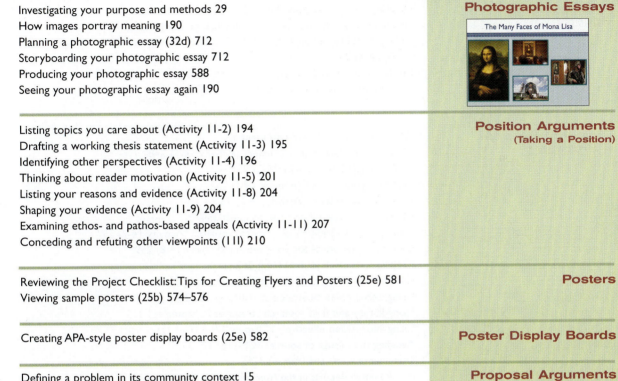

A Proposal to Clean Up Our Streets

Writing Projects

Recommendation Reports

Research Reports: A Process

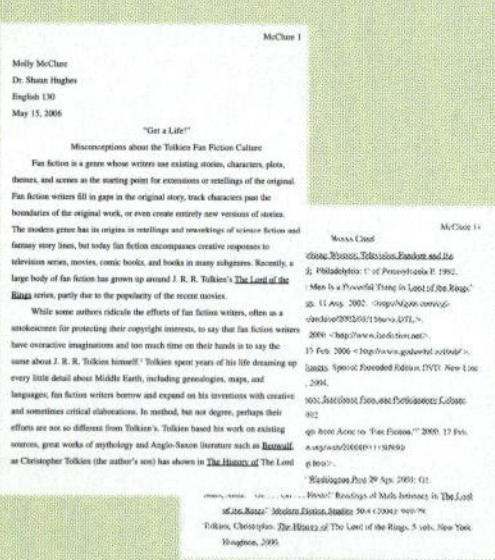

McClure 1

Molly McClure

Dr. Shaun Hughes

English 130

May 15, 2006

"Get a Life!"

Misconceptions about the Tolkien Fan Fiction Culture

Fan fiction is a genre whose writers use existing stories, characters, plots, themes, and scenes as the starting point for extensions or retellings of the original. Fan fiction writers fill in gaps in the original story, track characters past the boundaries of the original work, or even create entirely new versions of stories. The modern genre has its origins in retellings and reworkings of science fiction and fantasy story lines, but today fan fiction encompasses creative responses to television series, movies, comic books, and books in many subgenres. Recently, a large body of fan fiction has grown up around J. R. R. Tolkien's The Lord of the Rings series, partly due to the popularity of the recent movies.

While some authors ridicule the efforts of fan fiction writers, often as a smokescreen for protecting their copyright interests, to say that fan fiction writers have overactive imaginations and too much time on their hands is to say the same about J. R. R. Tolkien himself.[1] Tolkien spent years of his life dreaming up every little detail about Middle Earth, including genealogies, maps, and languages; fan fiction writers borrow and expand on his inventions with creative and sometimes critical elaborations. In method, but not degree, perhaps their efforts are not so different from Tolkien's. Tolkien based his work on existing sources, great works of mythology and Anglo-Saxon literature such as Beowulf, as Christopher Tolkien (the author's son) has shown in The History of The Lord

Resume

See Job Search Process and Documents.

Rhetorical Analysis

Scannable Resumes

See Job Search Process and Documents.

Technology Autobiography

Websites, Simple

Websites, Complex

White Papers

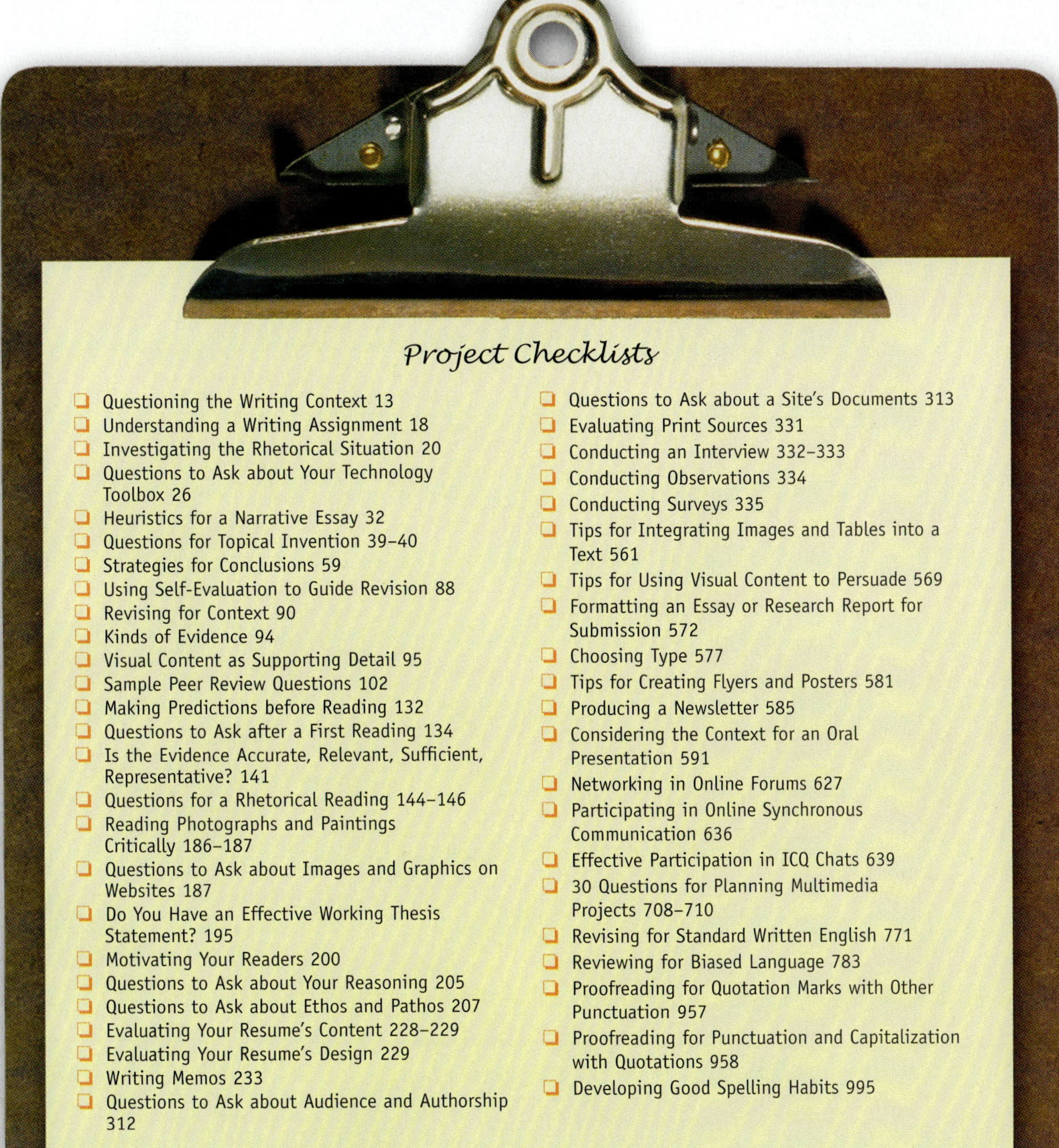

Project Checklists

At the heart of *Writing: A Manual for the Digital Age* is our belief that rhetorical principles are flexible and powerful enough to teach writers how to write effectively in any context or medium. Contexts change from moment to moment, but the study of rhetorical principles helps students learn how to gauge situations and formulate effective responses to them by asking and answering questions about contexts, texts, purposes, and readers. The principles of rhetoric—as their endurance and appeal across time and place suggest—*are* transferable. They stick. They make as much sense today as they did a couple of thousand years ago. They expand a writer's capacity for responding to new situations with confidence and eloquence.

See page 8.

Writing in the Digital Age

Our digital age poses tremendous opportunities and problems for every writer and reader. We are excited by the rapid emergence in the past twenty years or so of new forms of electronic communication and literacy. One major goal of this handbook is to show students how to adapt the new tools of technology to support their writing across a broad range of situations in college and beyond. Throughout the book, Technology Toolboxes show students how to use software to accomplish rhetorical goals. We do much more than simply recommend that students "save a backup copy" or "add a visual to enhance a presentation." We show students how to accomplish such tasks and provide our explanations not as prescriptive rules, but as the result of the kind of rhetorical questioning that ought to guide any pragmatic or creative use of technology. You will find that, for us, writing and reading happen in print *and* online. It's no longer the case that printed text is the ur-form, the primary medium or interface for literate activity. This is not to say that it is secondary, either. Awareness of the multiple contexts for reading and writing is sifted finely with our discussions of rhetorical principles, with print and digital forms each playing their important roles.

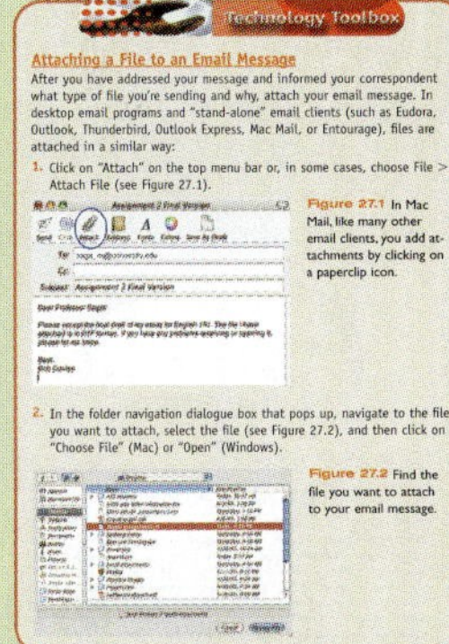

Technology Toolbox

Attaching a File to an Email Message

After you have addressed your message and informed your correspondent what type of file you're sending and why, attach your email message. In desktop email programs and "stand-alone" email clients (such as Eudora, Outlook, Thunderbird, Outlook Express, Mac Mail, or Entourage), files are attached in a similar way:

1. Click on "Attach" on the top menu bar or, in some cases, choose File > Attach File (see Figure 27.1).

Figure 27.1 In Mac Mail, like many other email clients, you add attachments by clicking on a paperclip icon.

2. In the folder navigation dialogue box that pops up, navigate to the file you want to attach, select the file (see Figure 27.2), and then click on "Choose File" (Mac) or "Open" (Windows).

Figure 27.2 Find the file you want to attach to your email message.

See page 612.

Information Architecture and Design

Reading habits have changed, partly as a response to the influx of information for the eyes to take in at a glance, in print and on screen. A writing handbook, especially, ought to take this change into account, and not simply for fashion's sake. *How* information is presented may be as important for learning as *what* is presented. Information architecture—the visual display of information to foster

See page 193.

learning—has been an overriding concern throughout the development of this book.

Handbooks especially need to communicate information efficiently, over time, and in a sufficiently interesting manner to encourage students to read, reread, and learn. The design of the book reflects these purposes. Visual content not only attracts the eye but also communicates information concisely and quickly. Readers remember challenging concepts more readily when they associate them with visual content, spatial location on the page, and even color. In classical terms, the visual display of information has mnemonic qualities, helping readers recall previous learning. So in the inner columns throughout the handbook, you will find a wide range of visual and verbal content, cast in ways that invite the attention, teaching core principles and providing concise guidelines for writing and reading. We also place real student writing in this spotlight because, in the end, it is students' work that matters most and that speaks most eloquently to other students.

Audience	General Purpose	Specific Purpose
People who hold views different from yours	To persuade people to change an attitude or behavior. Changing someone's attitude is possible only when knowledge is uncertain and there are multiple perspectives.	▪ To change people's minds and attitudes ▪ To solve problems ▪ To resolve conflict ▪ To build consensus ▪ To create community
People who share your view	To reinforce shared convictions. When people already agree, the purpose of argument may be to turn that agreement into action—for example, working to support a cause. In college classes, you typically won't argue issues on which your readers already agree. Instead, find the basis for disagreement on a subject, and build an argument from there.	▪ To reinforce belief ▪ To move people toward commitment and action ▪ To foster identification (see page 191)
People who wish to understand multiple views	To inquire into the shades of meaning in a subject so that you can open it up to reflection and reconsideration. It is often necessary to demonstrate that a subject lends itself to multiple perspectives. Help your audience understand that the subject is more complex than they had imagined.	▪ To open up a topic for discussion, debate, and further inquiry ▪ To question common knowledge ▪ To stimulate further research

See page 197.

At the same time, there are finer distinctions to be made, definitions to be learned, and a broader context to be considered. The verbal content in the outside columns throughout the book glosses and extends what you read and see in the inner columns. In many respects, the content of these outer columns is much like what you would find in any good handbook with rhetoric at its core. At the same time, we have composed that running narrative in concert with the content of the inner columns. The illustrations, for example, are not secondary, nor are they the whole story. Instead, the two columns work together on the page. In an age when much of our reading is, by necessity, composed of glosses, chunks, blocks, and images, this book's information architecture is coherent, organizing ideas in ways that make it easier for students to learn to write well and for instructors to show them how.

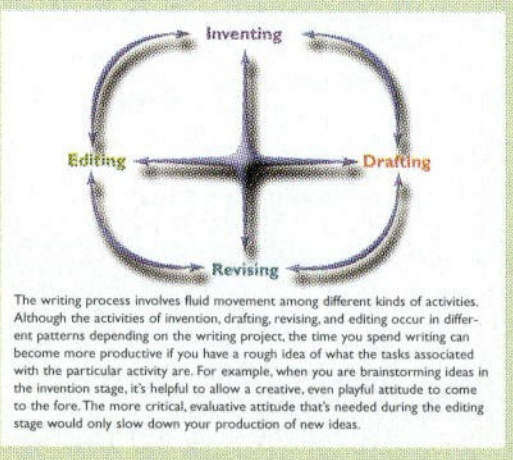

The writing process involves fluid movement among different kinds of activities. Although the activities of invention, drafting, revising, and editing occur in different patterns depending on the writing project, the time you spend writing can become more productive if you have a rough idea of what the tasks associated with the particular activity are. For example, when you are brainstorming ideas in the invention stage, it's helpful to allow a creative, even playful attitude to come to the fore. The more critical, evaluative attitude that's needed during the editing stage would only slow down your production of new ideas.

See page 24.

Visual Rhetoric

The information age, as we have suggested, has given way to a visual age. In introductory composition courses across the country, students still need to understand how to write effectively in traditional printed forms. Increasingly, they are also being asked to integrate their words into the flow of visual information that now surrounds all of us.

It is vitally important that writers appreciate the power of images to inform, persuade, and move. At the same time, as readers, they need to understand how images communicate meaning so that they can interpret them and, thus, respond critically.

As a field, rhetoric and composition has made good progress in explaining how to analyze images—including the display of visual information—in print and on the Web. We have struggled to find ways to teach writers how to create visual content, design it, and integrate it with their writing to create rich and persuasive texts.

As we have mentioned, the visual design of the handbook stands as an example in its own right. We have included, as well, chapters on the use of visual content to inform and persuade, ways to interpret and write about visual content, and how to make documents for print and the Web that meet these rhetorical goals. We show how images function as arguments and even how graphic design can enhance and structure information so that it can be understood and believed.

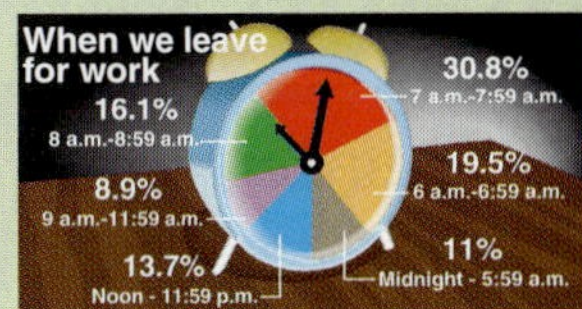

When we leave for work
16.1%
8 a.m.-8:59 a.m.
30.8%
7 a.m.-7:59 a.m.
8.9%
9 a.m.-11:59 a.m.
19.5%
6 a.m.-6:59 a.m.
13.7%
Noon - 11:59 p.m.
11%
Midnight - 5:59 a.m.

See page 565.

Take inventory of your skills, experiences, and goals.
Find and analyze job ads in your search, learn about and use various Web-based resources for job seekers, and ultimately select one job to pursue.
Write a resume suitable for such a position.
Compose a cover letter that identifies your reasons for applying and highlights your qualifications.

See page 220.

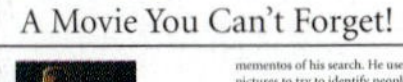
A Movie You Can't Forget!

This could be the best movie you will ever see all year, if you're looking for something intense, suspenseful, and different than your usual effects-packed thriller. This is the kind of movie that you will be talking about at work, at the bank (to total strangers!), and at the corner coffee shop.

The movie starts with a murder -- a revenge killing, in fact. But was the right person killed?

The main character, Leonard Shelby (Guy Pearce), is a man with no short-term memory. He hasn't been able to form new memories since the night his wife was murdered. On a hunt to find the murderer, but with no way of remembering names, dates, places, facts and faces, he tattoos mementos of his search. He uses pictures to try to identify people who know his name. Does he like this person? Does he trust this person? Is this the killer? He doesn't know unless he's written a note.

Writer/director Christopher Nolan puts you right in Leonard's shoes, living the story in reverse order. This ingenious method of story-telling means that you never know more than Leonard does. In one scene you see Leonard getting information from a person who knows him -- maybe a good person; maybe bad. In the next scene you see a previous meeting between the two which sheds more light on their relationship. Later still you see how they met. You, like Leonard, have no knowledge of what came before.

This film will leave its own memento on your mind, and you'll have a hard time forgetting how much you enjoyed it.

See page 130.

Unique Features of *Writing: A Manual for the Digital Age*

Writing instructors across a broad range of courses and college settings will find a wealth of features to help them achieve course outcomes; make the teaching of writing more effective, if not any easier; and instill in writers the rhetorical fluency that will serve them well in college and beyond.

Writing Projects

Consistent with our call for writers and instructors to apply rhetorical principles in situations that matter, we have provided a wide range of sample writing projects—thirty in all—that offer occasions for applying principles learned in each chapter. Writing projects cover traditional genres such as informative essays, position and proposal arguments, personal essays, critical reviews, and rhetorical analyses; forms that focus on or tend to include more visual content, such as photographic essays, brochures, and flyers; job search documents; research papers; and digital and multimedia projects such as simple Web pages, complex websites, and multimedia essays.

Writing projects are woven together with writing project threads, which are summarized in the table of contents beginning on page xv. Writing project threads suggest to students and instructors alternative pathways through the book. It is possible, for example, for an instructor to use the handbook to support a writing course that makes service learning or civic action its focus, with writing projects threaded from chapter to chapter and describing the wide variety of documents students will want to learn to produce. Writing projects also provide helpful direction to students who are using the handbook independently.

Project Checklists

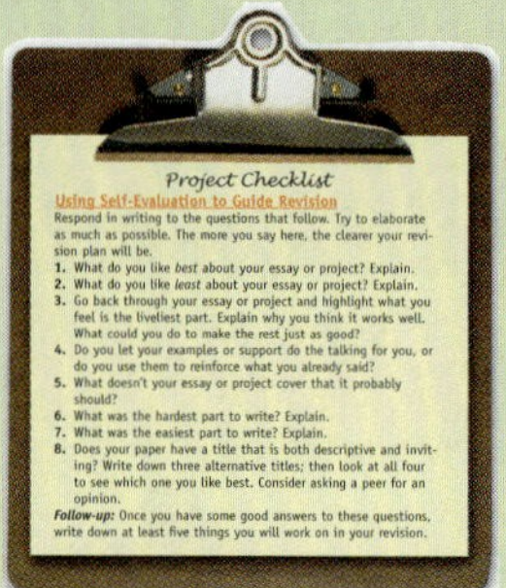

Project Checklist

Using Self-Evaluation to Guide Revision

Respond in writing to the questions that follow. Try to elaborate as much as possible. The more you say here, the clearer your revision plan will be.

1. What do you like *best* about your essay or project? Explain.
2. What do you like *least* about your essay or project? Explain.
3. Go back through your essay or project and highlight what you feel is the liveliest part. Explain why you think it works well. What could you do to make the rest just as good?
4. Do you let your examples or support do the talking for you, or do you use them to reinforce what you already said?
5. What doesn't your essay or project cover that it probably should?
6. What was the hardest part to write? Explain.
7. What was the easiest part to write? Explain.
8. Does your paper have a title that is both descriptive and inviting? Write down three alternative titles; then look at all four to see which one you like best. Consider asking a peer for an opinion.

Follow-up: Once you have some good answers to these questions, write down at least five things you will work on in your revision.

See page 88.

Most chapters contain clipboards with checklists that help writers ask detailed questions about the rhetorical situation or the aspect of writing or reading that is the focus of the chapter. The questions reinforce key principles as they provide students with additional means of inventing, elaborating, and evaluating content.

Activities-Based Learning

Activity 1-1: Thinking about Contexts: Asking a Favor by Email

Suppose you wrote an email message to a peer asking for feedback on a personal essay. Use the pictures below as you consider the questions on page 7, which ask you to put yourself in the role of both a writer and a reader.

Scenes for writing and reading email.
How would your message change if you knew it would be read in the contexts pictured here?

See page 6.

Principles, like concepts, are not static ideas to be learned about. They are the instruments of thought and, thus, writing. In each chapter, students and instructors will find numerous activities that directly encourage students to apply what they have learned in a wide variety of ways. We have always thought that learning comes from doing, and our activities form the basis for understanding and trying out new skills in a variety of different ways. As much as possible, we designed these activities to build on rather than simply rehearse knowledge. The Instructor's Manual, expertly conceived and written by Erin Karper, includes sample responses to each activity, many of which she developed.

Technology Toolboxes

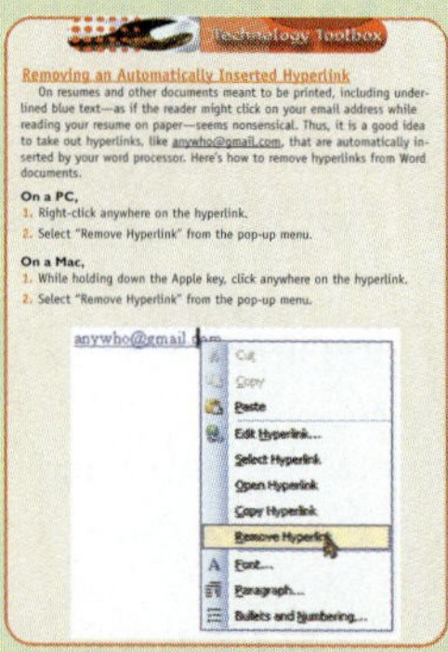

Technology Toolbox

Removing an Automatically Inserted Hyperlink

On resumes and other documents meant to be printed, including underlined blue text—as if the reader might click on your email address while reading your resume on paper—seems nonsensical. Thus, it is a good idea to take out hyperlinks, like anywho@gmail.com, that are automatically inserted by your word processor. Here's how to remove hyperlinks from Word documents.

On a PC,
1. Right-click anywhere on the hyperlink.
2. Select "Remove Hyperlink" from the pop-up menu.

On a Mac,
1. While holding down the Apple key, click anywhere on the hyperlink.
2. Select "Remove Hyperlink" from the pop-up menu.

See page 230.

The overriding concern in the Technology Toolboxes has been to show students how to use software and hardware to accomplish their writing goals and how new tools can help them manage some of the challenges posed by computers, websites, and competing user interfaces across browsers, platforms, and software. We have created all of the screenshots ourselves and have run each through careful usability tests, conscious that people choose different operating systems and software to perform similar tasks, even down to the number of buttons they prefer on a mouse. We have also been careful to include suggestions for using nonproprietary and open source software, some of which will perform writing and design tasks as well as or better than more expensive counterparts.

Words about Words

There are moments when we must pause to provide a nuanced explanation of how we are defining key terminology. For example, first-year students may not grasp the distinctions among analysis, interpretation, and evaluation or between paraphrase and summary. Multilingual writers may find the explicit definitions and comparisons in the Words about Words boxes particularly useful.

How Can You Identify . . .

Sometimes a writer needs an extra push to get going again. How Can You Identify . . . boxes give students suggestions for writing and reading, which they can turn to when they are stuck or at a loss for how to write about and interpret their experience. In Chapter 2, for example, we help students identify subjects for writing when their instructors give them the freedom choose their own topics. While that sort of freedom, we believe, produces some of the most effective writing, it is still daunting to most writers. How Can You Identify . . . boxes are also provided throughout the style and grammar chapters to help students locate certain sentence elements.

New Contexts for Writing

At the beginning of each part is a one-page presentation of a new context for writing. Our aim is to show students just a few of the new and interesting situations that may move them to write. Some of these contexts, such as weblogs and podcasts, are digital, but others suggest how writing functions in collaboration, civic action, volunteerism, gaming, and the creation of image-rich texts like comic books. Each part opener defines new terminology and suggests resources for additional inquiry.

Disciplinary Spreads

The disciplinary spreads in Chapter 14, Conceptualizing the Research Project, are two-page discussions and illustrations of key principles and methodologies in different fields of study. We start at the most general level, with one spread each on the humanities, the social sciences, and the sciences. Our goal is not to capture all the complexity of a discipline but to give students and instructors some insight into how specialists in a discipline think about their subject matter, what evidence they value, and what sorts of subjects they find interesting. An additional six example spreads—two in each of the broader disciplines—show students more specifically what writers and researchers do in the representative fields of film studies and history (the humanities), psychology and sociology (the social sciences), and biology and astronomy (the sciences). These snapshots help students understand that writing and rhetoric are not uniformly conceived and applied across fields. Instructors may find them helpful in introducing students to the broad range of intellectual life in college.

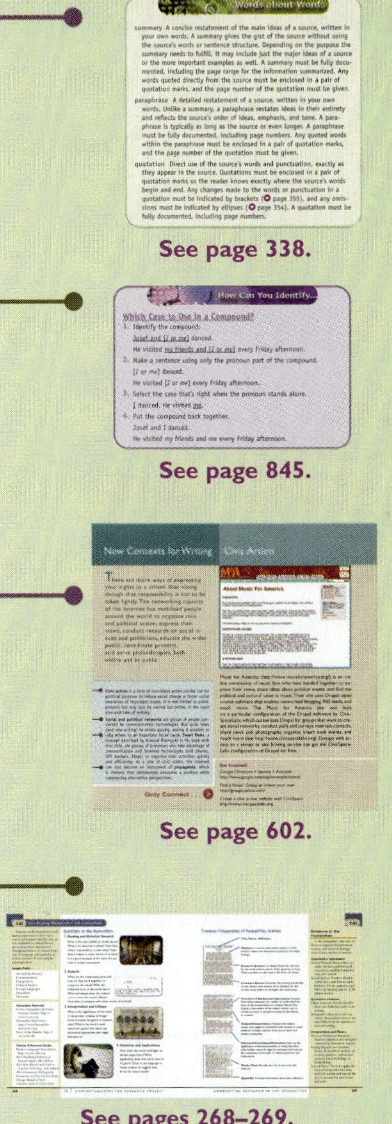

Words about Words
summary A concise restatement of the main ideas of a source, written in your own words. A summary gives the gist of the source without using the source's words or sentence structure. Depending on the purpose the summary needs to fulfill, it may include just the major ideas of a source or the more important examples as well. A summary must be fully documented, including the page range for the information summarized. Any words quoted directly from the source must be enclosed in a pair of quotation marks, and the page number of the quotation must be given.
paraphrase A detailed restatement of a source, written in your own words. Unlike a summary, a paraphrase restates ideas in their entirety and reflects the source's order of ideas, emphasis, and tone. A paraphrase is typically as long as the source or even longer. A paraphrase must be fully documented, including page numbers. Any quoted words within the paraphrase must be enclosed in a pair of quotation marks, and the page number of the quotation must be given.
quotation Direct use of the source's words and punctuation, exactly as they appear in the source. Quotations must be enclosed in a pair of quotation marks so the reader knows exactly where the source's words begin and end. Any changes made to the words or punctuation in a quotation must be indicated by brackets (page 355), and any omissions must be indicated by ellipses (page 354). A quotation must be fully documented, including page numbers.
How Can You Identify...
Which Case to Use in a Compound?
1. Identify the compound:
Josef and [I or me] danced.
He visited my friends and [I or me] every Friday afternoon.
2. Make a sentence using only the pronoun part of the compound.
[I or me] danced.
He visited [I or me] every Friday afternoon.
3. Select the case that's right when the pronoun stands alone.
I danced. He visited me.
4. Put the compound back together.
Josef and I danced.
He visited my friends and me every Friday afternoon.
New Contexts for Writing
Civic Action

See page 338.

See page 845.

See page 602.

See pages 268–269.

The Organization of *Writing: A Manual for the Digital Age*

Context is the organizing principle that ties all of the parts together. As we move from the general to the particular through the parts, we show how rhetorical principles can help writers make good decisions sensitive to shifting contexts across the curriculum and into digital spaces. Our overriding concern has been to demonstrate that even though the territory may be new to many students—and may sometimes feel like an unexplored wilderness—they can learn to write effectively by always bearing in mind that diligent attention to the rhetorical situation can help them chart their course. Such attention will ensure they are habitually effective writers and aren't merely successful by chance or good luck.

Part 1, Managing Your Writing, introduces students to the idea that rhetorical context shapes readers' responses, meaning, and the writer's purpose. Detailed information on planning to respond to writing assignments and specific strategies for inventing, drafting, revising, and editing follow. Two student papers, one a response to an article (in Chapter 4) and the other a personal essay (in Chapter 6), are annotated to demonstrate the writer's rhetorical moves and organizational strategies.

Part 2, Reading and Writing Critically, helps students understand how to construct genre knowledge (in Chapter 7), read actively and critically and perform rhetorical analysis (in Chapter 8), read literature critically (in Chapter 9), and read images critically (in Chapter 10)—both inside the frame and beyond it. Chapter 11, Writing Arguments, emphasizes understanding multiple perspectives and considering audience and aims. Chapter 12, Writing for Business and the Workplace, includes extensive information on documents written in the job search and on other genres such as memos, case analyses, white papers, and recommendation reports. A chapter on writing effective essay exams (Chapter 13) ends the section.

Part 3, Conducting Research, provides information on how to conceptualize a research project and plan and keep track of the process. The chapter on online research (Chapter 15) includes an unusually diverse selection of strategies to accommodate different kinds of research situations, and the chapter on library and field research (Chapter 16) takes into account both print and electronic sources of information. A guide to integrating source material includes step-by-step guidelines on writing summaries and paraphrases and using quotations effectively. Chapter 18 definitions and comparisons in the Words about Words boxes particularly useful.

How Can You Identify . . .

Sometimes a writer needs an extra push to get going again. How Can You Identify . . . boxes give students suggestions for writing and reading, which they can turn to when they are stuck or at a loss for how to write about and interpret their experience. In Chapter 2, for example, we help students identify subjects for writing when their instructors give them the freedom choose their own topics. While that sort of freedom, we believe, produces some of the most effective writing, it is still daunting to most writers. How Can You Identify . . . boxes are also provided throughout the style and grammar chapters to help students locate certain sentence elements.

New Contexts for Writing

At the beginning of each part is a one-page presentation of a new context for writing. Our aim is to show students just a few of the new and interesting situations that may move them to write. Some of these contexts, such as weblogs and podcasts, are digital, but others suggest how writing functions in collaboration, civic action, volunteerism, gaming, and the creation of image-rich texts like comic books. Each part opener defines new terminology and suggests resources for additional inquiry.

Disciplinary Spreads

The disciplinary spreads in Chapter 14, Conceptualizing the Research Project, are two-page discussions and illustrations of key principles and methodologies in different fields of study. We start at the most general level, with one spread each on the humanities, the social sciences, and the sciences. Our goal is not to capture all the complexity of a discipline but to give students and instructors some insight into how specialists in a discipline think about their subject matter, what evidence they value, and what sorts of subjects they find interesting. An additional six example spreads—two in each of the broader disciplines—show students more specifically what writers and researchers do in the representative fields of film studies and history (the humanities), psychology and sociology (the social sciences), and biology and astronomy (the sciences). These snapshots help students understand that writing and rhetoric are not uniformly conceived and applied across fields. Instructors may find them helpful in introducing students to the broad range of intellectual life in college.

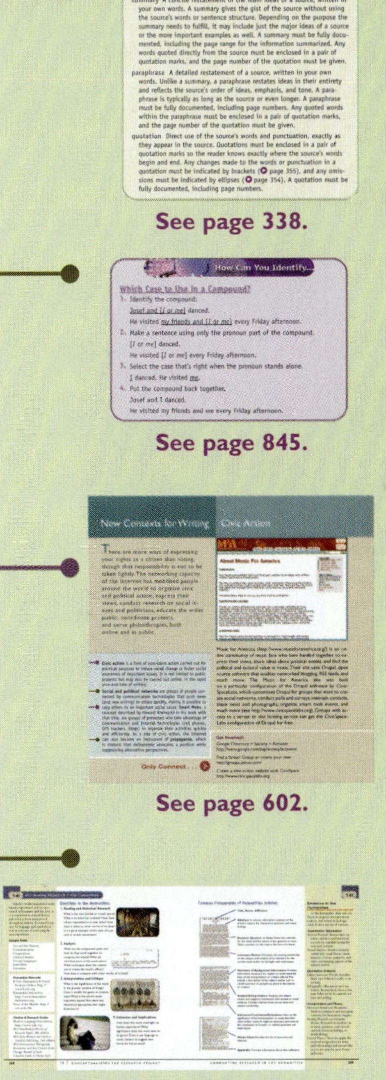

See page 338.

See page 845.

See page 602.

See pages 268–269.

The Organization of *Writing: A Manual for the Digital Age*

Context is the organizing principle that ties all of the parts together. As we move from the general to the particular through the parts, we show how rhetorical principles can help writers make good decisions sensitive to shifting contexts across the curriculum and into digital spaces. Our overriding concern has been to demonstrate that even though the territory may be new to many students—and may sometimes feel like an unexplored wilderness—they can learn to write effectively by always bearing in mind that diligent attention to the rhetorical situation can help them chart their course. Such attention will ensure they are habitually effective writers and aren't merely successful by chance or good luck.

Part 1, Managing Your Writing, introduces students to the idea that rhetorical context shapes readers' responses, meaning, and the writer's purpose. Detailed information on planning to respond to writing assignments and specific strategies for inventing, drafting, revising, and editing follow. Two student papers, one a response to an article (in Chapter 4) and the other a personal essay (in Chapter 6), are annotated to demonstrate the writer's rhetorical moves and organizational strategies.

Part 2, Reading and Writing Critically, helps students understand how to construct genre knowledge (in Chapter 7), read actively and critically and perform rhetorical analysis (in Chapter 8), read literature critically (in Chapter 9), and read images critically (in Chapter 10)—both inside the frame and beyond it. Chapter 11, Writing Arguments, emphasizes understanding multiple perspectives and considering audience and aims. Chapter 12, Writing for Business and the Workplace, includes extensive information on documents written in the job search and on other genres such as memos, case analyses, white papers, and recommendation reports. A chapter on writing effective essay exams (Chapter 13) ends the section.

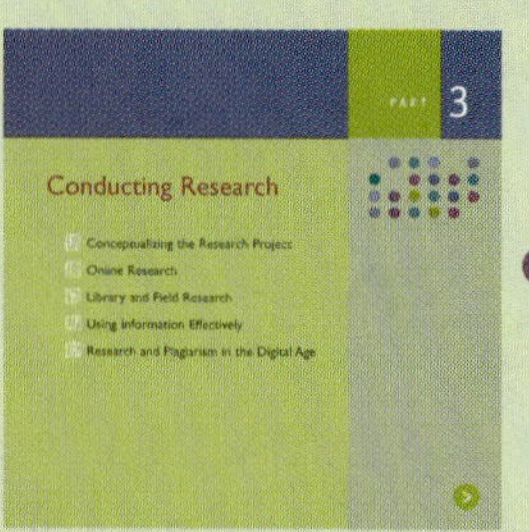

Part 3, Conducting Research, provides information on how to conceptualize a research project and plan and keep track of the process. The chapter on online research (Chapter 15) includes an unusually diverse selection of strategies to accommodate different kinds of research situations, and the chapter on library and field research (Chapter 16) takes into account both print and electronic sources of information. A guide to integrating source material includes step-by-step guidelines on writing summaries and paraphrases and using quotations effectively. Chapter 18 on plagiarism offers a question-and-answer session on how to avoid plagiarism as well as examples of common knowledge and citation problems.

Part 4, Citing Sources, outlines five documentation styles used across the curriculum. A running index in the outside margins makes citation models particularly easy to find. The MLA chapter (Chapter 19) includes a special section on how to format an MLA paper using Microsoft® Word®, with specific directions on creating running heads, indenting block quotations, placing images and adding captions, and creating hanging indentations on the Works Cited page. Sample papers are provided for the MLA, APA, and CMS styles.

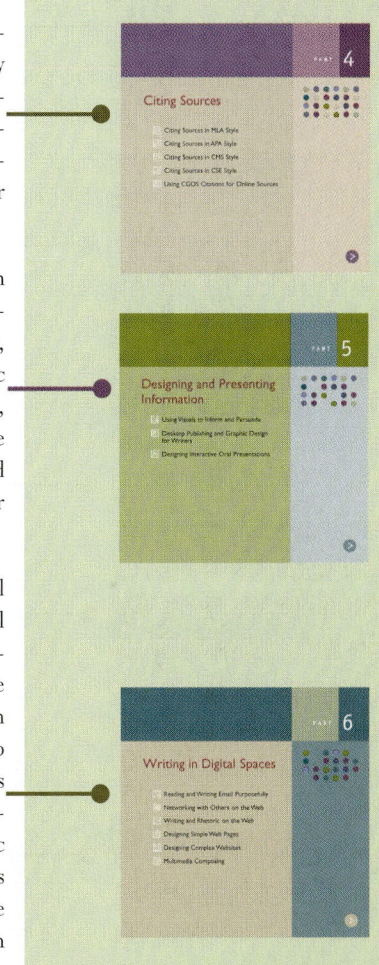

Part 5, Designing and Presenting Information, starts with a discussion in Chapter 24 of how to choose, integrate, and cite visuals that will inform and persuade readers. The contexts and basic principles of graphic design, typography, and color are described in Chapter 25, along with academic and non-academic applications of graphic design, such as poster display boards in APA style, posters, flyers, newsletters, and brochures. The chapter on designing interactive oral presentations (Chapter 26) covers contexts, content, the advantages and disadvantages of visual aids, and strategies for using technologies as support for presentations.

Part 6, Writing in Digital Spaces, starts by showing students the rhetorical considerations important in drafting and sending email and participating in email discussion groups. Chapter 28 covers networking with others on the Web, including asynchronous and synchronous forms, with particular attention to the blogging community and to participating in class discussions online. A chapter on writing and rhetoric on the Web (Chapter 29) helps students decide whether to create their work in print or digital format (or both), shares the W3C guidelines for writing style and for accessibility, and devotes a section to intellectual property and copyright issues. Two chapters on Web design, one that lays out basic considerations and strategies for simple pages (Chapter 30) and one that describes in detail more advanced strategies (Chapter 31), provide students with the rhetorical and technical information they need to create websites. A chapter on multimedia composing (Chapter 32) provides a checklist of 30 questions for planning multimedia projects and describes the process and the recordkeeping necessary to track them.

Part 7, Making Choices about Style, encourages students to make their writing clear, using the five basic principles of readability. Chapters on parallelism, coordination and subordination, concise sentences, variety and emphasis, effective word use, and language and diverse audiences provide comprehensive instruction, numerous examples, and revision activities to help students make their writing more polished and to give them more control over the effects they have on their audiences.

Part 8, Understanding and Revising Sentences, provides a very clear and comprehensive discussion of the parts of speech and sentence structure, as well as separate chapters on fragments; run-ons and comma splices; pronouns; verbs; subject-verb agreement; and adjectives, adverbs, and modifying phrases. "How Can You Identify" boxes are used throughout to help students with tricky points: how to identify dependent clause fragments, for example. Five principles of bias-free language are taught to help students transfer their learning to new rhetorical situations.

Part 9, Punctuating with Purpose, demonstrates the rhetorical and conventional uses of punctuation marks. Separate chapters on end punctuation marks, commas, semicolons, colons, apostrophes, and quotation marks emphasize the purposes of each mark. A final chapter covers dashes, parentheses, brackets, ellipsis points, and slashes.

Part 10, Understanding Mechanics, includes chapters on abbreviations, numbers, italics, capitalization, and spelling and hyphenation, which provide succinct coverage of the conventional usages.

Part 11, Grammar for Multilingual Writers, written by ESL expert Colleen Brice, offers four chapters that address rhetorical and grammatical questions multilingual writers may have. Chapter 59 discusses general academic expectations regarding paper structure and shows students how to learn from an instructor's comments on a paper. A chapter on nouns and articles, a chapter on verbs and verbals, and a chapter on English sentence structure provide detailed and specific information for multilingual writers.

The Glossaries consist of a glossary of technology and Web terms, a glossary of grammatical terms, and a glossary of usage.

Teaching and Learning Resources

Instructor Flex-Files. Designed to give you maximum flexibility in planning and customizing your course, the Instructor Flex-Files provide an abundance of helpful materials, including answers to activities, sample syllabi, pedagogical questions and solutions, an ESL insert, and more. Part II provides a wealth of resources for instructors interested in incorporating technology into their composition course.

Writing: A Manual for the Digital Age Workbook. This printed workbook combines exercises with clear examples and explanations of grammar, usage, and writing to supplement the information and exercises found in the handbook. It also covers technology in Part IV, "Make Your Rhetoric Electric."

Technology Tools

You can learn more about these technology tools at
cengage.com/English/Blakesley

CengageNOW™ for Blakesley and Hoogeveen's *Writing: A Manual for the Digital Age.* This powerful online teaching and learning tool features reliable solutions for delivering your course content and assignments, along with time-saving ways to grade and provide feedback. **CengageNOW** assists with the most common grading and reporting tasks that instructors perform every day. For students, **CengageNOW** provides an integrated ebook, diagnostic self-assessment, and Personalized Study that enables them to focus on what they need to learn and guides them in selecting activities that best match their learning styles. To package access to **CengageNOW** with every new copy of ***Writing: A Manual for the Digital Age,*** contact your representative from Wadsworth, a part of Cengage Learning.

CENGAGENOW™

English21: Composition for the 21st Century. Through interactive instruction, this groundbreaking online tool teaches students how to analyze the various texts that inundate their lives, and demonstrates how to use rhetorical devices in writing.

English21

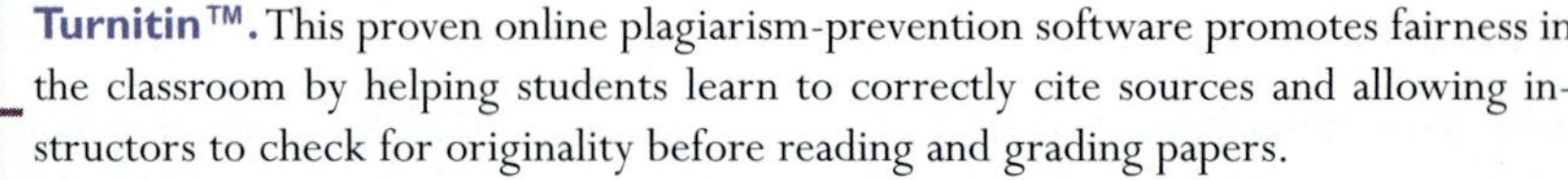

Turnitin™. This proven online plagiarism-prevention software promotes fairness in the classroom by helping students learn to correctly cite sources and allowing instructors to check for originality before reading and grading papers.

Cengage Learning InSite for Writing and Research™. This multi-functional online writing and research tool includes electronic peer review, an originality checker, an assignment library, help with common errors, and access to InfoTrac College Edition. InfoTrac College Edition provides nearly instant access to more than 18 million reliable, full-text articles from 5,000 academic and popular journals.

WriteNote®. This Web-based research and writing tool helps students search for and organize references used in their academic papers, so that they can focus on the content of their research and the presentation of ideas.

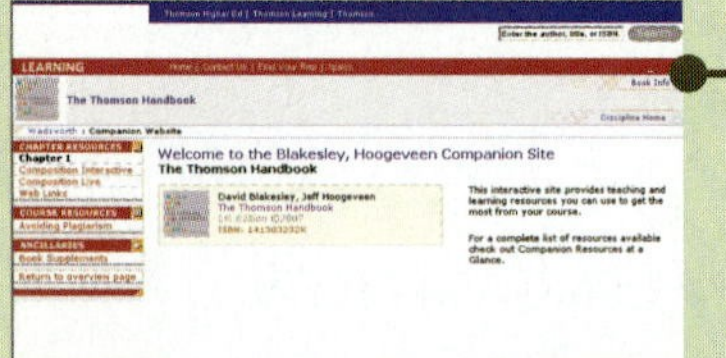

Book Companion Website. This site contains many interactive resources for students, including libraries that offer animated tutorials and information on diction, grammar, mechanics, punctuation, and research, as well as examples of student papers.

Acknowledgments

We have many people to thank for their help in making this book possible. Because it's a book that breaks the mold in many respects, all of them deserve credit for their vision and persistence. We would like to thank Leslie Taggart for her expert stewardship of this project from its inception. Leslie's eagerness to take risks, her willingness to experiment with new forms of presentation, and her patience and perseverance have always been inspiring. The finest qualities of this book are largely due to her expert guidance. We will take all the credit for every instance when it falls short of her high standards.

Michael Rosenberg, Publisher at Wadsworth, a part of Cengage Learning, has likewise supported our work enthusiastically. Dickson Musselwhite helped launch the project and remained an enthusiastic supporter of the project throughout. During production, Samantha Ross kept us on track as our production editor, overseeing all the details of writing, designing, and publishing a comprehensive and innovative handbook—no small feat. Sally Lifland, our project manager, oversaw all of the aspects of copyediting and proofing with the precision and talent that writers can only hope for in their editorial team. Linda Beaupré translated our ideas on information architecture into a beautiful book design, and Bill Reuter created the cover. The team at Graphic World carefully composed the pages and the extensive art program. Our researchers, Sheri Blaney, Francelle Carapetyan, Isabel Alves, and Marcy Lunetta, worked diligently and resourcefully to clear permissions. Karen Judd managed the process of creating a brief version of the handbook, which, because of the tight integration of verbal and visual content, posed considerable challenges. She is the editor of editors and—probably no thanks to us—has retained her great sense of humor. Star MacKenzie Burruto and Mandee Eckersley organized all of our focus groups and workshops, which helped us improve the book significantly.

The many reviewers and focus group participants who have had a hand in shaping this handbook deserve special recognition and thanks. The handbook benefited greatly from reviewers' responses to both the evolving manuscript and the design concept. We thank you for your patient reading and your insightful comments. In meetings with the development team in Miami, Houston, and Chicago, the focus group participants (whose names are indicated with an asterisk in the following list) provided many comments about the scope and sequence and the design of the handbook, which were helpful as we finished our work on this first edition. Thank you for your thoughtful collaboration.

Liz Ann Aguilar, *San Antonio College*
Preston Allen, *Miami Dade–North**
Sarah Arroyo, *University of Texas at Arlington*
Martha Bachman, *Camden Community College*
John Barber, *University of Texas at Dallas*
Bryan Bardine, *University of Dayton*
Papia Bawa, *Purdue University**
Kristina Beckman, *University of Arizona*
Michael Benton, *University of Kentucky*
Emily Biggs, *University of Kentucky*
Samantha Blackmon, *Purdue University*
Jennie Blankert, *Purdue University**
Bradley Bleck, *Spokane Falls Community College**
Anne Bliss, *University of Colorado at Boulder**
Beverley Braud, *Texas State University*
Anthony Campbell, *Eastern Kentucky University*
Geof Carter, *Purdue University**
Melvin Clarkheller, *South Texas Community College**
John Comeau, *Ivy Tech Community College of Indiana at South Bend*
Sean Conrey, *Purdue University**
Jennifer Consilio, *Lewis College**
Linda Coolen, *North Central Texas College**
Romana Cortese, *Montgomery College**
Emily Cosper, *Delgado Community College*
Nancy Cox, *Arkansas Tech University*
Paul Crawford, *Southeastern Louisiana University**
Linda Daigle, *Houston Community College, Central*
Dale Davis, *Northwest Mississippi Community College*
Marcia Dickson, *Ohio State University at Marion*
Carol Dillon, *University of Nebraska at Omaha*
Huiling Ding, *Purdue University**
Shannon Dobranski, *Georgia Institute of Technology*
Keith Dorwick, *University of Louisiana at Lafayette*
Marilyn Douglas-Jones, *Houston Community College*
Rebecca Duncan, *Meredith College*
Dawn Elmore-McCrary, *San Antonio College**
Joshua Everett, *Central Texas College**
James Fenton, *Delgado Community College*
Jane Focht-Hansen, *San Antonio College*
Murray Fortner, *Tarrant County Community College*
Judith Gardner, *University of Texas at San Antonio**
Dianna Gilroy, *Purdue University**
Mary Godwin, *Purdue University**
Anissa Graham, *University of North Alabama**

Andrew Green, *University of Miami**
Magnolia Hampton, *Hinds Community College*
Christopher Harris, *University of Louisiana–Monroe**
Carolyn Harrison, *Oakland Community College*
Betty Hart, *University of Southern Indiana*
Scott Hathaway, *Hudson Valley Community College*
Cynthia Haynes, *Clemson University*
Rebecca Hite, *Southeastern Louisiana University**
Carolyn Ho, *North Harris College*
Megan Hughes, *Purdue University**
Joanna Johnson, *University of Miami**
Rick Johnson-Sheehan, *Purdue University**
Rachel Jordan, *Hudson Valley Community College*
Paul Karpuk, *Central Connecticut State University*
Rick Kemp, *University of Maryland, University College*
Malcolm Kiniry, *Rutgers University*
Jessica Kohl, *Purdue University**
Cindy Konrad, *Purdue University**
Martina Kusi-Mensah, *Montgomery College**
Kathy Lattimore, *State University of New York at Cortland*
Mary Ann Lee, *Longview Community College*
Stephen Leone, *Westchester Community College*
Mia Leonin, *University of Miami*
Robert Leston, *University of Texas at Arlington*
Mike Lohre, *Ohio State University at Marion*
Charlie Lowe, *Grand Valley State University**
Clark Maddux, *Tennessee State University*
Gina Merys Mahaffery, *St. Louis University*
Carolyn Mann, *Morgan State University*
Gina Maranto, *University of Miami*
Rebecca Marez, *Del Mar College*
Mike Matthews, *Central Texas College**
Pat McMahon, *Tallahassee Community College*
Alisa Messer, *City College of San Francisco*
Susan Miller, *Mesa Community College*
Homer Mitchell, *State University of New York at Cortland*
Michael Mizell-Nelson, *Delgado Community College*
Kevin Moberly, *University of Louisiana at Lafayette*
Samantha Morgan-Curtis, *Tennessee State University*
Ed Moritz, *Indiana University–Purdue University at Ft. Wayne*
David Mulry, *Longview Community College**
Marshall Myers, *Eastern Kentucky University*
Mary Anne Nagler, *Oakland Community College*
Kathryn Naylor, *Purdue University**
Sally Nielsen, *Florida Community College at Jacksonville*

Matthew Novak, *California Polytechnic State University*
Carla Nyssen, *California State University at Long Beach*
Melinda Payne, *Houston Community College*
John Pekins, *Tallahassee Community College*
David Peterson, *University of Nebraska at Omaha*
Tim Poland, *Radford University*
Judie Rae, *American River College; Sierra College*
Kathryn Raign, *University of North Texas*
Colleen Reilly, *University of North Carolina*
Teresa Reynolds, *Indiana University–Southeast*
Melissa Richardson, *Central Texas College**
Thomas Rickert, *Purdue University*
Jared Riddle, *Ivy Tech State College–De La Garza*
Rochelle Rodrigo, *Mesa Community College*
Brooke Rollins, *University of South Carolina*
Linda Rosekrans, *State University of New York at Cortland*
Jill Terry Rudy, *Brigham Young University*
Kathy Sanchez, *Tomball College*
Joy Santee, *Purdue University**
John Schaffer, *Blinn College**
Susan Sens-Conant, *Johnson County Community College**
Annabel Servat, *Southeastern Louisiana University**
Barry Seyster, *Orange Coast College*
May Shih, *San Francisco State University*
Catherine Shuler, *Purdue University**
Susan Slavicz, *Florida Community College at Jacksonville*
Andrew Strycharski, *University of Miami*
Barbara Szubinska, *Eastern Kentucky University**
Chris Thaiss, *George Mason University*
Valerie Thomas, *University of New Mexico*
David Tietge, *Monmouth University*
Carla Todaro, *Walters State Community College*
Linda Toonen, *University of Wisconsin at Green Bay**
Alice Trupe, *Bridgewater College*
Sam Umland, *University of Nebraska*
Ralph Velazquez, *Rio Hondo College**
Kathryn Waltz-Freel, *Ivy Tech Community College of Indiana*
Colleen Weldele, *Palomar College*
Cornelia Wells, *William Patterson University*
Natasha Whitten, *Southeastern Louisiana University**
Sallie Wolf, *Arapahoe Community College**
Peggy Woods, *University of Massachusetts at Amherst*
Maria Zlateva, *Boston University**

In 2003, we conducted a survey of English instructors to find out what technology questions their students asked them so that we could develop our Technology Toolboxes to cover those topics students need help with. We thank you all for sharing that information with us.

James Allen, *College of DuPage*
Dana Anderson, *University of Indiana*
Kristina Beckman, *University of Arizona*
Anne Bliss, *University of Colorado at Boulder*
Vince Bruckert, *Wilbur Wright College*
Mattavia Burks, *Calhoun Community College*
Anthony Campbell, *Eastern Kentucky University*
Constance Chapman, *Clark Atlanta University*
Janice Clayton, *San Antonio College*
Taylor Emery, *Austin Peay State University*
Karen Gardiner, *The University of Alabama*
Baotong Gu, *Georgia State University*
Magnolia Hampton, *Hinds Community College*
Betty Hart, *University of Southern Indiana*
Scott Hathaway, *Hudson Valley Community College*
Matthew Higgs, *Northeastern University*
Klint Hull, *Spokane Community College*
Tim Lindgren, *Boston College*
Clark Maddux, *Tennessee State University*
Rebecca Marez, *Del Mar College*
Brett Millan, *South Texas Community College*
Susan Miller, *Mesa Community College*
Samantha Morgan-Curtis, *Tennessee State University*
Mary Anne Nagler, *Oakland Community College*
Troy Nordman, *Butler County Community College*
Matthew Novak, *California Polytechnic State University*
Ruth Oleson, *Illinois Central College*
John Pekins, *Tallahassee Community College*
Susan Sens-Conant, *Johnson County Community College*
Susan Slavicz, *Florida Community College at Jacksonville*
Monica Smith, *University of Georgia*
Peggy Woods, *University of Massachusetts at Amherst*

We also want to thank the students who filled out another version of the technology survey. Since several students expressed concerns about their privacy, we will not mention them by name, but instead offer a general thank-you for taking the time to complete the survey.

Additional Thanks from Jeff

I would like to first thank Dave, co-author extraordinaire, whose ideas, skills, friendship, and good humor made drafting this first edition a pleasure and a learning adventure. Ron Shelly, Cengage Learning sales rep, was incredibly generous with his time and resources as this idea became a manuscript over the last several years. Dr. Gladys Willis, who has been a mentor to me since I began at Lincoln and whose professional and collegial support have kept my ambitions harnessed to productive projects like this one, has my gratitude. Thanks to all my colleagues at Lincoln, who have supported my efforts since the project began, and to my students, who have listened, offered suggestions for examples, and provided writing for this book. Thanks to my wife, Kathy, who has offered numerous suggestions, listened and responded to drafts, and read the manuscript time and time again. Jean and Chet Hoogeveen, Diane Hallmann, and Neil and Marge O'Kane have always given me their unflagging support. I would also like to remember two generous friends and humble mentors who recently passed away: Scott Christianson of Radford University and Bill Mensel of the University of Rhode Island.

Additional Thanks from Dave

I would like to first thank the many students who contributed their fine writing, ideas, and suggestions: Lauren Armenta, Jessica Hary, Franklin Jewell, Molly McClure, Chris McKibbin, Eugene Rhee, Cas Riddle, Wyatt Roth, Jacob Warrington, Kristofer Whited, and Gina Wolf. Gina was especially generous, allowing us to use her photographs and notes, which proved invaluable in helping us show how writers adapt to new contexts. Dr. Erin Karper deserves enormous credit for writing most of the handbook's activities and the Flex-Files Instructor's Manual. In the time it has taken for us to complete the book, Erin has completed her doctoral work and launched a successful career at Niagara University. Her experience as the webmaster of Purdue's OWL and as a technology coordinator for professional writing made her the perfect contributor to the project, and her writing and insights were always first-rate. Prior to completing their doctoral degrees at Purdue, Dr. Jonnika Charlton and Dr. Colin Charlton shared assignments and ideas that proved enormously helpful early in the process. Karl Stolley—the current OWL webmaster and designer extraordinaire—influenced all of the writing on graphic design and multimedia with his ideas. Karl also helped with the early development of our online resources.

All of my colleagues in Rhetoric and Composition and Linguistics at Purdue have been wonderfully supportive and enthusiastic about all of my work. Jenny Bay, Linda Bergmann, Margie Berns, Tammy Conard-Salvo, Richard Johnson-Sheehan, Janice Lauer, Charlie Lowe, Thomas Rickert, Shirley Rose, Michael Salvo, Tony Silva, Pat Sullivan, and Irwin ("Bud") Weiser set very high standards for me to meet, and I can only hope this book passes muster with them. I need to thank Shirley, Pat, Bud, and Interim Dean (and my colleague) Thomas Adler for helping make this year one to remember. Charlie's deep knowledge of computers and writing pedagogy, the collaborative principles of open source, and software has helped me understand (as much as it's possible to do so) the importance of reconceptualizing writing in the digital age. Tarez Graban, Rebecca Longster, and Jeremy Tirrell helped us map the handbook to outcome goals for Purdue's Introductory Composition program. Thanks also are due to Jill Jordan, who keeps us all properly caffeinated and the shelves cleared for the handbook.

How does one properly thank a co-author? Jeff Hoogeveen had the original idea for this book and invited me to join him, for which I am grateful. It has always been a pleasure to work with Jeff. His wit and sense of humor are unbounded and abundant. Jeff is an unwavering supporter of students and obviously takes great pride in their work. Purdue alum Colleen Brice, now an assistant professor at Grand Valley State University, brought her expertise on second language writing and linguistics to Part 11, composing each of those excellent chapters.

While we were completing work on the book, I was saddened by the loss of my parents' greatest friend, Francis ("Smitty") Smith. Smitty was the punster to beat all, and I remember fondly the advice he gave me about writing term papers when I was young. He never liked his writing textbooks too much; this one, I hope, would pass muster with him. Luckily, everything passes muster with my mom, Pearl, and brother, Roger.

While this book has been underway, my twins—Meagan and Matt—have grown from toddlers to tweeners, and even as I write this they wonder, "So when is the handbook coming?" Well, here it is! They are making their own books now, so maybe they think we're doing something interesting. My smart and beautiful wife, Julie, brought them into the world all at once, which makes the accomplishment of writing a handbook pale in comparison.

Writing: A Manual for the Digital Age

PART 1

Managing Your Writing

>

New Contexts for Writing Weblogs

Weblogs have spawned a new generation of writers, journalists, knowledge experts, and social networks. The millions of bloggers around the world have proven that the Internet is a hive of active and participatory culture, rather than the isolating cave that some commentators feared. Social relations and knowledge—the glue of our culture—develop and grow through weblogs. For these reasons, writers need to understand this new context for writing. The character of our culture depends on it.

- You can think of a **weblog** as an online journal with accumulating content. The entries in a weblog, however, are not just written text; weblogs may include any kind of writing, photos, videos, software programs, or other multimedia projects. The term *weblog* is a fusion of *Web* (as in World Wide Web) and *log* (a record of activity). The term has been shortened further to *blog* (a noun), and the related verb is *to blog*. *To blog* something means to write about it in a weblog.
- An **RSS feed** connects remote blogs together across the Internet. RSS stands for "Really Simple Syndication." (*To syndicate* means to distribute content for republication.) RSS feeds are collected by **aggregators,** which are a part of the blogging software that scours preselected blogs elsewhere for new posts and collects them for presentation at the local weblog.
- The advantages of blogs are that bloggers can create content using a browser interface, don't have to worry about designing each new post, and can choose keywords to categorize content. All content is automatically archived. When you read a blog, you'll see the most recently posted entries first.

What a Powerful Web We Weave . . .

Perhaps the most important aspect of blogging is its connection across time and space to the wider world of the Internet. With RSS feeds and aggregation, bloggers network effortlessly with others around the globe, building the Internet from the inside with shared content and richly linked information. Much like weblogs, new Web browsers and even email programs will aggregate RSS feeds automatically. Whereas the first generation of the Internet was connected by hyperlinks to remote content, the next generation of the Internet, sometimes called the *Semantic Web* or *Web 2.0*, is constructed on the fly, instantaneously and automatically, from bits and pieces of information authored around the globe, giving the average person an important role in creating the Internet.

Only Connect . . .

Anyone with an Internet connection can get started reading and writing weblogs. Remember that the Internet—like a street corner, a mall, a bazaar, a cathedral, or a carnival—may be filled with strange people and unfamiliar ideas. One goal of the "New Contexts for Writing" part openers is to teach you how to navigate this world intelligently and enjoyably.

Weblog Services: Google these names to learn more: Blogger, Drupal, ELGG, ExpressionEngine, Greymatter, LiveJournal, Moveable Type, MySpace, TypePad, Wordpress, Xanga.

Syndicator: Technorati (http://www.technorati.com) tracks more than 26 million weblogs and 1.9 billion links.

Every piece of writing develops in a context that influences how we respond to what we read and how we compose what we write. Readers interpret writing and images in the contexts of a place and a time, attitudes, memories, and even other words. Writers draw from experience and memory to imagine what these contexts are and how they might influence readers. In one sense, being an effective writer means that you know how to imagine the many contexts in which your writing may be read. You can anticipate different or complex contexts and understand how your meaning may be shaped by them and even how you can reshape contexts to suit your purpose. You can use your knowledge of possible contexts to make good decisions about your content and to shape it for readers to teach, persuade, or move them.

One of the great challenges of writing effectively is to decide what to write. But it is just as difficult and important to know the contexts that influence how others interpret the signs you send them. What are the circumstances for writing and reading? Regardless of what situation calls you to write, each situation has a context that should be considered carefully before you start writing and while you are writing and revising. When you consider contexts as a writer, you practice the art of rhetoric, which involves discovering ideas and using words and images designed to persuade, inform, or move readers.

1 WRITING AND RHETORIC IN CONTEXT

Suppose you want to ask a peer to give you feedback on a personal essay before you submit it to your instructor or to your campus literary magazine. Your essay brings up some memories that you feel deeply about but that you also want to share with others.

The hard part about asking for a favor is not the gist of what you will say or write—"Would you please give me feedback on this essay?"—but figuring out *how* you will say or write it (the style, the words), what medium you should use (spoken words, a handwritten note, an email message, an instant message), under what circumstances your message will be read, and how the person will respond (yes, no, maybe, why? what?). You decide that you'll ask for help via email.

You write your message, struggling to find the right words and to imagine the response to them. You realize that you're asking someone to give up time. You also want to make sure your reader gives you more than a pat on the back, which is nice but will not help you improve your writing for a broader audience. You worry about whether your work is too personal and the story, uninteresting—or whether "you had to be there." Should you send the essay as a file attachment with your first message? In other words, you have a variety of concerns and intentions.

Activity 1-1: Thinking about Contexts: Asking a Favor by Email

Suppose you wrote an email message to a peer asking for feedback on a personal essay. Use the pictures below as you consider the questions on page 7, which ask you to put yourself in the role of both a writer and a reader.

Scenes for writing and reading email

How would your message change if you knew it would be read in the contexts pictured here?

As a Writer

1. How would the contexts suggested by these images affect your writing? What scenarios provide the most comfortable contexts for writing your email? Why? Which would be the least comfortable context? Why?

2. Which of the scenarios would you most like to be the context in which the intended recipient read your email? Why? Which would be the least comfortable context? Why?

3. How do you think these different contexts would affect your reader's interpretation of and response to your message?

4. If you were asking your correspondent out on a date rather than for feedback on a personal essay, how would these reading contexts affect your writing? Why?

As a Reader

1. Which of the pictured scenarios would provide the most comfortable context for reading an email asking you for a favor? Why? Which would be the least comfortable context? Why?

2. Would your response to the message change depending on the context you were in? If so, how would it change? Why would it change?

3. Would the context in which you read the email affect the response you gave to the writer? Why or why not?

4. If you were asked out on a date via an email that you read in one of these scenarios, how would context affect your interpretation? Why?

You also need to take into account your reader's context. Under what circumstances will he or she read your request for a favor? In the midst of a busy day, among lots of spam email? On a busy commute home on a wireless PDA? As a friend or mild acquaintance? What does your reader already know about you? Will he or she be inclined to respond? What might he or she expect in return?

Context Shapes Meaning 1b

Context is an important concept for understanding reading and writing. A common term, *context* is often used synonymously with terms like *scene, situation,* and *circumstance.* It is a combination of the prefix *con-* or *com-,* meaning "together," and the Latin word *texere,* meaning "weave." Context is a weaving together. In certain variations in Latin, *texere* also referred to woven material and then later, by analogy, to literary compositions or *texts.* Texts may be words, images, or any other phenomenon that can be viewed as a composition of elements. For example, *Moby Dick* and *The Adventures of Super Diaper Baby* are easily recognizable as texts, different as they are in many ways. Films as distinct as *The Return of the King* and *Austin Powers: International Man of Mystery* are texts. Television shows from *The Apprentice* to *Gilligan's Island* are texts. Even social practices and groups—hip-hop culture, MP3 culture, blog culture, or any subculture—are texts. All may be seen as a composition of elements and thus may be "read." Meaning (and hence interpretation) can be thought of as the relationship between *text* and *context,* which includes the situations of readers and writers, the historical and physical circumstances, other texts, and even the broader systems of meaning like ideology that "contain" the text. You can read books, films, TV shows, and cultures as texts that have contexts that shape meaning.

Whenever you write for readers, you should bear in mind how all these aspects of **context** might shape your meaning and thus how your words will be interpreted by others:

- the subject or topic
- the nature of the audience
- the conditions of reading or viewing
- the medium
- the timing
- what others have said about the subject
- the wider culture in which it plays a part

Expressing ideas verbally or visually is a social act in which these aspects of context shape meaning.

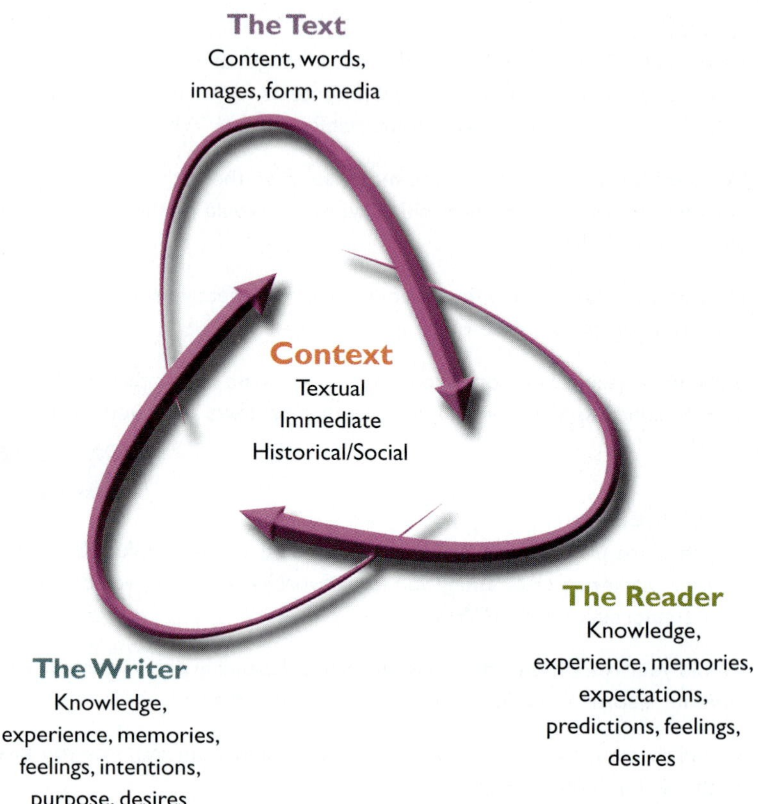

The Rhetorical Situation

At the start of any writing project, think through your writing in context, as a **rhetorical situation** involving your own ideas, the words and media that you will use to express them, and the ideas and expectations of your readers. The elements of context will shape your thinking at each node of this rhetorical triangle.

Activity 1-2: Meaning Depends on Context

What a word, phrase, or sentence means will vary depending on context.

1. How would you describe each of these contexts?
2. Imagine that "Are we having fun yet?" is the caption for each image. How might the meaning of "Are we having fun yet?" change if it were read or heard in these contexts?
3. How does context—even when it's only imagined—influence interpretation?

Context refers to all the situational elements that might shape a writer's intentions or purpose, whether or not they are conscious. A purpose is a motive—some situation that "moves" you to write (hence the word *motive,* which is related to *motion* and even *emotion*). When you have or discover purpose, you act on the world in a deliberate way—through writing, art, the spoken word. You feel compelled to "size up" a situation and respond to it. You can also intentionally shape contexts so that, for example, you have some say in the circumstances and media in which your writing is read.

As a writer yourself, you already know that one of the greatest challenges is to use the right word at the right time in the right place. How do you make these difficult decisions? How do you know what to write? Where do you find purpose? Every writing situation is different to some degree, so learning to draw on elements of the context in order to shape your purposes and your subject is a strategy you'll need in every situation that calls for you to communicate your ideas to others.

Context shapes your motives for writing about and, thus, acting on the world. When sensitive to context, your writing becomes a deliberate and active process. When your writing is not attuned to context, you miss the opportunity to act on real people in real situations that matter.

It is customary to think of the elements of context that contribute to meaning in terms of the textual context, the immediate context, and the social and historical context.

The Textual Context

When people use the term *context* with regard to writing, they often have in mind the text that immediately surrounds a given idea or sequence of words. Those who market films sometimes take liberties with the textual context, quoting single words out of context. For instance, a film review that says "It's amazing that this stupid and violent film was ever made in the first place" suddenly becomes "Amazing . . ." in the film's newspaper promos. Taking amazing out of its local textual context and inserting it in the new textual context of the film's marketing blitz suggests that the reviewer of the film believed it was "amazing" and distorts the reviewer's meaning.

Global Contexts

John F. Kennedy's 1963 Berlin Speech

Words usually have multiple meanings and those meanings depend on context, so it can be very challenging to use the words of another language in unfamiliar situations. In a famous speech in Berlin in 1963, during the height of the Cold War, President John F. Kennedy spoke to Berlin citizens about his belief that all Americans stood with Berliners for the cause of freedom. He was speaking to people in West Berlin, separated from communist East Berlin by the Berlin Wall, which became the symbolic dividing line between West and East during the Cold War. To make his point, Kennedy used this sentence:

> Two thousand years ago, the proudest boast was *civis Romanus sum*. Today, in the world of freedom, the proudest boast is *Ich bin ein Berliner.*

When you are in Berlin, *Berliner* means "a person from Berlin," but outside of Berlin, *Berliner* means "jelly doughnut." To an audience of German speakers outside of Berlin, Kennedy seemed to be boasting, "I am a jelly doughnut!" Of course, Kennedy knew that he was speaking to Berliners in Berlin, and so he chose his words well: "We are all Berliners." The excerpt on the next page shows how writers at Wikipedia (**http://www.wikipedia.com**) explain that context is all-important in judging Kennedy's meaning. Wikipedia is a free content encyclopedia written collaboratively by contributors around the world. It is a "wiki," which means that anyone can contribute. Over time—and given sufficient numbers of readers and contributors—Wikipedia's information will make gains in status. See **http://en.wikipedia.org/wiki/Wikipedia:About** for more information about the project.

Ich bin ein Berliner

From Wikipedia, the free encyclopedia.

"Ich bin ein Berliner" is a famous phrase by John F. Kennedy. On June 26, 1963 in West Berlin, he made a speech containing the sentences:

> "Two thousand years ago the proudest boast was *civis Romanus sum*. Today, in the world of freedom, the proudest boast is "*Ich bin ein Berliner.*"
>
> "All free men, wherever they may live, are citizens of Berlin, and, therefore, as a free man, I take pride in the words "*Ich bin ein Berliner!*"

According to the context of the speech, Kennedy meant that he stood together with West Berliners in their struggle to maintain their freedom against Communist aggression.

Jelly doughnuts are called *Berliner* outside Berlin (but usually referred to as *Pfannkuchen* in Berlin itself). This has led some people to believe that the phrase Kennedy uttered was amusingly ambiguous ("I am a jelly doughnut"), which is, for the most part, incorrect. While the phrase *could* possibly be understood that way, both the context of the quotation and the fact that jelly doughnuts are not actually called "Berliner" in Berlin made this unlikely. Normally a Berliner would say "Ich komme aus Berlin" ("I come from Berlin"), but because Kennedy wanted to emphasize the common identity among people of the "world of freedom", that usage would have been misleading. "Ich bin Berliner" (cf. "Ich bin Amerikaner", "Ich bin Deutscher" etc.) would be preferred in common usage. This sentence is about as likely to be misinterpreted as the following analogous example: suppose that the speech had taken place in Frankfurt instead, and Kennedy had said "I am a Frankfurter." While it is *possible* that a native English speaker would mistake his meaning for "I am a hot dog," given the context most would understand the president to have meant, "I am a citizen of Frankfurt."

The jelly doughnut urban legend apparently arose in Florida in the 1980s and culminated in a letter to the editor to *The New York Times* in 1987 which claimed that the error was embarrassing and resulted in laughter. The context made the meaning very clear, though, so nobody misunderstood Kennedy when he delivered his speech. He did however pronounce the sentence with a very strong American accent, reading from his note "ish bin ine bear-LEAN-ar". Contrary to the urban legend, it was not followed by a roar of laughter. Audio and film recordings show the remark was followed by applause and cheers, as was witnessed by television audiences in Europe and the United States at the time.

Interestingly, Kennedy did get a laugh a moment after he first used the phrase, but deliberately. His speech was being translated into German for the crowd phrase-by-phrase. "Ich bin ein Berliner" was "translated" to itself, resulting in the interpreter parroting what Kennedy had just said a moment before. As the applause died down, Kennedy paused for a moment, then said: "I appreciate my interpreter translating my German", a quip which did receive a solid laugh from the crowd.

The Immediate Context

This aspect of context refers to the text, the author(s), the reader(s), and the immediate situation to which the text responds. The rhetorical situation of our hypothetical film review includes the review itself; the reviewer, her taste in films, previous reviews she has written, and so on; the particular newspaper in which the review appears; the newspaper's readership; and even the people responsible for making the film. All these components are aspects of the review's rhetorical situation.

The Social and Historical Context

Any particular film review also acquires meaning as part of a broader context of cultural and social attitudes and practices that have histories associated with them. So, for example, our film review might be read in the context of conflicting cultural attitudes about violence in the media, in the context of previous films that treat the subject more intelligently, or in the context of film reviews of the past.

The questions you ask and the rhetorical decisions you make with regard to the context and your subject matter for a given occasion should be governed by a sense of *kairos. Kairos,* a Greek concept meaning "timeliness" and "suiting the word to the occasion," is central to understanding rhetoric (and writing generally) as a method of discovering the available means of persuasion in any situation.

For example, suppose you are in charge of stopping an out-of-control eighteen-wheeler driven by a mad trucker who refuses to put on the brakes. Given this tough situation—its "kairotic" moment—what could you do to stop the truck? Would you build a huge brick wall? Persuade the driver over a cell phone not to hurt others, to give himself up peacefully? Can you reason with him at all? Will regret, guilt, or other emotions influence him to stop? (You can't use road spikes because you fear that the truck's cargo will explode and cause more damage.)

Given these circumstances, you shrewdly conclude that placing an innocuous road sign, "Bridge Out," in the right location might do the trick. *Kairos*—your sense of the driver's state of mind, the physical scene, the timing—helps you reach this conclusion.

"Put on the Brakes!"

Which road sign would be more likely to persuade, given the circumstances of our mad trucker? Why?

"Bridge Out" "Seismic Retrofitting"

Activity 1-3: Exploring Contexts in Which You Write

You already write in many different contexts, and throughout your life may find yourself writing in many more. Make a list of the different contexts in which you write in the following aspects of your life:

- School
- Community
- Personal life
- Work

1. What do the contexts in which you write have in common? How do they differ?
2. Why do you write in these contexts?
3. Do you approach the contexts differently as a writer? Why or why not?
4. What kinds of readers do you expect for each context?

Project Checklist

Questioning the Writing Context

Use this list to guide you as you begin thinking about the ways that context can shape your project.

Textual Context

1. What is my purpose? To inform? Entertain? Persuade? Or something else?
2. What are the important terms and concepts associated with my topic?
3. What style and arrangement are best suited to my project?
4. What genre (or genres) will best represent my project? An essay, a Web page, a brochure, a letter?
5. What media will I use? Paper, website, poster display, oral presentation? Will my project be published or presented somewhere?

Immediate Context

6. What are the important facts about my topic?
7. Who will read what I write, and what do they already know about my subject? How do they feel about it?
8. What do these readers know about me or about my purpose for writing?
9. What will the situation be when readers respond to my work? How will the interface (paper, screen, event) affect what I write?
10. Should I expect my readers to respond to me directly or in some other way?

Social and Historical Context

11. Why is now a good time to write about this topic?
12. Have there been recent and relevant news reports or current events that make my timing good?
13. What have others written about my topic, recently and throughout history?
14. What other writers have successfully addressed this subject, and how did they pull it off?
15. What social or political issues does my project raise, and how do my readers feel about them?

We can persuade in subtle ways, sometimes by indirection. Use your knowledge of your audience's expectations—their personal contexts—to move them with words they can appreciate! The BRIDGE OUT sign will persuade if the trucker can read it and if he's concerned for his safety or that of his truck and its cargo. If the sign works, the situation will be a good example of words as instruments of power and persuasion.

Context has an enormous impact on the composition and reception of meaning. An understanding of context will help you, as a writer,

- choose your words and structure your writing to convey meaning
- create and meet the expectations of your primary and secondary audiences
- evaluate the effects of time and place on your readers' interpretation of your meaning and purposes
- choose what subject matter to include and how to arrange and convey it to suit the place and time (*kairos*)

Gina Wolf, a student at Purdue University, is the author of the autobiographical narrative "Still Guarding the Fort," printed in Chapter 6 (▶ pages 114–117). Gina had written a letter to her friend Jamie, part of which she later turned into an essay for her composition class. In addition to changing the genre from letter to essay, Gina had to make several other kinds of changes so that the piece would work in its new context. In her composition course, and for a new audience, she found that she needed to re-create some of the original context because her readers wouldn't share her memories, as Jamie had.

Gina Wolf on the New Context for Her Narrative

Here is Gina's description of how the new context and more public, unfamiliar audience guided her writing and revision.

> The basis of the Fort story was actually a part of a longer letter I wrote as a high school graduation present for my friend Jamie (the girl in the essay). I took the basic narrative and revised it to add a lot more detail about how everything looked and was. Obviously the random reader would have no clue what I was talking about by saying "The Fort," whereas with Jamie, none of the description was necessary. The writing assignment I responded to asked us to recall some event that had made an impact on our lives . . . so I deleted some of the nonpertinent memories, changed it to give it a different tone, and added in the beginning and ending to make my point clear.

The context of memories shared by Gina and Jamie, pictured here as youngsters in front of the Fort, is deeper and richer than the context of the first-year composition course for which Gina later wrote her essay.

A table of contents for writing project threads appears on pages xv–xxii.

Proposal Arguments

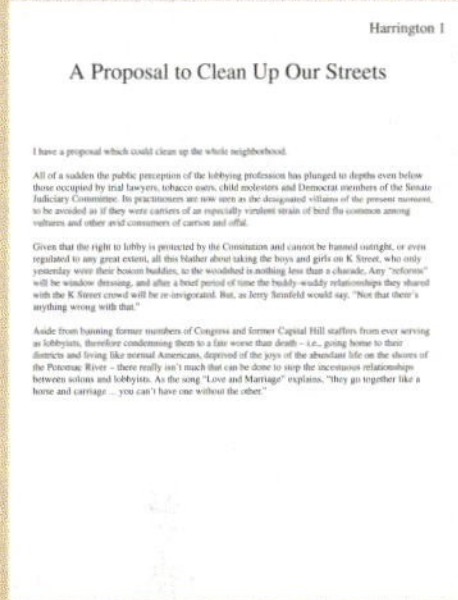

Harrington 1

A Proposal to Clean Up Our Streets

I have a proposal which could clean up the whole neighborhood.

All of a sudden the public perception of the lobbying profession has plunged to depths even below those occupied by trial lawyers, tobacco users, child molesters and Democrat members of the Senate Judiciary Committee. Its practitioners are now seen as the designated villains of the present moment, to be avoided as if they were carriers of an especially virulent strain of bird flu common among vultures and other avid consumers of carrion and offal.

Given that the right to lobby is protected by the Constitution and cannot be banned outright, or even regulated to any great extent, all this blather about taking the boys and girls on K Street, who only yesterday were their bosom buddies, to the woodshed is nothing less than a charade. Any "reforms" will be window dressing, and after a brief period of time the buddy-wuddy relationships they shared with the K Street crowd will be re-invigorated. But, as Jerry Seinfeld would say, "Not that there's anything wrong with that."

Aside from banning former members of Congress and former Capital Hill staffers from ever serving as lobbyists, therefore condemning them to a fate worse than death – i.e., going home to their districts and living like normal Americans, deprived of the joys of the abundant life on the shores of the Potomac River – there really isn't much that can be done to stop the incestuous relationships between solons and lobbyists. As the song "Love and Marriage" explains, "they go together like a horse and carriage ... you can't have one without the other."

Defining a Problem in Its Community Context

In a proposal argument, you will be asked to identify a problem, propose a solution, and justify your solution with reasons and evidence. Often you will need to support your line of argument with the ideas and work of others. For questions you can use to approach a proposal argument, see the Problem and Solution section in Chapter 5 (▶ page 81).

In a proposal argument, you might write about

- possible solutions to problems on campus, such as unequal treatment of students, lack of parking, rising tuition, overcrowded dormitories or campus facilities, or a shortage of funds for student activities
- possible solutions to problems in your neighborhood, hometown, or county, such as lack of medical insurance, poverty, racism, or homelessness
- possible solutions to problems in your country, such as the budget deficit, inequities in the tax system, or election irregularities
- possible solutions to problems in the world related to international relations or environmental issues, such as global warming

Communities define problems based on how they manifest themselves within the community's context. For example, the problems listed above can be seen as examples of how context shapes the problems that communities identify as important.

Begin by considering a general problem, such as poverty, racism, gender inequality, or human rights violations. Write down how this problem manifests itself in local, national, and global communities. How would each community define the problem within its specific context?

Finally, choose a specific problem, within a specific community context, that you would like to investigate. (If you're having trouble coming up with problems, try some of the brainstorming strategies in Chapter 3.) ▶ page 43.

Brochures

Contexts for Brochures

A key consideration in writing and designing a brochure is the context in which you are writing. Here are some sample contexts for creating brochures. How would the brochures created be different from one another because of their contexts? What context(s) does your brochure fit into?

School

Information about recreational sports at your school
Information about your school's first-year writing program

Community

Information about a local crisis prevention or pregnancy counseling center
Information about a local animal shelter

Workplace

Information for employees about this year's United Way campaign
Information for customers or clients (about programs, services, or products)

In order to develop a clear picture of the context and to explore ideas for your brochure's creation and development, review the Project Checklist on page 13. To what contexts does your brochure belong? page 30.

Research Reports

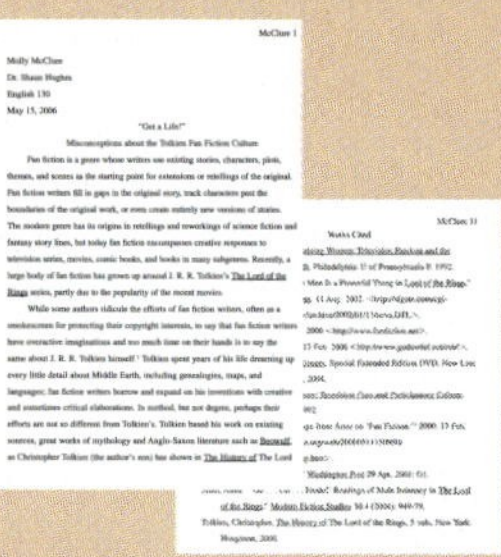

Considering the Rhetorical Moment

When you write a research paper, you'll want to begin by considering the rhetorical moment that you've been placed in and how that affects what you can and will write about in your paper. Reread section 1d on how *kairos* allows you to choose and use words that are suitable for a specific occasion. Then do some freewriting about the rhetorical moment that you find yourself in with this assignment.

- What topics and ideas do you think are particularly suited to this assignment and to the time and place where you are right now?
- How would you characterize and describe the rhetorical moment that you're in?
- How do you think it will shape your creation of a research paper? page xx.

2 PLANNING YOUR WRITING PROJECTS

PROJECT PLANNING SOFTWARE 27

Any writing task, assignment, or project offers an occasion that calls you to write, much as a hail grabs your attention or an invitation presents a social opportunity. To answer the call successfully, you need to understand not only why you've been hailed but also the best way to respond. You need to think about your motives for writing. You also need to create a process that helps you achieve your purpose, whatever it may be.

Writing projects include your motives and writing processes, but also your research, your invention of content, your interaction with peers, and your systematic efforts to revise and craft your writing. Successfully managing all the tasks involved in completing a project requires careful planning. In this chapter and the others in Part 1, you will learn effective ways to plan and manage writing projects so that you can develop this ability into a craft. Once you understand the processes involved, you will be able to respond effectively to any of the writing tasks, assignments, and opportunities you face in college and beyond.

Writing is motivated by the need to respond to a demand (such as an assignment) or by the internal desire to communicate something to another person or even to oneself. This motivation is called *exigency,* a term that comes from the Latin *exigere,* which consists of *ex-* ("out") and *agere* ("to drive") and is related to "act" and "agency." Writing is an act of will and requires some agency, or means for carrying it out. As a writer, you need to have or find reasons for writing and a process for fulfilling your purpose.

2a Writing to Respond to a Need

In college, your motives for writing either will arise naturally as a result of your interests or will result from assigned coursework. Even when you write because you've been assigned to do so, you can discover a personal motivation to make the enterprise more interesting—to express yourself, examine what you know, or "set the record straight," for example. Whatever the circumstances of your writing, one key to success is to approach any writing situation as an opportunity to learn, as well as to teach, persuade, or move others.

When your motivation is internal—when you have what psychologists call a "felt need" or there is some imbalance you need to respond to—you can still be systematic about the process you follow to produce good writing. For example, you may want to voice your opinion on a community problem in a letter to the editor of a newspaper, or you may want to post a review of a book you recently enjoyed on your reading blog at Blogger.com or Reger.com. Your reasons for writing may arise out of your own experiences and motives, but you will still need to examine the editorial policy of the newspaper or the blogging practices followed by others so that your writing will communicate effectively with readers. You will need to understand your writing in context.

Project Checklist

Understanding a Writing Assignment

1. **The prompt or topic.** What topic, question, or situation have you been asked to write about or respond to? How much freedom do you have to pick a specific subject or approach?
2. **The background information.** Assignments often discuss the prompt by explaining the context, providing more information about how to approach the topic or why the topic is important.
3. **Steps in the process.** Some assignments spell out what steps you need to follow to complete the writing project and even list due dates for completing intermediate steps, such as doing research, participating in peer review, and turning in rough drafts.
4. **The audience.** The assignment might identify a specific audience. For example, you might be asked to address your argumentative essay to readers who haven't yet made up their minds on a subject. Your sense of audience should help you guide your invention of subject matter and your methods of developing and organizing your content.
5. **Grading criteria.** To help you set your goals, assignments may provide you with specific criteria for measuring your success (called rubrics), or more general expectations regarding the form of your writing and its effectiveness in elaborating the subject, explaining information, or arguing a point.
   - ❑ Does your assignment discuss what kinds of evidence will be needed? Will details come from personal experience, talking with others, or conducting more formal research?
   - ❑ Does your assignment discuss what final form the project should take? For example, does it call for a five-page printed essay, a brochure, a Web page, or a lab report?
   - ❑ Is there a specific length requirement for the final project?
   - ❑ Are you required to cite or refer to a specific number of outside sources of information?
   - ❑ For projects that draw on outside sources, which documentation style should you use?

Activity 2-1: Examining Writing Assignments from Across the Curriculum

Read each short assignment listed below. With a classmate, make a list of all the key terms used to indicate the subject, details, form, and required sources for each project. Then discuss how you would approach working on each assignment.

1. We've been reading the memoirs of people who often seem to be able to identify key turning points in their lives. Can you identify moments of decision or fate that have changed the course of your life? Discuss the impact one such moment has had on your life. Why do you consider this turning point important? (Composition)
2. In a paper of no more than five or six pages, describe the major trade routes to and from the East African coast in the fourteenth century and evaluate which was the most important. Give your rationale. You may include a map, but it is not required. (History)
3. Each group will design a poster for our upcoming film series on vampire movies. Be sure to include the titles of all four movies, as well as dates, times, locations, and cost. We will put the posters up around campus, so make sure your poster is eye-catching and interesting. (Film Studies)
4. Compare Freud's theory of psychosexual development and Erikson's theory of psychosocial development in terms of stages. Which theory makes more sense to you? Why? (Psychology)
5. Summarize the information from the three sources we have read on the Gross National Product (GNP) from 1980 to the present and present your summary as either a 1- to 2-page report or as a graph or chart. (Economics)
6. Of the five types of interactions of poverty, welfare, and crime we have studied, which one do you believe is most important for further research, and why? (Sociology)

When writing is motivated by the need to respond to an assignment in a class (or even on the job), you can follow some steps to ensure that you understand what you have been asked to do, why, and what your goals should be. If you are responding to a writing assignment in a college course, pay close attention to its wording. College instructors craft most assignments carefully.

2c Considering the Rhetorical Situation

Every call to write has a rhetorical situation. Analyzing it can help you make smart choices about how to approach your subject matter and present it to readers. In addition to considering the elements of context (discussed in Chapter 1), develop an understanding of the rhetorical situation—your subject, purpose, and audience—as you analyze your writing assignments.

Project Checklist

Investigating the Rhetorical Situation

Take notes to identify the major aspects of the rhetorical situation to which you are responding.

Subject

- ❑ What do you already know about the subject?
- ❑ What have others said about it?
- ❑ What does your audience know about it?
- ❑ To develop your understanding of the subject, use the invention methods discussed in Chapter 3.

Purpose

- ❑ What are your purposes for writing this assignment? Will you analyze a trend, inform readers of a new policy, entertain them with a story, or persuade them to take action?
- ❑ What tone—your attitude expressed toward the subject—will best accomplish your purpose? Do you want to sound formal and distantly polite, informal but engaged with your subject, lively, reasoned, expert, or inexperienced but curious?
- ❑ What genre will best help you accomplish your purpose?

Audience

- ❑ Who is your **primary audience**—the people you want to influence most directly? Consider traits such as the age, gender, economic class, region, ethnicity/race, previous experiences, education, reading ability, and likely interests of your intended readers. Which of these (or other) traits of your audience is most important in this particular writing situation?
- ❑ Do you have a **secondary,** or **subsidiary, audience,** and if so, whom does it include? The subsidiary audience for your writing consists of readers who may read your work but who will do so with less investment than your primary audience. What audience expectations should you address in order to fulfill your purpose for writing? As your writing becomes more public—on the Web, for instance—you will find it increasingly important to consider how both primary and subsidiary audiences might respond to you.

Activity 2-2: Considering the Rhetorical Situation in a Writing Assignment

Using a writing assignment that you have been given for a course or one of the sample writing assignments from Activity 2-1, answer the questions in the Project Checklist on page 20.

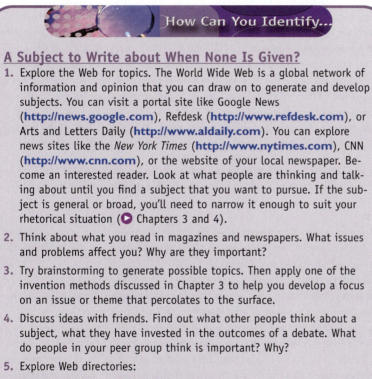

A Subject to Write about When None Is Given?

1. Explore the Web for topics. The World Wide Web is a global network of information and opinion that you can draw on to generate and develop subjects. You can visit a portal site like Google News (**http://news.google.com**), Refdesk (**http://www.refdesk.com**), or Arts and Letters Daily (**http://www.aldaily.com**). You can explore news sites like the *New York Times* (**http://www.nytimes.com**), CNN (**http://www.cnn.com**), or the website of your local newspaper. Become an interested reader. Look at what people are thinking and talking about until you find a subject that you want to pursue. If the subject is general or broad, you'll need to narrow it enough to suit your rhetorical situation (▶ Chapters 3 and 4).
2. Think about what you read in magazines and newspapers. What issues and problems affect you? Why are they important?
3. Try brainstorming to generate possible topics. Then apply one of the invention methods discussed in Chapter 3 to help you develop a focus on an issue or theme that percolates to the surface.
4. Discuss ideas with friends. Find out what other people think about a subject, what they have invested in the outcomes of a debate. What do people in your peer group think is important? Why?
5. Explore Web directories:

   Google Directories: **http://directory.google.com**

   Yahoo! Directories: **http://dir.yahoo.com**

   Wikipedia: **http://en.wikipedia.org/wiki/Main_Page** (also **http://www.wikipedia.org**)

   SciTech Daily: **http://www.scitechdaily.com**

As you plan your writing projects, you will need to consider genre. A *genre* is a type of writing (or, more broadly, composition) used in a particular situation for a certain purpose and often with a conventional form, style, or subject. Your understanding of genre will color many of your decisions throughout the planning, inventing, drafting, revising, and editing phases of your writing process. What expectations about your purpose, form, style, and subject matter will your audience bring to your work?

The features of any given genre are not fixed in stone; they change over time, and any one composition may not perfectly fit the genre's mold. There are genres and subgenres of nonfiction (such as biography and the personal essay), literature (poetry, fiction, drama), music (classical, country, punk, hip-hop, rap, rock), and art (still life, portrait, landscape, abstract).

Genre becomes critically important as you write in classes across the curriculum: people learn to value a certain type of writing for certain purposes and in particular contexts. Readers bring expectations that help them decide how to read and respond to your writing. For example, the conventional form of an argumentative essay changes somewhat as you move from writing about literature to writing about science. A **thesis**—a statement to be proven—might organize your argument in an essay on literature, but in psychology, a **hypothesis** might organize a study whose results argue that the hypothesis itself is true or false.

Genres arise because of patterns in human activity and so are much more complex than readymade forms or recipes for success. You learn to use your knowledge of genre to your advantage by writing and reading with and to others over time, in situations that matter. As you plan your writing projects, you should from the start try to learn the conventions of the genre so that you know what expectations your readers will bring to your work and how they are likely to respond to what you write.

The Academic Essay as a Genre

The genre of the academic essay has features that help readers distinguish it, for example, from a blog posting, a note between friends, a business letter, or a screenplay. Like any genre, it has conventions of form, style, and subject matter that distinguish it from personal narrative, fiction, poetry, or drama.

Genre Notes on the Academic Essay

A genre needs to be learned and practiced; no list of features can fully define it. The following guidelines are meant only as a starting point.

Form

- A *descriptive title* that suggests the subject and, if possible, the writer's perspective or position.
- *Introductory paragraphs* that invite readers into the subject by providing them with background information, context, and a thesis to be argued or a problem to be posed and explored.
- *Body paragraphs* that develop the reasons and evidence needed to support the thesis or elaborate the problem. Each body paragraph typically offers a full explanation of one major reason, idea, or example that supports the thesis statement or extends the inquiry.
- *Concluding paragraphs* that return to the thesis or problem, explain the implications of the argument or new ideas, or raise questions for further consideration.

Not all academic essays will be organized in this fashion, but if you are unsure how to organize your thoughts, these guidelines suggest a form that will be useful.

Style

- A *formal* or *semiformal* style in which the writer addresses a knowledgeable but unknown reader. Academic essays typically avoid slang and the colloquial language people use in everyday speech.
- *Specialized terms* that clarify or explain the subject. Be careful about your use of jargon, the field-specific words that people who share knowledge use to simplify their exchange of information. Good academic essays are not so jargon-laden that only a few people in the world can understand them. As academic essays have both primary and subsidiary audiences, you should define specialized terms so that all educated readers will understand your meaning.
- *Well-developed paragraphs and sentences* that help readers ponder meaning and follow a line of reasoning or explanation.

Subject

- *Subject matter* that people have conflicting opinions about, that is timely, that can help us solve or understand problems, or that inspires deeper understanding of the human condition.

- *Connections and circulation* with the ideas of others, whose work is cited. Academic essays join an ongoing conversation about the subject matter and so will typically acknowledge what others have written previously.
- *Citation style* appropriate to the given field of study.
- A *tone* of confidence in the writer's attitude toward the subject. Good academic essays show their writers to be careful, knowledgeable, and trustworthy. It is clear that the writer has thought carefully about the subject.

Analyzing Genre Requirements and Learning Specialized Terms

When analyzing and completing assignments, writers using English as a second language sometimes face additional challenges, especially regarding genre.

- **Analyzing genre requirements.** If you have questions about what is expected of you when you are given an assignment, ask your instructor for help. If you can point to specific aspects of the assignment that you don't understand, write your questions down before you talk to your instructor. You can also ask to see examples of effective writing projects that were responses to similar assignments. Carefully examine the samples you are given and take notes on the features of the writing. Share the samples with peers in or out of class and discuss what they think is expected. After you look over the samples, go back to your instructor and share what you have learned about the assignment. Instructors will appreciate your early attempts to understand assignments and will help when they can.
- **Learning specialized terms.** Part of the difficulty of studying a new topic or a new academic discipline is learning the precise meanings of words or phrases that mean something different in general usage. For example, when you are asked to write a *critical analysis* in a composition course, that usually means more than criticizing something (as in finding fault with it). Critical analysis involves breaking a subject into its parts and explaining how and why these parts add up to something of value (or not). (See Key Terms for Understanding Exam Questions on page 241.) When you are dealing with complicated concepts and language, take the time to check your understanding of ideas and language with someone who knows your subject matter well, such as a tutor in the writing center.

Developing Content in Context: Understanding Ethos, Logos, and Pathos

Regardless of the genre in which you compose, three rhetorical concepts can help you decide how to develop your subject: ethos, logos, and pathos. In rhetoric, ethos, logos, and pathos describe the three kinds of proof, or rhetorical appeals, that a writer can draw on when deciding what to say about a subject and how to say it. Because they help writers make decisions about what to write and how to write it, ethos, logos, and pathos are considered aspects of **rhetorical invention.**

Ethos is the appeal to the character of the writer and his or her attitude toward the subject. Writers convey ethos with their depth of knowledge about a subject, tone or attitude toward the subject, awareness of alternative viewpoints, manner of addressing readers, and fairness and trustworthiness. **Logos** is the use of content as a form of proof or appeal and may include ideas, images, information, and evidence. **Pathos** is the appeal to the emotions of the audience. Writers use pathos to encourage readers to attach emotional responses to the content (logos) or writer (ethos) and thus to feel moved to action or belief.

Much of this book includes information about the writing process, which is the systematic craft of developing and presenting textual, visual, or other content to an audience in any rhetorical situation. The writing process is the agency—the means—with which you act in response to a call to write. Generally speaking, the process includes the acts of inventing, drafting, revising, and editing. They are not always performed in linear order, and each will occupy more or less attention, depending on your context and purpose.

Inventing

Inventing is figuring out what you and others know about the subject and what more there is to learn. An assignment may require research in the library or online. Or it may require fieldwork, such as conducting interviews. Can you use your own experiences (in the first person) as a basis for presenting information?

Drafting

At some point, you need to assemble what you know and have learned about your subject into a composition—an organized set of

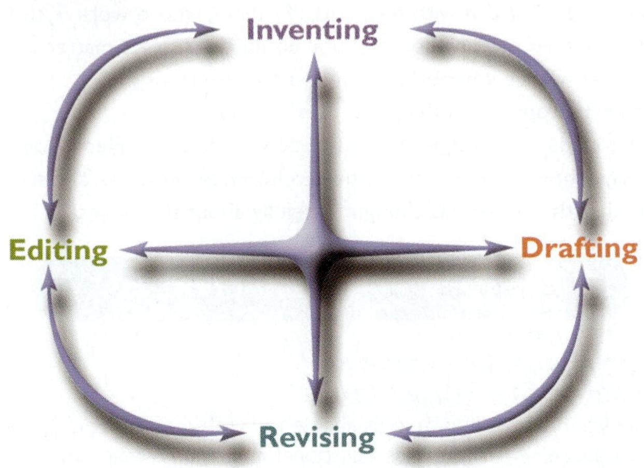

The writing process involves fluid movement among different kinds of activities. Although the activities of inventing, drafting, revising, and editing occur in different patterns depending on the writing project, the time you spend writing can become more productive if you have a rough idea of the tasks associated with each stage. For example, when you are brainstorming ideas in the invention stage, have a creative, even playful attitude. The more critical, evaluative attitude that's needed during the editing stage might slow down your production of new ideas.

Activity 2-3: Thinking about Your Writing Process

Describe the process that you normally go through when writing in the following situations. Include information about the various stages or steps you might take, the technologies you use, how much time you take, and the final form(s) that the documents take.

- Writing a letter or an email to a friend, relative, or discussion list
- Writing a research paper for a school assignment
- Writing an essay exam in a course
- Writing a college application essay
- Writing at a job you have (or have had)
- Writing a resume
- Writing the content for a Web page
- Writing an entry in your weblog

Does your writing process change depending on the type of project on which you are working? How do the context and rhetorical situation affect your writing process?

elements—with a form that readers can understand and that helps you accomplish your purpose. Drafting may include informal and formal outlining, composing good sentences and paragraphs, storyboarding, and building a tentative argument.

Revising

For good writers, revising, or "re-seeing," is a critical step because it is when they develop their drafts into more precise compositions that reflect sharp awareness of the rhetorical situation—the subject matter, purpose, and audience. Revision may occur at any stage during the process. For example, sentences and paragraphs may be reworked as it becomes clearer to the writer how readers will receive them or what they will expect. Revision often involves discovering what you really mean once you see what you've written, then returning to your writing to make it better.

Editing

Many writers edit their work as they go, but they also spend concentrated time polishing their work. They clarify meaning and usage, punctuate and cite according to accepted guidelines, and double-check to make sure all components of an assignment have been addressed.

2f Considering Technology Needs

Sometimes your writing assignment will contain directions about the tools you need to use to research information, how to record and transmit it, and how to design it for readers. If effective use of technology is a critical component of your assignment, do you understand how to use the tools? For example, many assignments today include requirements that you present your writing visually, using presentation software or a website. Sometimes an assignment needs to be submitted to others for peer review by email or through a course management tool. Over time, you will learn to use these technologies efficiently and critically. When planning a project, you should consider well in advance any technology issues that are likely to come up as you develop and share your work.

For a list of topics addressed in Technology Toolboxes in the handbook, see the inside rear cover.

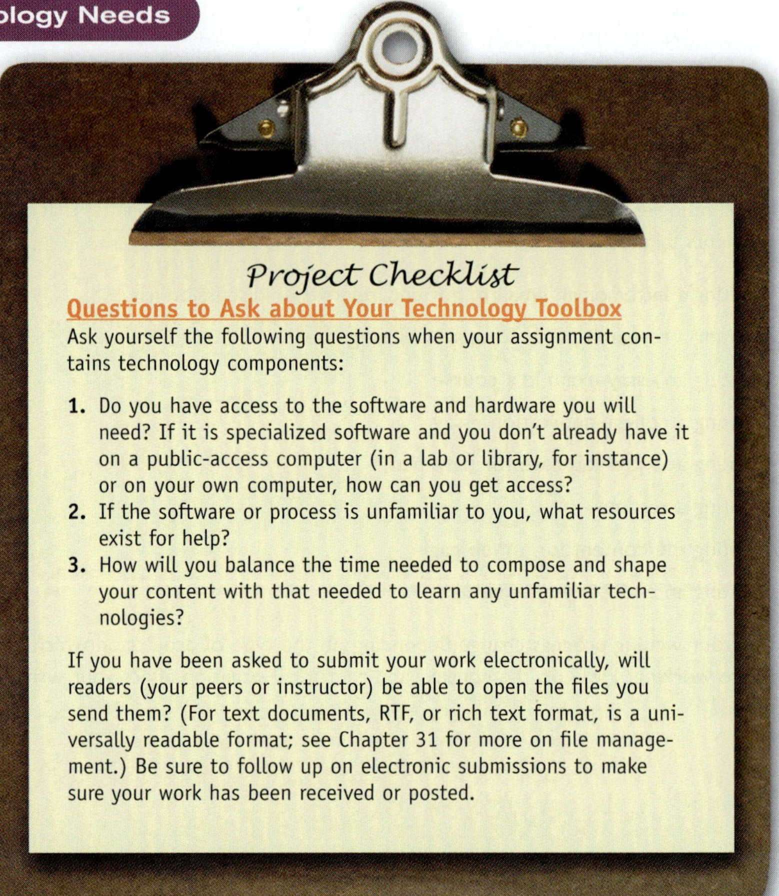

Project Checklist

Questions to Ask about Your Technology Toolbox

Ask yourself the following questions when your assignment contains technology components:

1. Do you have access to the software and hardware you will need? If it is specialized software and you don't already have it on a public-access computer (in a lab or library, for instance) or on your own computer, how can you get access?
2. If the software or process is unfamiliar to you, what resources exist for help?
3. How will you balance the time needed to compose and shape your content with that needed to learn any unfamiliar technologies?

If you have been asked to submit your work electronically, will readers (your peers or instructor) be able to open the files you send them? (For text documents, RTF, or rich text format, is a universally readable format; see Chapter 31 for more on file management.) Be sure to follow up on electronic submissions to make sure your work has been received or posted.

Activity 2-4: Researching Technology Resources

Create a two-column grid on a piece of paper. On the left, list the hardware (computers, printers, scanners) and software (Web browsers, word processing software, Web authoring tools) you expect you might need for writing and researching. On the right, list places you can gain access to each technology (on campus, on the Internet). Compare your lists in a group, and draft a master list of resources to share with the class.

Project Planning Software

Email programs, word processors, and weblogs often include tools that you can use to plan important steps in a project, keep the tasks of individual group members organized and on track, and take notes as you go. In Microsoft® Outlook®, for example, you can use the Task Manager and Calendar to schedule meetings and other steps in a project, even generating automatic reminders. You can also share these calendars and task lists with group members. You can create customized tables in your word processor to add notes, due dates, and other important project information. Learning to use tools like these early in your college career can be a great timesaver.

Month/Year

Sunday	Monday	Tuesday	Wednesday	Thursday	Friday	Saturday
				Month and Day Assignment received and discussed in class.	Month and Day Review assignment and analyze it for task-related verbs.	Month and Day Create a list of 5 possible topics.
Month and Day	Month and Day Narrow list of topics to 1 and write a short paragraph explaining my reasoning.	Month and Day Submit topic proposal to instructor.	Month and Day Begin researching topic in 1) library; 2) online. Check any key terms in the *Oxford English Dictionary*.	Month and Day Get feedback in class from peers regarding choice of topic. Ask for advice about how to elaborate the topic. Also, what interests them about my topic?	Month and Day Categorize notes and begin planning draft 1.	Month and Day
Month and Day	Month and Day Complete draft 1.	Month and Day Peer review. Visit writing center to get feedback on draft.	Month and Day Revise draft and then save time for copyediting.	Month and Day Submit the project to the instructor. Check to make sure the format of the document is correct, that I include all required steps, and that it has submission notes (if required).	Month and Day	

This is a five-row, seven-column table created in a word processor for use as a three-week planning calendar. Once you have the table set up, you can save it as a document template for use in later projects. (Select Save As and then choose "template" (or the equivalent) in the Save as Type drop-down box.)

The ability to work and write with others is one of the most important skills to develop if you want to participate successfully in academic, civic, and professional contexts. Group writing projects are often more complex than those assigned to individuals, so the group will need to analyze the assignment carefully and then decide how to proceed. Ultimately, everyone bears responsibility to contribute actively to the team, and you should volunteer if there's ever a feeling that you're not doing enough to help or to be evaluated fairly by your instructor.

Some teams elect group leaders, or they rotate the job of project leader. To stay organized, it's helpful to have a recorder for each group meeting to take notes on important decisions and then summarize them for the others. Rotate the role of recorder among group members as the project progresses.

Project responsibilities need to be defined and a schedule set up, with due dates for each important step toward the final draft. Plan to have a group meeting at least once before each major step or draft is supposed to be completed. Group meetings should be devoted to planning, not production. Take the time to discuss individual roles and tasks and manage other group activities. (See also section 32c.)

2h A Student Shapes Her Writing to Suit the Assignment

Gina Wolf, author of the autobiographical narrative "Still Guarding the Fort," reprinted in Chapter 6 (pages 114–117), repurposed her letter to a friend from high school when she responded to an assignment for her Composition 101 class.

Gina already knew that she wanted to write her essay about her friend Jamie (page 14), so she needed to consider how she could add details that would help a reader not familiar with the fort understand its significance for the two girls. She had to dramatize some scenes to help her reader see the nature of their relationship. To help the reader understand why the experiences with Jamie were meaningful, she wrote an ending that showed how the loss of their imaginary world had meant the loss of their innocence, but not Gina's need to care for her friend. A letter of reminiscence became a reflective essay on friendship, loss, and responsibility in which Gina's readers experience the events of the narrative.

Composition 101 Assignment

Write an autobiographical essay about a significant event or person in your life. Choose the event or person with your readers in mind. The subject should be one that you feel comfortable presenting to others and that will lead readers to reflect on their own lives or on the difference between their personal experiences and your own. Present your experience dramatically and vividly so that readers can imagine what it was like for you. Through careful choice of words and details, convey the meaning and importance in your life—the autobiographical significance—of this event or person.

Questions to Think about for 101 Essay

—Why was Jamie so important to me?

—How did all the experiences that Jamie and I shared at the Fort affect me (aside from just the fun of it all)?

—What kinds of details will help readers understand the Fort and our time there?

—What was my relationship with Jamie? What was it later?

—What events from those years could I show readers to help them understand our relationship?

A table of contents for writing project threads appears on pages xv–xxii.

Critical Reviews

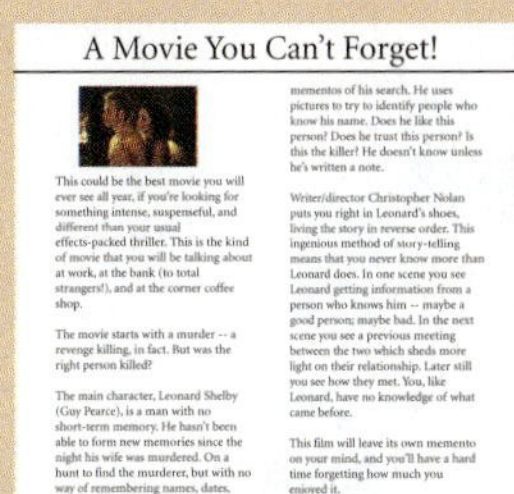

A Movie You Can't Forget!

This could be the best movie you will ever see all year, if you're looking for something intense, suspenseful, and different than your usual effects-packed thriller. This is the kind of movie that you will be talking about at work, at the bank (to total strangers!), and at the corner coffee shop.

The movie starts with a murder -- a revenge killing, in fact. But was the right person killed?

The main character, Leonard Shelby (Guy Pearce), is a man with no short-term memory. He hasn't been able to form new memories since the night his wife was murdered. On a hunt to find the murderer, but with no way of remembering names, dates, places, facts and faces, he tattoos mementos of his search. He uses pictures to try to identify people who know his name. Does he like this person? Does he trust this person? Is this the killer? He doesn't know unless he's written a note.

Writer/director Christopher Nolan puts you right in Leonard's shoes, living the story in reverse order. This ingenious method of story-telling means that you never know more than Leonard does. In one scene you see Leonard getting information from a person who knows him -- maybe a good person; maybe bad. In the next scene you see a previous meeting between the two which sheds more light on their relationship. Later still you see how they met. You, like Leonard, have no knowledge of what came before.

This film will leave its own memento on your mind, and you'll have a hard time forgetting how much you enjoyed it.

Subject, Purpose, Audience

As you've seen in your genre analysis, reviews can take many different forms, depending on the review's subject, purpose, and audience. For example, to help them decide what movie to see, many people read short blurb reviews in the paper before heading out to the theater. On the other hand, people who enjoy discussing films would want to read a longer, more in-depth review in a magazine or on a website.

Work through the Project Checklist on page 20 to help you consider the rhetorical situation for your review. Pay special attention to the purpose of your review (Why are you writing it?) and the audience (Who are your readers? Why would they read your review? What do you think that they would want to know?). ▶ page 151.

Photographic Essays

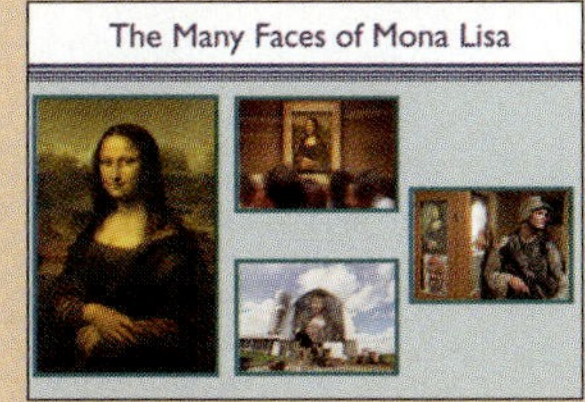

Investigating Your Purpose and Methods

A photographic essay includes images taken (or sometimes found) by the writer as well as explanatory or connecting text. It might take the form of photos and words printed on paper, digital work in Flash or another animation program, or a website. Any of these media can provide a forum for sharing information, narrating a story, or persuading readers to change their opinions or enact a solution to a problem.

Make sure that you understand your instructor's criteria for the assignment. Within those guidelines, consider how adding visuals to a text changes the methods you can use to explain an idea, tell a story, or persuade readers. What new questions do you need to ask or what new decisions do you need to make in order to take best advantage of the visual dimension? What kinds of images have you seen—in magazines, on TV, in video games, in advertisements, in photo albums, on CD covers—that were effective in provoking learning, grabbing attention, or changing your behaviors? ▶ page 190.

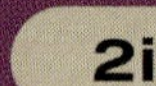

Brochures

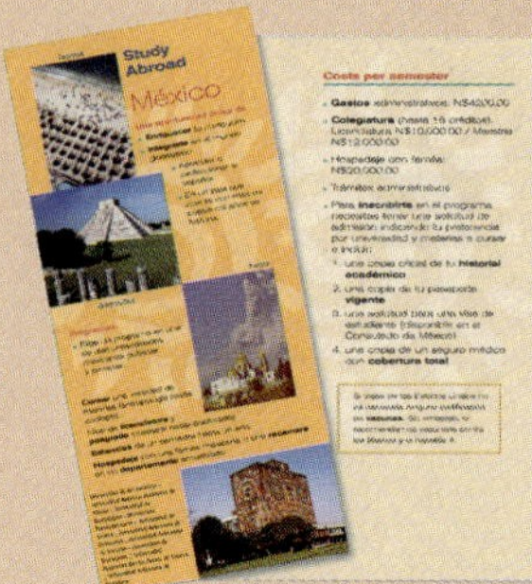

Analyzing Sample Brochures

A brochure is a specific genre of writing. To understand the generic features of a brochure, you can analyze some samples and see what they have in common. Acquire some sample brochures from various contexts. Make sure to include brochures that are similar in terms of rhetorical situation to the brochure you will be creating. Make a list of their similarities and differences in terms of how they

- address their audience
- work within their described context
- present information using text and images
- condense information to fit into a limited amount of space

How will your brochure be similar to and different from the sample brochures you have collected? page 287.

3 INVENTION AND INQUIRY

Writing is an act of discovery and elaboration. Ideas don't often spring, fully developed, from a writer's mind, to be written down in a flurry of genius. Sometimes great or interesting ideas will pop into your head when you least expect them. At other times, they won't be anywhere you can find them, at least not when you look inward. We know from experience, however, that writers can follow some principles that, used systematically, can help nurture ideas by capturing the depth and texture of experience and knowledge. In this chapter, you will learn strategies for inventing and shaping ideas for your writing.

Experience also tells us that writing usually doesn't happen in neat stages or in one-two-three fashion. Instead, it unfolds in stops and starts and turns back on itself, at various times rushing forward furiously (when the moment is right), plodding along painfully, and not moving at all (when procrastination takes over). We know that writing begins somehow, and that experienced writers follow some general principles that help them get from beginning to end more or less successfully and consistently, in a series of stages that have identifiable characteristics. There is, in other words, a writing process. Writers can take deliberate steps to understand stages of the writing process and to learn how to work the process in order to be successful as a writer more often than not. Invention is the stage that is the subject of this chapter. In Chapters 4 through 6, you will find strategies for drafting, developing, and elaborating paragraphs (the smaller units of a larger whole), reviewing and revising your work on your own and with others, and editing and proofreading.

Invention is a richly rewarding aspect of writing that involves discovering, creating, and elaborating ideas. It is a form of inquiry, an art, that usually takes center stage early in the writing process and may also influence how content is shaped and revised later. In the writing process, invention has three facets:

1. *Discovering* what you and others already know about a subject and how you and they feel about it. Writers need to understand what they already know, which is not as easy as it sounds. Sometimes you aren't sure what you think until you see what you say. If you are writing to readers, you also need to have some idea of what they bring to your text.
2. *Creating* new ideas and describing new relationships among existing ideas. So much has already been written and researched that it may seem challenging to come up with entirely new ideas, but because you have a unique set of experiences, you can find ways to add new ingredients to existing knowledge in order to flavor it in new ways.
3. *Elaborating* and developing what you and others know about a subject by connecting it with other subjects, analyzing a subject's parts and how they are related to one another, showing how the subject changes in different contexts, and finding examples that bring ideas to life.

In some respects, the craft of invention acts like a prism or diamond, which refracts white light (a mixture of all colors) into its component parts. As a writer, you observe the world as a unity. To see all of its colors, you need to interact with it, turning the diamond this way and that. *Heuristics,* a term from Greek meaning "discovery," are methods of invention that guide this interaction.

Project Checklist

Heuristics for a Narrative Essay

Asking questions is an effective way to start developing content for a piece of writing. The questions here could be used to get started on writing a narrative essay, for example, about a life-changing event or an influential person in your life.

Discover

1. What specific details do you remember?
2. What have others said or written about the event or person, in personal accounts, newspapers, blogs, or other forums?
3. How have other writers written about similar subjects?

Create

4. What made the event or person unique, unusual, or profound?
5. How did the event or person affect you? Why? Is there something unique in your experience that made the timing just right?

Elaborate

6. Can you make a point about the event and then find examples that will help readers appreciate its impact?
7. Why does this event or person stand out from all the rest? What difference has this event or person made for your life in the present? What can you point to in your life that shows this change?

Gina Wolf on Sitting in a Lawn Chair, Looking at Photos, and Reading Old Journal Entries

Gina Wolf, author of the autobiographical narrative "Still Guarding the Fort" in Chapter 6 (▶ pages 114–117), drew from her memories of the fort and her friend Jamie to re-create important scenes, images, and details for her readers. Here is how she described her process of stepping from images and journal entries to the wider significance of her story.

When I decided that I was going to go away for college, I began to realize towards the end of my senior year how much my time spent on the farm meant to me, particularly the time in the Fort—a feeling of simple clarity and happiness. It didn't even cross my mind that Jamie would look upon that portion of her childhood with such fondness until she told me "You know, the only time I've ever been truly happy was in the Fort." Even then, I couldn't really remember what we all did out there or why it was so precious to me until I ran across the few entries that we made in the Fort Diary. The entries aren't very long or very detailed, but something struck me with importance and urgency. So, a senior, I went out and sat in the pink lawn chair with that Diary and just tried to listen and hear the World that we had created and abandoned. Much like when I realized for the first time that none of it was real, only silence answered. However, my memory did me justice by allowing me to glimpse small images of what our childhood was consumed by through the Diary and by sitting quietly and willing myself to remember.

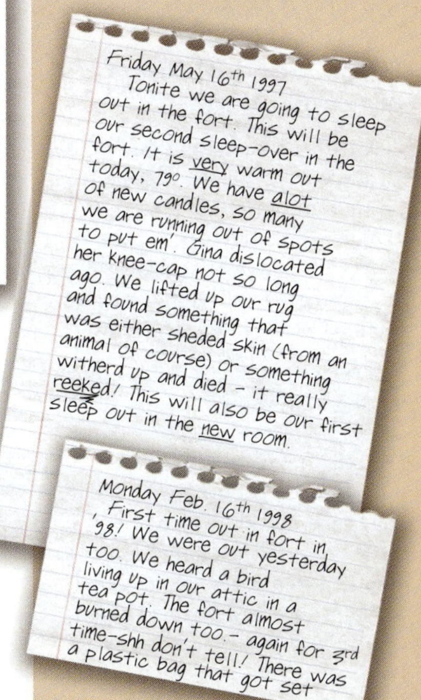

Friday May 16th 1997
Tonite we are going to sleep out in the fort. This will be our second sleep-over in the fort. It is very warm out today, 79°. We have alot of new candles, so many we are running out of spots to put em'. Gina dislocated her knee-cap not so long ago. We lifted up our rug and found something that was either sheded skin (from an animal of course) or something witherd up and died – it really reeked! This will also be our first sleep out in the new room.

Monday Feb. 16th 1998
First time out in fort in '98! We were out yesterday too. We heard a bird living up in our attic in a tea pot. The fort almost burned down too.– again for 3rd time–shh don't tell! There was a plastic bag that got set

Photographs help us recollect the past and reinvent the people, places, and events they portray. Music and even scents can have a similar effect on invention.

When you need to discover what you know, generate new ideas and relationships, or decide on a way to frame your perspective on a general subject, you can practice *freewriting,* a popular method of getting ideas down on paper or on screen. Although freewriting is free in the sense that it liberates you to invent ideas and take inventory of what you know without risk, there are some strategies that help make it work.

Three General Rules of Freewriting

1. Give your full attention, focus, and energy for the short amount of time you write (usually 5–15 minutes).
2. Write quickly without rushing.
3. Never stop for long to correct, think of the exact word, etc.

Freewriting helps because during the time you write, you turn off the editor or monitor in your head that tends to censor everything you say or write. You deliberately turn off, in other words, all those questions and doubts about whether your ideas are any good, are in proper grammatical form, and so on. Often when we write we are so afraid of making mistakes that we reject many potentially good ideas. We also edit unacceptable thoughts and feelings, as we

Freewriting on the Computer

Freewriting can be especially fun on a computer because if you're a good typist, you can (perhaps) keep up with the flow of your thoughts.

1. Open a new word processing document. Write your initial topic at the top, skip a space, and then position your cursor as if you were about to write as usual.
2. Turn off your monitor (not the computer itself) so that it doesn't display anything. Start your freewriting session.
3. After ten minutes or so, turn your monitor back on to read what you wrote.
4. Save your freewriting as a file if you want to keep it.

How did freewriting on your computer with the monitor turned off feel different from freewriting on paper? Was it difficult? Successful?

Activity 3-1: Focused Freewriting

Following the guidelines for freewriting, practice some focused freewriting.

1. Start with a topic.
2. With your topic in mind, freewrite for ten minutes or so. When finished, reread your meanderings, tracing the development of your thoughts, and underline, circle, or highlight any interesting or surprising phrases or ideas.
3. After exploring the connections and pathways in your first session, start a freewriting that focuses on an idea, scene, or event that began to emerge in your first session. You may want to choose one particularly surprising statement in your first session to begin your second. Write that topic down, and then focus your next freewriting session on it.
4. After you have done three or four of these sessions, perhaps spaced out over a day or two, freewrite a paragraph describing what it feels like to freewrite. (In thinking about this process, you make it familiar and habitual.)

A Sample of Focused Freewriting

Angela used freewriting as she searched for a way to focus her paper on an important event. The annotations are her notes as she went from session to session.

Session 1 Topic: Important Event

Write for 5 minutes she says. On an important event . . . (for me) . . . let's see. It's easy for me to remember how much fun I had playing games with my brother, Andy, when I was little. These were not one important event but a series of them over time that feel important now. I was lots younger than ~~Andy, 8 years~~ younger, and he ~~is smart.~~ So most of the time he'd clean my clock at Risk, Monopoly, or even Pac-Man when we played video games. He taught me how to play "by the rules" even if they were sometimes his rules. Ha ha. I just remember these being fun times and I even forget some of the details about which games we played. Maybe I'll email him to find out what he remembers.

war game

Session 2: Why are games fun?

This is a hard question to answer. They just are. Well maybe not all of them are. I remember how awful it feels to lose, especially when someone rubs it in. I can understand losing and can take it as long as I can say ~~I tried my best~~ or it was luck on their part. It's fun to play video games with yourself when you can solve them without pulling your hair out or when they take your hair out. (I like The Sims because of how unexpected things get.) Even when I played with Andy though I had the most fun just hangin out with him. It didn't matter what game we played. So it was social. I haven't tried online gaming yet, but maybe that's why people like it.

What was I thinking there?!

Session 3: Games as social engagement

This is getting deeper but I had the thought that playing games taught me to enjoy dealing with other people and (hehe) even how to fake them out or trick them into thinking they knew better. There are "rules of engagement" that you can bend to your will, but you have to be careful that you don't bend them too far or else no one will play with you again and being social will be impossible, which gives me an idea for how to organize my essay around the title "Rules of Engagement." I think that's a phrase from a movie or something, so I will have to look it up. I think it's also something from the military. Maybe there's a link here about games and war, even, and about playing by the rules or something.

social rules?

Could this be my thesis or main point?

do in speaking in public. Freewriting can help you develop a writer's voice, an important source of power in writing. Freewriting helps you find the sound, texture, and rhythm of your thoughts.

Some of your freewriting will probably be garbage. That's okay. Everyone writes garbage once in a while. But you'll also find some good writing lurking among those canned ideas. There will be moments when your writing will mysteriously become more coherent and thoughtful than you could have imagined. You'll produce words that seem to grow organically out of a thought, feeling, or perception. Your words will be permeated by meaning, blended more finely because you didn't let the editor in you take over.

Focused Freewriting

Once you have gotten some thoughts on paper by freewriting, you can go back and examine what you wrote to look for ideas to use as seeds for your next freewriting session. This method, which is shown in Angela's writing, allows thoughts to percolate and evolve.

When you brainstorm, the goal is to come up with as many ideas as possible in a short time, with little or no concern for putting these ideas into sentences. The point is to come up with lists, words, images, drawings, or anything else related to your subject. You can start by writing your possible subject at the top of a sheet of paper or word processing document. Then generate as many different ideas as you can. Your lists may consist of various perspectives on the subject: How would other people, especially people who might not agree with your interpretations and ideas, approach it? Or you may list different ways of phrasing and therefore thinking about your subject. Jot down as many different aspects of the subject as you can. You can also brainstorm lists of questions you have about your subject.

Group Brainstorming

Early in a collaborative project of any kind, it is helpful for all members of a group to contribute thoughts and ideas without worrying too much about whether they will pan out into something useful or profound later on. Or if you and your peers are responding individually to the same assignment, you may be able to brainstorm about possible approaches.

Activity 3-2: Generating Alternatives with Group Brainstorming

1. With a group, decide on a subject and write it on a whiteboard or chalkboard. You may find it helpful to consider the subject as a noun—a "thing."
2. Break the subject into parts or features. What are its main components or features? Write these main features across the top of the board.
3. Under each feature, list any alternatives that come to mind, as your group members shout out possibilities.
4. Once you have generated a list under each feature, choose one word/feature in each column to circle, and then draw a line connecting the circles.
5. As a group, discuss how the subject changes when you think of its key features in this way.

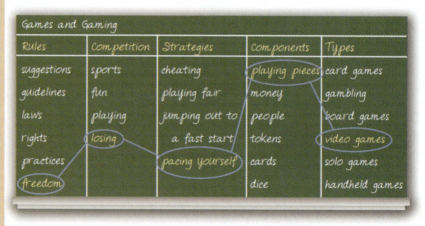

Games and Gaming

Rules	Competition	Strategies	Components	Types
suggestions	sports	cheating	playing pieces	card games
guidelines	fun	playing fair	money	gambling
laws	playing	jumping out to a fast start	people	board games
rights	losing	pacing yourself	tokens	video games
practices			cards	solo games
freedom			dice	handheld games

What happens when you think of games in the terms highlighted? What would a game be like if there were no rules? If the object were to lose? What if the only way to win were to pace yourself? Or to create your own pieces? Can you think of any games like that? Can you create one? Would it be fun?

Activity 3-3: Writing Dialogue to Represent Multiple Perspectives

Choose an issue that is unsettled or open-ended or a question that lends itself to alternative viewpoints. Create a written dialogue that represents a conversation among characters who take different views of the issue. To help you generate full and useful points of view, follow these guidelines:

- Create at least four voices, each one with a different perspective on the issue.
- Write a full description of each character/voice at the beginning of the dialogue, one that explains the character's position on the issue or conveys important biographical information.
- Each character speaks at least twice, for at least 100 words at each turn. That means there shouldn't be any throwaway lines like "Sounds good to me."
- No one "wins"; no point of view seems inherently better than the rest or more persuasive.
- No one makes silly statements that seem to violate the position taken previously.

When you compose multiple viewpoints on a subject, you are practicing the rhetorician's art of exploring the many sides of an issue—the heart of rhetorical invention.

You might scare your friends and family if you start talking to yourself, but the benefits may be worth it, given how easily you can develop a subject by speaking and writing freely about it to yourself. You can take debating with yourself one step further by actually acting out different points of view to try to understand what perspectives readers may bring to a subject. You can role-play members of your audience or different perspectives on an issue. As you develop a more nuanced idea about the people and perspectives involved in the debate, take into account the various personal agendas readers might bring to the subject, as well as their ages, sexual orientations, genders, ethnicities, and socioeconomic classes.

However, be careful not to overgeneralize (or rely on stereotypes) about your audience based just on their backgrounds. Role-playing is only a starting point for a project. As you read and research your subject, you'll begin to discover the wide range of responses your subject provokes.

Clustering is a method of developing a visual landscape of your ideas and how they break into categories and subcategories, without the pressure to get everything perfectly in place at the start. To create a cluster of ideas, write your idea or subject in the center of a sheet of paper, circle it, and then see if you can think of three or four subcategories of this larger subject. Write those in their own circles, with connecting lines to the center. Each subcategory may also divide into even narrower subjects. As you think of ideas, you will begin to generate more details and may see more readily where to place them, since you have a visual map before you that can be taken in at a glance.

Search Engine Clustering

New developments in the visual representation of data provide some useful models for imagining how topics and subtopics may be connected. The KartOO search engine (http://www.kartoo.com) will visually represent the results of an Internet search so that you can see how elements of your topic may be related. Enter a term related to your topic and not only will you see that topic represented visually on a clickable map, but you will also see subtopics that may give you research leads for further invention and elaboration.

Sample Cluster on How Self-Image Is Manipulated by Various Media

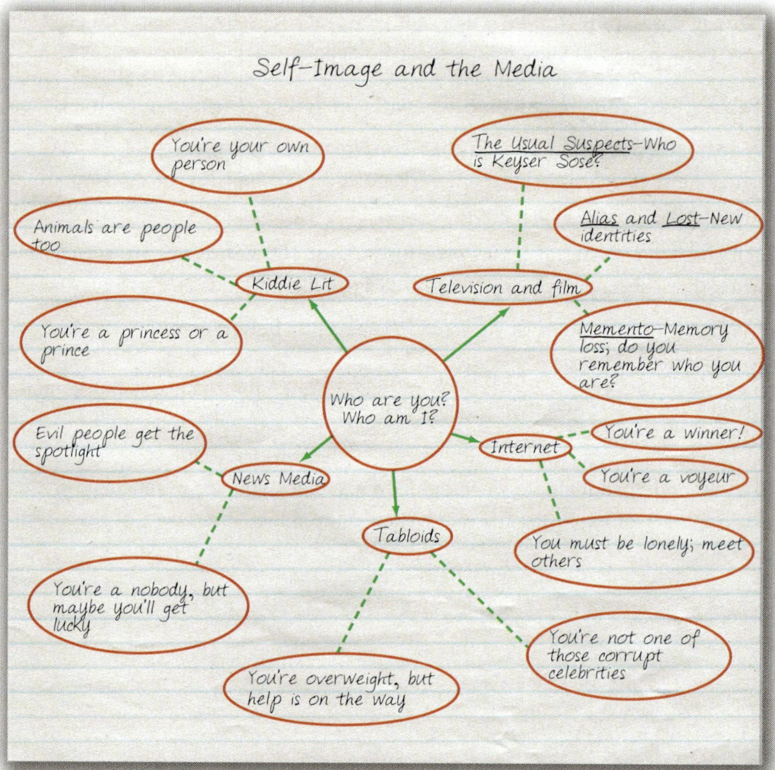

Here is some invention clustering on the topic of how self-image is manipulated by various media. Notice that each subcategory could also be expanded further. Any one circled item could itself become the center of a new cluster as well.

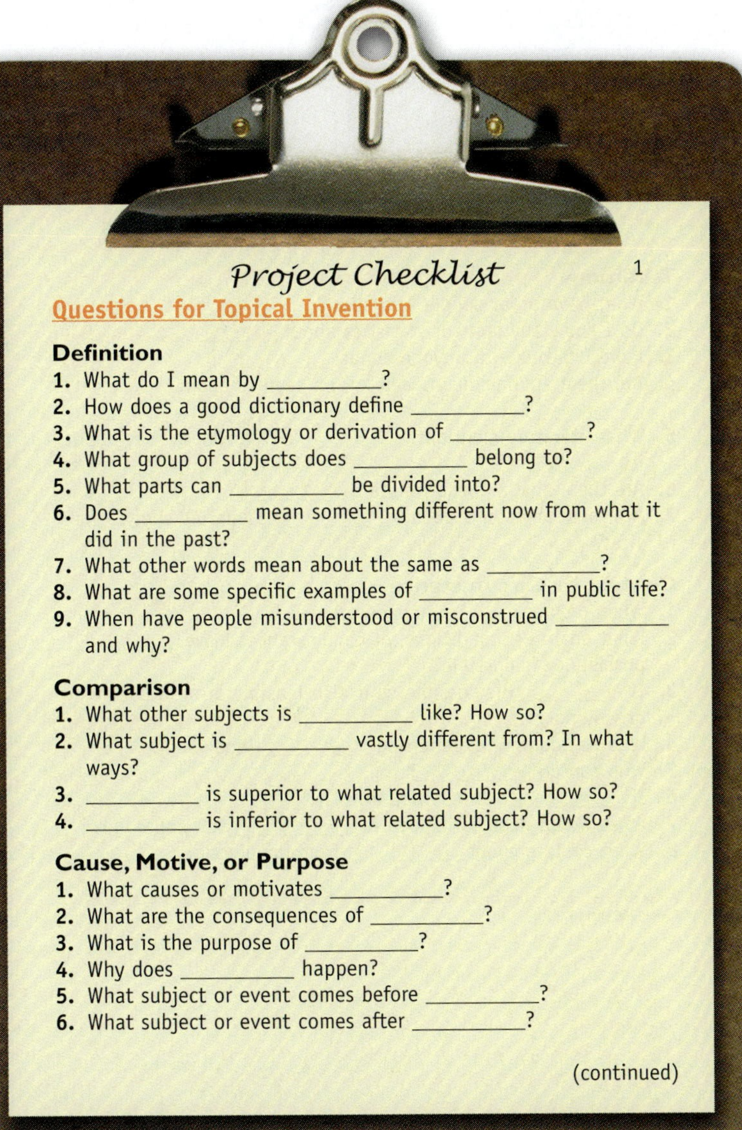

Project Checklist 1

Questions for Topical Invention

Definition

1. What do I mean by __________?
2. How does a good dictionary define __________?
3. What is the etymology or derivation of __________?
4. What group of subjects does __________ belong to?
5. What parts can __________ be divided into?
6. Does __________ mean something different now from what it did in the past?
7. What other words mean about the same as __________?
8. What are some specific examples of __________ in public life?
9. When have people misunderstood or misconstrued __________ and why?

Comparison

1. What other subjects is __________ like? How so?
2. What subject is __________ vastly different from? In what ways?
3. __________ is superior to what related subject? How so?
4. __________ is inferior to what related subject? How so?

Cause, Motive, or Purpose

1. What causes or motivates __________?
2. What are the consequences of __________?
3. What is the purpose of __________?
4. Why does __________ happen?
5. What subject or event comes before __________?
6. What subject or event comes after __________?

(continued)

Likely the oldest method of rhetorical invention, topical invention comes from classical rhetoricians and logicians such as Aristotle, Cicero, and Boethius. Aristotle, for example, listed 28 common topics (or *topoi*) when discussing how ideas can relate to one another or to their context.

For the purposes of inventing and elaborating content, it is helpful to divide these topics into basic categories that arise when you ask about what a subject means (definition), how it relates and compares with other subjects (comparison), what it results from or causes (cause, motive, or purpose), what people say about it (testimony), and where and when it has meaning (context or circumstances).

Under each category in the Project Checklist, you see questions that come to mind, with blanks inviting you to plug in your subject. If you answer these questions with a few sentences or more, you will have collected a broad range of information about your topic that could be used in an essay or project.

Topical Invention for Narrowing a Subject

You can also use the questions for topical invention in reverse. Instead of using them to elaborate a subject, you can use them to narrow a subject that is too broad for the length of the project you are producing or the amount of time you have to write. Once you have explored your responses to some or all of the categories of questions, select one to consider in more detail. Responses to any one of the categories will supply plenty of options for narrower subjects.

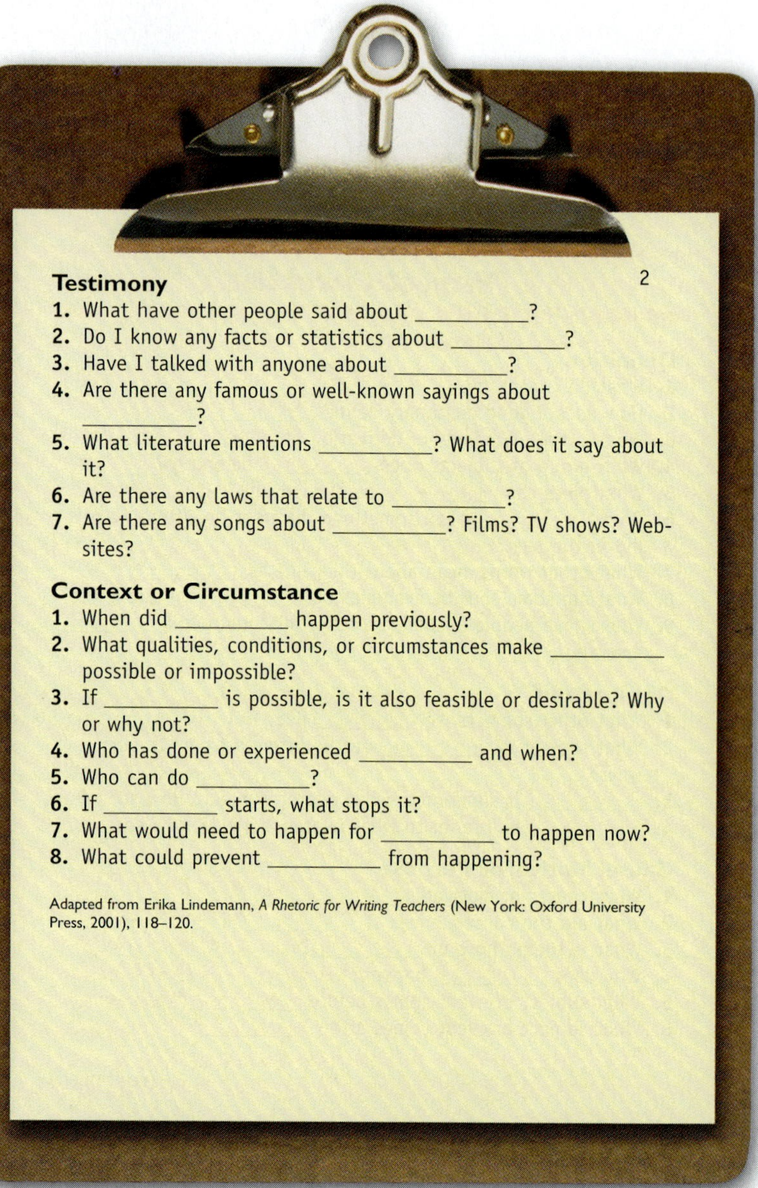

2

Testimony

1. What have other people said about __________?
2. Do I know any facts or statistics about __________?
3. Have I talked with anyone about __________?
4. Are there any famous or well-known sayings about __________?
5. What literature mentions __________? What does it say about it?
6. Are there any laws that relate to __________?
7. Are there any songs about __________? Films? TV shows? Web-sites?

Context or Circumstance

1. When did __________ happen previously?
2. What qualities, conditions, or circumstances make __________ possible or impossible?
3. If __________ is possible, is it also feasible or desirable? Why or why not?
4. Who has done or experienced __________ and when?
5. Who can do __________?
6. If __________ starts, what stops it?
7. What would need to happen for __________ to happen now?
8. What could prevent __________ from happening?

Adapted from Erika Lindemann, *A Rhetoric for Writing Teachers* (New York: Oxford University Press, 2001), 118–120.

You Might Know Jack, but You're Not Sure . . .

Suppose you realize that you're interested in focusing on how television can sometimes fool people into thinking that what they see on screen is "real." You recall hearing the story about how radio listeners once thought that a dramatization of H. G. Wells's *The War of the Worlds* was a news broadcast of a real alien invasion. But that's about all you remember. What can you do?

You decide to look up the film *The War of the Worlds,* using the A9 search tool, **http://www.a9.com**, and see what you can find. With a few clicks in the right places, you can hear the original radio broadcast and read the headlines from news organizations. One thing leads to another, and suddenly what once was an inkling can serve as a well-researched example for your essay on realism in television programs.

Top: Complete War of the Worlds Website, http://www.war-of-the-worlds.org. Center and bottom: http://www.waroftheworlds.org.

One of the great benefits of systematic invention is that it will give you a good idea of what you need to know more about if you hope to cover your subject with the attention it deserves. It can be a humbling experience to discover that you don't know as much as you thought you did. Take heart. The first step in learning is to be aware of your own ignorance.

Take the invitations to conduct research prompted by your invention. When you don't know something but it seems clear that you need to know it, go to the library, talk to people who might know more than you do, or visit one of the useful resources on the Internet. Encyclopedias and dictionaries are good places to start because they will point you in new directions. Online communities and collaborative knowledge bases—like Wikipedia (http://www.wikipedia.com) or the Internet Movie Database (http://www.imdb.com)—can be resources as well. Use the guidelines for conducting online and library research discussed in Chapters 15 and 16 to track down what you need to know.

A table of contents for writing project threads appears on pages xv–xxii.

Personal Essays

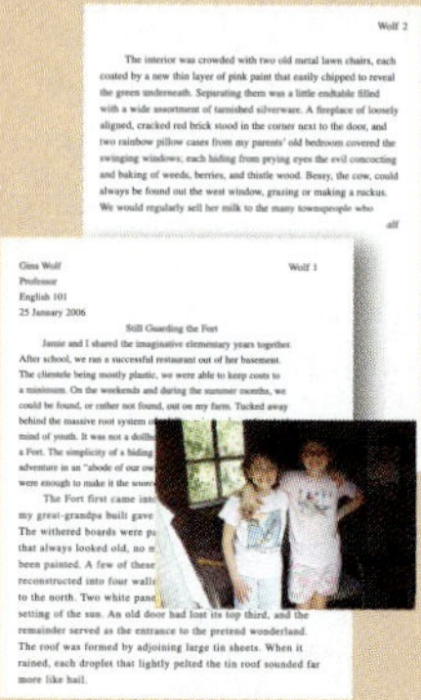

Wolf 2

The interior was crowded with two old metal lawn chairs, each coated by a new thin layer of pink paint that easily chipped to reveal the green underneath. Separating them was a little endtable filled with a wide assortment of tarnished silverware. A fireplace of loosely aligned, cracked red brick stood in the corner next to the door, and two rainbow pillow cases from my parents' old bedroom covered the swinging windows; each hiding from prying eyes the evil concocting and baking of weeds, berries, and thistle wood. Bessy, the cow, could always be found out the west window, grazing or making a ruckus. We would regularly sell her milk to the many townspeople who

all

Gina Wolf

Professor

English 101

25 January 2006

Wolf 1

Still Guarding the Fort

Jamie and I shared the imaginative elementary years together. After school, we ran a successful restaurant out of her basement. The clientele being mostly plastic, we were able to keep costs to a minimum. On the weekends and during the summer months, we could be found, or rather not found, out on my farm. Tucked away behind the massive root system o
mind of youth. It was not a dollh
a Fort. The simplicity of a hiding
adventure in an "abode of our ow
were enough to make it the sourc

The Fort first came int
my great-grandpa built gave
The withered boards were p
that always looked old, no m
been painted. A few of these
reconstructed into four walls
to the north. Two white pane
setting of the sun. An old door had lost its top third, and the remainder served as the entrance to the pretend wonderland. The roof was formed by adjoining large tin sheets. When it rained, each droplet that lightly pelted the tin roof sounded far more like hail.

Finding Out about You

Writing a personal essay can give you a reason and a method for exploring your attitudes and beliefs and for making meaning from your experiences. The process can also help you connect with others through sharing stories about your life. More publicly, personal essays are often published in magazines, on websites, and in anthologies. Many people now share their life stories online through personal journals or blogs, both of which can be seen as extensions of the personal essay. If you already keep an online journal or a blog, consider using material from it as a source for a personal essay.

Use the strategies in this chapter (freewriting, clustering, topical invention, brainstorming) in conjunction with the following activities to help you generate ideas for a personal essay.

1. Draw your family tree (as far back as you would like to go). How does the family group you belong to affect who you are? Add descriptive words or notes about various family members by drawing clusters off of their names.
2. Collect some pictures of yourself. Freewrite for five minutes on each picture.
3. If you keep a journal, read over past journal entries. Do any entries inspire you to write more from a later perspective?
4. Make a list of adjectives and nouns that you feel best describe you. What do these words say about you? What patterns do you find? page 336.

Informative Essays

Garrison 1

Angela Garrison

English 101

Dr. Simpson

September 26, 2005

From Over There to Over Here:

War Blogs Get Up Close, Personal, and Profitable

Blog was the word looked up most often in the online *Merriam-Webster's Dictionary* in 2004 ("Blog"). What's all this fuss? When you read someone else's personal blog, you find out what they like and don't like, what they're doing, and maybe other bits of gossip offered at random. You can read news blogs to find out what's going on lately, what other people think about it, and why it matters. You can keep your own blog to share your thoughts and feelings, to tell your friends and family what you're up to, and sometimes to capture the interest of someone you've never met. When you read and write blogs, you join, or even create, a community. Blogs are also an efficient way to break news, spread rumors, and glorify causes. In short, blogs help people do what they've always done as social beings, just more quickly now, and from almost anywhere on Earth. Soldiers on the ground fighting in Iraq are writing blogs from the front lines. But a review is now under way at the Pentagon to "better understand the overall implications of blogging and other Internet communications in combat zones," according to John Hockenberry in his *Wired* article "The Blogs of War." The benefits of blogs written by U.S. soldiers in Iraq far outweigh the hypothetical risks of revealing sensitive or strategic information. Those benefits, however, aren't as obvious as they might seem.

In spite of what the imagery of smart bombs and predator drones might lead television viewers to believe, wars are fought by people, not just technology. Most blogs start out as efforts to stay in touch with family and friends, but they quickly turn into

Discovering Your Interests

Writers of informative essays seek to explain a concept or teach readers about a specific topic, often for a specific reason. Even when the writer knows a fair amount about the topic, research is typically needed at least to confirm the details. But more often, research—in the library, online, or in the field—is the basis of such an essay.

Your first task in writing an informative essay is to discover what you are interested in writing about. What more do *you* want to learn about your . . .

- major field of study?
- current or future career?
- hobby or interests?
- areas of expertise?
- concerns?

Or consider narrowing one of these general ideas:

- stories or urban legends that you have heard or read about
- old documents, photographs, or vinyl records that you've discovered
- local events, current or historical
- the history of a location or place
- fascinating people (inventors, travelers, artists, philanthropists, activists)
- how something you use is made (clothing, houses, cartoons, video games)

Try at least two of the invention strategies given in this chapter to help you generate ideas. You may want to work with a partner or some of your classmates to generate and talk over topics. ▶ page 286.

Brainstorming Possible Solutions

After you've chosen a problem, consider a variety of ways to solve it. Most problems have more than one solution. Use the clustering techniques in this chapter to help you think about possible solutions for your problem.

1. Write your definition of the problem in the center of a piece of paper. Draw a circle around it.
2. Draw lines out from the problem and write down a possible solution for the problem at the end of each line.
3. Add details to each solution by adding circles and lines to each solution cluster.

Show your cluster to a partner. Does she or he have any suggestions for additional solutions? ▶ page 287.

Proposal Arguments

Harrington 1

A Proposal to Clean Up Our Streets

Brochures

Making a Mockup

The layout of text and graphics is especially important in a brochure, since you have limited space. Therefore, it's important to keep layout in mind throughout the entire writing process, even at the invention stage.

Take a piece of paper the same size as your brochure (usually brochures are printed on $8\frac{1}{2}$" by 11" paper, but some brochures are printed on larger paper), fold it into thirds, and sketch a mock layout for the brochure. Or you can use a computer program to draw a mockup.

Draw boxes to show where text and graphics could go, and write a few descriptive words about each one. It's a good idea to draw several layouts and experiment with where and how you think important ideas (whether they're in text or images) should be placed. Show your sample design(s) to a partner and get some feedback on what he or she thinks would be most effective. ▶ page 68.

Email Letters to the Editor

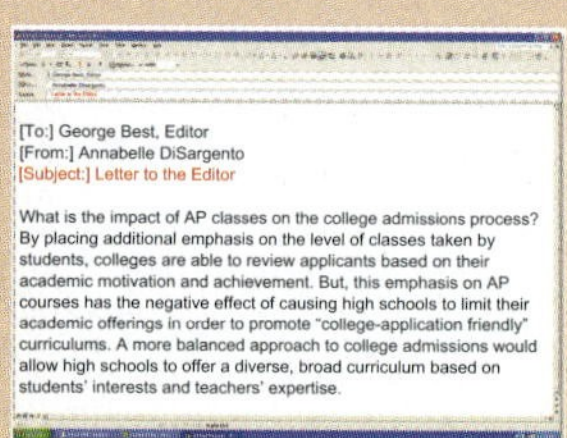
[To:] George Best, Editor
[From:] Annabelle DiSargento
[Subject:] Letter to the Editor

What is the impact of AP classes on the college admissions process? By placing additional emphasis on the level of classes taken by students, colleges are able to review applicants based on their academic motivation and achievement. But, this emphasis on AP courses has the negative effect of causing high schools to limit their academic offerings in order to promote "college-application friendly" curriculums. A more balanced approach to college admissions would allow high schools to offer a diverse, broad curriculum based on students' interests and teachers' expertise.

Considering Your Response

When you send a letter to the editor of a newspaper, magazine, or online publication, you're generally responding to an article, editorial, or letter that you read there. Or you may be writing to make people who read the publication aware of issues or problems. Why are you responding to this text? And why now? Use the Project Checklist on pages 39–40 to help you consider different aspects of your response. ▶ page 130.

4

DRAFTING AND SHAPING CONTENT

In the simplest terms, composition involves finding out what to write and then writing it. We see two ways to approach this challenge: (1) compose by chance, hoping that more often than not you will stumble upon a subject and happen to address it in a way that makes sense; or (2) compose deliberately, developing your writing process as a method and a craft so that it is effective repeatedly, not by chance, but because you know what you are doing. We believe it is better to be a habitually good writer than a lucky one.

Good writers make their own luck. They systematically create the circumstances that help them discover what they know or need to know (invention) and how to shape and develop their ideas (compose) to suit any situation (context, audience, purpose). In Chapters 1, 2, and 3, you learned how the rhetorical situation influences the circumstances of your writing and guides invention to help you appreciate the depth and complexity of your subject matter. In this chapter, and then in Chapters 5 and 6, we present strategies for developing and shaping content more precisely and on a broader scale.

Once you have generated some ideas about your subject, begin organizing your ideas into a draft. If your invention has been successful, you will probably have more ideas and content than you will ultimately use, so start drafting with the following goals in mind.

- **Limit the scope of your topic.** To limit scope, you can qualify your topic by putting it into some context, writing for a particular audience, or analyzing just one of its aspects.
- **Keep your main points in mind.** Once you've limited scope, break your subject matter into logical parts, and then draft paragraphs that touch on the main idea of each part.
- **Give each main point about the same amount of discussion.** Aim for balance so that no one part of your essay overshadows all the others and so that you cover your (well-focused) subject fully.

For example, . . .

Suppose your task is to write an essay about how a novel has been adapted into a film. It would be difficult to write a short, strong essay about "Adapting Novels into Film," which is a complex subject with many possible examples. Instead, you can limit scope by focusing on one particular adaptation of a novel into film. Better yet, you can focus on how one important scene in the novel is adapted to the screen. In the act of writing about this scene, you may also come to some general conclusions about adaptation in general.

For example, . . .

You could choose to examine how the film director focuses on a particular character in the scene from the film you're analyzing, comparing and contrasting that focus with the novelist's depiction of the character. In subsequent paragraphs, you could focus on how the casting of the character suits your understanding of the character in the novel. Or the focus might be on how the use of close-ups, lighting, or even music reveals aspects of the character that reflect or differ from the novelist's characterization. In each case, you discuss each point with an eye on how the adaptation compares to, contrasts with, or extends its source.

For example, . . .

You wouldn't want to spend most of your time writing about how the casting of the lead character in the film violated the meaning of the novel and then devote just a few sentences to other qualities of the adaptation. Instead, give each part its due. If one point is a complex or especially interesting one, you can give it more weight, as long as you don't neglect other key points.

Activity 4-1: Narrowing Your Topic

1. Write your topic at the top of a piece of paper.
2. Under your topic, make a list of specific questions that you have about different aspects of your topic.
3. Trade lists with a partner. Add the questions you have about your partner's topic to his or her list.
4. On your own list, circle the question that you would most like to answer in your essay. Use this question to guide the beginning of your research.

Characteristics of Effective Thesis Statements

They single out an aspect of the subject and define a position toward it.

> The American labor movement is in a mess, and the current leadership doesn't seem to have a clue what to do about it.
>
> From Linda Chavez, "Lack of Union in the Labor Movement."

They focus on the subject matter, not on the act or piece of writing.

> L (Revised to focus on the subject.)
>
> ~~*I am going to argue that*~~ ^language police are not as concerned about usage as they are consolidating power to control the words of others.

The following sentence just announces the subject of the essay without stating a position about it. It is an example of the shaky practice of "tellin' 'em what you're goin' to tell 'em" that won't hold much interest for the reader.

> *In the following essay, I discuss* the motives of language police.

Here it is revised to include the writer's claim about the subject:

> Language police are motivated by a desire to control the natural forces of change, which have always been resistant to organized or governmental control.

In its original context in ancient Greece and Rome, a *thesis* was a "lowering of the voice" and came to mean "the act of laying down" or "putting." In music, the thesis was the accented part of the musical measure, the downward movement that draws attention to itself quietly, without being overly strident. The meaning of *thesis* has evolved to include "claim" and "position." A thesis in writing is something to be proven, demonstrated, or advanced. Sometimes the thesis is called a *controlling idea* because it has a shaping influence on everything else, even when it is not explicitly present but only alluded to in other terms or demonstrated by example. Reflecting the earliest meaning of *thesis,* a thesis statement guides and directs the attention of readers.

While you are drafting your project, your thesis statement can also guide and direct your attention, helping you decide what is important to include and how best to arrange your ideas. You can expect your thesis to evolve along with the rest of your project. If your best ideas seem to be taking the project in an unexpected direction, don't hesitate to revise your thesis.

What Do Thesis Statements Do?

Thesis statements are concise expressions of a writing project's controlling idea or central argument, including both the subject and the writer's approach toward or claim about the subject.

- **An effective thesis statement singles out some aspect of a subject for attention and clearly defines your approach to it.** It says "Look at *this* rather than *that*" or "Think about *that* in *this* way."
- **An effective thesis statement focuses on the subject, not on the act of writing itself or the piece of writing.**

Avoid phrases like these:
My firm belief is that . . .
In this essay, I am going to . . .
I am going to discuss . . .
It seems to me . . .
I want to show that . . .

This "blueprint" could be a thesis if there were a claim about these aspects of culture:

> The essay below discusses the three aspects of culture—high-, middle-, and low-brow—and then explains how each affects class relationships.

How *are* class relationships affected?

> High-, middle-, and low-brow culture are concepts used by social critics who too easily dismiss class conflicts in American society as a sign of moral decline and who ignore the economic causes of the culture wars.

They raise expectations about what comes next.

> Copyright was once a means to guarantee artists a decent income. Aside from the question as to whether it ever actually functioned as such—most artists never made a penny from the copyright system—we have to admit that copyright serves an altogether different purpose in the contemporary world.
>
> From Joost Smiers and Marieke van Schijndel, "Imagine a World without Copyright."

With this thesis, Smiers and van Schijndel implicitly promise to explain what the purpose of copyright is now, as opposed to what it used to be. Sure enough, they go on to discuss how the entertainment industry has exploited copyright law for corporate gain.

> Peer-to-peer file sharing on the Internet has prompted some changes to copyright law that are unconstitutional and, sadly, supported by music-industry lobbyists who don't understand the positive benefits of word-of-mouth for offline sales of music.

This thesis makes several claims about peer-to-peer file sharing: that laws against it are unconstitutional, that it could increase offline music sales by stimulating chat, and that the music industry doesn't understand how word-of-mouth online can work to quickly generate the kind of buzz that sells CDs. Readers will expect to read reasons why changes to copyright law (for example, the Digital Millennium Copyright Act) are unconstitutional, how those changes affect file sharing, why sharing files is any different from sharing a book, and what evidence exists that online chatter can increase desire for offline purchases.

They may share how a personal insight fits into a larger context.

> I learned from watching *Gilligan's Island* reruns that it's not so much the accomplishment of a common goal that has enduring value for the castaways, or any of us, but rather the act of overcoming catastrophe and hardship creatively and collaboratively.

This sentence shapes a narrative essay about "something learned from popular culture." It avoids being too explicitly argumentative. Instead, it describes an experience of watching a television show.

- **An effective thesis statement creates expectations.** Readers look for thesis statements and for topic sentences in paragraphs to help them understand the gist of a piece of writing. A good thesis statement arouses in readers expectations that help them predict what might come next. It creates an appetite, in other words, and keeps readers on the lookout for content that satisfies it.
- **An effective thesis statement may sum up or interpret a personal insight in a broader context.**

What Kinds of Projects Need a Thesis?

Most formal academic writing includes a thesis. In short interpretive or argumentative writing, the thesis often comes near the end of the first paragraph, where many readers will look for it by convention. Since short essays need to grab a reader's interest quickly, an early thesis statement is critical. Avoid thinking of your thesis as a hidden gem that you will only gradually reveal. Readers aren't that interested in critical essays written as if they were mystery novels.

In most situations in which thesis statements are not explicitly stated, both in college projects and in more public genres of writing, they still have their counterparts. An editorial in the newspaper will argue a point, often expressed in a headline. A narrative essay about a profound experience might tell of a lesson learned or of some subtle insight, without stating the point outright. An entry in a weblog might take a position on some subject in the news or (in the give-and-take of online dialogue) argue against another's position. A novel has a plot, which is not just a sequence of events, but some theme or insight that rises above the details and functions much like a thesis to organize or explain the events of the story.

Does the Project Need a Stated Thesis?

Probably Needs a Thesis	May Not Need a Thesis
Critical essays that interpret literature, film, art, social movements, political events, or other phenomena	*Informative essays* that cover a subject as fairly and as thoroughly as possible
Problem-posing or problem-solving essays that point to the presence of problems and/or means of solving them	*Reports* that record but do not interpret the results of fieldwork, lab research, or other studies
Research papers that report on a subject, cite sources, record and interpret data, and/or take a position on an issue	*Informal response writing* in a journal or on a weblog
Poster presentations that outline a perspective on an issue that lends itself to alternative viewpoints	*Websites* that function as portals or windows on a subject or organization
Narrative essays about a profound experience, important person, or social issue	

Activity 4-2: Which Writing Situations Call for a Thesis?

Discuss with a small group of peers which of the following writing situations seem to call for a thesis. Start by making your judgment individually; then share your responses. Which situations prompt the most disagreement? Why?

- Letter to the editor
- Email message to a parent or guardian asking for money
- Film review
- Poster for a club event
- Analysis of a molecular process
- Discussion of a scientific principle
- Discussion of a poem
- Description of the process of using some software
- Photographic essay
- Hypertext fiction
- Scholarship application letter

Activity 4-3: Creating Your Own Thesis

1. Think about the question you circled in Activity 4-1 and any research you have done to explore it. Draw a box on a piece of paper, and in it write a phrase or sentence that states your major claim or contention about the question.
2. Draw other boxes around, under, or beside the claim box to represent the reasons that support your claim or statement, and connect them to the claim box with lines. Write the various reasons and pieces of evidence that you will be using to support your claim in these boxes.
3. Examine your diagram, and write a sentence that encapsulates the claim and reasons that you have written down. Use this as your tentative thesis statement.

Sample Opening Paragraph

Creates connection with readers by acknowledging that recycling takes effort but is worth doing

Uses familiar categories of recyclable materials to help readers move from known information to new information

Introduces some new information about one category

Although it is not always easy, recycling offers many benefits, among them the peace of mind that comes from using resources wisely. Newspaper can be turned into pulp immediately, and pulp's uses are many. Glass too can be melted and reused immediately. The benefits of recycling some materials, though, might have to be put off for a little longer. Unfortunately, many kinds of plastics are expensive to recycle right now, and the current recycling methods for certain plastics generate almost as much pollution as creating plastic from scratch. However, reverting back to throwing away plastic products in overfilled landfills is not environmentally sound, either. Since there are so many recycling programs run by large corporations and municipal entities (like towns and cities), plastic does not have to be recycled right now.

States thesis, which readers are now prepared for

To be whole, any work needs a beginning, middle, and end. For that reason, it's helpful to think of a draft as having three sections—introduction, body, and conclusion—each of which performs a different function in giving a work its unity. All the parts of the whole should somehow explain, elaborate, or qualify the work's thesis.

The most important goals of an introduction are to spark your readers' curiosity about your subject and to provide them with sufficient background so that they can understand your thesis.

Suppose you have found through research that recycling certain plastics is too labor intensive to save resources. You want to persuade your readers that it makes better sense to store certain plastics than to try to recycle them now. In the future, when new technologies for their integration into recycling processes become available, the plastics can be recycled. How much background information will you need to give before you state your thesis?

You do not need to compose your introduction first just because it comes first in the final paper. Many experienced writers organize their body paragraphs before they begin writing an introduction. That way, they have a better sense of where they are headed and can write an introduction that effectively prepares the reader for what follows.

Consider these strategies for introducing your controlling idea.

- Startle your readers with an astounding piece of information or a distinctly unusual point of view designed to make them take notice.

- Provide a range of viewpoints that people have on the subject, and then reveal your own.

- Begin with a quotation that reveals an important aspect of your topic.

Sample Introductions

We are all being robbed, and most of us don't realize it. Today, 12.4 percent of every dollar we make is siphoned into a pyramid scheme called social security—from which our generation is unlikely to see much benefit.

From Hunter Williams, student at the University of Florida, "Prof Potpourri," *The Independent Florida Alligator Online* 18 Feb. 2004.

Higher education has changed dramatically due to the influence of the markets. In particular, the American system of higher education has become significantly competitive and this has reshaped institutions like Purdue. The intensity of this transformation has been addressed by authors like Stanley Aronowitz in *The Knowledge Factory* and Bill Readings in *The University in Ruins.* Terms in the titles of these books are somewhat alarming: "Knowledge Factory" suggests that universities have been reduced to mere vocational centers where little more than the training of future employees happens. "Ruins" implies that higher education is no longer valuable. It is true that market forces have changed the system of higher education, posing threats as Aronowitz and Readings argue, but they also create opportunities for improvement.

From Felipe Camacho, student at Purdue University, "The Market-Driven University."

"Every woman has a well-stocked arsenal of anger potentially useful against those oppressions, personal and institutional, which brought that anger into being." So writes Audre Lorde in a keynote presentation given at the National Women's Studies Association Conference. . . . It is this anger's applications in fighting for women's causes and particularly the responses that it draws from a patriarchal society that I believe are well worth examining in a critical light. From the women's lib movement to the resurgence in the popularity of anger as a tool in the early 1990s, anger has always been a subject of contentious debate in the struggle to further women's causes.

From Jesse Conrad, "Lorde and Rich and Spice Girls, Oh My! The Commercialization of Feminist Anger" *New Views on Gender* 5 (Spring 2000): 3.

Linda Segar defines "hero stories" as those in which we root for the hero and celebrate what he has accomplished because of our own experiences (Segar 123). Hero stories contain a healing phase; Segar defines it as "a hero being broken through physical, emotional, or psychological [means]." The hero "must find and balance himself" (Segar 127). From every myth there are life morals that a person can learn. The movie *Initial D* contains a hero myth, including a healing phase that transforms the main character.

From Jammy Inton, student at Florida Community College, Jacksonville, "*Initial D*'s Myth."

- Begin with a definition of an important term so that your readers will understand an analysis based on it.

"Good morning, rocketeers! The first flight of the day is ready to go. Out on pad 24 we have Nichole Eastman's Tethys. She is going for her level two certification. Flying on a J350, this one's going to go somewhere in the neighborhood of 5,200 feet. Let's see how she flies! We are clear, T-five, four, three, two . . . ." The countdown finishes and within seconds, the rocket ignites and lifts off the pad. Within a couple of seconds the rocket is out of sight, but the crowd waits in silence. Everyone is waiting . . . for the parachute.

When I first entered the world of rocketry, I barely understood a word of what anyone was saying, so it wouldn't surprise me if you, too, right now know only that a rocket was launched, but not the details of a "Tethys" flying on a "J350." When I first began building rockets, I didn't understand them, either. Perri Klass shares a similar experience of being thrown into a world with a language she didn't speak in "Learning the Language." Over time, she learned medical talk and was able to fit into the everyday life of a hospital, and I too have learned the lingo of the field I love.

From Nichole Eastman, student at Arapahoe Community College, "Rocket Challenge."

- Open with a real anecdote that uses action or dialogue to exemplify the problem you will address, the solution you support, or the case you will study.

The body of an academic essay explains and develops the thesis. The longest section of the paper, the body offers a line of reasoning and a sufficient amount of information—evidence, facts, anecdotes, examples, statistics—to support, extend, or elaborate it. Chapter 5 discusses particular rhetorical strategies for paragraphs. Here we will discuss a general pattern that is useful to know, especially in academic writing.

Try T-R-I: Topic-Restriction-Illustration

Well-organized paragraphs normally develop one primary idea, even if several examples, illustrations, or qualifications are used to elaborate that one idea. The form of a paragraph should be emergent and relevant to the subject under discussion. In academic writing, however, many paragraphs include a topic sentence, one or more restrictive sentences, and illustrations. You can remember this pattern with the acronym T-R-I, or "try."

A **topic sentence** states the main subject or focus of the paragraph. A well-written topic sentence

- signals the reader about the focus of the paragraph
- supports or extends the thesis
- unifies and summarizes the paragraph's content

Typical Paragraph Structures in Academic Essays

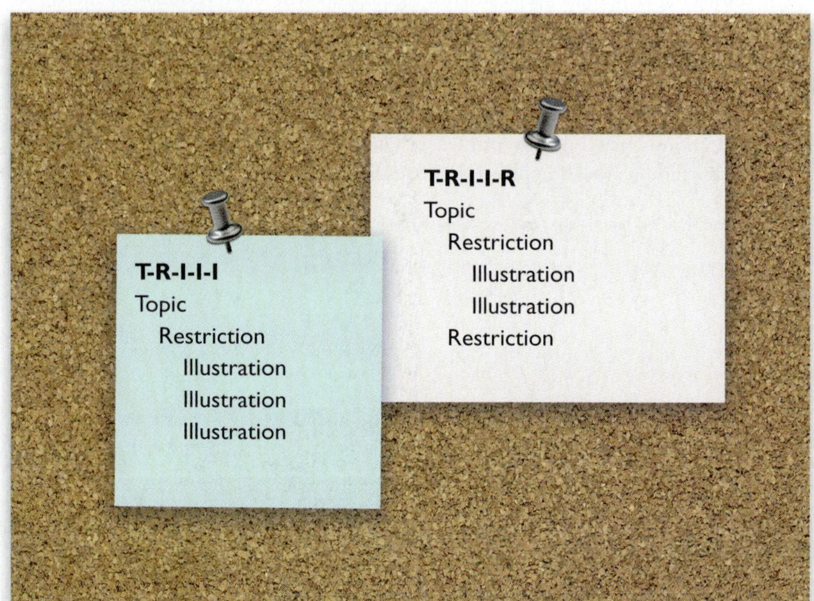

These are basic patterns, so they should be adjusted to fit when the logic of your subject matter and the circumstances of your rhetorical situation call for a different arrangement. Vary the order and number of the components in the T-R-I pattern, depending on what is needed to develop your topic properly.

Activity 4-4: Identifying Paragraph Structure

Read each sample paragraph on pages 76–84 and identify its T-R-I pattern. If a paragraph doesn't have a topic, restrictive, or illustrative sentence, discuss the possible reasons and give reasons why the paragraph still works effectively. The paragraph samples show these methods of developing and organizing content: description, process, cause and effect, definition, comparison and contrast, problem/solution, narration, exemplification, classification/division, and analogy.

Example of T-R-I

Fear thrives best in the present tense. That is why experts rely on it; in a world that is increasingly impatient with long-term processes, fear is a potent short-term play. Imagine that you are a government official charged with procuring the funds to fight one of two proven killers: terrorist attacks and heart disease. Which cause do you think the members of Congress will open up the coffers for? The likelihood of any given person being killed in a terrorist attack is infinitesimally smaller than the likelihood that the same person will clog up his arteries with fatty food and die of heart disease. But a terrorist attack happens *now;* death by heart attack is some distant, quiet catastrophe. Terrorist acts lie beyond our control; french fries do not. Just as important as the control factor is what Peter Sandman calls the dread factor. Death by terrorist attack (or mad-cow disease) is considered wholly dreadful; death by heart disease is, for some reason, not.

From Stephen D. Levitt and Stephen J. Dubner, *Freakonomics: A Rogue Economist Explores the Hidden Side of Everything* (New York: William Morrow, 2005), 151.

Here, the topic sentence is in red, the restrictive sentence is in black, and the illustrations are in green.

Activity 4-5: Writing Paragraphs of Your Draft

1. Write two body paragraphs for your draft in which you try the two T-R-I structures presented on page 54.
2. Trade paragraphs with a partner. Label the T-R-I patterns in your partner's paragraphs.
3. Examine your labeled paragraphs. Did your partner correctly identify the patterns you were creating?

Readers look for a topic sentence early in the paragraph to help them comprehend the significance of individual sentences, so consider placing your topic sentence first. Sometimes you may want to start with a sentence that captures your audience's attention or a transitional sentence that links to the previous paragraph to help readers shift from one topic to the next. You can do that, but readers will expect to find a topic sentence next. Your readers' needs and your purpose for writing should be the primary considerations in deciding where to locate topic sentences.

Restrictive sentences explain or narrow the focus of the topic sentence by adding qualifying information. They take the more general assertion and channel it in a way that will make illustrative sentences the logical next step. Restrictive sentences may also function as concluding sentences, easing the transition to the topic in the next paragraph. There may be more than one restrictive sentence in a paragraph.

Illustrative sentences may provide examples that clarify the meaning of topic sentences and restrictive sentences, or they may show how the topic relates to a particular context or idea. Any number of illustrations may be used.

4d

Although most paragraphs should have a topic sentence, some do not need one. You might be able to omit a topic sentence in a paragraph that narrates a series of events. Or you may not need a topic sentence when a paragraph continues developing an idea that you introduced (with a topic sentence) in the previous paragraph or when all the sentences and details in a paragraph clearly refer—perhaps indirectly—to a main point. The vast majority of your paragraphs, however, should have a topic sentence.

Paragraph with No Topic Sentence

Linda Thurston is trim and pretty, a dark strawberry blond given to large, swinging earrings; today she wears a pair of silvery stars almost of a size to be hoisted atop the courthouse cupola for Christmas. She sits down across from me to see what I'm scratching in my notebook. Now I'm copying what is on her coffee mug:

I HAVE A B.A., M.A., PH.D.
ALL I NEED NOW IS A GOOD J.O.B.

The doctorate is in child psychology, she is thirty-nine, divorced, and has a son, John. She calls across the little café to the new waitress, *We can't do scrambled eggs over easy.*

From William Least Heat-Moon, *PrairyErth* (New York: Mariner Books, 1999), 124–125.

4e Threading the Thesis through the Paragraphs

A thesis should function as the organizing principle or controlling idea for developing paragraphs in a project that argues a point or makes an interpretation. The thesis is not merely repeated, but extended into relevant contexts or supported by examples or statements from authoritative sources. Key aspects of the thesis should be threaded through the paragraphs so that readers will understand how each part relates to the whole. To do this, use key terms in your thesis statement and then repeat them, with variations, throughout the work to keep readers on track.

Using Key Terms to Keep Readers on Track

Thesis statement:

The **organic standards** that the Department of Agriculture recently tried to water down must be **maintained** to protect the **viability of small farms.**

Topic sentences and other sentences repeat the key terms:

These standards . . .
Organic crops provide . . .
Maintaining the standard . . .
In order to remain economically viable, small farms . . .

Activity 4-6: Identifying Key Terms in Your Thesis Statement

1. Highlight or underline the key terms in your tentative thesis statement.
2. Examine the draft you created in Activity 4-5. Try to work each key term into an existing sentence where it makes sense to do so, or write a new sentence that could be incorporated in your draft.
3. Read your draft out loud to yourself. Wherever there seems to be a break in the pattern of thought, consider whether using a key term or a variation on it might make the ideas more coherent.

Threading a Thesis Statement through an Essay

Take, for example, our thesis statement regarding the controversy over peer-to-peer file sharing from page 49. Notice how the topic sentences from later paragraphs repeat or rephrase key points suggested in the thesis.

Peer-to-peer file sharing on the Internet has prompted some changes to copyright law that are unconstitutional and, sadly, supported by music industry lobbyists who don't understand the positive benefits of word-of-mouth for offline sales of music.

Thesis statement

The Internet makes it possible for remote users to share files of almost any type easily and without the usual barriers of reproducing content on physical media.

Body paragraph topic: Background information

The Digital Millennium Copyright Act of 1998 included an important provision making it illegal for anyone to create a process for sharing files even when he or she doesn't actually share any copyrighted content.

Body paragraph topic: Copyright law

It is unconstitutional to charge someone with a crime for sharing a process unrelated to the copyrighted material and that may be designed for other purposes, such as sharing ideas via text files.

Body paragraph topic: Unconstitutionality

Some musical artists have recognized that file sharing actually increases sales of their work in the same way that radio broadcasts create buzz about a new song and prompt people to buy a CD.

Body paragraph topic: Increasing sales

A free society depends on the democratic principle of an educated citizenry, so the government should not sacrifice this broader ideal of free speech to appease a music industry that has failed to recognize the power of the Internet to promote their product.

Conclusion topic: Limitation of free speech

Transitional expressions can be used to help readers move from point to point. Transitions are words and phrases that reveal the connections among parts of a larger whole—the patterns of organization in your writing.

Transitions

To give additional information or support:

Additionally, again, also, and, besides, equally important is, furthermore, in addition to, incidentally, in the first place, moreover, more so, next, otherwise, too

To provide examples:

Another example of this/that is, examples include, for example, for instance, in fact, in particular, one example of that/this is, specifically, that is, to illustrate this/the point

To compare and contrast:

Also, although, and, at the same time, but, despite (that), however, in a similar way, in contrast, in spite of this/that, likewise, nevertheless, on the contrary, on the other hand, similarly, still, though, yet

To indicate chronology or order:

After, afterward, and then, as, at last, before, during, earlier, finally, first/second/third, formerly, immediately, in the meantime, later, meanwhile, never, next, now, once, shortly, since, subsequently, then, thereafter, until, when, whence, while

To indicate placement or location:

Above, atop, below, beyond, close, farther, here, in, nearby, on, on top of that, opposite, over, south/north/east/west, there, to the right/left, underneath

To show logic:

Also, and, as a result, because, because of, but, consequently, for this reason, hence, however, if, otherwise, since, so, then, therefore, thus

To summarize:

Finally, in closing, in conclusion, in other words, in short, in summary, on the whole, so, that is, then, therefore, to close, to sum up, to summarize

An effective conclusion satisfies readers that they are finished reading, encourages them to reflect further on the issues, or urges them to act based on their new understanding. A conclusion usually does more than repeat the thesis or summarize what's already been written. In a shorter academic essay, a summation is not necessary; focus instead on extending the significance of the issue or even making a call to action that lets readers know what they might do (or think) next. In a very long essay or report or when the information is especially technical or complex, you should synthesize for your readers what they have just read and emphasize what is most important.

Don't offer entirely new material in the conclusion. If at the end of your draft you think of new material that seems important, then when you revise your first draft, move the point earlier and develop it in the body paragraphs.

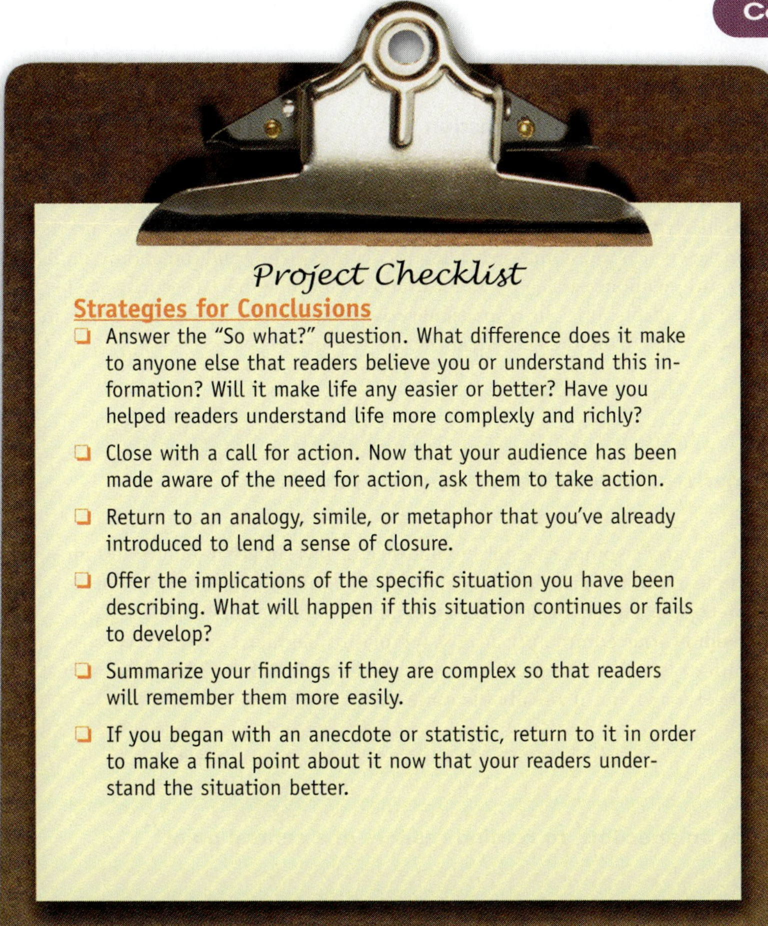

Project Checklist

Strategies for Conclusions

- Answer the "So what?" question. What difference does it make to anyone else that readers believe you or understand this information? Will it make life any easier or better? Have you helped readers understand life more complexly and richly?
- Close with a call for action. Now that your audience has been made aware of the need for action, ask them to take action.
- Return to an analogy, simile, or metaphor that you've already introduced to lend a sense of closure.
- Offer the implications of the specific situation you have been describing. What will happen if this situation continues or fails to develop?
- Summarize your findings if they are complex so that readers will remember them more easily.
- If you began with an anecdote or statistic, return to it in order to make a final point about it now that your readers understand the situation better.

Activity 4-7: Writing Alternative Conclusions

Consider which strategies from the project checklist you might use to conclude your essay. Choose two of them, and draft two conclusions. In a group, compare your conclusions. Group members should vote for the conclusion they prefer for each essay and explain why. Using this feedback, decide which conclusion to use and then revise it.

You may want to examine the conclusions of the student work throughout the handbook:

- Gina Wolf, in "Still Guarding the Fort," closes her essay by reminding readers of the relationship she and Jamie had while children and how that bond has now reasserted itself in a grown-up context (page 117).
- L. Franklin Jewell begins his concluding paragraph to "Things We Carry" by summing up in the first few sentences what he has learned. The remainder of the paragraph describes what "things" the people in his life have carried with them, with references to the portraits he painted earlier in the essay (page 150).
- Angela Garrison, in "From Over There to Over Here: War Blogs Get Up Close, Personal, and Profitable," finishes her essay by noting that regardless of the motives behind the blogs of soldiers, they still provide us with a rare glimpse of what life in a war zone is like, and for that reason, they may influence those who don't appreciate the great tolls of war on everyone (page 66).

Sample Conclusions

Answers the "So what?" question

After everything they have done for us throughout the years, we owe it to our elderly to ensure their retirements are comfortable and secure. We need to make certain the system providing for them is strong and can endure until we retire, without passing on an unsustainable burden. Social security can be saved if it adapts. It is our responsibility as young people to encourage reform because, otherwise, the consequences will be ours to bear.

From Hunter Williams; see his introduction on page 52.

Summarizes the topic's contemporary relevance

To today's volunteers, the significance of this suburban hilltop lies most particularly in the fact that the defenses were built by ordinary citizens to protect their city in a crisis. "It's an example of homeland security, of defending your community against terrorism," said Fort Wright city administrator Larry Klein. "They may not have thought of it in those terms 150 years ago, but it's really the same thing."

From Andrew Berg, "The Best Offense," *Smithsonian*, Sept. 2005, p. 42.

Relates an anecdote to remind readers of a central point

[The play] ends with a crowd-pleaser: Mary Poppins departs the Banks family by soaring up and into the rafters, borne aloft by her umbrella and by the forgiving enthusiasm of the audience, which often includes ample representation from the under-ten set. She has been more punitive and frightening than Julie Andrews ever was, but she has nonetheless managed to evoke the powerful emotions—in particular, children's deep fear of abandonment—that have always been at the story's core. On one occasion, when the beloved nanny was making her getaway, a middle-aged man was heard to cry out in anguish, "Mary Poppins, don't leave!"

From Caitlin Flanagan, "Becoming Mary Poppins," *The New Yorker*, Dec. 19, 2005, p. 46.

Example of a Working Outline

April Massiter, a second-year student, based her working outline on a tentative thesis statement.

Heart disease is on the rise in the United States because people are bombarded by advertising for fast, unhealthy food, making people associate being an American with being super-sized.

Intro:

—There has always been unhealthy food in abundance. Why should fast food chains be to blame? What is the difference between them and the typical supermarket? Or a classier restaurant?

—Mention the film Super-Size Me.

—Define fast food and give brief overview of history of fast food.

Body:

—Growth of fast food and franchise restaurants

—Fast food at school, prepared food at home, and thus, not much control over intake of fattening foods

—Rise of fad diets, especially Atkins, which encourage people to eat high-fat foods

—People seem to lack personal responsibility. They would rather sue fast food restaurants and cigarette manufacturers instead of watching what they put in their bodies. Be careful not to equate cigarettes—addictive—and French fries—delicious, but addictive?

—Diabetes, high blood pressure, lack of exercise, and cardiac problems

End:

Tell readers to pay attention to what they eat so that they can live healthy, long lives.

April noticed that her working outline suggested a historical progression and decided to try to arrange her ideas chronologically in her first draft.

Some writers like to organize their thoughts before drafting, and others prefer to write a draft first and then check the organization before writing another. When you need to check the organization of your writing project, an outline can be a helpful tool. Three kinds of outlines are the working outline, the topical outline, and the sentence outline. Your instructor may ask you to submit an outline with your project, so be sure to clarify which kind of outline is required.

Working Outlines

The **working outline** is a very rough guide to organization. Writers who want to get a quick handle on how they will organize (or how they have organized) their writing might jot down a working outline with just a few points.

Formal Topical Outlines

More extensive than the working outline, the **topical outline** includes all the topics that the project will cover, written in phrases. Like the working outline, the topical outline shows how the project will support the idea in the working thesis. It uses a conventional format that gives the writer a chance to check the logic and consistency of the plan for writing.

Format for Formal Topical and Sentence Outlines

Thesis statement
I. First major idea
    A. First supporting idea
        1. First detail
        2. Second detail
            a. First minor support
            b. Second minor support
    B. Second supporting idea
        1. First detail
        2. Second detail
II. Second major idea

Notice that for every I, there is a II, and for every A, there is a B. If there aren't at least two points to make at a given level, the idea should be handled at the next level up. This constraint of a formal outline can help you find the gaps in your plan where you need more ideas or details. If you have only one piece of evidence to support a major point, you should do more research to find additional support. If you cannot find additional support, you should revise your major point.

I. Social concerns of psychology
II. Philosophical concerns of psychology
III. Moral concerns of psychology
    A. First supporting idea
    B. Second supporting idea
    C. Third supporting idea

At each level of a formal outline, such as I, II, III (or A, B, C), the entries should be in parallel grammatical form. In this topical outline, the three major points each start with an adjective-noun phrase.

Sample Topical Outline

Thesis: Although Roger Wilkins might argue that the advantages to society as a whole outweigh the disadvantages of using affirmative action to achieve more racial and cultural diversity on college campuses today, Shelby Steele and John Leo would vehemently argue that affirmative action should not be used for this purpose.

I. Definition of affirmative action
   A. Purpose of affirmative action
   B. Actual uses of affirmative action, according to Steele and Leo
   C. Use of affirmative action to promote diversity
II. Wilkins
   A. Disadvantages to white men
   B. Benefits of affirmative action to society
      1. Increased opportunity for individuals
      2. Broader array of skills available in the American population utilized
III. Steele
   A. Detrimental effect on children who are not well off, but not "disadvantaged"
   B. Unfair process of admissions
   C. Misuse of affirmative action
IV. Leo
   A. Use of affirmative action to evade laws or court rulings against quotas
   B. No racial and ethnic preferences allowed in the public sector in California
V. Conclusion

The outline to the left was drafted by Brad Redrow, a first-year student at Camden County College, who was preparing an argument in response to the following assignment by Martha Bachman:

> Suppose someone argued that affirmative action is a necessary tactic to achieve more racial and cultural diversity on college campuses today. Referring to the essays by John Leo, Roger Wilkins, and Shelby Steele, how do you suppose they would respond to such an argument?

Formal Sentence Outlines

The **sentence outline** is the most comprehensive kind of outline. It follows the same conventional format as the topical outline, but instead of using a phrase for each listing, it includes complete sentences. The sentences at each level are often written in parallel form. If you create a formal sentence outline, your first draft will be easy to write, since you can use sentences straight out of your outline in the draft. If your instructor requires that you submit a formal sentence outline with your project, double-check that the points in the outline and in the final project are arranged in exactly the same order.

Activity 4-8: Writing an Outline

Draft a sentence outline for your essay and ask a partner for feedback. Have your partner answer the following questions:

1. Can a reader follow the organization of the paper as shown in the outline? If so, what strategies has the writer used to make the organization clear? If not, what about the organization is difficult to understand?
2. Are there any places where the outline seems to be lacking evidence or explanations of an idea?
3. What do you think the writer needs to add to or take away from the outline to make it more coherent or interesting?

Angela Garrison's class was asked to write a brief paper in response to an article by John Hockenberry called "The Blogs of War," which appeared online at *Wired* magazine. Although the assignment did not specifically require writers to consult other sources, she decided that to understand Hockenberry's article fully she should examine some of the blogs soldiers were posting online. She cites all her sources in the Works Cited list on the last page of her paper.

Garrison 1

Angela Garrison

Dr. Simpson

English 101

September 26, 2005

From Over There to Over Here:

War Blogs Get Up Close, Personal, and Profitable

The opening provides background information about the popularity and uses of blogs.

Blog was the word looked up most often in the online *Merriam-Webster's Dictionary* in 2004 ("'Blog' Most Popular Word on Web Dictionary"). What's all this fuss? When you read someone else's personal blog, you find out what they like and don't like, what they're doing, and maybe other bits of gossip offered at random. You can read news blogs to find out what's going on lately, what other people think about it, and why it matters. You can keep your own blog to share your thoughts and feelings, to tell your friends and family what you're up to, and sometimes to capture the interest of someone you've never met. When you read and write blogs, you join, or even create, a community. Blogs are also an efficient way to break news, spread rumors, and glorify causes. In short, blogs help people do what they've always done as social beings, just more quickly now, and from almost anywhere on Earth. Soldiers on the ground fighting in Iraq are writing blogs from the front lines. But a review is now under way at the Pentagon to "better understand the overall implications of blogging and other Internet communications in combat zones," according to John Hockenberry in his *Wired* article "The Blogs of War." The benefits of blogs written by U.S. soldiers in Iraq far outweigh the hypothetical risks of revealing sensitive or strategic information. Those benefits, however, aren't as obvious as they might seem.

Restricts the focus to war blogs

States the main focus of "The Blogs of War" article

The thesis statement makes a claim that the author will support in the rest of the response essay. The last sentence then functions as a transition that piques the readers' interest.

Topic sentence for the paragraph

In spite of what the imagery of smart bombs and predator drones might lead television viewers to believe, wars are fought by people, not just technology. Most blogs start out as efforts to stay in touch with family and friends, but they quickly

Garrison 2

turn into a kind of citizen-on-the-street journalism. Blogs humanize soldiers by showing others what their lives are like on the front lines. One told the story of how "the braver [Iraqi] children will approach and try to practice their English skills, which usually revolves around the phrase 'Mr., Mr., Saddam is a dork'" (Bout). Naturally, the stories milbloggers (short for "military bloggers") tell are not always pretty, and many don't have happy endings or show people in their best light. One milblogger and doctor, Michael Cohen, wrote gripping accounts of the carnage following the suicide bombing of a mess tent and described the doctors' efforts to save the wounded (Hockenberry). Another milblogger, Neil Prakash, writes about how "the poetry of warfare is in the sounds of exploding weapons and the chaos of battle" (Hockenberry): "So far there hadn't been a single civilian in TF2-2's sector. We had been free to light up the insurgents as we saw them. And because of that freedom, we were able to use the main gun with less restriction" (Prakash). Danjel Bout, another milblogger, sums up the purpose of these front-line messages: "For people to really understand our day-to-day experience here, they need more than the highlights reel. They need to see the world through our eyes for a few minutes" (qtd. in Hockenberry).

The understanding Bout has in mind may be more than just appreciation for the tough and harrowing lives of the soldiers fighting for their country thousands of miles from home. Some milblogs exploit this realism for ulterior motives. If you visit these milblogs, you see that some of them have become vehicles for all kinds of propaganda on behalf of political views, serving both conservative and liberal agendas. Other milbloggers do everything they can to profit from their popularity--in the grand American tradition. Still others play up their role as unobstructed news from the front lines and become the examples used by Washington think-tanks to make their arguments, pro and con, for how the war is going. For example, "Blackfive," as he is known, kept his blog during his time as an intelligence officer in

These sentences restrict the topic by explaining how blogs humanize the war.

Example 1

Example 2

This sentence sums up the reasons for humanizing the war with milblogs.

This transitional sentence introduces a contrast, suggesting other motives for milblogs.

Topic sentence

The sentences that begin "If you visit . . . ," "Other milbloggers . . . ," and "Still others . . ." restrict the topic.

Extended example of how one person uses a milblog for profit.

Addresses the thesis statement and provides a reason that benefits outweigh security issues. This is also the topic sentence of the paragraph.

The sentences following the topic sentence restrict the focus of the topic to the DOD's position.

The concluding sentences "raise the stakes" by arguing that the benefits are more than just "staying in touch." Instead, milblogs offer insight into the day-to-day realities of war that may help us understand how to avoid it in the future.

Garrison 3

Iraq and has continued it now that he has become an IT officer for a high-tech firm (Hockenberry). Blackfive's blog is

> nearly as cluttered with ads as the Drudge Report, and the sales pitches mostly hawk "liberal-baiting merchandise." There are pictures of attractive women holding high-powered weapons, dozens of links to conservative books and films, and even the occasional big spender like Amazon.com. Blackfive also sells his own T-shirts to benefit military charities. (Hockenberry)

Right next to such ads, you can read the stories of distraught parents hearing the news that their son or daughter has been killed in action. The impression you get is not so much a sense of the human price of war, but the willingness of anyone to exploit and glorify pain and suffering to sell an idea or a t-shirt.

Because there are so many milbloggers and their messages range from personal stories to propaganda, it is unlikely that the enemy will monitor milblogs for clues about the American military's next move. The Department of Defense (DOD) realizes this, of course, so the milbloggers will no doubt continue their work to humanize the war, even as others profit from it. The DOD knows also that milblogs build the morale of the soldiers over there by giving them an outlet to express and share their fears with others, even opportunities to think about something other than what's around the next bend. The milblogs show us the heroes as well as the profiteers. Regardless of the purity of the motives of milbloggers, readers over here see a side of the war reported not by professional journalists but by the actors themselves. Although the function of these blogs has become much more than maintaining ties with friends and family, they still help all of us understand how our soldiers feel, how they respond to their situations, and how they confront and explain them. That insight can benefit everyone, especially those who instigate or prosecute war.

Garrison 4

Works Cited

"'Blog' Most Popular Word on Web Dictionary." *MSNBC.com.* MSNBC, 2 Dec. 2004. Web. 15 Sept. 2005.

Bout, Danjel. "Snapshots." *Frontline Blogs.* N.p., 21 Aug. 2005. Web. 15 Sept. 2005.

Hockenberry, John. "The Blogs of War." *Wired.com.* Wired, Aug. 2005. Web. 14 Sept. 2005.

Prakash, Neil. "11 November: Tank Mines." *Armor Geddon.* N.p., 23 Jan. 2005. Web. 15 Sept. 2005.

The Works Cited section includes listings for all sources of outside information in the essay, including the citation for the term *blog*'s popularity, Hockenberry's article, and two milblogs that the writer tracked down through a Google search.

Writing Project Threads 4j

A table of contents for writing project threads appears on pages xv–xxii.

Deciding on a Solution and an Argumentative Thesis

Your research activities will have provided you with a lot of information about possible solutions and their feasibility. Based on your research and your perspective, choose the solution that you think is the best one possible. Freewrite a list of reasons why your solution is better than others. Then follow the strategies in section 4b to develop a thesis statement that states the problem, your solution, and your reasons for choosing it. ▶ page 119.

Proposal Arguments

Harrington 1

A Proposal to Clean Up Our Streets

Writing Your Life

Once you've collected and organized information about yourself, write your first draft. What aspect of your experience—an event, perhaps—should you focus on first in order to interest readers and help them understand the point of your narrative? Consider how you will describe your experiences. ▶ page 86.

Personal Essays

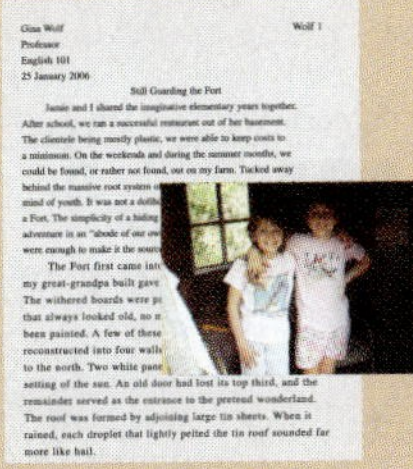

Informative Essays

Garrison 1

Angela Garrison
English 101
Dr. Simpson
September 26, 2005

From Over There to Over Here:
War Blogs Get Up Close, Personal, and Profitable

Blog was the word looked up most often in the online *Merriam-Webster's Dictionary* in 2004 ("Blog"). What's all this fuss? When you read someone else's personal blog, you find out what they like and don't like, what they're doing, and maybe other bits of gossip offered at random. You can read news blogs to find out what's going on lately, what other people think about it, and why it matters. You can keep your own blog to share your thoughts and feelings, to tell your friends and family what you're up to, and sometimes to capture the interest of someone you've never met. When you read and write blogs, you join, or even create, a community. Blogs are also an efficient way to break news, spread rumors, and glorify causes. In short, blogs help people do what they've always done as social beings, just more quickly now, and from almost anywhere on Earth. Soldiers on the ground fighting in Iraq are writing blogs from the front lines. But a review is now under way at the Pentagon to "better understand the overall implications of blogging and other Internet communications in combat zones," according to John Hockenberry in his *Wired* article "The Blogs of War." The benefits of blogs written by U.S. soldiers in Iraq far outweigh

Planning and Presenting Information

After researching and taking notes, you'll have a wealth of information with which to answer your research question. You then need to figure out how to share this information with your readers.

- Create a tentative thesis statement using the information in section 4b.
- Think about which ideas are related. Draft a plan to show these groupings. Section 4h can help you with outlining strategies.
- Draft your essay, drawing on sections 4c–4g as needed.

Will you need to include images in your essay to help elaborate ideas? If so, refer to Chapter 24 for guidance. ▶ page 314.

Proposal Arguments

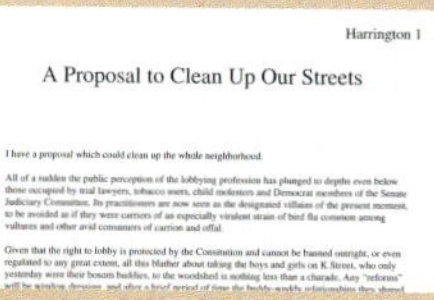

Harrington 1

A Proposal to Clean Up Our Streets

I have a proposal which could clean up the whole neighborhood.

All of a sudden the public perception of the lobbying profession has plunged to depths even below those occupied by trial lawyers, tobacco users, child molesters and Democrat members of the Senate Judiciary Committee. Its practitioners are now seen as the designated villains of the present moment, to be avoided as if they were carriers of an especially virulent strain of bird flu common among vultures and other avid consumers of carrion and offal.

Given that the right to lobby is protected by the Constitution and cannot be banned outright, or even regulated to any great extent, all this blather about taking the boys and girls on K Street, who only yesterday were their bosom buddies, to the woodshed is nothing less than a charade. Any "reforms"

Outlining and Drafting Your Proposal

Once you have talked over your solution and reasons with interested community members, create an outline of your proposal. Lay out the problem, solution, and reasons, as well as counterarguments against your solution. Then write a first draft. In your draft, do your best to show how your solution addresses more aspects of the problem than other solutions do. ▶ page 86.

Brochures

Drafting "Infochunks" for Your Brochure

A brochure is very different from an academic essay in terms of how information is organized and presented. Instead of breaking information up into an introduction, a body, and a conclusion, a brochure presents chunks of information in neatly arranged blocks. Sometimes key information is presented as an image or a graphic to provide visual interest. Review the material in section 25b on graphic design principles, and then draft the "infochunks" that will make up your brochure. Start by listing all the critical topics to cover. Then write an infochunk of no more than two or three sentences for each one. Put them in a logical order, which, in a brochure, usually means from the general to the particular. Print them and then manually place them in your brochure mock-up—or, if you're working in a desktop publishing program, cut-and-paste or import them into the brochure template that you've created. ▶ page 588.

Critical Reviews

A Movie You Can't Forget!

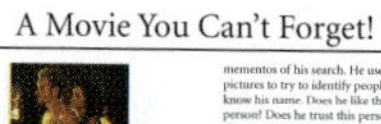

This could be the best movie you will ever see all year, if you're looking for something intense, suspenseful, and different than your usual effects-packed thriller. This is the kind of movie that you will be talking about at work, at the bank (to total strangers!), and at the corner coffee shop.

The movie starts with a murder -- a revenge killing, in fact. But was the right person killed?

mementos of his search. He uses pictures to try to identify people who know his name. Does he like this person? Does he trust this person? Is this the killer? He doesn't know unless he's written a note.

Writer/director Christopher Nolan puts you right in Leonard's shoes, living the story in reverse order. This ingenious method of story-telling means that you never know more than Leonard does. In one scene you see Leonard getting information from a person who knows him -- maybe a good person; maybe bad. In the next scene you see a previous meeting between the two which sheds more light on their relationship. Later still you see how they met. You, like

Getting to the Point

A review needs to clearly answer two questions for the reader: What are the criteria for evaluating this work? Did the work live up to these criteria? Your review should include a thesis statement that summarizes your responses to these two questions. A review makes an assessment or a recommendation that readers will look for. Don't be afraid to take a position, but be sure to support it as well. ▶ page 86.

5 DEVELOPING PARAGRAPHS

Writers use paragraphs to organize their ideas. Each paragraph performs a certain kind of work in the larger piece of writing—for example, to advance the argument, to provide illustrations and examples, to discuss the effects of a solution the writer is proposing. Paragraphs also have an internal logic; they focus attention on one idea at a time, along with a cluster of closely related sentences that explain, extend, or support that idea. See pages 54–55 for a general discussion of the paragraph structure T-R-I, which includes the topic sentence, restrictive sentences, and illustrative sentences.

Visually, a paragraph break gives readers' eyes a brief rest, and readers can take advantage of the break to reflect on what they have read or even to scribble notes. Paragraphing chunks information into manageable units and gives the reader a starting point when returning to read.

The form, length, style, and positioning of paragraphs will vary, depending on the nature and conventions of the medium (print or digital), the interface (size and type of paper, screen resolution and size), and the genre. For example, paragraphs in a newspaper are quite a bit shorter, typically, than paragraphs in a college essay because of the newspaper's narrow columns. On a website, paragraphs on the opening page may consist of more signposts than would be typical in a printed work, allowing readers to select which direction to track via hyperlink. Paragraphs in a work of creative nonfiction will likely include transitional words and sentence structures not often found in lab reports.

In short, the rhetorical situation should always guide your use of paragraphing. When you understand paragraph conventions, your audience and purpose, your rhetorical situation, and your writing's subject matter, you will be in the best position to decide how to use paragraphs strategically and effectively to teach, delight, or persuade with your writing.

Paragraphs are formatted in different ways, depending on the medium and genre. In printed text, paragraphs usually begin on a new line, with the first line indented. In some block formats, such as the memorandum format, new paragraphs aren't indented but have an extra space above and below. On websites, paragraphs usually take the block format because there is no TAB character in HTML code and the paragraph tag <p> automatically double-spaces after a paragraph break (or ENTER).

A typical paragraph in academic writing is composed of five or more sentences, depending on sentence construction and length. Shorter paragraphs are used on occasion to add emphasis. Longer paragraphs are sometimes necessary when the topic is complex or requires precise argument or numerous examples.

The size of the visible space matters. Paragraphs on an $8\frac{1}{2}" \times 11"$ sheet of paper with double-spacing rarely run longer than a page. On a computer screen, text that runs from one edge of the screen to the other and down without any breaks is extremely difficult to read. Printed newspapers often use short paragraphs and narrow columns to allow the reader to jump from one story (or point) to the next. Short paragraphs in newspapers also allow more flexibility for breaking stories across pages.

Paragraph Breaks Make Text Easier to Read

As Ellen Lupton notes in *Thinking with Type* (Princeton Architectural Press, 2004), "Paragraphs do not occur in nature" (102); they are used deliberately to make text easier to read. Both of the examples that follow are from the ebook of Jane Austen's *Pride and Prejudice* (1813), available online at Project Gutenberg, **http://www.gutenberg.org**. In the top sample, the paragraph breaks have been removed. The sample at the bottom includes them. How do paragraph breaks improve readability?

It is a truth universally acknowledged, that a single man in possession of a good fortune, must be in want of a wife. However little known the feelings or views of such a man may be on his first entering a neighbourhood, this truth is so well fixed in the minds of the surrounding families, that he is considered the rightful property of some one or other of their daughters. "My dear Mr. Bennet," said his lady to him one day, "have you heard that Netherfield Park is let at last?" Mr. Bennet replied that he had not. "But it is," returned she; "for Mrs. Long has just been here, and she told me all about it." Mr. Bennet made no answer.

It is a truth universally acknowledged, that a single man in possession of a good fortune, must be in want of a wife.

However little known the feelings or views of such a man may be on his first entering a neighbourhood, this truth is so well fixed in the minds of the surrounding families, that he is considered the rightful property of some one or other of their daughters.

"My dear Mr. Bennet," said his lady to him one day, "have you heard that Netherfield Park is let at last?"

Mr. Bennet replied that he had not.

"But it is," returned she; "for Mrs. Long has just been here, and she told me all about it."

Mr. Bennet made no answer.

Activity 5-1: Revising a Paragraph for Unity

Read the following paragraph and check the relationship that each sentence has to the topic sentence. Cross out irrelevant sentences. Then make any other needed revisions.

While some people associate penguins exclusively with the frigid Antarctic continent, there are actually many species of penguin which inhabit warmer climates. Penguins have heavier bones than some of their bird cousins, which allow them to dive easily. Their heavy bones evolved over time as they lost their ability to fly. However, penguins are exclusively confined to the Southern Hemisphere; the only ones in the Northern Hemisphere are in captivity. Penguins enjoy a varied diet of fish and krill. Penguins inhabit various countries in South America, including Peru and Chile, build colonies along the African coast, and nest on beaches in New Zealand. There are even penguins in the Galapagos Islands, which are close to the equator! Penguins tend to hatch only one egg a year.

Activity 5-2: Revising Your Writing for Unity

In a paragraph that you have written recently, highlight the topic sentence. How does each of the other sentences in the paragraph relate to the topic sentence? If the relationship is difficult to describe, rewrite the sentence to make the connection clear, or if there is no relationship, take it out completely. If many of the sentences seem to relate to one another but not to the topic sentence, revise the topic sentence to make it more accurate.

In academic writing, readers expect a paragraph's sentences to cluster around a central idea or theme. This tight focus on one main idea is known as paragraph *unity*. The topic sentence states the subject and the approach to the subject, just as the thesis statement does for some longer pieces of writing. The other sentences all stick to this idea and this approach. Check to be sure each sentence has a direct relationship with the topic sentence. If it doesn't, you should take it out, perhaps saving it for another paragraph if the idea is important to your project. If several sentences seem to go off the topic, you may need to develop them into a separate paragraph.

Coherence in a paragraph is derived from the network of relationships between the topic, unifying idea, or theme and the other sentences, as well as the flow of information from one sentence to the next. Coherent paragraphs have sentences that flow easily and effectively, and the connections between the sentences and their ideas remain clear at all times.

Coherence can be hard to maintain, especially when the unifying idea is abstract. Narratives tend to be easier for readers to follow because they (usually) follow a chronological sequence, although even in narratives, coherence must be checked. But in other forms of writing, coherence has to be managed by attending carefully to sentence and paragraph topics, making sure that readers understand how each sentence connects with a unifying idea.

Stay with the Topic from Sentence to Sentence

A topic is the focus of a sentence; it is what your reader remembers about the sentence. When you keep the same topic in the forefront of a reader's mind, shifting only slightly to variations as a paragraph develops, your writing will be more coherent. When writers shift the topic in sentence after sentence, the writing becomes incoherent.

Keeping the Topic in the Forefront of the Reader's Mind

The topic—Hush Puppies—is introduced, defined

Topic shifts slightly, from type of shoes to brand of shoes

And from brand to sales of the brand

From sales of the shoes to the company that sells the shoes

And from the company to its executives

For Hush Puppies—the classic American brushed-suede shoes with the lightweight crepe sole—the Tipping Point came somewhere between late 1994 and early 1995. The brand had been all but dead until that point. Sales were down to 30,000 pairs a year, mostly to backwoods outlets and small-town family stores. Wolverine, the company that makes Hush Puppies, was thinking of phasing out the shoes that made them famous. But then something strange happened. At a fashion shoot, two Hush Puppies executives—Owen Baxter and Geoffrey Lewis—ran into a stylist from New York who told them that the classic Hush Puppies had suddenly become hip in the clubs and bars of downtown Manhattan. . . .

From Malcolm Gladwell, *The Tipping Point* (Boston: Little, Brown and Co., 2002), 3.

Activity 5-3: Revising a Paragraph for Topical Flow

Revise the following paragraph for topical flow, rearranging sentences so that topic shifts are in logical order and adding phrases to help smooth the flow where necessary.

Allusion is the practice of making references to other literary or cultural figures within a work. Readers must be familiar with other literary works to recognize allusions. The main characters in the three books find themselves in situations which covertly or overtly resemble *Paradise Lost.* An example of allusion in children's literature is the references to Milton in Pullman's *His Dark Materials* series. Writers must take care to avoid alienating or confusing readers who are unfamiliar with the work to which the allusion is being made. The epigraphs for each book also refer explicitly to the poems as well. Why has Pullman used a poem meant for adults in a work meant for children?

Coherence: Transitions, Pronouns, and Lexical Ties

Another characteristic of the creative person is that he is able to entertain and play with ideas that the average person might regard as silly, mistaken, or downright dangerous. All new ideas sound foolish at first, because they are new. (In the early days of the railroad, it was argued that speeds of twenty-five mph or over were impractical because people's brains would burst.) A person who is afraid of being laughed at or disapproved of for having "foolish" or "unsound" ideas will have the satisfaction of having everyone agree with him, but he will never be creative, because creativity means being willing to take a chance—to go out on a limb.

From S. I. Hayakawa, "What It Means to Be Creative," *Through the Communication Barrier* (New York: Harper & Row, 1979).

Transitions are marked in blue, lexical ties in green, and pronouns in red, to illustrate how the three coherence devices thread through the paragraph. Note that many people consider use of the pronoun *he* to mean "a person" sexist usage—see section 39c. See page 57 for an example of how lexical ties keep a whole essay coherent.

Use Transitions and Punctuation Precisely

Transitions are words or phrases that connect your ideas. Normally, when new information is given, a transition cues your reader how to interpret it. For example, the word *because* lets readers know that a cause is next; the word *however* that a contrast is coming. The phrases *the point is, the important thing to note,* and *what strikes me most is* all say "pay attention now." (A list of transitions appears on page 58.)

Punctuation performs similar functions but more quietly. A colon emphasizes important information, a semicolon shows that two ideas are closely related in content, and commas can show that a series of ideas are distinct yet similarly important. (See the introduction at the beginning of each chapter in Part 9.)

Use Pronouns to Create Ties to Previous Words and Sentences

Pronouns function like threads in a cloth, linking new information to old information. When you use a pronoun, you ask the reader to keep its antecedent in mind. For information on using pronouns, see Chapter 43.

Use Synonyms and Repeat Important Words as Necessary to Create Lexical Ties

A lexical tie works like a pronoun, placing familiar words in new contexts or sentences where they take on added meaning.

Use Parallel Structures across Sentences to Create a Framework

Repeat grammatical patterns within and across sentences to create a consistent and familiar framework for reading your ideas. Using parallel structure—a kind of repetitive form—builds expectations in your readers so that, as they move forward, they catch the rhythm and swing along for the ride. See Chapter 34 on parallelism.

Be careful not to overuse this strategy, however. If all of your sentences have the exact same structure, you'll bore your readers. When you find yourself lapsing into overuse of a particular parallel structure, see how you can combine sentences to improve sentence variety and texture.

Activity 5-4: Identifying and Adding Lexical Ties in Your Writing

Mark the lexical ties in a paragraph that you've written, using the example in this section as a model. In your notes, answer the following questions:

1. What lexical ties do you use most often?
2. How effective are they?

Rewrite your paragraph to experiment with different kinds and uses of lexical ties.

Coherence: Creating a Framework with Parallel Structures

Topic sentence, echoed in the last sentence

The first item in the list, not parallel with the rest

This and next four sentences are parallel: "As . . . , they . . ."

It is no accident that all our social institutions—including science, law and government, religion, education and the arts, commerce and administration—rely on the stabilizing power of documents to accomplish their ends. In the form of books and journal articles, documents are carriers of scientific knowledge. As sacred scripture, they are the central artifacts around which many religious traditions have been organized. As written statutes, charters, and contracts, they play a crucial role in constructing and regulating lawful behavior. As works of literature, paintings, and drawings, they are the tangible products of artistic practice. As textbooks and student notes, they are crucial instruments around which learning practices are organized. As receipts and accounts, memos and forms, they are crucial ingredients in the way commerce, and indeed all bureaucratic conduct, is organized. In each of these cases the ability to hold talk fixed—to provide communicative stability—is crucial.

From David M. Levy, *Scrolling Forward* (New York: Arcade, 2002) 37.

Activity 5-5: Revising Your Writing for Coherence

Highlight parallel structures in a paragraph that you've written, using the example in this section as a model. In your notes, answer the following questions:

1. How often do you use parallel structure?
2. How effective is your use of parallel structure in the paragraph?

Rewrite your paragraph or the sample paragraph to experiment with different types of parallel structure.

Activity 5-6: Understanding Meaning and Coherence

Read the paragraph that follows. The transitions appear in blue, and synonyms are in green. We've added transitions and synonyms to exaggerate what happens when we don't trust our readers to remember information.

> To begin with, Sandburg College's buildings can be divided into three categories of structure. First, there are the academic buildings, such as University Hall and Carl Sandburg Hall, structures where classes are held during the daytime at the academic institution. Second, there are additional buildings like Milhous Building and Whitmore Annex where administrative offices, such as the Registrar and Financial Aid, are housed at the college. Third, there are dormitory buildings as well, such as Reginald Hall and the Living Center, where students live on campus. In conclusion, therefore, these three categories cover the main kinds of buildings on Sandburg's campus.

Delete all the transitions and synonyms in this paragraph, and then read it aloud. Is the paragraph coherent? What is the relationship between coherence and meaning?

Coherence and Prior Knowledge

Effectively managing coherence involves more than just connecting ideas clearly, because clarity depends on prior knowledge. Thus, coherence depends on what your audience already knows about your controlling idea and what information you provide.

Knowledge Readers Bring

Sometimes paragraphs that are too coherent seem dull to readers. Has anyone ever asked you a question that you knew the answer to, only to go on to tell you in detail things that you already know? For instance, suppose someone asked, "Do you know anything about hip-hop music?" and you responded, "Yes, I listen to it all the time." Then you would probably be bored by a paragraph that began "Hip-hop is a new kind of music" and included eight or nine sentences of information better suited to someone who had never heard—or heard of—hip-hop.

Information You Provide

Even if your topic is new to readers, they will accumulate information as they read your sentences. Trust your readers to remember basic facts and concepts from sentence to sentence. Reread each paragraph to see whether you have overused transitions or synonyms. They can obscure the flow of meaning by becoming distracting.

Description

Writers use description to help readers see, hear, taste, smell, and feel the particulars of a scene or subject. Descriptive details are chosen to help readers form a dominant impression or an emotional sense of the subject. At times, however, description is used objectively; for example, you might write an objective description of damage done to your car as part of an insurance claim.

To craft evocative descriptions, ask

- What is the most interesting thing about this subject, or what is most important to convey, given the larger purpose for sharing the description?
- Which of the many details that are part of the subject will best convey this important point?
- What does this subject look like? Sound like? Smell like? Taste like? How does it feel?

Description can be used . . .

- to supplement narratives, so that readers can "see" the setting or the people
- to augment a complex function in a process
- to illustrate the similarities among items grouped in a classification

Sample Description

As you read, consider how word choices contribute to your dominant impression of Darlington and the Deluxe Café.

> Then Darlington, a town of portico and pediment, iron fences, big trees, and an old courthouse square that looked as though renovated by a German buzz bomb. But on the west side of the square stood the Deluxe Café. The times had left it be. The front window said AIR CONDITIONED in icy letters, above the door was neon, and inside hung an insurance agency calendar and another for an auto parts store. Also on the walls were the Gettysburg Address, Declaration of Independence, Pledge of Allegiance, a picture of a winged [J]esus ushering along two kids who belonged in a Little Rascals film, and the obligatory waterfall lithograph. The clincher: small, white hexagonal floor tiles. Two old men, carrying their arms folded behind, stopped to greet each other with a light, feminine touching of fingertips, a gesture showing the duration of their friendship. I went in happy.
>
> From William Least Heat-Moon, *Blue Highways* (Boston: Houghton Mifflin Co., 1982), 67–68.

Description in a Drawing

Information that is very complex to describe in words may be better described in a diagram or illustration or in a combination of image and word, as practiced so frequently by Leonardo da Vinci. Da Vinci included detailed descriptions in drawings to make sure that his designs and inventions were conveyed as accurately as they could possibly be, as is illustrated in this diagram of the light of the sun and moon from Codex Leicester.

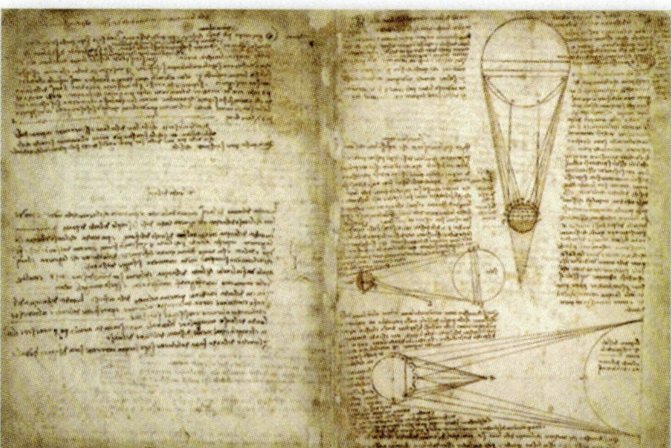

Sample Process Analysis

If you happen to like avocados, does this paragraph make you want to eat one? How do the writers use chronological transitions to describe each step?

How to eat an avocado (you think you know how, but you don't). First of all, it must be a perfectly ripe Hass avocado (small, dark green, and with an alligator's crumply skin). Cut it in half and gently pop out the seed. Set each half, cut side up, in a shallow bowl. Now, in a separate dish, mix together (for every two halves) about a spoonful of olive oil, a good squeeze of fresh lime, a few drops of Tabasco, and a pinch of coarse salt. Mix this well and dribble a fair share into each avocado half. Now fall to, eating the avocado out of its skin with a teaspoon, catching a bit of the dressing with each bite. A little buttered bread is good with this; the oil and lime juice can be further enhanced, if you like, with a morsel of crushed garlic and, instead of the Tabasco, a sprinkle of powdered cayenne. God didn't make the avocado just for guacamole.

From John Thorne, with Matt Lewis Thorne, *Outlaw Cook* (New York: Farrar, Straus and Giroux, 1992), 20.

Describing a Process to Different Audiences

The degree of detail necessary to successfully describe a process depends on the nature and prior knowledge of the audience. Chimpanzees know how to use sticks to catch termites: they insert a narrow stick into a hole in a termite mound and then pull it out, to find juicy termites clinging to it. How would your description of termite hunting change if you wanted to describe the process to a child? To a primate behaviorist? To a chimpanzee? For the latter, what rhetorical resources would you use? Words? Sign language? Images? Modeling? A stick and some termites?

Process Analysis

A process is a series of events that can be replicated to produce a certain result. A process analysis often describes the sequence of events, the instructions, and any procedures to be followed, in as precise detail as necessary for the reader to successfully complete or understand the process. A process analysis often closely resembles step-by-step instructions.

To craft a useful process analysis, ask

- What is to be done, or what should happen?
- How long will it take?
- What will be needed?
- What are the steps required to complete the action?
- In what order do they occur?

Process analysis can be used . . .

- to explain a complex set of procedures
- to make sure that something is assembled or completed properly
- to model an action or event
- to describe how one thing leads to another (in a short story, for example)

Cause and Effect Analysis

A cause and effect paragraph answers the question "How did this come to be?" or "What happened because of this?" Be careful to base conclusions on adequate, reliable evidence from multiple sources. Most events or actions have multiple causes and effects, so avoid oversimplifying.

To discover causes and effects, ask

- What exactly happened, to whom, where, and when?
- How did the events unfold over time?
- What are the other possible causes or effects of this event?
- What are the causes and effects of similar events that have occurred?
- What do other people with knowledge of the subject say about its causes and effects?

Cause and effect analysis can be used . . .

- to explain why something happened and how it will affect people or future events
- to rationalize behavior or other events when a cause is not obvious
- to predict how one thing will lead to another given an original set of circumstances or causes (as with law)

Sample Cause and Effect Analysis

Provides necessary background information

Statement of the cause

Initial effects

Possible long-term effects

Soon after a baby was born, it was swaddled tightly into a basketry cradle. There were practical reasons for restraining a child: California had grizzly bears, rattlesnakes, scorpions, poisonous plants, rushing water, and numerous other dangers. Also, a swaddled baby seldom cried or fussed. Yet surely those early months packed into a basketry cradle must have greatly influenced personality. The severe restriction of movement curbed independence and a sense of experimentation. A child *watched* the world rather than acted upon it. Perhaps in the process the child developed an attitude of acceptance toward the world—an attitude that throughout a person's life would be amplified by other cultural experiences, until in the end *acceptance of the world* would become the very center of a complex system of belief and value.

From *The Way We Lived: California Indian Reminiscences, Stories, and Songs*, edited with commentary by Malcolm Margolin (Berkeley, CA: Heyday Books, 1981), 11.

Cause and Effect in Images

Does the first image of cradles by itself provide any evidence for the reasons why babies were bound this way? Is there anything in the desolateness of the setting or the simple dress of the grownups? In the painting, is there any evidence for why the baby is bound as it is? Does either image suggest effects of this practice? What reasons might there be other than the ones offered in the passage from *The Way We Lived?*

Sample Definition

In this paragraph, Richard L. Gregory defines perception using the method of analogy: perceptions are "like the predictive hypotheses of science."

Paragraph begins with a clear and direct topic sentence

Illustration from experience

Restrictions of the topic sentence

Illustrations

Extension of the topic sentence explains significance

A central notion here is that perceptions are *hypotheses.* This is suggested by the fact that retinal images are open to an infinity of interpretations, and from the observed phenomena of ambiguity. The notion is that perceptions are like the predictive hypotheses of science. Hypotheses of perception and of science are risky, as they are predictive and they go beyond sensed evidence to hidden properties and to the future. For perception, as for science, both kinds of prediction are vitally important because the eye's images are almost useless for behaviour until they are read in terms of significant properties of objects, and because survival depends on behavior being appropriate to the immediate future, with no delay, although eye and brain take time to respond to the present. We behave to the present by anticipation of what is likely to happen, rather than from immediate stimuli.

From Richard L. Gregory, *Eye and Brain: The Psychology of Seeing,* 5th ed. (Princeton, NJ: Princeton University Press, 1997), 10.

A Test Picture: Gregory mentions the phenomena of ambiguity, by which he means the ways perception fills in the details in a mental image when the source is unclear or ambiguous. He uses this famous test picture to illustrate the process. Can you see the Dalmatian?

And a Question: William A. Covino has defined *literacy* as "alertness to linguistic ambiguity," or an ability to recognize multiple meanings (*Magic, Rhetoric, and Literacy* [Albany: SUNY Press, 1994], 31). We normally think of literacy as relating to reading and writing. How is perception (or seeing) related to literacy as an "alertness to ambiguity"?

Definition

Writers define terms to establish common ground with readers and to direct their meaning in particular ways. If a reader accepts your definition of important terms, your chances of persuasion improve dramatically. When we define a term, we necessarily do so in terms of *what it is not.* That is, all words "mean" by virtue of their relations to other words.

To craft a definition, ask

- What cluster of words is this term associated with? With what words is it customarily defined? To what words is it closely related in meaning (e.g., *craft* and *skill, ideology* and *belief*)?
- What analogy, or comparison to another word, can be used to define this term? What perspective can be gained by taking the term out of its usual context and placing it among other terms with which it is not usually associated?

Definitions can be used . . .

- to establish common ground with readers as a lens, filter, or screen for explaining or generating new ideas
- to show how objects, events, acts, people, or other subjects are related to one another

Comparison and Contrast

The technique of comparison and contrast draws out the similarities and distinctions between two or more objects, events, texts, people, or methods. Two methods may be used to organize the comparison. The **subject-by-subject method** discusses each subject or particular features of the subject in its own section or paragraph. The **point-by-point method** features the points of comparison, with the comparison and contrast moving back and forth between subjects on each point.

To compare and contrast, ask

- How is A different from B?
- What does A have in common with B?
- What advantages are there to considering A in concert with B?
- Is A better than B, or vice versa? Why?

Comparisons and contrasts can be used . . .

- to understand a subject more complexly
- to create richer perspectives on alternative viewpoints
- to show how ideas, objects, people, events, or other subjects are related

Sample Contrast

In this paragraph, Cornel West uses the subject-by-subject method to introduce some distinctions between two ways of discussing the plight of African Americans. His use of the transitional expressions *on the one hand* and *on the other hand* sets up the contrast.

Recent discussions about the plight of African Americans—especially those at the bottom of the social ladder—tend to divide into two camps. On the one hand, there are those who highlight the *structural* constraints on the life chances of black people. Their viewpoint involves a subtle historical and sociological analysis of slavery, Jim Crowism, job and residential discrimination, skewed unemployment rates, inadequate health care, and poor education. On the other hand, there are those who stress the behavioral impediments on black upward mobility. They focus on the waning of the Protestant ethic—hard work, deferred gratification, frugality, and responsibility—in much of black America.

From Cornel West, *Race Matters* (New York: Vintage Books, 1994), 17–18.

Contrast in a Painting

In *The Consequences of War* (1638), Peter Paul Rubens uses the left and right sides of the canvas to compare and contrast consequences of war. In the center, Venus (the goddess of love) tries to restrain Mars (the god of war). Visually, Rubens suggests contrasts with his use of the canvas space, the content on each side, color, and the dialectic between Venus and Mars, as well as what they represent.

Sample Problem-Solution Paragraph

It's hard enough to endure plunging temperatures if you can find shelter. Plants have evolved ingenious ways to survive winter. Many strategies will work, and here are just a few: Some plants hide out underground—as roots, bulbs, and tubers crammed with food—until it's safe to grow leaves again; many plants secrete alcohols and sugars as a kind of antifreeze to lower the temperature at which cell walls would burst; lichens dehydrate over the winter; some plants grow low to the ground to avoid windchill; others create their own microclimates underground; some flowering plants (like mountain laurel) grow hairs along their stems and fruit as insulation; arctic flowers often use large petals as sun traps; some just sink their roots deeper; plants that live in extreme cold (such as red algae, which can grow on top of ice) sometimes use a color like red to convert light into heat. The plants in my yard are luckier—I cover some with pink sheets for a short spell, then bundle them in parkas of canvas and pine needles and dry leaves. It's a symbiosis as dear as the one between dogs and humans. I nourish them and they nourish me.

From Diane Ackerman, *Cultivating Delight: A Natural History of My Garden* (New York: HarperCollins Publishers, 2001), 171.

Thinking about Unstated Problems

Ackerman intervenes in the plant world's problem solving by introducing a solution of her own to help them along—and possibly for another reason as well. In addition to the problem of keeping her plants warm in winter, what other problems might Ackerman be attempting to solve? How might plants nourish people (in ways other than as food)?

Although this solution—protective sheeting placed over a small peach tree—might not be as lovingly applied as Ackerman's solution to her own plants' problem, it may work just as well for the plant.

Problem and Solution

The questions posed in the problem and solution method are "What problems exist?" and "What will solve these problems?"

To pose problems, ask

- What are the most obvious problems associated with the subject?
- What problems have other people noticed about it?
- Who is affected by the problem?
- What difference would solving the problem make?

To think of solutions, ask

- What is the fairest solution to the problem?
- Who will be most affected by the solution to the problem?
- What are the less obvious solutions to the problem?
- How much will solutions cost, or what implementation will they require?
- What solutions to the problem have failed in the past?

Problem posing and problem solving are used . . .

- to make decisions
- to better understand, use, or manage life's problems
- to expose problems no one has noticed
- to explain unintended consequences or byproducts of human invention or action

Narration

A narrative normally makes a point; that is, the story carries some sort of message for the audience. This message need not be a moral. Rather, a narrative essay can be used to evoke in readers a strong understanding of the events described in it and perhaps empathy with the people involved. Narratives allow readers to see, hear, experience, and maybe even live in a story.

To create a narrative, ask

- What happened to make the story worth telling?
- Who was involved?
- When did it happen, and over how long a period of time did it happen?
- Why did the events happen?
- What is the scene?
- What can be learned from the experience or event?

Narratives can be used . . .

- to show how one person's experiences can be compared to another's
- to illustrate why someone did something
- to show what the effect of something was upon someone
- to show the real consequences of an argument
- to entertain readers with interesting stories

Sample Narration

Touch the Clouds, Crazy Horse's seven-foot Miniconjou friend, asked that Crazy Horse be allowed to die in an Indian lodge. Dr. McGillycuddy carried the request to General Bradley, adding that violence might result from putting Crazy Horse in the jail. Bradley said, "Please give my compliment to the officer of the day, and he is to carry out his original orders, and put Crazy Horse in the guard house." Dr. McGillycuddy relayed this to Kennington, who tried again. American Horse, who had recently conspired against Crazy Horse's life, protested that Crazy Horse was a chief, and could not be put in prison. Dr. McGillycuddy returned to Bradley and told him it would be death to try a third time. Bradley finally agreed to compromise and allow Crazy Horse to be taken to the adjutant's office, a small room with a desk, a kerosene lamp, and a cot. Several Indians carried him in a blanket and set him on the floor. He refused to lie on the cot.

From Ian Frazier, *Great Plains* (New York: Penguin Books, 1989), 112.

Narration in a Cartoon

Cartoons are often mini-narratives that make us laugh (if the artist is successful, that is). What narrative is told here? Suppose you were the artist and had to put this narrative into words. What would you say?

"On the Internet, nobody knows you're a dog."

Sample Exemplification

In this example, Carl Sagan uses a narrative example to help readers imagine how people rationalize behavior by explaining away normally solid evidence.

Topic and claim that alibis were hard to come by

Example showing difficulty of creating alibi and the consequences

In the witch trials, mitigating evidence or defense witnesses were inadmissible. In any case, it was nearly impossible to provide compelling alibis for accused witches. The rule of evidence had a special character. For example, in more than one case a husband attested that his wife was asleep in his arms at the very moment she was accused of frolicking with the devil at a witch's Sabbath; but the archbishop patiently explained that a demon had taken the place of his wife. The husbands were not to imagine that their powers of perception could exceed Satan's powers of deception. The beautiful young women were perforce consigned to the flames.

From Carl Sagan, *The Demon-Haunted World: Science as a Candle in the Dark* (New York: Random House, 1996), 121.

A Photograph as an Example

In the summer before the assassination of President John F. Kennedy, Lee Harvey Oswald had this picture taken of himself holding a Mannlicher-Carcano rifle and a copy of *The Daily Worker,* a communist newspaper. How does a photograph serve as an example that explains a person's character? What did Oswald do to make sure that character came out? How might others interpret such an example as evidence that demonstrates a point, perhaps one not intended by the subject?

Exemplification

Exemplification provides readers with examples to illustrate a larger point. Examples help to demonstrate the validity and believability of a claim; they are especially useful when you need to explain complicated, abstract, or new ideas. Examples can be quotations, facts, narratives, statistics, details, analogies, opinions, or observations. Most generalizations you make need to be supported by plenty of examples so that your readers will appreciate your point.

To think of good examples, ask

- What in my own experience am I basing my conclusions on?
- What does someone need to know to appreciate my point?
- What examples from my reading (or viewing) can I draw on to illustrate the point?
- What experiences do I have in common with my readers that might exemplify my point?

Exemplification can be used . . .

- to explain and clarify complex or new ideas
- to demonstrate that something is true based on shared experience with readers
- to establish your credibility by showing that your ideas have a basis in experience
- to help readers imagine circumstances when your subject may be relevant to them

Classification and Division

The method of classification and division involves dividing a subject into its parts and then grouping (classifying) them on the basis of similarities. Writers choose a principle of classification—the means of dividing the subject—and communicate that principle to readers. The ability to divide a subject into its component parts and then determine how those parts might be classified has been seen, since classical times, as one of the most important for any writer to acquire. Especially helpful in dividing a subject so that you can begin to see patterns emerge is the method of contextual invention called tagmemics.

To classify and divide a subject, ask

- What are the most important or obvious features of the subject?
- What aspects of the subject are not as obvious?
- What do these features have in common with one another, and how do they differ?
- How have others classified and divided the subject?
- What other subjects is your subject like, and what features might they have in common?
- What features of your subject change over time? What features remain the same?

Sample Classification and Division

Clear statement of topic

Describes historical context and previous types

Origin of the hybrid cycle-rickshaw

Division of cycle-rickshaws by type and according to geographical origin

The rickshaw designs are as widely variable as their riders. Hong Kong still has a handful of the old hand-pulled rickshaws and Calcutta is the only city on earth where they are still in use as everyday transport. In the other cities the rickshaw, a creation of the 1880s, gave birth to the cycle-rickshaw during the 1930s and 1940s but no standard pattern developed for this new-fangled device. In Manila, Rangoon and Singapore the cycle-rickshaws are standard bicycles with attached sidecars. The Manila versions with their mini-bikes and youthful riders look like a toytown model, while in Rangoon the passengers ride back-to-back. In Ara, Beijing, Dhaka and Macau the rider is out front and the passengers sit behind, as if the front part of a bicycle was mated with an old hand-pulled rickshaw. In Hanoi, Penang and Yogyakarta the meeting of bike and rickshaw produced precisely the opposite result, as if the back part of a bicycle had been joined to the old rickshaw seating; as a result the passengers sit, sometimes frighteningly, out front, watching on-coming traffic hurtling towards them.

From Tony Wheeler, *Chasing Rickshaws* (Melbourne: Lonely Planet Publications, 1998), 7.

Cycle-rickshaws are classified as variations of a bicycle, divided into various types depending on how they differ from each other and from the familiar two-wheeled bicycle. Here, the bicycle serves as a class and the rickshaws as sub-types, but with their own distinctiveness.

Diagrams That Classify and Divide

Diagrams are a useful way to quickly show relationships among the constituent parts of a complex subject. Below, the subject of digital cameras has been divided into two categories, and then one of the categories has been broken down into four subcategories. A diagram like this will teach the basic framework of a subject quickly. One danger, of course, is that the diagram, which is a synthesis of a process of classification and division, may leave out or obscure important subtleties. Can you think of any digital cameras that might not fit neatly into this scheme?

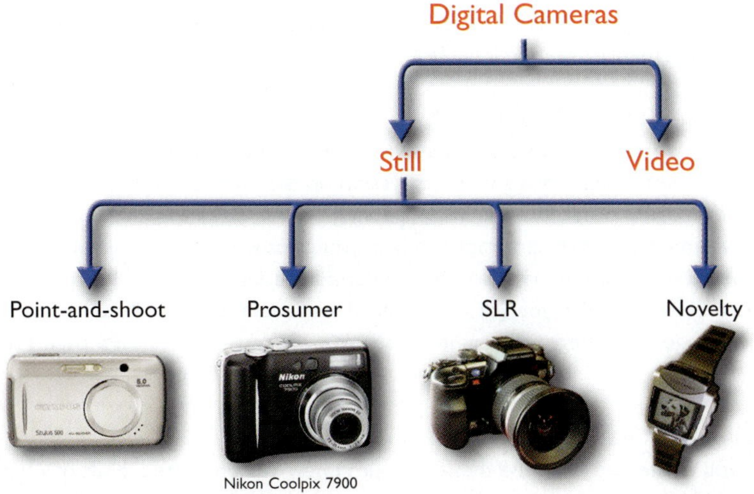

Nikon Coolpix 7900

Classification and division can be used . . .

- to show that a topic may be (and usually is) more complex than it initially appears
- to identify a pattern or schema that can help classify aspects of a new subject or situation
- to help readers understand what might otherwise appear as unassociated ideas

Writing Project Threads 5e

A table of contents for writing project threads appears on pages xv–xxii.

Shaping Information: Revising Paragraphs

A key strategy for communicating information clearly is creating good paragraphs that each communicate one main idea. Use the strategies in this chapter to help you think about the structure and purpose of each paragraph in your draft. Does each paragraph present one idea? Do any paragraphs need to be split? Combined? Consider the patterns for developing paragraphs in section 5d. Can you take advantage of these familiar patterns to make your information more understandable to readers?

Informative Essays

Garrison 1

Angela Garrison
English 101
Dr. Simpson
September 26, 2005

From Over There to Over Here:
War Blogs Get Up Close, Personal, and Profitable

Blog was the word looked up most often in the online *Merriam-Webster's Dictionary* in 2004 ("Blog"). What's all this fuss? When you read someone else's personal blog, you find out what they like and don't like, what they're doing, and maybe other bits of gossip offered at random. You can read news blogs to find out what's going on lately, what other people think about it, and why it matters. You can keep your own blog to share your thoughts and feelings, to tell your friends and family what you're up to, and sometimes to capture the interest of someone you've never met. When you read and write blogs, you join, or even create, a community. Blogs are also an efficient way to break news, spread rumors, and glorify causes. In short,

Proposal Arguments

Harrington 1

A Proposal to Clean Up Our Streets

I have a proposal which could clean up the whole neighborhood.

All of a sudden the public perception of the lobbying profession has plunged to depths even below those occupied by trial lawyers, tobacco users, child molesters and Democrat members of the Senate Judiciary Committee. Its practitioners are now seen as the designated villains of the present moment, to be avoided as if they were carriers of an especially virulent strain of bird flu common among vultures and other avid consumers of carrion and offal.

Given that the right to lobby is protected by the Constitution and cannot be banned outright, or even regulated to any great extent, all this blather about taking the boys and girls on K Street, who only yesterday were their bosom buddies, to the woodshed is nothing less than a charade. Any "reforms" will be window dressing, and after a brief period of time the buddy-wuddy relationships they shared with the K Street crowd will be re-invigorated. But, as Jerry Seinfeld would say, "Not that there's anything wrong with that."

Aside from banning former members of Congress and former Capital Hill staffers from ever serving as lobbyists, therefore condemning them to a fate worse than death – i.e., going home to their districts and living like normal Americans, deprived of the joys of the abundant life on the shores of the Potomac River – there really isn't much that can be done to stop the incestuous relationships between solons and lobbyists. As the song "Love and Marriage" explains, "they go together like a horse and carriage ... you can't have one without the other."

Addressing Counterarguments Using Paragraph Strategies

Part of your essay should address any strong arguments against your solution that arose in your community discussion or your research. In a counterargument paragraph, you present the counterargument and then explain why it doesn't make sense, why it doesn't matter, or why it doesn't outweigh the value of the solution you propose. This may involve comparing and contrasting your solution with another solution, explaining the problems with another solution, narrating what happened when something was tried, and so on. Review the paragraph writing strategies in section 5d. Then use these strategies to help you develop appropriate counterargument paragraphs. (If you are having trouble understanding what a counterargument is, see section 11k.) ▶ page 216.

Personal Essays

Gina Wolf Wolf 1
Professor
English 101
25 January 2006

Still Guarding the Fort

Jamie and I shared the imaginative elementary years together. After school, we ran a successful restaurant out of her basement. The clientele being mostly plastic, we were able to keep costs to a minimum. On the weekends and during the summer months, we could be found, or rather not found, out on my farm. Tucked away behind the massive root system ... mind of youth. It was not a dollh... a Fort. The simplicity of a hiding ... adventure in an "abode of our ow... were enough to make it the sourc...

The Fort first came int... my great-grandpa built gave ... The withered boards were p... that always looked old, no m... been painted. A few of these ... reconstructed into four wall... to the north. Two white pane... setting of the sun. An old door had lost its top third, and the remainder served as the entrance to the pretend wonderland. The roof was formed by adjoining large tin sheets. When it rained, each droplet that lightly pelted the tin roof sounded far more like hail.

Telling Parts of Your Story

In a personal essay, most paragraphs serve at least two purposes: they provide descriptive details that leave a vivid impression on the reader, and they narrate events in a logical order. Use the information in section 5d of this chapter about narrative and descriptive paragraphs to help you create effective paragraphs for your personal essay. You may also want to consider using photographs of people, places, or events to help you tell your story. If so, review section 24b to help you choose images and integrate them into your story. ▶ page 118.

Critical Reviews

A Movie You Can't Forget!

This could be the best movie you will ever see all year, if you're looking for something intense, suspenseful, and different than your usual effects-packed thriller. This is the kind of movie that you will be talking about at work, at the bank (to total strangers!), and at the corner coffee shop.

The movie starts with a murder -- a revenge killing, in fact. But was the right person killed?

The main character, Leonard Shelby (Guy Pearce), is a man with no short-term memory. He hasn't been able to form new memories since the night his wife was murdered. On a hunt to find the murderer, but with no way of remembering names, dates, places, facts and faces, he tattoos mementos of his search. He uses pictures to try to identify people who know his name. Does he like this person? Does he trust this person? Is this the killer? He doesn't know unless he's written a note.

Writer/director Christopher Nolan puts you right in Leonard's shoes, living the story in reverse order. This ingenious method of story-telling means that you never know more than Leonard does. In one scene you see Leonard getting information from a person who knows him -- maybe a good person; maybe bad. In the next scene you see a previous meeting between the two which sheds more light on their relationship. Later still you see how they met. You, like Leonard, have no knowledge of what came before.

This film will leave its own memento on your mind, and you'll have a hard time forgetting how much you enjoyed it.

Shaping and Sharing Your Ideas

After you've decided what the thesis of your review will be, write a draft of your review. Use the paragraphing strategies in this chapter to help you describe events, scenes, or features of the work (description); present criteria (classification and division); provide examples (exemplification); and compare and contrast ideas (comparison and contrast). Remember to think about the subject, purpose, and audience as you shape your review. ▶ page 152.

6 REVISING, EDITING, AND PROOFREADING

Revision is an act of discovery. When they revise, writers find out whether their draft matches their intentions and meets their expectations. Revision is a process of fine-tuning and elaborating meaning in a continual act of invention. Revision takes place whenever it needs to, not simply at the end of the process or in the eleventh hour before an essay or project is due.

Successful revision makes average writing into great writing. Even accomplished and successful writers don't get it right the first time and dribble out some horrible prose. However, they have strategies for raising the stakes, for re-seeing their writing and re-thinking their subject matter, for re-imagining their purpose and the expectations of their readers, and for adding, deleting, changing, or rearranging their words so the piece of writing can work its magic on others.

As you approach revision, you can ask yourself, "What do I want my writing to do?" "What have I done?" "What can I do now to meet my goals and reach my audience?"

Revision focuses on content and form and usually involves adding, deleting, changing, and rearranging—all acts that require careful thought and even new research and writing. Editing, in contrast, typically focuses on sentence-level and formatting issues at that point when a work has already undergone deep revisions that have made it better suited to its context and more likely to achieve its purposes. When you revise, you consider global issues—those qualities of your writing that suit it to the rhetorical situation. When you edit, you fine-tune, correct, and improve your writing with a careful eye for the particular. When you proofread, you double- (or triple-) check your writing systematically, looking for mistakes such as typos, unusual formatting, punctuation mistakes, spelling errors, and citation problems. Proofreading is the final stage of the process, when all that remains is to dot your *i*'s and cross your *t*'s.

6a Assessing Your Writing to Aid Revision

Effective writers are often their own harshest critics. Rhetorician Kenneth Burke once wrote that "some people write poems on paper, and others carve theirs out of jugular veins" (*Permanence and Change,* 76). As a writer, you will need to be thick-skinned.

It is almost always helpful to receive feedback on your writing from others. But when you revise your writing, you need to decide on your own whether it achieves its purpose and rises to the level of quality that you envision for it. It may not at first, but it will eventually if you keep asking questions of it, if you become a good judge and reviser of your own work, and if you raise the bar for yourself and don't settle for mediocrity. Eventually, you will learn to predict how your readers will react as well.

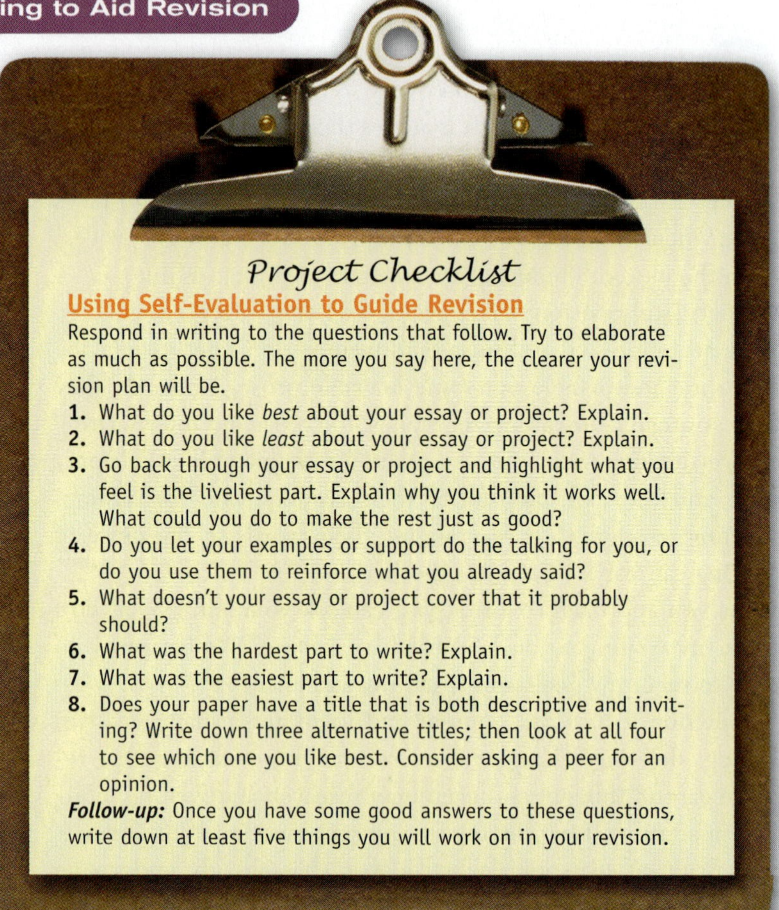

Project Checklist

Using Self-Evaluation to Guide Revision

Respond in writing to the questions that follow. Try to elaborate as much as possible. The more you say here, the clearer your revision plan will be.

1. What do you like *best* about your essay or project? Explain.
2. What do you like *least* about your essay or project? Explain.
3. Go back through your essay or project and highlight what you feel is the liveliest part. Explain why you think it works well. What could you do to make the rest just as good?
4. Do you let your examples or support do the talking for you, or do you use them to reinforce what you already said?
5. What doesn't your essay or project cover that it probably should?
6. What was the hardest part to write? Explain.
7. What was the easiest part to write? Explain.
8. Does your paper have a title that is both descriptive and inviting? Write down three alternative titles; then look at all four to see which one you like best. Consider asking a peer for an opinion.

Follow-up: Once you have some good answers to these questions, write down at least five things you will work on in your revision.

Activity 6-1: Thinking about Revision

Reflect on the following questions in your writing notebook.

1. Have you ever revised a piece of writing that you wrote for a class or for your own use? What was the process like in each case? What changes did you make to your writing?
2. Have you ever participated in peer review or peer editing with classmates? What did you like best about it, and what did you like least?
3. What kinds of feedback help you to understand what to revise?

As a reader:
- What excites your curiosity or makes you want to read this piece?

As a writer:
- How can you build on this aspect of the writing in your next draft?

As a reader:
- Is there anything—an idea, a detail, a choice of words—that might cause you to stop reading or feel defensive?

As a writer:
- What changes can you make to entice readers to keep reading even when they disagree with your ideas?

To evaluate a draft, the writer steps into the reader's experience. Then the writer returns to his or her own perspective to build on the draft's strengths and solve its problems.

In most cases, first drafts (and often even second, third, and fourth drafts) require deep revision. As we begin to learn more about the subject in the act of writing, it becomes clearer how we ought to shape our knowledge to suit the context, which consists of the audience we're writing to, our purpose, and the rhetorical occasion, or *kairos*. What do you know about your subject now that you didn't know when you started? And how can you use your new level of awareness to improve your work?

Audience

Step into the experience of at least one typical reader as you ask yourself how your draft would be read. For example, if you have written a first draft of a persuasive essay arguing that reality television actually does have some redeeming qualities, have you considered how people who have never seen these shows might respond? Or about how people who like *Survivor* but not *The Bachelor* might take your enthusiasm? If you have drafted an editorial for the morning newspaper, imagine you are a reader encountering the piece while you're drinking coffee at your kitchen table or cooling down after your morning run. If you are working on a brochure for a county historical museum, imagine you are a reader scanning a shelf full of brochures at an information kiosk or public library. What would make you decide to pick this one up? What would make you decide to start and continue reading it? Reading your work from the point of view of an audience member will help you revise your project in a way that will make sense to readers.

Purpose

You set out to achieve a purpose when you created your first draft. Has your purpose changed since you first started? As you reread your work, evaluate how close you have come to achieving your goals. For example, if you have written a cover letter to accompany a resume, how persuasively have you described your main qualifications for the specific job? In a newsletter article about an upcoming walk-a-thon to benefit people who have AIDS, have you given readers all the information they need in order to participate? In a poster presentation designed to share the details of your research study, have you presented the information in a way that will catch the eye of people walking through the conference room and then allow them to grasp the gist of your study in less than five minutes?

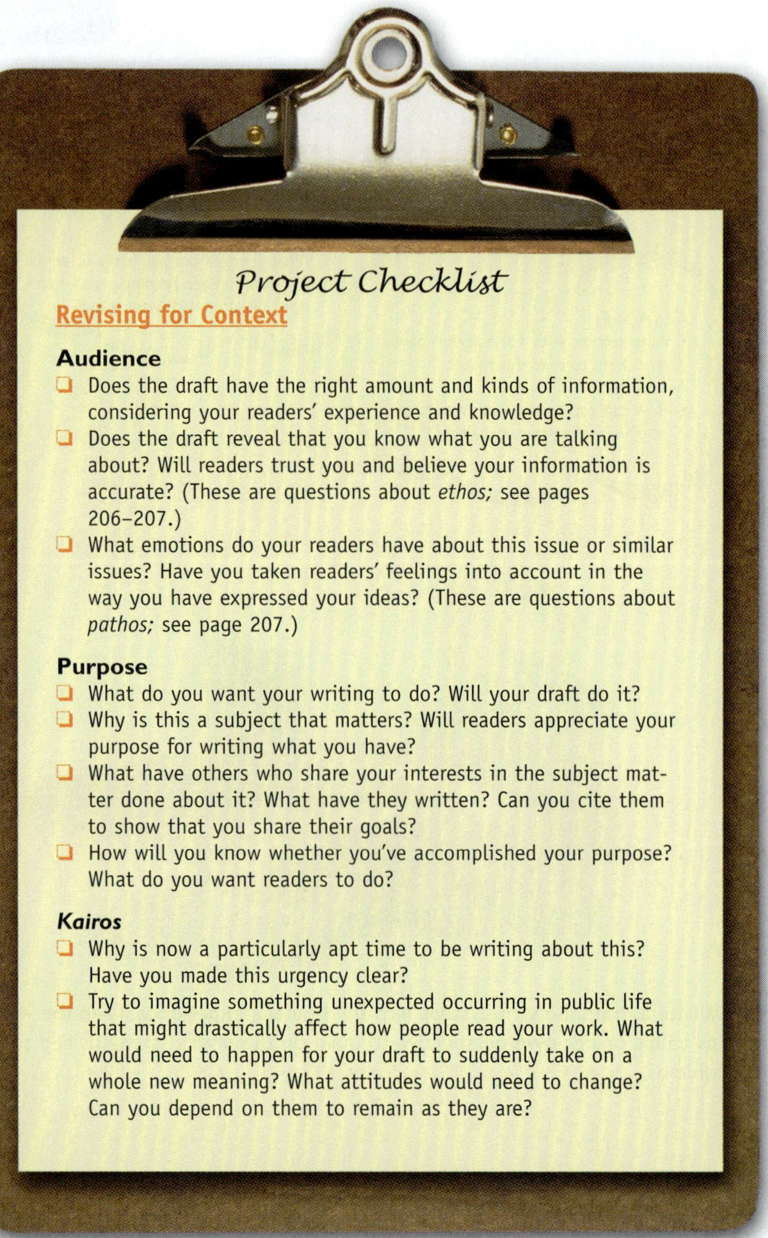

Project Checklist

Revising for Context

Audience

- ❑ Does the draft have the right amount and kinds of information, considering your readers' experience and knowledge?
- ❑ Does the draft reveal that you know what you are talking about? Will readers trust you and believe your information is accurate? (These are questions about *ethos;* see pages 206–207.)
- ❑ What emotions do your readers have about this issue or similar issues? Have you taken readers' feelings into account in the way you have expressed your ideas? (These are questions about *pathos;* see page 207.)

Purpose

- ❑ What do you want your writing to do? Will your draft do it?
- ❑ Why is this a subject that matters? Will readers appreciate your purpose for writing what you have?
- ❑ What have others who share your interests in the subject matter done about it? What have they written? Can you cite them to show that you share their goals?
- ❑ How will you know whether you've accomplished your purpose? What do you want readers to do?

Kairos

- ❑ Why is now a particularly apt time to be writing about this? Have you made this urgency clear?
- ❑ Try to imagine something unexpected occurring in public life that might drastically affect how people read your work. What would need to happen for your draft to suddenly take on a whole new meaning? What attitudes would need to change? Can you depend on them to remain as they are?

Activity 6-2: Responding from a Reader's Point of View

1. Write a description of one member of your audience. What does he or she know? Why is this person reading your piece of writing? What opinions does he or she already have about the topic you are writing about? Be as detailed as possible in your description.
2. Re-read your draft from the perspective of that audience member. Take notes from this new perspective. Do your best to role-play the audience member and to think from his or her perspective, not yours.
3. If possible, give your draft and your audience member description to a partner and ask the partner to respond as if she or he were part of that audience.
4. Make any revisions suggested by your analysis.

Activity 6-3: Thinking from a Broader Perspective

Consider your writing project in terms of *kairos*.

- Is there a current event that you can use to interest readers in your topic?
- Can your topic shed light on an event in the public eye right now?
- Is your topic an example of something larger that people are talking about?

Think through the connections between your topic and the events of the day, whether on your campus or in more encompassing communities, to see if you can make use of them to spark readers' interest and attention.

Kairos

As you write your draft on a computer at home by yourself or in a computer lab on campus, it is easy to forget that real people will read and respond to your writing later. But now it's time to think carefully about your timing and the circumstances of the act of reading itself and what people are likely to know about your topic. How will these more public circumstances affect responses to your work?

For example, suppose you have created a website that documents some historical event, using some of your own photography, and the website is now ready to be uploaded to a server. You planned for just your peers and instructor to be the readers, plus maybe a few friends. But suddenly you realize that outsiders may be interested, especially if the event you describe parallels something now in the news or if people you wrote about suddenly become famous or notorious. You worry that you might be (as they say when a website suddenly becomes hit by a lot of traffic) "slash-dotted." Should you plan ahead for these changing circumstances? Would you create your website differently once you realized the potential for a wide audience?

First drafts are a medium for figuring out what you want to say and how to say it. Rarely does a first draft reflect the best way to make your main point to readers; many times, your words won't even represent your thoughts accurately. Mine the first draft for ideas you intended to convey and those you can develop. It is at this point that revision becomes an act of discovery—the moment when you suddenly begin to see language not merely as a means of representing what you know but as a lens for seeing more deeply into your experience.

Sharpening the Focus

First drafts are often filled with generalities that represent several different approaches to the topic or even, on closer examination, completely different topics. If you find more general statements than details, you should focus your draft. Which general statement seems most interesting? Which one suggests an intriguing path to explore? If your draft wanders among competing generalities, select one that makes you curious and explore it (◀ section 3a).

Revision Example: Focusing an Introduction

Wyatt Roth, writing in a first-year composition course at Purdue University, chose to draft his essay straight through from beginning to end. But he revised his introductory paragraph radically based on feedback from his instructor, Colin Charlton. Wyatt's first draft started out very generally, a typical feature of first-draft writing.

First Draft

Competition at Its Best

Most people have at least one very distinct quality about them that sets them apart from everybody else. Sometimes it is something as obvious as a physical condition: obesity, hair color, freckles, or glasses. But more often than not, it is something that you cannot see by just looking at the person. Perhaps it is something about their personality or something they like to do. Regardless of what the defining characteristic is, everybody has one, and for me it is competitiveness. Ever since I was a young boy, I loved to turn even the smallest of things into a competition. I would say to my brothers, "Hey, I'll race you to the end of the road," or "I'll bet I can beat you in a game of Monopoly." It didn't matter what the scenario was, but rather how can I turn it into a game? Through this portrait I hope to show that I am a competitive person.

Why this explanation of universality? I like the move from physical to personality, but I'm wondering why you make the case for all of us having that distinct quality. How else could you frame your competitiveness in this beginning?

Wyatt threw away his first-draft introduction. In the second draft, he introduced his essay with specific details about the injuries he and his brothers have sustained while playing sports. This approach gave Wyatt a dramatic way to emphasize his love of sports and competition.

Second Draft

> Competition at Its Best
>
> Three broken collarbones, a torn ACL, a broken ankle, a separated shoulder, two torn hamstrings, a torn rotator cuff, and countless bumps, cuts, and bruises. It sounds like a list of injuries that you might see at a sports medicine clinic in a single day. These injuries, however, are a list of all of the things that have happened to my brothers and me over our football careers. The grand total for all of the expenses is estimated at around $85,000 (thank God for insurance). It sounds very painful and agonizing to many people, but if we were asked to do it all again knowing that we were going to have to go through all of these injuries the answer would be the same for all of us: "In a heart beat." So why would we do it all again? The enormous cost and wear and tear to your body would be enough to make most people hang it up. What was different about us? The answer is twofold: a deep love of football, but an even deeper love for the competition that it brings.

Activity 6-4: Looking Closely at Revision

Read the two drafts of Wyatt's essay and answer the questions below.

1. What is the focus of Wyatt's first draft? Is it easy or difficult to determine the focus from his introductory sentences? Why?
2. What is the focus of Wyatt's second draft? Is it easy or difficult to determine the focus from his introductory sentences? Why? How has the focus changed since the first draft?
3. Which introduction do you like better? Why?
4. What can you learn from this example about focusing your writing?

Most of the time, a thesis statement is predictive of the overall form of a work. If the thesis statement is unclear, missing, tentative, or noncommittal, the draft will probably reflect that. Examine all the other general statements in the draft to see whether they support and develop the working thesis statement. If they don't, you can rewrite them to link them more closely to the thesis, or you can discard them. Or you may find that your thesis statement needs to become more specific in order to perform its function as a focal point. You may even find a mechanical or grammatical problem in your thesis; once it is cleared up, you may be able to see more clearly what you meant to express. If you don't yet have a thesis statement, reread your draft and then write one to serve as the focus for your next draft (◀ section 4b).

Adding Details and Evidence

Readers want to be shown the evidence on which you base your position. Knowing the details, they can then decide whether they agree with your central point in an argumentative essay or the gist and insights of a narrative. What kind of evidence or events you need to include depends on the point you are asking readers to accept or the feelings and thoughts you want them to keep in mind.

In many academic projects, evidence will emphasize the *why* and *how* of your thesis. If you write, "Even though it is not a poem, the film *Rabbit-Proof Fence* has many important qualities of an epic," then you will need to tell readers why you think so. How do several specific aspects of the film correspond to important qualities of an epic poem? The amount of supporting information you will need to support a given thesis will vary, too. If your readers hold a view contrary to yours, you will need more evidence than if they are likely to agree.

Project Checklist

Kinds of Evidence

If you find that your draft needs more details, evidence, scenes, or texture to draw out and elaborate its main points, consider these kinds of evidence, taking into account the rhetorical situation:

- *Sensory details*—visual details and contrasts, sounds, aromas, textures, and tastes—can all add atmosphere to a scene.
- *Facts* that go beyond common knowledge and that are properly cited show that you have done your research. (For more about common knowledge, see pages 359–362.)
- *Statistics* can appease readers who wonder whether your numbers really add up when you make generalizations about, for instance, how many people think this or that. In science and social science fields, statistical evidence can be especially important.
- *Voices of authority* and *expert opinion* can add credibility to your claims, improve your own ethos, and show that you know what others have already written about your topic. But don't let the voices of authority smother your voice. Be certain to cite direct and indirect uses of another's words and ideas.
- *Visual presentations*—graphs, charts, illustrations, tables, screenshots, and photographs—are useful ways to summarize data and show relationships across sets of data over time. Be sure that your visual information doesn't simply stand by itself but that you weave its meaning into your draft (▶Chapter 24).
- *Experiential evidence* can be used when you have insider knowledge of an event, know how something works, or have acquired information over time. Draw from personal experience.

It is very likely that you will want to do additional research in order to find appropriate support for your thesis and details for your narratives. Conducting focused research at the stage of revision can be fun. You know what you need, and it's exciting to find it. (For advice on conducting research online, see Chapter 15; for library research, see Chapter 16.)

Visual content—photographs, charts, graphs, illustrations, cartoons, advertisements—serves as supporting material in many kinds of writing projects. In college writing, follow the conventions of your discipline in using visual content; for example, lab reports sometimes include diagrams of apparatus, and essays may use images as a subject of analysis. Projects such as brochures, newsletter articles, Microsoft® PowerPoint® presentations, and websites often include images and other design elements. (See Chapter 24, Using Visuals to Inform and Persuade.)

If you use visual content, scrutinize every instance to be sure it is suitable for your purpose and audience. Don't presume that readers will see what you want them to see; they rarely will. Does the visual content work as evidence? Does it illustrate a point? Since visual content naturally draws the eye and attention, does it merit the attention it will get? Or is it more decorative than informative? Is it sharp and clear? Make sure any compressed images are not overly pixellated. (An image is said to be "pixellated" when the individual dots that make it up are big enough to be seen by the viewer.) All visual content needs to be cited properly.

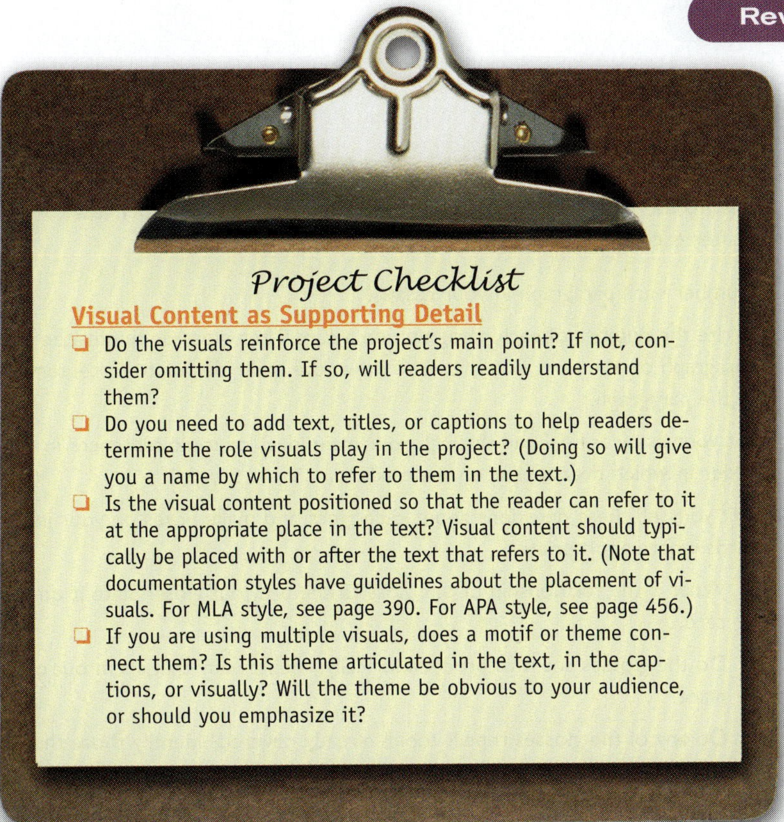

Project Checklist

Visual Content as Supporting Detail

- ❑ Do the visuals reinforce the project's main point? If not, consider omitting them. If so, will readers readily understand them?
- ❑ Do you need to add text, titles, or captions to help readers determine the role visuals play in the project? (Doing so will give you a name by which to refer to them in the text.)
- ❑ Is the visual content positioned so that the reader can refer to it at the appropriate place in the text? Visual content should typically be placed with or after the text that refers to it. (Note that documentation styles have guidelines about the placement of visuals. For MLA style, see page 390. For APA style, see page 456.)
- ❑ If you are using multiple visuals, does a motif or theme connect them? Is this theme articulated in the text, in the captions, or visually? Will the theme be obvious to your audience, or should you emphasize it?

Activity 6-5: Considering Your Need for Evidence

1. Write down or highlight the thesis or focusing statement in your piece of writing. Make note of each reason or category of evidence that you provide to support your claim, and give each one an identifying number or symbol.
2. Sentence by sentence, read through your draft. Next to each piece of evidence, place the number or symbol that corresponds to the relevant reason for your claim.
3. Note which reasons are supported by the most evidence and which reasons have the least. Then decide where you need to provide more support.

Check your draft to see how easy it is to follow your ideas.

Paragraph Glossing

Paragraph glossing is a method of evaluating your work to see if your essay is structurally coherent, if your argument proceeds logically, if your writing is repetitive, and if your paragraphs are in the right order.

Posting Signs for Your Readers

Give your readers directions to help them find their way through your writing:

- **Key terms** deliberately repeated throughout the work to keep readers focused (◀ page 56)
- **Transitions** to help make your pattern of organization evident (◀ page 58)
- **Headings** (sometimes called *headers*) to name the sections in long or complex documents. Headings should act as summaries of a part's major focus. So, rather than using headings like "Introduction," "Background Information," and "Conclusion," use headings tied to your topic. In an essay on "The Benefits of Celebrity Charity," you might have headings like "The Recent History of Celebrity Charity" and "When Does Charity Become Promotion?"

Activity 6-6: Paragraph Glossing

It's best to use index cards for this exercise. If you use regular paper, leave 3–4 lines after each gloss for your notes.

1. Number each paragraph in your essay.
2. Write the number of each paragraph on a card. Then gloss or summarize the paragraph on the card. (That is, write down the main idea or topic sentence of the paragraph.)
3. Set your essay aside. Read through your main ideas or topic sentences in the order in which they appear on the cards.
4. Ask yourself these questions about each gloss, and make notes on your index cards where appropriate:
   a. What is the relationship of this gloss to the previous gloss? State it on the card.
   b. Do the glosses seem to proceed logically? Identify any that seem out of place.
   c. Do any of the glosses repeat topics already covered? Identify those that do and consider either deleting the associated paragraph or combining the paragraphs on the same subject.
   d. If a gloss you have just written does not appear in its associated paragraph, would it work as the topic sentence? If so, add it to your draft.
5. Identify those glosses/paragraphs whose order troubles you. Try reading the glosses in a different order—for example, 1, 2, 3, 5, 4, 6, 9, 7, 8, ... Does anything change? If the order doesn't seem to matter, then your essay probably needs a controlling purpose or idea that will give it momentum or direction.
6. Describe briefly what you have learned about your original paper after completing steps 1–5. What changes will you make? Why?

Cutting, Copying, and Pasting Text and Images

1. Position your cursor where you want to begin cutting or copying.
2. To cut or copy, hold down the left mouse button (on a two-button mouse) or press the Command key (⌘) and click the mouse (on a Mac). Highlight the text or image by dragging the cursor over it. Then use the commands in the table below.
3. To paste, position the cursor at the insertion point and then key the paste command shown in the table.

Function	Windows Keystroke	Mac Keystroke
Cutting deletes the text or image and places it on the clipboard in your computer's memory for later pasting. Only the most recent cut is saved on the clipboard, so be careful!	Ctrl + X	Command (⌘) + X
Copying leaves the original text or image where it is but copies it to the clipboard for later pasting.	Ctrl + C	Command (⌘) + C
Pasting takes the content of the clipboard and inserts it at the location of the cursor.	Ctrl + V	Command (⌘) + V

Using the cut, copy, and paste keystrokes is the quickest method, but you may be more comfortable using a toolbar or menu to perform these functions. In Microsoft® Word® 2007, look for these functions on the Home ribbon: . In Microsoft® Word® Mac 2008, look under the Edit menu. Most word processors will also copy and paste the formatting styles of the source. Sometimes you will not want to preserve the original formatting in your new document, in which case you should use the Paste Special command (Alt + Ctrl + V in Word® 2007 or Edit > Paste Special in Mac Word® 2008), which allows you more control over exactly what gets pasted and how.

For instructions that apply to Microsoft® Word® 2003, visit the handbook's website: **cengage.com/english/blakesley**

Writers working on a computer can experiment freely with revisions because word processing software allows for quick manipulation of text and images. For example, to create an informal outline of your first draft or to gloss your paragraphs when revising, you can use the cut, copy, and paste functions to capture the topic sentences and paste them into a new document. Cut-and-paste makes it easy to move paragraphs and sentences around within a document and between documents if you need to adapt your writing to other contexts or media (such as a Web page). You can also use the cut, copy, and paste functions in Windows Explorer (PC) or Finder™ (Mac®) to move and delete files. Cut, copy, and paste also are useful for copying and moving text from email messages, browsers (URLs and page content, for example), and chat boxes. Although there may be some variation across programs, Windows® and Mac operating systems generally use a standard set of keystrokes for the cut, copy, and paste functions.

As you work with documents on a computer, it is important to use what's called "version tracking" by naming your files carefully. When you revise, for example, it is useful to save the original copy of your draft and then use the Save As command to save the new copy with a different name so that you can easily see later which version is which. You may, later on, find that a paragraph used in the original draft and then deleted is useful after all, so it is handy to keep both versions.

Document Cycling and File Naming Conventions

Here is a sample of how one student named a first draft and then a revision:

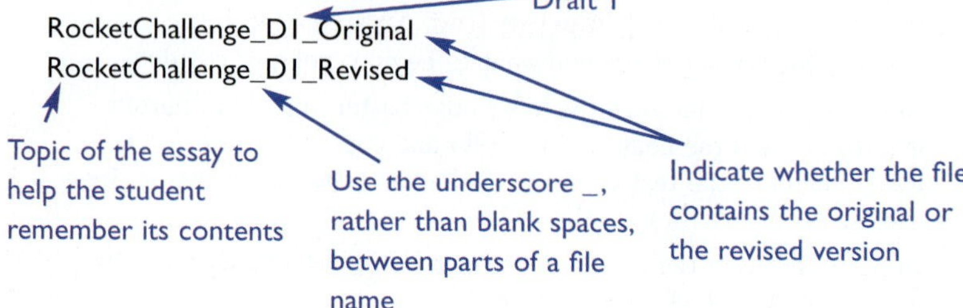
Draft 1
RocketChallenge_D1_Original
RocketChallenge_D1_Revised
Topic of the essay to help the student remember its contents
Use the underscore _, rather than blank spaces, between parts of a file name
Indicate whether the file contains the original or the revised version

Activity 6-7: Revising with Cutting and Pasting

1. Swap electronic copies of your draft with a partner.
2. Open your partner's draft and save it using a different file name (such as one that includes your initials).
3. Using the cut-and-paste function of your word processor, change the order of your partner's paragraphs. Don't change anything but the paragraph order.
4. Send the paper back to your partner.
5. Examine your paper as revised by your partner. What do you like (and not like) about the new paragraph order? Do any ideas arise that you can use to make your writing more effective?

Using the Paramedic Method to Analyze and Revise Sentences

Using a double-spaced copy of your draft, do the following.

1. Underline the prepositional phrases (such as *of the night, for his work*).
2. Circle the "to be" verbs (*am, is, are, was, were, been*).
3. Find the action or state of being in the sentence. (Look for nominalizations, such as *description* rather than *describe,* since nominalizations often disguise the action in a sentence.)
4. Put this action in a simple (not compound) active verb.
5. Determine the agent of the action, and then compose the base clause.
6. Start fast—avoid long introductory phrases.
7. Try to keep the subject/agent of the sentence close to the action.
8. Vary the lengths of your sentences; go for rhythm and balance.
9. Read the passage aloud with emphasis and feeling. Revise sentences to improve rhythm and put stress on key ideas. (Information that comes last in a sentence is remembered most clearly.)

Use this method judiciously, depending on your rhetorical situation. Certain purposes require more linking verbs than others. Basic description, for example, often requires a simple verb, as in "The sky was blue." So does a sentence that defines a state of being, such as "The Fourth of July is a national holiday in the United States." In much expository prose, however, a ratio of no more than one "to be" verb to every five sentences is about right. In any event, be aware of your style and know that you have options.

Activity 6-8: Revising with the Paramedic Method

Apply the steps of the paramedic method to these sentences to revise them.

1. Having this particular self-investigation to perform as an assignment enabled me to get some concrete ideas about myself that were formerly all in my head, down on paper in a cohesive way.
2. From the beginning, the writing of this paper was marked by reluctance.
3. After all the mechanical devices were put into place, it was hoped that his interest would be aroused for the world of the mysterious.

Sentences rarely come out finely tuned in a first draft, so experienced writers have learned to revise when their stylistic habits lead to unreadable or unnecessarily wordy prose. The paramedic method, first devised by Richard Lanham in the 1970s, helps writers revise what he called the official style.

The official style (the kind used so often in badly written formal reports, company memos, and other public documents) uses **passive** constructions, **nominalizations,** and long strings of **prepositional phrases** and nouns joined rather loosely with "to be" verbs. A nominalization is a noun that should be written as a verb for clarity's sake. In the following sentence, the nominalization is in boldface: *The story caused me to experience **confusion***. Revised, the sentence is easier to understand: *The story **confused** me.*

In the official style, concepts or inanimate objects often appear in the subject position in a sentence. Writers can improve the clarity and grace of their writing by using an agent-action style and putting people in the subject position whenever possible (see the five general principles of readability in section 33d).

If you apply the paramedic method consistently to every one of your sentences, your writing will be clearer, more concise, and, most importantly, readable. You will also develop a sharper sense of what you have already written and thus clearer ideas about how to revise your writing so that it better accomplishes your purposes.

Sample Application of the Paramedic Method

Here's a sample of some writing that sorely needs the paramedic method. First, read the passage aloud to hear the awkwardness of the style and rhythm. Then apply the nine steps of the paramedic method to revise it. See if your revision turns out like the revision we offer.

Draft

For readers of today, the practice of bad writing is harmful when it results in an inhibition of the reader's responses to intellectual and imaginative stimuli. There are several factors existing that readers are inhibited by and which create the dulling of the senses. The causes of these inhibitions should be considered by writers to avoid the decline of their clarity into the deep morass of jargon. On the one hand, it is an easy mistake for writers to use jargon to appear to be saying a lot when in actual fact very little of real import has indeed been actually imparted by them. Secondly, it is a bad habit to have one's writing become too monotonous. Primarily, it is a fault to make one's sentence forms repetitive. Mainly, it creates a feeling of sleepiness in the reader. Imagine what it would be like to read these sentences out loud, too! (151 words)

Revision

Bad writing dulls the senses and stifles the imagination of readers. Writers should consider the causes of these inhibitions. First, if you want to preserve clarity, don't use jargon. Some writers mistakenly use jargon to present the "appearance" of depth. Second, avoid monotonous repetition, which makes readers fall asleep. Imagine reading your sentences aloud! (54 words)

In the revision, we managed to preserve much of the meaning of the original but eliminated 97 of the 151 words. This means that 97 of the 151 words in the original paragraph, or 64% of its content, were useless. Lanham referred to such stylistic excess as "lard content." In most cases, you should try to keep your sentences as lean as possible.

Responding as a Reader: Pointing, Summarizing, Reflecting

It is sometimes helpful to respond to a draft as a reader, without the compulsion to offer specific suggestions for improving it. Writers find it valuable to know what their readers remember, what they felt as they read, and what they want to know more about. To give writers this kind of response, you can respond by pointing, summarizing, and reflecting.

- **Pointing.** What one idea or image really stands out? What is the most striking sentence? What do you remember most about it?
- **Summarizing.** What is the writing about? Give the most direct answer, and try to elaborate as much as possible. The idea is to give the writer a good sense of what readers remember about the work.
- **Reflecting.** If you have a chance to annotate the work, let the writer know what you are thinking as you read. For example, if you are lost, write "I am lost here." If you feel sad, write "This scene makes me feel sad." It's enough to reflect these kinds of responses back to writers. They may decide that you were lost because you weren't paying attention, or they may realize that they need to work a little harder to give you something that keeps your interest.

Activity 6-9: Peer Review: Point, Summarize, and Reflect

Make two copies of your paper. In a small group, exchange papers. Give a classmate feedback on his or her draft by pointing, summarizing, and reflecting. Then trade a second copy of your paper with another classmate and provide the same kind of response. When you have received two responses to your writing, read your classmates' notes. Consider what revisions you'd like to make.

Peer review of writing is a critical component of revision. Not only will your reading of another's work help the writer, but you will find yourself sharpening your critical reading ability in ways that help you evaluate and revise your own work. As a peer reviewer, you will also see options that you hadn't considered previously for approaching a topic.

As a writer, you will receive the valuable responses of real readers, who may be different from the ones you imagined while you were drafting. Reader feedback—when it is careful and reflective—almost always will help you improve your work. Knowing that real readers will care about what you say may also motivate you in other ways. (It can be a terrible feeling to have something that is not your best effort responded to by readers who really care about what you say.)

From the Reviewer's Perspective

As a reader helping a writer revise his or her work, you should keep some general principles in mind.

- Find out about the context.
- Read carefully.
- Make constructive comments.
- Be a reader, not an editor.
- Suggest specific improvements.

Find out about the context. Before you begin, ask the writer about the work's context. What is the assignment, or what is the writer trying to achieve? Who is the audience? Once you understand the context, you'll be in a better position to provide useful feedback.

Read carefully and attentively. Give the writing your full attention. Most reviewers find that two readings are necessary. First, read through the whole work to get the gist. Then read it again more slowly, making notes as you go. Put a check mark next to each part of the draft that you think is particularly good. If you are reading the work electronically, consider using the word processor's comment function (page 104).

Make your comments constructive. The work is a draft and as such is unfinished. Remember that it can be difficult to receive feedback, especially on a draft that took a lot of time and effort to write. So be supportive instead of negative, and offer suggestions as well as critical comments.

Be an interested reader, not an editor. At the drafting and revision stages, writers need feedback on the big issues: content, structure, flow, persuasiveness, examples, style, and so on. It's more important that you read as a reader than as an editor. (See page 106 for strategies for reading as an editor.)

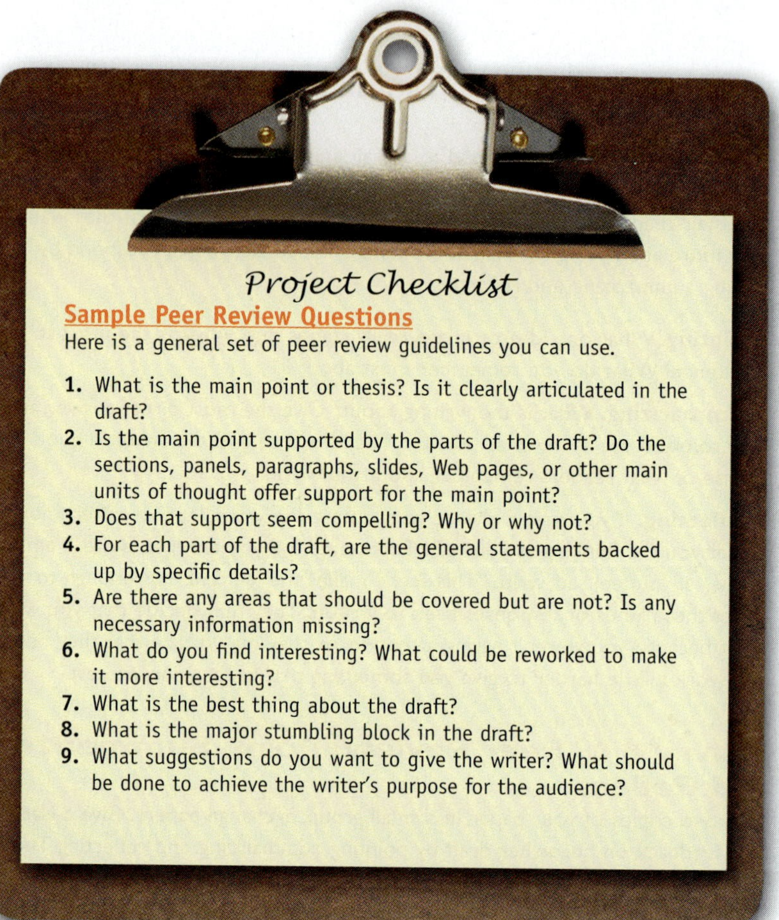

Project Checklist

Sample Peer Review Questions

Here is a general set of peer review guidelines you can use.

1. What is the main point or thesis? Is it clearly articulated in the draft?
2. Is the main point supported by the parts of the draft? Do the sections, panels, paragraphs, slides, Web pages, or other main units of thought offer support for the main point?
3. Does that support seem compelling? Why or why not?
4. For each part of the draft, are the general statements backed up by specific details?
5. Are there any areas that should be covered but are not? Is any necessary information missing?
6. What do you find interesting? What could be reworked to make it more interesting?
7. What is the best thing about the draft?
8. What is the major stumbling block in the draft?
9. What suggestions do you want to give the writer? What should be done to achieve the writer's purpose for the audience?

Activity 6-10: Questions for Peer Review of an Analysis Paper

In groups of three, exchange drafts so that each person has a paper to read. Read the draft and respond to the following questions in detail. When finished, sign your name to your comments and return them to the writer. If time permits, discuss each writer's draft as a group.

1. What do you like best about this piece of writing? Explain.
2. What do you like least about this piece of writing? Explain.
3. Does the writer tell you enough about the subject or the content of the text analyzed for you to decide whether the analysis is legitimate and perceptive? Explain.
4. What doesn't the writer tell you that you would like to know more about?
5. How would you say this person feels about the subject in general? Briefly explain how you came to your conclusions.
6. Go back through the paper and bracket and initial what you feel is the liveliest part. Explain why you think it works well.
7. Does the analysis lead to any conclusions? What are they? What is the most important conclusion and why does it matter?
8. Does the paper have a good title? Suggest two or three good alternative titles, and then circle the one of your suggestions that you like best.

Provide specific suggestions for improvement. Writers need specific feedback. Sometimes they need a pat on the back or a reminder that they have a lot of work to do. But most of the time, writers want to know how readers reacted and what suggestions they have for making improvements in later drafts. "I don't like this!" or "This doesn't sound good" is not specific enough to be useful. Nor is "I liked your essay." Whether you do or don't like something, you should explain why and offer a suggestion for improvement: "The anecdote at the beginning is priceless! I can hear the voices of your aunts as they complain. But I think you need to add some kind of transition to get us from Mississippi to Florida, since your thesis focuses on the family you are part of now."

From the Writer's Perspective

As a writer . . .

- Don't make disclaimers about your writing.
- Be receptive to feedback.
- Ask follow-up questions.
- Revise with reviewers' comments in mind.

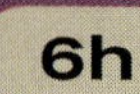

Don't preface the peer review with disclaimers. A disclaimer is a statement like "I only spent an hour on this draft" or "I didn't understand the assignment." Such disclaimers may be true, but the point of peer review is to give readers a chance to respond to what is actually written.

Be receptive to feedback. Don't be dismissive about any reader's feedback. Sometimes people will read differently than we expect, but use that to your advantage. Why did that happen? What might you have written to prevent a misreading?

Ask follow-up questions. Readers probably won't mind if you ask them questions about comments you don't understand or if you ask for a response to a particular aspect of your writing (its conclusion, for example).

Revise with your reviewers' comments in mind. Keep the peer reviews next to you when revising. Read through them again as you plan your revision so that you remember what aspects you want to address in a second draft.

Balloon Commenting in Microsoft Word 2007

To make sure that your comments on a text appear as balloons, follow these steps:

1. Select the Review tab and then the down arrow on the Track Changes icon, which then allows you to choose "Change Tracking Options." (See Figure 6.1.)

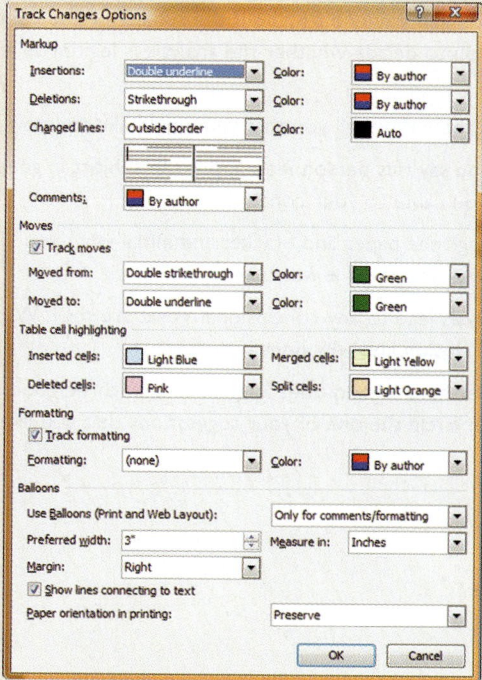

Figure 6.1 Setting the Options for Commenting and Track Changes in Microsoft Word 2007

2. In the Options dialogue box, set "Use Balloons (Print and Web Layout)" to "Only for comments/formatting" in the drop-down menu.
3. Click OK.
4. Set your view to Print, Full Screen Reading, or Web Layout using the View ribbon: Choose View > Print Layout in most cases.

To insert balloon comments, follow these steps:

1. Choose the Review Tab.
2. Highlight the text you want to comment on.
3. On the Review ribbon, click on the New Comment button. (See Figure 6.2.)

Figure 6.2 Inserting a Comment in Microsoft Word 2007

4. Type your comment in the balloon.
5. To insert another comment, repeat steps 2–4.

For instructions that apply to Microsoft® Word® 2003, visit the handbook's website: **cengage.com/english/blakesley**

Commenting on a Document in a Word Processor

Most word processors allow writers and peer reviewers to comment on a text without changing the original text itself. In Microsoft Word, WordPerfect®, and OpenOffice.org Writer, the process works similarly. (Each has additional tools for making and recording changes to the text itself. To track changes throughout a document, see section 6j, Proofreading on a Computer.) As different readers respond to a draft, their comments appear in different colors, and the initials of the respondent help writers identify who said what.

Reading as an editor requires shifting the focus of your attention from that of writer to that of reader. When editing, you pay deliberate and systematic attention to the ways your work communicates with readers. How will they respond to your writing? You may find that a deep edit prompts you to return to revising in order to work out some of the problems that have surfaced. Like revision, editing may prompt rewriting.

To help you see (and hear) your writing in ways that help draw out issues for editing, try these strategies.

Read Your Writing Aloud

When you read your work aloud, even by yourself, you will see and hear problems with the text. The act of translating the words to speech will help you notice awkward phrasings, repetition in word choice, problems with coherence, lapses in tone, and other stylistic problems that should be addressed. Read with pen in hand so that you can place a check mark next to sentences and sections that need further attention.

Getting Ready to Edit

Use these strategies when you edit.

- **Let it be.** Set your work aside. Let it rest for a few hours or days, and return to it with fresh eyes. You'll be surprised by how differently it reads after you've achieved some critical distance.
- **Edit on paper and screen.** Consider editing first on screen and then on paper, which will help you see your writing in two distinct ways. On screen, consider tracking the changes you make to your document so that you can read these changes as both a reader and an editor.
- **Edit your editing.** It may seem like overkill to suggest that you edit your revision and editing. However, writers often introduce new problems into their work with the corrections they make. Read your additions with an editor's eye.
- **Avoid distractions**. If you are distracted or daydream when you edit, you will overlook mistakes.
- **Change the look of your text.** Professional editors fear looking at that first copy of the finished magazine or book because they know that errors sometimes leap right off the page, making them wonder how on earth they missed them. When a familiar text has new haunts, it will look different and you will notice mistakes more readily.

Having Your Computer Read Aloud

Some software programs, such as Adobe Acrobat and Adobe® Reader®, will read your writing (or any writing) aloud so that you can follow along as if you were in the audience. It will be helpful to have a printed copy to mark up as you listen.

If you have the ability to make your text file into a PDF (portable document format) file, then you can open it in Acrobat or Reader and have the program read your text aloud. To convert a text file to a PDF file without having Acrobat installed on your computer, use a free program like CutePDF Writer (**http://www.cutepdf.com/Products/CutePDF/writer.asp**) or Adobe's online service, Create Adobe PDF Online (**http://createpdf.adobe.com/?v=AHP**), which has a free trial for the first five conversions. The computer's voice will sound machine-like, but you can trust that it will read exactly what's written. If it can't recognize a word because of a spelling mistake, you will hear it stumble.

With your PDF document open in Acrobat or Reader,

1. From the top menubar, choose View > Read Out Loud and then select whether you want it to "Read This Page Only" or "Read To End Of Document."
2. Press and hold Shift + Ctrl + C (Windows) or Shift + Apple + E (Mac) to pause the reading or restart it.
3. To end the reading, press and hold Shift + Ctrl + E (Windows) or Shift + Apple + E (Mac).

A computer lab on your campus may have Adobe Acrobat; check to see whether you can convert your documents to PDF there.

Activity 6-11: Evaluating Editing Strategies

1. Use two of the editing strategies discussed in this section, such as changing the background color of your draft, printing the draft on colored paper, or having a friend or your computer read the draft aloud to you.
2. Write a paragraph that compares the two strategies. What types of changes did each method lead you to make? Which one helped you more? Why?

Read Line by Line

When you are editing at the sentence level, reducing the amount of text you see at any one time will help you focus your attention.

1. On screen, minimize the size of the window so that you see only a few lines of text at a time. Then do your editing.
2. On paper, use a colored piece of paper to cover up all but a few lines of text. Then do your editing.

Read Sentences in Reverse Order

Read the text from the last sentence to the first, reading each sentence out loud. When you read backwards, you divorce yourself from the logic and flow of your text's delivery and are more likely to locate problems and weaknesses. It will take some time for you to read this way, but if you have time, especially with shorter texts, try it.

Focus Your Editing

When you edit your work, try to focus on one feature at a time. When you look for something in particular—such as tone or your use of sources—you are much more likely to notice issues that need to be addressed by some editing. When you try to pay attention to everything, you may not notice much of anything.

Pay Special Attention to Beginnings and Endings

Professional editors know how common it is to make mistakes in the first and last sentences of a document, section, or even paragraph. At the beginning of a new section, the eye tends to jump ahead and move rapidly down the page, so obvious mistakes may be missed. At the end of a section, the eye senses that the end is near and rushes to finish. Read your opening and concluding sentences carefully as you edit and proofread. There are few feelings more awful for a writer who has spent hours revising and editing than discovering an obvious mistake in the very first line of an essay or, worse, the title itself. There's a story about a famous linguist who, having written a fine essay on the use of the definite article in English (the word *the*), mistakenly titled his work "Use of Definite Article in English" before sending it off to the publisher. What error did the linguist make?

Focal Points for Editing

Global Issues

If you have revised carefully, you may have already addressed most of the global issues that will affect the reception of your writing. However, at the editing stage, it is important to reconsider these issues as a final check. Use the Project Checklists on pages 90, 94, and 95 to check global issues once again. Also take this opportunity to think about your title. Does it accurately reflect the work's content or purpose? Will it appeal to the intended audience? Check the title for spelling and grammatical mistakes.

Local Issues

- **Transitions.** Check to make sure that you use effective transitions across paragraphs. If transitions between sentences aren't necessary, eliminate them (◀ sections 4f and 5c).
- **Metadiscourse.** Eliminate statements that merely announce your intentions, such as "In this paper, I will . . . ." These references to the act of writing itself—called metadiscourse—focus readers' attention on you rather than on the subject matter, where it belongs (◀ section 4b).
- **Coherence.** Read through your essay to see if you have good sentence-to-sentence coherence (◀ section 5c). Are there any abrupt leaps that need to be fixed?
- **Diction.** Make sure that you use terms that your audience will understand and that are appropriate to the subject matter and rhetorical situation (▶ Chapter 38).
- **Usage.** Check to see that you have followed usage guidelines for special or unusual terms, nonsexist language, spelling, and other conventions appropriate to the genre or discipline.

Software for Editors

If you do a lot of editing, you may find it useful to try out some software that makes routine editing tasks easier, especially when working with long and complex documents. One possibility is

Editor's ToolKit: **http://www.editorium.com**

(A free 45-day trial is available.)

Style, Mechanics, and Spelling

- **Agent-action style.** Wherever possible, use an agent-action style. Use simple action verbs to add concreteness and liveliness to your writing (Chapter 37).
- **Repetition.** Eliminate unnecessary repetition of words and ideas (Chapter 36).
- **Parallel structure.** Use parallel structure with a series of items, phrases, or sentences when you want to establish a consistent pattern (Chapter 34).
- **Sentence fragments.** Use complete sentences; if you use any fragments, make sure you have a rhetorically sound reason to do so (Chapter 41).
- **Comma splices and run-ons.** Make sure that you don't use commas where periods or semicolons are needed (Chapter 42).
- **Dangling modifiers.** Make sure that modifying phrases are next to the terms they modify (section 46n).
- **Subject-verb agreement errors.** The verb should agree with the subject in every sentence. Double-check your sentences, especially when there is a prepositional phrase or modifier between the subject and the verb (Chapter 45).
- **Pronoun reference and agreement.** All pronouns should have a clear antecedent and agree in number with that antecedent (Chapter 43).
- **Clichés.** Eliminate clichés, as well as idiomatic phrases that some readers won't understand (section 38g).
- **Homonyms.** Don't confuse homonyms, such as *to, too,* and *two* (section 58c).
- **Missing words.** Make sure that you haven't left out any words needed to complete the meaning of a sentence (Chapter 41).
- **Spelling.** Run your document through a spell checker *and* read through it one last time so that you catch the errors that spell checkers almost always miss, such as homonyms (Chapter 58).
- **Citation style.** Check all the entries in your works cited or bibliography to make sure they include the required information, use the required form and style, and are listed in the required order (Part 4).
- **Punctuation.** Check punctuation throughout. Double-check the opening and closing sentences of all paragraphs (Part 9).

Make a List of the Words You Commonly Misspell

Keep a list of words you often misspell and refer to it as you edit and proofread. You can use your word processor's Find function (usually Ctrl + F on a PC or Apple + F on a Mac) to search for them. You can also add these words to your AutoCorrect dictionary if you are using Microsoft Word.

Keep Track of Your Most Common Grammatical, Mechanical, and Punctuation Errors

If you have learned from your instructor's feedback or your own editing that you have trouble with particular kinds of sentences, grammatical constructions, or comma rules, make a reference sheet to use while editing. Hang it somewhere where you'll see it as you edit. Make a notecard to keep in your purse or wallet so that you'll have your list handy. Often, you will learn quickly to reduce these errors and thus won't have to carry the list with you for the rest of your life.

See the Editing Symbols chart on the last page of the book. It will help you understand your instructor's comments and respond to them.

When you proofread, you examine your document carefully to make sure that you haven't left anything out, that the pages are formatted correctly, and that you haven't misspelled words or made any typos. Proofreading is the last step in polishing your work for readers, who will appreciate the extra care you have taken. Word processing programs include a variety of useful tools for checking your writing during this final stage.

Tracking Changes to a Document

Microsoft Word, WordPerfect, and Writer in OpenOffice.org each allow users to track changes to a document and to compare documents so that the writer or the group members on a collaborative project can see what changes have been made. Tracking changes to a document can help you make sure that you haven't accidentally deleted important information from one draft to the next. You can also use the tracked changes to help you write submission notes, which instructors sometimes require with revisions.

Tracking Changes in Microsoft Word 2007

Note for Mac users: The Command key (⌘) on a Mac keyboard is the equivalent of the Ctrl key on a PC keyboard. To make the equivalent of a right click on a one-button mouse, hold down the Mac's Command key (⌘) while clicking; then select the function from the pop-up menu.

1. With your document open, choose the Review tab on the top menu bar.
2. Set your Track Changes options:
   a. Select the Review tab and then the down arrow on the Track Changes icon, which then allows you to choose "Change Tracking Options." (See Figure 6.3.)
   b. Set the options for displaying the types of changes you make to your document, including the appearance of comments. For editing purposes, we recommend using settings like those shown in Figure 6.3, which help you see changes, deletions, and comments most clearly.
   c. Click OK when finished.
3. On the Review ribbon, you can adjust the location of balloon comments, which kind of markup to show (e.g., Insertions and Deletions, Formatting), whether you view Final Showing Markup, Final, Original Showing Markup, or Original. The Review ribbon also includes handy commands for using Track Changes, including icons for accepting and rejecting changes, new comments, and comparing two documents.
4. Click on the Track Changes icon on the Review ribbon or press and hold Ctrl + Shift + E to start tracking changes to the document.

As you add and delete text, move it around, or change its formatting, Word will record these changes. Turn to page 112 to see your options for viewing the changes.

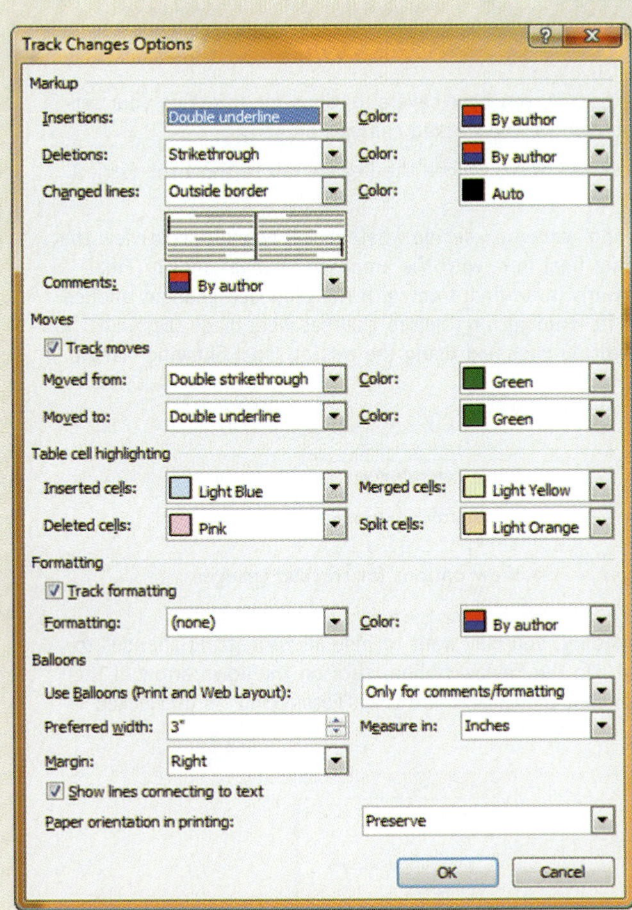

Figure 6.3 Recommended Settings for Track Changes in Microsoft Word 2007

For instructions that apply to Microsoft® Word® 2003, visit the handbook's website: **cengage.com/english/blakesley**

The actual steps will vary slightly from program to program and from Windows to Mac to Linux, but the general principles will be the same. These directions show you how to use the Track Changes tool in Microsoft Word in Windows XP.

Bookmarking Useful Reference Sites

In your Web browser, bookmark useful online reference sources so that you can access them easily as you check your facts and proofread. Here is a short list of writer's reference tools we find handy for this and many other purposes:

Merriam-Webster Online Dictionary:
http://m-w.com

Online Etymology Dictionary:
http://www.etymonline.com

RefDesk:
http://www.refdesk.com

Britannica Encyclopaedia:
http://www.britannica.com

Purdue's Online Writing Lab:
http://owl.english.purdue.edu

Viewing the Changes

In Microsoft Word 2007, you have several options for adjusting your settings so that you can see the tracked changes properly.

1. With the document open, choose the Review tab to show the Review ribbon.
2. In the "Tracking" category, decide whether you would like to view the document in its final form with the proposed changes shown (Final Showing Markup), in its final form with the proposed changes applied (Final), or in its original form before changes were made (Original). We recommend editing your text using the setting Final Showing Markup (Figure 6.4).

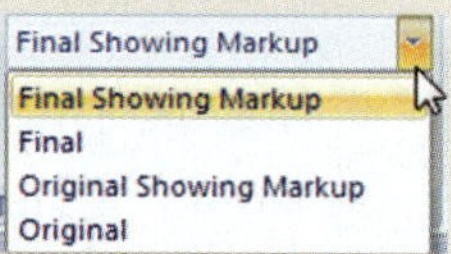

Figure 6.4 View options for tracked changes.

3. For ease of reading, you may want to hide all Formatting changes to the document. On the Review ribbon, click on the down arrow of the Show Markup icon, then make sure that "Formatting" is unchecked (Figure 6.5).

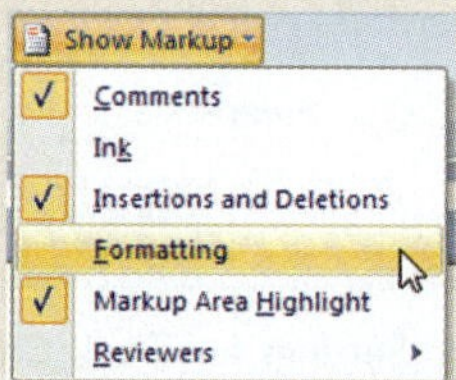

Figure 6.5 Show Markup options, here set to hide formatting changes.

For instructions that apply to Microsoft® Word® 2003, visit the handbook's website: **cengage.com/english/blakesley**

Sample Text with Track Changes

Track Changes helps you see which words have been added or deleted:

and musicians use "outlines" or "blueprints" ~~by~~ with which to perform text, to

Above, the black vertical line in the margin indicates that there is a change on the line. The word *by* has been deleted (indicated by the strikethrough), and the word *with* has been inserted.

In the text body, the material to which the comment refers is shaded, with a line connecting the comment to the location.

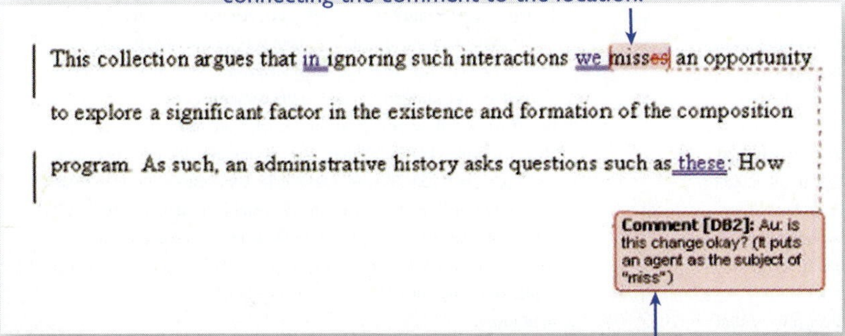

This collection argues that in ignoring such interactions we miss~~es~~ an opportunity to explore a significant factor in the existence and formation of the composition program. As such, an administrative history asks questions such as these: How

Comment [DB2]: Au: is this change okay? (It puts an agent as the subject of "miss")

In this comment balloon, "DB" is the initials of the person making the comment. A unique number is assigned to each comment; this is comment number 2.

Spelling- and Grammar-Checking Resources Online

To find out how to use spelling and grammar checkers in your word processing program, visit cengage.com/English/Blakesley. You will also find lessons in

- how to customize your spelling and grammar checker
- how to add terms to your Auto-Correct dictionary in Word
- what happened when we applied all suggested grammatical changes to the Gettysburg Address

6k A Student's Narrative Essay

Here is the final draft of Gina Wolf's autobiographical narrative essay, which she wrote in response to the assignment reprinted on page 28.

Wolf 1

Gina Wolf

Professor Larsen

English 101

25 January 2006

Still Guarding the Fort

Jamie and I shared the imaginative elementary years together. After school, we ran a successful restaurant out of her basement. The clientele being mostly plastic, we were able to keep costs to a minimum. On the weekends and during the summer months, we could be found, or rather not found, out on my farm. Tucked away behind the massive root system of a fallen oak stands a palace in the mind of youth. It was not a dollhouse or a castle or a tree house, but a Fort. The simplicity of a hiding place made out of scrap wood, the adventure in an "abode of our own," and the seclusion in the grove were enough to make it the source of dreams.

The Fort first came into being when an old granary that my great-grandpa built gave way and crashed into rubble. The withered boards were painted a distinctive rust color that always looked old, no matter how recently they had been painted. A few of these boards were relocated and reconstructed into four walls that seemed to slightly slant to the north. Two white paned windows faced the rising and setting of the sun. An old door had lost its top third, and the remainder served as the entrance to the pretend wonderland.

Wolf 2

The roof was formed by adjoining large tin sheets. When it rained, each droplet that lightly pelted the tin roof sounded far more like hail.

The interior was crowded with two old metal lawn chairs, each coated by a new thin layer of pink paint that easily chipped to reveal the green underneath. Separating them was a little endtable filled with a wide assortment of tarnished silverware. A fireplace of loosely aligned, cracked red brick stood in the corner next to the door, and two rainbow pillow cases from my parents' old bedroom covered the swinging windows; each hiding from prying eyes the evil concocting and baking of weeds, berries, and thistle wood. Bessy, the cow, could always be found out the west window, grazing or making a ruckus. We would regularly sell her milk to the many townspeople who happened by our Fort, which was in the middle of a dense grove, half a mile from any other farmhouse, and eight miles from three tiny rural towns.

We would be out there ten minutes after we woke up, doing our daily chores, such as dumping out Bessy's surprisingly stale, full water bucket and replacing it with fresh water. We had many discussions about how we were going to get that cow to drink more. A popular chore was to search for the ripe berry patches and pick the reddest and most plump of the fruit until our hands and clothes alike were stained purple. However, the most disputed and prized job was to go shopping, which included loading yourself up with money of

6k

Peer Review Question
Which parts of the description seem most effective? Why?

Wolf 3

the green, leafy kind and starting on the adventurous task of making your way to the junk pile. Being watchful of the broken glass and random nails, one of us would creep along and find an intact old jar or bowl, pick it up, and place our money into the sunken hole from where we had bought it. Many of our prized possessions were found on that heap, and many of them were very expensive, requiring many leaves to pay for them. Luckily, whenever there was an item that we just needed to buy, there always was an influx of Bessy's milk and of milk-thirsty passersby.

The fallen oak itself provided much entertainment. Not only did it conceal our whereabouts but it also served as a massive jungle gym. The trunk, right above the roots, rested on the ground and became our entrance to the winding maze. We were tightrope walkers daring to go on the small limbs and branches. We were mountain climbers adventurous enough to go higher and higher. We were egg hunters, trying to get to the eagle's nest. However, we never went on a branch too small or a limb too unsteady. Our fears were imagined, just like how the rope or nests were equally intangible. Yet sometimes, when I was out doing a chore, Jamie would release a resounding screech that pierced through the grove, a noise that seemed so foreign and shrill to the nature scene. No matter where I was, I could hear it and would go sprinting through the low branches and tangled weeds to her aid. Every time. It was just part of the game, of course. Perhaps she was bored with her current imaginary chore; perhaps she just wanted to portray the

Wolf 4

damsel in distress. However, when I was alone in that toppled tree, I never faked a scream. I never imagined falling. Maybe it is because I never became bored. Maybe it's because I could not imagine her rescuing me. Maybe it is because I could not conceive of failing and needing a savior.

As all Minnesotans know, the green leafy summer is not meant to last and eventually is overtaken by crystal. That did not deter our young minds. We had a mission of making it out to that Fort, and no one was going to stop us. Realizing our already evident headstrong nature, my parents did not dispute our quest but instead helped us along the way. Of course, before we left the house, my mother saw to it that we had enough layers of clothes on to be mistaken for marshmallows. The snow banks seemed to be especially high in those years, or it could just be my own height that made them seem so. To get into the Fort, we often had to crawl up a snowdrift to the west window, where I would use my expert survival skills, along with a butter knife, to unlatch it. We would then proceed to throw our blankets and extra candles in the window and step down onto the pink lawn chair. The rest of the day we would just sit there and hover over our candles in a vain attempt to steal their warmth. Each of us was only allowed one heat source at a time. The rest had to be conserved in case a snowstorm suddenly hit and forced us to wait it out inside the Fort. Meanwhile the drift that already led up to one window would grow so high that the Fort would be encased in white!

6k

Peer Review Question
Why do you think the author put the heater incident in her essay? What does this scene reveal about Gina's and Jamie's characters?

Wolf 5

"Better safe than sorry," I can hear Jamie's wise words, even now. Once my parents were overcome with the fear of us freezing our petite fingers and toes. They helped us in our creativeness and upgraded the Fort with a fish-house heater. This was a definite improvement because it allowed us to conserve more candles.

There is something that should be noted about the old heater; after all, it caused the first scenario to ever test my courage, a trial that I won't soon forget. My father was very wary about that heater, which was fueled by propane and probably too close to the flammable curtains, blankets. The design of the Fort itself worried him also. So, he put responsible-me in charge of our safety, a task that I did not take lightly. Jamie's often too-carefree attitude, which she still carries today, kept me constantly fussing over how close she was to it and that the blankets needed to be moved a few more inches away. Perhaps she found amusement in my nervousness, or maybe it added some adventure to the crystal stillness. She insisted on provoking a reaction from me. On a particularly quiescent day, she blew into the coils of the heater, and it retaliated with a repulsive sound while slightly changing in color. Of course, I sprang into action and ordered her plainly, "Don't do that again!" in the most stern and authoritative voice I could muster. She innocently smiled and attempted to be taken aback by my supposedly unwarranted outburst. A few moments later, not surprisingly, she blew into it again. This time, however, she made it very angry, and it burst into flames! Now, I was young, but not so stupid

Wolf 6

as to not realize that the rusty tank was filled with an explosive substance. I grabbed Jamie and dragged her to the window amidst her hysterical screeching and forced her outside, dumping her into the snow pile. Then I told her, "Go get Dad." I turned back to the growing flames and decided that I would rather die than have my father know that I let that thing start on fire. Rushing toward it, I frantically tried to remember which way I needed to turn the knob to stop the flow. "Lefty Loosey, Rightie Tightie, LEFTY LOOSEY, RIGHTIE TIGHTIE," my small mind cried, and I made a decision. The flames sucked back into the coils and all was deadly quiet as I waited for it to become angry again. It didn't. A few moments later, Jamie came crawling back through the window crying. Arm in arm, we sat down on our makeshift couch, stared at what seemed to be an evil intruder, and vowed to never tell my father what happened.

The winter passed and the summer returned. Now that we had conquered the snow, we found a new challenge in taking on the darkness. In these days, some of the escapades to our sanctuary took place in the eerie night. Flashlights and candles in hand, we would creep past the frozen monsters and outrun ghosts as we made the flight to our Fort. Once inside our haven, the candles would be lit and every faint rustle of weeds or groaning of trees would bring a tale of our certain doom. Between the scary ghost stories and shrills of childish fear, we talked about our three other close friends, and how this place was to be just for us, the one thing that was totally ours and would not be shared. To this

Peer Review Question
How does the mood of the essay shift as the narrator feels the loss of her imaginary world? What has she learned?

Wolf 7

day, so many years later, I don't think any of them have seen that place which they envied for so very long.

It is a fact of life that all things come to pass. I do not know precisely when it happened, but I gazed into the fallen oak and there were no tightropes or nests cradled in its arms. The rustling of leaves was not a bear coming to gobble me up, but just a squirrel jumping from one perch to the next. Jamie and I sat in the Fort and she coldly looked at me and asked, "Gina, don't you hear the knocking at the door? Let our guests in!" I obediently went to the withered door and opened it in a grand, sweeping motion, but was oddly disturbed when I did not see anyone there. Of course I would let them in anyway and set a cup of tea on the end table for them. However, I found it hard to follow Jamie's surprisingly one-sided conversation. For some reason I could no longer see who she was addressing, nor hear their reply. When our guest departed, I was equally confused as to why the teacup was still full. When the weight of these observations came bearing down upon me, I physically crippled and mentally screamed. My mind gave an outcry able to pierce time and flesh. At some moments I can still feel it echoing through me. It was the first time that I ever wanted to be saved.

After that, I became an actress in the very place that I had created. My world, my safe haven, was ripped from me, and I fully realized that I would never be able to go back. I was like a Lost Boy who left NeverLand, now doomed to the fate of being tied to this

Wolf 8

world. It took Jamie a longer time to come to the realization that I faced, but when she did, it did not seem to affect her in the profound way that it did me. For a long time, I was angry that she could so very easily dismiss the majesty of the world we had created together. Time passed, things changed as they always do, and she moved to another town close by.

We swiftly grew apart and have had very little in common these past few years. Though, oddly enough, she always seems to call me when something in her life takes a turn for the worse, seeking my counsel or just my presence. This action greatly confused me until the last month before I departed for college. She called me late one night, obviously intoxicated, and asked me to come and pick her up. I hate being used by drunken people as their chauffeur, but, in honor of our long, almost forgotten friendship, I went. On the way to her house I had to pull the car over twice for her to throw up, but when we finally did arrive, she just sat in the passenger's seat and rolled her head back. To my amazement, silent tears were running down her cheeks, and her surprisingly steady voice held a dismayed tone as she said, "You know, the only time I've ever been truly happy was in the Fort." Then I understood. We were eight again and candid friends. She was screaming and I was still saving her.

A table of contents for writing project threads appears on pages xv–xxii.

Personal Essays

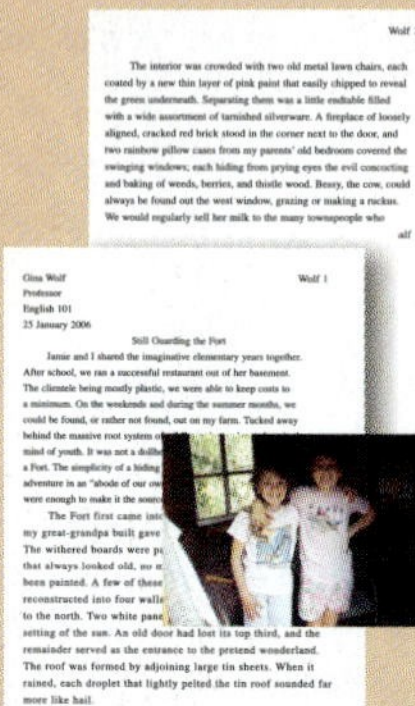

Wolf 2

The interior was crowded with two old metal lawn chairs, each coated by a new thin layer of pink paint that easily chipped to reveal the green underneath. Separating them was a little endtable filled with a wide assortment of tarnished silverware. A fireplace of loosely aligned, cracked red brick stood in the corner next to the door, and two rainbow pillow cases from my parents' old bedroom covered the swinging windows; each hiding from prying eyes the evil concocting and baking of weeds, berries, and thistle wood. Bessy, the cow, could always be found out the west window, grazing or making a ruckus. We would regularly sell her milk to the many townspeople who

Gina Wolf
Professor
English 101
25 January 2006

Wolf 1

Still Guarding the Fort

Jamie and I shared the imaginative elementary years together. After school, we ran a successful restaurant out of her basement. The clientele being mostly plastic, we were able to keep costs to a minimum. On the weekends and during the summer months, we could be found, or rather not found, out on my farm. Tucked away behind the massive root system o… mind of youth. It was not a dolib… a Fort. The simplicity of a hiding… adventure in an "abode of our ow… were enough to make it the sourc…

The Fort first came into… my great-grandpa built gave… The withered boards were p… that always looked old, no m… been painted. A few of these… reconstructed into four walls… to the north. Two white pane… setting of the sun. An old door had lost its top third, and the remainder served as the entrance to the pretend wonderland. The roof was formed by adjoining large tin sheets. When it rained, each droplet that lightly pelted the tin roof sounded far more like hail.

Sharing Stories

After you've completed your first draft, ask your classmates for feedback. Consider using one of these strategies.

1. Have a classmate read your essay out loud to you while you read along silently. As he or she reads to you, take notes about places where something seems to be missing or needs improvement.
2. Ask your classmate to use the strategy of pointing, summarizing, and reflecting (◀ page 101).
3. If your piece depends on chronology for organization, ask classmates to create a timeline of events in your essay. Does their assessment of what happened when agree with what you were trying to present in the essay?

In addition to getting your classmates' responses, use the Project Checklist on page 88 to evaluate the draft on your own. Then use both peers' and your own responses to decide how best to revise your work.

Informative Essays

Garrison 1

Angela Garrison
English 101
Dr. Simpson
September 26, 2005

From Over There to Over Here:
War Blogs Get Up Close, Personal, and Profitable

Blog was the word looked up most often in the online *Merriam-Webster's Dictionary* in 2004 ("Blog"). What's all this fuss? When you read someone else's personal blog, you find out what they like and don't like, what they're doing, and maybe other bits of gossip offered at random. You can read news blogs to find out what's going on lately, what other people think about it, and why it matters. You can keep your own blog to share your thoughts and feelings, to tell your friends and family what you're up to, and sometimes to capture the interest of someone you've never met. When you read and write blogs, you join, or even create, a community. Blogs are also an efficient way to break news, spread rumors, and glorify causes. In short, blogs help people do what they've always done as social beings, just more quickly now, and from almost anywhere on Earth. Soldiers on the ground fighting in Iraq are writing blogs from the front lines. But a review is now under way at the Pentagon to "better understand the overall implications of blogging and other Internet communi-

Seeing from a Peer Reviewer's Perspective

As you've been writing this essay, you've become an expert on your particular topic. When you become an expert, it can be difficult to remember what readers don't know or won't understand about a topic. Everything in your essay probably seems obvious to you. Getting some perspective from readers can help you to understand if you're communicating information clearly in your writing. Using the Project Checklist on page 102, work with a partner or in a small group to receive and give feedback on a draft of your essay. Be sure to ask specific questions you have about your work so that you can elicit good feedback. ▶ page 119.

Critical Reviews

A Movie You Can't Forget!

This could be the best movie you will ever see all year, if you're looking for something intense, suspenseful, and different than your usual effects-packed thriller. This is the kind of movie that you will be talking about at work, at the bank (to total strangers!), and at the corner coffee shop.

The movie starts with a murder -- a revenge killing, in fact. But was the right person killed?

The main character, Leonard Shelby (Guy Pearce), is a man with no short-term memory. He hasn't been able to form new memories since the night his wife was murdered. On a hunt to find the murderer, but with no way of remembering names, dates, places, facts and faces, he tattoos mementos of his search. He uses pictures to try to identify people who know his name. Does he like this person? Does he trust this person? Is this the killer? He doesn't know unless he's written a note.

Writer/director Christopher Nolan puts you right in Leonard's shoes, living the story in reverse order. This ingenious method of story-telling means that you never know more than Leonard does. In one scene you see Leonard getting information from a person who knows him -- maybe a good person; maybe bad. In the next scene you see a previous meeting between the two which sheds more light on their relationship. Later still you see how they met. You, like Leonard, have no knowledge of what came before.

This film will leave its own memento on your mind, and you'll have a hard time forgetting how much you enjoyed it.

Getting Reviews of Your Review

Your review can benefit from being reviewed! It's helpful to get another person's perspective on whether or not your review is comprehensible and helpful and whether it treats its subject matter carefully and ethically. Use the Project Checklist on page 102 to help you give and receive feedback on your reviews. Don't be afraid to ask your reader specific questions about your review. Readers will give you direct feedback if you ask, "Do you think that I should avoid critiquing the ending so that I don't spoil it for viewers? Or can I preface my analysis with a note about a spoiler coming?" If you ask, "Can you give me some feedback?" your readers might get back to you in a week or two if you're lucky.

Talking Over Your Reasons with Other Community Members

You will want to support your solution with research, but just as important, you will need to make sure that you provide reasons for your solution that appeal to community members who are affected by the problem and the solution you propose. If your reasons are unappealing, no amount of research can make your essay persuasive.

Work in groups of four. Explain the context for your problem and solution to your classmates, and ask them to role-play members of your community who are (a) in favor of your solution, (b) opposed to your solution, and (c) neutral about your solution. Discuss the reasons you recommend your solution, and note each community member's response. Are there places where you need to add additional reasons or change the reasons that you provide? page 68.

Proposal Arguments

Harrington 1

A Proposal to Clean Up Our Streets

Revisiting Information and Revising Your Draft

After you receive feedback from a peer review, revise your draft to incorporate suggestions made by your readers, to add, move, or remove information, and to make your meaning clear with word choices.

In addition to getting perspective from others on the content and features of your draft, you'll want to revisit the information you've included and consider its effectiveness. Use the following project checklists to help you think about how you are presenting and using information in your essay:

- Project Checklist: Revising for Context (page 90)
- Project Checklist: Kinds of Evidence (page 94)
- Project Checklist: Visual Content as Supporting Detail (page 95)

page 85.

Informative Essays

Garrison 1

Angela Garrison

English 101

Dr. Simpson

September 26, 2005

From Over There to Over Here:

War Blogs Get Up Close, Personal, and Profitable

Blog was the word looked up most often in the online *Merriam-Webster's Dictionary* in 2004 ("Blog"). What's all this fuss? When you read someone else's personal blog, you find out what they like and don't like, what they're doing, and maybe other bits of gossip offered at random. You can read news blogs to find out what's going on lately, what other people think about it, and why it matters. You can keep your own blog to share your thoughts and feelings, to tell your friends and family what you're up to, and sometimes to capture the interest of someone you've never met. When you read and write blogs, you join, or even create, a community. Blogs are also an efficient way to break news, spread rumors, and glorify causes. In short, blogs help people do what they've always done as social beings, just more quickly now, and from almost anywhere on Earth. Soldiers on the ground fighting in Iraq are writing blogs from the front lines. But a review is now under way at the Pentagon to "better understand the overall implications of blogging and other Internet communications in combat zones," according to John Hockenberry in his *Wired* article "The Blogs of War." The benefits of blogs written by U.S. soldiers in Iraq far outweigh the hypothetical risks of revealing sensitive or strategic information. Those benefits, however, aren't as obvious as they might seem.

In spite of what the imagery of smart bombs and predator drones might lead television viewers to believe, wars are fought by people, not just technology. Most blogs start out as efforts to stay in touch with family and friends, but they quickly turn into

Printing, Revising, Editing, and Sending

Print out your email and review it (or have a partner review it) for content and length. Do you have enough evidence to convince your reader? Does your letter meet the length requirements specified by the publication? Revise your email to make it as complete and concise as possible. Edit your email carefully for spelling and punctuation. Then locate contact information for the editor and send your email. Sometimes, the email address for an editor will be included in a publication; other times, you'll have to search for it on a publication's website.

Email Letters to the Editor

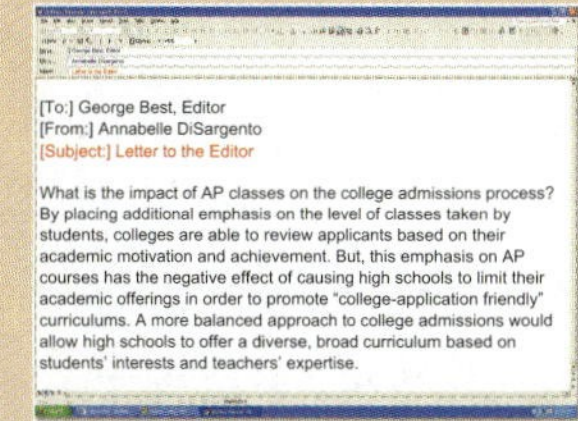

[To:] George Best, Editor

[From:] Annabelle DiSargento

[Subject:] Letter to the Editor

What is the impact of AP classes on the college admissions process? By placing additional emphasis on the level of classes taken by students, colleges are able to review applicants based on their academic motivation and achievement. But, this emphasis on AP courses has the negative effect of causing high schools to limit their academic offerings in order to promote "college-application friendly" curriculums. A more balanced approach to college admissions would allow high schools to offer a diverse, broad curriculum based on students' interests and teachers' expertise.

PART 2

Reading and Writing Critically

Collaboration in the Knowledge Universe

The Internet has the capacity to connect people with information and ideas, and search engines like Google and Yahoo! have made accessible more information than most people can handle. What's next? What is emerging as a way to manage information overload? We need readers who can evaluate information, and writers who can put it together in ways that make sense and that are accessible to everyone. In short, we need writers and "knowledge experts" who can create and synthesize content that is reliable, rich, and enduring.

Collaboration is the process of planning, creating, and writing with others to achieve a goal. It is, literally, a "working together." **Knowledge** is not simply a collection of facts or information, but a perspective on information, an attitude about how facts and information can be put to use to explain phenomena. A **knowledge network** is a system for relating ideas, usually facilitated by a **discourse community,** a group of people with shared interests and ideals who use a common language and set of perspectives, a kind of specialized literacy. A guiding principle of robust knowledge networks is the idea of **emergence,** a theory of knowledge production that says new knowledge and patterns of order can result from the uncoordinated but useful contributions of individuals, not unlike the emergent order in an ant colony.

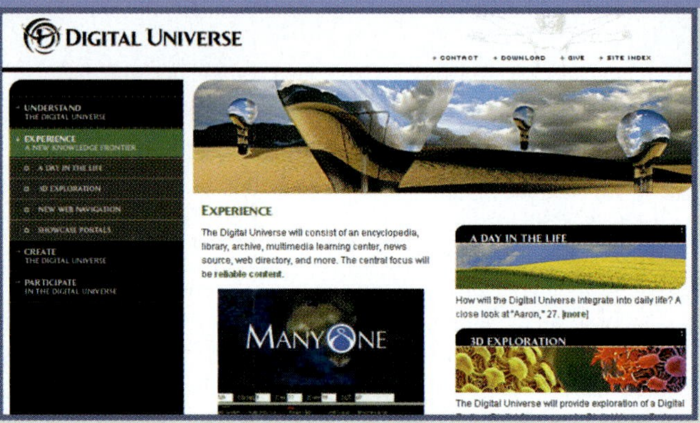

The Digital Universe (http://www.digitaluniverse.net) is an initiative with high aspirations: to use an open collaboration system to build the world's largest and most reliable information resource on the Internet. In that respect, it competes with Wikipedia. By allowing users to contribute and edit content, Wikipedia has quickly built the world's largest encyclopedia. The Wikipedia model depends upon the integrity and knowledge of its contributors, so there are times when its information is not as reliable or as balanced as it could be. (Erroneous information tends to be weeded out quickly with the help of volunteer reviewers and editors.)

At the Digital Universe, the model is similar but with some additional features. The site will combine open collaboration with review by editors and "stewards," who are widely acknowledged experts in the subject matter. Stewards will map the direction of content areas and enlist writers to help create and improve it. Customized software will allow people to learn in visually rich ways. The public will play an important role in this collaborative effort.

Collaborative Knowledge Networks

The Digital Universe | http://www.digitaluniverse.net
Internet Movie Database | http://www.imdb.com
EServer TC Library | http://tc.eserver.org
Wikipedia | http://www.wikipedia.org

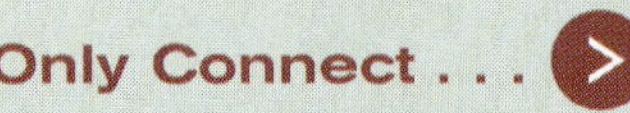

7 UNDERSTANDING ACADEMIC GENRES

Genres are types of writing, painting, music, or any other symbolic human action whose specific examples share style, form, content, or purpose. Some genres of writing you've probably encountered are, for instance, the short story, the job application letter, and the news story. Each of these diverse categories of writing is a genre. You have probably heard people talk about genres since you were in grade school, and you have no doubt used the concept to talk with your friends, family, or classmates about what kind of movies, books, or music you like.

Genres are an important concept in academic writing because people use these familiar forms to share knowledge, tell stories, and conduct research in ways that other people respect and value. When you're a newcomer to the university—to *this* rhetorical situation and context—it may take a while to learn how people talk and write about what interests them. When you understand academic genres—through practice, exposure, and experience—you will be able to understand better what knowledge people want to share and why that knowledge is valued. You will also learn how to use the conventions, or familiar patterns, of genre to express yourself more clearly, persuasively, and profoundly.

Understanding genres is a social process that involves people sharing, discussing, interpreting, composing, performing, and making use of different kinds of writing, music, art, or other products of human ingenuity. To know enough about "college research papers" so that you can write effectively in that genre, for example, you will need to spend some time reading, talking, and writing about them with others.

To learn a genre, you need to write about and discuss the following points:

- what genres contain (their *content*)
- what genres do (their *purpose*)
- how genres present content (their *form* and *style*)
- why genres are valued (they advance or report knowledge, entertain or move the reader)
- when and where genres are used (their contexts and *kairos*)
- how different fields of study or disciplines organize knowledge (genres as analytical)

Activity 7-1: Connecting Genres to Daily Life

In the opening to her book *Writing Genres,* Amy Devitt explains how genres work in our daily lives.

What expectations might you have about your favorite kind of music? What do you expect, for example, that a country song will sound like? What expectations do you have about its content? About the instruments used? What happens when a song doesn't meet your expectations? Can that surprise be good? How much surprise can you accept? How might a song "redefine the genre"?

How do jokes usually work? Is surprise a key feature? A play on words? How might jokes be a way to play with audience expectations? What other rhetorical aspects of jokes as a genre can you think of?

> Genre pervades human lives. As people go about their business, interacting with others and trying to get along in the world, they use genres to ease their way, to meet expectations, to save time. People recognize genres, though not usually the power of genres. People say, "I heard the best *joke* today," "I have to give a *lecture* at nine thirty," "I've gotten into *mysteries,*" and "Do you have a *travel brochure* for the Apostle Islands?" Genres have the power to help or hurt human interaction, to ease communication or to deceive, to enable someone to speak or to discourage someone from saying something different. People learn how to do *small talk* to ease the social discomfort of large group gatherings and meeting new people, but advertisers learn how to disguise *sales letters* as *winning sweepstakes entries.* Outraged citizens can express themselves in *letters to the editor,* but first-year college students may struggle to dissociate their personal experience from their *research papers.* Genre has significance for people's lives.
>
> From Amy J. Devitt, *Writing Genres,* Rhetorical Philosophy and Theory Series (Carbondale: Southern Illinois University Press, 2004), 1.

Personal experience may provide a strong motive for research, but personal experience is usually separated from the reports of that research in academic or professional writing. Why do you think that is? Where should the lens of the researcher be focused? What about types of research that focus on the researcher—when personal experience *is* the subject—such as some forms of psychological and ethnographic research?

Academic Genres by Type and Purpose

Types of Genres

Annotated bibliographies
Argumentative essays
Articles and reviews
Business letters and memos
Case studies or ethnographies
Email messages
Essay exams/timed writing
Field research
Interviews
Multimedia essays
Multimedia oral presentations
Narratives
News articles
Online forum postings
Oral presentations
Outlines
Personal essays
Poems
Poster sessions
Proposals and/or abstracts
Recommendation reports
Reflective or learning journals
Research notes
Research reports
Short stories
Technical or lab reports
Usability studies
Web pages and websites

Purposes of Genres

Amuse
Announce
Argue
Assure
Beguile
Cajole
Charm
Convert
Delight
Demonstrate learning
Discourage
Dissuade
Entertain
Gratify
Guide
Impress
Introduce
Lead
Make and change policy
Notify
Organize
Persuade
Plan
Please
Rejoice
Teach
Test
Wheedle

Activity 7-2: Matching Genre Type to Purpose

A genre may have multiple subtypes and purposes, but it is useful to think about how particular genre types can be associated with a particular purpose. For example, you could argue that the purpose of a short story is to entertain and that we read short stories mostly for pleasure. Do short stories ever teach as well? How about personal narratives? Do they teach? Entertain? Persuade? For each genre type, what corresponding purpose(s) would you consider to be its primary, or most important, function? Do any of the genre types have important secondary purposes?

People use genres to get along in the world, as Amy Devitt tells us (see Activity 7-1). It follows that if you want to get along in the world, you'll need to investigate genres and use genre knowledge to your advantage when you write. The process of learning genres begins when you read, write, and talk about them. Throughout the handbook are examples, discussions, and directions for writing in many of the academic genres that you will come across in college. Some of these are included in the list to the left.

Genres have features, purposes, and styles that sometimes can be bewildering because they vary so much as you move from field to field.

- The *content* of a scientific research report might include data analysis, but it might also include discussion of the social value of the research, moving it more into the realm of ethics or philosophy. A research essay in philosophy might involve analysis of the history of scientific research as it zooms in on the ethical issues in contemporary research. Both research genres might include a "review of the literature" that covers existing scholarship on the central issues.
- The *purpose* of a research report in a scientific field might be to test a hypothesis and report the results of quantitative research. The purpose of a research essay in a philosophy course might be to argue for an interpretation of a philosophical work or to show how and why an author shapes the work to express some insight (▶Part 3).
- The *form* and *style* of a research essay will vary across the curriculum as well. Disciplines follow different citation guidelines (▶Part 4) and different conventions of style, tone, formal-

Do you see a vase or faces?

What you see depends on what you're looking for. If you look for two faces, you'll see them. If you look for a vase, that's what you'll see. You probably won't see both simultaneously. Both the vase and the faces are "there" all the time, of course, and will come to light depending on your angle of approach. Genres help focus attention as well, drawing out subtleties of a subject that might otherwise remain hidden from view.

ity, and presentation. Even within a discipline, people may vary significantly in what genres they value and how they understand or employ them.

Genres focus your attention. What you see (and write about) when you look at your subject depends on what the genre predisposes you to look for and explain. When you use a genre to focus your attention, what you're looking for has a major impact on what you find, as illustrated in the "vase or faces" illusion.

Activity 7-3: Comparing Research Essays and Reports across the Curriculum

Sections 19e, 20d, and 21d each present a student research paper. The MLA-style paper on page 432 was written for a composition course, the APA-style paper on page 478 was written for a psychology course, and the CMS-style paper on page 516 was written for a history course.

Read the first two pages or so of each research paper. Then get together with several classmates to discuss the similarities and differences between the papers. Consider the following questions:

- Do the three papers represent three distinct genres? Why or why not?
- What can you figure out about the genre: What does it contain? What does it do? How does it present content? Why is the genre valued?
- What can you determine from the research papers about how each discipline—composition, psychology, and history—organizes knowledge?

Genres Convey Attitudes toward Knowledge 7c

The genre you choose to represent your subject matter implicitly brings with it an attitude or orientation to knowledge. One reason so many different genres are used in academia is that different fields of study value different forms of knowledge-making. By approaching a subject from many viewpoints, we learn more than we would by taking a single approach. To take a simple example, we might explain *oranges* by talking about how they look, what they taste like, where they grow, who uses them, how to plant and grow them, how to cook with them, what their history has been, what their chemical composition is, their value for human health, their place in the ecological system, and so on.

Assumptions Underlying Genres

- A narrative essay about a personal experience suggests that writing about personal events is a way of sharing experience that can teach us something of value.
- A scientific research report conveys that knowledge is cumulative (builds over time), corrective (fixes errors in previous studies), and verifiable (can be demonstrated or discovered by others).
- An analytical essay suggests that we can understand a subject by dividing it into its parts and then asking questions about how each part relates to the whole.
- A literary or film review suggests that one way to know is to evaluate a performance's (or text's) value.
- A timed essay exam conveys that knowledge is learned and demonstrated by explanation and synthesis.
- A fictional work implies that we can create knowledge through acts of imagination.

Three Ways of Writing about Déjà Vu

One way to understand how genres work is to notice how the same subject is treated differently in a variety of forms, using the terminologies and perspectives of various fields of study, for different purposes. Here we reprint three works that focus on *déjà vu* (French for "already seen"), an experience that many people report having had, sometimes with unsettling or profound feelings.

Suppose you want to write about déjà vu in a serious and sustained way. You want to tell people a story about an amazing experience you had (*entertain*), teach people what déjà vu means (*inform*), or settle once and for all the issue of what déjà vu really is (*persuade*). Perhaps you want to do a little of all three: entertain, inform, and persuade. How will you go about it? How will your context affect what you write, how you write it, and your appeal to an audience? How do the selections on déjà vu illustrate possible approaches to these questions?

Poem: Description of Experience

IV
Emily Dickinson

A thought went up my mind to-day
That I have had before,
But did not finish, some way back,
I could not fix the year,

Nor where it went, nor why it came
The second time to me,
Nor definitely what it was,
Have I the art to say.

But somewhere in my soul, I know
I've met the thing before;
It just reminded me—'t was all—
And came my way no more.

Psychological Explanation: Formulating Hypotheses

From "Déjà Vu"
Graham F. Reed

[W]hy is the experience so rare? Perhaps the problem is not why déjà vu occurs, but why it does not occur more frequently. There are several possible answers. One is that perhaps it does occur commonly, but that we only register it under certain conditions. But at the same time, it is probable that there are relatively few occasions when we can be objectively certain that we have not experienced the criterion situation previously. A first visit to a geographic area is one such example. Other cases where the total situation may be labelled emphatically as a personal 'first time' event are often ones of a heightened emotive nature, where we are likely to be more sensitive to our subjective state and more vulnerable to feelings of anxiety and perplexity. It should be noted that while we may be acutely aware that a given situation is a personal 'first', we have almost certainly experienced it at second hand, through descriptions, literary accounts, or films. Perhaps the obvious examples are marriage ceremonies, job interviews, and funerals. And it is of interest that, after the 'strange town' example, these are the very situations in which people most commonly report experiencing déjà vu.

From *Oxford Companion to the Mind,* ed. by Richard L. Gregory (Oxford: Oxford University Press, 1987), 183–184.

Technical Report of Research: Summary with Visual Explanation

3 MODELS OF DÉJÀ VU

The Victorian-era British psychologist Sir James Crichton-Browne suggested that déjà vu is caused by a tri fling and transitory" brain disorder, "like cramp in a few fibers of muscle." Here are three modern attempts to explain the phenomenon:

Spontaneous neural activity in the parahippocampal gyrus

According to this theory, the brain suffers a small seizure in the parahippocampal system, which is associated with spatial processing and our sense of familiarity.

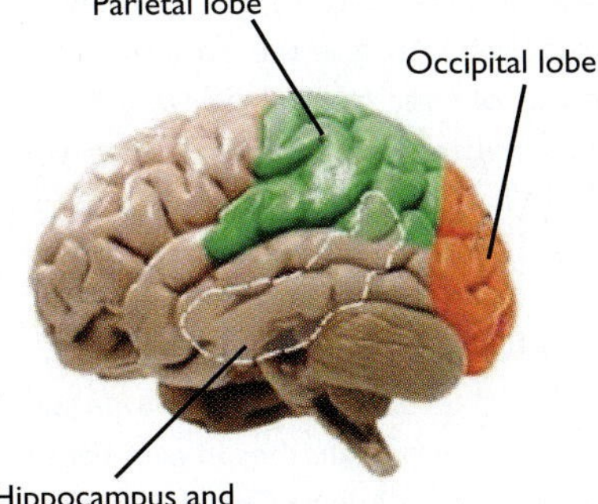

Slowdown in the secondary visual pathway

It is well established that we process visual information through two pathways. One goes directly to the visual cortex, in the occipital lobe. The secondary pathway, which is infinitesimally slower, is routed through various other areas of the brain, notably the parietal cortex, on its way to the occipital lobe. Some researchers believe that a déjà vu experience occurs when signals on the secondary pathway move too slowly, and the brain interprets this secondary wave of data as a separate experience.

Inattentional blindness

Imagine that you drive through an unfamiliar town but pay it little attention because you are talking on a cellphone. If you then drive back down the same streets a few moments later, this time focusing on the landscape, you might be prone to experience déjà vu. During your second pass, the visual information is consciously processed in the hippocampus but feels falsely "old" because the images from your earlier drive still linger in your short-term memory.

From *Chronicle* 50 (46):A12 <http://chronicle.com>.

More writings on déjà vu, accompanied by questions for analysis, are on the book's website at cengage.com/English/Blakesley:

- A journalistic report on déjà vu for a general audience
- A travel narrative about a déjà vu experience by Nathaniel Hawthorne
- A literary analysis of the treatment of déjà vu in Don DeLillo's novel *White Noise*
- A definition of déjà vu from Sigmund Freud

Help for ESL Writers

To see some of the genres, such as travel writing and personal narratives, that second language writers have found useful for talking about their experience, see *Topics: An Online Magazine for Learners of English,* at http://www.topics-mag.com.

A table of contents for writing project threads appears on pages xv–xxii.

Critical Reviews

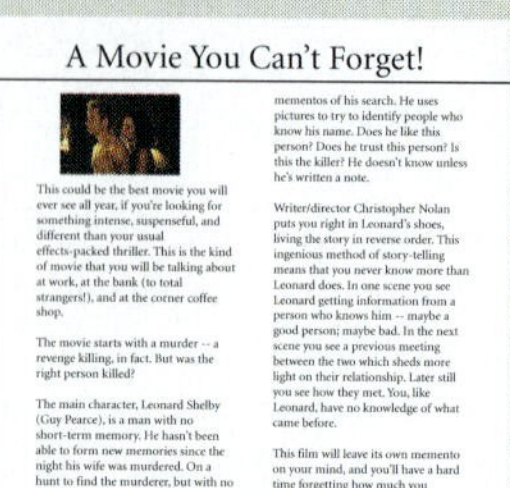

A Movie You Can't Forget!

This could be the best movie you will ever see all year, if you're looking for something intense, suspenseful, and different than your usual effects-packed thriller. This is the kind of movie that you will be talking about at work, at the bank (to total strangers!), and at the corner coffee shop.

The movie starts with a murder -- a revenge killing, in fact. But was the right person killed?

The main character, Leonard Shelby (Guy Pearce), is a man with no short-term memory. He hasn't been able to form new memories since the night his wife was murdered. On a hunt to find the murderer, but with no way of remembering names, dates, places, facts and faces, he tattoos mementos of his search. He uses pictures to try to identify people who know his name. Does he like this person? Does he trust this person? Is this the killer? He doesn't know unless he's written a note.

Writer/director Christopher Nolan puts you right in Leonard's shoes, living the story in reverse order. This ingenious method of story-telling means that you never know more than Leonard does. In one scene you see Leonard getting information from a person who knows him -- maybe a good person; maybe bad. In the next scene you see a previous meeting between the two which sheds more light on their relationship. Later still you see how they met. You, like Leonard, have no knowledge of what came before.

This film will leave its own memento on your mind, and you'll have a hard time forgetting how much you enjoyed it.

Investigating the Genre

A critical review asks you to create criteria for evaluating a work (such as a book, short story, play, essay, article, movie, website, or game) and then to judge how well the work meets these criteria. We read and write reviews to evaluate all sorts of things. Before you become a reviewer, you'll want to think about how reviews work.

Gather some reviews similar to the one you are going to write. (For example, if you are reviewing a movie, you might want to get movie reviews from several different websites or compare movie reviews in the newspaper with movie reviews on the Web.) Analyze the reviews and write a paragraph that explains the major features of your type of review as a genre. What expectations do the review authors create? How are the reviews you read similar to and different from each other? What conclusions can you draw about reviews as a genre? ◀ page 29.

Email Letters to the Editor

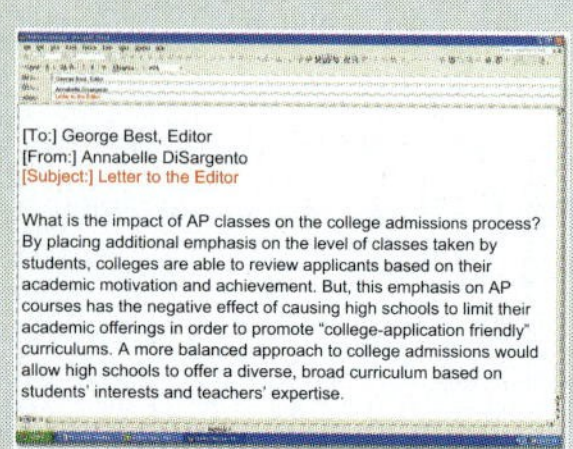

[To:] George Best, Editor
[From:] Annabelle DiSargento
[Subject:] Letter to the Editor

What is the impact of AP classes on the college admissions process? By placing additional emphasis on the level of classes taken by students, colleges are able to review applicants based on their academic motivation and achievement. But, this emphasis on AP courses has the negative effect of causing high schools to limit their academic offerings in order to promote "college-application friendly" curriculums. A more balanced approach to college admissions would allow high schools to offer a diverse, broad curriculum based on students' interests and teachers' expertise.

Becoming Aware of Genre Conventions

Letters to the editor share certain conventions regarding content and format, but they also differ from one another, in part because of the guidelines that publications provide for writers to follow. One publication may allow letters to be any length (and then edit them to fit the space available); others may have a word limit. Guidelines for email letters to the editor may differ from guidelines for print letters to the editor. Select three sample letters to the editor from different publications, and examine each publication's guidelines for letter writers. How are the letters similar and different? What do all the letters have in common? Make a list. How are the writers' guidelines similar and different? What do all the guidelines have in common? Make a list.

Compare lists with a classmate, and come up with a description of letters to the editor as a genre. Also, try to explain the differences that you see—what factors are causing the differences? Which letter to the editor do you think is most similar to the letter to the editor that you will write? Why? ◀ page xvi.

8 READING CRITICALLY

Nonfiction refers to prose texts whose subject matter is the so-called real world—the world that can be experienced by others. Nonfiction takes many forms, including biography and autobiography, travel guides and travel narratives, pop culture magazine articles and how-to books, public policy arguments, and "true stories" of personal tragedies. You can read nonfiction from a variety of perspectives to gain insight into the author's intentions and to understand the role you play in creating meaning.

When you read, paying close attention to your purposes for reading and your state of mind will help you understand what you have brought to the text. The first time you read a text, your experience and knowledge affect your interpretation of its meaning at least as much as the words and sentences you see on the page or screen. Other people's ideas affect how meaning is made, too: hearing what others say about a text may change what it means to you and will no doubt influence what meaning you derive from a second reading. These processes of *encoding*—what reading expert Frank Smith calls "the theory of the world in our heads"—help us convert information on the page into something familiar.

When we read, we also *decode* text, deciphering letters and their arrangement into familiar words that add up to something meaningful. Readers who have different purposes for reading attend to different aspects of a text in order to fulfill their needs. For example, you can focus on what a text meant historically or what it means now, to you or to others. You can study the techniques that writers use to influence your analysis, interpretation, and evaluation. You can reflect on the writer's aims or read as a writer to see whether you can learn by example. You may read to assert your point of view or to believe someone else's; you may read for information but also to create worlds in your imagination. You may simply read for pleasure.

To get the most out of your reading in college, read actively. Active reading begins with curiosity. By engaging your curiosity, you become alert to the possibilities of the text and your response to it. As you read, make predictions and see whether the text fulfills them in the way you anticipated. Argue with the author and ask questions about what you don't understand. Write down your thoughts and feelings about the text. Read the text carefully several times to extend your understanding of what it says, what it means, why it's important (or not), and what use you can make of it.

Making Predictions

You will find the text more engaging, and understand it more easily, if you spend a few minutes preparing to read by looking over key elements in order to make predictions about what is coming. Start by looking over the text from beginning to end, taking 5 or 10 minutes to gather information from its title, table of contents, abstract, section headers, jacket copy (or commentary), length, author biography, and any other features that frame or structure the text. If you are reading a text on a website, be sure you know where you are and who the author is—a person, a group, or a corporation, for example. Make note of any advertising.

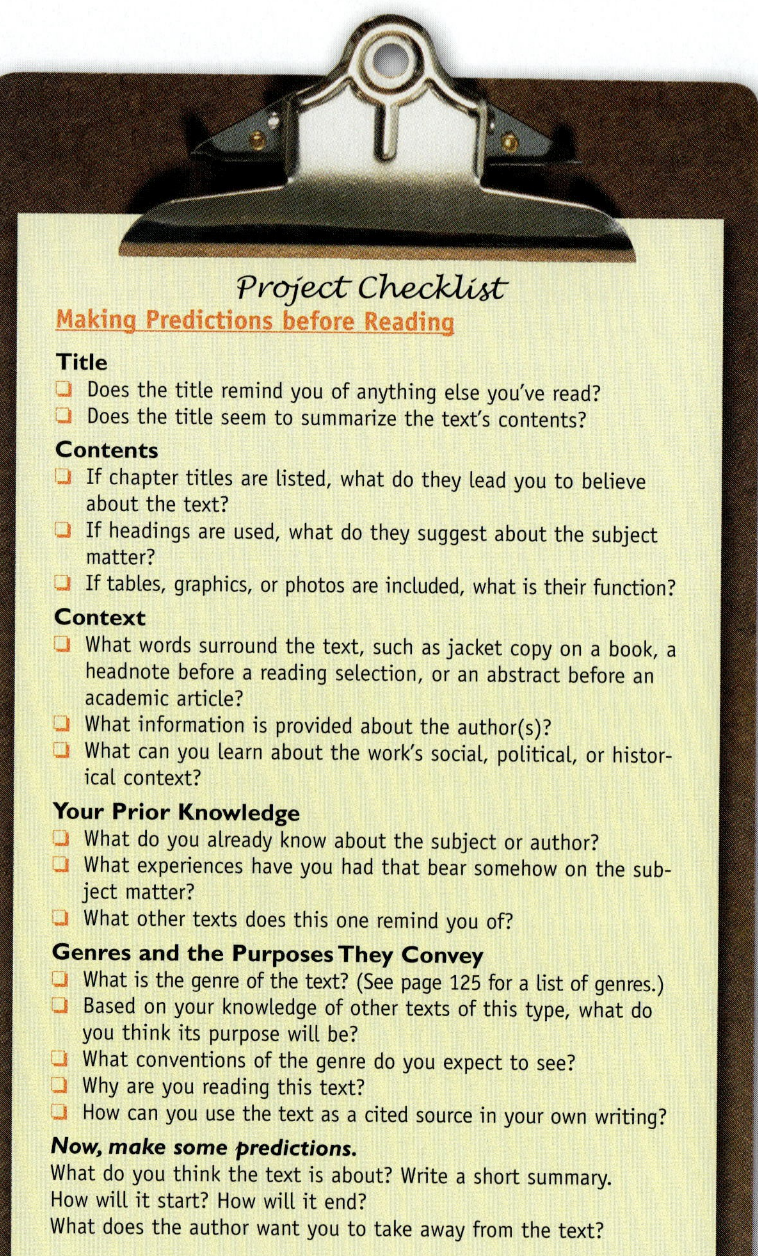

Project Checklist

Making Predictions before Reading

Title

- ❑ Does the title remind you of anything else you've read?
- ❑ Does the title seem to summarize the text's contents?

Contents

- ❑ If chapter titles are listed, what do they lead you to believe about the text?
- ❑ If headings are used, what do they suggest about the subject matter?
- ❑ If tables, graphics, or photos are included, what is their function?

Context

- ❑ What words surround the text, such as jacket copy on a book, a headnote before a reading selection, or an abstract before an academic article?
- ❑ What information is provided about the author(s)?
- ❑ What can you learn about the work's social, political, or historical context?

Your Prior Knowledge

- ❑ What do you already know about the subject or author?
- ❑ What experiences have you had that bear somehow on the subject matter?
- ❑ What other texts does this one remind you of?

Genres and the Purposes They Convey

- ❑ What is the genre of the text? (See page 125 for a list of genres.)
- ❑ Based on your knowledge of other texts of this type, what do you think its purpose will be?
- ❑ What conventions of the genre do you expect to see?
- ❑ Why are you reading this text?
- ❑ How can you use the text as a cited source in your own writing?

Now, make some predictions.

What do you think the text is about? Write a short summary.
How will it start? How will it end?
What does the author want you to take away from the text?

Activity 8-1: Making Predictions about a Text

Consider the questions in the Project Checklist as you examine the following pages from Malcolm Gladwell's book *The Tipping Point.* Write a summary of your predictions and then share your responses in a small group. How did readers' predictions vary? Why?

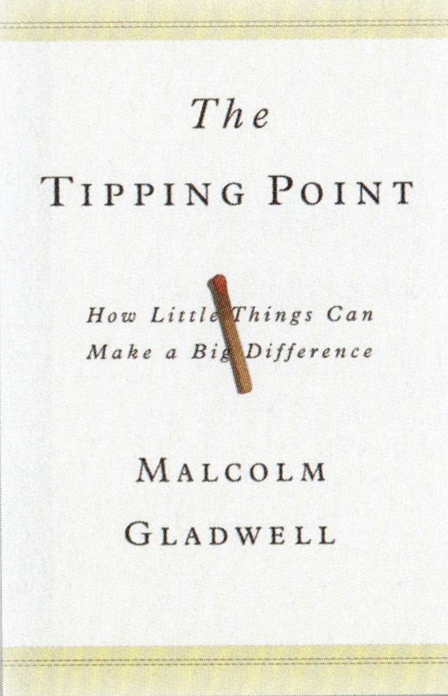

Contents

CURRENT AFFAIRS / BUSINESS

Why did crime in New York drop so suddenly in the mid-nineties? How does an unknown novelist end up a bestselling author? Why is teenage smoking out of control, when everyone knows smoking kills? What makes TV shows like *Sesame Street* so good at teaching kids how to read? Why did Paul Revere succeed with his famous warning?

In this brilliant and groundbreaking book, *New Yorker* writer Malcolm Gladwell looks at why major changes in our society so often happen suddenly and unexpectedly. Ideas, behavior, messages, and products, he argues, often spread like outbreaks of infectious disease. Just as a single sick person can start an epidemic of the flu, so too can a few fare-beaters and graffiti artists fuel a subway crime wave, or a satisfied customer fill the empty tables of a new restaurant. These are *social* epidemics, and the moment when they take off, when they reach their critical mass, is the Tipping Point.

Gladwell introduces us to the particular personality types who are natural pollinators of new ideas and trends, the people who create the phenomenon of word of mouth. He analyzes fashion trends, smoking, children's television, direct mail, and the early days of the American Revolution for clues about making ideas infectious, and visits a religious commune, a successful high-tech company, and one of the world's greatest salesmen to show how to start and sustain social epidemics.

The Tipping Point is an intellectual adventure story written with an infectious enthusiasm for the power and joy of new ideas. Most of all, it is a road map to change, with a profoundly hopeful message—that one imaginative person applying a well-placed lever can move the world.

Jacket design by Michael Ian Kaye
Jacket photograph by Dan Bibb

Visit our Web site at www.twbookmark.com
Printed in the U.S.A.

Reading for the Gist

If your text is relatively short—something you can read in a half hour or so—then read the text straight through to get the gist, or central idea. Reading for the central idea will help you find out more about the text's subject matter, purpose, and genre. You will find it easier to catch the broad outlines of the topic, story, or argument when you move forward without pausing to jot notes, look up words, or annotate the text.

If your text is longer, you should pause at points that seem to be natural stopping places, such as the end of a chapter, section, or scene, and write a brief note about the gist of the section you have read. This will help you retain the main thread of the ideas as you proceed.

Rereading for Depth

After you've made predictions about a text and read it through once to get the gist, read more carefully and deeply, pausing to reflect on what the text says, what it reminds you of, how it connects to other texts, and what expectations it creates and satisfies. Respond to the text as you read. You will probably need to look up key or unfamiliar terms in a college dictionary.

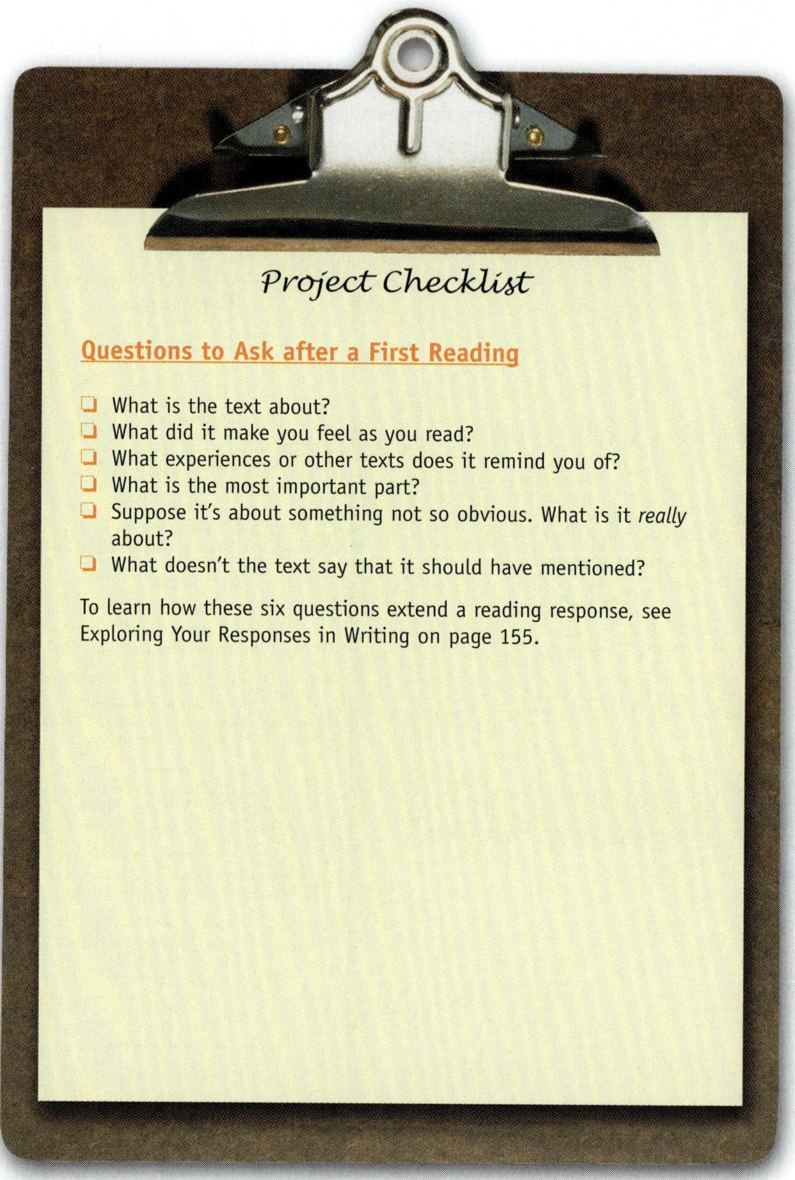

Project Checklist

Questions to Ask after a First Reading

- ❑ What is the text about?
- ❑ What did it make you feel as you read?
- ❑ What experiences or other texts does it remind you of?
- ❑ What is the most important part?
- ❑ Suppose it's about something not so obvious. What is it *really* about?
- ❑ What doesn't the text say that it should have mentioned?

To learn how these six questions extend a reading response, see Exploring Your Responses in Writing on page 155.

Illustration: Strategies for Annotating a Text

Observation about genre
He's playing on the saying "Food for Thought," which suggests this is a reflective essay.

Connection to other texts
We also read a selection from his book, Mind Wide Open.

From "Tool for Thought" by Steven Johnson

Question
What did people used to think about word processors? It's hard to imagine being without them.

[I]f the modern word processor has become a near-universal tool for today's writers, its impact has been less revolutionary than you might think. Word processors let us create sentences without the unwieldy cross-outs and erasures of paper, and despite the occasional catastrophic failure, our hard drives are better suited for storing and retrieving documents than file cabinets. But writers don't normally rely on the computer for the more subtle arts of inspiration and association. We use the computer to process words, but the ideas that animate those words originate somewhere else, away from the screen. The word processor has changed the way we write, but it hasn't yet changed the way we think.

Summary
Weaknesses of word processors

Tell me about it!

Experience
This reminds me of invention and the idea that analogy is a way of making connections among ideas.

Summary
We only use word processors to get our ideas down, not to create them.

Extension to big ideas
Thesis. I'll bet he's going to show us a tool that might help change the way we think!

From Steven Johnson, "Tool for Thought," *New York Times* 30 Jan. 2005 <http://www.nytimes.com>.

Annotating a Text

Active readers usually interact with the text by annotating it with a pencil, pen, highlighter, or sticky note as they read. They note agreements, disagreements, questions, connections they are making, and other reactions in the margins to help illuminate the text and to stay engaged. If you feel yourself drifting off and after a minute or two cannot remember what you read, then you should be annotating the text in addition to making predictions and forming expectations about the reading. Annotating the text will help you keep track of your thoughts.

When you annotate while you read, you can . . .

- ask questions of the text
- connect the subject matter to your knowledge and experience
- make connections to other texts
- mark important or unfamiliar terms, look them up, and summarize their definitions in the margin
- number the major examples or parts of the argument the writer is making
- summarize paragraphs or difficult sentences
- offer alternative perspectives to the writer's point of view or assumptions
- extend the meaning of the text by considering how it relates to or explains big issues

Forming Expectations

An expectation is like an appetite waiting to be fulfilled. Writers deliberately create expectations in their readers to keep them hungry for more.

As a reader, respond to these attempts by making predictions and annotating the text whenever possible. You should also think consciously about the expectations you have formed as you read. They will not only help you stay focused but also help you analyze, interpret, and evaluate what you read.

Your expectations and then your consideration of how they have been met (or not) give you valuable knowledge about what a text says, what it means, how well it achieves its purpose, and whether it merits even closer attention. This kind of knowledge also motivates your writing about reading and helps you recognize, appreciate, and make use of new information as you come across it in everything you read in the future.

"Is this text meeting my expectations?"

How do these new events or new information relate to previous events or old information?
Say what? That's a surprise! How did the text create a certain expectation without my noticing?
I'll make a note of this—it's just what I expected.
What did the author have in mind in structuring the text this way? What is the author's purpose?

Activity 8-2: Reading Actively

Read the following article, first published in *Forbes* magazine, using the active reading process described throughout this section. Then draft a summary, using the guidelines on page 340.

Illusions Are Forever

Jay Chiat

Jay Chiat founded the advertising agency Chiat/Day in 1968, with Guy Day. It became one of the most influential ad agencies in the world, creating cutting-edge advertisements for clients such as Apple Computer, American Express, Nike, and Energizer. Chiat/Day created the 1984 Super Bowl commercial to introduce Macintosh computers, shown only once to a national audience but widely considered to be the best commercial ever made.

I know what you're thinking: That's rich, asking an adman to define truth. Advertising people aren't known either for their wisdom or their morals, so it's hard to see why an adman is the right person for this assignment. Well, it's just common sense—like asking an alcoholic about sobriety, or a sinner about piety. Who is likely to be more obsessively attentive to a subject than the transgressor?

Everyone thinks that advertising is full of lies, but it's not what you think. The facts presented in advertising are almost always accurate, not because advertising people are sticklers but because their ads are very closely regulated. If you make a false claim in a commercial on network television, the FTC will catch it. Someone always blows the whistle.

The real lie in advertising—some would call it the "art" of advertising—is harder to detect. What's false in advertising lies in the presentation of situations, values, beliefs, and cultural norms that form a backdrop for the selling message.

Advertising—including movies, TV, and music videos—presents to us a world that is not our world but rather a collection of images and ideas created for the purpose of selling. These images paint a picture of the ideal family life, the perfect home. What a beautiful woman is, and is not. A prescription for being a good parent and a good citizen.

The power of these messages lies in their unrelenting pervasiveness, the twenty-four-hour-a-day drumbeat that leaves no room for an alternative view. We've become acculturated to the way advertisers and other media-makers look at things, so much so that we have trouble seeing

(continued on next page)

Writing to Remember and Understand Content

To help you remember the content of a text, you can write a summary, reducing the text to its main points. Think of a summary as a set of topic sentences intended to jog your memory. Each sentence can be unpacked to reveal more details. To get an idea of how much to condense ideas in a summary, consider that most academic articles, running from 2,000 to 10,000 words, contain an abstract or summary of only about 250 words. For information on how to write a summary, see section 17c.

Writing a summary will ensure that you know the material well and can explain it. As you examine each paragraph (in a short work) or section or chapter (in a longer one) and boil it down to its essence, you review the subject matter and its organization once again. You then write a summary using your own words, not the original author's. Even though it is written in your words, a summary does *not* include your interpretation of the text or your evaluation of its value. Stick to the material in the text. Finally, since the ideas are not your own, a summary must be documented. Note the complete publication information for the reading you are summarizing.

things in our own natural way. Advertising robs us of the most intimate moments in our lives because it substitutes an advertiser's idea of what ought to be—What should a romantic moment be like?

You know the De Beers diamond advertising campaign? A clever strategy, persuading insecure young men that two months' salary is the appropriate sum to pay for an engagement ring. The arbitrary algorithm is preposterous, of course, but imagine the fiancée who receives a ring costing only half a month's salary? The advertising-induced insult is grounds for calling off the engagement, I imagine. That's marketing telling the fiancée what to feel and what's real.

Unmediated is a great word: It means "without media," without the in-between layer that makes direct experience almost impossible. Media interferes with our capacity to experience naturally, spontaneously, and genuinely, and thereby spoils our capacity for some important kinds of personal "truth." Although media opens our horizons infinitely, it costs us. We have very little direct personal knowledge of anything in the world that is not filtered by media.

Truth seems to be in a particular state of crisis now. When what we watch is patently fictional, like most movies and commercials, it's worrisome enough. But it's absolutely pernicious when it's packaged as reality. Nothing represents a bigger threat to truth than reality-based television, in both its lowbrow and highbrow versions—from *Survivor* to A&E's *Biography.* The lies are sometimes intentional, sometimes errors, often innocent, but in all cases they are the "truth" of a media-maker who claims to be representing reality.

The Internet is also a culprit, obscuring the author, the figure behind the curtain, even more completely. Chat rooms, which sponsor intimate conversation, also allow the participants to misrepresent themselves in every way possible. The creation of authoritative-looking Web sites is within the grasp of any reasonably talented twelve-year-old, creating the appearance of professionalism and expertise where no expert is present. And any mischief maker can write a totally plausible-looking, totally fake stock analyst's report and post it on the Internet. When the traditional signals of authority are so misleading, how can we know what's for real?

But I believe technology, for all its weaknesses, will be our savior. The Internet is our only hope for true democratization, a truly populist publishing form, a mass communication tool completely accessible to individuals. The Internet puts CNN on the same plane with the freelance journalist and the lady down the street with a conspiracy theory, allowing cultural and ideological pluralism that never previously existed.

This is good for the cause of truth, because it underscores what is otherwise often forgotten—truth's instability. Truth is not absolute: It is presented, represented, and re-presented by the individuals who have the floor, whether they're powerful or powerless. The more we hear from powerless ones, the less we are in the grasp of powerful ones—and the less we believe that "truth" is inviolable, given, and closed to interpretation. We also come closer to seeking our own truth.

That's the choice we're given every day. We can accept the very compelling, very seductive version of "truth" offered to us daily by media-makers, or we can tune out its influence for a shot at finding our own individual, confusing messy version of it. After all, isn't personal truth the ultimate truth?

Jay Chiat, "Illusions Are Forever," *Forbes* 2 Oct. 2000 <http://www.forbes.com/asap/2000/1002/138.html>.

Activity 8-3: Thinking Critically about Chiat's "Illusions Are Forever"

Reread Chiat's article on pages 137–138 and your summary, as needed, to answer the following critical thinking questions.

1. Analyze Chiat's presentation of himself. Why do you think he begins the article the way he does? Does Chiat create a believable *ethos*? How?
2. Analyze the organization of the article. What purpose does each section serve? Does the organization help make for a convincing argument? Why or why not? How would you describe the argument in one sentence?
3. Consider your own experiences, both mediated and unmediated. Does Chiat accurately describe your experiences—or some of them? Why or why not?
4. Is your truth different from your neighbor's truth or your parent's truth? Is truth unstable and personal? How do you know?
5. What is the value of Chiat's article?

analysis To *analyze* a text, break it into its component parts, aspects, or features and then show how they relate to one another. *Key Questions:* What choices did the writer make about content, organization, and language? How do these choices relate to one another?

interpretation To *interpret* a text, find points, issues, or events whose meaning may be ambiguous or open to different points of view and then decide where you stand. *Key Questions:* What elements of the text are open to multiple viewpoints? Where would you disagree with the author or with other readers? Why is your interpretation better than any other?

synthesis To *synthesize,* put the elements of your analysis back together to see what they mean as a whole. *Key Questions:* Do you see any patterns or shades of meaning that you didn't see before your analysis? If, after reading your analysis and interpretation, someone asked "So what?" how would you respond?

evaluation To *evaluate* a text, make a judgment about its value. *Key Questions:* Is the text good/bad, worthwhile/unimportant, or better/worse than others of its kind? Why?

Critical reading is thinking while reading: questioning the author's intentions, line of argument, evidence, and choice of words, for example, and staying alert for what is going on below the surface. Do two parts of an argument seem contradictory? The critical reader will notice such instances and will try to figure out whether his or her interpretation is faulty or biased and, if it isn't, whether the author intended the contradiction or didn't realize there was one. If the author intended the two parts to clash, why? What purpose would be served by such a conflict? Does the author have an agenda that only alert readers will notice?

To investigate a text, you can use four interrelated thinking processes: analysis, interpretation, synthesis, and evaluation. For example, in an American history course, suppose you are curious about how the Declaration of Independence was received by the British. You could analyze the text for statements that challenge British rule or in some way go against what British readers at the time might have considered common sense. You could analyze actual published newspaper editorials of the time. You could then interpret this evidence to see whether there were any common reactions and thus synthesize the reception of the text. Once you have analyzed, interpreted, and synthesized, you can evaluate whether the British reaction was justified or not.

Critical reading involves carefully distinguishing fact, opinion, and belief; evaluating the evidence the writer puts forth; and evaluating the assumptions that underlie the writer's argument.

Distinguishing Fact, Opinion, and Belief

Facts are true statements that can be verified by multiple trusted sources. **Opinions** are interpretations of facts, and any set of facts may yield multiple interpretations. **Beliefs** are deeply held convictions. Beliefs can't be proved or disproved, no matter how many facts and reasons are piled up. Neither facts nor beliefs can act as the claim of an argument (Chapter 11).

Examples of Facts, Opinions, and Beliefs

A fact is a true statement that is specific and verifiable.

- On average, women tend to outlive men in the United States.
- In 2002, the life expectancy at birth for black women was 75.6 years; for white women, it was 80.3 years.
- For men, those figures were 68.8 (for black men) and 75.1 (for white men) years.

(Source: National Center for Health Statistics)

An opinion is based on facts, but also includes the writer's interpretation.

- The life expectancy for people in the United States has as much to do with social opportunity as with genetic factors.
- Men tend to live shorter lives than women in the United States because men's lives are more stressful.

(Note that to support either of these opinions adequately would require many facts not stated above.)

A belief is a deeply held conviction that cannot be proved or disproved.

- All people should have an equal opportunity to live a long and healthy life.

Activity 8-4: Distinguishing Fact, Opinion, and Belief

Determine whether each statement is a fact, an opinion, or a belief. Be prepared to explain your reasoning.

1. It's important that we protect the planet for future generations to use and enjoy.
2. Architects and builders have the power to help preserve the planet's energy resources.
3. The U.S. Green Building Council (USGBC) defines how environmental protection standards should be applied to various kinds of building projects.
4. For example, in November 2005, the USGBC published their LEEDS-NC version 2.2, a set of standards that can be applied to the construction and renovation of large commercial buildings.
5. Of course, "green" residences that use less energy than conventional houses are also being built.

Activity 8-5: Evaluating Evidence in Chiat's "Illusions Are Forever"

In "Illusions Are Forever," what evidence does Chiat provide to support his claim? Divide the evidence into the following categories:

- facts
- statistics
- opinions (Chiat's opinions and the opinions of others)
- beliefs (Chiat's beliefs and the beliefs of others)

Based on the Project Checklist below, do you think that Chiat provides adequate evidence to support his claims? Why or why not?

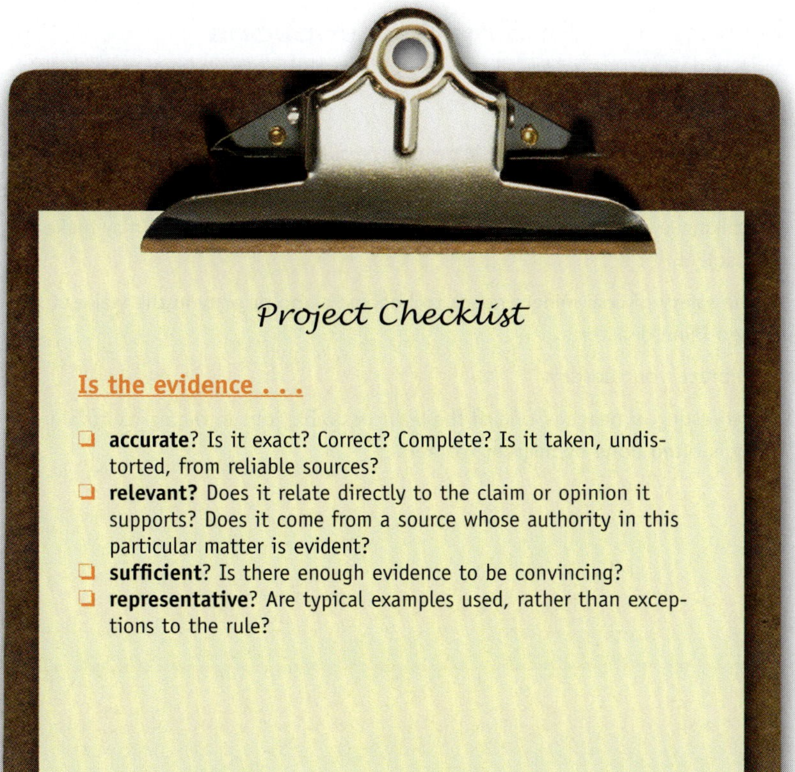

Project Checklist

Is the evidence . . .

- ❑ **accurate**? Is it exact? Correct? Complete? Is it taken, undistorted, from reliable sources?
- ❑ **relevant?** Does it relate directly to the claim or opinion it supports? Does it come from a source whose authority in this particular matter is evident?
- ❑ **sufficient**? Is there enough evidence to be convincing?
- ❑ **representative**? Are typical examples used, rather than exceptions to the rule?

Evaluating Evidence

Facts are one kind of evidence that writers can present to support an opinion or claim. Other kinds of evidence are statistics (facts stated as numbers), specific examples, and expert opinion. Judge each piece of evidence, and the evidence as a whole, to decide whether it is accurate, relevant, sufficient, and representative. Note that the sources of evidence are important. (For information on evaluating sources, see sections 15h and 16g.)

Not just any evidence will do, in spite of what the tabloid newspapers might suggest. Every once in a while, a tabloid will claim that John F. Kennedy survived his assassination attempt or that Elvis is still alive and in seclusion. You will almost always see fuzzy photos to support the story (a problem of accuracy), quotations from one or two unidentified witnesses and experts (problems of relevance and sufficiency), and suggestions that these facts are representative of some big government conspiracy (a problem of using flimsy evidence as representative of some larger, unexamined truth).

Evaluating Underlying Assumptions

When anyone makes a proposition about a subject—as in a thesis statement or an assertion of opinion—there are always underlying assumptions. Writers depend on readers' sharing some beliefs with them so that they can build an argument. Writers need this common ground and rely on readers' granting it to them, at least while they read. For example, if I argue that humans should return to the moon to build agricultural stations and thus spare the Earth further ecological destruction, I make the underlying assumptions that (1) humans have visited the moon previously, (2) it is possible to build such a station without further depleting natural resources in the effort, and (3) the Earth is suffering ecological destruction. These assumptions may or may not be valid, but for the argument to work, writers and readers need to share them.

You can evaluate texts to see what assumptions they make about their subjects:

1. What assumptions does the author make in the thesis?
2. Which assumptions are valid?
3. Which assumptions do you think some people could fairly challenge?
4. Has the author failed to assume shared beliefs, values, or even facts that might help the argument? What are they?

Activity 8-6: Evaluating Assumptions in Chiat's "Illusions Are Forever"

Refer to Chiat's "Illusions Are Forever" to answer the questions below.

1. What is Chiat's claim? What assumptions about the world does he present in his claim? What assumptions does Chiat present in the rest of his essay?
2. Which assumptions presented or assumed in the essay do you think are valid? Why do you think they are valid?
3. Which assumptions presented or assumed in the essay do you think some people could fairly challenge? Why do you think people might challenge them?
4. Do you notice any places where Chiat has failed to assume shared beliefs, values, or even facts that might help the argument? What are they?

Activity 8-7: Finding Assumptions

Work with a partner to list all the assumptions that underlie each of the following statements.

1. It is difficult for people who grow up in a culture of honor to participate effectively in a culture of law.
2. Walking is a natural and necessary activity that the Segway HT may make obsolete.
3. The safety of coal miners needs to become a top priority in the wake of the Sago Mine disaster.
4. Embrace your destiny.
5. Harvesting of peaches, one of the least desirable jobs in the agricultural industry, is often done by migrant workers.

ethos The appeal to the character of the writer and his or her attitude toward the subject as a means of cultivating readers' trust. Ethos may be conveyed by tone (the writer's attitude toward the subject as expressed in the language), identification with readers, and even the writer's reputation (if the writer is known to the audience).

logos The use of content as a form of proof or appeal. Logos includes all of the content of a work—not only ideas, images, information, and evidence, but also diction, style and sentence structure, and arrangement of parts.

pathos The appeal to the emotions of the audience. These emotions are used to deepen an effect.

purpose The writer's aims, how others use or refer to the text, and its consequences.

context The rhetorical situation, consisting of the circumstances of the writer, the historical situation of the text, and the nature of the audience addressed.

Learning to analyze other people's texts can help you become a better writer. As you become more aware of how other writers achieve certain effects, your increased flexibility and control as a writer will help you make more purposeful rhetorical decisions.

Rhetorical analysis is a systematic method of analyzing the effects of a text and how the writer achieves them. The key question for a rhetorical analysis is "What effects does the writer achieve, and how exactly does the writer achieve them?"

Writers use the rhetorical appeals of *ethos* (presentation of character), *logos* (content, arrangement of ideas, evidence, language choices), and *pathos* (emotional pleas), and so a rhetorical analysis will focus on how these appeals create effects. Rhetorical analysis also examines purpose (intention, if it is announced or implied) and context (the immediate social and historical circumstances of the text). For more on ethos, pathos, and logos, see pages 204–207. For more on purpose and context, see pages 9–11.

Reading Any Text as an Argument

When reading rhetorically and when writing a rhetorical analysis, it is helpful to think of the text as an argument that makes appeals to readers and thus to focus on this element of logos. The text may be a straightforward argumentative essay that attempts to persuade readers to adopt a particular point of view or to take some action. But a text that aims to inform or entertain can also be considered an argument because in singling out a subject for the reader's attention, it says, "Pay attention to *this*" and, by default, diverts attention from other subjects. That deflection of attention is a rhetorical move that influences our responses to the world and functions much like an argument. Rhetorical analysis can help you appreciate the presence of influence and persuasion where it is not easy to spot. It can also help you adapt your own writing to new situations and subject matter.

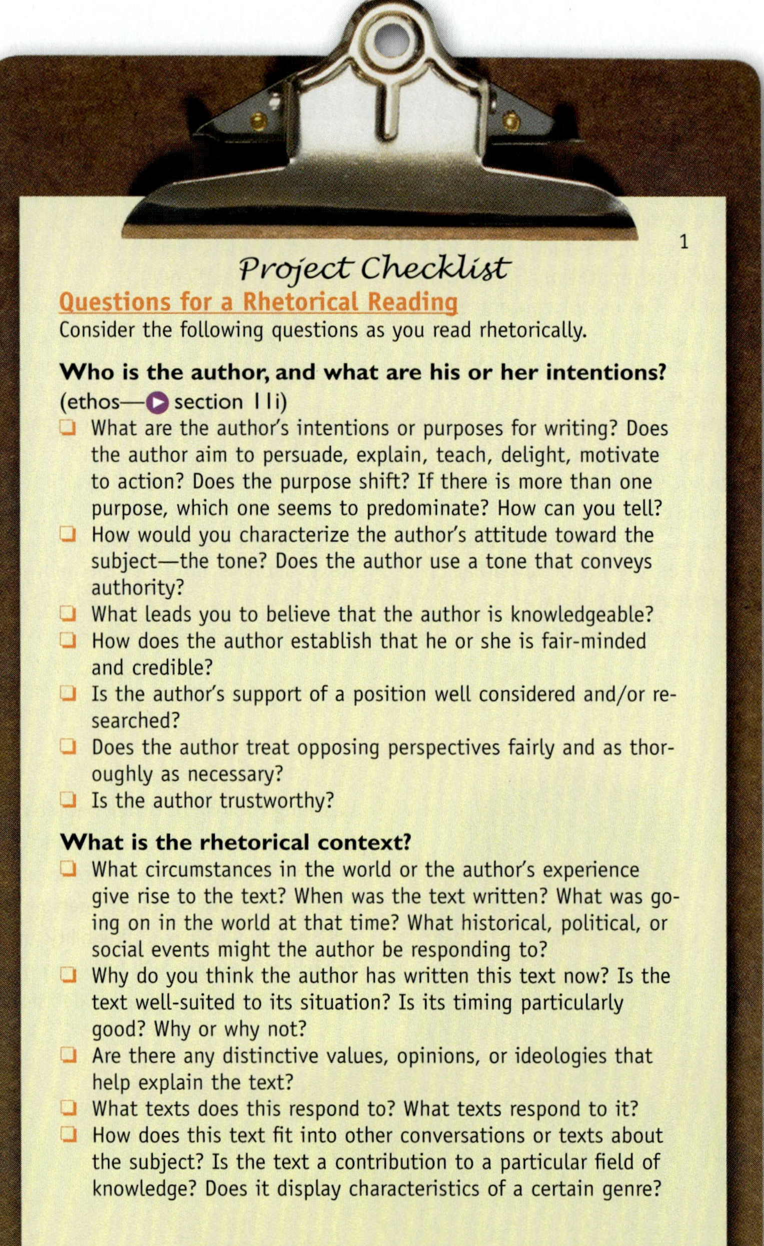

1

Project Checklist

Questions for a Rhetorical Reading

Consider the following questions as you read rhetorically.

Who is the author, and what are his or her intentions?
(ethos— section 11i)

- ❑ What are the author's intentions or purposes for writing? Does the author aim to persuade, explain, teach, delight, motivate to action? Does the purpose shift? If there is more than one purpose, which one seems to predominate? How can you tell?
- ❑ How would you characterize the author's attitude toward the subject—the tone? Does the author use a tone that conveys authority?
- ❑ What leads you to believe that the author is knowledgeable?
- ❑ How does the author establish that he or she is fair-minded and credible?
- ❑ Is the author's support of a position well considered and/or researched?
- ❑ Does the author treat opposing perspectives fairly and as thoroughly as necessary?
- ❑ Is the author trustworthy?

What is the rhetorical context?

- ❑ What circumstances in the world or the author's experience give rise to the text? When was the text written? What was going on in the world at that time? What historical, political, or social events might the author be responding to?
- ❑ Why do you think the author has written this text now? Is the text well-suited to its situation? Is its timing particularly good? Why or why not?
- ❑ Are there any distinctive values, opinions, or ideologies that help explain the text?
- ❑ What texts does this respond to? What texts respond to it?
- ❑ How does this text fit into other conversations or texts about the subject? Is the text a contribution to a particular field of knowledge? Does it display characteristics of a certain genre?

2

Who are the intended readers, and how does the writer address them? (pathos—section 11i)

- Who is the author's intended audience?
- What knowledge and expectations do readers bring to the text?
- How are readers likely to feel about the subject matter or the author's presentation of it?
- What values do readers and the author seem to have in common? How does the writer appeal to these values?
- Does the writer have secondary (or subsidiary) audiences in mind? (See Investigating the Rhetorical Situation, on page 20.)
- If the audience for the text is not obvious, who do you think the writer wants it to be?

What is the subject matter of the text, and how is it arranged? (logos—section 11i)

- Does the author use examples or illustrations to prove points (argument), show events (in narrative), or explain methods (hypothesis testing)? (induction)
- Does the author build a case for his or her position by starting with widely accepted knowledge and then moving toward new insights or claims? (deduction)
- Does the author appeal to reason?
- Does the author use or invoke emotion to help make the point or show the story? (pathos)
- Does the author rely on his or her reputation or authority to garner the reader's interest or support? (ethos)
- Is the subject matter complemented by reference to outside sources, including other texts and voices?

(continued)

Reading for the Use of Language

Writers choose words and adopt a style that helps them achieve their purposes and create effects in their readers. Word choice, or **diction,** has a major influence not just on meaning but on how a text is received. For example, it makes a great difference whether a change of government is labeled a "victory for the people" or a "disaster for freedom."

Diction conveys a writer's purpose and tone as well. Writers usually choose **formal diction** when the occasion for writing is a serious one (as in a research paper) or is part of a ritual (as in a speech to a graduating class). Writers use **informal diction** when they want to identify with their readers and cultivate trust and familiarity (section 38c).

Style is the arrangement of words into sentences in a sequence and form. No one style is naturally better than any other; the use of each should be judged by how well it is suited to the circumstances.

Reading for the Writer's Purposes

Your judgment about a writer's purposes can be formed by paying attention to the author's announcement of his or her **intention(s)** (if any are stated), by asking whether the readers' **expectations** are fulfilled (and thus anticipated by the writer), and by analyzing whether the **rhetorical context** provides any clues about what the writer might be trying to accomplish. A writer's purposes are not always clear, and they may be contrary to the effects that are actually achieved. Nevertheless, writers usually write with a purpose in mind that shapes their decisions, and so readers should try to discern it.

Reading for Rhetorical Context

Every text is part of some wider conversation that you can learn about and use to attribute motive to a writer and assign meaning to a text. A text is written at a unique time and place, usually for a specific purpose, and addressed to an audience. The more you know about a text's historical circumstances, the circumstances of the writer, the subject and form of the text, and the intended audience, the better sense you will have of its overall meaning.

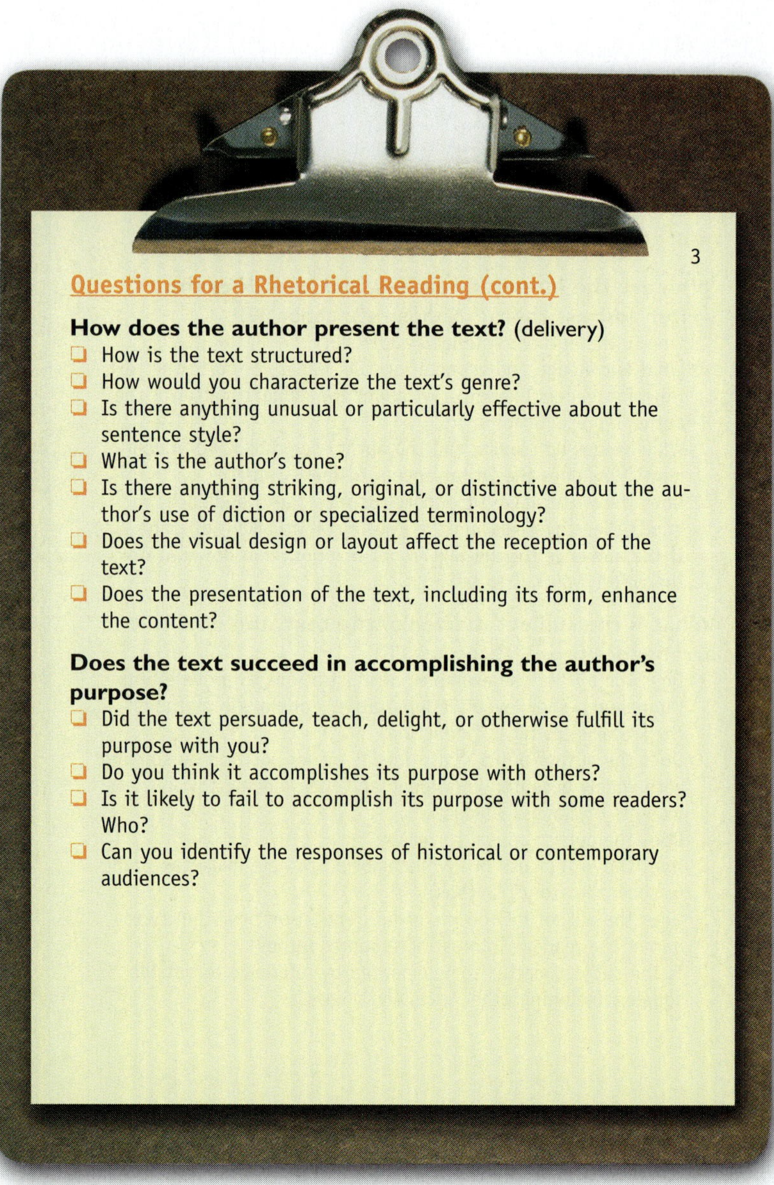
3

Questions for a Rhetorical Reading (cont.)

How does the author present the text? (delivery)
- ❑ How is the text structured?
- ❑ How would you characterize the text's genre?
- ❑ Is there anything unusual or particularly effective about the sentence style?
- ❑ What is the author's tone?
- ❑ Is there anything striking, original, or distinctive about the author's use of diction or specialized terminology?
- ❑ Does the visual design or layout affect the reception of the text?
- ❑ Does the presentation of the text, including its form, enhance the content?

Does the text succeed in accomplishing the author's purpose?
- ❑ Did the text persuade, teach, delight, or otherwise fulfill its purpose with you?
- ❑ Do you think it accomplishes its purpose with others?
- ❑ Is it likely to fail to accomplish its purpose with some readers? Who?
- ❑ Can you identify the responses of historical or contemporary audiences?

Activity 8-8: Analyzing an Ethnography

L. Franklin Jewell wrote the following autobiographical essay in an anthropology class, as a response to an assignment that called for "an ethnography." An ethnography is, in a nutshell, "writing about people or race" (combining *ethno,* "race" or "people," with *graphie,* "to write"). Ethnographies try to capture the essence of human culture not by "summing it up" but by presenting the details of people's words, lives, and interactions with others.

Using the Project Checklist on pages 144–146, read and respond to Franklin Jewell's essay. You can choose one subset of questions for your analysis or handle each set more briefly as part of an overall rhetorical analysis.

Read Actively

Before you read, remember to make predictions based on the title, contents, context, your prior knowledge, and the genre (◀ page 132).

Jewell 1

Things We Carry:
A Multicultural Awakening
L. Franklin Jewell

When I think about the events in our lives that shape us, I think about the things we carry. In 1998 I read Tim O'Brien's *The Things They Carried,* a story of the physical and emotional burdens that O'Brien's platoon buddies carried on the battlefields of Vietnam. I reflect on the way my life has been molded by my own memories and the enduring impressions of the people who left them. The impressions of our past are like footprints in our mind, always present as we adapt to or rebel against each new event.

My mother and father carried our family from the hills of Kentucky to the plains of Indiana. My mother recalled that on the morning after their arrival, as she swept the sidewalk in front of our house, she overheard the conversation of two neighbor women across the street. Both women were partially deaf, and they were unaware of the volume of their speech—my mother heard every word.

Mrs. Gilkey asked Mrs. Pevler, "Who are the new neighbors?"

Mrs. Pevler replied, "Probably some more of that Kentucky white trash."

My older sister, who witnessed the event, said my mother pretended not to hear but added more energy to her sweeping. Over the next twenty years, an inseparable bond was formed among these women and my mother. The societal prejudice disappeared as our families shared economic hardships and personal tragedies, each family clinging to the support of the other. My street became a street

Jewell 2

of widows: Mrs. Pevler, Mrs. Gilkey, Mrs. McKnight, Mrs. Irvin, Mrs. Marquess, Mrs. Hutcheson. They came to rely heavily upon the take-in meals from my Kentucky mother and the handyman skills of my Kentucky father. When we were older, my brother and I mowed the grass and shoveled the snow for these widows. We did it for no wages. My father said it was wrong to take money from them, and it was always wrong to take money from people who had less money than we had.

We lived in a small house sided with shiplap siding, covered with brick-colored tarpaper. It was a three-bedroom house. My mother and father slept upstairs. I slept with my younger brother Don in the east bedroom, and my sisters, Margaret and Mary, slept in the west bedroom—one bed per bedroom. My father said that's the way it should be. He said, "One bed per bedroom—if we had two beds in a bedroom, we'd have to call them *bedsroom.*" It always made my brother and me laugh, but my mother and sisters only smiled. I believe it was my father's sense of humor that helped my family bear our shared poverty.

My mother's name was Nellie and my father's name was Lester, but because of his Kentucky roots everyone called him "Tuck." Although my parents left the woodlands of Kentucky, they never left their love for the music of Kentucky. Sneaking from my bed on winter evenings, I sat on the kitchen floor out of sight in darkened shadows. I peeked around the door, watching two mahogany fiddle bows, rising and falling like slender tree limbs, lifting and swaying with the wind. My father and his friend Frosty played tight

Read Actively
Remember to annotate the text while you read (page 135).

Jewell 3

harmonies, their twin fiddles playing sad Appalachian ballads, Cherokee reels, and happy Irish jigs. On weekday evenings after work, family and friends joined in our living room for jam sessions or gathered outside for front-porch concerts. Neighbors brought lawn chairs to our red brick sidewalk, and people in passing cars slowed, then circled the block before parking along our street. On Saturday nights my parents played their music at American Legion Halls and square dance parties in the barns of local farmers. Bankers, barbers, farmers, and teachers—they all danced to the tunes of my mother and father's music.

My father carried his pride like the tools of his carpentry trade. Although he had only a sixth-grade education, he was proud that he was employed by the university. When anyone asked him of his profession he replied, "I'm a carpenter at the university." A hammer hung from the loop of his worn bib overalls and a flat red pencil was half-tucked inside the rim of his billed cap. His gray shirt carried the smell of a carpenter's sweat. He carried a small notebook under the button flap of the front pocket in his overalls with scribbles of board feet, cubic yards, and square feet. He called it his "figurin' book."

My mother carried a threadbare canvas bag to her job at the high school cafeteria. The bag contained band-aids, aspirin, needle and thread, safety pins, Pepto Bismol, a wet wash cloth in a plastic bag, pliers, a screwdriver, a blue bottle of Vicks VapoRub, and a spare hair net. She toted the bag to baseball games, 4-H fairs, and music contests, and it gave her great pleasure that she might ease anyone's pain with the things she carried in her worn canvas bag. She had a

Jewell 4

high school diploma and was my editor for high school essays and my math tutor for seventh grade algebra.

In part because of the community concerts, I came to know every person in the town of Wingate, population 409. In the 1950s, an African American was called Negro; a Caucasian was called white. The town and surrounding community were not predominantly white—they were all white, with the exception of one African American, Ike Mitchell. Ike was an elderly bachelor and a hired hand of several local farmers. In the winter, when farm work was scarce, Ike was a grave digger at the local cemetery. Another man, Hap Deering, was also an aged bachelor. Hap, like Ike, was also a hired hand and grave digger. Both men were befriended by my father. They were illiterate and poor, and my father often sent me on errands to deliver bacon and biscuits to their room behind the barbershop. One cold autumn evening when I delivered corn bread and pinto beans from Mother's kitchen, Ike invited me in by their stove. I stood with my back to the stove, staring between my ankles at the nameplate below the orange glowing burner.

Hap said, "So you're Tuck's boy?"

I nodded.

"What grade you in?"

"Second grade," I said.

Ike walked closer and slid open one of the dampers on the stove. He turned to me and said, "Can you read?"

I said, "Yes."

He pointed down at the nameplate on the stove and said, "What do those words say?"

Read Critically
Remember to distinguish facts, opinions, and beliefs and to evaluate the author's underlying assumptions (pages 140–142).

I looked down at the two words on the plate. The first word was a short word; the second word was longer—what my teacher, Mrs. Bradley, called a two-syllable word. I said, "Warm Morning. It says Warm Morning." Ike smiled at me and looked down at the plate.

He said, "All of these years, and I always wondered what that stove said." He reached in his pocket and tried to put a nickel in my hand. I pulled back and told him that Mom didn't want any money for the food. He said the money was for reading.

"You take it," he said. "You earned it for readin'." I looked around the room at the two wooden chairs and two small beds with a pile of dirty clothes on the one by the wall. One light bulb hung from a braided wire from the ceiling and reflected on Ike's pink palm. I took the nickel, but I never told my mother and father. I reasoned that Ike was right; I earned it. But I never forgot the poverty of Ike and Hap, and I never forgot the nickel that was given to me by someone who had less than my family did.

In my junior year of high school my father announced that the university offered a fifty percent tuition discount for students of university employees. My mother's eyes were brighter than the bare light bulb in Ike's room, but my hands trembled. Mother saw opportunity for her Kentucky children, but I felt the fear of possible failure at the university. In that same year, the summer of 1966, I won a high school essay competition and was awarded a trip to Mexico as an exchange student.

In the rural countryside and small towns of Michoacan the people harvested grain from yellow wheat fields and hoed weeds

from the green corn. They baled purple bloomed alfalfa in green fields speckled with the white frames of buzzing bee hives. Brown-skinned Mexican women baked bread and corn cakes in their bakeries of sweltering heat. Mexican mechanics wiped their foreheads with greasy forearms and filled gas tanks from Texaco gas pumps. In that summer of '66, I witnessed the working men and women from a foreign culture. But some things were not foreign. I felt the fatigue from their labor and the pride in their work. I smelled the scent of baked tortillas and the odor of cornfield sweat. In the evenings after work I saw the carnival lights of summer night fiestas and heard the neighborhood mariachi bands of trumpets, guitars, and fiddles. Old women clapped their hands to the staccato notes of the trumpets. Dark haired girls danced and twirled in the summer moonlight, their skirts rising up and down like colored parasols on the tile plaza. And I remembered the barn dances and summer night concerts on the sidewalks of my hometown. Although we were one thousand miles apart, we were different. But we were also alike.

My younger sister's husband died in 1968 at the age of twenty-six. In January of that year, I quit school at the university to work on her farm. The farm was heavily mortgaged, and I spent a quarter of a century trying to resuscitate it until the spring of 1993 when I entered a factory as a temporary worker from a local employment service. I was an engine assembler in the factory—called an assembly temp. A temp was a subclass employee, with low wages and no benefits. At lunch time and breaks, temps sat at the temp table, and factory employees sat at the other tables. As temps, we knew our job security

Read Rhetorically

Remember to ask the key question for a rhetorical analysis: What effects does the writer achieve, and how exactly does the writer achieve them (page 143)?

Jewell 7

was tentative; we were only needed as long as demand was at its peak. In any economic decline we were expendable.

There was one other table for the other temps. They were from another employment agency, one that contracted workers for service jobs: window washing, floor scrubbing, and restroom cleaning. None of the tables had a label, but their table was marked by color. I saw the brown faces and arms of the Mexican workers. I said, "Hola," and one of the men smiled and nodded, then bowed his head toward me. A few days later, I spoke to him in the washroom. His name was Nicholas. He spoke more English than I spoke Spanish. We developed a routine of daily salutations and discussions on the weather. Each day I watched him buff water-speckled mirrors and oily wash basins into shiny new fixtures. He introduced me to Rosa and Daisy, two middle-aged single mothers who waxed the floors and cleaned the toilets in the employee restrooms. I gained hero status with Rosy and Daisy, who called me "Pancho Rey de Agua!" because I had repaired a broken water line for them. I was Pancho, King of Water! Through our broken language and awkward translation, we became friends: Nicholas, Rosy, Daisy, and Pancho, the agua king. I sat at their table of color, but they never felt comfortable sitting at mine.

During my months as a temp I enrolled at the university where I gradually completed my studies in English and history. At the university I saw many tables of color. I saw Peruvians, Colombians, Chileans, and Brazilians. I saw Indians, Pakistanis, Koreans, and Chinese. I was ashamed of my nationality classification by color. I asked myself, "Isn't white a color?" And I believed that diversity in

Jewell 8

color could not exist without the color white. I confessed to myself, feeling guilty for my own passive prejudices of race, religion, and nationality. But I believe my cultural awareness of global diversity had awakened my desire to be a citizen not of my country or race, but a citizen of the world.

Today, as I sit at the factory break table I reflect on where I have been and where I am going, and I remember the things people carry. I know that each individual carries a unique set of values, formed from his or her experiences in the world. I know that I carry the memories and values of my parents and all of my struggles and observations along the way. In Tim O'Brien's story, the soldiers carried 223-caliber ammo and letters from mom and dad. They carried pictures of family and ghosts of dead comrades. In the factory, I know that Shawn had been divorced for two years, but he still carried his wife's picture in his wallet; he gets "the boys" on Saturday and Sunday. I know that Leo's daughter has cancer, but Leo says, "Only God knows best." I know that Nicholas carries a small English/Spanish dictionary in his work satchel, and I think of my mother's canvas bag. Daisy carries a small notebook of "ounces per gallon" for the soap and wax in her floor scrubber, and I think of my father's "figurin' book." Rosy carries an A+ paper from her daughter's spelling book, along with her lucky buffalo nickel, and I think of Ike's nickel and the Warm Morning stove. The break is over and I watch the stream of passing workers file along my table. I look into their eyes and I wonder what things they carry.

A table of contents for writing project threads appears on pages xv–xxii.

Forming a First Impression

In a review, you are asked to examine and evaluate a text or product with a critical eye. Before you begin to analyze a work, it can be useful to consider what preconceptions might be guiding your thinking or what you think the text or product might be about. Use the Project Checklist on page 132 to help you think through these ideas. Before you dig deeper, what's your first impression?

Listing Criteria and Examples

What criteria will you use to judge the work you are reviewing? What does a work of this particular type have to do—or what features does it have to have—in order to be effective or worthwhile? Think about similar works and what makes them effective (or not). Make a list of your criteria.

Use the critical reading strategies in this chapter to help you apply the criteria to the work. Read and reread the work in order to find examples to justify your opinions about whether or not the work meets the criteria. Under each criterion, note at least one example (and preferably more) from the work that could be used to illustrate it. (If you are writing about an image or a work that uses images extensively, consult the Project Checklist on pages 186–187. If you are writing a review of a book, poem, play, or other literary work, Chapter 9 can help you analyze texts and clarify your ideas.)

◀ page 68.

Critical Reviews

A Movie You Can't Forget!

This could be the best movie you will ever see all year, if you're looking for something intense, suspenseful, and different than your usual effects-packed thriller. This is the kind of movie that you will be talking about at work, at the bank (to total strangers!), and at the corner coffee shop.

The movie starts with a murder -- a revenge killing, in fact. But was the right person killed?

The main character, Leonard Shelby (Guy Pearce), is a man with no short-term memory. He hasn't been able to form new memories since the night his wife was murdered. On a hunt to find the murderer, but with no way of remembering names, dates, places, facts and faces, he tattoos mementos of his search. He uses pictures to try to identify people who know his name. Does he like this person? Does he trust this person? Is this the killer? He doesn't know unless he's written a note.

Writer/director Christopher Nolan puts you right in Leonard's shoes, living the story in reverse order. This ingenious method of story-telling means that you never know more than Leonard does. In one scene you see Leonard getting information from a person who knows him -- maybe a good person; maybe bad. In the next scene you see a previous meeting between the two which sheds more light on their relationship. Later still you see how they met. You, like Leonard, have no knowledge of what came before.

This film will leave its own memento on your mind, and you'll have a hard time forgetting how much you enjoyed it.

Evaluating Facts, Opinions, Beliefs, and Assumptions

Before you write a letter to the editor, you'll need to consider how other writers have responded to the topic you want to write about in the publication to which you will send your letter. What facts do writers agree or disagree about? What opinions, beliefs, and assumptions do they hold in common (or not)? Which of these opinions, beliefs, and assumptions do you agree with, and which do you disagree with?

Use the Project Checklists in this chapter to help you position the facts, opinions, beliefs, and assumptions you consider to be important to your letter so that you have a clear perspective from which to draft your letter.

◀ page 44.

Email Letters to the Editor

[To:] George Best, Editor
[From:] Annabelle DiSargento
[Subject:] Letter to the Editor

What is the impact of AP classes on the college admissions process? By placing additional emphasis on the level of classes taken by students, colleges are able to review applicants based on their academic motivation and achievement. But, this emphasis on AP courses has the negative effect of causing high schools to limit their academic offerings in order to promote "college-application friendly" curriculums. A more balanced approach to college admissions would allow high schools to offer a diverse, broad curriculum based on students' interests and teachers' expertise.

Informative Essays

Garrison 1

Angela Garrison

English 101

Dr. Simpson

September 26, 2005

From Over There to Over Here:

War Blogs Get Up Close, Personal, and Profitable

Blog was the word looked up most often in the online *Merriam-Webster's Dictionary* in 2004 ("Blog"). What's all this fuss? When you read someone else's personal blog, you find out what they like and don't like, what they're doing, and maybe other bits of gossip offered at random. You can read news blogs to find out what's going on lately, what other people think about it, and why it matters. You can keep your own blog to share your thoughts and feelings, to tell your friends and family what you're up to, and sometimes to capture the interest of someone you've never met. When you read and write blogs, you join, or even create, a community. Blogs are also an efficient way to break news, spread rumors, and glorify causes. In short, blogs help people do what they've always done as social beings, just more quickly now, and from almost anywhere on Earth. Soldiers on the ground fighting in Iraq are writing blogs from the front lines. But a review is now under way at the Pentagon to "better understand the overall implications of blogging and other Internet communications in combat zones," according to John Hockenberry in his *Wired* article "The Blogs of War." The benefits of blogs written by U.S. soldiers in Iraq far outweigh the hypothetical risks of revealing sensitive or strategic information. Those benefits, however, aren't as obvious as they might seem.

In spite of what the imagery of smart bombs and predator drones might lead television viewers to believe, wars are fought by people, not just technology. Most blogs start out as efforts to stay in touch with family and friends, but they quickly turn into

Reading Research Critically

As you collect and read information for your essay, be sure that you read each source carefully to determine whether facts and evidence in one source correspond to or contradict those in another; which statements are facts, opinions, and beliefs; and what each author's underlying assumptions seem to be. (Consult section 8b as you read.) How do the sources help you define or refine the areas of the topic in which you are interested? ◀ page 68.

Critical Reviews

A Movie You Can't Forget!

This could be the best movie you will ever see all year, if you're looking for something intense, suspenseful, and different than your usual effects-packed thriller. This is the kind of movie that you will be talking about at work, at the bank (to total strangers!), and at the corner coffee shop.

The movie starts with a murder -- a revenge killing, in fact. But was the right person killed?

The main character, Leonard Shelby (Guy Pearce), is a man with no short-term memory. He hasn't been able to form new memories since the night his wife was murdered. On a hunt to find the murderer, but with no way of remembering names, dates, places, facts and faces, he tattoos mementos of his search. He uses pictures to try to identify people who know his name. Does he like this person? Does he trust this person? Is this the killer? He doesn't know unless he's written a note.

Writer/director Christopher Nolan puts you right in Leonard's shoes, living the story in reverse order. This ingenious method of story-telling means that you never know more than Leonard does. In one scene you see Leonard getting information from a person who knows him -- maybe a good person; maybe bad. In the next scene you see a previous meeting between the two which sheds more light on their relationship. Later still you see how they met. You, like Leonard, have no knowledge of what came before.

This film will leave its own memento on your mind, and you'll have a hard time forgetting how much you enjoyed it.

Checking Fairness and Accuracy

Reviews need to be accurate and fair; otherwise, readers won't trust the reviewer. Could someone who holds a different view accuse you of providing a one-sided review—have you ignored any details from the work that would contradict your claim? Use the Project Checklist on page 141 to help you evaluate the use of evidence in your first draft. You may also find the Project Checklist on page 94 helpful in learning more about supporting evidence and its accuracy.

◀ page 118.

What is literature? This deceptively straightforward question has been asked and answered in many ways through the years. Traditionally, literature has been defined as fiction, poetry, drama, or other forms of written or spoken artistic expression that are widely considered to be excellent. According to literary critic Kenneth Burke, literature is "designed for the express purpose of arousing emotions" (*Counter-Statement* [Berkeley: University of California Press, 1968] 123). Its purpose may be to spark some desire or interest in readers; to entertain, delight, or move them; to make them despair or cause them pain. Or a literary work may move readers toward a particular way of judging experience, some way to sum up an attitude about life that has value. Literature, it has been suggested, speaks to universal human themes.

From a more overtly political angle, cultural theorist Terry Eagleton calls our definitions and value judgments about literature "the assumptions by which certain social groups exercise power over others" (*Literary Theory* [Minneapolis: University of Minnesota Press, 1996] 16). We *use* literature, in other words, to influence each other, as well as to help us adjust to the human situation. For this reason, Kenneth Burke also called literature "equipment for living" (*Philosophy of Literary Form* [Berkeley: University of California Press, 1973] 293). And writer Salman Rushdie, responding in a public lecture to the fatwa issued against him by the Ayatollah Khomeini in response to his 1988 novel *The Satanic Verses,* says, "Literature is the one place in any society where, within the secrecy of our own heads, we can hear voices talking about everything in every possible way" ("Is Nothing Sacred?" *Guardian,* 7 Feb. 1990; also *Granta* 31 [1990]: 97–110). As the death threat against Rushdie so graphically illustrates, literature can have a profound effect on our lives and on its times. As you approach literature as a writer, bear in mind that a work of literature gains power and meaning as much from your angle of approach as from its form and content.

Literature—as a form of writing—always has some context, a situation that accompanies the act of the writer and the reading of the work. Writers work hard to establish that context because it establishes verisimilitude, the appearance of truth that helps sustain the illusion of fiction. Readers likewise use context to give literature significance and meaning.

For example, any reader who picked up Don DeLillo's 1997 novel *Underworld* after September 11, 2001, probably noticed its striking cover image. In the foreground stands an old church. Behind it are the looming towers of the World Trade Center shrouded in fog. A solitary bird glides next to one of the towers. DeLillo's sweeping novel is about the contradictions in American life and the power of history in a post-nuclear age. Read in the context of 9/11—which is unavoidable and necessary given both its theme and its cover—it gains significance and meaning. In fact, DeLillo himself wrote about this context in "The Ruins of Terror," available at http://www.guardian.co.uk/Archive/Article/0,4273,4324579,00.html.

More about his efforts to re-create the American scene, with audio readings and images, can be found on the Web at http://www.nytimes.com/books/97/03/16/lifetimes/delillo.html.

The Rhetorical Situation of a Literary Work

The Text

What is the work about?
What genre of literature is it?
What do we know about the genre?
What can we say about the language?
What is the situation *in* the work?
Is the work addressed to someone?
What other works is it like?

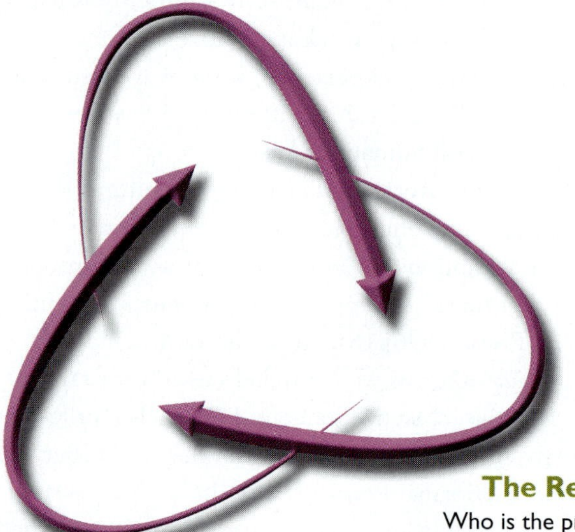

The Reader

Who is the primary audience for the work?
What are readers likely to know about the author or the content?
What demands does the author make of the reader?

The Writer

Who is the writer?
What do we know about the writer's life?
What other works has the author written?
What can we learn about the author from the work itself?

Exploring Your Responses in Writing

Writing in response to these questions one by one should give you plenty of ideas to build upon if your goal is to write an essay about a particular literary work.

- **Restatement.** What is the text about? Try to be as accurate as possible.
- **Affective response.** What did you feel as you read? Explain the reasons you felt as you did.
- **Associative response.** What does the text remind you of? Does it remind you of any personal experiences? Of anything else that you have read or seen?
- **Decisions about literary importance.** What do you think is the most important word, line, or scene in the text? People will naturally disagree about what is most important, so dont worry about making incorrect choices.
- **Imitation and parody.** Write about an event or person in your own experience as if you were this author. Imitate the author's style. Or exaggerate the author's style in a parody.
- **Extensions of your response.** Suppose that the text is not about what you said it was in your restatement above—that it's about something deeper, more complex, or less obvious. What is it *really* about?

You will find writing about literature more enjoyable, and even easier, once you understand that all of these types of responses add to our appreciation of literature's value. Especially when the work is fresh to you, see whether you can respond in multiple ways. More varied and rich responses will leave you more options for developing your initial responses into essays or other projects.

When you read a work of literature, you consider within your own reading context whether the work is successful in achieving its apparent aims and the ways it goes about accomplishing them. You can ask, for example,

- What effects does the work of literature have?
- How does it achieve these effects?
- What does it teach us, and why does or doesn't that lesson matter?

Noticing Your Responses

The key to developing an understanding of a work of literature is to be aware of what you think about and feel as you read, and then to try to discern later if the thoughts and feelings add up to a meaningful pattern. Very often, they will. You can start by writing about what you perceive in a text, how you feel about what you see, and then what associations the text stirs in you.

Making Predictions and Forming Expectations

When you read literature with the plan of writing about it later, you should be prepared to *analyze, interpret,* and *evaluate.* When you analyze a story, for example, you break it down into its components—such as plot, point of view, and character—and consider how these features fit together in meaningful ways. When you interpret a story, you come to some conclusions about what the story means. When you evaluate a story, you consider its strengths and weaknesses. (See Words about Words on page 139.)

To better comprehend what you read and thus prepare yourself for analyzing, interpreting, and evaluating, spend at least a few moments thinking and even writing about the work before you start reading. *Anticipation* and *prediction* are two important steps in getting ready to read. Spend a moment pondering the title of the work, try to recall what you know about the author or any of the author's works, read the "About the Author" note if one is present, and scan the work to see how long it is and whether it consists of chapters or other sections.

As you read, you can *form expectations* about, for example, what will happen next, how a character might change, or what problem a character faces. You can make predictions based on these expectations, as well. Good writers understand that readers form expectations, and they take advantage of those expectations to make the story more dramatic or meaningful or suspenseful, by using techniques

Activity 9-1: Reading a Short Story

Explore your thoughts and feelings about the following short story. Before reading, make predictions about the work. After you read, respond to the questions in Exploring Your Responses in Writing (page 155). Then share your responses with a small group of classmates. Once everyone has shared responses, ask again, "What is the story *really* about?"

The Story of an Hour (1894)

Kate Chopin

About the Author: Kate Chopin (1850–1904) grew up in St. Louis, Missouri, and lived there for the greater part of 40 years. Chopin was raised by her mother, Eliza, who sent her to a Catholic school. There, she was taught to be submissive and modest, to look forward to a life of marriage and motherhood, and to desire what was—the reasoning went—women's natural role in society. She began writing seriously in 1884 and published her great novel, The Awakening, *in 1899. Five years later, she died unexpectedly of a brain hemorrhage.*

Knowing that Mrs. Mallard was afflicted with a heart trouble, great care was taken to break to her as gently as possible the news of her husband's death.

It was her sister Josephine who told her, in broken sentences, veiled hints that revealed in half concealing. Her husband's friend Richards was there, too, near her. It was he who had been in the newspaper office when intelligence of the railroad disaster was received, with Brently Mallard's name leading the list of "killed." He had only taken the time to assure himself of its truth by a second telegram, and had hastened to forestall any less careful, less tender friend in bearing the sad message.

She did not hear the story as many women have heard the same, with a paralyzed inability to accept its significance. She wept at once, with sudden, wild abandonment, in her sister's arms. When the storm of grief had spent itself she went away to her room alone. She would have no one follow her.

There stood, facing the open window, a comfortable, roomy armchair. Into this she sank, pressed down by a physical exhaustion that haunted her body and seemed to reach into her soul.

She could see in the open square before her house the tops of trees that were all aquiver with the new spring life. The delicious breath of rain was in the air. In the street below a peddler was crying his wares. The notes of a distant song which someone was singing reached her faintly, and countless sparrows were twittering in the eaves.

There were patches of blue sky showing here and there through the clouds that had met and piled one above the other in the west facing her window. She sat with her head thrown back upon the cushion of the chair, quite motionless, except when a sob came up into her throat and shook her, as a child who has cried itself to sleep continues to sob in its dreams.

She was young, with a fair, calm face, whose lines bespoke repression and even a certain strength. But now there was a dull stare in her eyes, whose gaze was fixed away off yonder on one of those patches of blue sky. It was not a glance of reflection, but rather indicated a suspension of intelligent thought.

There was something coming to her and she was waiting for it, fearfully. What was it? She did not know; it was too subtle and elusive to name. But she felt it, creeping out of the sky, reaching toward her through the sounds, the scents, the color that filled the air.

Now her bosom rose and fell tumultuously. She was beginning to recognize this thing that was approaching to possess her, and she was striving to beat it back with her will—as powerless as her two white slender hands would have been.

When she abandoned herself a little whispered word escaped her slightly parted lips. She said it over and over under her breath: "Free, free, free!" The vacant stare and the look of terror that had followed it went from her eyes. They stayed keen and bright. Her pulses beat fast, and the coursing blood warmed and relaxed every inch of her body.

She did not stop to ask if it were or were not a monstrous joy that held her. A clear and exalted perception enabled her to dismiss the suggestion as trivial.

She knew that she would weep again when she saw the kind, tender hands folded in death; the face that had never looked save with love upon her, fixed and gray and dead. But she saw beyond that bitter moment a long

(continued on next page)

such as *foreshadowing* (hints or other content that prepares readers for later events). Paying attention to how your expectations take shape during your reading—even by jotting notes in the margins of a story—will help you focus your attention on the work as it unfolds and will make your interpretation more a result of your reading experience than a matter of guesswork.

Critical Frameworks

Researchers and scholars in the humanities acknowledge that it is virtually impossible to approach a work of literature without some preconceptions about what is important in literature, what its role in personal and social life might be, and how it achieves its effects. When you write about literature, the terms and concepts you use act as filters that let new detail shine through. Your prior beliefs and values will also influence what meaning you derive from a text, as will its situation in history. *Literary theory* is an attempt to make such knowledge explicit *and* to use these insights to gain perspective when interpreting complex works.

Historical criticism examines the work of literature in its place and time, with reference to the social, political, and historical contexts that influence the author and readers.

Cultural studies takes a broad view of what counts as "literary" and so draws concepts from a variety of philosophical, theoretical, historical, and rhetorical perspectives to examine a wide range of texts from popular culture.

Marxist criticism explores literature as a response to the negative effects of class division, which leads to alienation and oppression. Social and political circumstances (ideology) shape how people (and writers) think about and respond to the world.

Feminist criticism studies cultural, political, and biological representations of women and men in literature. Feminist critics believe that gender and sexuality are central themes in literature.

Reader-response criticism studies the literary work as an appeal to readers in a rhetorical situation. With its form and content, literature creates expectations in readers, and interpretation focuses on how the work creates and satisfies those expectations.

Formalist criticism studies the literary work as an artifact that communicates meaningfully without the need for relating its meaning to historical, biographical, or social contexts.

Postmodernist criticism studies literature as not merely an artifact but also a self-referential act that contests its own function

procession of years to come that would belong to her absolutely. And she opened and spread her arms out to them in welcome.

There would be no one to live for her during those coming years; she would live for herself. There would be no powerful will bending her in that blind persistence with which men and women believe they have a right to impose a private will upon a fellow creature. A kind intention or a cruel intention made the act seem no less a crime as she looked upon it in that brief moment of illumination.

And yet she loved him—sometimes. Often she had not. What did it matter! What could love, the unsolved mystery, count for in the face of this possession of self-assertion which she suddenly recognized as the strongest impulse of her being.

"Free! Body and soul free!" she kept whispering.

Josephine was kneeling before the closed door with her lips to the keyhole, imploring for admission. "Louise, open the door! I beg; open the door—you will make yourself ill. What are you doing, Louise? For heaven's sake open the door."

"Go away. I am not making myself ill." No; she was drinking in a very elixir of life through that open window.

Her fancy was running riot along those days ahead of her. Spring days, and summer days, and all sorts of days that would be her own. She breathed a quick prayer that life might be long. It was only yesterday she had thought with a shudder that life might be long.

She arose at length and opened the door to her sister's importunities. There was a feverish triumph in her eyes, and she carried herself unwittingly like a goddess of Victory. She clasped her sister's waist, and together they descended the stairs. Richards stood waiting for them at the bottom.

Some one was opening the front door with a latchkey. It was Brently Mallard who entered, a little travel-stained, composedly carrying his grip-sack and umbrella. He had been far from the scene of accident, and did not even know there had been one. He stood amazed at Josephine's piercing cry; at Richards's quick motion to screen him from the view of his wife. But Richards was too late.

When the doctors came they said she had died of heart disease—of joy that kills.

Activity 9-2: Reading a Second Time

Using the list of terms and questions on pages 160–161 as a guide, reread the story. Consider which elements of the story seem most important or interesting. Now that you know what happens at the end, watch for any foreshadowing to see how Chopin sets the theme of the story from the beginning. How does she create and satisfy the reader's expectations?

Activity 9-3: Researching an Author's Biography

Knowing about an author's life often can help us see how (and why) themes emerge from his or her writing. From a critical edition of Kate Chopin's *The Awakening,* one student discovered these additional (and remarkable) details about her life:

- When she was 5 years old, her father, Thomas O'Flaherty, died tragically in a train accident, one of several city dignitaries who perished when the Gasconade Bridge collapsed under the weight of the first train to cross it.
- She married Oscar Chopin in 1870 and moved with him to New Orleans.
- In 1874, her older brother, Tom, died after falling from a buggy.
- She had borne six children by the time she was 29.
- She had an extramarital affair not long before her husband died suddenly of malaria in 1882.

The Dictionary of Literary Biography, searchable through InfoTrac Online, is an excellent resource for learning more about literary authors and their work. Track down information about an author whose work you are currently reading. How does the biographical information illuminate the work?

When you are thinking and writing about a work of literature, be sure to distinguish between the author and the narrator (in prose) or the speaker (in poetry). See page 168.

and status as art. A novel or short story, for example, can also be said to be about the act of writing itself: how fiction communicates meaning (or not) and the techniques it uses to move the reader.

Deconstruction studies the ways that a work of literature undermines itself in its reliance on binary oppositions. For example, "The Story of an Hour" includes oppositions between woman and man, freedom and oppression, and life and death. The story privileges one side of the opposition in making its case for Mrs. Mallard's suffering. Deconstruction points out how these oppositions, which are embedded in language and culture, limit perspective, and it is the critic's job to build up the ignored term in the binary pair.

The function of these approaches to literature is not to demonstrate that the "theory" itself is true, but to show that a literary work achieves its meaning in any number of ways for many different reasons. Taken together, these approaches confirm our common sense that works of literature speak to readers in multiple ways and at a variety of levels. One of your aims as a writer and critic should be to choose an angle of approach to literature that helps you appreciate its value and complexity.

9b Terms for Understanding Fiction

When reading fiction, consider the terms and questions below.

Terms and Definitions	Questions to Ask about Fiction
PLOT The pattern of events of the story, with an emphasis on cause and effect.	What is the initial conflict in the story? How is it resolved?
CHARACTERS People, animals, aliens, or other beings who act on the world in the story.	Are the main characters in the story fully fleshed out ("round") or one-dimensional ("flat")? Static (unchanging) or dynamic (growing, changing)? What do you know about them? What role do the minor, or flat, characters play? Do you empathize with any of the characters? Do any make you feel angry or disappointed?
SETTING The place and time of the story.	Where and when does the story take place? What do you know about the social or historical circumstances of the story? How does the setting influence the plot?
IMAGERY Vivid language that helps readers imagine the visual or emotional qualities of objects, people, events, or places.	What are the most striking or memorable visual or emotional images in the story? How do these images comment on or develop the theme?
POINT OF VIEW The perspective or vantage point of the narrator.	How does the narrator's point of view give you insight into the characters or theme? Does the narrator use the first-person point of view ("I"), or does the narrator refer to characters in the third person ("he" and "she") and thus act as an outsider to the plot? Does the narrator seem all-knowing, or are certain characters or events outside of the narrator's range of knowledge? Is the narrator reliable or unreliable?
STYLE AND TONE *Style* refers to the overall flavor and texture created by the writer's word choices and sentence structures. *Tone* is an attitude toward the events of the story—humorous, ironic, cynical, and so on.	Does the author use a complex or straightforward style? How do you think the author feels about the story or particular characters in it? What word choices and sentence structures lead to that impression?
SYMBOLISM The use of one thing to stand for another, usually a larger or more abstract concept.	Does the author use any symbols that seem especially striking or memorable? Are the symbols woven into the story, or do they depend on your prior knowledge of their meaning (or both)?
THEME The central point(s) the work makes about some aspect of life or human values.	What theme or themes does the story confront? What do you think the central theme is? What elements of the plot or characterization support this central theme?

When you interpret and write about literature, critical approaches such as those outlined on pages 157–159 can help you appreciate a work's multiple layers of meaning. It's also helpful to follow a story's lead. For example, "The Story of an Hour" lends itself especially well to feminist criticism because of its themes of gender relations, marriage, power, freedom, loss, and "imposing of will." Here is how one student initially approached her interpretation in some notes that she later used to write her essay on the story (printed starting on page 169):

> Louise feels free for the one time in her life and is almost beside herself with joy. She feels her husband has been controlling her and even that she has been controlling him a bit, since that's what seems to have happened in their marriage. She suddenly feels alive again. Everything outside her window is green and lush and quivering. It's almost as if Louise has been reborn. Her so-called freedom is not so easily won because we see Brently come strolling in. I wanted to blame Louise for being so happy at first, but then I felt how awful it would be to have your freedom suddenly taken away from you again. The battle of the sexes in this story is all about power and bending of wills. Louise loses in the end.

Questions about "The Story of an Hour"

Why does Louise Mallard react as she does to news of her husband's death? How does she react at first? Later? Does the surprise at the end suggest anything about the "appropriateness" of her initial and later responses to her husband's death?

Do you think that Louise Mallard changes during the course of this (very short) story? Is her sudden realization believable? Why or why not? What do you know about Brently Mallard? Josephine? Richards?

Why is all the action of the story inside the house? If you did not know the date when the story was written, could you tell when the story takes place? How?

What does Louise Mallard see when she looks out her bedroom window? How does the description suggest her state of mind? How do these images contrast with how she imagines her husband at his funeral?

What is the point of view of "The Story of an Hour"? Why is it important that we know Louise Mallard's thoughts? How do you think Richards or Josephine would view her, not knowing her thoughts?

Knowing what you now know about the sudden death of many of the men in her life, how would you characterize Kate Chopin's attitude toward Louise Mallard? Are there indications in the story that we should view her sympathetically or with disdain?

What does Louise Mallard observe outside her bedroom window? How does the description symbolize her state of mind?

Is the theme about the constraining and demoralizing effects of patriarchal culture on women? The vanity of people who see only advantage in the suffering of others? Something else? Why do you think so?

9d Terms for Understanding Poetry

These terms will help you know what to look for when you read, analyze, and interpret poetry.

Terms and Definitions	Questions to Ask about Poetry
IMAGERY A pattern of images that creates meaning. For example, imagery with contrasting themes may suggest difference or disruption.	Is there a pattern of imagery in the poem? What is the most important or most emphasized image? How would you characterize the imagery in terms of tone?
SOUND How a poem sounds when read aloud. *Meter* is the poem's sound pattern, especially its sequence of stressed and unstressed syllables. *Rhyme* is the sound similarities across words or lines.	Does the poem have a regular pattern in its meter, rhyme, or sounds? What is the mood of the poem?
FORM A pattern of line length, rhyme, and meter. In open forms, the pattern varies across lines. Closed forms have regular patterns. Form in poetry may also be considered an appeal consisting of the arousal and fulfillment of the reader's or listener's desire.	Does the poem have an open or closed form? If it is open, are there any places where a pattern in line length, rhyme, or meter stands out? If it is closed, does the pattern depend on line length, rhyme, meter, or some combination of these? In this closed form, do any lines in particular have a special function?
DICTION AND SYNTAX *Diction* refers to word choice, which may be formal, informal, or varied in formality. Some words or phrases may be repeated several times, placing stress on their meaning and sound. The sequential patterns of the words are known as *syntax*.	What words in the poem seem most important or memorable? Are any words repeated? Is the diction formal or informal? If the poem is addressed to someone, does the speaker use everyday or elevated speech? Is there anything unusual about the poem's syntax or word order? Why does the poet vary the syntax?
RHETORICAL SITUATION Most poems can be considered events involving a speaker, an audience, a text, and a situation or context.	What is the rhetorical situation of the poem? What do you know about the speaker? Whom does the speaker address? What can you learn about the speaker's audience? What is the context of the poem? Is a conflict or crisis represented in the poem?

Reading a Poem

Anne Sexton (1928–1974) is widely regarded as one of the major American poets of the twentieth century and is noted for her incisive and deeply personal reflections on her recovery from a nervous breakdown. "The Starry Night" is inspired in part by Vincent Van Gogh's famous painting. Sexton invests the image with emotional qualities and symbolism, reflecting her own state of mind and her identification with Van Gogh's famous suffering and despair as the tortured artist.

The Starry Night (1962)

Anne Sexton

The town does not exist
except where one black-haired tree slips
up like a drowned woman into the hot sky.
The town is silent. The night boils with eleven stars.
Oh starry, starry night! This is how
I want to die.

It moves. They are all alive.
Even the moon bulges in its orange irons
to push children, like a god, from its eye.
The old unseen serpent swallows up the stars.
Oh starry, starry night! This is how
I want to die:

into that rushing beast of the night,
sucked up by that great dragon, to split
from my life with no flag,
no belly,
no cry.

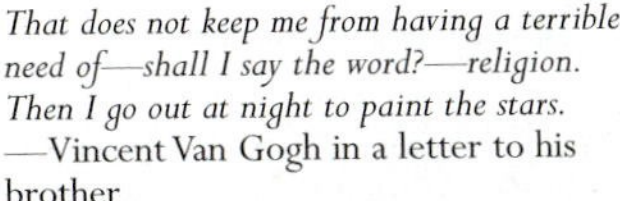

That does not keep me from having a terrible need of—shall I say the word?—religion. Then I go out at night to paint the stars.
—Vincent Van Gogh in a letter to his brother

Excerpts from a Student's Notes on "The Starry Night"

Imagery: tree is like "a drowned woman"; night boils; moon bulges in its orange irons

The images suggest movement and life. Something in this representation of stars is spiritually renewing for Sexton . . . Maybe she's saying the power of art is to represent life as fully as possible?

Symbolism: unseen serpent, beast of the night, great dragon

Sexton may not be as calmed by the image of Van Gogh's painting as he may have been. Perhaps she sees Van Gogh's demons creeping through—the vitality, the intensity of the swirly, boiling shapes. Or are these her own demons?

Form: three stanzas, an open form.

The first two have six lines and end in "I want to die"; this last line continues the sentence that starts "This is how." Curious that Sexton separates the sentence because "I want to die" (a suicidal wish) seems to be dampened by the wish to be one with the stars and the heavens. (So it is uplifting, too.) . . .

Working Thesis: Sexton's "The Starry Night" shows how the work of an artist, using visual symbols or words, can stir more profound feelings than the "real thing."

9e Terms for Understanding Drama

Reading a play is perhaps as common as watching one performed, but it is always important to remember that plays are written to be acted out on stage (dramatized).

Terms and Definitions	Questions to Ask about Drama
CHARACTERS Characters in plays may be flat or round, dynamic or static (◀ page 160). Usually, no narrator comments on characters' actions, so we have to infer their motives from what characters say and do and from how others respond to them.	Who are the most important characters in the play? Do any of them change significantly during the course of the play and, if so, how? What conflict do the important characters face? What roles do the minor characters play?
PLOT Like fiction, drama has plot (◀ page 160). Plays are divided into acts and scenes. Many plays are performed in five acts, each having a unified structure of its own (a conflict and crisis, for example).	What is the conflict in the play? What is the play's crisis? How is it resolved? Does the resolution turn out differently than you expected?
STAGING Playwrights usually include stage directions that indicate the characters' entrances and exits, physical gestures, and setting. Staging also includes costumes and scenery.	What stage directions does the playwright include? How much interpretation of the staging is left to the actors and the director (and, thus, the readers when the play is read)? How does the staging help draw out the theme(s) of the play?
THEME Like fiction (◀ page 160), plays have themes that are explored in the action. It can be helpful to think of a play as a question about a complex issue that lends itself to multiple responses. Characters act out possible responses on stage, and the audience is invited to decide which responses seem best.	What is the central theme of the play? What questions does the play ask? What answers, if any, to these questions are offered by the characters or in the resolution of the conflict?

Film Adaptations of Shakespeare's *Hamlet*

Three film adaptations of *Hamlet*—directed by Sir Laurence Olivier (1948), Franco Zeffirelli (1990), and Kenneth Branagh (1996)—have each framed the scene leading to Hamlet's famous "To be or not to be" speech to evoke a different mood.

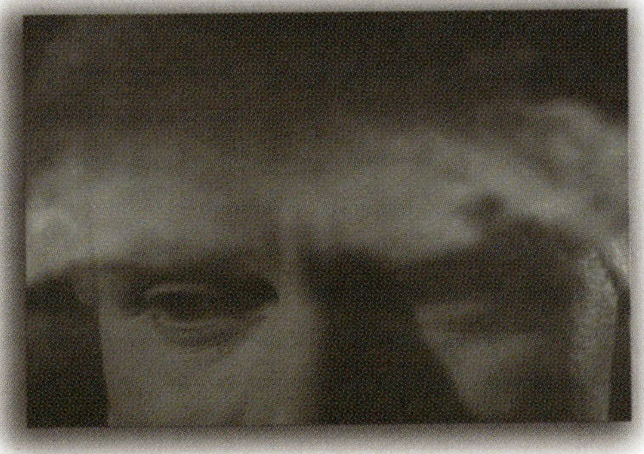

In the Olivier version (J. Arthur Rank Films, adapted by Sir Laurence Olivier, starring Sir Laurence Olivier as Hamlet), the scene includes a series of rapid cuts, rising from a tomb up to the parapet overlooking the ocean, where the camera takes us into Hamlet's mind in turmoil. The scene is accompanied by a loud musical score that reinforces the dramatic tension.

In Branagh's adaptation (Sony Pictures Entertainment, screenplay by Kenneth Branagh, starring Kenneth Branagh as Hamlet), the scene includes two quick shots of others eavesdropping on Hamlet's speech (first Ophelia and then Polonius). Hamlet looks over his shoulder several times, suggesting he knows of their presence, and then delivers the speech in the mirror.

Zeffirelli's version (Carolco Pictures, screenplay by Christopher DeVore, starring Mel Gibson as Hamlet) is a simpler, muted staging of Hamlet's speech. There are no cuts, and there is no musical score. Hamlet descends into a tomb; the camera pans the room and then zooms in for a closeup as the speech begins. The scene suggests Hamlet's isolation and despair.

Staging

Shakespeare's stage directions for Act 3, Scene 1 of *Hamlet* are minimal. The scene takes place in "a room in the castle." Immediately preceding Hamlet's speech, Claudius (Hamlet's uncle and murderer of King Hamlet, Hamlet's father), Polonius (advisor to King Hamlet and Claudius), Queen Gertrude (Hamlet's mother), and Ophelia (Hamlet's lover) discuss Hamlet's apparent madness. Gertrude exits, and then we read:

LORD POLONIUS:
I hear him coming: let's withdraw, my lord.
Exeunt KING CLAUDIUS and POLONIUS
Enter HAMLET
HAMLET:
To be, or not to be: that is the question . . .

Adaptation

A film version of a dramatic play is called an adaptation. An adaptation calls for the director, writer(s), cinematographer, and actors to interpret how lines are delivered and staged. In both the Olivier and Zeffirelli versions, Hamlet is depicted alone. Olivier places him on a ledge overlooking the ocean. Zeffirelli puts him in a tomb. Each version conveys a different sensibility about the events of the play, what they mean, and how we should interpret them.

For writing strategies you can use to brainstorm ideas, organize, and draft your essay, refer to Chapters 2–6. Also consider the following aspects of writing about literature.

Use Summary and Paraphrase Sparingly

Avoid summarizing or paraphrasing large portions of the work for readers who are very familiar with the work. If you need to refer to details of a long or complex work that readers might have trouble remembering, summarize enough so readers will be able to put your interpretation in context. In reviews written for a general audience, you will probably need to recount events of the story so that your readers can understand the basis of your interpretation or evaluation.

Document All Uses of Source Material

Every source you quote, paraphrase, or summarize in your essay must be documented. See Chapter 17, especially pages 338 and 339, for specific information.

- **Quoting fiction.** In the parenthetical citation after a quotation, use page numbers to refer to the original. If the original includes quoted dialogue, use single quotation marks to represent that dialogue within your double quotation marks. See section 19b for treatment of quotations of four lines or more.

> At the end of "The Short Happy Life of Francis Macomber," Wilson accuses Margaret of deliberately shooting her husband: "'He would have left you, too'" (48).

- **Quoting poetry.** Use a forward slash with a space on each side to indicate line breaks in a poem. Use line numbers (not page numbers) in your parenthetical citation.

> Williams breaks compound nouns into separate words in "The Red Wheelbarrow" to show that it is in the particulars of experience that we find meaning. The red wheelbarrow is "glazed with rain / water / beside the white / chickens" (5–8). Rainwater and white chickens are single things, but here Williams divides them across line breaks to make his point.

- **Quoting drama.** Include the act, scene, and line numbers in your parenthetical citation. Use Arabic numerals.

> In Shakespeare's *As You Like It,* Jacques utters the famous lines that suggest life is like a play: "All the world's a stage, / And all the men and women merely players" (2.7.149–50). In its time, this well-known saying referred to two ideas. First, it was used as a metaphor to describe the dramatic nature of life itself. . . .

- **Additions to quotations.** If you need to add any words to a quotation, put them in square brackets to show that they are not part of the original.

> In the third book of *Gargantua and Pantagruel,* Rabelais begins—as he usually does—by inviting his readers to imbibe while they read along: "I will tell you a story about him [Diogenes] presently, while we start on the wine—Drink up, my boys—and I start my argument" (281).

- **Omissions from quotations.** If you omit any words from a quotation, use an ellipsis (three spaced periods: . . .) to show where words were removed.

> Poe shows Montresor's diabolical nature right from the beginning of "The Cask of Amontillado": "neither by word nor deed had I given Fortunato cause to doubt my good will. I continued~~—as was my wont~~ . . . to smile in his face, and he did not perceive that my smile now was at the thought of his immolation" (154).

For a complete list of rules related to ellipses, see section 53d.

- **Titles.** Italicize the titles of novels, novellas, and plays. Put the titles of short stories, poems, and essays in quotation marks.

> D. H. Lawrence's most famous works include the novel *Lady Chatterley's Lover,* the poem "Whales Weep Not!," and the play *A Collier's Friday Night.*

Quote from the Work

Quote from the work to support and extend your analysis, interpretation, or evaluation. Let your readers know what has captured your attention and led you to your interpretation. (For an annotated example, see the sample essay in section 9g.)

Every time you quote from a primary or secondary source, be careful to explain how the quotation contributes to your interpretation. Be especially thorough in your explanation if you include a quotation of more than four lines from a source. Explain what your readers should see by explaining how you read the quotation.

Be Assertive

Present your interpretation without qualifying it with subjective statements such as "I believe that," "I think . . .," or "I feel . . . ." Your readers understand that your interpretations are yours; you don't need to remind them. Your writing will be more concise and persuasive if you come out and make the proposition.

Use Present Tense Verbs

Use the *fictional present* (present tense verbs) when discussing what happens in a literary work or when describing the author's act of writing it. Use the past tense when describing events surrounding the work—for example, the work's impact or reception in its time.

Don't Mistake the Narrator or Speaker for the Author

Bear in mind that the narrator of a work of fiction or the speaker in a poem or play does not necessarily speak for the author's point of view.

Writing about Literature

State your point with confidence

~~I believe that~~ Anne Sexton saw Van Gogh's *Starry Night* as a dreamy contemplation of eternity, not merely a depiction of a sleepy town.

Use present tense verbs

Describing a character's actions:

In *To Kill a Mockingbird,* Atticus Finch defends Tom Robinson not only on the charge of rape but also against widespread racial prejudice.

Describing an author's actions:

In *Snow Crash,* cyberpunk author Neal Stephenson depicts a world ravaged by the unintended by-products of technology.

Keep narrator (or speaker, in poetry) and author distinct

Inaccurate:

"We're waiting for Godot," says Samuel Beckett, alluding to humanity's need for hope.

More accurate:

In *Waiting for Godot,* Samuel Beckett's Vladimir speaks the hope of humanity: "We're waiting for Godot" (1).

Caliandro 1

Kim Caliandro

Dr. Sarah Applebaum

English 230

May 14, 2005

"Who's that bell tolling for?":

The Vanity of Freedom at Any Cost in "The Story of an Hour"

In "The Story of an Hour," Kate Chopin shows us the rise and rapid fall of her main character, Louise Mallard. Louise, who is "afflicted with a heart trouble" (198), learns that her husband, Brently, has been killed in a railroad disaster. We later find out, however, that she imagines a bright future for herself now that Brently is supposedly dead. "The Story of an Hour" shows how the desire to be free at any cost is vain when it must depend on the suffering of others.

From the very beginning of this story, we come to expect that something unusual will happen because Louise does not take the news as a widow might normally (by expressing disbelief or shock). She "did not hear the story as many women have heard the same, with a paralyzed inability to accept its significance. She wept at once, with sudden, wild abandonment" (198). Chopin wants us to consider why Louise reacts so differently. Could it be that she has already (so soon) accepted the significance of Brently's death? Does she already know what Brently's death will mean for her? Has she imagined or wished for his death in the past? We have no way of knowing with certainty what Louise might have imagined previously.

When she retreats to her room, leaving her stunned sister, Josephine, to worry about her, Louise sinks into a comfortable armchair near the window, feeling a "physical exhaustion that haunted her body and seemed to reach into

A good title reveals the writer's perspective and so focuses the reader's attention.

Too general:
The Use of Point of View in "The Story of an Hour"

Specific enough:
Liberation Fantasies in Kate Chopin's "The Story of an Hour"

The title should not be the same as the title of the work you plan to write about; that title has already been used, after all.

The thesis statement argues a point that can be debated.

This quotation from the story is introduced and then used to support the claim that Louise did not react normally. The page number of the quotation is given in parentheses.

This line and the following questions elaborate on the significance of the quotation.

Mentions Chopin's use of symbolism

Discusses how point of view gives readers unique insight into Louise's thoughts

These lines connect the topic to important but more abstract issues.

The thesis is woven throughout the essay.

Caliandro 2

her soul" (198). Her "heart trouble" (198) may be the cause of her tired body, but Chopin also suggests that it may be symbolic of the absence of love in her marriage because immediately she seems rejuvenated. Chopin uses the third-person, limited omniscient point of view to put the reader in Louise's mind, using adjectives and phrases to help us feel her dramatic turnabout. The tree tops are "aquiver" (198). There is the "delicious breath of rain" in the air (198). Someone is singing a "distant song" (198). Sparrows are "twittering in the eaves" (198). All of these details help us feel Louise's renewed life. Her transformation is so sudden that it must be because she feels as if she has escaped from a prison.

Marriage (or any relationship, even one between countries) may feel oppressive or threatening. We are born into social structures that control our lives one way or the other, so it is somewhat natural for Louise to feel her new freedom deeply. That feeling doesn't come to her immediately. It creeps up on her as something unknown, but when it takes over her, it is as if it is something she has been waiting for all over her life: "'Free, free, free!' The vacant stare and the look of terror that had followed it went from her eyes. They stayed keen and bright. Her pulses beat fast, and the coursing blood warmed and relaxed every inch of her body" (199). Her first taste of freedom causes a physical reaction. She is coming back to health from her broken heart. At that moment in the story, we feel for her.

It is in her next thoughts that we see Louise fall prey--perhaps innocently--to the vanity that later proves to be her undoing. "She did not stop to ask if it were or were not a monstrous joy that held her" (199). Instead, she thought briefly of Brently in his casket, but then imagined "a long procession of years to come that would belong to her absolutely" (199). From then on, she would take control of

Caliandro 3

her own life and would be free of Brently's will: "There would be no powerful will bending her in that blind persistence" (199).

We cannot know for sure whether Louise's feelings are caused by Brently's ill-treatment of her. In fact, he had never "looked save with love upon her" (199). There's the suggestion that the powerful will-bending is not Brently's act, but more a consequence of social norms that force people to marry when they may not be in love or ready for such a commitment. There are marriages of social convenience. Louise's big mistake is that she seems to heap the blame for all of this on Brently, who may also have been living according to custom. Is it his fault?

Considers wider social issues

Vanity is having excessive pride. The most powerful impulse of Louise's being is her "possession of self-assertion" at this moment in her life. Her vanity is no less a crime than Brently's tragic and accidental death. Louise's vanity sneaks up on her because her sense of self had almost been extinguished. Brently's death is the catalyst for sparking it back to life. However, as we see at the end when Brently comes strolling in the door, there is a price to pay for her being too eager to embrace this new freedom. Louise sees him and dies on the spot. The doctors say that she died of "heart disease--of joy that kills" (200).

Defines key term

Louise's vanity is not of her own doing but a natural and even physical response to a social system that teaches women to sacrifice their identity for the sake of getting along. For Louise, it seemed to be all-or-nothing. If she remained trapped in an unloving marriage, she had no sense of self. When that marriage dissolved because of Brently's death, her feelings shot to the other extreme--where there was no one else to live her life for her.

Connects theme of vanity to social responsibility

In any social system--or to support any institution, for that matter--people need to depend on each other. We live our lives for others, too, not just for

Connects the theme of this story to previous reading

Explains the title of the essay

Caliandro 4

ourselves. In her self-absorption, Louise forgets that until it is too late. She has learned the hard way that we are all connected. As John Donne put it, "No man is an island entire of itself; every man is a piece of the Continent, a part of the main . . . . Any man's death diminishes me because I am involved in Mankind; and therefore never send to know for whom the bell tolls; it tolls for thee" ("Meditation 17"). Louise asked one too many times whom that bell was tolling for, hoping to set herself free not just from Brently, but from marriage and even her family. Chopin may see that as a desire that cuts too deep.

The Works Cited includes the short story itself and the source for the quotation from John Donne.

Caliandro 5

Works Cited

Chopin, Kate. "The Story of an Hour." 1894. The Awakening *and Selected Stories of Kate Chopin*. Ed. Barbara H. Solomon. New York: New American Library, 1976. 198–200. Print.

Donne, John. "Meditation 17." *Devotions upon Emergent Occasions.* Anglican Library, 2000. 1624. Web. 12 Feb. 2005.

An asterisk * indicates that the database resource is also available online.

CONDUCTING RESEARCH ON LITERATURE	Writing about Literature: A Guide to Research (University of Minnesota Libraries): **http://subject.lib.umn.edu/hum/writinglit.html** *MLA International Bibliography of Books and Articles on Modern Languages and Literatures** *Literary Research Guide* (Harner, MLA) *Characters in 20th Century Literature* (Harris) *Dictionary of Literary Biography** *Masterplots Cyclopedia of Literary Characters* (Magill) *Oxford English Dictionary** *The New Princeton Encyclopedia of Poetry and Poetics* *Book Review Index**
FINDING SOURCES IN JOURNALS	*Humanities Index** *British Humanities Index**
LITERARY TERMS AND PERIODS	*A Handbook to Literature* (Holman) *Oxford Companion to American Literature* *Oxford Companion to English Literature* *Cambridge Guide to Literature in English* Glossary of Literary Theory (Henderson and Brown): **http://www.library.utoronto.ca/utel/glossary/headerindex.html**
LITERARY AND CRITICAL THEORY	The Johns Hopkins Guide to Literary Theory and Criticism: **http://www.press.jhu.edu/books/hopkins_guide_to_literary_theory/** *Literary Theory: An Introduction,* 2nd ed. (Eagleton) Guide to Literary and Critical Theory: **http://www.cla.purdue.edu/academic/engl/theory/**
LINKS TO LITERARY RESOURCES ON THE WEB	Voice of the Shuttle: **http://vos.ucsb.edu/browse.asp?id=2718** Sarah Zupko's Cultural Studies Center: **http://www.popcultures.com**

10

READING IMAGES CRITICALLY

An image in your mind is not exactly a picture, any more than a song playing in your mind is an MP3. People think of images as pictures, however, because the two have a similar connection to the world of visual sensation. A picture is a representation of the visual world that has been framed for the attention of a viewer by a photographer, painter, cartoonist, or other visual artist. An image is a visual interpretation and representation of an idea. In fact, the word *idea* means, in its original Greek form, *idein,* "to see."

It's important to think of images as ideas so that you can appreciate that the pictures and other visual elements you see on a page, a screen, or a museum wall are an artist's or designer's framing of experience. In reading images critically, you learn also to think, create, and communicate graphically and visually. In this chapter, you will learn to read images critically and to consider how others use images to persuade, inform, or move readers.

Like any text, an image is a stylized response to a rhetorical situation. The response is "stylized" because it attempts to create or frame a visual experience for the viewers. For this reason, images can also be viewed as **rhetorical appeals,** involving many of the same elements as you find in written texts but expressed through visual means.

Images set before the mind's eye what others want us to see. Pictures, paintings, and other graphical representations may be examined critically as rhetorical appeals, as unique interpretations of visual experience. A photograph, for example, says, "Look at this." In leaving out the world beyond the edges of the photograph (and any movement that may be part of the picture's context), the photographer implicitly singles out the framed subject for our attention. It is important to learn to read such images critically because they are not simply unbiased representations of what's real. They are selections meant to reflect reality, but as reflections they are also deflections or (sometimes) distortions.

The key concept for interpreting the visual content inside a frame (what has been singled out) is *composition*, the organization of various elements into an artistic form. When you write about pictures, graphics, or other visual content, you can focus on the composition of elements—those aspects of the image that can be singled out for attention and that the artist, photographer, or writer has used to compose the image.

The Elements of the Rhetorical Situation

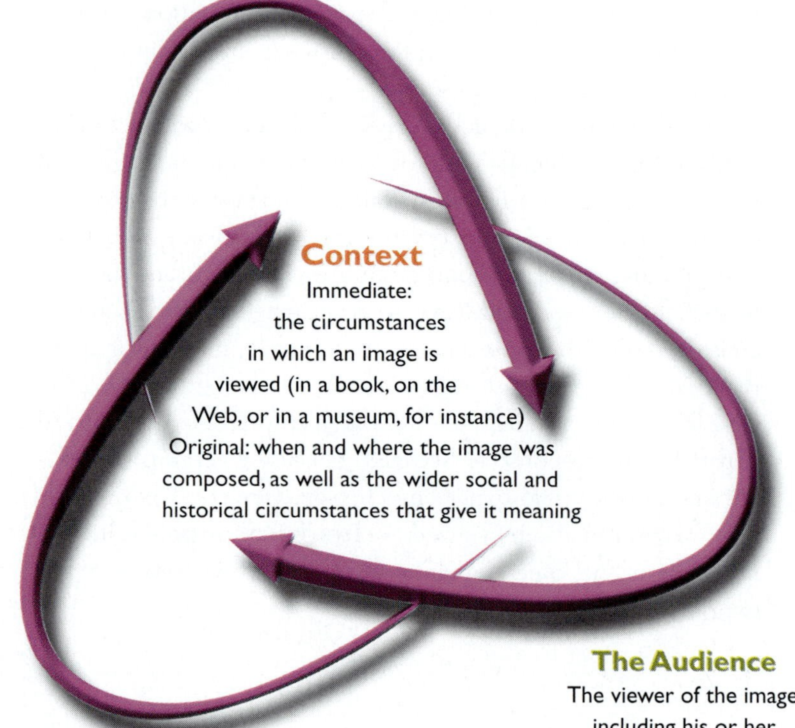
The Content
All the visual content, including its subject matter and its composition
Context
Immediate: the circumstances in which an image is viewed (in a book, on the Web, or in a museum, for instance)
Original: when and where the image was composed, as well as the wider social and historical circumstances that give it meaning
The Audience
The viewer of the image, including his or her expectations and prior knowledge
The Artist
The person who composed the image, his or her intentions, and past work

The Elements of Composition in the Frame

Here, the photographer has rotated the angle of the camera about 30° clockwise so that the two people remain the center of attention. The subjects, in this case, have an oblique relationship to the viewer. The tilted shot also conveys some disorientation.

In this still shot from Alfred Hitchcock's *Psycho,* Norman Bates is positioned on the right side of the frame and shot from a low angle, with a stuffed bird of prey hovering at the top of the frame. In the film, you also see more stuffed birds and two pieces of art depicting nudes in the center. Thus, Hitchcock invites the association between Norman and the birds, his sexual obsession, and possibly his own victimization by the voice of "Mother" inside his head. The low angle makes Norman look dominating even though most of his body is outside the frame.

Spatial Relationships

Visual elements in a frame have a spatial relationship with one another and with the viewer. They appear near or far apart from one another, larger or smaller, closer to the viewer or farther away.

Placement in the Frame

Content is positioned to draw your attention to certain elements—in the center of the frame or near an edge, for instance. Sometimes, objects are placed at the edge of the frame, with part of the content outside of it. Viewers are expected to complete the picture by "filling in" the rest of the detail.

Color, Shapes, Textures

Painters, photographers, and graphic artists use color to convey mood, to show contrasts between elements, and to create visual appeal. The human eye can detect millions of variations in color, so the artist's choices are vast. Nevertheless, color contrasts and shades tend to convey certain feelings or invoke associations in the viewer.

Painters use color palettes and different application techniques and brushes to mix color and texture. American painter Jackson Pollock used a wide variety of colors, techniques, and brushes. He applied (or dripped) paint with sticks, with cooking basters, and even straight from the can. He also included glass, cigarette butts, and other objects to add more texture to show the energy of composition and the depth in his paintings.

Graphic artists use color guides like the one shown below to help them evaluate how color communicates. Photographers use lighting and color filters to convey mood and draw out detail.

Geometric shapes, such as lines in parallel, establish patterns and relationships among the subjects in a picture or graphic. They may also be used to show depth (as when parallel lines seem to converge in the distance), to convey movement or energy, and to draw contrasts.

Photographs depict objects with different textures to create patterns and contrasts. Painters use different kinds of paint and brushstrokes to add texture to the surface of the art. (Jackson Pollock's paintings usually have a lumpy surface—a result of the drip method—and René Magritte's paintings are so smooth that you can hardly tell they are painted at all. For more on Magritte, see section 24b.)

Jackson Pollock, *Blue Poles: Number 11, 1952*

Jackson Pollock's technique is illustrated in this photograph from the Library of Congress's exhibition "The Work of Charles and Ray Eames." Pollock liked to literally step inside his paintings, where all meaning was on the surface and in the act of painting itself.

"Playful" colors from the *Pantone Guide to Communicating with Color.* These colors are "outgoing, comical, fun-loving, joyful, childlike, noisy, active, spontaneous."

Photographer's caption: Specialist Lucas Vogt clowns around with Specialist Sarah Baker by showing her his "sunshine face," which routinely makes her burst out laughing. The soldiers, who are mechanics with Bravo 20th Engineers, were just hanging out following another hot day of turning wrenches at Camp War Eagle, adjacent to Sadr City. Although this camp is fired on daily and is the most dangerous of all the 1st Cavalry bases in Iraq, the soldiers are trying to take the danger level in stride. Baker, one of the few women soldiers at Camp War Eagle, says, "He, SPC Vogt, makes me laugh with that out of control face every time."

Mt. Williamson, Sierra Nevada, from Manzanar, CA, 1945. Photograph by Ansel Adams. Adams uses an extreme closeup with a deep focus shot so that the rocks in the foreground and the majestic mountains in the background are in clear focus. The image contrasts the immediacy and familiarity of the rocks with the grandeur of the mountains shrouded in clouds and illuminated by the sun.

Content of the Frame

Of course, the subjects represented in the frame are critically important in judging its overall meaning. What a photographer, for example, chooses to include within the frame (or "shot") focuses our attention. In this picture, we see a soldier taking a silly pose in front of a woman, who is laughing boisterously. It is a lighthearted moment. We notice that the soldier is in camouflage fatigues and has an M-16 slung over his shoulder. The "scene" represented is in stark contrast to the mood conveyed by the specter of war.

Technique

Photographers, painters, and graphic artists use a wide variety of techniques and technologies to render images in a particular way. For example, a painter might use particular kinds of paint, media (type of canvas, for instance), or brushes to achieve certain effects. Photographers use filters to enhance or subtract detail and different lenses to draw aspects of the subject into relief (wide-angle or telephoto, for instance). Graphic artists use a variety of software tools, which include layering, masking, and other filters, to create stylized images.

Dominant Contrast and Intrinsic Interest

The subject matter in the frame draws attention because of its inherent interest or because of its placement in relation to other objects in the frame. The dominant contrast in a frame is what draws the eye first because of its visual appearance (it may be brightly colored, standing off by itself, or in some other way drawing the eye). Intrinsic interest refers to the visual appeal of an object because of what we already know about the subject matter.

In the film *Schindler's List,* director Steven Spielberg used color to show dominant contrast. The film was almost all in black and white, except for one scene of a little girl in a red coat being led away by Nazis.

The Elements of Context

This photograph depicts one dramatic scene during the Elian Gonzalez case (April 22, 2000). In the original context, there was a custody battle over the young boy. Elian's father, a Cuban citizen, wanted Elian returned to Cuba after the boy's mother had drowned in her attempt to bring them both to the United States, but Elian's cousins insisted he stay in the United States. U.S. Attorney General Janet Reno ordered that the boy be taken forcibly from his cousins' home and returned to the custody of his father in Cuba. The political context included strained relations with Cuba, divisions among the Cuban-American community in Florida, and debates in Congress about granting Elian asylum in the United States.

This photograph depicts the actual armed seizure. So that you don't misunderstand what it means, you should consider the circumstances under which it was taken. It was shot by a professional photographer who had positioned himself in the room so that he would have a good angle to capture the moment. Elian was kept in the closet until the federal agents found him. How much of this event, and thus this image, was scripted in advance? It seems to document a spontaneous and frightening moment. But it may also be a scene manipulated for propaganda purposes. What else would you need to know to decide what this photograph shows? For further information, see "The Elian Gonzalez Case: An Online NewsHour Focus" (PBS), at **http://www.pbs.org/newshour/bb/law/elian/**.

What lies beyond the frame of an image is just as important in reading images critically as what is inside the frame. An image is part of a situation that shapes the intentions of the artist and its reception by viewers. To read images critically and to avoid limiting your interpretation to content within the frame, you can consider the ways the elements of context shape meaning.

Original Context

The original context refers to the personal and social situation in which the artist created the image. When was it created? What are the historical and social circumstances? Is there a particular style to the period? What shaped the artist's response? Under what conditions was the image produced?

Consider, for example, a photograph, which depicts a moment frozen in time. To understand what it means, you can identify its subject matter, form, and style (the elements of composition in the frame). But you also can gather information about when and where the photograph was taken, how its style fits with the artist's other work or the photographic style of the times, what has been happening in the world, and—especially in the case of documentary photographs (as in news photography)—the conditions under which the photograph was taken, including what might lie just beyond the frame.

Immediate Context

The immediate context refers to the conditions under which the image is viewed, including where it is viewed (on a Web page, in a museum, in a book), its surrounding context (other images and text), and the physical circumstances of the viewing (lighting, frames, the presence of other people).

Leonardo da Vinci's *Mona Lisa* is easily the most recognizable painting in the world. It has been viewed in the Louvre in Paris by millions of people. In its immediate context in the Louvre, the *Mona Lisa* rests behind bulletproof glass. There are almost always crowds, so people are lucky to get a good glimpse of the painting as other people rush by or stand on their toes in front of them. This context certainly affects our interpretation. In fact, while our appreciation of the painting itself might be diminished, its staging in the Louvre and its familiarity give the *Mona Lisa* another meaning as a cultural icon. To some it might symbolize the commodification of art; to others, the power of art to move millions.

Actvity 10-1: Reading Images in Context

Consider the ways in which the immediate contexts, as depicted in this series of images, affect your interpretation. Discuss your ideas with a partner.

1.

Leonardo da Vinci's *Mona Lisa*

2.

Museum visitors view the *Mona Lisa.*

3.

4.

This *Mona Lisa* was painted on a barn by Dennis Wiemer of Ladysmith, Wisconsin, after the University of Wisconsin won the Rose Bowl in 1994.

A soldier in the U.S Army's 4th Infantry Division (Task Force Ironhorse) stands next to pictures of Saddam Hussein and the *Mona Lisa* as he secures a house during a raid in the town of Baquba in central Iraq on December 14, 2003.

5.

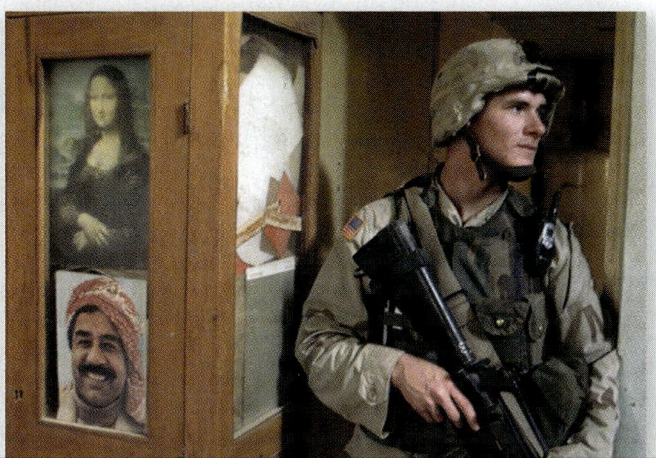

As you know from watching movies, images shown one after the other convey meaning. Photographs presented sequentially—such as the five photographs depicting the *Mona Lisa*—can also express meaning in this way. In this case, a common subject is represented in each photograph, but the context changes. In image 1, the *Mona Lisa* is pictured alone, with no intervening or surrounding context. In images 2 and 3, the painting is obscured by greater and greater numbers of people, making it seem distant and now including people (and the idea of spectatorship—the act of viewing itself) as part of the visual composition. In image 4, you see the *Mona Lisa* painted on a barn, suggesting its status as a familiar cultural icon (a visual sign expressing some value). In image 5, the *Mona Lisa* is depicted on a door window, above a picture of Saddam Hussein—the deposed ruler of Iraq—and next to a U.S. soldier. Each image captures a moment in the life of a cultural icon, from its beginning as a work of art to its status as an object to be viewed to its ultimate role as a cross-cultural icon.

Graphic artists use images on websites to add visual appeal, but images often have other uses that help Web authors create meaning and that guide critical analysis.

1. As *navigational aids* (buttons and rollover images, arrows, menus, image maps, thumbnail images). Website authors and designers use images to structure information so that it is accessible quickly to readers. Text alone is often not enough to provide direction or explain a process; visual cues—in combination with text—train the reader's eye to make quick associations and thus help the reader learn to interact with the website. (See pages 686–687 for an illustration of how the David Bowie website uses a visual theme to aid navigation.)
2. As illustrations that complement the text or serve as examples (user documentation, photographic essays, hypertext commentary, photo galleries, museum exhibits).

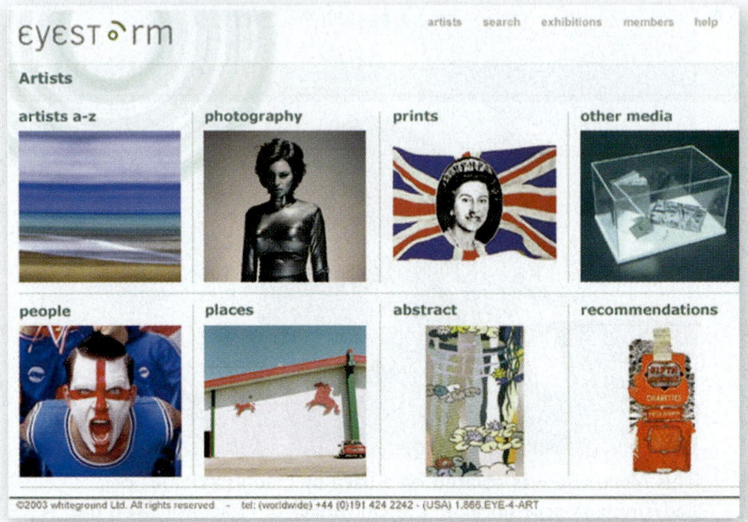

Here, words and images are linked by position, with the image itself creating visual interest and correspondence to the link (for example, "people" appears above a photograph of Robbie Williams as an excited soccer fan). From Eyestorm (Gallery of Artists): http://www.eyestorm.com/artists/

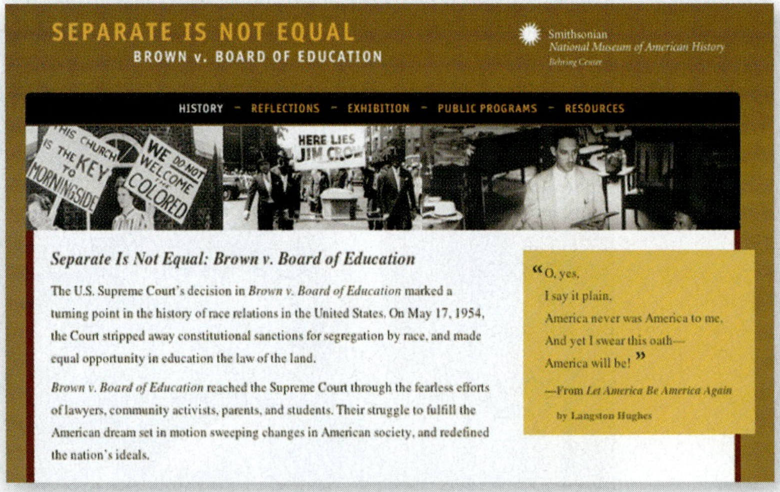

From http://americanhistory.si.edu.

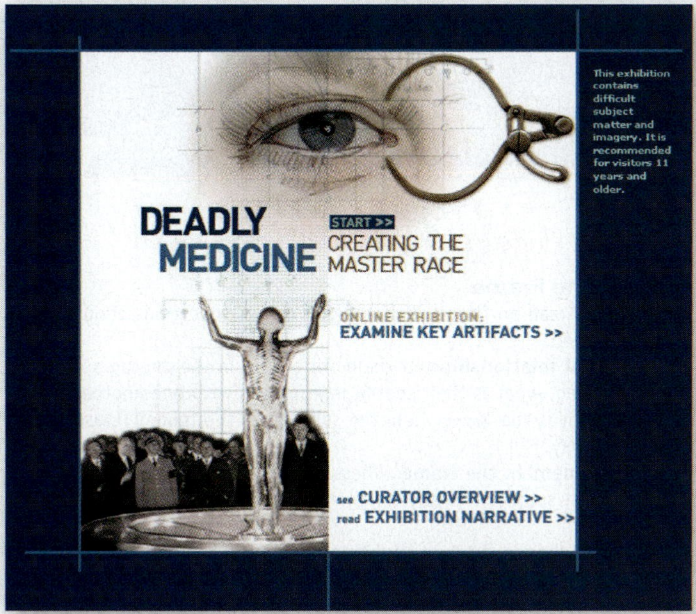

From United States Holocaust Memorial Museum: http://www.ushmm.org.

Here the text takes the form of an image symbolizing a pip on a playing card. By graphic designer John Langdon: http://www.johnlangdon.net.

In this logo for San Diego State University Press's imprint Hyperbole Books, the word *hyperbole* (which means overstated comparison) is in the shape of an exclamation mark, which adds further emphasis! From http://www-rohan.sdsu.edu.

3. As primary material explained by the surrounding text (paintings on museum websites, for example).
4. As iconic symbols that have meaning in their own right and that make a point or convey an idea. (In the case of the *Mona Lisa,* discussed earlier, the painting is often used to represent status, refinement, and artistic genius.) An *iconic symbol* is an image used as a direct representation of the thing it represents, or a modern hieroglyph, such as the image of a speaker on a radio's volume control.

An **icon** is a pictorial representation of an object or idea. Website authors use icons to structure information for readers. The website of the Department of English and Comparative Literature at San Diego State (http://www.rohan.sdsu.edu/dept/english/engl.html) has a visual theme that is echoed strongly on pages deep in the site. The homepage is a cornucopia of visual allusions to pop culture and literary figures, relying heavily on readers' ability to learn to navigate the site by exploring these icons and discerning their meanings. Web pages on which visual content emphasizes verbal content are good examples of using images to convey meaning that text alone might not fully represent.

Icons (such as a pointing finger) and logos (visual signs associated with an organization or company) may speak for themselves but may also represent some idea or feeling. Interestingly, over time—as we saw with the *Mona Lisa* images—elements of our culture gain status as icons so that whenever we see them we have particular ideas. The images/icons represent not only the original object but also abstract ideas. During the Middle Ages and the Renaissance, artists used iconology—the study and use of icons—to create complex depictions of religious ideas.

1

Project Checklist

Reading Photographs and Paintings Critically

Inside the Frame

When you read an image critically, you can ask questions about its composition.

- ❑ **Spatial relationships.** If there are people in the photograph or painting, what is their spatial relationship with one another? How far is the viewer from the subjects in the frame? (Close? Far away?)
- ❑ **Placement in the frame.** Where in the frame are the most important subjects? Is anything important on the edge of the frame?
- ❑ **Color, shapes, texture, lighting.** What stands out about the use of color? Is there a wide range of color? How do the colors contrast with one another? Is there any relationship between color and the work's meaning? Are there any noticeable patterns in lines, edges, or other geometric shapes? Is the scene or object brightly illuminated, or are there heavy shadows? Are there sharp contrasts between light and dark? Do color, shape, texture, and lighting create a realistic or more abstract image?
- ❑ **Content of the frame.** Who or what does the image show? What is happening in the image? Why do you think the photographer or painter chose to show this content? Does the photograph or painting seem to leave anything out, or is there any indication that something important may be just out of view?
- ❑ **Technique.** Are there any regions or elements that are in sharper focus than others? *Photos:* Does the photographer use an unusual angle? Why or why not? Does the photographer use any filters to affect the colors or details? *Paintings:* Does the painter use any unusual means of applying paint or other material? What kind of paint does the artist use? How would you describe the painter's brushwork?
- ❑ **Dominant contrast and intrinsic interest.** Where does your eye land first when you look at the photograph or painting? What is the most important object depicted? If characters or people are in the image, where are they looking?

2

Beyond the Frame

You can also ask questions about context.

- **Original context.** What can you learn about the photographer or painter? When and where was the photograph taken or the painting made? Are there any social, political, or other circumstances that "contain" the image in the photograph or painting?
- **Immediate context.** How is viewing a photograph or painting in a textbook different from viewing one in a museum? Would the photograph or painting have a different meaning if it were on the cover of *Life* magazine? *Cosmopolitan*? On display at a yard sale? Hanging in a Barnes and Noble coffee bar?

Questions to Ask about Images and Graphics on Websites

- Do the images and graphics help explain the verbal content, or are they the primary content of the website?
- Does the image have a clear purpose or meaning in relation to the verbal content of the site?
- Does the image overpower the rest of the content on the Web page, or is there a good balance between verbal and visual information?
- Does the image set the proper tone for the content?
- Does the graphical material complement the site's content?
- Do the images and graphics establish a consistent identity for the website?
- Are the images and graphics original, or do they appear to be borrowed from another source?
- Why is this graphic here? What is the motive or purpose for this graphic?
- Could the images and graphics be of better quality? How so?

When you write about an image, you probably will not have room to provide full answers to all of the questions in the checklist. Your aim should be to form a judgment about what a photograph or painting means or what it shows and why it is important. You then support your interpretation (your thesis) by drawing on your answers to these kinds of questions. If you believe that a work is significant and achieves its effects in interesting ways, you should be able to point specifically to the elements of composition and context that lead you to your interpretation. Very often you will find from a careful analysis that there's more in the image than you noticed at first glance.

To guide your writing, use the principles and concepts discussed in this chapter. You can also discover useful guidelines on the Web at The Analysis of Visual Images (School of Fine Arts, University of Newcastle, Australia): http://www.newcastle.edu.au/discipline/fine-art/theory/analysis/analysis.htm.

When you write about images, you inform and analyze. Suppose you are asked to write about art or about the use of images in advertising, for example. Your main goals will likely be to describe carefully what you see (the elements of composition in and outside the frame—a focus on information) and to interpret it for your reader (its significance for understanding artistic intention or its meaning in relation to the wider culture). Here are some principles to bear in mind:

1. Include the image with your writing or point your readers to it on the Web or in an easily accessible archive so that they can see what you are referring to.
2. List all citation information about the image's source. In educational contexts, it is acceptable to include the image in a printed document as long as the source information is also included (artist/photographer, title of work, date, copyright owner or museum, location, and—if found on the Web—the date of access).
3. Include a well-focused thesis statement that can be supported with evidence and analysis—for example, "The artist Chuck Close chose himself as the focus of all of his paintings to show how technique transforms the meaning of the subject matter."

Activity 10-2: Analyzing Website Images

The screenshot below shows the navigational system for a website of the Professional Writing major at Purdue University: **http://pw.english.purdue.edu**. The banner contains a sequence of images that express a theme. From left to right, three paintings are depicted: Giuseppe Arcimboldo's *The Librarian,* Jan Steen's *The Rhetoricians,* and René Magritte's *The Human Condition.* Other images and icons also appear. Altogether, what theme do these images and graphics represent? Find another website that uses a similar method to establish a visual theme and explain why you think it is or isn't effective.

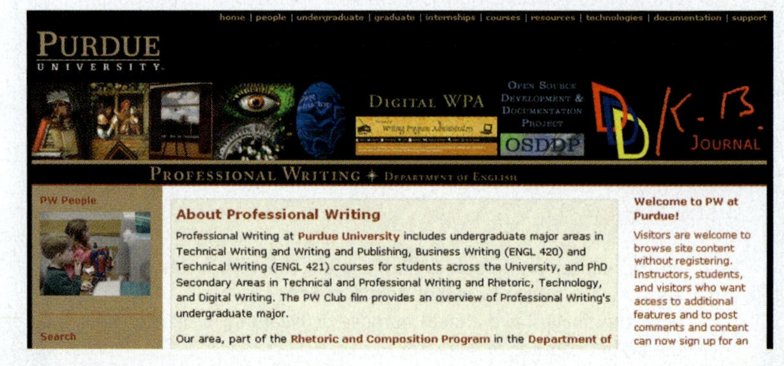

While a sophomore at Lincoln University, Kathy O'Kane wrote about a series of paintings by African American artist Jacob Lawrence for her art history class. Here is a brief excerpt from her work.

O'Kane 1

The Migration of the Negro's Place
in the Harlem Renaissance
Kathy O'Kane

The Migration of the Negro is the first narrative series completed by an African American, and it consists of 60 panels of the same size, painted with tempera on masonite. Each panel has the frame painted into the picture. The panels have an accompanying narrative written by Lawrence. These narratives are very short and direct, as if the reader were viewing a child's book. What struck me about the narratives is that in spite of Lawrence's difficult time reading about the harsh lives of terror and misery that were endured in the South, his text is written in such a nondescript way so as to let the power of the images speak for themselves. To me, the pictures relate so much information because of the way the characters are portrayed.

The subjects were painted in a semi-abstract form, but you can still interpret their mood, whether joyous, scared, or sad, because of the way Lawrence constructs their body language. In Panel number 10 (see fig. 1), the narrative reads "They were very poor." In this panel, the eye focuses first on the dominant contrasting object in the frame, a white bowl in front of the woman. From there, the eye is drawn to the woman's face; a look of exhaustion is seen but also a sense of faith and determination, as she sits next to her husband. The man and woman appear to be tired and beaten, but there is a sense of hope as

O'Kane 2

they pray over small portions of food. Behind them, the wall is empty except for a hanging cooking pot. The feeling conveyed by the images is that the couple never knows where the next meal might come from. With heads hung low, you can feel their heavy hearts. They are seated at a table with no other apparent furniture in the room. Perhaps they are praying for the answer to come of whether or not they should embark on their own migration.

Fig. 1. Jacob Lawrence, *The Migration Series, Panel No. 10: "They were very poor"* (1940-1941). Tempera on gesso on composition board. 12 x 18 in. (30.5 x 45.7 cm). Museum of Modern Art, New York.

10f Writing Project Threads

A table of contents for writing project threads appears on pages xv–xxii.

Photographic Essays

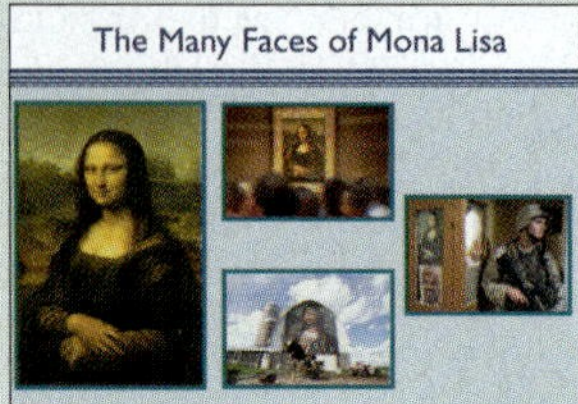

How Images Portray Meaning

Images portray meaning by offering the reader a visual experience that is different from the experience of reading the paragraphs of an essay. A photographic essay is likely to use a series of images to portray meaning, like the series of *Mona Lisa* photos on pages 182–183. Review the introduction on page 175, and think about the rhetorical situation you are attempting to create with images in your own essay. Then review sections 10a and 10b about reading images critically. How do you want people to read and interpret the images that you create? What techniques will you need to use to create these readings and reactions?

◀ page xix.

Personal Essays

Connecting through Pictures

One of the ways we record and remember our lives is through pictures.

- Collect some pictures of yourself or of the event or aspect of your life that you're writing about. You might also want to collect other related pictures, such as pictures of places, people, or other events that had an impact on you during that time.
- Use the strategies in sections 10a and 10b to read these images and think critically about them and about what they tell you about your life. Write about the images.
- Consider whether to use the images or their descriptions, depending on your purpose. ◀ page 67.

Photographic Essays

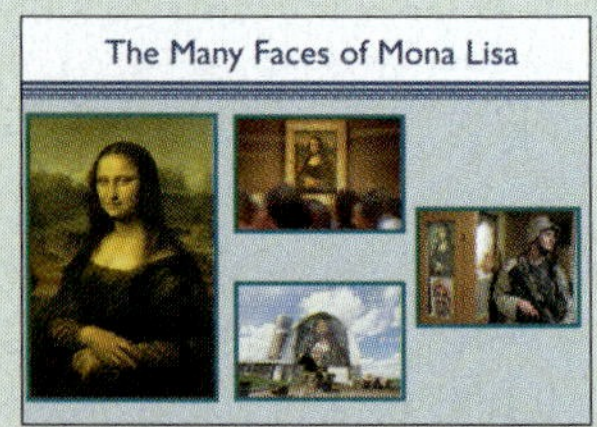

Seeing Your Photographic Essay Again

Revision literally means "seeing again." In a photographic essay, this is an important part of the process! Use the Project Checklist on pages 186 and 187 to assess your own photographic essay, or ask a classmate to apply the checklist to your essay. Are there any revisions you need to make?

11 WRITING ARGUMENTS

Differences of opinion arise for practical and often unavoidable reasons. Most questions that vex people lend themselves to alternative perspectives. We are naturally divided over issues because each of us has a unique set of experiences that influences how we make sense of the world and how we act on it.

Yet our division from one another is not absolute. We share experiences, sensations, and knowledge. There is a margin of overlap, in other words, that makes identification with one another possible and even desirable (page 192). Identification is a "coming to terms" among people that enables them to act and think together. While argument begins with uncertainty and even disagreement, it fosters identification among people by showing that we do have some bases for cooperating with each other and that it is in our best interest to keep looking for reasons to get along. Argument plays a critical role in social and political life because it is our means of acting together, of negotiating across our differences in the interest of building community. Argument is an important genre in our culture and in college because most of what we know is built on consensus (agreement) and not absolute certainty.

The process of writing to persuade begins the moment you, as a member of a community, feel *exigency*—the desire to set things straight or to make your position known. The call to write, in other words, comes from an urge to speak out about some imbalance or injustice in the world. For an argument to be persuasive, its writer needs to feel the exigency of a situation.

As a genre defined by social practice, arguments vary in form and content as you move across the curriculum and into new fields of practice. (For more on genre, see Chapter 7.) Conventions of form, for example, create expectations among readers in a given academic field that an argument—whether a report of research findings in the sciences or a literary interpretation in the humanities—will proceed in a certain way.

Conventional Forms

The conventional form of an argument within a discipline serves a purpose. For instance, a scientific research report includes certain sections because each one helps persuade other researchers that the hypothesis was a good one, the methods of testing it and studying the results were sound, and the analysis and conclusion are thus worth considering. A research report, when persuasive, will prompt other researchers to replicate the study or even to apply its conclusions to solve or explain other problems. In contrast, a research report that used an unfamiliar structure might catch readers by surprise, possibly even causing them to miss important information entirely. Sections 11f and 11g detail two structures often used in arguments written in introductory composition.

The Writer
Every writer has a unique set of experiences, memories, knowledge, physical circumstances, and feelings.
The Margin of Overlap
The writer and the readers share some experiences, knowledge, beliefs, terminologies, desires, and physical needs.
The Readers
Each reader has a unique set of experiences, memories, knowledge, physical circumstances, and feelings.

To persuade your readers, you look for common ground—points on which you agree or are likely to agree. Once you have established this connection, you can ease readers toward new insights or changes of attitude. The connection you have made shows readers they can trust you, and you can then widen the margin of overlap by providing authoritative information, good reasons, and vivid examples to support your position. This process makes it easier for readers to believe or learn what might have been beyond their experience previously.

Identifying Common Ground with Readers

What does your audience care about? See whether you can find a way to link your concerns, which they may not have thought about yet, to their existing concerns.

I want to show my friends that volunteering for Public Interest Research Group is worthwhile, but all they seem to be interested in is getting their careers started.

So how will volunteering help them in their careers? They might . . .

— develop research and presentation skills that they will be able to use on their jobs.

— be able to promote themselves as people who follow through to reach important goals.

— show potential employers they are willing to contribute toward the common good.

Maybe I should argue that they should each choose an organization to volunteer for, not just promote PIRG. Since my friends are going to be searching for different types of jobs, I'll bet they can each find an organization particularly suited to their interests.

Claim and Support

In the academic community, a successful argument includes a claim about a contested issue and support for the claim in the form of good reasons, examples, expert knowledge, and verbal and visual evidence. A claim is a position the writer stakes out in the thesis statement. Most issues that are considered worth writing arguments about are disputed; reasonable people disagree about them. When planning an argument, consider the many sides of a contested issue and then make smart and ethical decisions about what claims to put forth, how to support them, and how to persuade others that your point of view is warranted and desirable.

11b Choosing a Topic

A good topic for an argument in a composition class has these important attributes:

- It is a contested issue. Reasonable people hold substantially different opinions about it. For example, people might use words indicating value judgments about the issue, such as *should be, should not be, the best, the worst, too much,* and *not enough.*
- It is an issue you care about, feel invested in, or find intellectually stimulating. Your sense of exigency, or motivated curiosity, drives you to learn more about the issue.
- It is limited enough in terms of the amount of research you'll need to do and the number of pages it will take to cover the topic adequately. The research and writing need to fall within the guidelines set by your instructor.

Activity 11-1: Identifying Good Topics for Argument

Discuss which of these topics would work well in an argumentative paper and which ones would be better suited for an informative paper.

1. The need to build a new bridge between the United States and Canada
2. Protecting endangered species from poachers
3. The process of becoming a wedding planner
4. The mating patterns of jellyfish
5. Mandatory drug testing for all professional athletes

Activity 11-2: Listing Topics You Care About

By answering the questions below, come up with a list of at least five topics that you could write about in an argumentative paper.

1. What are some problems or issues on my campus? In my hometown? In my state? In my country? In the world? How would I solve these problems?
2. What are some issues or arguments that come up often in my community that I feel strongly about?
3. What are some issues that have come up in the news recently that have made me react or respond?

Decide which ones would make good topics for argument. From that narrowed list, choose one topic to work with throughout this chapter.

Conventional Forms for Argument Claims

Basic Form	Examples
Something (Topic) should (or shouldn't) be done. (Claim)	Toxic waste disposal needs to be reconsidered because containers have a finite lifetime.
Something is good (or bad).	Hackers who expose security flaws in popular software protect consumers.
Something is true (or false).	Contrary to urban legend, alligators do not roam the New York City sewers.

Activity 11-3: Drafting a Working Thesis Statement

Using your topic from Activity 11-2, develop a working thesis statement. Use the questions below to decide whether it is effective, and if it isn't, revise it.

Project Checklist

Do You Have an Effective Working Thesis Statement?

Answer the following questions to decide whether your working thesis is effective.

- ❑ Does it indicate that the issue is contestable? Consider which people or groups of people would not agree with your working thesis. Write down their objections. If you find at least a couple of substantial objections, the issue is contestable.
- ❑ Does it give a sharp focus to the topic? Does it provide a specific claim and possible reasons and evidence that support that claim?
- ❑ Does it have the potential to change as new information comes to light through research? How might it change in the future? If you can think of how and why it might change, then your thesis can be deliberated and debated.
- ❑ Does it point you to the premises that you will need to explain or demonstrate and those that will likely be accepted by the audience? Premises that don't need support—that everyone agrees with already—are a sign that your thesis argues a point no one will contest (a "moot point") (see Activity 11-10, Identifying Premises and Conclusions).
- ❑ Does it help you map out the structure of your argument?
- ❑ Does it invite more information? Can you clearly see what you would need to include in order for it to be believable?

The thesis statement in an argument is composed of (1) the topic and (2) your claim about the topic. The claim is the assertion that your paper will support with reasons and evidence. It's the opinion you develop about the topic as you think and conduct research.

As you start your project, developing a working thesis statement will help you learn more about your rhetorical situation and your topic. For instance, you might think, "Anger management classes should be required for people who display road rage." This idea is your working thesis. As you research the problem of road rage and some of the solutions that have been proposed, you may discover that several states already have anger management programs in place. In other states, community service is seen as a more effective way to treat those guilty of the crime. You may decide that community service shouldn't be associated with punishment. You decide that you will argue against community service as a "penalty" handed out by courts for a wide variety of minor offenses. You realize, however, that you will need to propose a way to encourage community service with a positive attitude—perhaps by letting road rage perpetrators choose among alternatives.

To write an effective argument designed to persuade, you need to develop a keen understanding of the beliefs of the people opposed to your position, what arguments they make to one another, and which arguments on the other side (your side) they distrust. Consider that there may be moderate positions somewhere in the middle.

For example, suppose you believe that the death penalty is cruel and unusual punishment under any circumstances. If you want to persuade death penalty advocates of your point of view, research their views. Visit the *Weekly Standard* (http://www.weeklystandard.com), the conservative, pro–death penalty journal, even if you prefer the position of the *New Republic* (http://www.tnr.com). See whether you can identify positions that have qualifications. Research the positions of people who believe there should be a moratorium while we learn more about the issues, such as the North Carolina Commission for a Moratorium (http://www.ncmoratorium.org/site/default.asp). Some people hold other views—for example, that the death penalty should not apply to juveniles or should be used only under extraordinary circumstances. Your best writing may emerge from using the evidence that others would use against you.

Activity 11-4: Identifying Other Perspectives

Think about your working thesis statement. Who *would agree* with it, who *might agree* with it, and who *would disagree* with it? Why? Divide the possible perspectives into at least two, and preferably more than two, camps. Set up a chart like the one below to help you keep track of them.

People who agree would think . . .	People who might agree would think . . .	People who disagree would think . . .

Then, using a key term on your topic, conduct an Internet search to find newspaper or online news source editorials that illustrate these positions. If you wanted to survey the range of opinion on file sharing of music, you could try these steps:

1. Go to Google News: **http://news.google.com**.
2. Type "*file sharing*" (in quotation marks) in the search box at the top of the page, and then click on Search News. Your search results will include a long list of editorials on this topic from various news sources around the world. You can tell from the title of the page and the brief summary whether it's directly related to your topic. Even the first few search results for "file sharing" reveal a broad range of opinion, with headlines like "File sharing is not the problem" and "File sharing online: Good or bad for the local musician?"
3. Add to your chart a summary of each position or each editorial that looks helpful. (Be sure to include the citation information.)
4. Analyze an editorial on your topic from each camp, focusing on questions like these:
   - What position does the editorial take?
   - What evidence or reasons does the editorial provide?
   - What are the stakes of the argument?
   - Does the editorial address the views of the other side?
   - What doesn't the editorial say that it might have said in the interest of arguing its position more effectively?

A Comparison of the Audiences and Aims of Argument

Audience	General Purpose	Specific Purpose
 People who hold views different from yours	To persuade people to change an attitude or behavior. Changing someone's attitude is possible only when knowledge is uncertain and there are multiple perspectives.	▪ To change people's minds and attitudes ▪ To solve problems ▪ To resolve conflict ▪ To build consensus ▪ To create community
 People who share your view	To reinforce shared convictions. When people already agree, the purpose of argument may be to turn that agreement into action—for example, working to support a cause. In college classes, you typically won't argue issues on which your readers already agree. Instead, find the basis for disagreement on a subject, and build an argument from there.	▪ To reinforce belief ▪ To move people toward commitment and action ▪ To foster identification
 People who wish to understand multiple views	To inquire into the shades of meaning in a subject so that you can open it up to reflection and reconsideration. It is often necessary to demonstrate that a subject lends itself to multiple perspectives. Help your audience understand that the subject is more complex than they had imagined.	▪ To open up a topic for discussion, debate, and further inquiry ▪ To question common knowledge ▪ To stimulate further research

Writing arguments involves developing, shaping, and presenting content to an audience for a reason. When you *develop* an argument, you take your subject matter into account in great detail through a process of invention and inquiry. When you *shape* an argument, you consider audience and purpose to decide how much of that content is relevant or useful. When you *present* an argument, you consider how your content should be arranged and what style, diction, and tone best convey it to readers.

Effective writers shape and refine subject matter to suit circumstances, which include the opinions and attitudes of the audience and the purpose for writing. Your consideration of what your readers already know about the subject, how they feel about it, and what contrary opinions they hold toward it should guide every decision you make as you shape and present your argument. The aim of your argument—to change minds, rally supporters, foster sympathy, and so on—should likewise guide your selection, shaping, and presentation of subject matter.

11f Arguing to Inquire: Rogerian Argument

Often an either/or argument not only presumes an issue has only two sides but also shows the amount of force holding people apart in the world. Sometimes people in ongoing debates and arguments become so defensive that they cannot even see the humanity of the people with whom they are arguing.

Arguing to inquire involves arguing ethically and intelligently in order to build grounds for consensus. One form of arguing to inquire is Rogerian argument, a method developed by Carl Rogers (1902–1987). The goal of Rogerian argument is to find as much common ground as possible so that parties in the debate or argument will see many aspects of the issue similarly. Believing that shared views of the world create more harmonious conditions, Rogers hoped that people would hold enough in common that they could be persuaded, through debate and dialogue, to allow differences to coexist peacefully. Rogerian argument seeks to resolve conflict by expanding the margin of overlap between people.

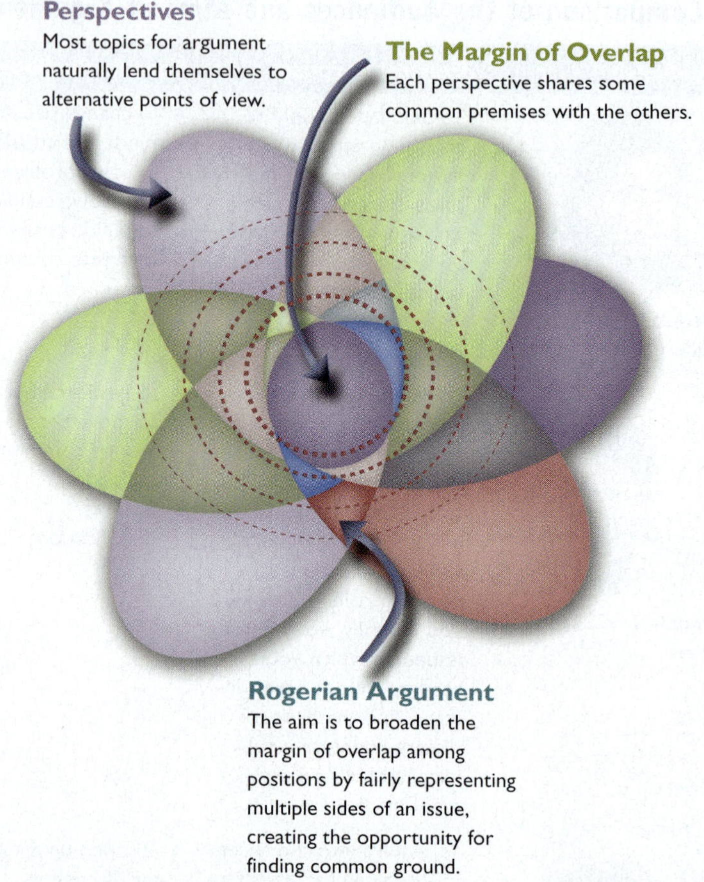

Perspectives
Most topics for argument naturally lend themselves to alternative points of view.
The Margin of Overlap
Each perspective shares some common premises with the others.
Rogerian Argument
The aim is to broaden the margin of overlap among positions by fairly representing multiple sides of an issue, creating the opportunity for finding common ground.

Rogerian argument acknowledges and accommodates alternative positions and perspectives. The purpose is not so much to settle an issue as to map the various positions that reasonable people might hold. Throughout a Rogerian argument, the writer emphasizes common ground, attempts to be objective and truthful about the alternative perspectives, and concedes the relevance of other points of view. The argument often provides background or context, in the hope that enlarging the frame of the argument will make it easier for the various disputants to find common ground. Rogerian argument is particularly useful when your audience is hostile.

The Classical Form of Argument

- **Introduction** (*exordium*). The introduction puts the reader in the right frame of mind and suggests, "Here comes something important." It might tell a story that illustrates the controversy or the need to resolve it.
- **Narration** (*narratio*). The narration provides background information necessary for understanding the issue or tells a story that makes a comparison, discredits opponents' views, or just entertains the audience. It often includes cited research and references to what other people have said about the topic in the past.
- **Partition** (*partitio*). The partition lists the points to be proven or divides the points into those agreed on and those in dispute. It is usually very brief, sometimes only a few sentences if the essay is short.
- **Confirmation** (*confirmatio*). The confirmation is the proof and thus argues the case, thesis, or main point of contention. It may include evidence, examples, and quotations from authoritative sources. Each premise or assumption may be unpacked, explained, and argued using deductive reasoning (arguing from accepted fact to implications) or inductive reasoning (arguing from examples). The confirmation takes up each of the points listed in the partition or implied in the thesis or controlling idea.
- **Refutation** (*refutatio*). The refutation takes the other side or sides and shows why they don't hold. It may dispute the positions of opponents, using anticipated or actual arguments; cite claims of inadmissible premises, unwarranted conclusions, or invalid forms of argument; or cite stronger arguments that nevertheless apply only in unrealistic circumstances. The refutation should address the most likely counterarguments, treating them fairly and accurately so as not to arouse the indignation of the audience.
- **Conclusion** (*peroratio*). The conclusion sums up or enumerates the points of the argument; it may appeal to the emotions of the readers, encouraging them to feel motivated to change attitudes and sometimes to feel resentful of opposing viewpoints or sympathetic to the writer's position. The conclusion should help people understand the significance of the issue and the importance of viewing it as the writer proposes. The conclusion may also rouse the audience to action or make a specific recommendation.

Aristotle described rhetoric as the art of finding the available means of persuasion in any particular case. This means, simply, that a speaker or writer needs to know what arguments to use and the best way to present them. Aristotle spent most of his time trying to identify how to invent arguments and how to determine their potential usefulness. Cicero, a Latin rhetorician, later described a generic form for the classical argument.

The classical form rests on the theory that we change our minds and come to believe in something new in a predictable pattern. First something needs to capture our attention. Then we need to learn more about it, analyze it, consider what others say about it, and interpret it. The chances of persuading others increase when a writer knows both how to "find the available means of persuasion" and how to present them in classical form.

The classical structure can be used flexibly, depending on the rhetorical situation. In most cases, though, each of the parts listed to the left appears in some form in an effective argument.

An effective argument includes reasons and evidence in support of the points you are asking readers to accept. Organized logically and presented persuasively, the reasons and evidence you provide make your case.

Research Your Topic

You need to find the background information and facts you can share with readers so that they will judge your argument as reasonable. What sources will help define and elaborate on your opinion? It's smart to know more about your subject matter than your audience does so that you can shape their responses to it. As you do research, be sure to gather all the information you will need to cite your sources accurately and completely. See Chapters 14–18 on conducting and reporting research. If you are not sure which citation style to use, ask your instructor.

Define Terms to Establish Common Ground

Defining the terms you will use in your argument is crucial because it helps you establish common ground with your readers. You can use this consensus to develop definitions in a way that supports your point of view. For instance, when

Project Checklist

Motivating Your Readers

How can you motivate your readers to identify with your position and change their actions or attitudes?

- ❑ **Consider the kinds of evidence that your audience will find persuasive.** Suppose you are against hunting animals for sport. Claiming that all animals should have the same rights as humans might not be persuasive with hunters, who might see their rights under the Constitution as superseding those of animals. Rather, you might suggest alternative sports that provide the same kind of satisfaction as hunting or demonstrate that, because of accidents and hunter-on-hunter violence, hunting is more dangerous to humans than to animals. You will need to include evidence that helps hunters see that it is in their best interest to try something else.
- ❑ **Treat your readers as intelligent and reasonable people, even if you think their positions are wrong.** Suppose you want to advance the cause of Students Against Drunk Driving. Saying that social drinkers are "incapable of knowing what is best for them" or calling them "future alcoholics" is likely to cause them to ignore the logic of your appeal.
- ❑ **Tell readers why they should consider your position, and be direct about what you want them to do or think.** What difference does it make if readers agree with you? What exactly should they take away from your argument? What do you want readers to do? How should they see the subject differently now?
- ❑ **Make the case for why the issue is important now.** Readers will want to feel some urgency. What difference does it make if they believe you now rather than later (or never)? What will happen if the situation is not resolved?

Activity 11-5: Thinking about Reader Motivation

Using your working thesis statement and the information you have gathered so far about alternative perspectives on your issue, answer the following questions about reader motivation as they relate to your topic. It will be important to keep your answers in mind as you shape your content to suit the occasion (*kairos*).

1. How do readers feel about the topic?
2. What would catch their attention in an introduction?
3. What background information will they need to grasp your claim? What points do the people involved in this debate seem to agree on, for the most part? What points do they disagree about? List these separately.

Use the Project Checklist on page 200 as you think about how you will motivate your readers to be persuaded by your argument. Be guided throughout by the contexts of your argument (◀ pages 9–11).

Activity 11-6: Crafting Definitions to Support Your Claim

Think about your claim and your audience. What terms do you need to define to make sure your audience understands your claim and argument? How do these definitions support your argument? Play with the definitions to see if you can make them better support your claim.

you write "education," some readers might think "public education"; others, "secondary education"; and still others, "on-the-job training." If you want to make an argument that universities should accept their function as a gateway to the professional world, then you might define education as a bridge to social and professional life, or as a set of practices that creates future opportunities. You might not want to define education as a body of knowledge, since doing so might undermine the idea that college is a place to apprentice in a field of study or work.

Use Evidence Effectively

One of the primary problems with reading other people's arguments as you develop your own is that you may be tempted to adopt someone else's argument and lose your own unique vision of the problem and solution. Spend the majority of your preparation time developing your position on your argument, and concentrate on supporting your sequence of logic. Draw on sources where necessary to bolster your case or to cite facts not commonly known. Verifiable facts and widely accepted truths are almost always the most effective kinds of support.

Distinguish Fact from Opinion

When you gather evidence for your arguments, it is helpful to distinguish between fact and opinion. Facts will usually be more persuasive if your audience is fair-minded. The opinions of others don't prove an argument's claims, but they do show that others have come to similar conclusions, making your argument more believable. As you collect your evidence, make a list of facts (which help make an argument valid and relevant, as well as giving readers essential information) and opinions (which bolster an argument) so that you know which to use at the opportune moment (*kairos*).

A *fact* is a statement whose truth can be verified by observation, experimentation, or research. It is a fact, for example, that Neil Armstrong and Buzz Aldrin set foot on the moon on July 20, 1969 (relative to Eastern Standard Time). You will find this fact mentioned in authoritative and independent sources—not just on the NASA website, but in dictionaries, encyclopedias, and museums around the world.

An *opinion* is an interpretation of evidence or experience. In academic arguments, support every opinion with enough facts or other evidence that readers can see why you hold your opinion. See pages 311 and 331 on deciding whether evidence is comprehensive, relevant, reliable, and balanced.

Example of Facts

Prevention of Art Theft

The biggest art heist in history occurred in Boston in 1990, when thirteen pieces of art, including three Rembrandts, a Manet, a Vermeer, and five Degas drawings, were stolen from the Isabella Stewart Gardner Museum. ("The Gardner Heist," by Stephen Kurkjian, Boston Globe at boston.com, Globe Special Report, March 13, 2005, accessed March 13, 2005.)

Source of the Facts

Stephen Kurkjian, a journalist who later reported these and many other facts about the Gardner theft, reexamined old interviews with museum guards, reviewed the leads FBI and other investigators have followed to recover the art, reviewed all known information about how the robbery occurred, including some not previously released to the public, and more. Kurkjian conducted enough research on the theft to become an expert on it.

Example of an Opinion

Prevention of Art Theft

Museums should do their best to prevent art theft, but if they cannot prevent it, they should be financially prepared to replace stolen art with art of similarly high quality when necessary.

Source of the Opinion

This opinion is that of a student who read Kurkjian's report and then did further research at the FBI's new "Art Theft Program" website. She acquired information from O'Connell International Arts, a firm that tries to prevent art theft. She read an article from the insurance industry's point of view in a trade publication, *Risk Management Magazine*. She read about museums' efforts to prevent theft and about other art thefts around the world. In short, she informed herself about why and how art theft happens and then developed her opinion. Doing research may not make you an expert, but if you are thoroughly informed, readers will have more reason to value your opinion. See the section on ethos on page 206.

Draw on Expert Testimony and Authoritative Sources

You can bolster your arguments by citing the opinions of those who have expert knowledge of the subject matter because they have published books or articles on the subject, have studied it professionally, or have some other insight not shared by the general population. Knowledge that has been vetted—screened, reviewed, and edited by experts—has an air of authority that can give added weight to a case. It's important to use such evidence to bolster but not to replace your own position. For help evaluating the quality and authority of your sources, see sections 15g and 16g.

Be Careful When Using Personal or Anecdotal Experience

Suppose you are against allowing any more casinos to be built in your state. You base your argument on your gambling problem and its horrific effects. Or you recount anecdotes from a couple of other people about how casinos have ruined their towns. A few personal experiences, no matter how poignant, are not enough support for an argument. While you can certainly recount personal experiences, base your argument against casinos mainly on statistics and other evidence that show how numerous other people have such a problem or how many towns have been ruined by casinos.

When you write an argument, you can make three general kinds of appeals to readers. They are usually named by the original Greek terms: logos, ethos, and pathos:

- *Logos* is the appeal to reason, logic, knowledge, truth, written evidence, and the facts of the case.
- *Ethos* is the writer's presentation of herself or himself as fair-minded and trustworthy, through the manner in which he or she treats the subject and, in some cases, by reputation.
- *Pathos* is the appeal to the emotions of the audience or the emotional content of the subject matter.

Logos: The Appeal to Reason

Logos should be the focus of an academic argument. Readers want good reasons why they should change their minds, and what qualifies as a good reason depends on what values you share with them, what they accept as truthful or believable, and what the evidence of experience and history shows. Two main types of logical appeals are the example (relying on inductive reasoning) and the enthymeme (relying on deductive reasoning). You can use both kinds of reasoning in your argument, choosing whichever pattern is more likely to persuade your audience of each of your points.

Activity 11-7: Identifying Appeals

Read the following paragraphs from a student paper on drinking problems on campus. Identify the places where the author uses the appeals of logos, ethos, and pathos.

> The sirens blare as the ambulance races toward the hospital, carrying John Doe, another victim of alcohol poisoning, found in his room this morning when he wouldn't answer his phone. John's roommates and friends follow him to the hospital, wondering if he'll be all right and what they'll tell his parents. Sadly, John dies without regaining consciousness, leaving a grieving campus community behind. John was a good student and friend who just wanted to have a little fun on the weekends. Like many college students, his fun came out of a bottle. What was the harm in that?
>
> In 2001, 33.5% of male college students in the United States had drunk five or more alcoholic beverages in a row on at least 1 day in the past 30 days (National Institute on Alcohol Abuse and Alcoholism). Many university representatives say that their schools have "created a climate that fosters acceptance of binge drinking" (Miller). Is Unseen University a school that encourages this type of climate where students drink irresponsibly and cause damage to themselves and others? What can we do to help students use alcohol responsibly and avoid more cases like John's?

Activity 11-8: Listing Your Reasons and Evidence

In a chart like the one below, list the reasons and evidence that you have compiled for the argument you have been working on.

Claim:

Reason	Evidence That Supports It
#1	
#2	
#3	

Activity 11-9: Shaping Your Evidence

Look over the Project Checklist on page 205, and answer the questions about the list of reasons and evidence you created in Activity 11-8.

Project Checklist

Questions to Ask about Your Reasoning

Ask these general questions about your reasoning. Refer to pages 311 and 331 for more information on evaluating research sources for comprehensiveness, reliability, and relevance.

- ❑ Have you supplied sufficient evidence to be convincing without boring your readers? Evidence is sufficient when it proves your argument but doesn't pile on unnecessary information that might distract readers from your point(s).
- ❑ Is the evidence you cite reliable and accurate? Can you confirm that the information is correct by finding it mentioned in other sources?
- ❑ Are the experts you cite in support of your argument knowledgeable, authoritative, and trustworthy?
- ❑ Are your examples relevant, sufficiently developed, and interesting?
- ❑ Does your argument proceed by sound logic? Have you avoided making logical fallacies (▶ pages 208–209)?

If your argument is based on examples, also ask

- ❑ Do the examples show what you say they do?
- ❑ Are the examples familiar or obscure? Are they memorable? Why?
- ❑ Have you used a sufficient number of examples to make your point, but not so many that you bore or insult your reader?
- ❑ Do you explain clearly what your examples prove or illustrate?

If your argument moves from general to specific, also ask

- ❑ Will readers agree with your premises? If not, should you explain them?
- ❑ Is it clear how your conclusion follows from your premises?
- ❑ Are there any other conclusions to be drawn from your premises? Should you mention them?

Induction: Reasoning from Examples to Conclusions

One form of reasoning is induction. **Induction** is the process of reasoning from experience, gaining insight from the signs and examples around us. Induction relies on examples to support or justify conclusions. The most important consideration with induction is to make sure that the examples support the conclusions—that they "exemplify" the case in the reader's mind. When the examples are valid and vivid, an inductive argument can be persuasive if you have properly gauged the rhetorical situation. When you give examples after a claim (in a paragraph, for instance), you may need only one or two to fix the point in the reader's mind. But when you present the examples first and then induce the conclusion from them, you will need to use more examples so that your readers can see how you came to your conclusion.

Deduction: Reasoning from General to Specific

In **deduction,** you argue from established premises, or truths about general cases, toward conclusions in more specific circumstances ("Given A, then B and C must follow"). A deductive pattern uses a syllogism or an enthymeme to draw a conclusion.

A **syllogism** is a form of logic that has a generalization (or major premise), a qualifier (or minor premise), and a conclusion. A syllogism starts with true statements from general cases and applies them to specific cases. A syllogism written in list form normally includes all the steps in the deduction, from the generalization to the conclusion, but when you write an argumentative essay, you won't include every step.

An **enthymeme,** which we have been calling a claim, suppresses one or more premises because the audience is likely to accept them. If you say, for example, that all curious people enjoy learning, so you do, too, then the unstated premise is that you are a curious person. If the audience is willing to accept that premise, your conclusion will ring true. If you presume too much and leave out a premise not accepted by the audience, you may fail to gain agreement.

The goal of the writer is to try to get readers to give a little each step of the way. A persuasive writer can systematically lead readers down a path by taking advantage of their willingness to agree with unstated premises.

Ethos: The Appeal of Being Trustworthy

Readers will look to see if the writer is someone they can trust. As a writer, you cultivate trust by showing readers that you know what you are talking about, have

Sample Syllogisms

A Valid Syllogism

Generalization (major premise):	All curious people enjoy learning.
Qualifier (minor premise):	You are a curious person.
Conclusion:	Therefore, you will enjoy learning.

An Invalid Syllogism

Generalization (major premise):	All curious people enjoy learning.
Qualifier not dependent on major premise:	Learning is naturally easy.
Conclusion:	Therefore, you will learn easily.

(There is no minor premise stating that "you" are a curious person, so the conclusion does not follow from the major or minor premise.)

Sample Enthymemes

Minor premise — Conclusion

1. I'm a curious person, so I enjoy learning new things.

Major premise — Conclusion

2. Curious people enjoy learning, so I do, too.

Activity 11-10: Identifying Premises and Conclusions

Identify the premise(s) and conclusion of each claim. Does the claim argue a point that can be contested? Proven?

1. When people try to place the Confederate flag in public places, they resurrect a painful history that stokes racial tensions.
2. Angry drivers who show road rage should lose their driving privileges.
3. Scientists tell us that you cannot avoid death and taxes because they are inevitable.
4. Toxic waste generated by unregulated factories and lax environmental controls will kill the planet.

Activity 11-11: Examining Ethos- and Pathos-Based Appeals

Take some time to draft those paragraphs of your argument that will include ethos- and pathos-based appeals. Exchange paragraphs with a partner. Read your partner's paragraphs and take notes on how your partner used ethos and pathos to appeal to the reader. (Use the Project Checklist below.) Tell the writer how these appeals work (or don't work) for you as a reader.

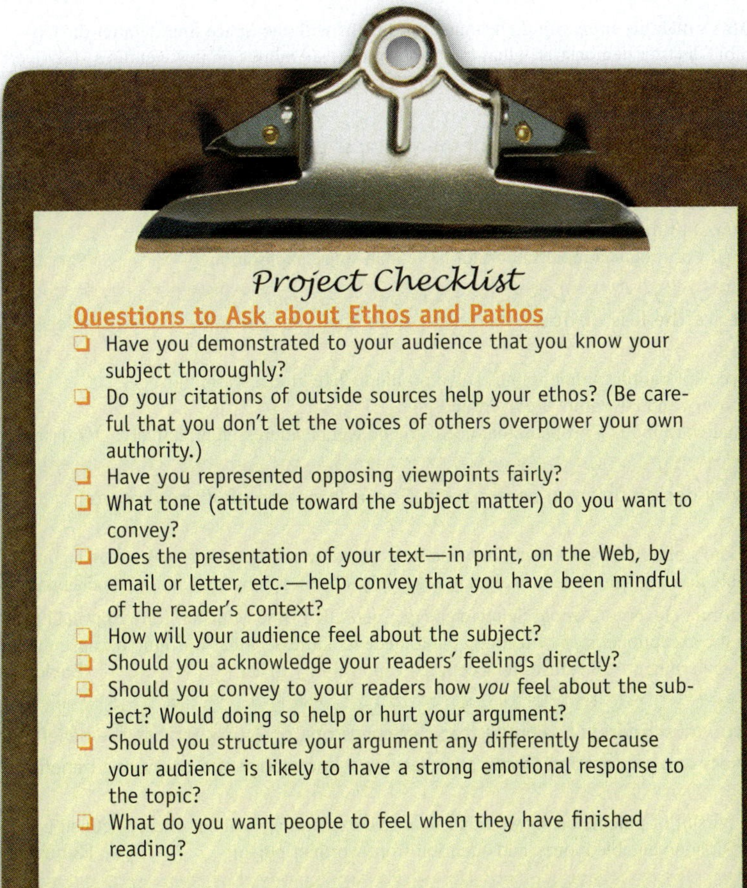

Project Checklist

Questions to Ask about Ethos and Pathos

- ❑ Have you demonstrated to your audience that you know your subject thoroughly?
- ❑ Do your citations of outside sources help your ethos? (Be careful that you don't let the voices of others overpower your own authority.)
- ❑ Have you represented opposing viewpoints fairly?
- ❑ What tone (attitude toward the subject matter) do you want to convey?
- ❑ Does the presentation of your text—in print, on the Web, by email or letter, etc.—help convey that you have been mindful of the reader's context?
- ❑ How will your audience feel about the subject?
- ❑ Should you acknowledge your readers' feelings directly?
- ❑ Should you convey to your readers how *you* feel about the subject? Would doing so help or hurt your argument?
- ❑ Should you structure your argument any differently because your audience is likely to have a strong emotional response to the topic?
- ❑ What do you want people to feel when they have finished reading?

carefully considered the evidence and other perspectives on the issue, and have the audience's best interests at heart. Your presentation of a strong ethos will help readers accept your argument. Practically speaking, ethical appeals tend to be very powerful and often trump appeals to logic or emotion. (That's one reason celebrities are commonly paid handsome amounts of money to endorse products on television.)

Pathos: The Appeal to Emotions

In most academic writing and in situations where, as Aristotle put it, the "truth alone should be enough to persuade," you won't need to appeal to the emotions of your readers. However, emotion is naturally a factor when people make judgments, so if you consider your audience carefully, you can use the emotional nature of a subject to move people to take action or change their attitudes. If your aim is to win readers over to your side, help them associate positive feelings with your position. Invite them to remember their own positive experiences, relate how others like them feel about the subject, and help them see how the subject relates to them.

The persuasiveness of your argument depends on a wide variety of factors: the willingness of your audience to assent and their motives for doing so, the common ground you establish, the effectiveness of your rhetorical appeals, and the context that defines all of these factors. Philosopher and rhetorician Stephen Toulmin recognized the importance of context in evaluating persuasion. He also developed a method for analyzing and mapping the structural basis and logic of persuasive arguments, what he called their *progression* (where an argument starts and how it unfolds). Writers can use the Toulmin method to analyze their own arguments or those of others.

Arguments proceed from **data** or **grounds** (facts, evidence, or reasons) that support a **claim** (a point of contention, a position on a controversial issue, a call to act, a thesis). Claims are based on **warrants,** the unstated premises that support a claim. Warrants require **backing** (support, additional data) when they are disputable. **Qualifiers** (terms like *some, most,* or *many*) may be used to soften the claim. **Rebuttals,** or challenges to the claim, focus on points that undermine the claim or invalidate the warrant.

Sample Toulmin Analysis

In your reading and research, you learn

> The U.S. government wants to spend billions of dollars to send people to the moon, once again, for the purposes of building a permanent colony there for scientific research and in preparation for sending astronauts to Mars. The government has also been slow to respond to the crisis of global warming. **Data**

So you claim

> NASA's inability to rectify the technical problems with the Space Shuttle after the Columbia disaster demonstrates that it is foolish to waste money on new ventures and divert taxpayer dollars from more pressing scientific problems like global warming. **Claim**

Then you ask: What are some of the warrants that support the claim?

> NASA has not fixed technical problems in the past.
> If you can't fix old problems, you shouldn't create new ones.
> Global warming is a more important issue than space exploration. **Warrants**

What are the less obvious warrants—ones that rest on value, belief, or ideology?

> Space exploration cannot help us solve problems like global warming.
> Discovery and adventure are overrated goals.
> Global warming is a problem that needs to and can be addressed effectively. **Warrants**

You may decide that you need backing for at least one of your warrants:

> Al Gore's film *An Inconvenient Truth* confronts global warming nay-sayers by showing indisputably that the phenomenon is already negatively affecting global agricultural production.
>
> California Governor Arnold Schwarzenegger and UK Prime Minister Tony Blair had to take the exceptional step of forming an alliance to address global warming because the U.S. government still refuses to accept its responsibility to act. **Backing**

And you must address a rebuttal that challenges one of your warrants, the belief that discovery and exploration always stimulate new knowledge and economic benefits:

> The pursuit of phlogiston showed that scientific exploration without clearly defined goals may siphon valuable money and attention from worthier pursuits. **Rebuttal**
>
> Qualifier ("may")

Fallacies of Relevance

1. **Personal attack *(ad hominem)*.** Discrediting the person making the argument to avoid addressing the argument

2. **Jumping on the bandwagon (*ad populum*).** Arguing that something must be true or good because a lot of other people believe it

3. **Nothing suggests otherwise . . . (*ad ignorantiam*).** Claiming that something is true simply because there is no contrary evidence

4. **False authority (*ad vericundiam*).** Suggesting that a person has authority simply because of fame or notoriety

5. **Appeal to tradition.** Claiming that just because something has been so previously, it is justified or should remain unchanged

6. **The newer, the better (theory of the new premise).** Claiming that because the evidence is new, it is the best explanation

Fallacies of Ambiguity

7. **Hasty generalization.** Making a claim about a wide class of subjects based on limited evidence

8. **Begging the question.** Basing the conclusion on premises or claims that lack important information or qualification

9. **Guilt by association.** Claiming that the quality of one thing sticks to another by virtue of a loose association

10. **Circular argument.** Concluding from premises that are related to the conclusion

11. **"After this, therefore because of this" (*post hoc, ergo propter hoc*).** Assuming that because one thing followed another, the first caused the second

12. **Slippery slope.** Arguing that if one thing occurs, something worse and unrelated will follow by necessity (one stride up the slippery slope will take you two steps back)

· A fallacy is an error in reasoning, whether deliberate or inadvertent. You can use your knowledge of fallacies to expose the problems in reading material, and you should check for fallacies in your own writing. *Fallacies of relevance* work by inviting readers to attach to a claim qualities that are not relevant to the subject. Fallacies of relevance bring unrelated evidence or information to bear on issues that are outside the scope of the subject matter or that have little or no bearing on our judgment of a case in its own right. *Fallacies of ambiguity* include ambiguous or unclear terms in the claim. Fallacies of ambiguity presume that something is certain or commonsensical when multiple viewpoints are possible.

For more on fallacies, visit The Writing Center of the University of North Carolina at Chapel Hill (http://www.unc.edu/depts/wcweb/handouts/fallacies.html).

When you *concede,* you give credence to an opposing or alternative perspective; you grant that some members of your audience might disagree with you and agree with another's point. When you *refute,* you examine an opposing or alternative point or perspective and demonstrate why it is incorrect or not the best response or solution. If you have researched and considered your argument, you should be able to conceive of many of the opposing and differing perspectives within your ongoing debate or argument. Rhetorically, concession and refutation give your writing a *gravitas,* or vital weight.

If you address possible objections in a fair-minded but direct way, you increase the likelihood that the opposition will understand and be won over to your position. Fair-mindedness will also enhance your ethos with neutral readers, who will consider you a reliable and trustworthy source.

Contending with Readers' Perspectives

Two methods exist for contending with readers with hostile or differing perspectives.

- You can demolish their arguments viciously (as many argument writers on unmoderated message boards do).
- You can anticipate their objections and refute them tactfully.

Where to Place Your Refutation

You should place your refutation at the spot in your argument where it will do the most good. If your readers are likely to have a refuting point in the forefront of their minds, then you need to address that opposing issue earlier rather than later. The longer you put off dealing directly with the likely objections of readers, the longer you postpone their possible agreement with your position. If there are important contrary views that your readers might not have made up their minds about, then your refutation will likely work best later in your essay. The important principle to remember is that effective writers raise issues (as in a refutation) at the opportune moment—just when readers expect them to be discussed.

As an undergraduate at Purdue University, Jacob J. H. Warrington wrote the following argument about the film *Fight Club* for a film course. One of his goals was to draw from what others had written about consumerism and film interpretation as he built his argument that *Fight Club* is an effective critique of modern capitalism.

Warrington 1

Jacob Warrington
Professor Felluga
Eng. 373
November 19, 2005

Postmodernism and the IKEA Nesting Instinct:
Consumerism and Commodification in David Fincher's *Fight Club*

"That condo was my life!"
Narrator, *Fight Club*

As the narrator of the 1999 film *Fight Club* succinctly illustrates, the definition of human existence via commercial purchases is an increasingly common occurrence in our modern culture. The film has as one of its central explorations this notion that acting the part of the consumer is a viable means of self-expression. More accurately, *Fight Club* challenges this typical notion, suggesting--and questioning--the possibility of rejecting a lifestyle so ingrained into capitalist culture as to border on subconscious instinct. This work seeks to analyze *Fight Club*'s commentary with the aid of postmodern theorists, in order to understand what the film communicates about the consumerist trend.

For a preliminary exercise, I should first carry out the important task of defining the central concepts of this work as they will be put to use. In this context, consumerism is a general theory of seeking gratification and/or stature through the act of making purchases. One can say, alternatively, that consumerism believes "my purchases define me." A complementary concept, and another central point of *Fight Club*, is that commodification is the seizure of benign goods (i.e., art), generally by corporations, in order to transform them into a

Warrington 2

marketable commodity capable of producing profit. Finally, there is the realm of postmodernism itself. While a discussion of what defines postmodernism is well beyond the scope of this endeavor, it is nevertheless useful to point out that postmodern theory is often interested in the rise of capitalism and the development of multinational corporate entities. Likewise, postmodern thought tends to be wary of humanity's ability to alter the ideologies that govern our everyday lives--these are the aspects of postmodernism that prove most useful in the analysis of David Fincher's *Fight Club*.

Consumerism as a Lifestyle, Commodification as Common Practice

Early in the film, as the narrator is describing the effects of his insomnia at work, we see a camera shot from the bottom of a trash can, pulling upward, while the narrator notes that the combination of deep space travel and corporate sponsorship will lead to realities of the "IBM Stellarsphere," the "Microsoft Galaxy," and "Planet Starbucks." This sequence vividly describes commodification at work, developing a scenario of corporate giants capitalizing on what is not even accessible with our current technology. The camera motion itself becomes an analogue to the commentary: after the shot begins at the center of this trash can "universe," the camera slides out, approaching the ends of the universe, capturing a gratuitous display of corporate logos as it travels. This general implication of growing corporate power is parallel to what Fredric Jameson described as "a network of power and control . . . difficult for our minds and imaginations to grasp: the whole new decentered global network of the third order of capital itself" (37). The scope of commodification is on display; it reveals the reach of a process

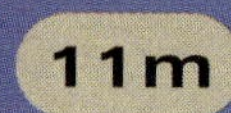

Audience and Purpose
Who seems to be the audience for this paper? List the features that lead you to this conclusion. How would you describe the paper's purpose?

where, as Dino Felluga puts it in his discussion of similar concepts in *The Matrix*, "the consumer product, itself defined by an involved commercial campaign, takes the place of 'the real thing'" (76).

Whereas the trash can sequence provides a keen description of commodification, the following scene addresses equally well the lifestyle of consumerism. The narrator goes so far as to describe his motivation, saying "if I saw something clever, like a coffee table in the shape of a yin-yang, I had to have it," adding "I'd flip through catalogs and wonder, 'what kind of dining set defines me as a person?'" This is precisely the cry of the individual caught in consumerism, searching for self-realization in the pages of a quarterly catalog. Jameson notes in his work *Postmodernism, or, the Cultural Logic of Late Capitalism*, that "what has happened is that aesthetic production today has become integrated into commodity production generally" (4), and this suggests how the narrator is satisfied to search for, simply, "something clever," purchasing these clever twists on true aesthetic work whenever possible.

In fact, Jameson adds, "The disappearance of the individual subject, along with its formal consequence, the increasing unavailability of personal style, engender the well-nigh universal practice today of what may be called pastiche" (16). The *Fight Club* narrator's practice of pastiche reflects in his addictively purchasing mass-produced décor based on hand-made creations of the past, or, in Jameson's words, his "neutral practice of . . . mimicry" (17). Again exciting is how the film techniques used in the scene directly reflect this condition. We do not simply have a shot of furniture in a condominium, but rather a live-action catalog, with the narrator walking *inside* the advertisement itself. He is living inside a construct

of commercial corporations: a furniture catalog, yes, but also consumerism itself. The scene uses this technique to provide ironic commentary, for while the narrator attempts to add commercial products to his home in order to individualize it, he only succeeds in making a more accurate copy of the mass-produced advertisements he orders from.

In several ways, the Fürni catalog scene additionally demonstrates Slavoj Žîžek's concept of "the world in which corporate Capital succeeded in penetrating and dominating the very fantasy-kernel of our being" (73). After the narrator says "we used to read pornography, now it was the 'Horchow collection,'" we can re-view the beginning to the scene, with the narrator in the bathroom, as parallel to Žîžek's description. As he sits on the toilet leafing through a catalog, we realize that this commercial tool has taken the place of what would have been pornographic fantasy. As he throws the Fürni catalog down, and the camera pulls into a photo with the tagline "Use Your IMAGINATION . . . ," we enter the narrator's own fantasy-kernel, filled with kitschy furniture and advertising descriptions. Thus, *Fight Club* proves its world is very much the one that Žîžek considered.

As a final exploration of *Fight Club*'s early introduction to the theory of its postmodern world, one should consider the montage of the film's narrator traveling on the job. The film introduces "the equation," an algorithm using three variables to estimate settlement costs of faulty car parts. If the costs of settlement are lower than the cost to recall flawed cars, no recall is performed. The mechanic actually at work under this veil of corporate villainy is the reduction of

Reasoning and Evidence
What is the claim? What evidence from the film and various outside sources does the writer use? How well do the examples used in the first major section, "Consumerism as a Lifestyle, Commodification as Common Practice," support the claim?

Warrington 5

human life to a number--precisely, a dollar amount. The prevalence of this postmodern symptom is brought up in Felluga's overview of exchange-value:

> According to Karl Marx, the entrance into capitalist culture meant that we ceased to think of purchased goods in terms of use-value, in terms of the real uses to which an item will be put. Instead, everything began to be translated into how much it is worth, into what it can be exchanged for (its exchange-value). Once money became a "universal equivalent," against which everything in our lives is measured, things lost their material reality (real-world uses, the sweat and tears of the laborer). *We began even to think of our own lives in terms of money rather than in terms of the real things we hold in our hands*: how much is my time worth? How does my conspicuous consumption define me as a person? (74, italics added for emphasis)

In this sense, the understanding of life as a dollar amount is symptomatic of modern capitalist culture, similar to the effect of consumerism, wherein one's worth is translated into the monetary values or those commodities they have purchased. Not surprisingly, this point is summed up nicely as the narrator reflects, in his skewed perspective, as he waits for his luggage in an airport terminal: "I had everything in that suitcase: my CK shirts, my DKNY shoes, my AlX ties . . . ."

Rise and Fall of Rebellion

After the film's narrator has been introduced to the character of Tyler Durden, a soap salesman, projectionist, and so-called "guerrilla

Warrington 6

terrorist of the food service industry," *Fight Club* provides viewers with a stance against consumerism. Primarily, we encounter Tyler's rebellious acts: splicing pornography into children's films, befouling banquet food with urine, etc. If he were asked the reasons for these choices, he could potentially quote the logic of Michel Foucault, who said "the analysis, elaboration, and bringing into question of power relations, and the 'agonism' between power relations and the intransivity of freedom is a permanent political task inherent in all social existence" (218). Spouting catch phrases like "Self-improvement is masturbation," Durden is a vigilante against corporate corruption, a sort of anti-hero for the disenfranchised.

The movie initially gives him latitude to convert mindless consumers with his appealing brand of misbehavior. When a police officer speaks with the narrator on the telephone about the explosion that destroyed his condominium, Tyler repeatedly interjects his spin:

> NARRATOR. Who would go and do such a thing?
> DETECTIVE. I'll ask the questions.
> TYLER. Tell him. Tell him the liberator who destroyed my property has realigned my perceptions. . . .
> DETECTIVE. Have you recently made enemies with anyone who might have access to homemade dynamite?
> NARRATOR. Enemies?
> TYLER. Reject the basic assumptions of civilization, especially the importance of material possessions! . . .
> NARRATOR. Yes, it's very serious. Look, no one takes this more seriously than me--that condo was my life!

Rhetorical Appeals
What kinds of appeals does the writer use—logos, ethos, pathos? Which appeal predominates?

Warrington 7

> Ok? I loved every stick of furniture in that place. That was not just a bunch of stuff that got destroyed. It was me!
>
> DETECTIVE. Is this not a good time for you?
>
> TYLER. Just tell him you f***ing did it! Tell him you blew it all up; that's what he wants to hear. . . .

While the narrator still plays the part of the devoted consumer ("I loved every stick of furniture in that place. That was not just a bunch of stuff that got destroyed. It was me!"), we see that Tyler exerts influence on him. When the narrator realizes he is a suspect for the crime, he accepts Tyler's pseudo-wisdom even more readily. Later, after we (and, concurrently, the narrator) realize that he did, in fact, destroy his own condominium, we might assume that the movie suggests this extreme rejection of consumer principles is a viable reaction to the rampant cultural commodification individuals face. When Tyler says we have become "slaves with white collars," adding "advertising has us chasing cars and clothes, working jobs we hate, so we can buy s*** we don't need," we want to believe his alternative will change it all.

However, *Fight Club* undercuts this notion. Especially toward the end of the film, we see signs that Tyler Durden's vision is not the perfect solution to all of postmodernism's problems. First, we have Tyler's "you are not your job" monologue. It echoes all of his previous condemnations of consumerism: "you are not how much money you have in the bank," and "you are not your car." At the end of the sequence, though, there is a strange occurrence. The frame blurs and shakes, and as it shifts, we can see around the film, noticing the edges

Warrington 8

of the frame, the reel tracks, and the light behind it. We are informed that, although Tyler speaks to us of shirking our reality of consumerism, it is through one branch of this reality, the mass media--the motion picture industry--that Tyler speaks to us. While he claims to be above and outside this realm of capitalist consumer concerns, he is, on the contrary, directly in the middle of it. It is essentially the same contradiction as in Linda Hutcheon's discussion on metafiction, where she notes "it always works *within* conventions in order to subvert them" (5). Here, the film has chosen to make viewers aware of Tyler's complicity with movie *in order to question* his reliability.

Further, as the development of Project Mayhem continues to expand the role of the "Fight Club" (this, the entity inside the movie), it becomes more apparent that Tyler Durden is unable to escape the ideology of consumerism. In Louis Althusser's discussion on ideology, he is able to point out that although individuals may wish to be outside systems of ideology, this is an impossibility (246). His understanding of how one acts in contradiction to ideology--"As is well known, the accusation of being in ideology only applies to others, never to oneself" (246)--is remarkably similar to how Tyler Durden treats the members of his Fight Club; while Tyler seeks to cure disillusioned men from "false consciousness" (borrowing a phrase from the Marxists), he is yet still caught in the commercial ideology himself.

So, what would *Fight Club* have us believe? Is there hope of escape from the lurking commodification of our culture? . . . Essentially, no; only awareness. Continuing with Althusser, the subjectivity of individuals is inherent: "Before its birth, the child is

Effectiveness
Do you find the argument effective? Why or why not?

Warrington 9

therefore always already a subject, appointed as a subject in and by the specific familial ideological configuration in which it is 'expected' once it has been conceived." This trait *subjects* us to the ideologies of the culture in which we live. As Althusser summarizes, "I only wish to point out that you and I are *always already* subjects, and as such constantly practice the rituals of ideological recognition, which guarantee for us that we are indeed concrete, individual, distinguishable, and (naturally) irreplaceable subjects" (245). In this context, we see that *Fight Club* admits we are all a part of the postmodern consumerist tradition, just as Tyler Durden remained a part, but it strives to make us aware of the condition. Although Althusser acknowledges the rarity with which individuals can consciously state "I am in ideology" (246), I argue this is precisely the conclusion *Fight Club* wants its viewers to reach. According to popular postmodern theory, though we might currently be unable to alter the ideological structures within which we live, awareness is a prerequisite of change. Although David Fincher's *Fight Club* may not have all the answers, it certainly has the presence to lay bare some of the central issues of the postmodern condition. If viewers can read between the lines (or perhaps, more accurately, *see between the frames*), they will be able to learn a great deal more about the commodification of our culture and the ideology of consumerism than the majority of contemporary film has ever attempted to communicate.

Warrington 10

Works Cited

Althusser, Louis. "Ideology and Ideological State Apparatuses." *Critical Theory since 1965*. Ed. Hazard Adams and Leroy Searle. Tallahassee: U Presses of Florida, 1986. 238–50. Print.

Felluga, Dino. "*The Matrix*: Paradigm of Postmodernism or Intellectual Poseur? (Part I)." *Taking the Red Pill: Science, Philosophy and Religion in* The Matrix. Ed. Glenn Yeffeth. Dallas: Ben Bella, 2003. 71–84. Print.

Foucault, Michel. "The Subject of Power." *Michel Foucault: Beyond Structuralism and Hermeneutics*. 2nd ed. Ed. Hubert L. Dreyfus and Paul Rabinow. Chicago: U of Chicago P, 1982. Print.

Hutcheon, Linda. *A Poetics of Postmodernism: History, Theory, Fiction*. New York: Routledge, 1988. Print.

Jameson, Fredric. *Postmodernism, or, the Cultural Logic of Late Capitalism*. Durham: Duke UP, 1991. Print.

Žîžek, Slavoj. *Tarrying with the Negative: Kant, Hegel, and the Critique of Ideology*. Durham: Duke UP, 1993. Print.

A table of contents for writing project threads appears on pages xv–xxii.

Proposal Arguments

Harrington 1

A Proposal to Clean Up Our Streets

I have a proposal which could clean up the whole neighborhood.

All of a sudden the public perception of the lobbying profession has plunged to depths even below those occupied by trial lawyers, tobacco users, child molesters and Democrat members of the Senate Judiciary Committee. Its practitioners are now seen as the designated villains of the present moment, to be avoided as if they were carriers of an especially virulent strain of bird flu common among vultures and other avid consumers of carrion and offal.

Given that the right to lobby is protected by the Constitution and cannot be banned outright, or even regulated to any great extent, all this blather about taking the boys and girls on K Street, who only yesterday were their bosom buddies, to the woodshed is nothing less than a charade. Any reforms will be window dressing, and after a brief period of time the buddy-wuddy relationships they shared with the K Street crowd will be re-invigorated. But, as Jerry Seinfeld would say, "Not that there's anything wrong with that."

Aside from banning former members of Congress and former Capital Hill staffers from ever serving as lobbyists, therefore condemning them to a fate worse than death - i.e., going home to their districts and living like normal Americans, deprived of the joys of the abundant life on the shores of the Potomac River - there really isn't much that can be done to stop the incestuous relationships between solons and lobbyists. As the song "Love and Marriage" explains, "they go together like a horse and carriage ... you can't have one without the other."

Thinking about Your Appeals in the Context of Community

Your essay needs to be appealing to community members so that they will be persuaded to accept your solution. Reread your draft to check how you have used ethos, pathos, and logos in your argument. Consider your essay from the points of view of community members who will feel they have something valuable to gain or to lose from your proposal. Have you effectively addressed their emotions and thoughts? page 374.

12

WRITING FOR BUSINESS AND THE WORKPLACE

Many professionals—regardless of their field, whether or not they consider themselves professional *writers*—will admit that writing plays an important role in their daily work. In this chapter we move beyond the classroom to the worldly contexts in which writers and writing work. The same rhetorical principles and writing practices that lead to effective college writing are used to create strong business letters and resumes, memos, case analyses, white papers, and recommendation reports. Writers must hone their sense of the rhetorical situation, whether it is in the workplace, on campus, or in the community, and whether the goal is to share information, analyze choices and make recommendations, or sell a product or service, such as their own talents. The principles of effective collaboration and project management also play critical roles in business and workplace writing.

Much of the writing that you practice in college reflects what people do in everyday life, so you will find that the principles and practices of professional writing described in this chapter will serve you well right now. In college, you often need to practice—as an apprentice of sorts—the kinds of writing that professionals in your field of interest successfully manage every day. In service learning courses, you need to communicate effectively with clients and with peers in a collaborative process. You may want to promote a student club, apply for scholarships or financial aid, persuade people to vote for a political candidate, or inform fellow students about a new service. You will almost certainly want to use your skills as a writer when you prepare to enter the workplace or—if you are already there—to improve your chances of securing a job that will make you happier, wealthier, or both.

Whenever you broaden the audience for your writing to include readers other than peers or instructors, you should bear in mind—perhaps with even more attention than usual—the nature of the rhetorical situation. Your writing will more often communicate beyond its usual borders the further you go in your education, and particularly when you seek employment during or after college. In the rhetorical situation of business writing and the workplace, your goals will be to

- develop and understand various strategies for planning, researching, drafting, revising, and editing documents that respond effectively and ethically to professional situations and audiences
- analyze professional cultures, social contexts, and audiences to determine how they shape the various purposes and forms of writing, such as persuasion, organizational communication, and public discourse

The Rhetorical Situation in Professional Writing

Purpose: What do you want your writing to accomplish?

Audience: What are the expectations and needs of your primary and secondary readers?

Context: What is the context in which your writing will be read?

Subject: What do you know and what do you want to say about your subject?

How Can You Identify...

The Professional and Social Culture of a Company or Organization?

1. Read the company or organization's mission statement, strategic plan, annual report, or other "constitutional" document that sets goals and priorities.
2. Find out how the company or organization represents itself publicly. Run a Google search on its name. At the physical site, find a brochure or other public-relations information that summarizes goals and activities.
3. Observe how people manage routine activities on a typical day. How do they spend their time? What tasks keep them the busiest?
4. Study the life of a collaboratively written document. Who drafts documents? Who reviews them? Who revises them? Who publishes them? Is the process divided among people with unique responsibilities, or does everyone play a role during each stage?
5. How does the company or organization interact with business partners or related organizations? Are these interactions a regular activity or not?
6. What "rules" or standard procedures seem to control how people (employees or volunteers) interact with each other? Are there ways for disputes to be resolved?
7. How much of the work people do takes place on a computer, using email, a content management system, or other communication technology? How important is this work to the company or organization's existence?

As writing technologies vary, so might the responses of your readers. A notepad, a book, and a laptop are all interfaces that shape the writing and reading process.

Much of your writing and reading in the workplace is mediated by technology. Anything you use to produce writing—from pen to typewriter to word processor—is a writing technology and as such governs how you write and affects how your readers read and respond to your writing. In this sense, technology is an *interface,* a screen through which readers and writers communicate. Each interface will have some effect on how your readers respond.

Saying that writing is *mediated* by technology suggests that your ability to use technologies to accomplish rhetorical tasks will be a critical factor in your success as a writer. In particular, you will need to learn to

- develop strategies for using and adapting various communication technologies to manage projects and produce professional documents
- design effective visual documents and argue with visual data, understanding and implementing principles of format, layout, and design to create documents that meet multiple user and reader needs (Chapters 24 and 25)

Learning to write effective cover letters and resumes is important because everyone will at some time apply for a new job, start a new career path, or move up the corporate ladder. To be successful, you need to let people know what you can do for them.

A **cover letter** is usually a one-page introduction (a "cover") to documents presented to readers, clients, or—in the case of a job search—a prospective employer. A **resume** is a summary of your qualifications for employment and usually includes information about your education, work experience, accomplishments, and professional interests. As genres of writing, cover letters and resumes follow conventions in terms of format and content, but their form and content should also be responses to particular circumstances. Your goal should be to portray yourself as a thoughtful, experienced, and highly qualified candidate for a job, scholarship, or other situation that calls for a cover letter and resume.

Writing Project: The Job Search

Suppose your goal is to locate a real and specific job for which you are qualified and to prepare the materials to apply for it. Here are the steps to take as you aim to represent yourself and your experience fully and effectively.

Take inventory of your skills, experiences, and goals.
Find and analyze job ads. In your search, learn about and use various Web-based resources for job seekers, and ultimately select one job to pursue.
Compose a cover letter that identifies your reasons for applying and highlights your qualifications.
Write a resume suitable for such a position.
Eugene Rhee

Job Search Activity 12-1: Taking Inventory of Your Skills, Experiences, and Goals

To help you decide what kind of job you want and to generate ideas for your cover letter and resume, write down answers to the following questions.

Work Experience

1. What work experiences have you had? List them all, with the title of your position, the name and location of the company or organization, your supervisor's name, the dates of your employment, and the job's requirements.
2. Have you ever volunteered with a nonprofit organization? List the details, as in item 1.
3. Have you had any internship experiences? Describe them in detail.

Educational Experience

4. What courses, projects, and other activities have taught you valuable skills? Describe them in detail.
5. Have you received any scholarships or awards? Describe them in full.

Skills

6. What skills do you have that rise above the ordinary? What do you do especially well? Do you have any special talents (think broadly)? How do your skills and talents relate to the kind of job you seek?
7. Do you have skills in working with particular groups of people? Do you speak more than one language?
8. Do you have computer skills? What software programs do you know well?
9. Do you have skills working with particular kinds of equipment?

To generate more specific ideas about the skills you already possess, review the extensive list of terms that name these skills on the "Job Skills Checklist" at Purdue University's Online Writing Lab: **http://owl.english.purdue.edu/handouts/pw/p_skillinv.html**.

Job Search Activity 12-2: What Do You Want from a Job?

Write down your criteria for a job. You may wish to consult "Job Search Self-Analysis: Finding a Position That Meets Your Needs" at Purdue University's OWL: **http://owl.english.purdue.edu/handouts/pw/p_slfana.html**.

Taking Inventory of Your Skills, Experiences, and Goals

"Know thyself" was the common refrain of the Greek philosopher Socrates. If you want to have good content to work with when you portray yourself to others, you need to be sure that you have explored your talents fully. Who are you? What have you done and what can you do? Those are not always easy questions to answer, even though your field of research (the self) is as close to home as it can get. You may have some work-related experience to list. You will also have educational experience: courses, class projects, and other educational activities. Take inventory of your skills and experience.

Consider, too, what you want from a job, not to mention from your life. Are you looking for a position that will teach you new skills, such as an internship or apprenticeship? Are you looking for a position that will prepare you for higher-level work in your field? What do you enjoy doing most? Do you prefer working alone or with people? Where do you want to work?

Finding and Analyzing Job Ads

Once you have found an ad for a job that interests you and for which you are well qualified, you should spend some time analyzing the ad to make sure you understand the nature of the position and its requirements. You should also spend some time researching the company itself. You will use information from this analysis as you tailor your cover letter and resume to the rhetorical situation.

Job Search Activity 12-3: Using Print, Campus, and Internet Resources

Once you've taken inventory of your skills, interests, and goals, begin to narrow your search for a suitable position. You can find job listings in your local newspaper (online or offline) and in your college's employment or career center. In addition, you may find these Internet resources helpful.

Background Information on the Job Search

The Riley Guide: **http://www.rileyguide.com**
Job Hunter's Bible: **http://www.jobhuntersbible.com**

Salary Comparisons

Salary.com: **http://www.salary.com**

Job Boards and Listings

Career Magazine: **http://www.careermag.com**
CareerBuilder: **http://www.careerbuilder.com**
Computerjobs: **http://www.computerjobs.com**
InternWeb.Com: **http://www.internweb.com**
Jobstar: **http://jobstar.org**
Journalism Jobs: **http://journalismjobs.com**
Manpower: **http://www.manpower.com**
Monster.com: **http://www.monster.com**
Net-Temps: **http://www.net-temps.com**
NicheBoards: **http://www.nicheboards.com**
Overseas Job Web: **http://www.overseasjobs.com**
Yahoo! HotJobs: **http://hotjobs.yahoo.com**

Job Search Activity 12-4: Analyzing Job Ads

Analyze two or three job ads that interest you. You may wish to consult "How to Read a Job Ad Carefully" at Purdue University's OWL: **http://owl.english.purdue.edu/workshops/hypertext/coverletter/read.html**.

Job Search Activity 12-5: Why Are You Interested? How Are You Qualified?

Respond to these questions in as much detail as you can:

- Why are you interested?
- How are you qualified?

Sample Job Ad

WE'RE LOOKING FOR AMERICA'S BEST
The Best Eyecare ... Every Day

Job Title: Receptionist
Department: Retail Operations
Reporting Relationships:
Reports to Assistant Manager–Eyeglasses and Assistant Manager–Contact Lenses
Summary of Position:
Ensures telephones are answered promptly in accordance with company telephone protocol and that customers receive courteous service.
Essential Duties and Responsibilities:

- Schedule and confirm appointments, follow-up visits, and classes.
- Maintain permanent records.
- Ensure smooth flow of patients through store.
- Notify customers when orders are in or of any delays.
- Maintain neat and orderly front desk and waiting room.

Experience:

- Experience preferred, but not required.

Benefits Include:

- Competitive Salaries
- 401K Plan
- Incentive Plan
- Health Insurance
- Dental Insurance
- Disability Insurance
- Paid Vacation
- Paid Holidays
- Employee Eyewear and Eyecare Discount Program

For consideration, send resume & cover letter with salary requirements to:
America's Best Contacts and Eyeglasses
7255 Crescent Blvd.
Pennsauken, NJ 08110
Attn: Human Resources
FAX (800) 555-1000
dlawson@twopair.com

No phone calls, please.
Proud to be an equal opportunity employer.

To learn more about us, visit www.twopair.com

Whenever you respond to a job ad or any "announcement" that requires a formal response, be sure to read the source carefully. After you are sure you know what it says or asks for, write down the reasons you want to respond to it. Then determine what will make your response—your cover letter and resume—relevant and important to your ultimate reader.

The ad asks for someone who excels at customer service.

The successful applicant will have good record-keeping skills, customer service experience, and phone skills.

They would like someone who has job-related experience, but other experience, such as volunteer work, may be acceptable as well.

Preparing the Cover Letter

Before you draft your cover letter, answer these questions:

- Why am I interested in this position?
- How am I qualified for it?

To prepare a cover letter, pay attention not only to the content of the ad but also to the circumstances of the company or organization. Think, too, about who might read your letter. What will they notice? What questions might they have?

In response to the ad she chose, Jessica Hary wrote the cover letter on page 225. Notice how she effectively addresses the two questions above, at least indirectly. In her first paragraph, she identifies her reasons for applying. She realizes that the employer might wonder why a student in optometry was applying for a job as a receptionist. She is careful in the following paragraphs to give details about her experience in customer service.

Sample Response: Why Am I Interested? How Am I Qualified?

Jessica Hary, the student who found the job ad on page 223, wrote her answers to these questions in preparation for writing a cover letter.

America's Best Contacts and Eyeglasses

This is a position for a receptionist at America's Best Contacts and Eyeglasses. The responsibilities of this position are that you answer the phones in the appropriate business manner and that you be courteous to the patients. The duties and responsibilities of this position are very general. These duties include but are not limited to scheduling and confirming appointments with the patients, keeping up-to-date records for each and every patient, letting the patients know when their orders are in or if they are back ordered, and maintaining an organized desk.

I chose this position because of the fact that I want to be an optometrist. I have six years left before I am completely done with my schooling, so it is hard to find a job that fits my major. In this case, I would get some experience in the field of optometry. This would allow me to be able to converse with the doctor and ask questions and maybe even get to sit in on a checkup. This would also allow me to see what actually goes on in an optometrist's office, so in the future, when I am an optometrist, I will have some insight into what should take place in the office.

I believe that I am qualified for this position for many reasons. One reason is that I consider myself a people person, and I have several communication and people skills. I have worked at a grocery store for the past five years. This has allowed me to be able to communicate with different types of people and has taught me how to deal with certain situations. Another reason I consider myself qualified is because I have experience with answering phones. I worked in my high school main office for two years, answering phones and taking messages. I am also a very organized and neat person. I would not have a problem with keeping my work area organized and presentable.

Sample Job Application Cover Letter

Jessica Hary
123 Anywhere St.
West Lafayette, IN 47906
(555) 555-5555
nobody@purdue.edu

May 19, 2006

Human Resources Manager
America's Best Contacts and Eyeglasses
7255 Crescent Blvd.
Pennsauken, NJ 08110

Dear Human Resources Manager:

I am currently a student at Purdue University majoring in General Health Science with a focus on Pre-Optometry. I am applying for the position as a Receptionist at your Indianapolis store, advertised on Yahoo! HotJobs, and I have enclosed my resume in application for this position. I believe that my experiences in customer service and public relations would make me a valuable addition to your company. I am very interested in this position because I hope to be an optometrist someday and this would be a great starting place for me to learn about the everyday life of an optometrist.

For the past five years, I have been employed at a local grocery store, and I also volunteered answering phones in my high school's main office. I have gained considerable experience in these roles, which would benefit your company and would allow me to make an immediate contribution if I were successful in obtaining this position.

I am enthusiastic and hardworking and have excellent communication skills. Furthermore, I am a skilled user of Microsoft Word, Excel, and Money, as you can see from my resume. In addition, I know how to deal with difficult situations with customers in a polite and well-mannered way. These qualities have allowed me to build and maintain excellent relationships with customers and my fellow workers in my previous jobs. I would like to bring these experiences and skills to your company; I want to benefit your company and in the process learn from my experiences to further help me in the field of optometry. My salary requirements are $25,000.

Please contact me at (555) 555-5555 or by email at nobody@purdue.edu. I look forward to speaking with you. Thank you for your time and consideration.

Sincerely,
Jessica Hary

Enclosure: Resume

Parts of the Cover Letter

Heading. The various items in the heading should appear in this order: sender's name, address, and any other contact information; date; recipient's name or title and address; and greeting. Each chunk of information is separated by a blank line.

Greeting. Try to find the name of a person to address your cover letter to. If you can't find a name by doing research, use the person's exact title. "Dear" is the standard way to begin.

Opening. Let your reader know why she or he has received your letter, who you are, and which ad you are responding to.

Persuasion. In this section, which may be several paragraphs in length, you should explain in detail what you want your reader to remember about you or the material you are introducing (here, your resume and qualifications for the position).

Closing. "Sincerely" is an accepted closing. Vary from it only if you have a clear reason for doing so. For example, if you know the person well, you might instead choose to close with "Best regards." Sign your cover letter, and identify any accompanying documents in an "Enclosure" line.

Writing a Resume

A resume, like a cover letter, should be tailored to a specific rhetorical situation—as announced by a job ad, for instance—instead of being one size fits all. Many job seekers prepare multiple versions of their resume in order to respond to a range of positions. The resume should make clear that the potential employee or intern is perfectly suited for the position or internship.

How Long Should a Resume Be?

Your resume should strike a nice balance between depth of content and visual appeal, with a length suitable to your experience and the requirements of the position. Early in your career, keep a paper resume to one page to help your reader focus attention on your skills and qualities. As your work experience grows, your resume will expand because you will have more relevant information to list.

Do not sacrifice appearance and readability in order to squeeze more information onto a page. The organization and appearance of a resume are at least as important as its content in appealing to readers. Readers usually do not spend much time reading a resume, especially when screening candidates early in the selection process, so resume writers need to catch readers' attention by highlighting critical information with effective layout and typography.

Draft Resume with Instructor's Comments

Is it conventional to list this information for government positions like this?

Put a space after the closing parenthesis.

Eugene Rhee
(US citizen)

Campus Address
123 Somewhere Dorm
West Lafayette, IN 47906
(765)555-1111

eugenerhee@purdue.edu

Permanent Address
456 Bonita Drive
Chula Vista, CA 91911
(619)555-2222

The font seems very small in your addresses.

Objective To obtain a position as a test engineer at Raytheon Company that utilizes ~~the~~ *my* technical skills and knowledge gained in Electrical Engineering and Communication coursework.

Good specific objective

Education
Purdue University West Lafayette, IN
Bachelor of Science, August 2004
Major: Electrical Engineering Minor: Management
Engineering coursework:
Signals and Systems
Digital Signal Processing
Electomechanical Motion Devices
Electomagnetics
Optics
Feedback Systems Analysis
Management coursework:
Financial and Managerial Accounting
Finance
Marketing
Organizational Behavior

Would listing GPA (ex. 3.4/4.0) be a good idea?

Skills
Operating Systems: Windows, Unix, Linux
Programming Languages: Matlab, C, HTML, ABEL, Basic
Applications: Excel, Matlab, Minitab, Microsoft Office
Testing Equipment: Spectrum Analyzer, Oscilloscope, Multimeter, Signal Generator, Power Meter, Analog Filter, Amplifier

Good detail!

Work Experience
Blockbuster Video [Aug. 2003 – Present] West Lafayette, IN, USA
Customer service representative – Ensured the satisfaction of customers.
Maintained organizational structure for effortless accessibility of company assets.
Collaborated with management to develop enhancements to the company's security system.
Excelled in promotional sales and achieved special recognition among employees.

Try to get these lines shorter so that the last word doesn't wrap (saves room and improves appearance).

You break the pattern here. The position description is in bold in the second item.

Office Assistant [June 2001 - Aug. 2001] Yongsan Military Base, Korea
Analyzed computer database program and made recommendations to change the software; changes were implemented shortly after internship.
Entered data into computer database of military housing information.
Filing and organization of military housing applications and miscellaneous requests.

If you can't get these to one line, then use hanging indents.

Activities
Korean American Students Association
Joined in order to establish relations with Korean-American students new to Purdue; also to maintain relations with Korean-Americans already at Purdue.
Cornerstone Fellowship
Helped organize and participated in special events such as Goodwill Games and Graduation Night.
Helped cook for students living in the dormitories when cafeteria food was not available (Sunday nights).

Try to make this more concise by combining the two parts of the sentence.

Good layout, Eugene. In addition to addressing the marginalia in your revision, you might think about ways you can bring in more of your experience with projects that have given you hands-on experience in testing. You could reduce the space devoted to Work or Activities that aren't quite as relevant (Blockbuster might get only one or two lines instead of the six it gets now).

Revised Resume

Eugene Rhee

Campus Address
123 Somewhere Dorm
West Lafayette, IN 47906
(765) 555-1111

eugenerhee@purdue.edu

Permanent Address
456 Bonita Drive
Chula Vista, CA 91911
(619) 555-2222

Objective To obtain a position as a test engineer at Raytheon Company that utilizes my technical skills and knowledge to assure quality engineering and safety.

Education

Purdue University — West Lafayette, IN
Bachelor of Science, August 2004
Major: Electrical Engineering — Minor: Management
Major GPA: 3.74/4.00 Grad GPA: 3.80/4.00 — Minor GPA: 4.00/4.00

Engineering Coursework: Signals and Systems, Digital Signal Processing, Electromechanical Motion Devices, Electromagnetics, Optics, Feedback Systems

Management Coursework: Financial and Managerial Accounting, Finance, Marketing, Organizational Behavior

Skills
Operating Systems: Windows, Unix, Linux
Programming Languages: Matlab, C, HTML, ABEL, Basic
Applications: Excel, Matlab, Minitab, Microsoft Office
Testing Equipment: Spectrum Analyzer, Oscilloscope, Multimeter, Signal Generator, Power Meter, Analog Filter, Amplifier

Projects
Created a communications device to transmit and receive binary data and displayed data on seven-segment LEDs.
Assembled a video processor and captured the image on a computer screen.

Work Experience

Customer Service Representative [Aug. 2003 - Present] — Blockbuster Video, West Lafayette, IN
Ensured customer satisfaction.
Maintained organizational structure for effortless accessibility of company assets.
Collaborated with management to enhance a security system.

Office Assistant [June 2001 - Aug. 2001] — Yongsan Military Base, Korea
Analyzed computer database program and made recommendations to change the software; changes were implemented shortly after internship.
Entered information in database of military housing records.
Organized and filed housing applications and other requests.

Activities

Korean American Students Association
Joined to establish and maintain relations with Korean-American students.

Cornerstone Fellowship
Helped organize and participated in special events such as Goodwill Games and Graduation Night.
Helped cook for students living in the dormitories when cafeteria food was unavailable.

References Available on request.

Eugene's revised resume has better column alignment, stronger emphasis in the right places, consistent use of active verbs, and a more direct objective statement.

Parts of a Typical Resume

Resumes typically contain contact information, career objectives, educational background, work experience, achievements, special skills, and a list of references or a statement that they are available. Precisely which headings you use to organize your resume will depend on the nature of the position you are applying for and the types of experience you have. If, for example, you are applying for a position that requires experience as a graphic designer, you might include a section called "Exhibitions and Portfolios." Or if you have substantial volunteer work experience, you might list that experience in its own section, "Volunteer Experience." The order of the sections will depend on which aspects of your qualifications you want to emphasize, with the most important aspects placed early in the resume.

Additional Headings That May Be Used in a Resume

The following headings are particularly useful for college students who don't yet have an extensive work history, homemakers returning to the paid workforce, and people changing careers:

Volunteer Service (or Volunteer Work)
Honors (or Achievements, Scholarships, Academic Recognition, Awards)
Technical Skills (or Software Skills, Equipment Skills, Certifications, Licenses)
Hobbies (or Interests and Activities, Extracurricular Activities)
Leadership Activities
Field Experience
Portfolios (or Exhibitions)
Languages

Designing the Resume

Resumes are challenging to design and present. They must include lots of information, presented logically in an aesthetically pleasing way, to readers who may not take more than a minute or two to read them. For these reasons, the design and layout of your resume are critically important.

Establish consistency among similar types or levels of information.

- All major section headings, such as "Education" and "Work Experience," should be in the same

1

Project Checklist

Evaluating Your Resume's Content

- ❑ **Contact information.** Your contact information should be listed prominently, usually near the top of the page, with no heading. Include your campus and/or permanent mailing address; your home and/or cell phone number; your email address (use a "professional" one); and, if appropriate, the URL for your home page or Web portfolio.
- ❑ **Objective** (sometimes listed as "Career Objective," "Objective Statement," "Career Goals," or "Philosophy Statement"). Resumes may include statements about career objectives, but in some occupations it is common practice not to include them, so find out whether others in your field do so. The objective should state clearly and concisely what you want to accomplish for yourself *and* for a company or organization. Remember: The reader wants to know what you can do for the company or the organization. Notice the difference.

  YES—What *you* can do for *them*

  Objective: To use my experience as a marketing strategist to help a fast-paced, creative ad agency in the fashion industry.

  NO—What *they* can do for *you*

  Objective: To obtain a high-paying position that will improve my skills as a marketing strategist in the fashion industry.
- ❑ **Education** ("Educational Experience"). Identify the level of education you have obtained and, if relevant, the degree you are working toward. If it is still early in your college career, list information about your high school diploma or equivalency; by the time you graduate, you probably won't need to include it. Some kinds of information are essential; others are optional, depending on how important they are to your case and to the specific rhetorical situation.

  Essential: Name and location of institution, inclusive dates of attendance, major, minor, degree obtained (or sought, with "date expected" listed)

  Optional: GPA, relevant courses taken, specializations, licenses and certificates obtained

2

- **Work Experience** ("Employment History" or "Employment"). Describe in detail any work experience that makes you a strong candidate and include all other experience relevant to the position. You needn't list every job you have ever had, but you do need to list all the recent ones. Employers will look for "gaps" in your employment history, so instead of leaving out recent jobs that seem irrelevant, list them briefly. A good "Work Experience" entry contains the position title, name and location of the company, dates of employment, and list of responsibilities.
- **References** ("List of References"). Employers expect you to provide references, either on request or on the resume itself. Be sure to talk to your references in advance, asking them if they can give you a good recommendation and letting them know what types of positions you plan to apply for. (If you are asking for letters of reference also, allow about 30 days for the letter-writing.)

Evaluating Your Resume's Design

Readers scanning a page tend to start in the top left corner and move down the page, left to right. Keep this in mind as you decide where to place information on your page and how to use typography and layout to draw the reader's eye.

- Is the contact information easy to find? Have you drawn the reader's eye to your name without overdoing it?
- Are columns of information aligned?
- Do section headings stand out clearly without taking too much space?
- Is each quarter of the page filled with about the same quantity of text?
- Have you used typography to draw attention to important information and to present detailed information legibly?
- Have you used white space (empty space) to help direct the reader's eye to important information? What will readers notice first?
- If readers had only 20 seconds to scan your resume, would they remember what you want them to remember?

typeface and font size, aligned consistently, and spaced the same distance from the text that comes before and after them.

- Group information to make it easier to grasp quickly. For example, consider using bulleted lists of your major responsibilities in your most relevant jobs to draw attention to each one.

Use contrast to show differences in the types or levels of information.

- The typefaces used for headings and body text should contrast with each other so that each type of information stands out. Sans serif typefaces such as Verdana, Geneva, Century Gothic, and Arial are good for headings in paper resumes, while serif faces like Times, Times New Roman, Garamond, and Palatino are easy enough to read to use as body text.
- Use indentations of various distances from the left margin to establish a visual hierarchy of information.

Make sure type is large enough to be legible. For serif fonts, use 11-point or larger type. You may be able to use 10-point sans serif fonts. For the body text, use a font no larger than 12 points. Do not try to squeeze in more information by reducing your font size.

Use white space to give readers' eyes a rest and to direct their attention. Your resume should have at least 1" margins all around, and within the text area there should be empty space around major headings so that they stand out from the rest of the words.

Maintain the right visual "attitude." For most applications, print your resume on a laser or high-quality inkjet printer, using only black ink on white or off-white paper. Most potential employers will not expect your resume to be flashy.

Removing an Automatically Inserted Hyperlink

On resumes and other documents meant to be printed, including underlined blue text—as if the reader might click on your email address while reading your resume on paper—seems nonsensical. Thus, it is a good idea to take out hyperlinks, like anywho@gmail.com, that are automatically inserted by your word processor. You can also turn off this automatic formatting function by clicking on the Office button and selecting Word Options > Proofing > AutoCorrect Options. Under the AutoFormat tab, uncheck the box next to "Internet and network paths with hyperlinks." Under the "AutoFormat As You Type" tab, also uncheck the box next to "Internet and network paths with hyperlinks." Here's how to remove hyperlinks from Microsoft Word 2007 or Word 2008 (Mac Office) documents with a mouse click:

On a PC,

1. Right-click anywhere on the hyperlink.
2. Select "Remove Hyperlink" from the pop-up menu.

On a Mac,

1. While holding down the Command key (⌘), click anywhere on the hyperlink.
2. Select "Remove Hyperlink" from the pop-up menu.

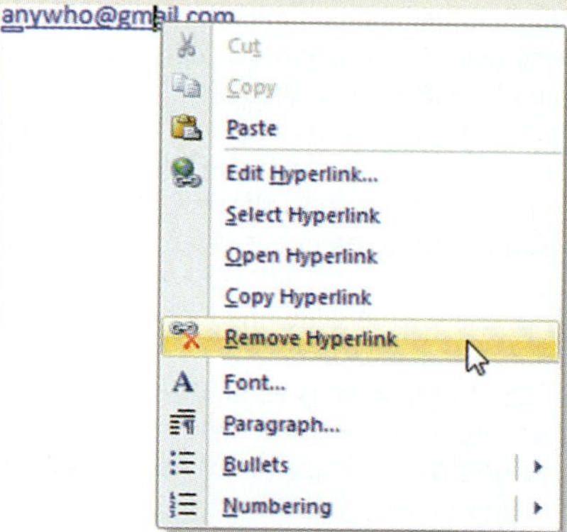

For instructions that apply to Microsoft® Word® 2003, visit the handbook's website: **cengage.com/english/blakesley**

Using Columns and Tables to Design a Resume

You can use your word processor's Table command to create perfectly aligned columns in your resume, rather than trying to use tabs or margin indentations. Once set in table columns, lists and other grouped information can be modified without much effort.

Suppose, for example, that you want to use two columns to list your relevant courses. In Microsoft Word 2007, you can do the following:

1. Place your cursor at the insertion point.
2. Select the Insert tab to show the Insert ribbon.
3. Select the down arrow beneath the Table icon.
4. Set the number of columns and rows; for a two-column list, you would choose two columns and one row. You can do this quickly by mousing over the boxes shown or by selecting "Insert Table," as shown to the right.
5. Leave "Fixed column width" set to Auto and readjust your column widths by placing your cursor over the table borders and dragging them to the desired width.

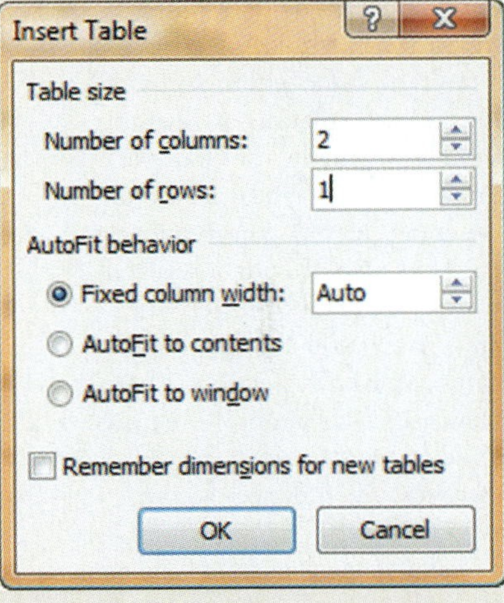

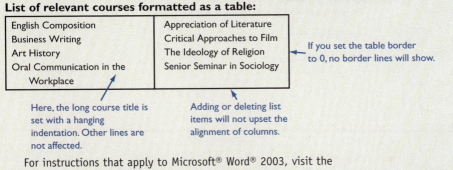

Word processors help you insert and format tables to control complex page layout precisely.

List of relevant courses formatted manually:

English Composition Appreciation of Literature
Business Writing Critical Approaches to Film
Art History The Ideology of Religion
Oral Communication in the Workplace Senior Seminar in Sociology

When you don't use a table, the long course title runs into the next column, forcing you to reformat all the lines.

List of relevant courses formatted as a table:

English Composition Business Writing Art History Oral Communication in the Workplace	Appreciation of Literature Critical Approaches to Film The Ideology of Religion Senior Seminar in Sociology

If you set the table border to 0, no border lines will show.

Here, the long course title is set with a hanging indentation. Other lines are not affected.

Adding or deleting list items will not upset the alignment of columns.

For instructions that apply to Microsoft® Word® 2003, visit the handbook's website: **cengage.com/english/blakesley**

Memoranda—memos, for short—are documents circulated within an organization that convey important information (announce upcoming events or policy changes, for example) or ask recipients to take some action (provide requested information or read the attached document, for example). Memos are important documents for keeping lines of communication open. They also provide a written historical archive of the activities of an organization and its people. In some well-known cases—the Enron case, for example—memos became the legal record of who knew what when during a company crisis.

Purposes of Memos

Your purpose in a memo should be to convey information or request action clearly and concisely. Your readers will likely spend only a few moments reading your memo, so it needs to get across the important information quickly. It may be tempting at times to be creative with your memos—to entertain as well as inform, for example—but realize that people may not respond positively to playfulness. Memos have a form and a moment, in other words, so careful writers use them judiciously to accomplish a specific purpose.

Sample Format for a Memorandum

Memorandum

To: List all primary recipients here, with full names, each separated by a comma
From: Author(s) of memo (Author should initial or sign here) *RP*
Author's title (if any and if customary in your organization)
Date: 23 February 2006
Subject: Concise but descriptive summary of memo's subject

Memoranda use a top-down structure, with the most important information listed first. In the introduction to your memo, you should state clearly what the memo is about. If you are writing an informative memo, you should give the most important information first. If you expect your readers to respond in some way, let them know what they need to do and, if relevant, the deadline they need to meet.

In your body paragraphs, provide further information or details regarding the subject of your memo, starting with the most important first. If you include dates, locations, or other information that you want people to access easily, you can use a list.

Event Title:
Time and Date:
Location:

You may have additional body paragraphs, but bear in mind that memos should generally be kept short so that readers can scan them quickly and access important information without misreading.

Close the memo with a short statement about how readers can request further information if any questions arise. You don't need to sign the memo at the bottom. However, you should identify any attached documents by title. If you are copying the memo to secondary recipients, you should identify them also.

Attachments: Planning Calendar

CC: John Jacob
Marisa Tomlinson

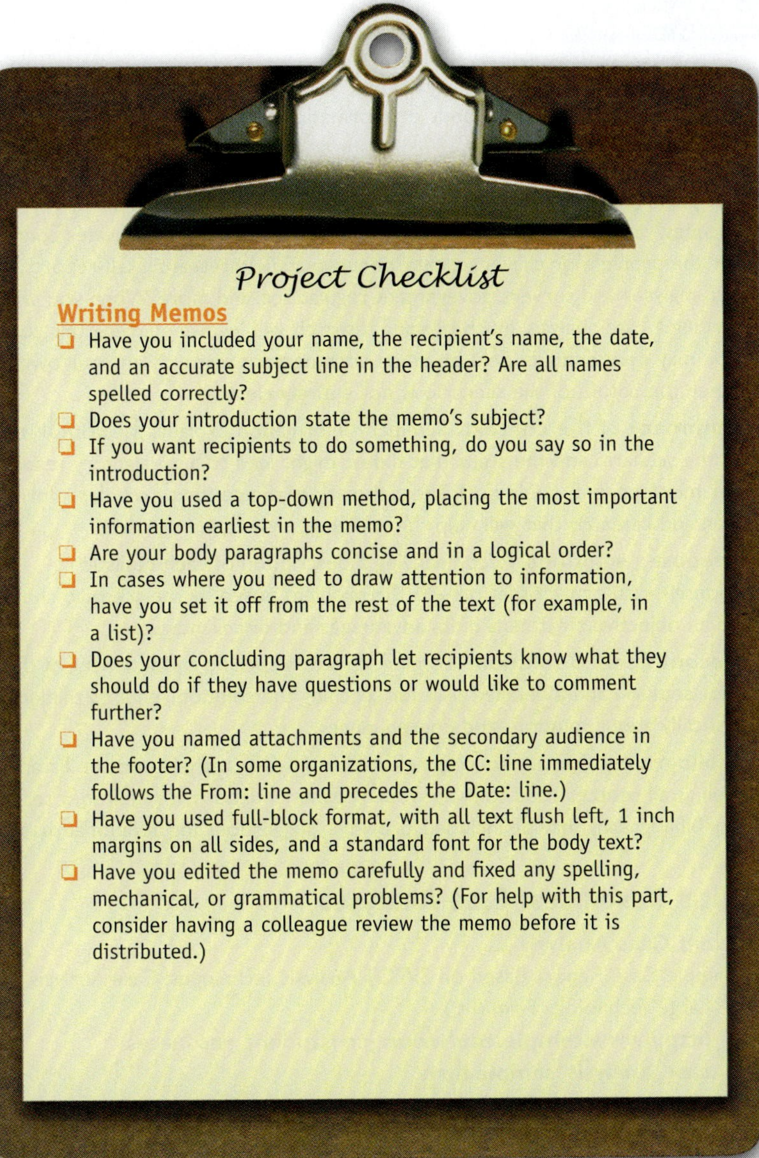

Project Checklist
Writing Memos
Have you included your name, the recipient's name, the date, and an accurate subject line in the header? Are all names spelled correctly?
Does your introduction state the memo's subject?
If you want recipients to do something, do you say so in the introduction?
Have you used a top-down method, placing the most important information earliest in the memo?
Are your body paragraphs concise and in a logical order?
In cases where you need to draw attention to information, have you set it off from the rest of the text (for example, in a list)?
Does your concluding paragraph let recipients know what they should do if they have questions or would like to comment further?
Have you named attachments and the secondary audience in the footer? (In some organizations, the CC: line immediately follows the From: line and precedes the Date: line.)
Have you used full-block format, with all text flush left, 1 inch margins on all sides, and a standard font for the body text?
Have you edited the memo carefully and fixed any spelling, mechanical, or grammatical problems? (For help with this part, consider having a colleague review the memo before it is distributed.)

Primary and Secondary Audiences for Memos

The primary audience for a memo consists of the person or people who have the responsibility to address the memo or make note of the information it contains. The primary audience should be listed in the To: line. The secondary audience consists of people who need to be aware of the contents of the memo but who do not need to act on it. The secondary audience is not directly responsible for responding to the memo.

In the workplace, you will likely spend time analyzing complex situations—for your managers or for clients—to support recommendations on policy changes, organizational action, or a formal response to some issue or opportunity. You may, for example, want to explore an opportunity to create a new product or implement a new process to improve production. When you write up the results of your analysis, your purpose is to persuade readers that your recommended solution is the best one.

Audience for the Case Analysis

The case analysis is a useful document for people who have the responsibility and the power to make important decisions. Your readers will rely on the accuracy of your research and the credibility of your analysis in making their decisions, so be especially mindful that your writing conveys an effective ethos.

Similar Genres

Feasibility studies are like case analyses, except that the focus is on studying the past to anticipate future costs and consequences. Market analyses focus on field research to determine whether a product is worth developing further. The results of such research are typically presented in a recommendation report (page 237).

Features of a Case Analysis

A case analysis provides five kinds of information within a persuasive framework:

- **Clear statement of the problem.** A scenario description explains or poses the problem, challenge, or situation that has been studied. Scenarios, or "scenes," can be constructed by drawing from anything that provides context for the problem or challenge: data, documents, field research, self-reports, market analyses and surveys, government regulations, and more. When you are writing a case analysis, much of your research will involve studying this context. You may even conduct field or other documentary research on your own when the nature of the scenario is not entirely clear.
- **Summary of the context.** Summary information explains the critical issues in the scenario and the steps that did or might lead to a satisfactory resolution (or missteps that would not). The summary of the context provides information and research that will help the audience understand the case.
- **Proposed solutions.** Accompanying a description of each realistic response—real or hypothetical—to the problem posed by the scenario should be an objective treatment of its advantages and disadvantages.
- **Recommended solution.** Coming up with a specific endorsement of the best solution and a detailed plan for reaching the solution requires thinking critically about solutions and consequences.
- **Bibliography.** Primary sources referred to in your analysis must be listed, as well as all sources used to make your recommendations. If required, a secondary bibliography may be included, providing suggestions for additional reading.

Digital Resources: Case Analyses

Student Case Analysis

Sample Case Report Based on SWOT Analysis Techniques: Case Analysis of a Large Technology Firm (Ltf):
http://www.temple.edu/writingctr/student_resources/case_analysis_sample.htm

How-To Guides and Professional Samples

A Model for Case Analysis and Problem Solving by Edward G. Wertheim:
http://web.cba.neu.edu/~ewertheim/introd/cases.htm

The Case Study by Robert W. Starinsky:
http://facweb.cti.depaul.edu/rstarinsky/case%20studies.htm

Features of White Papers

White papers have several important components, each of which should be clearly identifiable so that readers can move quickly through the document the first time and review its major components later with a glance.

- **Title page.** The title page lists the official title and subtitle, the names and professional titles of the authors, and any sponsoring organizations or companies. Some writers include a short table of contents on the title page or the page immediately following.
- **Executive summary.** The executive summary is often placed on the title page so that readers can decide quickly whether they need to read further. These summaries are *informative* (listing the essential points) rather than *descriptive* (announcing what the white paper will cover without giving precise details). (For further discussion of the differences between the two types of summary, see section 17c.)
- **Body or argument.** The body of a white paper is broken into chunks, each representing one piece of the larger puzzle. The body of a white paper may have several levels of headings, which clearly divide and subdivide information into logical units. All heads should be descriptive rather than generic. (Turn the page to see a comparison of descriptive and generic heads.) Descriptive heads help readers remember the main points of the white paper.
- **Conclusion.** A white paper may or may not have a formal conclusion that sums up the topic. If the issue remains unsettled, it can be helpful to readers to indicate that in a concluding section. The conclusion may mention what questions remain to be answered. Above all, it is important not to take sides on an issue too obviously, lest a reader believe all of the information presented is biased (even if it may indeed be so).

White papers are used in business, industrial, and governmental contexts to sum up what's known about a subject. The subject matter of white papers is often technical, and therefore writers have to pay special attention to the needs and expectations of readers. A white paper's credibility should be unquestioned; ethos is a major rhetorical appeal.

Purposes and Contexts of White Papers

In spirit, at least, a white paper represents the most accurate information—the facts—about a subject. A white paper appeals to a reader's desire for accurate and unbiased information. As you might expect, however, in practice white papers are not always as objective or factual as they seem to be. In fact, many organizations, including governments, use white papers to stake out a position on an issue by presenting information as if it were unambiguous or inarguable. Nowadays, organizations use white papers in their own self-interest to try to establish that their service or product represents the best—or only—solution to a problem. This tactic may be misleading because of the nature of the genre of white papers, but it is certainly understandable that an organization would be an advocate for its own service or product. As always, the decision about which type of white paper is most appropriate for a given situation depends on the purpose, the audience, and the rhetorical occasion.

White papers range in length from a few pages to hundreds of pages. In most cases, they are short documents; brevity best serves their purpose of explaining something clearly and convincingly.

Headings in a White Paper Should Be Descriptive

Effective Descriptive A- and B-Level Headings	Ineffective Generic Headings

Domestic and Foreign Economics of Open Source Software
  Open Source Software Is Economically Beneficial
  Open Source Software Benefits Programmers in Several Ways
  Open Source Software Benefits Big Business
Open Source Software on the Domestic Front
  Open Source Software Competes Effectively with Proprietary Software
  Microsoft Responds Negatively to Open Source Software Usage
  Government Uses Open Source Software to Save Money
	Economics of Open Source Software
	  Economics
	  Benefits
	  Effects
	Open Source Software on the Domestic Front
	  Competition
	  Microsoft
	  Government Use

Digital Resources: White Papers

Student White Papers

Government initiatives regarding open source and their successes and failures:
http://osddp.org/node/186

IBM and Novell: Investing in an Open Source Future:
http://osddp.org/node/242

How-To Guides and Professional Samples

How to Write White Papers, by Stelzner Consulting:
http://www.stelzner.com/copy-g-HowTo-whitepapers.php

White papers on environmental and consumer topics by the Public Interest Research Group (PIRG):
http://uspirg.org (select "Reports")

Parts of a Recommendation Report

- **Title page.** Include the title of the report, the name of the client for whom the report was written, the authors' names, and the submission date.
- **Overview.** In a brief description of the report, include a general analysis of the client's needs and the consulting team's proposed responses.
- **Background.** Naturally, clients like to know the foundations of the recommendations. Include information about the research conducted and the sources considered when formulating the recommendations.
- **Recommendations.** Divide the recommendations into explicit points, highlighted (with major headings, for example) so that the client will not miss any. Recommendations should be realistic, given the client's resources, and achievable with a reasonable amount of work and time. Often each recommendation has three components: (1) a description of the recommendation, including how it will help the client meet goals; (2) a rationale and explanation for the recommendation, including foreseeable benefits; and (3) an action plan describing exactly what steps the client would need to take to proceed.
- **Cost analyses.** Include an analysis and estimate of the cost factors involved. Visual representation of these costs in a table or chart will help clients understand at a glance how much they should expect to spend if they follow your recommendations. (For a discussion of the persuasive use of visuals in documents, see Chapter 24.) Break down costs for each recommendation and its components. Where possible, recommend vendors to your clients.
- **List of sources.** Properly cite all the sources used in writing the report, and also provide your client with a list "for further reading." Chances are that clients will want to verify and learn more about your recommendations. Giving them a head start will further demonstrate your commitment to them.
- **Appendixes.** Include further instructions, samples, glossaries, illustrations, and diagrams in separate appendixes.

Recommendation reports are detailed documents written directly to clients; as their name suggests, they make recommendations for taking action on some issue of importance. Recommendation reports, like case analyses, are built on detailed research, which may include field observations, client interviews, document analysis, surveys, and other means of gathering information. Recommendation reports are often written by a team of consultants who complete the research and write the report collaboratively.

Digital Resources: Recommendation Reports

Student Recommendation Report

OpenOffice.org Target Market Research and Analysis Report:
http://osddp.org/node/217

How-To Guide

A Model for Case Analysis and Problem Solving by Edward G. Wertheim:
http://web.cba.neu.edu/~ewertheim/introd/cases.htm

A table of contents for writing project threads appears on pages xv–xxii.

Scannable Resumes

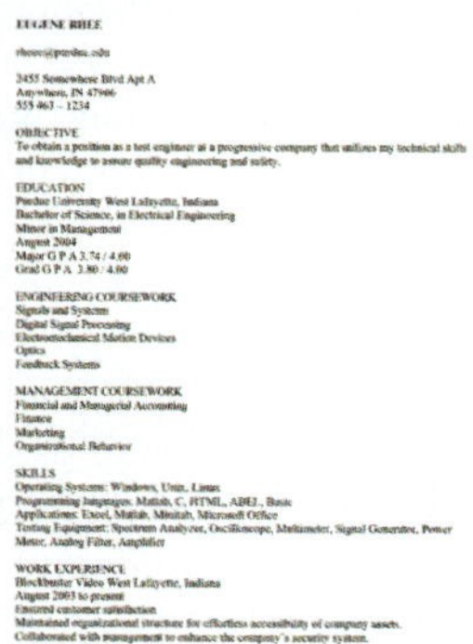

EUGENE RHEE

[illegible]

2455 Somewhere Blvd Apt A
Anywhere, IN 47906
555 463 – 1234

OBJECTIVE
To obtain a position as a test engineer at a progressive company that utilizes my technical skills and knowledge to assure quality engineering and safety.

EDUCATION
Purdue University West Lafayette, Indiana
Bachelor of Science, in Electrical Engineering
Minor in Management
August 2004
Major G P A 3.74 / 4.00
Grad G P A 3.80 / 4.00

ENGINEERING COURSEWORK
Signals and Systems
Digital Signal Processing
Electromechanical Motion Devices
Optics
Feedback Systems

MANAGEMENT COURSEWORK
Financial and Managerial Accounting
Finance
Marketing
Organizational Behavior

SKILLS
Operating Systems: Windows, Unix, Linux
Programming languages: Matlab, C, HTML, ABEL, Basic
Applications: Excel, Matlab, Minitab, Microsoft Office
Testing Equipment: Spectrum Analyzer, Oscilloscope, Multimeter, Signal Generator, Power Meter, Analog Filter, Amplifier

WORK EXPERIENCE
Blockbuster Video West Lafayette, Indiana
August 2003 to present
Ensured customer satisfaction
Maintained organizational structure for effortless accessibility of company assets.
Collaborated with management to enhance the company's security system.

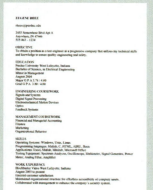

Understanding Key Differences between Traditional and Scannable Resumes

Many employers like to scan resumes into a digital database that they can search using keywords. Thus, a computer, not a person, will read your words. A scannable resume presents the same content as a traditional resume, but has two key differences:

- To ensure that the resume includes keywords that employers might look for, nouns and noun phrases are used instead of verbs to describe jobs, skills, and responsibilities. Read job ads in your industry to see which keywords to use.
- Formatting is removed.

Rewriting Your Resume for Scannability

1. Turn important verb phrases that describe your jobs and skills into nouns. For example, the phrase "wrote advertising copy" would become "advertising copywriter."
2. Remove commas between the items in lists and periods after lists or phrases. Place spaces between the words.
3. Create a keyword summary that describes your major qualifications in terms your industry would use, and place it at the end of the resume. Check the spelling of all key terms several times.

Don't worry if the content of your scannable resume seems less coherent than that of your traditional resume. Employers will be looking at specific qualifications, not at your scannable resume as a whole.

Reformatting Your Resume for Scannability

1. Remove all tables, columns, and special text positioning.
2. Place each element (such as a line of an address, a phone number, or a skill) on its own line. Remove all bulleted lists. (Replace bullets with asterisks [*].) Left-justify all content.
3. Change all text to a 10- or 12-point serif font such as Times New Roman.
4. Remove italics, underlining, and boldface.

The scannable version of your resume may be longer than your traditional resume; this is perfectly acceptable.

13

WRITING ON THE SPOT: ESSAY EXAMINATIONS

The ability to write well under pressure is an important skill. Not only are timed essay exams a part of college writing for most students, but the ability to write well and write quickly is important in many professions as well. This chapter focuses on the kinds of essay exams you'll be asked to take in college classes, but the skills you develop will serve you well in any number of other settings.

Two things are critical to doing well on essay examinations: (1) knowing the subject matter and (2) adopting a sensible approach to writing timed essays. Knowing the subject matter—that is, engaging with the course materials so that you are prepared to be tested—is outside the scope of this chapter. If you need more help learning the subject matter, you should consult your instructor or take advantage of the study skills resources found on your campus. Developing a sensible approach to writing timed essays is a relatively straightforward matter.

Common sense tells you that in a timed situation you want to understand the rules of the game before you begin. Ask your instructor any questions you have about the test before you take it—questions about whether the test is open or closed book, if you can bring a dictionary, whether you're supposed to use a blue pen or a number 2 pencil or if you can take the exam on a computer, if you can see sample questions or answers ahead of time, if the test will be given in a special location, or if you have to use a special kind of notebook.

Map out a schedule so that you will use your time wisely. You need to allot time for planning your response, time for writing your response, and time for proofing your response, giving the greatest priority to writing, the second to planning, and the least to proofing. Allot approximately one-quarter to one-third of your time for planning, including outlining your response; leave two-thirds to three-quarters for writing the exam, paring off a smidgeon of that time for proofing your work. Use your knowledge of your own writing processes as an aid in deciding how to proceed.

If an exam includes multiple short essay questions, you'll want to figure out how much time to allow for each, based on how heavily each question is weighted in your final score. Also, different instructors place different weights on spelling and punctuation in essay exams; clarify beforehand what your instructor wants so you'll know how much time to allot for proofreading.

Look at the clock, consider the number of questions you have to answer and the different amounts of time you want to allow for the different stages of the exam-writing process, and quickly jot down a schedule. Be somewhat flexible, but keep yourself on track.

Map Out a Schedule

Plan for a Single Question in a Two-Hour Exam

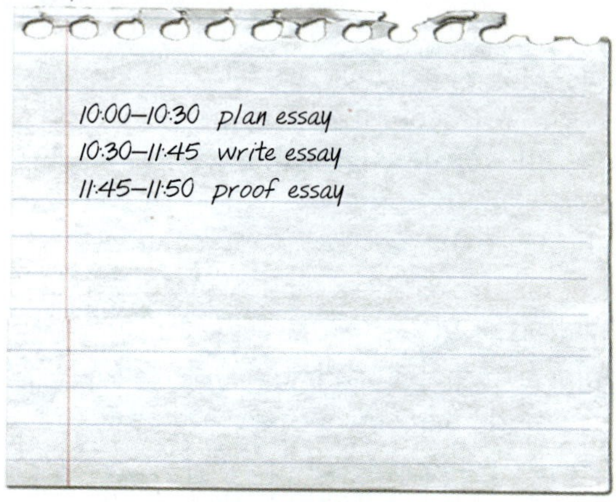

10:00–10:30 plan essay
10:30–11:45 write essay
11:45–11:50 proof essay

Plan for Multiple Questions in a Two-Hour Exam

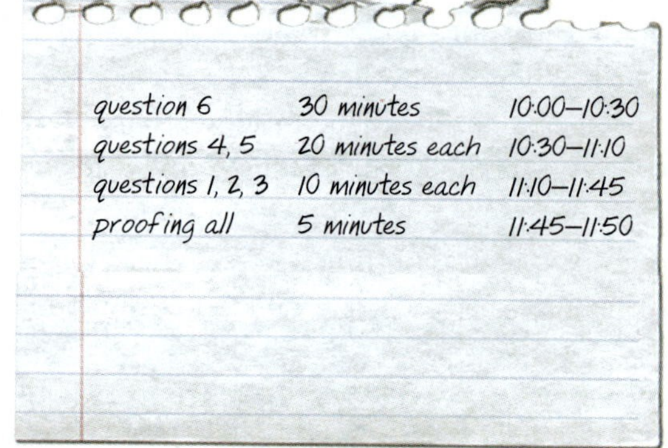

question 6 30 minutes 10:00–10:30
questions 4, 5 20 minutes each 10:30–11:10
questions 1, 2, 3 10 minutes each 11:10–11:45
proofing all 5 minutes 11:45–11:50

Key Terms for Understanding Exam Questions

Analyze: Divide a subject into its important parts, and examine each part separately and as it relates to the whole.

Argue: Take a position and support it with clearly articulated reasons and evidence.

Classify: Divide a large group into smaller groups based on shared characteristics.

Compare and contrast: Examine the similarities and differences between one thing and another.

Define: State the precise meaning of something and describe its essential properties. A definition is often followed by an example.

Describe: Systematically explain something, with attention to facts, details, and particulars. The term is often used to elicit a recounting or summarizing of course content.

Discuss: Present a close examination of something, considering as many important elements as you can. The term is often used to prompt an original argument and a demonstration of breadth of knowledge of a subject.

Evaluate, critique, assess: Give a reasoned, informed opinion, providing ample justification for your point of view.

Explain: Make a process, event, or idea clear and understandable. An explanation often breaks a subject into steps or categories, which are then appropriately amplified, illustrated, or supported by examples.

Explicate: Analyze a passage from a source text, explaining what lines or sentences mean in context, while also noting the ways in which the source text may be interpreted (or has been interpreted by others). An explication is sometimes referred to as a "close reading" of a text.

Illustrate, give examples: Develop, support, or clarify by providing examples.

Review: Provide a general survey (sometimes chronological, sometimes organized by other principles), critically evaluate, or reexamine. The term has different meanings depending on the context. Make sure you understand how it's being used before you answer the exam question.

Review the literature: Name and summarize the major sources of information and research on the subject. A review of the literature usually evaluates sources critically in light of their relevance and importance to the topic at hand.

Summarize: Present the substance of the material in a condensed form. Summaries are comprehensive but brief—often just a paragraph or sentence.

Begin planning your essay by carefully evaluating the exam question. What precisely is the instructor asking for? Rewrite, underline, or highlight keywords as necessary. If your essay—however well informed or well written—fails to address the exam question, you will not meet the terms of the assignment. Don't get ahead of yourself and rush through the question in a panic to begin, only to find you've written on the wrong topic entirely. In some cases, the time you take to understand the question—and even to take issue with some of the terms it uses or the perspective it seems to present—can be the most critical step of the process because it helps you shape your approach carefully and thoughtfully, which leads to good writing.

Outlining your response and drafting a thesis statement are perhaps the most critical steps for keeping your essay on track. They are combined here in recognition that different writers work differently. Some do their strongest work if they first draft an outline, then write the essay, and only then write the thesis paragraph. Others work best by first drafting the thesis statement and then outlining the more detailed progression of their ideas in response to the thesis paragraph. In either case, you'll need to approach the task in a compressed and straightforward manner. In a timed essay, you should be as deliberate and matter-of-fact in your approach as possible. There's not much wiggle room for false starts or feel-your-way-as-you-go wanderings.

A timed essay response should present a clear argument in a well-organized and well-supported fashion. In essence, you want to observe the guidelines for writing a strong essay or research paper in miniature. Begin with a strong thesis statement; advance your argument step by step logically; signal the progression of the argument clearly with appropriate transition phrases or other rhetorical strategies; support each point appropriately as you advance; finish with a strong conclusion that summarizes your points.

A Comparison of Successful and Unsuccessful Responses

Sample Exam Question

You are a biologist in charge of managing an oak-forest ecosystem in the northeastern United States. Citizens in your state are concerned about Lyme disease. What factors must you consider in managing outbreaks of Lyme disease? Describe the relevant ecological web in as much detail as possible and evaluate the pros and cons of various management strategies. Use scientific terminology as appropriate.

Excerpt from Successful Student Essay

First paragraph sets up the factors to be considered.

Although Lyme disease is carried by ticks, researchers have determined that major outbreaks of Lyme disease in oak-forest ecosystems in the northeastern United States result from complex interactions among oaks, ticks, and deer and rodents. These interactions can in turn affect gypsy moth, song bird, and predator populations. Balancing the effects of these interactions is a complex matter. While reducing the mouse population does reduce incidence of Lyme disease, it also increases incidence of gypsy moth outbreaks, which are especially devastating to oaks (oak leaves being one of the gypsy moth's favorite foods). While citizens want less Lyme disease, they also want healthy oaks and—oaks being the dominant species in the oak-forest system—healthy forests. Current research suggests that the best approach is to maintain both mice and gypsy moths at reasonable population levels by enhancing biodiversity.

The Ecological Web of Lyme Disease

Oaks and Acorns. The ecological web of Lyme disease begins with the dominant species in the northeastern oak-forest system, the oak. One of the oak's strategies for escaping seed predation is masting: every so often oaks produce a bumper crop of acorns. Masting helps oaks reproduce successfully by outsmarting animals that feed on acorns. Take mice as an example. Mouse populations fluctuate in response to the availability of acorns. In bumper acorn years, there are more mice. In leaner acorn years, there are fewer mice. Likewise, in leaner acorn years, most of the acorns get eaten; but in mast years, so many acorns are produced that there are not enough mice to eat them all. In mast years, more acorns are left to become oak seedlings. . . .

Response is well organized, and transitional phrases and headings help the reader follow the train of thought.

Main assertion for the paragraph

Appropriately supported by evidence and detail

The student went on to describe the major relationships among species that lead to an increase of Lyme disease. A second major section, called "Expanding the Web," then included strategies for managing Lyme disease, the pros and cons of management choices, and a more complete description of the web of ecological interactions.

A timed essay exam is not the place for dramatic rhetorical flourishes. It's not the place to worry about whether a sentence is elegant, so long as it is grammatical. Make the points you need to make, paragraph by paragraph, in the clearest and simplest language possible. Certainly, you should write as well as you possibly can under the circumstances, but for the most part a timed essay is a place to demonstrate knowledge rather than a place to show what a great writer you are. Use clear, grammatical sentences and correct spelling and punctuation. Say what needs to be said in response to the question.

Although the bulk of your attention must go to preparing for and writing the essay, in most cases you'll want to leave some time at the end to reread what you wrote, make simple insertions or changes, and correct grammar, spelling, and punctuation. Different instructors weight these kinds of errors differently—you may want to consult your instructor beforehand so you'll know how much time to allot to this stage of the process.

Don't waste time recopying your writing onto a pristine sheet of paper. Instead, show changes as neatly and clearly as possible with carets, lines, and inserted punctuation. Don't get sidetracked trying to make major changes in your argument—clarify your argument before you write. Finally, if you must leave an essay or part of an essay unfinished, try at least to jot down your ideas or sketch a simple outline at the end so the instructor can see where your response might have headed.

Unsuccessful Student Essay

Vague opening doesn't suggest a specific approach to the question →

More and more people are concerned about Lyme disease in more and more parts of the country. And the consequences are serious: arthritis, heart damage, nerve damage. Many people are now afraid to go hiking because of Lyme disease. Deer contribute to Lyme disease, as do mice. Both are hosts to the vector for the disease, which is ticks. Acorns are an important food source for mice and deer, which is one reason why oaks are the dominant species in forests that have ticks. The more acorns there are, the more mice there are, and the more mice there are, the more ticks there'll be. But mice also eat gypsy moth larva, which is a good thing.

Irrelevant detail → (afraid to go hiking because of Lyme disease.)

The response would be more successful if specific processes were described in detail. →

Deer carry ticks in the fall and thereby contribute to Lyme disease. As with the mice, the more deer you have, the more ticks you'll get too.

Nobody likes Lyme disease, but if the gypsy moths get out of hand they can ruin the forest because they'll eat all the oak leaves right off the trees.

This short paragraph just restates part of the question rather than providing an answer to it. →

Biologists who manage forests try to maintain a balance between the mice and the moths and the ticks. And this just shows the web of life, with each species affecting the others.

PART 3

Conducting Research

New Contexts for Writing

Hypertext and the Semantic Web

The Internet is evolving into a new digital ecosystem where everyone plays a part in writing, developing, sharing, and learning new content. The Semantic Web, also called Web 2.0, is a new vision of the Internet. Originally, the Internet was a collection of millions of pages on thousands of servers around the globe, connected only by hyperlinks. In the Semantic Web, writers, bloggers, and Web authors have their content (or data) networked—connected and refreshed automatically and quickly.

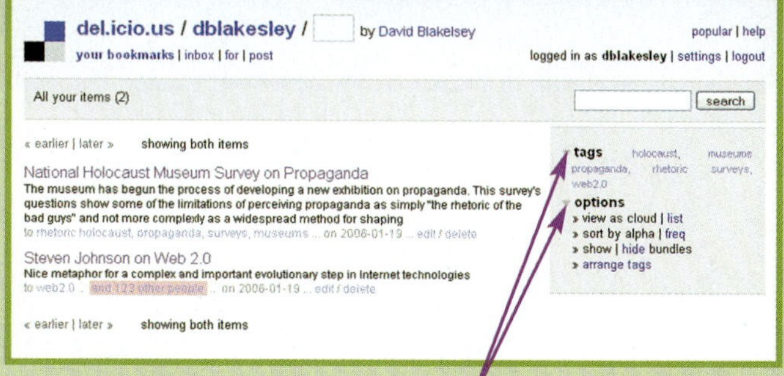

This image of **del.icio.us,** a Web 2.0 free service for "social" (shared) bookmarking, shows tags and bundles in action. Users can track keywords as they appear in other sites in del.icio.us and on the Internet with just a few clicks.

Hypertext is text and information connected across Web pages and websites by **hyperlinks.** Hyperlinks, or **links,** are the directional pointers that, when clicked, tell a Web browser to retrieve new content from an Internet server. In **Web 1.0,** information was interconnected through these links, which function like signposts pointing the way.

In **Web 2.0,** or the **Semantic Web,** information is still linked, but sharing and republishing links is automated, allowing new content to be assembled, distributed, and linked on the fly by **RSS** ("Really Simple Syndication") feeds that scour the Web for new content, **aggregators** that assemble this new content, and **social networks,** where people connect with information and each other. Information is connected semantically using **keywords** and **metatags,** both of which function like terms in an index and help people locate shared interests and allow computers to create "bundles" of meaning.

Information Flows

In the Web 2.0 model, we have thousands of services scrutinizing each new piece of information online, grabbing interesting bits, remixing them in new ways, and passing them along to other services. . . . Information in this new model is analyzed, repackaged, digested, and passed on down to the next link in the chain. It flows.

— Steven Johnson
"Web 2.0 Arrives"
Discover 26.10 (October 2005)
http://www.discover.com/issues/oct-05/departments/emerging-technology/

Link, Ping, and Tag Your Way to a Research Network

Share bookmarks and network with other researchers on your topic:
del.icio.us: http://del.icio.us

Tap some RSS feeds or feed some content yourself:
Technorati: http://www.technorati.com

Tag your digital images in a folksonomy:
FlickR: http://www.flickr.com

Only Connect . . . >

14

CONCEPTUALIZING THE RESEARCH PROJECT

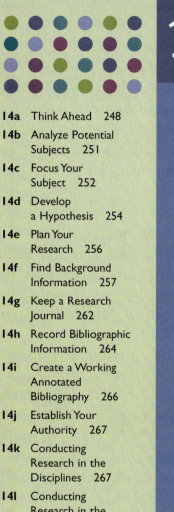

Research projects typically involve posing problems and answering questions about a subject that you want to learn about or that you think others should understand better. You may find it hard to sustain your own or your reader's interest without this exigency, which is the feeling of urgency, curiosity, and need that motivates good writing. It's hard to write well about subjects that you don't care about or that no one else wants or needs to know about. Sometimes it's also hard to care about every subject that crosses your path or to ask questions about subjects you have never encountered. Nevertheless, we do and must write every day—in courses, to friends and family, to others who share our interests, and even to ourselves. So what can you do?

Get motivated to do research. The urgency associated with writing from curiosity and need doesn't just arise magically. Good writers learn how to care about their subjects by exercising their natural inclination to learn new things, right wrongs, uncover new truths, or discover complexity in the superficially obvious aspects of everyday life. There's always more there than meets the eye. For example, the writer John McPhee began to write about oranges for a short magazine article in the mid-1960s but soon learned that even with something as familiar as an orange you find histories, stories, and significance. He ended up writing an entire book called *Oranges* (1967) because he learned more as he dug further. He learned to care. Oranges *are* interesting!

In the end, McPhee's book, *Oranges,* says much about our relationship with nature, about ecology, and about the human struggle to survive. Perhaps most important for our purposes, it was by approaching his subject methodically that McPhee learned to care.

By researching his subject carefully, taking notes, and being open to new connections, he found that there was more to oranges than he (or anyone) might ever have imagined.

For McPhee and all good writers, the research process is a craft. This chapter will teach you what its components are and how to make it work for you as well as it has worked for others.

Activity 14-1: Getting Motivated to Find a Subject

Get motivated by responding in writing to the following questions about possible research subjects.

1. What subjects are you passionate about or would you like to learn more about? (List at least three.) Why do you care about these subjects? How did you learn to care about them?
2. What subjects do you *need* to know more about? (List at least three.) How do you know you need to know more about these subjects?
3. Why would anyone want to learn about these subjects?
4. What would someone need or want to know about these subjects?

From your writings, choose three subjects to explore in later activities.

14a Manage the Research Process by Thinking Ahead

Many writers view research projects with fear and trembling. When you are asked to write a dozen pages or write and design an informative website about an unfamiliar topic, the research process can seem daunting, even overwhelming. One natural reaction is to procrastinate, postponing the bulk of the work until just before the project's due date. If instead you plan ahead and immerse yourself in your subject early—right after you receive the assignment, for instance—you'll find managing the research project far less intimidating than it initially appears to be.

By planning your time and undertaking your project systematically, you will learn to conceptualize the research process. Planning will help you discover what research is and how to do it, and we hope you will look forward to it

Develop a research hypothesis.
Select a research subject.

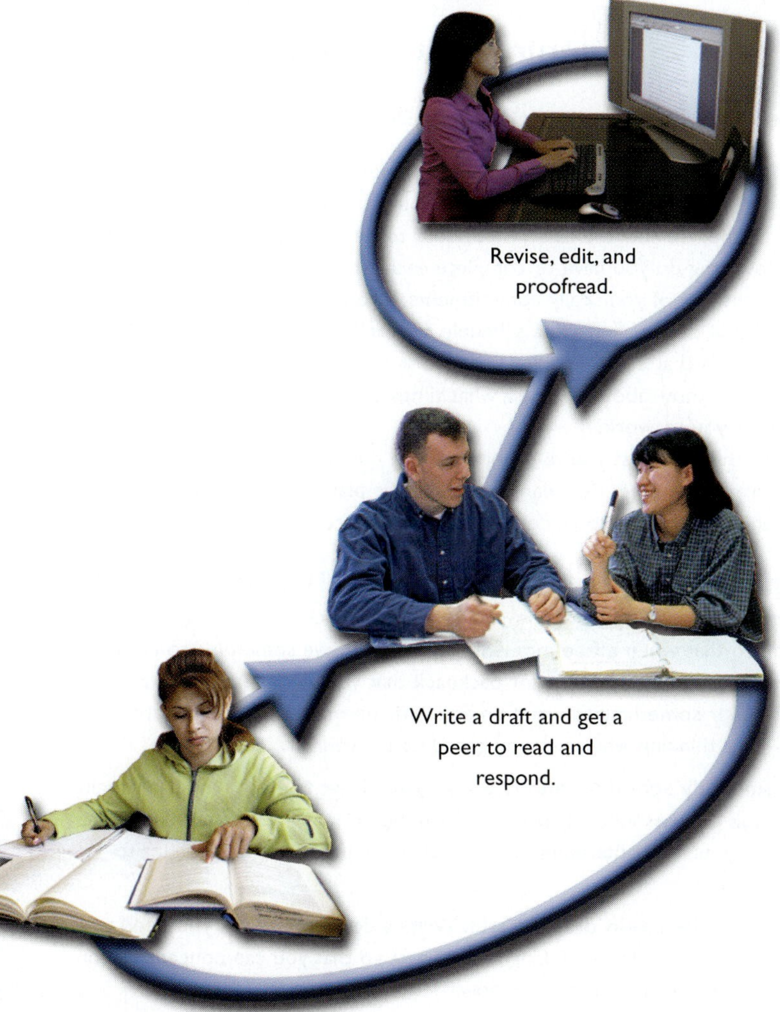
Revise, edit, and proofread.
Write a draft and get a peer to read and respond.
Conduct background research and think. Then do focused research.

next time as an interesting challenge. When you've reached that point, you will be ready for new research projects as they come your way in college, and afterward in your professional and civic life.

Take It One Step at a Time

There's a saying, "A journey of 1000 miles begins with a single step." A research project can seem intimidating, but, in reality, like almost everything else you have done so far, it is easily broken down into manageable steps and processes. By focusing on one small part at a time, you can complete even the most complex projects.

Make Research a Habit

Be realistic about time management. There are only so many hours in the day that are going to be useful for managing a research project. Some people like to get up early and write for a couple of hours in the morning when they feel most creative. They may do online searching and emailing in the evening because it does not require quite the same attentiveness as crafting sentences does.

Ask questions about your daily and weekly schedule:

- What do I have to do during the day?
- During each day, when are my free hours or free minutes?

- What days or times during the day can I be alone or can I go to the library?

Most people with busy lives benefit from making a daily list of things to do. Computers, PDAs, handhelds, and even cell phones now typically have calendaring functions that can help you plan your day. Use one of these calendars or a printed day-planner. And take the bold step of adding "Research __________ today for one hour." Taking the initiative to write down your intention will help make it happen: writing motivates more writing. By planning and tracking the stages of the project, you'll also know when it's time to move from one stage to another. You'll learn as you go how to gauge what you can accomplish in an hour or two. But accomplish something. It may be a small breakthrough, such as a new way of seeing your topic, or it might be five pages of brilliant prose. Either way, the incremental gain is important. Establish momentum.

Make the research and writing into a routine. Like starting to exercise, establishing a writing routine may be difficult at first, but after a while you won't be able to function until you've had your research fix. Write or read on the bus. Talk to a friend about your research subject. Email a question to someone. Keep the subject alive in your mind so that you give it a chance to grow.

Activity 14-2: Planning Your Research Process

Make time for your research by completing the following steps.

1. Using as a guideline the stages of the research process shown in the graphic on pages 248–249, create a to-do list for your current research project. After you've finished, review the list: What needs to be done first? In the middle? Last? How long do you have to complete each step?
2. Make a schedule of your daily commitments. If your schedule changes based on the day of the week, make a schedule for each day that is different. Where are there gaps that could be filled with work on your research project? Based on what you know about yourself, what times of the day would be most productive for you to work?
3. Combine the to-do list you've generated with the available time you've identified to create a project calendar. Write specific plans, goals, and deadlines on the calendar, and use it to guide your research process.

Strategies for Developing a System for Time Management

- **Plan for the unexpected.** Always keep a book, article, or printed Web pages with you so that when a free moment arises you'll have something to read. Carry writing with you in a bag or backpack that you always use. Have a laptop, a PDA, or something to write on and with, no matter where you are. Record your thinking whenever you get ideas for your project.
- **Plan your daily schedule and then do your best to keep to it.** Maintain a date book that has a lot of space for each day so that you can take notes, summarize your thoughts, and make lists of other things you don't want to forget.
- **Write out daily to-do or task lists.** Writing down the things you need to remember helps you stop thinking about them so that you can concentrate on what you need to pay attention to now.

Activity 14-3: Analyzing Subjects

Take notes as you ponder these questions relative to three of the potential subjects you wrote about in Activity 14-1.

The Rhetorical Situation

1. What is going on—on campus, in your community, or in the world—that relates to these subjects?
2. What purpose will you ultimately have in communicating your research? Will you teach readers? Persuade them? Delight them?
3. What period of time do you have to complete the project?
4. How long should your final project be?

Analyze the Subject

5. Given the rhetorical situation, is your subject too large and unwieldy? (Even writing about oranges and their history can get out of hand, so be careful to focus. Good writers can make sharp ideas go a long way.)
6. Is your subject too narrow? Or is it irrelevant to the assignment? (For instance, why *you* like oranges may be personally interesting, but you'll find it hard to prove that you actually do like them or to persuade anyone else that learning more about why *you* like them is worth the effort.)
7. Is this subject something that you can find information about—more than what is commonly known? (For example, many book writers have tried to explain the Kennedy assassination, but at some point they all run up against the fact that much of the information is still protected in the National Archives or otherwise not easily retrieved. In the film *JFK,* director Oliver Stone had to invent a character, X, who could reveal top-secret information.)
8. Will your subject interest your readers *and* fulfill the assignment? (For instance, how sneakers are made in Asia in horrible working conditions by children who are paid meager wages might be a subject that you can learn more about and that will be interesting to sneaker owners and to those concerned about the exploitation of children.)

You can choose one of the three potential subjects from Activity 14-1 to work on now, or you can take more time to think about your choice. Remember that your research subject should interest you because you will be working on it in depth and perhaps for quite some time.

Once you have chosen several potential subjects to research, ask questions like those in Activity 14-3 about your subject, the assignment context (including its purpose), the broader social context of your writing, and your audience.

You should learn enough about your subject so that you can pose and respond to a problem. For instance, suppose you have decided that national security is a decent topic; you want to focus on the invasion of civil liberties or on how much privacy a person is entitled to in the face of threats to national security. Since your intended audience already knows that these concerns relate to the topic of national security, you will want to find a unique approach or a problem that has not yet been considered. Perhaps you could focus on threats to the privacy of online communication. Can the government eavesdrop on people's email without their knowledge? Let's say that the information you find suggests that clandestine eavesdropping on email is something that is already happening. You might want to craft a survey to ask people what level of privacy they think they should have in the face of threats to national security. Alternatively, you might want to conduct research to find out what countermeasures are being taken to protect email privacy. Perhaps some new technology has been introduced that will increase the level of privacy.

Activity 14-4: Exploring Your Subject

As you refine your subject, use these strategies to learn more about it.

1. Discuss possible topics with your instructor, classmates, friends, family, or other interested people.
2. If you know people who are knowledgeable about your subject, ask them whether they know of any hot issues that you could explore.
3. Do Web and/or library searches for popular news articles about your subject.
4. Using search engines such as Google, search for websites about your topic.
5. Look through Internet discussion groups such as Yahoo! Groups, located at **http://groups.yahoo.com**, or L-Soft's CataList, at **http://www.lsoft.com/catalist.html**, to see if there are any mailing lists that relate to your subject.
6. Use a search engine such as the Google Glossary™ to locate definitions of important terms or phrases. Go to **http://www.google.com**; then, in the search box, enter define:*yourterm*. Google will return a list of definitions drawn from reliable websites and provide links to those sites where you can learn more about the terms and phrases you're looking for. Let serendipity guide you early in the process. Be open to new discoveries.
7. Browse the library or a bookstore for magazines, newspapers, or books related to your topic.

Activity 14-5: Collaborative Practice: Focusing Subjects

Consider the following list of possible general research topics. Select three and, individually or in a group, narrow each one down into a more manageable research subject.

Advertising and its effect on society
Affirmative action and minorities
Agriculture in today's world
Business and ethics
Celebrities and the law
Changing gender roles
Contemporary architecture
Contemporary journalism
Crime, the justice system, and prisons
Domestic abuse
Domestic responses to terrorism and other emergencies
Forms of communication
Gambling addiction
Homeschooling and social life/sports
Immigration and the law
International relations and war
Job market, the loss of American jobs overseas, and international trade

National economy
Politics and the media/the politics of the media
Private versus public education
Proliferation of television channels
Religion in America and the world
Resource conservation
Single parents and traditional families
Taxes, income levels, and fairness

This is the way you begin formulating a research problem. Out of the problem, there should emerge a research hypothesis or a potential solution to the problem.

Activity 14-6: Focusing Your Subject

As you think about your approach to your research topic, consider these questions, which will help you focus your subject.

- **Brainstorm.** What do people think about it? Why? How long has this topic been an issue in society? How does it affect people's lives?
- **Review texts that discuss your topic.** What has already been said? What solutions have been proposed to problems associated with your topic? Have any solutions been tried? Are people satisfied with the state of your issue/topic?
- **Consider the elements of your issue.** How long has it been an issue? Who is affected? Where and when does the problem occur? Does it primarily affect a certain group of people? Is money involved? How? Is money part of the problem, or is money a possible solution to the problem?
- **Compile ideas about problems and solutions.** What have you discovered so far about your issue? What new questions do you have in light of your recent discoveries about the topic?
- **Rethink whether the problem is important and your response is realistic.** Is this problem significant? Is your solution feasible? Who will fund your solution if it needs financial support? Would you pay extra taxes for the solution? Would others? Where and when are the benefits going to emerge? Who will be affected primarily if your problem is solved? Are there any secondary benefits?

The process of narrowing a broad subject into a hypothesis—a tentative proposition about the subject—requires time for reading, thinking, and writing. Once you have figured out what subject you want to research, begin considering the various elements or aspects of that subject. Look for new angles, trends, and ideas concerning your subject. It may help to consider what local perspectives there may be on your subject or how your subject affects you, your family, and/or your social group. Move toward discovering a unique angle or perspective that offers you a problem to solve or an opportunity to analyze your subject in a new light. This may sound time-consuming, but it makes common sense: You want to develop a research subject that is focused enough to be manageable in the limited time you are offered. You also want to find a way of writing something fresh about your subject.

Example: Developing a Hypothesis about Online Communities

Here's an example of one way to develop a hypothesis on the subject of online communities.

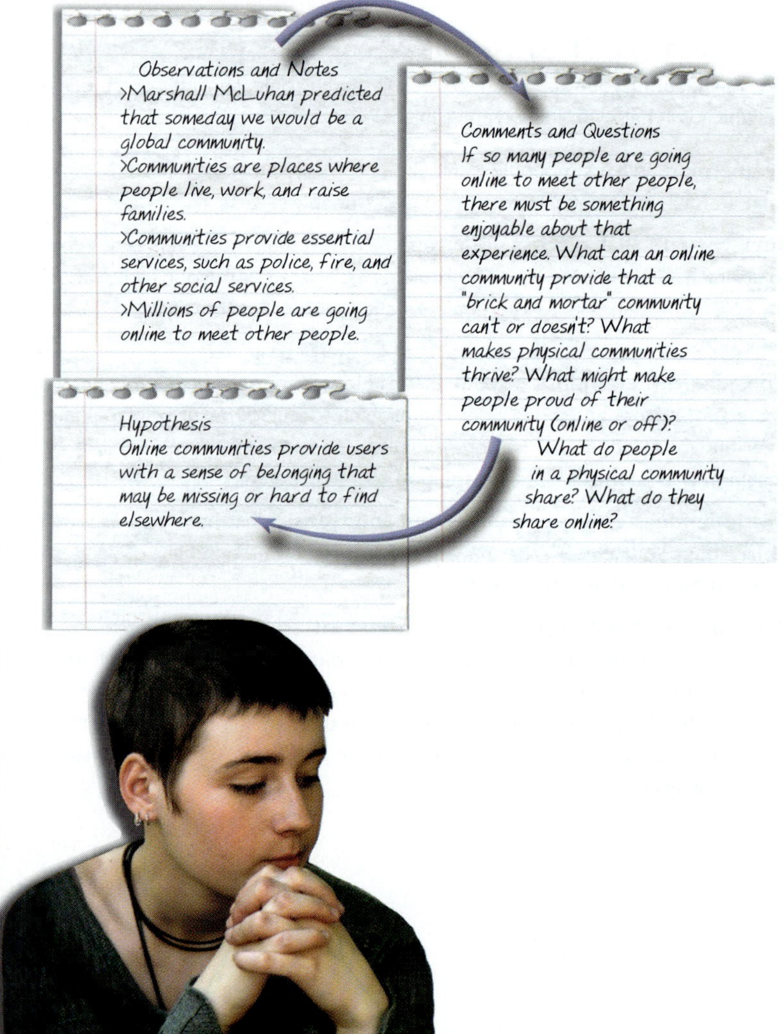

Observations and Notes
>Marshall McLuhan predicted that someday we would be a global community.
>Communities are places where people live, work, and raise families.
>Communities provide essential services, such as police, fire, and other social services.
>Millions of people are going online to meet other people.
Comments and Questions
If so many people are going online to meet other people, there must be something enjoyable about that experience. What can an online community provide that a "brick and mortar" community can't or doesn't? What makes physical communities thrive? What might make people proud of their community (online or off)? What do people in a physical community share? What do they share online?
Hypothesis
Online communities provide users with a sense of belonging that may be missing or hard to find elsewhere.

Student Example: Shanti Kanwar's Research Problem

Standardized test scores continue to fall for high school students, yet college admissions continue to rise.	Subject
Have the tests changed over time? Are the tests tougher? Do the tests assess what is taught? What groups are affected by test scores? Do some groups remain constant in their scores? Have certain groups underscored historically? Why is this? What has been done to correct this? Why are more students attending college? How do they pay for college? Do they take out loans? How do college educated workers fare in this job market compared to non-college educated workers? What do employers look for in college graduates? Future employees?	Questions that research into this topic provoked
More and more colleges are offering basic skills courses that help students catch up and become prepared for college.	Issue discovered while considering the questions
Are there more underprepared students today than there were ten years ago? Are these students from certain geographic areas, socioeconomic classes, or ethnicities? Are the basic skills courses really a problem for anyone? Do they work? How do these students do in college after taking the courses?	More questions that this research provoked
Why are these college students unprepared? Is this a political issue? Is there more than one side debating this issue? How has politics caused this problem? Can politics answer this problem? How will political factors cloud the issue and color the information?	Focus developing out of questions and research
How many students entering college take basic skills courses? How many students are underprepared for college? What kinds of academic support are they offered?	Revised research question
Basic skills courses work better when there is a support network of peers and tutors. Summer programs that help prepare students for college seem to work even better than regular semester basic skills courses. These summer programs are often called bridge programs.	Proposed research hypothesis after further research
The percentage of students who remain in college and graduate is higher for students who take summer bridge programs than for students who take basic skills courses during the regular semester.	Research information discovered
Because they more often lead to college graduation, summer bridge programs are more effective than basic skills courses.	Research hypothesis

Consider where and how you will find information related to your research hypothesis. This is the stage that might cause you to abandon an unwieldy research topic. If you have dreams of using this research project to fulfill your goal of conducting field observations on the parenting rituals of Midwestern American prairie dogs but you live in North Carolina, now is the time to be realistic about the challenges of getting to your observation site. Similarly, if you want to find out what Langston Hughes thought of another writer but you live in Arizona, you will need to determine whether the information will be accessible by some means other than by perusing his personal library at Lincoln University.

When researching, start with the most general ideas and move to the particular. Find broad overviews and definitions first and then look for recent, specific information in articles, in books, and on websites.

With online research in particular, sometimes people get sidetracked very early in the process by overly particular information and never get to see the "big picture" that books and magazine or journal

Moving from General to Specific Ideas

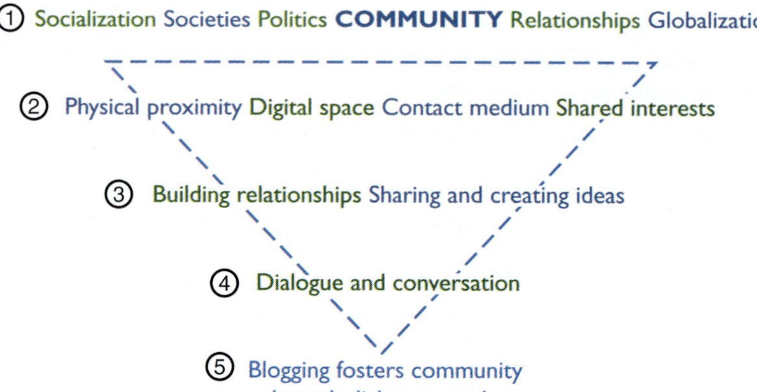

This inverted pyramid shows how you can move from general to particular topics and ideas. Here, the top-level terms describe general notions of human community. Level 2 describes how that community takes shape and why. Level 3 shows some effects of community. Level 4 lists an important part of the process of building community. The bottom level comes to a more specific topic and thesis: the idea that weblogs build community only when they encourage dialogue among bloggers, not when they focus exclusively on reporting public (or even personal) news.

Activity 14-7: Considering the Logistics of Potential Research

Consider the logistics of your potential research. Think about how you will handle the research, from finding information and equipment to traveling to locate information.

- Is the subject currently in the news?
- Which media are covering the topic the most?
- Is the topic so recent that finding sources might be difficult?
- Where will I find the most complete information about the topic?
- How will I initially determine the best sources so that I can learn more?
- Has this topic been selected by half the class already? Will I have to compete with others for materials?
- If the subject includes extensive visual elements (such as modern art or film), can I find the equipment necessary to view and analyze it? Do I need access to a DVD player or a microfiche machine? Can I find and use this equipment?
- Will I need to conduct field research to find more information?

articles offer. That happens in part because Internet search engines don't pay much attention to information architecture (how information is structured, arranged, and presented); they focus more on where information is located and how many other sites link to it (referred to by Google as "page rank"). So be careful when you're conducting research online that you also find general sources. If you want to write about digital communities on the Internet, the first source you read should probably not be a three-year-old discussion of Apache release Beta 1.84 at Slashdot (http://www.slashdot.com).

Find Background Information 14f

Once you have established your research question or problem, start gathering information. The following methods can help you establish a context for your hypothesis.

Track the Names of People Associated with Your Subject

Begin by noting, as you come across them, the names of people and texts that are cited in articles and stories about your topic. Some people or sources will emerge as authoritative after you've learned more about the subject.

Generate Keywords

Use keywords to look on the Web for information. **Keywords** are words or phrases, often nouns or noun phrases, that describe an element of your research question. Write down important words that appear in the hypothesis, important words from texts that you read as you do research, and synonyms for these terms. (Chapters 15 and 16 provide more information about how to use library resources and search engines effectively.)

Define Terms

Start with a good dictionary. *Merriam-Webster's Unabridged Dictionary* and the *Oxford English Dictionary* (*OED*) are the standard reference works for researching the meaning and derivation of terms. College libraries often make these works available electronically, so you may be able to search them by looking on your library's website under categories like "Resources and Databases." You can find Merriam-Webster's Online Dictionary at http://www.m-w.com.

Sample List of Keywords on "Online Communities"

If you were working on a research project on the nature of online communities (or a particular online community), you might include these terms on an initial list of keywords:

community	online	Usenet newsgroup
blogs	space, spatiality	chat (IM, iChat, Netmeeting)
network	geography	
email	discussion lists, listserv	

Merriam-Webster's Online Dictionary Entry for *community*

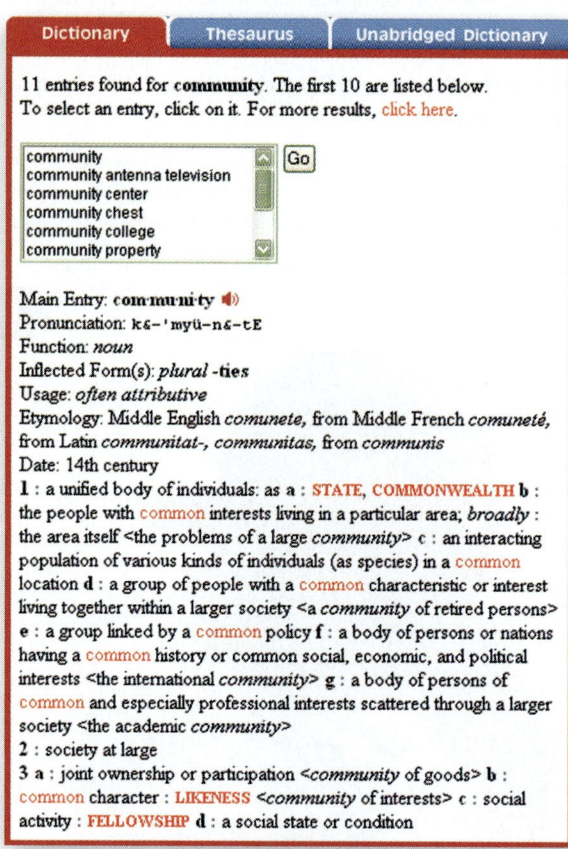

Dictionary | Thesaurus | Unabridged Dictionary

11 entries found for **community**. The first 10 are listed below.
To select an entry, click on it. For more results, click here.

community
community antenna television
community center
community chest
community college
community property
Go

Main Entry: **com·mu·ni·ty**
Pronunciation: k&-'myü-n&-tE
Function: *noun*
Inflected Form(s): *plural* **-ties**
Usage: *often attributive*
Etymology: Middle English *comunete,* from Middle French *comuneté,* from Latin *communitat-, communitas,* from *communis*
Date: 14th century
1 : a unified body of individuals: as **a** : STATE, COMMONWEALTH **b** : the people with common interests living in a particular area; *broadly* : the area itself <the problems of a large *community*> **c** : an interacting population of various kinds of individuals (as species) in a common location **d** : a group of people with a common characteristic or interest living together within a larger society <a *community* of retired persons> **e** : a group linked by a common policy **f** : a body of persons or nations having a common history or common social, economic, and political interests <the international *community*> **g** : a body of persons of common and especially professional interests scattered through a larger society <the academic *community*>
2 : society at large
3 a : joint ownership or participation <*community* of goods> **b** : common character : LIKENESS <*community* of interests> **c** : social activity : FELLOWSHIP **d** : a social state or condition

Activity 14-8: Generating Keywords for Your Subject

Generate a list of ten keywords about your topic. Then do some quick searches on the keywords, either in the library or using Web search engines, to determine whether they generate any specific and relevant information for your topic.

The Google Glossary Search on *craft*

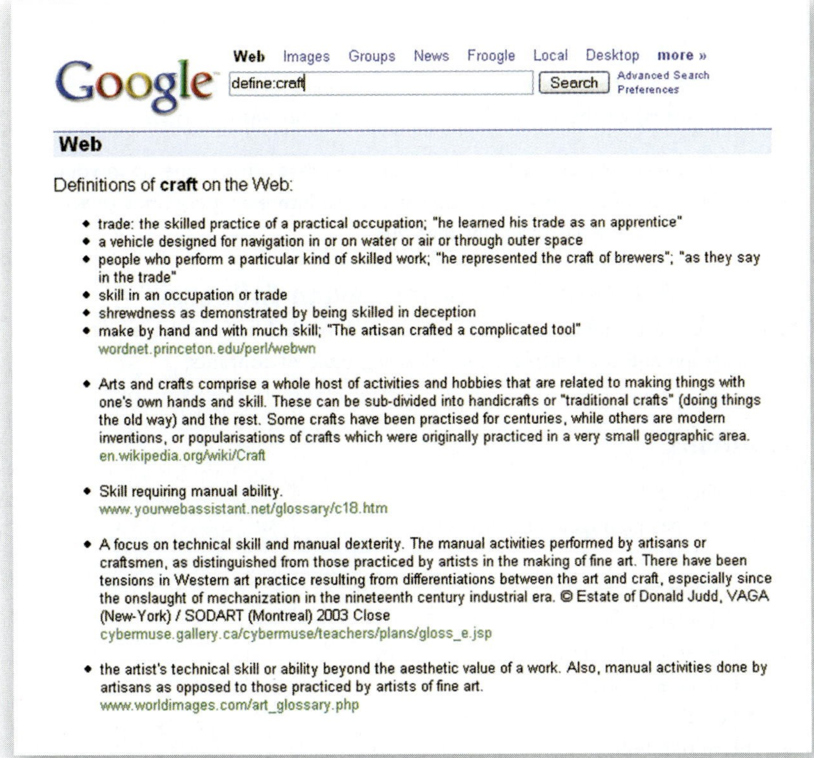

Google
Web Images Groups News Froogle Local Desktop more »
define:craft | Search | Advanced Search Preferences

Web

Definitions of **craft** on the Web:

- trade: the skilled practice of a practical occupation; "he learned his trade as an apprentice"
- a vehicle designed for navigation in or on water or air or through outer space
- people who perform a particular kind of skilled work; "he represented the craft of brewers"; "as they say in the trade"
- skill in an occupation or trade
- shrewdness as demonstrated by being skilled in deception
- make by hand and with much skill; "The artisan crafted a complicated tool"
wordnet.princeton.edu/perl/webwn

- Arts and crafts comprise a whole host of activities and hobbies that are related to making things with one's own hands and skill. These can be sub-divided into handicrafts or "traditional crafts" (doing things the old way) and the rest. Some crafts have been practised for centuries, while others are modern inventions, or popularisations of crafts which were originally practiced in a very small geographic area.
en.wikipedia.org/wiki/Craft

- Skill requiring manual ability.
www.yourwebassistant.net/glossary/c18.htm

- A focus on technical skill and manual dexterity. The manual activities performed by artisans or craftsmen, as distinguished from those practiced by artists in the making of fine art. There have been tensions in Western art practice resulting from differentiations between the art and craft, especially since the onslaught of mechanization in the nineteenth century industrial era. © Estate of Donald Judd, VAGA (New-York) / SODART (Montreal) 2003 Close
cybermuse.gallery.ca/cybermuse/teachers/plans/gloss_e.jsp

- the artist's technical skill or ability beyond the aesthetic value of a work. Also, manual activities done by artisans as opposed to those practiced by artists of fine art.
www.worldimages.com/art_glossary.php

See **http://www.google.com** and type define:*yourterm*

Write down the definitions of your keyword, not so that you can cite the dictionary in your research project (an awkward tactic, especially for familiar words) but so that you understand the range of the word's meaning and what other words it may be related to. Knowing this will help you guide further research.

Another method is to plug your keywords into a search engine and look for basic definitions. Try entering a keyword, the Boolean operator AND, plus the word *definition*. You'll be surprised at how many websites offer definitions; remember to visit several of them so that you don't start out your research with a marginal definition. The Google Glossary is an excellent resource.

Talk Like an Insider

Use the terminology that people who know about your subject use to discuss it: If you are using one term and you find that other people tend to use a different one, switch to that term. If, for instance, you are using the term *hacker* to research that social and technological phenomenon, you should know that there are several types of hackers and "missions," such as "hacktivism," which refers to the socially conscious brand of hacking meant to disrupt (presumably) unjust social practices.

Locate Encyclopedias

Find an encyclopedia (online or in print) and use it to develop an expanded understanding of your subject, keywords, and important phrases. One of the better sites is Encyclopedia.com (http://www.encyclopedia.com). Although this site has a subscription service, you can search and find excellent results without subscribing initially. Additionally, links to other useful sites that have information related to your search words are provided. Webopedia (http://www.webopedia.com) provides detailed definitions of terms related to computer and Internet technologies. A search using the term *digital,* for example, will return a very detailed discussion, some illustrations, and links to other related terms, such as *quantum computing.* Wikipedia (http://en.wikipedia.org) is a community-developed free encyclopedia that contains a vast collection of very current articles, to which you might also contribute as you learn more about your subject. With its many links to online sources, Wikipedia is an excellent place to launch your research. Like all encyclopedias, it is most useful as a stepping stone to more authoritative sources and not an end point for research. (Note that Wikipedia articles may be revised frequently; for example, by press time the article "Avian Influenza" mentioned here was titled "Avian Flu" and listed new external links.)

Activity 14-9: Looking Up Your Topic in Online Dictionaries and Encyclopedias

Take one or two keywords for your topic and look them up online in the following resources:

1. An online dictionary such as Merriam-Webster (**http://www.m-w.com**), a set of dictionaries such as Dictionary.com (**http://www.dictionary.com**), or an online glossary such as Google (**http://www.google.com**; type: define: *yourterm*)
2. An online encyclopedia such as Britannica (**http://www.britannica.com**) or Wikipedia (**http://en.wikipedia.org**)
3. A hierarchical directory such as the Google Directory (**http://directory.google.com**) or the Yahoo! Directory (**http://dir.yahoo.com**)

Note the synonyms or specialized words or phrases that come up in your searches. Print out your results, or copy and paste interesting portions of your results into a separate file and print that out.

Example: Wikipedia's Entry for "Avian Influenza"

The entry for "avian influenza," also known as "bird flu," begins with an introductory paragraph and then displays the following table of contents:

Contents

- 1 Infection
- 2 Subtypes pathogenic to humans
  - 2.1 H1N1
  - 2.2 H5N1
  - 2.3 Other strains
- 3 Prevention and treatment
- 4 Potential pandemic
- 5 See also
- 6 External links
  - 6.1 General
  - 6.2 News
  - 6.3 Preparing
  - 6.4 Web logs

Each topic listed in the contents is covered in its own section. External links lead to other sources of information.

External Links

General

- "The Threat of Bird Flu": HealthPolitics.com (**http://www.healthpolitics.com/archives.asp?previous=bird_flu&bhcp=1**)
- CDC page about avian influenza (**http://www.cdc.gov/flu/avian**)
- "Defying Death": An award-winning round table discussion on viral diseases including avian flu by the Vega Science Trust (**http://www.vega.org.uk/video/programme/6**)
- WHO avian influenza frequently asked questions (**http://www.who.int/csr/disease/avian_influenza/avian_faqs/en**)
- Bird Flu Timeline (**http://www.twoop.com/medicine/archives/2005/10/avian_influenza.html**)
- Avian-Influenza.com—a website with information on control, preparation, and the latest news on outbreaks. Sponsored by Intervet (**http://www.avian-influenza.com**)

Activity 14-10: Specialized Terms for Your Topic

Make a list of specialized words, terms, and phrases related to your topic. If you have not conducted specific searches using these terms yet, conduct some library or Web searches to see whether they provide relevant results related to your topic.

One way of minimizing the time you spend searching for sources is to highlight in your research journal the terms that continue to come up in abstracts, articles, and books. For instance, if you are researching how affordable homes can be built in your area, you may encounter terms like *home equity, real estate values, mixed housing,* and *variable-use dwellings.* If you begin to list them or highlight them, you can return to these terms and use them as search terms if sources prove to be difficult to find.

Find Bibliographies

Bibliographies, which are lists of sources about a research subject, have probably already been compiled on your subject by others. If you need help tracking down a research bibliography, ask a reference librarian. Or look on your library's website under categories like "Research Guides" or "Bibliographies." After you've tracked down an article or two, you can also find good bibliographies in academic journals on your subject.

Annotated bibliographies, which are lists of sources with short descriptions, are an even more useful tool in the early stages of research. Online, you can get a head start by probing information portals (like Yahoo! or Google). To use Google, for example, go to http://directory.google.com/Top/Reference/Bibliography and enter your keywords in the search box.

If you locate a bibliography, you can save a lot of time and find yourself with a rather decent-sized stack of books and articles (and URLs for websites) that are relevant to your subject.

Use a research journal to keep track of the places you have searched, the information and sources you have found (and how to find them again), and your thoughts about your research process. Your research journal may be in a word processing file, in a paper notebook, on a PDA, or even on one of several websites that help users keep track of research processes, such as WriteNote® at http://www.writenote.com. Above all, while you're conducting your research, take note of every interesting detail you can, even if it seems unimportant. If something captures your interest, unrelated or not, it might become useful later.

It's common to feel rushed in the early stages of a research project, but it's worth taking the time to be methodical. Tracking down missing or inaccurate information later will cost you a lot of time, probably at a moment when you don't have very much time to spare. Now's the time to "sweat the details."

Student Example: Excerpts from Alejandro Covas's Research Journal

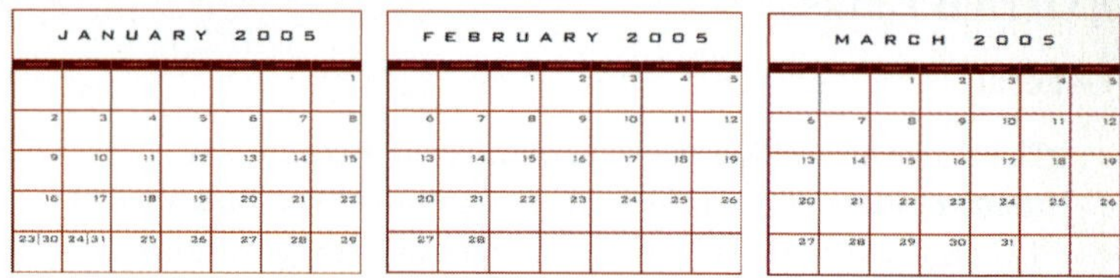

January 5th
This is my first day of researching and I spent most of the afternoon in the library. I didn't do much more than read a lot of magazines and some of these school magazines called journals. Since Music Education is my major I decided to find stuff on music and was I already lost in all that I found. If it weren't my major I would never have gone on. But I think I will do some reading on music therapy and see what turns up. This report is due March 10, 2005!

January 8th
I spent the last two days doing two main things. I found and cut and pasted about ten pages of an annotated bibliography I found online at the music and dance library of Brigham Young University into a Word file that I called "Music_Therapy_Research_Spring_2005." I also went down to the journals room and asked this guy named Neal Larson for help, and he found me two journals on Music Therapy.

January 11th
I've been taking this laptop with me everywhere and I hooked up in the library today and did something that I think was pretty darned smart. I set up a yahoo email account called Alexandmusictherapy@yahoo.com. I have been cutting and pasting a lot of stuff into the Music Therapy file and I have been saving it on my hard drive mostly, except for when I get back to the room and remember to store it on CD. So every day now I send an email from my real account to this yahoo account. Nobody else knows about it and nobody uses it, so I can store backup copies of my files there.

APRIL 2005						
					1	2
3	4	5	6	7	8	9
10	11	12	13	14	15	16
17	18	19	20	21	22	23
24	25	26	27	28	29	30

MAY 2005						
1	2	3	4	5	6	7
8	9	10	11	12	13	14
15	16	17	18	19	20	21
22	23	24	25	26	27	28
29	30	31				

JUNE 2005						
			1	2	3	4
5	6	7	8	9	10	11
12	13	14	15	16	17	18
19	20	21	22	23	24	25
26	27	28	29	30		

January 27th
I have focused my research on a controversy about music therapy for children who have been traumatized. I have cut and pasted a bunch of articles from EBSCOhost and InfoTrac (where Neal the library guy showed me all the journal articles are) that are talking about how this school district in Texas has completely cut the music and other art curriculum, even the support things like music therapy. Turns out that they needed more money for their football team or something. Some parents sued the school district and all these music therapy experts testified in the case. I bet there are a dozen articles from these online sources that mention something about that lawsuit. Most people (DUH!) in the journals are for music therapy but there were a few people who said it was useless. I have been really looking into their arguments since most of the stuff I can find says otherwise. My research project is now about the value of music therapy in public schools when it comes time to cut school budgets.

January 28th
I have started to create annotated bibliographies (see file Music_Therapy_Research_Biblios_ Spring_2005) that summarize and give all the bibliographic information for my sources.

February 2nd
Another lawsuit! This time in Pennsylvania. Some kid's parents think that the music therapy caused him to fight another kid and the kid's ear was bitten off. Now my whole research paper has to be rethought since someone is claiming not that music therapy is useless but that it causes anti-social behavior. I am using the online versions of the Philadelphia Inquirer for stories about this case, and I have decided to lead my paper off with this case and show how wrong the parents are and then move to how effective and useful music therapy really is.

14g

How to Keep a Research Journal

- **Keep a record.** Keep a record of the places you go and the dates. Take a few minutes to record your steps so that you will not have to retrace them later.
- **Track your evolving understanding.** Record the ways your research process changes your understanding of your subject and your ideas about its key terms. You could include running notes under each term, for example. Or use a double-entry notebook. Divide the page in half, with factual information on the left side and running notes and commentary on the right.
- **Write down quotations and ideas** that intrigue you on 3" × 5" index cards, which are easy to sort (▶ section 14h). Microsoft Outlook has a useful Note function. On Macs, you'll find "Stickies." Post-it® Notes offers a free "Lite" version of "Post-it Software Notes" for PCs at http://www.3m.com/market/office/postit/com_prod/psnotes/index.html.
- **Record complete publication information.** Always note precise publication information about each work that you examine (▶ section 14h).

Always record the citation information for sources you find, including as much information as is available in the three main categories of all bibliographic references:

1. Authorship
2. Title information
3. Publication information

Even if the source you are reading doesn't seem to apply to your research project, take a moment to record the information on your source list. If your research focus changes (which is likely), having these other sources may prove valuable. In addition, at times you will need to let readers know what information you've considered and dismissed; this helps build your ethos.

Note the following kinds of information for each source:

- Quotations—enclosed in a pair of quotation marks so you will know later that they are another person's wording, rather than a paraphrase or summary of source material
- Complete bibliographical information, including the page number(s) of material you have quoted, paraphrased, or summarized
- The date you found the source (especially important for online sources)

Compile Information on Index Cards or in a Text File

Some people like to record their research on paper index cards, finding them easy to deal with at the library and easy to rearrange later in organizing their paper. If you work on your computer, you may prefer to set up a text file for tracking your sources.

Sample Book Entry in a Text File

Topic: Subtopic
Identity: National

Author — Title — Publication information

Kidder, Tracy. *Mountains Beyond Mountains*. New York: Random House, 2003. Print.

Summary

A book about Paul Farmer, a doctor who lives and works in Haiti several months out of every year (he volunteers)

Paraphrase of an event; quotations in quotation marks

Dr. Farmer talking with another doctor getting ready to leave Haiti. Farmer wondered if it would be difficult, but the other doctor couldn't wait to get back to America. He said, "I'm an American, and I'm going home." Farmer thought about this into the night: "What does that mean, 'I'm an American'? How do people classify themselves?" (page 80)

Reader's note to self, kept separate from summary

Compare with other accounts of Americans working abroad, such as those by Peace Corps volunteers: How much do they feel their "Americanness" and what impact does this have on how they view the people they work with?

Read 9/18/05 — Call number: R154.F36 K53 2003

Sample Index Card for a Magazine Article

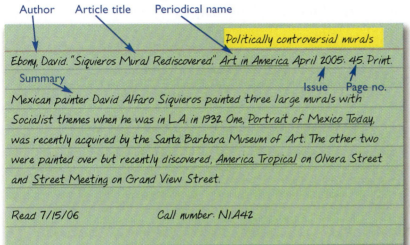

Author — Article title — Periodical name

Politically controversial murals

Ebony, David. "Siqueiros Mural Rediscovered." Art in America April 2005: 45. Print.

Summary — Issue — Page no.

Mexican painter David Alfaro Siquieros painted three large murals with Socialist themes when he was in L.A. in 1932. One, Portrait of Mexico Today, was recently acquired by the Santa Barbara Museum of Art. The other two were painted over but recently discovered, America Tropical on Olvera Street and Street Meeting on Grand View Street.

Read 7/15/06 Call number: N1.A42

Sample Index Card for a Website

Web page title — Access date — Website name

Textile trade in mid-19th century

"Emigrants of 1843." End of the Oregon Trail Interpretative Center. Historic Oregon City, 2004. Web. 20 Nov. 2007. <http://www.endoftheoregontrail.org/piofam/famhewit.html>.

URL of specific page for student's own reference.

Summary

This page tells the story of the Hewitt and Methany family journey on the Oregon Trail in the Great Migration of 1843. Mary Cooper Methany took many kinds of seeds to see what would grow in Oregon. Among them were flax seeds; linen comes from the flax plant. "Flax was a major cash crop in the Northwest for many years." Includes dour photos of family members.

Site includes a history center that outlines the overall history of the Oregon Trail.

Visited 11/20/07

You can record information on index cards or in a text file.

Here is some practical advice for using index cards:

- Use the same sized index cards and use only one side.
- Rewrite a card if it is overcrowded or illegible.
- Leave some free space on the card so you can add comments later.
- Use numbers or colors (with highlighters) to organize your index cards around subtopics.
- Alphabetize your index cards by author's last name within the subtopics.
- Read through your index cards often, and add comments and further questions.
- When writing out source information by hand, underline titles that you will later italicize on your computer.

Your index cards will be useful when it comes time to locate the most effective sources for your research project. Some people put their index cards in piles by subtopic to help them organize their drafts. Robert Pirsig, author of the interesting books *Zen and the Art of Motorcycle Maintenance* (1974) and *Lila* (1991), its sequel, used index cards (thousands of them) to organize his entire life, including the elaborate philosophy that he developed over a thirty-year period!

As you collect information from a variety of sources, recording all the bibliographic information as described on pages 264–265, one useful strategy is to incorporate a short summary of the work after the bibliographical information. Normally, annotations are brief; try to keep a summary of an article or book chapter to a paragraph or so.

In your annotation, describe and evaluate the potential of the source:

- Make your annotation descriptive. Information that might not seem relevant early on may become critical later, so try to relay accurately the content and scope of the work.
- Provide an analysis of the quality of the source and its relevance to your research project. Discuss how it might fit into your work.
- Don't focus on your emotional responses to the reading. For instance, don't write that the article makes you angry. However, do make the annotation serve your purposes.

You are likely to review, skim, and read dozens of sources. Your annotated bibliography will provide you with a descriptive trail back into areas of your research that you may need later.

Student Example: An Entry in Juliette Ludeker's Working Annotated Bibliography (MLA)

Simpson, Philip L. "*Copycat*, Serial Murder, and the (De)Terministic Screen Narrative." *Terministic Screen: Rhetorical Perspectives on Film*. Ed. David Blakesley. Carbondale: Southern Illinois UP, 2003. 146-62. Print.

Simpson's essay is as much an exploration of the role society has in the formation of serial killers as it is a critique/exploration of the film *Copycat*. Using Kenneth Burke's notions of the terministic screen and of humans as symbol-using animals, Simpson posits, "Human beings (including serial killers) reconstruct reality into the narratives through which they make sense of the world" (147). Therefore, the tendency exists for humans to write themselves into a particular narrative they are experiencing. Film and visuals can cause a strong sense of identification in the viewer because they mimic (or might be understood as) "experiencing." Simpson posits that, in one argument, critics of media point to a killer's strong identification with the violence narrative constructed by the media. The serial killer is, in effect, created as a killer by the media—becoming a "copycat" of what in popular culture (movies and literature) is given space and glorified in cinematic storytelling. Simpson counters this argument by stating that this claim is a narrowing of Burke's "selection-and-deflection strategies" of the terministic screen. It assumes behavior is determined only by environmental influence and not by psychology or motivation.

Checking Your Knowledge

The first stage of managing the research project will be complete once you have gathered and learned from a sufficient number of sources to really know your subject.

1. You should have an expert's sense of the history, current events, and likely future trends of your narrowed subject. You will know you are at this point when you can talk about your subject to someone you don't know for 15 minutes, without stopping, authoritatively.
2. You should be able to show that you are aware of the existing literature on your subject, that you understand the relationships among your ideas and that literature, and that you can elaborate on the implications of your work for understanding the subject or for projecting it into the future.

Managing the research project well in its early stages is critical to establishing your ethos, or credibility, so that, in the end, your readers believe that you know what you're talking about and that the information you provide is trustworthy. If you follow the steps outlined in this chapter, you'll have a good chance of developing your authority. You'll find that you won't have to rely only on the content of your final draft when asked questions about the subject; you will be able to recollect everything that led to that stage.

Conducting Research in the Disciplines 14k

Scholars in the humanities, the social sciences, and the sciences approach research from different but not entirely dissimilar perspectives. All fields value ethical, rigorous, and interesting research, but each focuses on different aspects of experience, uses unique vocabularies to talk about the subject, and ranks some questions as more important than others. The next nine spreads offer a brief introduction to the questions asked across these broad fields of study and provide examples of how two specific disciplines in each broader field attempt to answer them.

This outside column identifies some of the fields, research networks, and citation guides used by researchers in the discipline.

This outside column identifies the nature and types of evidence that researchers in the discipline use to support their findings

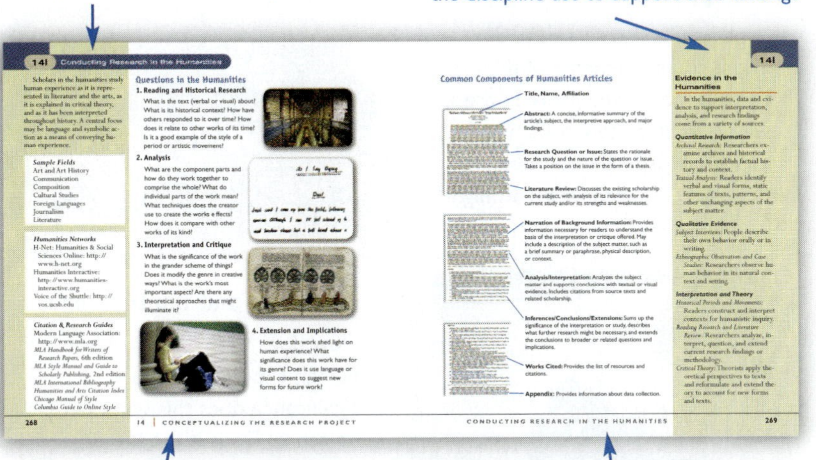
14l Conducting Research in the Humanities

Scholars in the humanities study human experience as it is represented in literature and the arts, as it is explained in critical theory, and as it has been interpreted throughout history. A central focus may be language and symbolic action as a means of conveying human experience.

Sample Fields
Art and Art History
Communication
Composition
Cultural Studies
Foreign Languages
Journalism
Literature

Humanities Networks
H-Net: Humanities & Social Sciences Online: http://www.h-net.org
Humanities Interactive: http://www.humanities-interactive.org
Voice of the Shuttle: http://vos.ucsb.edu

Citation & Research Guides
Modern Language Association: http://www.mla.org
MLA Handbook for Writers of Research Papers, 6th edition
MLA Style Manual and Guide to Scholarly Publishing, 2nd edition
MLA International Bibliography
Humanities and Arts Citation Index
Chicago Manual of Style
Columbia Guide to Online Style

Questions in the Humanities

1. Reading and Historical Research
What is the text (verbal or visual) about? What is its historical context? How have others responded to it over time? How does it relate to other works of its time? Is it a good example of the style of a period or artistic movement?

2. Analysis
What are the component parts and how do they work together to comprise the whole? What do individual parts of the work mean? What techniques does the creator use to create the works e ffects? How does it compare with other works of its kind?

3. Interpretation and Critique
What is the significance of the work in the grander scheme of things? Does it modify the genre in creative ways? What is the work's most important aspect? Are there any theoretical approaches that might illuminate it?

4. Extension and Implications
How does this work shed light on human experience? What significance does this work have for its genre? Does it use language or visual content to suggest new forms for future work?

268 | 14 | CONCEPTUALIZING THE RESEARCH PROJECT

Common Components of Humanities Articles

Title, Name, Affiliation

Abstract: A concise, informative summary of the article's subject, the interpretive approach, and major findings.

Research Question or Issue: States the rationale for the study and the nature of the question or issue. Takes a position on the issue in the form of a thesis.

Literature Review: Discusses the existing scholarship on the subject, with analysis of its relevance for the current study and/or its strengths and weaknesses.

Narration of Background Information: Provides information necessary for readers to understand the basis of the interpretation or critique offered. May include a description of the subject matter, such as a brief summary or paraphrase, physical description, or context.

Analysis/Interpretation: Analyzes the subject matter and supports conclusions with textual or visual evidence. Includes citations from source texts and related scholarship.

Inferences/Conclusions/Extensions: Sums up the significance of the interpretation or study, describes what further research might be necessary, and extends the conclusions to broader or related questions and implications.

Works Cited: Provides the list of resources and citations.

Appendix: Provides information about data collection.

14l

Evidence in the Humanities

In the humanities, data and evidence to support interpretation, analysis, and research findings come from a variety of sources.

Quantitative Information
Archival Research: Researchers examine archives and historical records to establish factual history and context.
Textual Analysis: Readers identify verbal and visual forms, static features of texts, patterns, and other unchanging aspects of the subject matter.

Qualitative Evidence
Subject Interviews: People describe their own behavior orally or in writing.
Ethnographic Observation and Case Studies: Researchers observe human behavior in its natural context and setting.

Interpretation and Theory
Historical Periods and Movements: Readers construct and interpret contexts for humanistic inquiry.
Reading Research and Literature Review: Researchers analyze, interpret, question, and extend current research findings or methodology.
Critical Theory: Theorists apply theoretical perspectives to texts and reformulate and extend theory to account for new forms and texts.

CONDUCTING RESEARCH IN THE HUMANITIES | 269

This inside column tracks the typical research process in the discipline, from the formulation of research questions and methodology through analysis, interpretation, and significance.

This inside column describes the genre of published research, focusing on important structural elements of discipline-specific articles.

Scholars in the humanities study human experience as it is represented in literature and the arts, as it is explained in critical theory, and as it has been interpreted throughout history. A central focus may be language and symbolic action as a means of conveying human experience.

Sample Fields
Art and Art History
Communication
Composition
Cultural Studies
Foreign Languages
Journalism
Literature

Humanities Networks
H-Net: Humanities & Social Sciences Online: http://www.h-net.org
Humanities Interactive: http://www.humanities-interactive.org
Voice of the Shuttle: http://vos.ucsb.edu

Citation & Research Guides
Modern Language Association: http://www.mla.org
MLA Handbook for Writers of Research Papers, 7th edition
MLA Style Manual and Guide to Scholarly Publishing, 3rd edition
MLA International Bibliography
Humanities and Arts Citation Index
Chicago Manual of Style
Columbia Guide to Online Style, 2nd edition

Questions in the Humanities

1. Reading and Historical Research

What is the text (verbal or visual) about? What is its historical context? How have others responded to it over time? How does it relate to other works of its time? Is it a good example of the style of a period or artistic movement?

2. Analysis

What are the component parts and how do they work together to comprise the whole? What do individual parts of the work mean? What techniques does the creator use to create the work's effects? How does it compare with other works of its kind?

3. Interpretation and Critique

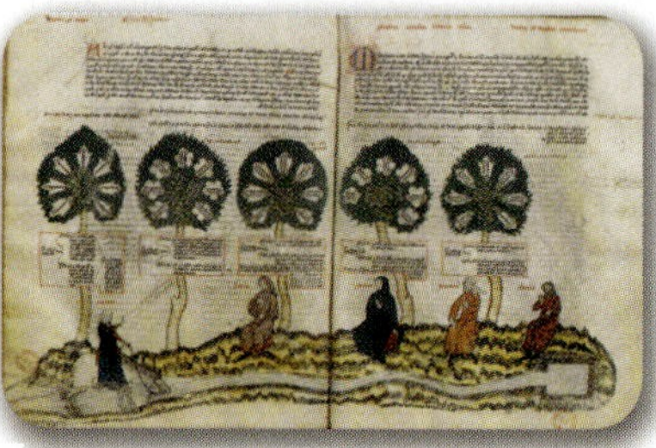

What is the significance of the work in the grander scheme of things? Does it modify the genre in creative ways? What is the work's most important aspect? Are there any theoretical approaches that might illuminate it?

4. Extension and Implications

How does this work shed light on human experience? What significance does this work have for its genre? Does it use language or visual content to suggest new forms for future work?

Common Components of Humanities Articles

Title, Name, Affiliation

Abstract: A concise, informative summary of the article's subject, the interpretive approach, and major findings.

Research Question or Issue: States the rationale for the study and the nature of the question or issue. Takes a position on the issue in the form of a thesis.

Literature Review: Discusses the existing scholarship on the subject, with analysis of its relevance for the current study and/or its strengths and weaknesses.

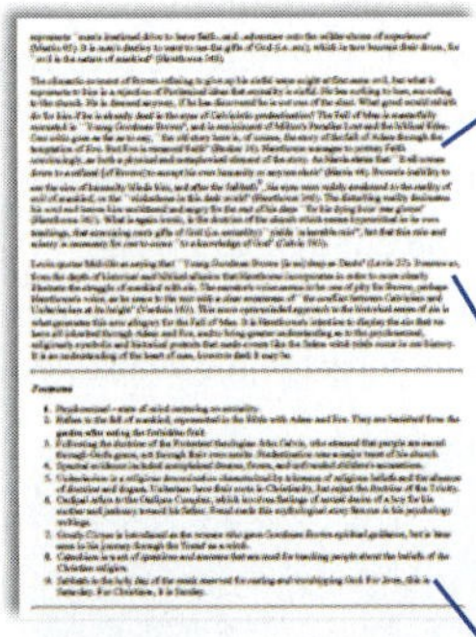

Narration of Background Information: Provides information necessary for readers to understand the basis of the interpretation or critique offered. May include a description of the subject matter, such as a brief summary or paraphrase, physical description, or context.

Analysis/Interpretation: Analyzes the subject matter and supports conclusions with textual or visual evidence. Includes citations from source texts and related scholarship.

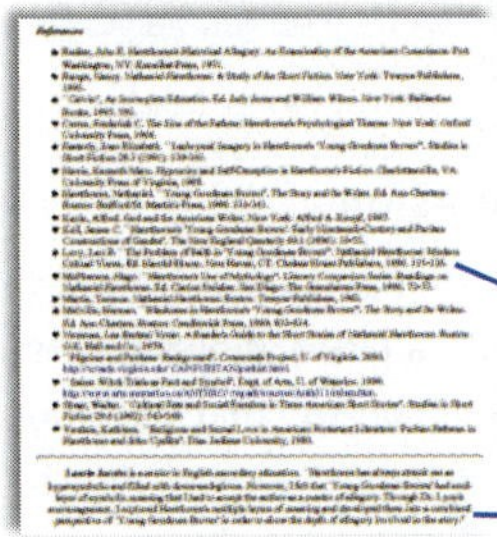

Inferences/Conclusions/Extensions: Sums up the significance of the interpretation or study, describes what further research might be necessary, and extends the conclusions to broader or related questions and implications.

Works Cited: Provides the list of resources and citations.

Appendix: Provides information about data collection.

Evidence in the Humanities

In the humanities, data and evidence to support interpretation, analysis, and research findings come from a variety of sources.

Quantitative Information

Archival Research: Researchers examine archives and historical records to establish factual history and context.

Textual Analysis: Readers identify verbal and visual forms, static features of texts, patterns, and other unchanging aspects of the subject matter.

Qualitative Evidence

Subject Interviews: People describe their own behavior orally or in writing.

Ethnographic Observation and Case Studies: Researchers observe human behavior in its natural context and setting.

Interpretation and Theory

Historical Periods and Movements: Readers construct and interpret contexts for humanistic inquiry.

Reading Research and Literature Review: Researchers analyze, interpret, question, and extend current research findings or methodology.

Critical Theory: Theorists apply theoretical perspectives to texts and reformulate and extend theory to account for new forms and texts.

Research in film studies focuses on how films achieve effects, how they reflect or challenge ideology, how they have progressed in technique or form, and how they contrast with other films in their genre. Researchers also are interested in how films function as cultural artifacts and as part of the larger industry of entertainment. Many films focus on the art of filmmaking or the act of viewing a film, inviting us to question the role of film as an art form that shares features with other art forms, like the novel, the short story, and various visual art forms.

Film Studies Networks

ScreenSite: http://www.screensite.org
Society for Cinema & Media Studies: http://www.cmstudies.org/scms_forums.html
American Film Institute: http://www.afi.com
Premiere Magazine: http://www.premieremag.com

Citation & Research Guides

Chicago Manual of Style Website: http://www.chicagomanualofstyle.org
Internet Movie Database: http://www.imdb.com
The New York Times Movies: http://movies.nytimes.com/pages/movies/index.html

The Art of Looking: Writing about Film as a Visual Medium

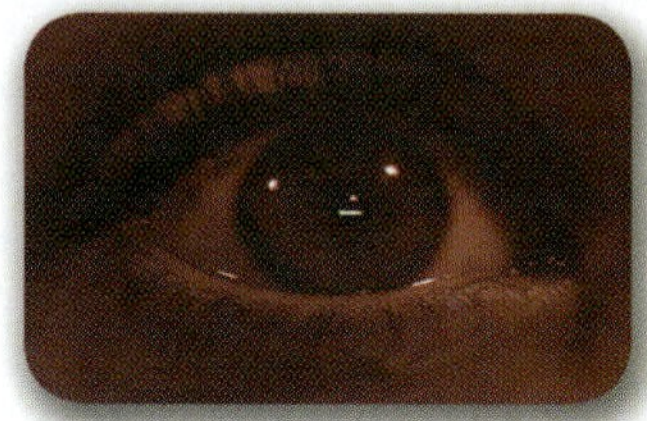

Opening credits, *Vertigo*, dir. Alfred Hitchcock

1. Working Thesis

Study a film or films and come to a provisional interpretation of their meaning and significance. *Sample Thesis: Many films portray the acts of watching and being watched to expose the power and danger of the gaze.* Why is this an important subject now? Are there also more innocent acts of watching? How can a person *being* watched wield power? How does this theme explain the pleasure of film viewing?

James Stewart as L. B. Jefferies in *Rear Window*, dir. Alfred Hitchcock

2. Approach to Gathering Evidence

To focus on film as a visual medium, you can draw from studies on visual rhetoric and the relationships among seeing, knowing, and power. Evidence can be gathered by using screen capture software (such as HyperSnap™) to take screenshots, carefully taking notes, and reading the script, if it's available.

3. Integration of Evidence

Build the argument by citing evidence from the film or films that illustrates the act of viewing and its function.

Guy Pearce as Leonard Shelby in *Memento*, dir. Christopher Nolan

4. Analysis, Inference, Extension

Break a film into its components and show how it "adds up." Does the film make a point about our "surveillance society"? Does it suggest that our ways of seeing are also ways of not seeing? Does it teach us how to read other films? Why is the thesis relevant to studies of visual culture?

Writing about Film Adaptations of Novels and Short Stories

In adapting a piece of fiction for the screen, directors, writers, and cinematographers face significant challenges, because film is primarily a visual medium while a novel or short story is purely verbal. Here are three approaches to film adaptation:

1. Fidelity: The film re-creates the plot as closely as possible, avoiding stylistic interpretation and divergence from the source text.
2. Interpretation: The film interprets the source text by stressing some aspects over others, exaggerating themes, or changing the plot and characters to make the film more dramatic or interesting for viewers.
3. Inspiration: The film draws thematic inspiration from its source but extends the themes to new contexts. A film may have fidelity to the source's themes while acting them out in completely new situations.

The excerpt below relates to the novel *Do Androids Dream of Electric Sheep?* (1968), by Philip K. Dick, and the films *Blade Runner* (1982) and *Blade Runner: The Director's Cut* (1992), directed by Ridley Scott.

> ...This novel's progression from print to screen is one of the better documented and most bitterly contested adaptations in film history. After producer Herb Jaffe's option to film Dick's novel ran out in 1978 (Dick thought the draft screenplay was "a bad joke"), the project was optioned to Hampton Fancher and Brian Kelly, then picked up by Universal. Fancher wrote increasingly variant screenplays of the novel, but when Ridley Scott, fresh off his success with *Alien*, was hired as the director, he began to convert the story into what Dick later called an "eat lead, robot!" screenplay, with Deckard as a "cliché-ridden Chandleresque figure" (Rickman).... Dick went public with his dissatisfaction, creating a nightmare for the film's publicist.... [E]ach of the collaborators had a distinct conception of what *Blade Runner* should be: Dick wanted the androids to be the catalysts for Deckard's and Isidore's moral and spiritual growth in facing evil; Fancher saw it as a love story about a man who discovers his conscience; Scott, a futuristic film noir set in a densely packed, garish cityscape (he wanted the final title to be Gotham City); Peoples, an exploration of the distinguishing qualities of humans and their replicants (Kolb). All four perspectives ultimately found their way into the film.... [I]n the end Dick believed that Peoples's revisions of the script made it a "beautiful, symmetrical reinforcement" of his novel's main theme. Ironically, Dick died suddenly of a stroke just a few months before the film's release....

Fidelity to the source

Interpretation of theme

Inspiration and extension

From David Blakesley, *Encyclopedia of Novel into Film,* 2nd ed., ed. John C. Tibbetts and James M. Welsh (New York: Facts on File, 2005).

Evidence in Film Studies

Evidence for analysis and interpretation, historical research, and film reviews comes from the films themselves and their context in the lives of artists and audiences. Films share qualities with other forms in terms of genre, style, and subject. You can draw on all these kinds of evidence.

Visual and Aural Evidence

Stills, Screenshots, Clips: Help explain complex descriptions of scenes. Clips (scene sequences) may be useful for multimedia essays.

Spoken Dialogue: Shows character or plot development and should be carefully transcribed.

Examples of Film Terminology

In addition to terms for literary analysis (◀ Chapter 9), film studies uses terms derived from film technique.

Editing: The way the sequences were put together.

Scene: A unified sequence of action.

Mise en scène: The arrangement of objects in the frame.

Contexts and Theory

Contexts and theory guide ways of reading by providing an interpretive lens. See the *Critical Dictionary of Film and Television Theory,* edited by Roberta E. Pearson and Philip Simpson (New York: Routledge, 2001).

Research in history focuses on documenting and interpreting the historical record of human social, political, and artistic life. Researchers use archival records and accounts to construct historical contexts, but they also draw on contemporary perspectives and values when selecting their subjects and when deciding on the relevance of historical research for our times. The work of historians both preserves and extends the record of human accomplishments—for good or ill—in the interest of divining the future by judging the past.

History Networks
Virtual Library History Central Catalogue: http://vlib.iue.it/history/index.html
Voice of the Shuttle: http://vos.ucsb.edu
PBS History: http://www.pbs.org/history/
Technology History: http://www.refstar.com/techhist/

Citation & Research Guides
Chicago Manual of Style Website: http://www.chicagomanualofstyle.org
Humanities Index
Historical Text Archive: http://historicaltextarchive.com

The Strange Uses of History: Was Albert Einstein Really a Bad Student?

1. Working Historical Question or Thesis

It's been said that Einstein was not always the best of students and that he failed math in high school. But by the age of 26 he had invented the general theory of relativity. Was he really a late-blooming student? What kind of student was he in high school and earlier? How did this experience lead him to become the greatest genius of his time? Where does this story come from, and why do people tell it?

2. Archival Research and Review of Primary and Secondary Sources

What have others said about this phenomenon? What do the primary sources say? Are there public records, personal memoirs and letters, or public accounts of Einstein's schooling? What do the formal histories say on this topic?

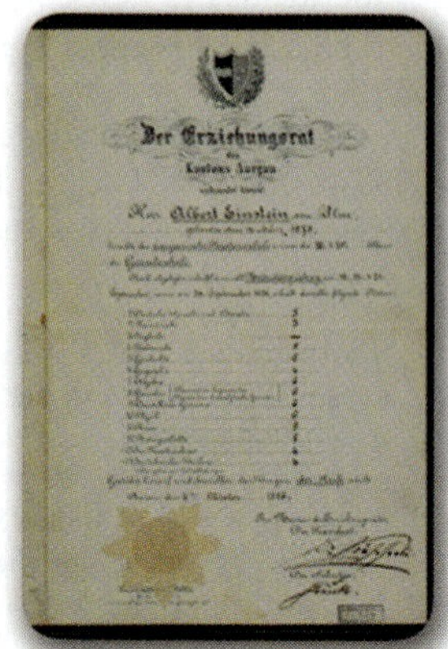
Der Erziehungsrat

Einstein's high school diploma shows sixes in math and physics, the highest score.

3. Evidence from Reliable Sources

Build the argument by citing evidence from Einstein's school records, his autobiography, and other biographies. Deal with evidence that may contradict your claim.

4. Analysis, Inference, Extension

How does the evidence about Einstein's early schooling contradict the mythology? Do people cite this story because they need to "bring him down to earth," as a kind of rationalization? What other figures have people explained in this way? Why is our construction of "fame" an important subject for history?

An interpretation, "Einstein's Dream Diptych" by Gerrit Greve

Deconstructing Urban Legends: *The Blair Witch Project*

Urban legends are stories that get passed among people but, when tested, prove to be based on unreliable historical evidence or unsubstantiated rumor. When questioning the truth of an urban legend, keep in mind the historian's need to depend on (1) reliable primary sources, (2) the factual historical record, and (3) secondary sources that have withstood the scrutiny of the scholarly community.

In some cases, people deliberately manufacture legends for entertainment, or even as hoaxes. One famous case concerns the film *The Blair Witch Project* and its supporting website, **http://www.blairwitch.com**. The legend is that a group of college students studying the history of the Blair Witch legend filmed their research but then disappeared. Their "found" film was shot as a documentary, lending realism to the legend. Haxan Films and distributor Artisan Entertainment built the legend by also creating a rich archive of primary sources, including images of the film reels that contained the original documentary evidence, diaries of the students completing the history project, and more. All of these elements drew their persuasive force from preconceived notions about what constitutes reliable historical evidence.

The excerpt that follows is from Redman Lucas Wells's *"The Blair Witch Project."*

> . . . it's quite surprising exactly how much of the Blair Witch story was fabricated by Haxan Films. Here's a quick introduction to some of the more basic facts behind the movie:
>
> - Yes, there is a real Burkittsville, Maryland (where the movie is set in the 'present day').
> - Burkittsville, however, was never known as Blair, Maryland.
> - In fact, there has never been a Blair, Maryland, past or present.
> - Burkittsville doesn't have a "real" Witch legend that bears even a remote resemblance to the tale unfolded in The Blair Witch Project.
> - The Witch legend, and all of the events associated with it in the movie, was manufactured entirely by the Haxan Film team. . . .
>
> So, unfortunately for those hunting for the "real" Blair Witch behind the hype of the movie treatment of the legend, there is no actual hidden substance to be found. The Blair Witch was entirely the product of the fertile minds of Haxan Films and may well go down as one of the most creatively marketed movies of the dying years of the 20th Century—if not of the history of cinema itself!

Factual record

This evidence relies on secondary sources that aren't mentioned

Analysis and implications of the evidence

Urban Legends Research Centre 1999, 6 Sept. 2004 <http://www.ulrc.com.au/html>.

Evidence in History

Evidence for history research comes from the historical record of facts, archival documents, images, and other artifacts. The chief task of the historian is to evaluate the integrity of the archival documents and to question previous interpretations.

Primary Sources

Archival Documents and Images: Libraries, museums, and other organizations keep original printed archives, which researchers may examine if prior approval has been granted.

Digital Archives: Online digital archives offer searchable databases of images of archival material.

Oral Histories: Sometimes, interviews can be or have been conducted with people involved in the events studied.

Secondary Sources

Original Secondary Sources: Use commentary and interpretation by others living at the time.

Subsidiary Contexts: People may have experienced the events secondhand or researched them.

Questions about Sources

Ask specific questions about the reliability and validity of your sources and the nature of their original contexts: What's the nature of the source? Is the source genuine? Who is the audience? Who is the author? When was the source produced?

Social scientists study society and the relationships and behavior of individuals within it. Research in the social sciences should be replicable, so the emphasis is on empirical methods, both quantitative and qualitative, that can be tested and improved.

Sample Fields
Anthropology
Archaeology
Economics
Environmental Science
Political Science
Urban Studies

Social Science Networks
Social Science Research Network: http://www.ssrn.com
Social Science Information Gateway: http://www.sosig.ac.uk
Social Sciences Virtual Library: http://www.clas.ufl.edu/users/gthursby/socsci/
Social Science at the Internet Public Library: http://www.ipl.org/div/aon/browse/soc00.00.00/

Citation & Research Guides
American Psychological Association: http://www.apa.org
Includes APA style helper, research and ethics guides, news, journals, books, and more. The official guide to APA style is the *Publication Manual of the American Psychological Association.*

Questions in the Social Sciences

1. Hypotheses

Based on experience, what do I expect to discover? How do behaviors or attitudes vary among subjects or across societies? What's wrong or inaccurate about historical accounts of this subject? How will people answer questions?

2. Research Method and Design

Should I use qualitative or quantitative methods or some combination of the two? What variables are there, and can they be isolated for study?

3. Data and Evidence

How will I collect the data and evidence? What practical challenges are there in conducting surveys, interviews, experimentation, testing, and research?

4. Analysis and Interpretation

What do the data and evidence show? How did subjects respond? What patterns are there? Do my hypotheses hold?

5. Conclusions

What type of report will best represent my findings? Can I contrast my results with other research?

Common Components of Research Reports in the Social Sciences

Title, Name, Affiliation

Abstract: A concise, informative summary of the report's hypotheses, methodology, and major findings.

Introduction/Hypotheses: Includes information necessary to understand the subject and working hypotheses, with reasons behind them.

Research Method/Design: Discusses in detail the methods used to collect data and/or gather evidence. Includes discussion of pros and cons of the methodology.

Data/Evidence: Provides the results of the qualitative or quantitative collection of data and evidence. Uses visuals such as charts and tables to show relationships in the data. Refers to appendix that shows the instrument of data collection.

Analysis/Interpretation: Analyzes the data and evidence collected. Explains what the visuals indicate. Discusses whether the data and evidence support hypotheses of the study.

Conclusions/Inferences: Sums up what the results indicate, describes what further research might be necessary, and extends the conclusions to broader or related questions.

Bibliography: Provides the list of resources and citations.

Appendix: Provides information about data collection.

Evidence in the Social Sciences

In the social sciences, data and evidence to support research hypotheses and findings come from a variety of sources.

Quantitative Data

Structured Observation: Researchers observe and measure social and individual behavior in controlled settings, where it can be isolated for study.

Experimentation: Researchers test hypotheses by creating artificial situations (scenarios) that can show the effects of variables on individual and social behavior, attitudes, and physiological responses.

Testing: Animal or human subjects are given behavioral tests whose results can be measured and compared under controlled conditions.

Qualitative Evidence

Subject Interviews, Self-Reports, Surveys: People describe their own behavior orally or in writing.

Naturalistic Observation: Researchers observe behavior in its natural context and setting.

Reading Research and Literature Review: Researchers analyze, interpret, question, and extend current research findings and methodology.

Psychologists study how human thought and action are affected by physiological and chemical processes, personality, and the environment. They study how the mind works and why, so that they can explain and influence behavior or improve mental health. Psychologists ask questions like these: How does trauma affect a person's personality? How do feelings of power affect altruistic behavior? How can depression affect learning? Why do sounds, such as music, evoke memories? How do people fall in love on the Internet?

Psychology Networks

Psychological Research on the Net: http://psych.hanover.edu/research/exponnet.html

PsychExperiments: http://psychexps.olemiss.edu/index.html

Citation & Research Guides

American Psychological Association: http://www.apa.org Includes APA style helper, research and ethics guides, news, journals, books, and more. The official guide to APA style is the *Publication Manual of the American Psychological Association.*

Psychology at Science Direct: http://www.sciencedirect.com/science/home/psychology

The Psychology Tutor (Nicole Sage): http://www.psy.pdx.edu/PsyTutor/

Conducting Qualitative Research in Psychology: Subject Interviews

1. Create Hypotheses

What do I expect to discover from my interview subjects? What causes the behavior or attitude? How do behaviors or attitudes vary among subjects? How does a change in one of these variables affect the others?

2. Formulate Research Method and Design

What questions shall I ask to draw out the attitudes and behaviors of my subjects? In what sequence? What will be my methodology for analyzing the contents of the interviews? Do I need approval to conduct human subject research? From whom? What type of report will best represent my results—formal research report, poster session, oral presentation, or thesis?

3. Collect Evidence and Data

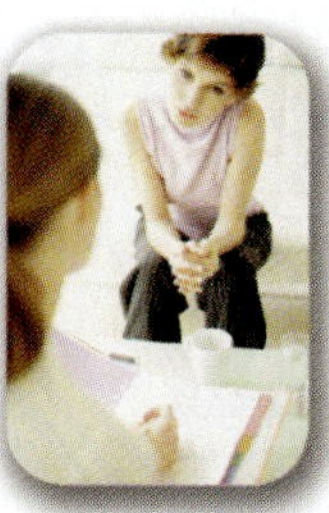

Should I record responses? Videotape them? How will I transcribe the interviews? Where will I conduct them?

4. Analyze, Infer, Extend

Do my hypotheses hold? How did my subjects respond? What patterns are there? What have I learned about their attitudes? About their behavior? What can others learn from my study? What inferences can I make about behavior? Can I contrast my results with other research?

Reading and Summarizing Research Reports

When you are reading research reports in the social sciences, you should keep your attention focused on these main questions, which will help you understand the report more quickly. You can also use them as an aid if you write a summary of the report.

1. What questions does this research address?
2. How did the researchers collect and analyze data?
3. What are the findings?

Neuron

The Neural Fate of Consciously Perceived and Missed Events in the Attentional Blink

Abstract

A glance at the February 5 issue of *Neuron:*

Seeing but not believing—or not noticing

Kellie Bartlett

You see more than you realize you do because two different parts of the brain are involved in recognizing scenes and consciously noticing them, according to a team of researchers led by René Marois, an assistant professor of psychology at Vanderbilt University.

In their study, members of Mr. Marois's team tried to determine what happens to visual information that a person is looking for, and sees, but does not report seeing. Researchers have noticed such "attentional blinks" in previous studies when people are focused on the first image they are looking for and miss the second, if it appears too quickly after the first.

Questions addressed by the research

Participants in the study were asked to look for two images, a face and a scene, among a series of scrambled scenes that were shown to them in quick succession. During that process, the participants were undergoing functional magnetic resonance imaging, which allowed the research team to see which parts of the participants' brains were activated during the test.

How the researchers collected data (methodology)

When participants reported seeing the face but missing the scene, seeing the scene "nonetheless activated regions of the medial temporal cortex involved in high-level scene representations, the parahippocampal place area," the researchers write. But "the frontal cortex was activated only when scenes were successfully reported," they say.

Analysis of data and findings

The article, "The Neural Fate of Consciously Perceived and Missed Events in the Attentional Blink," is available online to subscribers. Information about the journal is available at http://www.neuron.org

From "Magazine and Journal Reader," *Chronicle of Higher Education,* 10 Feb. 2004 <http://chronicle.com>.

Data and Evidence in Psychology

In psychology, evidence and data to support research hypotheses and findings come from a variety of sources.

Quantitative Data

Structured Observation: Researchers observe behavior in a controlled setting, where variables can be isolated for study.

Experimentation: Researchers test hypotheses by creating artificial situations that can show the effects of variables on behavior.

Testing: Animal or human subjects are given behavioral tests whose results can be measured and compared under controlled conditions.

Qualitative Evidence

Subject Interviews, Self-Reports, Surveys: People describe their own behavior orally or in writing.

Naturalistic Observation: Researchers observe behavior in its natural context and setting.

Reading Research and Literature Review: Researchers analyze, interpret, question, and extend current research findings and methodology.

Sociologists study group and social life, particular cultures and their history, and broader patterns in the development of society. Sociologists ask questions like these: How has the Internet affected social life? What is the relationship between violence and gender? How does socioeconomic class affect racial attitudes? How have conceptions of family changed? What is the role of culture in shaping attitudes toward aging?

Sociology Networks

Sociology Online: http://www.sociologyonline.co.uk
American Sociological Association Resources for Students: http://www.asanet.org/student/student.html

Citation & Research Guides

American Sociological Association: http://www.asanet.org
Electronic Journal of Sociology: http://www.sociology.org
Style Guide for the Electronic Journal of Sociology: http://www.sociology.org/styleguide.html
Sociological Data Resources: http://www.asanet.org/student/data.html
Pew Internet and American Life Project: http://www.pewinternet.org

Internet Globalization: Using Data Resources in Sociology Research

1. Create Hypotheses

The emergence of the Internet has negatively affected urban life and caused population decline in large cities. If this is so, what are the causes? If not, why might the availability of online meeting spaces lead to more clustering of populations offline? What variables are there with regard to access to the Internet? What will I contribute that isn't already present in the existing analysis of the data?

2. Formulate Research Method and Design

What questions shall I ask of the data resources? What will be my methodology for analyzing the data? Are there any methodological flaws in the design of the original study (or studies) that might compromise the data? How large was the sampling, and what is the margin of error? Shall I present my work as a formal research report, poster, oral presentation, or thesis?

3. Gather Data and Review Existing Research

What data resources are there for studying the effects of the Internet? Can I use multiple sources? What do the data show? Are there differences across socioeconomic class, gender, or age? What have others written about this topic?

PEW/INTERNET
U.S. Census Bureau
Computer Use and Ownership

4. Analyze, Infer, Extend

Does my hypothesis hold? Why has broadband Internet capability actually contributed to population growth in cities like New York, Boston, and San Francisco? What patterns are there in the data? Why did people think that the reverse would be the case? Can I contrast my results with other research?

Writing Informative Abstracts in Sociology

An abstract for a formal article or report on a sociological subject represents in compact form the context, purpose, methods, results, and conclusions of research. It typically runs no more than 250 words in length.

1. Objective: States the central issue, research topic, or purpose of the research.
2. Methods: Describes the population studied, how subjects were selected (sampling), and the design of the study.
3. Results: Summarizes the quantitative and/or qualitative results of the research.
4. Conclusion: Interprets the results in light of the hypotheses and suggests implications of the study for future research.

Collegiate Academic Dishonesty Revisited: What Have They Done, How Often Have They Done It, Who Does It, and Why Did They Do It?

Eric G. Lambert, Nancy Lynne Hogan, and Shannon M. Barton

Abstract

Academic dishonesty is a serious concern on most college campuses as it cuts to the heart of the purpose of higher education and the pursuit of knowledge. This study examined twenty different types of academic dishonesty as well as potential correlates of academic cheating by surveying 850 students at a four-year Midwestern university. While most past studies have used bivariate analysis, this study expands the literature by also including a multi-variate analysis to determine which correlates were most important in accounting for collegiate academic dishonesty. The results indicated that most of the bivariate associations were not observed in the Ordinary Least Squares analysis, suggesting that after controlling for shared effects, many variables have little overall effect on the summed measure of academic dishonesty. Specifically, only college level, membership in a fraternity or sorority, cheating to graduate, cheating to get a better grade, and past cheating in high school had a significant impact.

Objective: States the central issue

Methods: Names the population, sampling method, and methodology design

Results: Describes the research findings

Conclusion: Describes how the results support the hypothesis

From *Electronic Journal of Sociology* 7.4, 2003 <http://www.sociology.org/content/vol7.4/lambert_etal.html>.

Data and Evidence in Sociology

In sociology, evidence and data to support research hypotheses and deductions come from a variety of sources. The process may begin with **sampling,** a method of choosing an appropriate group of people for further study.

Quantitative Data

Analysis of Data Resources: Researchers study demographic and other statistical information gathered from a variety of sources: census data, statistical reports, and prior research.

Qualitative Evidence

Interviews, Self-Reports, Surveys, Questionnaires: People describe their own attitudes orally or in writing.

Ethnography: Researchers study cultures and subcultures in their natural context and setting from multiple perspectives, including those of participants and nonparticipants.

Reading Research and Literature Review: Researchers analyze, interpret, question, and extend current research findings (secondary data), theoretical positions, and methodology.

The sciences study the processes and laws of the natural world to explain its origins, how it functions, and how it will change over time. Scientific research also predicts the behavior of the natural world based on mathematically expressed laws formulated from observation, testing, and analysis. Research in the sciences should be replicable, so the emphasis is on quantitative empirical methods that can be tested and improved.

Sample Fields

Chemistry	Medicine
Ecology	Physics
Genetics	Zoology

Science Networks

National Science Digital Library: http://www.nsdl.org
National Science Foundation: http://www.nfs.gov
Voice of the Shuttle: http://vos.ucsb.edu

Citation & Research Guides

Scientific Style and Format: The CBE Style Manual for Authors, Editors, and Publishers: http://www.councilscienceeditors.org/publications/style.cfm
AIP Style Manual (Astronomy, Physics): http://www.aip.org/pubservs/style/4thed/toc.html
The ACS Style Guide (Chemistry): http://pubs.acs.org/books/references.shtml

Questions in the Sciences

1. Hypotheses

Based on observation, what do I expect to discover? How has the phenomenon behaved previously, and what predictions does this help me make? What's wrong or inaccurate about prior research on this phenomenon?

2. Research Method/Materials/Design

What variables are there, and can they be isolated for research? Will the research involve measurement, observation, or testing? What protocols will be followed? What's the best way to study the phenomenon?

3. Data and Evidence

How will I collect the data and evidence? What instruments can I use to take measurements? What can I use as a control in order to measure the effect of variables on the processes I measure?

4. Analysis and Interpretation

What do the data and evidence show? What patterns are there? Do my hypotheses hold? Why is this research important?

5. Conclusions

What type of report will best represent my results? Can I contrast my findings with other research?

Common Components of Research Reports in the Sciences

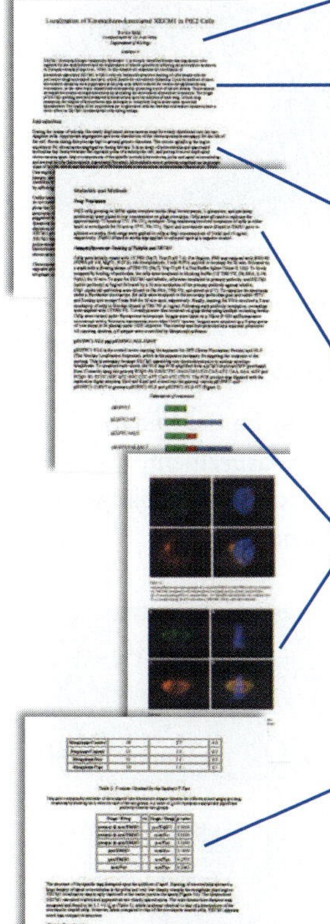

Title, Name, Affiliation

Abstract: Provides a concise, informative summary of the report's hypotheses, methodology, and major findings.

Introduction/Hypotheses/Review: Includes information necessary to understand the subject and working hypotheses, with reasons behind them. Reviews previous research.

Research Method/Materials/Design: Discusses in detail the methods used to collect data and/or gather evidence. Includes discussion of pros and cons of these methodologies.

Data/Evidence: Provides the results of the collection of data and evidence: observations, experiments, measurement, testing, and modeling. Uses visuals such as charts and tables to show relationships in the data. Refers to appendix that shows data instruments and models.

Analysis/Interpretation: Analyzes the data and evidence collected. Explains what the visuals indicate. Discusses whether the data and evidence support hypotheses of the research.

Conclusion/Inferences: Sums up what the results indicate, describes what further research might be necessary, and extends the conclusions to broader or related questions.

Bibliography: Provides the list of resources and citations.

Appendix: Provides information about data collection.

Data and Evidence in the Sciences

In the sciences, data and evidence to support research hypotheses and findings come from a variety of sources.

Quantitative Data

Measurement: Researchers measure change over time or the effects of introducing variables or materials.

Experimentation: Researchers test hypotheses by creating artificial situations that can show the effects of variables on natural processes.

Structured Observation: Researchers observe and measure phenomena in controlled settings, where they can be isolated for study.

Prediction, Modeling, Testing

Prediction: Drawing from research and extrapolating from mathematical principles, scientists predict the behavior of unexplained phenomena.

Modeling: Using extrapolations from mathematics and established scientific models, scientists test new models to measure and predict change and performance.

Testing: Animal or human subjects are given physiological tests whose results can be measured and compared under controlled conditions.

14n Science Example: Research in Biology

Biology research employs empirical methods to study living organisms in all of their forms and complexity. Researchers in biology conduct experiments that require attention to detail, as well as recording and interpreting data. They also synthesize the work of other researchers to address new questions. The experiments and methods of biologists need to be replicable so that other researchers can build on previous findings.

Biology Networks

BioTech Resources Web Project: http://biotech.icmb.utexas.edu
Human Genome Research Institute: http://www.nhgri.nih.gov
Voice of the Shuttle: http://vos.ucsb.edu
Science Direct: Digital Library of the Future: http://www.sciencedirect.com

Citation & Research Guides

Scientific Style and Format: The CBE Style Manual for Authors, Editors, and Publishers: http://www.councilscienceeditors.org/publications/style.cfm
Museum Stuff (Biology): http://www.museumstuff.com/links/science/biology.html

Conducting Research in Biology: The Behavior of Slime Molds

1. Hypotheses

Based on observation, what do I expect to discover? How have the biological processes of slime molds been measured previously, and what predictions can I make? Is there anything wrong or inaccurate about the idea that slime molds are complex, adaptive systems?

Researchers for the Human Genome Project are sequencing the genome of this type of slime mold.

2. Research Method/Materials/Design

What variables are there, and can they be isolated for research? Will the research involve measurement, observation, or testing? What protocols will be followed? What's the best way to study the process?

3. Data

How will I collect the data and evidence? What instruments can I use for the experiment? What can I use as a control in order to measure the effect of variables on the processes I measure?

4. Results

What do the data and evidence show? What patterns are there? Do my hypotheses hold? What do related studies show?

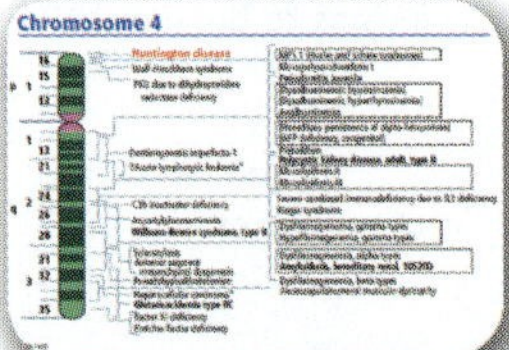

The slime mold genome may help us understand the human genome better.

5. Discussion

Interpret the data and make inferences about what the data show and why the results are important. Contrast the results with other research. Identify the ethical issues of the research.

Bioethics: Genetic Savings and Clone

Bioethics is a subdiscipline in biology dealing with the ethical implications of biological research and applications. Bioethicists examine implications of research whose methods and results may evolve faster than expected. Social and political systems need time to adapt as people grasp the full significance of their scientific discoveries. Bioethicists consider what's next in biology and how culture will be affected if the research proceeds and succeeds. Major laboratories and projects devote resources to studying the ethical implications of their research. It's their responsibility to communicate effectively with the public, which provides funding for efforts like the National Human Genome Research Institute. As a biologist, you need to represent your research accurately and consider its ethical and moral implications seriously.

Consider the following example of one company's effort to address issues of bioethics. Contrast it with what you find at the Human Genome Project: **http://www.nhgri.nih.gov/PolicyEthics/**

"CC" (short for "Carbon Copy") was the world's first cloned cat.

Ethics and Discussion

Genetic Savings & Clone, Inc.

The subject of cloning has long inspired writers and artists. Their work, in turn, has shaped popular myths and beliefs about cloning. Those myths and beliefs then affect public attitudes and expectations about the science.... Genetic Savings & Clone must routinely correct the misconception that a cloned pet will enter the world full-grown and equipped with the memories and precise personality of its genetic predecessor. It won't! The cloned pet will be a unique, newborn animal that will share genes and probably behavioral tendencies, but not memories, with its genetic predecessor.

GSC must also respond to the popular misconception that we'll increase the overpopulation of homeless cats and dogs, when in fact we'll reduce it ... or the misconception that pet cloning will diminish canine and feline genetic diversity, when it will more likely preserve or expand that diversity.

But many people have legitimate concerns about cloning. Some clones produced to date — especially those created using pre-CT cloning methods — have had health problems that appear to be cloning-related. Yet some scientists are already attempting to clone humans. What are the implications of cloning for society? How can we ensure that the technology is not abused?

GSC welcomes questions and discussion on these and other issues. Feel free to explore this section of our web site and participate in our discussion forums.

From http://savingsandclone.com/ethics/index.html.

GSC provides a link to its explanations, which come on a FAQ node.

Cloning methods are explained on this node.

The link to the discussion forums was dead in September 2004.

Data and Evidence in Biology

In the sciences, data and evidence to support research hypotheses and findings come from a variety of sources.

Quantitative Data

Measurement: Researchers measure change over time or the effects of introducing variables or agents to which the organism reacts.

Experimentation: Researchers test hypotheses by creating artificial situations that can show the effects of variables on natural processes.

Prediction, Modeling, Testing

Prediction: Drawing from biology research and extrapolating from previous studies, biologists predict the behavior of unexplained processes.

Modeling: Using extrapolations from previous studies, the laws of biochemistry, and established scientific models, biologists create new models to measure effects and predict change.

Testing: Animal or human subjects are given physiological tests whose results can be measured and compared under controlled conditions.

Astronomers study the stars, planets, galaxies, and universe—including its current state, its motion and evolution, and its origins. Astronomy is the oldest of the empirical sciences, dating back thousands of years to early use of the stars for navigation and timekeeping. A branch of physics, which studies matter and energy, astronomy relies on observation, measurement, and mathematical proof to generate knowledge.

Astronomy Networks
NASA: http://www.nasa.gov
NASA's Jet Propulsion Laboratory: http://www.jpl.nasa.gov
Astronomy Magazine: http://www.astronomy.com
Space.com: http://www.space.com

Citation & Research Guides
AIP Style Manual (Astronomy, Physics): http://www.aip.org/pubservs/style/4thed/toc.html
Chicago Manual of Style
Columbia Guide to Online Style
Writing about Science for General Audiences: http://www.stc.org/confproceed/2000/PDFs/00114.PDF

Seeing into the Past

1. Hypotheses

Based on prior observation and experience, what do I expect to discover? Would it still be possible to detect "light halos" from the supernova of 1054 C.E. that created the Crab Nebula in the constellation Taurus? Is the light from the blast only now illuminating distant objects, some 951 light-years distant?

2. Prediction

Calculations suggest that gaseous matter that comes into contact with light from the original Crab Nebula supernova will illuminate, even when the light source has dispersed so widely.

3. Research Method/Equipment/Design

Select for observation nebulous objects from the Crab supernova that are no greater than 951 light-years away. Schedule telescope viewing and data recording time. As a control, select an object more than 951 light-years away, with celestial coordinates similar to those of the target objects.

4. Evidence/Data

Record light data from target nebula. For comparison purposes, collect light data on target from 10 years prior to contact with light source.

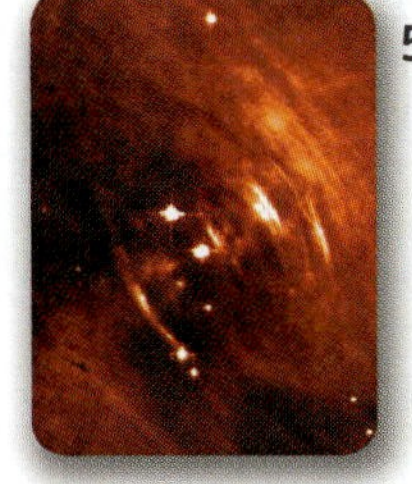

5. Analysis and Inference

The model predicts that light halos from the Crab supernova are detectable. Variations allow us to precisely chart the date and progression of the event. Contrast also with Hubble's recent measurement of the Crab pulsar's wave phenomenon.

Science Writing for General Audiences: SETI (The Search for Extraterrestrial Intelligence)

In translating specialized astronomical knowledge for general audiences, writers should be mindful to (1) establish context, (2) explain difficult concepts and specialized terminology, and (3) relate that knowledge to what readers will find familiar and interesting.

IT & SETI: The Role of Computer Technology in the Search for Extraterrestrial Intelligence
Kamil Z. Skawinski

SETI@Home is one unique undertaking that uses Internet-connected computers in the search for extraterrestrial intelligence. Launched on May 13, 1999, this best-known SETI endeavor consists of a special screensaver that computer users can readily download from the project's website setiathome.ssl.berkeley.edu. This special software, in turn, helps researchers at the University of California, Berkeley, efficiently evaluate the vast quantities of radio data received from the world's largest radio dish, the Arecibo Observatory in Puerto Rico. Faced with 50 terabytes of information to analyze, Berkeley's SETI team eventually turned to the public for help, which ultimately led to the launch of SETI@Home. . . .

> Explains the context of the SETI@Home project and provides necessary background information.

The distributed computing approach taken by SETI@Home, simply put, allows Berkeley's SETI researchers access to an enormous amount of essentially free computing power to evaluate the massive amount of data collected by the Arecibo dish. Every SETI@Home participant receives a "work unit" from the project's lab (consisting roughly of about 300 kilobytes of data), which is then processed by the PC whenever that user's machine is idle. Once the SETI@Home screensaver completes its analysis, the client then relays that processed information back to the lab at UC Berkeley. . . .

> Clarifies the concept of "distributed computing" and its significance.

Humans have been transmitting radio signals for a little over a century, and our high-powered signals have been generated only during the past 50 years—a blink of an eye in cosmic terms—and our radio emissions really have not traveled very far, astronomically speaking. Even if our broadcasts had encountered some civilized species some 50 or 60 light-years away, it will take any "reply" another 50 or 60 years to travel back to Earth. Therefore, patience and perseverance are musts in SETI research, for we simply do not know when we might discover that long-sought yet elusive signal from the stars.

> Connects SETI@Home to aspirations to make contact with intelligent life elsewhere in the universe.

From *California Computer News* 2 July 2002, 7 Sept. 2004 <http://www.ccnmag.com/index.php?sec=mag&id=156.0>.

Data and Evidence in Astronomy

In astronomy, data and evidence come from a variety of sources.

Quantitative Data

Observation: Astronomers use optical and radio telescopes to gather information about celestial bodies. Observations are recorded by computers and photographic equipment.

Measurement: Astronomers use equipment such as spectrometers to measure the results of observational data and to determine the distance, chemical composition, and rate of acceleration of objects.

Mathematical Proof: Astronomers use integral calculus, spherical trigonometry, and quantum mechanics to predict the behavior and motion of objects in space.

Information Processing: Relying on distributed computing power, researchers run complex calculations on data to produce usable results.

Modeling

Using extrapolations from mathematics and established physical models, astronomers create and test new models of the universe to explain observations and unexplained phenomena. Models guide observational methods and are verified or dismissed on the basis of further evidence.

A table of contents for writing project threads appears on pages xv–xxii.

Informative Essays

Garrison 1

Angela Garrison

English 101

Dr. Simpson

September 26, 2005

From Over There to Over Here:

War Blogs Get Up Close, Personal, and Profitable

Blog was the word looked up most often in the online *Merriam-Webster's Dictionary* in 2004 ("Blog"). What's all this fuss? When you read someone else's personal blog, you find out what they like and don't like, what they're doing, and maybe other bits of gossip offered at random. You can read news blogs to find out what's going on lately, what other people think about it, and why it matters. You can keep your own blog to share your thoughts and feelings, to tell your friends and family what you're up to, and sometimes to capture the interest of someone you've never met. When you read and write blogs, you join, or even create, a community. Blogs are also an efficient way to break news, spread rumors, and glorify causes. In short, blogs help people do what they've always done as social beings, just more quickly now, and from almost anywhere on Earth. Soldiers on the ground fighting in Iraq are writing blogs from the front lines. But a review is now under way at the Pentagon to "better understand the overall implications of blogging and other Internet communications in combat zones," according to John Hockenberry in his *Wired* article "The Blogs of War." The benefits of blogs written by U.S. soldiers in Iraq far outweigh the hypothetical risks of revealing sensitive or strategic information. Those benefits, however, aren't as obvious as they might seem.

In spite of what the imagery of smart bombs and predator drones might lead television viewers to believe, wars are fought by people, not just technology. Most blogs start out as efforts to stay in touch with family and friends, but they quickly turn into

What Do You Need to Find Out?

After you've chosen a subject, review sections 14c and 14d to help you focus your subject and develop a hypothesis or research question. Then determine which types of research would best suit the needs of your project. Would it be helpful to . . .

- talk to someone to get information about your project? If so, whom could you talk to and what would you want to know?
- conduct a survey to get information about your project? If so, which group of people would you survey, and why?
- observe events or to take notes in a particular location to get information? If so, where would you go and what exactly would you watch?
- read books, magazine articles, newspaper articles, or other sources of information about your topic? If so, what would you want to read about your topic?
- find information on the Web about your topic? If so, what websites would provide you with good information? Where could you start your search?

Use the answers to these questions to help you develop a research plan that indicates what types of sources you should locate. Depending on your answers and the requirements of your instructor, work through the activities in Chapters 15 and 16 to find out more about conducting different types of research.

Now is also a good time to ask your instructor which documentation style you should use. Find out, and then use the appropriate chapter in Part 4 to format your in-text citations and the references list at the end of your paper. Knowing the citation style, you can be sure to collect all the information you will later need to cite your sources correctly. ◀ page 152.

Collecting Information

You will need to include information in your brochure in order to inform and/or persuade your audience. Since different disciplines use information in different ways, looking at sections 14l–14n will help you think about what types of information you need to collect.

Create two columns on a piece of paper or in a word processing program on your computer. In the first column, make a list of the types of information you will need in your brochure. In the second column, make a list of the possible sources that you could use to get each type of information. Use this list as a checklist for gathering information and including it in your brochure.

▶ page 570.

Brochures

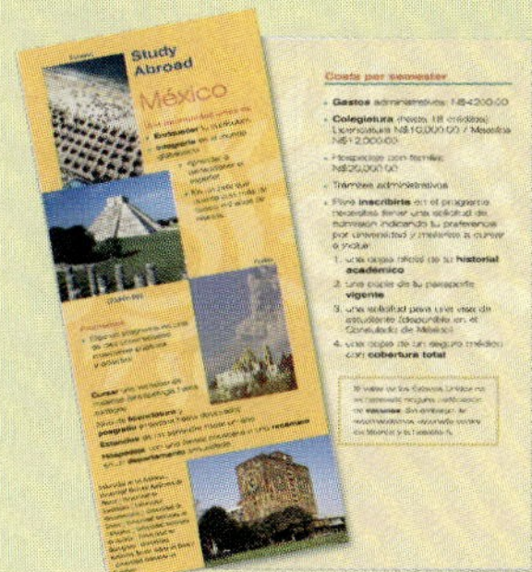

Investigating and Evaluating Past and Present Solutions

Chances are that you're not the first person to identify and attempt to solve the problem posed by your topic. As part of your research, identify the solutions others have thought of and tried. Were the solutions accepted by decision makers or not? If they were, how did they succeed or fail (or partly succeed or fail)? You'll also want to evaluate any solutions that are currently being implemented and decide whether or not they are good ideas. Use the strategies in section 14e to help you develop a research plan. Then use Chapters 15 and 16 to help you conduct research.

◀ page 67.

Proposal Arguments

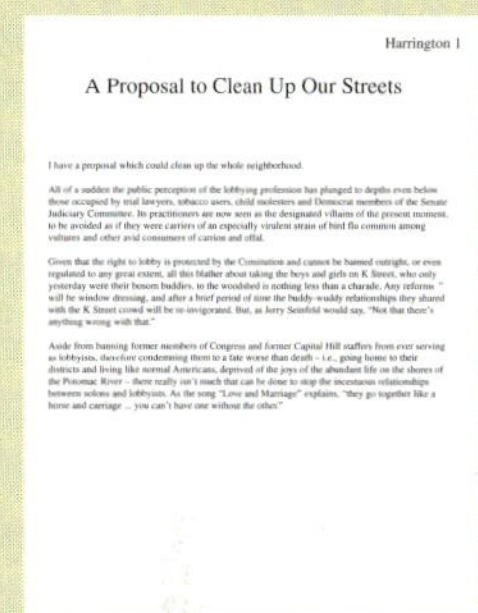

Harrington 1

A Proposal to Clean Up Our Streets

I have a proposal which could clean up the whole neighborhood.

All of a sudden the public perception of the lobbying profession has plunged to depths even below those occupied by trial lawyers, tobacco users, child molesters and Democrat members of the Senate Judiciary Committee. Its practitioners are now seen as the designated villains of the present moment, to be avoided as if they were carriers of an especially virulent strain of bird flu common among vultures and other avid consumers of carrion and offal.

Given that the right to lobby is protected by the Constitution and cannot be banned outright, or even regulated to any great extent, all this blather about taking the boys and girls on K Street, who only yesterday were their bosom buddies, to the woodshed is nothing less than a charade. Any reforms " will be window dressing, and after a brief period of time the buddy-wuddy relationships they shared with the K Street crowd will be re-invigorated. But, as Jerry Seinfeld would say, "Not that there's anything wrong with that."

Aside from banning former members of Congress and former Capital Hill staffers from ever serving as lobbyists, therefore condemning them to a fate worse than death – i.e., going home to their districts and living like normal Americans, deprived of the joys of the abundant life on the shores of the Potomac River – there really isn't much that can be done to stop the incestuous relationships between solons and lobbyists. As the song "Love and Marriage" explains, "they go together like a horse and carriage ... you can't have one without the other."

15 ONLINE RESEARCH

A survey by the Pew Charitable Trust in 2002 indicated that 66 million Americans used the Internet on a typical day. That number has continued to rise since then. Increasingly, research, personal writing, and communication of all kinds—once strictly the domain of the word processor, the pad of paper, and the library—are being carried out digitally, with much of the work accomplished on Web-connected platforms. On PDAs, at Internet cafes, on Web-enabled cellular phones, and on tablet computers, digital (and now wireless) communication has become the new mode of communication, with important social, political, and practical implications. You will find that information on many of the subjects that interest you can be found online in Web forums, ezines, newspapers, subject-specific discussion groups, and bulletin boards. You can find out about subjects in more ways than you can probably imagine at media sites, research hubs, libraries, government sites, professional and scholarly journals, and other digital archives. Much of your research will likely be conducted online.

Researching online is convenient and fast, but there are some precautions to bear in mind and some instances when there will be no substitute for a visit to the library, which now functions not only as a repository of printed (or filmed) information but also as a gateway to the digital world. This chapter will provide you with tools and techniques for locating and evaluating online information. Then Chapter 16 will provide detailed information about how to navigate both the physical and the digital spaces of modern libraries.

Many of us conduct basic searches for information and services every day—looking for news, weather, shopping, sports, recipes, music, and movies, for example—by going to our home page on a Web portal like AOL, MSN, or Yahoo!. We often begin by simply typing into the search box words that describe what we're looking for. We rarely consider how the words we use for searches (called queries) are used and arranged, nor do we spend much time thinking about how information has been arranged for us. We just type and click, rushing to one site after the next, hoping to find something relevant.

But you should be more careful about how you search for information. Not only can you save a lot of time, but you can also avoid relying on faulty or unreliable information or too eagerly accepting the highest ranked results from a query (they may have gotten that high because of advertising dollars!). Search engine technology has developed so much in the past few years that, with a few good strategies, you can find first-rate information quickly and without the distractions of advertising or irrelevant search results.

Web Portals

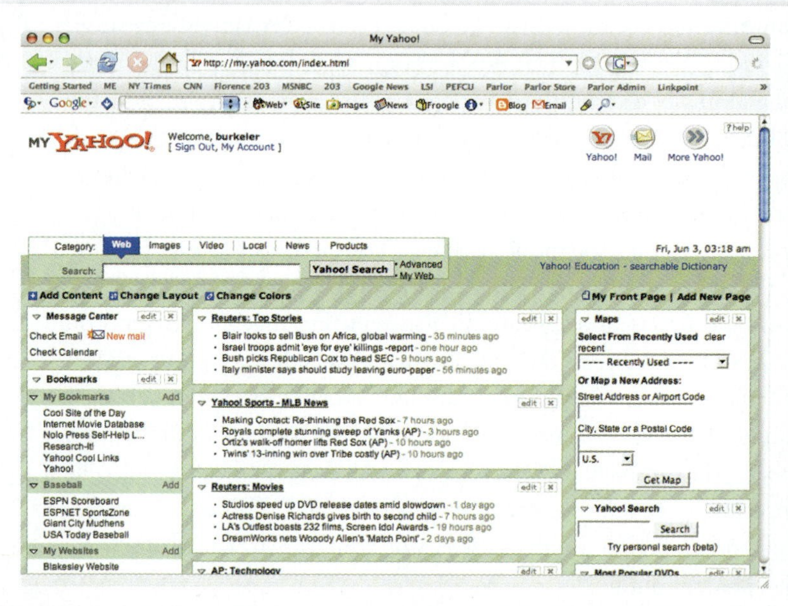

The Yahoo! Web portal

Perhaps the most commonly encountered search engine is one located on a Web portal, which is a website that provides many different services that you can customize to your own preferences. Many portals are designed to make money for the companies that offer them, so you need to judge the content in that context. It's not necessary to conduct searches through portals. As a savvy Web user, you'll want to know ways of searching outside of your portal (if you use one). For a list of helpful research portals, see page 306.

Open Sites in New Window or Tab

To open new windows or tabs (if the browser has that feature) with a two-button mouse, right-click and hold while you're over a link and choose "Open in New Window" (or similar wording). On a one-button mouse, hold the click until the pop-up menu appears, and then make your selection.

Open Link in New Window
Open Link in New Tab

Bookmark This Link...
Save Link As...
Send Link...
Copy Link Location

Properties

Web Developer ▶

Using "Open in New Window" or "Open in New Tab"

You will find it much easier to manage your online research if you learn to actively manipulate the size and number of browser windows or tabs open at any one time. All browsers allow you to choose a "New Window" (or similar) command from the file menu, and you can also open the links that you click on in new browser windows. Some browsers—like Firefox®, Opera, and Safari™—let you open new pages in a tab so that you can see all open windows in a tab bar from the current window. Using new windows or tabs, you can keep multiple websites open at any given time. Firefox allows you to save all open tabs as a session so that when you return to work on your project, you can reopen all of them with one click. We recommend that when you are conducting online research, you keep your search engine results list open in its own window or tab and open new links in new windows or tabs.

Results List

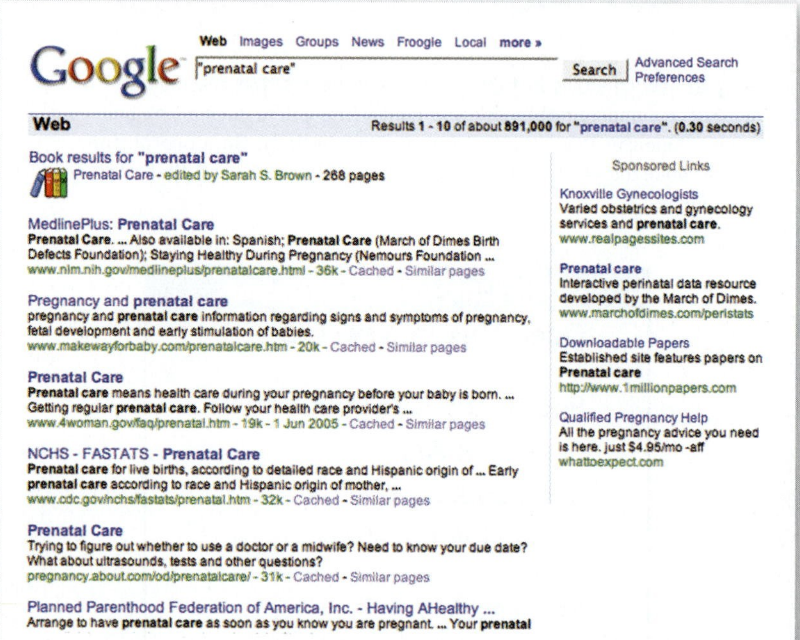

After you enter the terms for a Web search, you'll receive a results list, giving the websites that meet your search criteria. The search engine uses an algorithm to put the results into an ordered list, based on relevance to your search criteria and (on Google, for example) a particular site's popularity, measured by how many other sites link to it. A basic results list shows the Web page title and a link to the site. More complex results lists may also show a description of the Web page, its first few lines of text, the date it was last archived, its size, and a percentage ranking (or other indicator) of the page's relationship to your search criteria.

Some search engines allow advertisers to buy a higher ranking on a results list, so be wary. Avoid search engines that manipulate the results list in this way. Google's strategy is to place advertisers' links in a separate section to the right of the results list.

Crafting Your Search

To help you see how to shape a search so that your results list provides you with useful resources, let's consider a sample search. Suppose you're interested in learning more about *family planning.* Before starting your search, you've narrowed your search to *prenatal care,* which is one aspect of family planning. Any of the larger search engines will look for those two words in that order; but the better search engines will also look for those two words in any order, and then for websites with either of those words. You can end up with thousands of results, many of which have little to do with prenatal care.

A Google search for *prenatal care,* without quotation marks around the phrase, turns up 2,990,000 results. That number is too high; you won't have time to look through screens and screens of results. Most users look through only one or two screens of the results list, even after setting preferences (at the search engine site) to show 50 or more results. You need to search more effectively so that your results more closely match your goals of learning about prenatal care and finding credible sources. (See section 15h for more on judging the credibility of Internet sources.)

Activity 15-1: Listing Keywords for Your Subject

Make a list of keywords related to your current topic that you might use to search the Web. Also make a list of terms related to your topic that you want to avoid. Share your list with a partner and review each other's list, looking for keywords that your partner might have missed. If any words could be combined into key phrases, list the phrases, too.

Activity 15-2: Narrowing Your Web Keywords

Look over the list of Web keywords you made in Activity 15-1 and mark any that you think might be too general. Run some sample searches to test your hunches. If the search results are too general, write down other descriptive terms you could use to narrow your search. In thinking of new terms to try, you might find the Project Checklist on page 39 helpful. Or you can consult the *Library of Congress Subject Headings* (▶ page 325).

Activity 15-3: Searching within Results

Make a list of different combinations of search terms to try in the general search box and the "search within results" box. Then methodically try each combination. Track your results to see which combinations seem most helpful. Try different phrase combinations until you hit on one that works for your search.

This activity—or Activity 15-4 on page 295—may reveal to you the tension between recall and precision. *Recall* refers to the total number of Web page results that match your search criteria, as analyzed by the search engine. *Precision* refers to the relevance, or usefulness, of the results list in finding the exact Web pages that you are looking for, as expressed in your search criteria. By using more search words and phrases you may think that you are increasing your search's relevance, since you are narrowing the recall; but this may also have the unintended effect of eroding the precision of your search. Remember that you are the only one who can judge how effective your results are. Understanding recall and precision allows you to widen or narrow your search criteria, and therefore control your results list.

Search for Phrases When Possible

On Google, if you place *prenatal care* inside quotation marks, your search will return a results list of only sites with those two words together, in that order. Even using such a phrase search, however, you will still have too many results to sift through. Here, "*prenatal care*" returns 891,000 results. To get this number down to a manageable size, on Google you can search within results.

Search within Results

Scroll down to the bottom of the results list. At the bottom, you will find a "search within results" link. Suppose that you want information on increased federal funding for prenatal care. You can click on the "search within results" link and, in the next search box, type "*increased federal funding.*" Make sure that you consider whether you want to search for a phrase or to search for one word. We recommend using no more than one word or one phrase when searching within results, because you can always click on the back button on the toolbar and type in another word or phrase.

When we typed *"increased federal funding"* (with quotation marks) into the new search box and clicked Search, we received 79 items on the results list, which means that there are 79 sites with the terms *prenatal care* and *increased federal funding* on them. Five of the eight use both terms sequentially (i.e., in a row) and may be exactly what we are looking for. Four of the sites provide decent information for a paper arguing for the need for increased federal funding of prenatal care. Two of these are medical organizations that provide examples of why prenatal care is crucial for mothers and babies. One site is written by a political think tank opposed to federal funding increases. This site may have some value for our research: it could provide statistics that we can check against other sources, for example. However, since the site has an overt political agenda, information might be one-sided (▶ section 15h).

Combine Phrases Initially

Once you gain experience at searching within results in this manner, you can shorten your work even further by entering two phrases in the general search box: *"prenatal care" "increased federal funding."* Your results list will include sites that use both of those phrases.

The Google Toolbar

Google, the most comprehensive search engine presently available, offers a free Google Toolbar that you can install as a browser plug-in for Firefox, Internet Explorer, Safari, or other browsers, enabling you to conduct Google searches no matter where you are on the Internet. (See **http://www.google.com/tools** for more information.) Google has become the preferred search engine of savvy Web researchers. It can be so effective when used smartly that some people have suggested that it may even eliminate the need for Web designers to create complex navigational schemes on their sites.

Google Toolbar

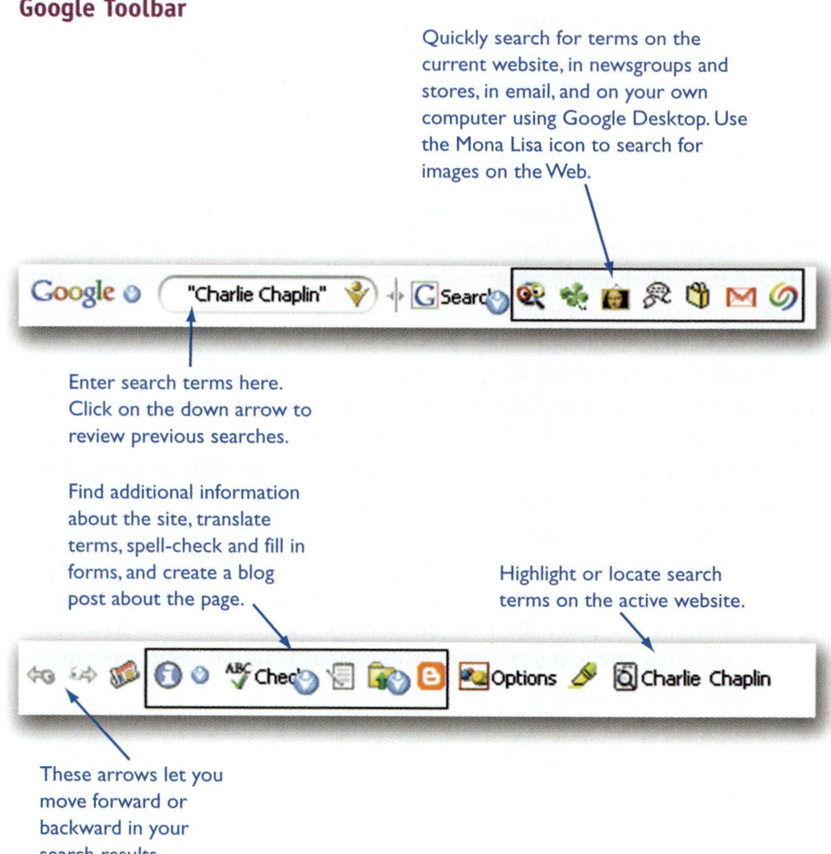
Quickly search for terms on the current website, in newsgroups and stores, in email, and on your own computer using Google Desktop. Use the Mona Lisa icon to search for images on the Web.
Google
"Charlie Chaplin"
Search
Enter search terms here. Click on the down arrow to review previous searches.
Find additional information about the site, translate terms, spell-check and fill in forms, and create a blog post about the page.
Highlight or locate search terms on the active website.
Check
Options
Charlie Chaplin
These arrows let you move forward or backward in your search results.

Boolean Operators

AND: Locates Web pages that contain all of the specified words or phrases. If you write *Music AND Videos,* then only Web pages with both words will be located.

AND NOT: Excludes Web pages that contain the specified word or phrase. If you write *Music AND NOT Videos,* then the search engine will return only those Web pages that contain the word *Music* and do not contain the word *Videos.* Make sure that you type in the two words *AND NOT,* rather than just typing in *NOT.*

NEAR and **W10:** Locates Web pages that contain both of the specified words or phrases within 10 words of each other. If you write *Music NEAR Videos,* then the search engine will return only those Web pages that have the word *Music* within 10 words of the word *Videos.* Using the W10 operator is another Boolean method of locating a word within 10 characters of another word on a Web page. You can also substitute other numbers for the 10. Both NEAR and W10 searches are called "proximity searches."

OR: Locates Web pages that contain at least one of the specified words or phrases. If you write *Music OR Videos,* then the search engine will return Web pages with either of those words.

Parentheses ( ): Allows use of two or more Boolean commands to locate Web pages. If you write *(Music AND Videos) AND (Eminem OR Rap),* then the search engine will return Web pages that contain either *Rap Music Videos* or *Eminem Music Videos.* If you changed the *OR* between *Eminem* and *Rap* to *AND,* then the search engine would return Web pages that contained *Rap Music Videos* and *Eminem Music Videos* and Web pages that contained *Eminem Rap Music Videos.*

Activity 15-4: Searching with Boolean Operators

Use Boolean operators to create different combinations of the search terms you generated in earlier activities. Conduct searches with them. Compare the search results you get from using Boolean operators with the search results you got from searching within results. How are the results similar, and how are they different? Write a paragraph articulating the similarities and differences and discussing which type of search seems more useful.

Search engines offer helpful search features: Boolean searches, which establish particular relationships among your search terms; directory searches, which use preorganized categories of information; and advanced searches, which include special options.

Using Boolean Searches

Boolean searches rely on a programming system for making logical comparisons created by mathematician George Boole. When you use certain *Boolean operators* between search words, you tell the search engine to look for words in certain orders and arrangements and to exclude other words from your results list.

A Boolean search is assembled by joining your search words with combinations of the Boolean operators *AND, OR,* and *NOT.* Some search engines allow you to manually click on the Boolean operators you want applied to your search. Other search engines can handle the Boolean operators written among the search words, as search commands. Some search forms match pages on any of the terms (*OR*) and require the searcher to add a plus sign (+) to indicate that a particular term is required. *Because search engines vary widely in their acceptance of Boolean operators, refer to the "About" or "> more" pages on each search engine site to see which ones will work for you.*

Accessing Cached Results

Good search engines offer you the ability to examine *cached results* as one option for viewing your search results. When the search engine collects its database of sites on the Web, it collects (or caches) a copy of each page as it exists at that moment in time. We recommend using the active results list for your research so that you are working with current information. However, if a new Web page loads slowly or can't be found, you can access the cached results. Cached results may be dated or may have been deliberately taken down by the authors, so we don't recommend citing them.

Still, cached results can save you time on occasion. When you use cached results in Google, for instance, you can see your search terms highlighted on the page, which is handy for assessing quickly whether a current Web page is a potentially good resource.

The Google Directory

Web Images Groups News Froogle Local **more »**

Search Directory

Preferences
Directory Help

The web organized by topic into categories.

Arts Movies, Music, Television,...	**Home** Consumers, Homeowners, Family,...	**Regional** Asia, Europe, North America,...
Business Industries, Finance, Jobs,...	**Kids and Teens** Computers, Entertainment, School,...	**Science** Biology, Psychology, Physics,...
Computers Hardware, Internet, Software,...	**News** Media, Newspapers, Current Events,...	**Shopping** Autos, Clothing, Gifts,...
Games Board, Roleplaying, Video,...	**Recreation** Food, Outdoors, Travel,...	**Society** Issues, People, Religion,...
Health Alternative, Fitness, Medicine,...	**Reference** Education, Libraries, Maps,...	**Sports** Basketball, Football, Soccer,...

World
Deutsch, Español, Français, Italiano, Japanese, Korean, Nederlands, Polska, Svenska, ...

In addition to using the directory at **http://www.google.com/dirhp** when you already know what your research question or hypothesis is, you can use the directory to generate ideas for topics. The section "Society – Issues" is particularly helpful for finding controversial subjects suitable for thesis-based research essays.

Sample Directory Search

Suppose you are doing research for a paper on contemporary female filmmakers. In a directory search, you would search smaller and smaller categories to find results:

Humanities
  Film
    Filmmakers
      Living filmmakers
        Female filmmakers, where you would find results for Web pages that contain information about international filmmakers, U.S. filmmakers, and so on.

At this point, you could continue refining your search by selecting smaller and smaller categories, or you could begin viewing your results, which you see at each directory level. (You will see the most items listed at the highest level of generality, and the results are usually alphabetized.) Use a directory search when you are not certain about the specific words and phrases that you want your Web pages to contain.

Advanced Search Options Typically Available

The advanced search feature of a search engine often includes the following options, though they may be configured differently on different engines.

- Search using "all of the words," "the exact phrase," "at least one of the words," and/or "none of the words," in any combination
- Search only pages updated within a certain time frame, with choices such as "anytime," "within the past three months," and "within the past six months"
- Search only pages written in certain languages
- Search only files saved in certain formats, such as those with .doc or .pdf at the end
- Search only certain domains, such as .edu, .com, or .gov
- Search only for search terms occurring in particular places, such as "in the URL," "in the title of the page," or "in the text of the page"

Conducting Directory Searches

A directory search uses pre-organized categories, such as the ones that you can find below the Yahoo! search box (◀ page 290) or the ones that you can find at Google. In directory searches, you rely on someone else's system of classifying information, which is fine for most purposes and will stimulate some connections for you. Instead of entering search words and phrases (which, in your search, are the smallest elements that you are looking for), you start with the largest category and search in increasingly narrower categories within it.

Conducting Advanced Searches

Some search engines have an advanced search feature. It may include options (generally separate search boxes) that allow you to search for words or phrases in the text of a website, in the URL, or in the titles of Web pages. We recommend using advanced search methods either at the very start or very early in your research process, once you know what you're looking for. You will soon be able to find exactly what you're looking for within seconds.

15b

Locating Similar Sites

Many search engines (Google, Yahoo!, MSN, A9, Ask) offer an option for follow-up searches called "More Like This" or "Find Similar." Clicking on "More Like This" will tell the search engine to locate Web pages that are similar to the ones shown. This is a method of refining your search without using specific words or phrases, since the search engines have similar search words and phrases already built into them. Sometimes the search engine has a more sophisticated method of searching, which is especially useful if you cannot think of any more search words.

WordNet: A Lexical Database for the English Language: http://wordnet.princeton.edu/

Trying to figure out synonyms for your search words?

Need to figure out the meaning of a word?

WordNet® is an online lexical reference system. English nouns, verbs, adjectives, and adverbs are organized into synonym sets, each representing one underlying lexical concept. Different relations link the synonym sets. The site has a simple, easy-to-use search engine for words.

15c Understanding the Kinds of Searches You Can Conduct

We've covered the basics of keyword and Boolean searches in sections 15a and 15b. This section discusses natural language searches, site searches, and wildcard searches. Metasearches are covered in section 15f.

Natural language search
Example: Typing into the search box *How many college students in the U.S. are enrolled in a degree-granting program?*

Site search
Example: Searching the White House site (**http://www.whitehouse.gov**) for current information on presidential speeches

Wildcard search
Example: Typing *lab*r* into the search box in order to find "labor" and "labour"

Metasearch
Example: Using a metasearch engine such as Dogpile, Mamma, or Ixquick to search other search engines and return one results list

The Parts of a URL?

A URL is the address for a site, file, or resource on the Web. A URL is made up of three main elements:

1. The protocol (that is, method of accessing the information), normally expressed as *http://* or, in some cases, *ftp://*.
2. The domain name, which is the main part of the address and can look like *purdue.edu* or *peta.org* or *creativecommons.org*. The domain name is the element of the name that most people remember.
3. The hierarchical name of the files on the site, such as *currentevents/listings.html,* in which the hierarchy is expressed with backslashes and the ending is often .html.

If you went to Yahoo.com (the domain), for example, and searched different protocols, such as *http://profiles,* you might find a specific place there where your friend's photo files were linked to her Yahoo! profile.

A URL identifies a folder structure targeting a particular file on a server. Sometimes that file is a static one (such as an .html file), and sometimes it is assembled from packets of information that depend on user input. Here's an example of a URL with the protocol, domain name, and folder structure indicated:

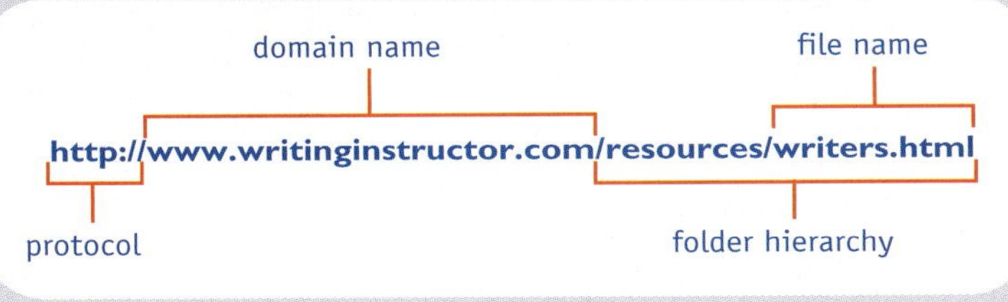

Using Natural Language Searches

Natural language searches (and search engines) were invented so that people would not have to memorize Boolean operators; they could use simple *natural language* for their searches. The best-known natural language search engine is Ask. When you use a *natural language search,* you can type in, for example, "How many people read the news online every day?" Some natural language search engines employ a vector search, which begins by using the language of your search to categorize results. In this case, it would begin by looking for indexed Web pages that answered questions beginning with *How many.*

Other natural language search engines use a statistical approach, in which sophisticated systems match the words and phrases in your natural language search sentence against a database of indexed Web pages. (In this case, the natural language search engine would look for pages that had a high statistical probability of matching *read* with *every day.*)

Using Site and Domain Searches

A site (or domain) search is one of the most effective methods of advanced searching. Site searches are handy when you know what sites should include information on your topic. For example, the CIA keeps track of vital statistics on every country in the world, so it's a good place to begin searching for country information. See the sample search of the CIA's World Factbook.

Including Stop Words in a Search

Stop words are common words (like *the, an, a, to,* and some numerals) that are often automatically deleted from searches in order to speed things up. If you need to ensure that a stop word isn't automatically deleted from a search, put the phrase in quotation marks. For example, if you're researching information about the poem "Ode on a Grecian Urn" by John Keats and want to find out how many times the poem is mistakenly titled "Ode *to* a Grecian Urn," then you should use quotation marks around the poem's title. When you do, you get hits that highlight this phrase without others mixed in because normally "to" would not be included in the search.

Sample Domain Search: Searching the CIA's World Factbook

Suppose you want to search for information about Afghanistan within the vast archives of global information on the CIA's website (**http://www.cia.gov**). For a site search of the CIA website from Google, type in the search box *afghanistan site:cia.gov,* where *cia.gov* is the domain and *Afghanistan* is the name of the country you want to research. *Site:* tells the computer to search only the CIA website. The search engine will locate and show only the pages relating to Afghanistan that it has indexed from the CIA.gov domain. If you wanted to find more specific information about the Taliban in Afghanistan, you would type in *Taliban Afghanistan site:cia.gov.* Notice the space after the words that precede "site." You can use this technique if you know the domain name of the website that you want to search. For example, *documentation site:owl.english.purdue.edu* will search the Online Writing Lab's website at Purdue University for all hits on "documentation."

Activity 15-5: Searching within a Site

Look over your search results from the last few activities and find a site that seems to be coming up often in your search results. Using Google's Advanced Search page (**http://www.google.com/advanced_search**), run a search in which you use your terms on just that site by entering the site's URL in the "Domain" box. How are your search results different from those of other kinds of searching? Is this kind of search helpful for your project? Why or why not?

Search inside the Book

In October 2003, Amazon.com created a searchable digital library that enables users to "search inside the book." The library originally included 120,000 full, searchable books that publishers had made available to Amazon for scanning and uploading to the site (the number has significantly expanded with time). If you're looking for a particular phrase or trying to track down the source of a quotation, the "Search Inside the Book" service can be a great help. In this example from Amazon.com, the researcher was looking for the source of a quotation from the book *The Devil in the White City* by Erik Larson. At that book's page, she searched inside the book for the phrase "Ferris Wheel" by mousing over the book's image. She also noticed additional information about the book—including a concordance, "statistically improbable passages" (SIPs), capitalized phrases (CAPs), other books cited, and readability statistics. The results list returned 44 instances of "Ferris Wheel" in the book.

SEARCH INSIDE!™
The Devil in the White City: Murder, Magic, and Madness at the Fair That Changed America (Hardcover)
by Erik Larson "A thousand trains a day entered or left Chicago..." (more)
SIPs: eastern architects, exposition directors, electric launches, furnace company, exposition work (more)
CAPs: Jackson Park, Chicago Tribune, Ferris Wheel, World's Columbian Exposition, Burnham Archives (more)
(402 customer reviews)
Inside This Book
New! Books on Related Topics | Concordance | Text Stats
Citations: This book cites 42 books | 4 books that cite this book
Browse Sample Pages: Front Cover | Copyright | Table of Contents | Excerpt | Index | Back Cover | Surprise Me!
Search Inside This Book: Ferris Wheel
Ferris Wheel
152 used & new available from $10.22
Share your own customer images

From http://www.amazon.com.

Using Wildcard Searches

A wildcard search uses an asterisk (*) to tell the search engine to look for a specific letter sequence plus any other letters. Wildcard searches are also referred to as *truncation* (when you search for any variation of the word's spelling) or *stemming* (when you use the stem of the word as a search term). The asterisk represents any letter or letters added onto your search words. Design* would cause the search engine to look for Web pages that contain *design, designer,* and *designing.* You should be thoughtful when using wildcard searches; in this example, the wildcard search would return a list of pages that contained *designation, designee, designator,* and other words that start with *design.*

Normally, you have to place three letters before the asterisk. You can put the asterisk anywhere inside the letters of your search word, which can help when you are uncertain about a search word's spelling or when another spelling can be used. For example, to cover both *theatre* and *theater,* you might type *theat**.

The search engines listed here are among the most effective now available.

Unless indicated, they automatically use the Boolean operator *AND* as a default when you write more than one search word. All of them also automatically use quotation mark phrase searches for proximity searching. All of them automatically sort your results by relevance or by a page's link frequency or popularity (how many other sites link to it). Some offer other ways of sorting the results list.

Search Engine Showdown

Search Engine Showdown is a website that ranks some but not all search engines. The site includes a chart organized by search engine, which can be found at http://www.searchengineshowdown.com/features/, and information organized by features (search capabilities), found at http://www.searchengineshowdown.com/features/byfeature.shtml.

Features of Popular Search Engines

Recommended Search Engines

Google: http://www.google.com
See also **http://www.google.com/intl/en/options/** for a list of special searches and tools that Google makes available, including the very useful Google Desktop Search™, which helps you quickly find files on your personal computer. (Apple makes a similar tool called Spotlight™ for OS 10.4 and higher.)

Google Scholar: http://scholar.google.com
Google Scholar™ enables you to "search specifically for scholarly literature, including peer-reviewed papers, theses, books, reprints, abstracts, and technical reports from all broad areas of research." If the work is published on the Internet, there's a strong chance Google Scholar will help you find it.

Google Images: http://images.google.com
Google Images™ enables Internet image-only searches.

Google Book Search: http://books.google.com
Google Book Search™ has begun digitizing the holdings of major libraries and publishers to allow full text searches of books, much like Amazon.com's "Search Inside the Book" feature.

Good Secondary Search Engines

Ask: http://www.ask.com
See **http://sp.ask.com/docs/about/tech_features.html** for a full list of features, including the new natural language question-asking tool, which analyzes search results for probable answers and categorizes them separately in your results list.

A9: http://a9.com
A9, developed by Amazon.com, is a good tool for researchers. Its integrative text and image search function allows users to sort results and add notes to them. See **http://a9.com/-/company/whatsCool.jsp** to learn more about A9's features and capabilities.

Clusty: http://clusty.com
Clusty groups the results list by topical categories. Clusty is a metasearch tool and so compiles results from MSN Search, Ask, Gigablast, Wisenut, and more. See **http://clusty.com/#** for a tour of Clusty's unique features.

International Search Engines

Search Engine Colossus: International Directory of Search Engines:
http://www.searchenginecolossus.com
Arnold Information Technology's List of International Search Engines:
http://www.arnoldit.com/lists/intlsearch.asp
The search engines listed in this chapter include options for searching in a wide variety of languages. Be sure that your instructor permits the use of research materials in languages other than English. Also be careful to evaluate such resources just as you would those written in English (section 15h).

Some of the major search engines have options for searching in French, Spanish, German, and Italian, and most will show only sites written in particular languages if you use the search engine's "preferences" settings. If you want to search in languages other than English, try the resources listed here, which include URLs to sites in English and other languages.

Activity 15-6: Searching Using Multiple Search Engines

Take one of your keywords or search phrases and use it to run a search on three different search engines from the list on these two pages. Print out the first page of search results from each search engine, and compare them. Write a paragraph that explains the similarities and differences between the search results, and explain which search engine gave the best results for your project.

Good Secondary Search Engines

KartOO: http://www.kartoo.com
KartOO groups results in topical clusters and includes a visual map to show the relationships across clusters. For more information, see **http://www.kartoo.net/a/en/aide01.html**.

MSN Search: http://www.msn.com
MSN Search includes image, music, and news searches. MSN Search users can get a free pass to search the Encarta encyclopedia. Tour MSN Search's features at **http://www.imagine-msn.com/search/tour/moreprecise.aspx**.

Open Directory Project (ODP): http://dmoz.org
Search results are sorted in advance by people, who help make results more precise. See **http://dmoz.org/about.html** to learn more.

Yahoo! Search: http://www.yahoo.com
Yahoo!'s search engine is powered by Google. Sponsored results are listed at the top of the results page.

A **metasearch engine** conducts a search for results by sending your search words or phrases to other search engines, which then search for your words or phrases. The metasearch engine assembles all the results for you. The results from all of the searches are shown on the first metasearch results page.

For example, if you entered *Violence AND Media AND Effect* into a metasearch engine (such as Ixquick, Metasearch, or Dogpile), then you would get results from different search engines (such as Yahoo!, Google, MSN, and iWon).

Some people prefer metasearch engines because they cover so much more than the databases of a single search engine (i.e., the totality of the Web pages that are indexed into, for instance, Yahoo!).

Metasearches are handy when you are uncertain about which specific words and phrases you should use to begin your search.

A List of Metasearch Engines

Mamma: http://www.mamma.com
Searches About.com, Open Directory, Mamma Collection, Business.com, Lycos, MSN, Ask, EntireWeb, Overture, LookSmart, FindWhat, Ah-Ha, ImageInclude, Kanoodle, Epilot, 7Search, and Search Engine Marketing.
Boolean operators: AND, OR, NOT, +, –, phrase

Search: http://www.search.com
Searches FindWhat, LookSmart, Business.com, Sprinks, Overture, Thunderstone, About.com, AltaVista, Galaxy, All the Web, Advice and Answers, Abika, EXP.com, QuestionExchange, webhelp.com, AskMe, CNET Shopper, Open Directory, Yahoo!, MySimon, CNET News.com, CNN, Yahoo! News, MSNBC, and more.

Ixquick: http://www.ixquick.com
Searches AOL, Ah-Ha, All the Web, Ask/Direct Hit, EntireWeb, FindWhat, Go, Hotbot, Kanoodle, LookSmart, MSN, Netscape, Open Directory, and Overture.

Dogpile: http://www.dogpile.com
Searches Ah-Ha, Ask, FAST, FindWhat, Inktomi, LookSmart, Overture, and Sprinks.

Activity 15-7: Conducting a Metasearch

Use one of your keywords or search phrases to run a search on two different metasearch engines from the list above. Print out the first page of search results from each metasearch engine, and compare them. Are they pointing you to similar results from similar search engines or to different results that you hadn't seen before? Write a paragraph that explains the similarities and differences between the search results, and explain which metasearch engine gave better results for your project. Did you find any new results by using a metasearch engine? Describe them.

Google Zeitgeist

Finding out what other people search for on the Internet can sometimes help you refine your own searches (or avoid advertisers, who often try to create sites that are based on popular search terms). Google's Zeitgeist™, at **http://www.google.com/intl/en/press/zeitgeist.html**, is a collection of data about how its users use the search engine, how terms come in and out of favor, and more.

As you can see, the terms are tied to current events, and they are words that you or I might use, without thinking about how attractive they may be to advertisers. So be as specific as possible with your terms. Our example on prenatal care led to results that were more specific than you would find with more general terms, such as *pregnant, baby, medical attention,* or *health*. But remember that overly precise language may limit your results prematurely. Our advice is to make multiple searches, on different search engines, with different combinations of words and phrases.

Zeitgeist This Week

Top 15 Gaining Queries: Week Ending September 5, 2005

1. hurricane katrina	6. fema	11. hurricane katrina pictures
2. red cross	7. us open	12. tulane university
3. new orleans	8. kanye west	13. fats domino
4. gas prices	9. sania mirza	14. cheap gas
5. salvation army	10. cnn	15. gas shortage

Be Creative When You Search for Information

It is often simple to determine what terms to use to find information. You know what you want to write, and, to a certain extent, you know the terms used for your subject.

For instance, if you were against abortion and you wanted some information to support a paper explaining your position, then you would naturally search for websites using a term like *pro-life*. However, if you were for a woman's right to choose, you would just as naturally use a search term like *pro-choice*. Sometimes, when we occupy one position, we forget the terms and kinds of language used by people who hold other beliefs. By understanding the language and the terms that are used by people who have different opinions or beliefs, you can search more effectively.

Be cautious about the most common search words. These words vary slightly over time; however, some search words are so commonly used in searches that they are sold to advertisers. If you use these words in your searches, you are typically going to find results that are driven primarily by the desire of an advertiser to sell you something.

Refine Search Terms by Investigating Results

As a general rule, for your first couple of searches, reduce the results to fewer than 10,000 entries by searching within results or by changing your search words. Then use different terms in the Search within Results function to reduce the four-digit number down to no more than 30 or 40 results, when you can begin examining pages by opening them in new windows (page 291). Open multiple windows, but eventually you might strain your computer's memory, so close the ones you have already bookmarked or no longer need.

Quickly Find What You Need on a Web Page

Sometimes your search terms are buried within the website, in which case it may be handy to use the Find command. Put your cursor near the top of the Web page, click on Edit, and then select Find. When the Find window appears, type in your search term(s). The Find function will search the Web page either up or down, depending on where your cursor is.

Also consider using the meta-search engine Ixquick (http://ixquick.com). It offers results pages with the search terms highlighted in yellow and in an enlarged font size.

Try a URL Search

Using a search engine when you already have a sense of the URL (the website address) is likely to waste time. Before conducting a search, simply write the name, as you think it is spelled, in the address box, after the *http://*. You'll quickly find out whether you need to search further.

Useful Research Portals

Research portals are sites that provide visitors with a collection of links and documents that are useful in research. Almost all of your research could start at **RefDesk** and you'd do well:
http://www.refdesk.com

Global Information (politics, culture, history, social sciences, humanities):
http://www.cia.gov/cia/publications/factbook/

Science Journals and Publications:
http://directory.google.com/Top/Science/Publications/Journals_and_Magazines/Free_Online_Journals/

Cultural and Social Issues:
http://directory.google.com/Top/Society/Issues/

Journal Archives:
You can search the EBSCOhost site either via the URL here or through your library's site if your college has a subscription to the service.
http://www.epnet.com/academic/default.asp

The Educational Resources Information Center (ERIC):
The national information system is designed to provide ready access to an extensive body of education-related research contributed by users.
http://www.eric.ed.gov

The Library of Congress:
Lists all books published in the United States and many published elsewhere.
http://www.loc.gov

Knowledge Network for Business, Technology, and Knowledge Management:
http://www.brint.com/interest.html

Activity 15-8: Using Research Portals

Use one of your keywords or search phrases to run a search using two different research portals from the list above. Compare the results you get from the research portals with each other, but also with the results you have gotten from searching on other types of search engines. Which results are the most relevant to you? What sites and sources of information did the research portals turn up that the other sites didn't? Write a paragraph explaining the similarities and differences.

Activity 15-9: Can You Verify This Information from Websites?

Below are four pieces of information from websites that could be used in different research projects. Use your online research skills to verify whether this information is accurate, partially accurate, or inaccurate. Write a paragraph on each piece of information, explaining why the information is accurate or inaccurate and citing the Web research that you used.

1. "It was Tim Berners-Lee who brought this all together and created the World Wide Web. The first trials of the World Wide Web were at the CERN laboratories (one of Europe's largest research laboratories) in Switzerland in December 1990." ("History of the World Wide Web," <http://www.nethistory.info/History%20of%20the%20Internet/web.html>)
2. "During a lecture I said 'If you are using aspartame (NutraSweet, Equal, Spoonful, etc.) and you suffer from fibromyalgia symptoms, spasms, shooting pains, numbness in your legs, cramps, vertigo, dizziness, headaches, tinnitus, joint pain, depression, anxiety attacks, slurred speech, blurred vision, or memory loss—you probably have Aspartame Disease!'" (Nancy Markle, <http://www.medical-library.net/sites/framer.html?/sites/_aspartame_disease.html>)
3. "The writer George Eliot was born on the Arbury Estate in Warwickshire in 1819. She was baptised with the name Mary Anne Evans and George Eliot was just one of five names she adopted through various periods in her life." ("George Eliot's Life of Sex and Scandals," <http://www.bbc.co.uk/coventry/features/george-eliot/eliot-scandals-and-rumours.shtml>)
4. "On 12 June [1776], one delegate from each colony was chosen to sit on a committee 'to prepare and digest the form of confederation' (38). The committee members were: Samuel Adams, Josiah Bartlett, John Dickinson (chairman), Button Gwinnett, Joseph Hewes, Stephen Hopkins, Robert R. Livingston, Thomas McKean, Thomas Nelson, Edward Rutledge, Roger Sherman, and Thomas Stone. Francis Hopkinson was added to the committee on 28 June." ("Articles of Confederation," <http://www.cr.nps.gov/history/online_books/dube/inde3.htm>)

Newspapers and magazines—if they hope to have the people's trust—must rely on their writers to carefully check every fact in an article. So much writing gets published so quickly that most news organizations don't have time to employ fact-checkers, though they will make attempts to confirm facts and get independent verification from alternative sources. When they do make mistakes, it can be embarrassing and expensive. If errors appear in published articles, the next issue must contain the correction. Newspapers also need to be wary of making libelous (untrue and harmful) statements about people, lest they be sued.

Most websites (and many printed publications) do not adhere to anything like these high editorial standards. The Web is especially likely to represent a very wide spectrum of opinions, "facts," and "truths," precisely because many Web page authors do not bother to check their facts. Evaluate the information you read online as carefully as possible.

Validate and Verify Your Information

Researchers often neglect one crucial stage of online research. You may have found decent results for your search, using specific terms and searching within results. However, it is a good idea to validate and verify your information by trying a new search, with different terms as starting points. For example, although we found thousands of results for *increased federal funding for family planning* and *prenatal care,* it would be a good idea to search again, using different terms or synonyms, such as *planned parenthood* or even *early pregnancy care.* You may end up with many of the same results. You may also find a wealth of new, supporting information. More importantly, you may discover an entirely new way of thinking about your subject, one that you have not yet considered. A second search, using synonyms, often helps widen the scope of both the information you find and the approach to your subject.

Search for Domain-Level URLs

To make sure you don't miss a major source of information on your subject, run a domain-level search for sites on your topic. For example, you could try entering *www.plannedparenthood.org* (or *.com*) in your browser's address bar to see what turns up. In many cases, organizations with much information to offer on a subject also have rights to a domain name associated with it, so you can guess at what the URL might be.

Beware of Para-Sites

In addition to interrogating the validity, reliability, and balance of the information you find online, you should be careful to consider the purpose of a website as a whole. Teachers have reported incidents of careless writers citing a website authored by a wing of the Ku Klux Klan in their papers on Martin Luther King Jr.'s life and accomplishments.

The Beloved Community

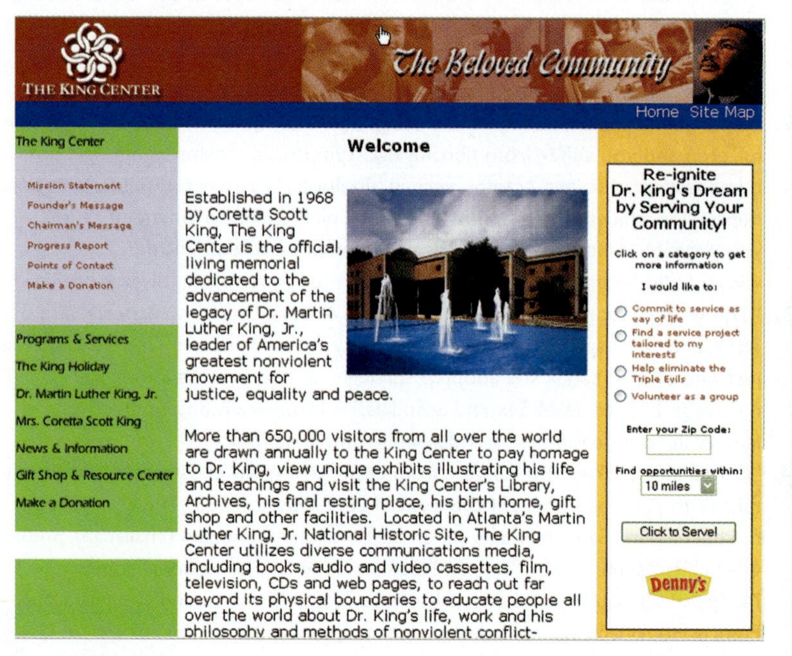

The authentic site of The King Center: **http://www.martinlutherkingjr.com** or **http://www.thekingcenter.org/tkc/index.asp**

Martin Luther King Jr. "Para-Site"

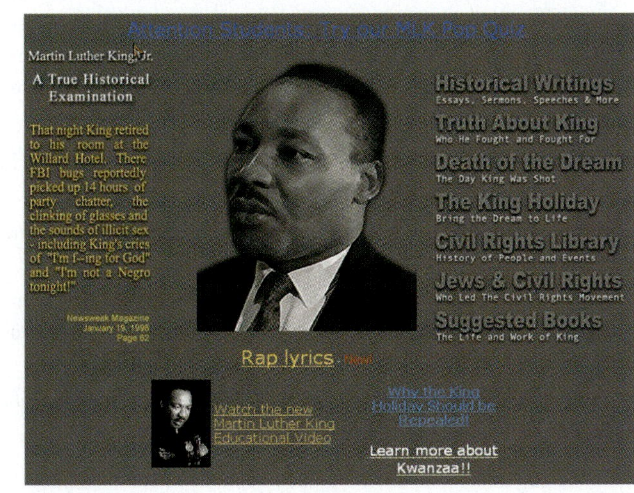

The para-site Martin Luther King Jr., which attempts to associate itself with the URL of the official voice of The King Center by using a similar URL: **http://www.martinlutherking.org**

If you pay attention to purpose, you can see rather easily that the para-site is affiliated with a hate group. Inserted into King's biography are rumors (unsupported by any documentation from reputable sources that can be validated), charges of sexual misconduct and excessive partying, and worse—all designed to suggest that Reverend King was not the great American so many admire for his message of peace and racial equality. If you look at other information on the site, you'll find people like David Duke, a well-known white supremacist, being praised. With experience, you should be able to recognize quickly when a website (or any other source) is offering you dubious information.

You have to be careful, however, because some domain names have been appropriated by groups with ulterior motives. For instance, the official website of the White House is at www.whitehouse.gov, but there is also www.whitehouse.com, a pornography site. Unscrupulous information providers know that many people don't pay much attention to the domain name suffix (.gov, .com, .org, and so on) and thus end up at "para-sites," which mimic a domain name in the interest of trapping unsuspecting Web travelers.

Evaluate the Motives and Purpose of a Site

Information is always manipulated to achieve certain ends, and the facts that are important to one person may be irrelevant to another. The information you find online is going to be channeled for a particular purpose and motive, and good researchers make sure they evaluate these motives when assessing whether or not to use such information. It's helpful, therefore, to perform some rhetorical analysis before you decide to cite sources.

If you need information on gun control, for example, you should understand that while the National Rifle Association (NRA) website will offer you more information on that subject than most others, it will be information designed to support the NRA's position on gun control. You could say the same for the Million Mom March or Handgun Control, Inc. websites. Information you find on partisan (or overtly political) websites may be useful, but remember that these groups provide information to the public to advance an agenda and so may shade facts in a particular hue. Use information, but don't get used by it. You still need to verify figures and check facts with other sites. (For more on rhetorical analysis, see sections 8c and 15i.)

Evaluating Online Information by Purpose

Websites typically fall into one of seven categories, so you can begin your evaluation of a source's reliability by identifying its genre or primary purpose. When evaluating an online resource according to purpose, remember to consider all of its elements: text, graphics, advertising, layout, links, authorship, currency of information, domain name suffix, and any other aspects that will help you contextualize the information it provides.

Before citing information from online sources (or from print sources, for that matter), consider the likely reliability of those offering it. Typically, educational, government, and news media sites offer the most reliable information, but you should always try to find multiple sources to confirm a site's validity. Each research subject will

Primary Purposes of Websites

No website gains or loses credibility simply because it falls into one or another of these categories. For example, e-commerce sites can be terrific sources of reliable information. At major corporations' sites, you can find news releases about products, "white papers," and user documentation. Just be aware that the information is meant to support a product or service, not necessarily to present a well-rounded discussion of an issue.

- **Navigational:** information portals or pathways (like RefDesk, Yahoo!, MSN, AOL, or even *Arts and Letters Daily*)
- **Educational and academic:** sites of educational institutions (with the .edu suffix), encyclopedias, and professional journals and organizations
- **News media:** sites of newspapers, magazines, and TV networks (for example, CNN, MSNBC, *New York Times, US News and World Report,* and *The Chronicle of Higher Education*)
- **Government documentation:** sites of the Library of Congress, branches of government, the FBI, the CIA, and state governments
- **Public advocacy:** sites that advocate for a position on social issues
- **E-commerce:** sites that offer services or products to consumers and businesses
- **Personal:** home pages, weblogs, personal journals, and camsites

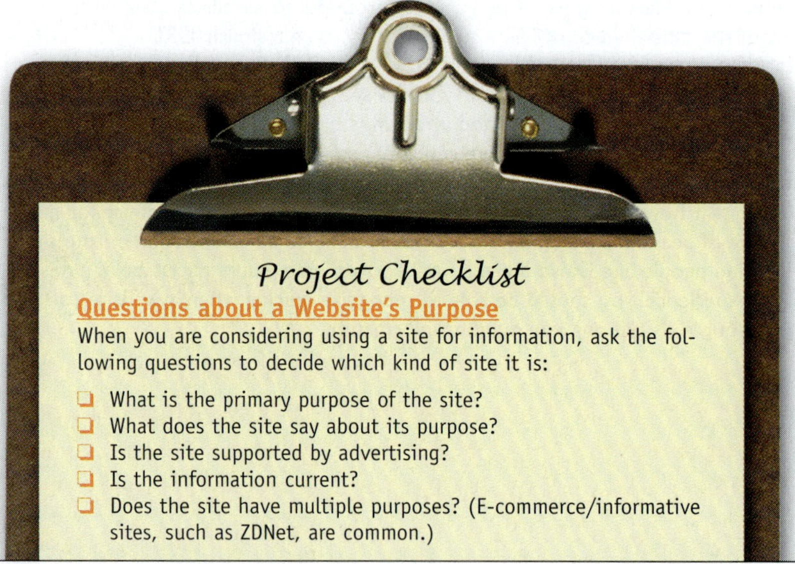

Project Checklist

Questions about a Website's Purpose

When you are considering using a site for information, ask the following questions to decide which kind of site it is:

- ❏ What is the primary purpose of the site?
- ❏ What does the site say about its purpose?
- ❏ Is the site supported by advertising?
- ❏ Is the information current?
- ❏ Does the site have multiple purposes? (E-commerce/informative sites, such as ZDNet, are common.)

Activity 15-10: Classifying Your Search Results

By now you should have a great many search results. Take a sample of five different sites from your search results, and evaluate them using the criteria presented in the Project Checklist on page 310. Answer the five questions, and then write a paragraph that describes each site's purpose for presenting information and puts the information in context.

Is the information . . .

- **valid?** Your information should be truthful. Example: If a website says that experiments with certain results were carried out at Columbia University in 1970, then, in fact, those experiments did take place and the results were as indicated.
- **reliable?** Your information should be consistent with that in other sources on the same subject. Example: You find the same facts in an encyclopedia and in a nonfiction book by a respected authority.
- **balanced?** Either your information should display no bias or its bias should be directly discussed as part of the presentation of the information. Example: You use information on the history of tobacco use in the United States, and the information serves neither to promote smoking nor to encourage smoking cessation.
- **comprehensive?** Your information should be essentially complete and not lack any valuable or integral elements. Example: In a critical review of popular diets in a nutrition course, you list all of the known drawbacks of each and don't let any escape notice.
- **relevant?** Your information should be appropriate to the situation. Example: You would cite a Shakespearean critic's analysis of Hamlet's character in a paper on the play *Hamlet,* but would probably avoid doing so in a paper on the children's book *Goodnight Moon.*
- **current?** Your information should be up to date. Example: With topics that are rapidly evolving, such as the development of digital media, you cite information that has been updated recently. On issues that have been settled, you use the most recent and frequently cited source for your information (▶ section 16g).

When your information does not meet these requirements, make sure that you discuss how it may fall short. This way, while your evidence might have problems, your use of it will not.

have its own best kind of site(s) to use for support.

You can use information from personal or e-commerce sites, but make sure your reader understands the nature of the source and its reliability. Although the value of a particular site primarily depends on your subject and purpose for writing, the sites on page 310 are ordered according to their general acceptability to readers, from most acceptable to least. By describing the sources of information in your writing, you engender your reader's trust.

Criteria for Evaluating Information

Information is useful for research when it is valid, reliable, balanced, comprehensive, relevant, and current. It is the researcher's task to make sure that all information meets these criteria. Unfortunately, not all of it will. When it doesn't, you must either find better sources or use good judgment about how you frame the information in your research project.

You can also evaluate your information resources by analyzing the rhetorical situation with respect to audience, authorship, and documents.

Project Checklist

Questions to Ask about Audience and Authorship

Questions about Audience

1. Who is the primary audience for the site? Is there any offensive or exclusionary language? (If so, consider using the information only to demonstrate how one person or group views your subject.)
2. What age/educational range does the site target? How valuable is the site for other ages/educational ranges?
3. Is the resource addressed to novices or experts on the subject?
4. Does the site provide a comment book or guest register? Does its content reveal anything about the audience?

Questions about Authorship

1. Who is the author or producer of the site? How does the author have the authority to provide this information? Has the author published anything else? Is the author cited by others?
2. Is the author associated with other individuals/groups? What do you find when you use the author's name as a search term?
3. What relevant professional, business, or political affiliations does the author have? Do any of these cast doubt on the author's objectivity, or do they add to the author's authority?
4. Who sponsors the site? Is the sponsor a nonprofit organization, a business, a government, or an educational institution? Does this sponsor's presence create bias?
5. Is the email address of a particular person provided, or is the person unnamed? (If there is no contact information, is this an anonymous site? If so, do not consider this source reliable.)
6. Who is the copyright owner of the site? If copyright is not listed, has the authorship of the information been clearly indicated otherwise? (If not, you shouldn't use it.)

Project Checklist

Questions to Ask about a Site's Documents

1. How accurate is the information provided on the site?
2. Are sources or citations given for any facts? (If not, be skeptical.)
3. What other kinds of information sources (i.e., books, journals) can you use to double-check the information?
4. Does this information appear only online or does it fit within an existing dialogue ongoing in other media?
5. Does the information appear too good to be true?
6. When was the document originally published? When was the site last updated? Can you find more up-to-date information elsewhere?
7. Are the links relevant and appropriate for the information? Are any links to sites that have moved? Are any of the linked sites out of date?
8. How well-rounded is the information on the site?
9. Is anything being sold at the page where you have found the information? Are there any connections between the information and the advertising that make the information seem dubious?
10. Does the site appear professional, or does it look hurriedly constructed?
11. Is the text grammatically and mechanically correct? Are there spelling errors?
12. Do the graphics relate to the site's content? Are any of the graphics simple clip art that doesn't serve an obvious purpose? Do the graphics complement the site's information well? Do they bias the information?
13. Is there an audio component? Does the audio produce any bias in relationship to the information? Does the audio interact appropriately with the site?
14. How convenient is the site to navigate?
15. Does the site have a search engine for internal elements on the site? Does it function properly? Or does the site use an external search engine?

Be among the 5%

Only about 5% of online researchers use any of the advanced search strategies we have discussed in this chapter. If you learn them well, you'll be able to conduct quick, focused, and productive searches through truly astonishing masses of information from around the world. If you then add rhetorical savvy by asking rigorous questions about the sources you find, you can be assured that your research projects will be based on accurate and reliable information.

15i

Activity 15-11: Evaluating Your Search Results by Asking Questions

Take a sample of five different websites from your search results. Analyze the information presented on them using the questions for rhetorical analysis of audience, authorship, and documents. How would you use the information from each site in your research paper? Which of the sites provides the most valid, reliable, and comprehensive information? Which of them provides the least valid, reliable, and comprehensive information?

15j Writing Project Threads

A table of contents for writing project threads appears on pages xv–xxii.

Informative Essays

Garrison 1

Angela Garrison

English 101

Dr. Simpson

September 26, 2005

From Over There to Over Here:

War Blogs Get Up Close, Personal, and Profitable

Blog was the word looked up most often in the online *Merriam-Webster's Dictionary* in 2004 ("Blog"). What's all this fuss? When you read someone else's personal blog, you find out what they like and don't like, what they're doing, and maybe other bits of gossip offered at random. You can read news blogs to find out what's going on lately, what other people think about it, and why it matters. You can keep your own blog to share your thoughts and feelings, to tell your friends and family what you're up to, and sometimes to capture the interest of someone you've never met. When you read and write blogs, you join, or even create, a community. Blogs are also an efficient way to break news, spread rumors, and glorify causes. In short, blogs help people do what they've always done as social beings, just more quickly now, and from almost anywhere on Earth. Soldiers on the ground fighting in Iraq are writing blogs from the front lines. But a review is now under way at the Pentagon to "better understand the overall implications of blogging and other Internet communications in combat zones," according to John Hockenberry in his *Wired* article "The Blogs of War." The benefits of blogs written by U.S. soldiers in Iraq far outweigh the hypothetical risks of revealing sensitive or strategic information. Those benefits, however, aren't as obvious as they might seem.

In spite of what the imagery of smart bombs and predator drones might lead television viewers to believe, wars are fought by people, not just technology. Most blogs start out as efforts to stay in touch with family and friends, but they quickly turn into

Uncovering Your Topic: Doing Online Research

Your research plans may include acquiring information online; use the strategies in this chapter to locate online sources. Be sure to use the guidelines in section 15h to evaluate the sources you are considering. Also, get complete citation information for every source you find and record it for safekeeping. You can use the table of contents inside the front cover for quick access to the citation style you need. You will also want to bookmark websites for later reference.

▶ page 336.

16 LIBRARY AND FIELD RESEARCH

The Internet has radically changed public access to information. Now whole libraries of information are just a click or two away. Does this make libraries obsolete? Not in the least. The library in the digital age has a critical role to play not only as a repository and archive of the printed content in books and journals that we need for research but also as a clearinghouse and filter for the best resources available.

- Librarians are highly skilled experts on finding and evaluating knowledge, and with the proliferation of information on the Internet, we need that expertise now more than ever.
- Libraries now serve as the gateway to the best that can be known, whether it's in print or digital form and whether you access that gateway online or by visiting the library—not to mention access to printed material that you can't find anywhere else.
- Libraries subscribe to hundreds of academic journals, indexes, databases, and data retrieval systems that the average person would never be able to access otherwise.

For today's savvy researcher, the library remains a primary site for college research. It is a place where smart people go to learn what they need to know, to make connections with other knowledge experts, and to tap what the wider culture deems important. Every researcher can benefit from frequent trips to the library, online *and* off.

This chapter shows you how to navigate a library. It also provides a brief introduction to conducting your own field research through interviews, surveys, and observations.

Before you begin your research project, take some time to familiarize yourself with the library (or libraries) on your campus. College and university libraries house a wealth of resources: not just books, although they will have these by the thousands, but newspapers; journals; reference works; CDs, DVDs, LPs, and other nonprint media; maps; music scores; government documents; special collections that might contain photographs, manuscripts, letters, artwork, or rare books; and—most importantly—librarians. Walk through the library and pick up helpful literature in the reference room. Take time, too, to tour your campus library's website. Library websites now act as portals not just to the library catalog but to all kinds of information, services, and retrieval systems.

Meet the Librarians

All kinds of librarians work at a library, but most important for the student researcher are the reference librarians. Reference librarians have special training in how to conduct research and may also have advanced degrees in individual subject areas. Their job is to help library patrons do research. Often, students feel as if they're not supposed to "bug" the librarians. Just the opposite: librarians are there to help you—no matter how narrow

The Library of Congress Classification System

A—General Works
B—Philosophy / Psychology / Religion
C—Auxiliary Sciences of History
D—History: General and Eastern Hemisphere
E-F—History: Western Hemisphere
G—Maps / Geography / Anthropology / Recreation
H—Social Sciences / Statistics / Economics / Sociology / Social History / Gender
J—Political Science
K—Law
L—Education
M—Music
N—Art / Architecture / Arts
P—Linguistics / Language Teaching
PA—Greek and Latin Language and Literature
PB-PM—Modern Languages (All) and Literatures Other than Those Listed Below
PN—Literature (General) / Performing Arts / Drama / Journalism
PQ—French, Italian, Spanish, and Portuguese Literatures
PR—English Literature from All Countries except US
PS—American Literature
PT—Germanic and Scandinavian Literatures
Q—Science: Math / Computer Science / Physics / Astronomy / Chemistry / Geology / Biology
R—Medicine
S—Agriculture
T—Technology, Including Environmental / Photography / Home Economics / Manufactures / Crafts
U-V—Military Sciences / Warfare
Z—Books / Libraries / General Bibliography

It's helpful to know that each book in a library has a unique call number. Call numbers are assigned according to the Library of Congress classification scheme. The subject categories shown here are further subdivided. Your library probably provides a map showing where each section is located.

or broad your question. So don't get stuck. Ask a librarian. The more you ask, the more you'll learn. The more you learn, the more fluent and effective you will be in techniques of library research.

Tour the Library's Website

While it's important to get comfortable in the library building, it's equally important to familiarize yourself with your library's website. College and university library websites offer online catalogs. They provide other means of searching for research sources, such as databases and indexes. They give users access to online reference works, ebooks, and full-text, partial-text, or abstract retrieval of articles from periodicals. Library websites provide lots of ways to get help: tutorials in basic research skills, guides to finding government documents, guides to the research process, guides to using citations, and online reference desks. Among the most important help resources are the online guides to researching in individual subject areas (section 16b). A library's website also provides basic information about the library system, such as how to request books through interlibrary loan. Library websites also provide links to the Web, along with guides to evaluating Web content.

Home Page of UMass Amherst Libraries

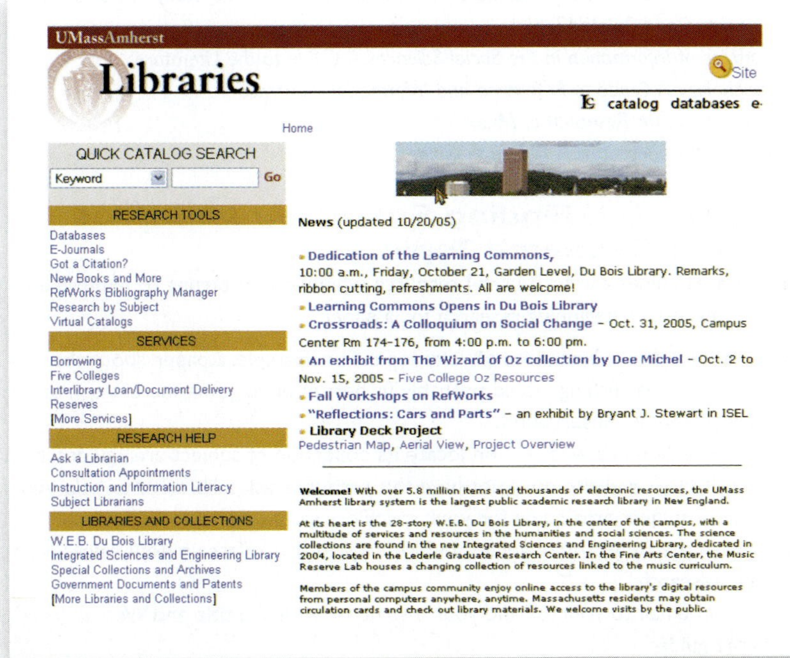

The home page for the University of Massachusetts Amherst library system provides numerous ways to search for information. Notice that "Ask a Librarian" is the first link from "Research Help." Under "Research Tools," "Research by Subject" links to subject area guides (section 16b).

An excellent way to begin your library research is to consult the research guide for your subject area, found on your library's website. Online guides might be called "guides by subject," "subject guides," "subjects a-z," "research and subject guides," "subject resource guides," "subject research guides," or "research guides." If you can't find a helpful guide on your own library's site, get help from a librarian and log onto another college's.

Book-length guides to research in individual subject areas can also be found in the reference area of your library. They may provide greater depth than the library's online handout, but the library's online subject guide will be more specifically tailored to resources available in your library.

Subject-area research guides will point you toward specialized reference materials:

- dictionaries, encyclopedias, handbooks, biographical resources, and atlases
- bibliographies and other kinds of specialized guides
- indexes and databases for finding articles and critical essays

Examples of Subject-Area Research Guides

Introduction to Library Research in Anthropology

Using the Biological Literature: A Practical Guide

Literary Research Guide: A Guide to Reference Sources for the Study of Literature in English and Related Topics

Sources of Information in the Social Sciences: A Guide to the Literature

Psychology: A Guide to Reference and Information Sources

Sourcebook for Research in Music

Medieval Iconography: A Research Guide

Activity 16-1: Finding Subject-Area Guides for Your Research Topic

Subject-area guides can be a useful resource when you're starting to explore an area of interest or beginning research for a paper.

1. Determine the subject area of your topic. For example, a paper about the dangers of overfishing would probably fit best in biology, marine biology, or environmental conservation.
2. Visit your library's website and locate its collection of subject-area guides. If your library's website does not have this resource, ask a librarian to help you locate a subject-area guide for your specific area.
3. Browse the subject-area guides and locate one that offers content relevant to your research.
4. Send an email to yourself and your instructor with the title and Web address of the guide.

"Reading the Media" Research Guide from Seattle Central Community College

research guide **the.Library.@.Seattle.Central**

Web: http://dept.sccd.ctc.edu/cclib

Reading the Media

Phone: 206-587-5421

Reference Books | Call Number Areas | Subject Headings | Periodicals
Periodical Indexes | AV/Multimedia | Web Resources | Evaluation & Citation

Reference Books

Encyclopedia of Communication a
Encyclopedia of Television, Cable
Dictionary of Media Literacy
From Talking Drums to the Intern
The Complete Film Dictionary
Magill's Survey of Cinema
Oxford Companion to Film
Filmmaker's Dictionary
Blacks in Film and Television
Images in the Dark; an encycloped
Women and Film: a bibliography
The Film Handbook
Reel Black Talk: Sourcebook of 50

Call Number Area

P90 – P120
PN1991 - PN2068

Subject Headings

Use the **Library of Congress Sub**
Film Criticism
Mass Media
Visual Communication

Periodical Indexe

Online: ProQuest Direct (with
Alt-Press Watch
Print: Reader's Guide to Peri

Periodicals

Film Comment	Film Quarterly
New York Times	Journal of Broadcasting & Electronic Media -ProQuest

AV/Multimedia

Color Adjustment	PN1992.8 .A34C64
Connections, #9	TR848 .C68
Graphic Design	PN1992.8 .G7.B34 1989
TV Gender Gap	PN4888 .W65
Writing for Film	PN1996 .W75 1989
Writing for TV	PN1992.7 .W75 1989

Web Resources

Yahoo's Film/Movie Resources
http://www.yahoo.com/Entertainment/Movies_and_Films/
CineMedia
http://www.gu.edu.au/gwis/cinemedia/CineMedia.home.html
Scarecrow Video
http://www.film.com/film/
Librarian's Index to the Internet: Motion Pictures
http://lii.org

Evaluation & Citation

Evaluate all information carefully. Web sites present additional challenges. Use the evaluation criteria below to determine the quality of information sources.

#1: Authority (who's responsible?)
#2: Accuracy (is this for real?)
#3: Objectivity (what's the bottom line?)
#4: Currency (how timely is this?)
#5: Coverage (what's included? excluded?)

A good researcher uses a standard citation format to identify the information used and give credit to its creator. Consistency is crucial. Find examples of MLA, Chicago, APA, and AAA formats at the library's **Citation Style Guides** web page
http://dept.sccd.ctc.edu/cclib/Research_Tools/Citation_Style_Guides/index.html

This subject-area research guide from Seattle Central Community College, at **http://dept.sccd.ctc.edu/cclib/Research_Tools/Research_Guides/Humanities/**, gives an overview of available resources in eight categories: reference books, call number areas, subject headings, periodical indexes, periodicals, AV/multimedia, Web resources, and evaluation/citation.

- special indexes (both print and online) for finding primary sources, such as individual songs or paintings, in fields like music or art history
- links to websites considered to be appropriate to research in the field
- special library holdings as well as digital resources in your library
- sometimes, style guides and citation styles appropriate to your field

Subject-area and course guides are both thorough and incredibly easy to use. While no guide created for all students in an academic field will hand you your research project on a silver platter, subject-area research guides provide an excellent roadmap to the steps you will likely want to take in your research and a working toolkit for conducting different kinds of searches along the way. Don't miss this resource.

Consulting reference works is a convenient way to get background information anytime you need a quick and clear overview of themes, questions, events, facts, or people. What they probably can't provide is the kind of in-depth information you'll need to adequately explain and support your research. Reference works have already synthesized a vast amount of content, and some of what's important to your project may have been left out.

General reference works address knowledge in all fields of inquiry. Specialized reference works are geared toward individual subject areas. Which reference works you choose will depend on your research area, your stage of research, the particular problem posed by your research, and your library's holdings. Many general and specialized references are also available online.

The Wide World of Reference Works

Reference Works	Examples
Almanacs, factbooks, news digests, and **yearbooks** provide country information and basic statistics. Facts and figures can also be found in **statistical abstracts** and **statistical indexes,** as well as in **books of historical statistics.**	*Statistical Abstract of the United States* *Facts on File: News Digest* *World Factbook* *World Almanac and Book of Facts* *Central Intelligence Agency Factbook on Intelligence* *ESPN Sports Almanac* *Fact Book on Higher Education*
Atlases are books of maps. Many also include statistical data. **Gazetteers** are geographical dictionaries.	*Dorling Kindersley World Reference Atlas* *Essential World Atlas* *Hammond Medallion World Atlas* *Maps for America* *Historical Atlas of South Asia* *Zondervan NIV Atlas of the Bible*
Bibliographic guides and **reference indexes** are indexed guides to available materials in individual subject areas.	*American Indian Studies: A Bibliographic Guide* *Guide to Reference Materials in Political Science: A Selective Bibliography* *Architecture: A Bibliographic Guide to Basic Reference Works, Histories, and Handbooks* *The Era of World War II: General Reference Works, Bibliography* *World Painting Index* *Popular Song Index* *Halliwell's Film and Video Guide*
Biographical reference works, often organized as either dictionaries or mini-encyclopedias, supply information about people.	*The Cambridge Biographical Encyclopedia* *Country Music: A Biographical Dictionary* *Who's Who in America* *International Women in Science: A Biographical Dictionary to 1950* *Distinguished Asian Americans: A Biographical Dictionary* *The Harvard Concise Dictionary of Music and Musicians* *Biographical Dictionary of Modern World Leaders, 1900–1991*

Reference Works	Examples
Concordances index every word in a particular book or body of work and show how each word is used contextually. For example, you could search a concordance of Shakespeare's work to find all uses of the word *dainty,* which could help you evaluate what the word meant in Renaissance England. (According to the Open Source Shakespeare concordance, the word appears 20 times, in 14 works.)	*Analytical Concordance to the New Revised Standard Version of the New Testament* *Harvard Concordance to Shakespeare* *Concordance to the Standard Edition of the Complete Psychological Works of Sigmund Freud* *Concordance to the Poetry of Robert Frost* *Concordance to the Correspondence of Voltaire* *Concordance to Beowulf*
Dictionaries define words and are arranged alphabetically. Dictionaries also provide guides to etymology, pronunciation, and usage. **Specialized dictionaries** define terms within a field of knowledge. Other language-usage reference works include **thesauruses,** which provide lists of synonyms.	*Oxford English Dictionary* *Random House Webster's Unabridged Dictionary* *American Heritage Dictionary of the English Language* *Dictionary of American History* *Dictionary of Archaeology* *Dictionary of Computing* *Dictionary of Plant Sciences* *Oxford Dictionary of Philosophy*
Directories include guides to colleges, internships, organizations, foundations, and grant resources, as well as telephone and zip code directories.	*Directory of International Internships* *Directory of Recycling Programs: Recycle and Save* *Directory of State Small Business Offices and Activities* *Directory of Foreign Firms Operating in the United States* *Directory of Museums & Living Displays* *Directory of National Fellowships, Internships and Scholarships for Latino Youth*
Encyclopedias, companions, and **reader's guides** contain short topic-specific articles and are arranged alphabetically. They can be single- or multivolume. **Handbooks** provide a concise reference in an individual subject area.	*Encyclopaedia Britannica* *Encyclopedia of Addictive Drugs* *Encyclopedia of Bioethics* *Encyclopedia of Human Rights* *International Encyclopedia of Statistics* *Blackwell Handbook of Social Psychology* *World Hunger: A Reference Handbook* *Reader's Guide to Lesbian and Gay Studies*

(continued)

Reference Works	Examples
Quotation books may be organized by author, by work, by keyword or subject area, or by chronology.	*Familiar Quotations* *Folger Book of Shakespeare Quotations* *Expanded Quotable Einstein* *The Words of Martin Luther King, Jr.* *Of the People, By the People, For the People, and Other Quotations from Abraham Lincoln* *Barbed Quotes: Mudslinging, Backstabbing, and Celebrity Dirt Dishing*
Timelines and **chronologies** provide a historical overview in a table or other largely visual format.	*Chronology of World History* *Timelines of Native American History: Through the Centuries with Mother Earth and Father Sky* *Timelines of the Arts and Literature* *Food Chronology: A Food Lover's Compendium of Events and Anecdotes from Prehistory to the Present* *People's Chronology: A Year-by-Year Record of Human Events from Prehistory to the Present* *Chronology and Fact Book of the United Nations*

Activity 16-2: Locating Reference Works for Your Topic

Consult the table starting on page 320. Write down the type of reference work that would allow you to locate each of the following:

1. Definitions of key terms related to your topic
2. Information about important people related to your topic
3. Short general articles about key ideas related to your topic
4. A chronology of key events in the history of your topic

Then use reference works in your library to help you locate sources that would provide these four types of information about your topic. Write down the titles of two or three works for each type.

Sample Search Results Page

You can sort the results of your search by relevance, title, author, publish date, and publish date descending.

Notice the large number of hits, which will make it difficult for you to sort through the entire list.

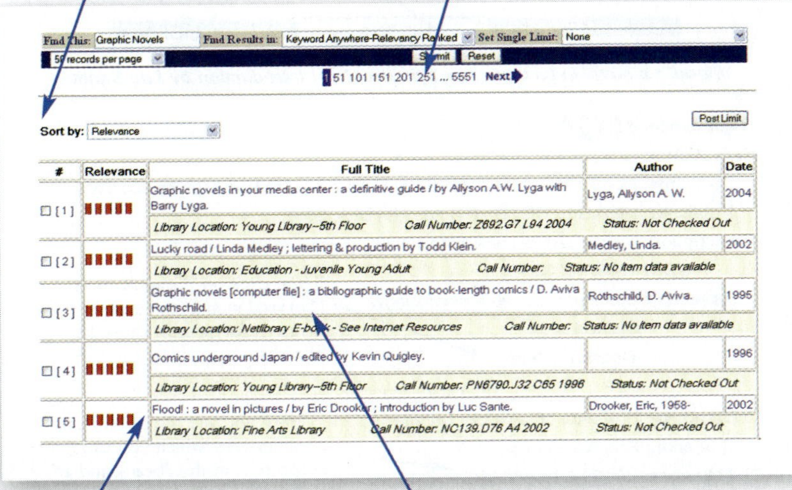

Find This: Graphic Novels
Find Results in: Keyword Anywhere-Relevancy Ranked
Set Single Limit: None
50 records per page
Submit
Reset
1 51 101 151 201 251 ... 5551 Next
Post Limit
Sort by: Relevance
| Relevance | Full Title | Author | Date
[1] Graphic novels in your media center : a definitive guide / by Allyson A.W. Lyga with Barry Lyga. | Lyga, Allyson A. W. | 2004
Library Location: Young Library--5th Floor | Call Number: Z692.G7 L94 2004 | Status: Not Checked Out
[2] Lucky road / Linda Medley ; lettering & production by Todd Klein. | Medley, Linda. | 2002
Library Location: Education - Juvenile Young Adult | Call Number: | Status: No item data available
[3] Graphic novels [computer file] : a bibliographic guide to book-length comics / D. Aviva Rothschild. | Rothschild, D. Aviva. | 1995
Library Location: Netlibrary E-book - See Internet Resources | Call Number: | Status: No item data available
[4] Comics underground Japan / edited by Kevin Quigley. | 1996
Library Location: Young Library--5th Floor | Call Number: PN6790.J32 C65 1996 | Status: Not Checked Out
[5] Flood! : a novel in pictures / by Eric Drooker ; introduction by Luc Sante. | Drooker, Eric, 1958- | 2002
Library Location: Fine Arts Library | Call Number: NC139.D76 A4 2002 | Status: Not Checked Out

Clicking on the title of the work leads to a new screen where you can view brief or full publication and other related information, as shown on the screen on page 324.

You discover several useful entries, one to a research guide on graphic novels and then another for "Graphic novels [computer file] : a bibliographic guide to book-length comics / D. Aviva Rothschild," which is available through the library's subscription to Netlibrary.

InfoKat (University of Kentucky Libraries Online Catalog and Gateway) search results for "Graphic Novels."

The library catalog is used for finding books primarily, but also for finding audio, video, and electronic resources, as well as a host of other kinds of materials. The catalog lists the *names* of all the periodicals in the library's holdings, but it will not point you to individual articles. Only indexes and databases do that (▶ section 16e).

Your library's online catalog might very well contain government documents, maps, slides, photographs, special collections, music scores, dissertations, theses, and other kinds of special materials; these might also be indexed in places other than the catalog. To search for these kinds of materials, you can ask a reference librarian, consult the online research guide for your subject area, or look through your library's website for more information.

The fundamental types of searches for books are by author, title, and subject. With the introduction of electronic catalogs, these three search categories have been joined by a fourth: search by keyword.

Basic Searching by Author, Title, or Keyword

Author searches generally require that you enter the author's name, last name first, as in "dickens, charles." You'll receive a list of author entries that will match. Some may be variations of the name, such as "Dickens, Charles" and "Dickens, Charles, 1812-1870." Enter the name as "charles dickens" and you're likely to get many hits on authors with the last name of Charles, but not the one you're looking for.

Title searches generally require that you begin with the first word of the title (except articles, such as *a, an,* or *the*). Enter "sun also" and you'll find Hemingway's *The Sun Also Rises* and any other titles beginning with the same phrase. Enter "also rises" and you'll come away empty-handed.

Keyword searches are the most flexible. Enter "charles dickens" in the keyword field and you'll find not only all catalog records in which "charles dickens" appears as an author, as a subject, or in a title, but also books of literary criticism of Dickens's works, biographies of Dickens's life, film versions of his novels, and sound recordings of *Oliver!* You'll find books on other subjects entirely but in which "charles dickens" is listed in the table of contents. You'll find Dickens's letters, reference works on Dickens's writing, and more. The beauty of the keyword search is that it is so far-ranging. The danger is that it casts too wide a net and makes it difficult for you to discern what's most important and relevant.

Sample Title Record

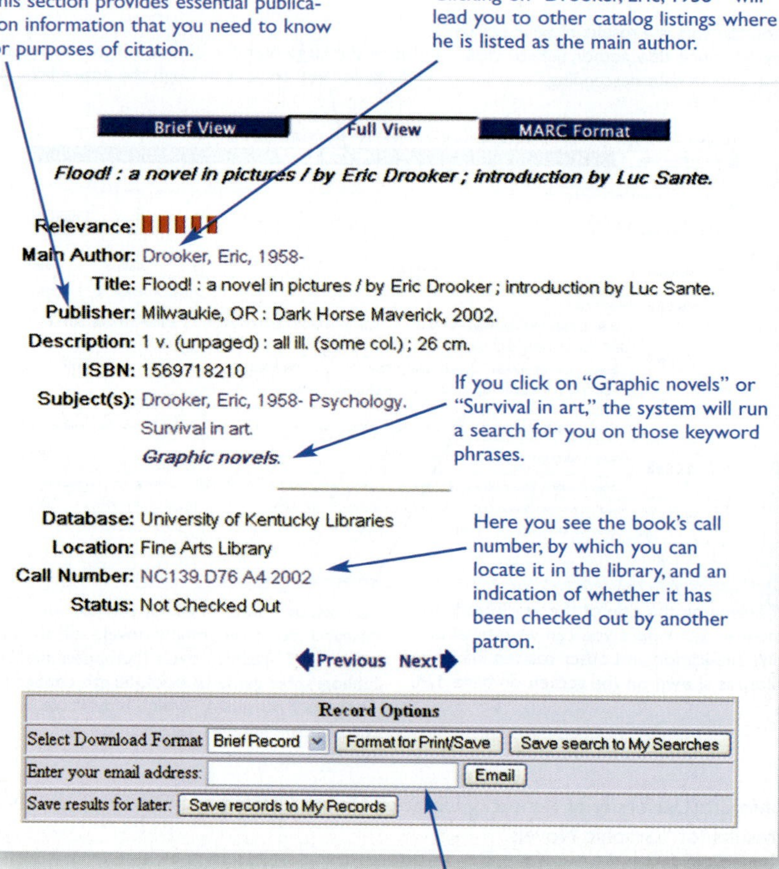

This is the full view of the record for *Flood! A Novel in Pictures* by Eric Drooker.

From InfoKat (University of Kentucky Libraries Online Catalog and Gateway), http://infokat.uky.edu.

Sample LOC Subject Headings Online

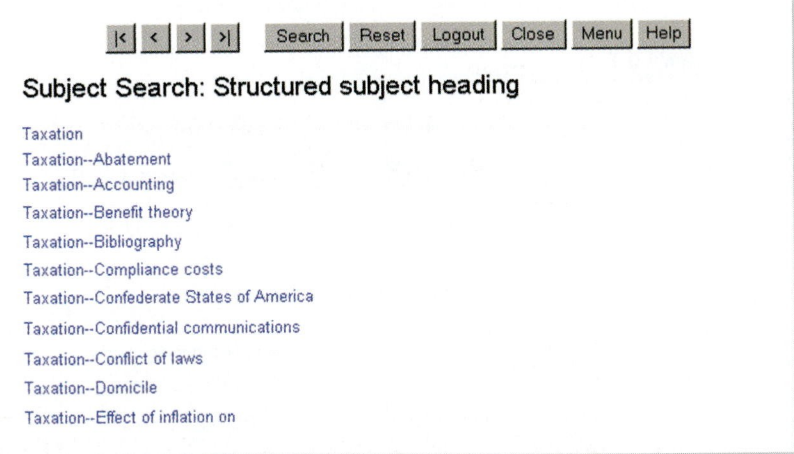

The subject heading search on the keyword *taxation* reveals the related subheadings, each of which in turn can be used to conduct a new search.

From http://www.loc.gov/catdir/cpso/classwebtutorial/illustrations/sh2007.gif.

Activity 16-3: Experimenting with Different Types of Searches

Author, title, and keyword searches can give you different results. Track your results in your research journal. See which type of search proves the most useful to you.

1. Conduct an author search for any important people related to your topic. This will turn up works that they have written. Are the results that you get useful?
2. Type one or two of your keywords into a title search. Do the titles seem related to your research topic? Why or why not? Try adding or removing keywords to see if that improves the relevance of your results.
3. Type the same keywords into a subject search. Do the materials returned seem relevant to your topic? How can you tell? Try adding or removing keywords and note how that changes your results.
4. Answer these questions in your research journal: Which type of search produced the most useful results for your topic? Why do you think this was true?

Searching by Subject

Subject searches are an important research tool, especially helpful when you're trying to figure out which books or other resources are available. Subject searches return all the library's entries in a given subject area. But subject searches are very literal. They use a *controlled vocabulary.* Fortunately for researchers, all library catalog subject searches use the same controlled vocabulary: the Library of Congress subject headings. As of the most recent edition of the subject-headings manual, there were over 270,000 official LOC headings and references, including over 7,000 new to that edition. Also fortunately, you needn't commit all 270,000 terms to memory. Try these strategies instead.

Consult the LOC Subject Headings

The five-volume, hardbound *LOC Subject Headings* is published annually and can be found in the reference section of your library. It's arranged alphabetically. Search the manual until you find the right subject category or cluster of categories for your research area. Make sure you write these down in your research journal! Now you're ready to go back to the online catalog and resume your search.

Think Concepts; Find Terms; Browse List

In a subject search, the library catalog looks only for LOC subject headings. It can't think outside the box. But you can. Keep brainstorming to generate different subject terms until you find one that works. Let's say you're interested in wolves. Try entering *wolf* in the subject field and you get lots of authors whose last name is *Wolf.* No good. Try entering *wolves* and you get a long list of wolf-related subject areas and links to titles in each area. Browse the list looking for the subject category or categories that fit your topic.

Work Backward and Forward

Sometimes you find a book that's exactly what you want. Use that book's LOC subject heading to find more books like it. You can find a book's LOC subject heading on the back of the book's title page, in a section called "Library of Congress Cataloging-in-Publication (CIP) Data." Or look the book up by title in the online catalog and go to the full citation, where you'll see the book's subject heading or headings. Click on a subject heading and you'll be linked to other titles with that same heading. Using these kinds of links in your catalog searches can be an easy way to find what you want.

Sample Results Page Using LOC Subject Heading Terms

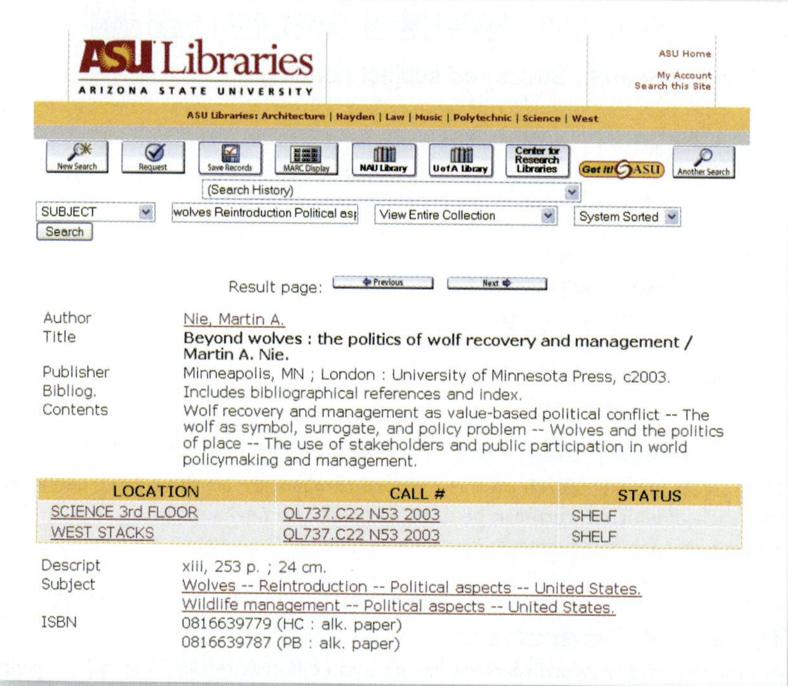

Once you find the appropriate subject descriptors in the *LOC Subject Headings,* plug them into the search box of your library's online catalog. In the Arizona State University library catalog, if you then click on the call number, you can scan the other books that surround your book in the stacks, which allows you to view other titles on the same subject.

Sample Results from Amazon.com

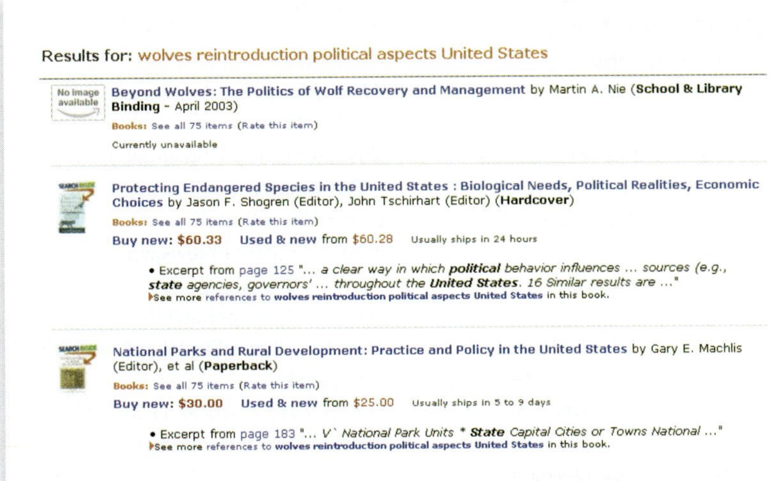
Results for: wolves reintroduction political aspects United States

Beyond Wolves: The Politics of Wolf Recovery and Management by Martin A. Nie (School & Library Binding - April 2003)
Books: See all 75 items (Rate this item)
Currently unavailable

Protecting Endangered Species in the United States : Biological Needs, Political Realities, Economic Choices by Jason F. Shogren (Editor), John Tschirhart (Editor) (Hardcover)
Books: See all 75 items (Rate this item)
Buy new: $60.33 Used & new from $60.28 Usually ships in 24 hours
• Excerpt from page 125 "... a clear way in which political behavior influences ... sources (e.g., state agencies, governors' ... throughout the United States. 16 Similar results are ..."
See more references to wolves reintroduction political aspects United States in this book.

National Parks and Rural Development: Practice and Policy in the United States by Gary E. Machlis (Editor), et al (Paperback)
Books: See all 75 items (Rate this item)
Buy new: $30.00 Used & new from $25.00 Usually ships in 5 to 9 days
• Excerpt from page 183 "... V` National Park Units * State Capital Cities or Towns National ..."
See more references to wolves reintroduction political aspects United States in this book.

The results page from selecting "Books" as our search area on Amazon.com and then using *wolves reintroduction political aspects United States* as the search phrase. The most relevant book is the same one that we found at the top of the list at the ASU library. Notice that part of the description of the second book is an excerpt from page 125 in which key terms from the search phrase are highlighted.

Activity 16-4: Subject Search Activity

Subject searches can allow you to easily locate relevant information about your topic.

1. Locate a book or other source in your library catalog that is relevant to your topic. Write down the subject headings from the library record in your research journal.
2. Use these subject headings to conduct three searches for related reference materials: in your library's catalog, in another library's catalog, and in a commercial bookstore's catalog. In each search, print out or write down the five most relevant results.
3. Answer the following questions in your research journal: What were the differences among the results of the three searches? Which catalog gave you the most useful information?

Searching Other Library Catalogs

Sometimes you want to know only what is available in your college or university library. Other times you may need a broader overview. Most library websites provide searchable links to other libraries' catalogs. The "Search Other Library Catalogs" feature might link you to the Library of Congress, WorldCAT, LIBWEB, or other libraries in your region. The Library of Congress is the world's largest library. It holds more than 17 million books and almost 95 million maps, manuscripts, photographs, audio and video recordings, prints, drawings, and other items. WorldCAT is a database that gives you access to the holdings of over 50,000 libraries worldwide. Its 56 million global information sources include books, journals, audio and video recordings, and electronic sources. LIBWEB provides access to library holdings in over 115 countries.

Another easy way to search all available books is to use the Amazon.com website, Google Scholar, Google Books, or (if available through your library's portal as a searchable database) Books in Print. (For more on Web-based research, see Chapter 15.)

To find articles in periodicals—newspapers, popular magazines, or scholarly journals—use indexes and databases. You'll see both "index" and "database" used on your library's website, often interchangeably, and they are closely allied. More precisely, a **database** is any electronically stored collection of information that can be retrieved and manipulated; a **periodicals index** is a listing of citations to journal, magazine, or newspaper articles.

Choosing Indexes and Databases

Determining which of the seemingly bewildering array of indexes and databases will best serve a particular research project is an advanced skill. **General-interest** or **interdisciplinary databases,** such as Academic Search Premier, Expanded Academic ASAP, FirstSearch, LexisNexis Academic Universe, and TDNet, index a wide variety of subject areas across the curriculum. **Specialized databases**, such as International Medieval Bibliography, CubaSource, or Oceanographic Literature Review, index particular subject areas. If you are unsure which databases to use for your research project, ask a reference librarian or your instructor, or consult the subject-area research guide on your library's website.

General Indexes and Databases

Some Interdisciplinary Indexes

Academic Search Premier
AccuNet/Associated Press Multimedia Archive
Alternative Press Index
Biography Index
Book Review Digest (Print Only)
Book Review Index (Print and Restricted Online Only)
Consumer Index
Expanded Academic ASAP
FirstSearch
Ingenta
JSTOR
LexisNexis Academic Universe
LexisNexis Congressional Universe
LexisNexis Statistical Universe
PCI: Periodical Contents Index
Project Muse

News Indexes, Current and Archival

AccuNet/Associated Press Multimedia Archive
African American Newspapers: The 19th Century
The Civil War: A Newspaper Perspective
Ethnic News Watch
InfoTrac Custom Newspapers
Harper's Weekly
LexisNexis Academic Universe
New York Times Digital Full-text Edition
NewsBank
Pennsylvania Gazette, 1728–1800
World News Connection

Specialized Indexes and Databases

Education

ERIC

Fine and Performing Arts

Art Index
Art Index Retrospective
Arts and Humanities Citation Index
International Index to Music Periodicals
Music Index
RILM (Répertoire international de littérature musicale)
RIPM (Répertoire international de la presse musicale)

Humanities

AfricaBib
America: History and Life
American Bibliography of Slavic and East European Studies
Arts and Humanities Citation Index
ATLA—Religion Database
Bibliography of Asian Studies
Clase
Hispanic American Periodicals Abstract
International Medieval Bibliography
Iter: Gateway to the Middle Ages & Renaissance
MLA Bibliography
Philosopher's Index

Math, Science, Medicine, Technology

Agricola (FirstSearch version)
Applied Science & Technology
Biological & Agricultural Index
BIOSIS
Chemical Abstracts
General Science Abstracts
Geobase
Internet & Personal Computing Abstracts
MathSciNet
Medline
Oceanographic Literature Review
OSTI
PubMed
Web of Science

Social Sciences

CubaSource
EconLit
Hoover's Online
NotiCen
NotiSur
PAIS
PsycINFO
RePEc (Research Papers in Economics)
Social Sciences Citation Index
Sociological Abstracts
SourceMex

Activity 16-5: Locating and Searching Databases

A successful database search relies on locating appropriate databases to search and generating appropriate keywords. Follow the steps below to help you accomplish both goals.

1. Look at the list of general and specific databases in this text or on your library's website. Identify two general and two specific databases that you could use to begin your search. Write down their names.
2. In your research journal, review the list of keywords and subject headings that you have generated on your own and through other activities. Circle the words and phrases that you want to track down in the databases.
3. Visit the databases you have chosen and run your keyword searches. Note the different and similar results you get from each database. Record any relevant materials in your research journal.
4. Answer the following questions in your research journal: Which database gave you the most relevant information? Which database gave you the least relevant information? Why do you think this was so?

Searching Databases and Indexes

The second great challenge in using databases and indexes is searching them. Though structured on common principles, each index or database is set up differently. And unlike library catalogs, which all use the Library of Congress subject headings for subject searches, each database tends to be a universe unto itself in this regard.

The easiest way to become adept is to practice with an index or database appropriate to your research area. Start with the basic search, then try the advanced. Familiarize yourself with the different search options that are available. Study the search tips. Drill yourself in the online tutorials. Most search vehicles have extensive help guides that are well written and easy to follow. Many provide a guide to their controlled vocabulary, often called a **thesaurus,** in the online help section.

Another important way to enhance your skill is by mastering Boolean logic (section 15b). Almost all search vehicles—indexes, databases, library catalogs, Web search engines—employ Boolean logic. So mastering this one skill makes you a better researcher with every conceivable kind of computer-assisted research.

The United States government is the world's largest publisher, producing thousands of books and reports each year. Government information can be found in books and other forms of printed media, microform, floppy disk, CD-ROM, videotape, databases, and online resources. Nationwide, 1,400 federal depository libraries have been designated to be special regional depositories for federal documents and to provide free public access to those documents.

But federal documents of various types can be found in most libraries, and electronic resources now make government information available in a multiplicity of ways. Consult the federal documents specialist in your college or university library before you begin your research. Federal documents might be indexed in your library's online catalog. They can be found indexed and shelved according to their own separate system: the Superintendent of Documents number, which catalogs them according to issuing government agency.

Where to Find Government Documents

A variety of electronic resources provide access to government documents or provide indexing services for government documents:

FirstGov, the U.S. government's official Web portal: **http://www.firstgov.gov**
GPO Access: **http://www.gpoaccess.gov**
Thomas—Legislative Information on the Internet: **http://thomas.loc.gov**
Government Information Locator Service (GILS): **http://www.gils.net**
Google Uncle Sam: **http://www.google.com/unclesam**
GovEngine.com: **http://www.govengine.com**
Federal Web Locator, Villanova Center for Information Law and Policy: **http://www.lib.auburn.edu/madd/docs/fedloc.html**
Enhanced GPO Catalog (U.S. government publications, 1976–present)
LexisNexis Congressional Universe
FindLaw

For more information, see *Using Government Information Sources: Electronic and in Print* (Oryx Press, 2001), as well as Richard J. McKinney's "Internet and Online Sources of U.S. Legislative and Regulatory Information" (available through **http://www.library.cornell.edu/olinuris/ref/usdocs.html**).

Activity 16-6: Locating Government Documents for Your Topic

Government documents can provide you with much useful and relevant information about a topic.

1. Visit FirstGov, the U.S. government's official Web portal (**http://www.firstgov.gov**), and conduct a keyword search on your topic. Note any results relevant to your topic in your research journal.
2. Visit Google Uncle Sam (**http://www.google.com/unclesam**) and try the same keyword search. Note any relevant results for your topic in your research journal.
3. Answer the following questions in your research journal: How did the results differ? How were they the same? Which search engine gave you better results for your topic?

Project Checklist

Evaluating Print Sources

For evaluating online sources, see section 15h.

- **Relevance.** Examine the title, table of contents, headings (if an article), index, and citations. What seems to be the slant on the general subject? Do any of your search terms appear in the index? Also, take care to differentiate general-interest works from scholarly works. Your own rhetorical situation will determine which is more appropriate for your project.
- **Timeliness.** Some projects require historical depth; others require current information. Most search vehicles let you screen by date.
- **Comprehensiveness.** A source that deliberately neglects significant information should be used with caution. However, you will often find a source that bears on only one aspect of your subject, and that's fine. Just be sure to use it within its own limits; don't overgeneralize any findings.
- **Balance.** There's nothing wrong with a biased source—as long as you know its flaws and can use it as an example of such. Authors who present only one side of an issue often haven't done their homework or have something to hide.
- **Reliability and validity.** Do you trust the information? Why or why not? Who is the author, and what are his or her credentials? Is the article from a scholarly journal? If it is from a popular magazine, what is the magazine's relation to its audience—does it inform, or is it mostly trying to stimulate consumption or amuse? Who is the publisher of the book? Is it a scholarly or university press, an alternative publisher, or a commercial publisher? Look also at a work's footnotes and bibliography. How extensive are they? Is the book well researched? Does the article's list of citations give you the impression that the author is steeped in the literature of his or her field?

At every stage of research, you must evaluate source materials—whether you're reviewing the results list from a search of an online catalog, index, or database; deciding which articles to scan briefly online, which to track down in bound periodicals, and which to read more closely; or examining a stack of books from the library shelves and choosing which to put back, which to take home, and which to read cover to cover. One of the researcher's most difficult tasks is choosing which resource materials to use and how to use them. As discussed for online sources in section 15h, one can evaluate material by analyzing it rhetorically in terms of authorship, audience, and purpose. Another way to evaluate material is to ask if it is valid, reliable, balanced, comprehensive, relevant, and current.

First Clarify Your Own Goals as a Writer

The question of relevance is irrelevant unless you have a sense of your own rhetorical situation: What is your purpose for writing? What do you want to say? What audience will you be addressing? What is the context? (If necessary, review the Project Checklist on page 13.)

Some research projects will require—or would benefit from—field research: an interview, observation, or survey. Many fields of study employ field research in their methodology. Take observation: Social sciences, life sciences, and fine and performing arts, as well as applied fields such as journalism and education, each have their own methodology (or methodologies) of observation. As a means of building a vocabulary of gesture and posture into a character, an actor might go to the zoo to observe how a particular animal moves. Someone interested in sports education might use CBAS, the coaching behavior assessment system, to observe and record how a particular coach employs positive and negative feedback in a practice session. Urban planners or architects might visit a particular plaza or neighborhood and observe how people relate to this physical environment. A wildlife biologist might visit a prairie dog town and record incidents of grooming, eating, resting, greeting, and so on, graphing behavior by frequency. A novelist might sit in a café and observe two lovers arguing.

1

Project Checklist

Conducting an Interview

Once you have clarified your purpose for conducting an interview, take the following steps to ensure that you find out what you want to know.

- ❑ **Plan ahead.** Know your subject matter and learn as much about your interviewee as you can before you conduct the interview. The purpose of an interview isn't to get basic information; it's to glean specifics from one person's knowledge or experience. The better prepared and informed you are, the better the quality of the information you'll derive from the interview.
- ❑ **Request the interview.** When you write to your prospective interviewee, take the time to introduce yourself and your research project. Be flexible about arranging a time at the interviewee's convenience. Let the person know how long you expect the interview to last, what questions you'd like to ask, and how you hope to use the interview results.
- ❑ **Construct questions carefully.** Brainstorm as many questions as you can. Set your timer to 5, 10, or 30 minutes and write down every question you can think of. Now go back and choose. Edit, select, and rearrange your questions so that the interview flows logically. Know which questions are the most essential. Avoid questions that can be answered with a simple yes or no.
- ❑ **Give and take.** Your carefully constructed series of interview questions provides an essential roadmap for the interview, but be prepared to adjust your questions to the flow of the conversation.
- ❑ **Consider the logistics.** Where will you interview the person? How will those surroundings affect the quality of the interview? Will you use a tape recorder? Will you be videotaping? If you'll be operating a tape recorder, are you sufficiently skilled? What's the condition of your equipment? Do you have the right kind of tapes on hand? Do you have pen and paper?

2

- **Hone listening and note-taking skills.** Listening is itself a skill. If you've never interviewed someone before, practice on a friend. Next practice listening and taking notes without losing track of the conversation or burying your face in your own papers. Add the tape recorder. Practice until you can juggle all three activities—listening, note-taking, and operating the tape recorder—at once, effortlessly.
- **Obtain appropriate permissions.** If the interview is to be videotaped, make sure the interviewee is well aware of this ahead of time and has agreed to it. If the interview is to be recorded, get the interviewee's written permission before you begin.
- **Observe interview decorum.** Dress appropriately. Be on time. Wear a watch and make sure that the interview goes only as long as scheduled. Thank the interviewee at the time and follow up with a written thank-you note.
- **Follow up promptly.** Go over your notes and write up what you want to use from the interview within 24 hours. Send your written thank-you note within two days, if not immediately. If you're transcribing the tape, listen to it right away to check for sound quality. It is ethical practice to send your results to the interviewee as well, particularly when you want to quote him or her directly. (Interviewees appreciate the opportunity to correct misstatements or other inaccuracies.)

Methods of field research vary with the subject area. A journalist will likely conduct a very different interview than a sociologist. And even the seemingly simplest method of field research can bring up complex questions about framing, assumptions, objectivity, and selectivity that are outside the scope of this section. What we can address, however, are certain commonsense guidelines that might be applicable to any number of situations in which you are called upon to conduct field research as part of an assignment. Finally, if you plan to publish your research outside of the immediate context of your class, then you should also check with your instructor to make sure that you adhere to the college's guidelines for research involving human subjects.

Conducting Interviews

Perhaps you want to talk with someone who is an expert in the field, hear about an event from an eyewitness, or listen to two sides of a controversy from two individuals involved. Perhaps you know of someone who has a unique or colorful story to tell and you want to capture his or her voice. Have a purpose for conducting an interview.

Conducting Observations

Who or what are you observing and why? An actor and an animal behaviorist might both go to the zoo to observe chimpanzees. But their purposes, the things they note, and the way they note them will be much different. Five psychologists or educators might visit a preschool classroom but conduct five different observations. One might observe gender-based behavior. A second might observe overall language use. Another might observe positive and negative reinforcement in teachers' discipline. Know your purpose.

How you conduct your observations depends on your purposes and the field of study in which you're conducting your observations. The actor watching the chimp might stand, move, and mirror. The animal behaviorist might choose one animal and note behaviors every 30 seconds:

15:20:00	feeding
15:20:30	feeding
15:21:00	grooming self
15:21:30	grooming juvenile

The novelist in the café might sit at a table sipping a cappuccino, her notebook open and pen in hand, as unobtrusively as possible writing down what the lovers say, how they're dressed, what kinds of gestures they use. Suit your methodology to your purpose.

Project Checklist

Conducting Observations

Once you have clarified your purpose and your methodology for conducting an observation, take the following steps to ensure that you find out what you want to know.

- ❑ **Obtain permissions as appropriate.** If your observation takes place in the campus lounge or a public park, you don't need permission. But if your site is one not open to the public—a classroom, a rehearsal, a labor-management contract negotiation session—obtain permission to observe and be prepared to take notes only. Audio or video taping usually requires the express written permission of all persons present.
- ❑ **Clarify context, using who, what, when, and where.** Label your observational context before you begin. Whom are you observing? What is the setting? Where are you? What time of day or season is it? The questions you want to address to clarify context will depend on your observation.
- ❑ **Be inconspicuous.** While observing, don't draw attention to yourself. Don't talk or engage with your subjects. If you have more detailed questions for someone in particular, set up a separate interview. If you find you need to survey a group of persons, conduct your survey at another time. Keep the process of observing distinct from other kinds of interactions.
- ❑ **Observe, don't interpret.** It sounds easy, but it's not. Study after study has shown how so-called observers' biases and preconceived ideas influence their research. When you construct your methodology, run it by your instructor for a bias check. Another easy technique is to set up your observation notebook in two columns: one for observations and one for questions, theories, and analysis.

Project Checklist

Conducting Surveys

Once you have clarified your hypothesis and your purpose for conducting a survey, take the following steps to ensure that you find out what you want to know.

- ❑ **Make the survey easy to take.** How long will it take someone to complete your questionnaire? The easier it is to take your survey, the more success you'll have in gathering a useful amount of data. If you can accomplish your research goal in a 10-question survey, don't ask 20 questions. Have all possible answers on the survey so that respondents can simply circle or check the correct answer. Try your questionnaire out on a small test group and get some feedback before launching the real thing.
- ❑ **Make it as easy as possible to tabulate,** given the kind of information you are searching for. Free-form comments are hard to tabulate. Fill-in-the-blank options are not. So design questions that have "yes" or "no" answers or a straightforward controlled range of responses, such as "strongly agree," "agree," "disagree," or "strongly disagree."
- ❑ **Make it fair and accurate.** Consider the range of opinions possible on the subject you are investigating. Design your survey to fairly and accurately accommodate opposite points of view (and all those in the middle). If you ask "Isn't the new parking policy unfair?" you've built your own bias right into the question. If you ask "Are you in favor of or against the new parking policy that assigns the closest spaces by lottery?" your survey will be more effective.
- ❑ **Make it representative.** If you think your survey might solicit different responses from different categories of people and if these differences are relevant to your research hypotheses, include checkable boxes for group identification. For example, is it important to your survey whether respondents are male or female? If so, include a checkbox for each group. Is income, class, or ethnicity important? Preserve anonymity when you gather demographic information.

Conducting Surveys

A survey is a means of sampling opinion in order to gather data representative of the larger group. You can conduct a survey by phone, by email, or by standing on the street corner. The two most important aspects of a survey are (1) whom you are asking and (2) what you are asking them. So consider carefully how you will make your sample reasonably representative of the group in question and how you will frame your questions so that your questionnaire most accurately reflects actual opinion. As in conducting an observation, perhaps the most difficult aspect of conducting a survey is designing a questionnaire free of your own biases and opinions.

Design your survey with a research hypothesis in mind. Ask yourself how the questionnaire will test your hypothesis and how your survey will advance your research.

16i Writing Project Threads

A table of contents for writing project threads appears on pages xv–xxii.

Informative Essays

Garrison 1

Angela Garrison

English 101

Dr. Simpson

September 26, 2005

From Over There to Over Here:

War Blogs Get Up Close, Personal, and Profitable

Blog was the word looked up most often in the online *Merriam-Webster's Dictionary* in 2004 ("Blog"). What's all this fuss? When you read someone else's personal blog, you find out what they like and don't like, what they're doing, and maybe other bits of gossip offered at random. You can read news blogs to find out what's going on lately, what other people think about it, and why it matters. You can keep your own blog to share your thoughts and feelings, to tell your friends and family what you're up to, and sometimes to capture the interest of someone you've never met. When you read and write blogs, you join, or even create, a community. Blogs are also an efficient way to break news, spread rumors, and glorify causes. In short, blogs help people do what they've always done as social beings, just more quickly now, and from almost anywhere on Earth. Soldiers on the ground fighting in Iraq are writing blogs from the front lines. But a review is now under way at the Pentagon to "better understand the overall implications of blogging and other Internet communications in combat zones," according to John Hockenberry in his *Wired* article "The Blogs of War." The benefits of blogs written by U.S. soldiers in Iraq far outweigh the hypothetical risks of revealing sensitive or strategic information. Those benefits, however, aren't as obvious as they might seem.

In spite of what the imagery of smart bombs and predator drones might lead television viewers to believe, wars are fought by people, not just technology. Most blogs start out as efforts to stay in touch with family and friends, but they quickly turn into

Uncovering Your Topic: Doing Library and Field Research

Using the strategies in this chapter for conducting efficient library research and working with the strategies given by your own library, locate books, periodicals, and other sources that could be useful for your project. Be sure to follow the guidelines given in section 16g to evaluate the sources you are considering. Also, collect complete citation information for every source you look up, and record it for safekeeping. You can use the table of contents inside the front cover for quick access to the appropriate citation style.

If your research plans call for talking to someone who is an expert on your research topic, observing a place or a practice, or conducting a survey in order to gather information, use the strategies in section 16h to conduct field research. Be sure to take good notes and to keep track of all important events.

▶ page 356.

Personal Essays

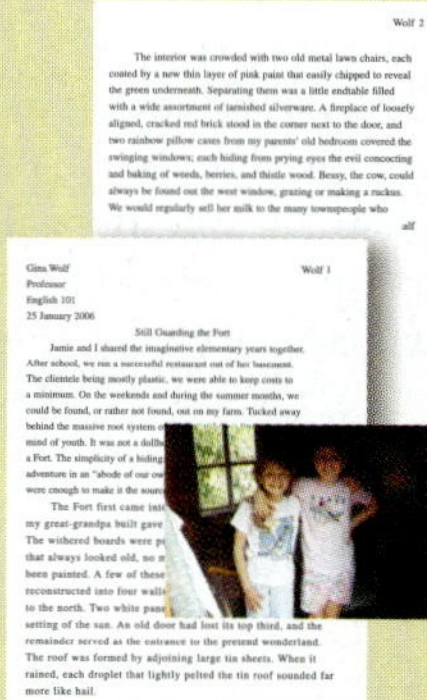

Wolf 2

The interior was crowded with two old metal lawn chairs, each coated by a new thin layer of pink paint that easily chipped to reveal the green underneath. Separating them was a little endtable filled with a wide assortment of tarnished silverware. A fireplace of loosely aligned, cracked red brick stood in the corner next to the door, and two rainbow pillow cases from my parents' old bedroom covered the swinging windows; each hiding from prying eyes the evil concocting and baking of weeds, berries, and thistle wood. Bessy, the cow, could always be found out the west window, grazing or making a ruckus. We would regularly sell her milk to the many townspeople who

Gina Wolf

Professor

English 101

25 January 2006

Wolf 1

Still Guarding the Fort

Jamie and I shared the imaginative elementary years together. After school, we ran a successful restaurant out of her basement. The clientele being mostly plastic, we were able to keep costs to a minimum. On the weekends and during the summer months, we could be found, or rather not found, out on my farm. Tucked away

behind the massive root system o

mind of youth. It was not a dollh

a Fort. The simplicity of a hiding

adventure in an "abode of our ow

were enough to make it the sourc

The Fort first came int

my great-grandpa built gave

The withered boards were p

that always looked old, no n

been painted. A few of these

reconstructed into four walls

to the north. Two white pane

setting of the sun. An old door had lost its top third, and the remainder served as the entrance to the pretend wonderland. The roof was formed by adjoining large tin sheets. When it rained, each droplet that lightly pelted the tin roof sounded far more like hail.

Interviewing a Family Member or Friend

Although a personal essay is about you, talking with a family member or friend can help you get perspective on the events or ideas that you're writing about.

1. Think of a family member or friend (or more than one) who would have information about the aspect of your life that you're writing about.
2. Using the interviewing strategies described in section 16h, develop questions to ask this family member or friend about the topic of your essay. What information can they give you that will help you understand and write effectively about this event or aspect of your life?
3. Finally, conduct the interview following the guidelines for interviewing in section 16h. Doing so will make even friends and family members more responsive and helpful.

◀ page 190.

17

USING INFORMATION EFFECTIVELY

Nearly all exchanges of written communication are persuasive in the sense that your goal is to have your audience understand what you are saying and find your ethos credible. Whether you are preparing a technical report, comparing two literary texts, describing classes of employers, or arguing for your position in a wider social debate, you will want to persuade your readers to be an attentive audience and to consider you a credible authority. In college, much of the writing you do will ask readers to assent to (agree with) your interpretation or assessment of your subject matter. One of the best ways of informing readers and persuading them to accept your ideas is to use evidence and information to bolster your position. When you provide evidence and examples, you demonstrate that you have listened to (and studied) the ongoing conversation of history in which we're all participants. You demonstrate that you have reflected on questions as yet unsettled, that you have some wisdom to share and deserve your audience's attention.

Your readers will naturally look for and evaluate your main idea or thesis (often without even recognizing that they are doing so) by considering the quality and quantity of the information you use to support it. You might use information from other sources to show the background or history of your topic, provide different perspectives on your topic, support your ideas with other people's insights, contextualize an argument by describing the contrasting positions, or show how other people disagree with your position and why they may be mistaken.

Your knowledge of your topic and your audience will help you decide how to use information from other sources most effectively.

Generally speaking, there are three ways to use information in your writing:

1. summary
2. paraphrase
3. quotation

Some writers and readers prefer one or another of these uses of information, but most writers employ all three to vary the rhythm of their prose and to ensure that their voice is not overwhelmed by the voices of those they cite. Keeping in mind your topic and the rhetorical situation, you should use information in ways that help you accomplish your purpose.

Throughout your research process, you will examine a wide variety of sources that will influence your ideas. Because most college writing projects call for you to emphasize your ideas, you will need to develop good habits for *assimilating* the ideas of others, blending them with your own to create new perspectives. A good research project does not merely stitch together sources into a narrative of what others say, which is an act of *appropriating.* Rather, good research projects take what is already known and has been said, channeling it in new directions to answer new questions or solve new problems.

summary A concise restatement of the main ideas of a source, written in your own words. A summary gives the gist of the source without using the source's words or sentence structure. Depending on the purpose the summary needs to fulfill, it may include just the major ideas of a source or the more important examples as well. A summary must be fully documented, including the page range for the information summarized. Any words quoted directly from the source must be enclosed in a pair of quotation marks, and the page number of the quotation must be given.

paraphrase A detailed restatement of a source, written in your own words. Unlike a summary, a paraphrase restates ideas in their entirety and reflects the source's order of ideas, emphasis, and tone. A paraphrase is typically as long as the source or even longer. A paraphrase must be fully documented, including page numbers. Any quoted words within the paraphrase must be enclosed in a pair of quotation marks, and the page number of the quotation must be given.

quotation Direct use of the source's words and punctuation, exactly as they appear in the source. Quotations must be enclosed in a pair of quotation marks so the reader knows exactly where the source's words begin and end. Any changes made to the words or punctuation in a quotation must be indicated by brackets (▶ page 355), and any omissions must be indicated by ellipses (▶ page 354). A quotation must be fully documented, including page numbers.

Examples of Summary, Paraphrase, and Quotation

Summary

This concept is called "slave Christianity": the religion of the oppressor was made into a safety net by and for the slaves (Simms 55).

In this informative summary, the writer captures the gist of the source material directly. The author's last name and the page number are required to cite this print source.

Direct Quotation

> When Africans arrived in America, there was a two-stage movement. The first stage involved destroying their original spiritual and religious systems. The second stage involved teaching them a form of Christianity, which served to keep them as slaves, but also, and not intentionally, contained the seeds of liberation. This is a concept called "slave Christianity": "In terms of subtle opposition, they used Christianity as an instrument of psychological and communal resistance, attempting to preserve both their individual and collective well being" (Simms 55). Slave owners selectively taught the parts of the Bible that reinforced slavery, but did not reveal to the slaves the parts of the Bible that would show them a way to be free.

This direct quotation of the source helps the writer define "slave Christianity." Notice that the quotation is carefully introduced and then is followed by a sentence that explains it further with an example. Because this is a print-based source, the author's last name and the page number are used for the parenthetical citation.

Paraphrase

> This is a concept called "slave Christianity": The slaves used the religion taught to them to create a sense of community and of individuality, both of which helped them maintain healthy personal and social attitudes (Simms 55).

In this paraphrase, the writer substitutes and rearranges some words to rephrase the original clearly. Notice that the writer uses about the same number of words in the paraphrase. Even with the paraphrase, the author's last name and page number are cited.

Work Cited

Simms, Rupe. "Slave Christianity." *The Western Journal of Black Studies* 22.1 (1998): 49-56. Print.

Most people see the wisdom of not shouting "fire" in a crowded theater when there's no fire and the prohibition against crying "wolf" when there's no wolf. People usually presume that you're telling them the truth and that what you tell them is relevant. Linguist H. P. Grice calls these two of the "cooperative principles" of conversational life.

These principles also apply to research and informative writing. Every writer has an ethical responsibility to the reader to write truthfully, to represent the work of others fairly and accurately, and to give credit where it is due. These are the general reasons why in college you're expected to be careful about citing sources and should under no circumstances misrepresent the work of another as your own.

By developing good habits for recording your research, you can ensure that you use information responsibly. Your notes should be detailed and precise from the beginning so that you won't need to waste time re-creating your research later and so that you can be certain that you have not misrepresented information in your sources. Whether you use index cards or a software program for taking notes, be sure that you practice the guidelines for effective note-taking discussed in section 14h.

When you summarize, you condense information, so a summary is considerably shorter than the original even though it still represents the original meaning as accurately as possible. You also put the original text into your own words. Normally, when you summarize, you include only the main ideas or only the main ideas that are relevant to your needs. A summary of another person's ideas must be documented with information required by the citation style that you're using. (If you don't know which citation style to use, ask your instructor.)

Quick Guide to MLA Style
To create an in-text citation, ▶ section 19b.
To create a Works Cited entry,
for a book ▶ page 392
for an article ▶ page 404
for an online source ▶ page 409

Quick Guide to APA Style
To create an in-text citation, ▶ section 20b.
To create a References entry,
for a book ▶ page 458
for an article ▶ page 466
for an online source ▶ page 469

When Should You Write a Summary?

1. Summarize when a quotation or paraphrase would give unneeded detail or distracting minutiae.
2. Summarize when several different kinds of information from the same source and author were provided over many pages in the original.

How Do You Write a Summary?

1. Read and reread the original until you are sure you understand it.
2. Identify the major ideas: the thesis statement, if there is one, and the topic sentences of paragraphs or sections. If the work is a narrative, write a very brief description of the major events in each section. If the work is very short, look for key ideas in repeated phrases. Annotate the pages if necessary to track the information.
3. Write one sentence that captures the main idea of the original. Rewrite the sentence as necessary until it works. Then write any supporting sentences that are needed so that your readers will grasp the major idea. Rewrite them until you have a summary that someone unfamiliar with the work will understand.
4. Check the summary against the source to make sure you have used all your own words. If you need to use any phrases from the source because they are unique, enclose the phrases in a pair of quotation marks. Note the page number of the material you have quoted.
5. Check to be sure you have not included your own thoughts and opinions in the summary. The summary should include only the source's ideas, not yours. (Your ideas are relayed before and after the summary. See pages 343, 345, and 351.)
6. Document your summary with the author's name, title of the work, and publishing information, including page numbers or URLs.

Sample Descriptive and Informative Summaries

Original

The Semantic Web will bring structure to the meaningful content of Web pages, creating an environment where software agents roaming from page to page can readily carry out sophisticated tasks for users. Such an agent coming to the clinic's Web page will know not just that the page has keywords such as "treatment, medicine, physical, therapy" (as might be encoded today) but also that Dr. Hartman works at this clinic on Mondays, Wednesdays, and Fridays and that the script takes a date range in yyyy-mm-dd format and returns appointment times. And it will "know" all this without needing artificial intelligence on the scale of *2001*'s Hal or *Star Wars*'s C-3PO. Instead these semantics were encoded into the Web page when the clinic's office manager (who never took Comp Sci 101) massaged it into shape using off-the-shelf software for writing Semantic Web pages along with resources listed on the Physical Therapy Association's site.

From Tim Berners-Lee et al., "The Semantic Web," *Scientific American,* May 17, 2001; also available at <http://www.scientificamerican.com>.

Descriptive Summary

Words that describe the act of the writers are highlighted.

In 2001, Tim Berners-Lee and his colleagues at W3C envisioned a new way to structure information on the Internet. They believed that content should be organized for users in terms of relations of meaning across databases.

Informative Summary

"The Semantic Web" is premised on the fact that users need to know how information is structured, not just where it is, and, crucially, how one bit of information is related to another, no matter where that information may be stored (Berners-Lee).

Descriptive vs. Informative Summary

There are two kinds of summaries: descriptive and informative. A *descriptive summary* explains the source from a reader's perspective, like a blow-by-blow description of what an author writes or what people do. It focuses on action. Descriptive summaries are most useful when the focus of your own writing is on something that has happened and the event (of reading, for example) is noteworthy in itself. For example, the sentence

> Faulkner begins his novel *Absalom, Absalom!* with a two-page-long sentence.

is a (very) short descriptive summary of how William Faulkner begins that novel.

An *informative summary,* by contrast, provides the content of a source in highly condensed form. So, for example, the descriptive summary above differs greatly from this short informative summary of the novel's beginning:

> Miss Coldfield knows from the very start why Quentin Compson has decided to go to Harvard.

Rhetorical Contexts for Descriptive and Informative Summaries

Descriptive summaries are useful for analysis and argument because they allow you to focus on another writer's act—what he or she has said, why, and how. You could use the descriptive summary of "The Semantic Web" in an essay on the evolution of search engines or on the nature of information on the Internet. Your focus might be on historical development, with key premises and events singled out for discussion and analysis.

The informative summary might be useful if, for example, you were writing to an audience that needed some background information on what "The Semantic Web" is. Informative summaries are often useful when you need to provide a context for later analysis, such as a plot summary at the start of a film review that may be read by people who have not seen the film yet. Informative summaries are somewhat like the abstracts that you often see at the beginning of scholarly articles. They help an audience learn enough about a subject so that they can understand your argument or analysis.

Activity 17-1: Writing a Summary

Using the guidelines for writing summaries on pages 340–341, write both a descriptive summary and an informative summary of the following excerpt from a news article.

Beagle 2's demise remains a mystery

15:37 24 August 2004

Hazel Muir, London

The team that led the doomed Beagle 2 Mars mission has done a thorough post-mortem of the project and published their speculations about why the lander might have disappeared. Their report—*Beagle 2: Lessons Learned*—aims to make the team's knowledge and experience available to the planners of future spacecraft missions. But it fails to give a clear answer to the one crucial question: why did the Beagle 2 lander fail?

Beagle 2 successfully separated from its mothership, the Mars Express orbiter, on 19 December 2003. At that time, its speed and spin rate were just right. But mission controllers heard nothing from the spacecraft after it entered the Martian atmosphere on Christmas Day.

A committee from the European Space Agency (ESA) and the British National Space Centre investigated the loss. Although they refused to make their findings public, they published recommendations for future missions that indirectly implied serious flaws in the Beagle 2 project. Future missions, the committee said, should be conceived and designed more carefully, and undergo more thorough tests.

No single answer

Now the Beagle 2 team have published their own appraisal, which attempts to identify all the possible reasons for failure and assess their likelihood. After months of analysis, there is still . . . no single compelling answer, according to the lead scientist on the mission, Colin Pillinger.

"It could have worked and it should have worked," Pillinger told a press conference in London on Tuesday. "It didn't work, and we don't know the reason why."

> The team were unable to rule out many possible problems. Tiles intended to prevent the lander overheating in the atmosphere might have broken off. Airbags designed to cushion the craft's landing might have punctured, or failed to inflate at all. Beagle 2 might have fallen down the side of a crater, or the lander's electronics could have malfunctioned for various reasons.
>
> And observations by Mars Express hint that the atmosphere above the landing site might have been unusually thin when Beagle 2 arrived. Because of that, its parachute could have opened far too late, in which case the lander might have hit the Martian surface at break-neck speed and shattered.

From Hazel Muir, "Beagle 2's Demise Remains a Mystery," NewScientist.com News Service 24 Aug. 2004, 11 Sept. 2005 <http://www.newscientist.com>

Activity 17-2: Summarizing a Research Source

From among the sources you are using for your research project, select one that you consider a good candidate for summarizing. Write a summary of it, either descriptive or informative. Be sure to document your summary in the appropriate style. Then respond to the following questions:

1. Why did you decide to summarize this source? How do you intend to use the summary in your project?
2. Did you write a descriptive or an informative summary? What rhetorical factors led to that decision?
3. Did you include any quoted material in your summary? Why?

Write the material that will surround or frame the summary in your research essay. Be sure to introduce the summary and then comment on it.

Framing the Source Material in Your Research Essay

All the source material you use in an essay needs to be framed so that readers will understand its purpose and significance. "Framing" it means surrounding it with words—putting it in a textual context—that lets readers know why it is important. Go back to page 337 and review the various purposes you might have for including source material in your essay. You may also think of other reasons not covered there.

Once you know why you are including a summary (or a paraphrase or quotation) in your essay, you are in a better position to know how to frame it. Introduce the summary in a way that helps readers focus on its importance to the point it is supporting. (See page 345 for a list of verbs that can help get your meaning across.) After the summary, refer back to it with some comments that will also lead readers to your next point.

When you paraphrase, you use your own words to accurately convey the meaning, order, and emphasis of the original. Because they include all the details and examples from the source, paraphrases are roughly the same length as or a bit longer than the original. It's critical that you remember that a paraphrase, like a quotation, must be documented with information required by the citation style you're using (for example, MLA or APA).

Quick Guide to MLA Style
To create an in-text citation, ▶ section 19b.
To create a Works Cited entry,
for a book ▶ page 392
for an article ▶ page 404
for an online source ▶ page 409

Quick Guide to APA Style
To create an in-text citation, ▶ section 20b.
To create a References entry,
for a book ▶ page 458
for an article ▶ page 466
for an online source ▶ page 469

When Should You Paraphrase?

1. Paraphrase when you need to discuss details from the source material rather than just the main ideas found in a summary.
2. Paraphrase when the author's ideas and facts are more important than the language used to describe them or when a quotation might be distracting.
3. Consider paraphrasing when the original text uses language that differs greatly in style, tone, or voice from your writing.
4. Paraphrase when the language of the original is technical, arcane, or complicated. You might encounter writing like this in any discipline; because jargon consists of terms and forms of language specific to an area of study, it usually speaks to only a restricted audience.

   Original (from Aristotle's *Rhetoric*):

   The duty of rhetoric is to deal with such matters as we deliberate upon without arts or systems to guide us, in the hearing of persons who cannot take in at a glance a complicated argument, or follow a long chain of reasoning.

   Paraphrase:

   The aim of rhetoric is to explore unsettled and important issues when there are no clear guidelines for making decisions and when people may not understand a complex argument.

How Do You Paraphrase?

1. Read the part of the source you want to paraphrase several times, until you are sure you understand not only its ideas but also its tone and emphasis.
2. Find the key terms and think of synonyms you could use instead. If you must quote a key term, enclose the quotation in a pair of quotation marks and note the number of the page on which it appears.
3. Write the ideas in your own words, using a tone of voice that is similar to the source's. Be sure that you emphasize the same ideas or examples the author did.
4. Check your draft against the source, and rewrite it as needed until it accurately represents the original. Be careful not to use the source's language.
5. Check to be sure you haven't included your own ideas or opinions in the paraphrase. (Your ideas are relayed before and after the paraphrase. See pages 343, 345, and 351.)
6. Document the paraphrase with the author's name, the title of the work, and publishing information, including page numbers or URLs.

Activity 17-3: Writing a Paraphrase

Using the guidelines for paraphrasing, paraphrase each of the following paragraphs.

Study: Misdiagnosis Led to Birds' Deaths

By KYLE WINGFIELD, Associated Press Writer

AUBURN, Ala. - When several birds fell ill last year at Auburn University's respected raptor center, experts were shocked and puzzled by the explanation that the culprit was a lethal disease never seen before in birds of prey. The disbelief has only magnified following an independent study that found the disease had been misdiagnosed—and that officials at the haven for hundreds of injured birds had hastily decided to euthanize "otherwise healthy animals."

"It just seemed like the trigger got pulled a little early, before they knew what they were dealing with," said Patrick Redig, director of the University of Minnesota's Raptor Center and one of the study authors.

The findings by Redig and a colleague were sent to Auburn and the U.S. Fish and Wildlife Service in January but were not released to the public.

From http://story.news.yahoo.com.

Activity 17-4: Paraphrasing a Research Source

From among your research sources, select one that you think would be a good candidate for paraphrasing, and paraphrase it. Be sure to document your paraphrase in the appropriate style. Then respond to the following questions:

1. Why did you decide to paraphrase this source? How do you intend to use the paraphrase in your project?
2. Did you include any quoted material in your paraphrase? Why?

Write the material that will surround or frame the paraphrase in your research essay. Be sure to introduce the paraphrase and then comment on it. Check your use of verbs to make sure that you are accurately describing both your source and your attitude toward your source.

Using Verbs to Frame Source Material

The verbs you use to introduce and comment on source material reveal your attitude toward the information itself, its author, or its importance. When possible, choose a verb that describes the nature of the original author's assertion. For example, if an author is *predicting* a future event, say "Jones *predicts,*" not "Jones *says.*" Each verb lends a different emphasis or tone. Saying that an author "insists" on a point suggests that you do not agree or that the author's tone is aggressive; "suggests" reveals a more tentative stance on the part of the author.

Verbs for Framing Source Material

argues	offers
asserts	predicts
believes	proposes
claims	questions
concludes	reasons
considers	refutes
disagrees	remarks
discusses	reports
emphasizes	responds
explains	says
imagines	shows
implies	states
indicates	thinks
notes	wonders
observes	

One of the most powerful ways of conveying information is to introduce a quotation that directly demonstrates or elaborates an important point. Many readers appreciate direct quotations of outside sources because they act as a sort of witness, testifying precisely to the validity or poignancy of your own writing. Quotations show readers that you have paid close attention to your subject and what others have said about it. When you use quotations ethically, they add another voice supporting or strengthening your ideas, which can improve your credibility and garner your reader's trust, two critical prerequisites of informative and persuasive writing.

Quick Guide to MLA Style
To create an in-text citation, ▶ section 19b.
To create a Works Cited entry,
for a book ▶ page 392
for an article ▶ page 404
for an online source ▶ page 409

Quick Guide to APA Style
To create an in-text citation, ▶ section 20b.
To create a References entry,
for a book ▶ page 458
for an article ▶ page 466
for an online source ▶ page 469

When Should You Quote?

Before using a quotation, you should be certain that the source is reliable and that the author you're quoting has some credibility or a favorable ethos (character of fair-mindedness) that will be persuasive.

1. Quote when the author's exact language will support your ideas better than a paraphrase or summary of the information.
2. Quote language that is striking or highly nuanced, allowing for multiple interpretations that you need to demonstrate for your readers.
3. Quote if you plan to spend time analyzing the quotation in your own text.
4. Quote when you need to demonstrate what other people feel or think about a subject.
5. Quote highly respected authorities whose words speak directly to one of your main points.

How Do You Quote?

1. Read the source carefully to understand the context of the words you are thinking of quoting.
2. Copy the quotation exactly, making sure to transfer the words, capitalization, punctuation, and even any errors in the source. If the source author has quoted someone else, enclose that quotation in a pair of single quotation marks (' '). Enclose the entire quotation you're using in a pair of double quotation marks (" ").
3. Check the quotation against the source word by word to make sure they match exactly.
4. Do not insert any other words into the quotation unless you enclose them in brackets (▶ page 355). (Your ideas are relayed before and after the quotation. See pages 343, 345, and 351.)
5. Document the quotation fully, including page numbers or URLs.

Irrelevant Quotation

> Many fish owners pride themselves on the environments they lovingly create for their fish, many of which are considered pets in the same way that another owner might love a dog or cat. "Ninety percent of all stock expires in transport due to customary industry irregularities" (Calolora 42). The level of affection shown toward their fish can come as a surprise to many non–fish owners.

The quotation isn't related to the paragraph's topic sentence, and its tone is different from Stuart's, which is slightly less formal and concerned with showing readers the relationship that fish owners have with their pets. In the revised paragraph, a new topic sentence and a frame for the quotation help the quotation function more effectively as support for the paragraph's new main idea, which is that loving pet owners would be shocked to learn how their pets are handled before they get to the store.

Revised Paragraph (New material is highlighted.)

> The importation of goldfish into the United States is often accompanied by a less noticed mortality rate for the goldfish that would horrify consumers. The level of affection shown toward their fish can come as a surprise to many non–fish owners. Many fish owners pride themselves on the environments they lovingly create for their fish, many of which are considered pets in the same way that another owner might love a dog or cat. Yet no cat or dog owner would tolerate the awful facts surrounding how many fish are brought into the United States just so that people can have a few in their tank. Philip Calolora, an expert in the fish importation industry, describes the incredibly high rate of mortality suffered: "Ninety percent of all stock expires in transport due to customary industry irregularities" (42). While Calolora's explanation is somewhat masked in industry jargon, the shocking truth is plain. Given fish owners' bond with their pets, outreach and education should cause the fish-owner community to address and correct the system of importation that supports their hobby.

You can see how the quotation blends in more effectively when it is subordinated to the author's ideas and language. The quotation is now introduced and woven into Stuart's sentence, not just dropped in with no explanation.

Make Relationships Clear

Introduce quotations so that their relevance is clear and their tone is consistent with your own writing. Readers are easily distracted when the tone or coherence of writing is broken, which can happen if the content or tone of quotations has no obvious relationship to the surrounding text. For instance, in the first example to the left, Stuart Larkin doesn't show how the information about "industry irregularities" relates to the behavior of fish owners.

17e

Don't Quote Too Much

To preserve coherence, use only the relevant parts of a quotation. Another kind of coherence problem arises when a quotation includes information that moves the topic in a direction you don't intend to pursue. Quote only what is necessary for your purposes. For instance, if Stuart used just one more sentence from the source, the relevance of the quotation would be called into question and the coherence of the paragraph would be seriously disrupted.

How Much Should You Quote?

1. Quote enough to make your point or elaborate your content *without drawing attention away from your own perspective.* Quotations shouldn't make your points; they should only validate or explain them.
2. Quote the least amount of material that will get your point across. Use ellipses so you can omit words that are unnecessary for your particular use.
3. Avoid using long quotations (in MLA style, that's more than four lines of your text or three lines of poetry) unless the quoted material is so important that you spend considerable time in your essay discussing and explaining it.

Too Much Material Quoted (The unneeded sentence is highlighted.)

The importation of goldfish into the United States is often accompanied by a less noticed mortality rate for the goldfish that would horrify consumers. The level of affection shown toward their fish can come as a surprise to many non–fish owners. Many fish owners pride themselves on the environments they lovingly create for their fish, many of which are considered pets in the same way that another owner might love a dog or cat. Yet no cat or dog owner would tolerate the awful facts surrounding how many fish are brought into the United States just so that people can have a few in their tank. Philip Calolora, an expert in the fish importation industry, describes the incredibly high rate of mortality suffered:

> Ninety percent of all stock expires in transport due to customary industry irregularities. At their annual industry meeting in Tampa, principal importation figures complained about the lack of support shown to their expedited import system by front line U.S. Customs workers, especially those in Atlantic cities, where the vast majority of stock arrives for movement throughout the country. (42)

While Calolora's explanation is somewhat masked in industry jargon, the shocking truth is plain. Given fish owners' bond with their pets, outreach and education should cause the fish-owner community to address and correct the system of importation that supports their hobby.

The additional sentence, while relevant in the original source, is not relevant in Stuart's paragraph, where it only pulls the reader's attention away from Stuart's main idea. Everything in the quoted material should either support or extend your main ideas.

Unnecessary Quotation (The unnecessary quotation is highlighted.)

The importation of goldfish into the United States is often accompanied by a less noticed mortality rate for the goldfish that would horrify consumers. The level of affection shown toward their fish can come as a surprise to many non–fish owners. Many fish owners pride themselves on the environments they lovingly create for their fish, many of which are considered pets in the same way that another owner might love a dog or cat. Christine Handy, a lifelong fish owner, claims, "I have never had a better, more affectionate pet, believe it or not, than my two goldfish." Yet no cat or dog owner would tolerate the awful facts surrounding how many fish are brought into the United States just so that people can have a few in their tank. Given fish owners' bond with their pets, outreach and education should cause the fish-owner community to address and correct the system of importation that supports their hobby.

The quotation from Handy supplements a secondary idea in the paragraph, which is that people who own fish have a strong bond with their pets. The quotation throws the paragraph out of focus and should be removed.

Don't Quote to Support Minor Points

When the relevance of a quotation to your main idea is not obvious, your audience may become confused and inattentive. If Stuart were to substitute a quotation that functioned as evidence of one of the paragraph's minor points (one that didn't need support), he would be overstating the case.

Position Quotations Carefully

There are no steadfast rules about using material from outside sources only in particular places in a paragraph, but quotations can be clumsy or distracting when used in parts of a paragraph conventionally reserved for other purposes. For instance, avoid using a quotation in either the topic sentence or transitional sentences. Readers use those sentences for cues about what comes next and to help them comprehend what they read. If all of your transition sentences are quotations, chances are that you're not doing a very good job of showing how one idea leads to the next.

Explain Every Quotation

When you use a quotation of a sentence or more, you should be careful to explain to your reader what the quotation means to you. Often, writers presume that there's only one way to interpret a quotation, but readers may interpret the quotation differently. As the writer, you want to steer the reader's interpretation, so take a moment to explain your quotations. Typically, you should provide at least one sentence of explanation for every sentence of quoted material.

Quotation Explained

(The sentence of explanation is highlighted.)

> People these days seem to respond to reality as if it were a TV show, especially when they face momentous events in their lives. In a CNN story about a tornado in Utah, here's what one witness reported: "As I'm watching, I'm watching it just tear the roof off Anderson Lumber . . . . It was like a Discovery Channel special on tornadoes." In our media-saturated world, we sometimes act as mere witnesses to our own lives, finding it more comfortable or manageable to respond to our own experience as if it were a TV show, something we might see on the Discovery Channel.

Note that the quotation of the tornado witness does not just confirm the point made in the first sentence. It becomes the basis for some interpretation in the last sentence. The writer interprets and extends the significance of the quotation.

Activity 17-5: Quoting a Research Source

From among your research sources, select one that you think would be a good candidate for quoting. Quote it, making sure the quotation you select is relevant as support for one of your ideas. Explain its significance, and make sure that the quotation doesn't interrupt the paragraph's coherence. Be sure to document your quotation in the appropriate style. Then respond to the following questions:

1. What particular reasons did you have for quoting from this source? How do you intend to use the quotation in your project?
2. Why did you select the particular words you chose to quote, instead of other words from the same source? What did you expect this particular quotation to accomplish?

Check your use of verbs to make sure that you are accurately describing both your source and your attitude toward your source.

Activity 17-6: Using Quotations

Suppose that you're writing a short paper about the use of online communication by teenage writers and its impact on their ability to succeed in college. Write a paragraph supporting the claim that online communication helps students become better writers. Use at least one quotation from the news article that follows to support your claim.

Blogging may make teens better writers

By JEAN NASH JOHNSON
Knight Ridder Newspapers

Someone in the academic world finally said it. Blogging, emailing and instant messaging among teens pay off. Despite punctuation lapses, grammar shortcuts and creative spelling, online communication invites critical thinking and better writing, says Purdue University English professor Samantha Blackmon. "Who cares if a student, to save time, types 'u' for 'you'? I want to see them writing more and if that means breaking a few rules, that's OK."

Students now come to college with years of online writing experience, putting them ahead of the game for research papers, says Blackmon, who studies computers and writing as well as minority rhetoric. The best part is when they get on the computer to write to friends. They don't view it as work or learning, but see it as fun, she says.

By routinely using a blog, a kind of cyber hangout for journaling and information gathering, young writers master sourcing and critical thinking. "Blogging forces students to be more accountable for what they say," Blackmon says. That leads to more solidly written papers.

Crandall High School senior Ansley Miller is on the computer hours at a time writing in her online journal and talking to her friends. Blogging and instant messaging have empowered her writing, she says. "When I write in my journal I feel comfortable with expressing myself."

From http://www.sunherald.com/mld/thesunherald/living/9480094.htm.

Choose Verbs Carefully

We've discussed the need to frame your source material (pages 343 and 350) and provided a list of verbs that can be used to introduce and integrate source material into your writing (page 345). When considering which verbs to use, don't use so many different verbs that you draw readers' attention to them.

The other issue to consider is whether verbs should be in the present tense (*suggests*) or the past tense (*suggested*). Use the present tense form to describe what the text is doing or to discuss the author's act of writing:

> Blass **describes** Milgram's approach to social psychology experiments as "sometimes playful" (xxiii) and Milgram's curiosity as "relentless" (xxiv).

Use the past tense form when you're writing about events that have already taken place or when chronology is important:

> Blass **notes** that Stanley Milgram **was** the first researcher to study national traits scientifically. Milgram's findings in France and Norway **confirmed** some of his own more casual observations while he was living in the two countries (53).

Use Signal Phrases to Integrate Quotations

Quotations, summaries, and paraphrases can't just be dropped into your project. They need to be integrated so that there are smooth transitions between your prose and your source material's.

Signal phrases—such as "Susan Orleans writes that" and "Glazier disputed her interpretation by noting"—introduce and integrate source material into writing. It's usually more graceful to cite the author of a quotation in a signal phrase than to name him or her afterward in parentheses. However, follow the preference of the documentation style. In APA style, writers are encouraged to cite the author by name after the quotation.

Consider whether you should provide a phrase that gives the quoted person's credentials as a way of improving ethos. The opinion of an expert in the field you are discussing will carry more weight with readers than that of a person whose credentials are unidentified.

Introductions to long, indented quotations are often whole sentences punctuated at the end with a colon. For an example, see the indented quotation on page 348.

Vary the position of signal phrases in different sentences to aid readability.

Where to Name the Author: Two Variations

MLA Smith-Johnson writes, "Being older is being in a situation where access to wisdom is granted more often" (35).

APA Aging has its benefits: "Being older is being in a situation where access to wisdom is granted more often" (Smith-Johnson 2005, p. 35).

How to Identify the Author: Credentials

When you quote experts with distinguished credentials that might add to their credibility, provide the reader with a phrase that identifies their expertise:

Michael Hudson, Distinguished Professor of Economics at the University of Missouri, . . .

Lynne Truss, author of three novels and book reviewer for *The Sunday Times*, . . .

Wangari Maathai, noted environmentalist and winner of the Nobel Peace Prize, . . .

Including Signal Phrases to Make Prose Read Smoothly

(Signal phrases are highlighted.)

Malcolm Gladwell describes his idea as "the theory of thin slices" (23). By using very small amounts of information, experts in various fields are able to make remarkably accurate predictions about people's behavior. They throw out the irrelevant material that might overwhelm the lay person, says Gladwell, in order to focus on the thinner slice of what really matters. For example, psychologist John Gottman focuses on what he calls "the Four Horsemen" of emotions in order to decide whether a couple is likely to stay together or divorce—"defensiveness, stonewalling, criticism, and contempt" (qtd. in Gladwell 32). But he can slice thinner than that, saying that if he knows whether the partners show contempt for each other he can tell if their marriage is in trouble. Through the use of numerous case studies, Gladwell demonstrates why he believes in the power of the unconscious to "[sift] through the situation . . . [and] zero in on what really matters" (33-34).

Punctuation with Quotations

Period after parenthetical citation at end of short, integrated quotation:

. . . zero in on what really matters" (33-34).

Period before parenthetical citation at end of long, indented quotation:

. . . the last word. (157)

Comma inside the closing quotation mark:

Jack Wilson writes that Bill Clinton "missed his father," especially when he was a young man.

Semicolon outside the closing quotation mark:

Wilson does not seem to respect Bill Clinton, calling him "[a]n outright liar"; it is obvious that Wilson is biased politically.

Above, the brackets indicate that a capital letter in the original was changed to lowercase.

Question mark inside the quotation mark only because it's part of the quotation:

Robert C. Allen, then the head of the honors program at University of North Carolina at Chapel Hill, describes a conversation he had with a venture capitalist. Allen asked Lucius Burch, "What made a difference to you when you were a student at Carolina?" only to find that Burch hadn't been a highly motivated student (B16).

Single quotation marks for a quotation that appeared in the original:

"Serious thinkers from both camps [liberals and conservatives] spoke against the principle of popular sovereignty," notes Lukacs, "and against what Tocqueville called 'the tyranny of the majority'" (15).

Above, brackets indicate material added by the writer to explain "both camps."

Slash with space on each side used to separate lines of poetry in a short quotation:

In "Ode on a Grecian Urn," John Keats describes the artist as one "who canst thus express / A flowery tale more sweetly than our rhyme" (3-4).

The numbers in parentheses are line numbers.

Punctuate Quotations Properly

Short quotations are set off from the rest of the sentence by a pair of quotation marks (▶ section 52a). Put periods and commas inside the quotation marks, and leave any other punctuation marks outside the quotation marks unless they appear in the quoted original. (See the Project Checklist on page 957.) A sentence that includes a short quotation ends after the parenthetical citation, not right after the quotation. The citation is part of the sentence that includes the quotation, so the period follows it. For punctuation of poetry in MLA style, see page 380.

Long quotations (in MLA style, more than four lines of prose or three of poetry) are set off by indenting them from the left margin. No quotation marks are used. If quotations appear in the original, use double, not single, quotation marks when reproducing them. To introduce long quotations, you may want to use a full sentence followed by a colon to help your readers move smoothly from your introduction into the quotation. Use a colon only if a full sentence introduces the quotation. If you use a phrase instead, you may or may not need a comma after it (▶ section 48c). In a long quotation, the parenthetical citation comes *after* the closing period of the quotation (▶ page 381).

Use an Ellipsis to Indicate an Omission

It is often advantageous to leave out words or sentences from quotations. For example, if an author refers to a portion of her work that you will not include in the quotation, readers wouldn't understand the reference. In the "tornado" quotation on page 350, we used an ellipsis (three spaced dots) to indicate that we had left out some material from the original. We chose not to include "said Carolyn Nordell, who lives a quarter-mile away" because that information was not necessary for us to make the point.

Whenever you remove words from a quotation, you should insert an ellipsis: . . . ; if the original already includes an ellipsis, then your ellipsis should be placed inside brackets to distinguish the two, according to MLA style: [. . .]. (For more examples, see section 53d.)

Examples of Ellipses

Ellipsis to indicate omission of material:

In a 1999 interview with Jacob Sullum and Michael Lynch, editors at *Reason,* economist John Lott said, "I was shocked by how poorly done the existing research on guns and crime was. . . . By far the largest previous study on guns and crime had looked at just 170 cities within a single year, 1980."

A period ends the first sentence, and then the three spaced dots of the ellipsis are given.

Ellipsis at end to show a sentence has been truncated:

Accompanying Paul Farmer on a trip to Matrosskaya Tishina (Moscow's Central Prison), Kidder found it easy to imagine getting thrown in jail: "In Russia just now, a young man could get thrown in jail for stealing a loaf of bread or a bottle of vodka . . ." (226).

Note that the period follows the citation. See more examples in section 53d.

Where Not to Use Ellipses

- **Ellipses are *not* used** to indicate that there are sentences before or after your quotation. Experienced readers bring a commonsense approach to quotations: they understand that something was written before and after the quotation you are using. However, **do** use an ellipsis at the end of a quotation to indicate that you have omitted part of the last sentence.
- **Ellipses are *not* used** to make a quotation say what you need said in your writing. If your quotation does not suit your needs, do not think that you have the liberty to change someone else's words to fit your purposes. Qualify the quotation by indicating that it supports just a portion of your idea, and then do further research to find other material to support your point. Using a quotation out of context not only misrepresents the intention of the original author, but also may harm your relationship with your readers if they know the original context of the quotation.

Examples of Brackets

Brackets used to alter the quotation so it will fit the grammar of the sentence:

In an appendix to the Anchor edition of *Under the Banner of Heaven*, Jon Krakauer wrote that "[b]ecause the Mormon leadership [was] so obsessed with controlling how the Mormon past was interpreted and presented, histories sanctioned by the LDS [tended] to be extensively censored" (364).

We can surmise from the use of brackets that, in the original, Krakauer used verbs in the present tense.

***[Sic]* used because correct title is "Ode on a Grecian Urn":**

"Keats's 'Ode to [sic] a Grecian Urn' is a poem about the timelessness of truth and beauty" (Schultz 19).

What to Do about Sexist Language in Quoted Material

At times the material you wish to cite may contain sexist or other discriminatory language, as described in Chapter 39. The general rule is not to change the source material by correcting such language—not to substitute nonsexist terms in brackets. Readers will understand that the language is that of the original source. When you do correct the sexist language in a source, you draw attention to it and may distract the reader from your main point in using the information in the first place. If necessary, you can use a note to explain to the reader that the sexist or other discriminatory language appears in the original.

Use Brackets When You Alter a Quotation

Do not change or add anything to a quotation unless you indicate the change with brackets. For instance, if you need to capitalize a letter to use a quotation to start your sentence, then indicate the change by placing brackets around the capitalized letter. (See the brackets in the punctuation examples on page 353.) You may also use brackets to change the tense or point of view in the quotation—if, for instance, the author writes in the first person and you use the quotation to describe her in the third person. (For more examples of brackets, see section 53c.)

Use *[sic]* to Indicate Errors in the Original

On occasion, you will discover an error in spelling or grammar in the material you want to quote. When that happens, you can indicate your awareness of the error by inserting *sic* in brackets next to it. That way your reader understands that you haven't accidentally made the error yourself. Don't be overzealous, however. Make sure that there is an error in the original before you use *[sic]*, and if there are several errors, consider not using the quotation at all. After all, how reliable is it if it contains so many errors?

17f A Process for Integrating Sources

The more you practice integrating sources into your writing, the more fluent you will become. We suggest that in writing where you have integrated source material, you first make sure your ideas predominate, not those of your sources. Second, check to see if your source material has the effect you intend: Does it provide the support for your assertions that will be needed to convince a reader in your particular rhetorical circumstances? Then go back and make sure that all quotation marks are in place, that authors and page numbers are cited correctly, and that periods and other punctuation make clear how you have used your sources. Check ellipses and brackets in a separate pass. Double-check your Works Cited or References list against the citations in your sentences. In short, use your knowledge of the writing process to divide up the tasks and make sure each one gets done well.

Activity 17-7: Integrating Sources

Suppose you are writing a persuasive essay for or against the use of Internet voting in future elections. Your readers are people who own computers. You read,

> It has been suggested that digital signature technology is the key to securing the internet voting process. Digital signatures provide the best level of security in electronic transactions, however they are not inexpensive. Questions raised about funding are important. If the government provides a digital signature for all voters the cost would be very high. Conversely, if voters who own or are willing to buy a digital signature are the only ones allowed to vote this way, then economic barriers to participation are being created. Additionally, there are several "classes" or security levels of digital signature. Some digital signatures are obtained without requiring any personal identification, others require high levels of ID including personal interviews. There is some irony in the fact that in order to register to vote a person only need fill in a form and mail it, but an in person interview may be required before a person could vote this way.

From David Elliot, "Examining Internet Voting in Washington," *Election Center* <http://www.electioncenter.org/voting/InetVotingWhitePaper.html>.

1. Write a sentence that provides an informative summary of the paragraph.
2. Write a sentence (or two) that incorporates a direct quotation.
3. Write a sentence that paraphrases the main point of the article.
4. Write a descriptive summary of Elliot's argument in the paragraph.
5. Write a paragraph about Internet voting that uses summary, quotation, and paraphrase from the article.

17g Writing Project Threads

A table of contents for writing project threads appears on pages xv–xxii.

Informative Essays

Garrison 1

Angela Garrison

English 101

Dr. Simpson

September 26, 2005

From Over There to Over Here:

War Blogs Get Up Close, Personal, and Profitable

Blog was the word looked up most often in the online *Merriam-Webster's Dictionary* in 2004 ("Blog"). What's all this fuss? When you read someone else's personal blog, you find out what they like and don't like, what they're doing, and maybe other bits of gossip offered at random. You can read news blogs to find out what's going on lately, what other people think about it, and why it matters. You can keep your own blog to share your thoughts and feelings, to tell your friends and family what you're up to, and sometimes to capture the interest of someone you've never met. When you read and write blogs, you join, or even create, a community. Blogs are also an efficient way to break news, spread rumors, and glorify causes. In short, blogs help people do what they've always done as social beings, just more quickly now, and from almost anywhere on Earth. Soldiers on the ground fighting in Iraq are

Weaving Together Your Ideas and Information from Sources

An informative essay relies on the accurate and even artful use of source material. Review sections 17a and 17b to help you think about the ways in which you will use sources in your essay. Then use the activities and information in sections 17c, 17d, and 17e to help you decide when to summarize, paraphrase, or quote from a source and how to integrate source material seamlessly into your own. Pay special attention to the sections on quoting and paraphrasing. page 374.

18

RESEARCH AND PLAGIARISM IN THE DIGITAL AGE

Citation has a rhetorical effect on readers. Citing the sources of your information and ideas is one way of persuading readers that you know what you are talking about and that your ideas have a basis in the writing and research of others. In academic writing, it's customary to cite frequently, whether to draw conclusions about common knowledge, to provide solid evidence for an argument, or to show that your work has precedents. When you use sources effectively to ground your research, advance an argument, or establish facts in contention, your research contributes to the advancement of knowledge.

Some people think that plagiarism is rampant on college campuses these days. New technologies do make it easier than ever before to find and repurpose useful information. They also speed up the pace at which students and researchers can disseminate new ideas. Those are the great benefits of the Internet. Some of your work as a researcher is easier now that vast amounts of information are available at the click of a mouse. At the same time, however, nothing has changed with regard to your responsibility to use your sources ethically. And while new technologies make more information available, they also make the process of checking and verifying source information much easier for those who review your work. In the end, the technologies are not the cause of citation problems. The causes are careless research, bad planning, and (often) a misunderstanding of the importance of representing your own work accurately. What should you do as a writer and researcher to use the ideas of others ethically and to make your research more effective?

In most contexts, plagiarism is understood to be a writer's deliberate misrepresentation of another's writing or ideas as his or her own. The principles and practices of academic integrity in your local environment will define plagiarism more precisely. As the contexts for your writing change and you communicate across fields with different groups of readers, the community's definition of sound research practice may change slightly. This can be true even at a college or university, where ethical standards for using information (or "intellectual property") may vary across different fields.

It's your responsibility as a writer to be aware of these issues and to ask questions when you're uncertain about the rules that define ethical academic conduct. You should review your own college's policies on plagiarism and academic honesty, which are usually published in the college catalog and on its website.

In this chapter, we help you understand what plagiarism is, how to avoid it by planning carefully and conducting research responsibly, and how to avoid misusing sources. The goal is to show you that you can integrate your own ideas with those of others to create effective research that others will want to read and cite themselves.

Activity 18-1: Examining Your School's Policy

Look up your school's academic honesty policy online or in a print publication. Write an informative summary of the policy. Next, write down any questions you have about the policy or terms that you don't understand. Bring your summary and questions to class, and compare them in groups. Do you all have the same understanding of how the policy works? What do or don't you understand?

Activity 18-2: Examining Examples of Acceptable and Unacceptable Uses of Sources

Visit the following websites to view examples of acceptable and unacceptable source use, with explanations:

Writing Tutorial Services at the Indiana University, Bloomington:
http://www.indiana.edu/~wts/pamphlets/plagiarism.shtml#plagiarized

"What Is Plagiarism?" from the Georgetown University Honor Council:
http://gervaseprograms.georgetown.edu/hc/plagiarism.html

Take Care to Avoid Plagiarism

1. Read carefully.

Ideas precede our understanding of facts, although the overabundance of facts tends to obscure this. A fact can be comprehended only within the context of an idea. And ideas are irrevocably subjective, which makes facts just as subjective.

2. Take notes carefully.

Wurman states that "[a] fact can be comprehended only within the context of an idea" (31).

Wurman, Richard Saul. Information Anxiety 2. Indianapolis: Que, 2001.

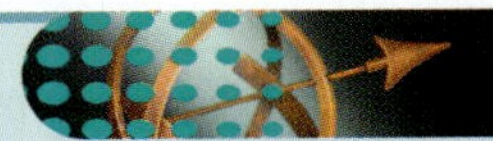

Global Contexts

Many students who have lived in different parts of the world find the idea of common knowledge confusing because information that is common knowledge in one part of the world may not be common knowledge in another. Common knowledge, as a concept, refers to the shared knowledge of your intended audience rather than just any group of people outside of a particular context. A group of people somewhere might know, for instance, all the procedures for currency devaluation by the World Bank, but if you're writing to an audience who doesn't, then you need to cite the sources of your information. In cases where you offer evidence and support but do not cite the source of your information, be certain that the information is common knowledge for your audience.

3. Use source information carefully.

Richard Saul Wurman notes that facts are subjective because they are always understood "within the context of an idea"; and ideas are always subjective (31).

OR

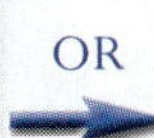

Each person screens reality through his or her own perceptions and beliefs. In the context of information delivery, Richard Saul Wurman agrees, stating that "[a] fact can be comprehended only within the context of an idea" (31).

In many definitions of plagiarism, the concept of *common knowledge* is used to determine what source information needs to be cited; if an idea is "common knowledge," then it doesn't need to be cited. But it's not always easy to determine what material falls in the domain of common knowledge. Here's how we define the concept:

> Knowledge is "common knowledge" when it's widely shared and known among a group of people and is a matter of the historical or factual record that no one would contest.

As researchers, we often communicate to diverse audiences that may not share the same body of common knowledge, hence the challenge of deciding what information needs to be attributed to a source and what information we can assume is widely known. Furthermore, if what you know with certainty is not common knowledge, then according to our definition of plagiarism, you still need to attribute it to a source (even when that source is your own experience). Sometimes information that is new to you falls within the scope of common knowledge, in which case citing it would be inappropriate.

If you understand why we don't cite common knowledge, you'll find it easier to judge for yourself whether information needs to be attributed to a source. In research writing, we cite sources to show how our own ideas are consistent with or contrast with those of other researchers—the place of our research in the larger conversation on knowledge. We also cite sources to express verifiability, which is one criterion for evaluating whether statements have validity. We want to show how new knowledge is constructed on existing knowledge. To ensure the assent of the community of readers, we want to establish that we're using information that others also deem to be credible.

When information falls in the realm of common knowledge, there's no need to reassert its credibility because people already believe it to be true. Common knowledge is often *uncontestable,* in other words. Since readers already presume common knowledge to be true, attributing common-knowledge

What Is Common Knowledge?

Here are some categories of information usually considered to be common knowledge, even though in some cases the information seems rather esoteric.

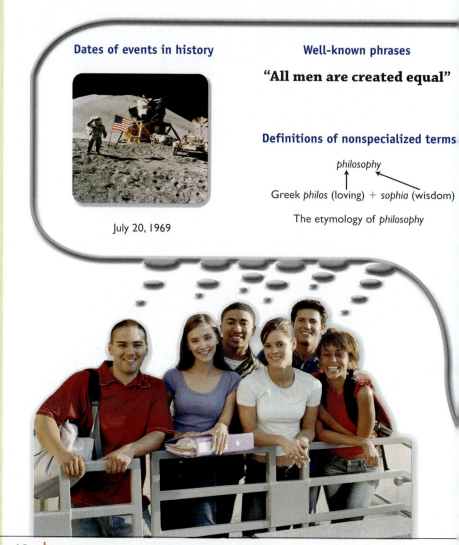

Dates of events in history

July 20, 1969

Well-known phrases

"All men are created equal"

Definitions of nonspecialized terms

philosophy

Greek *philos* (loving) + *sophia* (wisdom)

The etymology of *philosophy*

material to a source (such as an encyclopedia or dictionary) actually harms the author's ethos; it implicitly suggests that the author and readers don't already share such knowledge, or that it can be contested in the first place. Citing common knowledge has the rhetorical effects of boring readers and inviting them to question the author's level of awareness regarding what the community already knows to be true. Furthermore, we don't cite common knowledge in academic writing because doing so would make the task of sharing new information impossibly complex.

As you can tell, there will still be instances when it's difficult to decide whether factual information falls in the realm of common knowledge. When you're uncertain about the information you are drawing from a source, you should cite the source. Over time, you will gain experience judging what information is common knowledge; early in the process, it's better to be safe than sorry.

Geographical information

Lake Tahoe straddles Nevada and California.

Names of people

Mahatma Gandhi

Genealogies

Princess Margaret
1930–2002
m. Anthony, Earl of Snowdon

David, Viscount Linley b. 1961

Lady Sarah Armstrong-Jones b. 1964

English royal lineage

Information gathered through the senses

The moon appears red during a lunar eclipse.

Sometimes you may be faced with a situation in which you already know something that wouldn't normally be considered common knowledge. Perhaps you know it from personal experience, learned it years earlier in a museum, or recall reading about it when you were a child. In these cases, you either need to cite that experience or verify the information by locating a source that will confirm its validity. Suppose, for example, that you know that the Eiffel Tower was considered a monstrosity when it was first built. If you want to make that point in a research paper, you should cite someone saying so at the time or cite a historian who has made such a claim.

Examples of Common Knowledge

Suppose that you find the following information during your research. Is it common knowledge?

> Both presidents named Adams lived in Quincy, Massachusetts. They had a relative named William Adams, one of the most respected American psychologists in his time, and another relative named Henry Adams, who was an author. The latter two had a sister named Alice, who was also a writer.

It's possible to know this specific information without having looked it up anywhere, but we can also find it in many different sources—in fact, thousands of them—as part of the historical record. In this case, the information is common knowledge and would not need to be cited. We could add dates of birth and death, span of the presidential terms, and even the title of one of Henry Adams's books, all without citing a source for the information, for it is part of the historical record and would not be contested.

While there would be no dispute that two presidents were named Adams, once we began to report judgments about their lives or challenge existing information, we would need to cite our sources, if any. For example, if you read that John Quincy Adams was the first Boylston Professor of Rhetoric at Harvard University and that during his tenure he revitalized the study of rhetoric in American colleges, you would need to attribute that assessment to a source because it would not be widely known and could be a matter of contention. (Maybe he didn't revitalize American rhetoric, for example.) If you knew this topic so well that you were able to make the assessment yourself, then chances are that you would indicate to your reader that you were doing so after reviewing Adams's papers at Harvard (for example).

Activity 18-3: Determining Common Knowledge for Your Project

Assume that you are writing an essay whose audience is composed of your classmates. Make a list of five facts or ideas that you believe to be common knowledge about your topic. Show them to a partner. Are they common knowledge to your partner? Are your partner's facts common knowledge to you? Identify the ones that you think might need a citation.

Show your facts to three other classmates, and examine theirs. What proves to be common knowledge?

The following table answers common questions that may arise in different contexts. As a rule, if you are unsure whether to cite a source, go ahead and cite it.

Writing Context and Possible Questions	How to Avoid Plagiarism
COLLABORATIVE PROJECTS How much help can I accept? What kind of help can I accept? How much credit should I give when someone gives me an idea? When someone does some writing?	▪ Follow your instructor's guidelines for tracking and reporting individuals' contributions. ▪ If yours is the only author name, this means that you have done all the writing, even though you may have benefited from advice, written feedback, and pointed questions from friends or writing center tutors. ▪ If others have written part of the project, they need to be listed as co-authors. ▪ If others have contributed ideas but not writing, they need to be cited as research sources. (But see "Ideas a Friend Gives You" on page 364 for help.) ▪ If you need extra collaboration or help in an area that chronically troubles you, ask your instructor for assistance.
SOMEONE ELSE'S EXACT LANGUAGE You have cut and pasted information from the Internet or email, or you have copied quotations into your notes from sources at the library. Do I have to cite the sources? What kinds of publication information must I note? How can I keep my sources' ideas and my own ideas distinct?	▪ You must cite all quotations. See pages 370–371 for examples of cited and uncited quotations. ▪ Include all source information in your notes: author, title, and publication information—location, publisher, date, page numbers (if applicable), and URL and date of access (if applicable). ▪ Put all the text you cut and paste inside quotation marks. ▪ Every time you integrate a quotation into your own writing, put the author's last name and the page number in parentheses at the end of the quotation. If you are using more than one work by the same author, include a short title. If you have two authors with the same last name, add their initials so you'll remember which author a quotation is from.

Writing Context and Possible Questions	How to Avoid Plagiarism
CHANGING "JUST ENOUGH" How much do I have to change to make the material my own, to avoid citing it? Where in my work do I cite a source?	■ It is plagiarism to alter a source's phrasing slightly and then integrate the material into your work without citation. Any deliberate attempt to blur the distinction between your ideas and those of your source is plagiarism. You should consider quoting if the source's language is so memorable that you want it in your essay. ■ The placement of your parenthetical citation is crucially important. Every sentence that includes a quotation must have at least a page number in parentheses before the sentence ends; if the author's name hasn't appeared recently, the last name should be in parentheses there, too. Every summary and paraphrase must be documented. ■ When you place a parenthetical citation, you are signaling to your reader that this point is the end of another person's ideas and the resumption of your thinking. Don't make the mistake of placing the citation too early, making it appear that later ideas in your work originated with you when in fact they are another author's. To avoid this kind of plagiarism, compare the original idea to your use of the source, word for word, to ensure that your ideas grow out of the other person's ideas but are not repetitions of them.
IDEAS A FRIEND GIVES YOU Suppose you are working on a position paper concerning diesel emissions and air pollution. A friend tells you that she read something on how types of respiratory distress (such as asthma) might develop around urban areas where diesel engines are used the most. Should I cite my friend? Is that good enough?	■ We strongly encourage you to discuss your projects with others; academic writing almost always emerges from discussion, consideration, and revision. You'll often get good ideas from discussions you have, and that is fine. ■ If you believe that the idea about a connection among diesel fumes, urban areas, and respiratory distress is worth including, then you need to cite the author of the original research, which means you have to find it. This might seem like a lot of trouble, but if the idea is a good one, it will be worth the effort. ■ You do not need to cite the person who suggested the idea to you, but if the idea is critical to your project, it wouldn't be a bad practice to thank the person for the input in a footnote or endnote, as often happens in published academic articles and in the acknowledgments section in a book.

Writing Context and Possible Questions	How to Avoid Plagiarism
IDEAS SIMILAR TO THE IDEA YOU HAD If I have an idea, but then I find someone else has had a very similar idea, do I need to cite the outside source? Why?	■ It is certainly conceivable that your good ideas have been thought by someone else previously. ■ Even if you've never read anything about your subject, it's your obligation as an academic writer to research ideas and review existing information when you are in a situation where you need to develop theories of your own or analyze the ideas of others. If you find information that is similar to what you have developed, then cite it. ■ By citing similar ideas, you are indicating that the idea is so worthy of consideration that other people have published research about it also.
NUMERICAL AND STATISTICAL DATA How do I cite research that I conducted? How do I cite other people's research? Do I need to cite another person's research when I just duplicated it and got the same results?	■ If you write, "Seventy percent of my friends have tried junk food but have not become addicted," you are reporting data entirely attributable to you because you conducted the research. There is no need to cite this category of data unless you previously published the research. ■ If you write, "Seventy percent of adults from 18 to 25 have tried junk food without becoming addicted," clearly someone else has done the research and needs to be cited in your writing. ■ If you know of existing research on the effects of eating junk food and then conduct your own survey, you should cite the original research. If you know that another study proved exactly or even essentially what you are attempting to prove and you have used this research as a foundation or starting point for your own, cite the original. Doing so will add credence to your findings.

Writing Context and Possible Questions	How to Avoid Plagiarism
DUPLICATE SUBMISSION If I wrote an assignment for another class, can I turn it in again for a different class? Can I rewrite it and turn it in?	■ If you write an assignment for one class and then submit it as new work for another class without the prior approval of your instructor, that's a form of academic dishonesty. However, you may pursue the same ideas in different disciplines, looking, for instance, at the ramifications of gender inequity in society in different classes as you progress through your studies. You may even develop a specialization if you pursue ideas with that level of rigor and enthusiasm, and your specialization may become something that your school, family, and friends take pride in. ■ Sometimes teachers will allow you to revise or modify work produced previously or elsewhere, but in every case you should be absolutely clear about the origins of your work. ■ The following tips will help you to avoid misrepresenting your work and to make existing ideas fresh once again: ***Reexamine familiar secondary sources.*** Even if you feel that you know the secondary source by heart or if you find yourself relying on the same quotation again and again as evidence, reread your sources. You are likely to find some aspect that is especially relevant to your current work. ***Keep up with publications in your area of interest.*** Staying current with scholarship in your area of interest will give you the opportunity to connect the theories you are learning about with the theories you encountered in earlier classes. ***Never cut and paste anything from a previous assignment,*** even if it would be convenient. Revisit your sources instead and rewrite the evidence and the bibliographies. Your writing will likely come out much better the second time around. ***Ask your instructor.*** Don't ask the instructor whether you can simply write the same paper for different classes, which would be insulting. Instead, mention that you completed a research project in another course that you now want to pursue further. Ask the instructor how you can tailor that research interest in ways that will meet the goals of your current course.

Writing Context and Possible Questions	How to Avoid Plagiarism

CITATION INFORMATION ISN'T AVAILABLE

What if I can't find the publication information that I am supposed to include?

- Consider not using the source at all. If it can't be attributed to an author or organization or if there's no telling when it was published, then it may be unreliable information. Unconfirmed sources are never very persuasive, as you know if you've read tabloids.
- There are occasions when some aspects of information are simply unavailable. For instance, some websites fail to provide information about date of publication, authorship, or copyright. But suppose you still want to use the source? Ultimately, you just may not find the information you need in order to construct a proper citation. All the citation styles have a procedure for indicating that some source information is unavailable. (See section 19c for MLA and 20c for APA.) If you have confirmed that the information you need doesn't exist, then consult the appropriate style manual (in print or on the Web), ask your instructor, or consult with a writing tutor.
- **Don't** attempt either of these ad hoc solutions, which are violations of basic academic integrity:

  Do not insert false information. Clearly, researchers do a disservice to readers and violate their ethical responsibilities as citizens in a social process of inquiry if they falsify information. For professionals, the penalties for doing so can be severe. Student writers will find that if citation information appears obviously wrong to their readers, their credibility (ethos) will be seriously compromised.

  Do not fail to take the time to track down citation information. If you create false citation information or claim that the information is unavailable because you do not have time to prepare an accurate bibliography, your readers will judge your writing harshly.
- Many readers of academic writing thumb immediately to the bibliography as a method of assessing the quality of the research as a whole. The bibliography for a research project should never be an afterthought, but its foundation.

Writing Context and Possible Questions	How to Avoid Plagiarism
AIDING IN THE MISUSE OF INFORMATION What do I do if a friend wants to copy my work? How can I protect my documents on a publicly accessible computer?	■ In college or high school, where the pressure to succeed is high and time is often short, you may have heard sob stories from desperate friends with deadlines to meet and no way of meeting them. Allowing another person to copy your work or aiding in the misuse of information is just as unethical as copying or misusing it yourself. It may not be plagiarism, but it will certainly be considered a violation of academic honesty policies. ■ Be careful to protect your own documents. If you write a paper on someone else's computer or a publicly accessible computer, don't leave the file on the computer—or, at the very least, protect the file with a password. Most word processing programs allow authors to protect documents in this way. ■ If you find you have been put in a tough situation by a peer, consider responding in one of the following ways: ***Encourage the person to discuss the problem with the instructor to see if a solution can be negotiated.*** In most cases, discussion with the instructor will yield a painless solution. Most writing instructors are eager to assist students when they're in tight spots. ***Provide some tutoring or refer the writer to a writing center.*** It's okay to tutor a friend, but one of the cardinal rules of tutoring is that you shouldn't do the work for the person, which prevents learning and thus does a disservice in the end.

As you can see from the list of questions researchers have about using source material, there are well-defined rules for using sources ethically. It may take some time to absorb all the rules; do your best to learn them thoroughly. Talk to your instructor or a writing center tutor any time you aren't clear on how to proceed.

Activity 18-4: Thinking about Plagiarism

Which of the following actions would be considered plagiarism?

1. Citing a survey you conducted without attributing it
2. Citing a survey published in an academic journal, newspaper, or magazine without attributing it
3. Using an idea that you got from talking with a friend about your paper without citing it
4. Using an idea you got from a book without citing it
5. Cutting and pasting other people's words into your paper
6. Cutting and pasting other people's words into your paper, and then surrounding them with quotation marks and adding a citation
7. Paraphrasing or summarizing someone's work without attribution
8. Paraphrasing or summarizing others' work and giving them credit for their ideas

Talk about your answers in groups. What are other examples of circumstances that could be (or could not be) considered plagiarism?

Quick Guide to Using and Citing Sources

Using and Citing Sources

Recording bibliographic information: 14h
Summarizing effectively: 17c
Paraphrasing effectively: 17d
Quoting effectively: 17e
Integrating sources: 17f
Citing visual content: 24c
Citing sources in a presentation summary of an oral presentation: 26c
Citing sources in an online posting to a blog or discussion board: 28e
Copyright issues for textual, visual, musical and audio, and adapted website content: 29e

Citation Styles

MLA ▶ Chapter 19
APA ▶ Chapter 20
CMS ▶ Chapter 21
CSE ▶ Chapter 22
CGOS ▶ Chapter 23

Here is an excerpt from a *New York Times* article on Web logs. Read it and then study the examples of misuses and effective uses of this source.

New York Times,
October 23, 2003

Blog Bog and an Email Pony Express

Pamela LiCalzi O'Connell

Are Web logs more fizzle than sizzle? A recent study by Perseus Development, a research firm and maker of software for surveys, finds that fully 66 percent of the 4.12 million blogs, or online journals, created on eight leading blog-hosting services have been "abandoned"—that is, not updated for at least two months. And 1.09 million of those were one-day wonders.

The study went on to puncture other bits of common wisdom about blogs, like the frequency with which they are updated. Fewer than 50,000 of the sites in the study were updated every day. As for the notion that most blogs comment on the news, only 9.9 percent had a main-page posting that linked to a traditional news site. Perhaps most biting, the study

Proper Citation of Source

Reference to publisher

Title of article

A recent *New York Times* article, "Blog Bog and an Email Pony Express," cites a study by Perseus Development showing that 1.09 million of the current blogs now published on the Internet were created and then abandoned after only one day (O'Connell).

Information drawn from article (and not common knowledge)

Parenthetical citation of author of the article (MLA style). Note that there is no page number listed because the source is online. The URL will be listed in the Works Cited under the entry for "O'Connell."

Failure to Cite Source

Of the current blogs now published on the Internet, 1.09 million were created and then abandoned after only one day.

This information clearly comes from the source and needs to be cited. Readers know that information like this stems from formal research.

Changing the Information Slightly and Failing to Cite the Source

Of the current blogs now published on the Internet, a million were created and then abandoned after only one day.

This information clearly comes from the source and needs to be cited. Readers know that information like this stems from formal research and needs to be cited.

Misleading Citation Information

Of the current blogs now published on the Internet, 1.09 million were created and then abandoned after only one day (Perseus Development).

This citation is misleading. It suggests that the Perseus research was cited directly, when actually O'Connell cited the research in her article.

Properly Cited Indirect Source

Original source of the statement is named

Even though many blogs are abandoned after just one day, the story, according to Jeffrey Henning, is "how many people are trying blogs, not how many are giving up" (qtd. in O'Connell).

Use indirect citations sparingly, but when you do, MLA recommends this format.

This is an indirect quotation because O'Connell cited it in her article.

Using Quotation Marks without Documenting the Source

Even though many blogs are abandoned after just one day, the story is "how many people are trying blogs, not how many are giving up."

Clearly, someone has been quoted here and should be cited.

Inaccurate Attribution of Source to Another Person

Even though many blogs are abandoned after one day, the story is "how many people are trying blogs, not how many are giving up" (O'Connell).

This citation is inaccurate because it implies that O'Connell made the statement when Henning actually did.

found that the typical blog is written by a teenage girl who uses it twice a month to update her friends. Are blogs just that old friend from the 90's, the Web diary, dressed up in new tools?

The answer is yes and no. Perseus itself offers some significant caveats to its study. For one, only blogs on blog-hosting services like LiveJournal were studied. Blogs maintained by individuals on their own servers were not included, and one could argue that the most influential blogs fall in that category.

"This study is like a Rorschach test," said Jeffrey Henning, chief operating officer of Perseus. "Some people see it as dismissive of blogs. I look at it and see an incredibly accessible technology. The story is how many people are trying blogs, not how many are giving up."

From Pamela LiCalzi O'Connell, Online Diary, "Blog Bog and an Email Pony Express," *New York Times,* 23 Oct. 2003, 12 Sept. 2005 <http://www.nytimes.com/>.

Rarely does a person intentionally set out to misuse sources. More often, good intentions are foiled when schedules become overcrowded or work is put off until the last moment. At times like these, misusing information seems like the only alternative. But if you follow the strategies in this section, you won't run into the problem of having too little time to complete your work properly.

Use Your Time Wisely

Don't underestimate the amount of time necessary to prepare, revise, and complete your writing assignments. Create a realistic work schedule for every assignment and stick with it. Plan to work on your current writing project for a half hour to an hour every day. If you absolutely cannot finish your paper on time, ask for an extension. If your request is denied, turn in an "A" paper a day or two late and suffer the grade consequences rather than turning in a plagiarized and probable "F" paper on time.

Stop "Frittering Behavior"

Don't spend time mindlessly browsing the Web (or doing anything else) when you should be writing. Psychologists who study people at work describe this as "frittering behavior." You can wait to clean your room until after you finish working on your project.

Activity 18-5: Citing Information Accurately

Read the following excerpt from a *New York Times* article about Marshall McLuhan.

New York Times April 3, 2003

McLuhan's Messages, Echoing in Iraq Coverage

Sarah Boxer

. . . So what happens when a cool medium like television is attached to a hot weapon like a tank or a Bradley fighting vehicle?

It exerts a powerful effect on the audience. Suddenly everyone watching television is dragged into war. When there is a sandstorm, you, the audience, can't see ahead any better than the troops. When the fight's going smoothly, you feel that maybe the war will be quick and easy. When the camera is attached to a smart bomb, you might feel that you have become the bomb.

McLuhan understood this kind of tactile television experience. "In closed-circuit instruction in surgery, medical students from the first reported a strange effect—that they seemed not to be watching an operation, but performing it," he wrote. "They felt that they were holding the scalpel." Television, he continued, "in fostering a passion for depth involvement in every aspect of experience, creates an obsession with bodily welfare."

With the war rolling ahead on television, you the viewer are made a part of the invading army. Even the local meteorologists participate in the illusion. They give two weather reports: sunshine in New York, sandstorms in Basra.

Meanwhile, just as the audience feels a part of the army, the army becomes part of the audience. American troops on an aircraft carrier watch CNN to see how the war is playing and progressing. Soldiers are watching other soldiers on television.

That is, there is general confusion as to who is acting and who is watching. And at the crux of the confusion are the traditional eyewitnesses to war, the journalists, "embedded" with the troops. Are the television cameras the witnesses to war, or are they part of the weaponry? Or both?

From Sarah Boxer, "McLuhan's Messages, Echoing in Iraq Coverage," *New York Times* 3 Apr. 2003, 4 Apr. 2004 <http://www.nytimes.com>.

The following statements use information from the article. Evaluate each statement and write a sentence that explains whether the statement shows accurate use of source material or misuse. For misuses, rewrite the statement to correct the problem.

1. According to Marshall McLuhan, "In closed-circuit instruction in surgery, medical students from the first reported a strange effect" (McLuhan).
2. Soldiers are watching other soldiers on television a lot these days now that the war in Iraq has started.
3. Ever since it was invented, people have questioned whether television could adequately represent reality.
4. Watching television is hardly passive. In fact, viewers play an active role in constructing and interpreting the events on screen, as do the people who create these images in the first place. This creates the dangerous possibility that unscrupulous people will manipulate the so-called objective images of television news for the purposes of propaganda. "Are the television cameras the witnesses to war, or are they part of the weaponry?" (Boxer).
5. Television exerts powerful effects on audiences.
6. People are naturally concerned about the recent escalation of conflict, so weather reports now include weather information about Iraq.
7. According to Sarah Boxer, American troops on an aircraft carrier watch CNN to see how the war is playing and progressing. Soldiers are watching other soldiers on television.
8. Modern warfare has evolved to the point where people begin to identify themselves with the bombs themselves, such as when the camera is attached to a smart bomb, you might feel that you have become the bomb (Boxer).

Be Realistic

Avoid situations where you feel that you must read numerous weighty secondary sources before you can even begin. When your topic seems to call for that kind of research, reconceptualize it.

Use Sources Judiciously

Don't rely so heavily on outside sources that your own perspective gets lost.

Gather All the Information You Need the First Time

Always include the full citation information when you gather research notes. What might take a minute or two to write down early in the process can take hours to relocate at the end of the process.

Back Up Your Work

If you cannot back up your file, email it to yourself and then copy the file elsewhere. Or use a portable USB (or pen) drive as a backup. USB drives can hold large quantities of information (anywhere from 16 MB to 6 GB), and they simply plug into the host machine's USB port without requiring any pre-loaded software. Backing up your files takes a minute or two at this early stage and can save you hours later if your computer crashes because of a hardware failure or a virus.

A table of contents for writing project threads appears on pages xv–xxii.

Informative Essays

Garrison 1

Angela Garrison

English 101

Dr. Simpson

September 26, 2005

From Over There to Over Here:

War Blogs Get Up Close, Personal, and Profitable

Blog was the word looked up most often in the online *Merriam-Webster's Dictionary* in 2004 ("Blog"). What's all this fuss? When you read someone else's personal blog, you find out what they like and don't like, what they're doing, and maybe other bits of gossip offered at random. You can read news blogs to find out what's going on lately, what other people think about it, and why it matters. You can keep your own blog to share your thoughts and feelings, to tell your friends and family what you're up to, and sometimes to capture the interest of someone you've never met. When you read and write blogs, you join, or even create, a community. Blogs are also an efficient way to break news, spread rumors, and glorify causes. In short, blogs help people do what they've always done as social beings, just more quickly now, and from almost anywhere on Earth. Soldiers on the ground fighting in Iraq are writing blogs from the front lines. But a review is now under way at the Pentagon to "better understand the overall implications of blogging and other Internet communications in combat zones," according to John Hockenberry in his *Wired* article "The Blogs of War." The benefits of blogs written by U.S. soldiers in Iraq far outweigh the hypothetical risks of revealing sensitive or strategic information. Those benefits, however, aren't as obvious as they might seem.

In spite of what the imagery of smart bombs and predator drones might lead television viewers to believe, wars are fought by people, not just technology. Most blogs start out as efforts to stay in touch with family and friends, but they quickly turn into

Citing Your Sources Correctly

Take great care to keep source material distinct from your own ideas and expressions. When you use information produced by others, make sure you provide correct attribution for your sources. Check each use of source material against the information in this chapter to be sure you don't inadvertently plagiarize anyone else's work. page 118.

Proposal Arguments

Harrington 1

A Proposal to Clean Up Our Streets

I have a proposal which could clean up the whole neighborhood.

All of a sudden the public perception of the lobbying profession has plunged to depths even below those occupied by trial lawyers, tobacco users, child molesters and Democrat members of the Senate Judiciary Committee. Its practitioners are now seen as the designated villains of the present moment, to be avoided as if they were carriers of an especially virulent strain of bird flu common among vultures and other avid consumers of carrion and offal.

Given that the right to lobby is protected by the Constitution and cannot be banned outright, or even regulated to any great extent, all this blather about taking the boys and girls on K Street, who only yesterday were their bosom buddies, to the woodshed is nothing less than a charade. Any reforms will be window dressing, and after a brief period of time the buddy-buddy relationships they shared with the K Street crowd will be re-invigorated. But, as Jerry Seinfeld would say, "Not that there's anything wrong with that."

Aside from banning former members of Congress and former Capital Hill staffers from ever serving as lobbyists, therefore condemning them to a fate worse than death – i.e., going home to their districts and living like normal Americans, deprived of the joys of the abundant life on the shores of the Potomac River – there really isn't much that can be done to stop the incestuous relationships between solons and lobbyists. As the song "Love and Marriage" explains, "they go together like a horse and carriage ... you can't have one without the other."

Double-Checking Any Uses of Source Material

If your proposal incorporates any material from outside sources, such as facts and figures you have used to support your thesis, double-check to make sure that you have integrated it carefully into your own writing; followed the guidelines given in this chapter for using quotations, paraphrases, and summaries; and cited each use correctly. Reread your notes against your final draft to be sure you haven't mistaken any information. If your notes are unclear, go get the source and check your draft against it directly. Make any adjustments that are needed to your final draft.

PART 4

Citing Sources

New Contexts for Writing

Podcasting Music, Film, and Video Game Reviews

You may soon be listening to podcasts of course lectures or producing and broadcasting your own audio content—and you won't need expensive equipment or complicated software to do it. If you like to review new music, movies, or video games, now you can share your reviews with others, just as you would if you hosted your own radio show. Your reviews—if they're engaging and thoughtful—might be heard by more people than watch the nightly news on television.

Podcasting, which first became popular in 2004, refers to the process of recording audio programs—music, lectures, readings, radio shows, interviews, and more—and then preparing them for distribution on the Internet. Podcasting involves recording an **MP3** file using a digital audio recorder or a computer with a microphone and sound editing software like Audacity (audacity.sourceforge.net) or Apple GarageBand™. The MP3 file (a common file format for audio) can then be uploaded to a free hosting service like Ourmedia.org.

Podcast files are distributed through syndicators like Podcast.net and services like Apple's iTunes® and can be easily accessed with podcast aggregator software (called **podcatchers**) like iPodder, Ziepod, or iTunes. Using an iPod® or another MP3 player, users can subscribe to **feeds** that will automatically update the list of available podcasts as they are published elsewhere.

With the emergence of Apple's video-playing iPod, podcasting may now include the syndication of video content also.

Writing Good Reviews

When you write, speak, or publish content for a public audience, you need to consider and define your audience, develop content that will be interesting, and bear in mind that your words and images have consequences for others.

Good reviews of music, film, and video games do more than summarize and analyze. They situate the subject of the review in its historical context (its predecessors), relate it to other familiar works, analyze its strengths and weaknesses, and take a position on whether it's worth listening to, watching, or playing. Script your podcast reviews as carefully as you would any other public document.

Podcast Clearinghouses

Podcast.net
http://podcast.net

IGN Entertainment (music, movies, and video games)
http://www.ign.com/index/podcasts.html

Only Connect . . . >

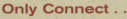

19

CITING SOURCES IN MLA STYLE

The citation style recommended by the Modern Language Association (MLA) is used to cite sources in research essays and other writing projects in the fields of English, rhetoric and composition, foreign languages, and literature. If you major in one of these fields, you may want to examine a copy of the *MLA Handbook for Writers of Research Papers,* 7th edition (New York: MLA, 2009), to become familiar with the citation style you will be using throughout your college career. This chapter focuses on the documentation of research sources and the format of MLA papers and projects.

The MLA style is widely known throughout the humanities. Using it allows your readers to easily identify the source of information or a quotation and find the relevant publication information. With publication information in hand, readers can locate the source when they want to conduct further research or when they want to evaluate the original context to see whether you've used the information effectively and ethically.

The MLA style includes two basic components: (1) citations of summaries, paraphrases, and quotations given inside parentheses in the body of the text and (2) an alphabetically organized Works Cited page at the end of the text, which provides the author, title, and publication details for each source used. The two components work hand in hand. The information that appears in your in-text citation leads readers to the corresponding entry in the Works Cited list. Typically, the author's last name is the link, but in certain circumstances a shortened version of the work's title will accompany the author's last name. In other cases, where no author's name is listed, the title will replace the author's name as the link to the Works Cited.

MLA INDEXES

In the example to the right, the author's last name links the in-text citation to the Works Cited entry.

Notice in the in-text citation:

- Both the author's last name and the page number of the quotation are given.
- The quotation is placed inside a pair of quotation marks.
- The page number is placed inside parentheses.
- The sentence ends after the in-text citation. The period follows the last parenthesis.

Notice in the Works Cited entry:

- The author's last name is used to alphabetize the entry. A comma separates the author's last name from the first name. A period ends the author portion of the entry.
- The book title is italicized. A period ends the title portion of the entry.
- The publication information includes the city of publication, followed by a colon; the name of the publisher, followed by a comma; the year of publication, followed by a period; and the medium of publication. The entry ends with a period.
- The first line of an entry starts at the left margin, but the second and subsequent lines are indented 1/2" from the left margin. (This is called a *hanging indentation.*)

The Link between the In-Text Citation and the Works Cited Entry

In-text citation of a work:

Jones 3

Hosseini has his protagonist, Amir, describe finding out how the Hazaras had been mistreated by the Pashtuns: "my people had killed the Hazaras, driven them from their lands, . . . and sold their women" (9).

Works Cited entry:

Jones 6

Work Cited

Hosseini, Khaled. *The Kite Runner*. New York: Riverhead, 2003. Print.

For information on using an ellipsis (three spaced dots) in a quotation, see section 53d on page 965.

Activity 19-1: Quick MLA Citation Practice

Referring to the example above, use the excerpt and publication information given below to create your own example of an in-text citation from a book and the Works Cited entry that would accompany it.

From the book *The Body: Photographs of the Human Form* by William A. Ewing
Published in San Francisco by Chronicle Books
Copyright 1994
Excerpt from page 10:

Photographers know all too well how easily their work can catapult them into the battles raging over the human body. Witness the storms of controversy which have surrounded the images of Robert Mapplethorpe, Sally Mann, Jock Sturges, or Andres Serrano in recent years; it is always some perceived transgression of conventional notions of the body, particularly issues relating to sexuality, that ignites public passions.

Two Ways to Identify the Source in the Text

Author's name in introduction:

> King 5
>
> In her remarkable autobiography, Jacobs writes that slavery was "demeaning to everyone involved in its vile operation" (124).

Author's name in parentheses:

> King 5
>
> Slavery was described by a former slave as "demeaning to everyone involved in its vile operation" (Jacobs 124).

Note: Do *not* put a comma between the author's name and the page number when both are included in your parenthetical citation.

MLA Tip

Be sure to include page numbers when taking notes from a source. The absence of a page number in a parenthetical citation (unless one is not available) will call into question your ability to handle evidence and support.

Parenthetical in-text citations should include the minimum amount of information—usually the author's last name and the relevant page number(s). That information helps the reader locate the source in the Works Cited list and then track down the precise location of the quoted material in the original source.

You have two choices about how to identify the source of the quotation (or paraphrase or summary):

- Use the author's name in your introduction to the quotation, in which case you place just the page number of the source in the parenthetical citation.
- Introduce the quotation without the author's name and then, before the sentence ends, place the author's last name and the page number of the source in parentheses.

In the second part of the example to the left, notice that even though the author's last name is not used in the introduction, the writer has included a phrase that identifies the author of the quotation: "a former slave." This phrase gives the quotation added impact, since its author was a participant in the subject she is evaluating.

If the author of the work you are citing is anonymous or if you are using more than one work by the same author, include an abbreviated version of the title. (See citation model 7 on page 384.)

Short Quotations

When you use a prose quotation of four or fewer of your lines (or a quotation of poetry that includes three or fewer lines of the poem), incorporate it as seamlessly as possible into your own sentence. Use quotation marks before the first word and after the last word of the quoted material to separate it from your text. Place the citation as close as possible to the material being quoted, either at a natural break in the sentence or at the end of it.

Remember that the sentence ends *after* the parenthetical information, so the period goes after the closing parenthesis, not within the last quotation mark. The exception to this rule is when your quotation ends with an exclamation point or a question mark. In this case, the punctuation mark stays within the quotation marks, and then you add the parenthetical citation followed by a period.

If you are quoting two or three lines of poetry, use a slash with a space on either side after each line to show the reader where the lines of poetry break. The citation gives the line numbers you are citing.

End punctuation after citation in short quotation:

Cervantes 2

Michael J. Fox describes his experiences with Parkinson's disease as "a situation of daily life that can seem both tragic and humorous at once" (196).

? or ! within the quotation:

Maclin 3

Most music reviewers have the same question about Vanilla Ice, the 1980s rapper with no street credibility: "Did he appropriate another culture's traditions when he began using the call and response rhythm of hip hop?" (Oakwood 101).

Slashes with spaces to indicate where lines of poetry break:

Hall 4

Coleridge's "Kubla Khan" demonstrates the use of inverted sentence structure: "In Xanadu did Kubla Khan / A stately pleasure dome decree" (1-2).

Hackman 7

McRobbie describes the punk rock phenomenon as mainly a consumer event:

> Punk was, first and foremost, cultural. Its self-expressions existed at the level of music, graphic design, visual images, style and the written word. It was therefore engaging with and making itself heard within the terrain of the arts and the mass media. . . . In the realm of style, the same do-it-yourself ethic prevailed and the obvious place to start was the local flea market. (198)

McRobbie's sense of the consumer ethic of punk differs from many cultural critiques of newer art and music movements. While purchasing the right kinds of clothing was essential for the punk fan, the main concept of consumerism was ironically ignored as punk's visionaries clothed themselves in used and vintage fashions.

Many writers use block quotations when a brief paraphrase or summary would achieve the same goal. Some mistakenly use block quotations simply to meet length requirements. Extensive use of block quotations may indicate that a writer is not using sources economically (that is, using brief examples from them to illustrate key points) or that the writer doesn't have much to say. If you are wondering about whether to use a long quotation, ask the following questions:

- Can you summarize the essential points instead of quoting them directly (◀ section 17c)?
- Can you use ellipses to cut out parts of the quotation that are not absolutely essential (▶ section 53d)?
- Can you integrate the source's ideas more smoothly into your prose while also clearly citing the source (◀ section 17f)?

Long Quotations

When a quotation takes five or more of your lines, omit the quotation marks, indent the entire quotation 1" (or 10 typewriter spaces) from the left margin, and double-space the lines just as you have in the rest of the paper. Often, an entire sentence, followed by a colon, is used to introduce a long quotation. The parenthetical citation is given after the last punctuation mark of the block quotation, with one space between them.

Whenever you use a block quotation, a careful explanation of its purpose or meaning is called for. While you should explain the significance of all uses of source material, a block quotation in particular requires ample discussion so readers understand why you found the material important enough to quote at length.

If you are quoting from a single paragraph, do not indent the first line even if it is the first line of the source's paragraph. If more than one paragraph is quoted, indent each paragraph an additional 1/4" (or 3 typed spaces) from the indented left margin.

MLA In-Text Citations Index

MLA In-Text Citation Models

1. Author named in your text

> Marsh tells us that the term "'Hooligan' derives from the name 'Houlihan,' a noticeably anti-social Irish family in nineteenth-century east London" (335).

The first time you use an author's name in your text, it's customary to use the first and last name. Then in subsequent references, such as the one above, you would use just the last name.

Notice that the original source included quotation marks already. Since the writer had to put all the source material in quotation marks, the ones from the original are changed to single quotation marks to distinguish them.

2. Author not named in your text

> The term "'Hooligan' derives from the name 'Houlihan,' a noticeably anti-social Irish family in nineteenth-century east London" (Marsh 335).

Readers will see the author's last name in parentheses, which cues them to the entry in the Works Cited list.

3. No author's or editor's name

Sometimes you may use a source that has no author or editor. Refer to it by title in the body of your text, or shorten the title to one or more words in a parenthetical citation, but make sure the first word is the same one you use when you alphabetize the title in your Works Cited list.

> In the article "Running and Health," a daily workout is described as "a mundane activity that generates health" (21).

Or you could write

> A daily workout is described as "a mundane activity that generates health" ("Running and Health" 21).

Notice that no comma is used between the title and the page number.

4. Two or three authors

When your source has two or three authors, use their names in the order in which they appear in the source. For the first reference in your text to two authors, use their first and last names; if there are more than two, you may want to use just last names. With two names, use the conjunction *and* between the authors' names:

> Trent Collins and Andrea Junkins describe the academic experience as a form of "systematic hazing" (31).

When there are three or more authors, punctuate the names like a series, with a comma after each name and the conjunction *and* between the last two names:

> Hollis, Johnson, and Ruotolo note that "binge drinking has emerged as the number one concern of university administrators" (111).

See citation model 5 on page 384 for an alternative style that can be used with four or more authors.

MLA In-Text Citations Index

MLA In-Text Citations Index

5. Four or more authors

When your source has four or more authors, you can either list them all as they appear in the source or use the first author's name followed by *et al.* (an abbreviation for the Latin term *et alii,* meaning "and others"). Note that there is no period after *et,* but there is a period after *al.*

> Some writers express discomfort at the label "poor" (Blinn et al. 119), preferring instead the expression "economically challenged" (Blinn et al. 120).

6. Two or more authors with the same last name

When you use two or more authors with the same last name as sources, use their first initials in your parenthetical citations to identify which one you are referring to. In the unlikely situation where the first initials are the same, use their middle initials also or the full name if no middle initial is available.

> Open houses were used to keep English language tutors motivated (J. Scott 1). As is pointed out in "Volunteer Motivation," it's crucial for refugees to build a network of reliable support, and one way to help achieve this goal is to ensure that volunteers serving a particular family continue volunteering (M. Scott 14).

7. More than one source by the same author

When you cite more than one source by the same author or authors, you should place a comma after the author's last name, shorten the title of the source, and insert that shortened title after the last name and before the page number or numbers—without a comma between the last two items.

> (Foucault, *Discipline* 198-202)
> (Foucault, *History* 32)

If you use the name of the author in the in-text citation, simply place the shortened title and page number or numbers in the parenthetical citation—with no comma between the two items.

> Foucault writes, "The Panopticon is a machine for dissociating the see/being seen dyad" (*Discipline* 201-02).

If you use the author's name and the shortened or full title in the introduction to your quotation, then use only the page number or numbers in the parenthetical citation.

8. Corporate author or government publication

When you cite a source with a corporate author or one written by a governmental entity, use the standard conventions. Treat the entity that wrote or sponsored the creation of the source as the author, and name it either in the parenthetical citation or in the introduction.

> The Federal Emergency Management Agency describes most toxic waste situations as "controllable and not a major problem to the nearby corporations" (22).

Or you could write:

> Most toxic waste situations are described as "controllable and not a major problem to the nearby corporations" (Federal Emergency Management Agency 22).

MLA In-Text Citations Index

MLA In-Text Citations Index

9. Two or more sources in the same citation

If you need to cite several sources in your parenthetical reference, include the author's last name and the page number or numbers for each, with a semicolon dividing the citations:

> (Highsmith 212; Hockley 23-45; McGrath 110-11)

Your readers might find this kind of in-text citation disruptive, so consider using an endnote. Don't forget to include the entries for these citations, as you would the entry for any other in-text citation, on your Works Cited page.

10. The entire work

To cite a complete work, use the author or other creator's name in the text rather than in parentheses:

> Allison's *Bastard Out of Carolina* provoked horrified tears and feelings of betrayal.

A work that does not have any page numbers can be referred to in this manner as well.

11. Multivolume work

If your source is from a work that includes multiple volumes, then your citation needs to direct readers to the correct volume. Between the author's last name and the page number or numbers, insert the volume number (as a numeral) with a colon after it—dividing it from the page number(s).

> "Truth is a fickle creature" (Wellman 2: 134).

Alternatively, you could write

> Wellman writes, "Truth is a fickle creature" (2: 134).

12. Source from an anthology or other collection

When your source is a text in an anthology or other collection compiled by an editor, use the author's name and the title in the text and the editor and the page number in the parenthetical reference:

> Walker's ode to womanism, "In Our Mothers' Gardens," fully elaborates upon her beliefs that gender and race create more new conditions of identity than previously realized (Moon 47).

(For correct citation in the Works Cited list, see citation model 9 on page 396.)

13. Literary source such as play, novel, or poem

When you cite literary sources, realize that they often come in several editions, so it is considerate to provide more information than just the author and page number to make sure readers can locate the information. Start by giving the page number, followed by a semicolon. Then you might include the chapter number or, in a poem, the stanza number. Use abbreviations for these parts of the text:

pt. for part	bk. for book	sc. for scene
ch. for chapter	sec. for section	st. for stanza

> Modern poets such as e.e. cummings always enjoyed what he called "the fortunate situation literature and poetry occupy in this culture" (22; st. 2, line 4).

Certain conventions and abbreviations are used for classic works. For example, the plays of Shakespeare each have a standard abbreviation; the one below refers to *Hamlet*. The act, scene, and line numbers are given, with periods in between.

> Shakespeare writes, "To be or not to be—that is the question" (*Ham.* 3.1.64).

MLA In-Text Citations Index

14. Sacred book

When you cite a sacred book like the Bible, the Talmud, the Vedas, or the Koran, use the name of the text (Bible, Koran, etc.) but do not italicize the title. (Sacred books are an exception to the rule; their titles are not italicized.) Also, provide the specific part of the book from which the quotation comes—for example,

> According to the Bible, "Any . . . foreigner among you who blasphemes the Lord's name will surely die" (Lev. 24.16).

When you create the Works Cited entry, provide as much detailed information about the specific edition as possible. Then provide additional information so that the reader can find the source in any copy of the text, even if it is not the edition you are citing from.

15. Indirect source

Try to avoid using indirect sources. Instead, using information from the indirect source's Works Cited page or bibliography, locate the original source, verify the quotation, and then cite the original source. However, if you must include indirect sources, insert *qtd. in* in the parenthetical citation immediately before the author's last name—the author, that is, of the indirect source. This way, your readers can still locate your information from the indirect source.

> The Dalai Lama says, "Holiness is a state of grace equivalent to any other kind of acting; it is a charade" (qtd. in Perry 244).

16. Electronic source with an author, title, and page numbers

When you cite electronic sources that have the standard author, title, and page numbers, follow the same conventions as you would for an equivalent printed text:

> In his online book *Modern Mystics*, Smith describes alchemy as "a modern science with ancient roots" (22).

How Can You Identify...

The Author of a Web Page?

Inexperienced researchers may think that a Web page does not have an author if the author's name is not readily available. To locate an author's name, look for a "contact us" or "about us" link in the site navigation or at the bottom of the home page. If you want to cite a single page inside a larger site, return to the home page by erasing the last parts of the URL in your browser's address bar. For instance, if you are at a page whose URL is http://mybandaids.tripod.com/bandaid_index.htm, you might "back up" to http://mybandaids.tripod.com to find more information about the site. Don't include a URL in your parenthetical documentation unless your text is electronic and you are creating a hyperlink.

17. Electronic source with numbered paragraphs

Some electronic sources use numbered paragraphs, which can be a great convenience for anyone who wants to locate the information on a lengthy Web page, for instance. In this case, cite the paragraph number in the parenthetical citation, preceded by *par.:*

> Octavia Deft, in her comprehensive website on modern dance, calls ballet "just so much courtesy and manners on sets of well-clad feet" (par. 17).

MLA In-Text Citations Index

MLA In-Text Citations Index

18. Electronic source without page or paragraph numbers

At times, the only information you will be able to glean from an electronic source such as a website will be the author's name and the work's title. Never use the URL as an in-text or parenthetical citation unless you want to create a hyperlink in an electronic document. Instead, use the information you have, beginning with the author's name and then the title.

> Sensenbrenner expresses doubt about "the road ahead for politics as usual, given the damage partisanship has already caused" (*Political Roundtable*).

We strongly caution you about sources for which you can't obtain basic information. Do everything you can to find out who has posted the material and what level of credibility or expertise that person has in your subject area.

19. Painting, sculpture, photograph, drawing, map, chart, or graph

In-text citation for images is handled in a caption printed below the image. Each image in your project is labeled *Fig.* (for *Figure*) and given a figure number; these run consecutively throughout the paper. A typical caption then lists the author's name (in regular order); the title of the work; the date of composition; the medium of composition; the source information, which may be the name of the museum, including the city, that holds the work; book information if the image was published in that format, or website information if the image was published online. (For information on positioning images in a document, see page 429.)

> Fig. 1. Leonardo da Vinci, *Mona Lisa*, c. 1503-05, oil on panel, Louvre Museum, Paris.
>
> Fig. 2. Michelangelo, *The Last Judgment*, 1536-1541, oil on wall, Vatican City, Vatican Palace, Sistine Chapel, from Roberto Salvini, Michelangelo (Danbury: MasterWorks, 1976; print; 125).

Sample Works Cited Page

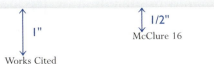

McClure 16

Works Cited

Bacon-Smith, Camille. *Enterprising Women: Television Fandom and the Creation of Popular Myth*. Philadelphia: U of Pennsylvania P, 1992. Print.

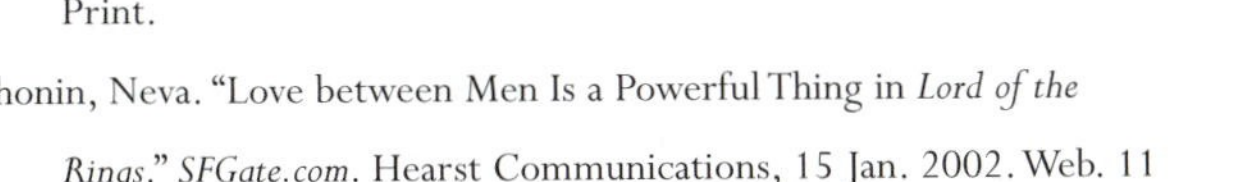

Chonin, Neva. "Love between Men Is a Powerful Thing in *Lord of the Rings*." *SFGate.com*. Hearst Communications, 15 Jan. 2002. Web. 11 Aug. 2002.

Green, Shoshanna, Cynthia Jenkins, and Henry Jenkins. "Normal Female Interest in Men Bonking: Selections from *The Terra Nostra Underground* and *Strange Bedfellows*." *Theorizing Fandom: Fans, Subculture and Identity*. Ed. Cheryl Harris. Cresskill: Hampton, 1998. 9-38. Print.

Irena. "For the Good of Gondor." *Fanfiction.net*. Xing Li, 21 June 2003. Web. 10 Dec. 2003.

Jackson, Peter, dir. *The Two Towers*. Special extended edition. New Line Cinema/WingNut Films, 2002. DVD.

Jenkins, Henry. *Textual Poachers: Television Fans and Participatory Culture*. New York: Routledge, 1992. Print.

LeGuin, Ursula. "Is Gender Necessary? Redux." *Dancing at the Edge of the World*. New York: Grove, 1989. Print.

Rose, Alix. "Slash Universe." *Soapbox Girls*. Lauren Bacon and Emira Mears, Mar. 2002. Web. 10 Nov. 2003.

The MLA Works Cited page offers readers a uniform system for locating the sources cited in your text. The Works Cited page follows the text, notes, appendix, bibliography, charts, and any other end matter except an index (if there is one). It should contain only the sources you have used for summaries, paraphrases, and direct quotations in your paper. (If your instructor asks for a complete list of works you have consulted, title it Works Consulted or Bibliography.) If you are citing only one source, your page will be titled Work Cited.

Format of an MLA Works Cited Page

Start your Works Cited list on the first new page immediately after the last page of your text, and continue the same page numbering system, with your last name and the page number in the upper right corner. Center the title Works Cited 1" from the top of the page. Each entry starts at the left margin. When an entry takes more than one line, indent the second and subsequent lines 1/2" (or five typewriter spaces) so readers see only the alphabetized last names as they scan down the list. Double-space between entries and within each individual entry. (See section 19d for specifics on how to format your essay using Microsoft Word.)

An important feature of the MLA Works Cited page is that entries are organized alphabetically by authors' last names. If there is no author, use the first word in the title (but not *A, An,* or *The*). This arrangement allows readers to easily thumb from a quotation, for instance, to the Works Cited page and find the full name of the author, the title of the publication, and its source so they can locate the original work.

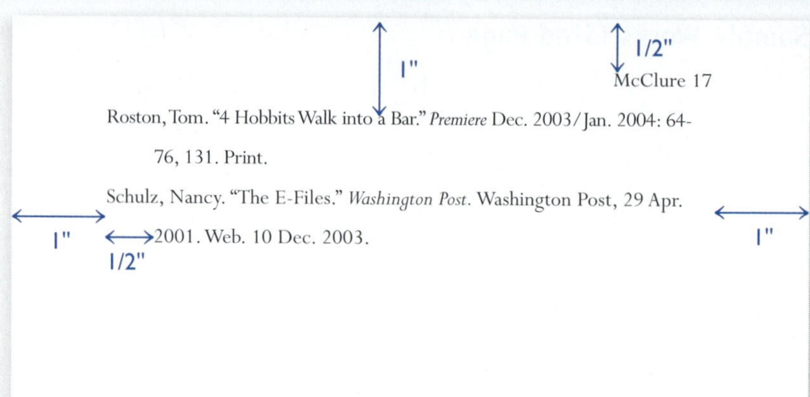

1"
1/2"
McClure 17
Roston, Tom. "4 Hobbits Walk into a Bar." *Premiere* Dec. 2003/Jan. 2004: 64-76, 131. Print.
Schulz, Nancy. "The E-Files." *Washington Post.* Washington Post, 29 Apr. 2001. Web. 10 Dec. 2003.
1"
1/2"
1"

Citing Books: General Information

Following are general guidelines. For models of specific kinds of book citations, see the index that begins on page 394.

Author's Name

Put the last name of the first or only author first, followed by a comma, and then the first and middle names or initials as they appear on the title page of the source. List multiple authors in the order in which they appear on the title page, and write the names of all the authors, reversing the name of the first author only. Use a comma after each author's full name, and use *and* before the final name, which is followed by a period.

Title of Book or Part of Book

Capitalize all significant words in a title, including the first and last words of the title and the subtitle.

Note: *Medium of publication.* Publications come in many forms. Note the medium of the entries on the Works Cited page (above) and those indicated with the entries that follow in this chapter. The medium consulted could be print, Web, LP, audiocassette, CD-ROM, DVD, and so on.

Basic Format for Authors of Books

One author	Allison, Dorothy.
Two authors	Levitt, Steven D., and Stephen J. Dubner.
Three or more authors	Yassin, Omar, George Goldberg, and Sunny Taylor.
Corporate author	Vermont Refugee Resettlement Program.

- Do not include an author's title or degrees.
- Do not abbreviate names to initials unless that is how the names appear on the book's title page.

Basic Format for Titles

Book	*Freakonomics: A Rogue Economist Explores the Hidden Side of Everything.*
Article	"Death of a Mountain: Radical Strip Mining and the Leveling of Appalachia."

Look for Publication Information on the Title and Copyright Pages

- **The city in which the work was published.** If several cities are listed, use only the first one. If the city is outside the United States and not well known, include an abbreviation for the country.
- **The publisher of the work.** Shorten the name of the publisher but make sure it will be easily recognizable to readers (e.g., *Random* for *Random House, Inc.* or *Simon* for *Simon and Schuster, Inc.*). Omit articles (*A, An, The*), business abbreviations (*Inc., Corp., Ltd.*), and words such as *Books, Publishers,* and *Press*. For university presses, use the capital letters *U* and *P* (without periods). If no publisher is named, use the abbreviation *n.p.*
- **The date of publication.** Write the date numerically (e.g., 2004). If no publication date is provided, use the abbreviation *n.d.*

When Publication Information Is Unknown

When you cannot locate elements of the publication information, use the following abbreviations:

n.p. for either no place of publication or no publisher
n.d. for no date
n. pag. for no pagination

> Foster, Thomas C. *How to Read Literature like a Professor: A Lively and Entertaining Guide to Reading between the Lines*. N.p.: Harper, 2003. Print.

When you are able to locate some of the information from some other source, include that information in brackets to indicate that the publication information came from somewhere other than the source you are using.

> Foster, Thomas C. *How to Read Literature like a Professor: A Lively and Entertaining Guide to Reading between the Lines*. [New York]: Harper, 2003. Print.

Significant words are all the nouns, pronouns, verbs, adjectives, adverbs, and subordinate conjunctions. The following kinds of words should **not** begin with capital letters:

- the coordinating conjunctions *and, but, or, nor, for, so, yet*
- the word *to* when it is part of a verb, as in *Born to Die*
- the articles *a, an,* and *the*
- prepositions such as *between, near, from, to, under, over*

But even these words should be capitalized when they appear first or last in the title or subtitle: *On the Run* or *The World Is Flat: A Brief History of the Twenty-first Century.*

Italicize the titles of longer works, such as books or journals, and use quotation marks around the titles of shorter pieces, such as poems, articles, or short stories. For detailed lists of works whose titles should be in quotation marks or italicized, see sections 52d and 56a.

Publication Information

You can usually find the publication information on the title page of a book or on the copyright page on the reverse of the title page. In your listing, you should include information about the city of publication, the publisher, the year of publication, and the medium of publication.

MLA Works Cited Index: Books and Other Print Nonperiodicals

1. Book by a single author
2. Book by two or three authors
3. Book by four or more authors
4. Two or more books by the same author
5. Book by an unknown author
6. Book with a corporate or group author
7. Book with an author and editor
8. Anthology or book with an editor
9. One selection from an anthology
10. Two or more selections from the same anthology
11. Translated book
12. Sacred book
13. Book in second or subsequent edition
14. Reprinted book
15. Book in more than one volume
16. Book in a series
17. Introduction, preface, foreword, or afterword
18. Article in a reference work (encyclopedia, dictionary)
19. Government publication
20. Published or unpublished dissertation
21. Published proceedings of a conference
22. Booklet or pamphlet

MLA Works Cited Models

1. Book by a single author

List the author's last name first, followed by a comma, the first and middle names or initials, and then a period. Underline the book title but not the period that follows the title. Next give the name of the city of publication, followed by a colon; the name of the publisher, followed by a comma; the year of publication, followed by a period; and the medium of publication, which ends with a period.

McCourt, Frank. *Teacher Man: A Memoir*. New York: Scribner's, 2005. Print.

Note: The seventh edition of the *MLA Handbook for Writers of Research Papers* now recommends using italics in place of underline.

2. Book by two or three authors

For books with two or three authors, list the names in the order in which they appear on the title page of the text, followed by a period. Only reverse the name of the first author; then list the other name or names, separating each using a comma and placing *and* before the last name.

Stevens, Mark, and Annalyn Swan. *De Kooning: An American Master*. New York: Knopf, 2004. Print.

3. Book by four or more authors

You can either list all the authors' names that appear on the title page, reversing only the first one, or write the first name followed by the abbreviation *et al.*

Bazerman, Charles, Joseph Little, Lisa Bethel, Teri Chavkin, Danielle Fouquette, and Janet Garufis. *Reference Guide to Writing across the Curriculum*. West Lafayette: Parlor, 2005. Print.

Bazerman, Charles, et al. *Reference Guide to Writing across the Curriculum*. West Lafayette: Parlor, 2005. Print.

4. Two or more books by the same author

List each source as a separate entry and alphabetize the entries according to the first major word of the second element of the entry (normally, the title of the text). List the author's full name only in the first entry. For subsequent entries, substitute three hyphens for the author's name, followed by a period (the three hyphens stand for exactly the same name given in the preceding entry). If the person edited or compiled the book, place a comma after the last hyphen and add the appropriate abbreviation (*ed.* for editor or *comp.* for compiler).

> Diamond, Jared. *Collapse: How Societies Choose to Fail or Succeed*. New York: Viking, 2004. Print.
>
> ---. *Guns, Germs, and Steel: The Fates of Human Societies*. New York: Norton, 1999. Print.
>
> ---. *Why Is Sex Fun? The Evolution of Human Sexuality*. Science Masters Series. New York: Basic, 1997. Print.

Note: If any of the books are co-authored, both authors' names have to be given in full, unless all of the authors are the same.

5. Book by an unknown author

If you cannot find the name of the book's author or the author is anonymous, alphabetize your entry using the first major word of the title, ignoring *A, An,* or *The*. Do not write *Anon.* or *Anonymous*.

> *Staying Clean: Living without Drugs*. N.p.: Hazelden, 1987. Print.

6. Book with a corporate or group author

Often books written by businesses and other kinds of organizations have no single author because many different people worked on them. In this case, list the institution, organization, or business as the author.

> American Association of Retired Persons. *Guide to Social Security Changes Enacted by the Congress in 2004*. Washington: AARP, 2004. Print.

MLA Works Cited Index: Books and Other Print Nonperiodicals

MLA Works Cited Index: Books and Other Print Nonperiodicals

1. Book by a single author
2. Book by two or three authors
3. Book by four or more authors
4. Two or more books by the same author
5. Book by an unknown author
6. Book with a corporate or group author
7. Book with an author and editor
8. Anthology or book with an editor
9. One selection from an anthology
10. Two or more selections from the same anthology
11. Translated book
12. Sacred book
13. Book in second or subsequent edition
14. Reprinted book
15. Book in more than one volume
16. Book in a series
17. Introduction, preface, foreword, or afterword
18. Article in a reference work (encyclopedia, dictionary)
19. Government publication
20. Published or unpublished dissertation
21. Published proceedings of a conference
22. Booklet or pamphlet

7. Book with an author and editor

List the author (last name first) and then the title. Use the abbreviation *Ed.* (short for *edited by*) and then the editor's name, in the usual first and last name order, followed by a period. Follow with any additional contributors.

> Lorde, Audre. *Marvelous Arithmetics of Distance: Poems, 1987-1992*. Ed. Daryl Cumber Dance. Fwd. Nikki Giovanni. New York: Norton, 1998. Print.

8. Anthology or book with an editor

Use the name of the editor as you would the name of an author, followed by a comma, and then write the abbreviation *ed.* for editor. If there is more than one editor, use the abbreviation *eds.* after the last name in the list.

> Garcia, Cristina, ed. *¡Cubanísimo! The Vintage Book of Contemporary Cuban Literature*. New York: Vintage, 2003. Print.

9. One selection from an anthology

When you cite a selection from an anthology or other collection, start your entry with the name of the author (in reverse order) who wrote the part you are citing from, followed by a period. Then write the title of the selection you are citing from (for example, a short story, poem, or reprinted article), followed by a period and enclosed in quotation marks. Next, provide the title of the anthology or collection, italicized and followed by a period. Write *Ed.* (short for *edited by*) after the title, followed by the name of the editor (in normal order), the publication information, the page numbers of the entire selection you are citing, and the medium of publication. (Do not use the abbreviation *pp.*)

> Connors, Brian R. "Principles of Legal Necessity." *Introduction to the Law*. Ed. Wendy Karlson. Chicago: Lighthouse, 2004. 22-28. Print.

Note: If the selection you are citing was originally published as an independent work, you should italicize its title.

10. Two or more selections from the same anthology

When you cite two or more anthologized pieces from the same text, you might wish to set up a separate entry for each source and then have each entry refer to an entry that cites the anthology. This saves space and avoids repetition. For instance, consider the anthology referred to in citation model 9. If you cited two articles from the same anthology, you would set up the entries like this:

Connors, Brian R. "Principles of Legal Necessity." Karlson 22-28.

Karlson, Wendy, ed. *Introduction to the Law*. Chicago: Lighthouse, 2004. Print.

Somers, Renee. "Purchasing a Home and Your Legal Rights." Karlson 29-36.

The second entry is for the anthology itself, and the other two entries are for the individual selections from it. Notice that no punctuation is inserted between the cross-referenced editor's name and the inclusive pages for each piece.

11. Translated book

When you cite a translated book, handle it as you would any other book, but insert *Trans.* and the translator's name (or names) after the title and before the publication information.

Djebar, Assia. *Women of Algiers in Their Apartment*. Trans. Marjolijn De Jager. Charlottesville: UP of Virginia, 1992. Print.

MLA Works Cited Index: Books and Other Print Nonperiodicals

MLA Works Cited Index: Books and Other Print Nonperiodicals

12. Sacred book

The titles of sacred books such as the Bible, the Koran, the Talmud, and the Upanishads are *not* italicized. When citing a standard version of the Bible, you do not need to include the version or publication information. However, if you are citing individual published editions of a sacred work, you should treat them as you would any other published book, italicizing as appropriate.

> *The New Oxford Annotated NRSV Bible with the Apocrypha*. Ed. Michael D. Coogan, Marc Z. Brettler, Carol A. Newsom, and Pheme Perkins. 3rd ed. Oxford: Oxford UP, 2001. Print.
>
> Upanishads. Trans. Eknath Easwaran. Tomales: Nilgiri, 1987. Print.

13. Book in second or subsequent edition

Indicate which edition you are using so your readers can locate information from your citations. Set up the entry as you would for any other book, and insert *2nd ed.*, *3rd ed.*, or whatever is appropriate after the title and preceding the publication information.

> Whitman, Walt. *Leaves of Grass*. Ed. Malcolm Cowley. 4th ed. New York: Penguin, 1976. Print.

14. Reprinted book

When your book is a reprint of an original printing, include the normal book entry information, and insert the original publication year, followed by a period, after the title of the book and before the reprint edition's publication information.

> Bradfield, Scott. *The History of Luminous Motion*. 1989. New York: Penguin Classics, 2001. Print.

15. Book in more than one volume

If you use information from only one volume of a multivolume set, write the capitalized abbreviation *Vol.* and the number of the appropriate volume right before the publication information in your entry.

> Dorfman, Rachelle A., ed. *Paradigms of Clinical Social Work*. Vol. 3. New York: Brunner-Routledge, 1988. Print.

Although it is not required, you can add the total number of volumes at the end of your entry.

If you are using material from more than one volume, cite the total number of volumes in the work immediately after the title (or after the editor's name or information about the specific edition), followed by the abbreviation *vols.*

> Guanzhong, Luo. *Three Kingdoms: Chinese Classics*. Trans. Moss Roberts. 4 vols. N.p.: Foreign Languages, 2001. Print.

If the volumes you cite were published over a period of years, give the inclusive dates at the end of the citation.

> Copelston, Frederick. *A History of Philosophy*. 9 vols. Garden City: Doubleday, 1946-75. Print.

If the volumes are part of an ongoing series, write the words *to date* after the number of volumes and leave a space after the hyphen when you write the publication date.

Note: Specific information about the volume you are referring to, including relevant page numbers, should be included in your in-text citation (see citation model 11 on page 386).

MLA Works Cited Index: Books and Other Print Nonperiodicals

MLA Works Cited Index: Books and Other Print Nonperiodicals

16. Book in a series

If you are citing information from a book that is one of a series (check the title page at the front of the book), insert the series name and the book number, if any, immediately after the medium of publication, at the end of the entry.

> Hay, Samuel. *African American Theater: A Historical and Critical Analysis.* Cambridge: Harvard UP, 1994. Print. The Harvard Series on American Culture 12.

17. Introduction, preface, foreword, or afterword

Start with the name of the author who wrote the specific part of the book. Give the name of the part you are citing (such as *Introduction, Preface, Foreword,* or *Afterword)*, capitalized but *not* underlined or in quotation marks, followed by a period. If the author of the part is *not* the author of the entire book, cite the name of the author of the work after the title, in normal order and preceded by the word *By.* If the author of the part you are citing is the same person who wrote the entire book, repeat the last name only, preceded by the word *By.* Provide the full publication information as outlined in the first citation model on page 394; end with the inclusive page numbers, followed by a period, and the medium of publication, ending with a period.

> McCourt, Frank. Foreword. *Eats, Shoots & Leaves: The Zero Tolerance Approach to Punctuation.* By Lynne Truss. New York: Gotham, 2004. xi-xiv. Print.

Note: If the introduction, preface, foreword, or afterword has a title, put it in quotation marks and place it immediately before the name of the part.

18. Article in a reference work (encyclopedia, dictionary)

When citing an article in an encyclopedia or an entry in a dictionary, follow the format outlined in citation model 9 (page 396) for listing a selection in an anthology, but omit the name of the editor. If the article is signed, alphabetize the entry using the last name of the author. If it is unsigned, give the title first. If entries in the work you are citing are arranged alphabetically, you do not have to cite page and volume numbers. If the reference work is frequently revised, do not provide full publication information; just list the edition and year published.

Chamberlain, Daniel. "Maurice Merleau-Ponty." *Encyclopedia of Contemporary Literary Theory: Approaches, Scholars, Terms*. Toronto: U of Toronto P, 1993. Print.

19. Government publication

Since there are so many different governments (municipal, local, state, federal) and agencies of government, citing the author of a government publication can be tricky. When you do not have a specific author, you should list the government and then the agency that produced the publication. For instance, you might cite the author like any of these:

Atlanta. City Commission on Historic Locations.
Minnesota. Dept. of Agriculture.
United States. Dept. of Homeland Security.

After you have cited the author, italicize the title of the publication (using *H* or *HR* for the House of Representatives and *S* for the Senate when citing congressional documents—for instance, *HR Bill 32.45*), and then write the publisher of the source. In the United States, most federal publications are produced by the GPO, the Government Printing Office, in Washington.

United States. Commerce Dept. Census Bureau. *Statistical Abstract of the United States, 2005: The National Data Book*. Washington: GPO, 2006. Print.

MLA Works Cited Index: Books and Other Print Nonperiodicals

20. Published or unpublished dissertation

If you are citing from a published dissertation, treat the entry like that for a book, but insert pertinent information about the dissertation before the publication information. If the dissertation was published by University Microfilms International (UMI) in Ann Arbor, then you can include the reference number after the publication information; the medium follows the reference number at the end of the entry.

Lavagnino, John. *Nabokov's Realism*. Diss. Brandeis U, 1998. Ann Arbor: UMI, 1999. AAT 9829823. Print.

If the dissertation has not been published, then enclose the title of the dissertation in a pair of quotation marks (do not italicize), write *Diss.* after the title, and write the name of the school that granted the degree and the year it was granted.

Schindler, Richard A. "Art to Enchant: A Critical Study of Early Victorian Fairy Painting and Illustration." Diss. Brown U, 1988. Print.

21. Published proceedings of a conference

For conference proceedings, create entries in the same way you would for a book. The only difference is that you include information about the conference, unless it is included in the title of the work.

Cozolino, Louis. *The Neuroscience of Psychotherapy: The Building and Rebuilding of the Human Brain*. Proc. of the 2002 Conf. on Neurology and the Future of Surgical Invasions. New York: Norton, 2003. Print.

22. Booklet or pamphlet

Treat pamphlets, even short ones, as you would a book. Include the author's name, the title of the pamphlet (italicized), and the publication information.

> United States Copyright Office. *Copyright Basics*. Washington: GPO, 2004.Print.

When there is no author, put the title first.

MLA Works Cited Index: Books and Other Print Nonperiodicals

Citing Periodicals: General Information

When you cite journal, magazine, or newspaper articles, note the following general considerations.

Author information. See citation models 1 through 8 (pages 394–396).

Article title. Capitalize all important words, including the first word of the subtitle.

Periodical name. Write out journal and magazine names in full. For newspapers, omit the initial *A, An,* or *The: New York Times.*

Volume and issue information. Provide this information only in citations to scholarly journals.

Date. The information you provide depends on how often a periodical is published; see individual citation models. Use abbreviations for all months except May, June, and July. September is abbreviated *Sept.*; other abbreviations consist of the first three letters of the name of the month. Follow an abbreviation with a period.

Inclusive page numbers. For numbers from 1 through 99, write both numerals out in full. For larger numbers, give only the last two digits of the second numeral, unless more are needed for accuracy or clarity: *367-73,* but *367-401*. When page numbers are not consecutive, write the first page number followed by a + sign: *52+*.

Medium of publication. See Note on page 392 for an explanation.

Basic Format for Scholarly Journal Articles

Author's last name, first name. "Article title: Subtitle." *Journal name* Volume number. Issue number (Year of publication): Inclusive page numbers. Medium of publication.

Basic Format for Magazine Articles

Author's last name, first name. "Article title: Subtitle." *Magazine name* Date: Inclusive page numbers. Medium of publication.

Basic Format for Newspaper Articles

Author's last name, first name. "Article title." *Name of newspaper* Date, edition name: Inclusive page numbers. Medium of publication.

MLA Works Cited Models

23. Article in scholarly journal with continuous pagination throughout annual volume

Most scholarly journals paginate consecutively from issue to issue throughout the course of a year. The year's issues make up one volume, which can be bound, and referred to, as a single entity. When citing an article from a continuously paginated journal, start your entry with the author's name, reversed and followed by a period, and then give the name of the article in quotation marks. Next write the name of the journal, italicized, and follow it with a single space. Add the volume number (do not use the abbreviation *vol.*) followed by a period and, when available, the issue number. Write the year in parentheses followed by a colon. End the entry with one more space, the inclusive page numbers for the entire article cited followed by a period, and the medium consulted and concluding period. (If page numbers are not continuous, give the number of the first page immediately followed by a plus sign.)

Walichinsy, Eileen. "Linguistic and Empathetic Understanding." *Distance Studies in Language* 16.1 (2002): 444-67. Print.

24. Article in scholarly journal that pages each issue separately

Some journals number the pages of each issue separately, starting each issue on page 1. For these journals, an issue number will almost certainly be available for you to include with the volume number.

Lassitor, Jules. "Cutting Short Communication When It's Painful." *Washington Regional Journal of Communication Studies* 21.3 (2004): 12-27. Print.

Note: Some journals number only the issues, not the annual volumes; when citing them, use the issue number as if it were a volume number.

MLA Works Cited Index: Periodicals and Print Correspondence

MLA Works Cited Index: Periodicals and Print Correspondence

25. Article in monthly or bimonthly magazine

If a magazine is published on a monthly or bimonthly schedule, use the format in citation model 24, but provide the month or months (abbreviated, except for May, June, and July) and year after the title, followed by a colon and the inclusive page numbers of the article. Do not include the volume or issue number.

> Stix, Gary. "Owning the Stuff of Life." *Scientific American* Feb. 2006: 76-83. Print.

26. Article in weekly or biweekly magazine

For magazines published every week or biweekly, provide the full date of the issue after the title. Begin with the day, abbreviate the month (except for May, June, and July), and give the year. Follow this information with a colon and the inclusive page numbers of the article. Do not include the volume or issue number.

> Wilkinson, Alec. "The Open Man." *Rolling Stone* 26 Jan. 2006: 31+. Print.

27. Article in daily newspaper

When citing a newspaper, give its name as it appears on the first page, omitting any introductory article (*A, An,* or *The*). Some newspapers do not include their home city in their titles. For these papers, put the home city in square brackets, after the title of the newspaper and before the period: *Journal Record* [Oklahoma City]. (This is not necessary for nationally published newspapers like the *Wall Street Journal.*) You do not have to include a volume number, an issue number, or a publication code. However, it is important to mention the edition (i.e., national edition, late edition, etc.) if it is listed at the top of the first page. Also, if the newspaper is divided into lettered sections and includes these designations before the page numbers, you need to do the same.

> Gonzalez, Juliet. "Scores for Sports." *Atlanta Constitution* 14 Apr. 2004, natl. ed.: C3-5. Print.

You would write *C3+* if the pages were not consecutive pages. If a paper is divided into numbered sections, provide the number of the section before the colon—for example, *sec. 4: 7-8.*

28. Anonymous article

When no author's name is given, use the title of the article. When you alphabetize, ignore *A, An,* or *The.*

> "Primary Care Reforms Are Urged." *Wall Street Journal* 31 Jan. 2006: D4. Print.

29. Editorial or letter to the editor

Use the letter writer's name, if available, and then the title of the letter in quotation marks. Next provide a description of the work, such as *Editorial* or *Letter.* Then insert the appropriate information from the newspaper or magazine and conclude with the medium consulted.

> Bennett, Jana M. "Doubting Thomas." Letter. *Harper's* Feb. 2006: 4-5. Print.

30. Review

Use the reviewer's name and then the title of the review, if any. After the title of the review, write *Rev. of* and then name the work that was reviewed (if it was another article, use quotation marks; if it was a book, italicize the title). Also include the name of the author of the reviewed work, preceded by a comma and the word *by.* Finish with the publication information.

> Pearson, Allison. "The Untalented Mr. Ripple." Rev. of *It's All Right Now*, by Charles Chadwick. *New York Times Book Review* 26 June 2005: 16. Print.
>
> "Revelation without Reflection." Rev. of *The Duff Cooper Diaries*, ed. John Julius Norwich. *Economist* 1 Oct. 2005: 80. Print.

MLA Works Cited Index: Periodicals and Print Correspondence

MLA Works Cited Index: Periodicals and Print Correspondence

31. Abstract of dissertation or article

When you create an entry for an abstract, start the entry with the author's name and the work's title, and include the publication information for the original work (the one the abstract summarizes). Finally, include the publication information for the abstract.

> Pender, Kelly. "Annotated Bibliography: Questions and Answers about the Pentad." *College Composition and Communication* 29 (1978): 330-35. Abstract. *Invention in Rhetoric and Composition*. West Lafayette: Parlor Press, 2004. Print.

32. Published or unpublished letter

Treat letters differently depending on whether they are published or unpublished. For unpublished letters—for instance, correspondence you received from another writer—cite the author and insert the words *Letter to* and the recipient, followed by the date and medium consulted. Use TS to indicate Typescript and MS to indicate Manuscript.

> Heckerling, Amy. Letter to the author. 23 May 2006. TS.

If the letter has been published, handle the letter as if it were an article, including the original date and then the publication in which the letter is now collected.

> Thomas, Edward. "Thomas to Frost." 1914. Letter 14 of *Elected Friends: Robert Frost and Edward Thomas to One Another*. Ed. Matthew Spencer. New York: Handsel-Other, 2003. 29-30. Print.

Basic Format for Digital Sources

See book models 1–8 for author information

Use quotation marks unless you are citing an entire site or ebook.

Consult the models for books and periodicals to find the right citation style.

Author's last, first name. "Title of work: Subtitle." Print publication information, if any. *Title of digital source*. Date of publication or update. Medium of publication. Access date <URL>.

Do this because e-sources can change quickly.

Do not add a hyphen when you break a URL at the end of a line.

Italicize the title of a website; give the date of e-publication or the date of latest update (use the abbreviation *n.d.* if not available); and name the organization that sponsors the site, if any (if none, use the abbreviation *N.p.*).

See citation model 33 on page 410 for general information about CD-ROM publications. See model 36 on page 411 for general information about online sources.

Note: Current MLA guidelines recommend including electronic addesses (URLs) as supplementary information only when the source would be difficult to find without one. If the URL takes up more than one line, it should be broken right after a slash. For examples of Web citations that include the URL, see citation models 53-55 on pages 418–419.

Citing Digital Sources: General Information

Some digital sources are published on CD-ROM and other portable media, such as diskettes and magnetic tape. For instance, databases are often provided in libraries on CD-ROM. Other digital sources are online: websites; various kinds of documents on websites; online magazines, newspapers, and journals; ebooks; message board postings; and so on. For almost all digital entries, you will need to cite

- the author's name(s)
- the title of the publication
- information about print publication (if applicable)
- information about electronic publication
- access information, including medium consulted, access date, and URL, if needed. (For more information on URLs, see Note on left.)

MLA Works Cited Index: Digital Sources, Online and Offline

MLA Works Cited Models

33. CD-ROM, DVD, or portable database

When you cite information from portable databases, CD-ROMs, and DVDs, provide the following information:

Author's last name, first name. Original publication data if the article was once a printed source (that is, "Title." *Name of periodical* (Date): Inclusive pages). Medium of publication (e.g., CD-ROM, DVD, portable database). *Title of database.* Name of computer service. Publication date.

"Windhover." The Oxford English Dictionary. 2nd ed. Oxford: Oxford UP, 2001. DVD-ROM.

Jackson, Peter. "Bullish on This Market." *Wall Street Journal* 12 Mar. 2003: 21-24. CD-ROM. *Wall Street Press*. SIRS. June 2004.

34. Source on nonperiodical database (CD-ROM, DVD, diskette, magnetic tape)

Cite a nonperiodical publication on CD-ROM, DVD, etc., the same way you would cite a book, but include the appropriate medium of publication.

Content Guide to Accompany NBC News Archive, Sociology Lecture Launcher, Collection 1.0. New York: McGraw-Hill, 2008. DVD-ROM.

35. Source on periodical CD-ROM database

If the CD-ROM is part of a periodical database, provide the author's name, the publication information from the printed source (including title and date of publication), the medium, the title of the database (italicized), the name of the vendor of the database, and the electronic publication date.

Hickoks, Helen. "Recovering Sociological Foundations." *Sociology Quarterly* 23.5 (2001): 123-32. CD-ROM. *InfoTrac: Magazine Index Plus*. Information Access. Jan. 2002.

36. Online source, in general

Online sources are found by downloading information through a computer service, rather than inserting a CD-ROM, diskette, or other portable medium. Because the sources in an online database are revised frequently, their Works Cited entries must include the date of access (the date when you found, read, printed, or used the source) as well as the date of publication or the most recent revision.

37. Entire website (scholarly, professional, personal)

When you cite an entire website, your entry should include the following information.

Author's last name, first name. *Title of site*. Name of the editor of the site (if provided), preceded by the abbreviation *Ed.* Version number, if it is pertinent and not included in the site's title (e.g., Vers. 3.5). Date of publication or of most recent update (day, abbreviated month, and year), if available. Use the abbreviation n.d. if no date is given. Name of the organization that sponsors the site, if available (if not available, use the abbreviation N.p. for No publisher). Medium of publication. Date you accessed the site.

Lowe, Charlie. *Cyberdash*. N.p., 11 Apr. 2004. Web. 28 Oct. 2005.

You may not be able to find all of the above information for your entries. Trying to find an author's name can sometimes be extremely frustrating. However, it is worth taking the time to follow hyperlinks and to closely examine the entire website in order to find the author's name. If you cannot find the author's name or, as may happen in some cases, a title or date of creation for the page, then you do not have to include this information in your citation. However, if the website has no authorship or other identifying information (called *provenance*), then you should strongly consider not using the source at all.

MLA Works Cited Index: Digital Sources, Online and Offline

MLA Works Cited Index: Digital Sources, Online and Offline

38. Short work from online site

Let's say you are using just one part or page of a larger website, and it has a different title from the main site. As you would for a collection of essays, put the part title in quotation marks and follow it with the title of the main page, italicized. Your complete entry would include the following information:

Author's last name, first name. "Title of page." *Title of site*. Sponsor, Date the page was created or last updated (day month year). Medium of publication. Date (in the same format) that you last visited the page.

Drudge, Bob. "Dictionaries and Language Resources." *Refdesk.com.* Refdesk, 2005. Web. 5 Nov. 2005.

39. Source from online service that your library subscribes to

When you use information from a service that your library subscribes to, follow the guidelines for citing articles in print periodicals, leaving out the medium of original publication (Print). Then provide the service title, medium consulted, and, finally, the date of access.

Hesten, Phillip. "Oscillations and the Global Weather." *Meteorology* 21 Mar. 2000: 122-28. *UNI-Information*. Web. 12 June 2002.

40. Source from online service that you subscribe to

When you use information from a source that you subscribe to (for instance, AOL), the major difference between this and other online source entries is the information you include about keywords, so that your reader can go back and find your information using your search method.

"18th Century Occidental Exploitation of Asian Resources." *Merriam Webster's Online Encyclopedia*. Merriam Webster, 2000. *America Online*. Web. 26 Sept. 2002. Keywords: Asian Resources and 18th Century.

41. Source from home page (academic department, course, personal)

When you cite information from an online personal or professional site, provide the name of the author (i.e., the person who created the site), if available; the title of the work (in quotation marks); and the title of the site (italicized) or, if there is no title, a description (Home page, Dept. home page, etc.). Provide the name of any organization associated with the page or site, the date of the last update, the publication medium, the date of your access, and the URL (if needed).

Barlow, John Perry. "Is Spalding Gray Finally Swimming to Cambodia?" *BarlowFriendz*. N.p., 16 Jan. 2004. Web. 22 Apr. 2004.

42. Online book

How you cite an online book depends on whether you used part of the book or the complete book. For complete online books, cite the author's or editor's name (last, first); the title (italicized); the name of the editor, translator, or compiler, if any; publication information, including version; medium of publication; and date of access.

Wynants, Marleen, and Jan Cornelis, eds. *How Open Is the Future? Economic, Social & Cultural Scenarios Inspired by Free and Open-Source Software*. Brussels: Brussels UP, 2005. Web. 6 Nov. 2005.

MLA Works Cited Index: Digital Sources, Online and Offline

MLA Works Cited Index: Digital Sources, Online and Offline

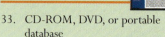

For parts of a book, insert the title of the part (if it is a chapter, use quotation marks; if it is an introduction, preface, or afterword, simply write that) after the name and before the title of the complete book.

> Rushkoff, Douglas. Introduction. *Open Source Democracy*. Project Gutenberg, 2003. Web. 6 Nov. 2005.

43. Article in online journal

Provide the following information when citing an article from an online journal:

Author's last name, first name. "Title of article." *Title of online periodical* Volume number.Issue number (Date of publication): Page (if not provided, write *n. pag.*) Medium of publication. Date of your most recent access.

> Weber, Brenda R. "Beauty, Desire, and Anxiety: The Economy of Sameness in ABC's *Extreme Makeover*." *Genders* 41 (2005): n. pag. Web. 6 Nov. 2005.

44. Article in online magazine

Provide the following information when citing an article from an online magazine:

Author's last name, first name. "Title of article." *Title of online magazine.* Sponsor of site. Date of publication. Medium of publication. Date of your most recent access.

> Saletan, William. "The Brontosaurus: Monty Python's Flying Creationism." *Slate.* Slate Magazine, 27 Oct. 2005. Web. 6 Nov. 2005.

45. Article in online newspaper or on online newswire

Provide the following information when citing an article from an online newspaper:

Author's last name, first name. "Title of article." *Title of newspaper.* Sponsor of site, Date of publication. Medium of publication. Date of your most recent access.

> McNerthney, Casey. "Seattle Landmark Set for Restoration." *Seattlepi.com.* Hearst Newspapers, 27 Mar. 2009. Web. 27 Mar. 2009.

Note: When citing a newswire article, substitute the title of the online wire service for the newspaper title.

46. Article from online government publication

When you create an entry for an online government publication, use the same information as you would for the printed government publication, and then insert the medium of publication and the date of access.

> United States. NASA. "Expedition 9 in Command of Station." 6 June 2004. Web. 6 Nov. 2005.

MLA Works Cited Index: Digital Sources, Online and Offline

MLA Works Cited Index: Digital Sources, Online and Offline

47. Online abstract

When you cite an online abstract, provide the author's name, the title of the work, the name of the publication, any volume and issue numbers, the date, and the inclusive page numbers (if none are given, use the abbreviation *n. pag.*) for the document the abstract summarizes. Then add the word *Abstract,* the medium of publication, and the date of access.

> Vandenberg, Kathleen M. "Sociological Propaganda: A Burkean and Girardian Analysis of Twentieth-Century American Advertising." *KB Journal* 2.1 (2004): n. pag. Abstract. Web. 6 Nov. 2005.

48. Online review

When you cite an online review, provide the reviewer's name; the title of the review (if any); the words *Rev. of* and the title of the work being reviewed; the word *by* and the author of the work; the name, any volume and issue numbers, and the date of the publication in which the review was originally published; the medium of publication; and the date of your access.

> Longaker, Mark Garrett. Rev. of *Rhetorical Landscapes in America*, by Gregory Clark. *KB Journal* 1.2 (2004): n. pag. Web. 6 Nov. 2005.

49. Article in online database (dictionary, encyclopedia)

When you create an entry for an online dictionary, encyclopedia, or other reference work, cite the entry title (e.g., "Digestion"); the name and version, if appropriate, of the online database; the sponsor of the site (if none is given, use the abbreviation *N.p.*); the date of the last update; the medium of publication; and the date of access.

> "Digestion." *Wikipedia*. Wikipedia, 12 Mar. 2003. Web. Nov. 2005.

50. Email

Provide the following information when citing an email communication:

Email author's last name, first name. "Title of email from subject line." Brief description of message (including the recipient). Day abbreviated month year the message was sent. Medium of delivery.

> Jacobson, Jack. "Re: Harassment in the Textiles Department." Message to the author. 18 Apr. 2003. Email.

Note: The seventh edition of the *MLA Handbook* (published in 2009) shows the word *email* with a hyphen.

51. Online posting/message board

Provide the following information when citing an online posting to a discussion list. If possible, cite an archival version of the posting to make it easier for your readers to find.

Author of posting's last name, first name. "Title of posting as given in subject line." Description of type of message (i.e., Online posting). Day abbreviated month year of posting. Name of message board/posting site. Medium of publication. Date of access.

> Greer, Michael Gordon. "Rhetoric Requires Magic." Online posting. 5 Nov. 2005. Kairosnews. Web. 6 Nov. 2005.

If you do not know the author's name, use the email address or screen name.

> AriAorta. "Oh, the Monorail." Online posting. 4 Nov. 2005. Music for America. Web. 6 Nov. 2005.

Note: If the name of the Internet site is unknown, give the email address of the moderator or list supervisor.

MLA Works Cited Index: Digital Sources, Online and Offline

MLA Works Cited Index: Digital Sources, Online and Offline

52. Posting to newsgroup or Web forum

When you cite a posting to a newsgroup or a Web forum, you need to create an entry that begins with the poster's name (or email or screen name, if the poster's name is not available). Then include the title, the words *Online posting,* the date of the posting, the site sponsoring the posting or news group, the medium of publication, the date of access, and the URL (if needed).

> Cypher. "Is Art Dead?" Online posting. 25 Oct. 2005. Art. Google Group. Web. 6 Nov. 2005.

53. Synchronous communication (chat)

Provide the following information when citing an online synchronous communication:

Author of posting's last name, first name. Description of event. Day abbreviated month year of posting. Forum for the communication (e.g., MUD, MOO). Medium of delivery. Date of access. <URL with prefix *telnet://*>.

Note: If the full name is not available, use the screen name.

> JaniceW. Editor's Mtg-2/12. 12 Feb. 2001. LinguaMOO. Web. 6 Nov. 2005. <telnet://lingua.utdallas.edu:7000/9879/>.

54. Computer software

When you cite information from a particular piece of downloaded software, include the name of the software or program (italicized), any appropriate information about versions, the medium consulted, the date you accessed the software, and the URL where you found the software.

> *TK3 Author*. Vers. 1.1. Web. 22 Mar. 2006. <http://www.nightkitchen.com/download/index.phtml>.

55. Online video, graphic, or audio source

When you cite information from an online film clip, picture or graphic file, or audio clip, include the author's name (if any), the title of the digital source (italicized if considered a long work, such as a film or computer game; within quotation marks if considered a short work, such as a song; see 52d and 56a), the title of the website (italicized), any appropriate information about versions, the site's sponsor (if not available, use "N.p."), the date of the digital source (if not available, use "n.d."), the kind of digital medium, the medium consulted (web), the date you accessed it, and the URL where you found the source, if your reader would have difficulty locating it.

> *The Gundertaker.* Machinima video. *Machinima.com*. Web. 29 Mar. 2009. <http://www.machinima.com/film/view&id=1357>.

56. Online conference presentation

Provide the following information when citing a conference presentation you accessed online:

Speaker's last name, first name. "Title of Presentation." Conference Presentation. Conference name, location, and date. *Title of database or website.* Medium consulted. Date of access.

> Williams, Evan. "Listening to Twitter." Conference Presentation. TED2009, Long Beach, CA. 3-7 Feb. 2009. *TED Blog*. Web. 3 Mar. 2009.

MLA Works Cited Index: Digital Sources, Online and Offline

WriteOnline

Citing Visual and Performance Media and Other Sources

Some sources of information do not easily fit into one of the preceding categories. Nevertheless, you have the same basic responsibility when using them as sources in your writing: you need to make it possible for your readers to locate and verify your sources.

MLA Works Cited Index: Visual and Performance Media and Other Sources

MLA Works Cited Models

57. Film, videotape, or DVD

Provide the following information when citing a film:

Title of film. Director's first name and last name, preceded by *Dir*. Main performers' first names and last names (usually no more than three or four), preceded by *Perf*. Name of distributor, year of distribution. Medium.

You can include other information you consider important, such as the name of the writer or producer, between the title and the distributor.

Pulp Fiction. Dir. Quentin Tarantino. Perf. Samuel L. Jackson and John Travolta. Miramax, 1996. Film.

If you are citing one person's contribution, begin the entry with the person's name (last name, first name), followed by a description of the person's role (e.g., *Dir.* for director or *Perf.* for performer).

Note: Other visual media such as DVDs, videocassettes, laser discs, slide shows, and filmstrips are cited in the same way, only you need to include the original release date (if relevant).

58. Sound recording

Provide the following information when citing a sound recording:

Last name, first name of the individual you are citing (this could be the composer, conductor, or performer, depending on the emphasis of your paper). "Title of song" (if you are citing a song or song lyrics). *Title of CD* (you do not italicize the titles of musical works identified just by form, number, or key). Performer(s) or conductor (if relevant). Manufacturer's name, year of CD's release. Medium.

To cite lyrics from the song "Milquetoast," from Helmet's album *Betty,* you would create the following Works Cited entry:

Helmet. "Milquetoast." *Betty*. Interscope, 1994.

Note: If you are not citing a CD (see above), you should indicate the medium the work appears in (e.g., Audiocassette or LP) after the date of release, *not* in quotation marks or italicized.

59. Live performance

When you are citing information from a live source, write the performer's name (last, first), the title (italicized), the place and date of the occasion, and then the word *Performance*.

Williams, Dar. *Dar Williams in Concert*. Scottish Rite Auditorium, Collingswood, NJ. 14 June 2004. Performance.

60. Television show or radio program

Provide the following information when citing a television or radio program:

"Title of episode, show, or segment." *Title of program*. Title of series (if any). Name of network. Call letters, City of the local station (if any). Broadcast date. Medium of reception.

Other information, such as the names of the producer, director, and performers, can be included as relevant.

"Backwards Episode." *Seinfeld*. Prod. Larry David. Perf. Jerry Seinfeld. WNBC, Baltimore. 10 Dec. 2003. Television.

If you are citing one person's contribution, begin the entry with the person's name (last name, first name), followed by a description of the person's role (e.g., *Narr.* for narrator or *Dir.* for director).

MLA Works Cited Index: Visual and Performance Media and Other Sources

MLA Works Cited Index: Visual and Performance Media and Other Sources

61. Painting, sculpture, or photograph

There are three major parts to an entry for a work of art: the artist's name (last, first), the title of the work of art (italicized), and the place where the work resides (the institution and the city, if the city is not a part of the institution's name). The date of composition and medium of composition, which follow the title, are also included in accordance with the latest MLA guidelines.

Nauman, Bruce. *Clown Torture*. 1987. Video (multimedia). Art Institute of Chicago.

If you are citing a reproduction of a work of art, include everything in the previous entry, and add the complete publication information (or the date of access, the medium, and the URL, if needed).

Nauman, Bruce. *Clown Torture*. 1987. Video (multimedia). Art Institute of Chicago. Web. 12 Apr. 2004.

62. Lecture or speech

Provide the following information when citing a lecture or speech:

Speaker's last name, first name. "Title of speech." Title of meeting. Name of sponsoring organization. Place of speech. Date of speech. Form of delivery.

Cone, James. "Black Theology/Black Pride." Larry Neal Lecture Series. Lincoln University School of Humanities. Mary Dod Brown Memorial Chapel, Lincoln University. 12 Mar. 2003. Lecture.

If the speech has no title, provide a concise description of it. Do not use quotation marks around your description.

63. Published or unpublished interview

Provide the following information for an unpublished interview you conducted:

Interviewee's last name, first name. Type of interview (e.g., Personal interview, Telephone interview, Email interview). Date of interview.

Soto, Dan. Personal interview. 21 Feb. 2006.

Published interviews are treated the same as other print sources. Broadcast or taped interviews are treated as broadcast programs. For both, provide the title of the interview if there is one, relevant source information, and the date the interview took place, if available.

Freedman, Jill. "Photographer." *Working: People Talk about What They Do All Day and How They Feel about What They Do*. By Studs Terkel. New York: Pantheon-Random, 1972. 153-54. Print.

64. Map, chart, or other illustration

When you cite a map, chart, or other illustration, include the name of the map, chart, or illustration; a description of the illustration (e.g., *Map, Chart, Illustration*); the title of the publication; the city of publication, publisher, year; the page numbers on which the illustration appears; and the medium of publication. If the work is online, write the appropriate medium (Web), the date of access, and the URL (if needed).

"Continental United States." Map. *Merriam Traveler's Guide*. Boston: Merriam, 2004. 22-23. Print.

MLA Works Cited Index: Visual and Performance Media and Other Sources

MLA Works Cited Index: Visual and Performance Media and Other Sources

65. Cartoon or comic strip

When you cite a cartoon or comic strip or include one in your work, create an entry that gives the artist's name and the title, if there is one, followed by the designation *Cartoon* or *Comic strip*. Then write the name of the publication in which it appears, along with the day month year of publication, page number, and medium of publication. Or write the appropriate medium (Web), the date of access, and the URL (if needed).

> Trudeau, Gary. "Doonesbury: The Daily Dose." Comic strip. *New York Times* 6 Nov. 2005: C4. Print.

66. Advertisement

When you cite an advertisement or include one in your work, start with the product or institution being advertised and then the word *Advertisement*. Next write the name of the publication in which the advertisement appears, along with the date of publication, inclusive page number(s), and medium of publication. If the ad is online, provide the appropriate medium, the date of access, and the URL (if needed).

> Palmolive Soap. Advertisement. *Ladies Home Journal* 1942. Digital Scriptorium. Web. 6 Nov. 2005.

This section shows you how to format your work for submission in MLA style using the software program Microsoft Word.

How to Create 1" Margins and Double-Space Your Essay

MLA style requires margins of 1" on all four edges of the page. The entire text must be double-spaced. With your document open in Word, follow these steps:

1. Place your cursor anywhere in the body of the text.
2. Select the Page Layout tab to show the Page Layout ribbon.
3. Select the arrow on the lower-right corner of the "Page Setup" category.
4. In the Page Setup dialogue box, adjust your settings so that they match those in Figure 19.1. Top, Bottom, Left, and Right all show 1". Orientation should be "Portrait." Pages should show "Normal," and Preview > Apply to: should list "Whole document."
5. Click on OK.

For instructions that apply to Microsoft® Word® 2003, visit the handbook's website: **cengage.com/english/blakesley**

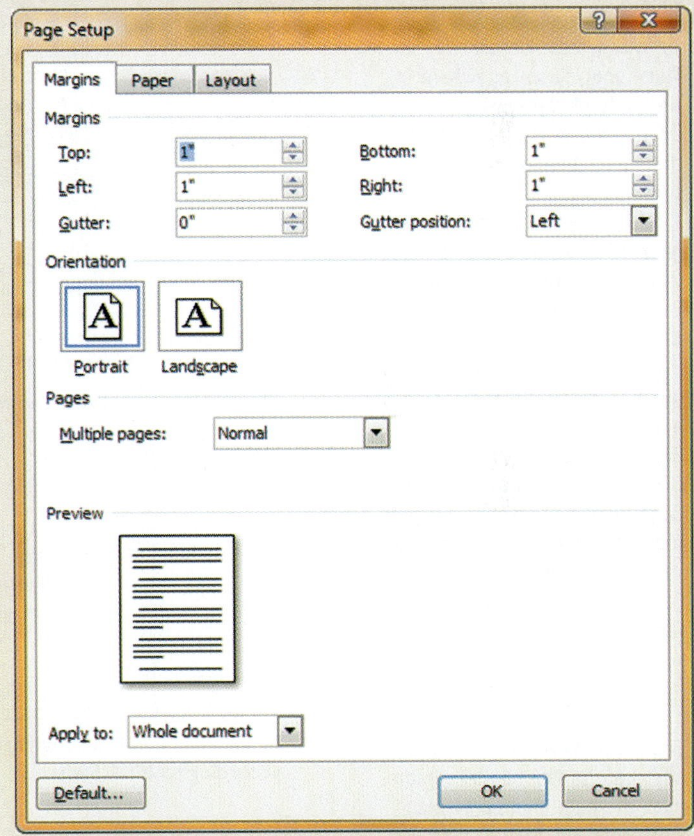

Figure 19.1 Setting Up Page Layout in Word according to MLA Style

How to Create Running Headers with Your Last Name and Page Number

MLA requires that each page of your essay include in the upper right corner a running header that gives your last name and the page number. With your essay open in Word, follow these steps:

1. Place your cursor anywhere in the body of the text.
2. On the top menu bar, choose the Insert tab to show the Insert ribbon.
3. In the Header & Footer category, click on the Page Number icon, and then choose Top of Page and select "Plain Number 3" (in the visual display of options), which will place the number in the upper-right corner of the page, as shown in Figure 19.2.
4. If needed, you can change the page numbering format by clicking on Page Numbers in the Design Ribbon in the Header & Footer category, as shown in Figure 19.3.
5. You now need to add your last name and also remove the header from the first page of your document. Double-click anywhere in the header region near the page number, which will reveal the Design ribbon automatically.

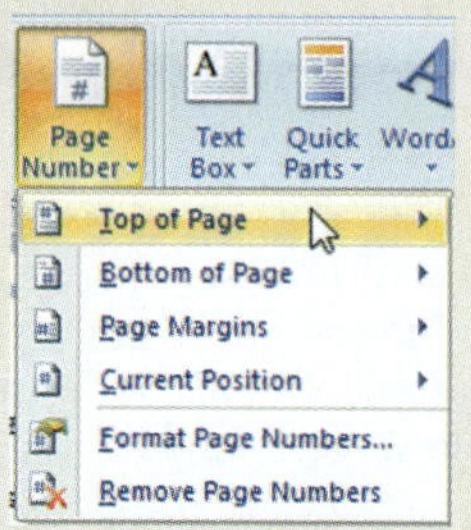

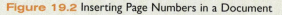

Figure 19.2 Inserting Page Numbers in a Document

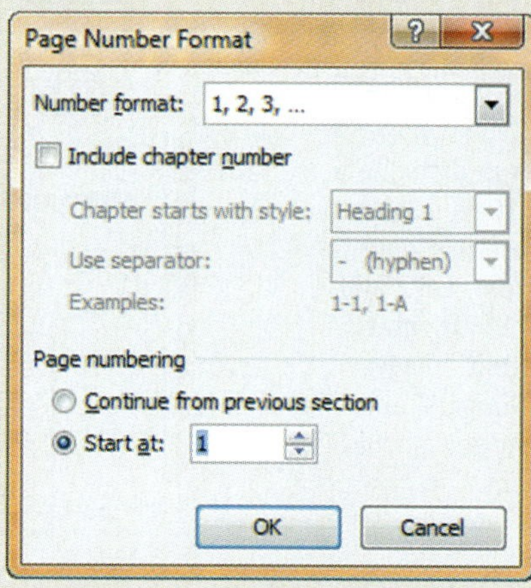

Figure 19.3 Adjusting Page Number Format in a Document according to MLA Style

6. In the Options category, check the box next to "Different First Page" to hide the page number and header on page 1 of your document. (You can also adjust this setting using the Page Setup dialogue box shown in Figure 19.5 (see Step 9).
7. To add your last name as the running header next to the page number, double-click in the header region, type your name as you would like it to appear, select "Insert Alignment Tab" in the Position category and select Right to position your name on the right side of the page to the left of the page number. Insert an extra space after your name to separate it from the number, as shown in Figure 19.4.
8. With the cursor still in the header region, you can change the font and style as needed. Choose the Home tab to make routing formatting changes.
9. Confirm that your page numbers and running headers are properly positioned by checking your Page Setup. Under the Page Layout tab, choose the arrow on the Page Setup category label. Your settings should look like those shown in Figure 19.5.

For instructions that apply to Microsoft® Word® 2003, visit the handbook's website: **cengage.com/english/blakesley**

Figure 19.4 Adding and Positioning Your Last Name in the Running Header

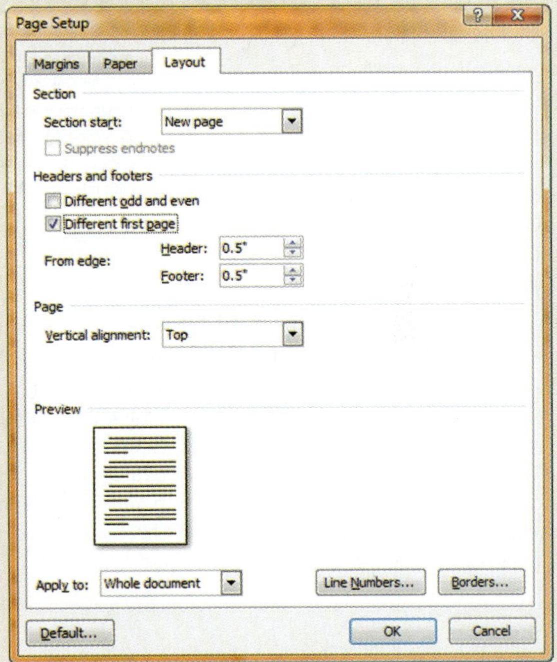

Figure 19.5 Setting the Header's Distance from the Top Edge

How to Create Block Quotations

MLA style calls for all prose quotations longer than four of your lines to be inset an additional 1" from the left margin. (The right margin remains at 1".)

1. Insert a return before and after your quotation so that it stands as its own paragraph. There should not be any extra line spaces above or below the quotation.
2. Place your cursor anywhere in the quotation paragraph.
3. On the Home ribbon in Word 2007, click twice on the Increase Indent button: ⇥. The quotation will be indented an additional 1" from the left margin.

moving on ma involve retracing our steps, returning to that alembic center, the molten mass

Left Indent

where all dist converge and of which he spoke in *A Grammar of Motives*:

Distinctions, we might say, arise out of a great central moltenness, where all is merged. They have been thrown from a liquid center to the surface, where they have congealed. Let one of these crusted distinctions return to its source, and in

Figure 19.6 Formatting a Block Quotation

First Line Indent

acc did see Julia again," he notes, "although by then no one, not even her own family back in Davenport, Iowa, could have been expected to recognize her." [. . .]

The book is no less vivid about its more solid citizens, the ones responsible for bringing the World's Columbian Exposition Company into being. Over the kind of menu that featured green turtle consommé and woodcock on toast, they laid glorious plans.

By citing Maslin as I have, I don't mean to suggest that anyone but Holmes is the devil referred to in the book's title. But I do think it's interesting to notice how the parallel themes in these two

Figure 19.7 Adding a Paragraph Indent Using the Margin Guide

Alternatively, on the top ruler bar, position your cursor over the small square box and then drag both arrows to the 1" mark. Since the page margin should already be set at 1", your indented block quotation will now be offset 2". See Figure 19.6. If you need to indent the first line of a paragraph in your block quotation, place the cursor anywhere in the paragraph you want to indent and then drag the top arrow of the margin guide .25" to the right, as shown in Figure 19.7. Note that you do not need to indent the first sentence of a paragraph if you are quoting from a single paragraph. If you are quoting from two or more paragraphs, indent those sentences that begin each paragraph in the source.

For instructions that apply to Microsoft® Word® 2003, visit the handbook's website: **cengage.com/english/blakesley**

How to Place an Image and Add a Caption

1. In Word 2007, place your cursor in your text where you would like to place the image.
2. Choose the Insert tab to show the Insert ribbon. Click on the Insert Picture icon. (If you want to include clip art, shapes, SmartArt, charts, Word art, or other images, you can choose to do so on the Insert ribbon.)
3. Navigate to the image, select it, and click OK. Your image will be placed in the text.
4. To adjust the precise placement and look of your image with a two-button mouse, click once on the image so that it's selected. The Format ribbon will appear. You can then adjust the alignment, position, text wrapping, and more. Figure 19.8 illustrates how to adjust the position. To add fills, lines, and other special effects, as well as adjust brightness, contrast, and more, right click on the image and select "Format Picture."
5. To add a caption, select the image with your mouse, right-click and choose Insert Caption. In the Caption dialogue box, enter the content of the caption in the "Caption:" box and adjust any other settings. See Figure 19.9. Then click OK. Once your caption has been placed, you can edit it just as you would any other text in your document. Word will keep track of the numbering sequence automatically.

For instructions that apply to Microsoft® Word® 2003, visit the handbook's website: **cengage.com/english/blakesley**

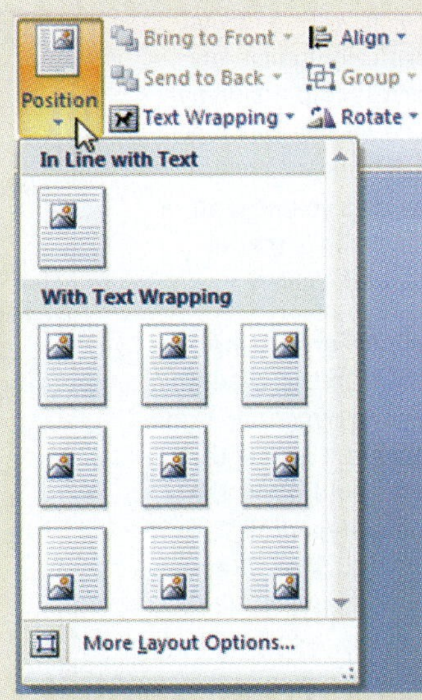

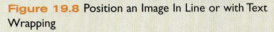

Figure 19.8 Position an Image In Line or with Text Wrapping

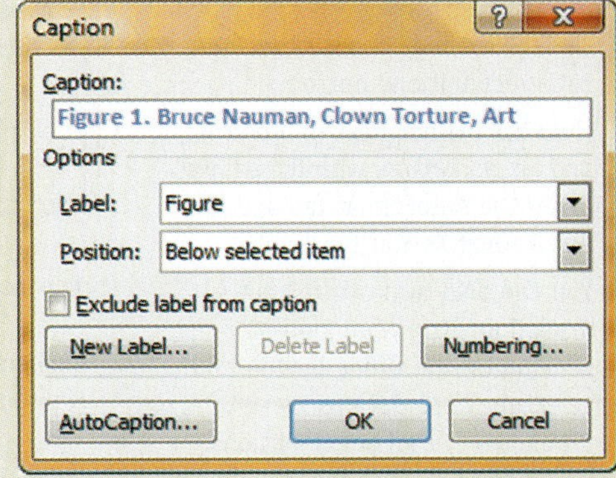

Figure 19.9 Adjusting the settings in the Caption Dialogue Box

How to Turn Off Automatic Hyperlink or Remove a Hyperlink

Microsoft Word comes with a default setting to automatically format any URL or e-mail address into a blue hyperlink. You should disable this function unless your document is online. You may also find that you need to remove formatted hyperlinks that already appear in your document.

Remove Hyperlink Formatting

On a PC, right-click on the hyperlink and choose “Remove Hyperlink” from the pop-up menu. On a Mac with a one-button mouse, hold down the Ctrl key and choose Hyperlink > Edit Hyperlink and then click on “Remove Hyperlink” in the Edit Hyperlink dialogue box.

Prevent Automatic Hyperlink Formatting

1. Choose the Office button and then Word Options.
2. Under Proofing, choose the “AutoCorrect Options button.
3. Unselect the box next to “Internet and network paths with hyperlinks” under the AutoFormat tab and the AutoFormat As You Type” tab.
4. You can also turn off this automatic formatting function by clicking on the Office button and selecting Word Options > Proofing > AutoCorrect Options. Under the AutoFormat tab, uncheck the box as shown in Figure 19.10.
5. Click OK.

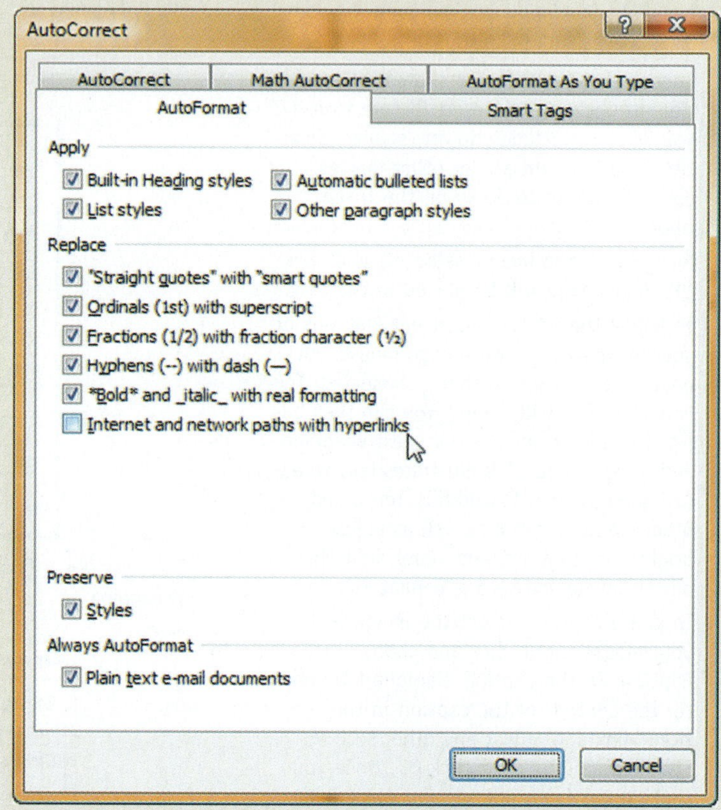

Figure 19.10 Removing the Automatic Hyperlink Insertion in Microsoft Word

For instructions that apply to Microsoft® Word® 2003, visit the handbook’s website: **cengage.com/english/blakesley**

How to Format a Works Cited Page with Hanging Indentations

MLA style requires that entries in the Works Cited section be formatted with hanging indentations, as shown in Figure 19.11.

1. Starting with your Works Cited entries in double-spaced, flush-left format, select all entries by placing your cursor before the first entry, holding down the left mouse button (or the only button on a one-button mouse), to select all the entries.
2. To use the default keyboard shortcut, press Ctrl + T (or Command + T on a Mac keyboard) and you will see the hanging indentation applied. Alternatively, drag the bottom arrow of the ruler guide .5" to the right so that it looks like what is shown in Figure 19.12.

For instructions that apply to Microsoft® Word® 2003, visit the handbook's website: **cengage.com/english/blakesley**

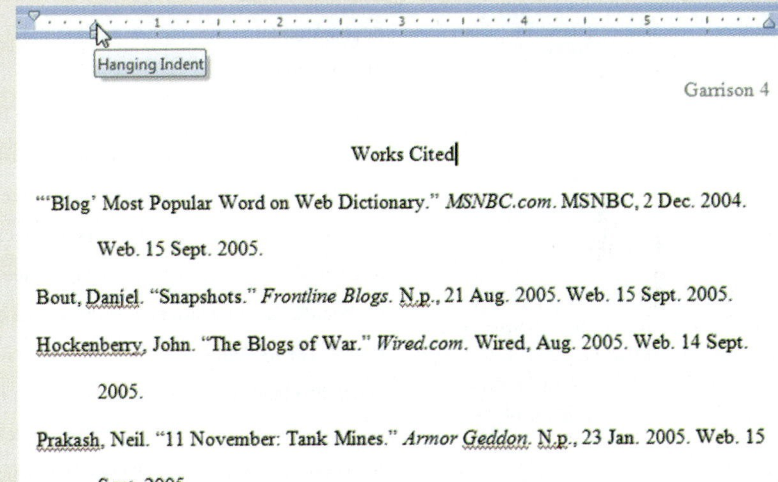

Hanging Indent
Garrison 4
Works Cited
"'Blog' Most Popular Word on Web Dictionary." *MSNBC.com*. MSNBC, 2 Dec. 2004. Web. 15 Sept. 2005.
Bout, Danjel. "Snapshots." *Frontline Blogs*. N.p., 21 Aug. 2005. Web. 15 Sept. 2005.
Hockenberry, John. "The Blogs of War." *Wired.com*. Wired, Aug. 2005. Web. 14 Sept. 2005.
Prakash, Neil. "11 November: Tank Mines." *Armor Geddon*. N.p., 23 Jan. 2005. Web. 15 Sept. 2005.

Figure 19.11 A Works Cited Page with Hanging Indentations for Each Entry

Figure 19.12 Dragging the Bottom Arrow of the Margin Guide to Create Hanging Indentations

Molly McClure's essay presents an argument using research from outside sources to build the case for correcting misperceptions about fan fiction, a wildly popular form of writing on the Internet. The title is an allusion to a famous *Saturday Night Live* skit in which William Shatner spoke to *Star Trek* fans at a convention and told them to "get a life."

The first paragraph provides some useful background information for understanding the basis of the argument, such as the definition of fan fiction.

This raised (superscript) number indicates that a note related to the sentence can be found at the end of the paper, after the main text and before the Works Cited page.

This general reference to an entire work includes the author's name and the title of the work, but not page numbers, which if included would indicate a more specific use of source material. Note, too, that the title of this work includes another book's title. The title within the title is not underlined or italicized.

McClure 1

Molly McClure

Dr. Shaun Hughes

English 130

May 15, 2006

"Get a Life!"

Misconceptions about the Tolkien Fan Fiction Culture

Fan fiction is a genre whose writers use existing stories, characters, plots, themes, and scenes as the starting point for extensions or retellings of the original. Fan fiction writers fill in gaps in the original story, track characters past the boundaries of the original work, or even create entirely new versions of stories. The modern genre has its origins in retellings and reworkings of science fiction and fantasy story lines, but today fan fiction encompasses creative responses to television series, movies, comic books, and books in many subgenres. Recently, a large body of fan fiction has grown up around J. R. R. Tolkien's *The Lord of the Rings* series, partly due to the popularity of the recent movies.

While some authors ridicule the efforts of fan fiction writers, often as a smokescreen for protecting their copyright interests, to say that fan fiction writers have overactive imaginations and too much time on their hands is to say the same about J. R. R. Tolkien himself.[1] Tolkien spent years of his life dreaming up every little detail about Middle Earth, including genealogies, maps, and languages; fan fiction writers borrow and expand on his inventions with creative and sometimes critical elaborations. In method, but not degree, perhaps their efforts are not so different from Tolkien's. Tolkien based his work on existing sources, great works of mythology and Anglo-Saxon literature such as *Beowulf*, as Christopher Tolkien (the author's son) has shown in *The History of* The Lord

McClure 2

of the Rings. To say that fan fiction is a passing fad would also be a mistake because its roots go back thousands of years, long before Tolkien inspired so many new authors. To say that fan fiction is not serious is to slight those who do take it seriously and to ignore that fan fiction may be one of the most popular and accessible forms of literary criticism in our culture. Like "remixing" and "sampling"—two popular forms of appreciating and extending music—good fan fiction requires practice, creativity, patience, and technical skill. Misperceptions about fan fiction writers, fan culture in general, and Tolkien fandom in particular prevent us from seeing its value as a form of critical literacy and a healthy form of literary appreciation.

The stereotypical—but by no means typical—fan fiction writer or reader is a heterosexual (predominantly but not exclusively) unmarried (sometimes) woman (usually true) with more time than she knows what to do with (definitely *not* true). Fan fiction writers and readers are women *and* men in every age group, every social class, every marital status, and every sexual orientation. These are not people with too much time on their hands; these are people who must make time to take part in their hobby. Reading and writing fan fiction are activities that require hours of thought and effort. Readers and writers of fan fiction cannot be dismissed as geeks, perverts, or sloths; to do so is to ignore the merit and worthiness of all types of fan fiction and to slight the value of literary appreciation itself.[2]

In literary history, Shakespeare and even his followers rewrote well-known plays to suit their present circumstances.[3] The impulse to reshape existing plots has an even longer history, however. Fan fiction writers are participating in a line of literary appreciation and intertextuality that extends back thousands of years, to times when stories and myths were preserved through successive retellings and elaborations. More so than people who simply read books or watch movies, fan

This thesis statement follows a series of points about some misperceptions of fan fiction. It makes an argument that can be debated and also emphasizes the importance of overcoming these misperceptions for important subjects like literacy and literary appreciation.

The first time a source is cited, it's common practice to include the author's full name and the title of the work. Since the author's name is given in the text, only the page number needs to be included in parentheses at the end of the sentence.

An ellipsis (three spaced dots) shows readers that some words from the source have not been reprinted in the paper. See section 53d for a discussion of using ellipses.

Molly lists the wide variety of sources for fan fiction to help make her point in the last sentence of the paragraph: fan fiction "is a widespread culture of literary appreciation." Simply saying so would not be enough, so she gives direct evidence. Lists like these are common knowledge (and available widely), so the information doesn't need citation.

McClure 3

fiction writers are active creators who deserve recognition, not ridicule, for their efforts. Henry Jenkins begins his well-known book on fan culture, *Textual Poachers*, by saying it "documents a group insistent on making meaning from materials others have characterized as trivial and worthless" (3). Jenkins goes on to say, "I want to participate in the process of redefining the public identity of fandom . . . and to encourage a greater awareness of the richness of fan culture" (7). Fan culture is indeed rich, and richly diverse. Some of the biggest and longest-lasting fandoms are in science fiction/fantasy: *Star Trek, Star Wars, The X-Files, Harry Potter, The Lord of the Rings, Buffy the Vampire Slayer, X-Men*. Fandoms have now sprouted around just about every TV show imaginable: *ER, The West Wing, MASH, Alias, Smallville, NYPD Blue, Gilmore Girls, JAG,* and *Xena: Warrior Princess*. The same goes for books and authors: *The Baby-Sitters Club*, the Bible, Charles Dickens, *The Diary of Anne Frank*, the *Hardy Boys*, Jane Austen, *Les Misérables, Lord of the Flies*, Shakespeare, *To Kill a Mockingbird*, and *Sherlock Holmes*. Still other fandoms are based on movies: *Nightmare on Elm Street, The Breakfast Club, Bring It On, Chicken Run, Rocky Horror Picture Show, Pirates of the Caribbean, Moulin Rouge!, Men in Black, The Magnificent Seven, The Fast and the Furious*. Fandom is not the realm of a few geeks; it is a widespread culture of literary appreciation whose writers find value in what some others might find "worthless" (Jenkins 3).

Fan fiction became hugely popular with the emergence of the Internet as a new venue for gathering information about books and movies and sharing writing related to them. The Internet has made information about such films, TV shows, and literature easily accessible to anyone. Email, instant messaging, weblogs, discussion forums, newsgroups, online journals and ezines, mailing

McClure 4

lists, and message boards now facilitate the kind of communication among fans that builds community and in turn nourishes fan fiction into existence. It's not surprising that fan fiction has evolved beyond its early focus on science fiction.

Today, one of the most popular and easily accessible websites for finding fan fiction is *FanFiction.Net*, which as early as April 2001, according to Nancy Schulz, already had "more than 41,000 stories in all, the work of 13,000 authors" ("The E-Files"). Those numbers have grown substantially in the last five years. One of the largest categories of stories at *FanFiction.Net* is based on *The Lord of the Rings (LOTR)*, partly because of the recent movies, which have made the *LOTR* trilogy more popular than ever. Although *LOTR* has been around much longer than many of the works common in fandom, there has not been much research into its particular nature, perhaps because until recent years the fandom was much quieter than others, with only the books to rely on. With the release of the movies, however, more and more people are reading and watching *LOTR* and becoming interested in the complex relationships among its characters. *The Silmarillion* category at *FanFiction.Net* has almost 1,000 stories, whereas *The Lord of the Rings* category is one of the biggest on the site: more than 36,000 stories are now posted.

Some of the popularity of writing about Tolkien's work has to do with the attractive actors in the films: there are more stories about Legolas than any other *LOTR* character at *FanFiction.Net*, due in no small part to Orlando Bloom's good looks. Many of these stories are "Mary Sues" written by "fangirls"; that is, the authors are girls and women who desire Bloom, so they write stories about Legolas in which he falls in love with original female characters who bear a striking resemblance to the story's author, sometimes even with the same name. These stories are some of the most despised in fandom, as the whole plot of the

The name of a website is sometimes the same as the site's URL (without the *http://www.*). Molly shows the title the way it is shown on the website, with each significant word capitalized. (Remember that current MLA guidelines no longer require a URL for Web sources unless it is needed for the reader to find the source or your instructor requires one.) If Molly had to use the actual URL (in this case, http://www.fanfiction.net), it would appear only in the Works Cited entry.

The quotation from Nancy Schulz illustrates effective use of an external source to help provide background information that is not common knowledge. The parenthetical citation doesn't include a page number because the entire article appeared on a single page. The page number is included in the corresponding Works Cited entry.

Molly gathered this information herself from *FanFiction.Net*. Since it's an observable fact (and therefore common knowledge), no citation is required.

Molly uses a complete sentence followed by a colon to introduce a block quotation. See page 381 for a discussion of block quotations.

At the end of a block quotation, a period ends the final sentence before the parenthetical citation is provided. This is one difference between citing a quotation that is run into your own sentence and one that is blocked off. See pages 380–381.

In this paragraph, Molly continues the strategy of defining strategies of fan fiction, using the Jenkins source, a recognized authority, to help guide the discussion and carefully citing it along the way. Examples are drawn from the Tolkien fandom.

McClure 5

story is for Legolas to fall madly in love with the perfect woman, marry her, father her children, and live happily ever after. Not all original characters are so stigmatized, but original love interests, especially Legolas's, are always looked on with suspicion lest Mary Sue/Marty Stu characteristics develop. Jenkins labels this writing technique "personalization":

> Fan writers . . . work to efface the gap that separates the realm of their own experience and the fictional space of their favorite programs. "Mary Sue" stories . . . constitute one of the most disputed subgenres of fan fiction. So strong is the fan taboo against such crude personalizations that original female characters are often scrutinized for any signs of autobiographical intent. (171-73)

Mary Sue stories are not the only kind of story popular with fan fiction writers. In addition to personalization, Jenkins explains some other strategies of writing fan fiction. He labels one popular subgenre "recontextualization," saying that "fans often write short vignettes ('missing scenes') which fill in the gaps in the original and provide additional explanations for the character's conduct; these stories focus on off-screen actions and discussion that motivated perplexing on-screen behavior" (162). In *The Lord of the Rings* fandom, stories detail scenes like the Fellowship's stay in Lothlorien, Aragorn's trip along the Paths of the Dead and up the Anduin, and the discovery of Pippin on the battlefield in front of the Black Gate. In *The Silmarillion*, popular topics include Feanor's sons' reaction to Fingon bringing Maedhros back to them. Jenkins also explains that "expanding the series timeline" is a common technique because "the primary texts often provide hints or suggestions about the characters' backgrounds not fully explored within the episodes" (163). It is common for writers to take these tidbits as starting points for writing prologues or counter

McClure 6

narratives. In *The Lord of the Rings* fandom, writers detail Legolas's life in Mirkwood before becoming a part of the Fellowship, or any of the characters' early lives: Boromir and Faramir as brothers in Minas Tirith, Gimli at the Lonely Mountain, and so on. Topics also include what happens next: What adventures do Aragorn, Gimli, and Legolas have as rulers of their own lands? Do Eomer and Faramir join them on these journeys? What happens once Frodo reaches Valinor? If Gimli really sails West with Legolas, how is he received? Alternate universe stories (AUs) fall within this category as well. For example, a story may posit that Elrond stays in Rivendell to see his grandchildren before sailing West. Frodo may live with Sam and Rosie and help them raise their children instead of leaving them at Bag End.

Another popular subgenre in fan fiction is "hurt/comfort," which falls under Jenkins's heading "emotional intensification" and "centers almost entirely upon such moments [of narrative crisis], sometimes building on a crisis represented within the series proper . . . other times inventing situations where the characters experience vulnerability" (174). A near brush with death or a serious revelation will allow two (normally male) characters to become closer to one another. Jenkins argues that the drives behind such stories "cut to the heart of our culture's patriarchal conception of the hero as a man of emotional constraint and personal autonomy, a man in control of all situations" (175). Hurt/comfort stories also reveal the natural and human weaknesses in larger-than-life heroes, which makes their recovery from near tragedy inspiring and all the more amazing. One favorite subject of hurt/comfort stories (commonly abbreviated as h/c) in the *LOTR* realm is Legolas, prompting fan fiction writers to invent the phrase "elf torture" as another name for stories in which he is in physical or mental distress. The character who seems to comfort Legolas the

The brackets around "of narrative crisis" indicate that Molly added words that did not come from the original source in order to make sure readers would understand the quotation in the context of her research paper. See page 964.

It's better to cite a source directly, rather than citing it as you saw it reprinted in another source. But sometimes you simply don't have access to the original source. In this case, you can note that you found the first source "quoted in" another. Notice in this paragraph how careful Molly is to distinguish the words of Henry Jenkins discussing David Bleich's study and the words of Bleich himself.

McClure 7

most is Aragorn, followed closely by Gimli. The popularity of this subgenre is also clear in the *X-Files* fandom, where there is an archive called "Mulder Torture Anonymous" that is filled with thousands of h/c stories.

How men and women might approach fan fiction differently has been the subject of interesting debates, reminiscent of those that have also focused on how women and men might read differently. Jenkins explores this subject by discussing studies done by David Bleich and Elizabeth Segel on the differences between male and female readers of literary texts. He claims that David Bleich's 1986 study found that "female readers entered directly into the fictional world, focusing less on the extratextual process of its writing than on the relationships and events" (108). In contrast, male readers "acknowledged and respected the author's authority, while women saw themselves as engaged in a 'conversation' within which they could participate as active contributors" (108). Male readers also "tended to maintain the narrative focus on a central protagonist, while female readers eagerly explored a broader range of social relationships" (Jenkins 109). Female readers, Bleich argued, sought to "retell the story more in terms of interpersonal motives, allegiances, and conflicts" (qtd. in Jenkins 109). Jenkins uses Elizabeth Segel's 1986 study of gender and reading to make the point that young girls are typically encouraged to "make sense" of male-centered narratives. Young boys, the study suggests, can't be coaxed into experimenting with female characters in their narratives, so their responses to fiction often focus on the weaknesses of female-centered stories (Jenkins 114). This certainly rings true when looking at *The Lord of the Rings*, in which there is a dearth of strong female characters. Women must interpret from the book what they can because there are hardly any women in the story to do it for them.

McClure 8

Anna Smol argues in "'Oh . . . Oh . . . Frodo!' Readings of Male Intimacy in *The Lord of the Rings*" that Tolkien fandom has intensified interest in exploring male relationships in ways that traditional criticism could not, adding to *LOTR*'s intertextuality (969). Fan fiction stories known as "slash," which focus on same-sex couples, also raise important social questions about gender identity. Jenkins explains his interest in slash in part by saying, "Slash . . . posits an explicit critique of traditional masculinity, trying to establish an homosocial-homoerotic continuum as an alternative to repressive and hierarchical male sexuality. Both partners retain equality *and* autonomy while moving into a more satisfying and committed relationship" (219). Slash may even have greater worth and value than "gen" (general, non-romance) or "het" (heterosexual romance) fan fiction. Certainly the reasons people write it and the questions it raises are just as interesting as, if not more interesting than, regular fan fiction. Whether slash fiction is considered perverted or not, often the politics behind slash fiction is fascinating. Neva Chonin wrote an article for *SFGate.com* in which she says a certain passage between Sam and Frodo in *The Two Towers* "illustrates one of the most basic and overlooked aspects of Tolkien's trilogy. Beneath its mythic layers of good and evil, wizards and kings and tyrants, . . . it's a tribute to love between men." It is not a great leap, then, for some writers to imagine physical expressions of two characters' love for each other. Camille Bacon-Smith says in *Enterprising Women* that "Many women perceive a deep and loving relationship between characters . . . because series creators put it there. The homosocial partnership has been a staple of Western romance tradition for at least two thousand years" (234). Strong relationships and bonds among men have been around for millennia, then, so perhaps it is understandable that women are writing about them in such large numbers.

This sentence and the discussion below raise the point that fan fiction tackles important social issues.

The first sentence of the conclusion explains how fan fiction worlds have social and personal value. It addresses the "so what?" question that readers sometimes expect to find answered by the end of an essay.

Molly uses a long quotation at the end of her essay to emphasize once again a point she made at the beginning: the same creative impulse drives fan fiction writers and the more famous authors whose work inspires them.

McClure 9

Works of fan fiction—like the stories on which they are based—ask us to imagine alternative universes so that we can gain perspective on our own. In the end, the reason people write fan fiction is simple, no different from the reason J. R. R. Tolkien wrote his epic novels. On the special extended DVD edition of *The Two Towers*, Brian Sibley (also author of *The Lord of the Rings: The Making of the Movie Trilogy*) shares this story:

> There was a conversation that took place between Tolkien and C. S. Lewis . . . in which they were talking about the fact that they felt a frustration that they couldn't pick up and read the kind of books and stories that they liked to read. And they both came to this conclusion that in the end maybe they had to write the books they wanted to read. (qtd. in Jackson)

Writers of fan fiction, whether they are writing gen, slash, het, h/c, or another subgenre, have come to the same conclusion, and they are no more worthy of scorn than Tolkien himself.

McClure 10

Notes

[1] Anne Rice, author of *Interview with the Vampire*, initially supported fan fiction based on her work, but when characters were developed in ways she disliked, she launched a "cease and desist" campaign that resulted in the removal of that novel as a source at *FanFiction.Net* and other sites. The forums at the website *Godawful Fan Fiction* include criticism of fan fiction in general and single out particularly bad examples for ridicule.

[2] Perhaps the best way to break down stereotypes is with knowledge. Although it should only be considered a starting point for further research and, like any such article, may contain inaccuracies, the Wikipedia article on fan fiction provides a lengthy and detailed overview of its major features, history, types, and devotees: http://en.wikipedia.org/wiki/Fan_fiction.

[3] See, for example, Nahum Tate's famous adaptation of *King Lear*, which has an alternative ending in which everyone survives, both happy and smarter, unlike in Shakespeare's original: http://andromeda.rutgers.edu/~jlynch/Texts/tatelear.html.

Notes serve two functions in MLA style: (1) they provide information relevant to the argument but not relevant enough to put in the body of the paper, and (2) they provide citations that would clutter the main text if placed there.

Here, note 1 adds information about critics of fan fiction that might have sidetracked Molly's main argument if it had been put in the body of the paper. Notes 2 and 3 also provide qualifying information and point to two websites.

The first line of each note is indented, and the note number appears in superscript (raised) style. A space follows the superscript number.

The Works Cited list includes all sources quoted, summarized, or paraphrased.

A book by one author

An article published in an online newspaper

Even though this source was discussed only in a note, it must be included in the Works Cited.

The title of this article from a scholarly journal includes a quotation enclosed in a pair of single quotation marks, as well as the title of the work being discussed, which is italicized because it is a book. The whole article title is then enclosed in double quotation marks. It's important to get these details right when preparing a Works Cited list.

McClure 11

Works Cited

Bacon-Smith, Camille. *Enterprising Women: Television Fandom and the Creation of Popular Myth*. Philadelphia: U of Pennsylvania P, 1992. Print.

Chonin, Neva. "Love between Men Is a Powerful Thing in *Lord of the Rings*." *SFGate.com*. Hearst Communications, 15 Jan. 2002. Web. 11 Aug. 2002.

FanFiction.Net. 2006. Web. 17 Feb. 2006.

Godawful Fan Fiction. 2006. Web. 17 Feb. 2006.

Jackson, Peter, dir. *The Two Towers*. Special Extended Edition. New Line Cinema/WingNut Films, 2004. DVD.

Jenkins, Henry. *Textual Poachers: Television Fans and Participatory Culture*. New York: Routledge, 1992. Print.

Rice, Anne. "Important Message from Anne on 'Fan Fiction.'" *AnneRice.com.* 2000. Web. 17 Feb. 2006.

Schulz, Nancy. "The E-Files." *Washington Post* 29 Apr. 2001: G1. Print.

Smol, Anna. "'Oh . . . Oh . . . Frodo!' Readings of Male Intimacy in *The Lord of the Rings*." *Modern Fiction Studies* 50.4 (2004): 949-79. Print.

Tolkien, Christopher. *The History of* The Lord of the Rings. 5 vols. New York: Houghton, 2000. Print.

20

CITING SOURCES IN APA STYLE

The citation style recommended by the American Psychological Association (APA) is used to cite sources in research essays and other writing projects in the social sciences—psychology, education, management, anthropology, political science, sociology, and economics. If you major in one of these fields, you may want to examine a copy of the *Publication Manual of the American Psychological Association,* 5th edition, to become familiar with the citation style you will be using throughout your college career. This chapter focuses on the documentation of research sources and the format of APA papers.

The APA style has two basic components: (1) citations of summaries, paraphrases, and quotations given inside parentheses in the body of the research paper and (2) an alphabetically organized References page at the end of the text, which provides the author, publication date, title, and other publication information.

In the social sciences, new research results frequently correct or replace previous knowledge. Research results are time sensitive, in other words, and can have a short shelf life. So it is important for readers to know when your cited source information was published. To establish this research timeline, the APA system includes the date of publication in the in-text citation. The author's last name and the date of publication are the two pieces of information that link the in-text citation to the References entry.

APA INDEXES

The author's last name and the date link the in-text citation to the References entry.

Notice in the in-text citation:

- The author's last name, the publication date, and the page number are all provided.
- The publication date is given in parentheses—often as you see it here, directly after the author's last name.
- The page number is given within parentheses, with the abbreviation *p.* used for "page" (and *pp.* used for "pages").
- The sentence ends after the in-text citation.

Notice in the References entry:

- The author's last name is used to alphabetize the entry. The author's first name is reduced to an initial. A comma and space separate the two.
- The publication date is given in parentheses. A period follows.
- The book title is given in italics. Only the first word of the main title, the first word of the subtitle, and any proper nouns (none here) are capitalized. A period follows.
- The publication information includes the city of publication, followed by a colon, and the name of the publisher, followed by a period.
- The first line starts at the left margin, but the second and subsequent lines are indented from the left margin.

The Link between the In-Text Citation and the Reference

In-text citation of a book:

Cultural Tasks 2

Woodman (1992) suggests that a main task in our culture is to learn to relate to archetypes without identifying with them (p. 13).

Reference entry:

Cultural Tasks 7

Reference

Woodman, M. (1992). *Leaving my father's house: A journey to conscious femininity.* Boston: Shambhala.

Activity 20-1: Quick APA Citation Practice

Referring to the example above, use the excerpt and publication information given below to create your own example of an in-text citation from a book and the References entry that would accompany it.

From the book *The Youth Charter: How Communities Can Work Together to Raise Standards for All Our Children* by William Damon
Published in New York by the Free Press
Copyright 1997
Excerpt from page 80:

There is a better way, for both the management of the home and the growth of the child: *authoritative parenting,* an approach that combines a firm enforcement of consistent rules with rational explanations for the purposes behind the rules. The child always knows what she is supposed to do and why. The child is respected, and her opinions are

Excerpt continues, from page 81:

heard, but at the same time, the child is expected to listen to the parent and follow the parent's lead.

Two Ways to Identify the Source in the Text

Author's name and date in introduction, page number in parentheses:

> Herbal Treatment 2
>
> Johnson (2004) shows us that "seizures can occur whenever other medications are not carefully considered" (p. 36).

Author's name, date, and page number in parentheses:

> Herbal Treatment 2
>
> Seizures are another possible outcome of mixing medicines (Johnson, 2004, p. 36).

For all source information that you summarize, paraphrase, quote, or refer to, you need to provide the author's last name and the date of publication. Page numbers are required for quotations and are recommended for paraphrased material. Usually, you provide the author's name, followed by the date in parentheses, in the body of your sentence and then put the page number(s) in another set of parentheses at the end of the quoted or paraphrased materials. However, you can also place the author's name, the date, and the page number(s) in one set of parentheses.

APA Tip

If page numbers are unavailable, provide paragraph numbers as a way to indicate to readers where source material is located, using the abbreviation *para.* or the paragraph symbol, ¶, before the paragraph number. In a long work, list the heading under which the material can be found, count the number of paragraphs up to and including the one you are referring to, and provide the information in your parenthetical citation: "(Simpson, 2001, Summary, ¶ 2)."

Short Quotations

Quotations of fewer than 40 words should be incorporated into the body of your text and enclosed in double quotation marks (" "). Place the citation as close as possible to the material being quoted, either immediately after the quotation if it will not distract the reader or at the end of the sentence. Page numbers are required, as are the author's name and the publication year.

Remember that the sentence ends *after* the parenthetical information, so the period goes after the closing parenthesis at the end of the sentence, not within the last quotation mark. However, when your quotation ends with an exclamation point or question mark, the punctuation mark stays within the quotation marks, and then you add the parenthetical citation followed by a period.

If the source you are quoting includes quoted sources or dialogue, change the quotation marks around the original quotation to single marks.

End punctuation after citation in short quotation:

> Genetic Basis 4
>
> Turner (2003) suggests that habitual behavior is often the "genius of genetic coding carried to an infinite degree of hereditary variables" (pp. 32–33).

? or ! within the quotation:

> Varied Intelligences 2
>
> Gardner (1983) asks, "What if one were to let one's imagination wander freely, to consider the wider range of performances that are in fact valued throughout the world?" (p. 4).

Original source includes quotation marks:

Here is what it says in the original source, *Family Therapy in Clinical Practice,* by Murray Bowen, M.D. (1985), page 348:

> The team-group meetings are commonly used for "training" inexperienced professional people who learn by participation in the team meetings, and who can rather quickly gain the status of "family therapist."

Here is what the text citation looks like, with double quotation marks changed to singles:

> Family Therapy 3
>
> Bowen (1985) describes one type of problem-focused family therapy: "The team-group meetings are commonly used for 'training' inexperienced professional people who learn by participation in the team meetings, and who can rather quickly gain the status of 'family therapist'" (p. 348).

Parenthetical citation after a long quotation:

Adoptive Family 9

Oxengale and Ferris (1999) cite disturbing trends in adoption:

> Unfortunately, the various entities of the states' DSS units often cull children from neglectful or absent parents, whose main offense seems to be more a medical one . . . than a criminal or DSS-related issue. During these periods of heavy growth in children taken into the custody of the states, foster parents are often even more difficult to locate. This causes systematic breakdown and overcrowding of wards best kept open for criminal-related individuals. (pp. 322–323)

Long Quotations

Quotations of 40 or more words should be set out in block format, *without* quotation marks. Block quotations should be started on a new line, indented 1/2" (five spaces) from the left margin, and double-spaced throughout. If the quotation is more than one paragraph, indent the first line of the second and any additional paragraphs in the quotation an additional 1/2" (a total of ten typewriter spaces). The parenthetical citation is given after the last punctuation mark of the block quotation, separated by one space.

Any quotation marks in the original can remain double, since the overall quotation is indicated by indentation, not by quotation marks.

Making Changes to Quotations

If you make any changes to quotations, you need to let readers know that you have done so.

Taking Words Out

Use an ellipsis (three spaced dots) to show that you have omitted material from a quotation. If you omit material from the beginning of a sentence that follows the end of another, use four dots—one for the period and three for the ellipsis. However, don't use ellipses at the beginning or end of the entire quotation, unless confusion would result if you didn't.

Adding Words or Explanations

Use brackets to indicate additions or explanations. For example, if you italicize a word that is important in the context of your essay, write *[emphasis added]* in your parenthetical citation. (See also section 17e.)

Changes You Can Make without Telling Readers

You can make *only* the following changes to quotations without telling readers:

1. The first letter of the first word can be changed from uppercase to lowercase, or vice versa.
2. The end punctuation can be changed to fit your sentence.
3. Single quotation marks can be changed to double, and double to single, to fit the context.

Here is what it says in the original source for examples on this page, *The Developing Person through the Life Span,* 5th ed., by Kathleen Stassen Berger (2001), page 423:

> Provocative international data from European nations show a negative correlation between hours of employment after school and learning in school (Kelly, 1998). Such correlations do not prove causation, but it is curious that U.S. fourth-graders, who obviously do not have jobs, score much closer to their European peers on standardized tests than U.S. twelfth-graders do.

Using Ellipses to Indicate Where Words Have Been Omitted

Ellipsis within a sentence:

Teenage Employment 5

Berger (2001) summarizes Kelly's (1998) European data and then cautiously notes that "such correlations do not prove causation, but . . . U.S. fourth-graders . . . score much closer to their European peers on standardized tests than U.S. twelfth-graders do" (p. 423).

Period and ellipsis between sentences:

Teenage Employment 5

Berger (2001) calls Kelly's (1998) European data "provocative"; they show a "negative correlation between hours of employment after school and learning in school. . . . it is curious that U.S. fourth-graders, who obviously do not have jobs, score much closer to their European peers on standardized tests than U.S. twelfth-graders do" (p. 423).

Using Brackets to Indicate Additions or Add Explanations

Teenage Employment 5

Berger (2001) rightly states that "[these negative] correlations do not prove causation" (p. 423), but suggests that increasingly divergent standardized test scores of U.S. and European students could be linked to the after-school employment of U.S. high school students.

APA In-Text Citation Models

1. Author named in your text

> Hillman (2004) says that we cannot understand war until we "understand the madness of its love" (p. 1).

Position the in-text citation so that it is clear to readers what information is being documented. Whenever possible, place the citation either at a natural break in a sentence or at the end of it. You should always provide a specific page number immediately after a direct quotation.

2. Author not named in your text

> Fascism is said to be "absolute politics for people with absolute agendas" (Hoskins, 2001, p. 21).

Note that commas separate the three elements in the parentheses.

3. No author's or editor's name or anonymous source

For texts with unknown authors, use an abbreviated form of the title, dropping *The, A,* or *An* from the beginning. Use quotation marks to enclose an article or chapter title; put the title of a book, periodical, or report in italics. Then in the References list, use the full title in place of the author's name.

> Binge drinking is cited as the most common form of teenage substance abuse ("Alcohol linked," 2002, p. 34).

Note: Although you do not use quotation marks around article titles in the References list, you *do* use them around article titles in your text.

APA In-Text Citations Index

APA In-Text Citations Index

If a source lists the author as "Anonymous," use that word as the author, along with the date:

> (Anonymous, 2004).

The References entry will be alphabetized under *Anonymous* in this case.

4. Two authors

Include both last names in your text each time you refer to the source. For in-text introductions, use the word *and* to join the names:

> Hollis and Ware (1994) felt confident that "hatred leads to aggression" (p. 11).

In parenthetical citations, use an ampersand (&) to join the names:

> Some reports suggest that "hatred leads to aggression" (Hollis & Ware, 1994, p. 11).

5. Three to five authors

Write all the authors' last names the first time you refer to the source, followed by the date of publication in parentheses. After that, include only the first author's last name in the text, followed by the abbreviation *et al.* (an abbreviation for the Latin term *et alii,* meaning "and others"), and provide the date only if you are citing the source for the first time in a paragraph.

> Hockney, Allison, Fielding, Johnson, and Glade (2003) indicate that "politics have been corrupted by wealthy individuals creating foundations with overly partisan agendas" (p. 12).

> Hockney et al. (2003) express their disdain in agreeing that "openness and candor are missing from some foundation sources this election cycle" (p. 33).

Note: If you use two sources published the same year and the last names of the first authors are also the same, cite the last names of as many of the other authors as needed to distinguish the sources from each other.

6. Six or more authors

For both introductory and parenthetical citations, use the first author listed and then the phrase *et al.*

> Ruotolo et al. (1985) lament the loss of "job and social stability when personnel depart the military" (p. 33).

In the References list, give the last names and first initials of the first six authors and then write *et al.*

7. Chapter in an edited book or anthology

Use the standard APA in-text citation format, giving the name of the author of the specific article or chapter you are referencing.

> Rogers (2004) noted . . . (p. 222).
>
> or
>
> (Rogers, 2004, p. 222).

APA In-Text Citations Index

APA In-Text Citations Index

8. Two or more primary authors with the same last name

The primary author is the first one listed for a particular source. Even if the publication dates of two works by primary authors with the same last name would distinguish the sources, use their initials each time you mention them in the text to avoid confusion.

> P. L. Knox and Allen (2004) found . . .
>
> A. J. Knox and Henry (2001) studied . . .

9. More than one source by the same author

If you are citing works by the same author(s) published in different years, including the dates in parentheses is enough to allow readers to identify the sources in your References. If the sources were published in the same year, alphabetize them in the References list according to title and then, in that order, assign each one a letter suffix (*a, b, c,* and so on) after the date.

> Surely, Smith (2001a) cannot be correct when she writes, "David Harris and other occupational therapists have violated their field's norms" (pp. 23–24).

Corresponding references list:

> Smith, J. D. (2001a). Occupational therapy and magnetic resonance . . .
> Smith, J. D. (2001b). Treating blood disorders . . .
> Smith, J. D. (2001c). Verification of patient responsibilities . . .

10. Corporate or other group author

Use the full name of the group or entity that created the source each time, unless the name is very long or unless an acronym for the group is well known—for instance, *CIA*. In this case, spell out the name the first time, along with the acronym, and use the acronym the second and subsequent times.

> The National Security Agency (NSA, 2004) identifies terrorism as "the major weapon of disempowered groups throughout the world" (p. 233).

Subsequent references:

> . . . (NSA, 2004).

11. Two or more sources by different authors in the same citation

In parentheses immediately following the use of the information (which often is not quoted but summarized), list the sources alphabetically by first author's last name and include the year of publication. Separate the information for each source with a semicolon. Include page numbers if they are known.

> Many researchers (Holtzbringer, 2001; Mallory, 2003, p. 99; Vickenstein, 2001, p. 76) have described rehabilitation as a painful, long, and grueling process. Holtzbringer (2001) has provided four criteria to use in judging how long rehabilitation is likely to take.

APA In-Text Citations Index

12. Two or more sources by the same author in the same citation

Write the author's name or authors' names only once, and then list the sources by year of publication, starting with the oldest. In-press publications are listed last. (These are works that aren't yet published but have been accepted for publication.)

> (MacKnight & Lovington, 1999, 2002, in press)

If two or more sources are by the same author(s) and have the same publication year, use suffixes (*a, b, c,* and so on) and repeat the year each time. (See citation model 9 on page 452.)

> Three surveys (Wangera, 2004a, 2004b, 2004c) . . .

13. Indirect source

When you cite an indirect source, provide the secondary source in the reference list. For your in-text citation, name the original source and then provide a separate citation for the secondary source.

For instance, if Cronenberg's quotation is found in an article written by Harding and Fields and you cannot locate the original Cronenberg source, list Harding and Fields in the in-text citation:

> David Cronenberg stated that "the future of Cinema is only limited by the dark imaginations of those involved in the production of filmic texts, while technology's role is overstated enthusiastically by those people with limited capacities for understanding the work of film in society" (cited in Harding & Fields, 2003, p. 34).

14. Electronic source

When you cite electronic data or information, include the author's last name and the publication date as you would for a printed source. If you directly quote material from an electronic document that numbers paragraphs rather than pages, use the abbreviation *para.* or the symbol ¶ before the number in your parenthetical citation. (See the box on page 445.)

> Horatio and Holder (2004) describe alternative treatments for sickle cell disease (Method section, para. 7).

Note: Because another researcher would not be able to locate the information later, informal electronic communications, such as personal email and posts to unarchived discussion groups, are only cited in the text and not listed in the References. Check with your instructor to be sure using such sources is acceptable.

15. Personal communication

When you cite personal communications (telephone conversations, emails, letters, and so on), write *personal communication* after the author's or speaker's name, followed by the full date of the communication.

> He describes *basic methods* as "facile and easily imitated versus more professional and less likely to be deviated from" (T. L. Scholder, personal communication, October 23, 2004).

Note: APA style calls for personal communications not to be listed in the References. However, your instructor may want you to list them anyway, so be sure to ask.

APA In-Text Citations Index

APA In-Text Citations Index

16. Photograph or figure

Copyright information for photos and figures is given at the end of the image's caption. (The caption explains the image and is placed after it.) Your entry will start a new line after the rest of the caption.

Format if the image is from a book:

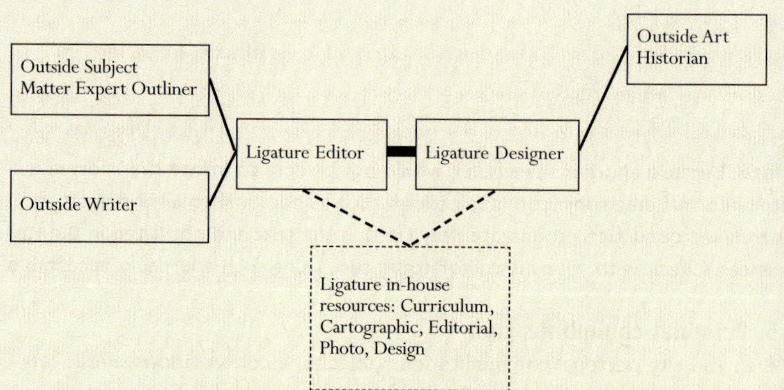

Figure 2. The Thumbnail Team. To develop a series of K–8 social studies texts, Ligature formed teams composed of editors and designers. The editor and designer were aided by subject matter experts, writers, art historians, and all the in-house resources at Ligature.

Note. From *The Visual Turn and the Transformation of the Textbook* (p. 17), by J. A. Laspina, 1998, Mahwah, NJ: Lawrence Erlbaum Associates. Copyright 1998 by Lawrence Erlbaum Associates, Inc. Reprinted with permission.

Format if the image is from an article:

Note. From "Article Title," by initials and last name of author, year, *Name of Journal, volume number,* page number(s). Copyright year by the copyright holder's name. Reprinted with permission.

If you make any changes to the image, write *Adapted* instead of *Reprinted.*

Sample References Page

Cultural Memory 8

References

Arkinson, R. C., & Shiffrin, R. M. (1971). The control of short-term memory. *Scientific American, 225*(2), 82–90.

Boire, R. G. (2003). Forget about it? *Corante.* Retrieved August 14, 2005, from http://www.corante.com/brainwaves/20030801.shtml#50203

Crowder, R. G. (1976). *Principles of learning and memory.* Hillsdale, NJ: Erlbaum.

Edwards, J. L. (2004). Echoes of Camelot: How images construct cultural memory through rhetorical framing. In C. A. Hill & M. Helmers (Eds.), *Defining visual rhetorics* (pp. 179–194). Mahwah, NJ: Erlbaum.

Gregg, V. H. (1986). *Introduction to human memory.* London: Routledge.

Hartman, G. H. (1995). On traumatic knowledge and literary studies. *New Literary History, 26,* 537–563.

Common APA Abbreviations Used in References Entries

chap.: chapter
ed.: edition
Ed. (Eds.): Editor (Editors)
No.: Number
n.d.: no date
p. (pp.) (include a space after the period): page (pages)
para: paragraph
Pt.: Part
Rev. ed.: Revised edition
2nd ed., 3rd ed.: second edition, third edition
Trans.: Translator(s)
Vol. (Vols.): Volume (Volumes)

The APA References page, like the MLA Works Cited page, includes only information on sources that are summarized, paraphrased, or quoted in your paper. The reference list starts on a separate page at the end of your text and is paginated consecutively in the same style as the rest of the work. It is helpful to prepare your reference list first so that you can accurately cite your sources in text. If you cite only one source, call the list *Reference*.

Format of APA References Page

Center the title *References* at the top of the page. Double-space the whole page, unless specifically told otherwise by your instructor. Arrange sources alphabetically, using the last name of the primary author. Start each entry at the left margin, and indent the second and any subsequent lines 1/2" (five typewriter spaces). Each element of an entry—the author, date, title, and publication information—is separated from the next by a period, followed by one space.

Citing Books and Other Nonperiodicals: General Information

Following are general guidelines. For models of specific kinds of book citations, see the index on page 460.

Author's Name
Put the last name of each author first, followed by a comma and initials for the first and any middle names, even if the names are provided in full in the text you are referencing. Provide this information for up to six authors, separating the names with commas and using an ampersand (&) before the name of the last author. For books with seven or more authors, see the third example.

Publication Date
Immediately after the authors' names, place the publication date in parentheses, followed by a period. For books, provide the year the book was copyrighted.

Title of Book or Part of Book
Book titles are italicized and followed by a period. Capitalize the first word of the title and the first word of the subtitle, if there is one. The only other words that are capitalized are proper nouns. If you need to include additional information, such as the editor's name, the translator's name, the edition number, or the volume number, provide it in parentheses after the title. The period should be placed after the last parenthesis.

Information about the Form of the Work
For nonperiodical works that are not books, place information about the form of the work in brackets after all the title information.

Basic Format for Books

Authors of Books

One author:	Diamond, J.
Two to six authors:	Levitt, S. D., & Dubner, S. J.
Seven or more authors:	Wattenberg, J. D., III, Mendoza, T. A., Murphree, D. C., Tilberg, W. P., Davis, M. L., Dalphin, S. T., et al.
Corporate author:	Justice Research and Statistics Association.

Note: If the author's name is followed by a suffix, such as *Jr., II,* or *III,* include it after a comma.

Publication Dates for Books

Book already published:	(2004).
Book accepted for publication but not yet published:	(in press).
No date available:	(n.d.).

Titles of Books

Title of a book:	*Voluntary simplicity: Toward a way of life that is outwardly simple, inwardly rich* (Rev. ed.).
Title of a chapter in a book:	Civilizations in transition.
Title of an article in an anthology:	What secrets tell.

The Form of the Work

Print:	[Advertisement].
	[Brochure].
Digital media:	[CD].
	[DVD].
	[Motion picture].
	[Videotape].

Publication Information for a Book

Boston: Harvard Common Press.

Washington, DC: National Academy Press.

Albany: State University of New York Press.

Note: Don't list the state if a work is published by a university press that includes the name of the state, such as University of Massachusetts.

Portland, OR: Graphic Arts Center.

Padstow, England: Tabb House.

Note: For cities that are not well known, give the name of the city, the state or province (if known), and the country if not the United States.

Publication Information

You can usually find the publication information on the title page of a book or on the copyright page on the reverse of the title page. Include the following information:

- **City of publication.** If the city is well known (for example, Chicago, New York, or San Francisco), use just the city name, followed by a colon. If the city is not well known or could be confused with another city of the same name, add a comma and the two-letter postal code abbreviation. Follow with a colon.
- **Publisher of the book.** Place the publisher's name after the colon following the city of publication. You can shorten the name and omit unnecessary terms like *Inc., Publishers,* or *Co.* However, provide the full names of associations, corporations, and university presses. Do not omit the word *Books* or *Press* from the publisher's name.
- **Page numbers.** Provide page numbers only if you are citing part of a book, such as a specific chapter or an article in an anthology. (See citation model 8 on page 462.) Use the abbreviation *p.* or *pp.* before the number(s). When you cite inclusive page numbers, always use full numbers: "pp. 762–769" (not "pp. 762–9").

APA References Index: Books and Other Nonperiodicals

1. Book by a single author
2. Book by two to six authors
3. Book by seven or more authors
4. Book by an unknown or anonymous author
5. Book with a corporate or group author
6. Book with an editor
7. Book with a translator
8. Chapter in an edited book or anthology
9. Two or more books by the same author published in the same year
10. Book in a second or subsequent edition
11. Work in more than one volume
12. Government publication
13. Report from a private organization
14. Report available from ERIC
15. Brochure

APA References Models

1. Book by a single author

List the author's last name first, followed by a comma and the initials of the first and any middle names. Then provide the year of publication in parentheses, followed by a period. Italicize the title, capitalizing only the first word of the title and the subtitle and any proper nouns, followed by a period. Then give the city of publication, followed by a colon and the shortened form of the publisher's name.

> Bazerman, C. (2002). *The languages of Edison's light.* Cambridge, MA: MIT Press.

2. Book by two to six authors

Separate the names by commas, and use an ampersand (&) immediately before the last author's name.

> Burawoy, M., Burton, A., Ferguson, A. A., & Fox, K. J. (1991). *Ethnography unbound: Power and resistance in the modern metropolis.* Berkeley: University of California Press.

3. Book by seven or more authors

Write the first six names and then *et al.,* followed by the year in parentheses. Then write the title, followed by the publication information.

> Delay, F., Deville, P., Echenoz, J., Greenlee, S., Mathews, H., Polizzotti, M., et al. (1997). *S: A novel.* Cambridge, MA: Brookline Books.

4. Book by an unknown or anonymous author

Write the title first, followed by any edition. Then include the date in parentheses; the translator, if applicable; and the city of publication and the publisher.

Rhetoric to Herennius. (1964). H. Caplan (Trans.). Cambridge, MA: Harvard University Press.

5. Book with a corporate or group author

Use as the author the name of the group or organization that created the document. When the publisher and the author are the same, use *Author* instead of repeating the group's name.

American Psychiatric Association. (1994). *Diagnostic and statistical manual of mental disorders* (4th ed.). Washington, DC: Author.

6. Book with an editor

Use names of editors as you would those of authors. Identify them as editors by putting *Ed.* or *Eds.* in parentheses after the name(s). **Note:** Use a period after the abbreviation *and* after the parenthesis.

Johnson, M. H. (Ed.). (1993). *Brain development and cognition: A reader.* Cambridge, MA: Blackwell.

7. Book with a translator

Write the name of the translator after the title, in parentheses, followed by a comma and the abbreviation *Trans.* Place a period after the parenthesis. **Note:** Use first and middle initials and then the last name.

Bertolucci, A. (2005). *Winter journey* (N. Benson, Trans.). West Lafayette, IN: Parlor Press.

APA References Index: Books and Other Nonperiodicals

APA References Index: Books and Other Nonperiodicals

8. Chapter in an edited book or anthology

Start the entry with the name(s) of the author(s) of the chapter and the date on which the *entire* work was published. Next, write the title of the chapter and follow with a period. Then write the word *In* followed by the name(s) of the editor(s) of the text, including first and any middle initials and giving the names in normal order. Continue with the abbreviation *Ed.* or *Eds.* in parentheses, a comma, the book or anthology title, page number(s) of the chapter in parentheses, and a period. Close with the publication information.

> LeBon, G. (1997). The crowd: A study of the popular mind. In C. D. Ellis (Ed.), *The investor's anthology: Original ideas from the industry's greatest minds* (pp. 6–12). New York: Wiley.

9. Two or more books by the same author published in the same year

When you use two or more books or other sources by the same author that were published in the same year, use lowercase letters—starting with *a, b,* and *c*—to differentiate them. The letter follows the year. Organize the works alphabetically by title, ignoring any initial article (*A, The, An*). Double-check your in-text citations to make sure you have labeled each source properly.

> Tufte, E. R. (1997a). *The visual display of quantitative information* (2nd ed.). Cheshire, CT: Graphics Press.
>
> Tufte, E. R. (1997b). *Visual explanations: Images and quantities, evidence and narrative.* Cheshire, CT: Graphics Press.

10. Book in a second or subsequent edition

For books in a second or later edition, provide the edition number and *ed.* in parentheses after the title, followed by a period. Use the abbreviation *Rev. ed.* for *Revised edition.*

> Patton, M. Q. (2002). *Qualitative research and evaluation methods* (3rd ed.). Thousand Oaks, CA: Sage.

11. Work in more than one volume

When you use only one volume from a multivolume work, cite the one volume.

Trumbach, R. (1998). *Sex and the gender revolution* (Vol. 1). Chicago: University of Chicago Press.

When you use more than one volume, cite all of the volumes you use.

Pelikan, J. (1975–1991). *The Christian tradition: A history of the development of doctrine* (Vols. 1–5). Chicago: University of Chicago Press.

12. Government publication

If no author is named for a government report, use the name of the sponsoring agency to start your entry. Include the publication number in parentheses after the title of the pamphlet or report, and show the U.S. Government Printing Office (GPO) as the publisher if the document is available from the GPO:

Office of Native American Programs. (1995). *Our home: Achieving the Native American dream of homeownership* (HH 1.6/3: H75/12). Washington, DC: GPO.

APA References Index: Books and Other Nonperiodicals

APA References Index: Books and Other Nonperiodicals

13. Report from a private organization

Use the standard book format. Use the author's name when available; otherwise, use the corporate name as the author. If there is a report or edition number, include it in parentheses immediately after the title:

> National Urban League. (2005). *The state of black America: Prescriptions for change.* New York: Author.
>
> Nierenberg, D. (2005). *Happier meals: Rethinking the global meat industry* (Worldwatch Paper #171). Washington, DC: Worldwatch Institute.

14. Report available from ERIC

Use the standard book format if the report did not originally appear in a journal. Add the ERIC reference number in parentheses.

> Hassel, B., Ziebarth, T., & Steiner, L. (2005). *A state policymaker's guide to alternative authorizers of charter schools* (ECS Issue Brief). Denver: Education Commission of the States. (ERIC Document Reproduction Service No. ED489327)

15. Brochure

After the title of the work, include information on the form of the work in brackets.

> University of South Carolina Office of Student Orientation and Testing Services. (2005). *Parent information 2005* [Brochure]. Columbia: Author.

Basic Format for Periodicals

Journal Articles

Author's last name, first and middle initial. (Year of publication). Article title: Subtitle. *Name of periodical, volume number,* inclusive page numbers.

Articles in Magazines or Newsletters and Papers Presented at Meetings

Author's last name, first and middle initial. (Year of publication, month). Article title: Subtitle. *Name of periodical, volume number,* inclusive page numbers.

Articles in Newspapers or Weekly Magazines

Author's last name, first and middle initial. (Year of publication, month day). Article title: Subtitle. *Name of periodical,* inclusive page numbers preceded by *p.* or *pp.*

Citing Periodicals: General Information

When you cite journal articles, create entries based on the basic format here. Also see citation models 16 and 17 on page 466.

When you cite articles in magazines or newsletters and papers presented at meetings, create entries based on the basic format shown. Also see citation model 19 on page 467.

When you cite articles in newspapers or weekly magazines, create entries based on the basic format given. Also see citation model 20 on page 467.

APA References Index: Periodicals

APA References Models

16. Article in journal with continuous pagination throughout annual volume

Start with the author's last name and then initials, followed by the publication date in parentheses. Titles of articles are never underlined or italicized; capitalize only the first word of the title and the subtitle and any proper nouns. Each important word in the journal name is capitalized, and the journal name *is* italicized, as is the volume number that follows it. Do not use the abbreviation *p.* or *pp.* before the page numbers. The title, volume number, and pages are separated by commas and end with a period. When an article is from a journal that numbers issues consecutively over the course of a year, you do not include the issue number.

Towler, A. J., & Schneider, D. J. (2005). Distinctions among stigmatized groups. *Journal of Applied Social Psychology, 35,* 1–14.

For author variations, see citation models 1 through 5 (pages 460–461) and 9 (page 462).

17. Article in journal that pages each issue separately

When an article is in a journal that paginates each issue separately (each issue starts with page 1), you need to include the issue number. Put it in parentheses immediately after the volume number (do not put a space between them), and do not italicize it.

Miles, L. (2000). Constructing composition: Reproduction and WPA agency in textbook publishing. *Writing Program Administration, 24*(1–2), 27–51.

18. Abstract of journal article

Write the author's name, the date (typically only the year), and the title of the article; then identify it with *[Abstract]*. Give the journal name in italics, and add the page number(s).

> Nespor, M., & Sandler, W. (1999). Prosody in Israeli sign language [Abstract]. *Language and Speech, 42,* 143.

19. Article in magazine

Start with the author's name and the date. If it's a monthy magazine, put the year, a comma, and the month. If it's a weekly or daily publication, put the year, a comma, the month, and the day. Then write the title of the article (without quotation marks or italics) and the magazine name (in italics). Write the volume number. Finish with the page number(s).

> Rosenwald, M. (2006, January). The flu hunter. *Smithsonian, 36*, 36–46.

20. Article in newspaper

Write the author's name, the date (year, month, and day), the title of the article, the newspaper's name (in italics), and the page number(s), preceded by the abbreviation *p.* or *pp.*

> Farrell, E. F. (2005, April 1). Starving for attention. *The Chronicle of Higher Education,* pp. A45–A46.

If no author's name appears, alphabetize by the first word of the title, excluding *A, An,* or *The.* If the page numbers aren't consecutive, give all page numbers, separated by commas: "pp. A2, A5, A7–A8."

APA References Index: Periodicals

APA References Index: Periodicals

21. Letter to the editor

Write the author's name, the date of publication (in parentheses), the title of the letter (if there is one), and *[Letter to the editor]*. Give the name of the journal or newspaper that printed the letter and the page number(s).

> Masterson, G. (2006, February 25). Coyote hunting I [Letter to the editor]. *The Addison Eagle,* p. 4.

22. Review

After the title of the review, in brackets add the words *Review of* and then give the kind of work reviewed—such as book, article, film, or CD—and the title of the work reviewed. Name the publication that printed the review, the volume number (if applicable), and the page number(s).

> Mondragon, T. (2004, March 29). Exposing the myth of the Matrix [Review of the motion picture *The Matrix Reloaded*]. *Contemporary Cinema, 13,* 32–57.

Basic Formats for Digital Sources

Online Periodical

Author's last name, first and middle initials. (Date). Article title: Subtitle. *Name of periodical, volume number,* page numbers. Retrieved month day, year, from URL

Online Nonperiodical

Author's last name, first and middle initials. (Date). *Source title.* Retrieved month day, year, from URL

Note: There is no period after the URL.

Citing Digital Sources: General Information

Include the following information about electronic sources on your References page:

- the name of the document or a description of it
- the date the material was published (or updated) and the last date on which you accessed it
- the address, or URL (uniform resource locator; see page 299). Preferably, provide the URL that links directly to the relevant document and not simply to the journal's home page. If the URL is too long to include on one line, break it before a period or after a slash. Do *not* add any hyphens to URLs. To ensure that your URL is correct, use the copy-and-paste function to move the URL from your browser's address bar to your document. **Note:** Double-check to make sure that the URL leads to the correct source page.

APA References Index: Digital Sources

APA References Models

23. Entire website

Albrecht, K. (2005). *Consumers against supermarket privacy invasion and numbering.* Retrieved April 22, 2005, from http://www.nocards.org

Unless you are referring generally to an entire website, make every effort to provide a URL that links directly to the specific content you are referencing.

If no author is listed (but see the box on page 390), start the entry with the name of the company, organization, or entity that supports the site's content. Or start with the site name if such information cannot be found. Include the date on which the page was written or last updated. Give the date on which you retrieved the material and the URL.

International Council for Caring Communities. (2005). Retrieved April 22, 2005, from http://www.international-iccc.org

24. Journal article that appears in print and electronic formats

When the online version is the same as the print version, use the same format as you would for an article in a journal. (See citation model 16 on page 466.) The only difference is that you place the words *Electronic version* in brackets after the title of the article.

Kensinger, E. A., Krendl, A. C., & Corkin, S. (2005). Memories of an emotional and a nonemotional event: Effects of aging and delay interval [Electronic version]. *Experimental Aging Research, 32,* 23–45.

If the online article is different from the print version—for example, the format is not the same—then you need to add the date on which you accessed the article and its URL.

Viano, M. (1999). *Life Is Beautiful:* Reception, allegory, and Holocaust laughter. *Jewish Social Studies, 5*(3), 47–66. Retrieved February 28, 2006, from http://muse.jhu.edu/demo/jewish_social_studies/v005/5.3viano.html

25. Article in online journal only

For articles published only in online journals, use the same format as in the example above.

Moss, S. A., & Ngu, S. (2006). The relationship between personality and leadership preferences. *Current Research in Social Psychology, 11*(6), 70–91. Retrieved February 28, 2006, from http://www.uiowa.edu/~grpproc/crisp/crisp11_6.pdf

26. Journal article retrieved from electronic database

Many articles are available in electronic databases. They can be accessed through a college library website or other websites and are sometimes in CD-ROM format. When citing these articles, provide the name of the database you used and the date you accessed it.

McArt, E., Shulman, D., & Gajary, E. (1999). Developing an educational workshop on teen depression and suicide: A proactive community intervention. *Child Welfare, 78*(6), 793–806. Retrieved January 3, 2006, from PsycINFO database.

APA References Index: Digital Sources

WriteOnline

APA References Index: Digital Sources

23. Entire website
24. Journal article that appears in print and electronic formats
25. Article in online journal only
26. Journal article retrieved from electronic database
27. Article in online newspaper
28. Article from university or government website
29. Part of an online document
30. Retrievable online posting (discussion group, online forum, electronic mailing list)
31. Email or nonretrievable online posting
32. Computer software
33. Information service

27. Article in online newspaper

For an online version of a newspaper, follow the directions for a print version (see citation model 20 on page 467), and then add the date on which you retrieved it and the full URL.

> Vedantam, S. (2006, March 1). Veterans report mental distress. *The Washington Post*. Retrieved March 1, 2006, from http://www.washingtonpost.com/wp-dyn/content/article/2006/02/28/AR2006022801712.html

28. Article from university or government website

For texts on university websites, write the host's name and the university program or department after the date of retrieval and before the URL. Place a colon between the host information and the URL.

> Felluga, D. (2003). *Introductory guide to critical theory*. Retrieved March 1, 2006, from Purdue University, College of Liberal Arts Website: http://www.cla.purdue.edu/academic/engl/theory/index.html

When you cite a text found on a government-sponsored website, make sure the URL you provide links directly to the search screen for the database.

> Federal Emergency Management Agency. (2003). *A citizen guide to disaster preparedness*. Retrieved March 1, 2006, from http://www.pueblo.gsa.gov/cic_text/family/disaster-guide/disasterguide.htm

29. Part of an online document

Your goal is to help your readers locate your sources, so provide the author's name, the date, and the title of the source and note the header, subheader, or section. Then write the title of the sponsoring organization, entity, or company, if available. Then write *Retrieved* and the date, followed by the full URL.

Hübler, M. (2005). The drama of technological society: Using Kenneth Burke to symbolically explore the technological worldview discovered by Jacques Ellul (header 2). *KB Journal 1*(2). Retrieved January 29, 2006, from http://kbjournal.org/node/60

30. Retrievable online posting (discussion group, online forum, electronic mailing list)

Be careful that any material you take from newsgroups, discussion groups, or online forums has academic value; articles from these sources have usually not been peer reviewed. Also, they must be archived if other researchers are to be able to access them. Many such sources are not archived for long periods of time.

If you are unable to locate the author's name, use the writer's screen name. Cite the exact date of the posting and the subject line of the discussion.

Downs, D. (2002, January 18). Re: inventing FYC. Message posted to WPA-L electronic mailing list, archived at http://lists.asu.edu/cgi-bin/wa?A2=ind0201&L=wpa-l&D=1&O=D&F=&S=&P=26473

APA References Index: Digital Sources

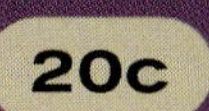

APA References Index: Digital Sources

Citing Visual and Performance Media and Other Sources

When you cite films, TV episodes, music recordings, and other diverse sources, you have the same responsibility as when using print media as sources. Your readers need to be able to locate and verify your sources.

31. Email or nonretrievable online posting

APA says that a personal communication or nonretrievable posting should not be listed in the References, since readers will be unable to locate it. If your instructor asks you to list it anyway, indicate that this was a private communication (such as email) or unrecorded or nonarchived chat. If you do not have the author's name, use the person's screen name.

Wellman, M. (2006, February 13). Tele-intern. Email to the author.

32. Computer software

When you cite information from computer software, provide the name of the author (if you can find it), the date (in parentheses), the name of the software (including the version number, if any), a description of the software (in square brackets), and the location and publisher of the software.

The Movies [PC video game]. (2005). Surrey, UK: Lionhead.

33. Information service

Write the name of the author or editor, if applicable, and the name of the service. Follow with the date in parentheses. Give the place of publication, followed by a colon, and the name of the publisher. Provide the date you retrieved the information, and end with a description of the medium or the URL.

SchoolMatters. (2005). New York: Standard & Poor's. Retrieved January 2, 2006, from http://www.schoolmatters.com

APA References Models

34. Film, videotape, or DVD

For movies, write the producer's and director's names (each followed by that designation in parentheses), the year of release (in parentheses), and the title, in italics. Follow with *[Motion picture]* in brackets, the country of origin, and the studio or production company that made the film.

> Eszterhas, J. (Producer), & Verhoeven, P. (Director). (1995). *Showgirls* [Motion picture]. United States: Universal Pictures.

35. Television show, series, or episode

When you cite a television show, consider whether you are citing a show, an ongoing series, or a particular episode.

A show:

> Shaffer, D. (Director). (2006, March 11). *Best friends: The power of sisterhood* [Television broadcast]. Alexandria, VA: PBS.

A series:

> Chase, D. (Producer). (2004). *The Sopranos* [Television series]. Hollywood, CA: HBO Productions.

An episode from an ongoing series:

> Weiner, M. (Writer), & Bogdanovich, P. (Director). (2004). Sentimental education [Television series episode]. In D. Chase (Producer), *The Sopranos* (Ep. 28). Hollywood, CA: HBO Productions.

APA References Index: Visual and Performance Media and Other Sources

APA References Index: Visual and Performance Media and Other Sources

36. Sound recording

Music:

Keenan, M. J., Jones, A., Carey, D., & Chancellor, J. (2001). The grudge [Recorded by Tool]. On *Lateralus* [CD]. San Diego, CA: Volcano Entertainment.

Other audio:

Wells, J., & House, J. (Speakers). (n.d.). *Sounds of the international phonetic alphabet* [Recorded by the Dept. of Phonetics and Linguistics, University College London]. London: International Phonetic Association.

37. Photograph or figure

Copyright information for photographs and figures you reprint is given in the caption to the figure or photo rather than in the reference list. See in-text citation model 16 on page 456.

38. Unpublished paper presented at meeting or symposium

When you cite an unpublished paper presented at a meeting, symposium, or conference, write the name of the author, the year and month of the gathering at which the paper was presented, the title of the presentation, and the name of the conference. Finally, indicate the location (city and state) of the conference.

Langtree, L., & Briscoe, C. (2001, December). *Calibrating the frontal trajectory of handgun entry wounds.* Paper presented at the meeting of the American Medical Association's 2001 Conference on Adolescent Health, San Francisco, CA.

39. Unpublished interview

When you cite an unpublished interview, you do *not* place an entry in the reference list, unless your instructor wants you to. Instead, insert a parenthetical in-text reference that includes the interviewee's name in regular order, the fact that it was a personal communication, and the precise date of the interview.

> (O. de la Hoya, personal communication, September 22, 2005).

APA References Index: Visual and Performance Media and Other Sources

Note that the information provided in section 19d can be used to format your APA paper using Microsoft Word. You will need to make the following changes to the MLA information to set up your paper in APA style:

1. The amount of space you indent a block quotation from the left margin is 1/2", or five spaces. If any new paragraphs begin in your block quotation, indent the first line an additional 1/2".
2. The page header includes a short version of your paper's title (two or three words), followed by five spaces and the page number.

Jenny Chow, Mira Zaharopoulos, Nancy Huynh, and Xin Xin Wu, psychology students at the University of California, Los Angeles, wrote the paper presented in this section as part of their participation in the Developmental Disabilities Immersion Program, a two-quarter program. Their paper was published in the *UCLA Undergraduate Psychology Journal*.

Parental Risk Factors 1

Running head: CONSTELLATIONS OF PARENTAL RISK FACTORS

A separate running head on the title page is required if you submit your paper for publication. It should be no longer than 50 characters, including punctuation and spaces.

A shortened version of the title is used as a page header on every page, along with the page number.

Constellations of Parental Risk Factors

Associated with Child Maltreatment

Jenny Chow, Mira Zaharopoulos,

Nancy Huynh, and Xin Xin Wu

University of California, Los Angeles

Advisor: Alexander Tymchuk, Ph.D.

The title and your name are typed, double-spaced, in the upper half of the page.

Abstract

Concern is widespread over the ability of parents with disabilities to care adequately for their children. The current study extends research previously conducted by Tymchuk, in the UCLA Parent/Child Health & Wellness Project. Data were collected on 261 cognitively impaired parents, with demographic characteristics included for determining health and safety knowledge and skills at the time of entry into the project. These data were analyzed in an attempt to identify parental characteristics that increase child risk for maltreatment. Cumulative risk indices within the three categories of family, parent, and child were correlated with performance variables relating to parents' medication usage, health and safety understanding, reading level, and the child's Alpern Boll score. The three cumulative risk indices were significantly correlated with low parental reading recognition and comprehension, which suggests that parents' reading abilities can be an important factor in providing adequate childcare.

Notice that the title of the research report is not printed on the Abstract page. The page does include the page header, with the page number 2, however.

The APA abstract accurately summarizes the content of the research report. Note that the abstract cannot be used to comment on the study; instead, it describes the research report.

The APA abstract must be concise: it should be no longer than 120 words. In this case, the students were following the guidelines of the journal to which they submitted their research report, the *UCLA Undergraduate Psychology Journal,* which requires that an abstract be fewer than 150 words.

The APA abstract must make sense on its own.

The introduction to a research report in psychology (here, paragraphs 1 through 6) introduces the problem, summarizes any background needed to understand the problem, and ends with a brief description of how the report addresses the problem.

Reference to a 2004 work with three authors. If the three authors had been named in the writer's sentence rather than in the parentheses, the word *and* would have been written out: "Ethier, Couture, and Lacharite (2004)." See in-text citation model 5 on page 450.

To find the complete publication information, the reader will examine the References list on page 489 for the entry that starts with "Tymchuk." See in-text citation model 2 on page 449.

Parental Risk Factors 3

Constellations of Parental Risk Factors

Associated with Child Maltreatment

Both laypersons and professionals have expressed concern that children of parents with cognitive disabilities may be more endangered than their counterparts without such disabled parents. Research has linked parental disability with heightened risk for child abuse and neglect (James, 2004). Because of this heightened risk, children of parents with disabilities frequently come to the attention of child protection services. However, research has also indicated it is not simply degree of intelligence that is a predictor of parental deficiency. It has been demonstrated that impoverished parents, and parents presumed to be mentally retarded, possess surprisingly similar—albeit limited—knowledge and skills concerning child healthcare and safety.

The best predictor for child safety is the adequacy of the parent's support system, regardless of parental knowledge and skill (Tymchuk, 1992). Further work has outlined risk factors that potentially increase probabilities of abuse and neglect. Such factors include (1) impoverished and chaotic living conditions, (2) the number of children in the household, (3) single parent status, and (4) the mother's history, such as foster home placement, reported sexual abuse, or status as a runaway (Ethier, Couture, & Lacharite, 2004).

These data suggest many factors affect parents' abilities in tending to the health and safety needs of their children across the development span. In an effort to reduce child maltreatment, various interventions have been implemented for enabling parents to provide more adequate care for their children. Recent empirical evidence has shown that tailoring educational intervention curricula to meet the needs of parents with cognitive disabilities can help these parents provide adequate health and safety care (Tymchuk, 1998).

Randomized clinical trials involving persons with cognitive disabilities exercised two particular interventions. A number of parenting assessment instruments were developed and validated in conjunction with these interventions. The assessment instruments were created both to study possible differential effects of the interventions and to create a systematic parenting approach based on practicability of suggested and analyzed parenting techniques (Tymchuk, 1992). The UCLA Parent/Child Health & Wellness Project provided support and education to low-income parents with mild cognitive limitations. The Project's intent was to increase parental awareness of both parental and children's health and safety, thereby reducing risks of child neglect and abuse. People with special learning needs often have substantial problems in reading recognition and comprehension, and in recalling complex written and spoken information. Tymchuk (1998) has demonstrated that tailoring instruction materials to parents' reading and processing level can help remedy learning needs. Simplifying language and utilizing illustrations further facilitate understanding.

In earlier work, Tymchuk and Andron (1992) systematically developed and validated measures designed to determine levels of parental knowledge and skill. Tymchuk, Lang, Dolyniuk, Berney-Ficklin, and Spitz (1999) also developed and validated health and safety instructional packages containing curriculum and parent-use materials. Based on work in which the parents' reading recognition and comprehension grade levels and learning styles were determined, the contents of these packages were presented in ways that would optimize parental learning. This accessible presentation style consisted of using (1) a large font, (2) uncluttered pages presenting single concepts, (3) language geared toward 5th-grade reading level, and (4) colored illustrations.

The current study extends the earlier project's pursuit of certain associative characteristics—namely, those characteristics that correlate inadequate self and

For works with two to five authors, cite all the authors' names on first mention. See in-text citation models 4 and 5 on page 450.

The Methods section tells readers how the research was conducted so that they can evaluate the method and, in some cases, replicate the research. Typically, this section is divided into subsections with headings: "Participants" (or "Subjects"), "Methods" (or "Materials" or "Apparatus"), and "Procedure" (or "Design and Procedure").

child healthcare with health and safety knowledge and skills. It was hypothesized that a constellation of risk factors would be significantly associated with inadequate healthcare knowledge. Specifically, it was hypothesized that parental economic impoverishment, fewer years of education than social norms, and limited opportunities for parents to participate in society would be associated with lower reading and comprehension levels and failure to recognize dangers in and around the home.

Methods

Participants

The UCLA Parent/Child Health & Wellness Project targeted parents from communities in Los Angeles and Ventura counties. These communities were notable for their high rates of economic impoverishment, reported crime, teen pregnancy, and physical injuries. Despite such conditions, families in these areas enjoyed few social services. Most parents were referred by community service agencies as being at high risk for child maltreatment and, as a result, for being declared unfit parents in danger of losing custody of their children. Such parents were primarily low-income, single Latina mothers, with a mean age of 19 years, who were assessed as having cognitive disabilities. Data analyzed in the present study derived from 261 such cognitively disabled parents who had children with average intelligence.

Materials

The present investigation utilized data obtained during pretesting in the Wellness Project. Investigative tools included those developed for the Wellness Project, as well as previously standardized techniques. Assessment approaches included (1) the Decoding Skills Test (DST), a standardized measure that was used to establish baseline reading recognition and comprehension levels of the parent (Richardson & DiBenedetto, 2004); (2) the Alpern Boll Developmental Profile, used for determining children's developmental performance in relation to IQ equivalency with parents (Malhi & Singhi, 2003); (3) the UCLA Parenting Reading Recognition List, in which the parent was asked to pronounce words from a word list organized with varying levels of difficulty; (4) the UCLA Parenting Reading Comprehension List, in which the parent was asked to read a short passage and answer questions pertaining to the reading; (5) the Home Danger and Safety Precaution Observation Scale, in which a health educator utilized a checklist to record the presence of any situation that could endanger the child or parent and the presence of any behavior or procedure that could prevent the occurrence of an accident; and (6) the Illustrated Home Danger and Safety Precaution Checklist, in which parents identified illustrated dangers in six home areas and suggested suitable precautions for each specified danger. The health educator determined suitability of parents' responses based on a previously devised checklist of dangers and precautions. Materials used for instructional purposes were matched to the participants' level of reading comprehension and were presented in a large font with headings and paragraphs. Illustrations were shown along with text to facilitate understanding. An illustrated Home Safety/Danger scale depicted possible dangers found in six areas in and around the home.

Design and Procedure

The Wellness study administered a battery of tests designed to determine parental demographic and background information, IQ, reading recognition and comprehension, and health and safety knowledge and skills. This information provided the basis for determining teaching materials for meeting the parent's specific learning needs. Guided by the work of Carta et al. (2001), cumulative risk indices were created using the pretest data from the previous Wellness study, in order to identify parental risk factors for child mistreatment. In order to ensure uniform scoring across demographic variables, all demographic variables were

Reference to a 2001 work with six authors. Only the first author's name is given, followed by *et al.*, which means "and others." See in-text citation model 6 on page 451.

Every table and every figure (charts, graphs, diagrams, photos) used to provide additional information must be referred to in the report. In this report, the tables are all collected in an appendix after the References page. For papers not being submitted to journals, an instructor might prefer to have tables and figures placed closer to where they are referred to in the text.

converted to values of 0 = no risk and 1 = risk. For instance, families with income levels below $19,000 were identified as at risk, and received a value of 1. Parents whose education level did not exceed high school were identified as at risk, and received a value of 1. Children who had never been sexually or physically abused were considered to be without risk, and received a value of 0. For the purpose of data reduction and analytical ease, composite variables were created from the original demographic variables. These composite variables were then grouped into three cumulative risk indices: (1) Cumulative Risk–Family—based on the composite family-level variables of parental income, number of children in the home, and living arrangements (single, married, living with guardian, etc.); (2) Cumulative Risk–Parent—based on the composite parent-level variables of parental abuse (the parents themselves were victims of abuse), parent education, parent health, parent daily activities (hobbies, exercise routine, social life, etc.), parent medical history, and prenatal risks (absence of prenatal healthcare); and (3) Cumulative Risk–Child—based on child disability and the composite child-level variables of child abuse (child is the victim of abuse) and child removal from the home (see Table 1). In addition, composite variables were also created from the original performance variables. In order to ensure uniform scoring across performance variables, all performance points were converted to scores ranging from 1 to 3. Points of 50 and below were assigned a score of 1. Points ranging from 51 to 75 received a score of 2. Points ranging from 76 to 100 received a score of 3. These performance composites included (1) parental medication usage (parent's understanding of prescription medication instructions and dosage), (2) reading recognition and comprehension, reading recognition total of Forms 1 and 2 (parent's identification of words from word lists Forms 1 and 2), DST total and grade equivalent, reading IQ of 85 or below, and (3) knowledge of illustrated home dangers and precautions (see Table 2). The three cumulative risk composites were correlated with the performance composites to test the hypothesis that greater cumulative risk in the above areas would be significantly associated with lower parental performance in reading and comprehension and inadequate healthcare knowledge. In order to determine the degree to which these risk indices were related to performance outcome, the Bonferroni correction for multiple correlations was employed, yielding calculated correlations between the data sets.

Results

Significant relationships were obtained between each of the cumulative risk indices and the performance composites. The relationships found are displayed in Table 3.

At the family level, greater cumulative risk is significantly associated with lower knowledge of proper medication usage ($r = -.212$, $p < .05$), lower parental reading scores ($r = -.201$, $p < .05$), and lower DST grade equivalent scores ($r = -.212$, $p < .05$).

At the parent level, greater cumulative risk is associated with lower levels of reading recognition and comprehension with respect to grade level ($r = .190$, $p < .05$), lower reading recognition with respect to age ($r = .278$, $p < .01$), lower reading comprehension ($r = -.260$, $p < .01$), lower Infant/Young Child Development scores ($r = -.242$, $p < .01$), lower reading recognition Forms 1 and 2 ($r = -.225$, $p < .01$), lower DST reading recognition and comprehension ($r = -.238$, $p < .01$), lower DST grade equivalent scores ($r = -.253$, $p < .01$), and reading recognition IQ of 85 or below ($r = .260$, $p < .05$).

At the child level, greater cumulative risk is associated with parental IQ of 70 or below ($r = .281$, $p < .05$). The child cumulative risk variable yielded surprising findings, indicating that greater child cumulative risk is associated with higher parental knowledge of illustrated dangers and precautions ($r = .307$, $p < .05$) and higher Child Alpern Boll IQ ($r = .268$, $p < .05$).

The Results section provides the data and statistical analysis needed to support the conclusions. If tables or figures are used to display information, be sure to discuss the most important information they reveal in your text also; don't expect readers to interpret them entirely on their own.

The Discussion section begins with a statement about whether the researchers' hypotheses were supported by the data analyzed. The Discussion should evaluate the research study and its results, and it should note any limitations of the study. This section can also refer to the larger issues at stake and further applications of the research.

Of the three cumulative risk indices, parent-level risk factors were most often associated with poor performance on reading recognition and comprehension tasks.

Discussion

Our hypotheses were partially supported in the present study. The hypothesis that cumulative risk variables would be associated with lower parental reading and comprehension levels was supported. Parent and family cumulative risk variables were significantly associated with lower parental reading and comprehension levels. Our hypothesis that parent and family risk factors would be directly associated with parental knowledge of health and safety was not upheld. There were nonsignificant correlations between the family and parent cumulative risk indices and the Illustrated Dangers and Precautions Checklist. Thus, the current study failed to find evidence that the family and parent cumulative risk indices were related to home dangers and precautions. While it is surprising that family and parent risk factors were not directly associated with recognition of home dangers and precautions, this suggests there may be other moderating variables that link risk factors with knowledge of health and safety, an important finding that should be explored in future research.

Each of the patterns of findings within the cumulative risk indices has significant implications. At the family level, greater cumulative risk is significantly associated with lower knowledge of proper medication usage. The correlation obtained between inadequacy of medical knowledge and increased family-level risk indicates a relationship that should be further explored. It may be that designing and implementing interventions that enhance and maintain medical knowledge could help to reduce maltreatment risk.

At the parent level, greater cumulative risk is generally associated with lower reading and comprehension levels. Greater cumulative risk is associated with lower levels of reading recognition and comprehension with respect to grade level, lower reading recognition with respect to age, lower reading comprehension, lower DST reading recognition and comprehension, reading IQ of 85 or below, and lower Infant/Young Child Development scores. Although the correlation was not significant between parent-level risk and the safety knowledge variable, it is known that reading and comprehension are important factors in dispensing safety knowledge. Without such skills, the child becomes at increased risk of maltreatment. This finding suggests that adequate reading recognition and comprehension are thus crucial, because the printed word continues as the favored medium for providing information about medicines, drugs, and other products. Tailoring health and safety materials to meet the needs of parents with poor reading skills could help to address this problem in communication. In addition, intervention to foster better reading skills might in turn improve parental knowledge and understanding of health and safety. Reading recognition and comprehension skills would therefore appear to be of priority for setters of social policies.

At the child level, greater cumulative risk is associated with parental IQ of 70 or below. Contrary to expectations, it was found that lower risk in the Child Risk index was linked to lower parental knowledge of illustrated dangers and precautions, and lower IQ scores. This unusual finding could be related to an artifact of measurement error.

Despite the significance of the present study, this study had several limitations. One limitation is related to the use of the original data set, which contained many variables. The large number of correlations examined can increase the probability of chance impacting findings. However, utilizing a Bonferroni correction for multiple correlations reduces this probability. A second possible limitation of the study is the correlational approach taken. This is because only relationships between the variables could be ascertained, without the possibility of inferring causation. Further work, using the posttest results obtained on the knowledge and

Discussion of the limitations of the study

Discussion of the relevance and applications of the study results

skill measures, is underway so as to facilitate the ability to infer causation regarding the mechanisms that link parent and family risk factors to performance outcomes.

Despite limitations, the present study embodies some important strengths. This population has rarely been studied; given the dearth of data regarding this population, the present study addresses a gap in previous research. The present results highlight the importance of identifying risk factors associated with substandard health and safety knowledge for parents with cognitive difficulties. These results help illuminate areas for further understanding, thereby opening the door for future study. These findings also suggest significant clinical relevance. Establishing risk of parental maltreatment of children is a primary task for all child-protective agencies. Yet, there are few empirically derived risk indices in this field of study. The current investigation's data will therefore assist in such work. Developing cumulative risk indices and identifying child maltreatment risk factors supplement a curriculum for addressing the educational needs of parents with mild cognitive impairments. These findings may therefore aid in creating and maintaining parental assistance programs for improved childcare, thereby reducing risks of child abuse and neglect.

References

Carta, J. J., Atwater, J. B., Greenwood, C. R., McConnell, S. R., McEvoy, M. A., & Williams, R. (2001). Effects of cumulative prenatal substance exposure and environmental risks on children's developmental trajectories. *Journal of Clinical Child Psychology, 30*, 327–337.

Ethier, L. S., Couture, G., & Lacharite, C. (2004). Risk factors associated with the chronicity of high potential for child abuse and neglect. *Journal of Family Violence, 19*(12), 13–24.

James, H. (2004). Promoting effective working with parents with learning disabilities. *Child Abuse Review, 13*, 31–41.

Malhi, P., & Singhi, P. (2003, May). Reply [Letter to the editor]. *Indian Pediatrics, 40,* 441–442.

Richardson, E., & DiBenedetto, B. (2004, January). (WPS-3) Decoding Skills Test. Retrieved May 25, 2005, from Slosson Educational Publications Website: http://www.slosson.com/item98689.ctlg

Tymchuk, A. J. (1992). Predicting adequacy of parenting by people with mental retardation. *Child Abuse and Neglect, 16,* 165–178.

Tymchuk, A. J. (1998). The importance of matching educational interventions to parent needs in child maltreatment: Issues, methods, and recommendations. In J. R. Lutzker (Ed.), *Handbook of child abuse research and treatment* (pp. 421–428). New York: Plenum Press.

Tymchuk, A. J., & Andron, L. (1992). Project parenting: Child interactional training with mothers who are mentally handicapped. *Mental Handicap Research, 5*(1), 5–32.

Tymchuk, A. J., Lang, C. M., Dolyniuk, C. A., Berney-Ficklin, K., & Spitz, R. (1999). The Home Inventory of Dangers and Safety Precautions—2: Addressing critical needs for prescriptive assessment devices in child maltreatment and in healthcare. *Child Abuse and Neglect, 23*, 1–14.

The References list starts on a new page. It includes all sources quoted, paraphrased, and summarized. See page 457 for general formatting guidelines.

Article from a journal with annual pagination. See citation model 16 on page 466.

Article from a journal with issue pagination. See citation model 17 on page 466.

Letter to the editor published in a journal. See citation model 21 on page 468 for a letter to the editor published in a newspaper.

Two entries by a single author are organized by date. The work that was published first is placed first in the references.

When several entries begin with the same author's name (as in the case of the articles by Tymchuk), those that are by that author alone precede any by the author and other writers. Entries that list the same first author but different additional authors are organized alphabetically by the second author's name (Andron before Lang).

Appendixes are used to provide detailed information that would be excessive in the body of the report. Here, the authors used an appendix to provide all the information they used to analyze the relationships between the cumulative risk indices (listed in Table 1) and the performance composite (Table 2). The results are shown in Table 3.

When there is a single appendix, it is labeled *Appendix*. If there are several appendixes, they are given letters to show the order in which they are mentioned in the paper: *Appendix A, Appendix B*. When an appendix includes only one table, the table doesn't need a separate title; it can be referred to by the appendix label. However, if several tables are in a single appendix, as in this paper, each table also needs to be numbered.

Appendix

Table 1

Cumulative Risk Indices: Family/Parent/Child

All composite variables listed below were derived from the original demographic variables in the UCLA Parent/Child Health & Wellness Project.

FAMILY (0=no risk, 1=risk)	PARENT (0=no risk, 1=risk)	CHILD (0=no risk, 1=risk)
Income: family yearly income, sources of income **Number of Children:** number of children in the home, number of children belonging to the parent **Living Arrangements:** where parent lives, with whom, parent's happiness regarding living arrangement	**Education:** parent's highest level of education attained, parent ever had special education, parent's previous job activity, parent's primary language, parent born and raised in the US **Activities:** parent participates in fun/relaxing activities, parent exercises, parent's current job activity, parent ever been incarcerated, parent makes decisions regarding the future **Health:** parent has disability (cognitive/physical), parent smokes, parent drinks alcohol, parent wears glasses, parent wears hearing aid, parent had/plans to have surgery, parent unfit, parent depressed, parent stressed, parent had any major illnesses **Parent Abuse:** parent ever been sexually abused/physically abused **Medical History:** parent has taken rx, parent has own doctor, parent has own health insurance, parent makes health decisions, parent takes medications **Prenatal Risk:** parent's current age, parent's age when pregnant with index child, presence of prenatal care, location of prenatal care	**Removal from Home:** child ever been removed from home, length of time child was removed from home **Child Abuse:** child ever been sexually abused/physically abused ***Child Disability:** child has a cognitive/physical disability

* Not a composite variable

Table 2

Performance Composite

All composite variables listed below were derived from the original performance variables in the UCLA Parent/Child Health & Wellness Project.

PARENT	CHILD
Medication Usage: parent's demonstrated knowledge of prescription medication and safe medication usage	***Infant/Young Child Development Score:** child's performance on developmental tasks
Reading Total: parent's performance scores on reading recognition Forms 1 and 2	
Reading Recognition and Comprehension: performance scores indicate parent is 2 grade levels behind in reading recognition and comprehension	
DST Reading Total: parent's DST reading recognition scores and DST reading comprehension scores	
DST Grade Equivalent: parent's DST reading recognition grade equivalent and DST comprehension grade equivalent	
Reading IQ 85 or Below: reading recognition performance scores indicate parent's IQ is 85 or below	
Illustrated Dangers and Precautions: parent's demonstrated knowledge of illustrated dangers and precautions (pretest scores)	
***IQ 70 or Below:** parent's IQ is 70 or below	
***Parental Age and Reading Recognition:** parent's reading recognition performance with respect to age	

* Not composite variables

Table 3

Cumulative Risk Indices Correlations (Risk Indices with Performance Composites)

Cumulative Risk Indices	Parents who are 2 grade levels below in reading recognition & comp	Parent age & reading recognition	Reading Comprehension	IQ 70	Child Alpern Boll IQ	Infant/Young Child Development
Family	0.103	0.142	−0.020	0.063	0.057	−0.155
Parent	0.190*	0.278**	−0.260**	0.203*	0.123	−0.242**
Child	0.106	0.216	−0.201	0.281*	0.268*	−0.164

*Correlations significant at .05 level
**Correlations significant at .01 level

Cumulative Risk Indices	Reading Recognition Forms 1 and 2	Medication	DST reading recognition and comprehension total	DST grade equivalent	Reading Recognition IQ 85 or below	Illustrated Dangers and Precautions
Family	−0.092	−0.212*	−0.201*	−0.212*	0.039	−0.056
Parent	−0.225**	−0.156	−0.238**	−0.253**	0.260*	0.056
Child	−0.153	−0.168	−0.110	−0.113	0.164	0.307*

*Correlations significant at .05 level
**Correlations significant at .01 level

21 CITING SOURCES IN CMS STYLE

CMS INDEXES

The Chicago Manual of Style (CMS), 15th edition, published by The University of Chicago Press, provides two documentation methods, one more suited to the humanities and the other more suited to the sciences. The sciences style is an author-date style similar to the APA style. If you are writing in the sciences, either use the APA style (◀ Chapter 20) or consult *The Chicago Manual of Style*. This chapter focuses on the CMS style more likely to be used in the arts, history, and literature.

In the CMS notes system, you can choose to use (1) concise footnotes or endnotes that relate to a complete bibliography of works cited in your paper or (2) detailed endnotes or footnotes that contain all the necessary bibliographic information, in which case a bibliography is optional. CMS recommends the first choice because it requires less duplication of information.

To use the recommended CMS style (option 1), place a superscript (raised) number immediately after the paraphrased, summarized, or quoted material you are citing:

> Hilary Siebert writes, "Short fiction as a genre is rapidly approaching the point at which its consumption is equal to its production."[1]

Then, either as a footnote at the bottom of the same page as the citation or as an endnote at the end of the document, provide concise bibliographic information, identified by the same number:

1. Siebert, "Be Careful What You Wish For," 213.

The first line of the note is indented one tab key (five spaces). The relevant number, not raised and in the same font size as the rest of the note, begins the entry. It is followed by a period. The source information follows.

The bibliography entry includes all necessary information:

Siebert, Hilary. "Be Careful What You Wish For: Short Stories and Consumer Economics." *Studies in Short Fiction* 36 (2000): 213–17.

In all CMS notes, the major elements—author's name, title of work, and publication facts—are separated by commas, *not* periods. The authors' names are given in normal order. All major words in book and article titles and in journal names are capitalized. Only the page numbers that relate directly to the information you are citing are given.

Detailed Notes

If you use detailed notes in your project, you do not need a separate bibliography. The first reference to a source, however, must be a detailed note. In second and subsequent notes, you can use a shortened version. Or, if the information is identical to that in the entry immediately preceding it or the same except for the page number, you can use the term *Ibid.*, which means "in the same place." If the page number differs from note to note, you add the page number after *Ibid.*

Don't use so many *Ibid.*'s in a row that your readers lose track of the original reference. If you draw heavily on one source, use the author's name in the text now and then to keep readers oriented or use a concise version of the note to ensure that they understand which source provided particular information.

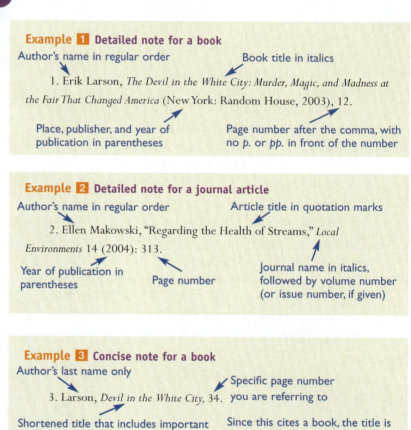

Example 1 Detailed note for a book

Author's name in regular order

Book title in italics

1. Erik Larson, *The Devil in the White City: Murder, Magic, and Madness at the Fair That Changed America* (New York: Random House, 2003), 12.

Place, publisher, and year of publication in parentheses

Page number after the comma, with no *p.* or *pp.* in front of the number

Example 2 Detailed note for a journal article

Author's name in regular order

Article title in quotation marks

2. Ellen Makowski, "Regarding the Health of Streams," *Local Environments* 14 (2004): 313.

Year of publication in parentheses

Page number

Journal name in italics, followed by volume number (or issue number, if given)

Example 3 Concise note for a book

Author's last name only

Specific page number you are referring to

3. Larson, *Devil in the White City,* 34.

Shortened title that includes important words of the main title

Since this cites a book, the title is in italics. For an article title, use quotation marks instead.

Example 4 Note with *Ibid.*

The word *Ibid.* is in regular type.

4. Ibid., 35.

A period follows *Ibid.*

A comma separates *Ibid.* and the page number.

Sample Footnotes

1. Kenneth Clark, *What Is Civilization?* (New York: Random House, 1981), 212.

2. Patrick Hartwell, "Grammar, Grammars, and the Teaching of Grammar," *College English* 47.2 (1985): 105.

3. Jane Blacque, "College Admissions and the New SAT," *Chronicle of Higher Education,* April 12, 2004, 12.

4. Clark, *What Is Civilization?,* 215.

5. Ibid.

6. "Representing College Life," in *Film Encyclopedia: The Most Comprehensive Encyclopedia of American Cinema in a Single Volume,* 4th ed., ed. Ephraim Katz, Fred Klein, and Ronald Dean Nolen (New York: HarperInformation, 2001), 192.

Concise Notes

If you choose to use concise notes in your project and a bibliography at the end, your footnotes or endnotes will look like the concise note in Example 3.

Whether you use concise notes or detailed notes, you can place them at the bottom (foot) of the page on which they are referred to (footnotes) or on a separate page at the end of the project (endnotes).

Footnotes and Endnotes

Footnotes are placed at the bottom of the page on which the source is cited. They may continue to the bottom of the next page if they are long. Double-space within and between footnotes.

Endnotes are placed on a separate page entitled *Notes* at the end of your project. Center the title 2" from the top of the page. List entries in numerical order as they appear in the text. Indent each entry five spaces (one tab space), write the relevant number, followed by a period, and then give the bibliographic information. Each line after the first one in an entry starts at the left margin. Double-space the entire list, both within and between endnotes.

See page 521 for an example of endnotes.

Author's Name
Entries are arranged alphabetically by the first author's last name, followed by the first name or initials. When there is no author name, start the entry with the name of the editor, translator, or compiler of the text.

Title
Titles of books and journals are italicized; titles of articles, chapters, short stories, and other short works are put in quotation marks. Capitalize all the major words in the titles of books, articles, and journal names. Use the same format when citing electronic material.

Publication Information
Provide the name of the city where the book was published, the name of the publisher, and the date of publication. You can omit abbreviations such as *Inc., Ltd., Co.,* and *& Co.* Do not omit the word *Press* when citing university presses.

Date of Publication
The year of publication is provided after the name of the publisher (for books) or after the name of the journal (for scholarly journals).

Format for CMS Bibliography

Authors

One author	Gore, Al.
Two to ten authors	Tucker, Robert W., and David C. Hendrickson.
More than ten authors	Jones, Kim, Ann Hertling, Scott C. Smith, Linda Conley, David Larson, Jim Karst, Pat Lynes, et al.
Same author as previous entry	———.

Titles

Book	*The Year of Magical Thinking*
Article	"Alternative Male Mating Strategies Are Intuitive to Women"

Publication information

New York: Harry N. Abrams

Lawrence: University Press of Kansas

Durham, NC: Duke University Press

- The place of publication is usually the first one listed on the title page or copyright page.
- For major cities and cities that wouldn't be confused with others, no state or country name is included. For example, since the name of the publisher in the second example above includes the name of the state, the state isn't needed after the city.
- However, if the state is not part of the university press's name, include the abbreviation for the state after the name of the city.

Date of publication

Book	Hargett, James M. *Stairway to Heaven: A Journey to the Summit of Mount Emei*. Albany: State University of New York Press, 2006.
Article	Harman, Heather. "Redefining *Ars Moriendi* in J. R. R. Tolkien's *The Lord of the Rings*." *The Oswald Review* 7 (Fall 2005): 47–60.

Sample Bibliography

Bibliography

Conklin, James. "The Theory of Sovereign Debt and Spain under Philip II." *Journal of Political Economy* 106 (June 1998): 483–513.

MacCaffrey, Wallace T. *Elizabeth I: War and Politics, 1588–1603.* Princeton, NJ: Princeton University Press, 1992.

McGurk, John. *The Tudor Monarchies, 1485–1603.* Cambridge: Cambridge University Press, 1999.

———. *The Elizabethan Conquest of Ireland: The 1590s Crisis.* Manchester, UK: Manchester University Press, 1997.

Nolan, John S. "The Militarization of the Elizabethan State." *Journal of Military History* 58 (July 1994): 391–420.

Shakespeare, William. *Henry IV,* Part I, 1598/1599. *William Shakespeare Literature.* 2003. http://www.shakespeare-literature.com.

Smith, Lacey Baldwin. *Elizabeth Tudor: Portrait of a Queen.* Boston: Little, Brown, 1975.

Wernham, R. B. *After the Armada.* Oxford: Oxford University Press, 1984.

Formatting
The word *Bibliography* is centered at the top of the page. The entire list is double-spaced.

Page Numbers
Do *not* give page numbers for books or popular magazines in the bibliography. For scholarly journals, provide the page numbers for the entire journal article. For electronic source material, for which page numbers are often unavailable, try to provide information such as a subhead or a paragraph number that would help your reader locate your exact source.

Electronic Source Information
When citing Internet sources, provide the URL. If you are citing other electronic sources, indicate the type—for example, *DVD* or *CD-ROM.*

The models illustrate the formats you would use for footnotes or endnotes and for entries in the bibliography. Remember that you must have a bibliography only if you use concise notes. With detailed notes, the bibliography is optional.

CMS Books Index

CMS Citation Models

1. Book with one author or editor

Note: For the general format, see Example 1 on page 494.

1. Van Burnham, *Supercade: A Visual History of the Videogame Age, 1971–1984* (Cambridge, MA: MIT Press, 2001), 25.

Bibliography: For the general format, see page 496.

Burnham, Van. *Supercade: A Visual History of the Videogame Age, 1971–1984.* Cambridge, MA: MIT Press, 2001.

2. Book with no (or an anonymous) author

Note:

2. *Jurisprudence and Individualism* (New York: Anchor Books, 1985), 63.

Bibliography:

Jurisprudence and Individualism. New York: Anchor Books, 1985.

3. Book with two or three authors or editors

Note: Do not use commas to separate the names of the authors in a note if there are only two of them; just use *and.*

3. Ellen Lupton and J. Abbott Miller, *Design | Writing | Research: Writing on Graphic Design* (New York: Princeton Architectural Press, 1996), 87.

Bibliography:

Lupton, Ellen, and J. Abbott Miller. *Design | Writing | Research: Writing on Graphic Design.* New York: Princeton Architectural Press, 1996.

4. Book with four to ten authors or editors

Note: Rather than list all the editors or authors in the note, write *et al.* or *and others* after the first editor or author. When there are multiple editors, write *eds.* after the last editor.

4. Marla Hamburg Kennedy and others, eds., *Looking at Los Angeles* (New York: Metropolis Books, 2005), 22.

Bibliography: Do list all authors or editors (up to ten) in the bibliography. When there are eleven or more authors, CMS recommends citing the first seven by name in the bibliography, followed by *et al.*

Kennedy, Marla Hamburg, Ben Stiller, David L. Ulin, Jane Brown, and Craig Krull, eds. *Looking at Los Angeles.* New York: Metropolis Books, 2005.

CMS Books Index

CMS Books Index

5. Book with a group or corporate author

Note:

5. National Geographic, *National Geographic Visual History of the World* (Hanover, PA: National Geographic Society, 2005), 16.

Bibliography:

National Geographic. *National Geographic Visual History of the World.* Hanover, PA: National Geographic Society, 2005.

6. Book with a translator

Note:

6. Paulo Freire, *Pedagogy of the Oppressed,* 30th anniv. ed., trans. Myra Bergman Ramos (New York: Continuum Press, 2000), 381.

Bibliography:

Freire, Paulo. *Pedagogy of the Oppressed.* 30th anniv. ed. Translated by Myra Bergman Ramos. New York: Continuum Press, 2000.

7. Second and subsequent editions

Note:

7. Jane Goodall, *My Life with the Chimpanzees,* rev. ed. (New York: Aladdin Books, 1996), 299.

Bibliography:

Goodall, Jane. *My Life with the Chimpanzees.* Rev. ed. New York: Aladdin Books, 1996.

8. Book in more than one volume

Note:

8. Sigmund Freud, *Collected Papers,* vol. 1, trans. Joan Riviere (London: Hogarth Press, 1950), 35.

Bibliography:

Freud, Sigmund. *Collected Papers.* Vol. 1. Translated by Joan Riviere. London: Hogarth Press, 1950.

9. Book in a series

Note:

9. Michael Carter, *Where Writing Begins: A Postmodern Reconstruction,* Rhetorical Philosophy and Theory Series (Carbondale: Southern Illinois University Press, 2003), 4.

Bibliography:

Carter, Michael. *Where Writing Begins: A Postmodern Reconstruction.* Rhetorical Philosophy and Theory Series. Carbondale: Southern Illinois University Press, 2003.

CMS Books Index

CMS Books Index

10. Chapter from an edited book or anthology

Note:

10. Heidi Julavits, "The Miniaturists," in *McSweeney's Enchanted Chamber of Astonishing Stories,* ed. Michael Chabon, 129–53 (New York: Vintage Books, 2004), 144.

Bibliography:

Julavits, Heidi. "The Miniaturists." In *McSweeney's Enchanted Chamber of Astonishing Stories,* edited by Michael Chabon, 129–53. New York: Vintage Books, 2004.

11. Article in a reference book

Note: Citations to general encyclopedias and dictionaries are usually given in notes only. Include the title and edition number. If the work is organized alphabetically, provide the article title after the abbreviation *s.v.,* which means "under the word."

11. *World Book Encyclopedia,* 2006 ed., s.v. "Olympic Games."

For more specialized reference books, you may want to include full publication information and have a bibliography entry.

11. *The Oxford Companion to the English Language,* ed. Tom MacArthur (Oxford: Oxford University Press, 1992), s.v. "Idiom."

Bibliography:

The Oxford Companion to the English Language. Edited by Tom MacArthur. Oxford: Oxford University Press, 1992.

12. Sacred work

Note:

12. The Upanishads, trans. Eknath Easwaran (Tomales, CA: Blue Mountain Center of Meditation, 1987), 241.

Bibliography:

The Upanishads. Translated by Eknath Easwaran. Tomales, CA: Blue Mountain Center of Meditation, 1987.

CMS Books Index

Periodicals: CMS Notes and Bibliography

When you cite a periodical, you should include some or all of the following information, as appropriate:

- the author's name or authors' names
- the article title
- the periodical name
- information about the issue (volume, issue number, date)
- page numbers

For online periodicals, see citation model 21 on page 509.

CMS Periodicals Index

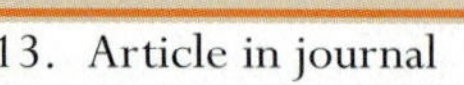
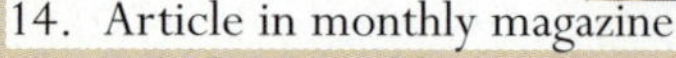

CMS Citation Models

13. Article in journal

Note: Give the author's name in normal order, the title of the article in quotation marks, and the name of the journal in italics. Next give the volume number, the issue number (preceded by the abbreviation *no.*), and the month or season and year (in parentheses), followed by a colon and the specific page on which the relevant information appears. Each major element of the entry is separated by commas *except* for the journal title and volume number, which are separated by a single space.

> 13. Collin Gifford Brooke, "Forgetting to Be (Post)Human: Media and Memory in a Kairotic Age," *JAC* 20, no. 4 (Fall 2000): 779.

Bibliography: Write the author's name (last, first, and any initials or titles), the title of the article in quotation marks, and the journal title in italics. Then write the volume number, the issue number (preceded by the abbreviation *no.*), and the month or season and year (in parentheses), followed by a colon and the page numbers for the article.

> Brooke, Collin Gifford. "Forgetting to Be (Post)Human: Media and Memory in a Kairotic Age." *JAC* 20, no. 4 (Fall 2000): 775–95.

14. Article in monthly magazine

Note: Give the author's name, the title of the article in quotation marks, the journal name in italics, the month, year, and the specific page on which the relevant information appears.

> 14. Michael Shermer, "Digits and Fidgets: Is the Universe Fine-Tuned for Life?" *Scientific American,* January 2003, 35.

Bibliography: Write the author's last name, first name (and, if applicable, any initials), a period, the title in quotation marks, the name of the journal in italics, the month, and the year. Page numbers for articles in popular magazines do not appear in the bibliography entry.

Shermer, Michael. "Digits and Fidgets: Is the Universe Fine-Tuned for Life?" *Scientific American,* January 2003.

15. Article in weekly magazine

Note:

15. Hugh Sidey, "Trying to Ensure an Epitaph," *Time,* August 19, 1974, 15B.

Bibliography:

Sidey, Hugh. "Trying to Ensure an Epitaph." *Time,* August 19, 1974.

16. Newspaper article

In CMS style, it is more common to cite newspapers in a note or in text than in a bibliography entry. If you do cite all the relevant information in your text (as in the following example), you do not have to include a citation in your bibliography.

In the article "Social Control and Welfare Reform" (*Providence Journal,* August 12, 2003), Robert Ethier notes, "Welfare reform has brought with it characteristics of surveillance and control that are a combination of Foucauldian terror and Orwellian drama."

CMS Periodicals Index

CMS Periodicals Index

Note: A note for a newspaper article would be formatted like this:

> 16. Robert Ethier, "Social Control and Welfare Reform," *Providence Journal,* August 12, 2003, metro section.

Bibliography: If your instructor requires a bibliographic citation, format it like this:

> Ethier, Robert. "Social Control and Welfare Reform." *Providence Journal,* August 12, 2003, metro section.

17. Letter to the editor

Note:

> 17. Carolyn Kay, letter to the editor, *Washington Times,* June 21, 2004, national edition, sec. A.

Bibliography:

> Kay, Carolyn. Letter to the editor. *Washington Times,* June 21, 2004, national edition, sec. A.

18. Review

Note:

18. Daniel Aaron, "The Letter and the Spirit," review of *The Selected Correspondence of Kenneth Burke and Malcolm Cowley, 1915–1981,* ed. Paul Jay, *New Republic*, March 13, 1989, 34.

Bibliography:

Aaron, Daniel. "The Letter and the Spirit." Review of *The Selected Correspondence of Kenneth Burke and Malcolm Cowley, 1915–1981,* edited by Paul Jay. *New Republic*, March 13, 1989.

CMS Periodicals Index

Digital Sources: CMS Notes and Bibliography

The CMS style requires that you provide complete URLs for books, articles, and other material you accessed via the Internet. Do *not* place angle brackets around URLs; write them exactly as they are given on the site. (Do not edit for capitalization, punctuation, or the like.) If you have to break a URL at the end of a line, do so *immediately after* a single or double slash; before a tilde, period, comma, hyphen, underscore, question mark, number sign, or percent symbol; or before or after an equals sign or ampersand. CMS does not generally recommend including access dates unless the material cited is time-sensitive (e.g., medical research) or likely to be periodically and substantially updated. It also does *not* require you to include revision dates.

CMS Index to Digital Sources

WriteOnline

CMS Citation Models

19. Website

When citing original content from a website (excluding online periodicals), include as much of the following information as you can locate: the name of the author, the title of the page, the name of the site, the date of publication, the URL, and the date of access (if time-sensitive). CMS recommends citing this information in a note.

Note:

19. Kathleen Fitzpatrick, "On the Future of Academic Publishing, Peer Review, and Tenure Requirements," *The Valve,* January 6, 2006, http://www.thevalve.org/go/valve/article/on_the_future_of_academic_publishing_peer_review_and_tenure_requirements_or/.

Bibliography:

Fitzpatrick, Kathleen. "On the Future of Academic Publishing, Peer Review, and Tenure Requirements." *The Valve,* January 6, 2006. http://www.thevalve.org/go/valve/article/on_the_future_of_academic_publishing_peer_review_and_tenure_requirements_or/.

20. Online book

Use the same format as for printed books (see the citation models on page 498), and add the URL. If the material is time-sensitive, provide the date of access in parentheses at the end of the citation.

Note:

20. Kate Agena et al., eds., *Digital Publishing F5 | Refreshed,* 2nd ed. (West Lafayette, IN: Parlor Press, 2003), TK3 Reader ebook, http://www.parlorpress.com/digital.html.

Bibliography:

Agena, Kate, Karl Stolley, Rita Wu, Christopher Eklund, Christopher Berry, Jingfang Ren, and Jennie Blankert, eds. *Digital Publishing F5 | Refreshed,* 2nd ed. West Lafayette, IN: Parlor Press, 2003. TK3 Reader ebook. http://www.parlorpress.com/digital.html.

If a book is available both in print and electronically, cite the source you used. If it would be helpful to your reader to be made aware that the material is available in another format, you can say that in your citation.

Blake, Marc. *How to Be a Sitcom Writer.* New York: Summersdale Publishers, 2005. Also available as PDF ebook at http://www.summersdale.com/product_info.php?products_id=409.

Note: The fifteenth edition of *The Chicago Manual of Style,* published in 2003, shows the word *ebook* with a hyphen.

21. Online article

Use the same format as for printed articles, and add the URL. If the material is especially time sensitive, provide the last date of access in parentheses at the end of the citation. Include page numbers if they are available. Otherwise, if the article is long, include information such as a subhead or paragraph number that would enable your reader to find your exact source.

Note:

21. Moya Ball, "A Response to Andrew King's 'Disciplining the Master: Finding the Via Media for Kenneth Burke,'" *American Communication Journal* 4, no. 2 (Winter 2001), http://acjournal.org/holdings/vol4/iss2/special/Ball.htm.

CMS Index to Digital Sources

CMS Index to Digital Sources

Bibliography:

Ball, Moya. "A Response to Andrew King's 'Disciplining the Master: Finding the Via Media for Kenneth Burke.'" *American Communication Journal* 4, no. 2 (Winter 2001). http://acjournal.org/holdings/vol4/iss2/special/Ball.htm.

22. Online government publication

Government documents are usually cited using notes and bibliographic entries. Information may include the name of the country, state, or government agency issuing the document; the legislative body, board, or committee involved; any subsidiary division; title, if available; author, editor, or compiler; number or other identifying information; publisher, if relevant; date; and URL.

Note:

22. Embassy of the United States, Islamabad, Pakistan, "212th Mobile Army Surgical Hospital Medical Outreach," press release, December 20, 2005, http://usembassy.state.gov/pakistan/h05122001.html (accessed January 3, 2006).

Bibliography:

Embassy of the United States, Islamabad, Pakistan. "212th Mobile Army Surgical Hospital Medical Outreach." Press release, December 20, 2005. http://usembassy.state.gov/pakistan/h05122001.html (accessed January 3, 2006).

CMS Index to Digital Sources

23. Information from database or subscription service

Use the same format as for a periodical article (see the index on page 504), and then provide the URL to the main page of the service. If the material is time sensitive, include the last date you accessed the material in parentheses at the end of the entry.

Note:

23. Melanie Ann Rosen Brown, "Posthumanity's Manifest Destiny: NASA, Its Contradictory Image and Promises, and Popular Culture," PhD diss., University of Central Florida, 2004, UMI ProQuest: AAT 3134675, http://proquest.com/products_umi/dissertations/disexpress.shtml.

Bibliography:

Brown, Melanie Ann Rosen. "Posthumanity's Manifest Destiny: NASA, Its Contradictory Image and Promises, and Popular Culture." PhD diss., University of Central Florida, 2004. UMI ProQuest: AAT 3134675. http://proquest.com/products_umi/dissertations/disexpress.shtml.

When citing scientific databases, CMS suggests that you include the following information in the order listed: the name of the database, the URL, information that indicates which part of the database you are citing (for example, a brief description or relevant file number), and the date you accessed the material.

24. Email

CMS recommends citing emails in your text or as a note:

24. Claire Rocheston, email message to author, December 15, 2003.

If you are citing an email message that has been archived online, include the name of the list, the date the message was posted, and the URL. Don't include email citations in a bibliography. **Note:** The fifteenth edition of *The Chicago Manual of Style,* published in 2003, shows the word *email* with a hyphen.

CMS Index to Visual and Performance Media and Other Sources

CMS Citation Models

25. Online multimedia

Note:

25. Martha Conway, *Girl, Birth, Water, Death*, 1995, http://ezone.org/ez/e2/articles/conway/jump1.html.

Bibliography:

Conway, Martha. *Girl, Birth, Water, Death.* 1995. http://ezone.org/ez/e2/articles/conway/jump1.html.

26. Video recording (movie, DVD)

Citations of recordings typically include some or all of the following information: the name of the person who created the content, such as a composer, writer, or performer; the title, in italics; the name of the recording company or publisher; the identifying number, if any; and the medium.

Note:

26. *Scream,* DVD, directed by Wes Craven (Burbank, CA: Dimension Films, 1996).

Bibliography:

Scream. DVD. Directed by Wes Craven. Burbank, CA: Dimension Films, 1996.

If the writer, producer, or director of a film is the focus of your paper, begin the entry with that person's name.

27. Audio recording

Note:

27. Jimi Hendrix, "Red House," MCA Records 11060, 1966, vinyl record.

Bibliography:

Hendrix, Jimi. "Red House." MCA Records 11060, 1966. Vinyl record.

Notice that "Red House" is a single song recorded on a 45 rpm record; thus it is considered a short work and its title is in quotation marks. For the titles of CDs and albums, which are considered long works, use italics instead.

28. Work of art

Copyright information about artwork is handled at the end of a caption to the piece of art, not in a note or bibliography entry.

Caption:

Figure 28. Matthew Barney, *Cremaster 2,* 1999. Photograph with Vaseline frame. New York, Guggenheim Collection. © 1999 by the Guggenheim Foundation. Reproduced by permission from the Guggenheim Foundation.

CMS Index to Visual and Performance Media and Other Sources

CMS Index to Visual and Performance Media and Other Sources

29. Lecture or public address

Note: Write the title of the lecture in quotation marks, followed, in parentheses, by the details of the event including the type of presentation (keynote address, lecture, paper, and so on), the name of the sponsoring organization, the location, and the date (month, day, year).

> 29. Virginia Anderson, "'The Perfect Enemy': Clinton, the Contradictions of Capitalism, and Slaying the Sin Within" (conference presentation, 1999 Triennial Conference of the Kenneth Burke Society, Iowa City, May 22, 1999).

Bibliography: Write the title of the lecture in quotation marks, followed by the type of presentation, the sponsorship information, the location, and the date.

> Anderson, Virginia. "'The Perfect Enemy': Clinton, the Contradictions of Capitalism, and Slaying the Sin Within." Conference presentation, 1999 Triennial Conference of the Kenneth Burke Society, Iowa City, May 22, 1999.

Papers published as part of the proceedings of a conference can be cited like chapters from a book (citation model 10 on page 502). If the paper is published in a journal, use the format for a journal article (citation model 13 on page 504).

30. Published or broadcast interview

An interview that has been broadcast or published is cited in the same way as an article in a periodical.

Note:

> 30. Lawrence Lessig, "Remixing Culture: An Interview with Lawrence Lessig," interview by Richard Koman, *O'Reilly Network,* February 2, 2005, http://www.oreillynet.com/pub/a/policy/2005/02/24/lessig.html (accessed May 20, 2005).

Bibliography:

Lessig, Lawrence. "Remixing Culture: An Interview with Lawrence Lessig." Interview by Richard Koman. *O'Reilly Network,* February 2, 2005. http://www.oreillynet.com/pub/a/policy/2005/02/24/lessig.html (accessed May 20, 2005).

If a live interview has not been published or broadcast, it is preferable to cite it in the text or as a note. You should include the names of the interviewer and interviewee, brief identifying information if necessary, the location and date of the interview, and, if a transcript or tape was made, where it can be located.

31. Personal communication (letter, phone call, memo)

Usually, refer to personal communications in your running text.

Carburg wrote me a letter on October 12, 2004, suggesting we . . .

You may use a note also:

31. Daniel Carburg, letter to author, October 12, 2004.

CMS Index to Visual and Performance Media and Other Sources

Michael Vogel wrote the following paper for a course in Tudor England at Indiana University South Bend. It was later published online in IUSB's *Undergraduate Research Journal*.

1

Michael Vogel
History 309
October 15, 2002

War on the Budget Plan:
The Elizabethan War with Spain

Queen Elizabeth's philosophy was that "English resources were to be committed only in the most necessary and desperate conditions, and then for the shortest time possible."[1] Though the war outlasted Elizabeth, she achieved her limited war aims and Philip II of Spain failed in his. Elizabeth didn't pursue glorious victories or territorial aggrandizement but simply a return to the previous status quo. War with minimum risk may have been unusual for the times, and the lack of glory frustrating to some of her subjects (such as the Earl of Essex), but in the end she won both the war against Spain and her battle against change. Amazingly, she used an outmoded feudal infrastructure, stretched far beyond any previous use, to wage and win a modern war.

Elizabeth I's long reign began with 30 years of relative peace. This ushered in a period of prosperity that Elizabeth's government did its best to prolong. The queen held true to her motto, *semper e adem*, "always the same,"[2] but the world changed even if England tried not to. As it would for centuries, English security depended on maintaining a balance between England's more powerful continental neighbors France and Spain. With

2

civil war raging in France after the collapse of the French monarchy in 1585,[3] Philip II of Spain became unquestionably the most powerful monarch in Europe. With a mixture of religious zeal and personal ambition, he seized the opportunity. This began an undeclared war between England and Spain that would last for 19 years.

With the introduction of firearms (matchlocks), a military revolution had occurred. This innovation changed the face of warfare, creating the first modern armies. The creation of a modern army, however, required an extensive bureaucratic infrastructure to support it. Elizabeth's government treated the war as a temporary phenomenon that made it unnecessary to alter the established peacetime routine of the state being simply an extension of the monarch.[4] Elizabeth I tried, and almost succeeded, in financing the war out of normal revenues and Parliamentary subsidies. In this way she could hold on to the previous control of the crown while combatting an empire with far greater resources than England's.

Compared to Philip II's Spain, England was rather underdeveloped.[5] During decades of almost continuous warfare between the Valois kings of France and the Hapsburgs of Spain and Austria, both monarchies developed institutions for waging large-scale and long-term warfare. They had professional standing armies and the fiscal and bureaucratic apparatus necessary to sustain a war machine indefinitely. In England, there was no

Michael chose to use the version of CMS style that includes detailed endnotes (page 493).

3

standing army, much less bureaucracy, and England had limited taxation ability.[6]

Philip's initial goal was to reestablish Spanish authority in the rebellious provinces in the Netherlands, a rich area comprising the modern-day Belgium and Holland, also referred to as the Low Countries. The Spanish would pursue this goal for 80 years and ultimately fail at it. Elizabeth, although willing to accept nominal Spanish sovereignty over the Low Countries, as in the time of Charles V, couldn't accept the risk of Spanish troops at nearby Dutch harbors. The coast of the Netherlands, as well as the French Channel coast, was referred to by the English as the invasion coast.[7] It was the best site from which to launch an invasion of England. The elimination of England would free Philip for what Wernham refers to as the "central element in the struggle," the attempt by Philip to gain control of France.[8]

Neither monarch ever declared war on the other. But with their aims so diametrically opposed over the status of the Netherlands, conflict was inevitable. It began with mutual trade embargoes, and Philip's involvement with the plot to replace Elizabeth with Mary, Queen of Scots. Between 1568 and 1585, Elizabeth unofficially sanctioned piracy against Spain, pocketing the proceeds.[9] This even included a Spanish pay ship taken in the Channel in 1569,[10] on its way to the Low Countries.

4

Elizabeth was "starkly modern in her realization that money was power."[11] This realization had much to do with why the English tended to overestimate Spain. Spain had twice the population of England.[12] With an annual budget of less than £300,000[13] the English watched as Philip's Plate fleet brought him an estimated £3,000,000 a year in silver from the New World, in addition to his regular revenues.[14] Philip had his own problems, though. Expenditures in the Low Countries consumed half of the annual royal budget.[15] An additional problem came with actually getting the money to the Low Countries to pay the large army stationed there. The shortest and fastest route was through the English Channel, but rough seas and the presence of English pirates made for an uncertain journey. To add to Philip's woes, the plague wiped out an estimated 8% of the Iberian population between 1598 and 1602.[16]

Elizabeth's long-term strategy was "the maximum disruption of her neighbors' dominions, with minimal cost or risk to England."[17] England's overriding fear was of Spanish invasion after the Armada. Wernham argues that England's war with Spain was primarily a land conflict, focused on the security of the Channel ports of France and the Low Countries.[18]

The war with Spain was fought on a much broader geographic scale than any previously known.[19] England faced commitments in the Netherlands, in Normandy and Brittany in France, expeditions against Spain and

5

Portugal, and expeditions against the Spanish West Indies. A prolonged series of revolts against English rule in Ireland consumed almost half of the English troops raised.[20] In addition, Elizabeth maintained a large part-time militia force.

Elizabeth operated under constant financial constraints throughout the war. Her allies from the United Provinces, as the rebellious Dutch provinces were known, Henry III and Henry IV of France, were in even worse financial straits. Henry IV at his accession controlled barely half the country and few of the large towns, which was where tax revenue came from.[21] Henry IV most often paid English troops sent to France, although this often involved loans from Elizabeth to cover the costs.

After the assassination of William the Silent in 1584, the United Provinces had difficulty in establishing a government with enough control to wage war. This lack of leadership led to the provinces being known as "the headless commonwealth." In 1585, Elizabeth brought her support for the Dutch rebels out in the open by signing a treaty with them and dispatching 7,000 men under the Earl of Leicester. As part of the treaty, the Dutch received a subsidy from England but had to pay the English troops stationed there. Generally, far more time was spent negotiating these financial concerns than was spent on strategy.

6

The costs of mobilizing the troops for overseas use were paid for locally, by the county or city, so that Elizabeth avoided the rather substantial costs involved with equipping them. In the actual raising of troops, Elizabeth made full use of the Lord Lieutenants, directly appointed by the crown. They had previously been used to raise troops in emergencies, but now they became a more permanent institution, still tied directly to Elizabeth's patronage. When a levy for troops was issued, the Lord Lieutenant used local officials to pick men. Many men were simply pressed into service. MacCaffrey says that levying soldiers meant clearing the cities of the homeless and unemployed.[22] McGurk argues that in practice "the rogues, vagabonds, and idlers were drafted in a policy of social cleansing, often at the expense of the army."[23] This led not only to a low quality of troops, but also to a high desertion rate, which peaked during the Nine Years War in Ireland. At one point in 1600, the Privy Council complained that out of 350 men, only 140 showed up for embarkation,[24] even though desertion was a capital crime. The saying at the time was "better to be hanged at home than die like dogs in Ireland."[25]

Sir John Falstaff, in Shakespeare's Henry IV (1598), gives us a thinly veiled contemporary perspective on the quality of soldiers in the 1590s and the corruption involved in their recruitment:

7

> I have misused the King's press damnably. I have got, in exchange of a hundred and fifty soldiers, three hundred and odd pounds. I press me none but good house-soldiers, yeoman's sons. . . . I pressed none but such toasts-and-butter, with hearts in their bellies no bigger than pin's heads, and they have bought out their services; and now my whole charge consists of ancients, corporals, lieutenants, gentlemen of companies, slaves as ragged as Lazarus in the painted cloth, where the glutton's dogs licked his sores; and such as indeed were never soldiers, but discarded unjust serving-men, younger sons to younger brothers, revolted tapsters and ostlers trade-fallen, the cankers of a calm world and a long peace, ten times more dishonourable ragged than an old faced ancient: and such have I, to fill up the rooms of them that have bought out their services.[26]

Prospects for survival for the Elizabethan soldier were grim. During 1588 and 1589, 24,000 men were sent on official expeditions to France and Portugal. Almost half never returned.[27] Disease was the greatest killer and crippler. In Brittany, Norris figured a force of 2,000 men would require 500 to 600 replacements every six months, whether or not they saw action.[28]

For the English expeditionary forces, the record of success was very limited. Elizabeth committed the absolute minimum of forces, seldom enough to achieve

8

victory, but usually enough to stave off the defeat of her allies. The expeditionary forces were more like mercenaries, usually being paid by the Dutch or the French king. The expeditions to Spain and the West Indies were very much entrepreneurial enterprises. In 1589, the army that accompanied the "Counter Armada" to Portugal included 9,000 government troops and almost 10,000 "volunteers" who joined in hopes of profitable plunder.[29] The operation was organized on a joint stock basis, with financing by the United Provinces, English merchants and other adventurers, and the queen. It was the only way that Elizabeth could afford the operation. Strategic aims and profit motives made for confused objectives. Often, as in this case, neither was achieved.

One area where this entrepreneurial spirit did function well was privateering. After the defeat of the Armada in 1588, at least 100, and in some years as many as 200, privateers were at sea.[30] On average, privateers made at least modest profits.[31] This helped to offset the loss of trade revenues due to the conflict and proved a constant annoyance to Spain.

For defense against invasion, Elizabeth relied on locally raised militia to deal with emergencies, in the time-honored feudal tradition of an army of peasants, poorly armed and untrained. Elizabeth, in 1573, turned this into a permanent part-time force, the Trained Bands. As the name implies, they were trained, and much care was given to equip them with up-to-date weapons.[32] Although occasionally used to add experienced men to a levy being sent to the continent, their primary mission was to repel a Spanish invasion. Nolan argues that Elizabeth's real army was these Trained Bands. Theirs was the all-important mission of guarding against the ever-present threat of invasion. The muster of 1588 involved over 40,000 trained troops and perhaps as many untrained levies,[33] compared to England's full-time army of 11,000.[34]

One area where the queen didn't skimp was her navy. Although smaller than the Spanish fleet, the English ships were far superior. This was due largely to Sir John Hawkins, Elizabeth's treasurer of the navy. Rejecting the accepted tactics of grappling and boarding, passed down since ancient times, the English ships were floating gun platforms able to engage at longer range.[35] In 1588, the queen had thirty warships but called on port towns to arm merchant vessels. Although such a call had been only rarely used since ancient times, she called on the ports again in 1589, 1595, 1596, and 1597.[36] This arming allowed Elizabeth to increase the size of her fleet with no additional cost to the crown.

The strain on the monarchy was great. The war cost England an estimated £4,500,000.[37] Over 100,000 men were raised and equipped during the war years.[38] From 1589 to 1603, taxes both direct and indirect were three times the amount raised in the previous 30 years.[39]

Parliamentary subsidies totaled £1,560,000 between 1585 and 1603, with requests becoming larger and more frequent through the 1590s to the end of her reign. Elizabeth had £300,000 in her coffers in 1585 and ended the reign £365,000 in debt.[40] The financial strain on the monarchy was great, but Elizabeth's limited war aims closely matched England's limited resources.

Luck may have been Elizabeth's greatest asset. Not only did storms wreck the Armada of 1588, but they also wrecked two other Spanish invasion fleets in 1596 and 1597, both headed for Ireland.[41] MacCaffrey refers to Elizabeth I as "Elizabeth the Fortunate."[42]

Elizabeth took the archaic feudal systems she had inherited and pushed them far beyond their former limits. By relying on a large part-time militia and using local governments to pay the costs of raising and equipping troops, England gained a much larger army than the Crown could afford. Arranging for many of these soldiers to be paid by foreign governments meant they could be maintained in the field. Elizabeth embraced privateering, which allowed for a self-financing naval war. The expeditions to Spain, Portugal, and the West Indies were run like business ventures in search of plunder, with Elizabeth as a minority shareholder. The expeditions kept the Spanish off balance at a low cost to the English Crown. Elizabeth creatively used conservative feudal systems to wage a war that required a modern state. After

11

her death in 1603, James VI inherited much of the structure of a modern state, but while Elizabeth was alive the entire government and its war machine were still based on time-honored feudal traditions and patronage. *Semper e adem.* Perhaps Elizabeth the Unchanging would be a more fitting title.

12

Notes

1. Wallace T. MacCaffrey, *Elizabeth I: War and Politics, 1588–1603* (Princeton, NJ: Princeton University Press, 1992), 217.

2. Ibid., 541.

3. R. B. Wernham, *After the Armada* (Oxford: Oxford University Press, 1984), 144.

4. MacCaffrey, *Elizabeth I,* 57.

5. Ibid., 20.

6. Ibid.

7. Ibid., 293.

8. Wernham, *Armada,* 555.

9. John McGurk, *The Tudor Monarchies, 1485–1603* (Cambridge: Cambridge University Press, 1999), 78–79.

10. James Conklin, "The Theory of Sovereign Debt and Spain under Philip II," *Journal of Political Economy* 106 (June 1998): 497.

11. Lacey Baldwin Smith, *Elizabeth Tudor: Portrait of a Queen* (Boston: Little, Brown, 1975), 175.

12. John S. Nolan, "The Militarization of the Elizabethan State," *Journal of Military History* 58 (July 1994): 403.

13. McGurk, *Tudor Monarchies,* 88.

14. Wernham, *Armada,* 15.

15. Conklin, "Sovereign Debt," 496.

13

16. John McGurk, *The Elizabethan Conquest of Ireland: The 1590s Crisis* (Manchester, UK: Manchester University Press, 1997), 14.

17. MacCaffrey, *Elizabeth I,* 558.

18. Wernham, *Armada,* 563.

19. Nolan, "Militarization," 408.

20. MacCaffrey, *Elizabeth I,* 10.

21. Ibid., 138.

22. Ibid., 43.

23. McGurk, *Elizabethan Conquest,* 33.

24. Ibid., 35.

25. Ibid.

26. William Shakespeare, *Henry IV,* Part I, 1598/1599, *William Shakespeare Literature,* 2003, http://www.shakespeare-literature.com.

27. Wernham, *Armada,* 18.

28. Ibid., 482.

29. Nolan, "Militarization," 406.

30. Wernham, *Armada,* 235.

31. Ibid., 249.

32. Nolan, "Militarization," 400.

33. Ibid., 405.

34. Ibid., 418.

35. McGurk, *Tudor Monarchies,* 87.

36. MacCaffrey, *Elizabeth I,* 32.

37. Ibid., 64.

38. Nolan, "Militarization," 408.

14

39. McGurk, *Tudor Monarchies,* 89.

40. Nolan, "Militarization," 413.

41. MacCaffrey, *Elizabeth I,* 439.

42. Ibid., 574.

22

CITING SOURCES IN CSE STYLE

CSE INDEXES

The CSE style is probably the most widely used documentation style in the natural and applied sciences. *Scientific Style and Format: The CSE Manual for Authors, Editors, and Publishers,* 7th edition (published in 2006) is sponsored by the Council of Science Editors. The manual offers three methods for citing sources: name-year, citation-sequence, and citation-name. Before choosing a method, analyze your assignment, check with your instructor as to his or her preference, and consider which style is more commonly used by your intended audience.

22a CSE Name-Year Method

The CSE name-year method of citation is similar to the name-year style used in APA documentation. The author's name and the year of publication are provided in text to refer readers to an alphabetized list of references. Unlike APA, however, CSE does not require that you include page numbers in your in-text citation. And in the CSE style, you do not place a comma between the author's name and the date in the in-text citation.

Sample In-Text Citation:
According to one study (Whorf 1964), Hopi has a prototypical eventness to its assertions in contrast to the prototypical thingness of English.

Sample Reference:
Whorf BL. 1964. Language, thought, and reality: selected writings. Carroll JB, editor. Cambridge: MIT Pr. 290 p.

The reference list will look like the APA reference list. See section 20c.

In the citation-sequence method, you place a superscript (raised) number immediately after the referenced material. (Use the superscript feature in your word processor, which is usually under the Format/Font menu.) If you are unable to produce a superscript, place the number in parentheses immediately following the material you are citing.

Sources are numbered in the order in which they appear in your text, so the first referenced source is 1, the second is 2, and so on. Once you have used a number to identify a source, you continue to use the same number to refer to that source throughout the course of your paper. These numbers correspond to a numbered list of references at the end of the work.

When you refer to more than one source at the same time, separate the numbers by a hyphen or en-dash if they are in sequence or by commas if they are out of sequence.

Organize the References page in the order in which sources were introduced. The source identified in the text as number 1 will come first, followed by number 2, and so on.

In-Text Citations for the Citation-Sequence Method

In their survey of recent parenting books, W. Hunter, G. Suluja, C. Runyan, and T. Coyne-Beasley found that none addressed more than half of the issues identified as critical by the American Medical Association[1].

The two most recent studies[2–4] found a similar trend.

Frequently, critics of diuretics[5,7,9] contend that dehydration is the sole bodily response.

Superscript numbers are separated only by hyphens (or en-dashes) or commas; there are no spaces between the numbers.

Sample Reference in the Citation-Sequence Method

2. Hunter W, Saluja G, Runyan C, Coyne-Beasley T. Injury prevention advice in top-selling parenting books. Pediatrics. 2005;116(5):1080–1088.

In-Text Citations for the Citation-Name Method

A new hypothesis developed . . . based upon positive relations between the areas with the highest CVD and infant mortality rates[2], and lower birth weight and increased risk of CVD mortality[3]. These historical cohort studies[1–3] and evidence from animal experiments[4] suggest that chronic diseases are biologically "programmed" in utero or in early infancy.

Sample References in Citation-Name Style

References

1. Barker DJP. Fetal origins of coronary heart disease. BMJ. 1995;311:171–174.
2. Barker DJP, Osmond C. Infant mortality, childhood nutrition, and ischaemic heart disease in England and Wales. Lancet. 1986;i:1077–1081.
3. Barker DJP, Winter PD, Osmond C, et al. Weight in infancy and death from ischaemic heart disease. Lancet. 1989;ii:577–580.
4. Nyirenda M, Seckl JR. Intrauterine events and the programming of adulthood disease: the role of fetal glucocorticoid exposure [review]. Int J Molec Med. 1998;2:607–614.

From M. R. Järvelin, "Fetal and Infant Markers of Adult Heart Diseases," *Heart* 84 (2000): 219–226 <http://heart.bmjjournals.com/cgi/content/full/84/2/219>.

To use the citation-name method, you must first create the references list, arranging entries alphabetically by the authors' last names. Then number the list. Once you have numbers for the alphabetical references, go back to your text and use the assigned numbers for the relevant sources.

In the text, place a superscript (raised) number immediately after the referenced material. (Use the superscript feature in your word processor, which is usually under the Format/Font menu.) If you are unable to produce a superscript number, place the number in parentheses immediately following the material you are citing.

If your first cited source is from an author named Tager and Tager is the fifteenth source in your references list, then the first citation in your project will be to [15]. If the second citation is to Jacobs, who is third in the references, the next citation will be to [3]. In other words, the citation numbers will not be in sequence.

When you refer to three or more sources numbered sequentially at the same place, separate the numbers by a hyphen or en-dash. When two numbers are in sequence, use a comma and no space. Use a comma and no space to separate numbers out of sequence.

Whether you use the name-year, citation-sequence, or citation-name method for in-text citations, list your sources at the end of your paper on a new page entitled *References* or *Cited References.*

The first line of each entry should begin at the left margin. In a citation-sequence or citation-name list, subsequent lines in the same entry should be indented so that they start directly below the first letter of the author's last name. In a name-year list, subsequent lines are indented five spaces.

If you are using the name-year method, list your sources in alphabetical order by the first author's last name. If you adopt the citation-sequence method, list your sources in the order in which they appeared in your text, starting with number 1. If you are using the citation-name method, organize your references alphabetically and then number them.

If you want to create a bibliography of sources you relied upon or used but did not cite directly, create a separate, alphabetized (but not numbered) list of the sources entitled *Additional References* and attach it after the Cited References.

Format for CSE Reference Entries

Number

In the citation-sequence and citation-name methods, start the entry at the left margin with the number, followed by a period and two spaces.

Author's name

Give the last name first, insert a space, and then provide the initials. Do not put spaces between initials or periods after any but the last initial. If a work has more than one author, place a comma after the initial(s) of each one to separate them. Do not use *and*.

Publication date

Citation-sequence and citation-name methods: Place the date after the publication information for a book or after the title for a periodical.
Name-year method: Place the date immediately after the last author's name.

Book title

Book and article titles are not italicized, underlined, or placed in quotation marks. Only the first word and any proper nouns are capitalized. Follow the title with a period.

Journal title

Journal titles are not italicized, underlined, or placed in quotation marks. Any title longer than one word is abbreviated. Abbreviate all significant words, and do not include the majority of prepositions, conjunctions, and articles. Do not use periods after individual abbreviations, but include a period at the end of the title. To download lists of abbreviations, go to **http://www.library.uq.edu.au/endnote**.

Nat Rev Sci. Chem Schol. Will Gde Tchng Chem.

Publication information for books

Citation-sequence and citation-name methods: Immediately after the title, provide the place of publication (followed by a colon), the name of the publisher (followed by a semicolon), the date (followed by a period), and the number of pages (use the abbreviation *p.* after the number).
Name-year method: Immediately after the name of the author, provide the date (followed by a period). Immediately after the title, give the place of publication (followed by a colon), the name of the publisher (followed by a period), and the number of pages (use the abbreviation *p.* after the number).

Publication information for journals

In both methods, the volume number is followed by the issue number (if there is one) in parentheses, then a colon, and then the inclusive page numbers. Do not use the abbreviation for page or pages, and do not leave spaces between any of the numerical elements.

Citation-sequence and citation-name methods: Place the date after the journal title and follow with a semicolon. Then give volume, issue, and page.

Name-year method: Place the date after the last author's name and follow it with a period.

The sample References page uses the citation-sequence method.

Sample References in Citation-Sequence Style

References

1. Kuh D, Ben-Shlomo Y. A life course approach to chronic disease epidemiology. New York: Oxford Univ Pr; 1997. 336 p.
2. World Health Organization. World health statistics annual 1989. Geneva: WHO; 1989.
3. Dobson A, Evans A, Ferrario M, Kuulasmaa KA, Moltchanov VA, Sans S, Tunstall-Pedoe H, Tuomilehto JO, Wedel H, Yarnell J. Changes in estimated coronary risk in the 1980s: data from 38 populations in the WHO MONICA project. Ann Med. 1998;30:199–205.
4. World Health Organization MONICA Project. Ecological analysis of the association between mortality and major risk factors of cardiovascular disease. Int J Epidemiol. 1994;94:705–716.
5. Rose G. Sick individuals and sick populations. Int J Epidemiol. 1985;14:32–38.
6. Annual report for 1913 of Chief Medical Officer of the Board of Education, Cd 7330. London: HMSO; 1914.
7. Barker DJP. Fetal and infant origins of adult disease. London: BMJ Publishing; 1992. 343 p.

Book with two authors; see citation model 2 on page 528.

Journal article with one author; see citation model 9 on page 532.

From M. R. Järvelin, "Fetal and Infant Markers of Adult Heart Diseases," *Heart* 84 (2000): 219–226 <http://heart.bmjjournals.com/cgi/content/full/84/2/219>.

CSE References Index: Books

CSE References Models

Each of the models includes examples of a book listed on a References page using the citation-sequence method and the name-year method. Note that if there is any possibility of confusion about where the city of publication is located, you should include the state or country in parentheses after the city.

1. Book with one author

Citation-sequence and citation-name:

1. Panno J. Animal cloning: the science of nuclear transfer. New York: Facts on File; 2005. 164 p.

Name-year:

Panno J. 2005. Animal cloning: the science of nuclear transfer. New York: Facts on File. 164 p.

2. Book with two or more authors

Author names are separated by commas, and you don't use *and* or an ampersand. If there are more than ten authors, you list the first ten and then, after the final comma, add the phrase *et al.*

Citation-sequence and citation-name:

2. Freitas RA, Merkle RC. Kinematic self-replicating machines. Georgetown (TX): Landes Bioscience/Eurekah; 2004. 341 p.

Name-year:

Freitas RA, Merkle RC. 2004. Kinematic self-replicating machines. Georgetown (TX): Landes Bioscience/Eurekah. 341 p.

3. Two or more books published by same author in same year

In the citation-sequence method, use the same format as for a book by a single author. In the name-year method, add lowercase letters after the year of publication, beginning with *a.*

Citation-sequence and citation-name:

3. Davis GA. Organic chemistry made ridiculously simple. New York: Medmaster; 2003. 228 p.

Name-year:

Davis GA. 2003a. Organic chemistry made ridiculously simple. New York: Medmaster. 228 p.

Each title is then identified in text by the same lowercase letter following the year in which it was published.

4. Book with an editor

Citation-sequence and citation-name:

4. Thistlethwaite SB, editor. Adam, Eve, and the genome: the Human Genome Project and theology. Minneapolis: Fortress Pr; 2003. 200 p.

Name-year:

Thistlethwaite SB, editor. 2003. Adam, Eve, and the genome: the Human Genome Project and theology. Minneapolis: Fortress Pr. 200 p.

CSE References Index: Books

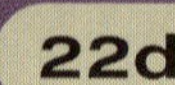

CSE References Index: Books

1. Book with one author
2. Book with two or more authors
3. Two or more books published by same author in same year
4. Book with an editor
5. Selection from a book
6. Book with a translator
7. Book in several volumes

5. Selection from a book

Write the title of the cited selection after the date (or after the author in citation-sequence or citation-name method), followed by a period. Then write the word *In* (followed by a colon), the names of the editors (followed by the word *editors* and a period), and the title of the text (followed by a period). Then add the publication information.

Citation-sequence and citation-name:

5. Hull DL. Scientific bandwagon or traveling medicine show? In: Gregory MS, Silvers A, Sutch D, editors. Sociobiology and human nature: an interdisciplinary critique and defense. San Francisco: Jossey-Bass; 1978. p. 50–59.

Name-year:

Hull DL. 1978. Scientific bandwagon or traveling medicine show? In: Gregory MS, Silvers A, Sutch D, editors. Sociobiology and human nature: an interdisciplinary critique and defense. San Francisco: Jossey-Bass. p. 50–59.

Abstracts can be cited in the same way as chapters or articles in edited books.

6. Book with a translator

The translator's name follows the book title. It is written last name first, followed by initials, a comma, and the word *translator* followed by a period. If there is also an editor, the editor's name, also in reverse order, follows that of the translator (after a semicolon) and is followed by a period.

Citation-sequence and citation-name:

6. Lukács G. Tactics and ethics: political essays, 1919–1929. McColgan M, translator; Livingstone R, editor. New York: Harper & Row; 1972. 257 p.

Name-year:

Lukács G. 1972. Tactics and ethics: political essays, 1919–1929. McColgan M, translator; Livingstone R, editor. New York: Harper & Row. 257 p.

7. Book in several volumes

Citation-sequence and citation-name:

7. Newton D. Linus Pauling: scientist and advocate. Volume 1, Makers of Modern Science. New York: Facts on File; 1994. 144 p.

Name-year:

Newton D. 1994. Linus Pauling: scientist and advocate. Volume 1, Makers of Modern Science. New York: Facts on File. 144 p.

CSE References Index: Books

CSE References Index: Periodicals

CSE References Models

8. Article in journal with continuous pagination throughout annual volume

Citation-sequence and citation-name:

8. Caldara R, Jermann F, Arango GL, Van der Linden M. Is the N400 category-specific? A face and language processing study. Neuroreport. 2004;15:2589–2594.

Name-year:

Caldara R, Jermann F, Arango GL, Van der Linden M. 2004. Is the N400 category-specific? A face and language processing study. Neuroreport. 15:2589–2594.

For journal articles with two or more authors, write the names in the order in which they appear, last names first followed by initials. Separate the names with a comma. For journal articles with organizational or corporate authors, use the full name of the organization or corporate entity in place of the author's name.

9. Article in journal that paginates each issue separately

Include the issue number in parentheses after the volume number, with no space between them.

Citation-sequence and citation-name:

9. Jacyna S. Jean-Martin Charcot's mechanisms of language. Cortex. 2005;41(1):1–2.

Name-year:

Jacyna S. 2005. Jean-Martin Charcot's mechanisms of language. Cortex. 41(1):1–2.

10. Magazine article (nonspecialized, mainstream periodical)

Include the month in the date and page numbers, but not volume or issue numbers.

Citation-sequence and citation-name:

10. Kinsley CH, Lambert KG. The maternal brain. Sci Am. 2006 Jan:72–79.

Name-year:

Kinsley CH, Lambert KG. 2006 Jan. The maternal brain. Sci Am. 72–79.

11. Newspaper article

Include full date, section letter, and page and column number.

Citation-sequence and citation-name:

11. Stewart J. Physiological dilemmas in public education. Atlanta Journal-Constitution. 2005 Jul 21;Sect. C:9 (col. 2).

CSE References Index: Periodicals

CSE References Index: Periodicals

Name-year:

> Stewart J. 2005 Jul 25. Physiological dilemmas in public education. Atlanta Journal-Constitution. Sect. C:9 (col. 2).

12. Editorial

Include the title of the editorial, the word *editorial* (in brackets and followed by a period), and then the publication information in newspaper format.

Citation-sequence and citation-name:

> 12. Science and the future of America's health industry [editorial]. Boston Globe. 2002 Oct 12;Sect. A:12 (col. 1).

Name-year:

> Science and the future of America's health industry [editorial]. 2002 Oct 12. Boston Globe. Sect. A:12 (col. 1).

13. Letter to the editor

Include the title of the letter, the words *letter to the editor* (in brackets followed by a period), and then the publication information in newspaper or magazine format.

Citation-sequence and citation-name:

> 13. Smith K. Humanity at the crossroads [letter to the editor]. Sci Am. 2006 Jan:12.

Name-year:

Smith K. 2006 Jan. Humanity at the crossroads [letter to the editor]. Sci Am. 12.

14. Published interview

In addition to the last name and initial of the interviewee, provide the title of the interview, the name of the interviewer (if not included in the title), and the information about where the interview was published. Use the relevant instructions from the kind or type of publication you found the interview in.

Citation-sequence and citation-name:

14. Hawking S. Reading Hawking's presence: an interview with a self-effacing man. Mialet H, interviewer. Crit Inq. 2003 Sum;29:571–598.

Name-year:

Hawking S. 2003 Sum. Reading Hawking's presence: an interview with a self-effacing man. Mialet H, interviewer. Crit Inq. 29:571–598.

CSE References Index: Periodicals

CSE References Index: Digital Sources

CSE References Models

When you cite Internet or other digital sources, include the standard author, title, place, publisher, and date information found in any reference, and add the URL for the site, the date you cited it, and the type of electronic medium involved.

15. Online book

For online books, put *Internet* in brackets after the title. At the end of the citation, write *Available from:* followed by the URL. Break URLs only after slashes.

Citation-sequence and citation-name:

15. Newton I. Observations upon the prophecies of Daniel, and the Apocalypse of St. John [Internet]. Project Gutenberg; 2005 [cited 2006 Jan 4]. Available from: http://www.gutenberg.org/etext/16878

Name-year:

Newton I. 2005. Observations upon the prophecies of Daniel, and the Apocalypse of St. John [Internet]. Project Gutenberg [cited 2006 Jan 4]. Available from: http://www.gutenberg.org/etext/16878

16. Online journal article

Citation-sequence and citation-name: Format the journal information using the guidelines for print journals. Put *Internet* in brackets after the title of the journal. Immediately after the date, provide the date of access, in brackets, following the word *cited* (give the year first, followed by the month, abbreviated, and the day). Immediately after the bracket, place a semicolon, the volume number, the issue number in parentheses (no space between them), a colon, and the page numbers, as best you can determine them. Follow the page numbers with a period and then write *Available from:* and the URL.

> 16. Brown E. Revenge of the dotcom poster boy. Wired [Internet]. 2006 Jan [cited 2006 Jan 4];14(1). Available from: http://www.wired.com/wired/archive/14.01/blogger.html

Name-year: The format is similar to that above, except the year of publication follows the names of the authors.

> Brown E. 2006 Jan. Revenge of the dotcom poster boy. Wired [Internet]. [cited 2006 Jan 4];14(1). Available from: http://www.wired.com/wired/archive/14.01/blogger.html

17. Entire website

Provide the author or organizational name and the name of the resource, and then put *Internet* in brackets. Placement of the date of creation depends on the method used. Give the date of your access, and after that write *Available from:* and the entire URL.

Citation-sequence and citation-name:

> 17. Liu A. Voice of the shuttle [Internet]. 2006 [cited 2006 Jan 4]. Available from: http://vos.ucsb.edu

CSE References Index: Digital Sources

WriteOnline

CSE References Index: Digital Sources

Name-year:

Liu A. 2006. Voice of the shuttle [Internet]. [cited 2006 Jan 4]. Available from: http://vos.ucsb.edu

18. Online database

Citation-sequence and citation-name:

18. Schelkunoff SA. Sailors, coconuts and monkeys. Sci Mon [Internet]. 1932 Sep [cited 2006 Jan 4];35(3):258–261. Available from: http://links.jstor.org/sici?sici=0096-3771%28193209%2935%3A3%3C258%3ASCAM%3E2.0.CO%3B2-E [Jstor]

Name-year:

Schelkunoff SA. 1932 Sep. Sailors, coconuts and monkeys. Sci Mon. [cited 2006 Jan 4];35(3):258–261. Available from: http://links.jstor.org/sici?sici=0096-3771%28193209%2935%3A3%3C258%3ASCAM%3E2.0.CO%3B2-E [Jstor]

19. Email

Indicate the author's name, the subject line and, inside brackets, the kind of communication (email, listserv, etc.), the person to whom the message was sent, the date and time that it was sent, and the date that you accessed the resource.

Citation-sequence and citation-name:

19. Connors B. Indications that health problems are imminent for patients with tuberculosis [email]. Message to: Nancy Ward. 2003 Jan 12, 9:30 am [cited 2003 Jan 24].

Name-year:

Connors B. 2003 Jan 12, 9:30 am. Indications that health problems are imminent for patients with tuberculosis [email]. Message to: Nancy Ward [cited 2003 Jan 24].

20. Retrievable online posting (newsgroup, discussion group, online forum, electronic mailing list, blog)

Citation-sequence and citation-name:

20. Ratliff C. Digital scholarly publishing: beyond the crisis [blog post]. 2006 Jan 2 [cited 2006 Jan 4]. Available from: http://culturecat.net/node/1005

Name-year:

Ratliff C. 2006 Jan 2. Digital scholarly publishing: beyond the crisis [blog post]. [cited 2006 Jan 4]. Available from: http://culturecat.net/node/1005

21. CD-ROM

Citation-sequence and citation-name:

21. Feynman R. The Feynman lectures on physics, Volumes 1–2 [CD-ROM]. New York: Basic Books; 2003.

CSE References Index: Digital Sources

CSE References Index: Digital Sources

Name-year:

Feynman R. 2003. The Feynman lectures on physics, Volumes 1–2 [CD-ROM]. New York: Basic Books.

22. Computer software

Citation-sequence and citation-name:

22. ChemDraw Standard [computer program]. Version 9.0. Cambridge (MA): CambridgeSoft; 2005.

Name-year:

ChemDraw Standard [computer program]. 2005. Version 9.0. Cambridge (MA): CambridgeSoft.

CSE References Models

23. Recording (audio, video, film)

Citation-sequence and citation-name:

23. Wise R, director. The Andromeda strain [film]. Los Angeles: Universal Pictures; 1971.

Name-year:

Wise R, director. 1971. The Andromeda strain [film]. Los Angeles: Universal Pictures.

24. Government publication

Citation-sequence and citation-name: Write the entry number and the names of the authors. Then write the title, with the first word and any proper nouns capitalized. Then write the name of the agency and any identifying information as to its nationality, even if it is from the United States; any other information needed about place of publication; and information about volumes, editions, and so on, if needed. Finally, write the date, the number of pages, *Available from:,* and the agency that made the publication available, followed by that agency's city, state (if in the United States), a semicolon, and the reference number of the work.

24. Metta G, Natale L, Rao S, Sandini G. Development of the "mirror system": a computational model. Genoa University, Italy; 2002. 1 p. Available from: NTIS, Springfield, VA; DABT-63-00-C-10102.

CSE References Index: Other Sources

CSE References Index: Other Sources

Name-year:

Metta G, Natale L, Rao S, Sandini G. 2002. Development of the "mirror system": a computational model. Genoa University, Italy. 1 p. Available from: NTIS, Springfield, VA; DABT-63-00-C-10102.

25. Report from a private organization

Citation-sequence and citation-name:

25. Teenage attitudes and behavior study. Richmond (VA): Phillip Morris USA; 2005. 1 p. Available from: http://www.philipmorrisusa.com/en/policies_practices/ysp/teenage_study.asp

Name-year:

Teenage attitudes and behavior study. 2005. Richmond (VA): Phillip Morris USA. 1 p. Available from: http://www.philipmorrisusa.com/en/policies_practices/ysp/teenage_study.asp

26. Technical report

Citation-sequence and citation-name:

26. Abad JL, Yacoub S. Ontology-based software development. 2005 Feb 1. Hewlett-Packard technical reports HPL-2005-13. 24 p. Available from: http://www.hpl.hp.com/techreports/2005/HPL-2005-13.html

Name-year:

Abad JL, Yacoub S. 2005 Feb 1. Ontology-based software development. Hewlett-Packard technical reports HPL-2005-13. 24 p. Available from: http://www.hpl.hp.com/techreports/2005/HPL-2005-13.html

27. Conference presentation

Citation-sequence and citation-name:

27. Zimmerman DE, Akerelrea CA, Smith JK, O'Keefe G. Assessing visualizations in public science presentations. STC 50th annual conference proceedings; 2003. 2 p. Available from: http://www.stc.org/ConfProceed/2003/PDFs/STC50-035.pdf

Name-year:

Zimmerman DE, Akerelrea CA, Smith JK, O'Keefe G. 2003. Assessing visualizations in public science presentations. STC 50th annual conference proceedings. 2 p. Available from: http://www.stc.org/ConfProceed/2003/PDFs/STC50-035.pdf

CSE References Index: Other Sources

CSE References Index: Other Sources

28. Dissertation or thesis

Citation-sequence and citation-name: Write the word *dissertation* in brackets after the title. Follow with the location of the institution granting the degree, a colon, the institution, a semicolon, and the year the degree was granted. Then insert the number of pages. If the dissertation is available from an agency, write *Available from:* and the name of the agency, its location (followed by a semicolon), and the document number (followed by a period).

28. Kleiber BA. Systematic analysis of language deficits related to cognitive functioning in Parkinsonian patients [dissertation]. Lubbock (TX): Texas Tech University; 1999. 142 p. Available from: UMI ProQuest, Ann Arbor, MI; AAT 9925615.

Name-year: The difference in this format is that the date is placed after the author's name (followed by a period), and the name of the institution is followed by a period, not a semicolon.

Kleiber BA. 1999. Systematic analysis of language deficits related to cognitive functioning in Parkinsonian patients [dissertation]. Lubbock (TX): Texas Tech University. 142 p. Available from: UMI ProQuest, Ann Arbor, MI; AAT 9925615.

The *Columbia Guide to Online Style* (CGOS*)*, 2nd edition, by Janice R. Walker and Todd Taylor (New York: Columbia University Press, 2006), provides a citation system designed specifically for documents published in digital form (such as websites, hypertext, digital presentations, and other forms of multimedia), which may not follow the conventions of printed documents. CGOS also presents commonsense practices for documenting electronic sources. It is usable with either a humanities (MLA or CMS) or a scientific (APA or CSE) style of documentation. CGOS will seem familiar if you already understand one or two of the major citation systems. The significant difference is that CGOS solves the problems of citing digital documents at the same time as it sets standards for handling a wide array of electronic sources.

The CGOS documentation system does not replace the other documentation styles but allows you to accurately cite electronic sources within the framework of the citation style you choose to use. It provides formats for citing electronic sources for both the major documentation systems, author-date (APA, CSE) and author-page (MLA, CMS). Just like other styles, CGOS requires that you provide an in-text citation for the source you quote from or refer to, as well as bibliographic information in a References or Works Cited list.

23a CGOS In-Text Citations

When you cite sources, you use parenthetical or in-text references. The principle, as for any documentation style, is to use in-text references to point to specific entries in your References or Works Cited list. When citing print sources, you use the last name of the author and the page number(s) of the source for humanities style or the last name of the author, the date of publication, and the page number(s) of the source for scientific style. When you cite electronic sources, you may not be able to identify some elements of traditional printed source information, in which case the parenthetical or in-text reference normally uses the last name of the author. When you cannot locate the name of the author or authoring organization, use the title of the source; for scientific style, also include the date of publication.

Humanities (MLA)

When citing print material using the humanities style, you should provide the author's last name and a page number in parentheses. Digital sources may not have page numbers, in which case you provide only the author's name.

If there is other information readers may need to locate specific text in a longer document (such as paragraph, part, or section number), include it after the author's name, separated by a comma.

If the digital source does not list an author, use a shortened form of the title—page or document title or file name—in your parenthetical citation.

Scientific (APA)

When citing print-based sources in the scientific style, you should include the author's last name and the date of publication in parentheses. For electronic sources, provide only the last name and the year of publication, even if more specific information is available. You can also name the author of the source in the body of your text and put the year of publication in parentheses immediately after the name. For electronic sources that do not include any information on date of publication, include the date (day, abbreviated month, year) you accessed the material: "11 Nov. 2006."

CGOS Humanities In-Text Citation Examples

Hockey has been "among the most popular sports for the northern tier states for over three decades" (Hochberg).

Associations can be a great source for locating "lists of members, rosters of committees, and other actionable information for marketing" (Sears, para. 4).

The new Medicare Bill has been described as "a giveaway for the pharmaceutical industry" ("The Loyal Opposition?").

Note: Do not include the URL or electronic address in the text for sources you cite; this information goes in the References or Works Cited list.

CGOS Scientific In-Text Citation Examples

Insurance regulation is "crippling the industry" (Smothers, 2003), say some members of the American Enterprise Institute.

Whether or not you ask direct questions, Allan Sweetwater (2004) believes that the best survey instruments contain "at least two or three open-ended questions."

Political donations are up this year, and "indications are that donations will be up again next year" (Holtry, 14 Jun. 2004).

CGOS Formatting Guidelines

Author's name

If an author's name is provided, you should list it. If the author's name is difficult to locate or absent, CGOS allows you to use whatever name is provided (including aliases, handles, email addresses, and login names). If there is no author information, list the source by its title.

Title of document

In CGOS style, titles are never underlined. However, since you will probably be adapting your electronic citations to fit within MLA or APA format, follow the conventions of the style you are using. For example, in MLA style, the titles of articles, Web pages, blog entries, and news articles are placed in quotation marks. In APA style, only the first letter of the title and any subtitle and any proper nouns are capitalized, and no quotation marks are used.

Sponsoring publisher or group

If any broader title is given to the publishing agency (such as the title of the journal or broader website or database), you should list it. If the publisher is a journal or similar entity, put the information in italics.

Date of publication

Provide the date of publication listed on the source document. On websites or blogs, the date of publication may be the "date last updated." Databases often list publication dates in their frontmatter. If no date is provided, you can still cite the source and use the abbreviation *n.d.* ("no date"). You should consider, however, that without a date of publication, a source's credibility and usefulness are in question and so it may not be legitimate enough to be worth citing.

Publication information

For most online sources, the electronic address (the URL—see page 660) is the most important publication information because it allows readers to find your sources for further research. An entry for a database may have a code or number assigned to it.

When you list your sources at the end of your document, you will usually title the page *Works Cited* (MLA), *References* (APA, CSE), or *Notes* (and/or *Bibliography*) (CMS), depending on which documentation system you are using. Electronic citations in the CGOS format should include the following information (although in scientific style the date of publication follows the author's name).

Format

Author's name. Title of document or site. Sponsoring publisher or group. Date of publication. Publication information such as URL (date of access).

Example

Ciesielski, Dennis. "Burke to Basics: Dialogue and Culture in Core Curricula and the First-Year Writing Program." *Burke Conference Paper Repository.* 1999. http://www.sla.purdue.edu/dblakesley/burke/ciesielski.html (12 Jun. 2005).

When your own document is a printed one, formatting of the References or Works Cited listings in CGOS is similar to that in other citation styles (use hanging indents, for example). However, if your own document is not print-based (such as a Web page), as is likely if you're using CGOS, then each entry is formatted flush left, with no hanging indentations. The simple reason for this variation is that basic HTML coding (the code that tells a browser how to display a Web page) does not include hanging indentations as an option. So for digital documents, each entry is flush left, with a blank line separating entries.

For each electronic source listed, examples of how to incorporate the CGOS format into the MLA and APA documentation styles are provided. The examples here use the flush-left, line-break formatting style common in digital documents.

Testing URLs

When you use a URL in your citation information, be sure to test it to make sure that it leads to your source. In some cases, the URL you see in your browser's address bar may lead only to the home frame of the website (if it uses frames, which is a way of loading multiple Web pages in a single window). You can load "framed" Web pages in a new window (with their correct URL showing) by placing your cursor on the page, either (with a two-button mouse) right-clicking or (with a one-button mouse) pressing and holding the Ctrl key while you click, and then selecting "Open frame in new window" in the pop-up menu.

Date of access

Provide an original publication date when it makes sense to do so—when you are citing an online version of a book based on a print source, for example, or an online magazine that appears in a dated format. If you are citing a website you can often find information about its original posting date and any updates on its home page. If you can't find the date a website was updated, CGOS allows you to use the date you accessed the website or page (day, month, and year). Since the goal of using CGOS is to make it easy for your readers to find your digital sources, any other information that would be necessary or helpful in retracing your steps to your source should be given at the end of a citation, immediately before the date you accessed it.

Note: In CGOS, the date of access appears in parentheses because it often follows a URL (in the publication information section of the entry). URLs do not end with periods, so be sure you don't add them. The parentheses help separate the date of access from the publication information.

CGOS Works Cited or Reference Models

1. Website or Web page

Humanities (MLA): Start your entry with the author's name (last name, first name), if it is available. Then, in quotation marks, write the full title of the particular Web page you are citing, followed by a period. Follow this with the name of the entire website (if available) in italics, any version or file numbers, and the date of publication or the last update or revision (whichever is most recent) followed by a period. Finally, write the complete Web address (URL) preceded by the protocol (often *http://* but perhaps *gopher://* or *ftp://*). Conclude with the date you accessed the source (day, month, year) in parentheses and followed by a period.

> Duffy, W. Keith. "Digital Recording Technology in the Writing Classroom: Sampling as Citing." *The Writing Instructor.* 2004. http://www.writinginstructor.com/duffy (5 Jul. 2006).

Scientific (APA): If you can find it, begin your entry with the author's name (last name first, followed by initials). Then give the year of publication, if available, in parentheses, followed by a period. Write the full title of the source, capitalizing only the first word, the first word of any subtitle, and any proper nouns. Give the name of the complete website in italics, capitalizing only the first word and proper nouns. Provide any version or file numbers in parentheses. Finally, write the complete Web address preceded by the protocol (often *http://*), any paths or directories necessary to find the site, and the date you accessed it (day, month, year) in parentheses. Follow the closing parenthesis with a period.

> Duffy, W. K. (2004). Digital recording technology in the writing classroom: Sampling as citing. *The writing instructor.* http://www.writinginstructor.com/duffy (5 Jul. 2006).

CGOS Works Cited or References Index

CGOS Works Cited or References Index

2. Online reference source or digital database

Humanities (MLA): Write the author's name, if available, and the titles of the article and the work it came from, followed by any publication information related to a print version (if there is one), including the date. Next provide any publication information related to the online source, as well as the name of the online service you used (in italics) or the protocol, address, path, or directories needed to access the source. Finally, give the date you accessed the material (in parentheses).

> Golden, Leon. "Aristotle." *The Johns Hopkins Guide to Literary Theory and Criticism.* Ed. by Michael Groden and Martin Kreiswirth. 1997. http://www.press.jhu.edu/books/hopkins_guide_to_literary_theory/free/aristotle.html (5 Jul. 2005).

Scientific (APA): Write the author's name if you can find it, the date of publication (if it's not available, use the date you accessed the material), and the title of the article. Then write the word *In,* the names of the authors or editors, and the title of the work you are citing (in italics). Next provide any publication information relating to a print version, the number of the online edition (if any), and either the name of the database or online source service (in italics) or the protocol, address, path, or directories needed to access the source. Finally, if you have not already done so, give the date you accessed the material (in parentheses).

> Golden, L. (1997). Aristotle. In M. Groden & M. Kreiswirth (Eds.), *The Johns Hopkins guide to literary theory and criticism.* http://www.press.jhu.edu/books/hopkins_guide_to_literary_theory/free/aristotle.html (5 Jul. 2005).

3. Software application or video games

Humanities (MLA): First write the name of the author or the corporation that produced the application or game. Then, in italics, write the title of the software or game. Include the version or edition number (if it is not a part of the title), followed by any publication information and the date of release.

> Bohemia Interactive. *Operation Flashpoint.* New York: Codemasters, 2001.

Scientific (APA): First list the name of the author or the corporation that produced the application or game, followed by the date of publication in parentheses. In italics, write the title of the software or game, capitalizing only the first word and any proper nouns. Then write the version or edition number (if it is not a part of the title), followed by any publication information.

> Bohemia Interactive. (2001). *Operation flashpoint.* New York: Codemasters.

4. Information accessed using file transfer protocol (ftp)

Humanities (MLA): List the author's name and the titles of the file and source you are citing. Then write the date of the document, if available, followed by the protocol (*ftp://*) and the full pathway used to access the information. Last, write the date you accessed the source (day, abbreviated month, year) in parentheses.

> Penn, Sean. "Iraq and the Rationale for War." *Sean's Home Page.* 26 Oct. 2000. ftp://ftp.Pennlinks.com/hepf/LaurieSean/0902 (22 Sep. 2004).

CGOS Works Cited or References Index

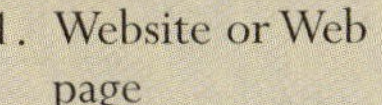

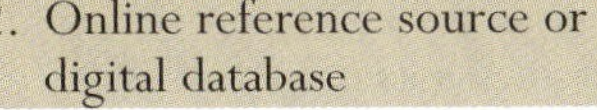

CGOS Works Cited or References Index

Scientific (APA): List the author's name, the publication date of the document, the title of the document or file, and the title of the source it came from. Next give any previous publication information, the protocol and address, the directory path, and the date you accessed the material (in parentheses).

> Penn, S. (2002, Oct. 26). Iraq and the rationale for war. *Sean's home page.* ftp://ftp.Pennlinks.com/hepf/LaurieSean/0902 (22 Sep. 2004).

5. Email, newsgroup, discussion list, forum, or blog

Humanities (MLA): When citing an email message sent to you or a discussion list, an online forum posting or RSS feed (see page 630), a message sent to a newsgroup, or an online posting in a blog or forum, start your entry with the author's name, if known (last name first). If the author's name is unavailable, use the handle, login name, alias, or email name (everything to the left of the @ sign). Follow by the subject line in quotation marks. Then write the date of the posting if it is different from the date on which you accessed it, the name of the listserv or discussion board (in italics), its address, and the date of access (in parentheses).

> Brooke, Collin. "Thinking Tools." 5 Dec. 2005. *Collin vs. Blog.* http://wrt-brooke.syr.edu/cgbvb/archives/2005/12/im_not_prone_to.html (4 Jan. 2006).

For an email message, write *Personal email.*

> Ethier, Robert. "SAT Scores and Your Admission." Personal email (20 Mar. 2002).

CGOS Works Cited or References Index

Scientific (APA): For listserv or discussion group entries, start with the author's name (last name first, followed by initials), if available. If it is not available, use the handle, login name, alias, or email name (everything to the left of the @ sign). Then, in parentheses, write the date of the posting if it is different from the date of access. Follow by the subject line (capitalizing only the first word and any proper nouns). Next write the name of the discussion group or listserv (again capitalizing only the first word and proper names) in italics. Finally, write the listserv or discussion group address and the date of access (in parentheses). For email, the term *Personal email,* in square brackets, is placed after the subject line and followed by a period.

> Brooke, C. (2005, Dec. 5). Thinking tools. *Collin vs. blog.* http://wrt-brooke.syr.edu/cgbvb/archives/2005/12/im_not_prone_to.html (4 Jan. 2006).

> Ethier, R. SAT scores and your admission [Personal email]. (20 Mar. 2002).

6. Chat or other synchronous communication transcript

Humanities (MLA): Write the author's name if you can find it (or alias), followed by the method of communication (e.g., Chat) or, if you are referring to a synchronous conference, its title in quotation marks. Next write the title of the website (if available) in italics, the protocol and address, relevant paths or directories, any necessary commands, and the date of the interaction.

> Gee, James Paul. "Video Games in the Classroom?" *Colloquy Live. Chronicle of Higher Education.* http://chronicle.com/colloquylive/2003/08/video/ (27 Aug. 2003).

CGOS Works Cited or References Index

Scientific (APA): Write the author's name or alias, followed by the method of communication (e.g., Chat) in brackets or, if you are referring to a synchronous conference, its title. Next write the title of the website (if available) in italics, the protocol and address, relevant paths or directories, any necessary commands, and the date of the interaction.

> Gee, J. P. Video games in the classroom? *Colloquy live. Chronicle of Higher Education.* http://chronicle.com/colloquylive/2003/08/video/ (27 Aug. 2003).

PART 5

Designing and Presenting Information

Comic Books and Graphic Novels

Comic books and graphic novels use images and words to tell stories. Writers now also use comic books to explain information and processes. In comic book format, for example, Scott McCloud, in *Understanding Comics*, explains how comics—with their tight integration of text, image, and iconography—create meaning. Descended from comic books, the graphic novel shares aims with the novel in its focus on character development and social critique.

- Writers use words, images, illustrations, and **iconography** (familiar symbols) to make comic books and graphic novels.
- **Comic books** are often serialized, with stories told over several issues. They have a wide range of content but usually focus on superheroes and their adventures. The comic book format has also been used as an effective way to explain complex subjects, as in the popular *Beginner Books* series. With comic book software, writers also now create user documentation and newsletters.
- **Graphic novels** are self-contained, full-length novels that reach beyond the traditional content of comic books (superheroes, for example), don't rely on serialization to keep an audience interested (they are self-contained), and display common features of the novel genre, such as complex character development and social commentary. **Manga** is the name given to Japanese comics, which have a distinct style (characters with large eyes, for example) and tell stories in the tradition of the epic and fantasy genres.

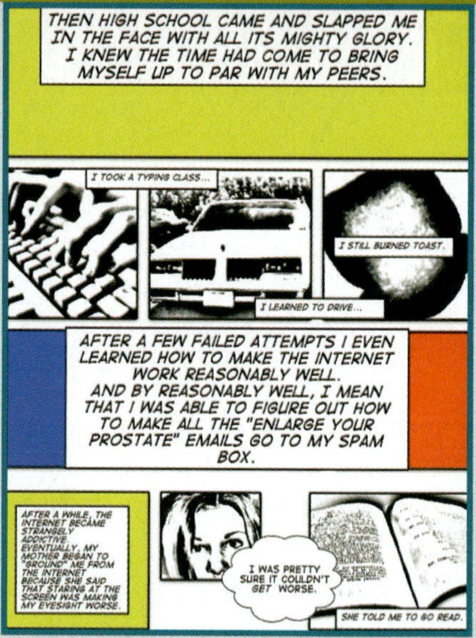

You can create comic books and graphic novels on your own using software that makes the process manageable. Comic Life (Mac; **http://plasq.com**) and Comic Book Creator (Windows XP; **http://www.mycomicbookcreator.com**) are good examples. Using a technology autobiography, her own photographs, and remixed found images, Cas Riddle used Comic Life to tell the story of her life with technology, as shown in this page from her comic book.

While comic book software may help, it won't do the really hard work for you. *You* must create the meaningful and interesting narrative with images and words. Nevertheless, comic book software makes the technical challenge of design and layout simple enough that you can spend more of your time on composing effective stories and creating or repurposing images and artwork.

Writing and Designing Comics

To create a comic book or graphic novel, you'll need to assemble images, drawings, icons, illustrations, and other visual content that you can then arrange to tell a story, explain a process, or communicate information. Textual content must work in concert with visual content.

Comic Life Gallery
http://plasq.com/comiclife/gallery/

Comic Book Resources
http://www.comicbookresources.com

Only Connect . . . >

Writers use visual content, such as photographs, illustrations, charts, graphs, and design elements, to inform and persuade readers, as well as to add visual interest to their documents. The emergence of new software and hardware technologies has enabled writers—not just graphic designers and programmers—to incorporate visual content into their work to help them achieve these important rhetorical goals. Writers are also now called upon to communicate with wider audiences in contexts beyond the walls of the classroom—on the Web, in student-produced magazines and ezines, and in service learning projects, for example—*and* to develop critical literacy themselves as readers in a visual culture. The occasions for producing visually rich documents have multiplied.

24a Informative and Persuasive Content vs. Design Content

The visual content you present in a document and the way you present it matter. Visual content plays two roles: (1) it presents information and arguments itself, and (2) it includes design elements that convey relationships between images and surrounding text.

Any arrangement of words, images, color, data, graphs, and charts presents information and makes appeals to readers. For example, consider a personal ad placed with an online matchmaking service. Personal ads typically contain verbal content about a person's personality, hobbies, interests, and so on, as well as a photograph. This is *informative content.* It is also *persuasive content* because it makes an appeal for action: "Contact me to see if we are compatible." The verbal and visual information work together. In a personal ad, the visual content is critical, since ads accompanied by photos are much more likely to garner responses than those that don't have photos.

Design Content

The arrangement and visual presentation of content shape how people perceive it—how they evaluate it, what relationships they perceive among its parts, and what verbal content they remember most. *Design content* refers to how and what the visual information in a document communicates to readers. Design content includes the arrangement of content on the page or screen, as well as the spatial and logical relationships between verbal text and visual content. Design content conveys an image and directs the reader's attention. It communicates attitudes toward the verbal content, and it sometimes makes arguments about the relative importance of information—in the form of visual hierarchies, for example. (For this reason, it is sometimes referred to as *information architecture.*) Design content also reveals the writer's assumptions about what an audience might be looking for in a document. (See Chapter 25 for more on design content.)

Images as Arguments

Visual content can stand on its own as information and as argument, without depending on its relationship with written text. In the image below, there is no verbal argument, but the action depicted makes an explicit argument nevertheless. The stack of books is being sawed in half. The books look like leather-bound volumes. It is hard to read the spine text, so we don't know what kind of books they are. The saw blade—with its shiny glint and the refracted rainbows—looks like a CD. The title of the image, *Computer Age Ending Literature,* makes the argument even more clear. Literature (represented by books) is being destroyed by the advent of the digital age (represented by the CD). Whether or not we agree with the argument, we can see how the image makes its point.

Computer Age Ending Literature by Chuck Savage.

Visual Content Serves Different Functions

Visual Form	Functions	Production
PHOTOGRAPHS	▪ Convey information and content ▪ May (like illustrations) be touchstones for analysis in the text ▪ Help your reader see what you mean ▪ Allow you to focus on discussing the meaning and significance of a photograph's content rather than merely describing it	▪ Take photographs yourself that express the information or argument ▪ Search for photographs in image archives
ILLUSTRATIONS	▪ Act as visual interpretations of textual content ▪ Explain complex tasks, equipment, or objects ▪ Clarify concepts or processes ▪ Prove a point by showing an example as evidence ▪ Add aesthetic appeal	▪ Draw or paint original art, digitally or by hand ▪ Search for illustrations in image archives ▪ Use a map to show a route ▪ Create a timeline that shows key events graphically
CHARTS AND GRAPHS	▪ Represent data visually ▪ Show trends and relationships among variables ▪ Draw attention to the most important conclusions to be drawn from an analysis of data	▪ Collect data through original research or at data repositories ▪ Use a spreadsheet program to create charts and graphs
DESIGN AND LAYOUT ELEMENTS	▪ Direct the reader's eye to the most important information ▪ Express hierarchies of value and categories across information ▪ Convey tone and mood (professionalism, artistry, playfulness) ▪ Express form as visual content (patterns, lines, etc.) ▪ Add aesthetic appeal	▪ Learn design conventions in the particular discipline, as described in style guides ▪ Study examples of effective design ▪ Use the layout and style features of a word-processing or desktop publishing program

Visuals should be chosen with consideration of how they will help you accomplish your rhetorical goals in a given context, and they should serve a specific purpose. You will need to decide whether to include visuals at all and, if you do include them, which kind of visuals you need and how to present them.

Words have a *dialectical* relationship with nearby images. Words comment on images; images help illustrate or explain verbal content. The viewer's eye tends to be drawn to the visual content, but words also shape the reader's perception. There's no guarantee that readers will see what you want them to see, so, as a writer, guide readers by using some basic principles for effectively integrating visual content into a text.

Visual content typically plays one of two roles in a text:

1. **Illustration and explanation.** Visual content may complement description or may help explain complex information. Visual illustrations and explanations serve as examples of content that has also been presented verbally. For example, *Computer Age Ending Literature* (page 558) could serve as an illustration in a text about the emergence of digital networking and the conservatism of neo-Luddites who see the computer age as destroying traditional print values.

Activity 24-1: Verbal and Visual Content in Concert

The Belgian surrealist painter René Magritte (1898–1967) is well known for pointing out the unusual nature of visual perception and the sometimes illogical presumptions we make about the visual world. One of his most famous works is *The Treachery of Images,* also commonly known as *Ceci n'est pas une pipe* (*This is not a pipe*).

René Magritte's *The Treachery of Images,* or *Ceci n'est pas une pipe (This is not a pipe).* Oil on canvas.

In this painting, Magritte makes a verbal assertion (*This is not a pipe*) right beneath a visual representation of a pipe. Then he titles the painting *The Treachery of Images.*

1. What do you think Magritte had in mind? It certainly looks like a pipe!
2. If we're to believe him, though, then what is it, if not a pipe?
3. How would you explain this painting as a visual argument?
4. Would the meaning be the same if the words weren't on the painting itself?
5. What do you think Magritte had in mind with the later painting shown below?

René Magritte's *The Two Mysteries.* Oil on canvas.

Project Checklist

Tips for Integrating Images and Tables into a Text

1. Every image should serve a specific function, as either illustration or content for analysis. When you use an image to bolster an argument or provide information, take the time to explain in your text how you want your readers to interpret the visual content of the image. Don't presume that everyone will see what you see or that the information graphic's point is self-evident.
2. Images and information graphics should be placed in the text after they are first mentioned and as near as possible to the point of reference. They should be referred to with labels such as *Figure 1* and *Table 2*.
3. Every photograph and illustration in a text should have a caption beneath it. In most cases, the caption begins with *Figure #* and a title or description. Captions are numbered consecutively throughout the text. Images that function only as design elements or visual cues (such as arrows) do not need captions.
4. Every chart, graph, and table needs a caption that summarizes its content. If it is a table of information, the caption should be placed above the table and begin with *Table #*.
5. All images should be accompanied by copyright or permission information and should be properly cited in the document's caption. (See Chapters 19–22 for information on documenting images and screenshots from films.)
6. Double-check your math to make sure that the information in charts, graphs, and tables makes sense. For example, the slices in a pie chart need to add up to a full pie (100%). Use clear and concise labels on the axes of a graph. Clearly identify what each portion of a chart indicates.
7. Leave enough padding (white space) around the image so that text doesn't run up against it.

Illustrations in novels—like the famous ones by John Tenniel in *Alice's Adventures in Wonderland*—usually function as an artist's interpretation of the written text.

An illustration by John Tenniel from *Alice's Adventures in Wonderland.*

2. **Content for analysis.** Information graphics and images serve as the source material for analysis and elaboration in the text. They are the primary content, in other words, with the verbal content meant to inform readers about what they see. In an essay on a painting, for example, the image of the painting serves as the subject for analysis. In an essay on a film, screenshots serve as content for analysis and also help readers remember important scenes.

Any visual content from outside sources needs to be cited in your text. While the Internet has made finding images much faster with tools like Google Images (http://www.google.com/images), image repositories, and clip art collections, it still remains the responsibility of the writer to provide documentation for visual content. Whenever you use visual content, you should keep records so that you have the information you will need later.

Record This Information

1. Name of the person who created the work
2. Title of the work
3. Publication date or date of creation of the work
4. Publication information, including URL (if the image was originally published on the Internet), name of the archive or print publication, and copyright holder and information (if available)

Part 4 provides specific details on formatting sources.

Permission to Republish Visual Content

Most images that you find are copyrighted, so not only do you need to cite their sources; you also need to request permission of the copyright holder before you republish them publicly, such as on your own website or in a student magazine.

Capturing Images from Your Computer Screen

Screenshots. Images that appear on your computer screen from any source can be "captured" and converted into an image file, called a screenshot or screen capture, that can be placed in a document or on a Web page for purposes of illustration, analysis, information, or evidence. Although it is possible to take a screenshot on Windows or Mac system software, the process is difficult and often time consuming. Mac OS 10.3 and higher comes with a utility called Grab (in the Utilities application folder) that makes the process straightforward. For a Windows-based PC, you can find shareware (low cost) or freeware (free) that makes taking screenshots a matter of a few keystrokes. HyperSnap DX-5 (or higher) is easy to use and powerful (see **http://www.hyperionics.com**).

Video capture. Some programs can grab images directly from film or video that plays on your computer using a different system (for example, DirectX on a PC) and are not capturable by the usual methods. For a complete listing of what's presently available, see ImagesPro.com: **http://imagespro.com/programs/capture/0-1.html**.

Animation capture. Movements and actions from animated visual content on a screen can be captured using software that converts them into Macromedia Flash Player or QuickTime® movies for delivery on the Web, in an ebook, or via other forms of multimedia. Both proprietary and freeware tools are available:

Camtasia: **http://www.techsmith.com** (proprietary)
Captivate: **http://www.macromedia.com** (proprietary)
Wink: **http://www.debugmode.com/wink/** (open source; freeware; also useful for still screen captures)

Giving Credit in a Caption

Any copyright information on images used under the provisions of visual content fair use should be listed right by the content, as in this example from an article "Defining Film Rhetoric: The Case of Hitchcock's *Vertigo*" by David Blakesley.

We watch Scottie watching Madeleine in an art museum. Copyright © 1986 Universal City Studios, Inc. Restored Version © 1996 Leland H. Faust, Patricia Hitchcock O'Connell, and Kathleen O'Connell Fiala.

Requesting Permission to Reprint

To request permission, you can write to the copyright holder. Let this person or organization know how you want to use the image, why, and where. In many cases, copyright holders will let you use the visual content if you agree to identify the copyright holder in your work.

In some cases, you may be able to claim "fair use," allowable under U.S. copyright law. Whether fair use applies in a particular case depends greatly on the nature of your use of the content and the nature of the source itself. Even if your use falls under fair use guidelines, you still must identify the copyright holder and cite your source. Generally speaking, it is allowable to

1. Use a small portion of a larger work in your own review or critical analysis of the original work.
2. Use visual content that has been substantially changed and thus bears little relation to the source.
3. Use or alter visual content for the purposes of satire.
4. Use a screenshot of a website for the purposes of analysis and demonstration.
5. Use a screenshot from a film or television show in the context of a review.

In all of these cases, you still need to name the copyright holder and cite the source in your text, but you may not need to request formal permission.

Visual content can be useful as information in a variety of situations that you're likely to come across as you create documents for your courses, including websites, magazines, photographic essays, and multimedia presentations. In any of these situations, be sure that the visual content pulls its weight; it should add and clarify information and not be used purely for decorative purposes.

Visual Content: Purposes, Situations, and Examples

Purpose	Situations and Examples
Provide readers with concise visual evidence of something referred to in the text	▪ You explain or analyze a painting, photograph, or other work of visual art in an essay and need to give readers an image so that they can see what you are referring to. ▪ You observe or participate in an event and need to show your readers what you witnessed or experienced. ▪ You write a critique of a scene in a film or TV show and want to help readers who may not recall the scene. ▪ In your archival research on a historical subject, you discover images that may help your readers understand the subject more clearly. ▪ In a magazine article, you report on a trend or event in the news.
Illustrate complex processes or sequences	▪ In a paper describing a process or series of steps, you want to show readers concisely what the steps look like when performed. ▪ In a science report, you need to illustrate the relationship between objects or the constitution of an object. ▪ In an engineering report, you want to provide a diagram of an instrument and how it works.
Summarize, explain, or interpret data	▪ You have collected data on people's attitudes toward a subject in your field of research and want to show how these attitudes are different now than they were previously. ▪ You find data on demographic variables at a data repository like the U.S. Census and want to show that they are related. ▪ You collect data over time indicating that a significant change has occurred, and you want to show this trend in a graph.

Activity 24-2: Analyzing Information Graphics

Examine the graphic and respond to the questions that follow.

More than 30% of commuters leave home for work between midnight and 7 a.m. Peak period is 6 to 8 a.m. when 50.3% of people get on the road.

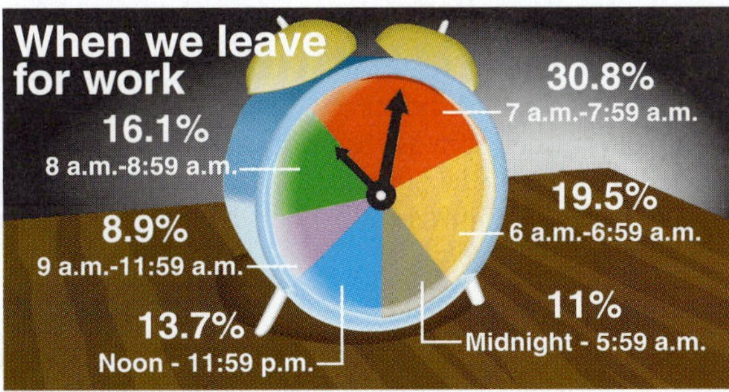

USA Today USA Snapshot. By Shannon Reilley and Gia Kereselidze. Source: U.S. Census Bureau.

1. Can a graphical illustration like the one above, standing by itself, convey accurate information? Why or why not? What factors make a difference?
2. Notice that the graphic cites the U.S. Census Bureau as its source. How is *USA Today*'s graphic an *interpretation* of the U.S. Census Bureau's 2000 data (shown in the table below)? Have the graphic's designers noticed a trend?
3. Compare the data depicted in the USA Snapshot with the Census Bureau data. Do you notice any discrepancies? Which source would you cite in a formal report? Why?
4. The clock is also being used as a pie chart, with its segments sized according to the percentage in a particular category. Is the visual presentation accurate? Why or why not?

TIME LEAVING HOME TO GO TO WORK

Workers who did not work at home	124,095,005	100.0
5:00 to 5:59 a.m.	9,440,321	7.6
6:00 to 6:29 a.m.	10,809,700	8.7
6:30 to 6:59 a.m.	13,386,429	10.8
7:00 to 7:29 a.m.	18,640,062	15.0
7:30 to 7:59 a.m.	19,665,861	15.8
8:00 to 8:29 a.m.	13,409,536	10.8
8:30 to 8:59 a.m.	6,528,339	5.3
9:00 to 11:59 a.m.	11,036,103	8.9
12:00 to 3:59 p.m.	8,522,829	6.9
All other times	12,655,825	10.2

From U.S. Census Bureau, "American Fact Finder" (2000 Census).

Using Graphics to Convey Information

When it first appeared on September 15, 1982, *USA Today* was not the first newspaper to introduce graphical information into its pages. However, it was the first daily national newspaper with wide distribution to use four-color graphical illustrations of information and polls throughout its pages, such as the illustration shown to the left, called "USA Snapshot."

Usually, graphics in the newspaper are tied to feature stories, so their relevance is evident to those who read the text. In other cases, however, the visual information is meant to stand alone. Critics have pointed out that standalone representations of visual information are often misleading because they condense complex information into nuggets that can easily be misinterpreted. Because of the power of the visual, such representations tend to be persuasive and memorable, even when the information they present may be interpreted in many different ways or is visually represented in a misleading way.

Types of Information Graphics

Line graphs show relationships among types of data, such as the change in a quantity (e.g., revenue) over time. Data are divided into logical units on the vertical and horizontal axes. A line graph showing revenue growth over time might have time units (e.g., months) placed horizontally and revenue units (e.g., dollars) vertically. You can graph several sets of data horizontally if they share a common reference (e.g., time).

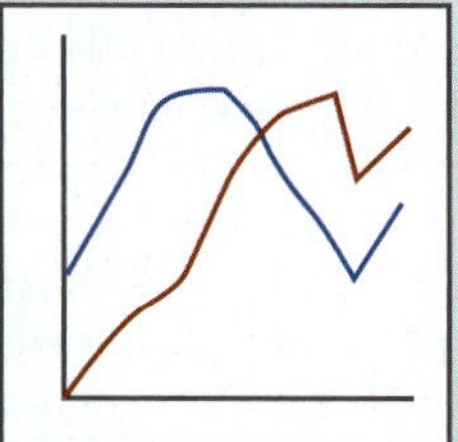

Bar graphs show comparative relationships across a data set, correlated with a common reference point. For example, a bar graph could show how much time people in different fields spent writing at their jobs. Each bar's height would be correlated with a certain amount of time, mapped on the vertical axis. A label for each bar would be placed on the horizontal axis, as in the example to the right.

Pie charts show the relative quantities of the components of

Inserting Graphs and Charts into a Document

Charts and graphs that have been constructed from data in a spreadsheet program can be inserted directly into a word-processing document. Some word processors, such as Microsoft Word 2007, allow you to construct the chart or graph in the program. The following steps describe the process of inserting a chart in Word 2007, but the process is similar in WordPerfect and in OpenOffice.org.

1. In Word 2007, place the cursor where you want to insert the chart.
2. Choose the Insert tab and then select the Chart icon on the Insert ribbon.
3. Choose the chart type that will best represent your data, then click OK. (See Figure 24.1.)

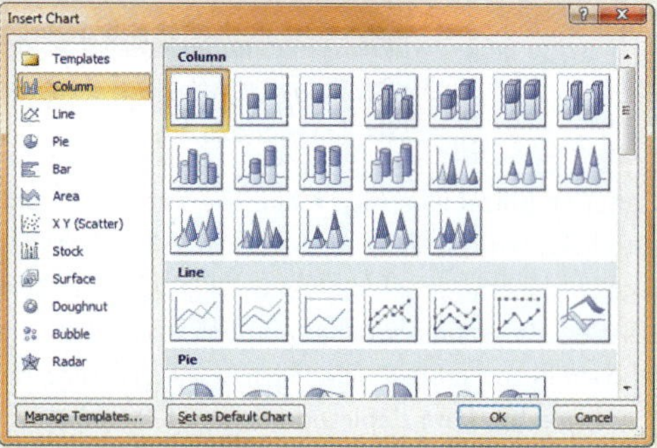

Figure 24.1

4. Microsoft Excel 2007 will open, allowing you to prepare your data. When finished, close the Excel document. Your generated chart will appear in your Word 2007 document. (See Figure 24.2.)

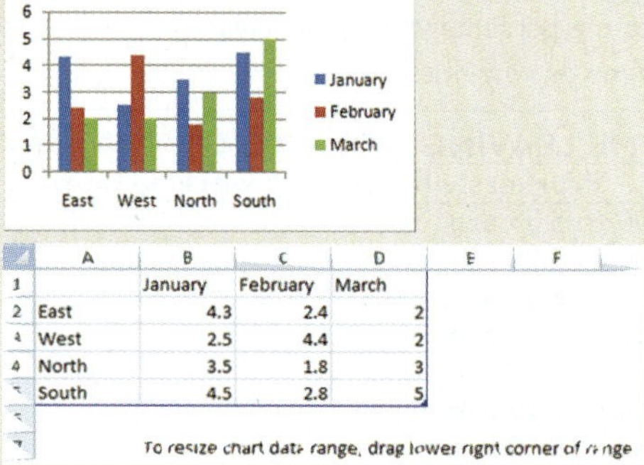

	A	B	C	D	E	F
1		January	February	March		
2	East	4.3	2.4	2		
3	West	2.5	4.4	2		
4	North	3.5	1.8	3		
5	South	4.5	2.8	5		

To resize chart data range, drag lower right corner of range

Figure 24.2

5. Adjust the appearance of the chart by double-clicking on any of its components.
6. Add a number and descriptive caption to the chart so that you can refer to it in your document. For tables and charts, the caption is placed above the object, as shown in Figure 24.3.

Table 1: Cost of Hiring Website Consultant for Nonprofit Organizations

	Cost per Hour	Total Hours	Total Cost
Option 1: Part-time employee, working in store and on website	$8 to $10	20 hours per week	$8320 to $10,400 per year
Option 2: Temporary skilled employee, contracted to reformat website	$20 to $30	40 hours	$800 to $1200 (one time)

Figure 24.3

The process of inserting tables, charts, and graphs is similar when you have already made them using a spreadsheet program. In cases where you want to publish the object in a printed document so a high-quality image is important, you can convert the object into an image (such as a JPG or TIF file) directly from the spreadsheet program.

For instructions that apply to Microsoft® Word® 2003, visit the handbook's website: **cengage.com/english/blakesley**

something. You could use a pie chart to show the makeup of a group of people, with each slice of the pie having a size corresponding to the percentage of people in that group. The slices in any pie chart must add up to 100 percent of the group. The "USA Snapshot" (page 565) is a pie chart.

Flowcharts include visual illustrations and arrows to show how a process unfolds over time or how one idea or action leads to another. Flowcharts help writers show the steps in a process. See page 220 to see how a flowchart illustrates the job search process.

Diagrams are illustrations of something that consists of parts (such as an engine). They provide readers with orientation and perspective. **Venn diagrams** use circles or arcs to show how one thing intersects or overlaps with something else. The "Margin of Overlap" (page 192) is an example of a Venn diagram.

Maps are visual illustrations of a physical space (such as a city or mall). Maps are also used to associate a region or idea with an event, action, or other phenomenon. So, for example, neuroscientists might develop a cognitive map that shows what parts of the brain perform which functions. The "3 Models of Déjà Vu" illustration (page 129) shows such a map.

Writers use visual content in their work to persuade people to take action or to change their attitudes. As you know from experience in our visual culture, photographs sometimes speak volumes, much more than a thousand words. They can be persuasive in their own right. Graphs and charts may present data strictly to inform, but they may also be manipulated in terms of design so that they argue a point. As a writer and a reader, you should be aware of how people use visual content to persuade—effectively or not, ethically or not.

Visual and Verbal Content as Argument

Visual content can make an argument on its own, without supporting text, as we saw in the image *Computer Age Ending Literature* on page 558. Often, however, visual content works in conjunction with printed text to inform and persuade readers, as in Magritte's *The Treachery of Images* on page 560. Artist Barbara Kruger is famous for making visual arguments that combine text and images.

Barbara Kruger's Visual Argument

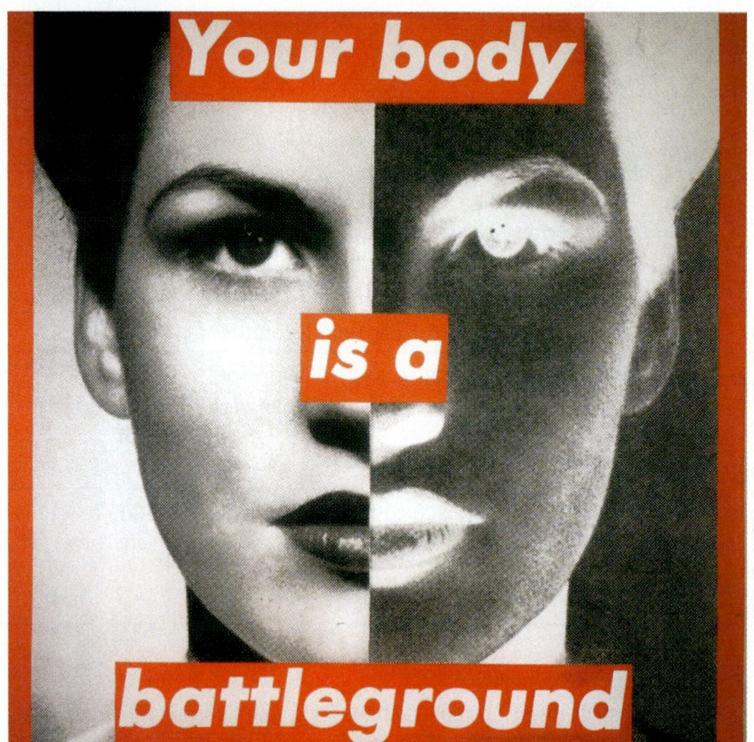

Barbara Kruger, *Untitled (Your body is a battleground)*, 1989. Photographic silkscreen on vinyl. 112 × 112 inches.

Activity 24-3: Analyzing Kruger's Argument

1. Kruger displays words prominently on her images. What do you notice about (a) the placement of the words, (b) the use of color, and (c) the use of contrast?
2. What is the argument in this image? How does Kruger's technique of arranging image and words support the argument?
3. Kruger uses red as the background for many of the words in her art. What effect does that have on you as a viewer?
4. How would your interpretation of this image change if the words were absent?

Visual Presentations of 2004 Presidential Election Results

For a fascinating look at different visual displays of election results and analysis of their impact, visit "Maps and Cartograms of the 2004 US Presidential Election Results" by Michael Gastner, Cosma Shalizi, and Mark Newman on pages hosted by Mark Newman, Department of Physics and Center for the Study of Complex Systems at the University of Michigan, at **http://www-personal.umich.edu/~mejn/election/**.

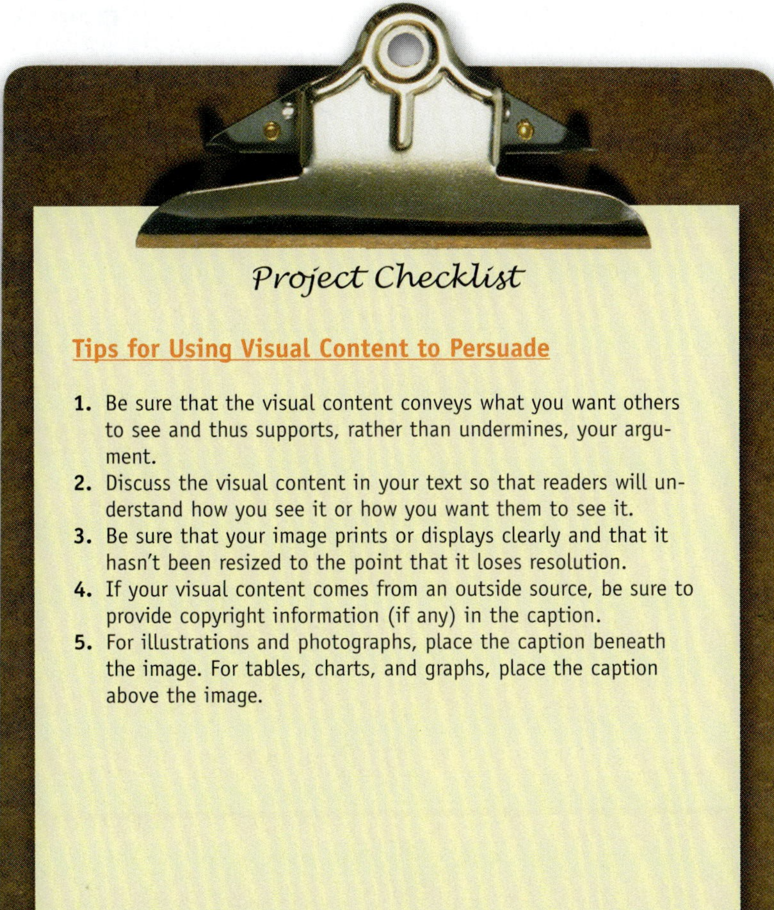

Project Checklist

Tips for Using Visual Content to Persuade

1. Be sure that the visual content conveys what you want others to see and thus supports, rather than undermines, your argument.
2. Discuss the visual content in your text so that readers will understand how you see it or how you want them to see it.
3. Be sure that your image prints or displays clearly and that it hasn't been resized to the point that it loses resolution.
4. If your visual content comes from an outside source, be sure to provide copyright information (if any) in the caption.
5. For illustrations and photographs, place the caption beneath the image. For tables, charts, and graphs, place the caption above the image.

Visual Content as Evidence in an Argument

Writers often use visual content as an example in an argument, to prove a point and to persuade a reader that a particular interpretation of an image (or of something the image represents) has merit. Visual content may serve as documentary evidence that something has happened or has happened as is argued in the text. It may also—as information—bolster an argument for changing course or for adopting new policies. Data from research are represented visually in charts, graphs, and tables for clarity but also to give the reader a snapshot that can be taken in at a glance and thus also function persuasively.

A table of contents for writing project threads appears on pages xv–xxii.

Brochures

Gathering Images

Images in a brochure can communicate information, express ideas and moods, and persuade an audience. If you are considering using photos in your brochure, consult the Project Checklist on page 186 to make sure each photo says what you think it does. If you are trying to determine which kinds of visuals would work best for your rhetorical situation, consult Chapter 24. Be sure to read section 24c on citing the sources of images. ◀ page 44.

25 DESKTOP PUBLISHING AND GRAPHIC DESIGN FOR WRITERS

Writing in college still includes writing essays and research papers printed on 8½" × 11" paper. But teachers also regularly encourage students to try their hand at new ways of expressing ideas in other forms people will read and value. You probably have seen beautifully printed documents created on simple word processors. Today, software tools for word processing, design and layout, and digital imaging are readily available. Hardware has advanced significantly as well, so now individuals—not commercial printers alone—have access to all the computing power they need to produce high-quality printed brochures, flyers, posters, magazines, and more on affordable color laser and inkjet printers. New developments in digital printing processes even enable print-on-demand book publishing and magazine publishing. Digital filesharing capabilities allow writers and designers to transfer their files to commercial digital printers and distributors via ftp uploads, reducing the time and expense of desktop publishing even further.

Because of these technological developments, the opportunity to manage all aspects of publishing, from the writing through the design, layout, and typesetting of printed documents, has shifted to content creators—that is, writers and designers. The democratization of desktop publishing has brought the creator of content potentially closer to the art of preparing it for publication. Whatever your field in college and beyond, it is likely that at some point you will be responsible for creating complex printed documents that twenty years ago would have cost thousands of dollars to produce, on printing equipment costing in the hundreds of thousands of dollars.

In college, you may find yourself participating in service learning projects that involve working with community organizations to help them produce documents like brochures and flyers. You may want to promote a student club or advertise a special event. You may work with peers to publish your writing or research project in a student magazine. You might start your own ezine in a creative writing class or create a poster board for display at a local conference.

After you graduate, you may be involved in preparing documents for an organization—either by contributing content or by managing the production and collaboration processes. These documents might communicate inside the organization or reach out to the general public. In any of these contexts, it will be useful to know how to represent your and others' work in print. Although it runs against common advice, people do often judge books by their covers, so it's worth your while to pay attention to what publishing and marketing specialists call "packaging," "branding," and "signage." Designers and writers present packaged products and content, aiming for brand recognition with logos or other visual design content that helps their work stand out. They also create informative and visual signs in printed material (books, magazines, etc.) and on display in physical spaces where it will be noticed.

Project Checklist

Formatting an Essay or Research Report for Submission

The style manuals described in Part 4 set standards for formatting essays and research reports for submission to an instructor or to a journal for possible publication. Instructors often require that you follow other formatting guidelines also. Take the time early in your projects to review these guidelines so that you can plan ahead to follow them. Then be sure to adhere to them when you print and submit your work. The guidelines make it easier for instructors and editors to process large quantities of information and to respond effectively. In the professional publishing world, editors evaluate an author's ability to format a submission properly as evidence that he or she will be able to manage the more complex tasks of revising a manuscript for publication. Your instructors will judge your ability to format a document as one sign that you have paid careful attention to all aspects of your work.

1. **Format.** Follow the formatting guidelines in the discipline's style manual or provided by your instructor, including those for placement of title, author, date, course, page numbers, and headers; size of margins; placement and use of visual content; footnotes or endnotes; and Works Cited or References.
2. **Legibility.** Use a font size that is legible. In most cases, 12-point Times New Roman is a good choice for printed essays and research projects.
3. **Printing.** Print your work using a good-quality printer on standard white paper, unless the situation calls for a specialty paper (for a flyer, for example). Double-check to make sure that all pages have printed and that the printer used sufficient ink.
4. **Submission requirements.** Instructors may ask you to submit your work in a folder with a title page, or they may have other requirements. The style guides for each discipline recommend how to submit work when no other guidelines are available. Many essays and research projects are bound with a paperclip, which allows the reader to separate pages and thus review the Works Cited or Bibliography while reading the paper.

Creating Proximity to Convey Meaningful Relationships

Visual Argument in the Digital Age:

Political Advertising as Propaganda in the

2004 Presidential Campaign

Andrea Wilson and Joe Malinger

April 1, 2006

No clear relationships exist among pieces of information.

Visual Argument in the Digital Age:
Political Advertising as Propaganda in the
2004 Presidential Campaign

Andrea Wilson and Joe Malinger
April 1, 2006

Relationships are created between the title and subtitle and between the authors and the date.

Brown 2

Alfred Hitchcock films are sometimes as famous for their openings as they are for their contents. Critics have noted how the themes of voyeurism and spectatorship have been illustrated by acts of spying, shown most directly in films like *Rear Window, Vertigo,* and *Psycho.*

They have also focused on how male characters often presume to speak for women, most memorably in *Psycho* when Norman Bates voices his mother. These themes work their way into the opening credit sequences. For example, the theme of voyeurism is expressed in the opening of *Vertigo* as the viewer seems to be spying on the woman, who seems fearful as the camera moves in. The Saul Bass/John Whitney credit sequence unfolds with an extreme close-up

Brown 3

of a woman's face, slightly off-center to the left. The viewer crosses the proxemic space of the familiar into the intimate. Then we see "James Stewart" appear above the woman's lips, with the implication that he (or his character) will speak for her, like a ventriloquist. (See Illustration 1.)

Illustration 1. Opening credits, *Vertigo.* © 1986 Universal City Studios, Inc. Restored version © 1996 Leland H. Faust, Patricia Hitchcock O'Connell, and Kathleen O'Connell Fiala.

The text that refers to the image precedes it, and the image is close to its description. Readers will understand the connection.

A primary goal of graphic design is to present content so that visual, design, and textual content work in harmony to convey information and create the desired effect. That goal is one to work for, whether your material is a brochure for a student club or program, a poster for a special event, a business card, or a research report that uses the visual representation of data to reinforce or extend an argument.

The principles of proximity, alignment, repetition, and contrast can be followed to make sure that your visual and design content works in concert with your verbal content so that you communicate efficiently or argue effectively.

Proximity

Proximity means closeness. Proximity is a familiar way to convey meaning, and as readers in a visual culture, we're so used to making judgments about meaning based on proximity that we often don't notice we're doing it. Readers expect images and text that are close to each other to have a meaningful relationship. As a writer/designer, try to put closely related images and text close to each other on the page.

Alignment

Alignment refers to the spatial layout of elements on a page in discernible patterns. Generally speaking, it is good practice to align every object on a page with the edges of other elements to establish a pattern and a relationship. Alignment helps create consistency and express relationships between pieces of information. Good page design often exhibits consistent alignment (in margins, for example) and sometimes draws attention to important information by deliberately misaligning it. Misaligned elements attract attention because of the effects of contrast, covered on page 575.

Repetition

Repetition of design elements conveys important structural information to a reader and thus can assist the writer in communicating information unobtrusively. When you repeat a design element—a typeface, an alignment, or a visual metaphor—you create meaningful connections among types of content, pages, or regions of a page. In a report, for example, it is common practice to use a consistent style for headers. A-level headers (like chapter titles or major sections) might be centered in 14-point type. B-level headers might be flush left in 12-point type.

Creating Alignment to Convey Meaningful Patterns

Here is information for an exhibit arranged in a logical order but without any design principles applied to its alignment:

Jennifer Sterling Design Exhibit
San Francisco, California
March 30 to June 24, 2001
San Francisco Museum of Modern Art

Below is a poster on which the designer, Jennifer Sterling, has realigned (and highly stylized) the information. On the left, you see the title and dates of the exhibit in a visual pattern that reflects the playfulness of her work. The eye leaps to the word *Exhibit* in the right column because of the large font, and then the artist's name is only partly revealed. People who know her work (professional designers) will complete the name. Those who don't may be curious. The bottom of the poster, where the eye moves last, repeats key information in a more familiar pattern so that there's no doubt about what the poster has announced.

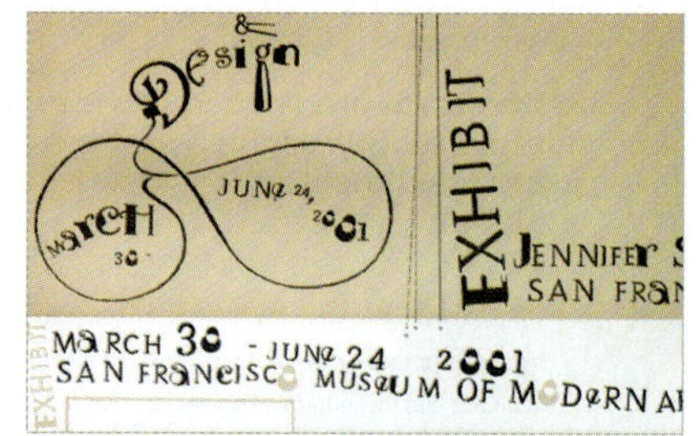

Final poster for the San Francisco Museum of Modern Art's exhibition of Jennifer Sterling's work.

Using Repetition to Convey Structural Information

A cover from a recording company's annual report, using repetition in the pattern to suggest the relationship between recordings and their musical sources.

Readers use this consistency to identify how sections of a document are related.

Repetition may involve more than the use of a consistent style for like elements. It may also involve modest variation on a design theme throughout a document, as shown on page 586, where pieces of the logo for the Human Relations Commission provide visual interest across the pages of the brochure.

In a tri-fold brochure, you might include a separator bar between columns (page 583). Or in a newspaper, you might consistently place visual data in the right column on the same page every day so readers know where to find it. On a website, you might provide a consistent visual cue such as an up-arrow (▲) to indicate where a reader should click to go to the top of the page.

Contrast

Contrast—sharp differences in color, typography, or other design elements—is used to highlight or prioritize information, and it adds visual interest. You can use contrast to direct your reader's eye where you want it to move first or to draw attention to some especially important elements on a page.

Contrast Used to Suggest a Close Relationship

This poster for the sociology department at Temple University uses an extremely large font size, with people cut-outs in a contrasting color, to suggest an equation between sociology and the study of group life.

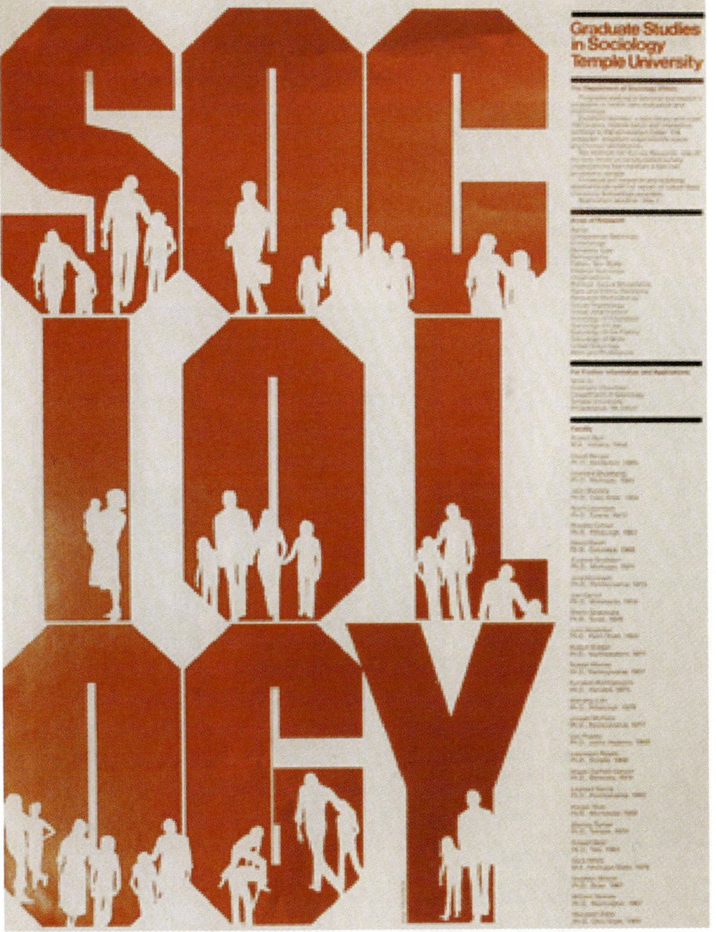

The large font size used for "Sociology" contrasts sharply with the people cut-outs and the smaller text on the right, which provides information about the department.

A Poster: Four Design Principles Working Together

This poster image is composed of three parts: the photograph and two lines of text. All are arranged using *contrast* and *repetition* to convey a mood of elegance.

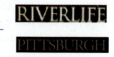

The top image of the sunset and skyline is rotated 180 degrees to imitate reflection on water, a good example of *repetition*.

The designers use a serif font in all capital letters, stretching across the poster and dividing the page in half. "Pittsburgh" is made transparent so that it appears to be a reflection of "Riverlife," even though that's impossible. *Proximity* helps equate the two and add to the illusion.

To give the impression that the bottom image is a reflection in water, it needs to be perfectly *aligned* with the top image.

The vertical lines of the suspension cables create a sharp visual pattern through *repetition*.

Project Checklist

Choosing Type

- Distinguish body text from headings by using contrasting fonts. Serif fonts are useful for body text on a printed page, and sans serif fonts are often used for headers.

Serif Fonts	Sans Serif Fonts
Times New Roman	Arial
Bookman Old Style	Century Gothic
Garamond	Tahoma
Book Antiqua	Verdana

- Check to be sure the font is legible.
  Not very legible, even at 12-point Quite legible at 12-point
- Make sure the tone and style of the type reinforce the message of your content. A script font like *Lucida Handwriting* would look odd in a formal research paper, but it might work well for a short header on a poster or a Web page.
- Use bold and italic for special purposes, such as to emphasize headings or words used in special senses (Chapter 56).
- Consider your audience when deciding on point size. In a newsletter for elders, for example, you might use 14-point instead of 10-point.

Typography refers to the overall balance and interplay of the letters on the page or screen. You can use typography to enhance the readability of information and to direct the flow of an argument by following design principles to establish a unified theme and style.

Attributes of Type

Type can be described by font family, typeface, and point size.

Fonts

Fonts are classified as serif and sans serif. Serif fonts have small strokes at the ends of some lines. Times New Roman is a serif font. Sans serif fonts do not have these additional strokes. For example, Arial does not. These two basic font styles (serif and sans serif) each include thousands of specific font families.

Typefaces

Use a normal typeface for most body text, and reserve special typefaces (bold, italics) for headings, titles, and other special elements.

Point Size

Most writers use 10-, 11-, or 12-point fonts for body text on paper documents, but for headings you can vary the point size modestly. For posters and other display documents, choose point sizes that will make the information stand out at the distance from which readers are likely to be viewing the piece.

Page Layout Issues

Line length, leading, margins and alleys, and justification all affect page appearance.

Line Length

Depending on the nature of the document (brochure, report, flyer, book, and so on) and the size of the paper, choose a line length for maximum readability. The upper limit for easy reading is 75 characters on a line, so keep your line length shorter than that.

Leading

Leading refers to the distance between successive lines of text. A double-spaced page of text has twice the leading of a single-spaced page of text, for example. Most word processors and desktop publishing programs use automatic leading, so you may not have to worry about it much in preparing familiar printed documents. But if you require more control over the visual design of your documents (in print or on screen), you will want to use a leading value that makes your text easy to read. A typical leading value for body text on a printed document is related to the point size of the typeface. So, for example, if you are using 12-point Times New Roman, the leading will likely be about 14.4 points.

Line Length in Two 5" x 8" Books

Notice how the line length in the following two excerpts affects your perception. The first is actually from the novel *The Kite Runner,* by Khaled Hosseini. The second shows how the book would look with a shorter line length.

24-pica line

What was I doing on this road in the middle of the night? I should have been in bed, under my blanket, a book with dog-eared pages at my side. This had to be a dream. Had to be. Tomorrow

22.5-pica line

What was I doing on this road in the middle of the night? I should have been in bed, under my blanket, a book with dog-eared pages at my side. This had to be a dream. Had to

Leading

14.4-point leading

These single-spaced lines of text have 14.4-point leading. This setting usually makes for comfortable reading, but in cases where you need more white space, want to create contrast, or need to make the text especially easy to read (on the screen, for example, or on a flyer viewed at a distance), you should increase the leading.

18-point leading

These lines of text have 18-point leading. This setting usually makes for comfortable reading on the screen or at a distance. Greater leading is useful for stylized text on presentation documents. It provides more white space when you need to create contrast or provide eye relief.

Justification

Fully justified text

This is fully justified text in a column with a short line length. Notice how there are rivers of white space that you can see traveling down the page. At a typical reading distance, these rivers can be very noticeable.

Left-justified text

This is left-justified text in a column with a short line length. Notice that here the letters are equally spaced across the line so that there are no discernible variations in distances between letters and words.

Margins and Alleys
Establish a consistent pattern with margins and alleys. A margin is the distance between the outer edge of text and the edge of the page. An alley is the distance between columns on a multi-column page. Margins and alleys create white space, which aids readability. They also help you manage line length. (Typical margins on a typed essay are 1"; a typical alley is 1/4" to 1/2", depending on the overall dimensions of the paper and the width of the columns.) The brochure on page 586 illustrates the use of margins and alleys.

Justification
Word processors allow you to set margins so that they are either aligned or jagged. For most informal writing, it's best to use a jagged right margin. For more formal documents, full justification (alignment) of the left and right margins is a good choice because it creates precise edges, improving visual appeal. However, most word processors do not create fully justified lines very well. To create them, the software may insert extra white space between letters, sometimes producing very awkward results, especially when the line length is very short. Managing fully justified text in a brochure with narrow columns may require that many words at the ends of lines be divided using hyphens.

25d Managing Color Effectively

Color adds life to display documents like flyers, posters, and brochures. Unfortunately, while graphics editors increase the range of options for incorporating color into designs, they also grant opportunities for designers to create awful color combinations. Furthermore, designers need to pay careful attention to ensure that color choices will be translated accurately by the printer that will run the job (page 584). Professional designers use color guides and palettes (collections of complementary colors). Color wheels show the spectrum of color and help designers choose analogous and complementary colors.

Analogous Colors

Analogous colors are next to each other on the color wheel. They usually go well together, both in print and in digital documents.

Complementary Colors

Complementary colors lie on opposite sides of the color wheel. They usually contrast well and print effectively, even though common sense might have prevented you from imagining such a combination.

Color wheel

Analogous colors

Complementary colors

Resources on Color

Color Matters: **http://www.colormatters.com**

This website includes detailed discussion of color theory, perception, design, and more.

Color Mixers: **http://colormixers.com**

This website allows users to enter a color number in hexadecimal format (each number is associated with a color) or RGB (Red-Green-Blue) format and get a palette of complementary colors.

Project Checklist

Tips for Creating Flyers and Posters

1. **Do your research.** Make sure that all the factual information you have about time, date, and location is accurate, that days and dates correspond, that you have identified the exact location (e.g., room number) of the event, and that people's names are spelled correctly. Also find out where and under what circumstances you are allowed to display your flyers or posters.
2. **Storyboard.** Create a mock-up of your flyer or poster, sketching out where you plan to place headers, images, and text. Tape your mock-up to a wall, and then stand back from it. Is anything about it unusual or striking? Will it grab your attention? If not, what can you do so it will?
3. **Grab attention.** Since a major goal is to catch someone's eye, you can be more assertive with your design than you might be in a handheld document. Grab attention with striking (but relevant) and larger-than-usual images, large headers or titles, and bold colors.
4. **Hold attention.** Once you have interested your audience, you need to give them useful and precise information. This information need not be presented as boldly as your header or title, but it should be legible from a short distance. Use subheads (fonts in larger point sizes) to make information stand out.
5. **Use graphic design principles to structure images and information.** Put related information close together on the page; align your edges; use sharp contrasts among white space, content, and images to add visual interest; and establish a color scheme that complements your images and content.
6. **Leave time to revise and edit text and design.** Ask at least one other person to read your flyer before you say "print it." Encourage reviewers to comment on your selection of images; sometimes the pictures we use suggest more than we intend or notice, and another reader can help you identify unintended connotations.
7. **Print your flyer on durable paper.** A coated, matte finish on card stock will help your flyer stand out from the rest and last.

Flyers, posters, poster display boards, and brochures are all documents that should be visually appealing, include ample white space, have highly readable typefaces, and be printed on (or mounted on) durable paper.

Flyers and Posters

Flyers and posters, two kinds of signs, share a common rhetorical goal. They need to catch the reader's eye—often from a distance—and make key information readily discernible closer up. The Sociology poster on page 575 effectively captures the eye from a distance and then provides detailed information once the viewer moves closer. Posters are typically large (at least 11" × 17"). They may be used for displaying information and images at an exhibit or other special event, such as a poster session. Flyers are used to announce events. Flyers are sometimes handed out, but more often they are posted in public places.

Flyers and posters can be used to announce events. Such announcements should include the following information:

- Title and nature of the event
- Time, date, and location
- Contact information for the organizers (people often have questions) and associated URL, if any
- Sponsorship information

Poster Display Boards

Like flyers, poster display boards at exhibits or special events need to be easily readable from a distance. However, the information they provide is usually more detailed—for example, summarizing the key findings of a research or lab project. Project display boards "tell the story" of a project and provide the audience with a snapshot or synopsis of the project's key points or features. Your local bookstore or art supply store may sell specially designed and foldable project display boards on which you can mount printed images and text.

Poster display boards are large, complex documents composed of images and text. In some respects, they function like a large page and thus need to guide the reader's eyes carefully to critical information. Plan your poster board in such a way that your reader will know how to read in sequence (if sequence matters). Don't be afraid to use numbers or other navigational cues to help people along. Some poster sessions or exhibits may have guidelines for the layout of posters, perhaps in the interest of keeping an audience moving along in a crowded space or in a competition.

Sample Poster Display Board in APA Style

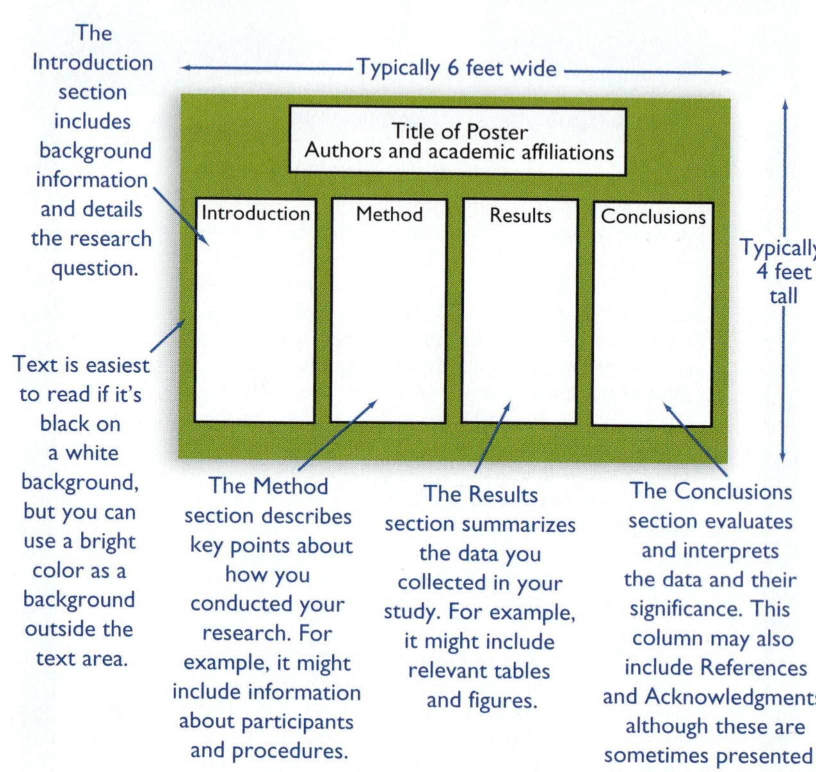
The Introduction section includes background information and details the research question.
Typically 6 feet wide
Title of Poster
Authors and academic affiliations
Introduction
Method
Results
Conclusions
Typically 4 feet tall
Text is easiest to read if it's black on a white background, but you can use a bright color as a background outside the text area.
The Method section describes key points about how you conducted your research. For example, it might include information about participants and procedures.
The Results section summarizes the data you collected in your study. For example, it might include relevant tables and figures.
The Conclusions section evaluates and interprets the data and their significance. This column may also include References and Acknowledgments, although these are sometimes presented in a handout that viewers can take with them.

Conference posters generally follow the same pattern as research papers formatted in APA style. (See section 20d for a sample APA paper.) They are prepared so that they can be read from the top of the left column down, from the top of the next column down, and so on.

This example shows the layout for a 6' × 4' poster, the recommended size in APA style. Another popular size for posters is 4' × 3'. They are designed as trifold display boards using three columns, with the center column measuring 2' and each side panel 1'. Presenters typically place the primary content in the center column and use the outer columns for related information or examples.

Sample Template for a Tri-Fold Brochure

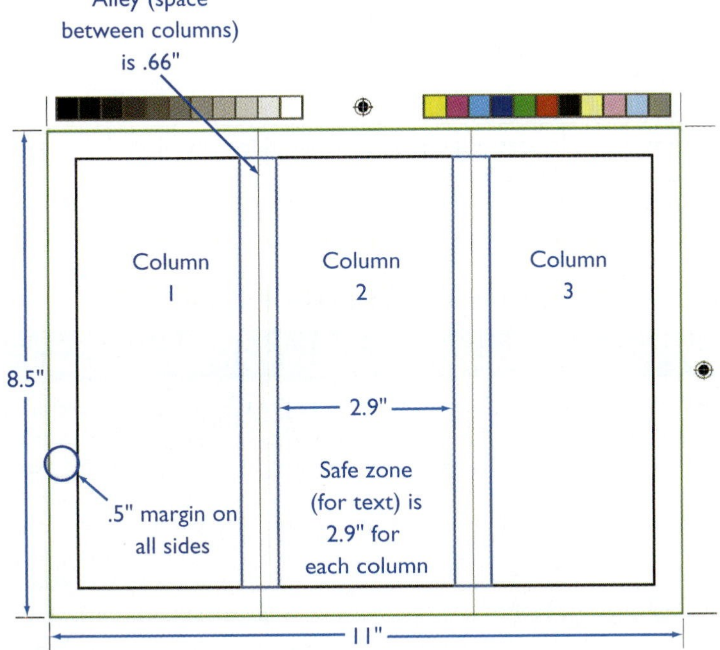

Sample layout specifications for a tri-fold brochure, with printer's marks.

Brochures

Brochures are pamphlets that contain only a few pages. They are often created by folding a single piece of paper into sections and having columns of text that correspond to the folded sections. Brochures can be informational, such as a brochure found in a hospital waiting room that describes the symptoms of a particular disease, or persuasive, such as a brochure that advertises a manufacturer's line of swimming pools.

One of the best methods of planning for a successful printing project is to prepare a prototype of what you hope to accomplish. That's especially true when you are working with unusual paper sizes or will be folding paper into its final form, such as when creating a brochure. Consider how you want the brochure to open and be read—in what sequence should the panels be read? Then fold a piece of paper and start blocking out sections of text and visuals. Note that it may be awkward for text to cross from one folded section to another, but photographs and illustrations can do so to good effect.

Papers and Printers for Display Documents

In printing flyers, posters, project displays, and brochures, your choice of paper is a critical one. Different papers will render colors differently, for example, depending on whether they are coated or textured, their brightness level (ranging from 87 to 110), their color, and their weight (from laser paper to cover stock). If you plan to use your own printer, experiment with a range of paper stock early in the process so that you can decide whether your images and text need any special handling. Words printed on glossy paper are somewhat more difficult to read when viewed from a distance, but the images will be brighter. Papers with matte finish work well for handouts to be distributed to people for personal reading and for flyers in which the legibility of the text is critical, as it often is.

Sample Paper Specifications for Flyer or Brochure

Weight: 44 lb (Flyers may use heavier stock, but brochures need to be folded, so the paper can't be too heavy.)

Finish: Glossy or matte

Color: White

Brightness: 100 or higher

Format: Inkjet or laser (Papers come designed for one or the other, so may not work well on both.)

Size: 8½" × 11", 11" × 14", 11" × 17", or 13" × 19"

A Comparison of Inkjet and Laser Printers

	Inkjet Printers	Laser Printers
EFFECTS ON TEXT AND IMAGES	Typically are used to print high-quality images on glossy paper.	Typically handle printed text and line art (drawings and graphs, for example) very well. Usually don't reproduce color images of photographic quality the way some inkjet printers can.
PAPER CONSIDERATIONS	Can handle a wide variety of papers.	May be more limited than inkjet printers in the range of paper sizes that they can handle.
INK SYSTEM	Use a three-color (or more) ink system called RGB mode (red, green, blue). Images and text should be created in (or converted to) RGB colors before printing.	Typically use a CMYK ink system with four cartridges (cyan, magenta, yellow, and black). Images and colors should be designed in or converted to CMYK mode in your production process.

Whether or not the paper is coated will affect the appearance dramatically, no matter what type of printing process is used. Paper with a matte finish tends to absorb ink and mute bright colors.

Project Checklist

Producing a Newsletter

The process of producing a newsletter includes many of the steps you follow to create a flyer or an even more complex document such as a multimedia essay (▶section 32d) or a website (▶Chapters 30–31).

1. **Storyboard** your newsletter so that you know how much space you have for each component (including a word count), how many images you need, and where you want to place text and images. Newsletters are typically in multi-column format, much like a newspaper, but it is common for images and other design elements to break across the columns to add visual interest.
2. **Create an assets list** that tells exactly which pieces of the newsletter you need to collect in advance (▶ page 713).
3. **Collaborate.** Ask for contributions to the newsletter from members of the group. Newsletters represent the group, so it is good (and ethical) practice to give others a voice. A newsletter should be the collective voice of the people it represents.
4. **Circulate a draft for revision suggestions.** Give some people the opportunity to read through the newsletter to make sure that it contains all the information it should, that it effectively represents the group, and that it is error-free. Allow time for feedback to come in and revisions to be made based on this feedback.
5. **Print** the newsletter on uncoated paper, with an opacity high enough that text and images don't show through the opposite side. A good weight to use is 44 lb paper stock. Textured papers work especially well for newsletters.

A newsletter is a multi-page publication—or at least one page printed front and back—that provides information about a group's activities to its members. Newsletters typically contain news about recent and upcoming events, notable achievements of individuals or the organization, profiles of new members, and other announcements. They are popular with student clubs and other organizations as a method of sharing information and building community.

When designing a newsletter, pay attention to design principles:

- Achieve a good contrast between images and text, leaving enough white space to provide eye relief but not so much that your reader's eye will get lost.
- Place bits of information of a similar kind in proximity (such as calendar items).
- Use headers to indicate new topics and to break column text into smaller units for easy reading.
- Use pull-out text to pique the interest of readers and reduce the monotony of text-heavy columns. Pull-out text consists of quotations pulled from the body text and repeated in larger type for contrast.
- Develop a visual theme (using typography and other design elements) to establish a consistent style.

One useful way to put your knowledge of desktop publishing to work is by helping a local non-profit organization develop documents that they can use to promote themselves in the community. Such projects require active collaboration among students and professionals. They also allow you to make design and content decisions in real contexts that matter to people, one of the best ways to learn complex principles.

The documents shown here were produced by a group of students working with three local human relations commissions, area high schools, and campus officials to help launch an awareness campaign. Their goals were to develop a logo and a range of documents: a flyer, a brochure, letterhead, a slide for a television ad, a press release, and a website. Early on, much of the process involved conducting research on the nature and function of human relations commissions and interviewing commissioners. This research was used to draft the documents that would later be discussed with the human relations commissioners.

Draft Brochure for the Human Relations Commission

Examples of Discrimination

- A potential employer asks questions of female applicants not asked of male applicants.
- You are fired from your job in retaliation for complaining about the company's discriminatory practice.
- You can't rent an apartment because, after learning you have children, the landlord tells you it is "for adults only." Or, when you begin to look pregnant, you are told you must vacate your apartment.
- A landlord tells you that a unit is no longer available for rental or purchase when he or she sees that you are not caucasian.
- You are denied seating in a restaurant because of your race when there is space available.
- You are denied access to a public facility because of a disability.

State and Federal Agencies

You can also seek assistance from State and Federal agencies when you feel you have been discriminated against.

Indiana Civil Rights Commission
http://www.in.gov/icrc/
800.628.2909 | 800.743.3333 (Hearing Impaired)

U.S. Commission on Civil Rights
http://www.usccr.gov/
312.353.8311 | 312.353.8362 (Hearing Impaired)

Fair Housing and Equal Opportunity Hotline
800.669.9777 or see
http://www.hud.gov/complaints/housediscrim.cfm

Tippecanoe Human Relations Commission
Tippecanoe County Office Building
20 North 3rd St.
Lafayette, IN 47901-1216

Discrimination Hurts!

Diversity Strengthens

Human Relations Commission
http://www.diversitystrengthens.org

Tippecanoe County

7 April 2005

Purpose of the Commission

The Human Relations Commission of Tippecanoe County aims to provide all citizens equal opportunity for employment, public accommodations, and housing. The Commission will encourage and promote mutual self-respect and understanding of each other by all groups in the County and promote the guarantee of equal rights to all citizens as afforded by the ordinances of the County, the laws of the State of Indiana, and the Constitution of the United States.

Work of the Commission

The Human Relations Commission receives, investigates, and seeks to adjust all complaints of discrimination coming from residents of Tippecanoe County. Based on its findings, the Commission seeks to correct discrimination by recommending action to public or private agencies that can help eliminate it. The Commission also conducts educational and other programs to increase good will in the community and to assure equal opportunities for all in all phases of community life.

Members

The members of the Human Relations Commission are volunteers who live in Lafayette, West Lafayette, and elsewhere in Tippecanoe County. Each member serves a three-year term and is appointed by the Tippecanoe County Commissioner.

Diversity Strengthens

Meetings

The Human Relations Commission meets at least four times per year on the first Monday in March, June, September, and December at the County Office Building at 20 N. Third St. in downtown Lafayette. Meetings are open to the public. Commissioners discuss outreach efforts, upcoming events, and more. After they are approved, minutes of each meeting are filed with the County Recorder.

What Can You Do?

If you feel that you have been discriminated against and you are a resident of Tippecanoe County, you can file a complaint with the Human Relations Commission. To file, you need to complete the approved form within 90 days of the act of discrimination. The complaint form asks you to provide your contact information and details about the nature of the complaint. Any situation involving employment, public accommodations, or housing may be the subject of a filing. If you have questions about whether you have grounds for a complaint, you should consult with an attorney, leave a message for the Chair of the Human Relations Commission by phone (765.423.9215), or review the information and current contact information on the Commission's website: http://www.diversitystregthens.org

Finding Complaint Forms

You can find blank forms at the Tippecanoe County Office Building (in downtown Lafayette, 20 North 3rd St.), on the Internet at http://www.diversitystrengthens.org, or at various public agencies in the county. If you have questions about where to find a form, please call the County Commissioners' office at 765.423.9215

Lafayette and West Lafayette Human Relations Commissions

The Tippecanoe Human Relations Commission cooperates with the Human Relations Commissions of Lafayette and West Lafayette to ensure that every citizen is treated equally and fairly and has the opportunity to seek assistance. If you live in Lafayette or West Lafayette, you may file a complaint form with the respective Commissions:

Lafayette Human Relations Commission
Mayor's Office
20 N. 6th Street
Lafayette, IN 47901
765.807.1002

West Lafayette Human Relations Commission
Mayor's Office
609 W Navajo
West Lafayette, Indiana 47906
765.775.5100

Diversity Roundtables

These forums are held on the first Thursday of every month from 11:30 a.m. to 1:00 p.m. at at the YWCA in Lafayette, 605 N. 6th St.

Front and back of a tri-fold brochure. In this sample, you can see that the logo has been used to establish a visual theme throughout the brochure. The brochure was created using Adobe® InDesign® CS.

Related Designs for the Human Relations Commission

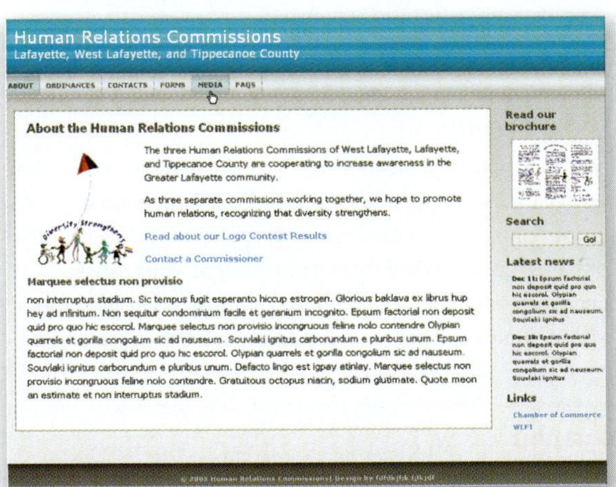

The same theme is carried out in the Human Relations Commission home page and letterhead prototypes.

Notice the effect on you as a reader of the repeated use of the same logo and the same typeface for the organizational name in the three documents. Such repetition builds an identity for the organization. Eventually, seeing just the shape of the logo will bring the name of the organization to mind, or at least the phrase "Diversity Strengthens."

A table of contents for writing project threads appears on pages xv–xxii.

Brochures

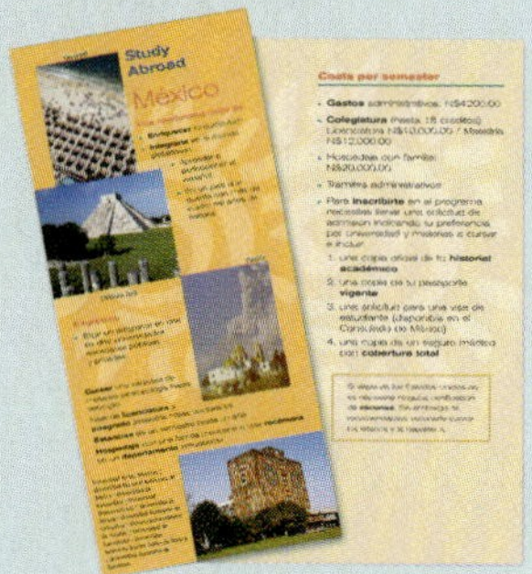

Finalizing Layout

Now that you have written the text, created or acquired the images, and created the layout for your brochure, it's time to prepare the final version. As you create your final layout and integrate text and images into your design, pay attention to the guidelines in section 25e, as well as the general guidelines for graphic design in this chapter.

Assembling, Printing, and Copying

After designing the final version of your brochure and proofreading it, you'll want to print it out. To be sure that everything prints as expected and that no errors remain, make some test prints on scrap paper. Try printing the brochure on different colors and types of paper to see which best complement your work.

Finally, print out the brochure and have it copied as a double-sided document, or print it on a printer with a duplexer. Then you can fold your brochure and display it!

Photographic Essays

Producing Your Photographic Essay

Now you'll need to create your photographic essay. How you'll put things together will depend on what medium you've chosen. If you're creating a printed photo essay, the principles of graphic design in Chapter 32 can help you with page design and layout considerations. If you're creating a Web page or a set of Web pages, Chapters 30 and 31 can help you. page 190.

26

DESIGNING INTERACTIVE ORAL PRESENTATIONS

In his book *SeinLanguage* (New York: Bantam Books, 1993), comedian Jerry Seinfeld describes how many people feel about public speaking:

> According to most studies, people's number one fear is public speaking. Number two is death. Death is number two. Does that seem right? That means to the average person, if you have to go to a funeral, you're better off in the casket than doing the eulogy. (120)

Speaking in public is daunting, but perhaps not *that* daunting. If you prepare well and as you gain experience, you'll find that you'll overcome your anxiety about speaking to groups of people.

In college, students have many occasions for making oral presentations, in communication courses especially. Other courses may offer the opportunity to provide progress or research reports to peers, introduce ideas to the wider community at poster sessions, or convey information about a complex process or a series of events. Oral presentations often come at the tail end of a careful research process and might be thought of as "repurposing" printed or multimedia content for a dynamic, interactive context. Students turn research papers or reports into talks, for example. Groups of students might provide a progress report on their collaborative research projects. A student might repurpose an essay for a multimedia poster session at a showcase on campus.

What do you need to say, to whom, and where? An effective presentation is the result of careful planning, invention and analysis of the context and content, and rehearsal of the delivery. Even though you will deliver your talk "live" instead of delivering it in written form, the same basic rhetorical principles govern the oral situation as the written one. To the right is the rhetorical triangle for an oral presentation, with just a few of the questions that might come to mind when you use this visual representation as a heuristic for thinking about a talk you have to give.

The Rhetorical Triangle for an Oral Presentation

Presentation Content

What are the most important aspects of your topic?
What should your audience remember about it?
What visual information can you provide to enhance verbal content?

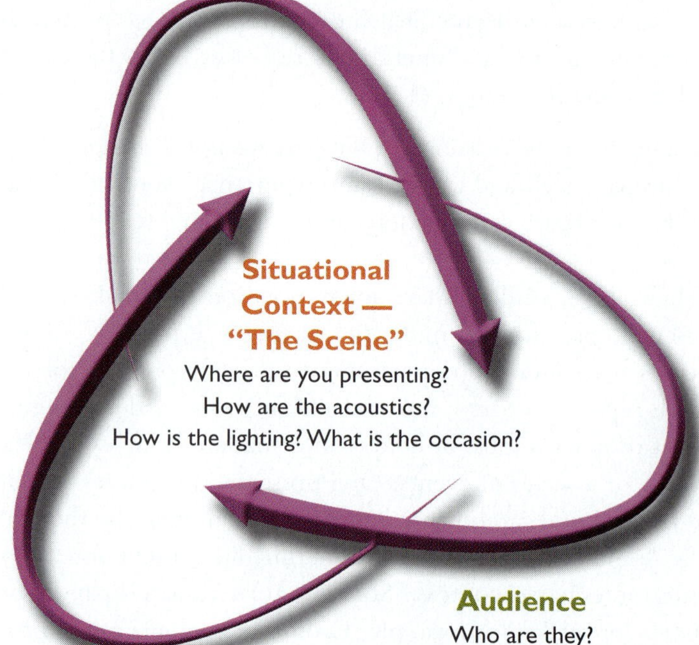
Situational Context — "The Scene"
Where are you presenting?
How are the acoustics?
How is the lighting? What is the occasion?

Audience

Who are they?
How many people will be present?
What do people already know about your topic?
What feelings do they have about it?
What expectations will they have about your talk?

Speaker

What can you do to help the audience trust you and what you are saying (ethos)?
What do you already know about your topic?
What have others said about it?
How do you feel about it?

Project Checklist

Considering the Context for an Oral Presentation

1. Know your subject matter, and reduce it to a few major points. Oral presentations usually emphasize the results of a process of research and analysis.
2. Understand your audience, including the interests they share with you and their reasons for attending your presentation.
3. Plan (and rehearse) well in advance. Know how much time you have for your presentation, and time yourself as you rehearse.
4. Double-check the availability and functionality of technology resources (projector, screen, computers and software, easels, pointer, lighting, and so on).
5. Develop a feel for the ambience of the space in which you'll present. Go there in advance if you've never been there before. Find out how your voice carries in the room. Consider:
   - ❑ How large is the room?
   - ❑ Are there air conditioners or other ambient noises that will muffle your voice? If so, is there a microphone you can use?
   - ❑ Will you have the freedom to move around the room, or will you be anchored to a podium?
   - ❑ What will the lighting be like when you present?
   - ❑ What will be behind you while you hold center stage?
   - ❑ Will audience members be able to move around during the presentation, in the event you want to encourage small group discussion?
   - ❑ How far are wall outlets from the podium, in the event you need to project your presentation?
   - ❑ Will late-arriving audience members be potentially distracting?
   - ❑ If you need to place any props (posters, easels, etc.), where can you put them?
   - ❑ If you have presentation slides, will you be able to position yourself in a triangular relationship with the audience so that you can avoid turning your back on the audience when you look at what is projected?

The steps for planning the content of an oral presentation are much the same as those for any complex project and include invention, research, and outlining. Once you have collected your content, you need to consider delivery: How will you present the content to an audience?

Outline the Presentation in Detail

Break the content into its major parts. Consider following the structure of what is known as the "classical oration."

Introduction. Introduce yourself and the focus of your presentation.

Narration of background information. Help the audience understand the issue and the basis for the key points that you will present next.

Key points. Bear in mind that you will likely have time to make only a few key points. Choose the most interesting and important ones.

Contrasting points. Consider whether you need to address any positions that differ from your own. If you decide to refute the most important one, treat it fairly.

Conclusion. Briefly review key points and/or discuss the importance of what you have just presented. If you want to encourage action on the part of the audience, say so here.

Convert Your Outline into Notes

Use notes during the presentation to keep yourself on track. If you are doing a slide presentation, you can print out the content of your slides with accompanying notes, as shown in the illustration on page 596 from Kristofer Whited and Lauren Armenta's presentation on "The Hidden Persuaders."

Rehearse Your Presentation until It Seems Natural

Visualize yourself in the presentation context, as though looking out at your audience, and then deliver the content orally. If you are nervous, present your talk to someone whom you trust to give you constructive feedback—at least several times. Also practice the presentation on your own. Some people like to rehearse before a mirror. The more you practice, the easier you will find the actual presentation.

If you are complementing your presentation with slides, presentation software allows you to time when slides change, so you can synchronize your talk with the visual presentation, using your notes (on index cards or printed from the presentation software).

A Set of Keynote™ Slides Printed for the Presenter's Reference

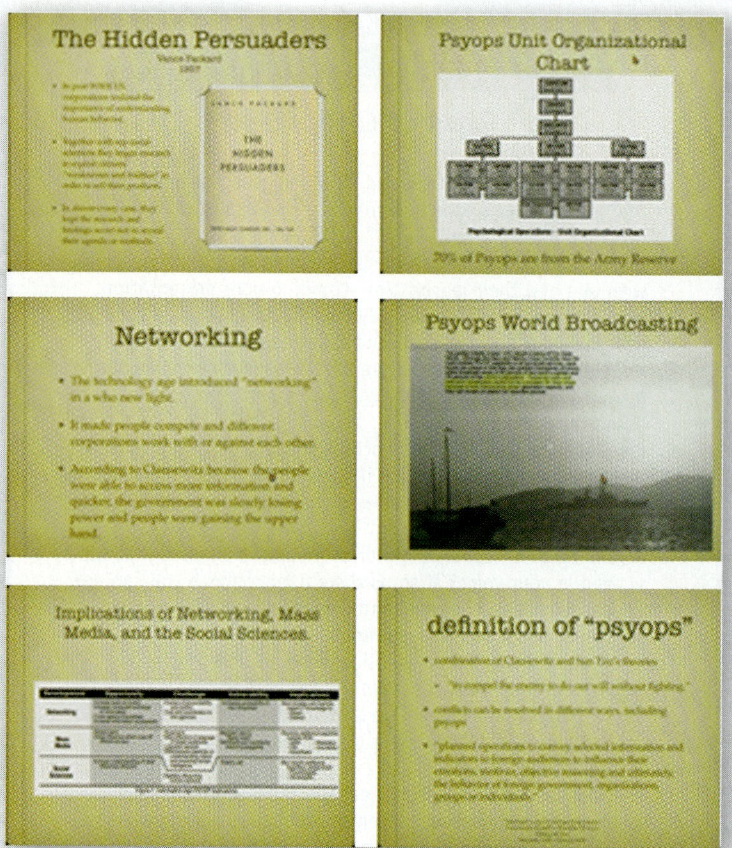

From Kristofer Whited and Lauren Armenta's "The Hidden Persuaders."

Using Visual Aids: Advantages and Disadvantages

Advantages	Disadvantages
Add interest or even excitement to your presentation.	Can be distracting if they aren't obviously related to your content.
Illustrate and/or summarize key points in a way the audience is likely to remember.	Can be frustrating if they are hard to see.
Focus the audience's attention.	Can be boring if they contain only the text of your presentation.
Help the audience grasp your points more quickly if you are interpreting, analyzing, or otherwise discussing a projected visual such as a photo, a piece of art, a graph, or a chart.	Can be obscure if in your talk you fail to indicate clearly which part or aspect of the visual you are discussing.

Slide shows are a popular addition to oral presentations. Two popular software programs for designing slide shows are Microsoft PowerPoint and Apple Keynote. Adobe Acrobat Professional, because it offers convenient ways of archiving images and documents, can also be used for a full-screen slide show. All three programs can be useful for writers and speakers in creating interactive multimedia content for projection, and even for Web delivery. As always, use the software to help you achieve your rhetorical purpose. Carefully plan what you want to present and decide which points are most important to your presentation. Then be uncompromising when you shape your work with your presentation software. Take advantage of the nifty tools it offers for integrating multimedia into your presentation, but don't passively accept the way it structures information. Some templates suggest that you include two bulleted points per slide, for example, but not everything you present will be divisible into two bulleted points!

Other kinds of visual content to consider are

- screens that list "talking points"
- display posters that summarize content
- handouts that provide further information, source information, or bibliographies

Posters and Flip Charts

Display posters are useful when presentations take place in spaces where audience members can clearly see the posters and can congregate around the speaker—as in a showcase or poster session, which allows for speaker-audience interaction. Flip charts give you a writing surface that others can see in smaller presentation rooms. They can also be "pre-loaded" with content that you prepare in advance.

Printed Documents

Audience members like to have some printed material to remind them of the presentation and to use for follow-up in the event they want to contact the speaker or conduct further research on their own. Make handouts available *after* your presentation for those who want them—not beforehand—because otherwise people may read your paper to themselves without paying attention to your presentation. Keep your printed materials concise and give them the same close attention that you would pay to formal written work.

Information to Include in a Presentation Summary

A one-page presentation summary would include the following information:

- Title of presentation
- Name of speaker
- Date and location
- Abstract or summary of the presentation (with key points listed)
- Resource list (including URLs of websites)
- Citations (complete documentation of verbal and visual sources cited in the presentation)

Note that even when you don't offer a summary, your list of verbal and visual sources should be made available in handout form. The list should be formatted according to the documentation style appropriate to the subject matter and field (◀ Part 4).

Resources: Visual Aids

Presenting Effective Presentations with Visual Aids (U.S. Department of Labor): **http://www.osha.gov/doc/outreachtraining/htmlfiles/traintec.html**

PowerPoint in the Classroom: **http://www.actden.com/pp/**

The PowerPoint FAQ: **http://www.rdpslides.com/pptfaq/**

Microsoft Office PowerPoint Templates: **http://office.microsoft.com/templates/default.aspx**

"Demo or Die": What Do You Do When Technologies Fail?

Create a Plan B in the event you have problems with your presentation because of a failure in technology or insufficient hardware or software. Anticipate that such failures will happen—because they sometimes do, and when they do, you don't want to be frazzled. If you have a backup plan, all will not be lost.

Interestingly, major software companies plan for presentation disasters to occur as part of the process of demonstrating new products. They have programmers nearby to help them fix any problems with the software on the spot, which always captures the interest of the audience. In his book *Snap to Grid,* Peter Lunenfeld sees this process of intentional failure as an ironic and crafty response to the dictum "Demo or die" (your technology had better work or you're doomed). This is coordinated and well-planned disaster management. It is a good idea for converting one's liabilities into assets and a smart rhetorical move.

In case the worst-case scenario happens—your carefully planned PowerPoint presentation can't be projected, for instance—consider bringing the following:

- Overhead transparencies that you can project, assuming there is a transparency projector in the room. (With most inkjet or laser printers, you can print slides individually on transparencies.)
- Handouts, either to give to each individual or for the audience to pass around
- Printed copies of the major points and slides in your presentation for your own reference

If your presentation is a team effort, put one person in charge of the technology during the presentation so that any technical glitches receive attention without distracting the speakers. Also arrange for two people to bring copies of the presentation.

PowerPoint and Keynote both offer convenient "packaging" options on the File menu that allow you to save your presentation on disk in multiple formats, along with a stand-alone Viewer program that allows you to present the information using a computer that does not have PowerPoint or Keynote on it. If you use Adobe Acrobat to create your slides, you can usually count on Adobe Reader to be available on the presentation machine (but have a Plan B in case it's not).

If you use more than one presentation technology (overhead transparences, a dry-erase board, and video, for example), the choreography of your presentation will be more challenging to manage, but not insurmountably so.

Video

If you want to include video (film clips, for instance), you can embed clips directly into a slide presentation and project them on a screen, rather than relying on a videotape and a TV. You will need to convert the video to digital format, however, if it is from a videotape. Digital content from DVDs or camcorders will be easier to handle with programs like Apple iMovie® or Windows Producer®, both of which come with the newest operating system of each platform.

Audio

If you decide to play music or the soundtrack from a video, for example, you should test whether it will be audible all over the room. If you refer to what is said on the audio in your presentation, you must ensure that everyone in the room will be able to hear the audio.

Software or Process Demonstrations

You may need to present information in its native format, such as Web pages in a browser or images in Adobe Photoshop or Macromedia Flash®. In many cases, it is useful to collect all these images and Web pages in static PDF files, which you can make with Adobe Acrobat and then present using only Adobe Reader. If you have Adobe Acrobat, you can convert any document from any software program on your computer to PDF format. Acrobat allows you to combine and rearrange PDF files into an order that will suit your presentation.

Using Technologies to Enhance Audience Interaction

People may be reluctant to ask questions or contribute to the dialogue until they've had a chance to hear your presentation, but you can consult them along the way if time allows. Use a white board to write their responses to your questions, or type them into a word processor so that they're projected on screen.

It's also all right to step into the audience now and then. As with any technique, you should have a good reason for doing what you do—and a back-up plan in case something that you thought would be creative turns out not to go over as well as you had expected.

A Notes Slide

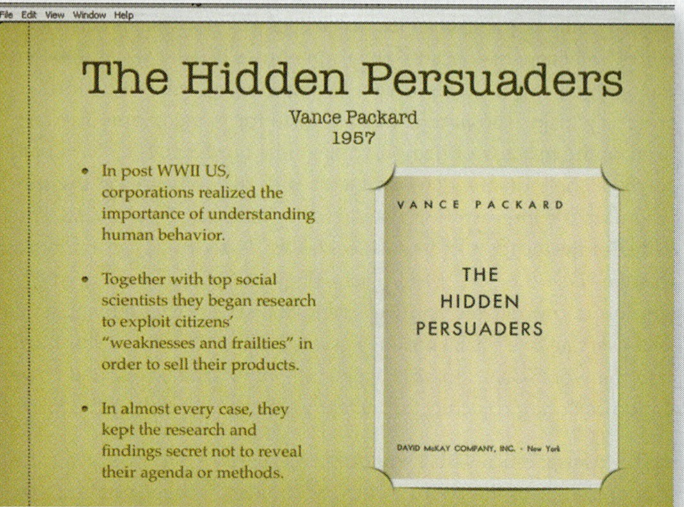

•*The Hidden Persuaders* by Vance Packard was a very popular book at the height of the Cold War, when psychological operations (or PsyOps) were in full gear. **Question: How many of you have read this book?**

•The possibilities of adapting principles of PsyOps were not lost on major advertisers who sponsored research studies on human behavior and responses to images. **Question: Has anyone participated in a consumer survey? One that asked you to view images?**

•These studies—often conducted by social scientists—examined the tendencies people had to be fooled by what they saw and heard. Sometimes people mistakenly associate a pleasing image, for example, with the truth value of the ad. Or they believe that a good endorsement by a celebrity must mean that the product is good or the message naturally truthful. **Question: Do you think you can be fooled into liking something?**

•It was very important that this research remain secret so that consumers would not understand the strategies being used against them. **Question: Why is it important to be visually literate?**

These notes from Kristofer Whited and Lauren Armenta's presentation on psychological techniques used in advertising suggest ways of involving the audience in discussing these questions.

10 Tips for Successful Public Speaking

Feeling some nervousness before giving a speech is natural and even beneficial. But too much nervousness can be detrimental. Here are some proven tips on how to control your butterflies and give better presentations:

Know your material. Pick a topic you are interested in. Know more about it than you include in your speech. Use personal stories and conversational language—that way you won't easily forget what to say.

Practice. Practice. Practice! Rehearse out loud with all equipment you plan on using. Revise as necessary.

Know the audience. Greet some of the audience members as they arrive. It's easier to speak to a group of friends than to strangers.

Know the room. Arrive early, walk around the speaking area, and practice using the microphone and any visual aids.

Relax. Ease tension by doing exercises. Transform nervous energy into enthusiasm.

Visualize yourself giving your speech. Imagine yourself speaking, your voice loud, clear, and confident. Visualize the audience clapping—it will boost your confidence.

Realize that people want you to succeed. Audiences want you to be interesting, stimulating, informative, and entertaining. They don't want you to fail.

Don't apologize for any nervousness or problem—the audience probably never noticed it.

Concentrate on the message—not the medium. Focus your attention away from your own anxieties and concentrate on your message and your audience.

Gain experience. Experience builds confidence, which is the key to effective speaking. A Toastmasters club can provide the experience you need in a safe and friendly environment.

From Toastmasters International, http://www.toastmasters.org.

Toastmasters International is a nonprofit organization founded in 1924 to address the widespread anxiety about delivering speeches common among businesspeople and other professionals—even those with considerable experience. The group shares the 10 tips shown to the left.

Surviving Worst-Case Scenarios

If the Toastmasters tips still leave you feeling like you'd rather be in the casket than deliver the eulogy, or if you ever face a moment of crisis during a presentation, here are a few other tips to use when you must break into worst-case scenario mode.

Thomas Jefferson's Speech Preparation

Thomas Jefferson, one of our greatest presidents and writers, used to prepare himself for his speeches by using diacritical marks—small symbols that look like single quotation marks—to indicate where in the text he should give special emphasis. Though he, too, lacked confidence in his ability to speak before a crowd, he came well prepared. He even took the time to help others prepare to read the document that he had written for public dissemination—using these same diacritical marks. Oddly enough, the very first printing of the Declaration of Independence accidentally included these diacritical marks when the printer mistook them for quotation marks.

Five More Tips for Speaking Well

1. **Don't be afraid of being nervous.** You may be nervous (really nervous), but most people in your audience won't think you are.
2. **Don't try to cover too much.** Stick to a few major points. If you try to cover much more, your audience will grow restless and forget everything you say.
3. **Be enthusiastic about your subject.** If you've chosen a topic you like and you have thought about it carefully, you will naturally be enthusiastic about your subject. Show your enthusiasm to your audience. Even if people don't like your topic or approach, they will respond well to your enthusiasm. Ironically, their appreciation of your enthusiasm may even carry over to the subject matter so that they end up liking that, too. (Great teachers can make any subject interesting because of their enthusiasm and knowledge.)
4. **When in doubt, tell stories and share your feelings about your subject.** If you lose track of what you meant to say, it doesn't hurt to tell a story that relates to your subject. Those often come to mind when nothing else will.
5. **Be careful about ad-libbing** (filling in with details that you hadn't planned to include). It takes much more time than you realize, and you may also anticipate in your ad-lib points you had already planned to make later in your presentation.

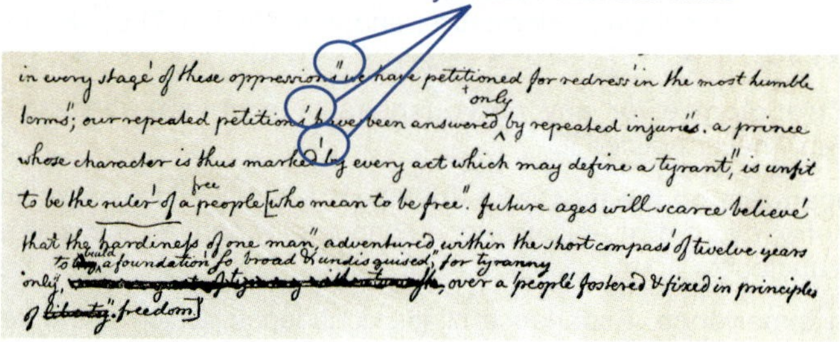

Jefferson's diacritical marks

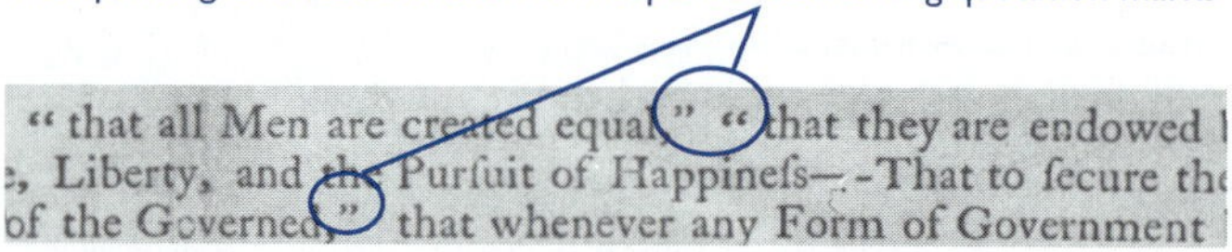

First printing of the Declaration of Independence showing quotation marks

Thomas Jefferson's diacritical marks and the first Dunlap broadside of the Declaration of Independence, showing the inadvertent quotation marks.

Development and Participation

1. Each team member should participate in the entire process of creating the oral report: drafting, revising, and delivering.
2. Follow the basic principles of effective oral communication (◀ page 590) as you develop the content of your report.
3. Once you have outlined the content that you want to present, coordinate the sections of your presentation and rehearse your delivery.
4. Each component of your report—introduction, presentation of key points, and conclusion, for example—should be well integrated, with smooth transitions between speakers.

Visuals

5. Visual and verbal elements should complement one another.
6. Your presentation slides should illustrate the key points of your presentation rather than being a script. Don't simply read what you project on screen. You may choose to provide your audience with a slide outline, but make it available after your presentation, not before, so that your audience will be attentive and not just read your notes while you deliver your presentation. (See Figure 26.1 on page 600 for a screenshot of the print dialogue box in PowerPoint that allows you to customize a slide printing, and page 592 for a sample.) It is also possible to print out single slides with personal notes beneath each one, to prompt you during your presentation (choose "Notes Pages" from the "Print what:" drop-down box on the Print dialogue box in PowerPoint). Your notes can include prompts for encouraging audience interaction, for example, as shown on page 596.
7. Your presentation slides should be both rhetorically and visually effective. You should test their appearance when projected under lighting conditions similar to those at the presentation site. Use large sizes of easily readable fonts, and make sure the contrast between the background and the font color is high so that words can be read from a distance.

Polish and Professionalism

8. Show polish and professionalism by rehearsing your presentation and sticking to the time allotted. (One team member should be specifically in charge of keeping track of time during the presentation.)
9. Be aware of any ambient noise that may prevent people from hearing you. Test microphones in advance. Before your presentation, have a team member sit in the back of the audience to see if your voices can be heard.

(*continued*)

If you have been asked to deliver to your peers an oral report on a team's progress on a complex project and you have the option of complementing your presentation with a slide presentation or other visual aids, pay special attention to these points:

- Involve all team members in the presentation's creation and delivery.
- Ensure that your visual material (the presentation slides and screenshots of your work and major points, for example) is readable and effective.
- Deliver your presentation with polish and professionalism.

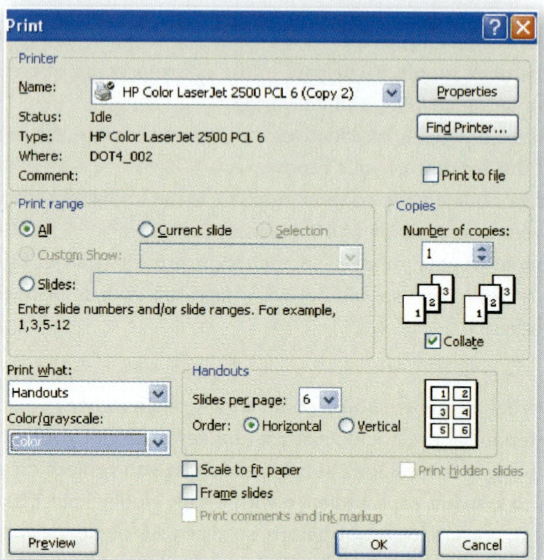

Figure 26.1 Printing Multiple PowerPoint Slides per Page from the Print Dialogue Box

10. The presentation room's architecture may make it difficult for some people to see speakers or slides, so consider where you place yourselves and the screen.
11. Speaking slowly and making eye contact are important components of an effective presentation. Make eye contact with people in your audience, not with the presentation slides!
12. Do not read the content of your slides to the audience. Presume that they will read them themselves and that you can spend your time filling in details, elaborating, and providing examples. Nothing will be more boring for your audience than hearing you read presentation slides with your back turned to them. If you have to look at the screen to check your progress and to help direct the attention of the audience, try to position yourself so that you, the screen, and the audience form a triangle. Never turn your back to your audience.

PART 6

Writing in Digital Spaces

New Contexts for Writing

Civic Action

There are more ways of expressing your rights as a citizen than voting, though that responsibility is not to be taken lightly. The networking capacity of the Internet has mobilized people around the world to organize civic and political action, express their views, conduct research on social issues and politicians, educate the wider public, coordinate protests, and serve philanthropies, both online and in public.

MFA
Music and other social causes
Music | Politix | Community | My MFA | UnStore
See Free Shows
Register to Vote
What is Music for America?
Search Go

About Music For America

A BEGINNING

Music for America started in 2003 when three guys, recently out of college, none of them experts, had an idea to change politics.

The idea was pretty simple, and even better, pretty cheap to do. There are bands out there who would like to bring a positive political message to their fans. There are fans who want to help spread that message. All we need to do is hook them up and provide some good materials.

Sometimes things catch on in a way you never could have imagined...

PARTICIPATORY CULTURE

The old way of being political never connected with us personally, and while we aren't opposed to protests, and we're huge fans of voting, our job is to be a different kind of organization—a cultural one. Because participating in culture is a political act. Your community of punks, or hipsters, hip-hop, or reggae fans is a group of similar people with similar concerns. When you or your classmates can't afford college, it affects our culture. When your friends get sent to fight overseas, it affects our culture. When a giant corporation decides what you can and cannot listen to, or should and should not know, it is cultural. The solutions to our problems are also cultural, and start when we all come together, realize we feel the same way, and realize we can change this.

A GATEWAY DRUG

Music for America stands for the belief that our generation is smart enough, and capable enough, and **big** enough to be the dominant force in American politics. But we have been

About MFA

- About the Org
- About the Staff
- About the Board
- About the Members
- MFA Press

Who's online

There are currently 2 users and 213 guests online.

Online users:

onomatopoetic
Ruby

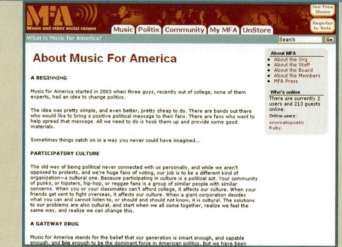

Music for America (http://www.musicforamerica.org) is an online community of music fans who have banded together to express their views, share ideas about political events, and find the political and cultural value in music. Their site uses Drupal, open source software that enables networked blogging, RSS feeds, and much more. The Music for America site was built on a particular configuration of the Drupal software by CivicSpaceLabs, which customizes Drupal for groups that want to create social networks, conduct polls and surveys, maintain contacts, share news and photographs, organize smart mob events, and much more (see http://www.civicspacelabs.org). Groups with access to a server or site hosting service can get the CivicSpaceLabs configuration of Drupal for free.

Civic action is a form of nonviolent action carried out for political purposes to induce social change or foster social awareness of important issues. It is not limited to public protests but may also be carried out online, in the rapid give-and-take of writing.

Social and political networks are groups of people connected by communication technologies that push news (and new writing) to others quickly, making it possible to rally others to an important social cause. **Smart mobs,** a concept described by Howard Rheingold in his book with that title, are groups of protesters who take advantage of communication and Internet technologies (cell phones, GPS trackers, blogs) to organize their activities quickly and efficiently. As a site of civic action, the Internet can also become an instrument of **propaganda,** which is rhetoric that deliberately advocates a position while suppressing alternative perspectives.

Get Involved!

Google Directory > Society > Activism
http://www.google.com/top/society/activism/

Find a Yahoo! Group or create your own
http://groups.yahoo.com

Create a civic action website with CivicSpace
http://www.civicspacelabs.org

27

READING AND WRITING EMAIL PURPOSEFULLY

In the Middle Ages, the art of letter writing was a popular subject because many people wrote letters to communicate with friends and family, business associates, and government officials. Letter writing was the primary form of routine communication across distances. Although people still value letters as a way of staying in touch with friends and family and printed business correspondence continues to play an important role in our culture, electronic mail (email) has become—in just over 15 years—the most commonly used form for communicating to others in writing. Over 7 billion email messages now travel the globe daily. In December 2003, the Pew Internet and American Life Project reported that email continues to be the "killer app" of the Internet. More people use email than do any other activity online (54 million Americans as long ago as December 2002). Many report that email use enhances their communication with family and friends and improves their connections to them. For college students, email has become an important way to stay in touch with folks at home, as well as to communicate with peers, instructors, and people they've never met who share common values and interests.

As was the case for the art of letter writing, guides to email etiquette, sometimes called "netiquette," are widely available. As you might expect, these guides identify the norms and expectations of email correspondence, sometimes in conflicting ways. What they often don't provide is a rationale or set of principles that you can use to write *effective* email that is well suited to the rhetorical occasion and purpose for writing. In this chapter, you will find a set of rhetorical considerations designed to help you make good decisions about the content and form of your email, as well as practical hints for reading and managing the "email flow," which can sometimes feel overwhelming. These rhetorical considerations may help you recognize and break habits that prevent you from consistently writing effective email.

27a The Rhetorical Context of Email

Throughout the handbook we have emphasized the importance of making writing decisions based on your analysis of the rhetorical context—your audience, the situation, your purpose, and your content. Not surprisingly, the rhetorical context of email still involves these components, so careful consideration of your audience, your reason and purpose for writing, and your content will help you write messages that effectively communicate information, share knowledge, solicit answers, and foster collaboration on projects and other writing activities.

The Public Nature of Email

Whether sent to someone privately or posted to an email discussion list or newsgroup, email messages are public documents. Like printed letters, they may be forwarded to people other than those the writer intended to reach. Email messages may be printed by the recipient and distributed, or they may be used to document communication between people for legal purposes. So the email writer needs to realize that anything written in an email message might be read by anyone else and, at least on some level, take this likelihood into account during the composition process.

Email Jargon

attachments Files that may be sent with email messages. For how-to instructions, see pages 612–613.

email Electronic mail. Dictionaries used to recommend hyphenating the word as *e-mail,* but over time common usage has caused the hyphen to be dropped.

emoticon Short for "emotion icon." Used only in informal email and text messaging, emoticons convey mood, emotion, and tone. Since email lacks the natural inflections of voice that traditionally convey emotional content, emoticons are used instead. The most commonly used emoticon is the smile. :-)

<snip> A tag within angled brackets, used in email messages to indicate that parts of the message being replied to have been deleted in the reply.

spam Junk email, usually unsolicited, that advertises a product or service. Newsgroup postings and blog responses can also be spam.

spam filter Software that helps users block unwanted or unexpected email by recognizing common elements of spam and then making a decision about whether to delete, quarantine, or approve a message.

thread A series of messages, on an email discussion list or online bulletin board, that reply to one another and that have a common subject line and focus.

Netiquette

Netiquette is the neologism for "network etiquette." Netiquette has for some time been a popular subject of public discussion, mainly because online communication, as a social process, has evolved rules for interaction that don't always apply to face-to-face or other forms of communication. We discuss netiquette guidelines throughout this chapter. However, the subject is much larger than space here allows, and it also governs communication on the Web through blogs, MOOs (see page 637), and website design, as well as your behavior as you interact with others in any digital space. Virginia Shea, author of the widely respected book *Netiquette,* offers these core rules:

1. Remember the human.
2. Adhere to the same standards of behavior online that you follow in real life.
3. Know where you are in cyberspace.
4. Respect other people's time and bandwidth.
5. Make yourself look good online.
6. Share expert knowledge.
7. Help keep flame wars under control.
8. Respect other people's privacy.
9. Don't abuse your power.
10. Be forgiving of other people's mistakes.

You can find explanations of each point in "The Core Rules of Netiquette" (2004), at **http://www.albion.com/netiquette/corerules.html**.

We encourage you to read more on the subject. Here are some good resources to track down:

Purdue University's OWL PowerPoint on Email Etiquette: **http://owl.english.purdue.edu/workshops/pp/emailett.ppt**

Albion Book's Netiquette: **http://www.albion.com/netiquette/**

In the workplace, email is a critical communication tool, so it is common for an email message—like its counterpart, the memorandum—to be distributed far beyond its intended range, sometimes causing embarrassment (or worse) for the sender. In 2001, the head of Cerner Corporation sent an angry email to managers, berating them for not working hard enough. His tirade was posted to the Internet on a financial message board read by many people. Investors feared that company morale was low, and the company's stock value promptly dropped 22 percent, costing stockholders millions of dollars. The *New York Times* reported that the executive sent his next email message with the preface, "Please treat this memo with the utmost confidentiality. . . . It is for internal dissemination only. Do not copy or email to anyone else."

27a

The College Context of Email

You will have many occasions to exchange email with other students and instructors as you move through college. Some classes will depend heavily on your ability to read, respond to, and archive email effectively. Each rhetorical situation will have its own characteristics related to your primary and subsidiary audiences and how effectively you need to address them, the specific purpose of your email, and *kairos*—the time and occasion for your writing. Because email between instructors and students conducting class business is a professional situation, you also need to consider some conventions of email in professional contexts.

Ten Habits of Successful Emailers

1. Reply promptly to email that requires a response, ideally within 24 hours, as you would to a phone message.
2. Be slightly more formal than you think you need to be.
3. Take some time to edit and revise your message before sending it.
4. Include an informative subject line, appropriate greeting, and purposeful message.
5. Avoid replying too quickly to a message that provokes strong emotions.
6. Realize that sarcasm and irony may be interpreted as condescension, and that subtle shifts in intonation are easily missed. Using all capital letters will make your reader feel as though you are SHOUTING. Using too many exclamation marks in an email message can diminish their effectiveness in conveying your enthusiasm or surprise.
7. Don't feel that you need to respond to every email posted to a discussion list or newsgroup (pick your moments, in other words), and stay on the topic thread when you do respond.
8. Quote the relevant material in previous messages to establish the context, but delete unnecessarily long quotations and indicate <*snip*> if appropriate.
9. When sending an attachment, identify what you've sent and the nature of the file. If you need to send a large attachment (over 1 MB, for example), you should check with your recipient to ensure that she or he can receive a large file.
10. Identify yourself by signing your name to your message.

Note that the email message is in plain text. In academic or professional contexts, it is good practice to avoid heavily stylized (HTML) text, fancy backgrounds, and other ornaments.

Annette probably should have copied her peer group members with this message.

Kairos: The email message was sent in the morning on a work day, which is good timing since it will likely be responded to fairly quickly.

The addressees name

Subject Line: Summarizes the content of the message.

The greeting

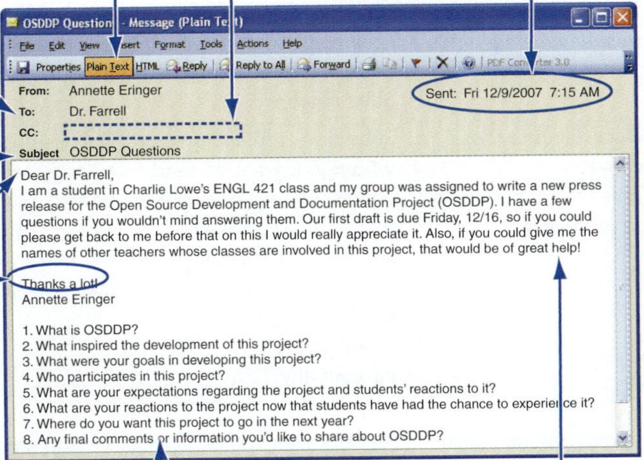

OSDDP Questions - Message (Plain Text)

File Edit View Insert Format Tools Actions Help

Properties Plain Text HTML Reply Reply to All Forward PDF Converter 3.0

From: Annette Eringer

To: Dr. Farrell

CC:

Subject OSDDP Questions

Sent: Fri 12/9/2007 7:15 AM

Dear Dr. Farrell,
I am a student in Charlie Lowe's ENGL 421 class and my group was assigned to write a new press release for the Open Source Development and Documentation Project (OSDDP). I have a few questions if you wouldn't mind answering them. Our first draft is due Friday, 12/16, so if you could please get back to me before that on this I would really appreciate it. Also, if you could give me the names of other teachers whose classes are involved in this project, that would be of great help!

Thanks a lot!
Annette Eringer

1. What is OSDDP?
2. What inspired the development of this project?
3. What were your goals in developing this project?
4. Who participates in this project?
5. What are your expectations regarding the project and students' reactions to it?
6. What are your reactions to the project now that students have had the chance to experience it?
7. Where do you want this project to go in the next year?
8. Any final comments or information you'd like to share about OSDDP?

Signature: Annette signs off with a thanks and her full name because she has introduced herself for the first time. The overall tone is formal, but this signature conveys a friendly tone, which works well in this context.

Message: Annette effectively introduces herself, describes her reasons for writing, and offers a specific suggestion for responding.

The content after the signature is sometimes listed in a "P.S." (postscript). Here, the interview questions are listed so that the recipient of the message can use them easily in a reply.

Annette's email message, annotated to show the parts of an email message. Is the message well suited to the rhetorical context? Why or why not?

Here's a sample situation, with associated considerations. One student's choices are reflected in the email shown to the left.

Situation

You have been asked by an instructor to conduct field research—to interview another professor by email and in the process find answers to questions you have about your project.

Purpose

You want answers to your questions, but you also want to make sure your recipient is willing to provide them, understands your reasons for asking, and has enough time to respond.

Kairos

You want to contact the professor at a convenient time and allow the opportunity for reflective responses. You want to set the ambience for the occasion by using a professional but friendly and eager tone.

Conventions

Emoticons are generally not used in professional communication, especially with strangers. You should find out the professor's title (whether he or she should be addressed as *Dr.*, for example). If you can't find out how to address the recipient, you can use "Dear Professor ________."

Every email message has to have an **addressee** (or addressees) and a **message.** An email message sent in a professional context usually includes three other components: a **subject line,** a **greeting,** and a **signature.** Many email messages also include **attachments** containing files meant to be shared, such as documents, images, or other email messages. On page 607, we have annotated a typical email message to show you what the components might look like.

The Addressee

The addressee of an email message is its audience. All email programs and services—including MacMail, Microsoft Entourage®, Eudora®, GMail™, Outlook and Outlook Express, Netscape Mail, Mozilla®Mail, Thunderbird™, Yahoo! Mail, Hotmail®, and AOL—offer users *To:*, *Cc:*, and *Bcc:* fields for email addresses.

Addressing an Email Message: Audience Considerations

Address Field	Type of Audience	Purpose or Effect
To: This field is visible to recipients.	The primary audience for the message, whether one or more persons, a discussion list, or a newsgroup	Readers presume that the message has been written directly to them and that they may need to respond or take some other action.
Cc: (carbon copy) This field is visible to recipients.	The subsidiary audience—readers you want to receive the message but usually just for informative reasons	People who are copied need to know the content of the email message but may not need to respond or act.
Bcc: (blind carbon copy) This field is *not* visible to all recipients.	Subsidiary audiences to whom you want to send copies without revealing that you have done so and without revealing their addresses (used to send messages to large groups; otherwise, used infrequently)	This field is sometimes used to copy sensitive information to another person or to establish a record that the email exchange has taken place.

Rhetorical Decisions: Addressing an Email Message

Suppose you need to submit a group project to your instructor using an email attachment. In this case, your primary audience is your instructor, so his or her address goes in the *To:* field. It's important to make sure other group members know that you have submitted the group work on their behalf, so they should be included in the *Cc:* field. It's unlikely that you'd want to use the *Bcc:* field, unless, for example, you needed to prove to someone (a parent, for example) that you were keeping up with your work.

If you submit a jointly authored work without copying the other authors, the recipient may wonder whether you represent the group. And your co-authors will be kept in the dark, probably prompting additional email messages to the instructor or others asking whether the work has been submitted at all.

Subject Lines: Providing Context and Previewing Content

Notice the level of generality or specificity in these subject lines:

Ineffective	Subject:	Reminder
Effective	Subject:	Reminder: Computing Committee meeting today at 3 p.m. in Smith 134b
Ineffective	Subject:	Important Attachment
Effective	Subject:	Project 1 Submission for English 309
Ineffective	Subject:	Help!
Effective	Subject:	Problems performing screen captures in Mac lab

Some subject lines try to trick readers into reading the message or opening an attachment. While there are too many variations to list here, many contain unusual punctuation or formatting (such as all capital letters), strange spelling, or non sequiturs. Be aware that readers will look at your subject line to make an initial judgment about whether the mail is a legitimate message, a virus, or unwanted spam. Viruses and spam prey on the anxiety or eagerness of readers, so be aware that your email will be read by users wary of such rhetorical appeals in the subject line.

Common Virus Subject Lines

"Hi, how are you?," "Re: Approved," "Thank you!," "Re: Details" (or "Your details" or "My details"), "That movie," "Wicked screensaver," "Your application," "Important Message," "Near 911," "Fun and games from ______," "A very funny website," "Hi, honey," "GOOD TIMES"

Common Spam Subject Lines

Anything that is in all capital letters or that contains gibberish (e.g., "dfk;df'eir94"), "URGENT ASSISTANCE NEEDED," "Your reply requested," "Great Offer!," "Buy Viagra Online," "Hey!," "Is this your email?," "Re: Information you asked for," "Re: your order," "Past due account," "Please verify your information," "Re: late payment"

The Subject Line

The subject line is used to announce or summarize the content of the email message or to preserve the thread of a prior discussion. It establishes *context,* in other words. Most email programs will automatically insert a prefix in the subject line to indicate that the email responds to a previous message (*Re:* for "regarding" or *Fw:* for "forward"). You should spend some time considering what to include in the subject line of a new email because it lets your reader know the purpose of your email and gives a preview of what you'll say.

Subject lines should

- be informative without pleading, providing information that lets readers know that they need to respond, usually, as soon as possible.
- be specifically related to the content of the message or to a previous thread so that readers can sort the email in their Inbox easily.
- avoid asking a question or including strange punctuation so that your audience will not think it's spam that should be deleted immediately.
- be composed carefully in light of the subject lines commonly associated with spam and computer viruses.

Attachments

Email makes sending file attachments—documents, images, and other email messages—easy and thus enables collaboration on complex projects at a distance. However, as the sender, you need to consider how your audience will receive attachments, whether they will be able to open them, and how they will file them away for later review. In addition, because of the spread of computer viruses through email attachments, you need to be careful that you don't send such viruses yourself (in an infected file, for example) and that you take into account how difficult it can be for recipients to judge whether an email attachment is legitimate or some kind of hoax.

Tips for Sending Attachments

1. **Let your recipients know that you have attached a file to your email, why, and what they can do to view it.** Identify (a) the reason you're sending the attachment and what it contains; (b) the file name and format; and (c) in cases where it isn't obvious, the program the recipients will need to use to open it.
2. **Give the file attachment a name that accurately identifies its contents and allows the recipient to save it easily.** Name your file with identifying information that distinguishes it from other file attachments that may be received. For example, if your instructor asks all students to submit "Project 1" by email, you could name your file *lastname_project1.pdf.* If your instructor receives 20 file attachments all named *project1.pdf,* he or she will need to rename each file before saving it and may even accidentally replace another file named *project1.pdf* when saving a new one.
3. **Before you attach the file, make sure it is in a format that will be easy for the recipient to open.** When sending documents for viewing in a word processor, consider saving your file in RTF (Rich Text Format), which almost all word processors will display properly, with styled text unchanged. (See the Technology Toolbox below.)
4. **Add the attachment!** Right after you write the recipient about the nature of the attachment, pause for a moment to attach it to your message (pages 612–613).

Technology Toolbox

Preparing Attachments for Easy Reading and Compatibility

Effective document sharing requires attention to the format of the files you plan to send to others. If you are writing an essay in a word processor such as WordPerfect, OpenOffice.org's Writer, or Word, you have the option to save your file in Rich Text Format, or RTF. These files will have the .rtf extension at the ends of their names. Here's how to make an RTF file in a word processor:

1. From the File menu, choose "Save As."
2. In the pop-up dialogue box, select "Rich Text Format," "RTF," or the equivalent from the drop-down menu box called "File Type" or "Type."

3. Name your file and then navigate to the folder where you'd like to save it.
4. Choose "Save."

Email Greetings

Notice that in the examples of messages addressed to specific people, we always use the person's name. Doing so conveys a positive tone. It also assures the recipient that the email message is not spam or a virus. Although viruses sometimes include the first part of the person's email address in the subject line, usually the person's name is not in the message greeting.

Greeting	Context
Dear _______ :	More formal situations, when you have never corresponded with or met the recipient and want to set a serious or professional tone
Dear _______ ,	Informal situations, when you have a close relationship with the person (as in "Dear Mom")
Hi, ______ — or *Hi, ______ :* or *Hi ______ ,*	More familiar situations, when it's appropriate to set an informal tone. Consider using a dash (or double hyphen) after the person's name to avoid the awkwardness of a double comma, as in "Hi, Ann," or simply omit the first comma.
To Everyone: or *Dear Everyone,* or *Hi, Everyone—*	Messages sent to a discussion list or a group of people
Firstname,	Informal situations, when the recipient knows you and (probably) expects messages from you
Dear Firstname (if I may),	When you have begun a formal correspondence with someone and feel the need to be more informal. If a person doesn't know you, asking permission to use his or her first name helps break the ice.

The Greeting

The greeting is an important component of an email message because it sets the tone for the message, shows recipients that the message is intended for them, and confirms (importantly) that the message was not randomly generated by a spammer.

Deciding which greeting to use is a matter of decorum and context. Careful email writers evaluate the situation and choose the greeting that sets the right tone and assists the recipient in identifying the intention of the sender. You should use a greeting that is well suited to your familiarity with the recipient and the formality of the occasion. As with the message body, it's probably a good idea to be slightly more formal than usual when you don't know your recipient well or haven't exchanged much email with him or her.

You should always double-check to make sure that you've spelled the person's name correctly and, if called for, used the person's title (e.g., "Dear Dr. Bliss"). Do not simply presume that the person's name is the first part of his or her email address.

In some situations, such as when you exchange multiple email messages with a person in a short time span, you don't need to use a greeting because the subject line will provide the recipient with the context immediately.

In the early Renaissance, Desiderius Erasmus's book *De Copia* included hundreds of variations on salutations to use in letters, each suited to a particular rhetorical purpose. Luckily, you don't need to have all of those on hand to compose effective email. Although there are certainly more than we list here, page 611 shows several greetings that you can use for specific situations.

The Message Body

What you say in the body of an email message will vary greatly with purpose and context. In all but the most informal situations, you should begin by establishing the purpose of your message and explaining the nature of any file attachments. Because active emailers read and write a lot of email, you should make sure that your message makes its point, asks its question(s), or shares information as clearly and concisely as possible. Of course, there are circumstances when you should take an informal tone and can afford to elaborate more than usual.

Attaching a File to an Email Message

After you have addressed your message and informed your correspondent what type of file you're sending and why, attach your file. In desktop email programs and "stand-alone" email clients (such as Eudora, Outlook, Thunderbird, Outlook Express, Mac Mail, or Entourage), files are attached in a similar way:

1. Click on "Attach" on the top menu bar or, in some cases, choose File > Attach File (see Figure 27.1).

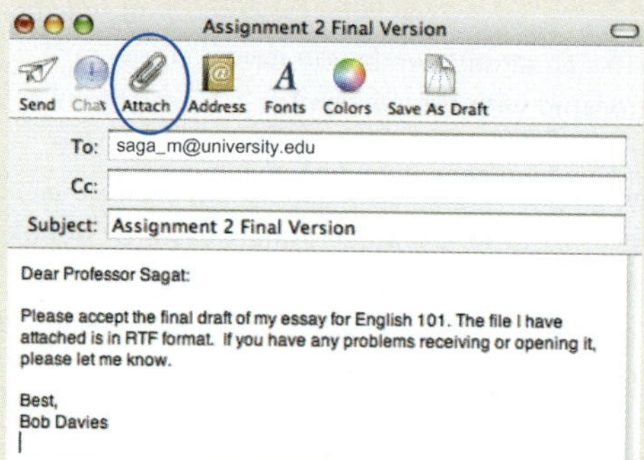

Figure 27.1 In Mac Mail, like many other email clients, you add attachments by clicking on a paperclip icon.

2. In the folder navigation dialogue box that pops up, navigate to the file you want to attach, select the file (see Figure 27.2), and then click on "Choose File" (Mac) or "Open" (Windows).

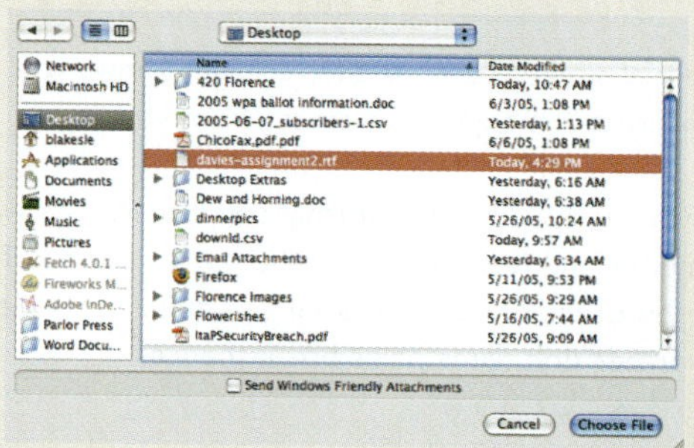

Figure 27.2 Find the file you want to attach to your email message.

3. Your file name will appear either in an attachment line near your address bar or in the body of your message (as shown in Figure 27.3).

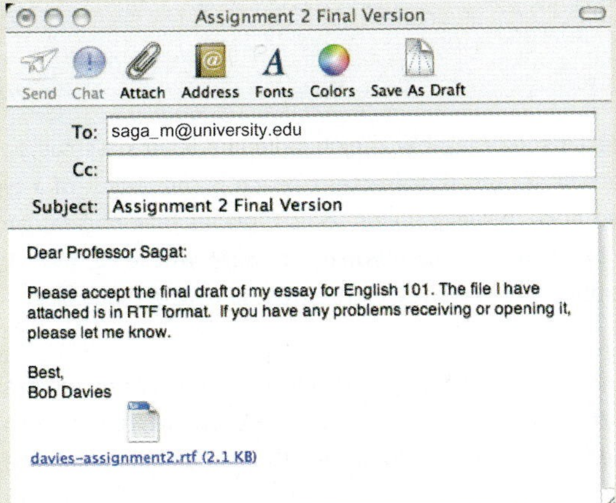

Figure 27.3 Check to see that the file has been attached to your message.

When using Web-based mailing services (like Yahoo! Mail or Google Mail), attach your file as follows:

1. Browse to and select the file you want to attach: In the Attach File box, click on "Browse" and then navigate to the file on your computer, select it, and click "Choose File" (Mac) or "Open" (Windows).
2. Upload the file by clicking on "Attach." Some Web-based mail services then require that you click on the Attach button right beneath the browser window. If yours does, click on it to upload your file, and then send your message when you're ready.

The important thing to remember is that you want your email messages to accomplish a rhetorical purpose: inform, persuade, entertain, invite, express feeling or attitude, and so on. Everything you write in your message body should help you accomplish that purpose.

In professional contexts—in college or the workplace, for example—there are some general guidelines you should follow to ensure that your email messages accomplish your purposes effectively. As a general rule, if you follow these guidelines, your email messages will be received favorably and will accomplish your goals.

Formatting

Most email programs give you the option of sending email in plain text or HTML format. Plain text messages are the most common, but improvements in email software have made it more feasible to format your messages and more likely that the recipient will see the message as you intended.

Formatting in HTML allows you to use alternative fonts, font styles (such as boldface and italics), and font sizes. Almost anything that can be embedded in a Web page can also be included in an email message. However, many people prefer to read email in plain text format because highly formatted email messages can be challenging (if not annoying) to read and respond to. For example, if you use a fancy font, there's no guarantee that the recipient will have the same font installed. The recipient's computer may substitute an alternative font that is nearly unreadable. Or the stationery or background color you use may make the message look nice when displayed on your monitor, but the recipient's monitor may render the font nearly invisible. These same complications can pop up in a variety of unforeseen ways because of wide variance in email programs and hardware.

Formatting messages in plain text will help you avoid these complications. Use plain text formatting in the message body unless you have a good reason not to do so. (Sometimes, for example, you know that your recipient wants HTML messages.) Because plain text formatting won't allow you to change font styles (from normal to italic, for example), there are a few conventions that you should know about.

Plain Text Formatting Conventions

- **Italics.** Indicate italics by using an underscore (_) to show where the italics should begin and end:

> I am reading Erik Larson's nonfiction book _The Devil in the White City_ for my Books and Coffee seminar.

- **Line length.** Email programs vary in how they handle line length. It's customary to set your line length at about 70 characters, which is the length of a typical line in a well-designed book (usually under Tools/Options/Mail Format or Preferences/Formatting, but consult Help if you're not sure where to find it). The reader's eye has trouble tracking back to the next line when lines are longer than that.
- **Headers.** Use headers in an email message to indicate new sections of text or to provide a list or other information that needs to be separated from the rest of the text, as in the following example, where the writer uses a header to introduce each URL:

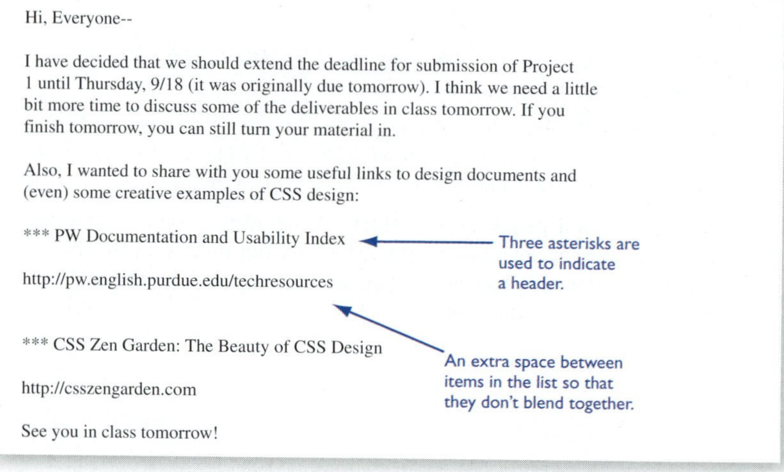
Hi, Everyone--

I have decided that we should extend the deadline for submission of Project 1 until Thursday, 9/18 (it was originally due tomorrow). I think we need a little bit more time to discuss some of the deliverables in class tomorrow. If you finish tomorrow, you can still turn your material in.

Also, I wanted to share with you some useful links to design documents and (even) some creative examples of CSS design:

*** PW Documentation and Usability Index

http://pw.english.purdue.edu/techresources

*** CSS Zen Garden: The Beauty of CSS Design

http://csszengarden.com

See you in class tomorrow!

Three asterisks are used to indicate a header.
An extra space between items in the list so that they don't blend together.

It is common in email messages to send links to websites. Identify the links with a clear header. To make sure you get the URLs correct, you can cut and paste the target URL from the address bar in your browser.

Quoting Previous Messages

Most email programs give you several options for handling quoted material in responses (see Figure 27.4). You can usually find these settings under Options > Preferences > Email Options (or something similar).

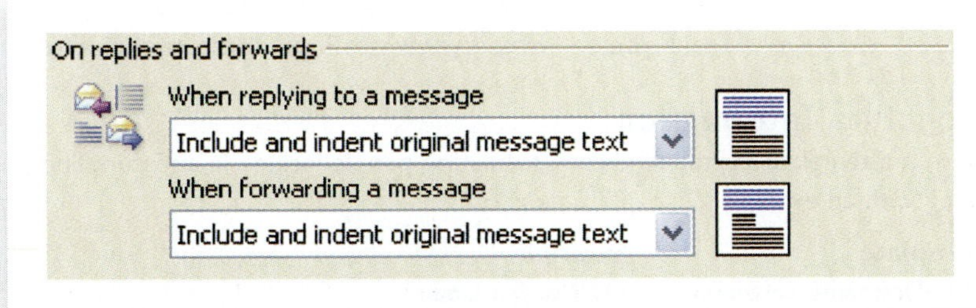

Figure 27.4 Sample Settings for Reply and Forwarding Options

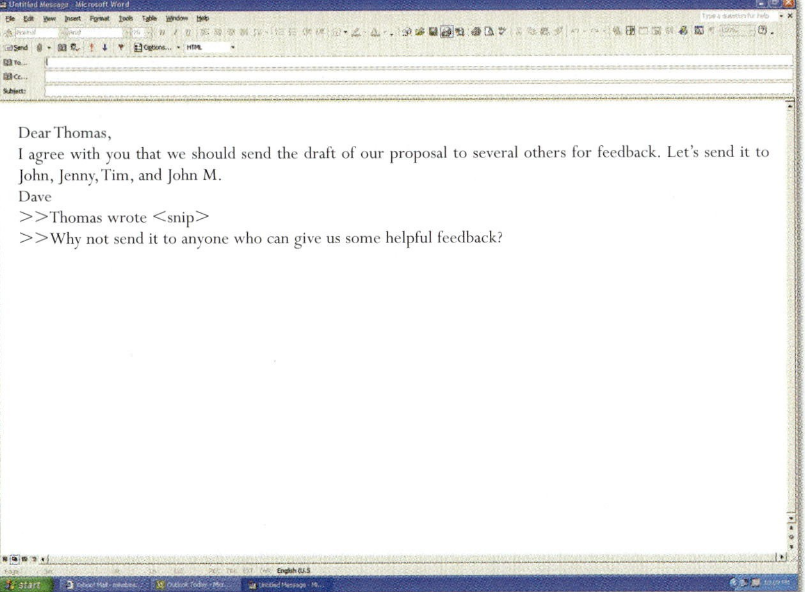

Length

Keep your email messages to under 500 words for most situations, especially when you want a quick response. It may be difficult for the recipient to respond to questions, for example, if they're embedded in long passages. For purely informative purposes, such as announcements, it's okay to write a longer message because you don't expect the recipient to respond. Excessively long messages can be confusing or feel oppressive to the recipient. Conversely, short, obtuse responses can leave readers wondering what you mean.

Quoting Previous Messages

When responding to an email, include the previous message as quoted material, usually at the end of your response after your signature. Recipients like to be reminded of the context of your response. When the quoted material contains multiple previous messages, review it and delete all but the most recent material unless there's a need to keep a precise trail of the exchange. (On discussion lists or newsgroups, eliminate all but the most recent message from the quoted material.) Trim quoted material to highlight the parts to which you're responding. When you trim quoted material, however, let your reader know you have done so by typing *<snip>* where you delete words.

Editing and Spell Checking

In the early days of email, it was common not to be too concerned about mechanics and spelling in email messages. As the purposes of email have expanded, however, it's now good practice to edit your email carefully before you send it. This includes checking for spelling mistakes, both by reviewing the message on your own and by letting your email program run a spell check if it has that capacity. When your email will be read in a professional or institutional context, you should be just as careful with your prose as you would in an essay submitted to an instructor, a cover letter with a scholarship application, or a flyer that you post in public.

Signature

The signature line(s) for an email message should, at the very least, include your name so that the recipient knows who is writing. In most situations, you'll also want to include a closing sentiment, such as one of those shown to the right, depending on the level of familiarity you have established with your correspondent.

In professional contexts, it's customary to provide additional information under your name: contact information, job title, URL of your website, and such. Limit your

Closing Sentiments: Degrees of Formality

Formal	Familiar	Casual
Sincerely yours,	Best,	Thanks,
Sincerely,	Yours,	Cheers,
Best regards,	Regards,	Later,
Best wishes,	Take care,	TTFN, CYA, etc. (see NetLingo at
	Thank you,	**http://www.netlingo.com/emailsh.cfm**)

Signature Information

Here is a template for the kinds of information people include in signature lines, along with an example.

Template	Example
Title Firstname Lastname	Ms. Maryan Liban
Job title/Major/Course	Coordinator of Special Services
Company/University	The University of Manitoba
Email address	Maryan.Liban@umanitoba.ca
URL	http://www.services.umanitoba.ca

Emailing on a PDA or a Cell Phone

Increasingly, people are reading and even writing email and instant messages on PDAs and cell phones. There is a wide variety of email software for Palm®, PocketPC, and BlackBerry™ platforms, and cell phone providers offer an array of systems for managing and receiving email. Wireless technologies have made it possible for people to send and receive email from anywhere they can receive a wireless or digital signal. This means that even if you don't use email on a PDA or cell phone, it's likely that you've received an email message, perhaps even one with an attachment, from someone who does.

Most of the guidelines for reading and writing email effectively apply to emailing with PDAs and cell phones, but there are a few additional considerations. Unless you have a full-size, attachable keyboard, your messages will usually be shorter because they take a long time to type. QWERTY keypads (small keyboards that allow you to enter text with your thumbs) simplify the process somewhat. Still, because of the smaller screen size, most messages sent from PDAs and cell phones will be short, so use them when a short message is enough to accomplish your purpose and use a laptop or desktop when you need to send longer messages or attachments. When sending messages to someone who is using a PDA or cell phone, you should realize that some of these same restrictions apply. It's likely that long messages will be hard for the recipient to read, and attachments sent to cell phones may not even be received. PDAs and cell phones can be especially useful for participating in chat and instant messaging, where all messages tend to be short and where it has become common practice for people to use abbreviations and acronyms for common sayings. (See Chapter 28 for more on participating in synchronous, real-time online conversations.)

signature to five or six lines, however, because such information is usually not critical in routine correspondence with colleagues or peers. When writing to people you don't know, use an informative signature so that they know more about you and how to reach you by means other than email.

Quotations

After their signature information, some email authors like to include witty, smart, or philosophical quotations from their favorite authors, in part to add some personality to their messages. It's understandable that this would become common practice, much as ASCII art was in the late 1990s. But quotations like these grow stale quickly, particularly for readers. Some email programs (especially online services like Yahoo! Mail) append a signature file after the message gets sent; as the author, you won't see the quotation as often as your readers will. So in all but the most informal email or groups that encourage swapping witty quotations, avoid using quotations in your signature, especially ones that are more than a few words.

Email discussion lists or newsgroups may be formed by people with similar interests or may be attached to college classes. Thousands of public lists revolve around topics ranging from hobbies to bands to scholarly and professional interests. Some discussion lists have been running for ten years or more, almost back to the days when people first started using email for social and professional communication. Discussion lists have endured because they are convenient ways to socialize and professionalize—to stay in touch with friends and network with others with similar personal or professional interests.

List members have adopted certain common practices to ensure that list discussion is (mostly) on topic and that list members enjoy the time they spend communicating with each other. Like any social group, networked communities have well-developed guidelines for interacting that you should understand and follow. Even if your discussion list is not a public one but, for example, attached to a course you're taking, you'll find that these guidelines can help you gain the most from your list participation as well as enrich the experience of others.

Guidelines for Participating on an Email Discussion List

1. **Research the list.** Before you join, take the time to find out as much about the list as you can to see if it matches your interests. Many lists have websites associated with them and searchable archives as well.
2. **Read the list FAQs.** After joining the list, you will receive instructions, often in the form of a set of FAQs, that you should read and save. They usually explain important details, such as how to adjust your subscription settings, how to unsubscribe, and how to receive the list email in digest form. Save this message for later reference, perhaps in an email folder named "Discussion Lists." Refer to it when you want to make changes to your subscription. It is a faux pas, and sometimes even a major professional gaffe, to send a message to 1000 or more people asking "How do I unsubscribe?" when you should already know how to do it or know where to find out how to do it. (Imagine interrupting the band at a concert to ask where the restroom is!)
3. **Introduce yourself.** After joining a list, it's a good idea to observe for a while (called *lurking*) before you put in your oar. Your first message to the list can be in response to another message that has been posted, but it's also accepted practice on most lists for your first posted message to be one that introduces yourself. Your message might go something like this:

> Hi, Everyone—
>
> I wanted to introduce myself to let you know that I've joined the list and look forward to listening to and joining the discussion. I'm especially interested in ______________.

4. **Preserve threads.** When you respond to what others have said, be sure that you use the same subject line (beginning with *Re:*) and that you quote the message thread you're responding to. It can be disruptive if, when the discussion is moving well in one direction, you ask a question or start an unrelated thread. Of course, there can be (and usually are) threads running simultaneously on a list, so use your best judgment, being mindful that you don't want to disrupt the flow for others.

5. **Don't respond to every new post.** Some people become so involved in list discussion that they fall into the habit of responding to every post or perhaps to multiple posts in any given day. Be careful about sharing an opinion on every subject because people will begin to wonder just how much you really know. (And don't forget, you don't want the ignominious distinction of having your email messages filtered automatically into everyone's Trash folder!) So be patient. Put in your oar when you have something useful, intelligent, or friendly to say, not at every turn. Give others a chance, too.
6. **It's fine to lurk.** Many people enjoy reading and thinking about what they read on discussion lists. You don't need to feel guilty about not posting your own messages. Lurking is fun. People who have always lurked and have never posted before often break their silence with a short line like "I've been lurking on the list and enjoying the discussion. I can't resist writing about . . . ."
7. **Don't post throwaway lines.** Even if you agree with someone strongly, it's inappropriate, in response to a long discussion, to post a message like "How true!" or "Me, too!" or "Well said!" If you feel compelled to say so, take the time to explain why you feel the way you do. Remember that your message may be going to thousands of people on a large list and you'll cause quite a lot of activity just to register your assent.
8. **Take the time to prune quoted material.** Typically, it's conventional practice to quote the previous message in your response. However, you can see that if everyone did that and a thread lasted for a while, every post to the list would contain numerous messages beneath it. So take the time to prune the amount of material you quote. You'll save bandwidth, and the people who subscribe to the list in digest form will like you. (Digests of a discussion list are daily messages that contain all the messages posted in a given day. It can be very difficult to find new contributions to a discussion when reading a digest because people don't prune quoted material. A typical digest might contain 90 percent quoted material and only 10 percent new material.)
9. **Don't post personal messages to the list, forward list messages to others not on it, or forward messages to the list from others not on it.** Sometimes people accidentally post personal messages to a list, because instead of using their address book to initiate a new message they reply to another message in a folder from the person they want to reach. (It can be so embarrassing to post a personal message to the list that you

(*continued*)

Participation on email discussion lists can be immensely rewarding, whether the members are all enrolled in a single small class or writing from all around the world. Public discussion lists in professional fields offer newcomers a chance to learn the ins and outs of specialized work from more experienced colleagues, whom they formerly would have encountered only at annual conferences or other meetings. Discussion lists also give people the opportunity to join a discourse community—to learn the "lingo" and ways of making meaning that can help them understand their subject more deeply and in the context of the concerns that others share.

To find out more about discussion lists that might interest you, try some of these clearinghouses:
Yahoo! Groups:
http://groups.yahoo.com
Topica: http://www.topica.com
Hotmail Groups:
http://groups.msn.com
AOL Groups:
http://groups.aol.com
L-Soft (Listserv):
http://www.lsoft.com/lists/listref.html

should just use your address book to initiate new messages in all circumstances.) A personal message that attacks a particular person (or post) with sarcasm or some other nasty response is called a *flame*. Most moderators these days won't tolerate even one flame, so be careful. In the early days of email, flames were common on discussion lists, but over time it seems that people have learned to restrain themselves when they feel the urge to be sarcastic.

10. **Ask the moderator if it's okay to post announcements.** Moderators appreciate such requests because announcements, even when well focused, are spam.
11. **Try to avoid being a hit-and-run commentator.** If you plan to participate on a list, read the messages in the thread carefully. It kills a discussion when people who haven't been paying attention post messages that repeat what has already been said or asked. If others can tell that you haven't been paying attention, they may resent you for it.
12. **Let the list moderator answer questions about the conduct of the list.** Discussions about list behavior often degrade quickly, so it's usually best to let the moderator address them publicly.
13. **Read the most recent messages before responding to older ones.** When a person asks a question that is fairly easy for others to answer, someone may answer right away. And then 18 others may answer, too, in a short time. There naturally will be some nearly simultaneous posts on the same subject because we receive email while we write it and because email programs only check for new mail now and then. However, do the best you can to stay current before posting the 19th message providing exactly the same answer.
14. **If a message to a list asks for data, provide the information off list (in a message to the requester of the data only) unless it's clear that others will want to read it.**
15. **Before posting open-ended research questions or surveys to academic lists, be sure to check with the list moderator and consult with others who may be able to advise you about how your request will be received.** Sometimes people will see a list as a perfect opportunity to tap a research pool, which can be fine, but do your homework first. Your research should be well advanced before you ask other people for new data.

28 NETWORKING WITH OTHERS ON THE WEB

The inventor of HTML and the World Wide Web, Tim Berners-Lee, imagines the Web as both a repository of information and a space for facilitating human communication. Here is how he put it in 1997:

> The Web was designed as an instrument to prevent misunderstandings.
>
> For this to work, it had to be not only easy to "browse," but also easy to express oneself. In a world of people and information, the people and information should be in some kind of equilibrium. Anything in the Web can be quickly learned by a person and any knowledge you see as being missing from the Web can be quickly added. The Web should be a medium for the communication between people: communication through shared knowledge. (Tim Berners-Lee, "Realising the Full Potential of the Web," 1997, *World Wide Web Consortium,* 26 Sept. 2004 <http://www.w3.org/1998/02/Potential.html>)

In the last ten years, with the rise of the Internet as a new technology for sharing information and communicating with others, *community* has become the popular term for describing one ideal of electronic communication. Since 1989, when Berners-Lee first envisioned this medium and space, many software technologies have been developed to help us connect with others on the Web and thus to realize this ideal of not only sharing and archiving information but building communities of people to help clear up misunderstandings and, importantly, develop new ideas in the presence of others who can offer their responses.

Over time, communities of users have come together online on the basis of shared interest or need. Because these communities have unique interests and goals, they use a wide variety of communication technologies, each of which offers a different experience for writers and readers. You can find online bulletin boards and forums on thousands of subjects, from home improvement and politics to desktop publishing and software. There are thousands of topical email discussion lists, many of which archive user posts on websites. In May 2006, for example, there were 73,946 public mailing lists using L-Soft's Listserv® software for managing discussion lists, out of 436,495 total Listserv email lists. There are many more email discussion lists that use other kinds of software, such as Majordomo or Mailman. As if that weren't enough, you can also find thousands (if not millions) of other groups using email servers, online bulletin boards and forums, and, in the past couple of years, weblogs (or, as they're affectionately known, blogs) and Wikis. Blogger, the major service provider for weblogs on the Internet, lists 1.1 million users and over 200,000 active weblogs. There are also now millions of users worldwide of

The terms *synchronous* and *asynchronous* refer to how communication online takes place in time.

synchronous communication Communication that happens simultaneously, in real time. When you talk to someone on a cell phone, your communication is synchronous because each party can hear the other at the moment words are spoken. On the Internet, technologies used in chat rooms (such as Instant Messenger) are called "synchronous" because they produce an exchange that takes place in real time. You type a message and click Send, and your message is received instantly. Clients like ICQ allow for a purer form of synchronous communication because the other person sees your words as you type them. (Clients are programs that request information or services from other computers.) In the film *The Matrix,* the people of Zion make their first contact with John Anderson via this kind of synchronous communication: "Wake up, Neo. . . ."

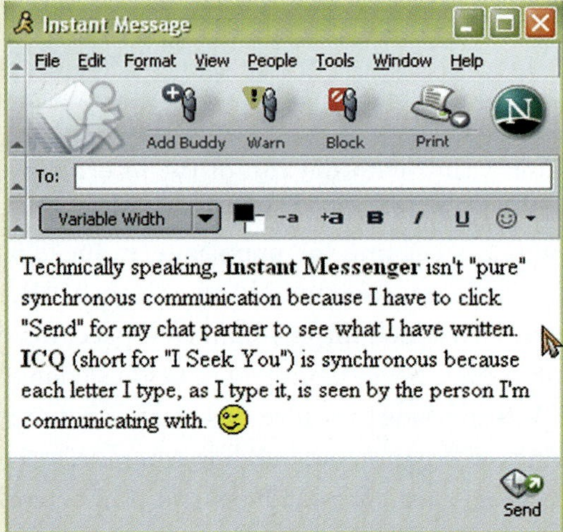

An instant message, a popular synchronous method of communication.

synchronous communication technologies, such as ICQ®, Instant Messenger™, and MSN® Chat. MUDs (Multi-User Domains) and MOOs (MUDs, Object-Oriented) have been popular for more than ten years. Many of these software technologies are in use on college campuses, so it's likely that you've already had occasion to use one or more of them and very likely that you will continue to use them in the foreseeable future.

Writing in online communities like blogs, MOOs, or discussion boards presents new challenges. It sometimes requires learning new software applications (or *clients*) and interfaces, and each tool may be used in particular rhetorical situations and sometimes for very specific purposes. As you learned about email in Chapter 27, writers need to be careful judges of the rhetorical situation—audience, message, and purpose—and to adapt the capabilities of the technologies in ways that help them write effectively in each situation. The same principles that we presented for writing effective email also apply to writing in online communities, but the circumstances and tools may be very different.

asynchronous communication Communication that takes place over an extended period of time. When you write a letter to a friend and send it via snail mail, you're communicating asynchronously. Likewise, when you post a message to an online bulletin board or a weblog, that's asynchronous communication.

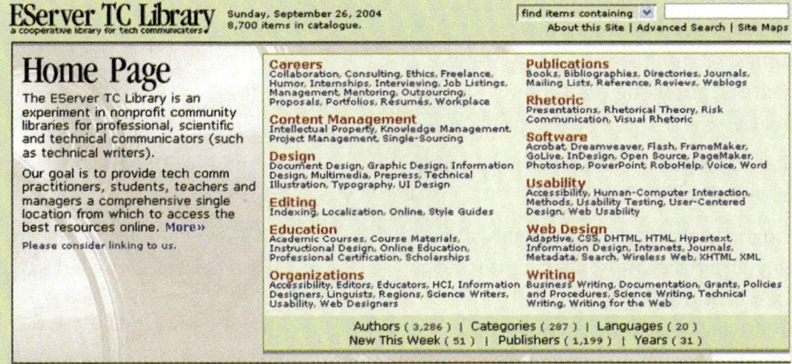

The EServer TC Library, a cooperative library for technical communicators. See **http://tc.eserver.org**.

The difference between synchronous and asynchronous communication matters because what we write and how we write it should be shaped by our understanding of how our readers receive our messages. Are they reading quickly? Are they composing their own responses even as they read ours? Are they holding multiple conversations simultaneously? Are they waiting and reflecting, then posting a response? How does the urgency of the synchronous context shape intention and message? What shortcuts (e.g., "TTFN!") do people use in synchronous situations to communicate more efficiently? Do you need to use them, too?

Online Communication: Uses, Tools, and Examples

Communication	Uses	Tools and Examples
SYNCHRONOUS		
Audio conference	Spoken conversation, meetings	Phones, conference calls, Skype
Chat	Real-time written conversation, planning meetings, interviews, group discussion	ICQ, iChat, Instant Messenger, NetMeeting
MOOs, MUDs	Chat, real-time writing conversation, group meetings, group analysis (using Web Projector), archiving documents, quick feedback	Telnet, Pueblo, enCore
Video conferencing	Spoken dialogue with a live visual feed, meetings, distance education	iSight, NetMeeting, ViaVideo, PicTel, Breeze
Whiteboard	Sharing screen space for collaborative writing, brainstorming, sharing desktops and applications	MOO (Projector), ClearBoard, WebCT, GRCLive
Web-based conference	Interactive presentations, meetings	Breeze, NetMeeting
ASYNCHRONOUS		
Email discussion lists, newsgroups	Group discussion, resource sharing, collaboration and planning, community-building (◀ section 27c)	Listserv, Mailman, Majordomo, Topic, Google Groups, Usenet Newsgroups, Yahoo! Groups
Bulletin boards, forums, threaded discussion lists	Focused group discussion, reading responses and discussion, project logs, information-sharing	Ultimate Bulletin Board, Ceilidh, Blackboard, WebCT, FirstClass, Sakai
Content management systems (CMSs)	Managing diverse content, documents, and discussion; weblogs, chat, peer review of documents, archiving; journals and ezines; digital portfolios	Drupal, CivicSpace, Mambo, Manila, Moodle
Weblogs and social networking services	Personal journaling and reflection, project logs, research notes, public discussion, dissemination of research, political action, information filtering, establishing a reputation	Blogger, b2Evolution, Drupal, FaceBook, Movable Type, LiveJournal, WordPress, ElGG, Orkut, MySpace, Friendster
Wikis	Collaborative authoring, resource-building, archiving, polling	Wikipedia, EServer TC Library, Wikibooks

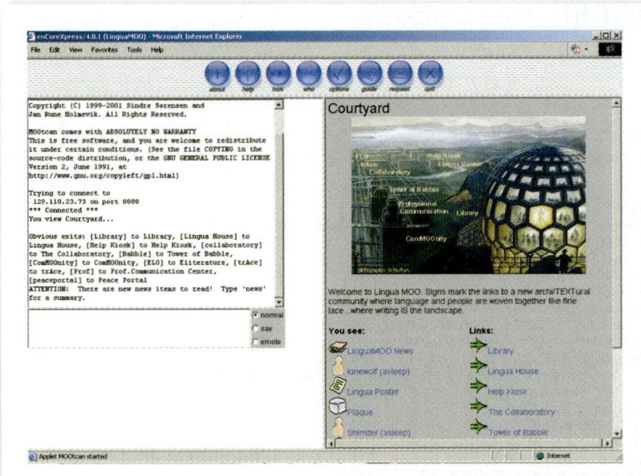

Synchronous communication: LinguaMoo, a MOO environment designed by Cynthia Haynes. See **http://lingua.utdallas.edu:7000/**.

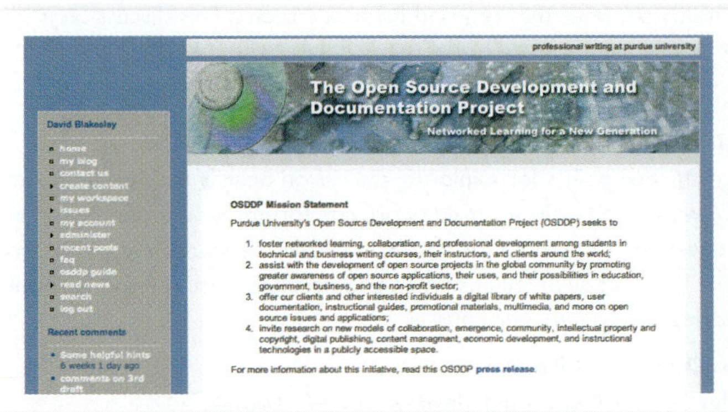

Asynchronous communication: This site is run by Drupal, a content management system and weblog. Drupal helps students manage their collaborative projects and link to each other's work and outward to the Internet, enhancing communication across classes and to the wider world. See **http://www.osddp.org**.

See section 27c for a description of email discussion groups.

Bulletin Boards, Forums, and Threaded Discussion Lists

Bulletin boards, forums, and threaded discussion lists allow users to post messages in threaded discussions, using a standard Web browser like Mozilla Firefox®, Netscape, Internet Explorer, Opera, or Safari as an interface. They have a wide variety of features, including automatic email notification when people respond to your posts, customizable "skins" (visual display settings), file sharing, and HTML-coded messages. They also usually allow the user to choose display options:

- "flat"—topics listed in the order in which they were posted
- "threaded"—posts grouped by thread, as shown in the screen capture on the next page
- "collapsed"—just headers
- "expanded"—full posts

Discussion boards and forums tend to be most useful for sustained discussion in close communities, as you find in class situations, when writers share ideas, responses, and feedback on work in progress. However, for these lists to work well, participants need to follow their user guidelines and return regularly enough to keep the discussion fresh. WebCT™, Blackboard®, First-Class, and Sakai are course management systems that include discussion boards. Ultimate Bulletin Board has been popular for many years because of its low cost and ease of use. Many networked learning environments, such as Drupal, include commenting and blogging functions that work much like threaded discussions.

Rhetorical Considerations in Discussion Networks

Most of the general guidelines or protocols for building community on bulletin boards, forums, and threaded discussion lists are derived from consideration of the ways in which rhetorical principles shape communication in this context. For example, because one of the main goals of a discussion board is to carry out sustained discussion on specific topics, users are encouraged to "stay on topic" and "keep the discussion relevant." Doing so will help others follow the written conversation without being distracted. If, as a writer, you violate these conventions, it is likely that your messages will be skipped over and your opportunities to contribute to the conversation seriously reduced.

Comment Viewing Options

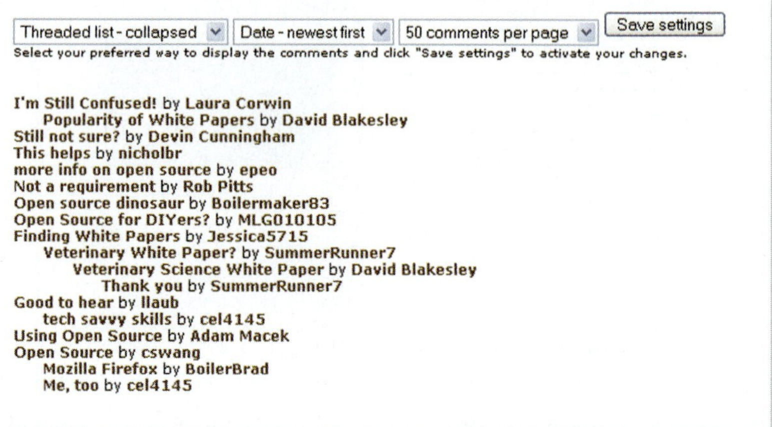

A "collapsed" threaded class discussion list. This one shows students discussing the genre of white papers and lists only the topic of the post and the writer. Indented items are ones that respond to thread topics. This discussion is occurring within a course site run by Drupal that encourages networking and peer response. See **http://joe.english.purdue.edu/fa05/420S1/**.

Resources on Discussion Boards and Forums

Here are starting points for exploring discussion boards and forums. In addition, many software and hardware makers provide forums where people can ask technology questions and search for answers offered previously. We highly recommend that you visit such forums when you have technical questions about the technologies you use in your courses:

Sample Discussion Boards

Motley Fool: **http://boards.fool.com/?ref=topnav**
Slashdot: **http://slashdot.org**

Directories

Google's Directory:
http://www.google.com/Top/Computers/Internet/On_the_Web/Message_Boards/
Big Boards: **http://www.big-boards.com**

Project Checklist

Networking in Online Forums

The following recommendations come from careful consideration of the typical rhetorical situation of discussion forums—public spaces where people with shared interests or values and special expertise gather to discuss the topics that interest them. The style and tone of posts are usually more formal than you might find in chat rooms, where the focus may be on immediacy and fast give-and-take.

1. Read the user guidelines for the board or forum and be sure to follow them.
2. Read through all the messages in a particular thread before posting a response.
3. Provide enough context in your message (by quoting from a previous post, for example) so that all readers understand what you're responding to or what you're proposing.
4. If you can't stay on topic, begin a new thread and give it a subject line that conveys the topic clearly.
5. If you want to reply to someone but your message seems somewhat personal or off topic, consider sending a personal message instead (through email or, if possible, the board's internal message server).
6. Take the time to preview and edit your messages before you post or publish them.
7. When your message is posted to the forum, open it and read it to see if it says what you intended. If it doesn't, re-edit it.
8. Return frequently to the forum to see how others have responded to your post or how the thread has continued. If the system has a "notifications" option that will send you an email when someone responds to your posts, turn it on.
9. If people respond to your post, keep the discussion going with another message (if appropriate).
10. Don't be so eager to reply to posts that you overwhelm everyone with responses to every message that gets posted. Give other people opportunity and time to reply.

Weblogs

Weblogs (blogs for short) have become popular as a form of publishing topical commentary unmediated by conventional media outlets, a kind of unfiltered civic discourse. Like discussion boards, blogs are online spaces that allow for reflection, discussion, and commentary among a variety of users, but they also differ in several ways:

- They are usually authored by one individual or a small group of people.
- Community networks—run by what's known as *social networking software*—collect multiple individual blogs together under one umbrella. MySpace (http://www.myspace.com) is a popular example.
- Readers are given permission (or not) to post comments that respond to the blog author(s).
- The software typically allows bloggers to share topics and RSS feeds (Rich Site Summary feeds), making content more dynamic and accessible.

A blog can "syndicate" the content from other blogs—the software will automatically scan for updated content on other websites that the blog can link to. News services like Google News (http://news.google.com) use RSS to gather news from hundreds of news sources around the world. Weblogs have thus become full websites in their own right, helping authors to integrate reflective commentary and research notes, archive information and documents, create lists of links to content and fellow bloggers, and collect (or aggregate) news from other weblogs. For a good example, see the news aggregator in action at Kairosnews: http://kairosnews.org/aggregator.

The Blogging Community

Content management systems and other blog management software allow bloggers to "subscribe" to or monitor other blogs with personalized news aggregators and RSS feeds, creating what are called *metablogs.* As a blog author, you may be able to collect blog postings from a variety of blog sites directly within your own blog portal, allowing you to easily find out what others have posted. Sometimes these services are provided by aggregators that tailor their choices to particular interests, such as Blogmob, a Seattle-based weblog portal. Participating in the blog community this way can help keep you "wired" to the conversations that already interest you, and thus you'll find yourself drawn to communicate with others in engaging and interesting ways.

Effective and Ineffective Blog Entries

A blog entry functions in many ways like the first post in a new thread in a discussion forum. The goal may be to write something interesting that will elicit good responses from your readers, to link to the wider conversations on the Web, or to keep a record of your thoughts—or all three at once. Here are some samples to consider. Notice how in the last one the writer goes out of her way to invite readers to respond. As a writer, don't be afraid to let your readers know how you'd like them to respond.

An uninspiring blog entry?

> Subject: Blogs
>
> Wartime weblogs have been discussed a lot lately now that the war in Iraq has lingered for so long. See http://discover.npr.org/rundowns/segment.jhtml?wfId=1212461 for a story about it.

Blogmob, at **http://seattle.blogmob.com**, is a good example of a weblog community portal that uses "trackbacks" to direct people to recently updated blogs.

An overly contentious entry?

> Subject: Blog Losers
> I heard a ridiculous story on NPR this morning that weblogs were having a significant impact on how Americans perceive the war in Iraq, in part because blog authors were writing from the scene and didn't have to run their commentary through media outlets or others who might censor their writing (see http://discover.npr.org/rundowns/segment.jhtml?wfId=1212461). How do we know who these goofballs are and where they're writing from? Isn't it the case that journalists are journalists because they verify sources and aren't free to write anything, true or not? Who cares what Joe Schmoe thinks? We see the pictures and know what's going on.

An entry people might respond to:

> Subject: Blogs in Wartime
> NPR reported this morning that weblogs were having a significant impact on how Americans perceive the war in Iraq. I see this as a good thing because it's important for us to weigh multiple perspectives on such weighty issues. It can be difficult to judge the integrity of the sources of information, but we should ask the same questions of media coverage also. It seems to me that one of the great benefits of a blog perspective is that it's personal and (somewhat) unscripted. We should know enough not to accept what we hear as "fact," but we can still begin to understand how one person experiences a significant event. That in itself is useful. What do you think? Should we trust bloggers from the war zone? What if they are soldiers? Should we care if they are biased? Could they NOT be biased?
> Link: http://discover.npr.org/rundowns/segment.jhtml?wfId=1212461

Rhetorical Considerations as an Author

Blogs are typically authored by a community of users, but sometimes the author is just one person. If you are the author of a blog and want to initiate new entries, consider the contexts in which others will read and (possibly) respond to your writing. As the author, it is likely that you can restrict who can respond to your entries and, if the blogging software allows for multiple user-roles, who gets to see your entries. These factors will help you decide how much to say, on what kinds of topics. If your blog is meant to be a "private" journal in public view, consider what ethos you present in your personal remarks. If you let readers post comments, weblogs can become give-and-take discussions.

As the one who sets the topic, a blog author who wants interesting or lively comments from users walks a delicate line between being overly contentious and being too timid. No one will want to respond if it's clear that you will leap on anyone who argues for a different view. Also, don't simply make observations—reflect on them in a bit of detail so that people who come to your blog have something to ponder. If you want them to return, give them something to think about, whether they are peers in your class or passersby who stumble upon your blog.

Rhetorical Considerations as a Reader Making Comments

Many of the same rhetorical considerations apply to blog commenting as to discussion board posting. First, you have some obligation to preserve the thread because readers typically read the author's posts and then the comments. It's easy to get carried away when responding, but bear in mind that these are public discussions and the purpose, even if it is only an ideal seldom attained, is to share ideas in an environment where debate and inquiry are valued. If you can't add anything, you don't need to post a response. But if you do have an opinion that you think others might want to hear or that is unique, share it. Be sure to explain yourself rather than simply making an observation and then quitting.

RSS Feeds Allow More People to Access Your Material

Depending on whom you ask, *RSS* stands for "Rich Site Summary" or "Really Simple Syndication." An RSS feed is an automated way for bloggers to make their content known to news aggregators, websites that index blog topics across the Internet. People used to think that if you published a Web page you would suddenly reach a wide audience—people you didn't even know would come to your site in droves. That doesn't necessarily happen. With millions of websites on the Internet, the likelihood of anyone but your friends or a search engine robot clicking through your site may not be high. RSS feeds, however, allow your blog content to be assembled and published elsewhere so that people can find it more easily.

To see how RSS feeds help spread the word about new blog content, go to Weblogs.com at **http://www.weblogs.com**.

To monitor blog traffic through an RSS compiler, visit Technorati at **http://www.technorati.com**.

Weblog Listings

Eatonweb Portal: **http://portal.eatonweb.com**

Al Macintyre's Radio Weblog: **http://radio.weblogs.com/0107846/stories/2002/10/03/blogSoftware.html**

Weblog Software and Hosting Services

Blogger: **http://www.blogger.com** (free hosting service from Google)

Greymatter: **http://www.noahgrey.com/greysoft/**

LiveJournal: **http://www.livejournal.com**

Reger.com: **http://reger.com/about/index.log**

TypePad: **http://www.typepad.com**

WordPress: **http://wordpress.org** (open source)

Hosting services allow writers to create nice-looking blogs in a matter of minutes with a unique URL and customizable features.

Rebecca Blood's Ten Tips for a Better Weblog

Blood is the author of *The Weblog Handbook: Practical Advice on Creating and Maintaining Your Blog* (Cambridge, MA: Perseus Books Group, 2002).

1. **Choose an updating tool that is easy to use.** Try out several services. Some are free, some cost a little money, but don't commit to a tool until you have had a chance to try it out. Pick the one that works best for you.
2. **Determine your purpose.** Weblogs are used to filter information, organize businesses, share family news, establish professional reputations, foment social

change, and muse about the meaning of life. Knowing what you hope to accomplish with your weblog will allow you to begin in a more focused way.

3. **Know your intended audience.** You conduct yourself differently with your friends than you do with professional associates, strangers, customers, or your grandmother. Knowing for whom you are writing will allow you to adopt an appropriate tone.
4. **Be real.** Even a professional weblog can be engaging. Avoid "marketese." Speak in a real voice about real things.
5. **Write about what you love.** A weblog is the place for strong opinions, whether about politics, music, social issues, gardening, or your profession. The more engaged you are with your subject, the more interesting your writing will be.
6. **Update frequently.** Interested readers will return to your site if there is likely to be something new. You needn't update every day, but try to post several times a week.
7. **Establish your credibility.** To the best of your ability, be truthful. Be respectful to your audience and to your fellow bloggers. Understand that on the Internet, your words may live forever, whether they are self-published or archived on another site. . . .
8. **Link to your sources.** The Web allows a transparency that no other medium can duplicate. When you link to a news story, an essay, a government document, a speech, or another blogger's entry, you allow your readers access to your primary material, empowering them to make informed judgments.
9. **Link to other weblogs.** Your readers may enjoy being introduced to the weblogs you most enjoy reading. The Web is a democratic medium and bloggers amplify each other's voices when they link to each other. Generously linking to other weblogs enlarges the grassroots network of information sharing and social alliances we are creating together on the Web.
10. **Be patient.** Most weblog audiences are small, but with time and regular updates your audience will grow. You may never have more than a few hundred readers, but the people who return to your site regularly will come because they are interested in what you have to say.

    Bonus tip: Have fun! Whether your weblog is a hobby or a professional tool, it will be more rewarding for you if you allow yourself to experiment a little. Even a subject-specific weblog benefits from a bit of whimsy now and again.

From Rebecca Blood, "Ten Tips for a Better Weblog," *Rebecca's Pocket,* 22 Mar. 2003, 26 Sept. 2004 <http://www.rebeccablood.net/essays/ten_tips.html>.

Blogs Integrated into CMSs

Weblogs are usually efficient at archiving previous discussions and may be integrated seamlessly with other elements of a website. Content management systems (CMSs) often integrate weblog features and so offer additional opportunities for combining the features of weblogs with the archival and document management features of a CMS. Popular open source (free) CMS software includes the following:

- Drupal: http://www.drupal.org
- CivicSpace: http://www.civicspacelabs.org
- Mambo: http://www.mamboserver.com
- Moodle: http://www.moodle.org
- Sakai: http://www.sakaiproject.org

Many students participate in online communities associated with classes or group projects. Because each communication technology has some unique features that shape how discussion unfolds online, student writers should take the time to establish guidelines for participation, including the expected frequency of posts, length, level of engagement, and more. These guidelines should be posted to the site so that people can refer to them later. By helping to establish *decorum,* a rhetorical concept related to *kairos* (◀ Chapter 1), such guidelines create conventions for lively and interesting discussions; they ensure that everyone understands how online conversations can develop fruitfully for all involved.

The screen capture to the right shows a list of seven guidelines that a group of students came up with and everyone in the class agreed to follow. Your class (or community) may generate guidelines of its own.

Here are some examples of a few of the guidelines in action:

- **No Phaedrus responses.** Phaedrus was one of Socrates's students and appears in Plato's dialogue named after him, *Phaedrus.* Throughout the dialogue, Socrates does most of the talking, on such subjects as the nature of love, madness, and writing. When he chimes in, Phaedrus says things like

WWWThreads Version 5.1.5 WWWThreads At Purdue University

Admin | Main Index | Search | Edit Profile | Send Private | Check Private | Who's Online | FAQ | Logout | User List

Archived Course Boards
>> English 680V: Visual Rhetoric & Composition (Spring 2002)

Thread views: 79 **Previous** **Index** **Next** **Flat** **Threaded**

Subject	**protocol for wwwthreads**
Posted by	**angela** *(Newcomer)*
Posted on	01/15/02 07:52 PM
From IP	128.211.135.107

Edit **Reply**

Here are the guidelines we discussed in class:

1) no phaedrus responses--elaborate on your responses--quote from a previous message if necessary
2) no sniper shots--no flaming--show respect
3) keep discussion relevant to the whole class--provide context for personal messages
4) reader responsibility--read a thread before responding to it--ask for clarification if necessary
5) brevity--one screen length--200 words or less
6) stay on topic to preserve the thread--begin a new thread if necessary
7) sign your messages

Enjoy!

Angela

Class guidelines developed by students for interaction in WWWThreads, a Web-based discussion board.

Example: No Phaedrus Responses

Original post:

> . . . for these reasons, I think it's important that we begin our project by first coming up with a good list of questions to ask our client.

Ineffective response:

> Exactly!

Effective response:

> Exactly! I have an idea for the first question we should ask: "What is the most important goal of your organization?" Do any others have some recommendations for possible questions?

In the effective response, the author develops the thread by coming up with a question and then asking others to do the same.

Example: Keep Discussion Relevant

Original post:

> Our client is really busy, so it's important that we are well prepared with our interview questions and thus don't have to ask too many follow-up questions later.

Ineffective response:

> I was really busy this weekend, I can tell you that! I went to a great movie on Saturday . . .

Effective response:

> Maybe we should also anticipate what our client's responses will be so that we can ask follow-up questions on the spot. If, for example, the client says that she enjoys the work "because she likes helping people," we should ask her to share a memorable example of when she made a difference in someone's life and how it felt.

Can you explain how the effective response shifts the course of the conversation? What kind of posts do you think might follow this one?

"How true. Tell me more!" The students in this course agreed that these kinds of responses don't add anything new to the discussion (an important goal for most posts in online communities) and should be avoided. Rather than simply registering agreement, these posts might better explain the basis for agreement. When you feel a Phaedrus response coming on, explain "Why?" when you post it.

- **Keep discussion relevant.** It's aggravating for participants to read personal messages exchanged between two people in a public forum. Sometimes people send a reply to everyone on an email discussion list, much to their own horror. (If you ever do this accidentally, it's common practice to send a quick, very short reply to the list expressing your apologies to everyone; see pages 619–620 for more on this subject.)

- **Stay on topic to preserve the thread.** You should always try to preserve the thread of a discussion by staying on topic. Threads are topical subject matter identified in the subject line (either of an email message or in a bulletin board posting). One of the main benefits of online discussion is that it enables us to follow and develop a train of thought with others so that, in pooling our ideas, we arrive at new and deeper insights or a more precise plan of action. If you intervene in such threads with posts that radically shift the topic, you may seriously hurt that effort. In cases where you find it necessary to take the conversation in a new direction, you can always post a new message, with a new subject line (i.e., start a new thread).

Example: Stay on Topic to Preserve the Thread

Subject line of thread: Using visuals in our client report

> Like Ann, I think we need to include visuals as more than fancy decoration in our report to our client. It would be helpful, for example, to give a screenshot of the parent organization's website so that the client can see what the catalog looks like, especially since they will have to develop their own catalog.

Ineffective response:

> I think our report should use APA style because that's what the client said she used in school and so she'll be familiar with it. What are we supposed to do?

Effective response:

> How about a screenshot also, of a catalog produced by another local organization with similar goals? I've found a website for an organization in Florida that provides people with a catalog of services that looks very nice and could be an excellent model. See http://fchr.state.fl.us/

How does the effective response both preserve the thread and create opportunities for others to respond?

What Should I Do If I Feel Threatened or Harassed in a Chat Room?

Unfortunately, the (apparent) anonymity allowed to users in chat rooms and other synchronous spaces means that some people violate common rules of decency and post threatening or harassing messages. If you feel uncomfortable in a chat *for any reason,* you can always leave immediately. However, if that feels like too drastic a step, especially if the discussion occurs in the context of class discussion or group work, you should first let the person (and others) know that the discussion is making you uncomfortable. A simple message like "This conversation has taken a turn that makes me feel uncomfortable" will often put a quick stop to such situations. If there is a moderator (or a teacher) who may be able to help, you can also let him or her know about the situation privately. Users who don't follow the community's guidelines for decorum can be banned from participating by the chat room administrators.

If a situation that makes you feel harassed doesn't stop, you can

1. Ignore the person's messages in the chat room by not responding to them.
2. Ignore any private messages sent to you by people you don't know.
3. Double-click on the person's chat room name and check the "Ignore User" box, if one exists for the chat client you're using.
4. Exit the chat room.

There may also be situations in which people say things that threaten others. In such cases, let a trusted peer or teacher know. You might also document the time, date, name of the chat room, and nature of the message so that the information can be reported to the chat room administrator.

Synchronous reading and writing take place quickly in unmoderated chat rooms, MUDs, and MOOs, so the rhetorical context that shapes these written conversations is very different from that in asynchronous environments. People don't have much time to think through topics, write or read extended responses, or revise their writing.

Because they unfold quickly in time, unmoderated synchronous discussions feel somewhat like conference calls. Several people (at least) are usually reading and posting messages at once, so the activity is often intense. You have to pay attention or else you'll lose the drift of the conversation. Often, people carry on multiple conversations simultaneously in a chat room or MOO, which can make things even more challenging (and interesting).

The fast action doesn't mean, however, that synchronous communication should be thoughtless or that sloppy prose and extensive use of acronyms (*lol*, etc.) are okay. Like discussion boards, chat or MOO communities develop explicit or implicit guidelines for decorum that you should learn, either by reading them or by sitting in on the conversation a bit (lurking) until you feel confident that you understand what people expect from your participation. When you use chat or MOOs in a class, take the time to discuss issues of decorum at the outset. The time you spend in the beginning managing the nature and conduct of your discussion is often well spent, before feelings get hurt or the discussion ceases entirely.

Chat

Chat rooms are popular because of the immediacy of contact they allow between participants. Like any communication medium, they have advantages and disadvantages. In writing courses, chat rooms allow for continued discussion of course content, brainstorming activities, group management, and live interaction when F2F (face-to-face) meetings may not be possible. Students who aren't comfortable expressing themselves in F2F meetings sometimes find chat a comfortable way to express themselves. At the same time, however, chat rooms typically don't offer much space for entering responses, require good typing skills, and favor frequent users who know the tricks of fast give-and-take, such as how to take turns. In public chat rooms, people may disguise their identities (including gender), which makes interaction interesting but also sometimes confusing.

Project Checklist

Participating in Online Synchronous Communication

1. Read the user guidelines for the community, or develop some with your group.
2. When you enter a live discussion, announce your presence with a short greeting to the list, when it seems appropriate to do so. (Example: "Hi, everyone. It's nice to be here.")
3. As messages are posted, try to read them all, but pay special attention to messages that are directed specifically to you or to something you've mentioned.
4. Try to stay on topic and preserve threads, but recognize that multiple threads may go on simultaneously.
5. If you can't stay on topic, begin a new thread and make sure that you announce how you'd like to shift the discussion.
6. If your post is meant for a particular person, preface it with that person's user name (e.g., "To MaryD:").
7. If you want to reply to someone but your message seems somewhat personal or off topic, consider sending a personal message instead (through email or, if possible, the board's internal message server). Many chat rooms and MOOs, for example, will also allow you to send private (backchannel) messages to other participants.
8. "Emoting" is a common practice that allows users to emulate physical gestures (e.g., "Joe waves to Dan") and helps establish group congeniality (▶ page 638).
9. Take a moment to read over your messages before you post them.
10. Watch to see if others respond to you. If they do—or ask questions—follow up. It's frustrating when people post messages and then leave the space or don't pay attention to the responses of others.
11. When you leave a synchronous conversation, it's customary to announce your exit. (Example: "Bye, everyone. Gotta run! TTFN.")
12. Don't be so eager to reply to every post that you overwhelm everyone else. Give other people opportunity and time to reply. Learn to take turns.

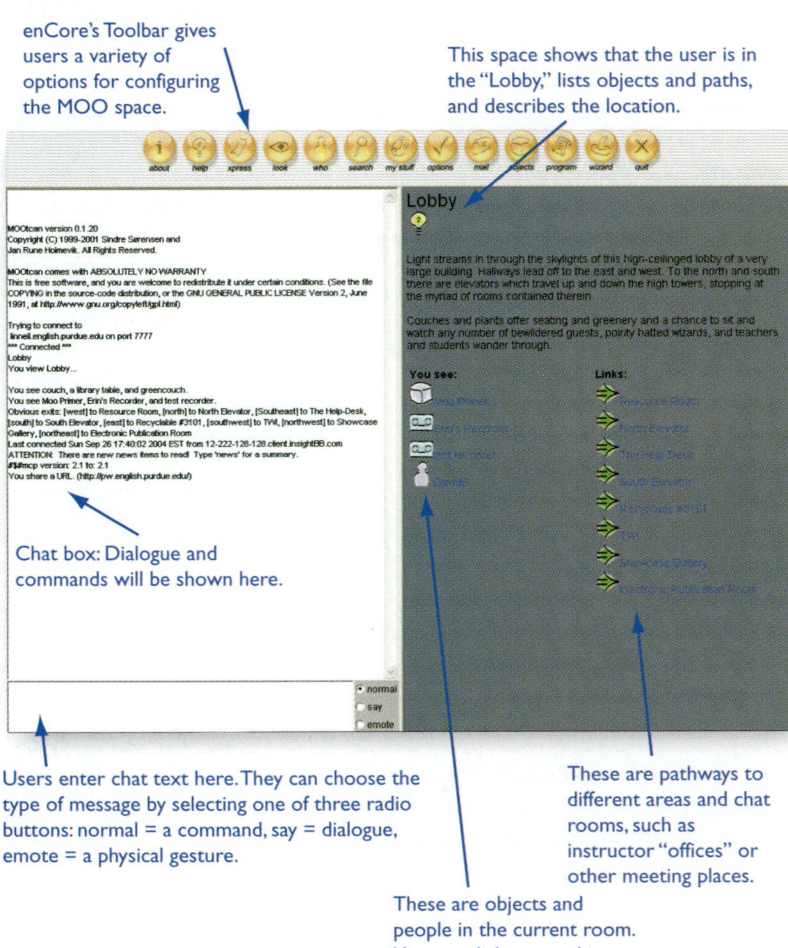

enCore MOO allows users to interact in a wide variety of ways. On the left are a chat box (bottom) and a chat transcript (top). On the right are tools (such as recorders, for "taping" chats; notebooks, for keeping journals and logs; and even projectors, for sharing images and websites with other users). Users can navigate to different spaces in the MOO where people gather to chat, share documents, archive material, and work collaboratively on ongoing projects.

enCore's Toolbar gives users a variety of options for configuring the MOO space.
This space shows that the user is in the "Lobby," lists objects and paths, and describes the location.
about
help
xpress
look
who
search
my stuff
options
mail
objects
program
wizard
quit
Lobby
Light streams in through the skylights of this high-ceilinged lobby of a very large building. Hallways lead off to the east and west. To the north and south there are elevators which travel up and down the high towers, stopping at the myriad of rooms contained therein.
Couches and plants offer seating and greenery and a chance to sit and watch any number of bewildered guests, pointy hatted wizards, and teachers and students wander through.
You see:
Links:
normal
say
emote
Chat box: Dialogue and commands will be shown here.
Users enter chat text here. They can choose the type of message by selecting one of three radio buttons: normal = a command, say = dialogue, emote = a physical gesture.
These are pathways to different areas and chat rooms, such as instructor "offices" or other meeting places.
These are objects and people in the current room. You can click on an object to see its description.

MOO Resources

See the Resources Guide at the enCore Open Source MOO Project (by Jan Rune Holmevik and Cynthia Haynes): **http://lingua.utdallas.edu/encore/**

MOOs

MOO stands for "Multi-User Domain, Object Oriented." MOOs provide a virtual space for chats, often situating them in "rooms" and "parlors" that give users the feeling that they're visiting a material space. The MOO uses virtual objects (such as rooms, recorders, and projectors) to help users navigate to chat rooms where they can meet privately, keep a transcript of their discussions, and discuss readings or websites.

To use a MOO, users need a MOO client such as enCore, which structures the interface through a Web browser, or an IRC (Internet Relay Chat) client, like Telnet. After logging in, users may visit places within a MOO space. Instructors often set up virtual offices in MOOs and provide student access to recorders (to produce a chat transcript), projectors (to show Web pages that all can see in a separate window), notebooks (to allow archiving of notes), and more. MOOs allow for immediate contact with others, who can respond quickly to your messages, communicate their observations of websites shared in the Web projector, or plan group work and manage projects.

ICQ

ICQ, which stands for "I Seek You," is the most popular software for synchronous communication on the Internet. (By June 2005, ICQ had amassed 180 million users in over 245 countries.) ICQ allows users to see messages as they are being typed by users, making communication even more immediate than with chats or MOOs. The software can be used as a portal to other forms of communication as well, such as email and audio or video messaging. Thousands of ICQ groups are organized around shared interests. (See http://web.icq.com/groups/ for a full listing.)

In writing classes and other courses, synchronous chat such as that enabled by ICQ may be used to facilitate group discussion, brainstorm, plan projects, and meet at a distance. Users can add one another to their contact lists, create personalized chat rooms, and tailor the experience in a variety of other ways so that students can connect directly with each other or even ask the teacher questions online at odd hours. It is common practice to arrange ICQ meetings in advance (especially with people you don't know well) or, at minimum, to invite someone to a live chat with an instant message or email. Student groups should make arrangements to meet online at scheduled times so that meetings don't interrupt other work.

Emoticons (Smileys)

Emoticons (short for "emotion icons"), or smileys, convey emotion and attitude. They are represented by keystroke combinations that pictorially represent the intended facial expression, albeit loosely. In informal contexts like chat and instant messaging, they are used frequently. Smileys are also used in email and on discussion boards when the situation is informal and their use has been established by convention.

In the Drupal networked learning environment and blog space, users can enter the typed smiley and the smiley icon will automatically be substituted when the message is posted. From http://www.drupal.org.

Emoticons and Smileys Resource:
http://www.muller-godschalk.com/emoticon.html

Project Checklist

Effective Participation in ICQ Chats

1. Plan your chat meetings in advance: when you'll meet, who will attend, what the purpose will be.
2. If you enter an ongoing chat, introduce yourself. (Example: "Hello, everyone. I'm here and will chime in as soon as I catch the drift . . .")
3. Stay on topic as best you can.
4. Take turns.
5. Wait for people to respond before posting messages that move the topic in new directions.
6. When you make a typing mistake that results in a confusing message, correct yourself so that people will understand your intentions.
7. Use acronyms to save time, but don't use so many that you confuse others.
8. If you don't understand someone's posting, ask for clarification.
9. When you leave, say goodbye so that other participants know you've left.
10. Invite strangers for chats only after you've sent a separate message requesting a meeting (via an instant message or email).

28e

Common Knowledge and Documentation in Networked Communities

Understanding the concept of common knowledge will help you decide when and how to cite your sources when you refer to or adapt the writing of others. **Common knowledge** refers to *what members of a discourse community in a specific context generally know: facts, information, concepts, terminologies, and practices.* A **discourse community** is a group of people who share values and beliefs about subjects and who converse about them in ways accepted as conventional within the group. Newcomers to a discourse community gradually learn its common knowledge and conventions by listening to and conversing with others, in much the same way that an infant gradually learns the meaning of words and what effects they might have on caregivers.

Citing Sources in Your Posting

In asynchronous communication contexts, such as blogs and discussion boards, citation practices are governed by context and purpose, as well as by the community's understanding of what qualifies as common knowledge. For example, in a weblog posting that refers to a news event, it is common practice to provide a link to the source in the form of a URL that readers can track if they want to learn more.

Direct quotations are indicated by quotation marks or block quotations (indented quotations enabled by the HTML tag <blockquote>). Weblog posts do not typically include parenthetical documentation (such as page numbers) or bibliographies. They do, however, name the authors and titles of the works they cite in their text. Information and terms that are common knowledge in a particular blogging network are not cited because the authors presume that the audience already shares that knowledge. On discussion boards, the practice is similar.

Citing a Posting as a Source

You may want to cite a posting as a source. Weblogs and discussion boards may occasionally offer information you will want to cite in your research projects—for example, when you want to explain a person's or group's attitude toward a given subject or describe how an event was discussed in online communities. Realize that common knowledge will be defined differently for this new discourse community, whose members may not be participating in the blog or discussion board. In deciding what needs to be documented, think carefully about what this audience knows and believes. For detailed information on how to cite online postings in MLA, APA, and other citation styles, see Chapters 19–23.

Documenting Sources in Your Online Posting

Title of post
Authors are cited indirectly and a link to the source is provided.
Money can't buy happiness
A new scientific study reveals that (shocker!) a nation's economic fortitude is not as tied tc the well-being of its citizens as previous believed. The results of the study--prepared by researchers at the University of Illinois and University of Pennsylvania--appeared in the latest issue of Psychological Science in the Public Interest.
"It has been assumed that money increases well-being and, although money can be measured with exactitude, it is an inexact surrogate to the actual well-being of a nation. In a 1985 survey, respondents from the Forbes list of the 400 richest Americans and the Maasai of East Africa were almost equally satisfied and ranked relatively high in well-being. The Maasai are a traditional herding people who have no electricity or running water and live in huts made of dung. It follows, that economic development and personal income must not account for the happiness that they are so often linked to."
Instead, the authors propose that a population's "engagement, purpose and meaning, optimism and trust, and positive and negative emotions in specific areas such as work life and social relationships" should be considered when measuring the strength of a nation.
Link
posted by David Pescovitz at 05:20:14 AM permalink | Other blogs commenting on this post
Author of post
Block quotation: Although quotation marks are used here, they are not needed because the material has already been formatted as a quotation.

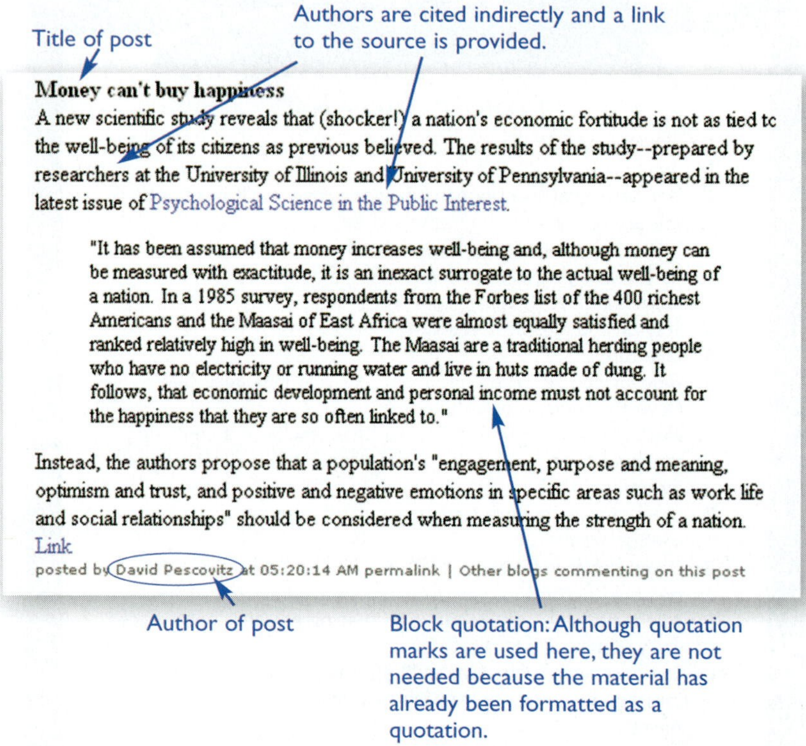

Sample blog posting at Boing Boing (**http://boingboing.net**). This is a good example of how a weblog posts reports on an issue, provides a link for users to track, and quotes from the source.

The World Wide Web is the new global marketplace for sharing information, buying and selling property, and influencing opinion. It is a public space much like the *agora* of ancient Greece, where people gathered to exchange goods, discuss ideas and politics, and form bonds with others in the wider community. (*Agora* is the Greek term for "gathering place.") On the Web, you will find amazing repositories of useful and current information on almost any topic. You will also run across content, discussions, and images that will make you wince because you strongly disagree or squint because the content is illegible. The Web can be a place for contesting and protesting, the scene for civic action, rhetoric, and propaganda. It is at heart a public space where rhetoric has a central role, as it does in any social situation that includes people with diverse interests, experience, and agendas who may identify with one another—or be dangerously divided. Whatever the Web's character and appeal, however, writers in the digital age need to know how to write and read effectively on it because it has become such an important part of everyday social life. In the chapters to follow, you'll find out how to make simple and complex websites, how to manage their many design elements, and how to test and evaluate them to make sure they accomplish your purpose.

Information technologies pose challenges for everyone. They also make it possible for anyone to express relationships among ideas in new or unusual ways. Through this process of restructuring knowledge—a metaphoric process at heart—writers learn to see subject matter in new ways, in other terms or images that can bring important information and nuances to light. Because information can be shaped in innumerable ways and for multiple purposes, it is not surprising that the Web has evolved into a scene of persuasion: of give-and-take and thrust-and-parry; of he said/she said; of revelation and fakery; of prideful boasts and shameful viciousness; of love and hate, pleasure and pain, and everything else that makes us social animals. The Web is a social space and naturally creates the conditions for persuasion to occur.

As you learn to write for the Web and to design websites, you should not forget that the Web is inherently a public space. In this chapter and the others on writing and designing for the Web, you will learn to shape information for a public audience. While it may be the case that only your primary audience—peers, teachers, co-workers, friends, family—will likely read your work, you should keep your subsidiary audiences in sight as you shape information for publication on the Web.

Information Literacy

Here are some questions that attentive writers and readers ask about information. You will notice that these are by now familiar questions about the rhetorical situation, couched here in the context of information literacy.

What Writers Should Ask

1. Is the information accurate?
2. Is the information useful?
3. What information is most important to readers?
4. What should readers understand most deeply after reading?
5. What can readers reference later, as the need arises?
6. How can I make information stick in the reader's mind?
7. What do I want my readers to do with the information?
8. What do my readers want to do with the information?

What Readers Want to Know

1. Is the information accurate?
2. Is the information useful?
3. What information is most important to me?
4. What do I need to remember most deeply?
5. What can I refer to later, as the need arises, and how can I find it again?
6. How can I remember so much information?
7. What does the writer want me to do with the information?
8. What do I need to do with the information?

In 1989, Tim Berners-Lee invented the World Wide Web. Since its inception, the Web has been conceived as a conduit for sharing information at unprecedented speeds. More recent developments in broadband technologies—T1 and T3 ethernets, DSL (digital subscriber lines), cable modems, and wireless networking—have made it relatively easy for people to transmit greater and greater quantities of information quickly and efficiently. While access to broadband technologies remains uneven across class, racial, gender, and cultural lines, this emphasis on information sharing has perhaps been the Web's lasting impact. We are only now beginning to grasp how dramatic this impact has been and to understand the demands it places on people to be literate in an information-saturated world.

Evaluating, Synthesizing, and Repurposing Information

Information literacy is the ability to evaluate, synthesize, and "repurpose" information. *Repurposing* refers to the process of revising a document or file that was created for one particular purpose and audience so that it will become better suited to a new rhetorical situation. Information literacy has become a necessary and valuable skill for writers and researchers in this digital age.

With new methods for conveying information made possible by Internet and digital technologies, we have come to realize that information architecture, or how we convey and organize information, is at least as important as the information we convey. Information architect Richard Saul Wurman, author of *Information Anxiety* and *Information Anxiety 2,* makes this point frequently: unorganized and unprocessed information is virtually useless. It is, rather, the power to convey and transform information that is valuable.

This is an astounding, even provocative, realization. Suddenly, *how* we say or write something is just as important as *what* we say or write. Shouldn't content always be more important than "mere" presentation? Of course it should! People have been saying so since, in *Phaedrus,* Plato had Socrates chastise the "writers of the handbooks" for placing more emphasis on "the niceties of the arts of rhetoric" than on "the truth." However, information has to be presented in ways that not only reach the audience but also help them learn. Information needs to be made manageable and useful by sorting, synthesizing, and assigning relative value to the content.

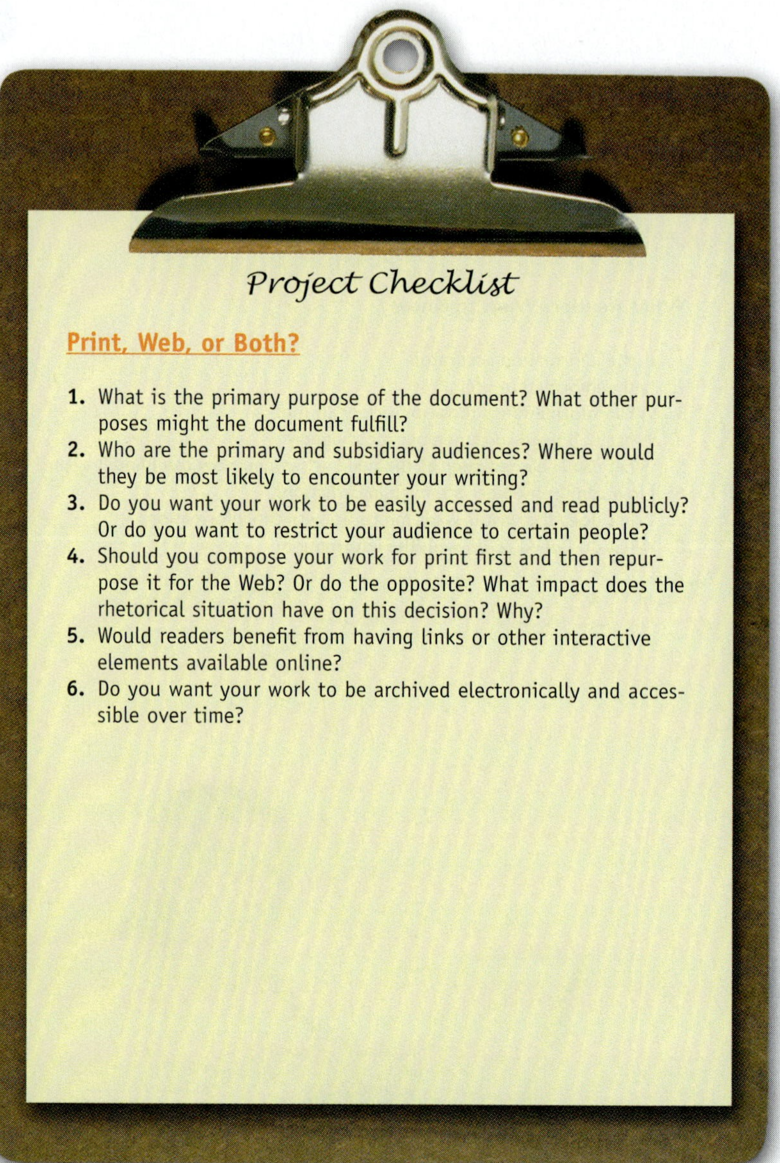

Project Checklist

Print, Web, or Both?

1. What is the primary purpose of the document? What other purposes might the document fulfill?
2. Who are the primary and subsidiary audiences? Where would they be most likely to encounter your writing?
3. Do you want your work to be easily accessed and read publicly? Or do you want to restrict your audience to certain people?
4. Should you compose your work for print first and then repurpose it for the Web? Or do the opposite? What impact does the rhetorical situation have on this decision? Why?
5. Would readers benefit from having links or other interactive elements available online?
6. Do you want your work to be archived electronically and accessible over time?

Web Publishing

Publishing on the Web would be a good choice in these situations:

1. Your assignment for a class is to compose an annotated bibliography on your topic and to include entries that can be accessed on the Web. You want your bibliography to be accessible to your classmates and others interested in the topic, and you think they will benefit from reading some of the works youve listed.
2. You want others (including people you may not know) to respond to and offer feedback on your writing, so you decide to create a weblog that will allow comments.
3. You want to develop a digital portfolio of your writing so that prospective employers will notice your work.
4. You have some special expertise on a subject and want to share your knowledge and establish your reputation as someone well informed on the subject.
5. You want to advertise and sell a product.
6. You want to create a journal or ezine of your own that collects articles and hypertexts submitted by others, but you don't have a budget to pay for printing and mailing copies.
7. You plan to present your work to a live audience at a poster session or conference and want people to have access to your work later.
8. You want to enlist the help of other people at a distance in creating a community website that provides up-to-date information.
9. You have created an ebook that includes multimedia components, such as video and audio, and have put it on a CD. You want readers to have access to it from anywhere.
10. You want to demonstrate a complex process to others, such as how to perform a task or make something, and can do so efficiently with video or other animation.
11. Your writing is about content easily accessible on the Web—at a museum website, for instance—and it would help readers to visit that website as they read your essay or hypertext.

Virtually any purpose that you can invent for print-based writing can also be applied to writing on the Web, and you can find examples of genres that have emerged in the digital age. Because they emerged as a result of a social process of sharing information and ideas, many of these genres resemble their counterparts in print, but with some important variations. When it comes time for you to decide whether to compose your work for print, the Web, or both, you will face a variety of questions whose answers will affect not only the final form of your work but also your decisions during invention, revision, and production.

Scenarios for Web Writing

Consider composing for the Web from the very start if you want your writing to

- be accessible to a wide and public audience
- network with what others have said on the Web
- offer readers choices about how and in what order to read
- evolve as you discover new ideas
- be accessible over time
- integrate multimedia components like video, audio, and animation

If *any* of these scenarios fit your circumstances, consider making a decision to publish your work on the Web at the point of invention and planning rather than later. You will find it easier to include Web-based components if you plan for them at the start.

Conventions for Web-based writing have evolved as we have come to understand more about how readers interact with texts in digital spaces, so you will need to compose your work from the start in a style that is suited to the medium. (See Writing Style on the Web, pages 648–651.)

Genres on the Web

Any writing that has a characteristic form and function in print can find its way to the Web. Google search results, for example, will often list websites and files in various formats that indicate how they were created: HTML—hypertext markup language; PDF—portable document format; RTF—rich text format; and so on. Many such documents were composed for print publication. Others were repurposed from print for the Web or were composed for the Web from the start. The difference between print-based and Web-based writing may seem subtle at first, but as a careful reader and writer of online content, you can learn to discern and appreciate content that has been composed specifically for the Web.

Characteristic Features of Digital Content in an Ebook

Multimedia content is included in a separate frame, and the user can view enlarged versions.

This page in the TK3 book has been "dog-eared," an effective simulation of a convenience available in a printed book.

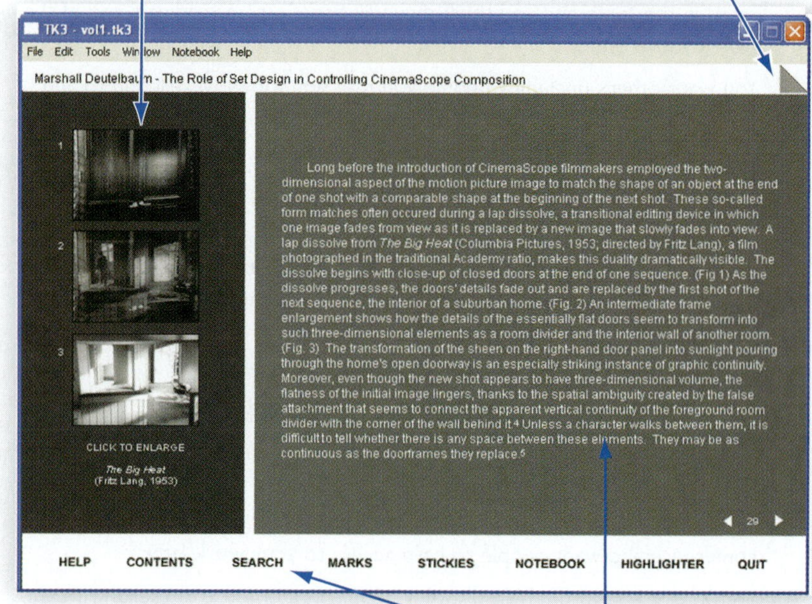

Navigational elements and tools allow readers to choose the reading sequence and enhance reading, notetaking, and bookmarking.

The text is broken into smaller chunks so that readers can focus on each text frame, much as they would a scene in a film.

From Marshall Deutelbaum, "The Role of Set Design in Controlling CinemaScope Composition," in Linda Lewis (Ed.) and Peter Henderson (Designer), *Filmbuilding: Selected Papers and Presentations*, Vol. I [Multimedia eBook on CD], 2001.

Characteristic Features of Digital Content in a Nonlinear Hypertext

The lead node for this hypertext essay explains the nature of the hypertext and provides notes to the reader. This sample internal node is very different, offering the reader a variety of choices about how to read further.

A key, associated with link color, provides information about the type of information.

Hypertext syntagmas: cinematic narration with links
revolver

While a node with a single word may not have the qualities that Metz attributes to the close up of the revolver (though given the fluidity of typography - face, size, weight, colour, movement - available that is questionable) it is apparent that the force of the node that results from the link is much like an order word or command There is an imperative attached to even a single word that is the destination of a link. There is some performative force that is the reult of a link, in some manner because a link always operates as a promise.

Adrian Miles: Hypertext syntagmas: cinematic narration with links A performative hypertext presented by Journal of Digital Information, 1(7), 20 Dec. 2000 <http://jodi.ecs.soton.ac.uk/Articles/v01/i07/Miles/>

Different-colored links lead to nodes containing different kinds of information.

From Adrian Miles, "Hypertext Syntagmas: Cinematic Narration with Links," *Journal of Digital Information,* 1(7), 20 Dec. 2000 <http://jodi.ecs.soton.ac.uk/Articles/v01/i07/Miles/>.

Text is presented in small chunks to help readers get the gist and then decide how to proceed. Note that the only navigational links are embedded in content, so the reader chooses the path, leaving open the possibility that the whole work will be read differently by different readers and that the experience may change dramatically on subsequent readings. There is also no guarantee that the reader will see every node in the hypertext.

Resource on Hypertext Style

For a style guide for online hypertext, see **http://www.w3.org/Provider/Style/Overview.html**.

General Characteristics of Print-Based Content

- Longer units of text with fewer breaks
- No links or multimedia content
- Minimal design elements
- Linear and sequential form; readers start at the beginning and read left to right down the page to the end, in serial fashion
- Content is fixed

General Characteristics of Digital Content

- Shorter units of text with more breaks
- Frequent use of links and multimedia content
- Design elements a critical component
- Nonlinear and nonsequential form; readers enter the text at different points, choose from multiple pathways, access content through an interlinked series of nodes
- Content may change

Printed content and digital content may each exhibit some characteristics of the other. Printed content may sometimes resemble a node (location) on the Web, and digital content may deliberately simulate characteristics normally found only in printed forms. As shown on page 646, for example, TK3 ebooks allow the reader, by clicking on the right corner of the screen, to "dog-ear" pages, creating bookmarks.

The writing style you choose for the Web depends on your purpose for writing, the nature of your content, and the motivation of your readers in reading and responding to it. On the Web, style—sometimes called "Web style"— refers to design content as well. Your decisions about composing, sorting, and presenting your writing will be informed by your knowledge of your audience: what they expect when reading on the Web, what they already know about your topic, and what others have said about it elsewhere. When you write and design for the Web, you will need to consider accessibility and usability in addition to writing style. (For more on accessibility and usability, see pages 656–658.)

Generally speaking, your writing should be composed so that it is well suited to the rhetorical context, which includes the interface and media through which your readers access your work. When you create content specifically for the Web, you can follow some guidelines that will help you keep the attention and interest of a wide audience. Websites that serve as navigation portals (such as the top-level node in a larger website or the first node of a hypertext) should include clearly written text presented in a logical arrangement, which will help site visitors easily find what you want them to find and what they are looking for. With this scenario in mind, and remembering that the true measure of ef-

W3C Guide to Writing Style

1. Strive for clear and accurate headings and link descriptions. Use link phrases that are terse and that make sense when read out of context or as part of a series of links. (Some users browse by jumping from link to link and reading or listening to only link text.) Use informative headings so that users can scan a page quickly for information rather than having to read it in detail.
2. State the topic of the sentence or paragraph at the beginning of the sentence or paragraph. Called *front-loading,* this will help not only people who are skimming visually but also people who use speech synthesizers. Users who "skim" with speech jump from heading to heading or paragraph to paragraph and listen to just enough words to determine whether the current chunk of information (heading, paragraph, link, etc.) interests them. If the main idea of the paragraph is in the middle or at the end, speech users may have to listen to most of the document before finding what they want. Depending on what users are looking for and how much they know about the topic, search features may also help them locate content more quickly.
3. Limit each paragraph to one main idea.
4. Avoid slang, jargon, and specialized meanings of familiar words, unless defined within your document.
5. Favor words that are commonly used.
6. Use active rather than passive verbs.
7. Avoid complex sentence structures.

From W3C, "Core Techniques for Web Content Accessibility Guidelines 1.0," 2000 <http://www.w3.org/TR/WCAG10-CORE-TECHS/#writing-style>.

Effective link:

At the Internet Movie Database, you will find useful information on the films of David Cronenberg.

Ineffective link:

David Cronenberg has made interesting films that you can read about online. (Click Here!)

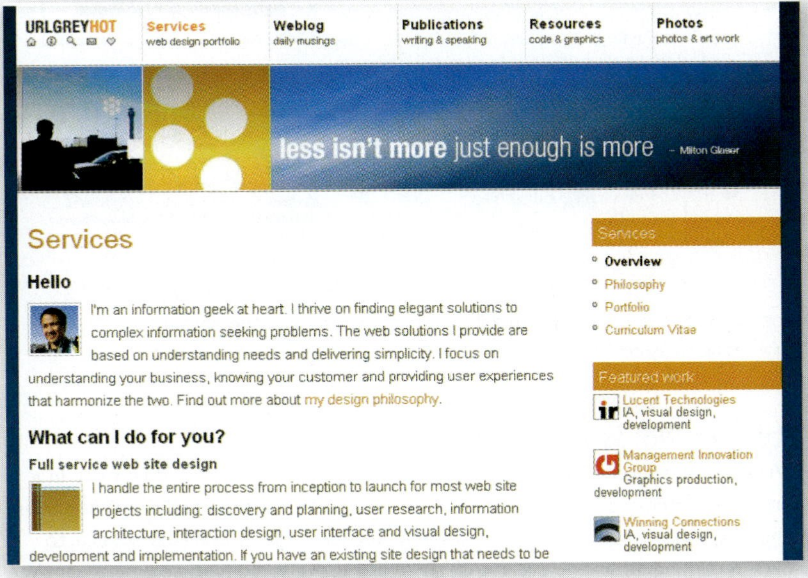

From Urlgreyhot, http://urlgreyhot.com/personal/services/overview.

fective writing style is whether it works, consider the W3C (World Wide Web Consortium) recommendations for Web style, along with our commentary.

Craft Links That Imply the Destination

Links should be integrated into the content and not simply be pointers. The destination should be implicit in the way the link is phrased so that readers understand (a) that it's a link and (b) where it is headed.

In the top example to the left, we can tell that the first link points to the Internet Movie Database (http://www.imdb.com) and can guess that the link on Cronenberg's name points to his filmography at the same site (http://www.imdb.com/name/nm0000343/). But in the bottom example, it's not clear where the link will lead, and the writer uses extra words to make the link.

Use Headings to Orient Readers Quickly

Headings (or headers) help readers see at a glance how information has been organized and allow them to follow their interests efficiently.

In the screenshot of a professional services portfolio, headers are used to direct the reader's attention to unique items in the suite of services. "Teaser" paragraphs give readers a preview, and "Find out more about" and image links let them know quickly where to click to learn more.

Front-Load the Topic

Readers scan nodes looking for information and signposts that will help them decide where to go next. They look for headings and links, but they also scan paragraphs to see if they need to read more deeply. Writers can make their navigational and content-heavy pages more accessible by placing main topics near the beginning of paragraphs and sentences.

Limit Each Paragraph to One Main Idea

If you give your readers too many topics in a single paragraph, they will have a difficult time remembering key information. When writing for the Web, keep your paragraphs fairly short and well focused. (For more on effective paragraph structure, see Chapters 4 and 5.)

Avoid Slang, Jargon, and Specialized Meanings of Familiar Words

Specialized terminology is useful when the community of readers shares common knowledge and experience. Your site's visitors may come from a wide cross section of the culture; not all readers interested in your topic will share knowledge and experience. You can provide a glossary of, and even links to, key terms that readers need to understand. You can also define terms in your text in parentheses or notes.

Paragraphs on the Web

Galileo and the Inquisition

Galileo's belief in the Copernican System eventually got him into trouble with the Catholic Church. The Inquisition was a permanent institution in the Catholic Church charged with the eradication of heresies. A committee of consultants declared to the Inquisition that the Copernican proposition that the Sun is the center of the universe was a heresy. Because Galileo supported the Copernican system, he was warned by Cardinal Bellarmine, under order of Pope Paul V, that he should not discuss or defend Copernican theories. In 1624, Galileo was assured by Pope Urban VIII that he could write about Copernican theory as long as he treated it as a mathematical proposition. However, with the printing of Galileo's book, *Dialogue Concerning the Two Chief World Systems*, Galileo was called to Rome in 1633 to face the Inquisition again. Galileo was found guilty of heresy for his Dialogue, and was sent to his home near Florence where he was to be under house arrest for the remainder of his life. In 1638, the Inquisition allowed Galileo to move to his home in Florence, so that he could be closer to his doctors. By that time he was totally blind. In 1642, Galileo died at his home outside Florence.

◀ Previous  Next ▶

Text, design, and layout by Megan Wilde for the Electronic Text Center. This biography is based upon information culled from The Galileo Project website.

The topic of the paragraph (highlighted) comes first in the paragraph.

From "Galileo," *The Internet Encyclopedia of Philosophy*, 2001 <http://www.iep.utm.edu/g/galileo.htm>.

Style in Words and Sentences

Writers use different levels of style, depending on the occasion and context. In a formal, commemorative speech before a public audience, the speaker might choose a high style, using words that you wouldn't normally find in everyday speech, to mark the grandeur of the event. A high style might also be marked by frequent use of passive verbs. A middle style uses more familiar terms, more active verbs, and simpler sentences, with an emphasis on clarity and grace, to inform readers. On the

Web, a middle style is often the most appropriate. A low style uses slang and other features of everyday speech to convey familiarity among friends, for example. Because it resembles speech and requires quick responses, instant messaging often uses a low style. (For more on levels of style, see Chapter 38.)

Active verb:

> Writers design websites to communicate with a broad audience.

Passive verb:

> Websites are designed to communicate with a broad audience.

The sentence with the active verb focuses attention on writers; the other, on websites. Readers remember people performing actions more easily than they do inanimate objects having something done to them by someone unknown. (See section 33d for a discussion of the principles of readability.)

Complex sentence:

> Long, complex sentences place demands on readers to pay close attention when they may not be ready to do so or may be scanning for key information, which is often difficult to synthesize and recall when it is embedded in complex sentences.

Simpler sentences:

> Long, complex sentences place demands on readers to pay close attention when they may not be ready to do so or may be scanning for key information. Readers often find the information in complex sentences difficult to synthesize and recall.

Favor Words That Are Commonly Used

For example, use *begin* rather than *commence* and *try* rather than *endeavor.*

Use Active Rather Than Passive Verbs

An agent-action style is clearer and more concise than a passive style. When the goal is to communicate with readers accurately and quickly, use verbs that express action, and make the subject of the sentence the actor.

Avoid Complex Sentence Structures

Long, complex sentences place demands on readers to pay close attention when they may not be ready to do so or may be scanning for key information. Readers often find the information in complex sentences difficult to synthesize and recall. Sometimes writers need (and expect) readers to pay close attention or to explore the complexity and nuances of a subject, in which case complex sentences may help. However, on the Web, you can help readers remember key information by breaking long sentences into shorter ones that may more easily be taken in at a glance.

In many contexts—business and academia, for example—ideas are considered commodities to be distributed, bought, and sold. People have certain rights over their work when it is published and may claim ownership of ideas and other content by establishing copyright. Copyrights are simply "rights to copy" content that is intellectual property. An essay or Web text is the intellectual property of the person or group who created it or who hired someone to create it. When you publish your own writing to the Web and when you evaluate and use online sources, you will need to pay attention to guidelines for fair use of sources and citation practices.

Textual Content

If you are the author of textual content, you own the copyright to your work even if you haven't officially registered the work with the U.S. Copyright Office. To reaffirm your rights to the work and your authorship, however, identify yourself as the author and include a copyright notice.

If you use source material, provide proper citation information for anything that is not common knowledge. (See sections 18b and 28e for a definition and examples of common knowledge.)

copyrights A collection of legal rights, conferred by governments, that relate to the reproduction, distribution, and performance of original literary, visual, artistic, or dramatic work.

intellectual property Copyrighted content as well as the more intangible property of trademarks, inventions and patents, ideas, and designs.

Sample Copyright Notice for Your Work Online

Here is a sample copyright notice for textual, visual, or audio content. You can include it in the footer area of each node or—when used with an image—immediately beneath the image.

"Title of Work" © Year by Author Name

Creative Commons License

This Creative Commons license icon indicates that others are allowed to use the content if the original author is credited or to adapt the work as long as the revision is also published under such license. For more information, see **http://www.creativecommons.org**.

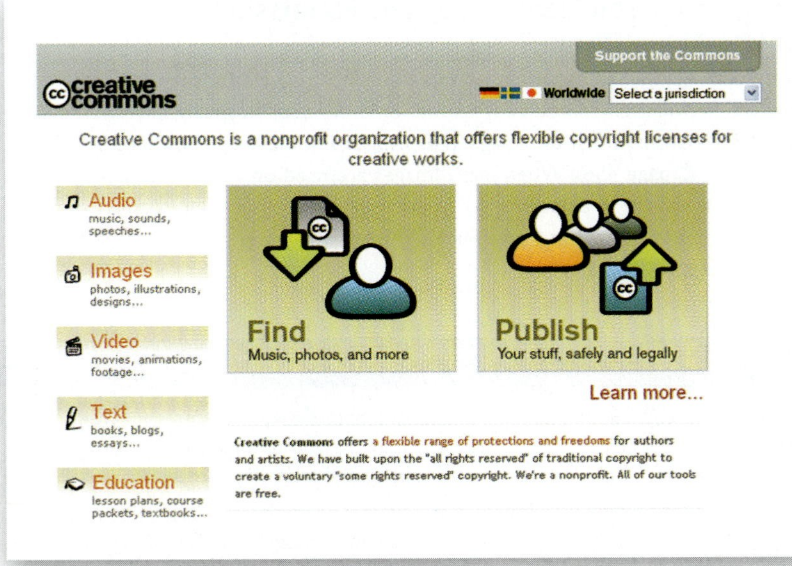

The Creative Commons directory of Creative Commons licensed content on the Web. See **http://creativecommons.org/getcontent/**.

Sample of Formal Acknowledgment

Here is a sample of an acknowledgment that thanks a copyright holder for permission to reprint lyrics:

> The author gratefully acknowledges Warner Records for allowing use of these lyrics on this website.

Suppose you want to quote a passage from another work on your website. Copyright law is somewhat imprecise on the issue of what constitutes "fair use" of already copyrighted textual content. Any use that infringes on another's right to earn income on his or her copyright is illegal, so even short phrases may be copyrighted (and sometimes trademarked). However, in critical reviews, scholarship, or informative research, it is acceptable to cite from previously published textual sources—provided you give complete bibliographic information.

In the case of poetry and song lyrics, which are highly condensed forms of writing, fair use guidelines apply, but with some restrictions. When reproducing significant portions of a poem or a song, for example, you should provide copyright information and, if you have asked for and received permission from the copyright holder to use the work, a formal acknowledgment somewhere in your text (in a caption or endnote, for example) that thanks the copyright holder. You will also need to provide the usual citation information in your Works Cited or References list. If you want to simply republish portions of poems or song lyrics outside of a formal review or critique, you will need to ask for permission from the copyright owner before you post them on the Web.

Visual Content

Images, such as photographs and illustrations, are special cases, and you are almost always required to secure permission to publish on your own website any images that you have not created yourself. If you are the photographer or illustrator, you own the rights to the content, but if you use an image that you find online elsewhere, permission is required.

There are two exceptions: (1) when the copyright holder has published the work under a Creative Commons license, which allows others to use the work, or (2) when advance permission has been granted. A Creative Commons license, which may be used for textual content as well, allows people to use the copyrighted material if the original author is credited.

Many Internet sites offer free stock photography that is copyright-free. Many software programs also include images (photographs or clip art) that can be used without risk of infringing on another's copyright. In addition to the resources listed under Resource Websites for Design Models and Tips (page 693), Creative Commons provides a comprehensive directory of quality work that you might find useful in developing your own content for the Web.

Images: Do You Need Copyright Permission to Use Them Online?

Note that even when copyright permission is not required, **citation is required.** Provide full source information for every use. Normally, give source information right beneath the image. (For captions in MLA style, ◀ page 390; for APA style, ◀ page 456.) When many images are used on a site, it is acceptable to identify the source in an acknowledgments section of your website, next to the image, or in the footer on a given node—unless the copyright holder specifies the placement of the notice.

Type of Image	Do You Need Copyright Permission?
Photographs someone else has taken	Yes, unless they are copyright-free, Creative Commons licensed, or provided with your software
Clip art someone else has drawn	Varies; check for copyright notices, usually prominent at clip-art sites
Illustrations someone else has drawn	Yes
Company logos	Yes
Screenshots from films or television shows	Not usually; see "Fair Usage Publication of Film Stills," an article in *Cinema Journal* that offers guidelines many publishers abide by: **http://www.cmstudies.org/cinema_journal_reports.html**
Screenshots of websites for the purposes of illustration and information	Not usually

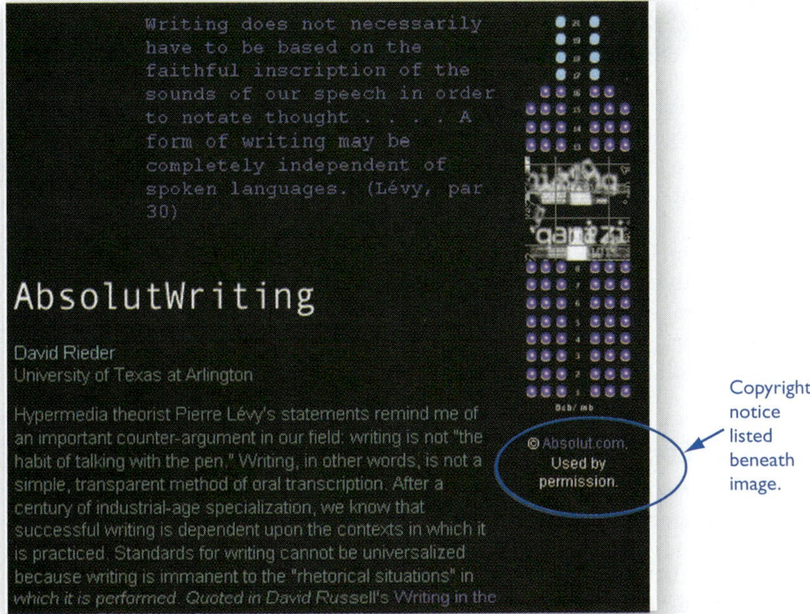
Writing does not necessarily have to be based on the faithful inscription of the sounds of our speech in order to notate thought . . . . A form of writing may be completely independent of spoken languages. (Lévy, par 30)

AbsolutWriting

David Rieder
University of Texas at Arlington

Hypermedia theorist Pierre Lévy's statements remind me of an important counter-argument in our field: writing is not "the habit of talking with the pen." Writing, in other words, is not a simple, transparent method of oral transcription. After a century of industrial-age specialization, we know that successful writing is dependent upon the contexts in which it is practiced. Standards for writing cannot be universalized because writing is immanent to the "rhetorical situations" in which it is performed. Quoted in David Russell's Writing in the

A screenshot from David Rieder's online article "AbsolutWriting" showing the use of a copyrighted image and the proper citation method. Rieder asked for and received permission to use this image from Absolut.com. From *The Writing Instructor*, Sept. 2001, 20 Oct. 2004 <http://www.writinginstructor.com/absolutwriting>.

Resources on Copyright and Intellectual Property

The U.S. Copyright Office: **http://www.copyright.gov**

- Copyright Basics: **http://www.copyright.gov/circs/circ1.html**
- Copyright FAQs: **http://www.copyright.gov/help/faq/**
- Digital Millennium Copyright Act: **http://www.copyright.gov/legislation/dmca.pdf** (PDF format)
- Copyright Searches: **http://www.copyright.gov/records/**

Stanford University Copyright and Fair Use Center: **http://fairuse.stanford.edu**

Copyright Clearance Center: **http://www.copyright.com**

Musical and Audio Content

With the rise and fall of Napster—the peer-to-peer music sharing network that caused such a stir in 1999—the rights to use and share copyrighted music became more strictly limited by copyright law and fair use guidelines. If you want to use music or audio content on your website, be sure to find sources whose use is unrestricted or is governed by a Creative Commons license or to gain permission to use them. If you want to use preexisting music in the soundtrack of a multimedia project, for example, you will need to get permission from the copyright holder and provide proper credit.

Adapting and Modifying Content

For the purposes of parody, a form of critique that sometimes falls under fair use guidelines, copyrighted content may be adapted and then republished. It is also possible to use image and audio editing software to substantially re-engineer source material—as in the technique of audio "remixing" or image filtering—and thus get around the usual copyright restrictions. However, it is ethical practice to cite your sources in every case.

The accessibility of your Web content will be affected by material conditions (hardware and software) and by the nature of your audience. The contexts for reading and writing online vary dramatically. Hardware and software will shape the context, for example, because they define the interface—the lens through which you view Web content.

- The nature, size, and screen resolution of your monitor affect how you see the content.
- The particular way your browser renders Web content may not be consistent with that of other browsers.
- The platform and operating system of your computer—Mac, Windows, or Linux, for example—also affect the interface context.

As a producer of Web content, you need to be aware of the effects of these different contexts on how your work is received. If your goal is to make your work public on the Web, you should not unnecessarily restrict your audience to, for example, users of Internet Explorer 6, as you will see some sites do. Instead, you should make your content accessible through usability testing, by following guidelines for accessibility, and by accepting peer feedback.

accessibility The degree to which Web content can be navigated and read by everyone, regardless of location, experience, physical ability, cultural background, or the type of computer technology used to access the content.

usability testing Systematic testing of the ease with which users can access and learn to use information. It involves checking to see whether usability guidelines have been followed, measuring how readers use a website, and testing that all elements of a website function as the authors intend and users expect.

Diverse Contexts for Visiting a Website

Many Web users will be coming to your website in contexts different from your own and from those in which usability testing was performed:

- They may not be able to see, hear, or move or may not be able to process some types of information easily or at all.
- They may have difficulty reading or comprehending text.
- They may not have or be able to use a keyboard or mouse.
- They may have a text-only screen, a small screen, or a slow Internet connection.
- They may not speak or understand fluently the language in which the document is written.
- They may be in a situation where their eyes, ears, or hands are busy or interfered with (e.g., driving to work or working in a loud environment).
- They may have an early version of a browser, a different browser entirely, a voice browser, or a different operating system.

From http://www.w3.org/TR/WAI-WEBCONTENT/.

W3C Priority 1 Principles of Accessibility

1. Provide equivalent alternatives to auditory and visual content.
2. Don't rely on color alone.
3. Use markup and style sheets and do so properly.
4. Clarify natural language usage.
5. Create tables that transform gracefully.*
6. Ensure that pages featuring new technologies transform gracefully.*
7. Ensure user control of time-sensitive content changes.
8. Ensure direct accessibility of embedded user interfaces.
9. Design for device-independence.
10. Use interim solutions.
11. Use W3C technologies and guidelines.
12. Provide context and orientation information.
13. Provide clear navigation mechanisms.
14. Ensure that documents are clear and simple.

*Tables and pages that "transform gracefully" will resize without drastically altering the display of text or images when the browser window is resized or when the page is viewed on monitors of varying resolution and size.

Take into account the challenges that persons with physical disabilities face in accessing Web content. People with impaired vision, for example, may use screen readers to access Web content. To make the site accessible, all images on a website should be tagged with an <alt> HTML tag, which displays the writer's textual description of the image, either when the user has set the browser to not load images or when the reader mouses over the image itself. Screen readers read the content of these <alt> tags. Web designers who take advantage of cascading style sheets (CSS) can make it possible for users to change how their websites appear; users can choose to apply alternative style sheets of their own for viewing content.

The governing organization of the Internet—the World Wide Web Consortium, or W3C—has published a wide variety of readability guidelines for ensuring that Web content is accessible across hardware and software platforms and to a wide variety of users. Following such guidelines—which include suggestions for arranging information and using design content to reinforce the message—will help you create effective websites for the widest possible audience.

Accessibility and Usability Resources

Definitive Guide to Accessibility Issues

Web Content Accessibility Guidelines 1.0: **http://www.w3.org/TR/WAI-WEBCONTENT/**

Will help Web developers create pages that everyone who browses the Internet can access and use efficiently and enjoyably.

Validating Services

W3C HTML Validator: **http://validator.w3.org**

Checks conformance of Web pages to W3C guidelines and recommendations.

WebXAct Accessibility Checker: **http://webxact.watchfire.com**

Allows you to check your page against various accessibility guidelines and points out areas for improvement.

CSS Validator: **http://jigsaw.w3.org/css-validator/**

Checks cascading style sheets for conformance to W3C guidelines.

Usability Websites

Usability.Gov: **http://usability.gov**

Provides an excellent collection of resources about all aspects of usability and accessibility, with explanations, research citations, and other useful guides.

Useit.com (Jakob Nielsen): **http://www.useit.com**

Presents excellent models of usability testing applied to corporate websites and high-tech products. Usability guru Jakob Nielsen has links to his Alertbox columns that discuss Web usability and list resources for usability and accessibility testing.

User-Centered Design (IBM's "Ease of Use"): **http://www-3.ibm.com/ibm/easy/eou_ext.nsf/publish/558**

Focuses on fundamental principles of shaping the user experience of websites and products. For suggestions that will make your website a disaster, see the "bad advice" document written by Peter Seebach, "The Cranky User: How Not to Make Your Site Accessible," at **http://www-106.ibm.com/developerworks/library/us-cranky1.html**. Seebach is, of course, being ironic.

30 DESIGNING SIMPLE WEB PAGES

The World Wide Web sometimes seems like a tangled web of information, overwhelming because of its sheer expanse and complexity. However, websites—even the most complex—are just collections of files stored on a computer and accessed by typing the right folder and file name into the browser's address bar. The Web is the network of servers that hosts these files, and the Internet is the pathway to each of them. When you publish your own writing and research to the Web, you make it public on a computer that is connected to this network and potentially viewable by anyone who has an Internet connection and a browser.

Before you begin creating websites, you should understand that the Web is not really a "place" in the sense that you can go to it, as you would the corner diner. It is a network of computers and files connected by an Internet that people navigate (like an "information superhighway"). Those long website addresses that you sometimes have to type into a Web browser's address bar—called URLs or Uniform Resource Locators—refer to specific computers on the network and to folders and files that are stored on them. When you tell people where to find your website, you are giving them an address that communicates to a browser what computer, folders, and files to look for among the billions of files out in cyberspace.

Uniform Resource Locators tell browsers where to look on the Internet for files that can be downloaded from another computer and viewed on a local machine. They may point to a wide variety of resources, including documents, images, email accounts, and anything else that can be stored in a file on a computer. Once you understand the basic information contained in a URL, you will be well on your way to a conceptual understanding of the Internet that will help you make good decisions about creating hyperlinks, managing your website, and navigating websites yourself.

As you browse the Internet, you will likely come across strange-looking URLs. Some of them may have the # character near the end. Much like a bookmark, the # character points to an **anchor**—that is, a location within a particular HTML file. For example, in the URL shown in the source line to the right, for Netspace's Guide to URLs, the # character points to the "What are URLs" section (anchor = what) of the file named url-guide.html, which is in the users/dwb subfolder of the netspace.org domain.

Protocol or Scheme:
http stands for "Hypertext Transfer Protocol" and describes the function of a server. Other protocols commonly used are *ftp* (File Transfer Protocol) and even *file* (to refer to a file on the local machine).

Path:
The path points to a file within a directory (or folder) on the particular server. Sometimes path names are much longer, meaning that the file (which is always the last part of the path name) is stored in a subfolder. In this case, the file *factbeg.html* is in the root (or main) directory. Sometimes a path will end in a forward slash, /, in which case the host will direct your browser to the default file (usually index.html or default.html). Shorter path names are convenient for users and also indicate a well-organized website.

http://www.refdesk.com/factbeg.html

Domain Name or Host:
The domain name is also called the Internet address. On the Web, most domain names look like this one, but sometimes the *www* is replaced by the name assigned to a computer. For example, *pw.english.purdue.edu* points to the server run by the Professional Writing program in the English Department at Purdue University.

The domain name in a URL points to a server, which is a computer that serves files over a network (like the Internet). Every domain name has an IP (Internet Protocol) address consisting of a unique number that other computers use to identify it. The IP address for www.refdesk.com is 216.40.241.219.

Domain names like *refdesk.com* are personalized identifiers. It's possible to create and use any domain name that's not already registered by someone else with a "domain name registry," which essentially tells other computers on the network that, in this case, www.refdesk.com = 216.40.241.219.

Adapted from Netspace Guide to URLs, at http://www.netspace.org/users/dwb/url-guide.html#what.

Resource on URLs

The "Official" Technical Source on URLs (Network Working Group; RFC 1738):
http://www.cse.ohio-state.edu/cgi-bin/rfc/rfc1738.html

The Web Design Process, Expanded

Planning, composing, designing, and publishing a website are creative processes that involve making numerous decisions based on how you want viewers to use your site and on the reasons they may have for visiting it.

Planning: What assets do you have (text, images, design elements)? Which navigational and page layout schemes will help you and your audience achieve your respective purposes?

Composing: Should you compose in a Web design and development program or Web authoring software? Or use HTML programming in a text editor? Or write with a word processor and then import the text into an HTML document? If your site has images, audio, or video content, what software can you use to prepare such content for easy access?

Designing: How can you make the site inviting and helpful? How will visual and design content complement and amplify the textual content to achieve your purpose? (See Chapter 25 for design principles to consider.)

Testing: Does your site display properly on different browsers and operating systems (Mac, Windows, Linux)? At different screen resolutions? Do all links work? Do all pages meet standard accessibility guidelines? How do your intended users interact with the site?

Publishing: What server should host your site? Which FTP program do you want to use to upload your files?

Updating: How often do you need to update your site? (The answer to this question will depend on how current the content needs to be.) How often should you check for broken links?

An effective Web design process consists of six steps:

1. **Planning** involves determining what you want to write about, deciding how you want to present the information to your primary and subsidiary audiences, and shaping your content and design so that you accomplish your purpose.
2. **Composing** involves crafting your textual, visual, and even aural content so that it suits your purpose, context, and audience. The composing process encompasses all the steps of the writing process described in Chapters 3–6, particularly regarding drafting, revising, and editing your writing so that it represents you well to a public audience, as well as to a narrower audience of peers.
3. **Designing** involves shaping your content for presentation on the Web.
4. **Testing** involves making sure that your website functions as it should and that your readers can access and interact with it.
5. **Publishing** involves finding a server to host your website and uploading the files to it.
6. **Updating** involves periodically checking to make sure that your website (or individual page) has the latest information and that all hyperlinks still work.

The content on a typical Web page (node) consists of written information, images, and hyperlinks. Good nodes have four components:

1. **Textual content** that is interesting, entertaining, or informative (including verbal and visual material)
2. **Visual and design content** that (a) is well suited to the textual content, (b) guides the reader's eyes to the most important information and keeps attention focused where it should be, (c) makes text legible, and (d) appeals in its own right as interesting content
3. A clear **navigation system** and, for complex sites, search tools that help people quickly find what they're looking for and what you want them to find
4. **Provenance information** that identifies copyright, dates published and modified, and authorship. Provenance establishes both the ownership and the value of the work and will be needed by others who want to refer to or cite it.

Textual Content

You develop textual content for a website in much the same way that you generate content for an essay or research paper. You think hard about what you want to say, whom you need to say it to, and what consequence you hope will

Converting Content from Word Processor to HTML Editor

You can take any content created in a word processor and convert it to HTML format so that you can import it into a Web design and development program like Adobe Dreamweaver® or NVu, a free Web authoring system (http://www.net2.com/nvu/).

To save your file in HTML (short for "Hypertext Markup Language") format, use the "Save as" command, available in most word processors. The following example uses Microsoft Word 2007 and Mac Word 2008.

1. Open your document in your word processor and then in Word 2007 choose the Office button > Save as > Other formats. In Mac Word 2008, choose File > Save as and choose the Save as Web Page button.
2. In the "Save As" dialogue box, first navigate to the folder where you want to save the file.
3. Name your file by typing its name in the "File name:" field. We recommend using the .html extension, which is the most common file name extension on the Web. Be sure not to use any spaces in the file name. The file name will ultimately appear as the last part of your Web page's URL.
4. In Word 2007, give your Web page a title by clicking on the "Title" field beneath the file name box.
5. In Word 2007, from the drop-down menu in the "Save as type:" field, choose "Web Page, Filtered (*.htm; *.html)" (see Figure 30.1). In Mac Word 2008, make sure that you select the radio button "Save only display information into HTML" (see Figure 30.2).
6. Word will save your file in HTML format. You can then open it in a Web authoring program, make adjustments as needed, and upload your file (along with any associated image files) to the Web.

Note: When saving in HTML, most word processors include style and formatting code that you won't need in your HTML file. Sometimes it causes Web pages to display improperly. Web editors like Dreamweaver have tools for cleaning up Word coding. (In Dreamweaver, choose Commands > Clean Up Word HTML to remove most of the extraneous HTML code.)

For instructions that apply to Microsoft® Word® 2003, visit the handbook's website: **cengage.com/english/blakesley**

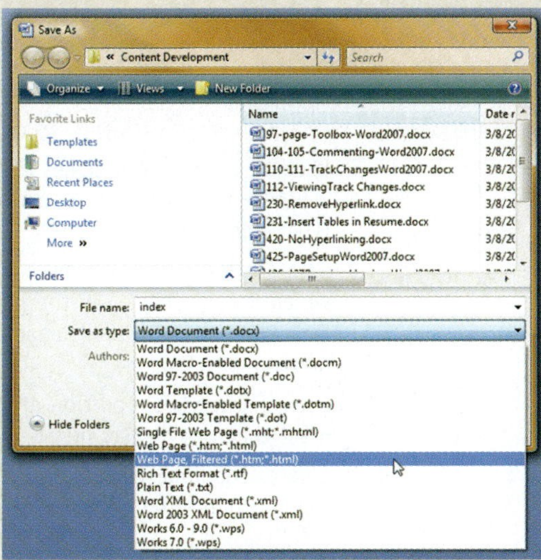

Figure 30.1 Converting to HTML in Microsoft Word 2007. Be sure that you select "Web Page, Filtered" in the drop-down menu.

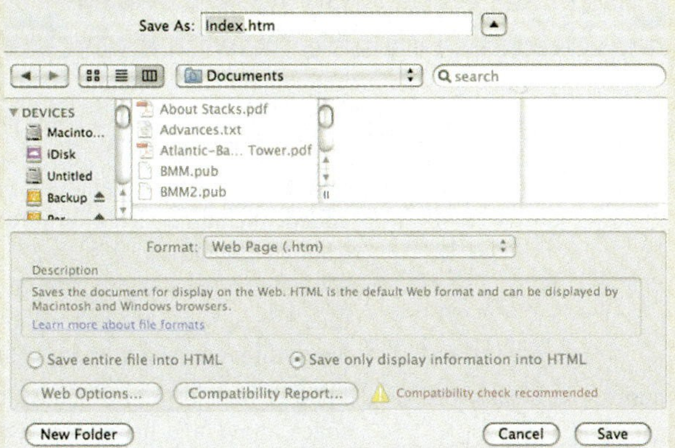

Figure 30.2 Converting to HTML in Mac-based Microsoft Word. Be sure that "Save only display information into HTML" is selected.

result, and then you write and plan. As with any complex project, it's likely that you will need to conduct research to verify facts and to support arguments.

Organize Interesting Textual Content with Readers in Mind

Make content relevant and sufficient. Give readers what they need to know and what you want them to know. Don't overwhelm them with information so unorganized that nothing stands out. On websites with long documents, for example, it's customary to give readers the choice of reading a long article all on one page or in chunks. If you have a lot of content to share, you will need to decide how your readers should receive it. All at once or in measured doses? A working rule among Web designers is that you should make your readers scroll down the page only when you have to or when they will want to. If your content is engaging, readers will scroll down. (They may not scroll to the right, however, if your node is wider than what their monitor can display.)

Provide Sufficient Information for Click-Through

Click-throughs, a measure of how many mouse clicks it takes to get to information from the parent page of a site, should be kept to a reasonable number—usually five or six at most. Your written information should be sufficient to

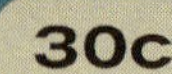

warrant clicking through to the next page. If your information is not relevant or sufficient, readers won't click *through;* they will click *out.* Their basic inclination is to not scroll down, so you need to garner their trust with your ethos and pique their interest with your visual design.

The Basics of HTML Coding

Hypertext Markup Language is programming code that helps browser programs interpret the information in an HTML file so that it can be displayed in the browser window. Knowing how such coding works will help you fine-tune your design, check for errors when a page doesn't display properly, and even examine the HTML code of Web pages that you want to use as models. HTML consists of *tags* that mark text and images and function as commands. For example, the HTML tag for creating italicized text is <em> (short for "emphasis").

WYSIWYG Web authoring programs, such as Nvu, work much like word processors because they allow you to open an HTML file and view an approximation of how the Web page will appear in a browser. (WYSIWYG stands for "What you see is what you get.") They also allow you to use command buttons to apply tags to your

Fifteen HTML Tags to Remember

HTML Tag	Function
<html></html>	Used to create a Web page. The <html> tag always starts and ends an HTML document.
<head></head>	Sets off the title and "head content," which doesn't display in the browser, from the body of the document, which does
<body></body>	Sets off the visible portion of the document that will display in the browser
<h1></h1>	Creates the largest headline. Related tags include <h2> (second largest headline), <h3> (third largest headline), etc.
<a href="URL"></a>	Defines a hyperlink. For example, <a href="http://www.wikipedia.com"> Wikipedia</a> tells the browser that what follows the equals sign is the URL for the text between the <a> and </a> tags. The URL is put in quotation marks.
<p></p>	Creates a new paragraph
<img></img>	Inserts an image. Parameters may be added, including size and border. For example, <img src= "http://www.mysite.com/myphoto.jpg"> tells the browser where to find the image file; *src* is short for "source."
<blockquote></blockquote>	Indents text from both sides and puts space above and below the text
 	Inserts a line break

(continued)

Fifteen HTML Tags to Remember (continued)

HTML Tag	Function
<strong></strong>	Creates bold text: <strong>boldface text</strong>
<em></em>	Creates italicized text: <em>italicized text</em>
<hr>	Creates a horizontal rule (or bar). Parameters may be added. For example, <hr width="200" size="1" noshade>
<table></table>	Creates a table. Parameters for size, border, background color, and more may be added in the start tag. For example, <table width="700" border="0" cellpadding="10" cellspacing="0" align="left">
<tr></tr>	Creates a row in a table. Parameters may be added. For example, <tr color="#999999">
<td></td>	Creates a column in a table. Parameters may be added. For example, <td width="200" height="400">

For a complete list of HTML tags, attributes, and parameters, see the HTML Reference Guide on the handbook's website:
cengage.com/English/Blakesley

Resources for Web Development Tools
You can get free Web developer tools for the Firefox browser (also free) that will help you test your Web pages for usability, accessibility, and more.
Firefox: **http://www.mozilla.org/products/firefox/**
Web Developer Extension:
http://www.chrispederick.com/work/firefox/webdeveloper/

document, rather than entering HTML tags manually. Even though this simplifies the process of tagging an HTML document, you should understand how these tags work. Some people prefer to compose their HTML documents in "Code View" (in Dreamweaver, for example) or directly in a text editor like Notepad (in Windows) or SimpleText (on a Mac).

All HTML tags have what amounts to an "on" switch such as <em>, which tells the browser when to start italicizing text, and an "off" switch such as </em>, which tells the browser to stop italicizing. The tag is enclosed in angled brackets. The closing tag includes a forward slash, /, to indicate a stop. To create italicized text in an HTML document, you can have the Web design and development program enclose the text in an <em> tag, or you can add the tag yourself directly in the code. Either way you choose to do it, here's what the code for *italicized text* looks like:

<em>italicized text</em>

Here's what it will look like in an HTML file viewed in a Web browser:

italicized text

The Code behind the Node

To better understand how a Web page is constructed, it's helpful to look at the HTML code used to create a simple node and its corresponding appearance in a Web browser.

Head content includes the page title and metatags that tell the browser how to respond to the page content.

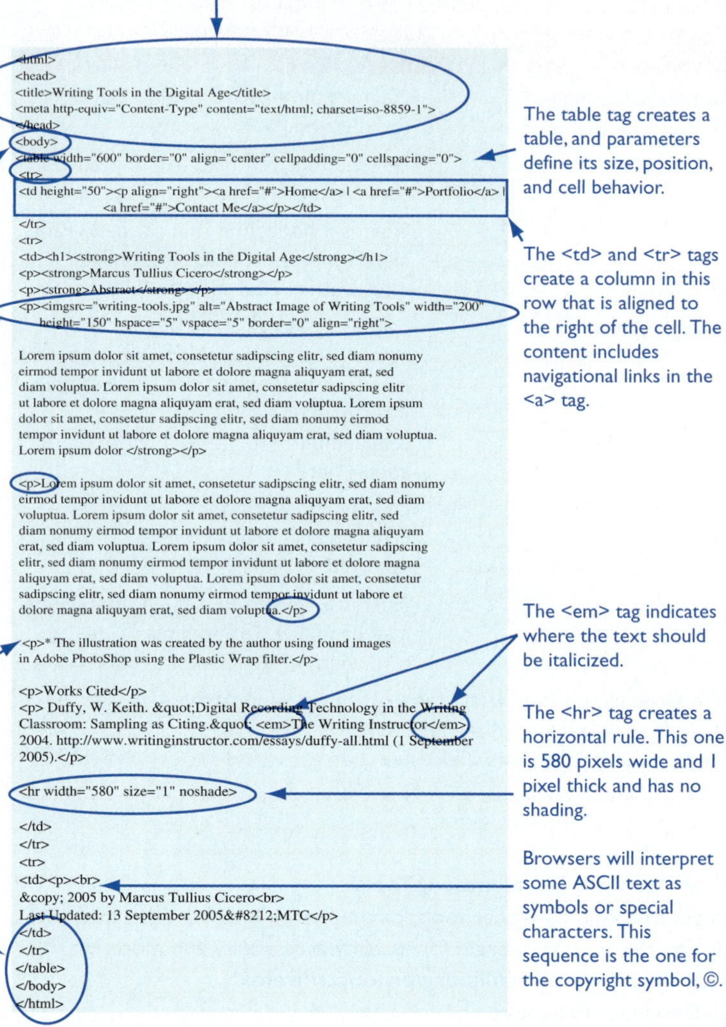

```
<html>
<head>
<title>Writing Tools in the Digital Age</title>
<meta http-equiv="Content-Type" content="text/html; charset=iso-8859-1">
</head>
<body>
<table width="600" border="0" align="center" cellpadding="0" cellspacing="0">
<tr>
<td height="50"><p align="right"><a href="#">Home</a> | <a href="#">Portfolio</a> |
            <a href="#">Contact Me</a></p></td>
</tr>
<tr>
<td><h1><strong>Writing Tools in the Digital Age</strong></h1>
<p><strong>Marcus Tullius Cicero</strong></p>
<p><strong>Abstract</strong></p>
<p><imgsrc="writing-tools.jpg" alt="Abstract Image of Writing Tools" width="200"
    height="150" hspace="5" vspace="5" border="0" align="right">

Lorem ipsum dolor sit amet, consetetur sadipscing elitr, sed diam nonumy
eirmod tempor invidunt ut labore et dolore magna aliquyam erat, sed
diam voluptua. Lorem ipsum dolor sit amet, consetetur sadipscing elitr
ut labore et dolore magna aliquyam erat, sed diam voluptua. Lorem ipsum
dolor sit amet, consetetur sadipscing elitr, sed diam nonumy eirmod
tempor invidunt ut labore et dolore magna aliquyam erat, sed diam voluptua.
Lorem ipsum dolor </strong></p>

<p>Lorem ipsum dolor sit amet, consetetur sadipscing elitr, sed diam nonumy
eirmod tempor invidunt ut labore et dolore magna aliquyam erat, sed diam
voluptua. Lorem ipsum dolor sit amet, consetetur sadipscing elitr, sed
diam nonumy eirmod tempor invidunt ut labore et dolore magna aliquyam
erat, sed diam voluptua. Lorem ipsum dolor sit amet, consetetur sadipscing
elitr, sed diam nonumy eirmod tempor invidunt ut labore et dolore magna
aliquyam erat, sed diam voluptua. Lorem ipsum dolor sit amet, consetetur
sadipscing elitr, sed diam nonumy eirmod tempor invidunt ut labore et
dolore magna aliquyam erat, sed diam voluptua.</p>

<p>* The illustration was created by the author using found images
in Adobe PhotoShop using the Plastic Wrap filter.</p>

<p>Works Cited</p>
<p> Duffy, W. Keith. &quot;Digital Recording Technology in the Writing
Classroom: Sampling as Citing.&quot; <em>The Writing Instructor</em>
2004. http://www.writinginstructor.com/essays/duffy-all.html (1 September
2005).</p>

<hr width="580" size="1" noshade>

</td>
</tr>
<tr>
<td><p><br>
&copy; 2005 by Marcus Tullius Cicero<br>
Last Updated: 13 September 2005&#8212;MTC</p>
</td>
</tr>
</table>
</body>
</html>
```

The table tag creates a table, and parameters define its size, position, and cell behavior.
The <td> and <tr> tags create a column in this row that is aligned to the right of the cell. The content includes navigational links in the <a> tag.
The <em> tag indicates where the text should be italicized.
The <hr> tag creates a horizontal rule. This one is 580 pixels wide and 1 pixel thick and has no shading.
Browsers will interpret some ASCII text as symbols or special characters. This sequence is the one for the copyright symbol, ©.

The <body> tag tells the browser to start displaying contents.

The image is defined with the <img> tag. Parameters include the alt attribute, which tells the browser to display the supplied text (for people who can't see the image in their browser and for automatic text readers); hspace and vspace, which define how much space there is between the image and text; and the image's border width and alignment.

Paragraph tags create blocks of text with spaces above and below.

These tags close the column, row, table, body, and page.

A page with HTML code.

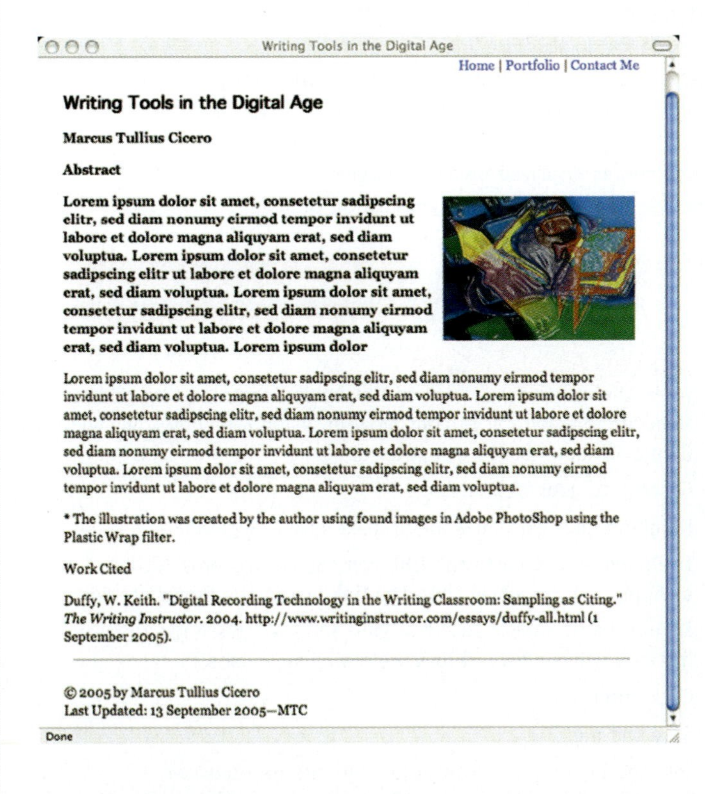
Writing Tools in the Digital Age
Home | Portfolio | Contact Me
Writing Tools in the Digital Age
Marcus Tullius Cicero
Abstract
Lorem ipsum dolor sit amet, consetetur sadipscing elitr, sed diam nonumy eirmod tempor invidunt ut labore et dolore magna aliquyam erat, sed diam voluptua. Lorem ipsum dolor sit amet, consetetur sadipscing elitr ut labore et dolore magna aliquyam erat, sed diam voluptua. Lorem ipsum dolor sit amet, consetetur sadipscing elitr, sed diam nonumy eirmod tempor invidunt ut labore et dolore magna aliquyam erat, sed diam voluptua. Lorem ipsum dolor
Lorem ipsum dolor sit amet, consetetur sadipscing elitr, sed diam nonumy eirmod tempor invidunt ut labore et dolore magna aliquyam erat, sed diam voluptua. Lorem ipsum dolor sit amet, consetetur sadipscing elitr, sed diam nonumy eirmod tempor invidunt ut labore et dolore magna aliquyam erat, sed diam voluptua. Lorem ipsum dolor sit amet, consetetur sadipscing elitr, sed diam nonumy eirmod tempor invidunt ut labore et dolore magna aliquyam erat, sed diam voluptua. Lorem ipsum dolor sit amet, consetetur sadipscing elitr, sed diam nonumy eirmod tempor invidunt ut labore et dolore magna aliquyam erat, sed diam voluptua.
* The illustration was created by the author using found images in Adobe PhotoShop using the Plastic Wrap filter.
Work Cited
Duffy, W. Keith. "Digital Recording Technology in the Writing Classroom: Sampling as Citing." The Writing Instructor. 2004. http://www.writinginstructor.com/essays/duffy-all.html (1 September 2005).
© 2005 by Marcus Tullius Cicero
Last Updated: 13 September 2005—MTC
Done

A screenshot of the page as it displays in the Firefox browser.

Early in the process of designing the layout of your Web page, it can be useful to use placeholder text, as we have done in this example. We used the Firefox extension Lorem Ipsum Generator, available at http://www.roundtwo.com/product/contentgenerator.

Making Hyperlinks

Hyperlinks—or links for short—are the steppingstones that make the Web a vast network of information and entertainment. They are used on websites to help people navigate to different pages within the site (relative links) or to pages elsewhere on the Internet (absolute links). A hyperlink consists of a URL and some HTML code that tells browser software what to look for and where and how to display it. Because the Internet evolves rapidly and files are moved around constantly, it is a challenge to keep the hyperlinks on your own site up to date.

If you browse the Web frequently, you know the frustration of following broken or "dead" links. Web design and development editors such as Composer, Dreamweaver, and FrontPage offer automated "link checkers" to help you test whether your links are still working properly. You should also do some manual usability testing of your hyperlinks.

Absolute Links to Other Sites on the Internet

An absolute link contains the full URL (protocol, host, and path—see page 660) for the file you want to link to. Absolute links need to be used for pages outside of your own website so that the browser software knows to look elsewhere for the file.

Example of an Absolute Link

HTML code for an absolute link:

```
<a href="http://enculturation.gmu.edu/4_1/style/" target="0">
Perspective: Notes Toward the Remediation of Style</a>
```

The same link, as displayed on a Web page:

<u>Perspective: Notes Toward the Remediation of Style</u>

Making an Absolute Link

1. Go to the website you want to link to and copy the Web address (URL) from the location bar in your browser, using the Copy command (Ctrl + C on a Windows-based computer or Apple + C on a Mac).
2. Go back to your Web editor.
3. Highlight the text you want to make into a hyperlink.
4. In Dreamweaver, paste the URL you copied in step 1 (Ctrl + V on a PC or Apple + V on a Mac) into the link box in the Properties window.

   In FrontPage, choose Insert > Link and then paste the URL into the link box. (Other Web editors use a similar process.)
5. Click Enter.
6. Save the file.
7. Test the link by previewing the HTML file in a browser.

Example of a Relative Link

HTML code for a relative link:

<a href="resources/index.html">Resources for Writers and Writing Instructors</a>

The same link, as displayed on a Web page:

Resources for Writers and Writing Instructors

Notice that the shortened URL tells a browser to look for the "index.html" file in a subfolder in the current location named "resources."

Making a Relative Link

In Dreamweaver:

1. Highlight the text you want to make into a link.
2. Click on the Properties window and then select the Folder icon, , next to the Link window. Browse to the file you want to link to and select it.
3. Hit Enter. Dreamweaver will automatically create the HTML code.
4. Save your file.
5. Test the link in your browser.

In Composer:

1. Highlight the text you want to make into a link.
2. From the top menu bar, choose Insert > Link.
3. In the "Link Properties" dialogue box, check the "URL is relative to page location" box and then click on the "Choose File" button.
4. Navigate to and then select the file you want to link to. Click on Open.
5. The relative path to the file and the file name should now appear in the Link Location window.
6. Click on OK or select "Advanced Edit" to add attributes, classes, or events (▶ Chapter 31).

Relative Links to Other Pages on Your Website

A relative link is different from an absolute link in that it includes only path information because the files being linked to are located within the same domain. Relative links are useful because they are shorter and because they are easy to update when you change the location of files within your website. (Dreamweaver, for example, will automatically update relative links in any pages within a website when you move or delete files that have links associated with them.) Such links are called "relative" because the actual URL depends on the location of the linked file relative to the page that contains the link (called the "referrer" page).

Email Links so Visitors Can Contact You

Email links are useful when you want visitors to be able to click on a hyperlink and have their default email program load automatically, with a message pre-addressed to you. The process of creating an email link is similar to that for making absolute and relative links. In this case, though, the URL uses the "mailto:" protocol. Microsoft FrontPage can be set to automatically make any email address typed in on your Web page into a "mailto:" hyperlink, but in most cases you will want to take charge of that process yourself.

Example of an Email Link

HTML code for an email link:

```
<a href="mailto:user@somewhere.edu">Email me! </a>
```

The same link, as displayed on a Web page:

Email me!

Making an Email Link

1. Highlight the text you want to make into an email link.
2. In Dreamweaver, click in the Properties window and then click inside the link box.

   In Composer, choose Insert > Link and then click inside the link box.

   In FrontPage, click on the hyperlink button on the toolbar, .
3. Type the word mailto: and then the email address in the link box (for example, mailto:user@somewhere.edu).
4. Click OK.
5. Test the link in your browser.

Inserting an Image on a Web Page

Inserting an image on a Web page involves establishing a link to it, in much the same way that you create a hyperlink to another document or website. In the case of images, the <img> tag tells the browser to "go get the image and put it here and make it this big." The browser will get the image from a folder within the current website or from another site.

Example of a relative link to a local image:

```
<img src="images/steenthumb.gif" width="30" height="39">
```

Example of an absolute link to an image at another website:

```
<img src="http://www.writinginstructor.com/images/epubcollage.jpg"
width="30" height="39">
```

(continued)

Inserting an Image on a Web Page(continued)

- In the relative link, the path, which is in quotation marks, points to the file "steenthumb.gif" in the images subfolder.
- In the absolute link, the path is to an image on another website, so the full URL is used: http://www.writinginstructor.com/images/epubcollage.jpg.
- The HTML tag is <img>.
- The first attribute is *src* for "source." The two other attributes used are *width* and *height*. You can use these attributes to specify the size at which the image should be displayed (the width and height will be in pixels, which is a unit of measure relative to the screen resolution on your monitor), but if you leave them blank, the image will appear at its original size. Dreamweaver, FrontPage, and other Web editors will create the HTML code for you.

To make a link to an image in a Web authoring program:

1. Place your cursor where you want the image to appear.
2. Click on the Insert menu and choose Image.
3. Navigate to the folder where your image is stored and then select it.
4. Click on the Open or OK button (depending on which editor you're using).
5. If you want the image to display at its normal size, leave the image dimensions unchanged. To make it smaller or larger, adjust the dimensions in the Properties toolbox. However, be aware that your original image may not appear as intended because the browser will resize it on the fly, which will also increase the time it takes for the page to load. Consider using dimension resizing to enrich the experience for visitors. For example, you might use thumbnails—small image links that take users to a larger image file for better viewing.
6. Test the link in your browser by opening the page to see if the image displays as you intended.

Visual Content

The visual content of a Web page consists of images and colors used for a variety of purposes, including the following:

1. to complement and extend the textual content
2. to direct the reader's attention with visual cues
3. to add information
4. to create visual interest
5. to establish a visual theme

During the planning stage, create or collect the images you plan to use. You may use a graphics editor to create images and drawings, take photographs of your own, or look for visual content that suits your purpose in repositories of ready-made images. Keep in mind that any image on a Web page should bear a clear relationship to textual content.

Placement of Images

When placing images on a Web page, keep in mind the principles of proximity, alignment, repetition, and contrast, covered more extensively in Chapter 25.

Proximity: Place images close to the textual content that refers to them or that the images complement.

Alignment: Align images on the Web page with the edges of text, and leave enough space between the images and the surrounding text. To place images precisely, use tables to manage your layout.

Repetition: Use images to create a visual theme that gives your Web page or website an identifiable character, one that reinforces its purpose.

Contrast: Use images to create visual contrast with the text—to provide eye relief and break up the monotony of lines of text running across the screen.

In addition, keep text and images in proportion. Be careful not to overwhelm your text by making images excessively large or using lots of images just to "spice things up." Avoid distracting animated graphics and elaborate background images that make textual content unreadable. Colors should likewise be chosen to highlight, not overwhelm, the content.

Activity 30-1: Gertrude's Pet Shop

Amy Kimme-Hea has devised an excellent project to help new Web designers appreciate the complexity and pitfalls of the craft while having some fun. The Gertrude's Pet Shop Web page shows what happens when you violate the principles of proximity, alignment, repetition, contrast, and proportion. In this case, the designer has deliberately exaggerated the effects of not heeding these principles. The screenshot of this Web page is admittedly painful to look at, but take a moment to identify where each principle has been ignored. Then discuss the effects. To feel the full effect of this design disaster and see the animated GIFs in action, go to **http://pw.english.purdue.edu/files/gertrude/gert.html**.

Optimizing Images for the Web

Images are usually larger in size than HTML files, so to make sure that your Web page loads quickly—especially for users with slow Internet connections—optimize your images for Web delivery. For most file types, you can reduce file size substantially without loss of image quality by using the graphics editor's "Save for Web" or "Export" command, usually found on the File menu.

Web browsers are capable of displaying JPG, GIF, PNG, and TIF images. JPG and GIF files are used most often because they offer a smaller file size.

JPG files. The JPG format works best with photographs. Images with the JPG extension ("Joint Photographic Experts Group") can usually be optimized at 80 percent without any degradation in quality. If your file is originally in another format, such as PSD (Photoshop®), CDR (CorelDRAW®), or PNG (Fireworks®), you can save a copy in JPG format that will be viewable in a browser and have a smaller file size. The original image below has a file size of 901 KB, but when optimized at 80 percent it has a file size of only 133 KB. In many cases, you should compress your images as much as possible, so use the Preview windows in your graphics program to evaluate the results at different compression percentages.

GIF files. The GIF format works best with text, color, line art, and other images that have been generated on a computer. GIF files can be given a transparent background so that the image will display well against any colored or patterned background (the transparent background of the image allows the background of the Web page to come through). GIF files can't be compressed like JPG files, but their file size will be naturally small.

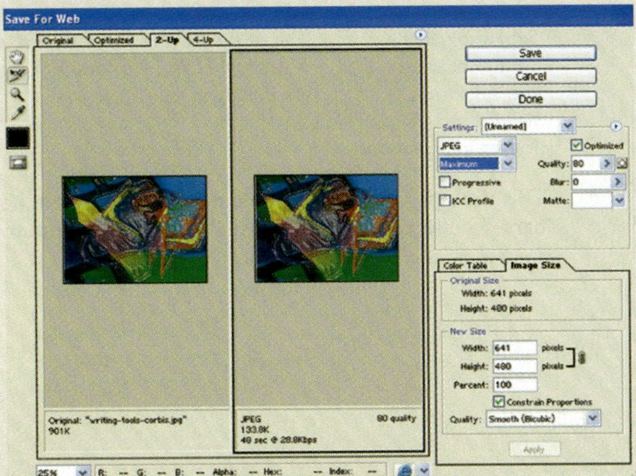

This Photoshop "Save For Web" dialogue box allows the user to adjust optimization level (here set at 80 percent), image size, and more.

Design Content

How best to select the design content of a website is a complex and controversial subject, with design styles going in and out of favor every few years. (See Chapter 31 for more on principles of organizing information visually.) When you're creating a website from scratch, rely on your own design sensibilities and experience as a reader to arrange visual elements, white space, and layout so as to structure information, guide the reader's eye to key components of the page, and add visual interest.

Banners and Headers

Web designers use banners and headers at the top of their Web pages to

- announce the title of the page or site
- establish a visual theme that gives the site a unique identity
- orient readers so they know what site they are viewing

Like the cover of a book, a banner draws the reader in and may also contain navigational elements, a search box, and (on commercial sites) advertising.

This Web page uses design elements, such as title headers, colors, and separator bars, to effectively arrange visual and verbal content.

From http://www.loc.gov/exhibits/blackburn/.

Creating Table Borders and Other Visual Elements with HTML

See pages 664–665 for a list of basic HTML tags.

- To add borders to a table to make its rows and columns stand out, use the border attribute within the opening <table> tag:

  <table border="size in pixels">
  <table border="5">

- To create a separator bar to divide regions of the page and set the bar's width, length, and shading, use the horizontal rule tag <hr>:

  <hr length="300" width="2" noshade>

  This tag will create a horizontal rule that is 300 pixels long and 2 pixels wide, with no shading.

- To make a bulleted list, use the tag for an "unordered list":

  <ul> begins the bulleted list
  <li> is used before each list item
  </ul> ends the list

- To make a numbered list, use the tag for an "ordered list":

  <ol> begins the numbered list
  <li> is used before each list item
  </ol> ends the list

HTML will insert a default bullet before each item in a bulleted list. With a cascading style sheet (CSS), you can make the bullet into an arrow or any other image you choose. For more on Cascading Style Sheets, see pages 697–700.

Borders, Separator Bars, Bullets, and Arrows

Decorative text elements can help structure information on a Web page and provide visual cues to readers about navigation.

Footers

Provenance and navigational links are typically included in footers, often with a separator bar above this information so that it isn't confused with body text. See page 677 for an example of provenance information in a footer with some decorative elements.

Navigation

Designing the navigational elements of a website seems simple, but it can get complex quickly as the website grows and the range of content widens. On a simple website consisting of only a few nodes, navigational elements are usually included in a side column or in the header and footer. They appear on every page in the site to help the reader navigate. In many cases, you should make it possible for readers to go directly from any node in a site to any other node.

To develop a navigational system, you need to organize the information that your site will contain. Here are four steps to follow in organizing information. It's helpful to sketch out this hierarchy using a grid, or template, like the one shown to the right.

1. Divide your information into logical categories.
2. Establish a hierarchy of importance and generality, moving from the most general to the most specific.
3. Use the hierarchy to create relationships or links across chunks of information.
4. Analyze your structure to see whether it will make sense to others. Move chunks of information to other branches if necessary.

Scenario for Developing a Navigational System

Susan is majoring in Art History and is hoping to someday be a museum curator. She wants to develop a Web portfolio to show to prospective employers. She has collected the best examples of her work from her courses and previous jobs, a resume (including lists of relevant courses and skills), and some links to favorite sites that have influenced her work. Her primary audience will be people in her field who may be in a position to judge whether or not she would be a suitable job candidate.

Here is her initial draft of a website structure.

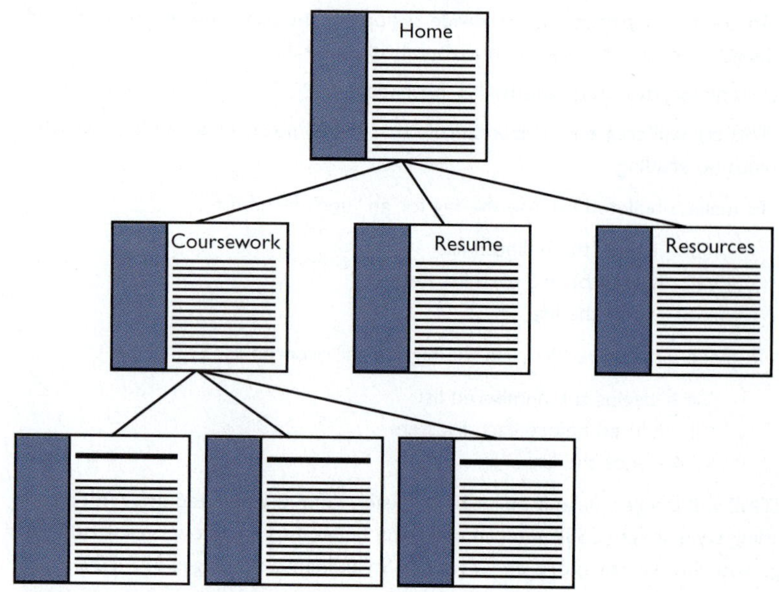

A tree diagram showing the site map for Susan's digital portfolio.

Susan's Navigational Decisions

Susan has a number of samples of her work that she would like to feature, so in the Coursework branch she has subcategories, with new pages devoted to major projects she has completed. She doesn't want visitors to go directly to the samples of her work because she would like them to first get a sense of the range and quantity of her work. So she settles on including three major links at the top level of her website, each to a B-level node. She will include these three links on each node of the website so that anyone can get back to the second level of the hierarchy. She also needs to have a "Home" link that will take readers back to the top level. So she needs a navigational system that has four links but also allows room for expansion later:

Home
Coursework
  Sample 1
  Sample 2
  Sample 3
Resume
Resources

On a navigation bar on each node of the site, she will create links to the four main nodes:

Home | Coursework | Resume | Resources

On her Coursework node, she will arrange thumbnail images of the samples, placing a brief description next to each to let readers know the nature of the sample.

Sample of Node Navigation

Node navigation is useful for long documents that should be broken into smaller chunks.

> properties we want students to learn about print literacy. Specifically it is important to explore television's qualities as a medium of popular response, distraction and simulation, and emotion.
>
> **continued**
>
> 1 | 2 | 3 | 4 | 5 | Works Cited | >>Next

Sample Footer

Provenance information is typically included in the footer of every page. Sometimes it is included with footer navigation, as in this example.

> Site content © 2004 - 2006 by *KB Journal*. Comments and forum messages © the individual author. Article content is published under a **Creative Commons** license attached to each article. *KB Journal* is sponsored by the Kenneth Burke Society and hosted at Purdue University by the Professional Writing Program. CMS theme design by **David Blakesley**. *KB Journal* is powerered by **Drupal**.

Readers sometimes resist reading a node that scrolls down for more than a screen or two, so you may want to lure them along in a longer document by breaking it up into pieces and providing navigational links at the bottom of each page. You can create a brief link to each node in the longer document and include a "continued" cue for the reader. Use the same list of links on each node, but disable (remove) the link for the active node. (For a more thorough discussion of website navigation and its importance, see Chapter 31.)

Provenance

Provenance establishes the ownership and authorship of a website. It is used not only by the author but also by others, and for multiple reasons.

- When people need to evaluate the nature, reliability, and timeliness of the content, they look to the provenance to see who authored the page and decide whether it's someone they can trust.
- When people have questions, they look for contact information so that they can write to website authors.
- When people want to cite the work in their own scholarship, they look for provenance information.

30d Publishing the Site to a Server

To publish your website to the Internet, you'll need to upload your files to a computer set up to serve Web pages, called a server. Web editors such as Dreamweaver and FrontPage have built-in functionality that allows you to "define a site" and then upload your files to the server after you've entered the information needed to make a connection.

To pass your files to another computer, you use FTP (File Transfer Protocol) or SFTP (Secure File Transfer Protocol). Standalone programs allow you to easily upload your files to other computers. Following are the most popular of these programs.

For PCs:

WS_FTP (see http://www.download.com)
SecureFX (see http://www.vandyke.com/download/securefx)

For Macs:

Fetch (see http://fetchsoftworks.com)
Fugu (see http://rsug.itd.umich.edu/software/fugu)

All come in fully functional versions that are free or available at low cost to college students. Windows XP and Mac OS 10.4 (Tiger) come with FTP functionality built into their own file management

Where to Publish a Website?

If you want to publish your website so that it can be accessed by others on the Internet, you will need to put your files on a server that has been set up to host websites. Check to see whether

1. your college or university provides you with free Web space or
2. the Internet Service Provider (ISP) through which you connect to the Internet at home—such as AOL, Insight Broadband, or EarthLink—provides a place to publish your files.

If you don't have access to an ISP, there are other good alternatives, some of which are free. In some cases, you may have to put up with a modest bit of advertising. All of these ISPs provide detailed directions for setting up your website on their servers:

Free (with advertising)

Geocities: **http://geocities.yahoo.com**
Google Page Creator: **http://pages.google.com**
Blogger: **http://www.blogger.com/start** (weblog hosting)

Low Cost (no advertising)

Active-Venture: **http://www.active-venture.com**

Low Cost, with Many Open Source Solutions for More Advanced Users (including blog-hosting and more)

Open Source Host: **http://www.opensourcehost.com**
Bryght: **http://www.bryght.com**
Site5: **: http://www.site5.com**

For examples of how to use FTP programs to upload files to a server, visit

WS_FTP: **http://pw.english.purdue.edu/techresources**
SSH Secure Shell 3.x: **http://www.ssh.com/support/documentation/online/ssh/winhelp/**
Fetch: **http://pw.english.purdue.edu/techresources**

Information You Need in Order to FTP Your Files to a Remote Server

Host: ____________________ ← For example, twi.english.purdue.edu

User Name: ____________________

Password: ____________________

Initial Remote Host Directory: ____________________ ← For example, /var/www/twi-html/upload

Sample Screen from an SFTP Program

You can drag and drop files from your local computer to the server, or you can use the download button to transfer files from the server to your local machine.

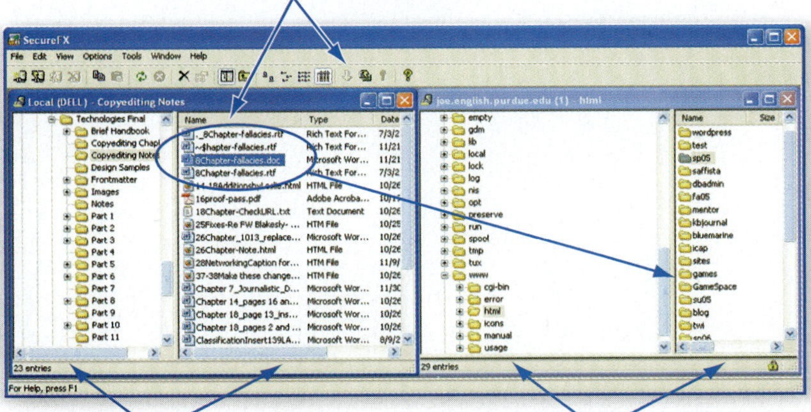

These panes show the folders, subfolders, and files on **your computer**.

These panes show the folders, subfolders, and files on **the server.**

SecureFX is an SFTP program that allows users to transfer files from their computer to a server securely, without risk of having their files intercepted by hackers enroute. Folders on the left are on the local computer. The server files are in the right pane. The user uploads files by selecting them in the left pane and dragging and dropping them into the proper folder on the right.

systems. The only trick is to make sure you have the settings you need to make contact with the server that will host your website.

To the left are the basic settings that you will need to specify in order to configure an FTP program to connect to a server. The specific information you need will be available from the hosting service you use.

31 DESIGNING COMPLEX WEBSITES

Complex websites consist of multiple nodes that connect a wide variety of information, such as digital archives, resource lists and links, articles, samples, products, forums, weblogs, and downloads—all in addition to textual and visual content. It can be difficult to manage all this information and all these functions. When designing a complex website—and even when creating a simple website that might evolve—you should consider the rhetorical situation, including your primary and subsidiary audiences, why readers will come to your website and what they will expect to find, how readers will interact with the information you provide, and how you will keep your content fresh so that they will return (◀ section 29c). Your writing should be clear and purposeful. Your visual and design content should complement and extend the textual information. Navigation should be user friendly. You should establish provenance—that is, provide information on authorship and copyright. Designing complex sites, in other words, requires all the same considerations as designing simple ones (covered in Chapter 30), with the additional need to plan each kind of content more carefully.

Complex websites require careful attention to information architecture—the organization of website content using logical categories, clear labels, effective navigation and search systems, and other cues that help readers locate and learn key information.

One important step in developing or overhauling a complex website is general planning with regard to purpose and audience. The *Web Style Guide,* 2nd edition (see http://www.webstyleguide.com) recommends taking the key steps listed to the right, and using the questions listed below each step as prompts when planning or analyzing a site for content and design (or form).

Questions to Ask When Planning and Analyzing a Site

Identify Your Goals (and Roles)

1. What textual, visual, and design content do you want to provide?
2. What is your timeline, from development through user testing?
3. How will you evaluate the success of your website?
4. What roles will there be for the Web development team (writers, designers, user-testers, etc.)?

Identify the Target Audience

5. Who is the site's primary audience? Subsidiary audience(s)?
6. Is that audience explicitly named or not? If not, how do you know who it is?
7. Based on its navigational design and use of browser technology, will the site be targeted to novices or "power users"?
8. Will the site make any appeals to casual visitors? If so, how? If not, why not?

Use Design Models

9. What successful models might help guide you in site development?
10. What does the design problem look like from the site user's point of view?

Define Your Purpose

11. Will the purposes of the site be explicitly stated? If so, what are they? If not, will they be evident from the textual, visual, and design content?
12. Will the primary purpose of the site be to teach (provide reference, training, or educational content)? Persuade (advertise and sell, move to action, promote)? Delight (entertain with content, including literature, games, images, video)? Network?
13. What other purposes might there be for the website (entertainment, business, promotion, news, reputation enhancement, etc.)?

Take Inventory of Your Content

14. Briefly, what is the nature of the information you plan to present on the website?
15. How will this information help achieve the website's purposes?
16. Will this information be presented in the form of a site map or set of FAQs?
17. Will the site offer links that take the user to other websites? If so, will these links be separate from the site content or will they be integrated?

Questions to Address in a Site Specification

Goals and Strategies

1. What is the mission of your organization, club, group, or department?
2. How will creating a website support your mission?
3. What are your two or three most important goals for the site?
4. Who is the primary audience for the website?
5. What do you want the audience to think or do after having visited your site?
6. What Web-related strategies will you use to achieve those goals?
7. How will you measure the success of your site?
8. How will you adequately maintain the finished site? (See question 15 also.)
9. How will you promote the site?

Production Issues

10. How many nodes will the site contain? What is the maximum acceptable count given your budget or time constraints?
11. What special technical or functional requirements are needed?
12. What is the budget for the site?
13. What is the production schedule for the site, including intermediate milestones and dates?
14. Who are the people or vendors on the development team and what are their responsibilities?
15. What provisions can you make now for future development and maintenance of the site?

A site specification is a concise statement of core goals, values, and intent. It is used to provide direction for making good decisions about the content, design, and navigation of a complex website. Ideally, a site specification document should include information about the scope of the content, the budget, the schedule, and technical aspects of the site (including where it will be hosted).

In the course of developing a website, you'll likely pass through six major stages.

1. Site definition and planning (site specification)
2. Information architecture (working with prototypes, models, storyboards, major interface questions, navigation, folder structure)
3. Site design (setting up page grid, page design, graphic design, templates)
4. Site construction (completing navigational elements, adding content, user testing)
5. Site marketing (advertising the URL, seeking placement on search engines, assigning metatags)
6. Tracking, evaluation, and maintenance (archiving, obtaining feedback)

Sample Site Specification Document

Site Specifications for the Greater Lafayette Human Relations Commissions

The team is creating a website for the integration of the Lafayette, West Lafayette, and Tippecanoe County Human Relations Commissions. To make sure that the class as well as the Greater Lafayette Human Relations Commission (GLHRC) has a definite idea of what the website's goal, values, and intent are, we have developed this site specification document. Here, we answer common questions in the process of developing and maintaining the website. We have included sections that address Goals, Audience, Site Success, Upkeep and Promotion, Site Design, and Deadlines.

Goals

The GLHRC has the mission of promoting better human relations in the Greater Lafayette area. The website will help the general public, as well as the Commission, meet the general goal of informing citizens about their rights. The new website should:

- Provide useful human relations information for the public
- Provide easy access to complaint forms
- Provide information about Federal, State, and Local law and regulations
- Provide contact information for Commissioners
- Make informationeasily accessible
- Help Commissioners organize their communication
- Announce and archive meeting minutes
- List special events
- Answer frequently asked questions

With an effective website, the GLHRC can provide needed information for the public's convenience. The website will organize the information to make it readily accessible to site users. It will provide understandable navigation and a consistent design them across the website.

Audience

Users of the GLHRC website vary. The primary audience is the general public seeking information about human relations. They will probably have an average level of user experience, meaning that they can navigate the Internet but may need instructions on how to download items, such as PDF files. Some users will be using a modem, so file sizes need to be kept to a minimum. We should design the website for a 17-inch monitor at 1024 x 768 resolution as this is the size most people are using. We probably want to include print-friendly versions of pages with instructions or reference material.

The secondary audience is the GLHRC itself. They can use the site to access meeting minutes and documents. We can provide the same level of guidance for the GLHRC as we do the general public.

When a member of the website's audience visits, we want them to be able to quickly access the information they are looking for. After they leave the website, we want them to feel that the we are working towards better human relations. We want the public to be willing to participate in the process by interacting with the GLHRC.

Site Success, Upkeep, and Promotion

The website's success can be measured in several ways:

- Increased human relations input from the public
- Number of visitors
- What other sites link to it

The finished site's upkeep will be managed by the GLHRC. Most of the information will be consistent and continuous, making for a site that needs little afterward involvement and only slight maintenance. The site will be relatively small, including probably less than fifty nodes. Because of the nature of the committees, the only website revisions necessary will be:

- postings of meeting minutes
- updating legal information and forms
- posting news about special events

Because of the concentrated Greater Lafayette audience, website promotion should not be a difficult task. Promotion of the GLHRC home page will result from word-of-mouth, promotional brochures, and public access advertising. Our promotion team and multimedia team may pool their resources to benefit advertising for the new site.

Site Design

The GLHRC's website should be designed to inspire confidence in the Commissions. We want people to feel that the Commission is fair and knows what they are doing while they serve the people. The tone should be official and serious. The website needs to be very functional. Graphics and design elements should not interfere with navigation or ease of use.

When designing the process of submitting complaints, we need to keep in mind that people like to complain and may see our site as the means to do that, even if their complaints don't fall under the purview of the Commissions. We need to build in a filtering system. They may consist of one of two things: (1) answering online questions about types of complaint to make sure citizen complaints meet our criteria for consideration; or (2) asks users to mail forms instead of submitting them electronically. Either one of these methods will make sure the site user is serious about filing a complaint.

Deadlines

Official deadline: End of semester
Preliminary site deadline: Presented at the meeting with GLHRC at mid-semester.

To structure information across a complex website consisting of many nodes, types of content, and features, Web developers focus on establishing an identity for the site—a look and a feel that help readers know where they are, what they can do, and what they can expect to find. Information architecture—the website's organization into a navigable and user-friendly structure—can be supported by

- a visual theme that complements and extends the site's purpose
- a layout that focuses the reader's attention on the most important content and makes it accessible
- a design that uses typography and color to enhance legibility and create visual interest
- a navigational system that directs readers through the site efficiently

Visual Design

The visual design of a website or Web page is complex. When you're creating a website from scratch and thus not using a template or predefined CSS (cascading style sheet), you need to rely on your own design sensibilities and experience as a reader, but there are also some criteria to bear in mind.

Designing to Establish a Visual Theme
In the BowieNet visualization to the right, you can see how the website uses design elements to establish a visual theme that, by means of repetition and consistency, is picked up on every node on the site. Readers quickly learn where to find information. Visual and graphical content can also be used to establish a visual theme that enhances the content and purpose. Visual themes give a website—and the organization or authors who publish it—a recognizable identity. In the corporate world, that's called branding, and it builds name recognition. If you want your website to have an impact beyond the moment, then you should think about creative ways to identify all of your work visually.

Close-ups of the upper left corners of several nodes from BowieNet appear on page 687. In each, you see the figure of a person, surrounded by icons that vary in color and shape but that give a contemporary, playful impression. The figure changes position and color across the nodes, helping to minimize the sense that these are static pages. There is a "retro" feel, but it is one that suggests that Bowie is comfortable in the

Visualization: Complex Visual Design Themes

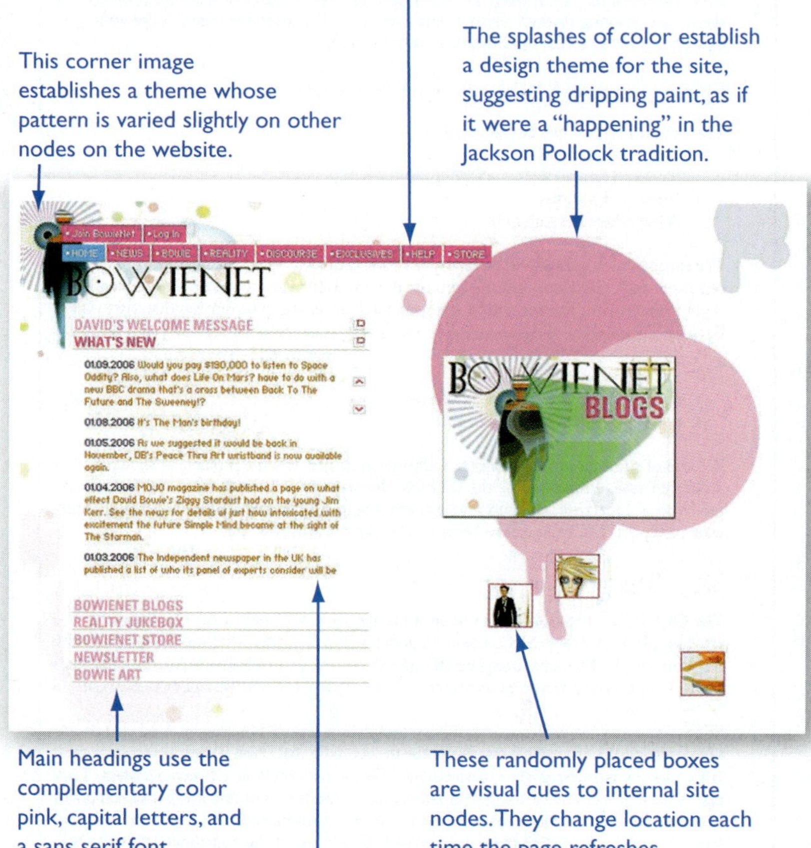

BowieNet uses a top navigation bar throughout the site in complementary colors.
This corner image establishes a theme whose pattern is varied slightly on other nodes on the website.
The splashes of color establish a design theme for the site, suggesting dripping paint, as if it were a "happening" in the Jackson Pollock tradition.
BOWIENET
DAVID'S WELCOME MESSAGE
WHAT'S NEW
BOWIENET BLOGS
REALITY JUKEBOX
BOWIENET STORE
NEWSLETTER
BOWIE ART
BOWIENET BLOGS
Main headings use the complementary color pink, capital letters, and a sans serif font.
These randomly placed boxes are visual cues to internal site nodes. They change location each time the page refreshes.
In this section, the headers expand to show more information after you click on them.

Annotated screenshot of BowieNet's home page at **http://www.davidbowie.com**.

BowieNet uses graphics to establish a visual theme. Visit the site at **http://www.davidbowie.com** to see how shapes, colors, and layout maintain a consistent look without causing the site to be repetitive or lose visual interest.

twenty-first century. This theme functions as effective design, but it also communicates a message about Bowie himself, regarding his talent for morphing his identity for almost 30 years as he seeks to stay on the cutting edge.

Using a Design Grid to Structure Information

Many of the principles of page design discussed in Chapter 24, Using Visuals to Inform and Persuade, can help you devise strategies for managing page layout for a website. Because screen space is usually at a premium, you need to plan carefully how you align your page elements (textual content, visual content, navigational elements, and provenance).

Layout

There are six overall schemes for managing all of the elements of a typical Web page:

1. **The inverted 7 grid** is useful for sites that contain numerous graphical elements and lots of information. The top and the left column are used for navigational or advertising elements, and the center is reserved for primary content.
2. **The L-shaped grid** is useful for text-heavy pages. In the example to the right, the entire page has a visual marker on the left margin, the primary text is in the middle, and the chief navigational elements are at the bottom.
3. **The double track grid** draws attention to the center of the page and usually includes hyperlinks on the left side and featured news on the right. There are few or no major elements at the top, except a logo or title.

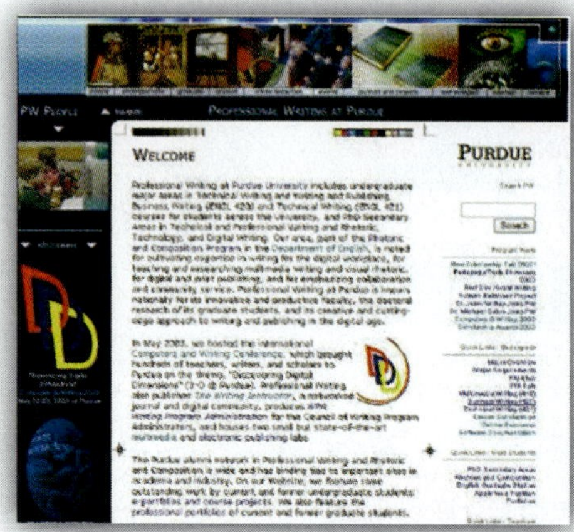

The inverted 7 grid.

From http://pw.english.purdue.edu.

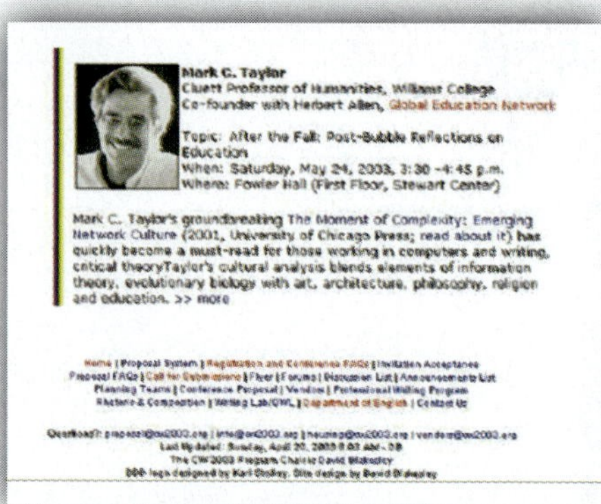

The L-shaped grid.

From http://cw.english.purdue.edu/speakers.html.

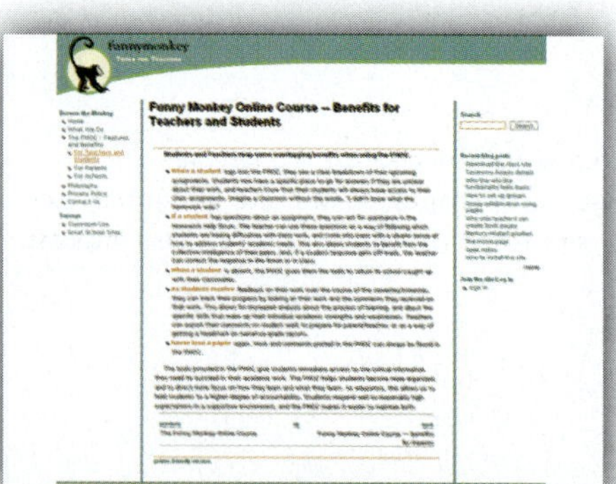

The double track grid.

From http://www.funnymonkey.com

The open grid.

From http://www.google.com (search on "Complexity Theory" and Emergence).

The invisible grid.

From http://www.arnoldproject.com.

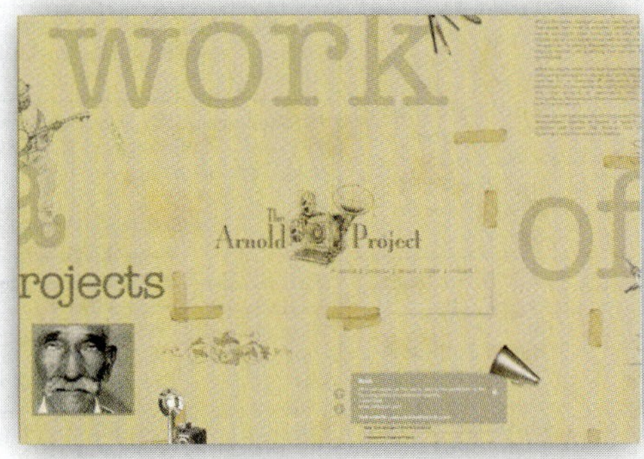

The visible grid of *Arts and Letters Daily.*

From http://www.aldaily.com.

4. **The open grid** is useful for sites that will change from day to day or moment to moment, such as search results pages. Google uses the open grid design to minimize the interference of advertising in search results while still placing it strategically.
5. **The invisible grid** is specific to sites that depict content graphically.
6. **The visible grid** is useful for sites where many hyperlinks or lots of advertisements are major components of a node.

Using Contrast to Emphasize Content

Contrast describes how effectively the individual and distinct elements of a page look in juxtaposition to one another. Such elements include visual information (images, colors, typography, organization) and textual information (text, headers, links). Contrast determines how these elements differ from one another and to what degree. In principle, it's useful to build contrast into your page design to highlight key information and direct your reader's attention. And it's important to make sure that contrast is not so low that nothing stands out. If all of the visual or textual information is similar—low contrast—then readers will have difficulty distinguishing the elements on a site and figuring out how to interact with it.

The contrast among key elements of your Web page should be sufficient to direct the reader's attention purposefully but not so jarring as to draw attention to the contrast in and of itself.

Low-Contrast Visual Information In the screenshot of Gertrude's Pet Shop (see page 672), one major problem is that the text does not contrast well with the background (or "wallpaper"). Some of the text is nearly invisible, especially the all-important links to the shop's products.

Low-Contrast Textual Information Link-heavy sites, like the Refdesk example to the right, can be difficult to read because most of the links look exactly the same. To counteract the effect of low-contrast textual information, Refdesk chunks types of links into clearly marked categories with logical titles and puts them in particular locations on the page. With only modest familiarity, readers come to know what kind of information to look for where. They can also distinguish one kind of information from another.

In situations where it is not possible to create high contrast among similar elements (as in lists of links), you need to find other ways to cue your readers, using the principles of *alignment* and *repetition*. Try grouping information into clearly marked categories or using other textual or visual cues such as arrows or pointers.

EURO Conversion Rates
Exchange Rates
FedEx
Find:
• Ancestors
• Birthdays
• College
• Doctor
• Elected Officials
• House
• Job
• Lawyer
• E-mail Addresses
• Government Stats
• Health Information
• Legal Information
• Lowest Prescription Cost
• Medical Information
• Military Information
• People
• U.S. Cities Guide
• U.S. Gov't Sites
• U.S. Representatives
• U.S. Senators
• Vital Records
Flags of the World
Foreign Words and Phrases

Grant Writing Guides
Gray's Anatomy
How Far Is It?
Kelley Blue Book
Language Translator
Legal Resources
List of Lists
Library of Congress
Maps: USA & World
Maps & Driving

• Business News: Barrons - Bloomberg - Business Daily Review - CBS MarketWatch - CNBC - CNN/Money - Financial Times - Forbes - Fortune - Investor's Bus. Daily - Kiplinger - Morningstar - Motley Fool - Red Herring - SmartMoney - TheStreet.com - WSJ - more >>

• Sports: CBS Sportsline - ESPN - GolfWeb - Inside Hoops - NASCAR.com - NBA.com - NFL.com - Sports HotSheet - Sports Illustrated - more>>

• Magazines: Atlantic - Bus. Week - CFOnet - Economist - Harper's - Nat. Review - Newsweek - New Yorker - People - Reader's Digest - Salon - Slate - Sci. Amer. - Time - TV Guide - US News - more >>

• Columns/Commentary: Dave Barry - David Broder - Dear Abby - William F. Buckley Jr. - Maureen Dowd - Matt Drudge - Ellen Goodman - Paul Harvey - Molly Ivins - Rush Limbaugh - George Will - WSJ - Yahoo Op/Ed - more >> #1 - #2

• Net/Tech News: c|net - CNN Technology - ClickZ - Net News - NewsLinx Web News - Slashdot - Wired - ZDNet - more >>

• Miscellaneous: Arts Journal - Editorials - **First Chapter:** NYT - WP - Movie Research - Movie Reviews - Opinion-Pages - Writ - more >>

Refdesk Subject Categories
Refdesk Site Map

Facts/Internet	Social Sciences	Applied Sciences
Agents/Robots	Business/Career	Automotive
Beginner's Guides	Crime/Law Enforce.	Aviation
Cool Site of the Day	Education	Career
Computer Graphics	Environment	Mental Health
Computer Hardware	Family Matters	Military
Computer	Food/Recipes	Pets/Animals
	Health	**Art/Entertainment**
	Homework	Arts & Culture

Perry-Castaneda Maps
Yahoo! Maps
Health
CancerNet
Mayo Clinic
MEDLINE Plus
WebMD
People Finder
Langenberg
WhitePages.com
World Telephone Directories
Quotations
Bartlett's
Quoteland.com
Style & Writing Guide
APA Style
Citation Styles
Elements of Style
Grammar, Punctuation, and Spelling
Guide to Grammar/Writing
Just For Fun
2003: Year in Review
Best Sites 2003: PC Magazine
Sci/Tech Awards 2003
Top 500 Search Keywords

A Game A Day
AirportMonitor: Real Time
Anagram Server
Analogy of the Day
Aphorisms Galore!
Classical Music Archives
Coffee Break Game Arcade
Cool Signatures

The Refdesk site manages to include a huge number of links on one page by carefully chunking resource links. Here is a close-up of a portion of Refdesk.com's home page.

From http://www.refdesk.com.

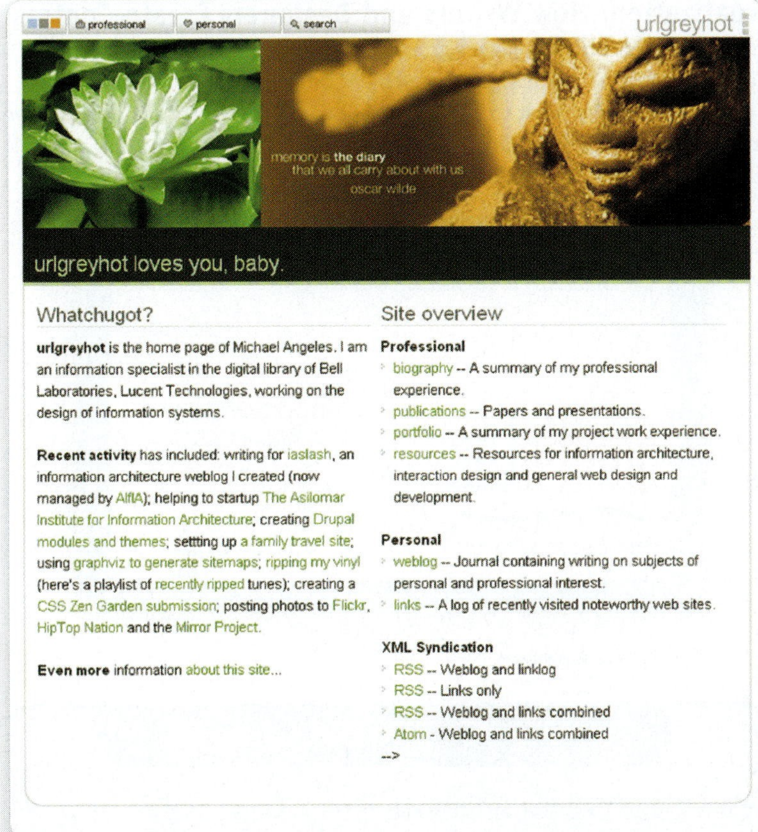

This node provides good contrast and visual interest with its banner, and the text is easy to read because of the visible grid, clear headers, and ample white space.

BOWIENET BLOGS
REALITY JUKEBOX
BOWIENET STORE
NEWSLETTER
BOWIE ART

Subtle horizontal bars help draw attention to the internal links on BowieNet.
From http://www.davidbowie.com.

High-Contrast Textual Information On websites with a large amount of textual information, it's important to find ways to provide contrast across categories of information; sometimes visual elements are needed to help provide that contrast. You can create high contrast in textual information by

1. organizing information carefully
2. providing clearly understood headers
3. associating visual cues with certain types of information
4. using white space to provide eye relief
5. keeping your line length relatively short, definitely no longer than 75 characters

High-Contrast Visual Information Sharp contrasts between pieces of visual information can help you move the reader's eye where you want it to go. They can also help individual elements of a page stand out from the rest. In the urlgreyhot screenshot to the left, interesting images appear in the banner, which includes the site slogan and is topped with navigational links. In the main body, textual information is clearly divided into a visible grid format, and each section has a clear header, drawing the reader's eye.

Dominant Contrast

In a written text, you create dominant contrast with good visual organization, sometimes called information architecture (◀ Chapter 24). The concept of dominant contrast—drawn from photography and cinematography—depends on a basic rhetorical principle worth keeping in mind: Direct your readers' attention strategically and carefully. When you distract them with unimportant details, you lose their attention, which makes persuading, informing, or moving them even more difficult than it already was. In an information-rich visual environment, the design of the page becomes as important (for comprehension and appeal) as the content itself.

Using Repetition and Consistency to Establish Patterns

Repetition can be an effective means of capturing someone's attention, a fact that advertisers know well and that some people use as their only design principle. Unfortunately, too much repetition can work against you by reducing contrast or by simply boring your reader.

Designers use repetition to establish patterns that readers can learn and then use to process complex information.

Visualization: How Writers and Designers Create Contrast

Contrast helps direct the reader's attention. For example, suppose you want readers to look first at a navigational element on your website, because otherwise they will wonder what to read or where to go. To draw attention, you have to create *dominant contrast.* On the DoodleLab site, the woman holding the child at the lower right is an animation that tells readers what to do first.

From http://www.doodlelab.com.

Managing Complex Information on a Large Scale

Large organizations have spent millions of dollars reorganizing websites that had grown into disorganized heaps of information with no coherent identity. By 1999, for example, International Business Machines (IBM) had amassed over 1 million nodes on its website, which had become a confusing labyrinth. Complex or nonexistent navigation made it difficult for customers to find information and make purchases. After careful usability testing that focused on user expectations and behaviors, IBM redesigned more than 150,000 nodes according to a detailed plan for their information architecture. Traffic to "Shop IBM" increased 120 percent immediately, access to Help nodes dropped dramatically, and the company's sales went up 400 percent, making IBM's huge investment in planning and redesign well worth the effort.

Resource Websites for Design Models and Tips

Website and URL	Description
Coolhomepages.com: **http://www.coolhomepages.com**	This site is a user-built community where you can see what others believe represents good website design and vote on the samples they provide. Coolhomepages.com includes a useful "Design Inspiration Gallery" that divides the sources of inspiration into many categories: by what software technologies or coding languages they use (Flash, cascading style sheets, rollovers, etc.) and by the purpose or genre of the site (e-commerce, education, ezines, etc.).
Web Design and Review: **http://www.graphic-design.com/Web/index.html**	Here, you can see what others say about Web designs and even submit your own for peer (and very public) review.
W3C (World Wide Web Consortium): **http://www.w3.org**	The W3C group sets standards for website design and elements, including standard coding protocols for HTML, stylesheets, and much more.
Builder.com ("Beyond the Code"): **http://builder.com.com**	Builder.com is a site and forum for advanced Web design (and coding, in spite of the slogan). It is a commercial site, but it contains many useful, sometimes dated, resources for Web design and development.
DevX, Project Cool: **http://www.devx.com/projectcool/Door/7051**	DevX's motto is "The know-how behind application development." This site is one of the most complete and useful of any focusing on Web design.
Open Source Web Design: **http://www.oswd.org**	At this resource site, designers contribute design templates that use standards-compliant cascading style sheets and that may be downloaded and repurposed.

Use repetition as you arrange the elements of each page. Whenever possible, navigational cues should be placed in the same location on each of your pages so that readers know where to find them. It has become common to place navigational elements on the left or top because readers expect to see them there.

Using Proportion to Indicate Importance

Proportion refers to the principle that every element of a Web page should have a presence in proportion to its importance or relevance to achieving the rhetorical purpose. Proportion will help you maintain balance among your rhetorical purposes and the elements of your website. Each element of a Web page should "pull its weight," performing a specific rhetorical or design function without drawing excessive attention to itself in the process and thus taking attention away from other important content.

Navigation

Useful websites include user-friendly, clear navigational aids that help readers find the information they are looking for and encourage them to return later. In addition to the principles discussed on pages 676–677, consider these guidelines:

1. **Cue readers with text and images.** For smaller sites, a simple navigation bar listing major categories is sufficient. On complex sites, you can create second-level links to nodes by using pop-up menus or, more simply, by including indented text on a sidebar.
2. **Provide redundant navigation.** To improve accessibility, include multiple ways for readers to navigate your site: (a) *navigation bars* (at the top and bottom, for example, when you have pages that scroll past one screen), (b) "*Quick Links*" menus on a sidebar, and (c) a *search tool*. For free search tools that you can use, see "Search Tools for Websites and Intranets" at http://www.searchtools.com/; the Google search tool is especially useful: http://www.google.com/services/websearch.html.
3. **Use persistent links.** Make links to major, top-level nodes *persistent,* which means that they appear on every node in the site.

Navigation on Complex Sites

The Library of Congress's Wise Guide provides several different ways to access sites. From http://www.loc.gov.

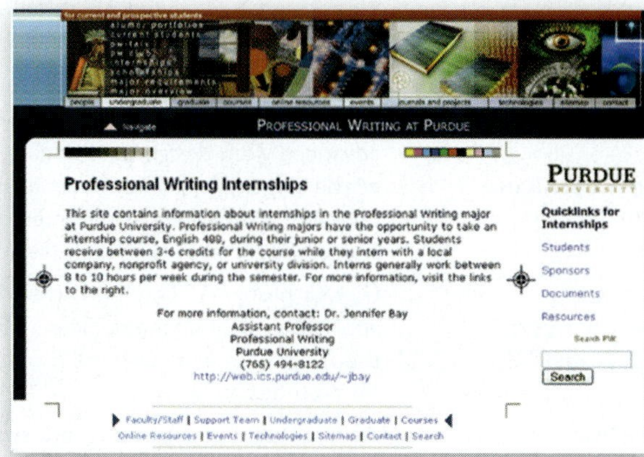

This small node on a website has a top menu bar with submenus, a list of links on the right to nodes relevant to internship information, and then footer navigation to major categories. A search tool is included at bottom right. The pop-up menus on the top were created with Macromedia Flash, but they could be created using Web authoring software and graphics editors such as Fireworks.

From http://pw.english.purdue.edu/undergrad/internships.shtml.

Adjusting Colors

You can adjust the colors of text, active links, and visited links by adding code in the <body> tag of your HTML document or by using a dialogue box in your Web authoring software.

- In Dreamweaver, choose Modify > Page Properties from the top menu bar.
- In Nvu, choose Format > Page Colors and Backgrounds.
- In FrontPage, choose File > Page Properties.

Creating Hyperlinks

- In Dreamweaver, choose Insert > Interactive Images > Navigation Bar, and then enter the text and link information.
- In any other program, create a table with the number of columns matching the number of links you want to include, add backgrounds or borders, and then create a hyperlink for each of the categories. (This method is the easiest and most straightforward.)

Home	Resources	News	Site Map	About Us

4. **Use color to cue readers.** For hyperlinks, use colors that contrast well with other colors on the node so that readers know that a link is a link. The default color for a hyperlink is blue and for a visited hyperlink is red. Some designers vary these colors to better suit their overall design theme, but be careful that you don't confuse readers.
5. **Minimize click-through.** It's helpful if a reader can find any node with just one or two clicks from any other node. If a node is on the eighth level of a website (eight clicks in from the home node), few people will find it except through an outside search engine.
6. **Use Web authoring design tools.** Use tools in your Web authoring software to make navigational aids.
7. **Study models.** Find examples of effective navigation on websites whose content and scope match your own, and emulate them.
8. **Learn from resources.** Review detailed instructions on creating effective navigation:

Web Style Guide: http://www.webstyleguide.com/interface/navigate.html

IBM's "Ease of Use" Document on Navigation: http://www-3.ibm.com/ibm/easy/eou_ext.nsf/publish/748

When you first set up your website, you'll need to decide how to organize all of its content. First plan your design and navigational system (pages 685–695) and complete a site specification (pages 683–685). It is helpful to match your folder structure to the major categories of information you have devised and to also include a folder (or more) for storing images, banners, navigational aids, and other design elements that will be used across a range of pages on your site.

A simple website folder structure may include only a few pages in the root, or main, directory (index.html, portfolio.html, and resume.html); an images folder and subfolders; a stylesheets folder; and a templates folder (used to store reusable page designs as you create new pages). This folder structure is for a small professional portfolio site:

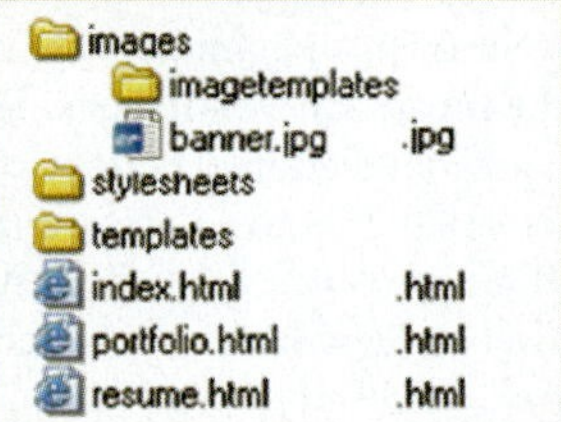

File and Folder Management for Complex Websites

The complex website file structure shown here contains folders that match the navigational structure of the website, but it also includes folders for storing PDF files, library items (elements used on multiple nodes), and templates. The file structure corresponds to the website shown at the bottom of page 694.

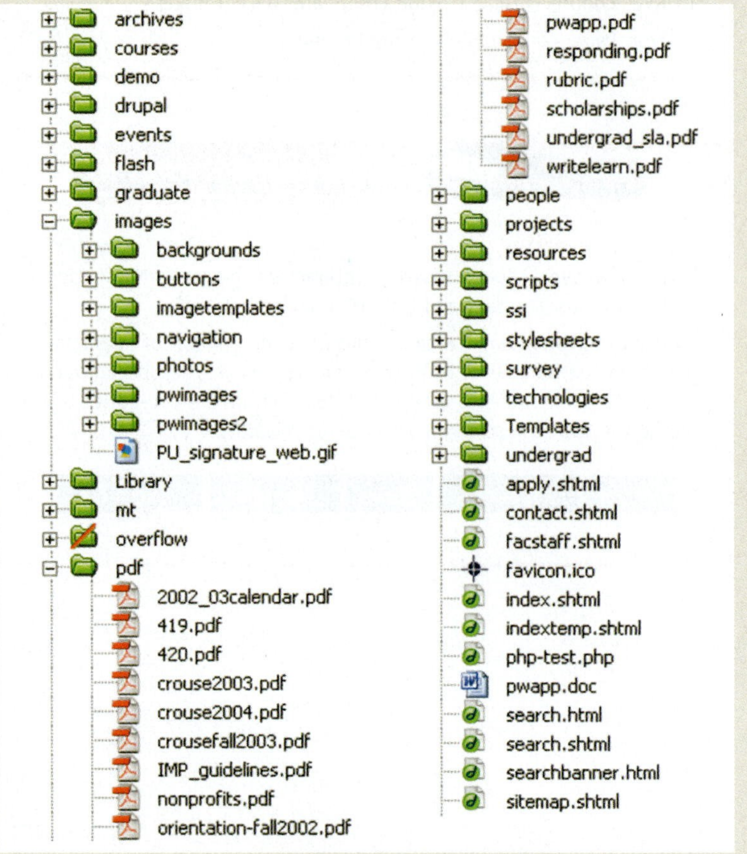

File-Naming Conventions

Don't use spaces in file names. Because a URL includes path information to files, you should not use any spaces when you name files and folders in your website. Browsers interpret a space in a URL as its end point, not as a character.

Use short descriptive file names. It's good practice to keep file names consistent, short, and descriptive so that URLs remain as short as possible and readers can understand where files reside in relation to the main nodes on the website.

Preserve file name extensions. Use standard file name extensions so that the server and readers' computers know which program to use to handle the file. As a general rule, keep your file extensions in the default format. For HTML files, the extension is usually .html, but it can also be .htm, .shtml (for "server-side include HTML"), or .xhtml (for XML-enhanced HTML pages). Image files are generally viewed in .jpg or .gif format. Flash files (.swf), text files (.txt), ZIP (.zip), MP3 (.mp3), movies (.mpeg, .mpeg2, .mpeg3), and Adobe Reader files (.pdf) are other common variants.

The principle behind a cascading style sheet (CSS) is that it is efficient to separate textual content from design content. Then, once a design for a website has been defined by a set of CSS codes, content can be added without the need to re-create the design each time. A CSS file can control the appearance of typography, tables, page colors, margins, and more. If you spend some time learning how to use CSS files, you will save enormous amounts of time when you want to change the color, layout, and typography of your website. It's now possible to change the look of a website dramatically (even one with thousands of pages) by changing just a few style definitions in a CSS file.

A CSS file is a collection of programming codes that tells a browser how to display aspects of an HTML or other dynamically created page (such as one generated from a database in XML or PHP, a scripting language that can be embedded in HTML). If a CSS file is attached to an HTML file, then each time that HTML file is opened in a browser, the browser reads the CSS file to determine how to display its elements. For example, suppose a CSS file says that all text inside the <p> tag (paragraph tag) should be displayed in Verdana font with a pixel size of 13 and a leading (distance between lines) of 17 pixels. All nodes on a website that contain text inside <p> tags and that use the CSS file definitions will display at 13-pixel Verdana with 17-pixel leading. You can achieve this same level of precision with almost any element of a Web page.

Web pages that are dynamically constructed (assembled from bits and pieces in a database) use style sheets, with marvelous and consistent results. Weblog software and content management systems use CSS files to control the look of a website so that the user can focus on contributing content. CSS files help create website "themes" that allow users to choose the look and feel that best match their purpose.

The effects of CSS can be dramatic. The screenshots to the right illustrate different CSS themes applied to a test site made in Drupal, a popular open source content management system.

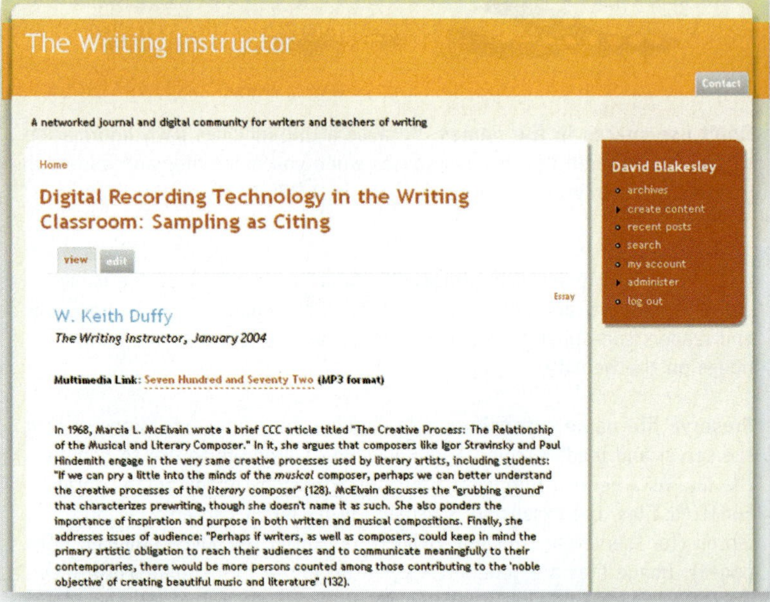

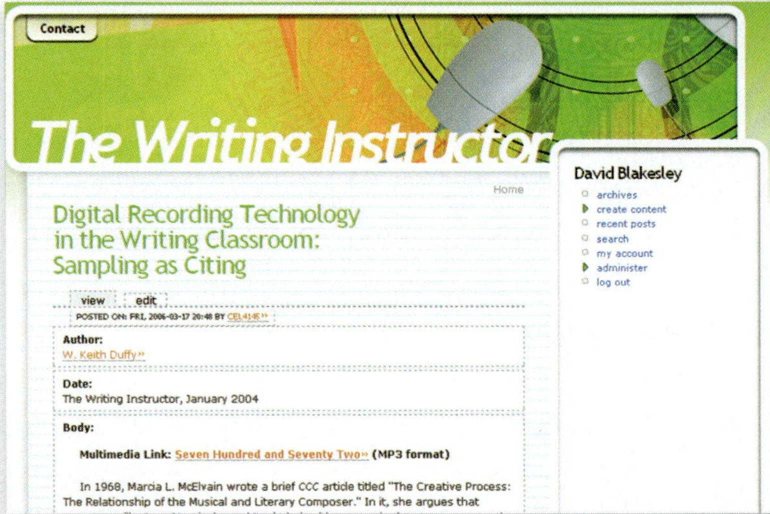

The textual content of these two screens is identical, but with CSS applied, the look is dramatically different.

Viewing a CSS File

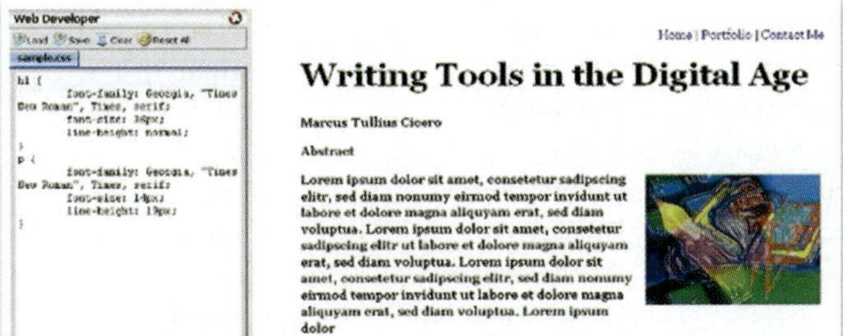

The CSS file for this HTML file consists of this code:

```
h1 {
        font-family: Georgia,"Times New Roman",Times, serif;
        font-size: 36px;
        line-height: normal;
}
p {
        font-family: Georgia, "Times New Roman",Times, serif;
        font-size: 14px;
        line-height: 19px;
}
```

This file tells the browser to treat all <h1> and <p> tags as indicated.

Resources for Cascading Style Sheets

W3C's Guide to Cascading Style Sheets: **http://www.w3.org/Style/**

W3C's CSS Tips and Tricks: **http://www.w3.org/Style/Examples/007/**

Web Design Group's Cascading Style Sheets: **http://www.htmlhelp.com/reference/css/**

Web Developer's Virtual Library: **http://www.wdvl.com/Authoring/Style/Sheets/**

Max Design (for creating stylized lists): **http://css.maxdesign.com.au**

Zen Garden: The Beauty of CSS Design: **http://www.csszengarden.com**

Cascading Style Sheets: The Definitive Guide, 2nd edition, by Eric Meyer (Sebastapol, CA: O'Reilly & Associates, 2004)

Programs such as Dreamweaver, FrontPage, and Composer have CSS capabilities built into them. If you plan to use CSS for your websites, you will find the Web development extension for Firefox very useful in testing how small changes in the CSS will affect your pages. Its CSS editor allows you to view a CSS file alongside the Web page, make a change (such as a change in font size), and see its effects immediately. To the left, you can see the CSS editor next to the Web page. You can use the Web Developer Extension for Firefox to examine and change CSS files (◀ page 665). Adjusting font size or adding styles immediately changes the appearance of the node.

In addition to letting designers redefine current HTML tags, CSS allows designers to create new tags with unique features, using the "class" and "div" attributes. An **attribute** is an HTML tag that defines the appearance of an element. The CSS and HTML resources listed to the left describe many of the attributes that can be assigned.

CSS Reference Guide

The table to the right shows the attributes that can be assigned to existing HTML tags or new ones (with "class" or "div" used to specify a unique style). Here is an example of what a redefined <p> tag might look like in a CSS file:

p { font-family: Verdana, Arial, Helvetica, sans-serif; font-size: 13px; line-height: 19px; }

Attributes, such as *font-family,* are followed by a colon and then the value or name. Each attribute in the redefined tag is separated from the others by a semicolon. The entire definition is enclosed within curly brackets, or braces: { }. When the browser is given this command by the style sheet, it interprets all <p> tag content in these terms.

CSS Level 1 Attributes

background
background-attachment
background-color
background-image
background-position
background-repeat
border
border-bottom
border-bottom-width
border-color
border-left
border-left-width
border-right
border-right-width
border-style
border-top
border-top-width
border-width
clear
color
display
float
font
font-family
font-size
font-style
font-variant
font-weight
height
letter-spacing
line-height
list-style-image
list-style-position
list-style-type
margin
margin-bottom
margin-left
margin-right
margin-top
padding
padding-bottom
padding-left
padding-right
padding-top
text-align
text-decoration
text-indent
text-transform
white-space
width
word-spacing

CSS Level 2 Attributes

background
border
bottom
clear
clip
color
content
cursor
direction
display
float
font
height
left
margin
marks
orphans
outline
overflow
padding
page
position
quotes
right
size
top
visibility
widows
width

Typography Considerations on the Web

1. Sans serif fonts such as Arial, Verdana, and Georgia are good choices for both headers and body text. (A sans serif font does not have the small strokes added to basic characters in serif fonts and therefore looks better on screens, where the resolution is not nearly as good as it is in print.)
2. The size of the typeface is critical. Because of cross-platform compatibility issues caused by different monitor resolutions, text that is defined as 13-point Arial in the HTML file or style sheet will vary in size from machine to machine. It is therefore common practice now to define sizes in terms of pixels and to consider which size will not look too small on a high-resolution monitor or too large on a low-resolution monitor. Test your choice of font sizes by viewing your pages at varying resolutions using different monitors. Programs such as Dreamweaver allow you to temporarily view a page at different resolutions so that you can evaluate how the fonts will appear.
3. Since text set in all capital letters is harder to read, avoid using all caps except for short strings of text, as in headers.
4. Keep your line length shorter than you think you need to. You can set tables at stable pixel widths rather than as a percentage of screen space to limit how far lines will stretch across the screen. It's good practice to keep line length to 75 or fewer characters so that readers can easily find the next line as their eyes move down the screen.
5. Use enough leading (pronounced "ledding") to create sufficient white space between your lines. The default value is often too little. Slightly more leading can make the text more readable, accessible, and visually appealing.
6. Use cascading style sheets to ensure consistency.

Resources on Typography

For a full discussion of designing with typography on the Web, see

The Web Style Guide: **http://www.webstyleguide.com/type/index.html**

To check how different font styles and sizes and other typographical elements display on screen, as well as to download the associated CSS code, go to

http://www.typetester.maratz.com

Fonts are sets of type, such as Times New Roman and Arial. **Typography** refers to the overall balance and interplay of the letters on screen.

Most Web pages are meant to be read as well as viewed, so choose the fonts for your Web pages carefully. Follow good design principles in using them. Text needs to stand out against the background, be legible, and cause minimal eyestrain. Choose fonts that make your website accessible to users using a wide variety of browsers, computers, and monitors. In order for a font to display properly on a local machine, that machine must have font files installed for each font used, so limit the number of fonts you use.

If you choose colors well, you can make your Web pages visually stunning and ensure that readers see what you expect them to see, no matter which operating system or monitor they have. Most graphics and Web authoring programs help by providing Web-safe color palettes.

The challenge is to select colors that complement one another and give your website a look and feel well suited to its purpose. Color symbolism is a complex and uncertain art (whether red makes people feel danger or passion can be disputed, for example). But color theory suggests that there are specific color combinations that work well together because of the eye's capacity for recognizing gradations in color. Also, readers get used to reading Web pages with consistent color schemes for new links, visited links, and active links, for example. Using color consistently across your pages will help readers make sense of complex information.

For more on managing color, see section 25d.

Managing Color on the Web

Visit Color Mixers at **http://colormixers.com**, which allows users to enter color codes or to select existing palettes that show a range of compatible colors and how they will look on a Web page.

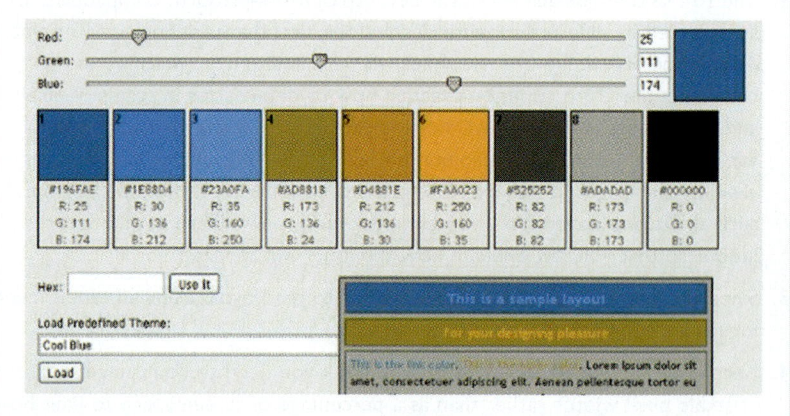

Complex Websites That Focus on Writing and That Use Weblogs or a CMS

Kairosnews: **http://kairosnews.org** (see especially the collection of "Rhetoric and Composition Weblogs": **http://kairosnews.org/node/3719**) (Drupal)

Open Source Development and Documentation Project: **http://www.osddp.org** (Drupal)

Weblogg-ed: **http://www.weblogg-ed.com** (Manila)

Council of Writing Program Administrators: **http://www.wpacouncil.org** (Drupal)

MetaFilter: **http://www.metafilter.com** (ColdFusion, MySQL)

Hosting Weblogs and CMSs

You may choose to run weblog or CMS software on your own server or through a hosting service (usually about $8 per month). Reasonably priced hosting services allow users to try weblog and CMS alternatives with free installation and no server maintenance:

OpenSourceHost: **https://www.opensourcehost.com**

Site 5: **http://www.site5.com**

Bryght: **http://www.bryght.com**

Many people choose to use free alternatives, such as Blogger (**http://www.blogger.com**), which allows users to customize themes and preferences. You can try out any open source CMS or weblog—and even work with a "live" site of your own immediately—through OpenSourceCMS (**http://www.opensourcecms.com**).

If you are developing a website that you expect to grow over time and that will feature interactivity and perhaps the archiving of documents, a weblog or CMS is a good choice because it lets you focus your attention on developing content and building a community of readers.

Weblogs—or **blogs** for short—are Web-accessible journals or commentary, usually authored by an individual or small group of people. Some blogs are contained within a larger **content management system (CMS),** which allows users to contribute to or create their own blogs, including journals and research logs, interview sites, and "link blogs" that collect and comment on other sites on the Internet (◀ section 28c). Content management systems help Web developers and users organize, categorize, and share information and commentary on a complex website, whose visual content and design content are either fixed or easily adjustable by individual users.

Content management systems, many of which are available to anyone for free download, run on servers and offer writers a wide range of options for managing information. A weblog or CMS will automatically archive new information and apply preset themes to it (using a CSS).

31j Analyzing the San Diego Zoo Website

Open the San Diego Zoo's website on your computer so that you get a full view of the home page: http://www.sandiegozoo.org. Answer the following questions and then discuss your answers in small groups. (It's likely that the page will look different than it does here, but the questions will still apply.) See if you can come to some agreement about whether this home page is an effective gateway to a complex website.

Content Questions	Visual Design Questions	Navigation Questions	Provenance Questions

Content Questions

1. How would you describe the balance of textual and visual information? Is the emphasis on textual information or visual information?
2. How many images do you see? How many design elements (lines, bars, colors, boxes, etc.)?
3. What is the focus of the textual content? Does it solely provide information? Is it a marketing pitch? How would you describe the balance between words that sell and words that inform?

Visual Design Questions

4. How would you describe the overall visual effect?
5. What design grid does the page use (◀ section 31d)?
6. What is the dominant contrast on the page? In other words, what draws your attention first? Does it serve the apparent purpose of the page? Is it well suited to the rhetorical situation?
7. Describe the color palette used. Is it effective? Does the text clearly stand out? Is it legible? How effective are link colors?

Navigation Questions

8. Describe the navigational system. Is it effective?
9. Does the page use any visual cues besides words or colors to indicate interactive navigation?
10. Are the categories used in the menu bar logical?
11. Are there multiple (e.g., redundant) navigation systems to allow readers multiple paths into the site?

Provenance Questions

12. Does the site provide information about its authorship, date it was last updated, privacy policy, and anything else that would be useful to identify it as the genuine site of the San Diego Zoo?
13. Could the site be an imitation or a "websquatter," only using a domain name likely to fool people? How do you know?

32 MULTIMEDIA COMPOSING

Multimedia composing is a set of skilled practices for integrating content that may appear in various forms—words, sounds, moving and still images, even physical objects—in the interest of communicating or entertaining. When you compose multimedia, you create content in a variety of forms; put it all together to persuade, teach, or delight; and use technologies, including physical media such as paper or printed pictures, that will help you share your content with your audience creatively, effectively, and richly.

An effective multimedia composition has tremendous power to persuade and move an audience. It appeals on many different levels, often simultaneously greeting the mind and the senses. Because we are a media-saturated society, most people have experienced the many ways in which images reinforce the meaning of words, and words add nuance, and sometimes explicit content, to images. Sounds, especially music, convey content, mood, and emotion. New technologies have made it possible for people who aren't technical specialists or professionals to compose multimedia. The creators of content, authors, designers, artists, musicians, are now closer than ever to the means of delivering rich multimedia content to audiences. In the end, the goal of the multimedia composer should be to create for the audience an experience that is appealing, while at the same time conveying content effectively and purposefully.

In the most general sense, *multimedia* means "multiple media." *Multimedia composing* refers to putting together several media elements to create a presentation, project, or performance. *Media* include printed text, of course, but also images and graphics (photographs, drawings, video) and audio (spoken words, music, sound effects). Multimedia composing may also involve communicating with tactile elements (things that you can touch and feel or that you interact with through bodily movements, called haptics). Taken together, these forms are sometimes called "the new media."

People have always communicated their ideas by means other than or in addition to writing—art and music, for example. Effective multimedia composing integrates text, image, sound, and sensation, using various technologies to accomplish familiar rhetorical purposes: to teach or inform, to delight or entertain, to move or persuade. Multimedia composing has become popular because new computing technologies have made it possible to combine these forms of communication purposefully in useful and interesting ways, without the need for equipment once found in production studios or print shops.

Activity 32-1: The Media of Multimedia Composing

Media is the plural of *medium,* and it refers to physical or digital means of representing texts, images, or sounds. A medium is literally a conveyance that transports or channels meaning from one place or person to another. Media are go-betweens or intermediaries. On computer screens, the media are the interfaces and the software that constructs them.

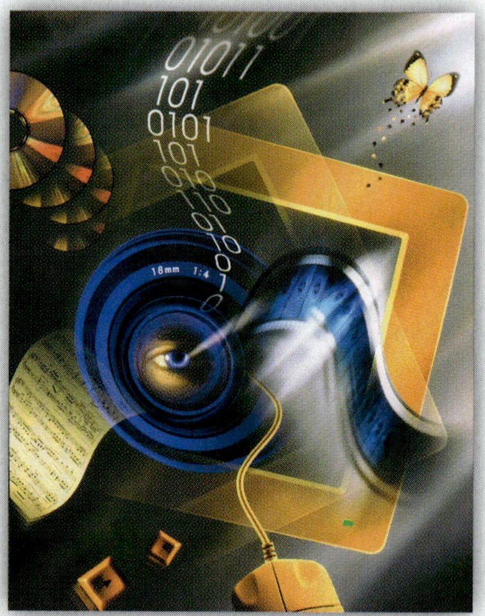

As a multimedia writer, you have various media to work with and numerous ways to make your content available to audiences. Here is a list of media in three categories:

1. **Print media:** paper, posters, cards, labels, banners, books, brochures, cloth, magazines, newsprint, postcards, greeting cards
2. **Graphical media:** photographs, slides, celluloid film, animation cells, drawings, paintings
3. **Digital and analog media:** computer screens, floppy disks, TVs, projection screens, CDs, DVDs, video- and audiotape, media cards

What other media have people found useful for conveying meaning? List five additional media types in each category. As a follow-up, over the next 24 hours, see whether you can identify five more types of media that compete for your attention on your way to and from your classes, work, or home.

The Multimedia Rhetorical Triangle

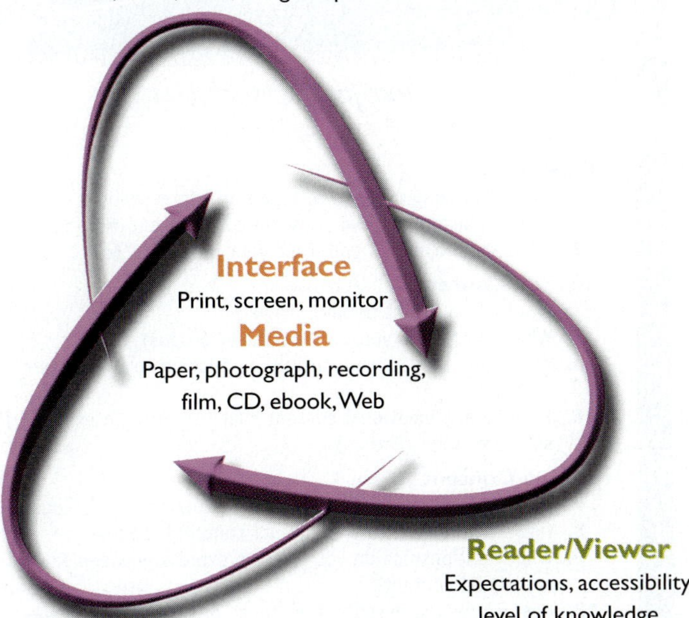

Media and interface balance relationships among authors, readers, and content.

For an interesting trip down memory lane, as well as articles on the development of multiple media, check out the "Chronology of New Media," written by Matthew Stanton, at the website Metro Memetics: **http://www.metromemetics.com/thechronology/index.asp**.

Like authors of many familiar forms of printed text, effective multimedia composers take into account the rhetorical situation and audience—the circumstances of writing and communicating to others—as well as all the means (ethos, logos, pathos, delivery, style, arrangement, memory) of accomplishing the purpose (to inform, delight, or persuade). When you compose in multimedia, you should first answer some questions about the rhetorical situation and the best means of accomplishing your goals. Because multimedia composing can be a complex multi-step process, it's important to develop the good habits of careful planning.

You should choose media to suit the occasion and your purpose, audience, and content, rather than letting the media dictate your rhetorical choices.

For example, if you want to share information about what students in your major or club do and their possible career paths, you might choose to make a QuickTime movie on the Web (reaching a broad audience and helping to recruit new students) or hold a special screening for current majors on a "movie night." You could even take screenshots from your video and surround them with text about your club—thus turning the video into a multimedia profile.

If you want to create a permanent record of student life on your campus, you will probably choose a print medium—a magazine or journal, for instance. If your goal is to reach out to students off campus, you might choose the Web as your medium—using an ezine or weblog, for example—and then repurpose the material as a printed document that can be archived in the library.

If you are looking for a job, you could prepare a printed resume to send to employers who request one and to take to job fairs. You could make an electronic version to email or fax to employers, presenting your experience as neatly as possible given the medium. Or you could integrate your resume into a larger

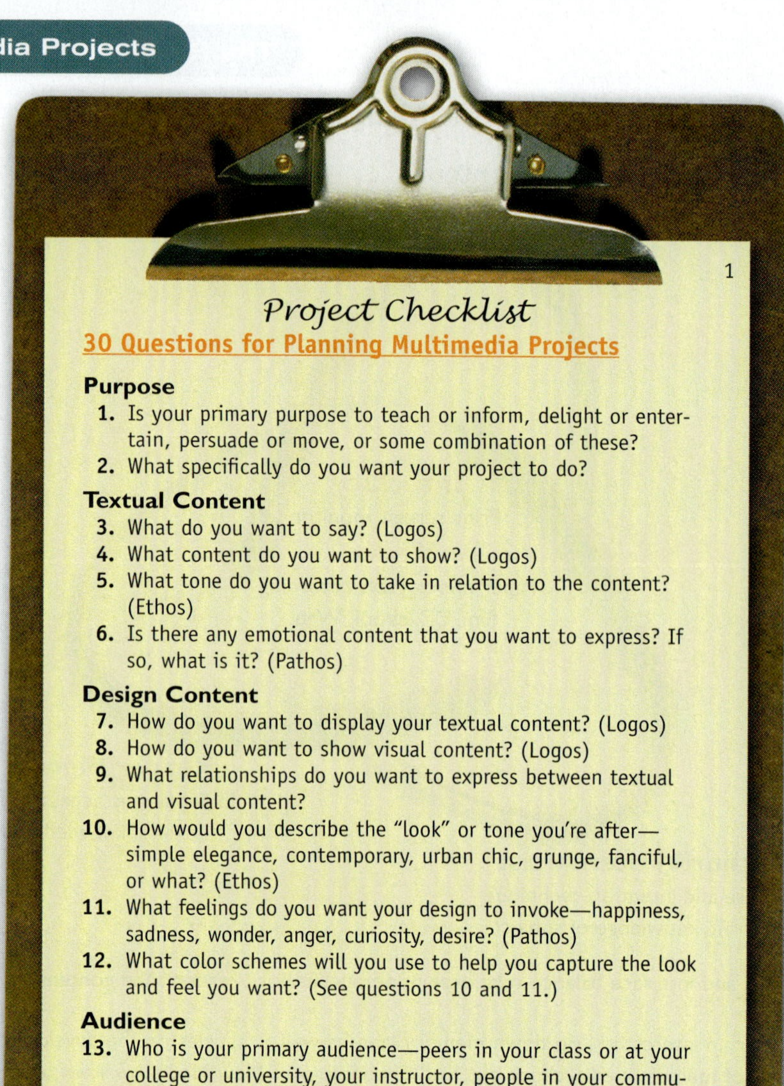
1

Project Checklist

30 Questions for Planning Multimedia Projects

Purpose

1. Is your primary purpose to teach or inform, delight or entertain, persuade or move, or some combination of these?
2. What specifically do you want your project to do?

Textual Content

3. What do you want to say? (Logos)
4. What content do you want to show? (Logos)
5. What tone do you want to take in relation to the content? (Ethos)
6. Is there any emotional content that you want to express? If so, what is it? (Pathos)

Design Content

7. How do you want to display your textual content? (Logos)
8. How do you want to show visual content? (Logos)
9. What relationships do you want to express between textual and visual content?
10. How would you describe the "look" or tone you're after—simple elegance, contemporary, urban chic, grunge, fanciful, or what? (Ethos)
11. What feelings do you want your design to invoke—happiness, sadness, wonder, anger, curiosity, desire? (Pathos)
12. What color schemes will you use to help you capture the look and feel you want? (See questions 10 and 11.)

Audience

13. Who is your primary audience—peers in your class or at your college or university, your instructor, people in your community, people with a contrary viewpoint, or like-minded citizens? What knowledge and experience will readers and viewers

2

bring to the work? (Recall that the primary audience is the group of readers or viewers most likely to interact with and respond to your work. You shape your textual, visual, and design content to appeal to your primary audience.)

14. Who are your subsidiary audiences? What knowledge and experience might they bring to the work? (Recall that the subsidiary audiences are the groups of readers or viewers who may also find your work appealing or at least be interested in your work. Very often, for example, an ezine will have as its primary audience peers in the same class, but its subsidiary audiences in the Internet community will include people from around the world.)

Media and Delivery

15. What media or interfaces will best convey your meaning under the circumstances? (*Kairos*)

16. What balance between print and other media do you want to achieve? (Proportion)

17. If your project is digital, what technologies will people need to read or view it? What directions will you need to provide for opening and viewing files, for example? If you're presenting your project orally, how will you project it? Will your project look different when projected than it does on your monitor?

18. If your project is in print, what kind of paper or other material do you want to use? How will you print visual material? Will you package or present your project in any way? If you're preparing a poster, for example, what material can you use? Does your bookstore or art supply store sell posterboard for live presentations?

19. If your project is print and digital, how will you package the two pieces together? Be sure also to address questions 17 and 18 if yours is a hybrid print-digital project.

(continued)

portfolio that includes printed samples of your work and a CD with more complex sample projects.

In the Project Checklist, notice that we have used the phrases *textual content* and *design content* to emphasize that both the textual and the visual elements of your multimedia projects convey messages. Contrary to some opinions, design or visual content is every bit as important as its textual counterpart. In other words, design content is not just ornamentation, but, as Marshall McLuhan suggested, part of the overall message itself. Design content conveys meaning by juxtaposing textual and visual information, by moving the eyes of the reader or viewer in strategic ways, and even by appealing to the emotions with color. For more on visual rhetoric, see Chapters 10 and 24.

Ask the questions in the Project Checklist not only as you start your projects but also as you come to key stages in production. In multimedia projects, for example, there may be instances when you need to provide background information—with a hyperlink, for example—for readers unfamiliar with a concept, so you will need to consider purpose, textual and visual content, audience, media, delivery, arrangement, and collaboration at many points in the project's development. The point is to use your answers to shape your decisions as you compose.

A multimedia essay integrates text and other media to accomplish its purpose, which may be to teach or inform, delight or entertain, or persuade and move an audience. You can write multimedia essays in any genre; you just need to adapt the form to the genre and the particular requirements of the assignment.

Multimedia essays can be constructed as a website. Alternatively, they may be packaged on a CD-ROM, a DVD, or, if the file sizes are small, a floppy disk. They can also be presented in printed format, with photographs, tape recordings, CDs, or podcasts used to supplement the textual content. We have also seen multimedia essays packaged in boxes or as well-designed posters that include printed text, visual and design content, and music. (At very low cost, you can buy nicely designed or blank cigar boxes for this purpose at Thompson Cigar: http://www.thompsoncigar.com. Search for item 994000: "Premium Empty Cigar Bxs-10.")

3

Arrangement

20. How can you arrange your textual and visual information in meaningful patterns or hierarchies? What do viewers need to notice first? What next?
21. What headings and subheadings can you use to help readers or viewers navigate through your project? Can you think of some headings and subheadings that will give readers or viewers a quick sense of the gist of your project?
22. Have you used print or screen space in ways that highlight the most important information?
23. Does your project have a clear beginning, middle, and end, with graceful transitions between parts?

Collaboration and Project Management

24. What are the steps you need to take to complete your project?
25. How much time will it take to complete each aspect of your project?
26. What information do you need to know (about technologies, for instance) before you get too far along in your project?
27. Does anyone on your team have particularly strong skills with certain technologies or media, such as Web design, video or audio production, photography, digital copyediting, file management?
28. What kinds of records should you keep of your collaboration—meeting notes, calendars, project plans?
29. If your project is a collaborative one, have you done all you can to complete the work you agreed to do on time and well, be a clear and responsive communicator, allow others opportunities to be as much involved as you are, and offer constructive feedback to team members?
30. How do you plan to evaluate your collaboration?

Useful Tools for Composing Multimedia Essays

Software

- Word processor (Microsoft Word, OpenOffice, WordPerfect, Notepad, SimpleText)
- Presentation software (PowerPoint, Apple Keynote, OpenOffice, Adobe Acrobat, Flash)
- Graphics editor (Photoshop, CorelDRAW, Photoshop Elements, Fireworks)
- Webpage editor (Dreamweaver, Composer, FrontPage, Nvu)
- Video editor (Adobe® Premiere®, Apple Final Cut Pro®, iMovie)
- Digital audio editor (Audacity, SoundEdit™, GarageBand, Pinnacle Studio)
- Comic book editor (Comic Life)
- Software for making CDs and DVDs (Roxio Easy CD Creator, Nero®, Toast®)
- Ebook authoring software (Sophie, TK3)

Hardware

- Mac or PC with Internet connection
- Video capture card for transferring video to your computer
- Sound card (for capturing audio from a digital recorder)
- Digital audio recorder
- Digital camera for still and video

Technology Resources

Multimedia essays can be challenging to compose, but if you have some experience incorporating visual content into your projects (Chapter 24) or designing websites (Chapters 30 and 31), then you already have the computer literacy you will need. The tools you choose to work with have a critical bearing not only on how you publish your work but also on how you plan and research your content. These tools make it possible to shape and render content, so you should have some idea from the outset about what form your writing will take.

Depending on the nature and format of your multimedia essays, you may use some of the software and hardware listed to the left. The titles listed in parentheses are recommendations for commonly used software, but many alternatives exist, and for most multimedia essays you don't need *all* this software. You also don't necessarily need to be an expert with any of it. However, you will need to spend some time learning how to use the software to accomplish basic tasks (image editing and optimizing, for example, in a graphics editor).

Planning Your Multimedia Essay

In addition to responding to the questions in the Project Checklist, you should also take a few more steps as you begin your multimedia essay.

Storyboard Your Project

It can be helpful to think of a multimedia essay as an unfolding sequence of events, like a film, and to plan each component or scene in some detail before you get too far into the project. Film directors and Web developers use storyboards to outline their projects in advance. Storyboards then help keep the project on track and the goals in sight. You will probably revise them as your project develops. Good storyboards make reference to the textual, visual, design, and audio content of your essay.

Five Steps of Storyboarding

1. Find or create a storyboard template that you can use to draft your outline, like the one shown below.

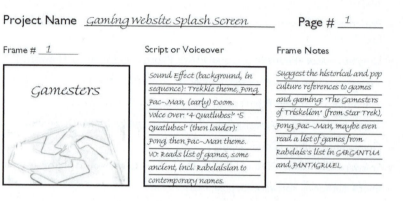

Project Name *Gaming Website Splash Screen* Page # *1*

Frame # *1*

Gamesters

Script or Voiceover

Sound Effect (background, in sequence): Trekkie theme, Pong, Pac-Man, (early) Doom. Voice Over: "4 Quatlubes!" "5 Quatlubes!" (then louder): Pong, then Pac-Man theme. VO: Reads list of games, some ancient, incl. Rabelaisian to contemporary names.

Frame Notes

Suggest the historical and pop culture references to games and gaming: "The Gamesters of Triskelion" (from Star Trek), Pong, Pac-Man, maybe even read a list of games from Rabelais's list in GARGANTUA and PANTAGRUEL

Sample storyboard frames and notes

2. Each frame of your storyboard should represent a unique page, a step in a sequence, or some other individual component of your work (such as a PowerPoint or Keynote slide, a keyframe in Flash, or a Web page).
3. In each frame, identify your content. Use shorthand to describe the content (including images and audio) that you want to include and approximately where it should be placed.
4. Add notes to each frame in your storyboard on design, source files, material, and anything else that will help you remember what each frame should contain and how it should be presented.
5. When you have completed a rough draft of your storyboard, read back through it to see whether it has an order that makes sense and includes the multimedia you want to use. Move frames around as necessary.

On the Web, you can find a free and useful planning and storyboarding tool called Denim, created by the Group for User Interface Research at Berkeley: **http://guir.berkeley.edu/projects/denim/**.

Sample Assets List

This assets list was generated for the multimedia essay "It's Dynamix, Dad," by Chris McKibbin. (See page 715 for a screenshot of the title page of this essay.)

Sample Assets List for a Multimedia Essay Writer: Chris McKibbin Project Title: "It's Dynamix, Dad" Last Update: May 5, 2004	
Textual Content	
	Paragraph introducing multimedia essay
	Paragraph on education
	Definition of "unique"
	Paragraph on literacy
	Paragraph on technologies
	Paragraph on work experience
Visual Content	
	9 navigation images for header (start, early, etc.)
	9 navigation images for rollovers in header ([start], [early], etc.)
	1 title image for header ("It's Dynamix, Dad")
	1 image of high school building
	1 image of home
	3 images of book covers
	1 image of me
	5 digital images of my dad from the time when I was ten years old
	5 digital images of my childhood home
	1 Flash movie (bookcovers.swf)
Audio Content	
	Missle.wav
	Laserfire.wav
	ZAP.wav
	laserfire3.wav
	laser.midi

Create an Assets List

An assets list itemizes all the textual, visual, and audio content that you might use in your multimedia essay. Assets lists can save you from wasting time later looking for or producing content for your project. Very often, writers get bogged down in the middle of composing a multimedia project because they didn't collect their assets before they began and thus, in the heat of the moment, made poor choices about what multimedia content to include.

In the beginning, use your assets list to identify what you want. When the list is complete, you can make sure you have all the assets. Don't waste time looking for images to use *as* you are completing your project; it's easy to get sidetracked when you acquire assets in mid-process. If you know in the beginning, after completing your storyboard, that you want to use some bird images (say, of peacocks) in your essay, then you should put "5 peacock images" on your assets list. You might need only one, but chances are you won't know exactly which one to use until you compose your essay. If you get five from the start (perhaps from a collection of stock photography on the Internet), you don't narrow your options too early. Or, for example, if you want to create a Flash interface on a Web page, you might list "3 Flash navigation bars" on your assets list, then find three templates that you can use for creating one (packaged with Flash, for example, or available on the Macromedia website or at one of the many Flash resource sites on the Internet).

Keep a Project Log to Document Your Work

As you work on your project, keep a running log of the decisions you make about particular images you will use (including resolution, file name and format, and source), design elements and color palette (each color will have a unique number associated with it, for example, in RGB format), and the citation information for any quotations or other copyrighted material you use. A project log will be useful for preparing your design notes, works cited, and protocol sheets—each of which is an important component in the final delivery or publication of your multimedia essay. Identifying file types, resolution, sources, and more will be very time-consuming if you wait until after you have completed your project. Project logs will also be important when it comes time to repurpose your content.

Sample Project Log

Sample Project Log for a Multimedia Essay
Writer: Chris McKibbin
Project Title: "It's Dynamix, Dad"
Last Update: May 5, 2004

Images

	Resolution	Format	Source
dynamix.gif	37.8 pixels/cm	.gif	Macromedia Fireworks MX
start.gif	37.8 pixels/cm	.gif	Macromedia Fireworks MX
startroll.gif	37.8 pixels/cm	.gif	Macromedia Fireworks MX

Color palette

	Background	Text	Links	Visited Links	Active Links
Top.html	#006699	n/a	n/a	n/a	n/a
main.html	#FFFFFF	#006699	#FF9900	#FF9900	#FF9900
books.html	#FFFFFF	#006699	#FF9900	#FF9900	#FF9900
computer.html	#FFFFFF	#006699	#FF9900	#FF9900	#FF9900
work.html	#FFFFFF	#006699	#FF9900	#FF9900	#FF9900
vacation.html	#FFFFFF	#006699	#FF9900	#FF9900	#FF9900
early.html	#FFFFFF	#006699	#FF9900	#FF9900	#FF9900

Copyrighted materials

Missle.wav	http://www.a1freesoundeffects.com/weapons.html
Laserfire.wav	http://www.a1freesoundeffects.com/weapons.html
laserfire3.wav	http://www.a1freesoundeffects.com/weapons.html
Definition of unique	http://www.bartleby.com/61/48/U0084800.html

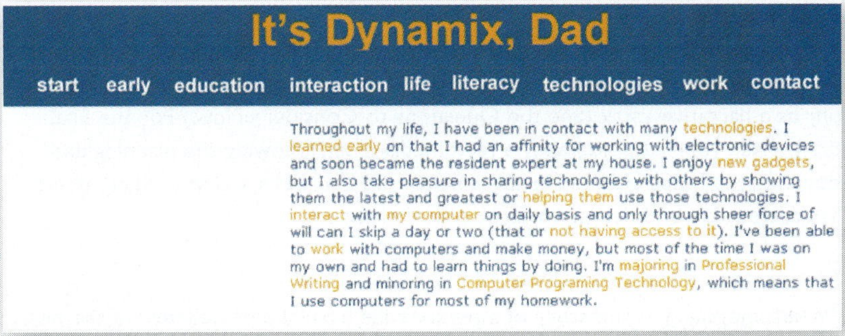

It's Dynamix, Dad

start early education interaction life literacy technologies work contact

Throughout my life, I have been in contact with many technologies. I learned early on that I had an affinity for working with electronic devices and soon became the resident expert at my house. I enjoy new gadgets, but I also take pleasure in sharing technologies with others by showing them the latest and greatest or helping them use those technologies. I interact with my computer on daily basis and only through sheer force of will can I skip a day or two (that or not having access to it). I've been able to work with computers and make money, but most of the time I was on my own and had to learn things by doing. I'm majoring in Professional Writing and minoring in Computer Programing Technology, which means that I use computers for most of my homework.

Chris McKibbin created a design with a top navigation bar and left a space for images on the left.

Write Design Notes or Protocol Sheets

Design notes are useful for documenting in summary fashion what the project log contains. They are especially important when projects involve multiple people and an extended period of time. Design notes provide explicit information about the nature of the media (website, type of paper, CD, etc.), about templates or style guidelines, and about fonts and color palettes. Here's an example.

Rubric for Design Notes on a Web-Based Multimedia Essay

URL of interface
Description of visual theme and design metaphor
Description of navigational system
Description of technologies used
Description of typography used
Description of colors used

Professor Richard Selfe has developed a useful project assignment that can be adapted for the multimedia essay form and that can serve as a model for planning other topical approaches.

Assignment

Write a technology autobiography that tells the story of the multiple roles that technology has played in your life. For the first draft, compose your autobiography as a narrative essay. (See the Questions to Consider below.) For the final draft, make your autobiography a multimedia essay, following the planning and documenting steps outlined in this chapter (30 questions, storyboarding, assets list, project log, and design notes or protocol sheet).

Discussion

An autobiography is the story of a person's life from the perspective of the person who lived it. A technology autobiography tells the story of a life with technology: the memorable experiences with and uses of technology throughout a person's life. Some writers focus on a particular kind of technology (writing technologies, household technologies, media technologies, computer technologies, or gaming technologies, for example). Autobiographies are normally written from the first-person point of view and depict specific instances or stories that illustrate the writer's experiences, usually to make a point about them or to show how the author learned from them.

Questions to Consider

As you plan the essay, you can jot down your thoughts about your life with technology. Here are some questions to help you discover what you have to say. In your essay, make sure you don't simply answer each question in succession without providing a thread or controlling idea in your narrative.

1. **Memory.** What childhood experiences with technological devices or artifacts do you remember? What do you recall about your earliest use of technologies? Were they positive or negative experiences? What stories do your parents tell about your interactions with technology? What were the popular gadgets in your household when you were young? Did you have access to the technologies you wanted to use? Who made sure that everything worked? How often did the technologies fail?
2. **Literacy.** Who is the most "technologically literate" person you know? What makes his or her relationship with technology unique? What behaviors or characteristics does he or she exhibit? What have you learned about your own uses of technology from him or her?

3. **Social consequences.** Are there social consequences for your lifestyle that hinge on your technological literacy? What are they? How would your relationships with others be affected if you suddenly had no access to technology?
4. **The future.** What do you think will be required ten years from now to be technologically literate? What positive or negative trends in technological development do you see unfolding? How do you think they will affect you?
5. **Learning.** How do you learn new technologies? Among your friends, are you considered an "early adopter," a "late adopter," or somewhere between?
6. **Access.** What technologies do you carry with you? Which ones do you have where you do most of your writing? What new technologies do you want to own? How will you use them?

Primary Audience

Think of your readers as your peers, people who likely have had some similar experiences with technology. It will help your audience to know what experiences you've had. Most people find that they are not alone in having confronted the complex demands of technology.

Purpose

The technology autobiography gives you a chance to reflect on your relationship to technology. To take advantage of new technologies and learn to use them critically and effectively, you should understand how technology has shaped your life this far, with an eye for controlling its use in your future. The process of composing a technology autobiography is designed to help you understand how you learn new technologies and, by extension, how you cope with technological impasses (those moments when things don't work as planned). Understanding your past experience with technology will help you become a better multimedia writer, as you will bring a critical eye to bear on the opportunities and challenges of writing in the new media.

Sample

Casandra Riddle composed a narrative essay entitled "Well, I'm Using a Computer." She later repurposed the essay, transforming the printed work into an electronic comic book. You can read both online at
cengage.com/English/Blakesley
For a screenshot, see page 556.

Multimedia or digital portfolios are quickly becoming an important means of featuring the work of students, artists, graphic designers, engineers—anyone who has samples to share with peers, potential employers, or the general public. A professional portfolio can serve as a repository where students archive class projects, essays, and any other work that illustrates the scope of their endeavors. In some courses, you may be asked to keep a portfolio of your work to demonstrate your accomplishments over the course of a semester.

Elements That Might Be Included in a Professional Portfolio

- **Background information:** a short narrative about who you are and what you do. In professional portfolios, it's often best not to share too much specific and sensitive information about yourself unless you don't mind being contacted by random visitors to your site.
- **Resume or vita:** a printable document stored as a PDF file, created with Adobe Acrobat or a PDF conversion plug-in such as PDF Maker for Microsoft Word or the stand-alone freeware CutePDF™ Writer
- **Sample publications and projects:** PDF versions of your printed work, screenshots of websites, video projects, scanned artwork, links to your work on the Web
- **Weblog:** your running commentary on current events in your field of interest, discussions of the work of others, etc. (◀ Chapter 28)
- **Links and resources:** a storehouse of links to websites that you find useful in your own work and that others might benefit from, a collection of documents that you have authored and that you can share with others, or a news aggregate

Visit These Multimedia Portfolios:

Mike Fortress: **http://www.fortressgraphics.com**
Dustin Hlava: **http://web.ics.purdue.edu/~dhlava**
Casey Cavanaugh: **http://web.ics.purdue.edu/~ccavanau**

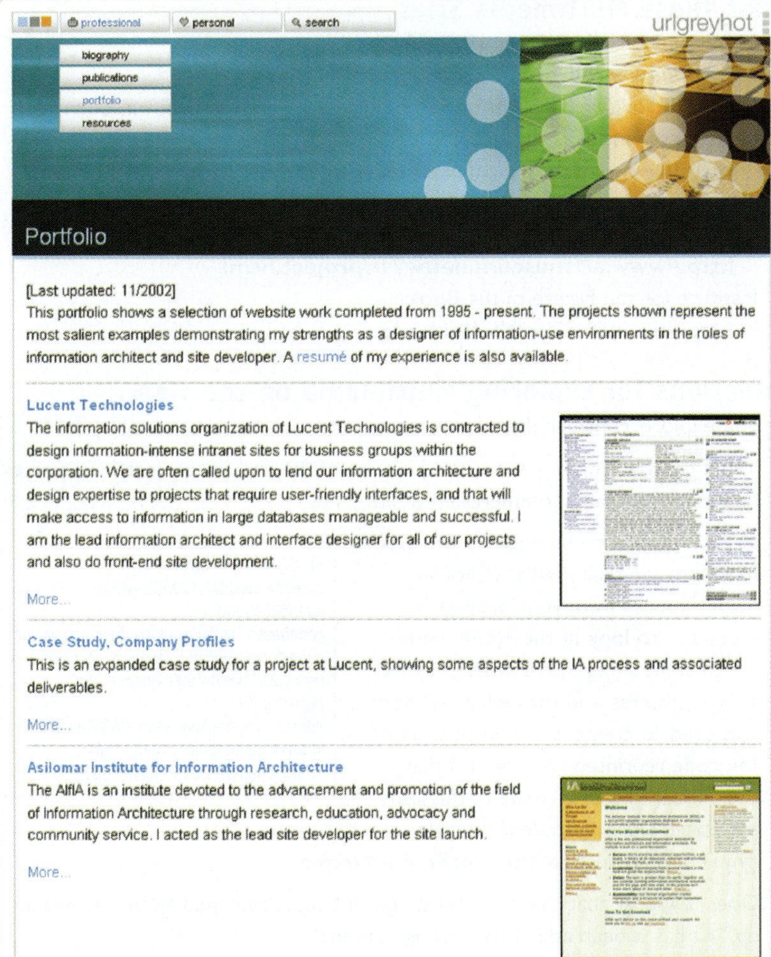

professional
personal
search
urlgreyhot
biography
publications
portfolio
resources
Portfolio
[Last updated: 11/2002]
This portfolio shows a selection of website work completed from 1995 - present. The projects shown represent the most salient examples demonstrating my strengths as a designer of information-use environments in the roles of information architect and site developer. A resumé of my experience is also available.
Lucent Technologies
The information solutions organization of Lucent Technologies is contracted to design information-intense intranet sites for business groups within the corporation. We are often called upon to lend our information architecture and design expertise to projects that require user-friendly interfaces, and that will make access to information in large databases manageable and successful. I am the lead information architect and interface designer for all of our projects and also do front-end site development.
More...
Case Study, Company Profiles
This is an expanded case study for a project at Lucent, showing some aspects of the IA process and associated deliverables.
More...
Asilomar Institute for Information Architecture
The AIfIA is an institute devoted to the advancement and promotion of the field of Information Architecture through research, education, advocacy and community service. I acted as the lead site developer for the site launch.
More...

This is the "Portfolio" node of Michael Angeles's Drupal website, which provides screenshots, short descriptions, and links to further information.

Michael Angeles's digital portfolio at http://urlgreyhot.com includes many of the components listed on page 718 in a nicely designed and professional package. He is a professional working in the design of information systems and websites. Notice how he has designed his portfolio so that it is easy to navigate. Each node presents summaries and samples of his work, with links offsite where appropriate. His site was constructed using a free (open source) content management system called Drupal, which includes a weblog: http://www.drupal.org.

Where can you find good examples of multimedia on the Web? They're all over the place! Here are some examples, representing the work of highly accomplished (and sometimes highly paid) professionals, as well as the work of people who compose multimedia simply to express themselves and their ideas. Explore these sites, but not just casually. Read and respond to them. Take special notice of the sites that allow you to practice your own skills in working with multimedia content to reshape it.

Visit These Multimedia Sites

The Remedi Project (Flash; 1997–2002):
http://www.theremediproject.com
Flinch Studios (Web Animation Technologies): **http://www.flinch.com**
Museum of Fine Arts, Houston:
http://www.mfah.org/microsites/IU/inverted_utopias_website/
The Alternative Museum: **http://www.alternativemuseum.org**
The Art Museum's Project "Multimedia: From Wagner to Virtual Reality":
http://www.artmuseum.net/w2vr/project.html
Institute for the Future of the Book:
http://www.futureofthebook.org

Questions for Exploring Multimedia on the Web

As you explore, consider these questions:

1. What can you find out about the purpose of the site (or project)—is it an exhibition, a journal, a commercial, a political ad?
2. What software technologies were used to create the multimedia? (Choose View>Source from your browser's menu bar to look at the HTML code, which sometimes shows what plug-ins a page requires, and thus what software was used to create it.) An inspection of the code reprinted here reveals that the "Visual Rhetoric" issue of the journal *Enculturation* (http://enculturation.gmu.edu/3_2/) uses a Macromedia Flash movie.

```
<p align="left"><object
classid="clsid:D27CDB6E-AE6D-11cf-96B8-
444553540000"
codebase="http://download.macromedia.com/
pub/shockwave/cabs/flash/swflash.cab#versio
n=4,0,2,0" width="590" height="393"
align="top">
<param name=movie value="VisRhe.swf">
<param name=quality value=high>
<param name="LOOP" value="false">
```

3. Does it appear that the multimedia content was developed from "the ground up," or has it been added to existing content?
4. How would you describe the reading/viewing experience?
5. What do you think projects like these are really about? (Suppose that they are not about the most obvious thing, but something more subtle.)

PART 7

Making Choices about Style

New Contexts for Writing

826 Valencia is the name of a public literacy project in San Francisco that focuses on helping students from 8 to 18 develop their writing ability by providing free tutoring, workshops, storytelling sessions, field trips, and facilities. It has become much more than that, however. It has become the catalyst for launching similar sites across the nation, with 826s now in Ann Arbor, Chicago, Los Angeles, New York City, and Seattle. Tutors, even some famous writers now and then, volunteer their time to help the young writers. Workshop topics include writing for the Web, filmmaking, bookmaking, and more.

Service learning projects in college involve students in working with clients, nonprofit agencies, and other community organizations on real projects that make a difference in people's lives.

Engagement is a movement among those in higher education to become partners in the wider community's cultural and social life. When you learn to apply your talents as a writer in contexts outside of the classroom, the rhetorical situation takes on added urgency. You are no longer writing merely for a grade (an important goal, of course); you are writing to and with people whose lives may change because of what you say. When you help others learn to write, you become a better writer yourself and have the satisfaction of knowing that you might have made someone else's life a little better.

826 Valencia

826 VALENCIA

Tutoring

Workshops

826 Valencia helps students, ages 8–18, w their writing skills, in the realm of creat writing, expository writing, or English a second language.

Field Trips

The idea for 826 Valencia was originally hatched and supported by Nínive Calegari and Dave Eggers, the author of *A Heartbreaking Work of Staggering Genius* and the co-founder of McSweeney's, which now publishes a literary and DVD magazine, books, a website, 826 Valencia student projects, and more. Eggers and Calegari, as well as many generous volunteers, have inspired others to join in, so plans to develop more 826 sites are in the works. College students can volunteer their time as tutors, writers, Web designers, and hardware specialists at 826 sites, and they might even organize efforts to start an 826 site in their own community.

What Can *You* Do?

Organize a student group project that helps a nonprofit organization build a website or weblog; make a brochure for a community organization; find out how you can volunteer in a local literacy campaign; ask your instructor what opportunities exist for you to tutor and mentor others; or even help launch a new 826 site.

826 and Related Sites on the Web

826 Valencia: http://www.826valencia.org
826NYC: http://www.826nyc.org
826LA: http://www.826la.com
826 Chicago: http://www.826chicago.org
826 Michigan: http://www.826michigan.org
826 Seattle: http://www.826seattle.org
The Pirate Supply Store: http://www.826valencia.org/store
McSweeney's Internet Tendency: http://www.mcsweeneys.net

33

SENTENCES IN CONTEXT

Try to imagine what an idea is like before it takes shape as a sentence or some other kind of symbolic representation (such as musical notes or a drawing). What does an idea feel like in your mind? Answering that question might not be as easy as it might seem, even though everyone has had ideas and most people share them all the time. Prior to the imposition of *some* formal pattern, ideas are like pre-formed thoughts in a molten state, unexplainable feelings, desires, or attitudes. They are pure potential, like seeds drifting in the wind, looking for fertile soil and water.

The challenge you face as a writer is to bring your ideas to fruition in good sentences that give them content and context for readers. The content of an idea consists of words that are signs pointing to things or to other words. The context of an idea is the situation that makes these words meaningful to readers who have experiences in common with the writer. When writers cast their ideas into sentences, they give them shape, a recognizable form that others can imagine and remember. Until shaped into sentences, ideas are shadows.

Sentences are the basic units of a language for expressing ideas. In the narrowest sense, ideas are relationships among things and representations of things (objects, actions, people, and so on). In this chapter, you will learn how to shape your ideas into effective, clear, and readable sentences. Good sentences are the lifeblood of good writing.

If you were baffled in grade school by the saying "A sentence is a complete thought," you are not alone. How do you decide if a thought is complete? Is a question ever complete? Is a question a sentence?

Fortunately, there are easier ways to understand what a sentence is. A sentence is *a string of words that obey the grammatical rules of a language.* Sentences are *grammatically complete,* meaning that they don't need any more words to make an assertion, state a fact, ask a question, or exclaim. Sentences can stand alone and make sense, or they can be combined with other sentences into larger units, such as paragraphs. In English, there may be well-formed sentences (ones that obey the rules of the language and make sense) and badly formed sentences (ones that obey the rules but don't make sense to anyone).

An Experiment for Deciding What Constitutes a Complete Thought

Here's an interesting experiment: If you approach someone and utter an incomplete or badly formed sentence or question, that person will spontaneously either

- look at you quizzically or
- ask what linguists call a "*wh-* question."

If you walk up to your friend and say, "The sun is . . . ," your friend will likely respond, "The sun is what?" Or if you say, "Do you know . . .?" she will ask, "Do I know what?" or "What are you talking about?" Commonly, a well-formed, complete sentence prompts the listener to speak more original sentences, but a badly formed or ungrammatical sentence prompts the listener to ask a question about the sentence itself.

Activity 33-1: Experimenting with Groups of Words

Suppose your friend came up to you and uttered the words in each of the following items. What would be your response in each case? What does your response indicate about the completeness and appropriateness of the word groups?

1. Will scientists ever be able to solve this problem?
2. Because she wanted to know.
3. The hurricane slammed into the island.
4. Finding the answer.
5. After the dance was over.

A sentence can be ill formed but clear

Sometimes sentences that might not make sense by themselves work quite well because of their context. For example, the first sentence ever uttered on the moon—"That's one small step for man, one giant leap for mankind"—doesn't quite make sense because the speaker, Neil Armstrong, left out the indefinite article *a*. Without it, if we interpret *man* as a pseudo-generic noun meaning "humanity," his sentence seems to say, "That's one small step for humanity, one giant leap for humanity," which is a contradiction.

What Armstrong meant to say was "That's one small step for *a* man [Neil Armstrong], one giant leap for mankind." Nevertheless, his sentence—well formed or not—did the trick. It was a grand pronouncement on a solemn occasion. If he had said "That last step was a doozy!" you can imagine how quickly his words would have been erased from the annals of history.

Good sentences are effective sentences. They take many forms, but they share these qualities:

- They are purposeful and timely—they are well suited to the rhetorical occasion.
- They are well suited to the ideas they represent. Simple ideas often require simple sentences; complex ideas may require more complex sentences.
- They express meaning that affects readers in ways the writer intended.
- Taken together, good sentences accomplish rhetorical goals such as teaching, persuading, delighting, cajoling, reporting, moving, and so on.

There is no ideal form for sentences—no definite structure that only the best sentences have—so crafting a good sentence is a slightly different experience each time you manage to do it. Sentences that are well formed grammatically may be ineffective nevertheless. You've probably had the experience of uttering sentences you wished you could withdraw after you saw the look on your friends' faces. Grammatically the sentences were probably fine, but rhetorically they were inept.

For something we read to be *clear,* we need to understand it. If we don't understand the meaning of a sentence, we say it is unclear. Once we understand it, however—perhaps have an "aha!" reaction or gather more information—it may become clear. Clarity, then, cannot be an intrinsic aspect of a sentence since sentences can be unclear one minute and clear the next, even though the words themselves or their order doesn't change. What changes to make a previously unclear sentence suddenly clear is the *context.* If you gain more knowledge, you become a different reader, however slightly, and your new awareness enables you to see with clarity where before there was confusion. The context (or situation) in which you read the sentence has changed.

When someone asks you to write clear sentences, he or she may not mean simple "short sentences," but sentences that are grammatical and meaningful in a given situation. Many grammatical, short sentences that make absolutely no sense are written all the time. (They are called *non sequiturs.*) There are also many long, complex sentences that make perfect sense because they are both grammatical and meaningful.

A sentence can be unclear but grammatical

The linguist Noam Chomsky used the following sentence to demonstrate that a sentence can be grammatical but meaningless and unclear:

> Colorless green ideas sleep furiously.

This sentence has a subject (*ideas*) and verb (*sleep*) and meets all the other criteria of a grammatical sentence. But it seems nonsensical. How can colorless ideas be green? If they're sleeping, how can they do that furiously? How can ideas sleep in the first place? And so on. But watch what happens when we create a context for such a sentence:

> Sometimes people come up with ideas that previously lay dormant in memory until the right situation comes along to spark them into awareness. Usually, such ideas lack flavor or color because they are empty of context or content. They are green—meaning "new" or "fresh"—when they are stirred by interesting situations or experiences. You could say that until that time, they sleep peacefully in the mind. They begin to stir as these new situations agitate them. It's not that hard to imagine that *colorless green ideas sleep furiously* until they are shaken and stirred, when that fury takes shape in a new sentence.

The additional sentences give enough context for Chomsky's nonsense sentence (in italics) that it's no longer impossible to imagine what it could mean; the sentence becomes clear in context.

The Five Principles of Readability

Readability is the general ease with which readers can understand and remember sentences. The words we choose affect readability, and so do our sentence structures, or style. Following the five principles of readability may help you communicate more effectively. These principles are not "rules" but general guidelines to follow unless circumstances demand some alternative. You should have a good reason for deviating from these principles.

1. Use an agent/action style.
2. Keep agent and action close together.
3. Put modifiers close to the words they modify.
4. When possible, put people in the agent position in a sentence.
5. Put old information first and new or most important information last.

Each principle is discussed in the following pages of this chapter. Chapters 34–39 then discuss these and related matters in detail.

Here is a sentence using the natural word order of English:

	S V O
Agent/action	John hit the ball. [This order is called the active voice.]

And here is a transformation of the natural order:

	O V S		O V
Action/agent	The ball was hit by John.	or	The ball was hit.
	[This order is called the passive voice.]		

The sentence with the O-V-S word order is a transformation of the natural word order that English grammar allows, but it makes more demands on readers, who must translate it into something like "John performed a hitting action on the ball." In the brief moment it takes the reader to gain clarity, some readability is lost. As the number of passive sentences in a passage increases, readability declines.

Whether readers understand a piece of writing obviously depends on many factors:

- the amount of background information they have about the subject (including the meaning of particular terms)
- their motivation for understanding it (i.e., we have to interest readers in what we have to say)
- their knowledge of the customs of the discourse community being addressed, including genre conventions and linguistic norms (spelling, syntax, punctuation)

Readers also must remember what they read and maintain their concentration as they translate our words into ideas and mental images.

Use an Agent/Action Style

Sentences that follow the natural word order of English (subject-verb-object, or S-V-O) can be understood more readily than can transformations of that order. In addition, readers understand sentences better when the verb is an action and the agent performing the action precedes it.

Keep Agent and Action Close Together

Sentences are easy to understand when the reader doesn't have to hold important information suspended while reading other words that come between the subject and the verb.

Put Modifiers Close to the Words They Modify

Group the information in your sentences into logical chunks so that readers can take in the whole chunk at once. For example, a noun may have some words that modify it: *the slightly balding, stooped* **man.** A verb may collect some modifiers: ***saw*** *quickly out of the corner of his eye.* Be sure to keep all the related words together.

When Possible, Put People in the Agent Position

It's easier to understand a sentence when a person or a character is performing an action than when the agent is an abstraction: ***Alexander*** *likes tennis* versus ***Socialism*** *is losing ground.*

Agent and action kept close together are easy to understand

Easier to understand	Knowing that her team depended on her, **Joan hit** the ball.
Harder to understand	**Joan,** knowing that her team depended on her, **hit** the ball.

The subject and verb are the two most important words in an English sentence. In the first sentence, they are close together, and the sentence is easy to understand. In the second sentence, the reader has to hold the thought of "Joan" suspended while awaiting the verb. This decreases readability.

Words and their modifiers kept close together are easy to understand

Here, the modifier is in italics and the word that it modifies is in bold:

Easiest to understand	*Feeling satisfaction for the first time in his miserable life,* **Fred** caught the ball that was hit.
Harder to understand	**Fred** caught the ball that was hit, *feeling satisfaction for the first time in his miserable life.*
Hardest to understand	Fred caught **the ball,** feeling satisfaction for the first time in his miserable life, *that was hit.*

Can you see how readability declines with each move away from keeping all the related words together as one chunk?

When people are agents, sentences are easy to understand

Easier to understand	Hitchcock implicates the viewer in Norman's Oedipal guilt.
Harder to understand	Hitchcock's implication is that the viewer shares Norman's Oedipal guilt.

Note here that the second sentence needs *is that* because the subject of the sentence is a noun phrase—*Hitchcock's implication* rather than *Hitchcock.* In the first sentence, not only is a person the agent, but the verb *implicates* conveys both that an implication is being made and that the implication involves some kind of sharing.

Help readers build their knowledge by giving old information first

Easier to understand:

> The Cassini spacecraft has beamed images back to NASA and ESA scientists, who now ask some astonishing questions about *the nature of Saturn's rings*. Once believed to be heated gases, Saturn's rings are composed of *dust, rocks, and crystalline ice that give clues to the nature of planetary formation*. If scientists can understand how frozen water became suspended in orbit around Saturn, they may be able to solve the *mystery of the migration of water through the solar system and thus the origins of life itself*.

Notice in the paragraph above how the new information (italicized) begins subsequent sentences as old information (underlined).

Harder to understand:

> The Cassini spacecraft has beamed images back to NASA and ESA scientists, who now ask some astonishing questions about *the nature of Saturn's rings*. *Dust, rocks, and crystalline ice give clues to the nature of planetary formation* and compose Saturn's rings, not heated gases. *The mystery of the migration of water through the solar system and thus the origins of life itself can be solved by understanding how* frozen water became suspended in orbit around Saturn.

Notice here how the second and third sentences begin with new information, which not only makes the passage read awkwardly but also taxes short-term memory.

Activity 33-2: Revising for Readability in Your Own Writing

Choose a recent piece of your writing. Does each sentence meet the five principles of readability? For any sentence that does not, consider whether revising it to meet the principles would improve the writing. Make any revisions you think would improve the sentences. What effect do your revisions have on your previous draft? Have you been able to make your revision easier to read? What did you do to make it easier to read for your audience?

Put Old Information First and New or Important Information Last

Suppose you are reading along and a woman's name, *Marcie,* appears. In the next sentence, you read the word *she,* and you understand that the writer is talking about *Marcie*. On first mention, *Marcie* was new information. By the next sentence, *Marcie* is old information, and thus the writer can refer to her as *she* with confidence. The same pattern holds true in general when people are reading. As they read each sentence, they build up a body of knowledge about the topic. What used to be new information becomes old information. A sentence that refers first to old information (as in the use of *she*) creates a bridge for readers to the new information.

34

PARALLELISM

Parallelism is one of the writer's most powerful tools for creating effective and eloquent sentences. At the most basic level, parallelism improves clarity. At a more advanced level, parallelism can also be used to create emphasis, rhythm, and grace. Writers use parallelism to draw the reader's attention, direct the flow of thought, relate ideas to one another, and give their writing stylistic power.

34a Understanding Parallelism

Parallel constructions hook up the same parts of speech in the same patterns: verbs with verbs, nouns with nouns, prepositional phrases with prepositional phrases, and so on. Even within these various categories, effective parallel construction requires matching of like with like—for example, pairing a gerund (an *-ing* verb form that functions as a noun) with another gerund, rather than with another kind of noun.

Examples of Parallelism

Martin Luther King Jr. used parallel words to highlight contrasts:

> Injustice anywhere is a threat to justice everywhere.

Abraham Lincoln wove parallel phrases throughout his famous Gettysburg Address; here is one instance:

> . . . and that this government of the people, by the people, for the people shall not perish from the earth.

Jim Bob Tinsley used parallel noun clauses to create a list in this excerpt from *He Was Singin' This Song:*

> Credit for saving [the cowboy song "Goodbye Old Paint"] from obscurity must be given to three Texans: a cowboy who sang it on trail drives, a cowboy who remembered it, and a college professor who put it down on paper.

Example 1 Parallelism in coordinated words, phrases, and clauses

Faulty — Cow power dairies **produce** milk and **are also generating** electricity.

Parallel — Cow power dairies **produce** milk and **generate** electricity.

Faulty — It may have been **a well-intended research design with a *clear* hypothesis,** but **the research design also needed more attention to formulation of a *significant* hypothesis.**

Parallel — It may have been **a well-intended research design with a *clear* hypothesis,** but it was **one with an *insignificant* hypothesis.**

Example 2 Parallelism with correlatives

Faulty — Neither **exercising** nor **to diet** appealed to him.

Parallel — Neither **exercising** nor **dieting** appealed to him.

Faulty — Whether it's **baseball players taking steroids to boost Major League performance** or **when students take Ritalin for improving SAT scores,** America has a drug problem.

Parallel — Whether it's **baseball players who take steroids to boost Major League performance** or **students who take Ritalin to improve SAT scores,** America has a drug problem.

Conjunctions should be placed logically

Make sure that conjunctions are placed logically to express the idea of the comparison you want to communicate.

Faulty — Buying cow power **supports not only** the development of renewable energy **but also reduces** pollution by turning waste into wealth.

Logical — Buying cow power **not only supports** the development of renewable energy **but also reduces** pollution by turning waste into wealth.

Buying cow power supports **not only the development of** renewable energy **but also the reduction of** agriculture-derived pollution.

Sentence elements—words, phrases, clauses—that are linked with coordinating conjunctions such as *and* and *or* need to be in parallel grammatical form. So do elements linked with pairs of correlative conjunctions such as *either . . . or.* When the word *than* or *as* is used to make a comparison, the items being compared need to be parallel.

Using Parallelism with Coordinating Conjunctions

Coordinating conjunctions—*and, or, not, for, but, yet, so*—signal a need for parallelism. One way to improve your sentence style is to look at sentence elements joined by a coordinating conjunction to see whether you've put them into parallel form.

Using Parallelism with Correlative Conjunctions

Correlative conjunctions also signal a need for parallelism. When revising, check sentences that use *both . . . and, either . . . or, neither . . . nor, not . . . but, not only . . . but also, just as . . . so, whether . . . or,* and similar constructions to see that parallel elements are treated in a parallel fashion.

Using Parallelism with *than* or *as*

Constructions using *than* or *as* to make comparisons require parallel treatment of the ideas being compared.

Repeating Function Words in Parallel Constructions

Be consistent in deciding whether to repeat function words, such as prepositions (*by, for, in, near, of, with*), articles (*a, an, the*), and the infinitive *to,* in parallel constructions. Whether or not you repeat function words is a matter of style. In some sentences, repeating a function word in a parallel construction adds emphasis and contributes to greater clarity; in others, such repetition just clogs things up. Inconsistency in including or excising these tiny words in a single sentence, however, is a grammatical and stylistic lapse.

The same rule about consistency applies to subordinating conjunctions (such as *after, although, while, since, because)* and to relative pronouns (such as *who, which, that*) in parallel constructions.

Example 3 Parallelism in comparisons

Faulty	Roger is as interested in **studying philosophy** as **to work.**
Parallel	Roger is as interested in **studying philosophy** as in **working.**
Faulty	In an ideal world, elected leaders would find **good government** more important than **getting reelected.**
Parallel	In an ideal world, elected leaders would find **governing wisely** more important than **getting reelected.**
	In an ideal world, elected leaders would find **good government** more important than **reelection.**

Be consistent when deciding whether or not to repeat function words

Inconsistent	While visiting temples in India, you will be expected **to remove** shoes and any leather items before entering, **dress** conservatively (women should ideally cover their heads), **stay out** of unauthorized areas, and **to ask** permission before photographing buildings, symbols of deities, or people.
Consistent	While visiting temples in India, you will be expected **to remove** shoes and any leather items before entering, **to dress** conservatively (women should ideally cover their heads), **to stay out** of unauthorized areas, and **to ask** permission before photographing buildings, symbols of deities, or people.

Be consistent when deciding whether or not to repeat other elements

Inconsistent	The child who is **nurtured, respected, who is listened to,** and **faces appropriate challenges** will develop self-confidence. The child **who is neglected, who is shamed, ignored, or is inappropriately coddled** will find his or her self-confidence undermined.
Consistent	The child who is **nurtured, respected, listened to,** and **appropriately challenged** will develop self-confidence. The child who is **neglected, shamed, ignored,** or **inappropriately coddled** will find his or her self-confidence undermined.

34b

Make sure all necessary function words are present

Unclear — The Supreme Court maintained its earlier position **by not hearing** the case and **returning** the matter to local jurisdiction. [Whether or not the matter was returned to local jurisdiction is unclear.]

Clear — The Supreme Court maintained its earlier position **by not hearing** the case and **by returning** the matter to local jurisdiction.

Unclear — Our dream is to sail to a tropical island near Tahiti or the Isle of Wight. [Is part of the dream sailing to a tropical island near the Isle of Wight, in which case the writer needs to check a map, or sailing to the Isle of Wight itself?]

Clear — Our dream is to sail **to** a tropical island near Tahiti or **to** the Isle of Wight.

In some sentences, omitting a function word can make a sentence unclear and thus incomplete. Be on the lookout for sentences in which function words must be included for clear communication.

Parallelism with Lists and Headings 34c

Faulty in first draft:

Guidelines for Participating in Email Discussion Lists

1. There should be no private messages.
2. Keep on topic by preserving the message thread.
3. Signatures are appropriate to identify yourself.
4. Responding promptly to others helps the discussion along.

Parallel in second draft:

Guidelines for Participating in Email Discussion Lists

1. **Send** private messages to the individual, not to the list.
2. **Keep** on topic to preserve the message thread.
3. **Use** a signature to identify yourself.
4. **Respond** promptly to keep the discussion lively.

The items in formal lists and outlines and the headings in a paper should be parallel in structure. See section 4h for sample outlines.

In the list to the left, notice how clarity improves when the items are made parallel.

The headings to the right are from a paper entitled "*Northanger Abbey* as Satire."

Faulty headings in first draft:	Parallel headings in second draft:
Jane Austen Pokes Fun at the Gothic Novel	The Gothic Novel Mocked
Some of the Gothic Elements Used in *Northanger Abbey*	Elements of the Gothic in *Northanger Abbey*
How Catherine Morland Is Like a Typical Gothic Heroine	Catherine Morland as Gothic Heroine
Seeing Catherine Morland as Herself	Catherine Morland as Herself

Activity 34-1: Revising Sentences for Parallelism

Revise each of the following sentences to make parallel the elements joined by a coordinating conjunction, a correlative conjunction, or *than* or *as*.

1. Opinions are divided as to whether children imitate television or are behaving in ways innate to human nature.
2. Unsurprisingly, most children are more interested in watching shows with action and adventure than to watch informational or educational shows.
3. It has been shown that both children who watch a lot of television and infrequent watchers of television can be affected by what they see.
4. Neither banning violence from television nor children being forbidden to watch certain television shows will completely eliminate the effects of media violence on society.
5. A solution to the problem must protect children from inappropriate content yet adults should be allowed content appropriate for them.

Activity 34-2: Revising Paragraphs for Parallelism

Revise the following paragraphs until no parallelism errors remain and the ideas are expressed clearly.

1. Whether they're from the fifth century or hailing from the nineteenth century, historical figures have become very popular detectives. Novelists such as Jane Austen and the author Charles Dickens both play detective in recent novels by other writers. Meanwhile, the Judge Dee novels offer a fictional look at ancient China, while presenting monastery life are the Brother Cadfael and Dame Frevisse books. Cicero assists in ancient Rome, and helping to solve mysteries in Ireland is Sister Fidelma. Authors seem to write more medieval mysteries than writing other time periods. Still, there are historical mysteries in almost every time period and located in every part of the world.
2. Toxic droppings from seabirds in the Arctic may explain mysterious and dangerous levels of pollutants in northern coastal ecosystems. The finding could help at-risk native communities create hunting strategies and in learning to modify their lifestyles to avoid risk. For years, environmental chemists have been watching as toxic chemicals—mercury, dioxins and polychlorinated biphenyls (PCBs)—accumulate in Arctic air, soils, presenting themselves in the water, and existing in people and animals. Neither being exposed to the air nor to swim in the ocean would cause the varying concentrations observed by scientists.

Activity 34-3: Revising for Parallelism in Your Own Writing

Print out a copy of a piece of writing you are working on, and set it aside. On screen, review your writing for parallel words, phrases, clauses, and sentences. Examine it a second time to identify any sentences that might benefit from parallelism. Using the methods outlined in this chapter, make revisions for parallelism and any other revisions you think strengthen the piece. Print out a copy of this version. Give both versions to a classmate. Discuss the effect that your revisions have on the clarity of the piece.

35

"Only connect," the epigrammatic theme from E. M. Forster's novel *Howard's End,* could well be the motto of every effective writer. Effective writing connects ideas and images and moves them forward. Among the writer's principal tools for connecting ideas within a sentence (and for advancing ideas from one sentence to another) are the various ways of coordinating or subordinating clauses, phrases, and words and of using transitional phrases. Coordination and subordination clarify the relationships between ideas, while also providing different possibilities for adding emphasis, varying sentence construction, and adjusting rhythm to more strongly present your point of view.

Coordination shows readers that related ideas are roughly equal in importance. When you use coordination, check to be sure that the two clauses, phrases, or words are written in parallel form (see Chapter 34). Subordination indicates that one idea is more important than the other.

Examples of Coordination and Subordination

Coordinated words:	The work was **hot** and **slow.** [adjective + adjective]
Coordinated phrases:	A cowboy **might find** himself out of work in the winter and **would go** from ranch to ranch looking for a job or a meal. [verb phrase + verb phrase]
Coordinated independent clauses:	**The Royal Governor recalled Randolph,** so **Jefferson went in his place.** [Each independent clause has its own subject-verb pair.]
One clause subordinated to the other:	When the Royal Governor recalled Randolph, Jefferson went in his place. [No longer grammatically parallel because the word *when* changes the first clause from independent to dependent]

First draft: Unconnected sentences in need of direction

Thomas Jefferson is the author of the Declaration of Independence. Jefferson was not considered an effective public speaker. He was a tall awkward man. He was not Virginia's first choice for the Continental Congress. The Virginia delegate was to have been Payton Randolph. Randolph was the Speaker of the Virginia House and had been reelected as President of the Continental Congress. Randolph was recalled by the Royal Governor and Jefferson went in his place. Jefferson was 33. He was so quiet that John Adams described him as the "silent member" of the Continental Congress. The committee called to draft the declaration was made up of Jefferson, John Adams, Benjamin Franklin, Robert R. Livingston, and Roger Sherman. The Declaration of Independence is the most important historical document in America. The Declaration of Independence is one of the most important documents in Western civilization. The Declaration of Independence is one of the most masterfully written documents in Western civilization. Most Americans agree with these statements.

Second draft: Focused paragraph with directions that help readers follow the argument

Today we consider the Declaration of Independence one of the most important documents in American history—indeed, one of the most important and most masterfully written documents in Western civilization. Yet Thomas Jefferson, the Declaration's primary author, was not even Virginia's first choice for the Second Continental Congress. The Virginia delegate was to have been Payton Randolph, Speaker of the Virginia House, who had been reelected as the Congress's president. When the Royal Governor recalled Randolph, Jefferson went in his place. He was 33. Though an awkward public speaker (and so quiet as to be described by John Adams as "the silent member" of the Continental Congress), Jefferson was acknowledged as a forceful writer. When the Continental Congress appointed a five-man committee to draft a declaration formally announcing the colonies' break from Great Britain, the committee—made up of Jefferson, Adams, Benjamin Franklin, Robert R. Livingston, and Roger Sherman—chose Jefferson to write the document.

The context for most sentences is the paragraph. Consider the first draft of the paragraph to the left. Do you find it clear or confusing? Why?

The sentences in this paragraph do little more than list a string of facts, leaving the reader utterly confused as to the purpose of the information. Such paragraphs—grammatically correct but rhetorically ineffective—are an unfinished connect-the-dots picture. The reader is left staring at the dots, but no picture emerges.

Coordination and subordination offer two methods of connecting the dots.

- Coordination emphasizes that the clauses, phrases, or words joined are rhetorically and logically equivalent. To join two independent clauses into a compound sentence, use a comma and a coordinating conjunction or use a semicolon.
- Subordination highlights one clause and suppresses another. To join an independent clause and a dependent clause to create a complex sentence, use a subordinating conjunction or a relative pronoun.

When rewriting a paragraph with disconnected ideas, you should be guided by your purpose for writing. The second draft shows one possible rewrite that relies mostly on subordination.

Activity 35-1: Comparing the Drafts

Reread four or five sentences from the first draft on page 737, and then locate them (or their revisions) in the second draft. Compare them, noting differences in sentence order, word order, and punctuation. What revisions were made? Which ones seem the most important for helping the reader understand the writer's thoughts? Why? What story does the revised paragraph tell that is concealed in the first draft?

35b Forming Compound Sentences

A compound sentence is formed by connecting two independent clauses with a comma and a coordinating conjunction or with a semicolon.

Using a Comma and a Coordinating Conjunction

The most common way to form compound sentences is to link two independent clauses with a comma and a coordinating conjunction: *and, but, yet, or, nor, for,* or *so.* These conjunctions have different meanings and function differently within a sentence:

and suggests addition or sequence
but and *yet* suggest contrast
or and *nor* suggest choice or alternatives
for suggests causes
so suggests effects or consequences

Example 1 Creating compound sentences by using coordinating conjunctions

Notice the comma that always precedes the coordinating conjunction in a compound sentence.

Addition vs. contrast:

Addition	Some dogs like to swim, **and** some dogs like to race in the snow.
Contrast	Some dogs like to race in the snow, **but** others prefer to snooze by the fire.

Two kinds of contrast:

Dogs can be pets, **but** dogs can also be workers.
Many dogs are workers, **yet** even workers need love and praise.

Addition vs. choice:

Addition	Train a large dog to be obedient, **and** it becomes a happy member of the family. Leave it untrained, **and** it becomes a nuisance and a danger.
Choice	Either a large dog is trained to be a happy and obedient member of the family, **or** it is left untrained and becomes a nuisance and a danger.

Addition vs. effect:

Addition	Border collies love to work, **and** most seem happier gathering sheep than playing with small children.
Effect	Border collies have a zealous drive to run, work, and herd, **so** it's better to keep them as working dogs than as family pets.

Activity 35-2: Choosing Logical Coordinating Conjunctions

In the following paragraph, select the more appropriate coordinating conjunction from each pair given in brackets.

In July 1942, magazines all across the United States displayed the U.S. flag on their covers. The publishers felt that the display was a way to demonstrate loyalty to the war effort, [and/but] the display had another meaning to the government. The U.S. government used the display to help boost morale, [and/so] government officials also hoped that the display would lead to the sale of more war bonds. The United States Flag Association selected ten judges to evaluate the five hundred entries, [for/nor] the display was also part of a contest among the editors. *House and Garden* magazine was awarded the cross of honor [and/nor] received hundreds of requests for cover reproductions.

Be precise when you choose which coordinating conjunction to use in forming a compound sentence. An imprecise choice can result in a vague sentence; an incorrect choice can result in a nonsensical one.

Example 2 Creating compound sentences by using a semicolon

Payton Randolph was recalled by the Royal Governor; the 33-year-old Jefferson went in his place.

As responsible custodians of the land, we must consume less fossil fuel; as responsible citizens of our country, we're told, we must use more plastic.

Using Semicolons

You can also create compound sentences by using a semicolon to join the independent clauses. This option works best to balance two short, direct statements that are closely parallel. Joining two independent clauses with only a semicolon is also effective when you want to use rhythm to create emphasis. The semicolon keeps the sentence shorter, which makes the rhythm sharp.

Activity 35-3: Combining Sentences with Coordination

Combine each pair of sentences using coordination. Be sure to use a comma before each coordinating conjunction.

1. Over the years, math teachers have used various aids to help students grasp abstract concepts. These devices have included the abacus, the slide rule, and the calculator.
2. In the nineteenth century, teachers wrote examples on blackboards. Students used slates to work out problems.
3. Teachers also used arithmetic charts. Students often preferred to use models and blocks to learn geometry instead of charts.
4. In the early twentieth century, math educators believed that students could better learn to graph using "squared lines." Graph paper was introduced to provide a way for students to work out mathematical problems.

Two common problems arise in creating compound sentences:

- excessive coordination
- illogical coordination

Excessive coordination occurs when you string too many independent clauses together, thus obscuring the logical relationships between thoughts. Faced with a muddle of loosely connected clauses, the reader doesn't see any formal relationship among ideas. The ideas simply pile up. Illogical coordination occurs when you either choose the wrong conjunction to support your meaning or yoke together two independent clauses that have no logical relationship.

Revising Excessive Coordination

First draft

Coordinating conjunctions between independent clauses are highlighted.

> The great cattle drives lasted but a few decades, yet the mythology of the cowboy remains one of the most compelling in American life, but most cowboys were far from the dashing heroes of film and television and more like what some have described as "the proletariat of the prairie." So what most cowboys' lives were really like is captured in such songs as "The Dreary, Dreary Life" and "The Old Chisholm Trail" and that life was mostly hard work and poor pay. For most cowboys earned on average a dollar a day and the work was seasonal and jobs were scarce.

Second draft

> The great cattle drives lasted but a few decades, yet the mythology of the cowboy remains one of the most compelling in American life. Most cowboys, though, were far from the dashing heroes of film and television and more like what some have described as "the proletariat of the prairie." What most cowboys' lives were really like is captured in such songs as "The Dreary, Dreary Life" and "The Old Chisholm Trail": hard work and poor pay. Most cowboys earned on average a dollar a day. The work was seasonal; jobs were scarce.

Example 3 Revising illogical coordination

Illogical	The great cattle drives lasted only a few decades, and the mythology of the cowboy remains one of the most compelling in American life.
Revised	The great cattle drives lasted only a few decades, yet the mythology of the cowboy remains one of the most compelling in American life.
Vague	The big cattle drives were seasonal, and cowboys were often out of work in the winter.
Revised	The big cattle drives were seasonal, so cowboys were often out of work in the winter.

Activity 35-4: Revising Faulty Coordination

Revise the paragraph that follows to remove excessive and illogical coordination. Rewrite it on a separate piece of paper, and exchange papers with a classmate. Discuss any differences you find.

The earliest method of voting was with ballot boxes, and the paper ballots listed names from just one party, yet these ballots were called party tickets. So ballot boxes and their ballots improved over time and other voting methods emerged as new technologies developed. Machines were used to capture votes and these machines proved to be faster and more secure than ballot boxes for security problems still existed. In the mid-twentieth century, computers changed the face of voting again for now people could fill out ballots with a number two pencil and these ballots would be read by a computer. Today, people cast their votes using computers by touching screens and they may yearn for the paper ballot again.

Forming Complex Sentences 35d

When you want to combine two simple sentences into a complex sentence, consider carefully which of the two ideas you want to highlight and which you want to suppress, which you want to make more important and which you want to make less so. In terms of grammatical structure, this means placing the idea you want to highlight, the more important idea, in the independent clause and the idea you want to suppress, the less important idea, in the dependent clause. Depending on your topic, the contrast in meaning can be subtle or substantial. The choice of which thought to emphasize and which to de-emphasize is entirely up to you, the writer.

Example 4 Combining two sentences with subordination

Jefferson was **an awkward public speaker.**
Jefferson was acknowledged as **an eloquent and forceful writer.**

Revision emphasizing Jefferson's skill as a writer:

DEPENDENT CLAUSE / INDEPENDENT CLAUSE

Although he was an awkward public speaker, Jefferson was acknowledged as an eloquent and forceful writer. [Notice the comma that follows the dependent clause when it precedes the independent clause. If the independent clause comes first, no comma is needed.]

Revision emphasizing Jefferson's awkwardness as a public speaker:

DEPENDENT CLAUSE / INDEPENDENT CLAUSE

Although he was acknowledged as an eloquent and forceful writer, Jefferson was an awkward public speaker.

Revision more strongly de-emphasizing Jefferson's awkwardness as a speaker:

APPOSITIVE (A PHRASE, NOT A CLAUSE)

Jefferson, an awkward public speaker, was acknowledged as an eloquent and forceful writer. [This sentence is not a complex sentence because it has only one subject-verb pair.]

35d

Using Subordinating Conjunctions

Be careful to choose the subordinating conjunction that best conveys the relationship you want to establish between the two ideas in a complex sentence. Subordinating conjunctions include *although, whereas, whether, because, since, while, even if, unless, wherever, after, before,* and *as.* (See page 806 for a more extensive list of subordinating conjunctions.)

Subordinating Conjunctions Indicate a Variety of Relationships

Comparison or contrast

Although most huskies need to be penned up or kept on a lead, my dog Bert never strays from my yard.

Rather than dashing into the next county, Bert just sits there and sniffs and waits for the squirrels.

Bert always stays put, **whereas** Champ takes off in a second if given half a chance.

Cause or effect

I made Champ the lead dog **because** he's faster, smarter, and stronger than all the others.

I let Bert chase squirrels **so that** he won't chase cats.

Since Bert is so happy being lazy, I just let him be.

Concession

I love my old mutt Bert, **even though** all he does is snooze by the fire.

Champ won't quit racing **even if** he's cold, hungry, and exhausted.

Condition

I love my husky Champ **whether** he wins or loses.
When he wins, I feed him raw steak. **When** he loses, he gets hamburger.
If I let Champ run loose, even for a second, he runs away.
Whenever Champ runs away, it takes hours to find him.

Time

After racing all day in the snow, Champ takes a nap.
While he's racing, Champ won't stop for anything.
I give him a dog biscuit **whenever** he asks.

Example 5 Subordinating with relative clauses

Bert never met a squirrel **that** he didn't like.

Chasing squirrels, **which** is Bert's favorite hobby, keeps him occupied.

Champ is the dog **who** is in the lead position.

Susan Butcher is the musher **whom** I most admire.

The musher **whose** team is strongest isn't always the one who wins.

In driving the Iditarod, you must be willing to take **whatever** punishment the weather delivers.

The race goes to **whoever** drives the fastest, smartest, and most determined race.

Whomever else she may have inspired with her determination and tenacity, she has certainly inspired me with her will.

Activity 35-5: Combining Sentences with Subordination

Combine each pair of sentences using either a subordinating conjunction or a relative pronoun. If you create a subordinate clause that comes before the independent clause, be sure to put a comma after the subordinate clause.

1. Many coins and denominations of bills have been around since the U.S. Mint was founded. American money has changed substantially over the years.
2. Gold was used in the production of American currency until 1933. The New Deal created by Roosevelt took the country off the gold standard.
3. The Bureau of Engraving and Printing has ceased production of all banknotes larger than the $100 Federal Reserve notes. Credit cards are believed to be safer to carry around than high-denomination banknotes.
4. Gold certificates were used for transfers of money until 1960. They were replaced by electronic transfers of money.
5. Electronic representations of money may replace the traditional bills and coins. Bills and coins still have their staunch admirers.

Using Relative Pronouns

You can also create complex sentences by using one of the relative pronouns.

Relative Pronouns

that	whose
what	whom
whatever	whoever
which	
who	

To decide whether to use a comma with *that* and *which*, see section 48f.

Two common problems arise in creating complex sentences:

- excessive subordination
- illogical subordination

Excessive subordination occurs when you jumble so many ideas into a sentence that the reader can no longer follow your meaning. Illogical subordination can occur when you choose the wrong subordinating conjunction or relative pronoun to support your meaning.

Revising Excessive Subordination

First draft

Subordinating conjunctions and relative pronouns are highlighted.

The Iditarod Trail Sled Dog Race, which officially began in 1973, honors the heroism of the some 20-odd mushers and their teams of dogs who crossed almost 700 miles in 127 hours (about six days) when the trip normally took around three weeks or more when in early 1925 a diphtheria epidemic threatened the isolated town of Nome. Although a Pony Express–type relay of dog teams rushed the serum along its path by far the longest and most treacherous leg was taken by Leonhard Seppala and his lead dog, Togo, who together drove 340 miles total while no other team drove more than 53 during which all dogs and men faced temperatures of around 40 degrees below zero and blizzards of up to 80 mph after which Togo's heroism left him permanently lamed because he never ran another long trip.

Second draft

The Iditarod Trail Sled Dog Race, which officially began in 1973, honors the heroism of the teams of dogs and mushers who in 1925 brought the serum needed to stop a diphtheria epidemic threatening isolated Nome. Some 20-odd mushers and their teams of dogs crossed almost 700 miles in 127 hours (about six days)—a trip that normally took at least three weeks. A Pony Express–type relay of teams rushed the serum along its path, battling temperatures that hovered at around 40 degrees below zero and blizzards of up to 80 miles per hour. By far the longest and most treacherous leg was taken by Leonhard Seppala and his lead dog, Togo, who together drove 340 miles total. No other team drove more than 53. Togo's heroism left him permanently lamed. He never ran another long trip.

Example 6 Revising illogical subordination

Illogical — **Because** the great cattle drives lasted but a few decades, the mythology of the cowboy remains one of the most compelling in American life.

Revised — **Even though** the great cattle drives lasted but a few decades, the mythology of the cowboy remains one of the most compelling in American life.

Example 7 Shifting the emphasis for logic's sake

Illogical	Buck was a greenhorn, **although** he surprised everyone with his skill in breaking broncos.
Revised	**Although** Buck was a greenhorn, he surprised everyone with his skill in breaking broncos.

In many sentences, choosing which clause to make more important (the independent clause) and which to make less important (the dependent clause) is a matter of personal preference. But some sentences become illogical if you place the less important information in the independent clause—that is, if you mistakenly emphasize what needs to be de-emphasized or vice versa.

Activity 35-6: Revising Faulty Subordination

Revise the paragraph that follows to remove excessive and illogical subordination. Rewrite it on a separate piece of paper, and exchange papers with a classmate. Discuss any differences you find.

Diamonds, which have long been considered a girl's best friend, may also be everyone's best friend since they can be used in many applications because they are useful. Many people want to develop synthetic diamond technology because the uses for diamonds are multiplying. One new technique for developing diamonds is chemical vapor deposition, which forms diamonds by a chemical reaction which is much more efficient than other methods for synthesizing then it can be used to create thin and thick layers of diamonds which can be used in microprocessors. The durability and stability of diamonds means that they could be used in an electric car which means that our dependence on fossil fuels could be lessened.

Activity 35-7: Revising Sentences in Your Own Writing

Choose a piece of writing you are working on. Using the methods outlined in this chapter, analyze five sentences in a row. Underline independent clauses in each sentence, and circle dependent clauses. Now consider the ideas in each sentence. Which sentences have a structure that connects particularly well with the meaning? Which sentences could you revise to make the structure more effectively reflect the meaning and logic of your ideas? Revise them. What effect does your revision have on the piece overall?

36

CONCISE SENTENCES

Writing concisely means making every word count. Some sentences need to be longer than others, as some thoughts take more words to express. But often sentences are weighed down by words and phrases that take up space without conveying meaning. Making your writing more concise will also make it livelier. Wordy prose is likely to be unclear, drab, or tedious. Concise prose carries the reader from meaning to meaning with energy, clarity, and purpose.

Sometimes revising for conciseness is simply a matter of spotting problem phrases or sentences. Wordiness often reveals a writer's overall struggle to express ideas. To produce their best prose, effective writers know that they must revise carefully, write and rewrite, draft and redraft. (For a broader discussion of revision strategies, including sentence-level revision methods, see Chapter 6.)

Examples of Making Wordy Sentences Concise

Wordy: Liebman presents the truth <u>in regard to what the experts really think</u> of the Atkins diet.
Concise: Liebman presents the truth about the Atkins diet.

Wordy: The <u>issue of</u> poverty is a big problem in our society <u>today</u>.
Concise: Poverty is a big problem in our society.
Poverty continues to plague us.

Example 1 Revising to make your prose concise

Wordy **Generally—though definitely not always the case—** students' happiness is determined by the friends they make and the social lives they develop.

Concise Students' happiness is determined by the friends they make and the social lives they develop.

Wordy **I know that** spelling and sentence structure are not a prerequisite for Mom's love, but it's still a shame that some people don't have the necessary skills **to use writing in an effective manner.**

Concise Spelling and sentence structure are not a prerequisite for Mom's love, but it's still a shame that some people don't have the necessary skills to write effectively.

Puffy Phrases to Cut

all things considered
as a matter of fact
for all intents and purposes
for the most part
in a manner of speaking
in a very real sense
in the case of
in the final analysis
in the process of
it is a fact that
it is clear/obvious that
it seems that
last but not least
more or less
that exists

Activity 36-1: Revising Puffy Connector Phrases

Revise the following paragraph to remove puffy connector phrases.

In my opinion, it is a fact that the giant Pacific octopus is one of the more intelligent aquatic creatures. For all intents and purposes, the octopus has been able to unscrew jars and more or less navigate mazes. As a matter of fact, it can also imitate other octopuses! It seems that the octopus has the ability to change colors by contracting skin cells filled with pigment. What I mean to say is that last but not least, the octopus is a truly amazing creature.

The editor's slogan "Cut deadwood!" suggests a good place to start revising for conciseness. In the same way a gardener prunes deadwood off a tree to keep it healthy and beautiful, a good editor cuts out words that do little but draw attention away from what matters most. Be on the lookout for these kinds of empty words and phrases:

- overused intensifiers, such as *very, really, definitely, actually*
- vague nouns, such as *factor, kind of, type of, thing*
- puffy connector phrases, such as *in the nature of, as a matter of fact, for all intents and purposes*
- phrases that unnecessarily draw attention to the writer, such as *the point I am making is, I think that, what I'm trying to say is*

Some phrases just need to be shortened. For example, use *although* instead of *in spite of the fact that;* use *because* instead of *by virtue of the fact that.*

How many meaningless words and phrases can you cut from the following sentence? When you have finished, what remains?

My point is that regardless of the fact that for all intents and purposes these types of words and phrases absolutely without a doubt convey little to no meaning, there is absolutely no question that in the very final analysis until such time as each and every writer prunes text more carefully these types of words and phrases will continue in a very real sense without a doubt to create quite extremely weak prose.

Revise for clarity, energy, and precision.

Phrases to Revise

Revise . . .	To become . . .
at all times	always
at a certain point in time, at that time	then
at the present time, at this time	now
because of the fact that	because
beyond the shadow of a doubt	certainly
by means of	by
by virtue of the fact that	because
despite the fact that	although
due to the fact that	because
for the purpose of	for
for the reason that	because
have a tendency to	tend to
in a slow [quick, etc.] manner	slowly [quickly, etc.]
in any case	anyway
in case	if
in connection with	with
in light of the fact that	because, since
in most instances	usually
in order to	to
in relation to	with
in some instances	sometimes
in spite of the fact that	although
in the event that	if
in the nature of	like
in this day and age	today
in those days	then
on an everyday basis	routinely
on the occasion of	when
regardless of the fact that	although
subsequent to	after
the reason is that	because
there is no question that	certainly
without a doubt	certainly, surely

Activity 36-2: Condensing Phrases into Single Words

Revise the following paragraph to make it more concise.

Does electronic mail have a tendency to make personal communication less meaningful? Beyond the shadow of a doubt, by virtue of the fact that email is more transient than a letter, it can be seen as less important. Due to the fact that many people receive a large amount of email on a daily basis, important messages can often get lost in the shuffle. In some instances, people find that email lacks the personal connection that a handwritten letter brings them. In this day and age, is it possible that the letter will become obsolete?

Unnecessary *I* Phrases to Cut

as far as I'm concerned	I think that
in my opinion	the point I am trying to make
in my mind	to my way of thinking
it is my opinion that	what I mean to say

Words to Cut

Cut vague nouns:

angle	element	quality
area	factor	scope
aspect	field	situation
case	kind, kind of	thing
character	nature	type, type of

Cut overused intensifiers:

absolutely	great	quite
awfully	hopefully	really
clearly	interestingly	totally
definitely	literally	undoubtedly
fine	major	very
fortunately	obviously	

Be Direct!

Writers may be justifiably tentative when drawing conclusions about knowledge that is relatively new to them or when making interpretations about complex subject matter, such as literature, historical events, or scientific findings. However, many times directness would be more appropriate.

- *I believe that* Emerson doesn't advocate exercising free will regardless of social consequences.
- *I feel that* the Vietnam War was the last one whose outcome was directly affected by social protest.
- *I think that* the discovery of life in underground water caves on Mars will shake the foundation of our world view.

Changing the second sentence to *The Vietnam War was the last one whose outcome was directly affected by social protest* (leaving out *I feel that*) makes the writing more concise and forceful. Readers *know* that you're expressing your feelings when you write, so you don't need to remind them. In fact, omitting expressions such as *I believe that* makes your writing more forceful and persuasive because your propositions will sound like indisputable facts, even if they might be debatable.

36b Eliminating Redundancy

Redundant phrases and word pairs, such as *circle around, final and conclusive, period of time, personal friend,* and *repeat again,* clog up prose. Once is enough. Prune this kind of deadwood as ruthlessly as the other types.

Common Redundancies
blue [red, etc.] in color: blue
large [small, etc.] in size: large
square [round, etc.] in shape: square
few [many] in number: few
seventeen [eighteen, etc.] years of age: seventeen

Example 2 Say it once!

Original	the **financial cost** to taxpayers
Revised	the cost to taxpayers
Original	When I was **about the age of twenty-three, . . .**
Revised	When I was twenty-three, . . .
	At twenty-three, I . . .
Original	They **carry a stigma** with them **that won't go away.**
Revised	They carry a stigma.
Original	**the low self-esteem** that young men **possess about themselves**
Revised	young men's low self-esteem

Redundant Phrases

Revise . . .	To become . . .
advance notice [planning]	notice [planning]
consensus of opinion	consensus
continue on	continue
cooperate together	cooperate
each and every	each, every [use either but not both]
final completion	completion
forever and ever	forever
important [basic] essentials	essentials
reason . . . is because	because

Activity 36-3: Revising for Redundancy

Revise the following paragraph to omit redundancies.

In addition to studying the letters of great historical figures for use in biographies of their lives, researchers are studying the letters of ordinary people. Researchers are studying letters that people wrote to relatives, families, and personal friends in order to gain insight into habitual customs. There is a consensus of opinion that these letters can provide a frank and honest perspective on the surrounding circumstances of great events in history and on what we all share in common with each other.

Example 3 Condensing clauses

Original The portrait **that I re-created was** a picture **taken of me** taken **while I was** wrestling **during** my sophomore year of high school.

Revised For the self-portrait, I chose a picture of me wrestling as a sophomore in high school.

Original **Having this particular self-investigation to perform as an assignment** enabled me **to get some concrete ideas about myself that were formerly all in my head** down on paper **in a cohesive way**.

Revised This "self-investigation" assignment helped me write concretely and cohesively.

Original HHS **will work to ensure** that men, including **teens and preteens**, **receive education and support** to postpone fatherhood until they are emotionally and financially ready to support a child. This will be **implemented in an adolescent male family planning initiative program**.

Revised The HHS initiative educates and supports male adolescents to help them postpone fatherhood until they are emotionally and financially ready.

Condense clauses and phrases whenever possible. Most paragraphs (if not most sentences) contain filler—words or phrases that add bulk but fail to clarify or convey meaning. Often, a clause can be reduced to a phrase and a phrase to a word. Pay special attention to prepositional phrases that not only add unnecessary words but also make your prose so convoluted that the reader can't follow the action.

Activity 36-4: Revising to Condense Clauses and Phrases

Revise the following paragraph to make it more concise.

For hundreds of years, people dreamed up many ideas about how to create a connection between the Atlantic and Pacific Oceans. One of the many ideas proposed by a multitude of engineers was to cut through the Isthmus of Panama. By late in the nineteenth century, engineers were ready to work to create the Panama Canal, which would implement a solution to the aforementioned problem of inter-oceanic travel. However, the projected canal would not be as easily accomplished as people thought.

36d Combining Sentences

Another way to achieve conciseness is by combining sentences. Often, sentences that need to be combined are found at a place in your draft where you were casting about to express yourself. Sometimes, two short sentences that share the same grammatical subject or some other element or information can be better and more economically phrased as one sentence. Two wordy, vague, or overly circular sentences can be condensed into one pithy sentence. Other sentences can be eliminated entirely, either because the information they deliver isn't important or because they are so vague as to deliver no information at all. Use the revision technique of sentence combining to tighten your prose and to clarify what you want to say.

Example 4 Combining sentences for conciseness

Original An antidote for arsenite poisoning in humans is British Anti-Lewisite (BAL) (Oehme, 1972). This drug was developed during World War I in response to gas warfare with arsenical compounds.

Revised One antidote for arsenite poisoning is British Anti-Lewisite (BAL), developed during World War I in response to gas warfare with arsenical compounds (Oehme, 1972).

Original The subjects were painted in a semi-abstract form. Even though the characters were painted in a simple form, you can still interpret their mood, whether joyous, scared, or sad, because of the way he constructed their body language.

Revised Even though the characters are painted in simple, semi-abstract forms, their mood—whether joyous, scared, or sad—is revealed in their body language.

Original A learning environment such as this does not promote good learning. It may only cause the intellectual ship to sink in a sea of ignorance.

Revised Rather than promote good learning, such an environment causes the intellectual ship to sink in a sea of ignorance.

Activity 36-5: Combining Sentences for Conciseness

Combine sentences to make the following paragraph more concise.

Seeing someone win at poker is not a rare event in Las Vegas. It is a rare event when done by a robot. Poker robots played each other. Upstairs, their human counterparts competed in the World Series of Poker. The winning poker robot was PokerProbot. PokerProbot was created by Hilton "Print" Givens. Many online poker players were angry at the creation of the poker robots. This is because they feel that poker robots will allow people to cheat at online poker. The creators of the robot say that their programs will help prevent cheating at online poker. This will be possible because they will allow online poker sites to test for errors.

Example 5 Cutting unnecessary expletives

Original	For as long as I can remember, **there was** a striving in the Roth household to be better than everyone else.
Revised	For as long as I can remember, the Roths strove to be better than everyone else.
Original	**It is true that** each teen birth costs taxpayers an estimated $37,000 over the lifetime of mother and child.
Revised	Each teen birth costs taxpayers $37,000 over the lifetime of mother and child.
Original	In Mamet's play *Oleanna,* **there exists** a rift between John the instructor and Carol the student.
Revised	In Mamet's play *Oleanna,* communication breaks down between the instructor, John, and the student, Carol.

Activity 36-6: Cutting Expletive Constructions

Revise the following paragraph to remove expletive constructions.

It appears that Danish scientists have created a new type of solar cell. This type of cell is made out of plastic. There is evidence that the cell lasts longer than previous versions. What this means is that the cell could pave the way for cheaper solar power. However, there exist claims that the cell needs to become more efficient before it can be adopted by consumers.

Strong verbs create lively prose. Weak (or linking) verbs create lifeless prose. In general, the three verbs *be, do,* and *have* are weaker than verbs that portray action. *Be, do,* and *have* show up in many kinds of clauses or phrases, but they are especially noticeable in sentences that include description or possession (*The house was green* or *I have the choice*), passive voice (*I was hit by the ball*), an expletive (*There was one reason for not quitting*), and nominalization (*Eowyn's implication was that Aragorn's reluctance to drink the soup was coyness*). When you revise, look through your writing to see how often *be, do,* and *have*—in all their grammatical forms—turn up. (Use the Search and Replace function in your word-processing program.) Sometimes forms of *be, do,* or *have* are the best choice, but if you find yourself using weak or linking verbs again and again, revise with stronger, more active verbs. (See page 99 in Chapter 6 for strategies for revising sentences with weak verbs; see Chapter 33 for a discussion of readability and active verbs.)

Cut Expletive Constructions

Expletive constructions begin with *it* or *there,* followed by a form of the verb *to be.* An occasional *it is* phrase can help slow the reader down and emphasize an important point. But in general, expletives unnecessarily clog your prose.

Choose the Active Voice

The sentence *I questioned him* is in the active voice. *He was questioned* and *He was questioned by me* are in the passive voice. The active voice is direct, uses vivid verbs, and clearly states who does what to whom; the passive voice is indirect, uses the weak *is* and *have* verbs (in all their grammatical forms), and often leaves the question of who initiated the action unanswered. Passive constructions are not only wordier but also vaguer, and they can make your prose seem muddled and uninteresting. Such constructions can signify that you haven't fully thought through your point, that you've not stated who did what to whom because you're not sure, or that you haven't chosen a specific enough focus for your sentence or paragraph. Choose the active voice unless you have good rhetorical reasons to do otherwise. (For helpful revision methods, see Chapter 6, page 99.)

Example 6 Changing passive to active voice

Original A recurring figure of a ladder **is seen** in the panels, signifying a bridge between past and future or perhaps the movement from South to North or moving up to a better life.

Revised The figure of a ladder recurs throughout the series, perhaps signifying a bridge between past and future, the movement from South to North, or progress from a more difficult life to a better one.

Original Poverty **has been looked at** in plays and short stories such as *A Raisin in the Sun* by Lorraine Hansberry, "Sonny's Blues" by James Baldwin, and "Everyday Use" by Alice Walker.

Revised Lorraine Hansberry's *Raisin in the Sun,* James Baldwin's "Sonny's Blues," and Alice Walker's "Everyday Use" all portray poverty.

Original It **was believed** that Atkins's heart problems **were caused** by his ingestion of steaks and cheese cubes, but his family maintained that that was a fallacious notion and that his heart **had been damaged** by a viral infection.

Revised Many believed that Atkins's fondness for steaks and cheese cubes caused his heart problems, but his family maintained that a viral infection disrupted his heart's rhythm.

Original My room **was so cluttered** with piles of mail and applications that eventually my mother bought me one of those rolling filing cabinets so that I could create a separate file for each prospective school.

Revised So many college applications and piles of mail cluttered my room that eventually my mother bought me a rolling filing cabinet.

Activity 36-7: Revising from Passive to Active Voice

Revise the following paragraph to change sentences from passive to active voice.

Pearls were attractive to people ever since they were first raised from the ocean floor by divers. It is known that pearls are produced by mollusks. The mollusk is infested by a piece of dirt or grit. Calcium carbonate is produced by the mollusks and is formed into the pearls. The mollusks that can produce pearls are mussels, clams, and oysters. The pearls are then harvested by divers.

Example 7 Recasting nominalizations as verbs

Original With the family's **declination** to have an autopsy done to prove critics wrong and **the cremation** of Atkins's body, suspicions were raised about whether the Atkins diet was indeed a healthy diet.

Revised The Atkins family **declined** to have an autopsy and then **cremated** Atkins's body, which raised suspicions about whether the Atkins diet was indeed healthy.

When the Atkins family **declined** to have an autopsy and then **cremated** Atkins's body, many became suspicious about whether the Atkins diet was indeed healthy.

Original My **assumption** was that the ceremony suffered a deliberate **disruption** at the hands of Malefoy.

Revised I **assumed** that Malefoy deliberately **disrupted** the ceremony.

Activity 36-8: Changing Nominalizations to Verbs

Revise the following paragraph to remove nominalizations by changing them to verbs. You can reorder the sentences as appropriate. (If you are unsure whether or not a word is a nominalization, check in a dictionary.)

In the early 1900s, there was a conception of a new art form by visual artists all over the world. The art was to be a representation of the energy and complexity of the new century. The artists searched for a transcendence of realistic representations and sought an elevation of the viewer's senses. Their belief was that music offered a model which could be an aspiration of visual art. Their work was given the appellation "visual music."

Revise Nominalizations and Verb Phrases

A nominalization is a verb turned noun, often ending in *-ance, -ment,* or *-tion:*

- The verb *to tolerate* becomes *tolerance.*
- The verb *to deviate* becomes *deviance.*
- The verb *to adorn* becomes *adornment.*
- The verb *to conceal* becomes *concealment.*
- The verb *to aggravate* becomes *aggravation.*
- The verb *to discuss* becomes *discussion.*

Nominalizations cause prose to be wordy because they lead to sentences with linking verbs. If you nominalize, you will have to use linking verbs to make your sentences grammatical, and these verbs often function like an equal sign, requiring both subject and object to be in noun (or noun phrase) form. Even more important, readers prefer to hear about a world of action where people do things rather than a world of inanimate or abstract concepts. So, if you find a verb hiding in a nominalization in one of your sentences, use it to recast the sentence. Your prose will become more dynamic and readable.

Revise wordy verb phrases when a simple verb will do: use *support* rather than *be supportive of, envy* rather than *be envious of, appreciate* rather than *be appreciative of,* and so on.

Example 8 Revising wordy verb phrases

Original	The candidate **is supportive of** health-care reforms.
Revised	The candidate **supports** health-care reforms.
Original	He **is capable of** much.
Revised	He **can do** much.
Original	The children **were appreciative of** the new backpacks.
Revised	The children **appreciated** the new backpacks.
Original	Many scientists think that the decline in amphibians **is indicative of** an overall breakdown in the environment.
Revised	Many scientists think that the decline in amphibians **indicates** an overall breakdown in the environment.

Activity 36-9: Revising for Concise Sentences in Your Own Writing

Choose a piece of writing you suspect may have problems with wordiness. Go through it looking for the empty and redundant phrasings listed. Decide which phrases can be cut altogether and which should be revised to be more concise. Make the revisions you've identified, and then reread your work. What effect does your revision have on the piece overall?

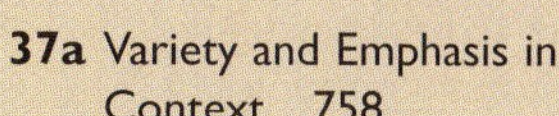

Sentence variety keeps writing lively and effective. Successive sentences of equal length and type with the same structure bore readers. When readers get bored, their attention drifts. Moreover, when sentences have the same form and length, it's impossible to know which ideas are the most important. Using emphasis to focus the reader's attention will help you achieve your broader rhetorical goal of informing, persuading, or entertaining.

Just as when you use any stylistic or formal strategy, when you strive for variety and emphasis, *kairos* should be your guiding principle. Make sure that the variety and emphasis in your sentences are well timed and suited to the context, taking into account the subject matter, the interests of your audience, and your goals. If, for example, you want your readers to be entertained by a narrative or informative essay and to relish the *telling* of the story, you should pay special attention to the rhythm of your sentences, your turns of phrases, and your dramatic emphasis. In a technical document, on the contrary, your sentences may need to establish a consistent pattern, with new information introduced carefully and explained fully, to reassure readers that they will find answers to questions that come up as they read.

Example of Variety and Emphasis

> He was very surprised when I tossed him in; for the first time in our association, I think, he was afraid. He looked afraid as he bobbed about on top of the water, looking up at me from ten feet below. Though we were both accustomed to his resistance and rigidity, seeing him still pitiful, I recognized that I must have done the wrong thing. At least the river was salty, but it was also bottomless; the waves were too rough for him, and the tide was coming in, bumping him against the pilings underneath the pier. Too late, I realized that he wouldn't be able to swim to a peaceful inlet in New Jersey, even if he could figure out which way to swim. But since, short of diving in after him, there was nothing I could do, I walked away.
>
> (From Edward Hoagland, "The Courage of Turtles," page 662)

Achieving variety and emphasis in your writing can be challenging, so this chapter assumes a working grasp of sentence style, as explained in previous chapters in Part 7. Many of the stylistic techniques described here build on topics like parallelism (Chapter 34), coordination and subordination (Chapter 35), and conciseness (Chapter 36). Use the table of contents, index, or glossary to find and review these topics as needed.

As you learn more about variety and emphasis, you will naturally pay more attention to them when you revise. Gradually, as the principles become part of your composing style, you'll also use these techniques more frequently while drafting. Even the best writers—perhaps *especially* the best writers—revise relentlessly to find the best word or the best way to recast a phrase, clause, or sequence of sentences. As you learn the principles of variety and emphasis, pay attention to how writers you admire use them to capture your interest. As a writer concerned with style, you'll learn to appreciate the effective use of variety and emphasis.

Activity 37-1: Thinking about Sentence Variety

Compare the following paragraphs. Which is more engaging? Which better holds your attention and directs your focus? Why?

Paragraph made up solely of simple and compound sentences:

Scarlett was a stray cat. She lived in Brooklyn. She saved her kittens from a fire. This made her famous. Firemen battled the flames, and Scarlett ran into the building repeatedly to save her five kittens. She was badly hurt, but she was happy to have saved her family. Fireman David Gianelli took Scarlett and her kittens to a shelter. There they recuperated and were adopted. Scarlett became a national hero.

Paragraph made up solely of complex and compound-complex sentences:

As firemen battled the flames engulfing an abandoned Brooklyn garage and alleged crack house, an alley cat ran back into the flames repeatedly and each time reemerged carrying a tiny kitten until she had saved her five kittens from the raging fire. Fireman David Gianelli, who's been nicknamed "the animal guy" by fellow firefighters for his many exploits in saving animals, found the kittens on the sidewalk across from the fire and found Scarlett, who was barely conscious, and took them all to the North Shore Animal League shelter, where they were treated for their injuries and where they received hundreds of fan letters and requests for adoptions.

Paragraph made up of a mix of simple, compound, complex, and compound-complex sentences:

Scarlett, the Brooklyn stray who saved her five kittens from a raging fire, is perhaps the most famous cat of the twentieth century. As firemen battled the flames engulfing an abandoned Brooklyn garage and alleged crack house, Scarlett ran back into the fire repeatedly and each time ran back out carrying a tiny kitten. Scarlett's heroism cost her dearly. She emerged from the fire more dead than alive—eyes blistered shut, ears burned to ragged nubs, fur scorched from most of her body—but when Fireman David Gianelli placed her with her kittens, she purred and gently touched each one by the nose as if counting to make sure all were there. Gianelli took Scarlett and her kittens to an animal shelter, and within three months all but one of the animals had recovered and were well enough to be adopted. Once a castoff, an alley cat, a stray, brave Scarlett became a national hero.

The Four Basic English Sentence Types

Simple	Few indigenous languages in North America are being taught to the next generation.
Compound	Numerous tongues—perhaps one-third of the total—are on the verge of disappearing along with their last elderly speakers, and many others are not far behind.
Complex	Even though the Navajos have been more successful than some other groups in keeping their language alive, the percentage of Navajos speaking only English more than doubled from 1980 to 1990 (Crawford).
Compound-complex	Some linguists mourn the loss of data implied by these languages becoming extinct, and others believe that this loss entails losing "intellectual diversity," while Crawford himself finds the most important issue to be "the human costs to those most directly affected."

Activity 37-2: Examining Sentence Variety in Your Writing

Examine a recent piece of writing you have done. Draw a large slash at the end of each sentence so that you can see the variety in sentence length. How varied are the sentences? Would more variety improve the readability of the piece? Use the techniques presented in the rest of this chapter to add variety.

Lively writing contains a mix of sentence structures: simple, compound, complex, and compound-complex. Let's review quickly:

- A *simple sentence* is made up of one independent clause.
- A *compound sentence* is made up of two independent clauses.
- A *complex sentence* is made up of one independent and at least one dependent clause.
- A *compound-complex sentence* is made up of at least two independent clauses and one dependent clause.

Overuse of any one type of sentence makes writing weak. Too many simple and compound sentences make writing choppy. Too many complex and compound-complex sentences make writing overly intricate and hard to follow.

Different kinds of thoughts require different kinds of sentences. If you use all simple (or all simple and compound) sentences, chances are you're not connecting ideas effectively. If you use almost all complex or compound-complex sentences, make sure that your subordinations aren't excessive, illogical, or beside the point—and that your meaning is not obscured in a fog of unnecessary words. The more clearly you understand your subject matter and your rhetorical purpose, the easier it will be to write sentences in a style well suited to the ideas they convey.

Paragraphs made up of sentences of equal length can easily become monotonous and difficult to follow. A paragraph with too many short sentences in a row sounds choppy and simplistic. If all your sentences are long, however, the reader is likely to get tired, lost, or distracted.

Like it or not, readers judge writing—or react to it—by how it sounds as well as by what it says. English is a highly rhythmic language, and meaning swings along with the form of sentences. Variation in length adds to the rhythm of the prose and can carry over to the meaning expressed in the sentences. Just as a piece of music might arouse your interest with its melody, sentences with rhythm and variety can mesmerize your readers into paying more attention and assigning greater value to your writing.

A sudden change in rhythm acts as a signal to the reader to sit up and pay attention. For example, writers often use a very short sentence as a means of placing emphasis on a key thought or theme.

Sentence Length

Be aware of your reaction to each sentence as you read this paragraph. Which idea is emphasized the most?

Today, when oral culture has been devalued for a culture of images, it is difficult to imagine the bygone skills of repartee or the delicate balance between self-effacement and self-aggrandizement. We tend to forget that before the advent of the mass press, let alone the free press, information divulged confidentially in private shaped ideas and their reception at large. Opinion evolved through collective voices; it was not dispensed in prepackaged formulas. The power of conversation—the ability to publicize and arbitrate, to shape consensus, to unite in dialogue those who would not normally meet—was key to the political politesse of the salon. As a result, the salon tradition of egalitarian sociability doubled in importance for Jewish women, who had not only their gender but also religious and ethnic difference to overcome.

From Emily D. Bilski and Emily Braun, Exhibition Catalog for "The Power of Conversation: Jewish Women and Their Salons," cited in "Salon Women," *The Chronicle of Higher Education*, Mar. 31, 2005 <http://chronicle.com/prm/weekly/v51/i30/30b02301.htm.>

Activity 37-3: Thinking about Sentence Length

Examine the third paragraph in Activity 37-1 on page 758 again, this time counting the number of words in each sentence. Which sentence is the shortest? What is the content of that sentence? What effect does this pairing of length and content have on you as a reader?

Five Standard Patterns of English Sentences

S V
Kate runs.

S V DIR OBJ
Tom throws the ball.

S V S COMP
Kate is Tom's friend.

S V IND OBJ DIR OBJ
Tom throws Kate the ball.

S V DIR OBJ OBJ COMP
Tom finds Kate entertaining.

Activity 37-4: Manipulating Word Order

How many different ways can you think of to vary the word order of the following sentence? You can make minor changes to words (such as changing their part of speech or changing their tense).

> Moving rapidly, the quick brown fox jumped over the lazy dog who was lying on the stoop.

One of the most important ways to achieve emphasis and variety in sentences is by manipulating word order. Two concepts underlie all such techniques. First, word order in English sentences is relatively fixed; the core pattern of English sentences is subject-verb-object (S-V-O). Second, the most prominent places to put information are at the beginning and the end of a sentence. Readers tend to remember endings especially clearly because that's where meaning reaches closure. (See the five general principles of readability on pages 727–729 for more information on how readers process subject matter.)

Notice that in each sentence to the left, the pattern is subject-verb (or agent-action) or subject-verb-object. Because the subject-verb pattern is so strongly fixed, understanding how to manipulate it effectively and grammatically will be enormously useful in improving the effectiveness of your writing, in any context. See section 40l for a detailed discussion of the five sentence patterns.

Readers focus on the grammatical subject, so one way to place emphasis in a sentence is through your choice of grammatical subject.

The examples to the right contain the same information, but emphasize different aspects of it by putting different words in the subject position. When the topic of the sentence—the focus of attention—changes, so does the rhetorical emphasis.

Example 1 Focusing attention by putting information in the subject

SUBJECT VERB

The Bureau of Labor Statistics found that employed women spend an hour per day more than employed men in doing household tasks and child care. [Focus is on the Bureau of Labor Statistics.]

SUBJECT VERB

Employed women spend an hour per day more than employed men in doing household tasks and child care, according to the BLS survey. [Focus is on the employed women.]

SUBJECT VERB

Household tasks and child care take up an hour more per day for employed women than for employed men, according to the BLS survey. [Focus is on the tasks of housework and child care.]

SUBJECT VERB

One hour per day more is devoted to household tasks and children by employed women than by employed men, according to the BLS survey. [Focus is on the greater amount of time allotted to the tasks.]

Activity 37-5: Testing Sentence Subjects

Revise each sentence in at least three different ways. Each revision should have a different subject. Then underline the subjects.

1. When they visit the beach, many people are afraid of the possibility of a shark attack.
2. Attacks have been increasing steadily throughout the 1990s and 2000s, leaving people unsure as to why.
3. The attacks seem to be coming in clusters, with multiple people being attacked in the same location over just a few days.
4. Scientists hope that the data from these attacks can help them understand shark behavior and prevent or warn about future attacks.
5. Still, a person's chance of being attacked by a shark is less than his or her chance of being hit by a falling coconut.

Varied Sentence Openings Allow for Smooth Reading

Which sentence openers in this paragraph work best? Try reading the passage without reading the sentence openers. How do the paragraph's rhythm and coherence change?

PHRASE In *Magnolia,* filmmaker P. T. Anderson looks at betrayal and forgiveness—especially that between parent and child. SUBJECT The film intertwines the stories of multiple characters: a day-in-the-life that becomes a day like no other. SUBJECT Frank T. J. Mackey is the self-made star of a men's how-to workshop called "Seduce and Destroy." PHRASE Prowling the stage as he instructs men in how to cheat and lie their way to seduction, Mackey displays a public persona constructed on a lie. PHRASE Behind the character's rage and cockiness lies a 14-year-old boy, abandoned by his father and left to care for his mother as she dies an agonizing death from cancer. CONJUNCTIVE ADVERB Now the father, TV producer Earl Partridge, is also dying. COORDINATING CONJUNCTION And Earl—through the pain and the morphine and the regret—wants one thing only: to see his son. SUBJECT Whether Earl's nurse can find his long-lost son before Earl dies and whether Jack/Frank can or should forgive the father who abandoned him are key plot elements that drive the story forward. TRANSITIONAL EXPRESSION Without a doubt, the scene of their reunion is one of the film's highlights.

Although most sentences begin with the grammatical subject, writing in which *all* sentences begin with the subject soon becomes tedious. To aid readability, vary your sentence openings by beginning with phrases, with dependent clauses, or with connecting words such as transitional expressions, coordinating conjunctions, or conjunctive adverbs. Introductory phrases should generally be fairly short so that the delay in getting to the core of the sentence—the subject-verb pair or the agent and action—does not suspend the reader's closure for too long. Readers look for that closure and depend on it to make sense of what they read.

Activity 37-6: Varying Sentence Openings

Revise each sentence in at least three different ways, experimenting with different sentence openings. Try opening with prepositional phrases or creating subordinate clauses for variety.

1. The Wachowski brothers brought the first *Matrix* film to theaters in 1999, and many were surprised by the commercial and critical reception of the film.
2. The film raised many philosophical and moral questions about who we are and what we do with our lives.
3. Many young professionals identified with Neo, seemingly stuck in a dead-end life until he is transformed by his decision to break out of the Matrix.
4. Others, of course, were attracted to the special effects of the film, including the now-famous "bullet time" sequences.

Reversing the strongly ingrained subject-verb pattern packs a strong punch. So, on occasion, you might want to try adding variation or shifting emphasis by using the sentence pattern verb-subject.

Take care when deciding to reverse the sentence pattern, however. Verb-subject reversal is not a technique to use arbitrarily, since many constructions won't yield gracefully to this shift. As Yoda of *Star Wars* might put it, "Confuse you it will."

Example 2 Using verb-subject order to emphasize the end of the sentence

Subject-verb	The sad collection (S) of hovels stood (V)—or rather leaned, drooped, and sagged—at the end of that dusty winding path.
Verb-subject	At the end of that dusty winding path stood (V)—or rather leaned, drooped, and sagged—the sad collection of hovels (S).
Subject-verb	The blizzard (S) of '78 was (V) particularly harsh (S COMPLEMENT), and stranded cattle died by the thousands.
Verb-subject	Particularly harsh (S COMP) was (V) the blizzard (S) of '78, in which stranded cattle died by the thousands.

Activity 37-7: Reversing the Usual Word Order

Revise the word order of each sentence so that the verb appears before the subject.

1. The blizzard of 1978 was one of the most horrible storms that attacked the East Coast.
2. Most of the population did not suspect that the storm was coming.
3. Those who knew about the storm assumed that it was not going to be severe.
4. The storm raged for three days, leaving a trail of destruction in its wake.
5. Many people were left stranded without power or heat.

Example 3 Changing from a cumulative to a periodic sentence

Cumulative — Earl (S) asks (V) to see his son, even though he is barely able to speak as he struggles against the pain and against the numbing effects of morphine.

Periodic — Struggling against the pain, through a morphine-induced fog, Earl (S) asks (V) to see his son.

Most sentences are cumulative; that is, the main subject-verb pair comes first, and the rest of the information follows. In contrast, periodic sentences withhold the subject-verb pair until the end. Although a periodic sentence maintains the expected subject-verb order, it places emphasis by making the reader wait until the end for the main information.

Activity 37-8: Crafting Periodic Sentences

Revise the following sentences to make them periodic. You can add or delete words and ideas if you need to.

1. Spielberg causes the shark to explode in the dramatic climax of *Jaws*.
2. Author Peter Benchley disagreed with this change from his novel.
3. Spielberg felt that the change made the film more dramatic and more powerful.
4. The director wanted audiences to be on their feet and cheering at the shark's demise.
5. Benchley ultimately conceded that the change did make for an exciting scene.

Using Climactic Order for Items in a Series

Readers naturally expect that ideas listed in a series will be arranged in climactic order—that is, that the ideas will progress from least important to most important. When this natural order is muddled, meaning gets muddled too. When you are listing ideas in a series, make sure that the ideas follow this expected progression. If you vary from this pattern, you should have a clear reason for doing so. In any case, the order of items in a series matters both for rhythm and for emphasis.

A highly skilled writer can exploit this natural progression to give additional punch to humor or irony. In the third sentence in Example 4, essayist Richard Rodrigues lays out a list that doesn't progress—its components being essentially equal—until the last word, *irony.* In doing so, he communicates the ways in which the kinds of artifice he has listed—ones that seem "fluffy" or unserious—are in fact part of the deadly serious business of survival.

Example 4 Using climactic order

My father, when drunk, was neither funny nor honest; he was pathetic, frightening, deceitful.

From Scott Russell Sanders, "Under the Influence," in *The Art of the Personal Essay: An Anthology from the Classical Era to the Present* (New York: Anchor Books/Doubleday, 1994), 735.

His short life read as a kind of catalogue of sin: Bromwell Bronte had been dismissed in disgrace, plunged into debt, wallowed in self-pity, fallen into alcoholism and addiction to opium, indulged in adulterous passion, and ruined himself utterly.

Homosexual survival lay in artifice, in plumage, in lampshades, sonnets, musical comedy, couture, syntax, religious ceremony, opera, lacquer, irony.

From Richard Rodrigues, "Late Victorians," in *The Art of the Personal Essay: An Anthology from the Classical Era to the Present* (New York: Anchor Books/Doubleday, 1994), 760.

Activity 37-9: Using Climactic Order in a Series

Arrange the following series of ideas in appropriate climactic order.

1. As Hobbes once remarked, life is short, brutish, and nasty.
2. The blogging phenomenon has been characterized as important, serious, world-changing, and frivolous.
3. The boss berated the plan as being wasteful, unnecessary, and irrelevant.

Example 5 Using questions, commands, or exclamations

"You ask girls here what they want to do and they'll tell you—'to be a Miss Venezuela.'"

But is the pressure too much?

Giselle Reyes, 38, who runs a beauty school and was once a beauty queen, thinks not. . . .

From Juan Forero, "A Bevy of Teeny Beauties, Minds Set on Being Queens," *New York Times*, April 15, 2005.

No, I can't see how it's a good idea. I would suggest that what's done is done, that you gave it a shot and it didn't work out and the best thing to do is let it go. Let him find someone else. And you find someone else as well. Don't fall for it. File for divorce. Get the papers signed. Forget about him.

From Cary Tennis, "Since You Asked . . ." column, *Salon*, April 14, 2005.

Well, when I had reached this period of silence, I was forced into a measure that no one ever adopts voluntarily: I was impelled to think. God, was it difficult! The moving about of great secret trunks. I wondered whether I had ever thought.

From F. Scott Fitzgerald, "The Crack-Up," in *The Art of the Personal Essay: An Anthology from the Classical Era to the Present* (New York: Anchor Books/Doubleday, 1994), 527.

Most sentences make statements; they are declarative. Occasionally, it's effective to use questions, commands, or exclamations to enhance variety.

Questions (interrogative sentences) can be an effective way to initiate a shift in thought, often at the beginning or end of a paragraph, or to emphasize an important point.

Commands (imperative sentences) tend to belong to how-to manuals, cookbooks, and advice columns, all challenging and often artful forms of nonfiction in their own right. Occasionally, imperative sentences can be useful in other types of nonfiction.

Exclamatory sentences get a lot of use in grocery store tabloids, but on rare occasions an exclamation can add the right bit of oomph to more serene or serious nonfiction.

Activity 37-10: Creating Emphasis by Varying Sentence Structure

Revise the following paragraph to vary sentence structure by using statements, commands, exclamations, and questions. You may change, delete, or add words as appropriate.

Many people argue that schools should stay open all year long. The current school year is based on the agricultural calendar, but most students no longer work on farms. The long gap decreases students' ability to retain information. Students have strong reactions to this: they don't want their vacation taken away. However, it's possible that summer vacation could disappear in our lifetime. People should voice their opinions on this issue.

The skillful, deliberate repetition of a word or phrase is an effective way to emphasize a key idea.

In this famous passage from a speech delivered to the British House of Commons on June 4, 1940, during World War II, Prime Minister Winston Churchill repeats the phrase "we shall fight" to rally Britain against what then seemed like grimly insurmountable odds. The Allies had just suffered a disastrous defeat at Dunkirk, and the Nazis had taken France, Belgium, Holland, and Luxemburg.

Repetition in a Famous Speech by Winston Churchill

We shall go on to the end, **we shall fight** in France, **we shall fight** on the seas and oceans, **we shall fight** with growing confidence and growing strength in the air, we shall defend our Island, whatever the cost may be, **we shall fight** on the beaches, **we shall fight** on the landing grounds, **we shall fight** in the fields and in the streets, **we shall fight** in the hills; we shall never surrender . . . .

Activity 37-11: Emphasizing an Idea Using Repetition

Revise the following sentences to repeat different sentence elements. You can combine sentences and add and delete words as needed.

> Lance Armstrong is most remembered for his remarkable endurance. People remember his grueling endurance in the Tour de France but also his status as a two-time cancer survivor. His amazing survival as both an athlete and a person has inspired both athletes and cancer sufferers to do their best.

Activity 37-12: Revising for Variety and Emphasis

Use any of the techniques from this chapter to improve the clarity and rhythm of the following paragraph.

> George Orwell wrote the novel *1984*. In this novel, people are subjected to horrible and invasive surveillance. Recently, papers have been released from one of Britain's archives. These papers show that Orwell himself was the subject of surveillance. Intelligence services were concerned about Orwell's activities. Most of these activities related to research for his essays and novels. Orwell was monitored and records were kept. It is ironic that someone who predicted and fought against surveillance was himself a subject.

Activity 37-13: Revising for Variety and Emphasis in Your Own Writing

Choose a piece of your writing that seems to have dull or boring parts. Go through these parts to see what kinds of sentence structures you've used. Using this chapter as a guide, revise some of your sentences for variety and emphasis. What effect does your revision have on the piece overall?

38

EFFECTIVE WORD USE

"Words, words, words," says Hamlet to Polonius. The English language is full of them—extraordinarily so. At somewhere over half a million words, English is generally considered to have the largest vocabulary of any language currently spoken. Ours is a polyglot tongue whose richness and variety reveal its history and sources: the gruff Anglo-Saxon of *pig, dog, gut, earth;* the elegant Norman French of *pork, nobility, attorney, chevalier;* the erudite Latin of *verisimilitude* and *intrepidity*. And along with all those words come all those rules: rules of spelling, rules of usage, rules of grammar. English is full of words that sound the same but mean something different, related clusters of words with almost infinitely nuanced shades of meaning, words that sound the way they are spelled and words that sound like something else entirely, words that mean just the opposite of what you think they would mean. Even the dictionaries don't always agree. What's more, the language is in constant flux. Words come and go, meanings change, usages become obsolete, and yesterday's prohibition becomes today's practice.

No wonder, then, that choosing the right word can seem both daunting and inspiring. Yet choosing and using words effectively is something we all do every day. We all use language to persuade, to amuse, to inspire, to give voice to what we want, dream for, and need. We all use language to communicate. The same impulse that drives our speaking drives our writing; it's just that writing requires us to pay more attention to what we're doing and how we're doing it.

Today English is spoken by more people than any other language. At least one quarter of the world's people speak English, roughly half as a native tongue and half as a second or foreign language. English acts as the *lingua franca*—common language of international exchange—in such fields as technology, business, and international relations. Around the globe—from England to India, from Australia to Africa, from Jamaica to Singapore—people speak a multiplicity of Englishes, each with its own character. American English itself is hardly monolithic: hackers, rappers, surfers; Down East lobstermen, Texas cowgirls, Georgia peanut farmers; college professors, cops, and cabbies all speak different variations. The vibrancy of American English, as captured in our literature, in music lyrics, in oral traditions, and in everyday speech, owes much to these distinctive voices.

Linguists confirm what we all hear—that language varies from place to place and from group to group—and tell us that there is no one and only "correct" English; rather, there are *varieties* of English. For a linguist, Standard Written English, Southern States English, Boston Brahmin English, American Indian English, Appalachian English, Spanish-influenced English, and African American Vernacular English, among others, are all equally valid varieties.

Regionalisms

As you move across the United States, you'll find that people use different words for the same thing. So, for example, a soft drink might be called a *soda* in one place and *pop* in another; the evening meal might be *dinner* in one place and *supper* somewhere else. In addition, groups of people—different socioeconomic classes or ethnic groups, for example—may also share speech patterns because of a shared cultural background. Along with variations in word usage, dialects may also exhibit grammatical variations. It is critical to note that these variations are each worthy of our respect. All dialects bind a people together, have a long and interesting history, and show regular and consistent grammatical principles at work.

Activity 38-1: Identifying Regionalisms and Dialects

Visit the following sites to learn more about regionalisms and dialects in U.S. English.

Dialect Survey Results: **http://cfprod01.imt.uwm.edu/Dept/FLL/linguistics/dialect/maps.html**

Pop or Soda Survey: **http://www.popvssoda.com**

Use them to help you answer the following questions.

1. How would you classify the English that you speak, given where you are from?
2. Select five questions on the Dialect Survey Results page and think about how you would answer them. Then compare your answers with the most common answers for your region. Are yours different or the same? How about a classmate's answers?
3. Is the term you use for a carbonated soft drink (such as *soda, pop,* or *Coke*) the term most commonly used in your state? If it isn't, why do you think your usage is different?
4. Do you use different terms than your parents or grandparents for the same concepts (such as soft drinks or sandwiches)? If so, why do you think your usage is different?

Using a Dictionary

When in doubt about a word or usage, consult your dictionary. Most dictionaries apply usage labels to words or usages of words that are likely to be questionable in Standard Written English.

- *Slang* is street talk, a word of recent coinage, often the specialized vocabulary of a particular group.
- *Nonstandard* means that a word or usage is unacceptable to educated speakers and writers.
- *Informal* or *colloquial* refers to language appropriate to everyday speech but unlikely to be appropriate to the more formal demands of writing.
- *Regionalism* or *dialect* indicates that a word or meaning is restricted to a particular group or area.
- *Archaic* refers to words or meanings now rare.
- *Obsolete* refers to words or meanings no longer in use.

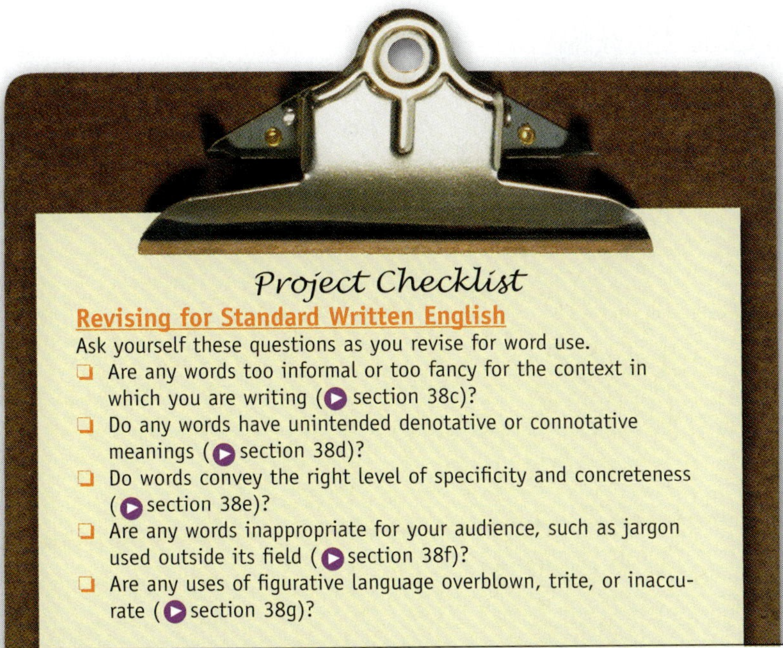

Project Checklist

Revising for Standard Written English

Ask yourself these questions as you revise for word use.

- ❑ Are any words too informal or too fancy for the context in which you are writing (▶ section 38c)?
- ❑ Do any words have unintended denotative or connotative meanings (▶ section 38d)?
- ❑ Do words convey the right level of specificity and concreteness (▶ section 38e)?
- ❑ Are any words inappropriate for your audience, such as jargon used outside its field (▶ section 38f)?
- ❑ Are any uses of figurative language overblown, trite, or inaccurate (▶ section 38g)?

Standard Written English (SWE) commands a special status as the medium of most public communication. It is the English of newspapers, books, and magazines; the English of government publications; the English of business and professional life and of academia.

As its name suggests, Standard Written English conforms to certain standards of grammar and usage (themselves the topic of this handbook), standards that have evolved and become codified as the language itself has evolved and changed. Although the idea of a standard has been wrongly used to treat other varieties of English as inferior, Standard Written English itself emerged (largely in the eighteenth century) as a growing class of professional writers sought to free the language from the tyranny of the court and aristocracy.

Whatever other varieties of English one chooses to use in daily life, a mastery of Standard Written English is imperative for having one's point of view or one's presentation of self given serious consideration in public contexts.

38c Understand the Levels of Diction

Most academic writing calls for the use of Standard Written English and a more formal level of diction than that found in everyday speech. *Diction* is just a fancy word for word choice, and *level of diction* refers to where your language sits on a continuum of least to most formal. Students writing in college should typically strive for a level of diction more formal than "What's up, dude?" but not so stuffy or overblown as to make them sound like pompous windbags. Readers of academic writing value above all clarity, simplicity, and intelligibility.

Diction on a Continuum from Informal to Formal

Least formal

Slang	Informal or Colloquial Diction
Street talk, a word of recent coinage, often the specialized vocabulary of a particular group, "lingo"	Language appropriate to everyday speech but unlikely to be appropriate to the more formal demands of college writing
"The Pit and the Pendulum" **creeps me out.** It gives me **the willies.**	"The Pit and the Pendulum" **scares me.** It gives me **goosebumps.**
Lots of companies treat the acid rain issue like a big **pain in the butt.**	Lots of companies treat the acid rain issue **as too big a hassle or too small to deal with.**
Jane's future **sucks.**	Jane is **doomed.**

Most formal

Formal Diction	Pompous Language
Language characterized by precise word choice, minimal use of contractions, formal but not pompous tone, terminology of a field	Language that uses long words where short ones will do, obscure ones where direct ones exist, old forms where new ones have become common, hyphenated words, nominalizations, and passive voice
In "The Pit and the Pendulum," Poe creates an atmosphere of **terrifying claustrophobia, torture, and suspense.**	"The Pit and the Pendulum" arouses **physiologically** a fight-or-flight reaction, **indicative of anxiety.**
Many polluting industries try either to **minimize the seriousness** of acid rain's devastating effect on the environment or to **overplay the costs of implementing environmental regulations.**	**Pollution-incognizant** companies overestimate their **inculpability** and exhibit reluctance to accept responsibility for the **infraction** of acid-rain build-up.
Jane's future **looks bleak.**	The **prognostication** for Jane's future was beset by **darkening clouds.**

Activity 38-2: Revising Slang and Pompous Language

Revise these sentences so that they are in Standard Written English.

1. Corporations act like it's no big deal when products have to be called back.
2. Allow me to chronicle this phenomenon with photographic equipment so that we may use it for later recollection.
3. The FBI dude said that this information was only to be eyeballed by peeps with top-secret clearance, who were to keep it on the down low.
4. The eventide abided stygian and tempestuous.
5. The head honcho of the corporation might have thought that he was, like, the awesomest, but not after he got sent to the slammer for totally ripping off those old ladies.

Even when you are writing in college, certain rhetorical situations may call for using diction other than Standard Written English. For example, if you are writing dialogue, you may want to represent a particular way of speaking in order to get across a speaker's tone, style, or background. In other rhetorical situations, you'll also vary the level of diction: if you are writing a survey for teenagers that will appear in a music magazine, your diction may well be slang. The point is not to restrict yourself to one level, but to become aware of which level of diction is most appropriate for a given context.

38d Consider Denotation and Connotation

Denotation is the meaning of a word. **Connotation** is an emotional association a word implies. To choose and use a word effectively, you must know what a word means and be aware of what it implies.

Denotation

Always look up words whose meaning you don't know. Find a word's denotative meanings in a good college-level dictionary, such as the *American Heritage Dictionary of the English Language, Merriam-Webster's Collegiate Dictionary,* or the *Random House Webster's College Dictionary.* Many words have more than one meaning, and sometimes these meanings are themselves contradictory. Usually, the primary, or most common, meaning is the writer's most straightforward choice. Using a more obscure meaning of a word might require additional clarification. Some dictionaries put the most commonly used meaning first; others put the oldest meaning (the one that's been in use the longest) first. You'll want to know how your dictionary is organized so that you can weigh your judgments accordingly. (You can find out by reading the dictionary's preface and notes in the beginning.)

Provide Context for Words with Competing Meanings

Let's take as an example the word *jargon* (also discussed later in this chapter). The *American Heritage Dictionary*'s first meaning (in this dictionary the most common usage) is "nonsensical, incoherent, or meaningless talk"; its third meaning is "the specialized or technical language of a trade, profession, or similar group." Depending on whether you go with the first or third meaning, *jargon* can legitimately be used to mean "words with no meaning at all" or "words with very precise meanings indeed." That's a big difference. If you use the word *jargon,* then, you should give readers enough context so that they will understand which meaning you intend:

> The mumbled jargon of the man on the corner at times became a shouted curse.
>
> Never having taken a college math course, we couldn't understand a single word of the engineer's jargon.

Many words require this kind of careful contextualization to make sure your denotative meaning is conveyed accurately to your readers.

Commonly Confused Words

Many words are commonly misused, especially words that sound similar but mean entirely different things, such as these:

- *Enormity,* which means "excessive wickedness or outrageousness," is frequently confused with *enormousness,* which means "great in size."
- *Disinterested,* which means "impartial," is frequently confused with *uninterested,* which means "not interested."

Whenever you are not sure about a word's meaning, check the Glossary of Usage in the back of this handbook or a dictionary.

Decide Which Synonym to Use by Checking Your Dictionary's Usage Notes

Consider a word's connotations when deciding which of several synonyms to use. They help set the emotional context of your ideas for readers. Here are some of the definitions and a list of synonyms for *easy* from the *American Heritage Dictionary of the English Language,* 4th edition.

eas•y (ē′zē) *adj.* **-i•er, -i•est 1.** Capable of being accomplished or acquired with ease; posing no difficulty; *an easy victory; an easy problem.* **2.** Requiring or exhibiting little effort or endeavor; undemanding: *took the easy way out of her problems; wasn't satisfied with easy answers.* **3.** Free from worry, anxiety, trouble, or pain: *My mind was easy, knowing that I had done my best.* **4a.** Affording comfort or relief; soothing: *soft light that was easy on the eyes.* **b.** Prosperous; well-off: *easy living; easy circumstances. . . .*

Synonyms *easy, simple, facile, effortless* These adjectives mean requiring little effort or posing little if any difficulty. *Easy* applies to tasks that require little effort: "*The diagnosis of disease is often easy, often difficult, and often impossible*" (Peter M. Latham). *Simple* implies a lack of complexity that facilitates understanding or performance: "*the faculty . . . of reducing his thought on any subject to the simplest and plainest terms possible*" (Baron Charnwood). *Facile* stresses readiness and fluency: *a facile speaker.* Often, though, the word implies glibness or insincerity, superficiality, or lack of care: *explanations too facile for complex events. Effortless* refers to performance in which the application of great strength or skill makes the execution seem easy: *wrote effortless prose.*

The Dangers of Using Biased Language

Be deliberate in your use of connotation, taking care not to undermine your own argument by sloppily using words with negative connotations to smear a person or position with which you disagree. Some words are especially loaded and, if used unthinkingly, can make your work seem biased. If, for example, all women politicians are *shrill* in your vocabulary or all union organizers are *bullheaded,* you might want to examine your writing for gender or class bias overall. The challenge here is not to censor your criticisms but to be aware that your argument will be undermined if you use emotionally loaded language or promote biased stereotypes rather than presenting your position objectively and reasonably. (For more on eliminating biased language, see Chapter 39.)

Activity 38-3: Understanding Connotations

Consult a dictionary to understand the connotations of each word below. Arrange each set of words so they are ordered from most to least positive.

1. dirt poor, destitute, hard up, impoverished
2. rude, primitive, uncivilized, boorish
3. immature, callow, young, childlike

Connotation

Connotation, what a word implies or suggests to the reader, also starts with the dictionary meaning but goes beyond it. Many words share a basic meaning but imply shades or differences of meaning that are distinctly important. Consider this quotation from the British journalist Katherine Whitehorn:

> I am firm. You are obstinate. He is a pig-headed fool.

Firm, obstinate, and *pig-headed* all mean "strong willed," but as Whitehorn's clever turn of phrase so aptly demonstrates, which of us would choose to label ourselves *pig-headed* rather than *firm*? The connotation of *pig-headed* is that one is stupidly obstinate; the connotation of *firm* is that one is admirably resolute. You can use a thesaurus to find synonyms (words that are alike in meaning), but to clarify differences in connotation, use a dictionary. Look at both a word's definition and the usage notes, if the dictionary provides any.

Good writing requires the deft balancing of the specific and the general, the concrete and the abstract.

- General words are used to define a category of thing: *vertebrates, American literature, undergraduates.* Specific words locate an item within that category: *aardvark; Toni Morrison's novel* Beloved; *Jane Smith, first-year student at Seattle Central Community College.*
- Abstract words identify concepts: *truth, justice, freedom, equality.* Concrete words create impressions based on our five senses (seeing, hearing, smelling, tasting, and touching): *yellow, loud, rank, sweet, soft.*

Specific and concrete words put readers in actual contexts, helping them identify people, actions, scenes, and the particularities of a moment. General and abstract terms stand above the immediacy of context, making it possible for readers to think about what many contexts have in common. We need all kinds of words to capture experience and reflect upon it.

A Sample Paragraph from Judith Ortiz Cofer

Color

In the animal world it indicates danger: the most colorful creatures are often the most poisonous. Color is also a way to attract and seduce a mate. In the human world color triggers many more complex and often deadly reactions. As a Puerto Rican girl born of "white" parents, I spent the first years of my life hearing people refer to me as *blanca,* white. My mother insisted that I protect myself from the intense island sun because I was more prone to sunburn than some of my darker, trigueño playmates. People were always commenting within my hearing about how my black hair contrasted so nicely with my "pale" skin. I did not think of the color of my skin consciously except when I heard the adults talking about complexion. It seems to me that the subject is much more common in the conversation of mixed-race peoples than in mainstream United States society, where it is a touchy and sometimes even embarrassing topic to discuss, except in a political context.

From Judith Ortiz Cofer, "The Story of My Body," in *The Latin Deli: Prose and Poetry* (Athens: University of Georgia Press, 1993).

The first three sentences are mostly general and abstract. The author makes generalizations about the significance and effects of skin color. Sentences 4–7 become more specific and concrete; the author shares her personal experiences with readers. The last sentence zooms out to abstraction again to compare the frequency of conversation about skin color in two cultures.

Activity 38-4: Making Language Concrete and Specific

Support each general statement with two more sentences that are more specific and concrete.

1. It was raining outside.
2. The butterfly took off from the flower.
3. Abuse is a problem.
4. The bird flew away from its nest.
5. The book was interesting.

Some Contemporary Buzzwords to Avoid

Nouns and Adjectives	Verbs Created from Nouns
action plan buy-in	to actualize
centers of excellence	to dialogue
core competencies	to gift
mission-critical	to disincent
pushback	to incentivize
thought leadership	to monetize
trend rifts	to operationalize
turnkey solution	to productize
value added	solutioning (a problem)
value proposition	

Bureaucratese, Revised

Bureaucratese	The experience of sudden hood fly-up may restrict the field of vision such that unfortunate circumstances result for the operator.
Revision	If the hood of your car opens while you're driving, you might not see where you're going and crash.

Activity 38-5: Revising Buzzwords and Bureaucratese

Revise these sentences so that they use strong, plain words.

1. We need to actualize our core competencies to achieve a value-added solution.
2. What happened at this point in time was that Joe utilized a corkscrew-shaped object to leverage the bottle of wine.
3. We struggled in solutioning the productivity enhancement cuts requested by our administrative supervisor.
4. My health-care provider has requested interpersonal communication where I will take her statements under advisement.
5. The sports supervisor incentivized his athletic unit to achieve success.

Don't confuse or mislead your reader with language that is overly specialized, obscure, pretentious, or archaic. Say what you mean in strong, plain words. Less experienced writers often use big words to impress their readers. Plain old English says *cat,* but in scientific Latin, it's *Felis silvestris domesticus.* Which kind of courage sounds more courageous to you, the Anglo-Saxon *guts* or the Latinate *intrepidity?* What will impress your reader most is clear thinking and clear writing, not multisyllabic utterances that take a dictionary to decipher.

Cut Buzzwords

Buzzwords are trendy words often chosen to signify that their users are in the know. In academic writing, use words to convey your thoughts rather than to signify your membership in the club.

Rewrite Bureaucratese

Bureaucratese is language that includes a high proportion of nouns and *to be* verbs; these make writing seem weighty and consequential, but that impression is false. This kind of writing obscures meaning rather than revealing it. Impress your readers instead with clear, direct, and vivid language.

Use the Jargon of Fields of Study with Care

One meaning of the word *jargon* is "the specialized technical language of a particular profession or pursuit." Specialized language does have a place in writing, depending on the context, including audience and purpose. Rock climbers know the difference between *scumming, smedging,* and *smearing,* but the ordinary person might not. *Spiders* and *cookies* are something quite different on the Internet than in ordinary life. And to the non-physician, a *capillary hemangioma* sounds much more ominous than a plain old strawberry birthmark. Specialists need specialized language to talk to one another with clarity and precision. But if you want to reach a general audience, you'll want to use a more accessible vocabulary.

Jargon in the Disciplines: An Example from Psychology

Every field of study uses a specialized vocabulary. If you were writing a paper on learning for a psychology class, for example, you might well need to use some of the following terms:

associative learning	extinction
classical conditioning	reinforcement
operant conditioning	avoidance conditioning
conditioned stimulus	partial reinforcement schedule
conditioned response	shaping
backward conditioning	modeling

Because these terms are jargon, you should refer to the glossary of your textbook for exact definitions when using any of them in your project. The meanings that a general dictionary includes will not be the same as those you find in a field-specific glossary. If your audience is only your instructor, you may not need to define these specialized terms, but if your audience includes others outside of the field, you may have to provide definitions for your readers.

Recognize Euphemisms

A **euphemism** is a word that is substituted for another in an attempt to make things "nice": *toilet* becomes *bathroom* becomes *washroom* becomes *restroom; undertaker* becomes *mortician* becomes *funeral director.* In these examples, the euphemisms are relatively benign, covering up our embarrassment about our bodies or our fear of death. Euphemisms can also be used to sell you a bill of goods, lit-

Using Euphemisms to Cover Up Embarrassment, Fear, and Disgust

At times euphemisms are appropriate—writing a note to a bereaved mother, you might well use the phrase *passed on* instead of *died.* In academic writing, however, it's best to be more direct. Each time you use a euphemism, consider what you are hiding from readers or yourself. Also, although the euphemisms listed below are at approximately the same level of diction as the words they are covering up, many euphemisms lower the level and thus become unsuitable in Standard Written English:

the facilities (the toilet)
know [someone] in the Biblical sense (have sex with)
passed on, passed away (died)
sanitary landfill (garbage dump)

Using Doublespeak to Evade the Truth

casualty (death or injury)
collateral damage (civilians killed)
downsizing or reduction in force (layoffs, itself a euphemism for mass firing of employees)
ethnic cleansing (genocide)
job flexibility (lack of job security)
negative health outcomes (death)
pre-hostility (peace)
servicing a target (killing)

Activity 38-6: Revising Euphemisms and Doublespeak

Revise the sentences to eliminate euphemisms and doublespeak.

1. In a statement, the CEO of the hospital said that he regretted the negative health outcomes caused by improper sanitation at his health-care complexes.
2. Last year, she lost her husband in the hurricane.
3. After Bill experienced involuntary job flexibility, he was forced to relocate to a corrugated living facility.
4. The economically diminished population has been forcibly encouraged to not maintain residence in the park areas.
5. I acquired a pre-enjoyed vehicle from the dealer.

eral or figurative: at the car dealership, every *used car* is a *pre-owned vehicle;* today's *biosolids* are yesterday's *sludge.*

Revise Doublespeak

The language of euphemism can take a sinister turn when used deliberately to evade or gloss over the truth (especially when this is done by members of large bureaucracies). In this case, euphemism becomes **doublespeak,** evasive language used intentionally to confound, cover up, or mislead. The bad guys have *weapons of mass destruction;* the good guys have *assets.* Up until 1949, we had the bluntly and forthrightly named Department of War; today, we have the Department of Defense.

Learn to identify euphemism and doublespeak used as part of another's argument. When writing, respect your readers enough to tell them the truth about what you think, in plain, strong words.

Figurative language engages our imaginations to more strikingly convey meaning. Figures of speech such as metaphor, simile, allusion, and hyperbole can help the reader see what you mean by creating word pictures.

Metaphor and simile both compare one thing to another. **Metaphors** are implicit; that is, they imply a comparison. **Similes** are explicit; that is, they spell out a comparison using the word *like* or *as.* "His mind is a steel trap" uses a metaphor; "His mind works like a steel trap" uses a simile.

An **allusion** refers to a familiar phrase or other part of a literary work, such as a character, storyline, or title. If you call something a "Sisyphean task," you're making an allusion to the myth of Sisyphus, who was condemned to endlessly roll a giant boulder up a hill only to have it fall down again each time he reached the top. If you write "The winter of 2003 was truly a winter of discontent for those citizens who faced soaring heating costs amidst a sinking economy and unprecedented job losses," you're alluding to the opening lines of Shakespeare's *Richard III,* "Now is the winter of our discontent / made glorious summer by this sun of York."

Metaphor, Mixed Metaphor, and Cliché

A metaphor implies a comparison by describing one thing in terms of something else, thus introducing a fresh perspective.

> The **demon of torture** returned to the police stations.
>
> From Robert D. Kaplan, *Balkan Ghosts* (New York: Vintage/Random House, 1993), 258.
>
> The young inventor followed in his father's **footsteps.**
>
> Philosophy is a **weighty** subject.

A mixed metaphor creates an awkward combination of images:

Mixed	The **burning anger** of the colonists **rained down** over Taxation without Representation. [Mixes metaphors of fire and rain]
Revised	The **burning anger** of the colonists **blazed** over Taxation without Representation.

A cliché is a metaphor that has worn out its welcome through overuse:

bent out of shape	grasping at straws
between a rock and a hard place	hard to swallow
cut to the chase	on a wing and a prayer

Similes

Similes make explicit comparisons between one thing and another using the word *like* or *as:*

> The man . . . had to walk half a mile to water, the weasel dangling from his palm, and **soak him off like a stubborn label.**
>
> From Annie Dillard, "Living like Weasels," in *Teaching a Stone to Talk* (New York: HarperCollins, 1982).

> The men who had stayed were doing their customary snake trading. One of them would offer a friend a rattlesnake, say, and the friend would reciprocate with a trio of copperheads. They were **like women swapping recipes after a church social.**
>
> From Dennis Covington, *Salvation on Sand Mountain: Snake Handling and Redemption in Southern Appalachia* (New York: Penguin Books, 1995), 190.

Don't stuff your writing with figurative language

Like any good thing, too much figurative language is apt to give your readers a kind of literary indigestion. Stick to the meat and potatoes of good plain prose when your aim is to inform or persuade your readers. Reserve figurative language for those times when your purpose is literary or when the rhetorical situation calls for elevated language and special emphasis, moments when the unexpected contrast between the things being compared or the shift in emphasis and added delight of alliteration convey meaning beyond the power of plain prose.

Hyperbole is the use of deliberate exaggeration to make a point; sentences such as "This book weighs a ton" or "I'm so hungry I could eat a horse" use hyperbole.

Alliteration differs from the above-mentioned figures of speech in that, rather than using startling contrasts or comparisons, it uses repeated sounds to create emphasis. Tom Paine's famous "These are the times that try men's souls" works through the alliterative use of "t" in *times* and *try*. Langston Hughes's "What happens to a dream deferred?" works through the alliterative use of "d" in *dream* and *deferred*.

Activity 38-7: Revising Mixed Metaphors and Clichés

Revise the sentences to eliminate mixed metaphors and clichés.

1. Like a hot sun, her happiness blew frostily over the assembled crowd.
2. With our team down by two runs, we were grasping at straws for a good play that would take us out from between a rock and a hard place.
3. The mayor, when speaking to the press about his plan for news conferences, said: "It has been our purpose all along to have a sort of a periodical potpourri to cover all of this flotsam and jetsam that flies through the media that can get nailed down on a regular, periodic track. So in a sense, that can be interpreted as open sesame, but don't throw darts."
4. It was a momentous decision; I was at a fork in the road where two paths diverged.
5. The pockets of corporations are bulging with the sweat of the working man.

Activity 38-8: Revising for Effective Word Use in Your Own Writing

Choose a piece of writing that you are working on. Visualize the audience you want to reach with your writing, whether it is your class, your instructor, or a different group. Examine your word choices while keeping your audience members firmly in mind. Using the chapter as a guide, revise your writing for effective word use. What effect does your revision have?

39

We live in a pluralistic society at a time of rapid social change. As society changes, so does our language. Seen as part of the ongoing challenge of dealing with pluralism, language strategies for including diverse audiences are not just about being nice—although common courtesy will take you a long way toward inclusive writing—or about being begrudgingly "PC." Eliminating bias from your writing—whether on the basis of gender, race and ethnicity, disability, class, creed, age, or sexual orientation—is about extending the ongoing dialogue of democracy; listening to and hearing voices other than your own; and extending your credibility as a writer by respectfully addressing audiences of people who may not be like you.

39a The Power of Words

One of the most devastating hurricanes of 2004 was named Ivan. Prior to 1979, all hurricanes were given women's names; today we alternate the gender of the name. Does it matter? In recent years, the Washington Redskins and other similarly named sports teams have come under increasing pressure to change their names. Does it matter? In Wounded Knee, South Dakota, a historical marker placed by the federal government once commemorated the "Battle of Wounded Knee"; it now marks the location of the "Wounded Knee Massacre." What cultural-historical assumptions are represented by the word *battle*? By *massacre*?

Examine Your Language for Bias: Is It . . .

- **fair and accurate?**

Yes . . . the ASG terrorist group, which operates in the southern Philippines, . . .
No . . . Islamic terrorists operating in the southern Philippines . . .
Biased language equates all believers in a particular religion with specific groups that use violence to carry out social or political objectives.

- **inclusive?**

Yes Birth partners are encouraged to attend the class.
No Husbands are encouraged to attend the class.
Biased language excludes unmarried partners, same-sex partners, and others.

- **relevant?**

Yes Jones most recently played the title role in *The House of Bernarda Alba.*
No The deaf actress most recently played the title role in *The House of Bernarda Alba.*
Yes Jones, who is deaf, most recently played Esther, a deaf linguist-anthropologist who has taught a gorilla, Graham, to communicate via sign language.
The actor's disability is irrelevant to her portrayal of a Spanish matron, but relevant to her role as a deaf researcher who teaches a gorilla to sign.

- **parallel?**

Yes Citigroup praised the Finance Minister and likened him to Margaret Thatcher and Ronald Reagan.
No Citigroup praised the Finance Minister and likened him to Mrs. Thatcher and former President Reagan.
The treatment of Reagan and Thatcher should be parallel: Mrs. Thatcher and Mr. Reagan, former Prime Minister Thatcher and former President Reagan, or Margaret Thatcher and Ronald Reagan.

- **respectful of preferences?**

Yes Gretchen Wilson's "Redneck Woman" stands traditional outsider criticism of blue-collar lifestyles on its head.
No Gretchen Wilson's "Redneck Woman" stands traditional outsider criticism of rednecks on its head.
The songwriter's self-identification of herself as a redneck is different from the commentator's use of the same term, which could be seen as disparaging.

We all know that the bad guy is the *villain* and that the good guy is *noble.* But do these words—whose roots lie in a medieval social structure in which all *villains* (literally, "peasants" or "farm servants," from the Latin *villanus*) were considered less worthy as human beings than their ruling-class counterparts—still promote a class-based value system? What about *fair* for beautiful or *black* for evil? Do these words promote racism?

Over 225 years ago, the founders of our nation declared that "all men are created equal." Was that language meant to label as nonpersons all women, all men who lacked the requisite economic status, and all nonwhites? Or does it set forth a standard for equality that we're still striving to achieve?

A group of schoolchildren, told by their teacher to build *snowmen,* built 11 snowmen and 1 snow woman; a group told to build *snow figures* built 5 snowmen, 3 snow women, 2 snow dogs, 1 snow horse, and 1 snow spaceship.

However you feel about these complex issues, clearly language wields great power. It both reflects and constructs our reality. Words matter.

39b What Is Biased Language?

All biased language is based on unstated assumptions that position one group as dominant and normative and give that group the right to speak and to name others, while denying equal voice or dignity to those others.

Biased language has many adverse effects.

- It promotes stereotypes and relies on unexamined assumptions: "All Latinos are hot-blooded." "All African Americans are great musicians and basketball players." "All persons in wheelchairs deserve our pity." "Women are domineering, but men are strong leaders."
- It excludes or marginalizes: "The founding fathers fought against taxation without representation." (Did women take no part in the struggle for independence?)
- It calls attention to differences that are irrelevant and treats people unequally: "The patient was tended by five nurses and a Jewish doctor." (Is the doctor's religion or ethnicity relevant?)
- It ignores people's preferences as to what they would like to be called or is deliberately demeaning: Inuits didn't ask to be *Eskimos*. Ugly words like *spic* and *fag* promote hatred.

Inclusive language respects differences and seeks to present them in nonjudgmental terms. Biased language harms your credibility with potential readers. Inclusive language widens your audience.

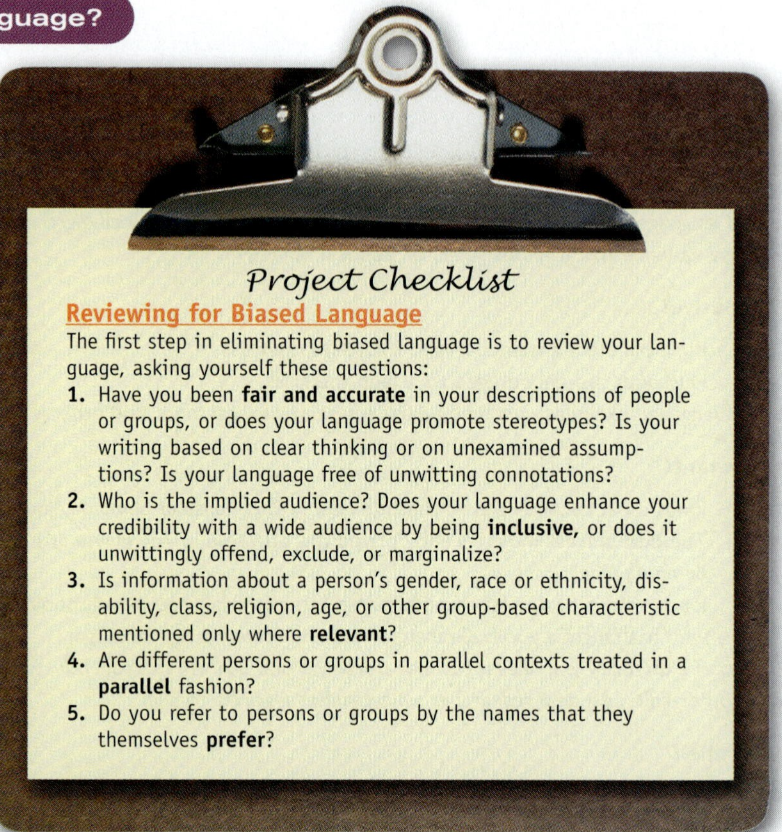

Project Checklist

Reviewing for Biased Language

The first step in eliminating biased language is to review your language, asking yourself these questions:

1. Have you been **fair and accurate** in your descriptions of people or groups, or does your language promote stereotypes? Is your writing based on clear thinking or on unexamined assumptions? Is your language free of unwitting connotations?
2. Who is the implied audience? Does your language enhance your credibility with a wide audience by being **inclusive,** or does it unwittingly offend, exclude, or marginalize?
3. Is information about a person's gender, race or ethnicity, disability, class, religion, age, or other group-based characteristic mentioned only where **relevant**?
4. Are different persons or groups in parallel contexts treated in a **parallel** fashion?
5. Do you refer to persons or groups by the names that they themselves **prefer**?

Activity 39-1: Revising for Inclusive Language Use

Revise the following sentences to make them appropriately inclusive.

1. Many communities provide an after-school program for working mothers.
2. The two senators from New York, Senator Schumer and Mrs. Clinton, attended the rally.
3. The Catholic terrorist group was accused of bombing another abortion clinic.
4. The hiring committee included two Asian women and three men.
5. The oncology conference was chaired by Mrs. Julia Jones, a lady doctor.

Approaches to Eliminating the Generic *he*

1. Eliminate the pronoun altogether.

a. Delete it.

b. Replace it with an article.

Original	Every citizen should cast **his** vote on November 2.
Deleted	Every citizen should vote on November 2.
Replaced	Every citizen should cast **a** vote on November 2.

Original	A zookeeper observes several precautions when **he** feeds the lions.
Deleted	A zookeeper observes several precautions when feeding the lions.

Original	The older child frequently expresses resentment toward **his** infant sibling.
Replaced	The older child frequently expresses resentment toward **an** infant sibling.

2. Change the person or number of antecedent and pronoun.

a. Use *we, one,* or *you.*

b. Make the antecedent itself plural.

Original	Every citizen should cast **his** vote on November 2.
Revised	**We** should each cast **our** vote on November 2.
Revised	**Citizens** should cast **their** votes on November 2.

Original	The savvy traveler packs **his** suitcase lightly.
Revised	Savvy travelers pack **their** suitcases lightly.
Revised	Savvy travelers pack lightly.

Original	A zookeeper observes several precautions when **he** feeds the lions.
Revised	**One** must observe several precautions when **one** feeds the lions.

Original	An older child frequently expresses resentment toward **his** infant sibling.
Revised	Older **children** frequently express resentment toward **their** infant siblings.

Eliminating gender bias in language is often a matter of addressing the ways in which women have been erased linguistically. Such a project requires grappling with core grammatical issues, such as pronoun use and subject-verb agreement, and rethinking words that have been in use since before the time of Chaucer. As with attempts to erase bias in other contexts, it also means examining one's writing for unintended use of stereotypes or assumptions about gender, examining the relevance of remarks about gender (including remarks about appearance and marital or family status), and treating men and women with equal respect. Today, most professional organizations, journals, and publishers demand that writers observe guidelines for nonsexist usage, so any writer who wants to be published will need to observe such guidelines regardless of personal politics. It's as simple as that.

The Generic Pronoun *he*

Twenty-five or thirty years ago, most handbooks would have told you to correct the sentence *Everybody paid for their ice cream* to *Everybody paid for* ***his*** *ice cream.* Man was indeed "the measure of all things," and the generic pronoun *he* was considered to represent women as well as men.

Today, most people agree that it's no longer acceptable to use a pronoun that leaves out half the human race. But steering a course between biased writing, on the one hand, and awkward prose, on the other, isn't always easy. Among the available strategies are

- removing the pronoun or replacing it with an article
- changing the person or number of the antecedent
- recasting the sentence altogether

A controversial solution is to use *their* after an indefinite pronoun: *Everyone returned to* **their** *ordinary routine.* The practice of using the singular *he* began in the eighteenth century as a decree by what were then known as the "prescriptive grammarians." Many writers and grammarians still argue that some indefinite pronouns—such as *anyone* and *everyone*—should take a plural rather than a singular pronoun, based on both logic and a desire to eliminate the generic *he*. Such practice, however, is far from being accepted in all quarters. Many instructors, for example, find it inappropriate for the level of diction expected in a college paper.

Other methods, however, are best avoided: among them, slashed constructions like *he/she* and *s/he* and prefacing your writing by saying that all references to *he* mean either *he* or *she*.

3. Recast the sentence altogether.

a. Use the imperative mood.

b. Use the passive voice.

c. Use entirely different wording.

Original	A zookeeper observes several precautions when **he** feeds the lions.
Imperative	**Observe** these precautions when feeding the lions.
Recast	Without proper precautions, feeding the lions can be dangerous.

Original	Every citizen must pay **his** taxes by April 15.
Passive	Taxes **must be paid** by April 15.
Recast	April 15 is the deadline for paying federal taxes.

4. Use the phrase *his or her* sparingly.

While too-frequent use of the combination pronoun *his or her* can result in unwieldy or awkward prose, sometimes it's the right choice for a particular context.

Original	Each child paid for his ice cream.
Revised	Each child paid for his or her own ice cream.

Activity 39-2: Revising to Eliminate the Generic *he*

Using the methods described above, revise the following sentences to eliminate the use of masculine pronouns.

1. Every child should be given an equal chance to achieve his potential.
2. A historian must study for many years to get his PhD.
3. Each person should pay his admission fee by October 22.
4. A college student needs to set aside plenty of time for sleep so that he can be rested and alert for exams.
5. Each cast member in this year's production of *Guys and Dolls* should pay for his own costume.

Eliminating *man* Words

Instead of . . .	Consider using . . .
man (n), mankind (n)	human beings, human race, humanity, humankind, humans, individuals, men and women, people, we
man's (adj)	humans', society's, our
manpower (n)	human energy, humanpower, personnel, work force, workers
to man (v)	to operate, serve, staff, work
-man, as in "four-man team"	-person
average man, common man, man in the street	the average person, ordinary people, workers
man-made	artificial, manufactured, synthetic
freshman	first-year
workmanlike	skillful, expert
fathers, forefathers	ancestors, forebears, founders, pioneers, trailblazers

Activity 39-3: Eliminating *man* Words and Revising Job Titles

Eliminate gender bias from the following sentences. Consult the lists above and on page 788 if necessary.

1. Our forefathers blazed a trail across the United States.
2. The reporter became famous for his "man on the street" reports, in which he recounted people's views about current issues.
3. Two men and two women were elected to man the bridge during the first shift.
4. On their visit to the base, Rep. Sally Smith and Rep. Bob Knowles, our state congressmen, were escorted by the city councilmen and the chairman of the Rotary Club.
5. Jane Lane, spokesman for the company, said that the cause of the blaze was under investigation.

Words with *man*

Another linguistic trouble spot is the word *man* used to represent all of humanity. Other *man* words, such as *manpower* or the verb *to man,* also require careful scrutiny, as do historical and cultural references to figurative *fathers* when what is meant is the more-inclusive *founders, innovators, pioneers,* or *ancestors.* Some categories of *man* words can be considered biased by some people but not by others, so you'll want to make up your own mind about words like *freshman, workmanlike, sportsmanship,* or *showmanship* based on your understanding of the rhetorical context and the conventions and usage that attend it.

Occupational Titles

Forty years ago, if you had been looking for a job, not only would you have found the want ads divided into two sections titled "Help Wanted, Male" and "Help Wanted, Female," but many job titles themselves would have been gender specific: *fireman, policeman, repairman, mailman, anchorman; cleaning lady, salesgirl, stewardess.* The Civil Rights Act of 1964 prohibited discriminatory language in job listings; by 1975, the U.S. Department of Labor had revised nearly 3,500 job descriptions. The movement toward inclusiveness now encompasses other categories of endeavor, such as *chairman, councilman,* or *spokesman.* Instead of the one-size-fits-all *businessman,* we might now refer to a *businessman* or *businesswoman* or collectively to *businesspersons.* For those who object to the *-person* suffix as too self-conscious or clumsy, there are other possibilities. A *congressman,* for example, might be a *congressman or congresswoman,* a *representative,* a *congressional representative,* or a *legislator.* A *chairman* might be a *chairman or chairwoman,* a *chair,* a *presiding officer,* a *convener,* or a *coordinator.*

Equally important is not labeling occupations as male or female, as in *male nurse, male secretary, female engineer,* or *female executive.* Refer to gender only when gender is relevant, and try to word your sentences to put the emphasis on accomplishment, not gender. One such strategy is to use *man* and *woman* as nouns rather than as adjectives—for example, *rise of women in aerospace engineering* rather than *rise of female engineers in the aerospace industry.* Avoid attaching diminutive suffixes, as in *author***ess**, *aviat***rix**, *poet***ess**, *propriet***ress**, *suffrag***ette**, or *sculpt***ress***;* instead, use the gender-neutral *author, aviator, poet, proprietor, suffragist,* or *sculptor.* Even customary holdouts to this rule—*actresses, hostesses,* and *waitresses*—are quite respectably referred to as *actors, hosts,* and *waiters* or *servers.*

Occupational Titles: Men and Women at Work

Instead of . . .	**Consider using . . .**
anchorman	anchor, anchorperson
businessman	businessman or businesswoman, businessperson
chairman	chair, chairman or chairwoman, chairperson, convener, coordinator, presiding officer
coed	student
congressman	congressional representative, congressman or congresswoman, legislator, member of Congress, representative
councilman	council member, councilman or councilwoman
draftsman	drafter
fireman	firefighter
foreman	foreman or forewoman, supervisor
housewife	homemaker, householder
layman	layperson, nonprofessional, nonspecialist
mailman, postman	letter carrier, mail carrier, postal worker (But use *postmaster* when referring to the person in charge of a U.S. Post Office.)
newsman	journalist, newscaster, reporter
policeman	police officer
repairman	repairer
salesman	salesperson
spokesman	representative, spokesman or spokeswoman, spokesperson, press agent, press officer, public relations agent
statesman	appointed official, elected official, leader, legislator
stewardess	flight attendant
watchman	guard, security guard
weatherman	weather reporter, weathercaster
workman	worker
workmen's compensation	workers' compensation

Clarifying Terminology: *woman, female, lady*

1. As a noun, the term *woman*, used in parallel with *man*, is preferred for general use:

   Yes Men still outnumber women in the Senate.
   No Males still outnumber ladies in the Senate.

   As adjectives, *woman* and *female* can be equally acceptable in specific contexts:

   Yes The search committee interviewed both men and women (or male and female) candidates for the new professorship.
   No The search committee interviewed both men and lady candidates for the new professorship.

2. The term *female*, used in parallel with *male*, is primarily biological in connotation and is generally used in technical, medical, or scientific contexts:

   A study contrasted 200 female and 200 male adolescents with bipolar disorder.

3. The term *lady*, used in parallel with *gentleman*, has a connotation of refined politeness or high social position and is also used in situations requiring special courtesy:

   She had the bearing of a lady.
   He was a gentleman in name only.
   Ladies and gentlemen, please direct your attention to the center ring!

   Lady is also used in specialized references to nobility or, as in *First Lady*, to refer to the wife of a president or other leader in her public role as spouse:

   First Lady Abigail Adams
   Marjorie Rendell, First Lady of Pennsylvania

   But as a singular noun, *lady*, once used to denote special courtesy, is now generally considered to be offensive when used in such phrases as

   lady engineers
   saleslady
   Hey, lady! Move your car!

Clarifying Terminology: *lady, female, woman*

When it *is* relevant to specify gender, which of these terms should you use: *female, lady, woman; male, gentleman, man?* Curiously enough, most problems arise in using words about women. Each of these words is most properly used in parallel, as follows: *female/male, lady/gentleman, woman/man*. Each has different connotations. And each is considered idiomatically appropriate in different situations. So be careful in your choice of words.

In scientific circles, the notion of race is an increasingly contested one, with current research showing that so profound are genetic interconnections around the globe that variation between individuals is more significant than variation among groups. A more current way of discussing our differences is by referring to the idea of *ethnicity,* which looks beyond skin color to ancestry, language, and custom. Nevertheless, discussions about race and ethnicity remain among the most difficult in contemporary America. And group differences remain a source of pride as well as prejudice.

Eliminating language bias in regard to race or ethnicity is a matter of applying the five guidelines—to be fair and accurate, inclusive, relevant, parallel, and respectful of preferences—and then stepping back to consider how your language might sound to another.

Writing about Ethnicity: Which Do You Prefer?

African American	Preferred by some groups and individuals
Afro-American	Considered dated
Black, black	Preferred by some groups and individuals; may be either lowercased or capitalized; consult a style guide
colored, Negro	Use only as part of the name of an organization (e.g., the National Association for the Advancement of Colored People, founded in 1909)
American Indian	Most widely used term; use a more specific description when appropriate; does not refer to Inuits or Aleuts
Eskimo, Inuit, Native Alaskan	Though still widely used and most recognizable, *Eskimo* is considered offensive by many; *Inuit* is preferred; some groups and individuals use *Native Alaskan*
Indian	Preferred by some groups and individuals; use a more specific description when appropriate
native, indigenous, aboriginal	As nouns, *native* and *aboriginal* can be considered offensive; as an adjective, *indigenous* is more widely preferred, but *native* (as in *Native American, Native Hawaiian*) and *aboriginal* are still widely used
Native American	Preferred by some groups and individuals; use a more specific description when appropriate
nation, people	Preferred to *tribe*
Chicana, Chicano	Derived from the Spanish term *mexicano;* preferred by some Mexican Americans but considered objectionable by others—use with care; *Chicano* refers to a man, *Chicana* to a woman, though specific English usage varies
Hispanic	Refers to persons descended from residents of Spanish-speaking countries or cultures, including Spain (cf. *Latino, Latina*); preferred by some groups and individuals; does not mean the person speaks Spanish; does not refer to race; use a more specific description when appropriate, such as *Mexican American, Puerto Rican,* or *Cuban American*
Latina, Latino	Refers to persons of Latin American origin; preferred by some groups and individuals; does not refer to race; *Latino* refers to a man, *Latina* to a woman, though specific English usage varies; use more specific description when appropriate, such as *Mexican American, Puerto Rican,* or *Cuban American*

Caucasian, Caucasoid	Derives from nineteenth-century pseudo-anthropological system of racial classification and refers to peoples from Europe, western Asia, northern Africa, and parts of India; has been misused as a synonym for European or white
Amerasian	Refers largely to children fathered by American servicemen during Korean and Vietnam wars
Asian	Preferred term to refer to residents of Asian countries (China, Japan, Korea, Vietnam, etc.) and to things relating to Asia; use more specific national descriptions when appropriate
Asian American	Preferred term; use more specific description when appropriate, such as *Korean American, Chinese American,* or *Filipino American*
Asiatic	Considered offensive; do not use
Oriental	Considered dated or offensive; do not use
hyphenated American	Disparaging; do not use
hyphen as punctuation	Open compounds are more widely preferred; but usage varies (e.g., the *New York Times* still hyphenates such terms as *Vietnamese-American*)
ethnicity	A group definition based on culture, geography, language, country of origin
race	A contested term, so use with consideration; avoid nineteenth-century pseudo-anthropological terms, such as *Negroid, Mongoloid, Caucasoid* (or *Caucasian*), and *Australoid*
minority	Considered offensive by some but appropriate and useful by others; use with consideration
nonwhite	Considered offensive by some but appropriate and useful by others; use with consideration
persons of color	Preferred by some groups and individuals as an alternative to *minorities* for referring to people other than whites
brown, yellow, red, white	Use with consideration; can be considered offensive

Using Preferred Terms

One issue that demands special attention is the importance of using preferred terms. Preferences aren't static; they change as the social landscape itself changes. As Harvard professor Henry Louis Gates Jr. wrote in his 1969 application to college, "My grandfather was colored, my father was a Negro, and I am black." Some Native Americans prefer to be called American Indians; some persons of Latin American origin call themselves Hispanic, some Latino, some Chicano, and others something else entirely, depending on gender, cultural identification, and country of ancestry. Do your homework: if you're writing about a particular group of people, know what they call themselves and prefer for others to call them, and use terms accurately.

It is also important to use more specific designations as appropriate. There are over three hundred American Indian nations currently identified in the United States alone. A Hispanic person might be from Spain, Paraguay, Cuba, Mexico, or any point in between. Asian Americans come from countries as diverse as India, China, and the Philippines.

A final usage note: Don't use hyphens in terms like Chinese American and Cuban American. The use of hyphens in such compounds, as well as the term *hyphenated American* itself, has increasingly come under criticism.

One of the most useful guidelines for eliminating bias in all writing has come out of the disability movement: the People First rule, which says to put the person first, not the disability (or any other qualifier, such as gender, ethnicity, age, or class). Rather than calling someone an *AIDS patient,* use *person living with AIDS;* rather than referring to an entire group of persons as *the learning disabled,* use *persons with learning disabilities* or, more specifically, *children with dyslexia.* Calling someone *a diabetic* equates the person with the disease; calling someone *a person with diabetes* requires more words, but it more fully recognizes that person's humanity.

In writing about disabilities, be specific and accurate. For example, *deaf* means that a person cannot hear; *Deaf* means that the person is self-identified as belonging to a community that uses American Sign Language as the primary form of communication. *Blind* refers to someone without sight; someone with *limited sight* might also be referred to as *visually impaired* or *partly blind.*

In writing about a particular group, do your homework: be informed enough to be current and accurate. Avoid terms that are unnecessarily emotional or negative, such as *victim of* or *cripple,* as well as euphemisms such as *challenged.*

Writing about Disability

Words to use

Preferred terms for talking about disability are *disability* (noun) and *disabled* (adjective); they are considered to be the most straightforward and hence respectful. Their English usage dates back to 1557.

Follow the People First rule: put the person first, then the disability.

Yes persons with disability
No the disabled, disabled persons

Yes person with paraplegia
No paraplegic

Yes person with cancer
No cancer patient

Yes person with bipolar disorder
No manic-depressive

Words to avoid

Though still widely used in law and in everyday speech, *handicapped*—as in *handicapped parking* or *handicapped accessible*—is considered by many to be offensive or euphemistic. For many disabled persons, the handicap is not the disability itself but the physical, legal, and social barriers they may encounter.

Challenged, differently abled, and *handicapable* should be avoided as condescending, awkward, or euphemistic.

Yes She uses a wheelchair.
No She is mobility challenged.

Afflicted with, crippled by, cripple, suffers from, sufferer, victim of, victim, and *deformed* should be avoided as unnecessarily negative or emotional.

Yes . . . the study found that those with arthritis . . .
No . . . the study found that arthritis sufferers . . .

Confined to a wheelchair should be avoided; wheelchairs are not necessarily confining to those who need them.

Yes . . . student Tom Baker, who uses a wheelchair . . .
No . . . student Tom Baker, who is confined to a wheelchair . . .

Other Resources to Consult on Eliminating Bias from Your Writing

- "Bias-Free Language" in the *Copyeditor's Handbook* by Amy Einsohn
- *The New York Times Manual of Style and Usage*
- *Talking about People: A Guide to Fair and Accurate Language* by Rosalie Maggio
- "Guidelines for Gender-Fair Use of Language" by the National Council of Teachers of English (2002): **http://www.ncte.org/about/over/positions/category/gram/107647.htm**
- "Guidelines to Reduce Bias" in the *Publication Manual of the American Psychological Association*
- "Avoiding Sexist Language," as well as entries for individual words, in the *Random House Webster's College Dictionary*
- Entries for individual words in the *American Heritage Dictionary of the English Language* and the *American Heritage Book of English Usage*

Along with references to gender, race, and disability, references to a person's age, sexual orientation, religion, and any of a host of other group identifiers and affiliations can be the source of bias. The resources listed here provide more specific information on eliminating bias from your language.

Activity 39-4: Revising for Inclusive Language in Your Own Writing

Choose a piece of writing that you are working on. Visualize the audience you want to reach with your writing, and visualize, too, the people you mention in your writing. Examine how you've identified the people you have written about—the nouns, verbs, and adjectives you have used to describe them. Using the Project Checklist on page 784, review your work for biased language. Make any necessary revisions. What effect does your revision have?

PART 8

Understanding and Revising Sentences

New Contexts for Writing

Bumper Stickers, T-Shirts, CDs, and DVDs

You might not normally think of the writing and visual content on bumper stickers, T-shirts, CDs, and DVDs as requiring very sophisticated composing processes or rhetorical awareness. But, for example, the rhetorical situation of a bumper sticker, as a claim frozen in time, poses all the usual problems for its creator, while also making unreasonable demands. The work must be concise and visually effective while also fostering identification between the speaker and the audience, presenting a trustworthy ethos, and appealing to the emotions and good sense of the audience.

A bumper sticker that says "A woman needs a man like a fish needs a bicycle" or "My honor student beat up your honor student" makes a political point (in the first case, about gender equity and feminism; in the second, about the proliferation of "honor student" bumper stickers, which may function as social-class markers). The person who owns this old Volkswagen van (itself a statement) has a lot to say. The sheer number of the bumper stickers, in fact, now makes the cumulative point that people should speak out and exercise their right to free speech, an American ideal.

Presentation or **display text** is a kind of advertising meant to catch the attention and hold visual interest. It has to be to the point (i.e., concise), catchy or witty without being too obscure (like a good metaphor), and able to be taken in at a glance. **Identification,** a primary aim of rhetoric, is the process of asserting identity between people or between people and ideas.

Genre Knowledge

Bumper stickers (and T-shirts) express identity, so while you have to worry about what to say and how to say it, you also need to realize that you will be identified with your words and images. In a nutshell, these are the same rhetorical challenges faced by any writer, no matter the genre and circumstances.

With CD and DVD packaging, you face similar challenges: to be concise while capturing visual interest, to represent the content of the CD or DVD accurately while also expressing its character visually, and to write and design within tightly controlled dimensions. CD and DVD packaging has become a genre all its own, with sleeve books and jackets telling more of the story, whether the content is music, movies, photographs, or other multimedia content.

Each of these genres may serve social and political purposes also. Bumper stickers announce political allegiances. T-shirts define identity and show solidarity with causes, groups, or products. CD and DVD packaging conveys the essence of content in ways that extend meaning. In writing in each of these contexts, you exercise rhetorical abilities that can serve you well in others.

Make Your Own!

- Buy blank bumper sticker labels for your printer.
- Create your own T-shirt design in a graphics editor and print it on fabric transfer paper.
- Design CD or DVD labels and write the content for the sleeve book using a free program like Avery's Design Pro Limited (http://www.avery.com).

40

PARTS OF SPEECH AND SENTENCE STRUCTURE

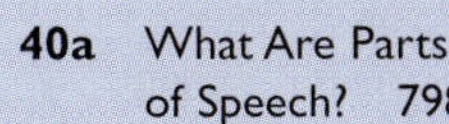

The sentence-level rules by which a particular language operates are known as grammar. If you're a native speaker, you know most of the rules of grammar already and did by the time you were three or four years old. You picked them up through observation and practice as an intrinsic part of acquiring language itself. You have, in other words, what's called *linguistic competence.* This chapter will help you sharpen your basic grammatical competence into effective *performance* as a writer who shapes language to the many complex contexts that call for effective and purposeful writing.

Grammar is all about sentences, not words or paragraphs. Although words do change (or *inflect*) according to the rules of grammar, they change in accordance with their use within a particular sentence and in relation to the words around them. Whereas the conventions of spelling and questions of correct usage apply to individual words, grammar by definition functions within the context of the sentence. In terms of the paragraph, while some paragraphs are clearly better written than others, there are no rules of grammar that apply to paragraphs per se—just to the sentences within them.

The first part of this chapter looks at how words function as parts of speech, focusing on their role within the sentence. In the second part, we'll look at syntax, or how sentences are structured.

40a What Are Parts of Speech?

At the most basic level, sentences consist of words that refer to or describe things (nouns, pronouns, and adjectives) and express or describe actions or emotions (verbs, adverbs, and interjections), connected by words that create relationships (conjunctions and prepositions). These building blocks of a sentence—the types of words people use to communicate ideas—are called the parts of speech. All the words you use to express your ideas are in fact parts of speech, and words can be classified into the major categories called "the parts of speech" based on their role in a sentence. The parts of speech are not specific words, but word functions defined by the context in which they are used. Very often, the same word can function as different parts of speech depending on how it is used in a sentence. You can *bake* (verb) a cake for a *bake* (adjective) sale. You can play with a toy *top* (noun), *top* (verb) a tree, or be a *top* (adjective) performer.

It's important to remember that the parts of speech aren't rules of usage that dictate how you should write. They are classifications of words by their function in a sentence.

The word *like* can function within a sentence as a(an) . . .

Verb	I *like* cake.
Noun	You don't see his *like* every day.
Preposition	They lived *like* royalty.
Adjective	in *like* manner.
Adverb	I ran *like* crazy.
Conjunction	She took to soccer *like* a duck to water.
Interjection (nonstandard)	Dude, *like*, let's get going!

Activity 40-1: Words Functioning as Parts of Speech

Use a college dictionary to determine which parts of speech each of the following words can be. Then choose one of the words, and see if you can write a sentence using it as each part of speech.

1. time
2. run
3. set
4. star
5. as

Examples of Nouns

Proper	Common	Concrete	Abstract
Linda Chavez	woman	bed	comfort
Vancouver	city	wind	anger
Hyundai	car	bells	belief

Collective	Countable	Uncountable
team	players	team spirit
faculty	classmates	homework
army	soldiers	equipment

Multilingual writers: Most errors in noun form result from problems in distinguishing between countable and uncountable nouns; see Chapter 60.

A Noun?

The following questions can help you decide whether a word is acting as a noun.

1. Can the form of the word be changed to indicate singular or plural (▶ section 60a)?
2. Can you make the word possessive (▶ section 51a)?
3. Can you insert *a, an, the,* or *some* directly before the word?
4. Does the word end with one of these suffixes, which usually indicate nouns: *-ance, -ence, -ment, -ness,* or *-ty*?

Activity 40-2: Identifying Nouns

Underline the nouns in the following paragraph. Then label them as being proper or common; concrete or abstract; collective, countable, or uncountable. A noun may be classified in several ways.

The International Olympic Committee released a decision from Singapore about the number of sports that would be allowed in the 2012 Summer Olympic Games in London, England. Karate, squash, and rugby were not admitted as sports. Baseball and softball were also cut from the competition. The games will have 26 sports, a decrease from the 28 sports of past games. The many players of these sports expressed disappointment that they would not be able to play them in the games.

A **noun** refers to a person, place, thing, quality, state, action, or concept: people, animals, locations, plants, insects, inanimate objects, collections of things, sensations, or actions (such as *jumping*). Anything that can be discretely isolated or referred to—pointed to or singled out—can be named with a noun.

- **Proper nouns** name a specific person, place, or thing. The first letter of a proper noun is capitalized. **Common nouns** name the types of things that a proper noun represents.
- **Concrete nouns** name things or objects that you can sense—see, hear, taste, smell, touch, or experience in the world. **Abstract nouns** name things that cannot be known through the senses, but can only be sensed internally as feelings or thoughts. They are intangible, even though they are real.
- **Collective nouns** name a collection or group: *police, faculty, team, family, army, class.* **Countable nouns** name things that may exist as distinct units and that may be counted: *voter, tree, shoe, byte.* Most count nouns can be made plural by adding *s: voters, trees, shoes, bytes.* **Uncountable nouns** name things that are usually considered wholes or abstract ideas and can't be counted: *mud, confusion, enthusiasm.* They normally can't be made plural.

40c Pronouns

A **pronoun** usually substitutes for a noun in a sentence. (The prefix *pro-* means "for," so you can remember that a pronoun stands in *for* a noun.) The noun that the pronoun refers back to or replaces is called the **antecedent.**

- **Personal pronouns** refer to people or things: *I, you, he, she, it, we, they, me, him, her, it, us, them.*
- **Indefinite pronouns**, such as *all, anyone, each, everybody,* and *some,* refer to unnamed or indefinite antecedents.
- **Relative pronouns,** including *which, that, who,* and *whom,* introduce a noun clause or an adjective clause. A list of relative pronouns appears on page 825.
- **Interrogative pronouns,** including *who, whom, which,* and *what,* as well as their corresponding forms *whoever, whomever, whichever,* and *whatever,* introduce questions.
- **Demonstrative pronouns**—*this, that, these,* and *those*—refer to a noun or pronoun antecedent.

Example 1 Pronouns

Personal pronouns:

Grace opened her book, but **she** couldn't find **her** place.

The picnicking *family,* who had gone swimming, returned to find **their** ham gone.

We wrote a book about *cognition* so that **you** would understand how **it** works.

Indefinite pronouns:

All it takes to succeed in this course is a little hard work.

Everyone driving through the neighborhood will see our yard sale signs.

Relative pronouns:

NOUN CLAUSE

She is the girl ***who* earned straight As in high school.**

ADJECTIVE CLAUSE

Go up the trail ***that* starts at the beach.**

Interrogative pronouns:

Which book will you read tonight?

I will read **whichever** one I like.

Demonstrative pronouns:

This is the best book I have ever read. [*This* refers to a book the speaker is holding.]

That one makes me fall asleep. [*That* refers to a book that is farther away.]

Indefinite Pronouns

all	each	more	one
another	either	most	several
any	everybody	neither	some
anybody	everyone	nobody	somebody
anyone	everything	no one	someone
anything	few	none	something
both	many	nothing	

Example 2 Demonstrative pronouns in topic sentences

Especially in topic sentences, consider replacing a demonstrative pronoun with a demonstrative adjective and a noun to make sure readers understand what other word is being referred to (the antecedent). Compare:

Einstein mistakenly put forth the notion of the ether as a way to account for all the matter in the universe that his theory of special relativity predicted. **This** was known as "Einstein's folly." [Does *this* refer to his theory of relativity or to his act of putting forth the notion of the ether?]

Einstein mistakenly put forth the notion of the ether as a way to account for all the matter in the universe that his theory of special relativity predicted. **This mistake** came to be known as "Einstein's folly." [The noun *mistake* clarifies that *this* refers to Einstein's notion of the ether.]

Example 3 More pronouns

Reflexive pronouns:

He hit **himself** in the foot with the puck.

After that party, they found **themselves** in trouble with their parents.

Intensive pronoun:

The author **herself** signed the book for me.

Reciprocal pronoun:

When two people are talking to **each other** at the same time, it's doubtful either one is listening.

Activity 40-3: Identifying Pronouns

Underline each pronoun in the following paragraph. Then label them as being personal, indefinite, relative, interrogative, demonstrative, reflexive, or reciprocal.

Identical twins may start to be less alike as they get older. Researchers studied forty pairs of twins; each was asked to fill out a questionnaire and give a genetic sample. Which twins most resembled each other? The results showed that younger twins were the ones who most resembled each other genetically. This research may contribute to an understanding of how our genes change as we get older as well as to research on how twins differentiate themselves from each other personally and psychologically.

- **Reflexive pronouns**—*myself, yourself, himself, herself, itself, ourselves, yourselves,* and *themselves*—refer back to nouns or personal pronouns when the subject of an action and the object of that action are the same.
- The same pronoun forms used to show the reflexive function can also be used for the purpose of intensifying an antecedent. When they are used this way, they are called **intensive pronouns.**
- **Reciprocal pronouns**—*each other* and *one another*—refer to an action that two antecedents perform mutually.

See Chapter 43 for more on pronouns.

40d Verbs

A verb is the central unit of any sentence or clause, and all the other words in a sentence take grammatical form based on how they relate to it. A **verb** can express action (*run, live, change*), states of being (*is, are*), or occurrences (*happen, become*). Sentences can have more than one verb. A clause is a sub-unit of a sentence that has one verb.

Action verbs express action by an agent in a sentence or clause. The agent needn't be present in the sentence, however. For example, in passive sentences agents may be deliberately omitted (▶ Chapter 44).

***To be* verbs** express states of being; they are sometimes referred to as *stative* verbs. *To be* verbs are *am, is, are, was,* and *were.*

See Chapter 44 for more on verbs.

Example 4 Verbs

Active sentence with action verb:

He *sat* quietly in front of the monitor.

Passive sentence with auxiliary and action verbs:

Mistakes *were made.*

Sentence describing state of being:

She *is* happy.

A Verb?

The following questions can help you decide whether a word is acting as a verb in a sentence.

1. Can you change the tense to indicate past time? Most verbs add *-ed* or *-d* to the plain form to indicate past tense: *played* (play + ed), *hiked* (hike + d). Some verbs form the past tense irregularly: *ride/rode, run/ran, eat/ate* (▶ pages 869–871).
2. If you put the word after a singular noun subject, would it change form in the present tense? *The child [swim]* → *The child swim***s**. Nearly all present tense verbs add *-s* or *-es* to the base form of the verb: *hugs* (hug + s), *kisses* (kiss + es). The two exceptions are *be,* which becomes *is,* and *have,* which becomes *has.*
3. Is the word one of two forms that can never be the verb in a sentence unless other verbs are helping them: infinitives (*to hug, to hit*) and *-ing* forms (*pleasing, writing*) (▶ section 41b)?

Activity 40-4: Identifying Verbs

Underline all the verbs in the following paragraph. Label each one as being active or a form of *to be.* Then determine which noun or pronoun each verb is working with.

The Pew Internet Project has released findings about how Internet users have changed their browsing habits. A survey of over 2,000 individuals revealed that many users are unhappy with spyware infestations. Half the respondents reported computer problems that were caused by spyware. While many acknowledge that some problems were their fault, all users insist that there should be more protection available for their computers.

Adjectives describe nouns and pronouns. Some adjectives limit or specify the noun or pronoun by showing its quantity, location, ownership, or other qualities.

- **Articles** are used before nouns. The articles are *a, an,* and *the.* The definite article *the* is used before a noun to indicate a specific item or items. The indefinite articles *a* and *an* indicate that a noun is used in a more general way.
- **Demonstrative adjectives**—*this, that, these, those*—emphasize a noun or pronoun.
- **Indefinite adjectives** are indefinite pronouns used to modify nouns and work much the same way as demonstrative adjectives.
- **Interrogative adjectives** go before a noun in a question.
- **Possessive adjectives** describe who possesses or owns the object named by a noun.
- **Proper adjectives** are proper nouns used to modify a noun.
- **Relative adjectives** are like relative pronouns, except they modify nouns instead of standing in for them.

Example 5 Adjectives

The **Lippit** *Morgans* are **beautiful** *horses.*

Articles:

The *teacher* used **a** laser *pointer.*

Demonstrative adjectives:

I'll carry **these** *boxes* if you take **that** *one.*

Indefinite adjectives:

Other *people* like these apples.

Each *kid* ran away from that school bus.

Interrogative adjectives:

What *kind* of motorcycle is that?

Whose *machine* broke first?

In **which** *tree* did you build a fort?

Possessive adjectives:

She hit **her** first *homerun* on the last day of the season.

Our *apartment* is too small for all of **your** *magazines.*

Proper adjectives:

Swedish *meatballs* are less popular with children than **Turkish** *taffy.*

Relative adjective:

If you would ask for directions, we would know **which** *road* to take.

Multilingual writers: Adjectives before a noun often need to be in a certain order; see section 62c.

Activity 40-5: Identifying Nouns, Pronouns, and Adjectives

In the following paragraph, underline and label each noun, pronoun, and adjective.

According to sleep scientists and doctors who specialize in sleep disorders, only fifty percent of Americans are getting enough sleep. Why are some people not sleeping well? Apparently, sleep quality is just as important as sleep length. For sleep quality, people need to make sure that they have enough time for sleeping as well as a soothing environment. To ensure a good night's sleep, experts recommend that people create an environment for themselves that is cool, dark, and comfortable, and also that they cut back on their intake of caffeinated drinks, especially shortly before their bedtime.

Adverbs modify verbs, but they also modify adjectives, other adverbs, and whole clauses. They answer the questions "When?" "Where?" "How?" "To what degree or extent?"

- **Adverbs of degree** answer the question "To what degree or extent?" Some adverbs of degree compare one item with a second; these are called **comparative adverbs.** Others compare an item with two or more other items; these are called **superlative adverbs.** For more on adverbs of degree, see Chapter 46.
- **Conjunctive adverbs** indicate specific relationships between sentences and ideas. They help show the relationships among sentences, and using them well can improve the overall coherence of your writing. Conjunctive adverbs create lexical ties, which are direct relationships of meaning across sentences (Chapter 5). You may want to memorize the conjunctive adverbs.

Example 6 Adverbs

I *ran* **yesterday**. [Modifies verb]
It was **really** *dark*. [Modifies adjective]
Hibiscus blooms **very** *profusely*. [Modifies adverb]
Quickly, the tourists *snapped* dozens of photos. [Modifies verb]

Adverbs of degree

Positive degree	I run **quickly.** I walk **fast.**
Comparative degree	I run **more quickly** than he does. I walk **faster** than she does.
Superlative degree	I run the **most quickly** of all the competitors. I walk the **fastest** of all.

Conjunctive adverbs and their meanings

	Conjunctive Adverbs
Comparing and contrasting	conversely, however, instead of, likewise, nevertheless, nonetheless, similarly, still
Adding information	additionally, also, besides, furthermore
Suggesting implications and results	accordingly, consequently, then, therefore, thus
Expressing time order	finally, first, meanwhile, next, second, subsequently, then
Making or emphasizing a point	always, certainly, definitely

Activity 40-6: Identifying Verbs and Adverbs

In the following paragraph, underline and label each verb, adverb of degree, and conjunctive adverb.

Stephanie Burns definitely recommends that you create habits for actions such as studying, brushing your teeth, and exercising, but also for long-term goals such as taking exams and saving money. Habits will keep you from having to struggle with certain decisions; you will be able to easily navigate through your day. How can you quickly instill a new habit? First, you must firmly decide on the specific behaviors that you want to be a habit. Second, you must decide on the triggers that you will use for the habit, and you must always use these triggers in order to more easily make the habit part of your life. Finally, you must carefully motivate yourself to act in ways that encourage the habit but do not discourage you from making changes.

Prepositions indicate relationships, often of space or time, between the nouns or pronouns that follow them and the other words in a sentence. Prepositions do not change form. English has many prepositions, but you can recall some of the most familiar ones if you imagine all the places you can be in relation to, for example, a house: *in, on, above, below, beside, around, between, over, under, at,* and so on. Some prepositions consist of more than one word.

Example 7 Prepositions

I ran **into** the *woods* and **across** the *stream* to escape my little brother.
The cat cackles **at** the *bird*.
I have everything my heart desires, **except for** *you*.

Common Prepositions

about	beyond	onto
above	by	out
according to	despite	outside
across	down	over
after	during	past
against	except	since
along	for	through
among	from	to
around	in	toward
aside from	in spite of	under
at	inside	underneath
before	instead of	until
behind	into	upon
below	near	with
beneath	of	within
beside	off	without
between	on	

Activity 40-7: Identifying Prepositions

Circle each preposition and underline the nouns or pronouns that come after it.

New York City requires that hotels and motels include all of the taxes in the final bill that you pay when checking out of the hotel or motel. The city also requires that safety, liability, and all incidental charges be explained on the inside of the room door. Unlike the situation in other countries, tips are never included in the final bill. For instance, the bellhop normally receives two dollars for each piece of luggage carried for you. As the bellhop exits your room or delivers you into your vehicle when you depart, you can give the tip. Unlike the bellhop, the housekeeper is not in sight, so you leave two or three dollars for each night in the room on the table or desk for the housekeeper.

40h Conjunctions

Conjunctions connect clauses, phrases, and individual words. Three types of conjunctions are coordinating, subordinating, and correlative.

- **Coordinating conjunctions** place words in a sentence in coordinate (that is, parallel) relationships. The seven coordinating conjunctions are *and, but, so, yet, for, or,* and *nor.* Notice that when the conjunction joins independent clauses, a comma must precede the conjunction.
- **Subordinating conjunctions** express a logical or temporal relationship among elements in a sentence or between ideas across sentence boundaries. If the subordinate clause precedes the independent clause to which it is attached, separate the clauses with a comma.
- **Correlative conjunctions** express relationships of contrast or similarity between different elements in a sentence. They come in pairs: *both . . . and, either . . . or, neither . . . nor,* and *not only . . . but also.*

Example 8 Conjunctions

Coordinating conjunctions:

He studies every afternoon, **but** he rarely passes his exams. [*But* joins two independent clauses. Notice the comma.]

I like to run marathons **and** lift weights. [*And* joins two phrases.]

Subordinating conjunctions:

Although he was quick on his feet, the attack surprised him.

You'd better have lots of money with you **when** you go shopping for a plasma TV.

Correlative conjunctions:

She **not only** *rose* to the top of her class **but also** *became* an ambassador for the school.

Notice that the words following each part of the correlative conjunction are of the same grammatical form (*rose* and *became* are both past-tense verbs). When you use correlative conjunctions, take care to preserve this parallel structure.

Subordinating Conjunctions

after	if	till
although	if only	unless
as	in order that	until
as if	now that	when
as long as	once	whenever
as soon as	provided (that)	where
as though	rather than	whereas
because (of)	since	wherever
before	so that	whether
due to	such that	which
even if	than	while
even though	that	why
how	though	

Interjections begin or interrupt sentences and express strong or sudden emotion, as well as attitude or tone, such as surprise, resignation, or irony. Interjections can also be words used to address someone, such as *hi, hello,* or *hey.*

Example 9 Interjections

Wow! That McDonald's coffee is hot.
Oh, how disappointing!

In the first sentence, the interjection is separated from the main sentence with an exclamation point. However, you can express a closer relationship between the interjection and the rest of the thought, and soften the expression of emotion, by including the interjection in the sentence, separated from it with only a comma, as in the second example.

Alas, poor Yorick. I knew him. [Hamlet's famous line expressing regret and irony, uttered while contemplating the skull of an old friend, now dearly departed]

Hi, _______ [common email salutation]

Activity 40-8: Identifying Conjunctions and Interjections

Read the following paragraph. Underline and label each conjunction and interjection, and note whether each conjunction is coordinating, subordinating, or correlative.

Although polio has now been almost eradicated in many countries, this was not the case in much of the earliest part of the twentieth century. Cases of polio happened most frequently in July, August, and September. The epidemics affected people of different economic classes as well as people in many geographic regions with different population densities. Although few people showed any symptoms and even fewer died or were paralyzed, people were still afraid of the disease since they did not understand how it was spread. Communities often overreacted to the disease because no one understood how or why people got it and also because children were the most frequently affected. Oh, if only the vaccine could have been discovered earlier!

40j What Is a Sentence?

A **sentence** is a string of words that obey the grammatical rules of a language. Sentences are grammatically complete, meaning that they don't need any more words to make an assertion, state a fact, ask a question, or exclaim. Grammatical completeness resides in the noun-verb pair that is the core of every sentence: someone or something carrying out an action or expressing a state of being. A sentence begins with a capital letter and ends with a period, question mark, or exclamation point.

A noun-verb pair is at the core of every sentence

N V
Reggie laughs.

N V
Darnelle was missed by her friends.

N V
Finding my long lost twin was like recovering a missing part of myself.

Notice that if you were to add a subordinating word such as *although* to the beginning of the sample sentences, they would no longer be complete, independent sentences. They would be incomplete thoughts: *Although Reggie laughs.*

40k Subject and Predicate

The grammatical terms for the noun-verb pair that is the core of every sentence are *simple subject* and *simple predicate.* Every sentence can be broken into these two parts.

- The **simple subject** is whomever or whatever the sentence is about; it and all the words that go with it are called the **complete subject.** In the complete subjects to the right, the simple subjects are in bold.
- The **simple predicate** is the verb that relays the subject's action or state of being. The verb and all the words that go with it are called the **complete predicate.** In the complete predicates to the right, the verbs are in bold.

Subjects	**Predicates**
Bao	**is** funny.
The beautiful **boat**	**sails** in the harbor.
Throwing pottery on a wheel	**takes** practice.
She	**has been thinking** about her family.
Suki and **Eriko**	**laughed** loudly.
Tomas's **car**	**skidded** and **flipped** over.

How Can You Identify...

The Subject of a Sentence?

1. Find the verb.

   The peacock **runs.** [Active voice]

   The research study **was conducted** by first-year students. [Passive voice]

2. Ask "Who or what . . .?"

   Who or what runs? [*The peacock* is the subject of the first sentence.]

   Who or what was conducted? [*The research study* is the subject of the second sentence.]

Activity 40-9: Identifying Subject and Verb Pairs

Underline each subject and verb pair. Be sure to underline both parts of any compound subject or verb.

I am writing this letter in strong support of the application of Karen Jones for the Sidney B. Williams Jr. Intellectual Property Law Scholarship. I have known Karen for about five years now, primarily as a colleague here at Lincoln. During that time, I watched as she developed a revamped curriculum for the Art Department, helping to make the program more technology-based and helping to make the program's graduates more marketable. To those ends, she worked with various committees, developed consensus with constituencies on and off campus, and, finally, worked with students to make it a meaningful program. It is my estimation, made during this long period of observation and interaction, that Karen Jones is a most capable person and is able to contend with unexpected scenarios and produce positive outcomes. I highly recommend her for your scholarship.

Sentences can also have compound subjects and compound predicates. **Compound subjects** consist of two or more nouns linked by *and*. **Compound predicates** include two or more verbs joined by *and*.

Five Basic Patterns of English Sentences 40l

Compare these two sentences:

The girl chases the boy. The boy chases the girl.

How do we know who's chasing whom? Only by word order.

Example 10 The five basic sentence patterns

1. The chain saws (SUBJECT) whined (VERB).
2. Volunteers (SUBJECT) were cutting (VERB) huge cedar logs (DIRECT OBJECT).
3. The cedar plankhouse (SUBJECT) would show (VERB) visitors (INDIR OBJ) traditional Chinookan life (DIRECT OBJECT).
4. Clark (S) had called (VERB) the Chinooks (DIR OBJ) "orderly." (OBJ COMPLEMENT)
5. The new plankhouse (SUBJECT) is (V) a monument to their culture (SUBJECT COMPLEMENT).

Word order is the primary means by which English sentences communicate meaning.

Given the dominance of word order, it makes sense that the kinds of sentence patterns the language employs are relatively fixed. Most English sentences can be shown to conform to one of five standard patterns. All are to a certain extent variants on the core structure of subject-verb-object: Someone (subject) does (verb) something (object).

All sentences require the fundamental subject-verb pair, which can then be followed or not (depending on the type of verb) by objects and complements.

Sentence Pattern 1

Subject + Verb

The predicate in the subject + verb pattern consists of the intransitive verb only. **Intransitive verbs** do not take objects or complements; their meaning is complete. You can add descriptive details, but they do not change the basic pattern.

Sentence Pattern 2

Subject + Verb + Direct Object

Transitive verbs require a direct object to complete the thought. Transitive verbs can be in the active voice or the passive voice. In the active voice, the subject of the sentence performs the action. In the passive voice, the subject receives the action (▶ section 44g).

In a sentence in the active voice, the **direct object** receives the action and is usually a noun, pronoun, or noun phrase. To find the direct object, turn the core subject-verb pair into a question ending with *what?* or *whom?*

Sentence Pattern 3

Subject + Verb + Indirect Object + Direct Object

Indirect objects indicate *to whom* or *to what* or *for whom* or *for what* an action is performed.

Pattern 1: Intransitive verbs don't need objects or complements

Subject	**Verb**
Lightning	**flashed.**
The clock	**ticks.**
The library	**will open** at 10 a.m. [*At 10 a.m.* is a prepositional phrase, not an object or a complement.]
Visitors	**should leave** now. [*Now* is an adverb, not an object or a complement.]

Pattern 2: Transitive verbs require direct objects

Subject	**Verb**	**Direct Object**
Alexander Selcraig	navigated [what?]	a British ship.
The sailors	ate [what?]	dried peas and salt meat. [Compound object]

Many verbs have both transitive and intransitive meanings. Consult a dictionary if you need to.

Intransitive	**Transitive**
The water **runs.**	Luca **runs** the drill press.

Pattern 3: The indirect object usually receives or benefits from the action of the verb on the direct object

An Indirect Object?

1. Find the direct object:

   David sent Angelina *The Secret Life of Bees.* [David sent what? *The Secret Life of Bees* is the direct object.]

2. Ask "to whom or what?" or "for whom or what?"

   David sent Angelina *The Secret Life of Bees.* [David sent *The Secret Life of Bees* to whom or what? *Angelina* is the indirect object.]

Multilingual writers: See section 62b on the order of direct and indirect objects following different verbs.

Pattern 4: The object complement renames or describes the direct object

SUBJECT VERB DIR OBJ OBJ COMP
The voters elected Hawley mayor. [Hawley = mayor]

SUBJECT VERB DIRECT OBJECT OBJ COMP
Environmentalists found McKibben's argument compelling. [argument = compelling]

Pattern 5: The subject complement renames or describes the subject

SUBJECT V SUBJ COMP
This forest feels lonely. [forest = lonely]

SUBJECT V SUBJ COMP
The conference was a disaster. [conference = disaster]

Activity 40-10: Identify Sentence Patterns in Your Own Writing

Take a paragraph or two from a writing project you are working on. Analyze each sentence to see which sentence pattern you used. Take notes. When you have identified the pattern of each sentence, count up how many times you used pattern 1, pattern 2, and so on. Did you rely on one pattern more than others to express your thoughts? If you find one or two patterns predominating, revise your passage in order to practice using the other sentence structures. Reread your revision to see what effects these changes had.

Sentence Pattern 4

Subject + Verb + Direct Object + Object Complement

Object complements add to, describe, identify, or rename the direct object. Complements can be nouns, noun phrases, or adjectives. Object complements help complete the meaning of transitive verbs such as *call, elect, make,* and *name.*

Sentence Pattern 5

Subject + Verb + Subject Complement

The **linking verbs** used in the subject + verb + subject complement pattern require a complement to complete the thought. The complement renames, identifies, adds to, or describes the subject. Complements can be nouns, noun phrases, or adjectives. The most common linking verb is *be* (in all its forms, such as *is, are, was, were, was being*). Other linking verbs include *appear, become, feel, grow, look, make, seem, smell, sound,* and *taste.*

40l

Word Order Shifts

Questions that can be answered with a "yes" or "no" are usually formed by inverting the subject-verb word order. **Multilingual writers:** For more on forming questions, see section 62d.

Occasionally, a declarative sentence will proceed in the order verb-subject, rather than subject-verb. (For more on this kind of sentence variation, see section 37g.)

In expletive constructions, the word *it* or *there* is used to postpone the subject.

Example 11 Word order shifts

Forming a yes/no question:

Statement Taxes are high.

Question Are taxes high?

Inverting a declarative sentence:

VERB SUBJECT

At the end of the elf's nose grew a large wart.

Expletive construction:

VERB SUBJECT

There are one hundred violinists in that orchestra. [One hundred violinists are in that orchestra.]

40m Phrases

Phrases are word groups that do *not* contain the subject-verb pair needed for a complete sentence. Phrases function as a single part of speech: as a noun, verb, adjective, or adverb. A phrase can be a *part* of a sentence, but it can never *be* a sentence. (For information on sentence fragments, see Chapter 41.)

Example 12 Phrases

S V

In summer she likes **getting chocolate ice cream cones from the vendor at the beach.**

Noun Phrases

Noun phrases function as nouns and are made up of the main noun and its accompanying modifiers (adjectives and adverbs).

Example 13 Noun phrases

NOUN PHRASE

Nineteenth-century author Charlotte Bronte lived

NOUN PHRASE

a very restricted life.

Verb Phrases

Verb phrases function as verbs and are made up of the main verb and any accompanying auxiliaries, including *be, can, could, do, have, may, might, must, shall, should, will,* and *would,* in all their forms.

Example 14 Verb phrases

VERB PHRASE

His many illnesses **might have been caused** by the approaching final exams.

Example 15 Verbal phrases

Infinitive phrases:

NOUN NOUN

To err is human; **to forgive,** divine.

ADJECTIVE

The *cakes* in the window were **only to look at.**

ADVERB

They were *afraid* **to speak.**

Gerund phrase:

SUBJ COMPLEMENT

SUBJECT OBJECT OF *OF*

Going to school is part of **growing up.**

Present participle phrase:

Swinging with all his might, *he* struck a homer into the bleachers.

Past participle phrase:

Chosen in a competition that included 1,421 submissions, Maya Ling Lin's *design* for the Vietnam Memorial was a V-shaped black granite wall etched with the names of the war's 58,000 American casualties.

Example 16 Prepositional phrases

PREP OBJ PREP PREP OBJ PREP

On NASA Road in Houston, Texas, is the Lyndon B. Johnson Space Center.

As adjective The *quest* **for greater knowledge** continues.

As adverb Everyone in the area *was evacuated* **to higher ground.**

As adverb The game *was canceled* **because of the rain.**

Verbal Phrases

Verbal phrases are made up of a verbal—an infinitive, gerund, or participle—and its accompanying modifiers, objects, or complements.

- **Infinitive phrases** can act as nouns, adjectives, or adverbs. The infinitive is made up of *to* plus the root form of the verb.
- **Gerund phrases** act as nouns. A gerund is formed from the *-ing* form of the verb.
- **Participial phrases** function as adjectives. A present participle is formed from the *-ing* form of the verb. A past participle is formed from the *-ed* form for regular verbs and variously for irregular verbs (the past participle of *to choose* is *chosen*). Irregular verbs are listed in section 44b.

Prepositional Phrases

Prepositional phrases consist of a preposition followed by a noun, pronoun, or noun phrase known as the **object of the preposition**. The prepositional phrase also includes any modifiers of the object of the preposition. Common prepositions include *as, at, by, for, in, instead of, of, onto, to, under,* and *without*. (For a list of commonly used prepositions, see page 805.)

Prepositional phrases can function as adjectives and adverbs.

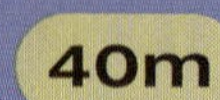

Absolute Phrases

Absolute phrases function as adverbs for an entire independent clause. An absolute phrase is usually made up of a noun and a present or past participle. (Sometimes the participle is understood but omitted.) Absolute phrases are set off from the clause they modify by a comma.

Appositive Phrases

Appositive phrases function as noun equivalents and restate, rename, or otherwise more fully define the noun immediately preceding.

- Most appositive phrases are **nonrestrictive**; that is, they are not essential to identifying the noun they rename. Nonrestrictive appositives are set off from the rest of the sentence by a pair of commas.
- **Restrictive** appositives—appositives essential to identifying the noun they rename—are not set off by commas.

For more examples of appositive phrases, see section 48f.

Example 17 Absolute phrases

The gold hidden, the pirates sailed away.

Example 18 Appositive phrases

Nonrestrictive (nonessential) appositive phrase with commas:

NOUN APPOSITIVE

Charlotte Bronte's *Jane Eyre,* **a novel that shocked Victorian England with its portrayal of a passionate, strong-willed woman,** made her both famous and infamous.

Restrictive (essential) appositive phrase with NO commas:

NOUN APPOSITIVE

The novels ***Jane Eyre* and *Wuthering Heights*** shocked Victorian England with their portrayals of passionate, strong-willed women.

In the first sentence, readers know exactly which novel the writer means, even if the appositive is removed; they even know the author's name. In the second sentence, the noun phrase is simply *The novels.* Here, we need the appositive, which includes the titles of the novels, in order to understand which novels the writer means.

Activity 40-11: Imitating Sentence Structure: Phrases

In each numbered item, a phrase modifies the basic sentence. (Phrases are shown in italics.) Write two sentences that imitate the sentence structure of each item. That is, use the same parts of speech and the same order of phrases and clauses. This practice will help you develop flexibility as a writer.

Examples based on #1 below:

The tree having split, the lightning arched back up into the sky.

The gate having broken, the horses pushed and shoved their way out.

1. *The film having concluded,* the audience gasped in relief.
2. The aisles, *coated with spilled soda and broken candy,* were treacherous.
3. The theater, *a cavernous and modern arena,* was dimly lit.
4. *On this sultry night,* the heat melted shoes to the floor.
5. *Enjoying the cool air outside,* people began animated conversations about the film's ending.

Example 19 Clauses

Independent clause as simple sentence:

I like chocolate ice cream.

Independent clauses as part of larger sentence:

Although I'm allergic to chocolate, **I like chocolate ice cream**.

I like chocolate ice cream because it is delicious.

Dependent clauses	although I'm allergic to chocolate because it is delicious
Noun clause	**What I love best about summer** is eating chocolate ice cream cones at the beach.
Adjective clause	The *ice cream* **that I love best** is chocolate.
Adverb clause	I *like* chocolate ice cream **because it is delicious.**

Relative Pronouns

that	which	whoever	whomever
what	whichever	whom	whose
whatever	who		

Example 20 Noun clauses

Noun clauses introduced by relative pronoun:

***That* men still make more money** is a fact. ***That* they deserve it** is not.

Noun clauses introduced by subordinating conjunction:

We can never know ***whether* he committed the crime or lied to the jury about his innocence**.

***How* we live** matters.

Noun clause as subject:

How wood frogs restart their hearts when unfreezing from hibernation is still a mystery.

Noun clause as direct object:

Scientists still don't understand **how wood frogs restart their hearts when unfreezing from hibernation.**

Noun clause as subject complement:

For scientists studying amphibians, one of the most intriguing questions is **how wood frogs restart their hearts when unfreezing from hibernation.**

Clauses are word groups that contain both a subject and a verb. An **independent clause**—as the name implies—can function independently as a simple sentence. It is grammatically *independent*. An independent clause can also combine with other clauses to form a larger, more complex sentence.

A **dependent clause**—as the name implies—cannot function independently as a simple sentence. It is grammatically *dependent*. All dependent clauses begin with a subordinating word, usually a subordinating conjunction or relative pronoun, that renders them unable to stand on their own as an independent sentence. Subordinating conjunctions are words like *because, as if, wherever,* and *even though*. A list of subordinating conjunctions appears on page 806.

Dependent clauses, like phrases, function as a single part of speech. They can be nouns, adjectives, or adverbs.

Noun Clauses

A **noun clause** begins with a relative pronoun (listed to the left) or a subordinating conjunction (usually *when, where, whether, why,* or *how*). Like all nouns, noun clauses answer the question "Who?" or "What?" in relation to the verb.

Like all nouns, noun clauses can function within a sentence as subjects, objects, or complements.

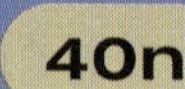

Adjective Clauses

Adjective clauses are usually introduced by relative pronouns and occasionally by *when, where,* or *why.* Like all adjectives, they modify nouns and pronouns and answer the question "Which one?" or "What kind of?" An adjective clause usually comes immediately after the noun it modifies.

Some adjective clauses are *elliptical*—that is, some part of the wording is understood rather than stated.

Example 21 Adjective clauses

According to a recent study, *athletes* **who wear red** win more often.

Revenge of the Sith, **which completes the *Star Wars* saga,** tells the story of how Anakin Skywalker becomes Darth Vader.

Manhattan's Lower East Side is a *place* **where many immigrants first began life in the United States.**

Elliptical adjective clause:

This is a *movie* [that] **everyone should see!**

Adverb Clauses

Adverb clauses are always introduced by subordinating conjunctions. Like all adverbs, adverbial dependent clauses modify verbs, adjectives, other adverbs, or even entire clauses. They answer the questions "How?" "When?" "Where?" "Why?" "In what manner?" "Under what conditions?" "With what result?" "To what degree?"

Some adverb clauses are *elliptical*—that is, some part of the wording is understood rather than explicit. In elliptical constructions in which both subject and verb are omitted from the adverb clause, watch out for illogical phrasings.

Example 22 Adverb clauses

They finally *left* the party **after eating all the food, drinking all the drinks, and monopolizing every conversation.**

At that moment, my father looked *older* **than he ever had before.**

The hair tonic never worked as *well* **as the advertisement promised.**

When the tornado sirens sound, *seek shelter.*

Elliptical adverb clauses:

George is just as *boring* **as Henry** [is].

Illogical — While mowing the lawn, a frog jumped in my way. [Here, readers may try to imagine just how frogs look while mowing the lawn, when you really intended one of the following.]

Logical — While I was mowing the lawn, a frog jumped in my way.

or

While [I was] mowing the lawn, I tripped over a frog.

Activity 40-12: Imitating Sentence Structure: Dependent Clauses

In each of the numbered items below, a dependent clause modifies the basic sentence. (Dependent clauses are shown in italics.) Using a piece of writing you have worked on recently as a starting point or starting fresh, write two sentences that imitate the sentence structure of each item. That is, use the same parts of speech and the same order and types of clauses. This practice will give you more choices of expression when you write.

Examples based on #1 below:

Penguins, which are a type of flightless waterfowl, live only in the Southern Hemisphere.

Red foxes, which are an endangered species, are being revived through zoo breeding programs.

1. Daylight savings time, *which requires people to shift their clocks forward and backward as the seasons change,* is practiced in most countries that are not located near the equator.
2. *What many people find attractive about daylight savings time* is their ability to do more in the evenings because of the extra hour of daylight.
3. However, many people are opposed to daylight savings time *because it can interfere with their sleep schedules or because they have to change their clocks.*
4. Two states *that do not observe daylight savings time* are Indiana and Arizona; however, Indiana has recently passed legislation in favor of adopting daylight savings time.
5. *Whether or not you agree with daylight savings time,* it seems that it is here to stay in most countries that are not near the equator.

Classifying Sentences by Grammatical Structure

Sentences can be classified by grammatical structure—that is, by the kinds of clauses they are built out of—as simple, compound, complex, or compound-complex.

Simple Sentences

A **simple sentence** consists of one independent clause. The essence of the simple sentence is the subject-verb pair. Although built on a single subject-verb pair, simple sentences can vary in length and complexity.

Compound Sentences

A **compound sentence** is made up of at least two independent clauses. In a compound sentence, the two independent clauses are usually joined by a comma and a coordinating conjunction (*and, but, or, nor, for, so, yet*). The two clauses can also be joined by a semicolon (◀Chapter 35).

Complex Sentences

A **complex sentence** consists of one independent clause and at least one dependent clause (◀Chaper 35).

Example 23 Simple sentences: one independent clause

S V
Snow is cold.

We saw the Grand Canyon.

Madame C. J. (Sarah Breedlove) Walker is considered to be America's first African American woman millionaire.

Example 24 Compound sentences

INDEPENDENT CLAUSE / INDEPENDENT CLAUSE
We saw the Grand Canyon / , and / they saw the ocean.

INDEPENDENT CLAUSE / INDEPENDENT CLAUSE
Madeleine is our calico cat / ; / she hates to catch mice.

INDEPENDENT CLAUSE / INDEPENDENT CLAUSE
Walker made millions / , and / she donated generously to African American causes, becoming one of the early twentieth century's most notable philanthropists.

Example 25 Complex sentences

DEPENDENT CLAUSE / INDEPENDENT CLAUSE
While we saw the Grand Canyon, / they saw the ocean.

INDEPENDENT CLAUSE / DEPENDENT CLAUSE
In visiting the rain forest, we at last saw the landscape / that we had imagined so vividly.

DEPENDENT CLAUSE
Although she was born to sharecroppers, orphaned at age seven, and

INDEPENDENT CLAUSE
widowed at twenty, / Walker made an independent fortune by developing and selling her own line of beauty products.

Example 26 Compound-complex sentences

INDEPENDENT CLAUSE

Walker used her wealth to support the preservation of African American history and the advancement of black culture / : /

INDEPENDENT CLAUSE

she helped to purchase the home of Frederick Douglass / , /

DEPEPENDENT CLAUSE

which is today a National Historic Site under the National Park Service /

INDEPENDENT CLAUSE

; and / the townhouse she built in New York City became an important gathering place for black artists during the Harlem Renaissance.

In the final independent clause, a dependent clause comes between subject and verb: [*that*] *she built in New York City.*

Compound-Complex Sentences

A compound-complex sentence is made up of two or more independent clauses and at least one dependent clause. To learn more about creating compound, complex, and compound-complex sentences, see Chapter 35.

Classifying Sentences by Discourse Function 40p

Sentences can also be classified by discourse function—that is, by considering one's purpose in writing or speaking.

Sentences Classified by Discourse Function

Declarative sentences give information:

Charlie found a worm in his apple.

Interrogative sentences ask questions:

Did he eat it?

Rhetorical questions, rather than being literal requests for information, are intended to engage or focus the reader's attention:

What is freedom? Freedom is a right and a privilege . . .

Imperative sentences issue commands; the subject, *you,* is usually implied:

Spit out that worm!

Exclamatory sentences express strong feelings or judgments; they usually begin with *what* or *how,* and they may be fragments rather than complete sentences:

How could he have done it! How disgusting!

41 FRAGMENTS

Sentence fragments are incomplete sentences, which many consider the most important errors to root out in college writing. Not only are they ungrammatical, but they can make your writing choppy and confusing, destroying the rhythm of your prose. Unintended fragments in writing result from an incomplete understanding of the grammatical structure of a sentence in English or from a failure to revise. If you revise too quickly, it's easy to miss a fragment in context. Basic English sentences include a subject, verb, and object, with some variations possible (in questions and orders, for example). Once you understand the grammatical structure and function of a sentence, you will have concrete strategies for identifying fragments and revising them to make effective sentences.

We often speak in fragments. Indeed, fragments are appropriate to spoken language, where the rhetorical purpose differs substantially from that of writing. Consider this exchange, conducted almost entirely in sentence fragments (underlined):

> "Where are you going?" says Jane.
> "<u>Home</u>," says John.
> "<u>OK</u>," says Jane.
> "<u>See you around</u>," says John.

In much the same way, fragments are appropriate in television shows, movies, plays, fiction—in any genre that seeks to capture the rhythms of everyday speech. In college writing, and even in more informal genres, such as email, sentence fragments are not the norm, and readers may judge fragments as a sign of carelessness or worse.

Fragments	Complete Sentences
No subject:	Who hid the diamond?
Hid the diamond.	Jane (S) hid (V) the diamond.
No verb:	What happened to the diamond?
The hidden diamond.	The diamond (S) was hidden (V).

A sentence is a grammatically and rhetorically complete unit that contains a subject and a verb. Whether a sentence is two words long or two hundred, the core of each sentence is someone or something (the subject) carrying out some action or expressing a state of being (the verb). A sentence begins with a capital letter and ends with a period, question mark, or exclamation point.

Sentence fragments are grammatically and rhetorically incomplete constructions, masquerading as sentences. Fragments lack a verb, a subject, or both. Or they have a subject and verb, but these appear in a subordinate clause that renders the clause dependent on another sentence for meaning. Even though fragments may be punctuated as if they were complete sentences, they are not.

Eliminate fragments by attaching them to complete sentences or by changing the fragment itself to a complete sentence.

Example 1 Revising fragments

FRAGMENT:
The hidden diamond.

REVISED TO BECOME A COMPLETE SENTENCE:
The hidden diamond (S) gleamed (V).

FRAGMENT:
After hiding the diamond.

REVISED TO BECOME A COMPLETE SENTENCE:
After hiding the diamond, Jane (S) ran (V) away.

FRAGMENT:
The diamond hidden.

REVISED TO BECOME A COMPLETE SENTENCE:
The diamond (S) hidden among the cinders gleamed (V) in the torchlight's glare.

FRAGMENT:
Jane hid the diamond. And ran away.

REVISED TO BECOME A COMPLETE SENTENCE:
Jane (S) hid (V) the diamond and ran (V) away.

41b Incomplete and Missing Verbs

A complete sentence requires a subject and a complete verb. Verbs define action and states of being. They tell you what someone or something does: Rover *runs,* Jane *laughed,* Tom *drinks.* Or they convey the subject's state of being: Sally *is* happy. Verbs answer the question "What is happening in this sentence?" A word group without a verb is not a complete sentence.

Verbals Aren't Complete Verbs

Some verb forms (called *verbals*) can act as nouns, adjectives, or adverbs but cannot function independently as verbs. Infinitives, gerunds, and participles are all verbals. Watch for these verb forms, either as single words or as part of verbal phrases, when revising to eliminate sentence fragments.

Infinitives

Infinitives, the root form of a verb such as *to run, to laugh, to drink,* or *to hit,* cannot act as verbs.

-ing Verbs

Verbs with the suffix *-ing,* such as *running, laughing,* and *swallowing,* cannot act as verbs unless paired with helping (auxiliary) verbs like *am* and *have.* Independently, they can function as adjectives (present participles) or as nouns (gerunds).

Some Fragments with Incomplete or Missing Verbs

Along the highway. [No verb; this is a prepositional phrase.]

Wishing for a miracle. [*Wishing* is an *-ing* verb.]

To run away together. [*To run* is an infinitive.]

Migration undertaken by birds and insects. [*Undertaken* is a past participle.]

Fears laid to rest. [*Laid* is the past participle of an irregular verb.]

Example 2 Revising a fragment caused by an infinitive

FRAGMENT:

The students to run in the halls.

REVISED BY ADDING A VERB BEFORE THE INFINITIVE:

The students ^want to run in the halls.

REVISED BY MAKING THE INFINITIVE PHRASE INTO THE SUBJECT:

~~The students to~~ ^To run in the halls~~.~~ ^is fun

Example 3 Revising a fragment caused by an *-ing* verb

FRAGMENT:

The python swallowing its prey whole.

REVISED BY ADDING A HELPING VERB BEFORE THE *-ING* VERB:

The python ^was swallowing its prey whole.

The python ^had been swallowing its prey whole.

REVISED BY CHANGING THE *-ING* VERB TO A SIMPLE PAST TENSE VERB:

The python ^swallowed ~~swallowing~~ its prey whole.

REVISED BY MAKING THE VERBAL PHRASE INTO THE SUBJECT AND ADDING INFORMATION:

The python swallowing its prey whole~~.~~ ^is an amazing example of nature's adaptability

Example 4 Revising a fragment caused by a past participle

FRAGMENT:

The blankets washed.

REVISED BY ADDING A HELPING VERB TO MAKE IT A COMPLETE VERB:

The blankets were washed.

REVISED BY MAKING THE PAST PARTICIPLE INTO A SIMPLE PAST TENSE VERB:

~~The~~ She washed the blankets ~~washed~~.

REVISED BY CHANGING THE PAST PARTICIPLE INTO AN ADJECTIVE AND THEN ADDING A NEW VERB:

The washed blankets smelled clean ~~washed~~.

Example 5 Revising a fragment caused by an absolute phrase

THE FIRST TWO WORD GROUPS ARE FRAGMENTS:

The blankets washed. The rugs hung out to dry. They paused for a snack.

REVISED BY CHANGING PERIODS TO COMMAS:

The blankets washed, the ~~The~~ rugs hung out to dry, they ~~They~~ paused for a snack.

Activity 41-1: Revising Fragments

Revise the paragraph below to eliminate fragments and to make complete sentences.

Many people believe that T. S. Eliot's epic poem "The Waste Land" was carefully planned by its author. Followed a careful plan when writing the long poem. However, Lawrence Rainey has discovered that the poem was not as carefully planned as people thought. How did Rainey discover that the poem was created out of multiple drafts? Using forensic analysis. The paper analyzed to determine age. The different types of typewriters and ink recorded. Allowed the professor to reconstruct a "timeline" of when each draft that made up the final poem written. Leading to a new vision of the poem. Will make many reconsider their analysis of "The Waste Land."

Past Participles

Past participles, usually formed by a verb plus *-ed,* can act as verbs only if paired with helping (auxiliary) verbs like *am* and *have.* By themselves, past participles act as adjectives.

Be careful! The same *-ed* word can function as both a simple past tense verb (*She* **boiled** *the eggs*) and a past participle (*She likes* **boiled** *eggs*), so you'll have to examine each construction individually to see if it's a sentence fragment or a complete sentence.

While past participles are usually created by adding *-ed* to the base verb, some common verbs form the past participle irregularly—for example, *hidden, bitten, slept, blown.* (For a list of irregular verbs, see section 44b.)

Absolute Phrases

One noun + participle construction often mistakenly used as a sentence is the *absolute phrase.* Absolute phrases are usually made up of a noun and a participle, plus any modifiers (they can also be a noun + a prepositional phrase). They modify an entire independent clause—they are not restricted grammatically to modifying a single word within that clause.

All sentences require a subject: a noun or pronoun that defines who or what the sentence is about. To find the subject, first find the verb and then ask, "Who or what is carrying out this action or is experiencing this state of being?"

Compound Predicates

Compound predicates are a common source of sentence fragments. A compound predicate consists of two verbs that belong to one subject: *She ate and drank.* The second verb sometimes gets cut adrift in its own sentence. To revise, either put the verbs back together again in one sentence or repeat the subject for one of the verbs.

Commands

Commands (also called *imperative statements*) might look like fragments, but they are in fact complete sentences. The subject (*you*) is implied. Commands are the only kind of sentence in English that can stand without a stated subject.

Some Fragments That Don't Have Subjects

Broke her heart. [Who or what broke her heart?]
Started to run. [Who or what started to run?]

Example 6 Revising a fragment caused by a compound predicate

THE SECOND WORD GROUP IS A FRAGMENT:

He broke her heart. And took her money.

REVISED BY PUTTING THE VERBS BACK TOGETHER IN THE SAME SENTENCE:

He broke her heart, ~~And~~ *and* took her money.

THE SECOND WORD GROUP IS A FRAGMENT:

The gambler grimaced and rolled again. Just needed two more points to win.

REVISED BY ADDING A SUBJECT TO THE FRAGMENT:

The gambler grimaced and rolled again. ~~Just~~ *He just* needed two more points to win.

Commands: Complete Sentences

Join the club.
Walk the dog.
Go to work!

Activity 41-2: Revising Fragments

Revise the paragraph below to eliminate fragments and to make complete sentences.

Recent medical technologies have told us more about the life and death of King Tutankhamen. Tutankhamen's short life and mysterious death have long fascinated people. And caused speculation about his cause of death. CT scans of the king's mummy have now shown us that the King was most likely not murdered. Instead died from pre-existing health conditions. Still, many people continue to theorize about how and why the king died. And how Egyptian history might be different had he lived.

A Dependent Clause Fragment?

1. Examine your writing for the subordinating conjunctions and relative pronouns listed below.

Subordinating Conjunctions

after	if	till
although	if only	unless
as	in order that	until
as if	now that	when
as long as	once	whenever
as soon as	provided (that)	where
as though	rather than	whereas
because (of)	since	wherever
before	so that	whether
due to	such that	which
even if	than	while
even though	that	why
how	though	

Relative Pronouns

that	whichever	whomever
what	who	whose
whatever	whoever	
which	whom	

2. When you find one, check to see how many subject-verb pairs are in the same sentence. If there is only one such pair, chances are you've written a fragment you need to revise.

   Although she knew him well.

3. If there are two subject-verb pairs, it may be that only one of them is part of the same clause as the subordinating word. If this is true, you have probably written a complete sentence.

   Although she knew him well, he didn't recognize her name.

While this method isn't foolproof, it will help you catch many dependent clause fragments.

All clauses—whether independent or dependent—contain a subject and a verb. But not all clauses can function as independent sentences.

A dependent (or *subordinate*) clause begins with a subordinating word that makes the clause function as a single part of speech: an adverb, adjective, or noun. Common subordinating words include *although, because, when, until, who, which, that, when, where, why,* and *how.*

A dependent clause on its own is a sentence fragment. To revise a dependent-clause fragment, either attach it to an independent clause, eliminate the subordinating words and make it into a complete sentence, or recast it entirely.

Dependent Clauses That Function as Adverbs

Adverbial dependent clauses are always introduced by subordinating conjunctions. Like all adverbs, adverbial dependent clauses modify verbs, adjectives, or other adverbs. They answer the questions "How?" "When?" "Where?" "Why?" "In what manner?" "Under what conditions?" "With what result?" "To what degree?"

If you decide to revise such a fragment by attaching it to an independent clause (complete sentence), think about whether it should come before or after the independent clause. If you attach it to the beginning, add a comma after the dependent clause.

Example 7 Revising a fragment caused by a subordinating word

THE FIRST WORD GROUP IS A FRAGMENT:

Because deforestation and pesticide use threaten the monarch butterfly. Its future is uncertain.

REVISED BY ATTACHING THE DEPENDENT CLAUSE TO THE COMPLETE SENTENCE WITH A COMMA:

Because deforestation and pesticide use threaten the monarch butterfly, ~~Its~~ its future is uncertain.

REVISED BY ELIMINATING THE SUBORDINATING WORD *BECAUSE:*

~~Because deforestation~~ Deforestation and pesticide use threaten the monarch butterfly. Its future is uncertain.

REVISED BY RECASTING THE SENTENCE:

Deforestation and pesticide use have made the monarch butterfly's future uncertain.

Example 8 Revising fragments caused by dependent clauses that function as adverbs

THE SECOND WORD GROUP IS A FRAGMENT:

Biologists predict that New England's maple sugar industry will move north to Canada. If global warming continues as currently predicted.

REVISED BY ATTACHING THE DEPENDENT CLAUSE TO THE INDEPENDENT CLAUSE; NO COMMA IS NEEDED SINCE THE INDEPENDENT CLAUSE COMES FIRST:

Biologists predict that New England's maple sugar industry will move north to Canada if global warming continues as currently predicted.

THE SECOND WORD GROUP IS A FRAGMENT:

The monarchs arrive at their winter homes in Mexico and California. After they make the arduous journey over plains, cities, deserts, and mountains.

REVISED BY MOVING THE DEPENDENT CLAUSE AND USING A COMMA TO JOIN IT TO THE INDEPENDENT CLAUSE:

After they make their arduous journey over plains, cities, deserts, and mountains, the monarchs arrive at their winter homes in Mexico and California.

Example 9 Revising fragments caused by dependent clauses that function as adjectives

THE SECOND WORD GROUP IS A FRAGMENT:

Many butterfly lovers join Monarch Watch. Which each year inspires monarch enthusiasts across America to observe and preserve this inspiring insect.

REVISED BY ATTACHING FRAGMENT TO THE COMPLETE SENTENCE WITH A COMMA:

Many butterfly lovers join Monarch Watch, which each year inspires monarch enthusiasts across America to observe and preserve this inspiring insect.

THE FIRST WORD GROUP IS A FRAGMENT:

The book that I want. It's on hold for another library patron.

REVISED BY ATTACHING FRAGMENT TO THE COMPLETE SENTENCE:

The book that I want is on hold for another library patron.

Example 10 Revising fragments caused by dependent clauses that function as nouns

FRAGMENT—THE WORD *WHY* IN THE SECOND WORD GROUP MAKES IT A FRAGMENT:

It's still unknown. Why the monarch migrates so many thousands of miles.

REVISED BY MAKING THE FRAGMENT INTO THE SUBJECT OF A COMBINED SENTENCE:

Why the monarch migrates so many thousands of miles is still unknown. [The dependent clause acts as the subject of the verb *is*.]

THE FIRST WORD GROUP IS A FRAGMENT:

What the owl eats. You can determine by examining its scat.

REVISED BY MAKING THE FRAGMENT INTO THE OBJECT OF THE VERB *CAN DETERMINE*:

You can determine what the owl eats by examining its scat. [The dependent clause *what the owl eats* acts as a noun.]

Dependent Clauses That Function as Adjectives

Adjectival dependent clauses are usually introduced by relative pronouns. Like all adjectives, adjectival dependent clauses modify nouns and pronouns and answer the questions "Which one?" "What kind of?"

Dependent Clauses That Function as Nouns

Dependent clauses that function as nouns can be introduced by relative pronouns and by subordinating conjunctions. Noun clauses function just like other nouns and represent a person, thing, or idea. They answer the question "Who?" or "What?" in relation to the verb.

Activity 41-3: Revising Fragments

Revise the paragraph below to eliminate fragments and to make complete sentences.

A solar spacecraft is being launched. That will orbit the Earth. Russian and United States scientists collaborated on the design of *Cosmos 1*. Which will use solar sails propelled by the streams of photons from the sun. Since this stream is always present. The spacecraft will always have a slow means of propulsion. It will be visible from Earth. As a bright point of light. Why this is important. Because the solar stream is always available. Scientists hope that this test will allow them to design future spacecraft. Which use this for controlled flight.

41e Missing Subjects and Missing Verbs: Phrase Fragments

A phrase is a group of words that lacks a subject-verb combination and that functions as a single part of speech. A phrase can be (and usually is) *part* of a sentence, but a phrase cannot *be* a sentence. An orphaned phrase is a sentence fragment.

Fragments	**Complete Sentences**
With the dawn.	~~With~~ The sun rose with the dawn.
To go home.	~~To~~ I want to go home.
Walking fast.	Walking fast is fun.

Prepositional and Verbal Phrase Fragments

A prepositional phrase is a preposition—a word like *at, by, during, toward,* or *with*—plus its object and any modifiers. Prepositional phrases can function as adjectives or adverbs.

A verbal phrase is a verbal (an infinitive, participle, or gerund) plus the relevant words connected to it. Infinitive phrases can function as nouns, adjectives, or adverbs.

Example 11 Revising prepositional and verbal phrase fragments

PREPOSITIONAL PHRASE FRAGMENT:

After walking down the street a little ways. She turned into the library.

COMPLETE SENTENCE:

After walking down the street a little ways, ~~She~~ she turned into the library.

INFINITIVE PHRASE FRAGMENT:

To walk down the street unhindered. It was a luxury she could scarcely imagine.

COMPLETE SENTENCE:

To walk down the street unhindered ~~It was~~ was a luxury she could scarcely imagine.

PARTICIPIAL PHRASE FRAGMENT:

People walking down the street. No one noticed the fire.

COMPLETE SENTENCE:

People walking down the street ~~No one noticed~~ didn't notice the fire.

GERUND PHRASE FRAGMENT:

What's my favorite pastime? Walking down the street and looking in the shop windows.

COMPLETE SENTENCE:

Walking down the street and looking in the shop windows is my favorite pastime.

See page 814 for a discussion of absolute phrases.

Example 12 Revising appositive and list fragments

THE SECOND WORD GROUP IS AN APPOSITIVE FRAGMENT:

To add a reddish cast to gold, medieval artists used dragon's blood. A darkish red paint made from palm tree resin.

COMPLETE SENTENCE:

To add a reddish cast to gold, medieval artists used dragon's blood, ~~A~~ a darkish red paint made from palm tree resin.

THE SECOND WORD GROUP IS A LIST FRAGMENT:

For my birthday I want four kinds of cake. Lemon, German chocolate, coconut with custard filling, and Boston cream pie.

COMPLETE SENTENCE:

For my birthday I want four kinds of cake: ~~Lemon~~ lemon, German chocolate, coconut with custard filling, and Boston cream pie.

Participial phrases always serve as adjectives. Gerund phrases always serve as nouns.

As with other types of fragments, revise by attaching the fragment to a complete sentence or by turning it into a complete sentence in its own right.

Appositive and List Fragments

Appositives, either as single words or as lists, are another common type of phrase fragment. An appositive renames or modifies a noun by giving examples of it, further defining it, or in some other way expanding upon it.

Lists are often introduced by transitional expressions, such as *besides, for example, such as,* or *especially,* so one way to spot list fragments is to be on the lookout for transitional expressions when revising. A list of transitional expressions appears on page 830.

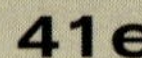

Use transitional expressions to help you spot list fragments.

Transitional Expressions

again	in other words
also	instead
and	like
as a result	mainly
besides	namely
but	on the contrary
consequently	on the other hand
especially	or
finally	specifically
for example	such as
for instance	that is
however	to be sure
in addition	therefore
in fact	

Example 13 Revising list fragments introduced by transitions

LIST FRAGMENT:

Monarchs require milkweed as the host plant for egg-laying and as food for their larvae. Plant a species appropriate for your region. Such as swamp milkweed (*Asclepias incarnata*), showy milkweed (*Asclepias speciosa*), common milkweed (*Asclepias syriaca*), or butterfly weed (*Asclepias tuberosa*).

COMPLETE SENTENCE:

Monarchs require milkweed as the host plant for egg-laying and as food for their larvae. Plant a species appropriate for your region, ~~Such~~ such as swamp milkweed (*Asclepias incarnata*), showy milkweed (*Asclepias speciosa*), common milkweed (*Asclepias syriaca*), or butterfly weed (*Asclepias tuberosa*).

Activity 41-4: Revising Fragments

Revise each of the following paragraphs to remove fragments.

1. Should you be able to communicate with your doctor by email? Many patients want to be able to email their physicians. To save time and frustration. Doctors claim that patients will bombard them with trivial concerns. Leaving them with little time to treat patients who really are sick. There are also other concerns. Privacy, liability, and reimbursement. Advocates say that solutions could be found. One solution might be to allow for virtual appointments. A scheduled time when doctors could be online and responding to patient queries. To email your doctor with questions instead of calling. Wouldn't that be worth getting sick?

2. The Sanilac Petroglyphs, rare American Indian carvings, created anywhere from 400 to 1000 years ago in soft sandstone. Drawn thousands of visitors over the years. Since they were discovered in the late nineteenth century. The carvings include many different types of representations. Birds, swirls, lines, handprints, and human figures. But the carvings are in danger of being lost forever. Unless something can be done to preserve them. There are many causes of this problem. Exposure to the elements and human vandalism. Local and state officials and local tribes trying to find solutions. That will preserve the carvings and allow people to see them. It's unsure what can be done. To preserve this part of our heritage.

Some Deliberate Fragments

Fragment in fiction:

[The peacock] shook itself, and the sound was like a deck of cards being shuffled in the other room. It moved forward a step. Then another step.

From Raymond Carver, "Feathers," in *Where I'm Calling From: New and Selected Stories* (New York: Vintage Contemporaries, 1988), 351.

Fragment in nonfiction:

It can be shown by infallible or at least official logic that values are all a matter of opinion, that what seems good in one culture (like eating babies to improve one's virility) seems unpleasant to another. It can be proved positively that everything is relative. But not to an artist.

From John Gardner, *On Moral Fiction* (New York: Basic Books, 1978), 172.

Fragment in nonfiction:

As we unroped and began to sort gear I dropped my hard hat. Johnny leapt down through the bushes after it. It is not easy to catch up with a ball-like object that's rolling downhill, but Johnny sprang over all obstacles and stopped my hard hat before it took its final plunge for the talus slope at the bottom of the cliff. Johnny could do this! Only Johnny.

From Laura Waterman, *Losing the Garden* (Washington, DC: Shoemaker Hoard, 2005), 146.

Activity 41-5: Revising Fragments in Your Own Writing

Choose a piece of writing you are working on. Using the methods outlined in this chapter, identify the complete sentences as well as any fragments. Were the fragments you found planned for effect, necessary, or appropriate in your writing context? If not, revise them to become complete sentences. What effect does your revision have on making your ideas more easily understood by your intended audience?

In general, it is best to avoid sentence fragments in formal and college writing. However, it's important to be aware that good writers do use fragments, sparingly but wisely.

In fiction (aside from dialogue, discussed earlier), a formal narrator will occasionally use fragments to create emphasis or a precise effect. In the passage to the left by Raymond Carver, one of the twentieth century's masters of short fiction, the fragment helps show the peacock's step-at-a-time, birdlike movements.

Nonfiction writers also use fragments occasionally in formal prose, most often as a technique to create emphasis through an abrupt change of rhythm. In many instances (including the examples on this page), the fragment is the last sentence of the paragraph. This allows the writer to underscore that he or she wants the reader to stop, look, and listen or to somehow pay special attention to the information in the fragment.

42

RUN-ONS AND COMMA SPLICES

Problems with run-on sentences and comma splices are problems of punctuation at sentence boundaries. A run-on sentence results when two independent clauses are joined with no punctuation; a comma splice results when two independent clauses are joined with only a comma. This sentence is a run-on sentence:

> *Rover is our dog she loves to chase cats.*

This sentence is a comma splice:

> *Rover is our dog, she loves to chase cats.*

Learning to eliminate run-on sentences and comma splices from your writing requires understanding the rules that govern how independent clauses are joined to one another. There are three ways to punctuate the boundary between independent clauses. First is with a period and a capital letter: *Rover is our dog. She loves to chase cats.* Second is with a comma and a coordinating conjunction, as in a compound sentence: *Rover is our dog, and she loves to chase cats.* Third is with a semicolon: *Rover is our dog; she loves to chase cats.*

Rules of punctuation aren't arbitrary constructions whose sole purpose is to torment writers. In the case of a compound sentence, for example, the comma and conjunction cue readers that there are two independent clauses, each communicating a separate but related idea.

This chapter will help you understand that run-on sentences and comma splices usually result from the writer's attempt to put two ideas together in a compound sentence, either without punctuation (the run-on) or with only a comma instead of a comma and a coordinating conjunction (the comma splice). Both are considered grammatical mistakes; they confuse readers and fail to show clear relationships between ideas.

Example 1 A compound sentence: two independent clauses

Each independent clause has a subject-verb pair and can stand alone as a complete sentence.

S V S V
Rover is our dog; / she loves to chase cats.

S V CONJ S V
Carlise sells software to businesses, / and / her friend Marcos installs it.

Activity 42-1: Identifying Independent Clauses

Identify the subject-verb pairs in these sentences by circling the subject and underlining the verb.

1. Scientists sampled brain cell activity in people.
2. They have made an important discovery, brain cells react to pictures of celebrities.
3. Individual cells react to specific images.
4. The brain uses only a few cells to record information, it was previously thought that the brain used a large network of cells.
5. No one could have predicted these findings they will lead to new research into how memory works.

Example 2 Run-on sentence

Two sentences with no punctuation separating them:

No one would be more surprised than Mary Shelley at the idea most immediately evoked by the name *Frankenstein* she intended her novel as a meditation on creativity, not creepy monsters.

Example 3 Comma splice

Two sentences with only a comma between them:

No one would be more surprised than Mary Shelley at the idea most immediately evoked by the name *Frankenstein*, she intended her novel as a meditation on creativity, not creepy monsters.

A compound sentence is made up of two or more independent clauses—that is, word groups that can stand alone as sentences. Run-on sentences and comma splices are the result of problems in punctuating compound sentences; both occur when you join independent clauses incorrectly. To find run-on sentences and comma splices, look for subject-verb pairs. When you find a sentence that includes more than one subject-verb pair, make sure that it is punctuated correctly.

A run-on sentence occurs when two independent clauses are joined without punctuation and without an appropriate conjunction. Like a grammatical train wreck, the first sentence *runs* right *on* into the second.

A comma splice occurs when two independent clauses are joined by a comma only; like a "splice" in a length of rope, this joining creates a weak spot.

Run-on sentences and comma splices are like badly marked roadways. Readers dutifully follow the road signs (the punctuation) but have to double back when they end up confused, with the purpose of the sentence unclear and the context lost. The punctuation leads readers to expect one thing (the continuation of a thought), but they receive another (a new thought entirely). Like all grammatical errors, run-on sentences and comma splices interrupt the flow of reading, which is already a difficult process without our making it a thornier path.

When you do spot run-ons or comma splices in your writing, you can use one of these strategies to correct them:

- separate the two clauses with a period and a capital letter
- separate them with a comma and a coordinating conjunction
- separate them with a semicolon
- subordinate one of the clauses or recast the sentence(s) entirely

The Grammar Checker

Most word processors include some form of grammar checker, a tool that allows the user to check a document for certain features that may or may not be signs of underlying grammatical problems. Use a grammar checker prudently, if you use one at all. (A grammar checker may help you check your writing, but it will not certify that your writing is grammatically correct in all instances.) You will find that grammar checkers make mistakes.

A grammar checker, for example, won't reliably recognize run-on sentences or comma splices. But you can try to get it to do so by checking the appropriate box in the options settings. In Microsoft Word 2007, select Office button and then Word Options. Under Proofing in the section on spelling and grammar (next to "Writing Style"), choose the Settings button. (See Figure 42.1.)

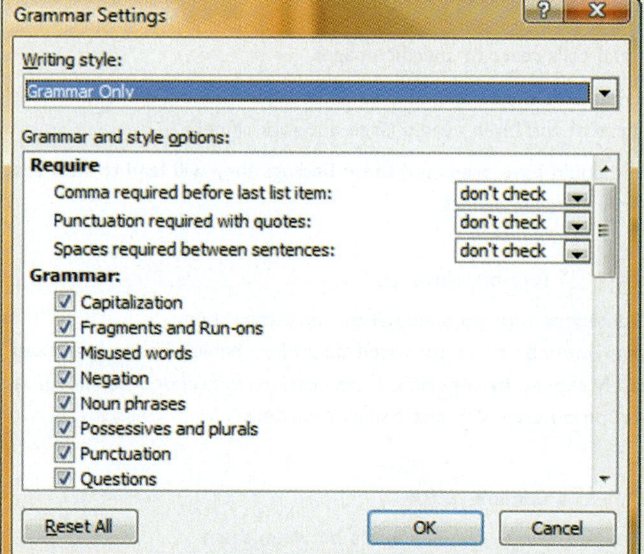

Figure 42.1 The Grammar Settings in Microsoft Word

For instructions that apply to Microsoft® Word® 2003, visit the handbook's website: **cengage.com/english/blakesley**

Revising by Separating into Two Distinct Sentences **42b**

Example 4 Forming two distinct sentences

Comma splice:

Ready-mixed paints weren't commercially available until the 1880s, before that time, artists had to mix their own colors, painstakingly grinding materials by hand.

Revised to become two distinct sentences by using a period and a capital letter:

Ready-mixed paints weren't commercially available until the 1880s. Before that time, artists had to mix their own colors, painstakingly grinding materials by hand.

If you want to emphasize the distinction between the ideas in the independent clauses, make each of the independent clauses into a separate sentence. A sentence is a logically and grammatically complete unit of thought that begins with a capital letter and ends with a period. (See section 41a for more about complete sentences.)

Revising by Using a Comma and Then a Coordinating Conjunction **42c**

Example 5 Using a comma and coordinating conjunction

Run-on sentence:

Galileo recanted his confirmation that the Earth revolves around the Sun in return the Pope commuted his sentence to house arrest.

Revised with comma and coordinating conjunction:

Galileo recanted his confirmation that the Earth revolves around the Sun, and in return the Pope commuted his sentence to house arrest.

Comma splice:

Galileo knew that the Earth revolved around the Sun, he recanted to escape Giordano Bruno's fate of being burned at the stake.

Revised with comma and coordinating conjunction:

Galileo knew that the Earth revolved around the Sun, yet he recanted to escape Giordano Bruno's fate of being burned at the stake.

Adding a comma and a coordinating conjunction is a good strategy when

- you want to give the ideas in each of the clauses equal weight
- you want to emphasize the parallel relationship between the two clauses
- the logic communicated by a particular conjunction (for example, addition, contrast, choice, or causality) is the most effective way to emphasize this relationship

The coordinating conjunctions are *and, but, yet, or, nor, for,* and *so.* To make a compound sentence, use the appropriate conjunction plus a comma. (See section 35b for more about using coordinating conjunctions to form compound sentences.)

Use a semicolon when you want to emphasize the continuity of thought between two closely related independent clauses. A semicolon implies a connection or a close relationship between the ideas in the independent clauses.

Example 6 Using a semicolon

Comma splice:

Ground bugs became crimson, mollusk shells became purple, lapis lazuli became ultramarine blue.

Revised with semicolons:

Ground bugs became crimson; mollusk shells became purple; lapis lazuli became ultramarine blue.

Run-on sentence:

Although Galileo never married, he had three children, Virginia, Livia, and Vincenzio he placed his two daughters in a convent and had his son legitimized and brought to live with him.

Revised with semicolon:

Although Galileo never married, he had three children, Virginia, Livia, and Vincenzio; he placed his two daughters in a convent and had his son legitimized and brought to live with him.

Using Colons between Sentences and to Introduce Lists

A colon may be used between independent sentences when the first sentence formally introduces the second. Colons are also used to introduce lists of related items (see Chapter 50 for more about punctuating sentences with colons). In some cases, a run-on or comma splice might best be recast with a colon between the two clauses.

Example 7 Using a colon

Comma splice:

Phyllis Wheatley's life story is an astounding one, born in West Africa, kidnapped, and sold into slavery, she distinguished herself as an internationally celebrated poet and as the first African American to be published.

Revised with colon:

Phyllis Wheatley's life story is an astounding one: born in West Africa, kidnapped, and sold into slavery, she distinguished herself as an internationally celebrated poet and as the first African American to be published.

Run-on sentence:

The medieval artist created paints out of natural materials ground bugs became crimson mollusk shells became purple lapis lazuli became ultramarine blue.

Revised with colon:

The medieval artist created paints out of natural materials: ground bugs became crimson; mollusk shells became purple; lapis lazuli became ultramarine blue.

Activity 42-2: Revising Run-On Sentences and Comma Splices

Revise the paragraph to correct run-on sentences and comma splices, using commas with coordinating conjunctions, semicolons, or colons.

Many people receive unsolicited email in their inboxes every day most delete it and move on with their lives. Unsolicited email is usually called spam, some forms of spam can be more harmful than others. Sometimes spam is just advertising for products other times it is an attempt to perpetuate a scam. Common scams are the "Nigerian email" this is when an unknown person wants your help in transferring money from a foreign country. Many people have fallen for this scam, they have lost thousands of dollars. Other scam email pretends to be from a credit union or bank it tells you that you need to update your account information. When you enter your account information, it actually passes the information on to scammers they can then use your bank information for their own purposes.

Punctuation with Transitional Expressions 42e

A semicolon or a period—not a comma—is required between two independent clauses joined by a transitional expression (see section 5c for more on transitional expressions). Common transitional expressions include *however, indeed, likewise, notwithstanding, for instance, subsequently, all in all,* and *consequently.* After the transitional expression, use a comma to separate it from the rest of the second independent clause.

Example 8 Punctuation with transitional expressions

Comma splice:

At Byron's challenge, the friends each wrote a ghost story, however it was Mary's creation—not the famed Shelley's or Byron's—that was published.

Revised as distinct sentences with period, transition, and comma:

At Byron's challenge, the friends each wrote a ghost story. However, it was Mary's creation—not the famed Shelley's or Byron's—that was published.

Run-on sentence:

Time has reversed the fame and status of Mary and Percy Bysshe Shelley indeed today *Frankenstein* is a household word, while such works as "Epipsychidion" have faded into relative obscurity.

Revised with semicolon between the clauses and a comma after the transition:

Time has reversed the fame and status of Mary and Percy Bysshe Shelley; indeed, today *Frankenstein* is a household word, while such works as "Epipsychidion" have faded into relative obscurity.

Activity 42-3: Revising Run-Ons and Comma Splices

Revise the following paragraph to add transitions and to punctuate transitions correctly.

The question of whether exposure to violent media makes children more violent has long been debated. It is a question that we may never be able to fully answer, research into how people's brains perceive virtual violence may help us to answer this question. Scientists wired young men to a scanner while they played violent video games they measured brain activity. Amazingly the subjects showed the same reactions as they would to a real violent situation, consequently they concluded that video games trained the brain to react with this pattern.

42f Revising by Recasting the Sentence

Depending on your purpose, sometimes the best strategy is to rewrite the sentence by making one clause subordinate, by making one clause a phrase, or by recasting in some other manner.

Example 9 Revising by recasting the sentence

Comma splice:

Reality TV draws on our collective desire for instant status and celebrity, it puts ordinary people in the spotlight.

Revised by changing the second clause into a phrase, thus de-emphasizing it:

Reality TV draws on our collective desire for instant status and celebrity by putting ordinary people in the spotlight.

Revised by making the second clause subordinate and changing the order of the two clauses:

Because it puts ordinary people in the spotlight, reality TV draws on our collective desire for instant status and celebrity.

Revised by removing *it* and using a compound predicate (i.e., having two verbs but one subject):

Reality TV draws on our collective desire for instant status and celebrity and puts ordinary people in the spotlight.

Activity 42-4: Revising Run-Ons and Comma Splices

Using all of the strategies in this chapter, revise the following paragraph to eliminate run-on sentences and comma splices.

The success of computer animation has left many traditional animators worried, will their skills still be useful in the twenty-first century. Companies such as Pixar Animation studios still find use for traditional animators however they use them in untraditional ways. Traditional animators work to create storyboards and pencil tests, their work is translated into pixels by computer animators. Computer animators are also encouraged to learn techniques of traditional animation this helps them to extend their creative range. Movies such as *Toy Story* are completely rendered on computers, traditional animation helps to shape them behind the scenes.

Exceptions to the Rule 42g

Two variations of the rules are sometimes considered acceptable.

Comma between Brief Parallel Independent Clauses

Some writers and editors consider brief parallel or balanced independent clauses joined by a comma to be an acceptable sentence. Others disagree.

She walks, she talks, she cries.

In college and other formal writing, use this kind of punctuation sparingly (if at all) and not until you've moved beyond the rules to a deeper understanding of how punctuation communicates.

Compare the rhythm of these sentences

The sun comes up, the sun goes down.

The sun comes up. The sun goes down.

The first example emphasizes the ever-changing cycle of nature. The rhythm is snappier and more unexpected, and the comma makes the sentence into a sort of endless loop (as soon as you say *down,* you're ready the start the whole thing all over again). The second example places a kind of final emphasis on *down.* It emphasizes that each day ends with night and the finality of that event.

Dash between Two Independent Clauses

A dash suggests a more abrupt or dramatic break in thought or shift in direction than a colon, but a dash is more commonly used to set off words or phrases *within* a clause than between independent clauses. So the dash is not only less formal than the colon; it's also less precise. Indeed, in many instances, writers and editors would consider a dash between independent clauses to be weak or incorrect punctuation.

Use the dash sparingly, for special effect only

Something was afoot—she just had to get back!

Activity 42-5: Revising Run-Ons and Comma Splices in Your Own Writing

Choose a piece of writing you are working on. Using the methods outlined in this chapter, identify several independent clauses you find especially well written. Write them out on a separate sheet of paper. Identify the subject-verb pair by circling the subject and underlining the verb. What makes these two sentences work well in their original context? Next, identify any run-ons and comma splices. What effect do these word groups have on readability? Revise them. What effect does your revision have on the piece overall?

43 PRONOUNS

Pronouns are among the little words that carry great weight in the English language. Consider the doomed Juliet on her balcony. Without pronouns, the mellifluous

> *What's in a name? That which we call a rose*
> *By any other word would smell as sweet;*

would become something like

> *Names are not important. Roses smell*
> *as sweet if called by other names than rose;*

which would just stink!

As important as pronouns are, they are frequently misused, especially with regard to issues of case, agreement, and reference. For example, it is not uncommon to hear people erroneously say, "Give it to her and I" instead of "Give it to her and me" (case); "Wallace and Simpson introduced himself right away" instead of "Wallace and Simpson introduced themselves right away" (agreement); or "Tom called Dick's father a liar, which made him so angry that they fought" rather than "Tom called Dick's father a liar, which made Dick so angry that Tom and Dick fought" (reference).

This chapter looks at how to use pronouns correctly and grammatically. Its discussion is framed within the context of the three areas of concern: case, agreement, and reference.

In general, a **pronoun** replaces a noun in a sentence. The noun the pronoun replaces is called the **antecedent.**

Most antecedents come before their pronouns (indeed, as an adjective *antecedent* means "going before"), but occasionally an antecedent can follow its pronoun.

While the various types of pronouns can take on various functions within a sentence, personal, possessive, relative, and demonstrative pronouns especially help to make sentences flow more smoothly by replacing nearby nouns.

Example 1 Pronouns

A pronoun replaces or refers back to an antecedent:

ANTECEDENT — PRONOUN — PRONOUN

Bruno was thrilled when **he** received **his** acceptance letter.

A pronoun may come before its antecedent:

PRONOUN — ANTECEDENT

Unlike **their** grandmothers' grandmothers, today's *women* can vote.

Types of pronouns

Personal	When elephants get hungry, **they** become unpredictable.
Possessive	When elephants get hungry, they stamp **their** feet.
Indefinite	**Everyone** gets hungry.
Relative	The elephants **that** were hungriest trumpeted the loudest.
Interrogative	**Who** is hungry?
Demonstrative	**That** elephant is very hungry.
Reflexive	The elephant injured **itself** in the mad rush for food.
Intensive	The keeper **herself** feeds the elephants.
Reciprocal	The elephants fed **each other** as part of the mating ritual.

Pronouns help streamline sentences and paragraphs

Awkward, wordy paragraph:

The archeologists were thrilled when the archeologists discovered the Mayan tomb. The Mayan tomb had lain undisturbed for centuries. The Mayan tomb contained the bodies of two women, and the two women were believed to have been sacrificed as part of a ritual marking the accession of a new king. In the ritual marking the accession of a new king, the women are believed to have symbolized the two helpers to the corn god.

More streamlined paragraph:

The archeologists were thrilled when **they** discovered a Mayan tomb **that** had lain undisturbed for centuries and **that** contained the bodies of two women **who** are believed to have been sacrificed as part of a ritual marking the accession of a new king. In **this** ritual, the women are believed to have symbolized the two helpers to the corn god.

Pronouns in the subjective case

Subject	**He** flew through the air.
Subject complement	The leading trapeze artist is **he**.
Appositive that renames a subject	The leading trapeze artists—Beaufort, Beaumont, and **he**—will be touring in the upcoming production.

Pronouns in the objective case

Direct object	She couldn't avoid **him**.
Indirect object	She gave **him** back his love notes.
Object of the preposition	She had seen enough *of* **him**.
Appositive that renames an object	Beaufort mistimed his somersault and dropped the *other two artists,* Beaumont and **him**, as the crowd gasped in horror.
Subject of an infinitive	She wanted **him** *to go* away.
Object of an infinitive	She wanted *to snub* **him** in front of everyone.

Activity 43-1: Identifying Subjective and Objective Pronouns

Underline the pronouns and indicate whether each is subjective or objective. For each subjective pronoun, determine whether it is a subject, a subject complement, or an appositive that renames a subject. For each objective pronoun, determine whether it is an object, an object complement, or an appositive that renames an object.

As an adult, Shirley Temple married, and she changed her name to Shirley Temple Black. In 1969, she became a delegate to the United Nations. In 1976, a great honor was given to her when she was named the first female Chief of Protocol of the United States. Many have praised her for her diplomatic style, saying that "one of the leading diplomats in the world was she."

The personal pronouns *I, we, you, he, she, it,* and *they* and the relative and interrogative pronoun *who* change their form, or **case,** to indicate how they function in a sentence.

Subjective Case

A pronoun that acts as the subject of a sentence, as a subject complement, or as an appositive that renames a subject or subject complement is in the **subjective case.**

Subjective Case
I
we
you
he/she/it
they
who

Objective Case

A pronoun that acts as the object of a verb, the object of a preposition, an appositive that renames an object, or the subject or object of an infinitive is in the **objective case.**

Objective Case
me
us
you
him/her/it
them
whom

Possessive Case

A pronoun that shows ownership is in the **possessive case.**

Possessive Case
my/mine
our/ours
your/yours
his/her/hers/its
their/theirs
whose

Some possessive pronouns have one form when used as an adjective and another when used as a noun.

Possessives Used as Adjectives and Nouns

my/mine
It's **my** *fault*.
The fault is **mine.**

your/yours
Your *cat* just ate my canary.
That bad animal is **yours**.

her/hers
Her *persistence* paid off.
The victory was **hers**.

their/theirs
Their *house* was painted.
Theirs is the unpainted house.

The possessive pronouns *its* and *whose* are commonly confused with contractions and vice versa.

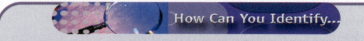

Example 2 Possessive pronouns

His tardiness was **our** undoing.

We made good use of **their** survival skills on **our** camping trip.

Whether to Use *its* or *it's*, *who's* or *whose*?

Possessive Pronouns

If the pronoun in question modifies a noun, then *its* or *whose* should not have an apostrophe:

__its__ color

its

Its fleece had been spun into wool.

The thrift shop committee decided on **its** annual division of profits to charities.

whose

Whose lamb is it?

Whose decision is it ultimately?

Contractions

If you can substitute *it is* for *it's* or *who is* for *who's*, then *it's* and *who's* should have an apostrophe:

__It's__ rainy. [It is rainy.]

it's [it is]

It's Mary's lamb at the door again.

It's our policy to give a full refund no matter when you return the merchandise.

who's [who is]

Who's at the door?

Before I buy presents, I'd like to know **who's** going to be there.

Activity 43-2: Identifying Possessive Pronouns

Underline possessive pronouns and circle contractions. For each possessive pronoun used as an adjective, note which noun it modifies. For each possessive pronoun used as a subject complement, note which subject it is linked to.

A new service has been introduced that allows parents to track their children using a mobile phone. The service is marketed to parents whose fears of child abduction or danger make them want to know where their children are at all times. Parents supply children with a mobile phone that has a transmitter in its innards. It's then simple for parents to "ping" their children and find their whereabouts. Still, the service raises questions: Who's responsible for supervising children?

How Can You Identify...

Which Case to Use in a Compound?

1. Identify the compound:

   Josef and [*I* or *me*] danced.

   He visited my friends and [*I* or *me*] every Friday afternoon.

2. Make a sentence using only the pronoun part of the compound.

   [*I* or *me*] danced.

   He visited [*I* or *me*] every Friday afternoon.

3. Select the case that's right when the pronoun stands alone.

   I danced. He visited me.

4. Put the compound back together.

   Josef and I danced.

   He visited my friends and me every Friday afternoon.

Pronouns that function as part of a compound word group are a common source of confusion. But fortunately, the rule is clear: a pronoun that is part of a compound word group takes the same case as it would take if it were standing alone.

A pronoun that is part of a compound subject takes the subjective case.

A pronoun that is part of a compound object takes the objective case.

Example 3 Pronoun case in compounds

Subjective case in a compound subject:

Scotty and **he** worked on the warp drive engines.

Uhuru and **they** finally conquered the Klingon invaders.

Objective case in a compound object:

Eyes narrowed, Spock considered Captain Kirk and **her**.

It was a sad day for Ivana and **me**.

Activity 43-3: Identifying Case in Compound Constructions

Make any needed revisions to pronoun case in the following compound constructions.

1. My professor invited Jennifer and I to work on a research project.
2. Her and me distributed surveys to various people on campus.
3. After that, the data were entered into a computer by Jennifer, I, and some other students.
4. Then I and the professor analyzed the data.
5. At a conference, the professor and me presented the results.

43d Pronoun Case after *than* or *as*

Which pronoun form should you use in a comparison after *than* or *as*? It depends on what you want to compare. Often such constructions are elliptical—that is, words are understood but left out. So to supply the correct case of the pronoun, you must decide what meaning you want to communicate.

To determine the correct case of a pronoun after *than* or *as,* supply the missing words:

> No one made us laugh as much as ~~him~~ he [did/made us laugh].

Example 4 Pronoun case when subjects or objects are being compared

Paulo likes Zack de la Rocha better than [*I* or *me*].

Revision if the comparison is between subjects *Paulo* and *I:*

Paulo likes Zack de la Rocha better than **I** [like Zack de la Rocha].

Revision if the comparison is between objects *Zack de la Rocha* and *me:*

Paulo likes **Zack de la Rocha** better than [Paulo likes] **me**.

Activity 43-4: Choosing Case in Comparisons

Select the appropriate pronoun from the choices offered in brackets.

1. James said he couldn't go to the basketball game because he had more homework than [we/us].
2. Sharon complained she couldn't see the court as well as [I/me].
3. The basketball team was determined to score more points than [they/them].
4. We made a valiant effort, but the opposing sports team was better than [we/us].
5. Still, no coach was as well loved as [he/him].

43e Pronoun Case and Appositives

Pronouns can function as part of an appositive that renames a noun or as the noun that an appositive renames.

Pronouns as Appositives

When you use a pronoun in an appositive, first identify whether the word it renames is a subject or an object. If the appositive renames a subject, use the subjective case. If the appositive renames an object, use the objective case.

Example 5 Pronouns in appositives

Appositive that renames a subject:

SUBJECT — SUBJECTIVE CASE

The class officers, Tamika and **he,** get together at least once a week.

Appositive that renames an object:

DIRECT OBJECT — OBJECTIVE CASE

The class officers chose my two friends, Raoul and **him,** for the faculty relations committee.

Example 6 Pronouns followed by a noun appositive

SUBJECT

We students asked for changes in the cafeteria food.

OBJECT

The cafeteria food's lack of variety prompted **us** students to ask for changes.

Activity 43-5: Selecting Pronouns with Appositives

Determine whether the pronoun should be in the subjective or objective case.

1. The commuter student subcommittee, Tamika and [him/he], reported to the larger parking committee.
2. The rest of the committee, Jane, Traci, and [I/me], listened to their report.
3. They presented a petition signed by many students that said: "[We/Us] commuter students deserve better parking access."
4. The Student Senate, the other senators and [we/us], voted on the proposal.
5. The text of the motion read: "Our concern about the availability of parking for [we/us] commuter students has led us to ask for this change."

Using *we* or *us* with a Noun Appositive

When *we* or *us* is followed by a noun appositive—*we students, us students*—the correct case is determined by the pronoun's function within the sentence. If the pronoun functions as a subject, use the subjective case; if the pronoun functions as an object, use the objective case.

To decide which pronoun to use, remove the noun that follows. Select the pronoun that best fits the sentence without the noun.

Pronoun Case with Infinitives 43f

Example 7 Pronouns as the subject or object of an infinitive

SUBJECT OF THE INFINITIVE

Zelda wanted **Scott** *to leave* that den of iniquity.

OBJECT OF THE INFINITIVE

Scott wanted *to leave* **Zelda.**

SUBJECT OF THE INFINITIVE

The reporters kept asking **her** *to comment* on the president's odd statement.

OBJECT OF THE INFINITIVE

But the secretary of state refused *to contradict* **him.**

The base or root form of a verb is called the infinitive: *to steal, to laugh, to run.* Infinitives can have both subjects and objects. The subject of the infinitive is the noun that does the infinitive's action. The subject of the infinitive usually comes after the main verb and directly before the infinitive.

The object of the infinitive receives the action of the infinitive.

Pronouns take the objective case when used as either the subject or the object of an infinitive.

The pronoun *who* functions both as an interrogative pronoun and as a relative pronoun. Like the personal pronouns (*I, we, you, he, she, it, they*), *who* has both a subjective and an objective form. Distinguishing between *who* and *whom* is one of the most baffling challenges in the English language. Not only is the distinction largely ignored in spoken English, but determining how the pronoun functions in a given sentence isn't always easy. Despite these difficulties and despite the centuries-old trend away from use of *whom* in spoken English, in formal written English it is important to use *who* and *whom* correctly.

General Guidelines for Using *who* and *whom*

Use the subjective case *who* for subjects and the objective case *whom* for objects.

Keep in mind that (as with all other pronouns) **case is determined by the pronoun's function within its clause,** *not* by that clause's function within the sentence.

In Example 9, although the clause *who did it* is the object of the verb *know,* the pronoun *who* functions as the subject of the clause *who did it.* So the correct form is *who.*

In Example 10, although the clause *whoever wants them most* is the object of the preposition *to,* the pronoun *whoever* functions as the

Example 8 The pronoun *who*

Interrogative pronoun	**Who** let the cat out?
Relative pronoun	The student **who** won the race lives in my dorm.

The words *who* and *whoever* are subjective; *whom* and *whomever* are objective

Subject	**Who** is he?
Subject complement	Madonna is **who** she is—no excuses.
Direct object	They brought **whomever** they wanted.
Object of the preposition	[A]nd therefore never send to know for **whom** the bell tolls; it tolls for thee. From John Donne, "XVII Meditation."

Example 9 *Who* as subject of clause serving as direct object

CLAUSE AS OBJECT
SUBJECT VERB
I know **who did it.**

Example 10 *Who* as subject of clause serving as object of preposition

CLAUSE AS OBJECT OF THE PREPOSITION
SUBJECT VERB
[You] Give the apples to **whoever** wants them most.

What is the pronoun's function within its clause?

I was delighted to interview a man **who** had entertained so many.

I was eager to interview a man **whom** so many had vilified.

Whether the Pronoun Is a Subject or an Object in Its Clause?

Sample sentence:

The star [*who* or *whom*] all the fans adored was the star [*who* or *whom*] finally retreated to a private island accessible only by helicopter.

1. Identify the clause that the pronoun is in.

   [*who* or *whom*] all the fans adored

   [*who* or *whom*] finally retreated to a private island accessible only by helicopter

2. Change the order, if needed, to subject-verb-object.

   All the fans adored [*who* or *whom*].

   [*who* or *whom*] finally retreated . . . .

3. Substitute in the appropriate personal pronoun (*he* or *him, she* or *her*).

   All the fans adored *her* (or *him*). [In other words, an object]

   He (or *she*) finally retreated. [A subject]

4. If the pronoun is an objective form, reassemble the sentence using *whom;* if the pronoun is a subjective form, use *who*.

   The star *whom* all the fans adored was the star *who* finally retreated to a private island accessible only by helicopter.

Activity 43-6: Choosing Forms of *who* in Dependent Clauses

Select the appropriate form of *who* from the choices in brackets.

Many people talk about the concept of infinite monkeys at infinite typewriters producing the works of Shakespeare, but [who/whom] originated the comparison is a matter of debate. [Whomever/Whoever] thought of it first deserves proper credit. Some say that A. S. Eddington is the one to [who/whom] the story should be attributed, while others say that Aldous Huxley is the one [who/whom] thought of the idea first. Regardless of [whoever/whomever] first thought of the idea, it remains a compelling image.

subject of the clause *whoever wants them most*. So the correct form is *whoever.*

Using *who* and *whom* in Dependent Clauses

The rule for using *who* and *whom* in dependent clauses is the same as the general rule: use *who* and *whoever* for subjects and *whom* and *whomever* for objects, based on the pronoun's function within its clause.

Using *who* and *whom* in Questions

In choosing between *who* and *whom* in questions, follow the general rule: use *who* or *whoever* for subjects and *whom* or *whomever* for objects.

You can use steps 2–4 of the process given on page 849 for finding the correct pronoun for a dependent clause.

The "How Can You Identify . . ." box on this page provides a second, sometimes simpler method for selecting the correct pronoun for a question.

Use *who* for subjects in questions

S V
Who was that masked man?

2. . . . was that masked man?
3. He was that masked man?
4. Who was that masked man?

Use *whom* for objects in questions

DIR OBJ OF *RESCUE*
Whom did that masked man rescue this time?

2. That masked man did rescue . . .
3. That masked man did rescue him.
4. That masked man did rescue whom?

When to Use *who* and *whom* in Questions?

1. Answer the question, using a personal pronoun.
   [*Who* or *whom*?] is ready to go to the park?
   She (or *he*) is ready to go to the park.
2. Notice the case of the personal pronoun. Use the same case of *who*.
   Who is ready to go to the park?

Activity 43-7: Choosing Forms of *who* in Questions

Select the appropriate form of *who* from the choices in brackets.

The terrible crime raised many questions among the community's residents. [Who/Whom] was responsible for the killings? [Who/Whom] did the police suspect? [Who/Whom] would find the murderers? To [who/whom] could the witnesses appeal for protection? Residents wondered [who/whom] would find the answers.

Use *whom* for subjects and objects of infinitives

Rodney wondered **whom** to blame for the debacle.

Rodney wanted to blame **whomever** he could.

Example 11 Using *who* and *whom* with certain expressions

[*Who* or *whom*] do you think is the greatest rock star of all time?

[*Who* or *whom*] . . . is the greatest rock star of all time?

Who do you think is the greatest rock star of all time?

[*Who* or *whom*] shall I say is calling?

[*Who* or *whom*] . . . is calling?

Who shall I say is calling?

[*Who* or *whom*] did Waldo say he was going to choose for his running mate?

[*Who* or *whom*] did Waldo . . . choose for his running mate?

Waldo did choose [*who* or *whom*]?

Waldo did choose *him*?

Whom did Waldo say he was going to choose for his running mate?

Most citizens would like to have legislators [*who* or *whom*] they know are trustworthy.

Most citizens would like to have legislators [*who* or *whom*] . . . are trustworthy.

Most citizens would like to have legislators **who** they know are trustworthy.

Activity 43-8: Choosing Forms of *who* with Infinitives and Certain Expressions

Select the appropriate forms of *who* from the choices in brackets.

[Who/whom] do you think invented the first board game? Historians want to credit [whoever/whomever] it might be, but defining what the first board game was is difficult to do. This means that it is difficult to decide [who/whom] should receive credit. [Who/Whom] should they choose as the inventor of the first modern board game, then? It is difficult to find evidence from sources [who/whom] they know are trustworthy, as many companies would like to have the honor of being the first.

Using *who* and *whom* with Infinitives

As with all pronouns, use the objective form, *whom,* for both the subject and the object of an infinitive.

Using *who* and *whom* with Expressions Such as *do you think*

Expressions such as *do you think, shall I say, they know,* and *she says* can sometimes make it more difficult to figure out how the pronoun *who* functions grammatically. But such expressions are in essence parenthetical. Simply ignore them in determining how the pronoun *who* functions grammatically.

Pronoun Case with Gerunds and Participles

A gerund is a noun made from the *-ing* form of a verb. Pronouns used to modify a gerund or a gerund phrase should be in the possessive.

A pronoun used with a present participle (a modifier made from the *-ing* form of a verb) does *not* take the possessive. If it is used as a subject, it takes the subjective case, and if it is used as an object, the objective case.

Use the possessive case for pronouns that modify gerunds . . .

POSSESSIVE PRONOUN — GERUND

His comings and goings mystified everyone.

The pronoun *his* acts as an adjective modifying the noun phrase *comings and goings*.

. . . but not for pronouns with present participles

PRESENT PARTICIPLE — SUBJECTIVE PRONOUN

Coming and going, **he** mystified everyone.

OBJECTIVE PRONOUN — PRESENT PARTICIPLE

We watched **him** coming and going.

Activity 43-9: Revising for Pronoun Case

Rewrite the following paragraph to fix any problems with pronoun case.

Chanelle is a generous student. Chanelle gives her free time at the local women's shelter where us students sometimes have a clothing drive to raise funds. Whom asked Chanelle to be so generous? Not anyone who we are aware of. Chanelle's roommate, Brie, has her own charities also. The two of them, Chanelle and she, are as likely to be found helping out during their weekends as they are to be found in the library working on their school work. Brie is no less generous with her time than she. Did I already tell you that Brie's involved with the animal shelter? Chanelle and her developed their volunteer hobbies after they took a class that asked Chanelle and Brie to get involved with the local community. I don't know whom does more, Chanelle or she. Either way, them two students are really the kinds of role models that incoming students should be aware of. They need to know about their good work.

Example 12 Agreement in gender

Feminine	Rosa washed **her** hair.
Masculine	Raymond shaved off **his** beard.
Neutral	The cat washed **its** paws.

Example 13 Agreement in number

Singular	Billy shouted as **he** raced onto the playground.
Plural	The children shouted as **they** raced onto the playground.

Example 14 Agreement in person

First person	We like washing **our** dishes the old-fashioned way.
Second person	How do you prefer to wash **your** dishes?
Third person	They would rather wash **their** dishes in a dishwasher.

Activity 43-10: Using Pronouns That Match Their Antecedents

Read the following paragraph and write the appropriate pronoun in the brackets.

In 1933, Charles Darrow invented the game of Monopoly. [ ] made the boards out of old oilcloths, and [ ] painted the properties on by hand. Parker Brothers Company rejected Darrow at first; [ ] said that the game wouldn't sell. However, people soon began to play the game regularly, and [ ] enjoyed it very much. Those of us playing the game today would find that the original version is very similar to the game [ ] play, but the game has changed slowly over time.

A pronoun must match its antecedent in gender, number, and person. (The antecedent, you will recall, is the noun that the pronoun replaces or refers back to.) This matching is called **pronoun agreement**.

The personal pronouns *he, she,* and *it* must take the same gender as their antecedents.

A singular antecedent requires a singular pronoun; a plural antecedent requires a plural pronoun.

A first-person antecedent requires a first-person pronoun; a second-person antecedent requires a second-person pronoun; a third-person antecedent requires a third-person pronoun.

First-person pronouns: *I* and *we*
Second-person pronoun: *you*
Third-person pronouns: *he, she, it,* and *they*

Compound antecedents joined by *and* require a plural pronoun, even if the antecedents themselves are both singular.

An exception is when the antecedents are preceded by *each* or *every.*

With compound antecedents joined by *or* or *nor,* the pronoun matches the antecedent nearest to it.

If one antecedent is singular and another plural, put the plural antecedent nearest to the pronoun. Doing so will make the sentence sound more natural.

If the antecedents differ in gender or person, it's often best to recast the sentence.

Use a plural pronoun with antecedents joined by *and*

As young boys, Wilbur and Orville Wright first became interested in flight when **their** father brought home a toy helicopter.

Unless the antecedents are preceded by *each* or *every*

Each cup and saucer was carefully dried and put back in **its** place.

Match the closer antecedent if antecedents are joined by *or* or *nor*

Neither Lucy nor Felipa brought **her** toothbrush to the campout.

Awkward Neither the hens nor the rooster liked **its** new pen.
Revised Neither the rooster nor the hens like **their** new pen.

Awkward Neither Mario nor Melissa got back to **her** work after the earthquake.
Revised After the earthquake, both Mario and Melissa left work for the day.

Activity 43-11: Using Pronouns with Compound Antecedents

Read the following paragraph and write the appropriate pronoun in the brackets.

Parents and teachers can work together to help young children become better readers and writers. Every boy and girl is different, and [ ] may require different strategies to help [ ] learn best. If parents and teachers collaborate, [ ] can find ways to help each boy or girl develop to [ ] full potential. A tutor or librarians can contribute [ ] expertise as well.

Example 15 Emphasizing the individuals or the group with the pronoun used with a collective noun

The flock resumed **its** journey north. [Singular; emphasis is on the flock as a unit.]

The lightning flashed, and the herd stampeded in all directions, **their** eyes wide with fright. [Plural; emphasis is on the individual animals within the herd.]

The committee brought **its** proposal to the larger assembly. [Singular; emphasis is on the committee as a unit.]

The committee found that **their** competing loyalties and ideologies kept **them** from working together effectively. [Plural; emphasis is on the individuals on the committee.]

A collective noun refers to a group of people, things, or animals.

Collective Nouns

audience	family
band	flock
bunch	group
choir	herd
class	jury
club	litter
committee	number
couple	pride
corps	public
crowd	team
faculty	

When used as an antecedent, a collective noun can take either a singular or a plural pronoun, depending on how the antecedent is being used. When the emphasis is on the group as a unit, use a singular pronoun. When the emphasis is on the individuals within the group, use a plural pronoun.

Activity 43-12: Using Pronouns with Collective Nouns

Read the following paragraph and write the appropriate pronoun in the brackets.

Emperor penguins don't create nests like other birds. After the females have laid eggs, the males incubate them on [ ] feet while the females return to the sea. After the eggs have hatched, the entire group participates in raising [ ] chicks. The flock of emperor penguins then resumes [ ] journey northward. When a single chick loses its way on the journey, [ ] may be left behind by [ ] mother. The colony then finishes [ ] journey at [ ] summer nesting grounds.

Indefinite pronouns (such as *anybody, each, none, someone*) refer to nonspecific persons or things. (For a complete list of indefinite pronouns, see section 40c.) Most indefinite pronouns are singular in formal written English.

However, the indefinite pronouns *both, few, many,* and *several* are always plural.

The indefinite pronouns *all, any, more, most,* and *some* can be singular or plural, depending on their meaning in a particular sentence.

Generic nouns (such as *dancer, lawyer, refugee, student*) refer to types or categories of persons or things and behave much the same way as do indefinite pronouns. A singular generic noun requires a singular pronoun. A plural generic noun requires a plural pronoun.

Treating singular generic nouns as plural is a common mistake.

Most indefinite pronouns are singular

Everyone has **his** or **her** favorite food.

Each of the ballerinas bowed after **she** completed **her** solo.

Each sumo wrestler bowed to **his** competitor at the start of the match.

But *both, few, many,* and *several* are always plural

Both strategies have **their** own merits.

Few thought that the president's proposal served **their** best interest.

Many thought **they** could have solved the problem better.

Several felt that **their** ideas had been overlooked.

And some vary depending on meaning

Most of the runway was impassable, **its** surface covered in several inches of ice and snow.

When the flights were canceled, most of the passengers found **themselves** stranded in the airport overnight.

Nouns used generically can be singular or plural, and pronouns match them

Singular	A person needs a goal if **he or she** wants to accomplish something meaningful.
Plural	People need goals if **they** want to accomplish something meaningful.
Incorrect	A person depends on **their** wits.
Revised	A person depends on **his or her** wits.
	People depend on **their** wits.

Activity 43-13: Using Pronouns with Indefinite Pronouns and Generic Nouns

Read the following paragraph and write the appropriate pronoun in the brackets.

Many people every year experience the death of a pet, and [ ] deal with it in different ways. Few people are unmoved when [ ] pet dies; both men and women grieve for [ ] pets. Each of the affected people deals with grief in [ ] own way. People depend on each other to help [ ] cope with [ ] loss.

Example 16 Revising for inclusiveness

Original — A zookeeper observes several precautions when **he** feeds the lions.

Revised — A zookeeper observes several precautions when **he or she** feeds the lions.

Zookeepers observe several precautions when **they** feed the lions.

A zookeeper observes several precautions when feeding the lions.

Contemporary speaking and writing call for gender-inclusive language. So in considering how to best match the right pronoun to a singular indefinite-pronoun or generic-noun antecedent, the careful writer will want to have more than one strategy at hand. An endless march of *his or her* and *to him or to her* and *he or she* can quickly become tedious.

Three strategies for avoiding sexist use of the pronoun *he* are to use *he or she,* recast the sentence as plural, and recast the sentence entirely to omit the pronoun. Avoid the nearly indecipherable *s/he.*

For more on this topic, including more detailed strategies for recasting sentences, see section 39c.

Activity 43-14: Revising for Pronoun Agreement

Rewrite the following paragraph to fix any problems with pronoun agreement.

A young child needs help if he or she is to reach his or her full potential as a writer. Each child has their own way of learning that is best for him. Many people think that he or she knows the best way to teach a child to write, but few theories survive when it is put to the test in the classroom. Every class is different, and they require different ways of teaching. A writing class may need different activities to help it learn best.

Understanding Pronoun Reference 43n

Example 17 Pronoun reference

Clear — I baked the cookies (ANTECEDENT) and put **them** (PRONOUN) in the cookie jar.

Confusing — To keep cookies (ANT?) away from children (ANT?), put **them** (PRONOUN) in the cookie jar. [What should you put in the cookie jar? Cookies? Children? The sentence is unclear.]

Revised — To keep cookies away from children, put **the cookies** in the cookie jar.

The reader must be able to easily identify which person, place, or thing a pronoun refers to.

Unclear pronoun reference usually results from there being

- more than one possible antecedent,
- an antecedent that is too far away, or
- an antecedent that is implied, vague, or missing.

Revise unclear pronoun reference by repeating the noun or by recasting the sentence.

Make sure that the pronoun clearly refers to one antecedent and only one.

Each pronoun can refer to only a single antecedent

Confusing	Frank (?) told Morris (?) that **he** didn't care. [Who didn't care: Frank or Morris?]
Revised	Frank told Morris that Morris didn't care. Frank told Morris, "You don't care."
Confusing	Charlotte (?) brought Anne (?) to the seashore to recuperate, but there **she** died. [Who died: Charlotte or Anne?]
Revised	Charlotte brought **her** sister to the seashore to recuperate, but there Anne died.

Activity 43-15: Making Pronouns Refer to a Single Antecedent

Revise each sentence to make pronoun reference clear.

1. Jane told Kelly that she didn't want to go to the dance.
2. To keep people from being injured by the ceiling fans, be sure to mount them as high as possible.
3. Bob explained to Steve that he wasn't going anywhere.
4. Help keep children from falling out of the shopping carts by strapping them in.
5. Kelly and Samantha went to the dance, but she left early.

An antecedent must not be too far away

Confusing — Charlotte Bronte wrote *Jane Eyre* while still surrounded by her close-knit family circle. Then less than a year after *Jane Eyre* was published, Branwell died. Emily followed soon after. And within six months, Anne too was dead. **She** was alone.

Revised — Charlotte Bronte wrote *Jane Eyre* while still surrounded by her close-knit family circle. Then less than a year after *Jane Eyre* was published, Branwell died. Emily followed soon after. And within six months, Anne too was dead. **Charlotte** was alone.

If antecedent and pronoun are too far apart, the reference is likely to be unclear.

To avoid confusion, it's generally necessary to place the pronouns *who, which,* and *that* directly after the word to which they refer.

The words *who, which,* and *that* need to follow directly after the antecedent

Confusing — Warren fed the cat some milk **that** followed him home. [The milk followed Warren home?]

Revised — Warren fed some milk to the cat **that** followed him home.

Confusing — The athlete won the pole vault **who** also won the high jump. [The pole vault won the high jump?]

Revised — The athlete **who** won the pole vault also won the high jump.

Activity 43-16: Keeping Antecedent and Pronoun Near

Revise each sentence to make pronoun reference clear.

1. The audience who were waiting for the speaker was crowded with people.
2. The speaker was well received by the audience who presented on theories of dinosaur extinction.
3. The different theories drew many questions from people that had evidence to support them.
4. Some people argued forcefully with the speaker who disagreed with his ideas.
5. At the end of the speech, people stayed who wanted to further discuss ideas.

In many cases, pronoun reference is unclear because the antecedent is implied, vague, or missing.

Do Not Use Possessives as Implied Antecedents

Technically, the possessive form of a noun cannot serve as an antecedent, unless both pronoun and antecedent are in the possessive case.

But of course a noun in the subjective case can function as the antecedent to a possessive pronoun.

Possessives can't be antecedents unless the pronoun is also possessive

	ANT ? ... PRONOUN
Confusing	Smith's appointment to the federal bench brought **him** to national attention. [*Smith's* cannot function as the antecedent to *him*—you couldn't write *brought Smith's to national attention.*]
Revised	Smith's appointment to the federal bench brought **his** judicial record and **his** personal history to national attention. [Both *Smith's* and *his* are in the possessive case: *brought Smith's judicial record and Smith's personal history.*]
	or
	Smith came to national attention when **he** was appointed to the federal bench. [Both *Smith* and *he* are in the subjective case: *when Smith was appointed.*]
	or
	When Smith was appointed to the federal bench, both **his** judicial record and **his** personal history came to national attention.

Activity 43-17: Revising Possessives Used as Antecedents

Revise each sentence to make pronoun reference clear.

1. John's job brought him new responsibilities along with an increased salary.
2. Shaquina's story reached the national press when she was picked up by the AP wire service.
3. Is it true that Jim's painting won a prize for his use of color?
4. Indira's sculpture gave her a chance to express her sorrow at losing her dog.
5. Jennifer's appointment as director allowed her to fullfill many of her long-term goals.

Example 18 Making broad references specific

Confusing What happened to the dinosaurs? The Alvarez hypothesis holds that the K-T extinction was caused by a collision between the earth and a giant asteroid. **This** threw up enough dust to cause massive climate change. [This what? The sentence is unclear.]

Revised What happened to the dinosaurs? The Alvarez hypothesis holds that the K-T extinction was caused by a collision between the earth and a giant asteroid. **This collision** threw up enough dust to cause massive climate change.

Confusing The Victorians found *Jane Eyre* vulgar and shocking. **This** is because they expected women to be demure and self-effacing at all times.

Revised The Victorians found *Jane Eyre* vulgar and shocking because they expected women to be demure and self-effacing at all times.

Confusing In this week's episode, the doctors tell Shereen her illness is terminal, **which** upsets her family. [Is the family upset because Shereen's illness is terminal or because the doctors tell her?]

Revised In this week's episode, the family become upset when they learn Shereen's illness is terminal.

or

In this week's episode, the family become upset when the doctors disregard their wishes and tell Shereen her illness is terminal.

Confusing I told Grover that I had voted for Smith, **which** shocked Sanders to no end. [Is Sanders shocked that you voted for Smith or shocked that you told Grover about it?]

Revised Sanders was shocked when he learned I'd voted for Smith.

or

Sanders was shocked when he learned I'd been brave enough to tell Grover how I'd voted.

Avoid Overly Broad Use of *it, this, that,* and *which*

Avoid using the pronouns *it, this, that,* and *which* to make broad references to an entire idea, phrase, statement, sentence, or paragraph. To ensure clarity, make sure that each pronoun has a clear and specific antecedent.

Activity 43-18: Making Broad References Specific

Revise each sentence to make pronoun reference clear.

1. Upper-level math courses are not required for the elementary education degree. This is so you will have time to complete other relevant coursework.
2. Many parents become angry when credit card companies woo their children into accepting credit cards. That results in students enrolling in money management classes.
3. Last week, Rebecca told Maria that her boss was resigning, which caused her to feel very disappointed.
4. This fraternity is concerned about excessive drinking and has chosen to ban drinking from the frat house. Students are surprised by it.
5. Shoshanna told Kari that she was going to be elected president of the student council, which surprised and amazed her.

Do Not Use *it, they,* or *you* as an Indefinite Pronoun

Only indefinite pronouns—such as *anybody, all, both, each, everybody, nobody, neither, none, somebody, something*—can be used without antecedents. But in informal speech, the pronouns *it, they,* and *you* are commonly left dangling, with no antecedent to be found. This misuse in writing is confusing and ungrammatical; it often makes sentences weak and wordy. The misuse can also reveal a poorly supported argument.

However, in all but the most formal writing, the pronoun *you* can legitimately be used in direct addresses to the reader.

Example 19 Revising uses of *it, they,* or *you* as indefinite pronouns

Weak **They** say that global warming demands our attention.

Revised Scientists from multiple disciplines—astronomy, biology, chemistry, climatology, environmental studies, geology, physics, and zoology, to name just a few—say that global warming demands our attention.

Weak In the news **it** says that more and more bike messengers are now entering the world of bike racing. [Use of the phrase *in the news it says* indicates a weak argument without proper citation. Grammatically, *the news* cannot function as the antecedent to *it* when it is the object of the preposition *in.*]

Revised A recent *New York Times* article describes how more and more bike messengers are entering the world of bike racing (Corder A5).

Weak In the *ancien regime,* **you** had to be a noble to have any rights.

Revised In the *ancien regime,* only nobles had rights.

Example 20 Addressing the reader as *you*

To make meringues, **you** will need good weather. Dampness defeats them utterly.

The word *it* can function within a sentence as a(an) . . .

Personal pronoun	When I fed the dog, **it** wagged **its** tail.
Expletive	**It** is a truth universally acknowledged, that a single man in possession of a good fortune, must be in want of a wife. From Jane Austen, *Pride and Prejudice*.
Part of an idiomatic expression	**It** is raining. **It** is a great distance from London to Beijing. **It** is almost dawn.

Example 21 Revising sentences in which *it* is used in multiple ways

Confusing	**It** was not surprising that when the thunder cracked **it** made us jump right out of our beds last night when **it** rained so heavily.
Revised	The <u>thunder</u> cracked so loudly last night **it** made us jump right out of our beds.

Activity 43-19: Revising *it*

Revise the following paragraph to correct uses of *it*.

It has been stated by many researchers that underage drinking is a serious problem on campus. It is true that it is a major issue for many college students who find it difficult to resist. In a recent study by the Harvard School of Public Health, it says that 40 percent of students binge drink regularly. It is clear from this study that something needs to be done about it.

Do Not Use *it* in Multiple Ways in One Sentence

Though one of the smallest words in the English language, the pronoun *it* can perform many functions:

- *It* is a personal pronoun and, with the addition of *s*, a possessive pronoun.
- *It* can function as an expletive.
- *It* is part of idiomatic expressions pertaining to weather, distance, and time.

To avoid confusion, use *it* in only one way in a given sentence.

A small handful of rules govern the use of the pronouns *who, which,* and *that.*

1. Use *who* for people and named animals and *which* or *that* for objects, unnamed animals, and abstract concepts.
2. Occasionally, you may need to use *whose* for animals and things to avoid an awkward *of which* construction.
3. *That* is restrictive: it introduces a clause, phrase, or word that tells you something essential to defining the noun it modifies.
4. *Which* is nonrestrictive: it introduces a clause, phrase, or word providing information that is parenthetical and hence *non*essential to defining the noun it modifies. Such phrases must be set off by commas.

Example 22 Using *who, which,* and *that*

Only people and named animals take *who*:

In the Bonampak murals, the ruler is the man **who** is wearing jaguar skin sandals.

The helmet **that** the queen is handing to him is made from the head of an actual jaguar.

Sammy, **who** has won multiple Best in Show awards throughout his career, is more officially known as Smithpom's Holly Go Lightly in Silver.

The dogs **that** I saw performed magnificently.

Whose can be used instead of *of which:*

Foxes, ~~the call of which~~ ^whose call^ is an eerie guttural bark, prey primarily on small mammals.

That is restrictive:

The book **that I returned** is the one your records still show as missing. [The book that I returned, and no other, is the one still shown as missing.]

Which is nonrestrictive:

This book, **which I just returned,** was outstanding. [The book was outstanding. The fact that I just returned the book is parenthetical and nonessential to its being outstanding.]

Activity 43-20: Revising *who, which,* and *that*

Revise the following sentences to correct pronoun problems.

1. The queen that survived the bombing gave an inspiring speech the next day.
2. The thunderstorm, who came through the area, last night caused massive power outages.
3. The raccoons, which had been eating our trash, scattered as soon as we turned on the porch light.
4. The performances which we saw last night were amazing.
5. Butterflies, the colors of which there are many and varied, live in many different parts of the world.

Activity 43-21: Revising Pronouns in Context

Revise the following excerpt from a student paper to take care of any misused pronouns.

It is clear that underage drinking is a serious problem on our campus. When a student that is drinking leaves the bar, they are likely to end up driving home drunk. This is a serious problem because he or she can get into an accident. Its a horrible thing to happen to someone that is young and just beginning their lives. These tragedies which could be prevented happen to we college students every day.

Whose responsible for students' decisions about drinking? It has been argued by many that the person whom is responsible is in fact the student themselves. Every person is responsible for his actions. Few people want to admit that it is their responsibility. To keep people's lives from being affected by alcohol and bad judgment, they must be educated. Us students need to work together to help them make responsible choices about drinking.

Activity 43-22: Revising Pronouns in Your Own Writing

In a piece of writing that you worked on recently, circle all the pronouns. Using this chapter as a guide, check to be sure your uses are appropriate in your writing context. Revise your pronoun use as needed, and then read your work out loud. How did your revisions affect the clarity and readability of the text? Is it clearer and shorter now? Why or why not?

44

VERBS

Calvin, the precocious prankster of the famous comic strip *Calvin and Hobbes,* used to go around "verb-ing" words, which he thought conveyed raw power. (Instead—as Hobbes, his imaginary tiger friend, knew—it made Calvin look silly.) In just a few short years, Google, the popular search engine, saw its name verb-ed. These days, if you're looking for something on the Web, you "google it."

Obviously, you shouldn't go around verb-ing every noun you come across. But you should recognize that verbs are extremely important not only because they convey action and experience but also because the grammar of the English sentence is built around them (English is called an S-V-O language, subject-verb-object, because that is its natural word order). Furthermore, verbs do more in a sentence than simply indicate what is happening or being experienced. Verbs can indicate when something happened, whether one or more people or things were involved, and whether an action comes as a request or an order. Many novice writers consider verbs to be the most problematic part of speech. To strip away some of the confusion regarding verb use, think of verbs as "doing or being" words. The goal of this chapter is to demystify what many people consider to be a bewildering array of tenses and aspects of verbs so that effective and conventional verb use comes as easily to you as use of other parts of speech.

The Five Forms of Regular Verbs

The first three forms are called the principal parts.

Plain (base) Form	-*s* Form (used with *he, she,* and *it* in the present tense)	Present Participle (*-ing* form)	Past Tense	Past Participle
walk	walks	walking	walked	walked
hope	hopes	hoping	hoped	hoped
classify	classifies	classifying	classified	classified

Example 1 Plain form verbs

I **want** to shop for shoes today.

You always **tell** me you **love** me after your dogs **do** something wrong.

Chew my Manolo Blahnik spiked heels again and **watch** my reaction.

Example 2 The -*s* form

He always **walks** the same route, and then he **eats** lunch down at the diner.

Delivering the mail **makes** his arm hurt after an hour or so.

Newman's apartment **needs** painting.

Activity 44-1: Verbs in Plain Form and -*s* Form

Determine the correct form of each verb in brackets. If a verb requires an -s ending, add it. Then underline the subject of each verb.

Many young filmmakers [find] that they are having trouble getting work these days. One young filmmaker [say] that he [send] up to twenty resumes a week, but [get] little response from companies. Why is this happening? Everybody [think] that making films is easy with the rise of digital technology. Chip Lord, chairman of the UC film school, [say] that his department has grown to over 500 students in the past ten years. As more people attempt to become directors, competition [grow] fierce.

All verbs except *to be* have five basic forms. Some forms can stand alone as the main verb of a sentence, but others need the help of auxiliary verbs in order to function as the main verb. See section 44c for information about auxiliary, or helping, verbs.

Plain Form

The **plain form**, or *base form,* of verbs is used to express actions, occurrences, or states of being in the present tense. The present tense can indicate actions that are happening now or actions that occur regularly. The plain form can be used as the main verb of a sentence.

The -*s* Form

The -*s* form is created by adding *s* or *es* to the plain form of a verb: *swim/swims, classify/classifies.* Use the -*s* form with subjects that are singular nouns *(cake, child, Margaret);* the pronouns *he, she,* and *it;* and indefinite pronouns such as *anybody.* The -*s* ending on a verb indicates the present tense. The -*s* form can be the main verb of a sentence.

Present Participle Form

Present participle verbs indicate action happening now. The present participle is formed by adding *-ing* to the end of the plain form: *singing.* To use this form as the main verb in a sentence, combine it with a form of the verb *to be:* **am** *crying,* **is** *encouraging,* **are** *going,* **will be** *arriving.* Present participles can also function as nouns (*Swimming* is fun) and adjectives (the *ringing* phone).

Past-Tense Form

The past-tense form indicates actions that happened before now. Normally, you form the past tense by adding a *-d* or an *-ed* to the plain form, but some verbs form the past tense irregularly (section 44b). The past tense can be used as a main verb.

Past Participle Form

Like the past tense, the past participle indicates actions that have already occurred. The past participle form is the same as the past form except in some irregular verbs (section 44b). If you want to use the past participle form as the main verb of a sentence, you also need to use a form of the verb *to be* or *to have:* We **have** *reported* the problem. Used without *be* or *have,* the past participle form acts as an adjective; it modifies a noun or pronoun: the *accepted* solution.

Example 3 Present participle form

He **is skiing** down the slope right now.

I **am running** for help.

We **are hoping** that your leg will heal before our ski vacation starts.

Singing in the rain can cause the common cold. [Present participle as a noun, not a verb]

Example 4 Past-tense form

You **rented** this apartment last year?

My car **died** on the Los Angeles freeway.

He **wrestled** the big masked man called the Undertaker.

Example 5 Past participle form

I **was fascinated** and **repelled** by the Michael Jackson documentary.

We **have operated** the heavy machinery for a month.

Jillian and DeShawn **had stopped** by the time we arrived.

Activity 44-2: Verbs in the Past and Past Participle Forms

Determine the correct form of each verb in brackets. If a verb requires a *-d* or *-ed* ending, add it. For each past participle, underline the form of *to be* or *to have* that helps it function as a verb.

A cache of letters written by a Civil War general have been [donate] to a museum in his hometown. Emory Upton was [locate] at West Point when the war [start]. Excerpts of the letters were [publish] in *The Life and Letters of Emory Upton* in 1888. The letters discuss the war and Upton's travels to Europe, where he [study] and [lecture] on military tactics. Historians also hope to uncover what [cause] Upton's suicide in 1881.

The Principal Parts of Common Irregular Verbs

Plain Form	Past Tense	Past Participle
be	was/were	been
beat	beat	beaten
become	became	become
begin	began	begun
bend	bent	bent
bet	bet	bet
bid	bid	bid
bite	bit	bitten
blow	blew	blown
break	broke	broken
bring	brought	brought
broadcast	broadcast	broadcast
build	built	built
burn	burned/burnt	burned/burnt
burst	burst	burst
buy	bought	bought
catch	caught	caught
choose	chose	chosen
come	came	come
cost	cost	cost
creep	crept	crept
cut	cut	cut
dig	dug	dug
dive	dove/dived	dived
do	did	done
draw	drew	drawn
dream	dreamed	dreamed/dreamt
drink	drank	drunk
drive	drove	driven
eat	ate	eaten
fall	fell	fallen
fight	fought	fought
find	found	found
flee	fled	fled
fly	flew	flown

You can tell the difference between regular and irregular verbs by how they are formed in the past tense and past participle. Almost all verbs are regular, which means that you form the past and past participle by adding *-d* or *-ed: laugh / laughed, arrive / arrived.* With irregular verbs, however, there is no general pattern to show you how to make the past and past participle forms. When you aren't sure whether a verb is regular or irregular, consult a dictionary. If the verb is irregular, the different tense constructions will be listed, often with a brief sample sentence to clarify the usage.

The Irregular Verb *to be*

The most widely used verb in the English language is also the most irregular.

***Forms of* to be**

Plain (base) form: *be*

Be ready at noon.

Past-tense form: *was* (singular); *were* (plural)

Was Jose unhappy yesterday?
Were Grant and Devon home?

Past participle: *been*

They have **been** friends since they were little kids.

-*s* form: *is*

That lifeguard **is** not paying attention.

Present participle: *being*

She is **being** a good sport.

Plain Form	Past Tense	Past Participle
forget	forgot	forgotten
forgive	forgave	forgiven
freeze	froze	frozen
get	got	got (preferred)/gotten (informal)
give	gave	given
go	went	gone
grow	grew	grown
hang	hung/hanged (if a person)	hung/hanged (if a person)
hear	heard	heard
hide	hid	hidden
hit	hit	hit
hold	held	held
hurt	hurt	hurt
keep	kept	kept
know	knew	known
lay	laid	lain
lead	led	led
learn	learned/learnt	learned/learnt
leave	left	left
lend	lent	lent
let	let	let
lie	lay	lain
light	lit (preferred)/lighted	lit (preferred)/lighted
lose	lost	lost
make	made	made
mean	meant	meant
meet	met	met
pay	paid	paid
prove	proved	proved/proven
put	put	put
repay	repaid	repaid
ride	rode	ridden
ring	rang	rung
rise	rose	risen
run	ran	run
say	said	said

Plain Form	Past Tense	Past Participle
see	saw	seen
sell	sold	sold
send	sent	sent
shake	shook	shaken
shoot	shot	shot
shrink	shrank/shrunk	shrunk
shut	shut	shut
sing	sang/sung	sung
sink	sank/sunk	sunk
sit	sat	sat
sleep	slept	slept
slide	slid	slid
speak	spoke	spoken
spend	spent	spent
spring	sprang/sprung	sprung
stand	stood	stood
steal	stole	stolen
stink	stank/stunk	stunk
strive	strove	striven
swear	swore	sworn
sweep	swept	swept
swim	swam	swum
swing	swung	swung
take	took	taken
teach	taught	taught
tear	tore	torn
tell	told	told
think	thought	thought
throw	threw	thrown
understand	understood	understood
wake	woke/waked	woken/waked
wear	wore	worn
weep	wept	wept
win	won	won
wring	wrung	wrung
write	wrote	written

The Irregular Verbs *to have* and *to do*

Forms of the verbs *to have* and *to do* can be used as main verbs or, as discussed in section 44c, as auxiliary verbs.

***Forms of* to have**

Plain (base) form: *have*
Past-tense form: *had*
Past participle: *had*
-s form: *has*
Present participle: *having*

***Forms of* to do**

Plain (base) form: *do*
Past-tense form: *did*
Past participle: *done*
-s form: *does*
Present participle: *doing*

Activity 44-3: Irregular Verbs

Choose the correct form of the irregular verb from the choices given in brackets.

Should soft drinks [come/comed] with warning labels? The director for the Center for Science in the Public Interest has [sayed/said] that yes, they should, and has filed a petition with the Food and Drug Administration. Although the calorie count of soft drinks is [gived/given] on the label, the director argues that most people do not [understand/understood] these labels. In the past, people [drinked/drank] less soda; now the average teen consumes two sugary sodas a day. The director of the center argues that a line must be [drawed/drawn] to encourage people to consume fewer sugary drinks. People must be [teached/taught] about how soda can be a part of balanced nutrition.

44c Auxiliary Verbs

Auxiliary verbs are often referred to as helping verbs. Auxiliary verbs help main verbs indicate shades of meaning, tense, voice, or mood. The main verb carries the basic meaning of the verb and can be in the plain form, the present participle form (the *-ing* form), or the past participle form (the *-ed* form for regular verbs). Together, the main verb and any auxiliary verbs are called the **verb phrase.**

Forms of *be, have,* and *do* are the most common helping verbs. They can be used as auxiliaries to other verbs, but in other cases they are used as main verbs. See pages 870 and 871 for a list of the forms of these verbs. The following pages discuss the most common uses for auxiliary verbs in verb phrases.

Example 6 Auxiliary verbs

Tense — She **was** (AUX.) **running** (MAIN (PRESENT PARTICIPLE)) for president.

Voice — He **was** (AUX.) **influenced** (MAIN (PAST PARTICIPLE)) by his colleagues.

Mood — She **might** (AUX.) **have** (AUX.) **run** (MAIN (PLAIN FORM)) for president if her friend **hadn't** (AUX.) [run] (MAIN (IMPLIED)).

Progressive Tenses: A Form of *be* + Present Participle

Notice that the *-ing* form of the main verb is used in the progressive tenses:

Present progressive	Lidia **is writing** her essay on the East African city-states.
Past progressive	She **was smiling** at the camera.
Future progressive	I **will be enjoying** my lunch for the next hour.

Modal + *be*

	MODAL	THE WORD *BE*
You	must	**be** waiting at the bus stop in the morning.
She	had better	**be** going home now.

Modal Auxiliary Verb	**Example**
be able to*	Someday you **will be able to run** a six-minute mile.
can, could	My dog **can smell** his favorite toy across the lawn.
had better	She **had better wear** sandals while walking across the hot beach sand.
had to, has to, have to*	We **have to swim** quickly in order to catch the wave.
may, might, must	**May** I **get** you a cold drink? No, I **must leave** now.
shall, should	I **should pick up** my brother at school.
be supposed to*	You **are supposed to drink** water with that aspirin. [Note the *-d:* suppose<u>d</u>.]
used to	He **used to take** his baby to the park every Monday. [Note the *-d:* use<u>d</u>.]
will, would	You **will meet** our manager before you begin working.

*These modals change form to indicate singular and plural subjects. For example, use

I (you/we/they) **have to** ask permission.

but

He (she) **has to** find out why. It **has to** be that way.

Progressive Tenses

When you use a form of the auxiliary verb *to be* and the present participle *(-ing)* form of a main verb, you create a progressive tense, which shows that an action is, was, or will be progressing over a period of time.

If you use the word *be* as an auxiliary verb, one of the modal auxiliaries needs to come before it. The modal auxiliaries communicate various shades of meaning, only a few of which are shown in the examples to the left.

Multilingual writers: See section 61e.

If you use the word *been* as an auxiliary verb, a form of the auxiliary verb *to have* (*has, had,* or *have*) is needed before it.

Any time you use a form of *to be* as a helping verb, you must use an additional auxiliary verb.

Form of *have* + *been*

	FORM OF *HAVE*	THE WORD *BEEN*
Ali	had	**been** experiencing problems with his computer.
Farhiya	has	**been** tired from all her studying.

Forms of *be* as auxiliaries require additional helping verbs

The tickets	*had, have*	**been** lost for days.
The tickets	*will have*	**been** lost for days.
I/We	*am, are, is*	**being** connected to the server.
She/He	*was, were*	**being** connected to the server.

Passive Voice

When you use a form of the verb *to be* with the past participle of a verb, you create the passive voice, which shows that the subject of your sentence is receiving the action of the sentence. Only transitive verbs (verbs that take an object) can be used in the passive voice (section 44g).

Passive Voice: A Form of *be* + Past Participle

Jackie **was taken** to the hospital. [Jackie is the recipient of the *taking* action.]

She **was given** an examination. [Someone gave her an exam.]

Uses of *to do* as an Auxiliary Verb

The auxiliary verb *to do (do, does,* and *did*) functions in three ways to aid the main verb.

Functions of *do* as an Auxiliary Verb

1. To ask a question: How *do* you *change* the car's oil?
2. To create emphasis: That dog *did bite* my neighbor!
3. With *not,* to negate the main verb: He *did not ask* for your help.

Multilingual writers: In sentence 1, notice how the subject, *you,* is located after the auxiliary verb *do* and before the main verb *change*. See section 62d for more information on forming questions.

Transitive verbs perform an action on an object

VERB OBJECT
I **uploaded** the files via FTP.

Intransitive verbs do not take direct objects—the action they express ends or is modified somehow

VERB
I **wonder** about that advice. [No direct object]

VERB
He **spoke** passionately about freedom. [*Spoke* is modified by the adverb *passionately.*]

Some transitive verbs can function intransitively in some contexts, especially when paired with an adverb or prepositional phrase

Transitive, with direct object	She **studies** calculus.
Intransitive, with adverb	She **studies** daily.
Intransitive, with prepositional phrase	She **studies** in the afternoon.

Transitive verbs take direct objects; intransitive verbs do not (◀ section 40l). Many verbs can be used both ways, and context determines whether they are working with an object or not.

The Pairs *lie* and *lay, sit* and *set, rise* and *raise*

The most common mistakes made with transitive and intransitive verbs occur with these pairs of irregular verbs: *lay/lie, raise/rise,* and *set/sit.*

Here is the standard written usage for each pair

lay To place, as in to put down. Does take an object.

He **laid** the <u>newspaper</u> on the table.

lie To recline. Does not take an object.

The dog **lies** by the door whenever Sergio says "Go **lie** down."

raise To lift up. Does take an object.

She **raised** the <u>standards</u> for everyone in the class.

rise To go higher. Does not take an object.

Her test scores **rose** all semester.

set To place (synonym of *lay*) or to configure. Does take an object.

Please **set** your <u>bookbags</u> in the hallway.

Please **set** the <u>clock</u> back an hour.

sit To sit down, to be seated. Does not take an object.

Will you **sit** at the table and eat?

Activity 44-4: Using *lay/lie, raise/rise,* and *set/sit*

Select the correct verb from the choices given in brackets.

"Won't you [set/sit] down for a moment?" Mom asked.

"I don't have time! I have to [set/sit] up my side of the room before my roommate arrives. If I don't get some of these boxes out of the way, neither of us will be able to [lay/lie] down tonight," Jennifer said.

"[Lay/lie] your clothes on the bed for now, and I'll hang them up," Mom said.

"Mom, do you think we could [raise/rise] my bed up on supports? Then I could store things under the bed," Jenn said.

"Maybe. We'll have to get rid of this [rising/raising] pile of boxes first," Mom said.

Verb Tenses of a Regular Verb (in Active Voice)

Name of Tense	Time of Action	Example
PAST TENSE		
Simple past	Action happened before now.	She *ran.*
Past progressive	Action continued during a time period in the past.	She *was running.*
Past perfect	Action was completed in the past before another past action.	She *had run.*
Past perfect progressive	Continuing action was completed before another past action.	She *had been running.*
PRESENT TENSE		
Simple present	Action happens now or habitually.	She *runs.*
Present progressive	Action continues during a time period in the present.	She *is running.*
Present perfect	Action happened in the past and may be continuing in the present.	She *has run.*
Present perfect progressive	Action happened in the past and is still continuing.	She *has been running.*
FUTURE TENSE		
Simple future	Action may happen in the future.	She *will run.*
Future progressive	Action will be happening during a period of time in the future.	She *will be running.*
Future perfect	Action will occur and end at some point in the future.	She *will have run.*
Future perfect progressive	Future action will have been completed before another future action.	She *will have been running.*

Tense is the form of a verb that communicates time. For example, time can be expressed in the past, present, and future tenses: *talked, talk, will talk.* These forms are the simple tenses. The perfect tenses usually indicate time completed before another time or action: *The farmer* ***had plowed*** *the field before she planted.* The progressive tenses indicate continuing action: *The council members* ***were considering*** *the zoning plan.*

Past Tenses

The Simple Past Tense
Use the simple past tense to express an action or state of being that began and ended in the past.

Past tense: plain form + *-d* or *-ed*

A spider **crawled** across my fork just a minute ago.

The plane **landed** and **burst** into flames. [*Burst* is irregular; see section 44b.]

The Past Progressive Tense
Use the past progressive tense to express actions that occurred in the past and were ongoing. The actions normally started at one point and finished later. There does not have to be any connection between those ongoing past actions and the present, since the actions are finished.

Past progressive: *was* or *were* + *-ing* form of main verb

Those men **were running** along the beach this morning.

One of them **was carrying** a backpack full of rocks.

The Past Perfect Tense
Use the past perfect tense to express actions or states of being that occurred in the past and were definitely finished in the past. People often use the past perfect to establish a chronology, so that they can show that one thing happened and then another thing happened.

Past perfect: *had* + *-ed* form of main verb

I arrived at school ten minutes late for class, and my instructor **had** already **marked** me absent.

Since the dog **had eaten** the entire turkey, we went out and ate duck at a Chinese restaurant. [*Eaten* is irregular; see section 44b.]

The Past Perfect Progressive Tense
Use the past perfect progressive tense to express ongoing actions that were completed before another past action.

Past perfect progressive: *had been* + *-ing* form of main verb

Those kids **had been running** around the cafeteria for twenty minutes before I stopped them.

Clark **had been meaning** to fix his CD player until someone stole it.

Present Tenses

The Simple Present Tense

The simple present tense describes actions or states of being that happen now. It is also used to describe

- regular or recurring (habitual) action
- with an adverb, actions in the near future
- general truths
- observations and judgments about conditions

The present tense is also used when referring to a literary text, a painting, or the like (◀ section 9f).

Present tense: plain form or *-s* form

Action happening now	The boat's sail **whips** in the wind.
With adverb, for the near future	The door **opens** promptly at eight o'clock tonight.
Habitual action	Every morning he **takes** his allergy medicine.
General truth	Water **freezes** at 32 degrees Fahrenheit. This temperature **is** its freezing point.
Observations	The five-year-old girl **picks** up a red balloon and **waves** it over her head.
Judgments	The waves **appear** to be about sixteen feet high.
Reference to a text	In her bestseller, Lynne Truss **gives** readers permission to love punctuation. Bilbo Baggins **sets off** from his cozy hobbit hole on a great quest.

The Present Progressive Tense

Much like the simple present tense, the present progressive expresses the ongoing nature of an action or state of being. You can also use the present progressive with an adverb or adverb phrase to indicate action in a future situation.

Present progressive: *am, is,* or *are* + *-ing* form of main verb

I **am running** a fever.

Holly **is thinking** about it right now.

They **are drawing** the winning ticket in the lottery drawing at noon.

The Present Perfect Tense

Use the present perfect tense to express action that

- started in the past and continues in the present
- has just stopped when you are describing it

Present perfect: *have* or *has* + past participle (with *-d* or *-ed*)

I **have received** those CDs from home that I want you to hear.

Jacques **has forgotten** what he is supposed to take to the picnic.

Present Perfect Progressive Tense

The present perfect progressive tense expresses an action that has happened in the past and is affecting the present. The present perfect progressive emphasizes the ongoing nature of the action or state of being.

Present perfect progressive: *have* or *has* + *been* + *-ing* form

Those neighbors **have been stealing** our mail for years.

Carmella **has been feeling** depressed since she found out she wouldn't get the promotion.

Future Tenses

The Simple Future Tense

Use the simple future tense to express actions or states of being that will occur in the future.

Future tense: *will* + plain form of main verb

She **will discover** your secret if you aren't careful.

Will you **drive** me to the movies tonight?

The Future Progressive Tense

Use the future progressive tense to express actions or states of being that will continue for a period of time in the future.

Future progressive: *will be* + *-ing* form of main verb

Trent Reznor **will be performing** with Saul Williams tonight from 8:00 to 11:00.

Will they **be discussing** the proposed teen center designs at the town meeting?

The Future Perfect Tense

Use the future perfect tense to express actions or states of being that will end before another action occurs.

Future perfect: *will have* + past participle (with *-d* or *-ed*)

Chris Rock **will have made** a couple of formulaic movies before the studios allow him to make something really funny.

They **will have taken** me to small claims court by then if I don't give them back their deposit.

The Future Perfect Progressive Tense

Use the future perfect progressive tense to express an ongoing action or state of being that will be finished at some point in the future.

Future perfect progressive: *will have been* + *-ing* form of main verb

The band **will have been singing** professionally for about three years by then.

If he keeps this up until tomorrow, Kevin **will have been ignoring** me for a full month.

Spanish-speaking writers: See "OM Verbs" for detailed information about constructing verb tenses; this site includes translations: **http://www.ompersonal.com.ar/omverbs/contenidotematico.htm**

Example 7 Verb tense shifts

Appropriate shifts:

PRESENT PERFECT
Several African artists **have donated** paintings to benefit the American

PRESENT PROGRESSIVE
Anti-Slavery Group. The organization **is hosting** an art auction on eBay.

FUTURE
Proceeds **will go** to their anti-slavery efforts in Africa.

Confusing shifts:

FUTURE
Andrej Mucic **is going to bicycle** 7,000 miles across Siberia to raise

PRESENT
$10,000 to support the American Anti-Slavery Group. Mucic **takes off** 100

PAST PRESENT
days of work from Home Depot, where he **worked.** He **spends** his whole summer biking.

Revised for clarity:

FUTURE
Andrej Mucic **is going to bicycle** 7,000 miles across Siberia to raise

FUTURE
$10,000 to support the American Anti-Slavery Group. Mucic **will take off**

PRESENT FUTURE
100 days of work from Home Depot, where he **works.** He **will spend** his whole summer biking.

Activity 44-5: Shifts in Verb Tense

Rewrite the following paragraph to omit any confusing shifts in verb tense.

Scientists have discovered the first planet to have three suns. The planet was a gas giant slightly larger than Jupiter, and it orbits the main star of a triple-star system called HD 188753. A person who stands on the planet's surface saw three suns in the sky. The largest sun would be orange and the other two are red. The new finding has upset theories that planets form only around single-star systems and leads to new discoveries in the future.

Avoiding Unnecessary Shifts in Verb Tense

You will often vary verb tenses in your writing to indicate different times. But when you shift verb tenses for no good reason, readers become confused. Your first sentence sets up an expectation about the time of the action; the time frame becomes known information. Each verb shift after that is new information that readers have to assimilate.

Understanding the Sequence of Verb Tenses

Every clause has a verb. Verbs in nearby clauses that relate actions occurring at about the same time should be expressed in the same tense. If clauses within the same sentence or in nearby sentences include actions happening at different times, then verb tenses, used precisely, can help readers sort out what happened when.

When one past event occurs before another past event, use the past perfect for the one that happened first.

When one future event happens before another future event, use the future perfect for the one that will happen first and the present tense (or the present perfect) for the one that will happen after it.

If you use the future tense in the independent clause, then use the simple present tense in the dependent clause to indicate an event happening at about the same time or the past perfect tense to indicate an earlier action.

Infinitives (such as *to walk, to look*) are used after verbs to indicate a sequence of time. Use the present infinitive to show an action happening at the same time as or later than the action expressed by the main verb.

Use the perfect infinitive if the action is earlier than the action of the main verb. The perfect infini-

Example 8 Using verb tenses to convey time sequence

Both verbs in present tense:

Joel **takes** avalanche gear when he **skis.** [Simple present tense for both verbs indicates habitual actions.]

Past perfect tense with past tense:

The last time he **went** telemarking, he **used** his probe to locate another skier who **had been buried** in a sudden snow slide. [The general time frame is the past. The past perfect tense in *had been buried* indicates that the skier was buried before being located. This phrase is also in the passive voice.]

Future perfect tense with present tense:

Joel **will have bought** a new DSP beacon by the time he **goes** into the backcountry again. [First he will buy the beacon; later, he will go.]

Future tense with simple present tense and present perfect tense:

On the anniversary of Martin Luther King's assassination, I **will walk** to Washington because I **want** to demonstrate that civil rights still **need** attention. I **will speak** to any groups I **have managed** to find.

Example 9 Infinitives

Present infinitive:

She <u>wants</u> **to perform** well tonight.

Paula <u>runs</u> **to meet** the mail carrier.

Perfect infinitive:

Rene <u>would like</u> **to have noticed** the rare bird first.

Example 10 Participles

Present participle:

Taking photos in the Arctic, Cherry Alexander <u>had shot</u> a closeup of a penguin family that won her the 1995 BBC Wildlife Photographer of the Year award.

Past participle:

Adopted by a Siberian woman, the orphaned baby reindeer <u>lived</u> a long and pampered life.

tive is composed of *to have* + the past participle.

The present participle is used to express action that happens at the same time as the action of the main verb.

The past participle is used to express action that happens earlier than the action of the main verb.

Activity 44-6: Sequence of Tenses

Make any needed revisions to verbs in the following paragraph so that the sequence of tenses is correct.

Many credit card companies give incentives such as free gifts to college students; they saw the gifts as another reason to sign up for credit cards. But by the time they left college, most students will aquire a lot of debt in exchange for their free gift. Some universities have reacted to this growth in credit card offers by teaching students about money management in first-year seminars. Still, many students would like to learn lessons about money management in a less painful way.

Mood 44f

Verb mood conveys a writer's attitude toward the subject.

The indicative mood is used to state facts, opinions, and questions.

Example 11 Indicative mood

Fact	Vietnamese writer Duong Thu Huong **was imprisoned** for nine months in 1991.
Opinion	Her refusal to shut up despite the Hanoi government's efforts **is** brave.
Question	How many other writers from Vietnam **have been silenced** by fear?

Use the imperative mood to request something or to make a command.

Example 12 Imperative mood

Request	Please **enjoy** yourselves.
	Send me an email with your resume attached.
Command	**Get** in, **buckle** up, and **keep** quiet!

Use the subjunctive mood to indicate conditions that are contrary to fact, desires, suggestions, and recommendations.

Use the subjunctive in subordinate clauses beginning with *if, as though,* or *as if* when the clause expresses speculation or a condition contrary to fact.

Use the subjunctive to make requests, demands, or suggestions in dependent clauses starting with *that.* Verbs that introduce such clauses include *request, invite, suggest, demand, insist,* and *require.*

Example 13 Subjunctive mood

Condition contrary to fact	The car seat seemed as if it **were** safer than a regular seat belt for children aged two to eight, but the FARS data indicate that this is not true.
Speculation	If the results **were** to become well known, children over two might not have to use car seats anymore.
Request	I ask that we **be** given the option of buying booster seats.
Demand	Parents are demanding that the agency **prove** the expensive car seats are needed.
Suggestion	In 2001, the Insurance Institute for Highway Safety was suggesting that the National Highway Traffic Safety Administration **reconsider** its call for booster seats.

Forming the Subjunctive Mood

Present subjunctive: Always use the plain form of the verb: *carry, be, do.*

> It is crucial that the bear **be** quarantined when it reenters the country.

Past subjunctive: Use the simple past tense, except for the verb *to be,* which in the past subjunctive is always *were* (even for singular subjects).

> Stephanie Allen wished she **had** a way to get families to eat dinner together again. She and Tina Kuna thought that if it **were** possible, they would like to be the ones to make it happen.

Activity 44-7: The Subjunctive Mood

Change any of the bracketed verbs in the following paragraph that should be in the subjunctive mood so that they are in the correct form.

> A society of virtual "agents" has been created by scientists from five European research institutes who would like to know if they [can simulate] how human societies evolve. If this simulation [was] possible, it could provide vital details about how culture grows and changes. Past research has suggested that agents [learned] about their virtual world quickly and easily. Other researchers have asked that they [are] given the option of contributing their own agents to the second version.

Passive verbs: a form of *to be* + past participle of transitive verb (with *-d* or *-ed*)

Other helping verbs may also be used, as in these examples:

was conducted
was being conducted
have been conducted
will be conducted

Example 14 Active vs. passive voice

	AGENT IS SUBJECT / ACTIVE VERB / DIRECT OBJECT
Active voice	Sara **hurled** the iron pot at the intruder.
	OBJECT IS NOW SUBJECT / PASSIVE VERB / AGENT IN PREP. PHRASE
Passive voice	The iron pot **was hurled** at the intruder by Sara.
Agent omitted	The iron pot **was hurled** at the intruder.

Example 15 Revising from passive to active voice

	PASSIVE VERB / AGENT IN PREP. PHRASE
Passive voice	Creative works **are protected** by copyright laws.
	NEW SUBJECT / ACTIVE VERB / NEW OBJECT
Active voice	Copyright laws **protect** creative works.

When a sentence is in the active voice, the subject performs the action. In passive voice, the subject is acted upon, and the performer of the action (called the *agent*) either is stated in a prepositional phrase or is missing from the sentence.

Active voice emphasizes the agent of the action, whereas passive voice emphasizes the action. Active voice sentences are written in the normal word order of English: subject-verb-object. They are easier to read and take fewer words than passive voice sentences. Sentences in the active voice are stronger and more direct than sentences in the passive. Unless you have a specific reason to use the passive, write in the active voice.

Revising Passive Voice to Active Voice

To convert a sentence from passive to active, make the agent into the subject of the new sentence, change the verb form to active voice, and use the subject of the original sentence as the object of the new one.

Passive voice is useful when the person who performed an action is less important than the action. For example, observations made in the social sciences and reports of experiments in the sciences often use the passive more frequently than writing in the humanities, which tends to emphasize the individual agent.

Uses of the Active and Passive Voices

- The active voice is strong and direct:

  The door **slammed** shut, and we **avoided** each other's eyes.
  Gil Scott Heron **recorded** the first rap album.

- The passive can be used to avoid responsibility by removing the agent:

Active voice	I **stole** your chocolate chip cookies.
Passive voice	Your chocolate chip cookies **were stolen.**

- The passive is used when the agents are less important than what they accomplished:

Active voice	Legislative assistants **wrote** the civil union laws.
Passive voice	The civil union laws **were written** by legislative assistants.
	or
	The civil union laws **were written.**

- The passive is used when giving "how to" directions:

  When the screw **has been tightened,** the guitar string should be in tune.

Passive Voice in the Sciences

Social Science Writing Sample
Actions are emphasized; agents are listed in the in-text citation.

Sets of data from surveys and interviews of American, Canadian, Japanese, Mayan, North African, Navajo, and Indonesian women **were compared** (Beyene, 1986; Flint & Samil, 1990; Lock, 1994; Walfish, Antonovksy, & Maoz, 1984; A. L. Wright, 1983).

Science Writing Sample
The information is the focus, not the people who gathered it.

Neuropeptides **could be found** not only in the rows of nerve ganglia on either side of the spine, but in the end organs themselves. . . . New peptide-containing groups of neuronal cell bodies . . . **are** now **being elaborated upon** every day.

From Candace B. Pert, *Molecules of Emotion* (New York: Touchstone/Simon & Schuster, 1997), 140.

Activity 44-8: Revising the Passive Voice

Revise the following paragraph so that most sentences are in the active voice.

> Many parts of the music industry are affected by music piracy. Music piracy happens when songs are downloaded illegally by Internet users. It has been argued by industry analysts that smaller record labels will be bankrupted by music piracy. It has been claimed by people who pirate music that their downloads actually lead to more exposure for the artists. Therefore, more concert tickets and other types of merchandise are sold by the musicians.

Activity 44-9: Revising Verbs in Your Own Writing

In a piece of writing you have worked on recently, circle the verbs. Using this chapter as a guide, check to be sure your uses are appropriate in your writing context. Revise the verbs as needed, and then read your work out loud. How did your revisions affect the earlier draft? Can you understand your writing more clearly now?

45

SUBJECT-VERB AGREEMENT

Subject-verb agreement is the backbone of sentence grammar. It is also a common source of error in college-level writing. Although the basic concepts of subject-verb agreement are part of beginning language acquisition (very young children already grasp the difference between *I go* and *he goes,* for example), subject-verb agreement can present any number of difficult and perplexing issues.

The subject and verb of a sentence must always agree in person. For example, although you use *run* with the first person *I* or the second person *you* (*I run, you run*), you use *runs* with the third person (*she runs*). The subject and verb must also agree in number. Whereas you use *runs* with the third person singular (*she runs*), you use *run* with the third person plural (*they run*).

This chapter explains the conventions for subject-verb agreement and looks at common problems in locating the subject and in deciding which subjects are singular and which are plural.

Example 1 Third-person singular subjects and verbs

My cat **catches** many mice.

The courthouse **stands** on the village green.

Three Irregular Verbs

The verb *to be*

First-person singular	I **am**	First-person plural	we **are**
Second-person singular	you **are**	Second-person plural	you **are**
Third-person singular	he/she/it **is**	Third-person plural	they **are**

The verb *to have*

First-person singular	I **have**	First-person plural	we **have**
Second-person singular	you **have**	Second-person plural	you **have**
Third-person singular	he/she/it **has**	Third-person plural	they **have**

The verb *to do*

First-person singular	I **do**	First-person plural	we **do**
Second-person singular	you **do**	Second-person plural	you **do**
Third-person singular	he/she/it **does**	Third-person plural	they **do**

Past tense forms of the verb *to be*

First-person singular	I **was**	First-person plural	we **were**
Second-person singular	you **were**	Second-person plural	you **were**
Third-person singular	he/she/it **was**	Third-person plural	they **were**

In every sentence, the subject and its verb must agree. **Subject-verb agreement** means that the noun and verb forms match in person and in number. A first-, second-, or third-person noun requires a first-, second-, or third-person verb, respectively. A singular noun requires a singular verb; a plural noun requires a plural verb.

In general, the first- and second-person singular forms of the verb and all plural forms of the verb are the plain form—for example, *run.* Variation appears in the third-person singular (as in *runs*)—the verb form that matches the pronouns *he, she,* and *it* and other third-person subjects, such as *the boy, the dog,* and *the car.* For regular verbs, the third-person singular is formed by adding *-s* (or *-es*) to the base verb form.

The verbs *to be, to have,* and *to do* are irregular. Unlike other verbs, the verb *to be* also varies in person and number in the past tense.

Subject-verb agreement remains one of the thorniest problems in English usage. Problems in subject-verb agreement arise when the subject is hard to identify, when the subject appears after the verb, when modifiers or prepositional phrases separate the subject from the verb, or when the subject is hard to identify as singular or plural.

Compound subjects can be either singular or plural, depending on the conjunction or conjunctions that join them. Some phrases appear to create compound subjects but do not.

Subjects Joined by *and*

Compound subjects joined by *and* are plural and take a plural verb.

The exception is two nouns joined by *and* that refer to a single person, place, or thing. Such a compound takes a singular verb.

Compound subjects joined by *and* take a singular verb if they are preceded by *each* or *every*.

However, if *each* or *every* follows a plural subject, the subject takes a plural verb.

Example 2 Subjects joined by *and*

Plural subject takes plural verb:

<u>The bride and groom</u> **cut** the cake together.

<u>Dick and Jane</u> **chase** Puff and Spot.

Singular subject takes singular verb:

<u>Rock and roll</u> **is** here to stay.

From David White, "Rock 'n' Roll Is Here to Stay."

Each or *every* + subject takes singular verb:

<u>Every hedge and tree</u> **is** pruned carefully.

<u>Each knife, fork, and spoon</u> **is** cleaned until it shines.

Plural subject + *each* or *every* takes plural verb:

<u>Knives, forks, and spoons each</u> **have** their own uses.

Activity 45-1: Making Subjects and Verbs Agree

Circle the subject in each sentence and select the appropriate verb form from those in brackets.

Why would sailors [pour/pours] oil onto the water? Historians and scientists [answer/answers] this question through careful research. Hurricanes [produce/produces] water droplets as they [move/moves] across the ocean. Each droplet and particle [become/becomes] suspended in the air, causing friction. Scientists and sailors each [suggest/suggests] that the oil [reduce/reduces] this spray.

Example 3 Subjects joined by *or*

Two singular subjects take singular verb:

The judge or her clerk **writes** the decision.

When one noun is singular and the other is plural, verb agrees with closer noun:

Neither the Pony Express nor the wagon trains **cross** Buzzard Pass during blizzards.

Neither the juvenile male gorillas nor the ranking adult male gorilla **likes** the new zookeeper.

When one noun is second person and the other is third, verb agrees with closer noun:

Either you or Ravi **is** going to drive the van.
Either Ravi or you **are** going to drive the van.

When subject is followed by *as well as* or a similar expression, verb matches subject:

The teacher, as well as her students, **enjoys** the field trip.

The proposed development, together with the added noise, pollution, and traffic it would bring, **dismays** many residents.

Example 4 Revising to a compound subject using *and* + plural verb

Original	Lead, together with air pollution, pesticides, environmental tobacco smoke, and drinking water contamination, **is** one of the top five environmental threats to children's health.
Revision	Lead, air pollution, pesticides, environmental tobacco smoke, and drinking water contamination **are** the top five environmental threats to children's health.

Subjects Joined by *or*

Compound subjects joined by *or* or *nor* can be singular or plural. If both nouns are singular, the sentence takes a singular verb.

If one noun is plural and one singular, the verb agrees with the noun closest to it.

Likewise, if the nouns are in different persons, the verb agrees with the noun closest to it.

Unlike compound subjects linked by conjunctions such as *and, or,* or *nor,* words or phrases introduced by *accompanied by* and similar expressions do not affect the number or person of the subject.

accompanied by
alongside
along with
as well as
besides
in addition to
including
no less than
plus
together with
with

When using such phrases, consider carefully whether a simple *and* would reflect your meaning more closely.

45c Words Intervening between Subject and Verb

Prepositional phrases and other kinds of word groups that intervene between subject and verb can mislead you into making an incorrect verb choice. But subject-verb agreement is not altered by these intervening words or word phrases. The basic rule remains unchanged: identify the subject and choose the verb form that agrees in person and in number. In Example 5, subjects are underlined, words that intervene between subject and verb are in italics, and verbs are in boldface.

Example 5 Ignoring intervening words

The list *of requirements* **is** daunting to many prospective majors.

Trophy hunting *of elephants for their tusks* still **claims** too many animals.

The child *of alcoholic parents* sometimes **overachieves** as a way of winning self-confidence.

The trees, *acknowledging the power of the protector,* **bow** in unison as she passes.

You may be interested to learn that multimedia books—*whether or not you like the feel of a printed book*—**are** here to stay.

Each *of the teams, including the Padres,* **plays** 162 games.

45d Linking Verbs Agree with Subjects, Not Subject Complements

In sentences in the subject–linking verb–subject complement pattern, the verb agrees with the subject, not the subject complement (◀ section 40l, pattern 5).

Common Linking Verbs

to appear	to remain
to be	to seem
to become	to smell
to feel	to sound
to get	to stay
to grow	to taste
to look	to turn
to prove	

Example 6 Agreement of linking verbs

Singular subject takes singular linking verb:

SUBJECT — LINKING VERB — SUBJECT COMPLEMENT

Her main research interest **is** ants.

Plural subject takes plural verb:

SUBJECT — LINKING VERB — SUBJECT COMPLEMENT

Ants **are** her main research interest.

Activity 45-2: Making Subjects and Verbs Agree

Circle the subject in each sentence and select the appropriate verb form from those in brackets.

Neither scientists nor the average person [understand/understands] what happens when we blink. Davina Bristow together with a team of scientists at University College London [have/has] found a reason why blinks go unnoticed. A collection of light-emitting optical fibers [was/were] placed in the mouths of volunteers. Their findings [prove/proves] that people do not notice blinking.

Example 7 Agreement when sentences are inverted

For effect:

V S
At the end of the hall **looms** the vampire.
At the end of the hall **loom** the vampires.

In questions:

AUX V S V
Does the train **stop** here?
Do the trains **stop** here?

In expletive constructions:

V S
There **are** few who know.
There **is** one who knows.
There **is** food to be cooked and beds to be made. [In this expletive construction, the first item in the compound subject is a singular noun.]

Although the subject comes before the verb in most English sentences, occasionally the subject comes after the verb. In such cases, the general rule still applies: the verb agrees with the subject in person and number. Inverted word order is used for emphasis or effect, in questions, and in expletive constructions (that is, constructions that begin with *there is, there are,* or *it is*).

In expletive constructions that have a compound subject, you may use a singular verb if the first element in the subject is singular.

Indefinite pronouns (*all, everybody, few, many, none, several,* and so on) pose problems for many writers, because some are singular, others are plural, and still others vary depending on context.

Most indefinite pronouns are singular and always take a singular verb.

Singular Indefinite Pronouns

anybody	everyone	nothing
anyone	everything	one
anything	much	somebody
each	neither	someone
either	nobody	something
everybody	no one	

Each **has** to take the exam.

A few indefinite pronouns are always plural and thus take a plural verb.

Plural Indefinite Pronouns

both many few several

Both **are** wrong.

Many **run** for office, but few **get** enough votes to win.

Several of the lamps **use** 40-watt bulbs.

A few indefinite pronouns can be either singular or plural, depending on the context.

Indefinite Pronouns That May Take Singular or Plural Verbs, Depending on Context

all	more	some	any
most	half	none	

Half of the children **were** overweight.

Half a loaf **is** better than none.

None of their new songs **are** any good.

None of the music **is** any good.

All **are** welcome.

All **is** well.

Activity 45-3: Making Subjects and Verbs Agree

Circle the subject in each sentence and select the appropriate verb form from those in brackets.

[Do/Does] you [think/thinks] that vampires are real? There [is/are] many who believe that vampires do exist. Several of these people [has/have] been the victims of unscrupulous charlatans who sell fake weapons. None of these solutions actually [work/works]. Most [is/are] too embarrassed to admit that they have been taken. Would you [report/reports] someone who sold you an anti-vampire charm?

Examples of Collective Nouns

audience	corps	herd
band	couple	jury
bunch	crowd	litter
choir	faculty	number
class	family	pride
club	flock	public
committee	group	team

Example 8 Agreement with collective nouns

If the faculty **decides** to change the student handbook, students will be appointed to the revisions committee.

The faculty **are** divided on this issue.

Based on the DNA evidence, the jury **finds** the accused innocent.

The jury **are** sequestered in various hotels throughout the city.

Example 9 Agreement with *a number* and *the number*

A number of pedestrians **are** jaywalking.

The number of pedestrians who jaywalk **is** shocking.

Example 10 Agreement with *media* and *data*

Emphasizes the multiple types of media—print news, television and radio news, magazines:

The media **are** accountable to the public good.

Emphasizes that there are pieces of information:

The data **show** a warming trend.

Emphasizes information as one entity:

Very little data **was** provided.

Collective nouns, such as *audience,* name a group of things or individuals and can be either singular or plural, depending on the context. A sentence that emphasizes the group's actions as a unit takes a singular noun. A sentence that emphasizes the actions of the individual members within the group takes a plural noun.

The collective noun *number* can be either singular or plural. Used in the phrase *the number,* it is treated as singular; used in the phrase *a number,* it is treated as plural.

The words *data* and *media* have caused grammatical controversy since they first entered English as the plurals of the Latin words *datum* and *medium,* respectively. Until recently, both were always treated as plurals in formal and academic writing, although they were used widely as singular in both spoken and written communication. Current usage guides like *The New York Times Manual of Style and Usage* call for treating *data* as a singular noun when it is a synonym for *information* and a collective plural noun when it refers to "a collection of facts and figures." *Media* is still considered plural, but its widespread use in spoken language as singular suggests that its usage will change fairly soon as well.

45h Measurement Words as Subjects

When measurement words function as subjects, determining whether they are singular or plural can sometimes be difficult. Most measurement words can be either singular or plural, depending on the context.

For indefinite pronouns that describe amounts (such as *each, both, half, all*), see section 45f. For phrases of the type *a number of* and *the number of,* see section 45g. For phrases of the type *one of* and *only one of,* see section 45k.

Example 11 Agreement with measurement words

After the sold-out concert was abruptly canceled, fully three-fourths of all ticket holders **were** demanding their money back.

Three-fourths of the fund **is** missing, and yet no one has been held accountable.

Five years **is** a long time to wait.

Five years **have** come and gone.

One hundred pounds **is** a lot to lose.

One hundred pounds of meat **were** consumed at the company barbeque.

45i Singular Words Ending in *-s* as Subjects

Words that end in *-s* but are singular in meaning, such as *physics, economics, politics, news, measles,* and *United States,* take a singular verb.

A few of these words can be construed as either singular or plural, depending on the context.

Example 12 Agreement with singular words ending in *-s*

Physics **is** required of all science majors.
The news **is** promising.
The United States **is** in the western hemisphere.
Statistics **is** a challenging field.

but

The infant mortality statistics **reveal** a region in crisis.

Activity 45-4: Making Subjects and Verbs Agree

Circle the subject in each sentence and select the appropriate verb form from those in brackets.

An audience [was/were] on hand to watch the latest shuttle launch. A number of them [has/have] never seen a launch except on television. One third of the audience [was/were] school-age children at Space Camp. The whole crowd [was/were] cheering as the shuttle blasted off successfully. The media [was/were] also on hand to broadcast news of the launch to a worldwide audience. The news [was/were] encouraging after many setbacks to the space program.

Titles, Names, Words Used as Words, and Gerunds as Subjects 45j

Example 13 Singular verbs with titles, names, and words used as words

Cats **plays** nightly at seven.

"The Snows of Kilimanjaro" **is** one of Hemingway's best known short stories.

Monument Farms Dairy **has been** in business since 1937.

Doctors without Borders **provides** volunteer medical assistance around the world.

The word *data* **comes** from Latin as the plural form of *datum.*

Titles of works, names of businesses and institutions, and words used as words are all singular and take singular verbs.

Example 14 Singular verbs with gerunds

Making homemade bread **is** a challenging and rewarding activity.

Training your new puppy **requires** patience and persistence.

Gerund phrases (the *-ing* form of the verb plus any accompanying complements or modifiers) function as singular subjects.

Agreement in Relative Clauses and with Clauses Beginning with *what* 45k

Example 15 Agreement with *who*

ANTECEDENT / RELATIVE CLAUSE

The student who **is** giving tonight's address comes from Africa.

ANTECEDENT / RELATIVE CLAUSE

The students who **attend** this school come from many countries.

ANTECEDENT / RELATIVE CLAUSE

She is one of those legislators who **have** integrity. [In this sentence, the antecedent of *who* is *legislators,* so *who* takes a plural verb.]

ANTECEDENT / RELATIVE CLAUSE

She is the only one of those legislators who **has** integrity. [In this sentence, the antecedent of *who* is *one,* so *who* takes a singular verb.]

In an adjectival dependent clause beginning with the relative pronoun *who, whom, whose, which,* or *that,* the relative pronoun requires the same verb form as its antecedent. A singular antecedent causes the relative pronoun to require a singular verb. A plural antecedent causes the relative pronoun to require a plural verb.

Constructions such as *one of the things that* or *one of the people who* require careful scrutiny to decide which noun is the antecedent of the relative pronoun (such as *who* or *that*).

In relative clauses introduced by the words *only one of,* the antecedent is almost always the word *one.*

In general, subject clauses beginning with *what* are singular.

Example 16 Singular verb with subject clause starting with *what*

What the committee recommended **is** at odds with what the students want.

Activity 45-5: Making Subjects and Verbs Agree

Circle the subject in each sentence and select the appropriate verb form from those in brackets.

The Public Health Association [has/have] announced that West Nile Virus [is/are] present in the mosquito population. The mosquitoes that are infected [appear/appears] no different from ordinary mosquitoes. West Nile Virus is one of the diseases that [do/does] significant damage to the elderly and children. Avoiding infection [is/are] possible if people follow precautions. What the association recommends [is/are] that people wear bug repellent and remove standing water from their property. People who suspect they may be infected [is/are] encouraged to see their health-care professionals.

Activity 45-6: Revising for Subject-Verb Agreement in Your Own Writing

Choose a recent piece of writing to work on. Circle the subjects of sentences and underline the verbs. Then, using the skills you have developed by reading and completing activities in this chapter, determine whether each subject agrees with its verb. Make any necessary revisions. Trade papers with a classmate and check each other's work.

46

ADJECTIVES, ADVERBS, AND MODIFYING PHRASES

Modifiers bring sentences to life by providing concrete detail about things and actions. All modifiers function as either adjectives or adverbs.

- Adjectives modify nouns and pronouns. In the phrase *a* ***lucky*** *man,* the adjective *lucky* modifies the noun *man*. In the sentence *He is* **lucky,** the adjective *lucky* is the subject complement to the pronoun *he*.
- Adverbs modify verbs, adjectives, other adverbs, and whole clauses. For example, the adverb *fast* modifies the verb *ran* in *He ran* ***fast,*** the adverb *very* modifies the adjective *fast* in *He was a* ***very*** *fast runner,* and the adverbial phrase *as the wind* modifies the adverb *fast* in *He ran fast* ***as the wind***.

Adjectives answer these questions:

Which one?	The *black* cat runs faster than the white cat.
What kind of?	I like *tortoise shell* cats best.
How many?	She called, and *several* cats meowed in answer.

Adverbs answer these questions:

How?	The cat crept up *slowly.*
When?	Cats hunt *at night*.
Where?	Our cats sleep *on the beds, the sofas, the floor, the tables—everywhere.*
Why?	Cats sometimes hunt mice *because they enjoy hunting for its own sake.*
How often?	My cats ask for food *continually.*
In what manner?	The cat batted the mouse *playfully.*
Under what conditions?	Cats will purr *if you scratch them behind the ears.*
With what result?	The cat ate *until it was so full it could barely walk.*
To what degree?	The cat stalked the mouse *very* stealthily.

46a After Linking Verbs

Use adjectives, not adverbs, as subject complements after linking verbs. Subject complements follow linking verbs and add to, rename, or otherwise complement the meaning of the subject. (For more on subject complements and linking verbs, see page 811.)

Linking Verbs

be	appear	prove
feel	become	remain
look	continue	seem
smell	feel	sit
sound	grow	stay
taste	make	turn
act		

Some verbs can function as linking verbs or as transitive or intransitive verbs, depending on the context. The verb's function and your intended meaning define whether a particular verb should be followed by an adjective or an adverb. To describe the subject following a linking verb, use an adjective. To describe the action of a verb following a transitive or intransitive verb, use an adverb.

Adjectives, not adverbs, act as subject complements

SUBJECT SUBJECT COMPLEMENT

The audience remained **silent** until one person broke out in wild applause.
Lata is **happy** that she is home again.
He looks **older** now.
The detective's hunch proved to be **true.**

Should you use an adjective or an adverb?

To describe a noun, use an adjective. To modify a verb, use an adverb.

Adjective — Suki felt **awful** after eating ten chocolate bars.
Adverb — Roger felt **cautiously** for the edge of the cliff.
[The adjective *awful* describes *Suki;* the adverb *cautiously* modifies the verb *felt.*]

Adjective — The lion appeared **nervous.**
Adverb — The rabbit **magically** appeared out of the magician's hat.
[The adjective *nervous* describes *lion;* the adverb *magically* modifies the verb *appeared.*]

46b After Direct Objects

A direct object can be followed by either an adjective or an adverb. Which you choose depends on the meaning you intend. To modify the direct object itself, use an adjective, but to modify the verb, use an adverb.

Should you use an adjective or an adverb after direct objects?

Use an adjective to modify the direct object itself; use an adverb to modify the verb.

Adjective — Brennan called the hawk **magnificent.**
Adverb — Brennan called the hawk **repeatedly.**

Adjective — Nora considered the project **completed.**
Adverb — Nora considered the project **carefully.**

Should you use *bad* or *badly*?

Adjective I felt **bad** when the pitcher sprained his ankle.
Adjective Lefty pitched a **bad** game after he sprained his ankle.
Adverb The pitcher played **badly** after he sprained his ankle.

Should you use *good* or *well*?

Adjective I feel **good.**
Adverb Though Katya's hands were numb with cold, she could feel just **well** enough to slip the key into the lock.

Adjective This year the Yankees have an exceptionally **good** pitcher.
Adverb This year the pitcher played exceptionally **well.**

Adjective **Good** education for our children is our top priority.
Adverb Educating children **well** is our top priority.

As an adjective, *well* means "healthy"

Adjective They are **well.**
Adjective After a year of battling a series of mysterious diseases, Fernando felt **well** at last.
Adjective He seems **well,** but doctors fear a relapse.

Should you use *real* or *really*?

Adjective Gregor drinks coffee only with **real** milk.
Adverb Gregor **really** detests nondairy creamer.

Activity 46-1: Selecting Adjectives and Adverbs

Choose the correct form of adjective or adverb from those in brackets.

A [recent/recently] survey from the Pew Internet Project reveals that teenagers [real/really] like communicating by text messaging and instant messaging. However, they find email to be [relative/relatively] useless; they think that email works [good/well] only for contacting [large/largely] groups of people. Otherwise, they consider email to be a [bad/badly] technology that only "old people" use. Use of the Internet by teenagers has grown [substantial/substantially] in the last five years. Most teens feel [good/well] about their Internet use, since it makes them feel [close/closely] to their friends and faraway relatives.

Although standard usage clearly dictates that only adjectives can modify nouns and pronouns and that only adverbs can modify verbs, adjectives, and adverbs, each is commonly misused for the other, especially in everyday speech.

Among the most commonly misused adjective-adverb pairs are *bad / badly, good / well,* and *real / really.*

Use the adjective *bad* as a subject complement or to modify nouns or pronouns. Use the adverb *badly* to modify verbs, adjectives, or other adverbs.

Use the adjective *good* as a subject complement or to modify nouns or pronouns. Use the adverb *well* to modify verbs, adjectives, or other adverbs.

Use *well* as an adjective when you mean *healthy.*

Use the adjective *real* as a subject complement or to modify nouns or pronouns. Use the adverb *really* to modify verbs, adjectives, or other adverbs.

46d Understanding Comparatives and Superlatives

Most adjectives and adverbs have three forms—positive, comparative, and superlative—used to compare degrees or amounts of a particular quality.

In general, use the comparative ending *-er* and the superlative ending *-est* with adjectives of one to two syllables and with one-syllable adverbs.

Use *more/most* and *less/least* with longer adjectives and with most adverbs.

The modifiers *good, bad, far, many, much, little, well,* and *badly* are irregular in the comparative and superlative forms.

Some adjectives can form the comparative and superlative either with *-er* and *-est* or with *more/less* and *most/least*. These include *able, angry, clever, common, cruel, friendly, gentle, handsome, happy, narrow, pleasant, polite, quiet, simple, tender,* and *yellow.* But don't use both methods together—for instance, don't write *more commoner.*

Because English is a language as notable for its exceptions as its rules, always check a dictionary if in doubt about the correct form of a comparative or superlative.

Positive	**Comparative**	**Superlative**
Adjectives		
fast	faster	fastest
brilliant	more brilliant	most brilliant
awkward	less awkward	least awkward
Adverbs		
steadily	more steadily	most steadily
carefully	less carefully	least carefully

Positive	**Comparative**	**Superlative**
Adjectives		
old	older	oldest
pretty	prettier	prettiest
Adverbs		
fast	faster	fastest
slow	slower	slowest

Positive	**Comparative**	**Superlative**
Adjectives		
terrible	more terrible	most terrible
palatable	less palatable	least palatable
Adverbs		
easily	more easily	most easily
accurately	less accurately	least accurately

Positive	**Comparative**	**Superlative**
Adjectives		
good	better	best
bad	worse	worst
far	farther/further	farthest/furthest
many	more	most
much	more	most
little (quantity)	less	least
Adverbs		
badly	worse	worst
far	farther/further	farthest/furthest
well	better	best

Use the comparative for comparing two items, the superlative for more than two

She is the **older** of the two sisters.
She is the **oldest** child in her family.

An **older** dog is harder to train than a **younger** one.
The bristlecone pine is Earth's **oldest** living organism.

Use *a, an,* or *the* with comparatives, *the* with superlatives

A **younger** bristlecone can be about 1,500 years old; an **older** bristlecone can be upwards of 4,000 years old. The **oldest** bristlecone, known as Methuselah, is dated at 4,767 years.

In formal writing, use the comparative for comparing two things or categories of things; use the superlative for comparing three or more things or for comparisons that imply that all items in a given category are being compared.

A comparative can be preceded by the article *a, an,* or *the,* but use *the* before a superlative.

Do Not Use Double Comparatives or Superlatives 46e

Ungrammatical comparisons: Don't use *more* and *-er* (or *most* and *-est*) forms together

Faulty	The pistachio is the more better flavor.
Revised	The pistachio is the better flavor.
Faulty	This must be the most hottest day of the year.
Revised	This must be the hottest day of the year.

Do not combine the *-er* or *-est* form with the *more/less* or *most/least* form in a single comparison. Such double comparatives and superlatives are ungrammatical.

Activity 46-2: Choosing Adjectives and Adverbs

Revise the following paragraph to correct any errors in the use of comparatives and superlatives.

Scientists have discovered some of the most older dinosaur eggs ever. These eggs are some of the goodest specimens of dinosaur embryos that have ever been discovered, since the eggs were just about to hatch and were therefore most much developed than other specimens. Researchers used the most delicatest of dental tools to most carefully crack open the eggs. Such a discovery is most excellent for learning about how young dinosaurs transitioned to their most adult forms.

46f Using Absolute Adjectives

Some adjectives cannot logically be compared. A *fatal* blow is just that, *fatal,* and can never be *more fatal* or *less fatal, the most fatal* or *the least fatal.* Other such **absolute adjectives** include *eternal, impossible,* and *unique.* Controversy exists over some usages, as in the United States Constitution's "more perfect union," but in formal writing it is best to avoid using absolute adjectives in comparative or superlative forms.

Illogical comparisons:
Don't use absolutes in the comparative or superlative

absolute	fatal	possible	unanimous
adequate	final	priceless	unavoidable
chief	ideal	principal	uniform
complete	impossible	round	universal
dead	incessant	simultaneous	unique
entire	inevitable	stationary	utter
equal	infinite	straight	whole
eternal	main	sufficient	
excellent	minor	supreme	
false	perfect	total	

46g Do Not Use Double Negatives

While it's okay for Mick Jagger to sing "I **can't** get **no** satisfaction," such double negatives are considered ungrammatical in standard written English.

Examples of Negative Modifiers	
no	never
none	neither
not	barely
nothing	hardly
nowhere	scarcely
nobody	the contraction
no one	*-n't (not)*

In other languages, the double negative is used for emphasis; in contemporary English, a double negative is logically construed to give a positive meaning. The only admissible double negative construction is *neither . . . nor.*

Ungrammatical *no*'s: Use only a single negative modifier

Faulty — We **can't** find **no** publisher for these magnificent poems.
Revised — We **can't** find **a** publisher for these magnificent poems.

Faulty — The citizens of this county will **never** vote for **no** new taxes.
Revised — The citizens of this county will **never** vote for new taxes.

Faulty — They **can't** give **no** reasons for their decision.
Revised — They **can't** give **any** reasons for their decision.

Only *neither . . . nor* is acceptable

Faulty — I **didn't** say yes **nor** no to their suggestion.
Revised — I said **neither** yes **nor** no to their suggestion.
I **didn't** say yes **or** no to their suggestion.

Activity 46-3: Revising Absolute and Negative Adjectives

Revise the following paragraph to correct any errors in the use of absolute adjectives and double negatives.

The most main problem that has seemed nearly eternal over the last twenty or thirty years is the way the glaciers are shrinking more inevitably than ever before. From 1500 to 1850, the Earth experienced a cooling trend during which it would have been most impossible for glaciers to retreat. From 1850 to 1940, the climate warmed; glaciers retreated most simultaneously. The world got slightly cooler from 1950 to 1980, reversing earlier glacial retreat. Since 1980, though, glaciers have never grown no larger; they get smaller and smaller, and some have disappeared completely. Glacial retreat can be more fatal than other planetary problems.

Understanding the Placement of Modifiers 46h

Where do adjectives go?

Before nouns:

I like the **blue** dress, not the **pink** one.

After linking verbs as subject complements:

He is **sad** today.

Bibi considers herself **lucky.**

Adjective clauses usually follow the word they modify

The pianist **who is now playing** is known for her technique.

The house **that I grew up in** has been demolished.

Adjectives placed for poetic effect

I am the River **Niger**—hear my waters!

From Joseph A. Walker, *The River Niger.*

We sail the ocean **blue,** and our saucy ship's a beauty;
We're sober men and **true** and **attentive** to our duty.

From W. S. Gilbert, *H.M.S. Pinafore, and Other Plays.*

Careful placement of modifiers is essential to clear and precise communication. The general rule is that modifiers should be placed near the word or words they modify. Adjectives almost always come directly before the word they modify. The exceptions are subject complements and adjective clauses introduced by relative pronouns. Adjectives functioning as subject complements come after the linking verb. (Yoda, from *Star Wars,* speaks distinctively in part because he places his adjectives functioning as subject complements *before* the linking verb, as in "Sad he is, today.")

Occasionally an author places an adjective directly after the noun it modifies for poetic effect, but this technique should be avoided in most ordinary prose.

Adverbs are considerably more flexible in their placement than adjectives. Although they usually go directly before or after the word they modify, adverbs can also go at the beginning or end of sentences.

Like single-word adverbs, adverbial clauses can go before or after the word they modify.

And like adverbs that modify verbs, adjectives, or other adverbs, conjunctive adverbs can often go several places in a given sentence.

Where do adverbs go?

Before or after the verbs they modify:

The car **quickly** sped down the road.

The car sped **quickly** down the road.

At the beginning or end of a sentence:

Quickly, the car sped down the road.

The car sped down the road **quickly.**

But ***not*** between a verb and its direct object:

Faulty	The snail crossed **slowly** the path.
Revised	The snail **slowly** crossed the path.
	The snail crossed the path **slowly.**
	Slowly, the snail crossed the path.

Adverbial clauses can go before or after the word they modify

When the music stopped, the children scrambled for the chairs.

The children scrambled for the chairs **when the music stopped.**

Conjunctive adverbs can be moved around

However, you did interrupt the senator, so customary procedure has not been observed.

You did, **however**, interrupt the senator, so customary procedure has not been observed.

You did interrupt the senator, **however**; so customary procedure has not been observed.

However, it is true that whales are not fish.

It is true, **however**, that whales are not fish.

It is true that whales are not fish, **however**.

Adjectives or adverbs placed too far away from the words they modify account for a fair number of unintentional gaffes. (A *gaffe* is a clumsy error.)

Confusing	The duchess pointed out the many pictures of her ancestors who had performed great and noble deeds **in the gallery.** [What had they been doing in the gallery?]
Clear	**In the gallery,** the duchess pointed out the many pictures of her ancestors who had performed great and noble deeds.
Confusing	Nala returned to the home in which she had experienced such poverty **in a private jet.**
Clear	**Traveling in her private jet,** Nala returned to the home in which she had experienced such poverty.
Confusing	**Roaring from a tremendous height,** Muir saw Yosemite Falls.
Clear	Muir looked at Yosemite Falls, **roaring above him from a tremendous height**.

Placing Limiting Modifiers Carefully 46j

Place limiting modifiers such as *almost, even, exactly, hardly, just, merely, nearly, not, only, scarcely,* and *simply* directly before the word they modify. In spoken communication, we can use tone of voice to clarify our meaning by emphasizing one word more than another. In written communication, however, the reader needs other guidelines. Be aware that small shifts in placement can radically change a sentence's meaning.

How does the placement of *only* affect meaning?

Only the red squirrels are seen on the eastern slope. [Implies that other kinds of squirrels, such as grey squirrels, are seen elsewhere]

The red squirrels **only** are seen on the eastern slope. [Implies that red squirrels are all there is to see—other kinds of animals seem to be elsewhere]

The red squirrels are **only** seen on the eastern slope. [Implies that they are seen there, but can be heard (for example) elsewhere]

The red squirrels are seen on the eastern slope **only.** [Implies that the only place to see red squirrels is on the eastern slope]

Activity 46-4: Choosing and Placing Adjectives and Adverbs

Revise the following paragraph, correctly placing adjectives and adverbs in order to clarify meaning. (You may rewrite parts of sentences if you need to.)

> On May 10, 1869, the golden spike was driven that united the two teams working on the transcontinental railroad. A telegraph operator signaled "Done!" excitedly. In cities from coast to coast, bells wildly rang out that were rung by citizens excited as they heard the news. Before this event, travel across the United States wasn't no easy feat. Travelers would take many months who traveled in wagons. The journey took now a little over a week. This also meant that freight could be shipped from one coast to the other as well as passengers.

46k Revising Squinting Modifiers

Sometimes a modifier is positioned so that it appears to modify two different words or phrases. Such misplaced modifiers are called **squinting modifiers.** Always revise sentences with squinting modifiers by repositioning the adverb so that it clearly modifies one word or phrase only.

Example 1 Revising squinting modifiers

Does the following sentence mean that you sometimes fed the cat or that the cat sometimes asked to be let in?

Squinting — The little stray cat we fed sometimes asked to be let in.

Notice the difference in the following revisions:

Revised — The little stray cat we **sometimes** fed asked to be let in.
The little stray cat we fed asked to be let in **sometimes.**

46l Revising Disruptive Modifiers

Modifiers that disrupt the logical connection between a subject and its verb, an auxiliary and its main verb, or a verb and its object sound awkward and can confuse the reader.

Disruptive modifiers are almost always adverbs or adverbial phrases. Adjectives that intervene between subject and verb typically don't cause such problems.

Example 2 Revising modifiers placed in a way that makes reading harder

Awkward — The conductor, **after wiping the sweat from his brow,** began the final movement.

Revised — **After wiping the sweat from his brow,** the conductor began the final movement.

Awkward — Children will, **if they get too tired or hungry,** become cranky.

Revised — Children will become cranky **if they get too tired or hungry.**

Faulty — Pele kicked **hard** the ball.

Revised — Pele kicked the ball **hard.**

Activity 46-5: Placing Adverbs and Adverbial Clauses

Revise the following paragraph to correctly place clauses in order to clarify meaning. (You may rewrite parts of sentences if you need to.)

As vaudeville, theater, and the music circuit centralized, the stage was set, which was at the end of the nineteenth century, for music to become a big commercial enterprise. Sheet music, if music was to succeed, needed in order to promote music's consumption to be published. Tin Pan Alley, located in New York City, was a part important of this enterprise. Scores sold to the public, although professional musicians used professional sheet music, had colorful illustrations and pictures of the artists.

Approaching Split Infinitives with Common Sense 46m

Avoid split infinitives when such constructions are awkward

Awkward — To, **as Pierre-Louis suggested,** visit the Louvre, we must skip the Eiffel Tower.

Revised — To visit the Louvre, **as Pierre-Louis suggested,** we must skip the Eiffel Tower.

But if splitting the infinitive helps you to communicate clearly and effectively, do so

To **really** enjoy a meal one must sit down at the table.

To **boldly** go where no one has gone before!

Motto from *Star Trek*.

Split infinitives (such as *to completely recognize* or *to joyfully sing*), in which a modifier comes between the infinitive *to* and the root form of the verb, continue to be the site of one of the ongoing "range wars" of English grammar. The idea that split infinitives are ungrammatical is a carryover from overzealous nineteenth-century grammarians who wanted to make English behave more like Latin, a language whose single-word infinitives are, obviously, unsplittable.

Revising Dangling Modifiers 46n

Modifiers are said to dangle when the word they are intended to modify is missing altogether. Dangling modifiers modify the wrong word, often with rather surrealistic results.

Among the constructions most likely to cause dangling modifiers are participial phrases, infinitive phrases, prepositions followed by gerund phrases, and elliptical clauses.

Example 3 Revising dangling modifiers

Dangling — As a little girl, my father liked to tell me stories about mermaids.

Literally, the sentence means that when your father was a young girl he told you stories about mermaids. Not too likely. The intended subject *I* is missing. To revise, supply the correct subject and place the modifier and the word it modifies in correct proximity, as below.

Revised — When I was a little girl, my father liked to tell me stories about mermaids.

As a little girl, I loved listening to my father's stories about mermaids.

Dangling — Driving out of the Channel Tunnel, France beckoned ahead. [France drove out of the Channel Tunnel?]

Revised — As we drove out of the Channel Tunnel, France beckoned ahead.

Driving out of the Channel Tunnel, we saw France beckoning ahead.

Dangling — To make a perfect soufflé, the eggs must be fresh. [The eggs are making a soufflé?]

Revised — To make a perfect soufflé, you must use fresh eggs.

Example 4 More dangling modifiers

Dangling	Upon entering the dance floor, the saxophone wailed loudly. [The saxophone entered the dance floor?]
Revised	As I entered the dance floor, the saxophone wailed loudly.
Dangling	Though fresh out of college, the firm hired Dario for a good salary. [The firm was fresh out of college?]
Revised	Though Dario was fresh out of college, the firm hired him for a good salary. The firm hired him for a good salary even though Dario was fresh out of college.

Activity 46-6: Revising Dangling Modifiers

Revise the following paragraph to correctly place clauses in order to clarify meaning. (You may rewrite parts of sentences if you need to.)

> In the 1920s, the ocean liner *Leviathan* ruled the waves; to as many have recounted sail on it was amazing. One of the largest and most recognizable passenger ships, on the Atlantic there was nothing like it. Upon entering the liner, luggage was taken by one of the many crewmen. Looking over the rail, England slipped away. Arriving in New York one week later, the view of skyscrapers beckoned you off the boat. Like all ocean liners, a stratified social network of people were present.

Activity 46-7: Revising for Adjectives, Adverbs, and Modifying Phrases in Your Own Writing

Choose a recent piece of writing to work on. Locate some sentences that include detail and description. Which sentences do you find especially vivid? Identify the adjectives and adverbs in them, and draw an arrow from each one to the word it modifies. Then find modifying phrases and do the same thing. If you find any words or phrases that don't work well with the words they modify, revise them. Make any other revisions that you think would improve the sentences. What effect do your revisions have on your earlier draft and your reader's understanding of your ideas?

PART 9

Punctuating with Purpose

New Contexts for Writing

Budding filmmakers can now write, produce, and distribute their videos with relative ease. The basic tools for making movies on a personal computer already exist, and now new software, including video games, and new distribution services, like Google™ Video, IndieFlix, and YouTube, give filmmakers all they need to make videos or films. You can create and edit your own digital video or adapt and remix digital content produced by others.

Digital video is film footage that has been converted to digital format, meaning it can be edited, reassembled, stored, and distributed electronically. You can shoot digital video with a camera and capture it on a computer using video editing software, which helps you add, delete, and rearrange scenes, add music and sound effects, edit dialogue, create special effects, and export video for others to view.

A **script** (or **screenplay**) is a detailed written account of the video's content. Scripting involves writing dialogue, describing settings, and providing stage (or scene) directions. **Storyboarding** involves sketching out events in a scene, showing how they will be filmed (camera angles, distance, and movement), and describing how sound, music, and special effects should be included. You can use screenwriting software like Movie Magic, Screenwriter, or Final Draft. Storyboard your video using printed templates or software designed to make storyboarding simpler, such as FrameForge 3D Studio. Try the free trial versions first.

Scripting and Directing Digital Video

Now you can create original movies in video game environments. In this screenshot from *The Movies* (Lionhead Productions), you see the crew and cast on a movie set, in this case a graveyard. The cast lineup is on the left. Directors can place actors, script dialogue, add a film score, and add scenes, transitions, and credits to create a feature film that can then be uploaded to the Web, where it will be viewed and rated by other filmmakers on *The Movies*'s community website. See http://movies.lionhead.com

Write a Screenplay and Storyboard Your Video

If you want to make a film that earns more than one star from reviewers and the audience, you'll want to write a good script and create storyboards that describe how each scene, and even each individual shot, in your film should be handled. To learn this process, most filmmakers start by making short videos (five to ten minutes) that show an interesting incident, provide information, or sell a product or service.

You'll want to start with a story concept—the gist of what you want to show or teach with your video. Even short videos will have a clear beginning, middle, and end.

Periods (.), question marks (?), and exclamation points (!), known as *end punctuation,* show the reader where statements, questions, and emphatic declarations end. More generally, they indicate how to interpret a sentence. If the writer is doing the equivalent of shouting on paper, an exclamation point might end the sentence; if the writer is making a matter-of-fact statement, this tone will be shown by the period at the end.

The context of the work also helps determine which marks are used. For example, in college research papers written in the MLA style, exclamation points are used only when they are part of a direct quotation. Other, more informal writing situations allow for more frequent use of the exclamation point, even though it is the least used of all the end punctuation marks. You can decide which type of end punctuation to use by considering what kind of sentence you need and what tone you wish to convey, within the constraints of the rhetorical context.

47a Using Periods

Use a period at the end of . . .

- **a statement:**
  Claire's results should help resolve her controversial hypothesis.
- **an indirect question:**
  Juan's research asks why the Dodo bird is extinct.
- **a mild command:**
  Be careful around that burner.
  You need to answer the survey.
  Give me the results.

Periods that end sentences are followed by one space (not two). Always capitalize the first word after a period so that your readers will understand that you are beginning a new sentence.

Always place periods inside quotation marks (double or single) at the end of a sentence.

Example 1 Using periods with quotation marks

I told him, "I need your results by Friday or the report will be late."

Periods to Punctuate Initials and Some Abbreviations

Periods are always used with initials and often used with abbreviations.

When a sentence ends with an abbreviation, the period that follows the abbreviation also serves as the end punctuation for the sentence.

Example 2 Using periods with initials and abbreviations

Use periods with . . .

- **initials:**

  George W. Bush   Carolyn B. Maloney   William J. Clinton

- **many common abbreviations:**

Mr.	Ms.	Dr.	Rev.
St.	Ave.	Sun.	Jan.
6:30 p.m.	etc.	9:15 a.m.	

But do not use periods with . . .

- **abbreviations indicating academic degrees:**

  PhD MA MS BA MD

- **postal abbreviations for states:**

  MA NC WA TX FL NY IL MN

- **abbreviations that appear in all uppercase letters (such as names of organizations, corporations, and government agencies):**

  NBA AFL-CIO PBS IBM FBI PDF ASAP

- **acronyms (pronounced as words, these abbreviations are formed from the first letters of the major words in longer names or phrases):**

  AIDS (Acquired Immune Deficiency Syndrome)
  OPEC NAFTA OSHA radar laser scuba

- **commonly shortened words and technical terms:**

  dorm math lab

Example 3 Using a single period to fulfill two functions

The research project requires lots of reading, note-taking, etc.

Example 4 Using a period with a question mark

Is it possible for both of them to make the rank of Brig. Gen.?

Example 5 Using a period with a comma

At 7:15 p.m., you need to reduce the temperature of the beaker.

Example 6 Using periods to mark divisions

Use periods with . . .

- **numbers with decimal places:**
  2.5 m $20.00 7.5 cm
- **URLs:**
  http://www.parlorpress.com
  (For an explanation of the parts of a URL, see section 30a, The Anatomy of a URL.)
- **email addresses:**
  Firstname.Lastname@anywhere.com

Example 7 Using a period in MLA style

According to Robeson, "Fear is a prominent feature of that discourse community" (22).

Example 8 Using periods to cite sections of literary works in MLA style

Use periods in . . .

- **act, scene, and line references for plays:**
  "Through tatter'd clothes small vices do appear;
  Robes and furr'd gowns hide all." (*King Lear* 4.6.152-153).
- **book and line numbers in long poems:**
  Virgil's *Aeneid* 2.12
- **book, chapter, and verse in biblical references:**
  Exod. 2.2-21

However, if the abbreviation at the end of a sentence is followed by a question mark or an exclamation point, the abbreviation retains its period.

When an abbreviation with a period is used within the body of a sentence, that period can be followed by additional punctuation, such as a comma.

Periods to Mark Divisions in Numbers, URLs, and Email Addresses

A period is used to separate the decimal portion of a number from the integer portion, as well as to separate parts of URLs and email addresses.

Periods in MLA Citations

If you refer to material from an outside source within a sentence of your own, place a period after the parenthetical citation at the end. But when you set off a long quotation in block format, place the period before the citation in parentheses. (See page 381 for an example.)

When citing specific sections of literary works in the body of an essay, use periods to show the relevant divisions.

Activity 47-1: Editing Periods

Edit the following paragraph and its Work Cited entry for appropriate use of periods.

Scientists have long speculated about the existence of life on Mars and were offered a rare chance to confirm its existence with the successful missions of N.A.S.A.'s twin rovers, *Opportunity* and *Spirit* The rovers' missions have been an unqualified success, unlike failed projects such as the European Space Agency (E.S.A.)'s failed Beagle mission and several other failed N.A.S.A initiatives The rovers work hard every day making new discoveries including findings about water, methane, and temperature readings Despite the rovers' findings which point to a wet past for Mars, the possibility of life on Mars is still debated by scientists. Dr Andrew Schuerger of the U of Florida said, "I believe there is life on Mars, and it's unequivocally there, because we sent it" (qtd in Chandler) More information about the Mars rovers can be found at http://wwwjplnasagov/missions/mer/

Work Cited

Chandler, David L "Life on Mars—But 'We Sent It'" *New Scientist* 25 Mar 2004 Web 15 Apr 2005

47b Using Question Marks

A direct question states someone's exact words. (Use a period after an indirect question in which the writer reports that someone else asked a question.) Note that a single word can be used as a question.

Use a question mark to indicate the end of a direct question within a sentence. Such a question will typically be set off by quotation marks, dashes, or parentheses.

Example 9 Using a question mark with a direct question

Do you think it's the heat or the humidity that makes it so uncomfortable?

She's running for reelection. Why?

Example 10 Using a question mark with a direct question within a sentence

She kept asking, "Who wrote that book?" even when it was clear nobody knew the answer.

Exams are early tomorrow morning—why are they always scheduled at eight o'clock?—and I need to study and sleep.

Example 11 Using question marks with a series of questions

Who wrote that article? When? Was it a reprint?

Question marks are also used to indicate the ends of questions in a series, even if the questions are not complete sentences.

Example 12 Using a question mark in a compound sentence that ends with a question

Our professor would really like to know something: Why did you miss class yesterday? When she asks you, what will you say?

Use a question mark to indicate the end of a question in a compound sentence that begins with a statement and ends with a question.

Question Marks with Other Punctuation

Do not use a question mark right next to a period or an exclamation point, except when the period ends an abbreviation. (For example, don't use an exclamation point and a question mark to try to indicate a surprised question.) Also, don't use more than one question mark.

Example 13 Using just a question mark

I don't agree with her, even when she asks, "Will this survey take more time than we have?"

Place a question mark inside quotation marks if the question is a part of a direct quotation.

Example 14 Putting a question mark inside quotation marks

I asked her, "Where did you go with my notebook last night after the power went out?"

Oates's stories answer the question "What is the meaning of the mundane life?"

However, if the question is not in the quotation but is a part of your interrogative sentence, place the question mark at the end of the sentence outside the quotation marks.

Example 15 Putting a question mark outside quotation marks

Is it true that Raymond Carver drank himself to what one critic called "a premature but not unexpected death"?

47b

Question Marks with Dates or Numbers

You may use a question mark to indicate that a date or number is unknown or uncertain. The question mark shows that knowledgeable people agree that a date or number is uncertain, not that the writer has done inadequate research. Put the question mark in parentheses if the dates aren't already in parentheses themselves.

Example 16 Using a question mark with dates

Aristotle wrote the *Rhetoric* (340–325? BCE) over a period of time; most experts agree that the text had parts added much later.

Another option is to use a word like *about* or *approximately* to indicate uncertainty about dates.

Question Marks and Tone

Don't use a question mark or more than one question mark to indicate irony or sarcasm.

Example 17 Avoiding question marks for sarcasm

No The Speaker sounds as if he's still teaching schoolkids???

Activity 47-2: Editing End Punctuation

Suppose that you are helping a classmate edit his or her research paper. Read the following paragraph and edit it for use of question marks. You may have to insert question marks or remove them.

The possibility of lowering the drinking age from 21 to 18 in the United States raises some important questions? First, would it be possible to convince lawmakers in every state to reverse their decision regarding the drinking age. Second, how would states deal with a possible increase in the amount of drinking-related problems such as drunk driving?. Third, would drinking problems among 18–20-year-olds really decrease once alcohol was no longer "forbidden fruit". Finally, how would we in that age group advocate for our rights and insist that we are no longer children??

47c Using Exclamation Points

Exclamation points may be used to indicate a strong emotion, to emphasize a point dramatically, to make a surprising or shocking statement, or to give a direct order.

Example 18 Using exclamation points for emphasis

STRONG EMOTION:

Grow up! Get over it! How dare you!

DRAMATIC EMPHASIS:

The governor was not even aware that his name was used for advertising face cream!

SHOCKING OR SURPRISING STATEMENT:

I like your parents!

In David Mamet's *Oleanna,* Carol exclaims, "I'm bad!"

DIRECT ORDER:

Don't yell at me!

Example 19 Avoiding overuse of exclamation points

OVERUSE:

Casual clothing at work is a relic of the 1980s! Only an idiot would think that he or she could get ahead by wearing torn jeans in Corporate America!!! These people need to be brought into today's world!

EMPHASIS CONVEYED BY DICTION:

Some workers still cling to the notion that Casual Friday exists. Casual Friday was a philosophy derived from business schools in the 1980s. The idea was that workers would increase productivity and engage one another more socially and more productively if they were comfortable in their clothing. Unfortunately, even though this philosophy seems archaic, some workers still abide by the idea of wearing clothing that is simply too casual for today's workplace.

Overuse of Exclamation Points

Use exclamation points sparingly. Overuse of the exclamation point diminishes its impact. Rely instead on choosing words carefully to add emphasis. Especially in business and academic writing, exclamation points are rarely used. The exception is when an exclamation point is part of a direct quotation. Never use more than one exclamation point at the end of a sentence.

Example 20 Avoiding exclamation points for sarcasm

SARCASM:

Hello! Get a life! Nobody wears Tommy anymore! Loser!

MORE SUBTLE SARCASM:

Good afternoon. I will venture to say that you are unaware that your brand of clothing is obsolete, charming as it is.

Inappropriate Use of Exclamation Points

Do not use an exclamation point to indicate sarcasm. Word choice will make your point more memorably.

Use with Other Punctuation Marks

When you use a quotation that ends in an exclamation point at the end of a sentence, use the exclamation point to end the complete sentence.

However, if the exclamation is a command and your sentence ends with the quotation, place the exclamation point outside of the quotation marks.

Example 21 Putting an exclamation point inside quotation marks

She kept yelling at Julia Fenn: "This is the third time!"

Example 22 Putting an exclamation point outside quotation marks

Follow this rule: "Do as I say, not as I do"!

Activity 47-3: Editing Exclamation Points

Revise the following portion of a paper so that it uses fewer exclamation points and is more appropriate as academic prose.

> Many teenagers who are in college report conflict with their parents, especially if they live at home, where parents must set the rules! Many teens find that their parents' rules are too restrictive, especially regarding curfew!! These rules are lame considering that 18-year-olds are adults! It is hard to believe that people old enough to die for their country must be in by 11 p.m.! Talking about these rules with parents only leads to fighting! What can we as teenagers do!!!

48 COMMAS: DEFINING BOUNDARIES WITHIN SENTENCES

Commas (,) are used to define boundaries within a sentence. They help readers understand how the writer has grouped ideas together or kept them apart. For instance, they set off the introductory words that come before the subject of a sentence so that readers can identify the subject more easily. Commas can also indicate whether the various parts of a sentence are crucially important for understanding the core meaning of the sentence or extra information that adds detail and texture. At other times, commas help readers see the boundary between the writer's words and quotations from research sources or spoken dialogue. Commas are also used in other situations to clarify meaning—for example, to make numerals easier to grasp at first glance.

48a Use a Comma between Independent Clauses

Use a comma *before* a coordinating conjunction (*and, but, or, for, so, nor,* or *yet)* when you join two or more independent clauses. An independent clause is one that can stand alone as a complete sentence. It has a subject and a complete verb (not an *-ing* verb or a *to* verb standing alone—see section 41c), and it does not begin with a subordinating conjunction (*because, since, while, even though,* and so on).

Note: Do not place the comma after the coordinating conjunction. The comma goes first:

My lab partner is late today, and she has our lab notes.

To link two independent clauses that already contain commas, use a semicolon instead of a comma. This usage is preferred in academic writing since it makes the grouping of ideas in the sentence clear.

Example 1 Link independent clauses

INDEPENDENT CLAUSE , [and, but, or, for, so, nor, yet] INDEPENDENT CLAUSE

This new style of music was unique, **and** it impacted music and culture for years after its creation.

From Nicole M. Walsh, Purdue University, "George Gershwin."

The pope did not mention the eccentricities of his predecessor, Urban VIII, **nor** did he directly criticize the behavior of the Inquisition.

From James B. Reston Jr., *Galileo: A Life* (New York: HarperCollins, 1994).

Multilingual writers: Note that in the example above, in the second independent clause after *nor,* the helping verb comes before the subject, just as in a question.

INDEPENDENT CLAUSE , INDEPENDENT CLAUSE , **and** INDEPENDENT CLAUSE

Paleobiologists study plant and animal fossils, paleoanthropologists study ancient humans, **and** paleoecologists study the interactions between ancient organisms and their environments.

Example 2 Place the comma *before* the coordinating conjunction

No Rupert bought everything in sight but, he still was not happy.

Yes Rupert bought everything in sight, but he still was not happy.

Example 3 Use semicolons when commas are used within the clauses

We oppose the proposed power lines, factory, and apartment building; we favor regulations to help our community maintain the feel of a traditional village.

Example 4 Omit the comma or coordinating conjunction in certain contexts

NO COMMA:

Feed the cat and walk the dog.

NO COORDINATING CONJUNCTION:

Very short, contrasting clauses	She lied, I did not.
Reported speech	Margaret says only a few students stayed in touch: "Some went back to their native country, some stayed here, some just lost contact." From Zhumei Meng, Purdue University, "Day in the Life."

Some writers omit the comma when the two independent clauses joined by a coordinating conjunction are very brief.

Depending on the context, some writers use a comma without a coordinating conjunction to join two very short contrasting independent clauses. In formal nonfiction writing, such as much academic writing, use a period or semicolon to separate the clauses. If you are quoting someone who is speaking informally, you can sometimes omit the coordinating conjunctions. But see section 42a on comma splices.

Activity 48-1: Editing Commas

Edit the following paragraph to correct the use of commas.

> Urban legends or urban myths have evolved out of the fears and hopes of modern-day culture and they mutate in accordance with changes in a culture as well. Some legends are funny some are grotesque. Different groups of people study urban legends: professional folklorists study how the legends change and grow and how the legends are tied into older mythical forms reporters and writers examine how the legends inform society and attempt to squelch possibly harmful rumors by bringing them to the attention of the public and amateur folklorists debate the origins of these legends in folklore society meetings and on the Internet.

48b Avoid Creating Comma Splices

Do not use a comma alone to join two independent clauses. A major sentence error called a comma splice results. See Chapter 42 for various ways to correct comma splices.

Example 5 Correct comma splices by adding coordinating conjunctions after commas

NO INDEPENDENT CLAUSE **,** INDEPENDENT CLAUSE

Maryam liked the look of the Liberty, ^but they decided to buy a Mini Cooper.

We don't know whether the recent slang term *phat* will last in the language as long as *cool,* ^yet it seems unlikely.

Activity 48-2: Editing Commas

Edit the following paragraph for use of commas. You may want to change punctuation, insert coordinating conjunctions, or break the sentences up to correct them.

One of the best known urban legends is the vanishing hitchhiker, this legend involves a driver who picks up a young girl at night. The driver gives the girl a ride home, she vanishes when they get to her place. The driver knocks on the door of the girl's house, her parents answer. They tell the driver that the girl died many years ago on prom night, her spirit often attempts to get home by asking for a ride.

48c Use Commas after Introductory Elements

Use a comma after an introductory word, phrase, or clause to link it to an independent clause that follows. If the introductory element is very short, some writers omit the comma as long as the meaning remains clear, but in college writing you can always use the comma.

Example 6 Use commas to set off introductory elements from independent clauses

INTRODUCTORY ELEMENT **,** INDEPENDENT CLAUSE

TRANSITIONS—USE A COMMA:

Sometimes the martial arts are taught as a form of combat. However, tai chi is used for self-defense and meditation. [Conjunctive adverb]

Many people around the world eat insects, many of which are high in protein. For example, grasshoppers are at least as nutritious as ground beef. [Transitional phrase]

OTHER INTRODUCTORY PHRASES—USE A COMMA:

Their historical reputation as winners finally secured by the victory over the Yankees, the Red Sox ran onto the field for an extended round of applause from their fans. [Absolute phrase]

To receive the best grades, you will need to take notes and stay organized. [Infinitive phrase]

Crying pathetically, the starving calico cat got our attention. [Participial phrase]

On the way to the Winter Carnival in Saint Paul, Silvio and Christopher could not resist taking some photos. [Prepositional phrase]

DEPENDENT (SUBORDINATE) CLAUSES:

After the holidays are over, we will visit our old neighbors.

When we run in the morning, we like to warm up and stretch briefly.

VERY SHORT INTRODUCTORY ELEMENT—SOME WRITERS OMIT THE COMMA:

In the 1950s, Moe Green controlled all the Las Vegas casinos.

INTERJECTION—USE A COMMA:

Wow, that beaker gets hot quickly on this Bunsen burner.

Note: If the interjection is emphatic, it can be set off with an exclamation point instead of a comma: *Whoa! I never agreed to that.*

If an interjection begins the sentence, set it off with a comma. An interjection is a word that expresses emotion, such as amazement or surprise, and that is not grammatically a part of the sentence.

Activity 48-3: Editing Commas

Edit the following paragraph for the use of commas.

While the vanishing hitchhiker serves as a good ghost story the legend about death from a tanning bed serves as a warning to men and women who like to get that golden glow. According to the story a woman visited several tanning beds for far longer than is recommended. Apparently she was trying to look good for her wedding. After a while she began to notice a horrible smell. When she went to the doctor she discovered that she had microwaved her insides by so much tanning! Of course nothing could be done and she died. While no one has ever verified this legend as being true it serves as a powerful example of an urban legend.

48d Use Commas between Items in a Series

Use commas to separate the items in a series of three or more words, phrases, or clauses of equal weight and grammatical structure. The last item in the list typically follows a comma and a coordinating conjunction, but in cases where the coordinating conjunction is omitted, the comma is still used.

The comma before the last item in a series is sometimes omitted in popular writing—for example, in newspapers and magazines—but in academic writing, the final comma is preferred.

Example 7 Use commas to separate items in a series

FIRST ITEM IN A SERIES , SECOND ITEM , [and, or] THIRD ITEM

SERIES OF NOUNS:

You can watch any of the following shows on MTV: *The Osbournes*, *Pimp My Ride*, *Punk'd*, or *Real World*.

SERIES OF GERUNDS:

The police ticketed him for speeding, driving to endanger, and obstructing justice.

SERIES OF VERBS:

Abdi likes to run, swim, and read.

SERIES OF OBJECTS:

To make an apple pie, you need baking apples, pre-sifted flour, and much patience.

Note: The phrases are parallel, including adjective + noun:

baking apples,
pre-sifted flour, and
much patience.

SERIES OF MODIFIERS:

Sleepless, cornered, and fighting mad, the soldiers hurled down the hill with muskets raised to their shoulders.

SERIES OF CLAUSES:

It didn't take me too long to figure out that Curly was the crazy one, Larry was the comic foil, and Moe was the ringleader.

SERIES WITH NO COORDINATING CONJUNCTION BEFORE THE FINAL ITEM:

Many chemistry majors enjoy the three basic chemistry courses: Anatomy and Physiology, Basic Chemistry, Introduction to Genetics.

SERIES OF NUMBERED OR LETTERED ITEMS WITHIN A SENTENCE:

Pacific Lutheran University's campus map clearly shows (1) McNabb House, (2) Park Avenue House, (3) Blomquist House, (4) Faculty House, (5) Knorr House, and (6) the Health Center.

Example 8 Use semicolons with series within series

Get me a beach sticker, good for the whole season; two inflatable rafts, preferably ones large enough for two kids; an umbrella, bright blue is best; and six beach towels.

When the items in a list or series include commas, use semicolons to separate the items.

Activity 48-4: Editing Commas

The following paragraph was written with no final serial comma, in the popular style. Rewrite the paragraph to use academic style for commas in a series.

Other types of urban legends involve childhood fears, confusions and wishes. For example, the Bloody Mary legend claims that if someone goes into the bathroom, turns the lights off and chants "Bloody Mary" a certain number of times, a witch will appear. The name used in the chant varies; it can be Bloody Mary, Mary Worth, Mary Worthington or Mary Whales. There are also a variety of events that follow a successful summoning: the "witch" may kill her summoner, injure her summoner, cause her summoner to go mad or pull her summoner into the mirror to take her place. Identities for the face in the mirror include Mary I of England, who was known as "Bloody Mary," and Mary, Queen of Scots, rumored to have taken part in the murder of her husband and other local villains, who range from demons to local murderers.

48e Use Commas between Coordinate Adjectives

Commas are used between coordinate adjectives. Coordinate adjectives in a series modify a single noun; they each add separate meaning: *honest, hardworking carpenter.* When adjectives are cumulative, however—that is, when the details accumulate or build toward a particular meaning—no comma separates them: *vivid blue eyes.*

A Coordinate Adjective?

1. Change or reverse the order of the adjectives. Does the sentence still make sense? If so, the adjectives are coordinate.
2. Join all the adjectives with the conjunction *and.* Does the sentence still make sense? If so, the adjectives are coordinate.

Are the adjectives coordinate?

That decrepit **[,]** unpainted house may be haunted.

1. Change the order of the adjectives: *That unpainted, decrepit house may be haunted.*
2. Join the adjectives with *and: That decrepit and unpainted house . . .*

The sentence still makes sense, so the adjectives are coordinate. Use a comma.

COORDINATE ADJECTIVE **,** COORDINATE ADJECTIVE NOUN

unpainted, decrepit house

Are the adjectives coordinate?

We rose to another day on the endless **[,]** African savannah.

1. Change the order of the adjectives: *We rose to another day on the African endless savannah.*

   The words cannot appear in this order, so the adjectives are not coordinate; do not use a comma.
2. Join the adjectives with *and: the endless and African savannah*

   The words cannot be joined with *and,* so the adjectives are not coordinate; do not use a comma.

   Note: Do not use a comma to separate the noun from the closest adjective:

COORDINATE ADJECTIVE, COORDINATE ADJECTIVE NOUN

Rex is a lovable, loyal dog.

Multilingual writers: For more on adjective order, see section 62c.

Example 9 Use commas with nonrestrictive elements

INDEPENDENT CLAUSE , NONRESTRICTIVE ELEMENT

I love to go camping, which I do every year with my family and friends. [You could remove everything after the comma and the core meaning of the sentence would remain intact: the writer loves camping. What follows the comma is simply additional information about the person's camping habits.]

NONRESTRICTIVE ELEMENT , INDEPENDENT CLAUSE

An enthusiastic speaker, Reverend Jones spoke during freshman orientation.

PART OF INDEPENDENT CLAUSE , NONRESTRICTIVE ELEMENT , REST OF INDEPENDENT CLAUSE

The west side of the city, which receives far fewer city services than the east side, has had a crime problem for over twenty years. [Without the highlighted nonrestrictive clause, the sentence still expresses the main idea.]

The rotisserie chicken, which is turning ever so slowly under the glass counter, makes her mouth water.

Lucia Hernandez, who is a good friend from college, just flew in from Miami. [A person's name precisely identifies the individual, so additional information placed after a person's name is typically nonrestrictive.]

Lucia Hernandez, a good friend from college, just flew in from Miami. [Without *who is,* this nonrestrictive element is an appositive, a noun or noun equivalent that follows a noun and describes it.]

The Lord of the Rings: The Return of the King, one of a series of movies based on J. R. R. Tolkien's famous trilogy, relates the final efforts of Frodo and Sam to battle the dark forces of Sauron. [Like a person's name, the title of a work usually identifies it exactly. The nonrestrictive element here, too, is an appositive.]

Remember: When the nonrestrictive element is in the middle of the sentence, two commas are needed to enclose it.

What Is a Nonrestrictive Element?

A **nonrestrictive element** is a word group that is not essential to the core meaning of the sentence. You can omit a nonrestrictive element from a sentence without changing its main idea. Nonrestrictive elements are often (but not always) signaled by the words *which* and *who.*

What Is a Restrictive Element?

Restrictive elements provide information that is crucial to understanding the sentence. Removing this information would make the sentence confusing or even nonsensical. Restrictive clauses literally restrict, or make more specific, the meaning of the sentence element they modify. Do not use commas with restrictive elements.

Example 10 Do not use commas with restrictive elements

PART OF INDEPENDENT CLAUSE | RESTRICTIVE ELEMENT | REST OF INDEPENDENT CLAUSE

A dog that bites children does not make a good family pet. [The meaning of this sentence changes dramatically if the restrictive clause is removed.]

My good friend Lucia Hernandez just flew in from Miami. [The name restricts the meaning of *my good friend.* It is not set off with commas, since it is essential information.]

Joyce Carol Oates's book *The Falls: A Novel* is set in Niagara Falls. [Oates has written many books; without the title, the sentence would not make sense. No commas are needed.]

Activity 48-5: Editing Commas

Correct the following paragraph for use of commas.

Horrible urban legends make us shiver or remind us to be cautious which is an important part of taking care of oneself in today's world. Some urban legends, that continue to circulate, use humor to deliver their message. The "kneeling myth" which was featured in many books and email forwards involves a group of American tourists visiting the British parliament. Sessions of Britain's House of Commons are called to order by the Speaker who marches into the halls in splendor. One day the Speaker saw Neal McLean a friend of his and called out to him: "Neal! Neal!" The American tourists who did not know the man interpreted it as an order and promptly fell to the ground.

Example 11 Use commas to set off parenthetical expressions

PARENTHETICAL EXPRESSION , SENTENCE

Understandably, she is happy about getting that promotion.

PART OF SENTENCE , PARENTHETICAL EXPRESSION , REST OF SENTENCE

For me, at least, chocolate is as valuable as gold.
That geology professor, of course, knows where granite is most prevalent.

Example 12 Use commas to set off transitional expressions

Jill, as a matter of fact, is returning to school next semester.

Braun's work validated many of Solms's findings; however, Hobson still maintained that those findings did not support a Freudian interpretation.

Parenthetical expressions offer extra information that isn't needed to understand the main idea of a sentence. (Unlike non-restrictive elements, parenthetical elements are typically words or phrases rather than clauses or appositives.) This information can be enclosed within commas or parentheses, depending on the degree of separation you want between the sentence and the extra information; commas suggest less separation than parentheses.

Transitional expressions move the reader from one idea to the next and show the reader how the ideas are related. (See section 41e for a list of transitions.) Conjunctive adverbs are one kind of transitional expression (◀ section 40f).

48h Use Commas to Set Off Contrasts, Interjections, Direct Address, and Tag Sentences

When the later part of a sentence offers information that contrasts with the information in the first part, use a comma to emphasize the contrast.

Example 13 Use commas to set off contrasts, interjections, and the like

TO SET OFF CONTRASTS:

We must address environmental issues now, not wait until there is a disaster later.

Female and young elephants stay together in groups, while males keep to themselves.

Use a comma to set off an interjection—a word that expresses emotion, such as amazement or surprise, and that is not grammatically a part of the sentence.

TO SET OFF INTERJECTIONS:

Whoa, you're running too fast for me to keep up.

Use a comma in direct address, when you the writer speak directly to the reader.

TO SET OFF WORDS IN DIRECT ADDRESS:

For your own good, you should pay close attention to the lab rules and procedures.

Stop, that flooring is likely to give way under your weight.

Use a comma to set off tag sentences and questions at the end of a sentence. If the tag is a question, the entire sentence ends with a question mark.

TO SET OFF TAG SENTENCES:

You have written your survey for Sociology 101, haven't you?

Commas separate quoted words from the words you use to introduce or explain them.

Example 14 Use commas to set off quotations

"I am starving," Pauline complained.

Maggie said, "Come back at noon and we'll have lunch."

"Get the sandwiches," Pauline yelled as she drove by, "and I'll meet you at the park."

When Representative Harold Velde writes, "Educating Americans through the means of the library service could bring about a change of the political attitude more quickly than any other method," he is referring to a change of politics more than a change in education.

"Anarchism is really a synonym for socialism," or so claims Daniel Guerin Jr., in his book *Anarchism,* where he also claims, "The anarchist is primarily a socialist whose aim is to abolish the exploitation of man by man."

Exceptions:

1. When a quotation blends smoothly into the grammar of your sentence, omit the comma.

   I believe that "the life well lived is the only one worth living."

   Where were you when the "lights went out in Georgia"?

2. When an exclamation point or question mark ends the quotation, do not use a comma.

   "Did you remember to lock the door?" Jonathan asked.

   "I don't want to leave!" she sobbed.

3. Use a colon, not a comma, to introduce a quotation when the introduction is a complete sentence, especially if the quotation is long.

   Faulkner's style is considered experimental: "Faulkner always strove to open new ground so his readers would experience his text as a world in a world."

Some uses of the comma are simply conventions that have developed over time. Forgetting to use a comma in one of these situations will not usually cause confusion for your readers, but it may cause them to question your grasp of punctuation rules. As you read and write, use these conventions and integrate them into your work and your memory.

Commas in Dates, Places, Addresses, and Numbers

- Use commas in dates . . .

  between date and year:

  January 1, 2006

  between day and date:

  Monday, February 14, 2005

  after the year in a full date within a sentence:

  Einstein was born on March 14, 1879, in Ulm, Germany.

- Do not use a comma in dates when . . .

  only the month and year are shown:

  November 2007

  only the month and day are given:

  September 17

  only the season and year are given:

  fall 2008

  the date is inverted:

  24 July 2006

- Use commas in places and addresses . . .

  to separate city and state:

  Tulsa, Oklahoma

  after the state within a sentence:

  American Forests' Historic Tree Nursery is a company located in Jacksonville, Florida, from which you can order a tree with historic significance.

  to separate the street address from the city, the city from the state, and the end of the zip code from the next word of the sentence:

  Send donations to the Heifer Project International, P.O. Box 8058, Little Rock, Arkansas 72203, to aid in the fight against hunger worldwide.

- Use commas in large numbers after each group of three digits (moving from right to left):

  3,456,789

  Commas are optional in most four-digit numbers, but be consistent:

  Of the 3,500 families served by the program, 2,899 live below the poverty level.

- Do not use commas in numbers of four or more digits when . . .

  the number is part of an address:

  35678 East Avenue

  the number is a page number:

  pages 1101–1134

  the number refers to a year:

  In 2004, there were 2,592 executives in the federal government.

Commas with Names and Titles and in Correspondence

- Use a comma between a name and a title or degree:

  Rene Sommers, PhD
  John O'Hara, MD

- Do not use a comma before *Jr., II,* and so on:

  Martin Luther King Jr.
  Ramses II

- Use a comma to separate inverted names, as in research paper bibliographies:

  Gladwell, Malcolm. *The Tipping Point: How Little Things Can Make a Big Difference.* New York: Little, Brown, 2000. Print.

- Use a comma after the greeting and after the closing in an informal letter:

December 7, 2006

Dear Dad,

It's Pearl Harbor Day, and I can't help but think of Grandpa . . .

Love,

Min

- Use a comma only after the closing in a business letter:

123 Court Street
Middlebury, VT 05753

December 24, 2005

Representative Harvey Smith
1 Main Street
Middlebury, VT 05473

Dear Rep. Smith:

Please vote "yes" on the education tax credit . . .

Sincerely,

Megan Flowers

Megan Flowers

Use a comma with a title or degree following a person's name. When a name is inverted so that the last name is given first, use a comma to separate the names.

You do not need to use a comma when a person's name is followed by *Jr.*, *Sr.*, *II, III,* and so on.

When writing an informal letter, use a comma after the salutation and the closing. In business letters, always use a colon after the salutation.

48l Avoid Misusing the Comma

Probably the most common misconception writers have about commas is that they should be used any time you would pause when uttering a sentence. This is not always the case.

Don't use a comma . . .

- **to separate a subject from a verb:**

  That man, allows his dogs to roam without supervision.
  What happened in 1857 to the Arkansas emigrants to Utah, may not have been sanctioned by Brigham Young.

- **to separate compound subjects, predicates, or objects:**

  Neither a young person, nor an older person can join that organization.
  Speeders will be ticketed, and will receive points on their licenses.
  Shanice had trouble distinguishing blue, from green.

- **at the beginning of a series:**

  Will you remember to buy, soap, detergent, and bathroom cleaner?
  Jack likes to, bring his books, read them whenever possible, and make notes about what he reads.

- **after the last item in a series:**

  Carol likes to read the *LA Times*, travel magazines, and short stories, before bed.

- **with essential (restrictive) modifiers:**

  Jackie brought the names of applicants, who are eligible for interviews.

- **after a coordinating conjunction between independent clauses:**

  Philip Foner was an excellent historian and, he worked on political justice for his whole life.

- **after a subordinating conjunction:**

  She did well on the history exam because, I helped her study.

- **with quotations that fit into the structure of your sentence:**

  I recall the lyrics that, "the best things in life are free."
  Ozzie keeps yelling for Sharon's dogs to, "shut up," even when they are not barking.

- **with quotation marks that enclose titles:**

  I love, "Dolan's Cadillac" by Stephen King.
  "Code Black," is the title of the most recent episode of *Grey's Anatomy.*

49

SEMICOLONS: EXPRESSING EQUAL RELATIONSHIPS AMONG CLOSELY RELATED IDEAS

The semicolon (;) is used to show that the phrases or clauses on either side of it are closely related and equally important. When a comma is too weak to separate the word groups and a period is too strong, the semicolon is used. For example, if you combine two independent clauses (complete sentences) into a single sentence, you can't show where one ends and the second begins with only a comma. The comma is too weak to mark this division; an error known as a comma splice would result. (And you wouldn't use a period if you wanted to show a closer relationship than a period would indicate.) Semicolons are also used to separate the items in a series of three or more items when one or more of the items already includes commas.

The semicolon is used in slightly different ways in technical, legal, and other writing contexts. For example, in programming languages like CSS (cascading style sheets), the semicolon is used to separate discrete formatting commands.

Semicolons are used between word groups that are grammatically equal: independent clause and independent clause, phrase and phrase, and one item in a series and another.

Between independent clauses:	Genuine tradition is not for sale, because no one needs to buy it; it's moored in the customs of one's own family (remember them?). (From Caitlin Flanagan, *To Hell with All That* [New York: Little, Brown, 2006])
Between phrases:	Early settlers had to know how to choose fertile land; how to build houses and barns; how to coexist with the local inhabitants; in short, how to live far from what they thought of as "civilization."
Between items in a series:	Photographs can be striking when the subject is doing something interesting, especially in closeups; when the photograph shows an unusual point of view; and when foreground and background offer a lively contrast.

49a Use a Semicolon between Closely Related Independent Clauses

When you want to show readers that independent clauses are closely related, and thus choose not to use a period to separate them into distinct sentences, you have a couple of choices. You can separate the clauses with a comma and a coordinating conjunction, or you can use a semicolon. Your decision may involve the larger context in which the sentence appears—the rhythm or the length of the surrounding sentences may help you determine which punctuation makes the sentence sound better or makes the paragraph more cohesive.

The semicolon is a particularly good choice when the two independent clauses provide either parallel or contrasting information.

Example 1 Using semicolons to link independent clauses

Parallel information:

INDEPENDENT CLAUSE

Horses frequently serve as ideals of human independence in works of art;

INDEPENDENT CLAUSE

the film *Spirit* is a good example.

Contrasting information:

Casual readers accept facts; critical readers evaluate them.

Example 2 The effects of using semicolons to link independent clauses

You had inputs from the outside world; you had memories of past inputs; and you had some kind of glorified calculator that would measure these inputs against each other and come up with a behavioral strategy.

From Steven Johnson, *Mind Wide Open: Your Brain and the Neuroscience of Everyday Life* (New York: Scribners, 2004), 52.

Note that Johnson uses three independent clauses, separated by semicolons:

1. All three independent clauses are written in parallel style.
2. The first and second independent clauses are short and refer to what's going on in the mind at any given moment.
3. The third independent clause is much longer and describes a third type of brain activity that stimulates action.

Punctuating the clauses as he does, Johnson conveys that the types of input and monitoring he describes happen all at once. He keeps the longest unit for last to enhance the rhythm of the whole.

Use a Semicolon between Independent Clauses Connected with Words Such as *however, then,* and *for example* 49b

Example 3 Using semicolons with conjunctive adverbs and transitional expressions to clarify the relationship between independent clauses

INDEPENDENT CLAUSE **;** CONJUNCTIVE ADVERB OR TRANSITIONAL EXPRESSION **,** INDEPENDENT CLAUSE

Napoleon was exiled to the island of Elba to remove him from world politics and spare France the wrath of Great Britain; nevertheless, he proceeded to make this small island in the Italian Riviera a kingdom all his own.

Jack the Ripper terrorized Whitechapel in the late nineteenth century while never revealing his identity in the busiest city on Earth; therefore, many Rip-perologists, as they are known, falsely believe that he must have either drowned in the Thames or been protected by royal connections.

Example 4 Conjunctive adverb or transitional expression within the second independent clause

FIRST PART OF SECOND INDEPENDENT CLAUSE **,** CONJUNCTIVE ADVERB OR TRANSITIONAL EXPRESSION **,** REST OF INDEPENDENT CLAUSE

Baseball, like many other spectacle sports, takes place over a certain time period between people in a confined space; its appeal, however, depends in part on how it flaunts Zen paradoxes with its timelessness (innings can last forever) and infinite space (the foul lines run to infinity).

To clarify how independent clauses are related, you can use conjunctive adverbs such as *however, consequently,* and *furthermore* or transitional expressions such as *for example, in addition,* and *as a result* (◀ section 41e).

A semicolon is used between independent clauses. A comma follows a conjunctive adverb or transitional expression when it begins the second independent clause. Some style guides recommend against using a comma after *then* when it begins the second independent clause; however, you should use the comma when it will prevent misreading.

Conjunctive adverbs and transitional expressions are moveable; they can be placed within the second independent clause as well as at the beginning.

Notice that a pair of commas encloses a conjunctive adverb or transitional expression when it is placed within a clause, setting it off distinctly from the body of the second independent clause.

Use a Semicolon between Items in a Series Containing Other Punctuation 49c

Example 5 Separating items in a series with semicolons

Lewis and Clark ventured into the Western wilderness fully loaded with all of the modern weapons technologies they could muster: military rifles, service muskets, and personal firearms; scalping knives and pipe tomahawks, which would be traded along the way for other supplies; and bullet molds, gun worms, ball screws, and other supplies that would help the expedition repair arms during its trip.

Items in a series of three or more are usually separated by commas. However, if an item in the series already includes a comma or other punctuation, use semicolons to separate the items.

49d Avoid Misusing Semicolons

Do **not** use semicolons in the following situations:

1. **To join unequal sentence parts.** For example, do not use a semicolon to separate an introductory phrase from the rest of a sentence, and do not use a semicolon to separate a dependent clause from an independent clause. Either use creates a sentence fragment. Similarly, do not use a semicolon between a phrase and a clause.
2. **To introduce lists or quotations.** When an independent clause introduces a list, a colon—not a semicolon—separates the introduction from the list (▶section 50b). Quotations are typically introduced with a comma (◀section 48i). If a complete sentence introduces the quotation, a colon is used (▶section 50c). Never use a semicolon to introduce a quotation.

Don't use a semicolon . . .

- **after an introductory phrase:**

  INTRODUCTORY PHRASE — INDEPENDENT CLAUSE

  With wide aperture lenses on binoculars and a steady hand, amateur scientists can observe Jupiter's moons.

- **between a dependent clause and an independent clause:**

  DEPENDENT CLAUSE — INDEPENDENT CLAUSE

  Since our classes ended at two o'clock, we shopped for the party.

- **to introduce a list:**

  Live 8 focused the world's attention for a brief spell on three kinds of poverty on the continent of Africa: excessive foreign debt, failing national economies, and widespread famine.

- **to introduce a quotation:**

  Fitzgerald concluded *The Great Gatsby* with the suggestion that the fight against vanity in a world of moral and spiritual decay never ends: "So we beat on, boats against the current, borne back ceaselessly into the past" (189).

Activity 49-1: Using Semicolons

Revise the following paragraph to use semicolons correctly. You may want to insert semicolons in place of commas and combine sentences with semicolons.

Personal computers have been around for only twenty years, however, they have become very important to all aspects of people's lives. Today, a computer normally consists of a case, which contains the motherboard, memory, hard drive, sound and video cards, a monitor, which allows users to see output from the computer, a keyboard, which allows for input, and a mouse or trackball, which is used as a pointing and clicking device, also users can attach devices such as digital cameras, scanners, and printers. When personal computers were first introduced, they were large and bulky. Today, computers are smaller, lighter, and cheaper than their earlier counterparts. In another twenty years, who knows what will happen?

50 COLONS: INTRODUCING EXPLANATIONS AND QUOTATIONS

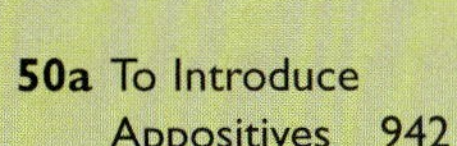

Colons (:) introduce information. In sentences, colons are almost always used to signal that the information to follow explains or elaborates previous information. A colon usually comes at the end of an independent clause (complete sentence) and draws attention to the example, explanation, quotation, or list that follows. Colons also have certain conventional uses in correspondence, titles of essays and other projects, expressions of exact time, Biblical references, and bibliographical citations.

How Colons Differ from Dashes:
Colons and dashes each have particular functions, so they are not interchangeable. To help you remember the differences, you might think of them this way:

: colons direct the attention forward →

← dashes direct the attention backward —

Colons forecast that new information will follow; dashes add information that might clarify or change information that came earlier.

50a Use Colons after Independent Clauses to Introduce Appositives

An appositive is a word or group of words that modifies or describes a noun, a noun phrase, or a pronoun. Colons introduce explanatory information, so it is natural to use one before an appositive phrase that modifies the independent clause that precedes it.

Example 1 Use a colon after an independent clause to introduce an appositive

INDEPENDENT CLAUSE : APPOSITIVE

Throughout my entire life, I have loved only one person: my mother. [Appositive: *one person I have loved* = *my mother*]

50b Use Colons after Independent Clauses to Introduce Lists

A list may be part of a sentence, or it may be set off from the running text, with list items formatted vertically and perhaps marked by bullets or numbers. In either case, if an independent clause introduces the list, you can use a colon to keep the introduction and the list separate.

At times, the independent clause that precedes the colon will indicate, with phrases such as the following, that a list follows:

as follows
the following
such as the following
including the following

But do **not** use a colon after expressions such as *for example, that is, namely,* or *such as*. The colon has the same function as these phrases: to point to and emphasize what comes next. It would be redundant to use them both.

Example 2 Use a colon after an independent clause to introduce a list

INDEPENDENT CLAUSE : LIST

Yes Three moisture-retaining media can be used to keep root crops crisp over the winter: sawdust, sand, or chipped leaves.

No Three moisture-retaining media can be used to keep root crops crisp over the winter, namely: sawdust, sand, or chipped leaves.

Use Colons after Independent Clauses to Introduce Quotations 50c

A colon is used at the end of an independent clause that introduces a long quotation. If the introduction is not a complete sentence, a comma is typically used instead of a colon (◀ section 48i).

Example 3 Use a colon after an independent clause to introduce a quotation

The opening paragraph of the 67-page essay is a model of reason and composition, repeatedly disrupted by that single obscenity:

> One of the most salient features of our culture is that there is so much [bull]. Everyone knows this. Each of us contributes his share. But we tend to take the situation for granted. Most people are rather confident of their ability to recognize [bull] and to avoid being taken in by it. So the phenomenon has not aroused much deliberate concern, nor attracted much sustained inquiry.

From Peter Edidin, "Between Truth and Lies, an Unprintable Ubiquity" [Review of *On [Bull]* by Harry G. Frankfurt], *New York Times*, Feb. 14, 2005, p. E1.

Use a Colon to Introduce a Second Independent Clause 50d

A colon is used between two independent clauses only when the second one illustrates or explains the first.

If the second independent clause is a question, you should capitalize its first letter. Otherwise, you can use a lowercase or a capital letter after a colon in such cases, but use one or the other consistently throughout your project.

Example 4 Use a colon to introduce a second clause that illustrates the first

Kate was the worst kind of neighbor: she once stole my lawnmower and used the engine for her go-cart.

ABC News took more than ideas from MTV: it hired one of the youth network's talented young producers, David Berrent.

From Mitchell Stephens, *The Rise of the Image, The Fall of the Word* (New York: Oxford University Press, 1998).

Men have to register with the Selective Service, but that doesn't mean they will be drafted if the draft is reinstated: clergy, conscientious objectors, men who are disabled, and others may be exempt from service.

The FBI has not yet managed to put into operation a modern computerized case management system: Why?

50e Conventional Uses of Colons

- **In correspondence.** Use a colon after the salutation in a formal letter or email. In an informal letter or email to a person you know well, use a comma rather than a colon. In memos, use a colon after each element in the memo header. (See page 232 for more information on memos.)

> Dear Doctor Williard:
> I am sorry to report that I could not attend your October 20 symposium on rat behavior in the East Science Building. . . .

> *Dear Dad,*
> *Could you send more money this week? I'm running on empty. . . .*

> **Memorandum**
> **To:** Public Relations Department
> **From:** Abi Baraka
> **Date:** November 11, 2005
> **Subject:** News Release Approval Procedure
> Follow this new procedure when members of other departments ask you to publish stories about their successes. . . .

- **In titles.** Use a colon to separate a title and subtitle. If the documentation style you are using requires titles to be italicized, italicize the colon as well as the words.

Example 5 Use a colon to separate a title and subtitle

Zambelli: The First Family of Fireworks

"Figure and Place: A Context for Five Post-War Artists"

- **In expressions of time**

Example 6 Use colons to separate hours, minutes, and seconds

It was exactly 1:26 a.m. when I heard the window shatter.

She gets up at 7:30 every morning.

Paula Radcliffe ran the London marathon in 2:15:25 in April 2003.

- **To indicate a ratio**

Example 7 Use a colon in a ratio

1:10 means "1 to 10" or "1/10."

Example 8 Use a colon to separate chapter and verse in CMS style

CMS Ezekiel 1:4 states . . .
MLA In Luke 1.1, . . .

Example 9 Use a colon to separate place of publication from the publisher's name

New York: Harcourt, 2004.
Forest Dale, VT: Paul S. Eriksson, 2003.

Example 10 Use a colon in a URL

http://www.fedstats.gov

Activity 50-1: Editing Colons

Suppose that your friend, a counselor in one of the residence halls on your campus, has asked you to proofread this memo, which will be sent to all students on her floor. Correct her use of colons.

To Fifth Floor Residents
From Jane Lane, Residence Assistant
Subject Noise Policies
Date February 20, 2006

I have been asked by the Residence Hall director to remind you about the noise policies in Sherlock Hall. The problems in Sherlock Hall can be eliminated by practicing one principle, respect. Loud noise—including the following types; music, screaming and yelling, large groups of people talking, TV, or movies—is not permitted after 11.00 p.m. Starting at 1115, counselors will make the rounds of the floors checking to make sure that residents are adhering to quiet hours. Daria Jones, the Residence Hall director, has asked us to tell you this "Adhering to these rules makes the hall a better place for everyone to live."

For more about quiet hour policies, please see the student handbook at http//www.university.edu/studentlife/handbook.pdf.

- **In biblical references.** If you are documenting your project in CMS style, use a colon to separate chapter and verse in references to the Bible. No space is used before or after the colon. (However, in MLA style, use a period to separate chapter and verse.)
- **In bibliographies.** In the works cited, references, or other bibliographical list in a project with research sources, use a colon to separate the city of a book's publication (and state, if needed) from the publisher's name.
- **In URLs.** When you use a colon in a World Wide Web address, do not put a space after it.

51 APOSTROPHES: SHOWING POSSESSION AND FORMING CONTRACTIONS

An apostrophe ('), usually with an *s* following it, indicates the possessive case of nouns, as well as the possessive case of some indefinite pronouns. Apostrophes also form contractions: they show where letters have been omitted from a word. Apostrophes create the plurals of numbers, letters, symbols, and words used as words. Missing or misused apostrophes can cause confusion for your readers, so be careful how you use them: *don't* use them to make personal pronouns possessive, to make nouns plural, or with verbs in the present tense.

51a Use an Apostrophe to Form the Possessive Case

The possessive case indicates ownership or possession: *Vikram's photograph of his sister.* In English, there are two ways to demonstrate that a noun or indefinite pronoun owns or possesses another:

1. You can use a phrase starting with the word *of: the eye of the storm; the voice of the singer.*
2. You can use the more common method of adding an apostrophe and the letter *s* to the end of the noun: *the cat's meow; the singer's voice.* When the noun is plural and ends in *-s,* the apostrophe follows the *-s*: *our mothers' responses.* When the noun is a singular proper name ending in *-s,* the apostrophe and *s* are added: *Elvis's peanut butter.* If the singular proper noun ends in *-s* but has a z sound, use an apostrophe only: *Socrates' scroll.*

Example 1 Forming the possessive case of inanimate objects

Yes The **door of the car** was left open all night.
Yes The **car door** was left open all night.
No The car's door was left open all night.

Yes The **fifth slide of the PowerPoint presentation** didn't display well when projected.
Yes The **fifth PowerPoint slide** didn't display well when projected.
No The PowerPoint presentation's fifth slide didn't display well when projected.

Example 2 Using *'s*

Use *'s* to form the possessive case of . . .

- **singular nouns:**

  Her mother's shawl was wrapped around the child's shoulders.
  Alice Smith's vocal range spans four octaves.

- **indefinite pronouns that end in *-body* or *-one:***

  I would like everyone's vacation requests on my desk by Friday.

- **irregular plural nouns that don't end in *-s:***

  The women's voting coalition meets Tuesdays at 7:00.

Example 3 Using only an apostrophe with plural nouns that already end in *-s*

The pilots' complaints about the airline have not been resolved.

The Joneses' house got an environmental award for its passive solar heating and wind-powered generator. [The house is owned by more than one person—perhaps a whole family—named Jones.]

Multilingual writers: In conventional usage, the possessive case of an inanimate object, such as a car, often does not take *'s.* Instead, a noun phrase is employed. Though there are exceptions, you won't be wrong if you use a noun phrase.

Apostrophe + *s*

Use an apostrophe and the letter *s* to form the possessive case of certain nouns and pronouns:

- singular nouns
- indefinite pronouns that end in *body* or *one*
- irregular plural nouns (irregular because they don't end in *-s,* such as *children, women, men, people, sheep, fish, deer)*

When a plural noun does end in *-s,* as most of them do, add only the apostrophe.

51a

Individual and Joint Ownership

When you want to indicate that items are owned or possessed individually, each noun gets its own apostrophe and *s*. When items are owned or possessed jointly, use an apostrophe and *s* only after the last noun. The same goes for compound words: to make them possessive, put the apostrophe and *s* on the last word.

Some Examples of Compound Words

in-laws' visit (plural)
sister-in-law's invitation
attorney general's indictment
anybody else's opinion

Example 4 Showing individual and joint ownership

INDIVIDUAL OWNERSHIP:

Tamora Pierce's and Garth Nix's young adult novels feature heroines who are intelligent and resourceful.

JOINT OWNERSHIP:

Ben and Jerry's first ice cream store opened in Burlington, Vermont.

Example 5 Making compound words possessive

My mother-in-law's brisket recipe is a family heirloom.

51b Use Apostrophes to Form Contractions

Apostrophes are used in contractions to take the place of one or more letters that have been omitted. Contractions are combination words that include a pronoun and a verb (like *she's* for *she is*) or the elements of a verb phrase (*aren't* for *are not*).

Contractions are a sign of informal writing; they are commonly used in emails, personal letters, and blogs, as well as in reported speech. Contractions are too informal for some types of college writing, such as research essays, but may be acceptable in others, depending on your audience's expectations about the rhetorical context and the genre in which you are writing.

Example 6 Making contractions

"It's a beautiful day in this neighborhood," Mr. Rogers used to sing at the beginning of his TV show for children.

Painter Roy Lichtenstein's cartoonish work *Drowning Girl* shows a woman in water exclaiming, "I don't care! I'd rather sink—than call Brad for help."

Some Common Contractions

I am = I'm
I will = I'll (similarly: you'll, he'll, she'll, we'll, they'll)
I have = I've (you've, we've, they've)
I would, I had = I'd (he'd, she'd, we'd, you'd, they'd)
you are = you're (we're, they're)
it is, it has = it's (he's, she's)
let us = let's
who is = who's
there is = there's
is not = isn't (aren't, don't, didn't, wasn't, weren't)
can not = can't
will not = won't

Contractions: with apostrophe	**Possessives: no apostrophe**
It's [it is] raining hard.	Its teeth were incredibly long and sharp.
Who's [who is] at the door?	Whose hat is this?
You're [you are] standing on my foot!	Your painting seems to be a forgery.
They're [they are] not trying to win.	Their father was ill.

51b

Take Care to Distinguish Contractions from Possessive Pronouns

Some contractions are frequently confused with possessive pronouns that sound the same—for instance, *it's* and *its, who's* and *whose.* Remember that a contraction is always written with an apostrophe, and a possessive personal pronoun never includes one. Readers get thrown off track when the two forms are confused, so double-check each use to be sure you're using them correctly.

Use Apostrophes to Form Plurals of Letters, Symbols, Words Used as Words, and Abbreviations

51c

Letters, symbols (for example, &, #, and @), words used as words, and abbreviations can be made plural either by adding an apostrophe and *s* or by adding only an *s.* (The decision may be dictated by the style you are following—for example, MLA style—or it may depend on your personal preferences.) The letter, word, or symbol should be placed in italics (or underlined), but the apostrophe and the *s* (or just the *s*) should be in roman (regular) type. Abbreviations do not need to be in italics.

Make sure that your usage is consistent throughout your project.

Example 7 Forming plurals

WITH APOSTROPHE AND *S:*

In England and Canada, z's are called zeds.

According to a concordance of *Death of a Salesman* compiled by Potter and Struss at Iowa State, there are 23,140 unique words in the play, which has 909 *you's* and 816 *I's.*

WITH *S* ONLY:

The Online Film Critics Society lists the top 100 overlooked films of the 1990s, including *Miller's Crossing* as number 1.

Since I am 19, I always get lottery tickets that have *1*s and 9s in them, but so far, I haven't had any luck.

Do you kids have proper IDs?

51d Avoid Misusing Apostrophes

An apostrophe is **not** used

- to make most nouns plural. Most nouns are made plural by adding only *s* to the singular form: *sisters.*
- to make personal pronouns possessive. Possessive personal pronouns do not need apostrophes because they are already possessive.

Possessive Personal Pronouns

mine	ours
yours	yours
hers	theirs
his	
its	

- to make present-tense verbs agree with *he, she,* or *it.* To make present-tense verbs agree with third-person subjects *he, she,* and *it,* just add *s* or *es.*

Example 8 Avoiding apostrophe errors

USE ONLY *S* TO MAKE MOST NOUNS PLURAL:

No Dog's are great company for kid's.
Yes Dogs are great company for kids.

ITS, YOURS, HIS, HERS, OURS, THEIRS ARE ALREADY POSSESSIVE:

Robert Frost begins the first two lines of his poem "Stopping by Woods on a Snowy Evening" with possessive personal pronouns: "Whose woods these are I think I know. / His house is in the village though."

USE ONLY *S* OR *ES* TO MAKE MOST PRESENT-TENSE VERBS AGREE WITH *HE, SHE,* OR *IT:*

No Codi say's she is carsick. She want's to go home.
Yes Codi says she is carsick. She wants to go home.

Activity 51-1: Editing Apostrophes

Suppose you are a literary editor who is preparing someone's diary for publication. Edit the following excerpts from the diary for correct use of apostrophes.

Its not funny how people laugh at my Dads car. Hes getting into his' 50s and his idea's of cool can sometimes embarrass the rest of the family. However, the family's been talking with him about his recent purchase of two Mazda Miata's, one for him and one for Mom. His and Her's Miata's, can you imagine? Since they are not going through mid-life crisis' right now, we all wonder whats on his mind.

That cat's kind of cute and kind of scary. I don't think that Iv'e ever seen a cat with those colors before. What do you call those colors'? Teal? Mauve? Henna? I bet her' cat glows in the dark. The veterinarian must laugh behind her back at her cats' strange fur.

That puppys foolish behavior would give it C's in any obedience school. Chasing its' tail, barking at the instructor, and running around without it's leash are just three of the several thing's it is doing to make things tough for all the other dogs, who's owners must wait until the puppy get's its behavior back in order.

52

QUOTATION MARKS: ATTRIBUTING WORDS TO PEOPLE AND CONVEYING TONE

Quotation marks signal to readers that the exact words between them come from someone other than the writer or the narrator. Quotation marks are used to present words taken directly from research sources or to report dialogue between speakers. They also enclose the titles of short works such as essays, songs, and short stories. (Italics or underlining is used for longer works; see section 56a.) Quotation marks can also set off words used in special senses (for example, ironically), although in academic writing, the preferred way of showing irony is to make careful use of sentence structure and to avoid relying on quotation marks to do the work for you.

Double quotation marks (" ") mark the beginning and end of most quoted material. The exception is when the quotation is long and, in accordance with certain citation styles, is presented in indented or block form, in which case the indentation itself marks the text as quoted material. When material is quoted within another quotation, single quotation marks (' ') enclose the material.

52a Use Quotation Marks to Enclose Short Direct Quotations

In MLA style, a prose quotation is considered "short" if it is four or fewer lines long. If you are quoting from a poem, three or fewer lines is considered short. In APA style, a short prose quotation is up to forty words. In either style, when you quote the exact words of a source, use double quotation marks at the beginning and end of the quotation. The ending quotation mark appears before the citation in parentheses, which in turn precedes the final end punctuation, such as a period.

For handling long quotations in MLA style, see page 381; for APA style, see page 447.

Example 1 Short quotations in MLA style

PROSE:

Lourie says, "It is to Pop I owe my love of wilderness" (34).

POETRY:

To show how the vision of natural beauty can foster reflection, Wordsworth writes, "While with an eye made quiet by the power / Of harmony, and the deep power of joy, / We see into the life of things" (47-49).

Example 2 A short quotation in APA style

By Bazerman et al.'s account (2005), "Writing across the Curriculum, like any academic program, arises out of a complex of institutional, intellectual, and social events and forces" (p. 5).

52b Use Single Quotation Marks for Quotations within Quotations

Material that you want to quote may itself include a quotation. In this case, use double quotation marks to indicate the beginning and end of the entire quotation and replace any quotation marks within the material with single quotation marks. (As described in section 19b, long quotations are set off from the text by indentation rather than by quotation marks. Thus, any quotations within the material should be reprinted exactly as they are printed in the original.)

Example 3 A quotation within a quotation

ORIGINAL SOURCE:

NEA chairman Dana Gioia, himself a poet, called the findings shocking and a reason for grave concern. "We have a lot of functionally literate people who are no longer engaged readers," Gioia said in an interview with The Associated Press.

From The Associated Press, "Report Shows Big Drop in Reading," *MSNBC*, 8 July 2004 <http://www.msnbc.msn.com/id/5389382>.

CHANGE TO SINGLE QUOTATION MARKS:

Each generation proclaims a literacy crisis, almost as a rite of passage. These days, the Internet is blamed, for example, for a whole host of declines both moral and intellectual. According to an anonymously written Associated Press article, "NEA chairman Dana Gioia, himself a poet, called the findings shocking and a reason for grave concern. 'We have a lot of functionally literate people who are no longer engaged readers'" ("Report").

Global Contexts

American vs. British Use of Quotation Marks

Because of England's colonial history, many people around the globe have learned to punctuate English writing the British way. If you learned British English but now attend college in the United States, you will need to make these adjustments in quotation mark usage:

1. Reverse the placement of double and single quotation marks: Often, British usage calls for using single quotation marks where Americans put double quotation marks and vice versa. American usage calls for double quotation marks for the entire quotation and single marks for any quotation within that quotation.
2. Put the period or comma inside the closing quotation marks, even if it doesn't seem logical. For example, write *We read "Hills Like White Elephants."*
3. Never put a period between single and double quotation marks. If both a single and a double closing quotation mark are used at the end of a sentence, the order is as follows: period, single quotation mark, double quotation mark.

Activity 52-1: Using Quotation Marks

Use the paragraph below to carry out the following activities with quotations, using either MLA or APA rules.

1. Incorporate a quotation from the paragraph into a sentence of your own.
2. Write a sentence of your own that includes a quotation within a quotation.

Wildlife smuggling usually doesn't provide a happy ending for either the smugglers or the animals. One animal has been extraordinarily fortunate, though; an infant pangolin recovered by U.S. Fish and Wildlife agents from a family who purchased it in Africa for a mere three dollars has been given a new home at the Los Angeles Zoo. Although they may appear reptilian, pangolins are "mammals with specially modified hairs that have evolved into hard, horn-like scales. They are insectivores and consume ants, termites, and other insects with their very long sticky tongues" (Campbell). Fed on a diet of high-protein kitten food, lovingly tended and admired by visitors, the pangolin is "Growing like a weed!" according to Zookeeper Greene.

Campbell, Will. "Pangolin Update: A Work in Progress." *Los Angeles Zoo* 5 Feb. 2005 <http://www.lazoo.org/zoo_headline2.asp?id=28>.

52c Use Quotation Marks in Dialogue

Enclose each speaker's words in a pair of quotation marks. When the speaker changes, start a new paragraph. If one speaker's words take more than a single paragraph, start each paragraph with a double quotation mark, but use an ending quotation mark only at the end of the entire speech, not after each paragraph.

Direct vs. Indirect Discourse

If you report a speaker's words but do not quote them, do not use quotation marks. Such reported speech is known as **indirect discourse.**

Multilingual writers: Notice the changes that need to be made in the shift from direct to indirect discourse. In direct discourse, the word *said* is in the past tense, but the quoted words are written using the verb that the speaker actually used. In indirect discourse, both the speaker tag *Sheila said* and the reported speech are in the past tense. The pronoun within the reported speech also shifts from *I* to *she,* since in the direct discourse, Sheila was referring to herself, but in the reported speech, the writer is referring to Sheila. The change in speaker is also the reason for the shift from *you* to *me* and *your* to *my.* The word *that* after the speaker tag is optional. If there is any chance your readers will become confused without *that,* however, be sure to include it.

Example 4 Using quotation marks in dialogue

In this passage from Edgar Allan Poe's story of revenge, "The Cask of Amontillado" (1846), each line of dialogue by a new speaker is treated as a new paragraph.

> Here I knocked off the neck of a bottle which I drew from a long row of its fellows that lay upon the mould.
>
> "Drink," I said, presenting him the wine.
>
> He raised it to his lips with a leer. He paused and nodded to me familiarly, while his bells jingled.
>
> "I drink," he said, "to the buried that repose around us."
>
> "And I to your long life."

Example 5 Direct vs. indirect discourse

DIRECT DISCOURSE:

Sheila said, "I want to help you decorate your new house." [Exact quotation]

INDIRECT DISCOURSE:

Sheila said *that she wanted* to help *me* decorate *my* new house. [Reported but not quoted exactly]

Activity 52-2: Editing Dialogue

Punctuate the following dialogue appropriately by inserting quotation marks and paragraph breaks.

> What did he want to know? Deanna asked. He wanted to know if he could borrow my trig notes, Sheila said. Did he say anything about me? Deanna said. He said that he was going to ask you but you'd left before he got a chance, Sheila said. Oh, Deanna said. Oh what? Sheila said. Oh, you know what, Deanna said.

Example 6 Quotation marks for titles of short works

DO NOT USE QUOTATION MARKS AROUND THE TITLE OF YOUR PAPER:

The Unveiling of the Ultra-Chic South Beach Diet

BUT IF THE TITLE OF A SHORT WORK IS PART OF YOUR TITLE, ENCLOSE THAT TITLE IN QUOTATION MARKS:

Selective Point of View in Hemingway's "A Clean, Well-Lighted Place"

Use quotation marks around titles of these types of short works

Short story	"A Good Man Is Hard to Find" by Flannery O'Connor
Short poem	"Leda and the Swan" by William Butler Yeats
Song	"The Last DJ" by Tom Petty and the Heartbreakers
Essay (other than your own)	"La Gringuita," an essay from *Something to Declare* by Julia Alvarez
Article in newspaper, magazine, or journal	"Buried Truths" by Benjamin Phelan in *Harper's Magazine*
Chapter or section of book	"Incommensurate Boundaries: Positivism and Darwinism in Victorian Biology" by Thomas M. Lessl, in *Rhetoric and Incommensurability,* edited by Randy Harris
Photograph	"Between Monsoons" by Alex Ambrose, in *25 under 25: Up and Coming American Photographers*
Unpublished speech	"Conservation in North Carolina in 2005: Our Success Stories"
Individual episode of television or radio series	"Homer the Moe," a *Simpsons* episode
Page or document on a website	"Health Promotion: Milestones on the Road to a Global Alliance" on the World Health Organization (WHO) site

Titles of longer works should be italicized (section 56a).

The titles of short works and works that are part of larger works, such as chapters of books, are placed inside quotation marks.

Important exception: Do not use quotation marks, italics, or underlining with the title of your essay. However, if the title of another work appears within your title, mark it appropriately. If it's a long work, italicize it; if it's a short work, put quotation marks around it.

52e Use Quotation Marks to Set Off Words Used in Special Senses

When a word is used as a word, either italicize it or enclose it in quotation marks.

Quotation marks are sometimes used to indicate irony or sarcasm, although this is not a preferred usage in college writing and other somewhat formal situations. Very often, the effect is different from the one the writer intended.

Don't use quotation marks around clichés, either. Instead, omit the cliché and use your own fresh language to say what you mean.

Quotation marks can be used to indicate the English translation of a word or phrase.

Example 7 Word used as a word

The word *idea* comes from the Greek verb *idein,* "to see."

What kind of "science" denies global warming?

Example 8 Avoiding clichés

No As they say, "A bird in the hand is worth two in the bush!"

Yes It would be a good idea to use the resources you have rather than waste all of your time in Photoshop trying to create something new.

Example 9 Avoid using quotation marks to indicate irony or sarcasm

No I'm glad your friend believes so strongly in your "innocence," Jack; otherwise you would be in jail right now.

Example 10 Quotation marks with English translations

Nemo me impune lacessit. ("No one injures or attacks me with impunity.")

Project Checklist

Proofreading for Quotation Marks with Other Punctuation Marks

- ❑ Are your commas and periods inside the closing quotation mark unless a citation in parentheses follows the closing quotation mark (in which case the period follows the parentheses)?

  Comma: She worried that we would "undervalue return investments," but I assured her we had high hopes.

  Period: Walter Mitty was overheard saying "puppy biscuits."

  But: Yeats describes "the great wings beating still" (1).

- ❑ Are your colons and semicolons outside the closing quotation mark?

  Colon: Renoir delighted in the peaceful moments of "companionship": people in a park, a mother and daughter, two friends.

  Semicolon: Hemingway bragged about "A Clean, Well-Lighted Place"; he felt it was one of his finer technical achievements.

- ❑ Are your question marks, exclamation points, and dashes inside the quotation marks if they are part of the quotation and outside if they are part of the larger sentence?

  Inside: Ophelia asks, "How does your Honor for this many a day?"

  "Watch your head!" she yelled, right after I'd bumped it on the cupboard.

  "Remember to flip the switch—the one for the lights—" was the last thing I heard her say.

  Outside: What does he mean when he warns about her "quaint honor"?

  If you want to be heard, "Take it to the streets"!

  Near the beginning of DeLillo's *White Noise,* the flight attendant—consulting the "Manual of Disasters"—has a complete breakdown of command presence.

Commas and periods are placed inside closing quotation marks. One important exception is when a citation in parentheses follows a quotation. In that case, the period is placed after the citation.

Colons and semicolons are usually placed outside closing quotation marks, but if they are part of the original material being quoted, they go inside.

Question marks, exclamation points, and dashes are placed inside closing quotation marks if they are part of the original quoted material; otherwise, they are outside.

52f

The punctuation and capitalization used in sentences with quotations varies depending on where the speaker is identified and whether the speaker is identified in an independent clause (complete sentence).

Project Checklist

Proofreading for Punctuation and Capitalization with Quotations

Is the speaker identified . . .

- **. . . before the quotation but not in a complete sentence?** A comma should appear between that information and the quoted material.

  Marie Antoinette is reputed to have said, "Let them eat cake."
- **. . . before the quotation in a complete sentence?** A colon (not a comma) should follow the speaker identification.

  Kenneth Burke had conflicting feelings about the human condition: "We stand nervously loquacious at the edge of an abyss" (272).
- **. . . between parts of the quotation within a complete sentence?** Two commas should be used (one after the first part of the quotation and the other after the interrupting speaker information), and a lowercase letter should begin the speaker information.

  "If you really need to know," said Maria, "you'll just have to google it."
- **. . . between parts of the quotation but with the second part of the quotation starting a new sentence?** A comma and end quotation mark should appear before the speaker information. A period ends the sentence containing the speaker information. The next sentence begins with an opening quotation mark and a capital letter.

  "Because film operates in real time, it is more limited," wrote James Monaco. "Novels end only when they feel like it" (45).
- **. . . after the quotation?** A comma should appear after the quotation. However, if the original includes a question mark or exclamation point that you want to use, don't add a comma.

  The charge of impeachment "might be an option," declared Senator Arlen Spector, Republican of Pennsylvania.

  "I have just begun to fight!" shouted John Paul Jones.

53 OTHER PUNCTUATION MARKS

The major punctuation marks, covered in Chapters 47–52, are unable to do all the different kinds of work needed to make sentences clear. This chapter covers other punctuation marks that help to accomplish that goal. Dashes, for example, dramatically emphasize the text they enclose. Parentheses are useful for enclosing information that is not essential to an understanding of the core meaning of a sentence. Brackets are used within quotations to show readers that you have added to or changed the text slightly so it will fit better into your context. Ellipsis points tell readers that you have omitted material from a source you are quoting, that a speaker in dialogue has left a statement unfinished, or (more rarely) that there is a pause or silence in spoken dialogue. Slashes separate the lines of a poem quoted in an essay and the parts of a URL, and they can indicate options. Each of these punctuation marks has specific purposes in writing.

A dash looks like this: —. It is keyed using two hyphens. (The use of hyphens is covered in Chapter 58.) The dash is also called an "em dash" because its length is approximately equal to the width of a capital M.

-- (dash formed by two hyphens)
— (em dash)

Dashes allow you to interrupt a sentence to provide and emphasize additional information. If the information falls in the middle of a sentence, it is set off with a pair of dashes. If it comes first or last in a sentence, it is followed or preceded by a single dash. When you use dashes, place the interrupting information as close as possible to the material it relates to. Dashes point backward in a text, modifying or clarifying information that has come before.

Dashes should be used sparingly—normally you should limit yourself to one set in a paragraph. Commas, which are less emphatic than dashes, are used more frequently. Compared with commas, dashes give readers the sense of a longer pause and greater emphasis.

Functions of Dashes

- **To set off material that interrupts the flow of a sentence:**

  It consisted almost entirely of repetitions of the word "whereas"—a typical Dada touch—and ended with declaring Greenwich Village a free and independent state . . .

  From "Dada Gets First Big U.S. Exhibit," *CNN.com,* 16 Feb. 2006, 17 Feb. 2006 <http://www.cnn.com/2006/US/02/16/dada.exhibit.ap/index.html>.

  Photographer Ansel Adams built on the traditions of painted landscapes but showed that the camera—even when dependent on black-and-white film—could reveal mysterious beauties that painting never had.

  From Philip Yenawine, *How to Look at Modern Art* (New York: Abrams, 1991), 69.

- **To emphasize appositives and examples:**

  The baby's favorite toys—the rattle, the teddy bear, and the blankie—are in the car still.

  Not even cities that are growing—southern and western boom cities—are keeping pace with their suburbs.

  From Bruce Katz and Jennifer Bradley, "Urban Affairs," *Atlantic Monthly* 284.6 (December 1999) <http://www.theatlantic.com/issues/99dec/9912katz.htm>.

- **To set off a term's definition:**

  SIM, like one version of TPF, is an interferometer—a set of small telescopes.

  From Tim Appenzeller, "Search for Other Earths," *National Geographic,* December 2004, p. 92.

- **To emphasize statements that summarize or describe a list of items:**

  Other fish, birds, even small mammals—the tigerfish of the Okavango Delta eats them all.

- **To set off an aside (a personal comment):**

  Nibiru is the planet which is the twelfth member of the Solar System—although technically it is, as a planet, only the tenth.

  From Zechariah Sitchen, *Genesis Revisited* (New York: Avon, 1990), 19.

- **To mark a shift in tone:**

  So many things have been produced and accumulated that they can never possibly all be put to use—certainly not a bad thing when it comes to nuclear weapons.

  From Jean Baudrillard, *The Transparency of Evil*, trans. James Benedict (London: Verso, 1993), 32.

- **To indicate a hesitation or a break in dialogue:**

  In the old man's obituary—cancer!—seven years later, Mary is listed as Executive Vice President and sole heir.

  From Katherine Dunn, *Geek Love* (New York: Warner Books, 1989), 150.

Example 1 Exclamation point inside dashes

Giving you some money—five hundred dollars!—is not high on my list of priorities.

Example 2 Quotation marks inside dashes

I've read that essay—"Have Typewriter, Will Travel"—and it was lively.

Parentheses also are used to indicate interruptions, but the material inside a pair of parentheses is not as integrally bound to the immediate context; instead, it functions more like an aside or a note. The use of parentheses suggests a sharper division between the main part of the sentence and the interrupting element.

Dashes with Other Punctuation Marks

If the material enclosed in dashes is a question or an exclamation, it can end with a question mark or exclamation point. Note that the exclamation point or question mark goes inside the dashes.

You can use quotation marks around material within dashes if the context calls for them.

Other than in the situations described above, do not use the dash next to other punctuation marks, including commas, periods, semicolons, or colons.

Parentheses are used to enclose material that interrupts the flow of a sentence or paragraph. Only material that is not essential to a sentence's meaning—that illustrates, supplements, clarifies, or expands on the main point being made—should be placed in parentheses. Parentheses can enclose a word, phrase, list, or sentence. Parentheses are also used to enclose citation information.

Compared to information enclosed by dashes or commas, material in parentheses is less necessary for understanding the sentence. Parentheses should be used sparingly. If you have many pairs of parentheses, you should reconsider how your information fits together and rewrite your sentences, either to integrate the information into the sentences or to omit some of it.

In legal and business writing, parentheses are used to enclose spelled-out versions of numbers so that there can be no mistake with figures: *Your contract states that you must work seven (7) hours daily.*

In technological and scientific writing that includes frequent references to measurements, parentheses are used to enclose comparative forms of numbers: *6 inches (152.4 millimeters).*

Functions of Parentheses

- **To enclose interrupting words:**

  Significantly, their intermediary in this was Jim Hickman of the Russian Exchange Program of the Esalen Institute in California (more on this later).

  From Lynn Picknett and Clive Prince, *The Stargate Conspiracy* (New York: Berkley, 1999), 149.

- **To enclose examples and explanations:**

  It is virtually impossible to determine the exact number of journalists on the CIA payroll—much less those who are informally slipped information (but in 1977 Carl Bernstein, in an article for *Rolling Stone,* estimated the number at that time to be about 400).

  From Jim Keith, *Mass Control: Engineering Human Consciousness* (Lilburn, GA: IllumiNet Press, 2002), 38.

- **To enclose citation information:**

  Slavery was described as "torturous, barbaric, counterproductive, and completely inhumane" (Smith 119).

  Notice that the parentheses are after the closing quotation mark and before the final end punctuation. In longer quotations (MLA, more than four lines; APA, more than forty words), the quotation is indented and the closing period comes before the parenthetical citation.

- **To enclose numbers or letters of items in a list:**

  The situational elements that may shape a writer's purpose include (a) the textual context, (b) the immediate context, and (c) the social and historical context.

- **To enclose numbers, dates, and cross-references:**

  During World War I (1914–1918), Australian solider Francis James Mack wrote a series of letters home that are collected at "Trenches on the Web."

  Gardner used eight criteria of "intelligence" as he reviewed the literature (see pp. 62–69).

- **To enclose examples, phone numbers, directions, and the like:**

  In addition, the bank would never use a cell phone number (514-588-5569) on their checks.

  From Wayne Madsen, "Texas to Florida: White House-Linked Clandestine Operation Paid for 'Vote Switching' Software," *Online Journal,* 12 Jan. 2004 <http://www.onlinejournal.org/Special_Reports/120604Madsen/120604madsen.html>.

Parentheses with Other Punctuation Marks

When you insert a complete parenthetical sentence within another sentence, do not capitalize the first letter of the enclosed sentence or end it with a period.

Example 3 Parenthetical sentence within a sentence

Educators worry about a growing gender imbalance in colleges (in 2000, women outnumbered men 128:100; by 2010, the proportion will be 138:100).

Adapted from Barrett Seaman, *Binge* (New York: Wiley, 2005), 50.

However, you can use an exclamation point or a question mark at the end of a parenthetical sentence placed within another sentence, even though the first word of the parenthetical sentence is not capitalized.

Example 4 Parenthetical question within a sentence

Repeated studies have shown that conflicts over gender (should the wife work? who should do what?) are leading causes of divorce.

From S. L. Nock, "The Consequences of Premarital Fatherhood," *American Sociological Review 63* (1998): 250–262.

When you insert a complete sentence enclosed in parentheses *between* two other sentences, capitalize the first word of the enclosed sentence and end it with a period inside the right parenthesis.

Example 5 Parenthetical sentence between sentences

More than once during World War II, Jack Kennedy courageously rescued enlisted men under his command. (Many officers were beloved by their subordinates and committed unrecognized heroic actions.) Kennedy was an example of the best that can emerge during war.

Do not use any punctuation before a parenthetical remark. A comma can follow the parentheses if the material before it would have required one.

Example 6 Punctuation with parentheticals

No Whatever the experiment's outcome, (and the boiling point must be reached before final analysis) the goal is the same.

Yes Whatever the experiment's outcome (and the boiling point must be reached before final analysis), the goal is the same.

Brackets are squared parentheses: [ ]. They are used less frequently than parentheses and only for specialized purposes.

A pair of brackets is used *within quotations* to show that you are making minor additions or changes to a source's words. Be careful that your changes don't alter the meaning of the original material. Use brackets to

- indicate that the words they enclose are yours and not those of the original author. For example, you might need to add a word or change a verb tense so the quotation will fit smoothly into the grammar of your sentence.
- indicate that you have changed a direct quotation. If you add italics to the quotation, for example, you should note in brackets that you did so.
- distinguish ellipsis points you have used to replace omitted material from ellipses already present in the original source (see also section 53d).
- point out or correct errors in source material (e.g., an incorrect date, fact, etc.). The word *sic* (Latin for "so" or "thus") in brackets indicates that the error (in spelling, grammar, or usage) is in the source.

Brackets are also used *within parentheses.* When one pair of parentheses falls inside another, change the inner set to brackets.

Functions of Brackets within Quotations

- **To indicate that the words they enclose are yours and not those of the original author:**

  As Terry Eagleton aptly points out, "An advertisement for a daily newspaper announces [as though we still believed in killing off unborn infants or putting the mentally ill on show], 'Times change, Values don't'" (11).

- **To indicate that you have changed a direct quotation:**

  In *The Book Club Companion,* Diana Loevy shares advice on running book clubs: which books to read, which thematic snacks to serve with different novels, and which pets to allow at meetings. On whether to give up a seat to a pet, she quotes Dr. Merry Crimi, a veterinarian, who says "Humans need to assert their rightful alpha position and seating is no different"; Crimi "tell[s] [her] dog occasionally, 'sometimes you just have to be the dog'" (27).

- **To distinguish ellipsis points you have used to replace omitted material from ellipses present in the original source, when using MLA style:**

  The introduction concludes with a quotation from Weinberger's multi-layered and richly textured pastiche of the beautiful city of Vienna: "The Vienna of popular imagination [. . .] does indeed exist, but no one really lives there . . . except the most willfully sentimental of foreign visitors" (xi–xii).

- **To point out or correct errors in source material:**

  In an attempt to gain the sympathy of the voters, the school board candidate spoke of the averse [sic] conditions under which he had been working for the past two years.

Function of Brackets within Parentheses

- **To add very brief additional information about the material in parentheses:**

  Three former members of the Black Panther Party famous today for their political activism are Danny Glover, board chair of TransAfrica Forum (also well known as a director and actor in more than 25 films, including the *Lethal Weapon* movies [1987–1998]); Malik Rahim, co-founder of the hurricane relief organization Common Ground Collective; and Aaron Dixon, candidate for U.S. Senate on the Green Party ticket in 2006.

Ellipsis points (also known as *an ellipsis*) are three spaced periods (. . .) that indicate omissions from quoted material or unfinished statements in dialogue.

Omission of Material from Quotations

Ellipsis points indicate the intentional omission of some amount of text from a quotation, whether a single word or whole paragraphs. An ellipsis is preceded and followed by a space. No matter how much material is removed, the omission should never change the fundamental meaning of the material being quoted.

In MLA documentation style, an ellipsis may be enclosed in brackets in order to differentiate it from ellipses in the original. The brackets make clear that the omission is the choice of the person quoting, not the person being quoted. In other documentation styles, brackets are not typically used to enclose ellipses used in quotations.

Prose Quotations

When you quote only a few words from another source, you don't need to use an ellipsis. Similarly, you don't usually need an ellipsis at the beginning of a sentence. If the quotation starts with a capital letter, readers assume that you are starting with a full sentence; if

Example 7 No ellipsis needed when it's obvious that only a few words are quoted

Describing custodial involvement in human activities, Robert Temple writes, "No doubt we are under routine monitoring" (313).

Example 8 Ellipsis to show an omission in the middle of a sentence

Investigative researcher Jim Marrs writes, "Various discrepancies in Oswald's military records . . . support the idea that Oswald was given secret intelligence training" (112).

Example 9 Ellipsis to show an omission at the end of a sentence

Roman Polanski recalls, "Although I was never questioned about the tape, I should no doubt be accused of concealing a significant aspect of our lifestyle . . ." (298).

IF CITATION INFORMATION HAS ALREADY BEEN GIVEN, THE PERIOD FOLLOWS DIRECTLY AFTER THE ELLIPSIS AND BEFORE THE CLOSING QUOTATION MARK:

On page one of *V.*, Pynchon writes, "Christmas Eve, 1955, Benny Profane, wearing black levis, suede jacket, sneakers, and a big cowboy hat, happened to pass through . . . ."

IF ANOTHER SENTENCE THEN APPEARS IN FULL, THE NEXT SENTENCE BEGINS DIRECTLY AFTER THE ELLIPSIS AND PERIOD:

That is what is meant here by "mythical knowledge . . . . It was only understood by a very few" (de Santillana, Giorgio, and Von Dechend 53).

Example 10 Ellipsis to show that an entire sentence has been omitted

As Pfaff points out, "But the meaning of class is dangerous ground for an American. . . . There is an identifiable upper class in Britain with an aristocratic ethos and a hereditary base" (39).

the quotation begins with a lowercase letter, readers will know you have started mid-sentence. Using brackets around the initial capital letter on the first word of a quoted sentence indicates that the word did not start a sentence in the original. The examples show various situations in which you do and do not need to use ellipses.

Poetry Quotations

When you omit words from within a line of poetry, the rules are the same as those for prose. When you omit an entire line of poetry and have indented the lines to preserve their original layout, show the omission with a row of spaced periods equal in length to the missing line or the one above it.

Unfinished Statements in Dialogue

An ellipsis can be used to indicate that a speaker's words are trailing off or that a speaker is hesitating.

Ellipsis Points with Other Punctuation

When you omit words from a quotation, you also omit any related punctuation, unless it is important to the structure of the sentence.

Example 11 Ellipsis to show omission from the middle of one sentence to the middle of another

Hancock concludes, "As at Giza, therefore, a real correlation exists between sky and ground . . . and this correlation only 'locks' perfectly at a very remote date" (133).

Example 12 Ellipsis points in quotations from poetry

ORIGINAL SOURCE:

Miss Nancy Ellicott smoked
And danced all the modern dances;
And her aunts were not quite sure how they felt about it,
But they knew that it was modern.

From T. S. Eliot, "Cousin Nancy," in *Prufrock and Other Observations* (London: The Egoist, 1917), lines 7–10.

ELLIPSIS TO SHOW OMISSION OF A LINE:

T. S. Eliot puts Nancy Ellicott under a microscope to show the difference between performance and authenticity: "Miss Nancy Ellicott smoked / And danced all the modern dances; / . . . / But [her aunts] knew that it was modern" (7–10).

Example 13 Ellipsis points in dialogue

Eric looked across the gorge and, with an air unequal to the gravity of the question, asked, "It is . . . safe?"

Example 14 Ellipsis points with other punctuation

ORIGINAL SOURCE:

However, it soon becomes apparent that fashion embraces more than the need to be seen in the right places, doing the right things with the right people, and wearing the right clothes.

From Neil Sammells, *Wilde Style: The Plays and Prose of Oscar Wilde* (New York: Longman, 2000), 100.

COMMAS IN THE SERIES DROPPED:

Sammells goes on to say, "However, it soon becomes apparent that fashion embraces more than the need to be seen in the right places . . . and wearing the right clothes" (100).

Functions of Slashes

- **To separate lines of poetry quoted in an essay:**

  In lines 39 through 41 from "Mending Wall," Robert Frost writes, "Bringing a stone grasped firmly by the top / In each hand, like an old-stone savage armed / He moves in darkness as it seems to me" (46).

- **To separate numerator and denominator in fractions:**

  3/5

- **To separate parts of a Web address:**

  Roald Dahl's *Charlie and the Chocolate Factory* is popular with children and adults, but if you want to know why, read this *New Yorker* piece: <http://www.newyorker.com/critics/atlarge/articles/050711crat_atlarge>.

- **To separate options:**

  The questionnaire was composed of ten yes/no questions.

Note: Current MLA guidelines recommend not using URLs in Works Cited entries unless they are needed for the reader to find the source or your instructor requires them.

Slashes are diagonal lines that look like this: /. They are used to separate the parts of a whole. Slashes are also used to indicate options.

Slashes Separate the Parts of a Whole

- Slashes are used between lines of poetry quoted in an essay. When you quote three or fewer lines of poetry, use a slash to indicate the end of each line. Each slash should be preceded and followed by a space. If you quote more than three lines, the poem appears as a block quotation and is printed without slashes (section 19b).
- Slashes are used to separate the numerator and denominator in a fraction written in numerals. No space separates the slash from the numerals on either side.
- Slashes are used in Web addresses (URLs). If a Web address runs onto a second or subsequent line, break it right after a slash.

Slashes Separate Options

Slashes are used to separate words that indicate a choice of options: *win/lose, pass/fail.* One such construction, *he/she,* should not be used in college writing; see section 39c for a detailed discussion of the nonsexist use of language.

PART 10

Understanding Mechanics

New Contexts for Writing

Writers these days have so many new contexts for writing that the choices are sometimes bewildering. Now, not only must you choose what to write and how to write it, but also you must choose how to present your writing—on paper or computer screen, animated, aurally, next to photographs or video, and, yes, even inside the world of a video game. Fear not! The auteurs are here.

Auteur, the French term for "author," was once used to describe a film director who had total control over a film's style, content, and delivery. In many respects, today's writers are auteurs, with more options now for controlling the reception of their work. Auteurs understand genres and conventions, but they know as well how to manipulate them, make games work to their purposes, and add some fun and even irony to their writing.

Machinima is a new form of auteurism that uses video game systems to produce animated movies. (*Machinima* is pronounced "machine-i-ma.") Writers script dialogue or record interviews, game players perform actions to suit the dialogue, and a sound person records and syncs the game play with the audio to produce a movie. With a video game machine and a computer, you can record it all, then publish it to the Web. Amateur machinima artists now make films for MTV, Spike TV, and other cable channels. *Red vs. Blue* (or RvB), made by RoosterTeeth, is the most popular machinima on the Web. Its website http://rvb.roosterteeth.com/home.php has 444,000 registered users who write more than 6 million forum messages per year. There are already 79 episodes of RvB.

Only Connect . . .

Machinima

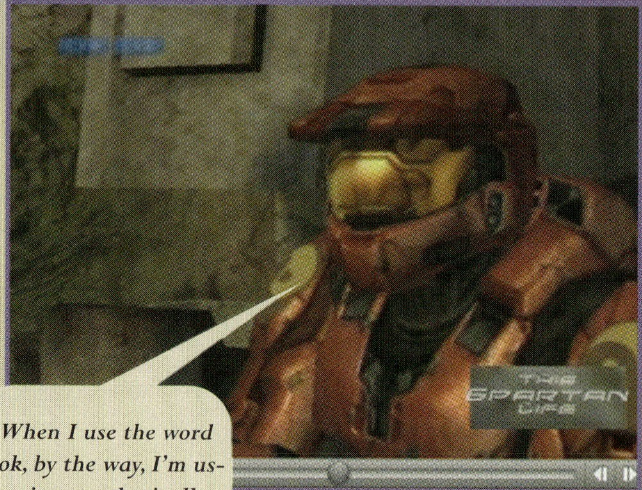

"When I use the word book, by the way, I'm using it metaphorically. Not the objects, but the vehicle that humans use to move heavy ideas around, big ideas around, and that vehicle is shifting from page to screen."
— **Bob Stein**

At **This Spartan Life: A Talk Show in Game Space** (http://www.thisspartanlife.com), Chris Burke interviewed Bob Stein, maker of the first multimedia CD ever, founder of the Voyager Company with its 300 films and 75 CD companion titles, creator of the TK3 multimedia ebook authoring software, and now director of the Institute for the Future of the Book, which has developed Sophie, the next generation of multimedia authoring tools. The setting is the video game *Halo 2*.

So, You Want to Be a Director?

Invent and **create** stories for machinima films:
Read Paul Marino's *3D Game-Based Filmmaking: The Art of Machinima* (2004)

Connect with machinimists
http://www.machinima.com

Read *Machinimag*
http://www.machinimag.com

Abbreviations are considerably shortened versions of words or brief phrases, typically ending with a period. Some abbreviations are used widely.

Titles:	Mrs., Ms., Mr., Dr., R.N.
Periods of the day:	11 a.m. (before noon), 11 p.m. (after noon)
Periods of history:	325 B.C.E. (before the common era)
	23 C.E. (common era)
	34 B.C. (before Christ)
	A.D. 783 (anno domini, "in the year of our Lord")
Time zones:	GMT (Greenwich Mean Time)
	PST (Pacific Standard Time)
	EST (Eastern Standard Time)

Other abbreviations, such as *mm* for *millimeter,* are most often used in specific kinds of writing, such as technical and scientific reports.

Acronyms are formed from the first letters of the major words that comprise longer phrases, and they are pronounced as words: *NATO* stands for *North Atlantic Treaty Organization.* You do not usually use periods with acronyms. **Initialisms** also consist of the first letters of a series of words. But unlike acronyms, which are pronounced as words, initialisms are pronounced by saying the letters individually, as in *FBI.* Initialisms are usually capitalized but do not usually include periods. If you do choose to use periods in initialisms, be consistent throughout the piece of writing.

Abbreviations save space and help writers avoid annoying repetition, but in academic writing clarity is more important than brevity, so use abbreviations sparingly in nontechnical academic writing. For example, spell out the names of disciplines (*sociology,* not *soc.*), and use the phrase *and so forth* or *and so on* instead of *etc.*

Use appropriate abbreviations in technical and scientific writing or research papers and in forms, statistics, graphs, and charts.

Spelling Out the Meaning on First Use

The first time you use an abbreviation, write the word or term out in full and put the abbreviation or acronym immediately after it in parentheses. After doing so, you can use just the abbreviation.

Use the standard form of abbreviation. For example, use *mph* (or *m.p.h.)* for *miles per hour,* not *MPH.*

Example 1 Writing out most words in formal academic writing

No Angela Davis taught philosophy at the **Univ.** of **Calif., L.A.,** from 1969–1970.

Yes Angela Davis taught philosophy at the **University** of **California, Los Angeles,** from 1969 to 1970.

No Benedict Arnold and Ethan Allen joined forces against **Ft.** Ticonderoga; later, Arnold destroyed a **no.** of ships in the **n. pt.** of **Lk.** Champlain.

Yes Benedict Arnold and Ethan Allen joined forces against **Fort** Ticonderoga; later, Arnold destroyed a **number** of ships in the **northern part** of **Lake** Champlain.

Example 2 Defining abbreviations on first mention

Many users expect that their Local Area Network **(LAN)** will function without fail; however, **LAN** administrators often experience daily troubles with their hardware.

- In long documents, consider writing out the full term, followed by its abbreviation, the first time the term is used in a major section or chapter.
- Don't use abbreviations or acronyms for words or phrases that appear only once or twice in your paper; spell them out. The exception is well-known abbreviations or acronyms such as *OPEC.*

Example 3 Making abbreviations plural

No internal punctuation	vols., HMOs, RVs, PhDs
Internal punctuation	*op. cit.*'s are rare in citation styles
Units of measure	ft. (for *foot* or *feet*), cm (for *centimeter* or *centimeters*)

- No internal punctuation is needed in abbreviations of academic degrees: *MA, PhD, JD*.
- Periods are used within abbreviations of proper names *(W. E. B. DuBois)* and time designations *(a.m.)*.

Making Abbreviations Plural

To form the plural of abbreviations or acronyms that do not use internal punctuation, simply add *s*. For those that do use internal punctuation, add an apostrophe and an *s*: *'s*. Usually, the plural of an abbreviation for a unit of measure is the same as the singular.

Abbreviating Titles, Ranks, and Degrees 54b

Example 4 Abbreviating titles, ranks, and degrees

- **Abbreviated:**

Rev. stands for *Reverend*	*PhD* stands for *Doctor of Philosophy*
MA stands for *Master of Arts*	*JD* stands for *Juris Doctor* (doctor of law)

- **Preceded by *The*:**

When preceded by the article *The*, *Reverend* is written out in full. The same is true for *Honorable*, used as a title of respect for high government officials:

Rev. Howard	but	The Reverend Howard
Hon. Gov. Rendell	but	The Honorable Governor Edward Rendell

- **Spelled out unless followed by a first name or initial:**

Senator	Senator Kennedy	Sen. Edward Kennedy
President	President Bush	Pres. George W. Bush
Professor	Professor Hatashi	Prof. K. Hatashi

- **Academic degrees standing alone:**

Madeleine Albright earned her **MA** and **PhD** from Columbia University, her **BA** from Wellesley College.

Titles commonly used either before *(Mr., Mrs., Ms., Rev.)* or after names *(Jr., MD, MA, PhD)* are regularly abbreviated.

Certain titles can be preceded by the article *The*. When they are, the title is spelled out.

Other titles are usually given in full, although they can be abbreviated if they are placed before a first name or initial.

Academic degrees are indicated either by an abbreviation before the name or by an abbreviation after it, but not both together. First letters are capitalized. Abbreviations for academic degrees can stand alone.

54c Abbreviating Names of Agencies and Organizations

Write out the names of organizations, companies, and government agencies in full, unless they are commonly referred to by abbreviations.

Example 5 Writing names of agencies and organizations

Write out the names of organizations:

Royal Geographic Society The Allstate Corporation
Pennsylvania Coalition Against Domestic Violence Avon Products

But use abbreviations for organizations known by their abbreviations:

USDA	United States Department of Agriculture
FedEx	Federal Express
NBA	National Basketball Association

54d Abbreviating Place Names

The names of states, countries, provinces, regions, and continents are not usually abbreviated unless they are part of an address, although some countries are commonly referred to by abbreviations: *UK, USA.* State names should be written out in full in formal writing, unless they are part of a specific address. When a state name appears in a sentence after a city name, it is preceded and followed by a comma.

Example 6 Writing place names

No	Sarita Perez lived on Euclid **Ave.** in Pittsburgh, **PA,** for three years.
Yes	Sarita Perez lived on Euclid **Avenue** in Pittsburgh, **Pennsylvania,** for three years.
Yes	Sarita Perez lived at 345 Euclid Avenue, Pittsburgh, PA, 15120, for three years.

When state names are part of a specific address, they are abbreviated using the United States postal codes. For a list of postal codes, go to the United States Postal Service website:
http://www.usps.com/ncsc/lookups/usps_abbreviations.html#suffix

54e Abbreviating Units of Measure

You can use abbreviations for units of measure that accompany numbers, but it is generally better to write both the number and the unit of measure out in full in nontechnical academic writing. However, in technical writing that

Example 7 Writing out numbers and units of measure in nontechnical academic writing

It took her **fifteen minutes** to complete the task.
He traveled over **fifteen thousand miles** during the **six**-month period.
The new wall was **twenty feet** taller than the old one.

includes numerous units of measure (*cm, mm*), periods of time (*yr*), and acronyms (*URL, LAN*), abbreviations are expected.

In scientific and technical writing, periods are usually omitted unless doing so would cause confusion (*in* versus *in.* for *inch*). Periods are not typically used with metric measurements.

When the unit of measure is not well known to readers, offer an equivalent, in familiar units, within parentheses immediately after the abbreviation.

Typical Abbreviations for Units of Measure

1 qt.	15 oz.	7½ in.	12° F (Fahrenheit)
3 yd.	3 tsp.	10 kg	–6 K (Kelvin)
750 lb.	30 mpg	15 km	33° C (Celsius)

Example 8 Providing a familiar equivalent for an unfamiliar unit

The first Olympic marathon was 40 km (24.85 **miles**). Today, the word *marathon* refers to a running event of 42.195 km (26 **miles** and 385 **yards**).

Using Signs and Symbols 54f

Use the dollar sign ($) as an abbreviation for the word *dollar* only when you are referring to a specific sum of money. Similarly, when you are reporting percentages in a nontechnical document in the humanities, spell out % as *percent*. In a document that reports data, use the percent symbol: %.

Use symbols such as +, –, =, and # only in tables, charts, and graphs or in technical writing. An exception is the @ sign, which you should use when you include an email address in your text.

Example 9 Using $ only with specific amounts

You had to pay **$7.50** for a movie ticket?

The Defense Department asked for an additional **$5 billion** for the war on terrorism.

How many **dollars** do you have in your wallet right now?

Example 10 Using % only in documents that report data

The news media report that fewer than **50 percent** of registered voters actually vote in the November elections. [Nontechnical source]

I think you will find that the **percentage** is far higher this year. [The % sign is never a proper replacement for *percentage*.]

In our survey of self-described "Internet junkies," **43%** of the respondents reported that they frequently google their last names, while another **32%** admitted that they compare numbers of hits with their friends. [Document that reports data]

54g Using Abbreviations for Latin Expressions

Use Latin abbreviations sparingly in your academic writing. Most can be easily translated into their English equivalents.

Note: You can use the abbreviations to the right when documenting sources or in parenthetical citations.

Abbreviation	Latin Term	English Equivalent
i.e.	id est	that is
N.B.	nota bene	note well
cf.	confer	compare
viz.	videlicet	namely
e.g.	exempli gratia	for example
et al.	et alia	and others
etc.	et cetera	and so on

54h Using Abbreviations for Book Divisions

There are a number of common abbreviations for parts of books. These can be used in footnotes, parenthetical citations, and works cited lists, but not in the body of your text.

Note: The MLA and APA documentation styles have different conventions regarding the use of these abbreviations, so check the style manuals to ensure correct usage.

Abbreviations for Parts of a Book

bk. (book)
vol., vols. (volume, volumes)
ch. or chap., chs. or chaps. (chapter, chapters)
p., pp. (page, pages)
pt. (part)
sec. or sect. (section)

Activity 54-1: Editing Abbreviations

Edit the following paragraph from the draft of a psychology paper. You may need to spell out abbreviations, add abbreviations, or add punctuation to abbreviations.

Subjects, all of whom attended the U. of Phil, were recruited from several states, including NY, PA, and OH. A no. of the subj. already had Ba degrees; several had M.A.'s. The Minnesota Multiphasic Personality Inventory (M.m.P.i.) was administered to each subject at the beginning of the study. Subjects were then asked to complete a puzzle; the average time of completion was fifteen min. Forty % of the subjects were able to complete the puzzle in under fifteen min.

55 NUMBERS

Numbers can be spelled out in words (*five, ten thousand, three-quarters*) or written as numerals (*17, 2001, 10,354*). Writers in scientific disciplines frequently use numerals in their texts; those in the humanities tend to use a combination of spelled-out numbers and numerals. Whatever the context, you want your use of numbers to be as clear as possible. The various conventions described in this chapter govern the use of numbers in academic writing.

55a Cardinal Numbers

Cardinal numbers are the numbers used in counting. They may be written either in words (*one, two, three*) or in numerals (*1, 2, 3*). The various style manuals have different recommendations for choosing between the two forms.

The context in which numbers appear will help determine whether they should be written as words or numerals. In writing for a general, nontechnical audience, use words for whole numbers, for numbers that can be spelled out in one or two words, and for inexact amounts. In technical contexts, use numerals before units of measurement, and consult the style manual for the field to make sure other uses of numbers conform to the expectations of your audience.

Example 1 MLA style for numbers

one	two hundred	three-quarters	55,372
fifteen hundred	thirty-five thousand	five-eighths	1,300,541
thirty-five	three million	six billion	1,095

- Spell out all numbers that are one or two words long and use numerals for those that are longer.
- Spelled-out numbers from 21 to 99 are hyphenated: *twenty-one, eighty-eight, ninety-nine*. Hyphenated numbers count as one word, so you would still spell out *thirty-five thousand*.

Example 2 APA style for numbers

one	11	5-mile race
99	1,200	16-year-old girl
300	13,466	

- Spell out the numbers from one to nine and use numerals for all numbers 10 and above.
- Spell out numbers at the beginning of a sentence and use numerals for measured amounts.

Example 3 Writing numbers

No	**3,705** people voted for the incumbent.
Awkward	**Three thousand seven hundred five** people voted for the incumbent.
Yes	The incumbent received 3,705 votes.

Ordinal Numbers 55b

Ordinal numbers are used to express the sequence or order of things. They too may be written either in words (*first, second, third*) or in numerals (*1st, 2nd, 3rd*). For ordinal numbers, follow the same rules as for cardinal numbers.

If you refer to centuries when writing in the humanities, spell them out.

Example 4 Writing ordinal numbers

I was in **second** place this year, but **first** last year.
He was the **fourth** in line to the crown.

Example 5 Referring to centuries in the humanities

The **twentieth** century was a period of extraordinary change and upheaval.

Combining Words and Numerals 55c

When you use specific numbers frequently—for example, statistics, temperatures, or percentages—it is acceptable to use numerals. Otherwise, combine words and numbers in order to make your writing as clear as possible to the reader.

Within a sentence or a longer passage when you are using numbers to refer to items that belong in the same category or to express a range, use numerals and be consistent. This allows the reader to more easily identify the numbers and make comparisons.

When numbers follow each other in a sentence, use a numeral for one and words for the other, for the sake of clarity.

In a sentence where one number stands alone and the others form a series of related numbers, it makes sense to spell out the single number and provide the rest as numerals.

Combine words and numerals to express large round numbers.

Example 6 Using numerals in comparisons

In April, the company produced **15** new models; in June, **2,000;** and by December, it was turning out **2,500** models per week.

Between **1,000** and **3,500** pedestrians cross that street every weekday.

Example 7 Combining words and numerals

Sixteen 18-wheeler trucks just drove by the house.
I'd like **one hundred 3⁄4-**inch nails, please.

Example 8 Distinguishing between types of numbers

Over the course of a month, the **three** friends each increased the distance they ran from **2,** to **5,** to **8** miles per day.

Example 9 Writing large round numbers

New statistics reveal that **1.7 million** jobs were lost last year.
The meteorite hit Earth approximately **300 million** years ago.

55d Punctuating Numbers and Making Them Plural

Commas

Use commas in numerals with four or more digits (five or more digits in CSE style). Starting from where the decimal point would be, place a comma after each group of three digits, to indicate thousands, millions, and so on. Don't use the comma in numbers used to express calendar years.

Example 10 Using commas with numbers

4,000 100,534 50,000 1,546,378

But 1066 CE

Hyphens

Don't use a hyphen to link a number or a fraction to the word it modifies if that word stands alone, but do use a hyphen to link a number and a word that together modify a following noun.

Example 11 Using hyphens with numbers

2.5 gigabytes	2.5-gigabyte memory disk
3/4 mile	3/4-mile road race

Example 12 Using hyphens to help distinguish numbers

She asked me to buy 3 six-packs of diet cola, 1 two-liter bottle of ginger ale, and 5 gallons of milk.

Spaces

Put a space between a number and the word it modifies, unless they are connected by a hyphen. If you are formatting your fractions as full-size numbers arranged horizontally, insert a space between the whole number and the fraction.

Example 13 Using spaces with numbers

There are four 1/8-inch drill bits missing from my toolbox.

The spider spun 14 1/2 feet of web in under a day. [Otherwise, the number could be read as $^{141}/_{2}$.]

Plurals

You can make a number plural by adding the letter *s*. When referring to decades, be sure to include the century.

Example 14 Making numbers plural

No I loved the 80's.

No I loved the eighties.

Yes I loved the 1980s.

 My wallet is full of 10s and 20s.

Using Numerals for Exact Measurements 55e

Numerals are typically used with abbreviations for units of measure and with exact measurements.

Numerals for Exact Measurements

Decimals	1.07		
Measured amounts	17° Celsius	3.5 gallons	12 feet
	32° F	25% (or 25 percent)	
Statistics, scores, ratios, surveys	8–5 (score)	a 3-to-1 ratio; 3:1	
	9 out of 10	a mean of 12	
Rates of speed	120 mph	4,500 rpm	25 kmh
Large or non-even amounts of money	$25,000	$1.5 million	
	$7.99		

Note: For nontechnical writing, most style guides allow the use of either numerals or words for percentages and even amounts of money. If you use a symbol (%, $, ¢) for the unit, however, you must use a numeral for the quantity.

For clarity, use numerals to express fractions, unless they are common fractions used in a nontechnical context.

Example 15 Writing fractions

Nontechnical	I will be home in half an hour. Make that a quarter of an hour.
Technical	Ground water indirectly contributes 1/4 of the water input to Calliope River.

Using Words for Inexact Amounts 55f

Spell out inexact or approximate numbers.

Example 16 Writing approximate numbers

The wall was about **five** feet tall.
There were approximately a **hundred** people at the demonstration.

Using Numerals for Dates and Times 55g

Dates and times should generally be written in numerals. But in nontechnical writing, spell out dates written in ordinal numbers and spell out times incorporating words like *past, after, to,* and *o'clock.*

Numerals for Most Dates and Times

Dates	35 BCE	AD 1666	350 CE	the 1960s
	the twenty-first century	April 15, 1955 or 15 April 1955		
	November fifth	from 1914 to 1918		
	between 1860 and 1923			
Time of day	11:15	2315 hrs	9 a.m.	3 p.m. (not three p.m.)
	three o'clock in the morning (not 3 o'clock)			
	half past seven			

55g

Note: When specifying a range of numbers in text, use the word *to* instead of a dash.

No — From **1954–1972,** Cold War fears found expression in science fiction films like *Them* and *Night of the Lepus*.

Yes — From **1954 to 1972,** Cold War fears found expression in science fiction films like *Them* and *Night of the Lepus*.

55h Using Numerals for Parts of Books and Plays

Use numerals to refer to parts of books (volumes, chapters, and pages) and plays (acts, scenes, and lines).

Numerals for Parts of Books and Plays

Volumes, chapters, pages	Volume 3 Chapter 10 page 205 or p. 205 or pp. 200–205
Acts, scenes, lines	*Oleanna* Act I, scene i, lines 5–10 or *Oleanna* I.i.5–10

55i Other Uses of Numerals

Use numerals for addresses, routes, phone numbers, television channels, radio stations, and social security numbers.

Numerals for Various Types of Numbers

Addresses	1600 Pennsylvania Avenue Washington, DC 20500	P.O. Box 312 Interstate 91
Telephone numbers	202-456-1111 (comments line for White House)	
Television and radio stations	Channel 22	WAMC FM 90.3
Social security numbers	101-01-1000	

Activity 55-1: Editing Numbers

Edit the following paragraph using MLA style for use of numbers.

The 1960's were a tempestuous time, as the novel clearly demonstrates. The novel begins with a diary entry of Anne's, dated January fifth, nineteen-sixty. In this entry, Anne 1st begins by describing the $one dollar she spent to purchase the diary and then moves on to summarizing the news. Anne's 3 younger siblings allow the author to explore the various aspects of at least 1-third of her childhood in the sixties.

Used for the first time in the early sixteenth century, italic is a style of lettering, or font style, that is slanted to the right: *this is italic.* Before the emergence of word processing, which made italicizing selected text a simple matter, italics were indicated by underlining. Current MLA guidelines recommend that italics be used in place of underlining.

56a Use Italics for Titles of Long Works

Use italics to indicate the titles of long works or of works that are subdivided into parts. (For short works, see section 52d.) For example, italicize these titles:

Book:	*The Eyre Affair*
Newspaper:	*New York Times*, *Washington Post*
Journal:	*A Cancer Journal for Clinicians*
Magazine:	*People*
Ezine:	*Y3K Software News*
Weblog:	*Shadow of the Hegemon*
Film:	*Wizard of Oz*
Television show:	*The Sopranos*
Radio program:	*Morning Sedition*
Play:	*Hamlet*
Long poem:	*In Memoriam*
Long musical work, CD, record album:	*And All That Might Have Been*
Painting, drawing, sculpture, dance:	*Ground Level Overlay*
Cartoon or comic strip that appears regularly:	*Doonesbury*
Computer game:	*Battlefield: Vietnam*
Pamphlet:	*Men 18–25 Years*

Note: Italicize an article (*A*, *An*, or *The*) only if it is part of the title. The definite article can be left off newspaper titles: *New York Times* instead of *The New York Times.*

56a

Don't italicize names of major religious works, books of the Bible, or legal documents.

Don't italicize the title of your own essay, story, or poem on the title page, but do put the title in quotation marks if you refer to the work elsewhere.

Do not use any italics or quotation marks for major religious works, books of the Bible, or legal documents

Major religious work	Bible, Qur'an, Torah
Book of the Bible	Leviticus, Nehemiah, James
Public, legal, or classic document	Declaration of Independence, Magna Carta, Charter of the United Nations

56b Take Care When Using Italics or Underlining for Emphasis

Be careful about overusing quotation marks or underlining to emphasize words; this practice can quickly become annoying to your audience. Instead, choose your words carefully and use sentence structures deliberately to indicate special emphasis.

Example 1 Using italics for emphasis

Original — He *says* he would never resort to *mere* rhetoric, but his *actions* speak louder than his *words*.

Revised — He claims he would never resort to mere rhetoric, but his actions speak louder than his words.

56c Use Italics for Words and Letters Referred to as Such

Italicize words, letters, and numbers when they are used to refer to themselves or when they are being defined.

Example 2 Using italics to refer to words, letters, and numbers

The word *weird* is derived from Old English.

Spell out *5* as *five* unless exact quantities are critical or you're reporting data.

Speakers of Maay-Maay from Somalia may have trouble distinguishing the English sound *b* from the sound for *p*.

56d Use Italics for the Names of Spacecraft, Aircraft, Ships, and Trains

Use italics for the names of specific trains and other crafts, but not for kinds of vehicles or craft.

Use italics for names of specific individual crafts

The *Columbia* disaster   H.M.S. *Queen Elizabeth II*   *Air Force One*

But do not italicize names of categories of vehicles or types of crafts

the Ford Mustang   a Baycraft sailboat   United Airlines DC-10

Use Italics for Some Foreign Words and Phrases 56e

Example 3 Using italics with foreign words and phrases

FOREIGN WORD IN COMMON USE—NO ITALICS:

When he missed the piñata, he struck me in the face with the stick.

FOREIGN PHRASE NOT IN COMMON USE—USE ITALICS:

He spoke *ad nauseam* about the state of his liver, so I wanted to bolt from the table.

LATIN NAME IN NONSCIENTIFIC WRITING—USE ITALICS:

While searching for rare birds, we saw a *Pterocles coronatus* alight nearby.

COMMON LATIN ABBREVIATIONS—NO ITALICS:

Q.E.D. (which has been shown)

N.B. (Note carefully)

viz. (that is to say or namely)

Italicize foreign words and phrases only if they are not in common use. If you don't know whether a term is in common use, consult a dictionary.

Italicize Latin names of plants and animals, except in scientific/technical contexts where they are more commonly used.

Substitutes for Italics in Email Messages 56f

Example 4 Substituting for italics in email

I want to read that book _The Monuments of Mars: A City on the Edge of Forever_ by Richard Hoagland.

Email programs that require plain text and thus limit text styling do not allow you to use italics or underlining, so use a pair of underscores to set off words or terms you would normally italicize.

Activity 56-1: Editing for Italics

Edit the following paragraph for the use of italics.

When surveyed about their news preferences, only a small percentage of people said that they read papers of national importance such as The New York Times or The Washington Post. More people read USA Today than either of those two papers. People also expressed a preference for reading news online—many of them said that they read the BBC News or Guardian Online websites to gain an international perspective on events. Online news has become almost as popular as television news broadcasts, although shows such as Nightline and Crossfire still remain popular. Few people pick up books on current events, although many in the study said that they had read Bill Clinton's autobiography, My Life, and James Cameron's account of the Titanic's treasures.

57

CAPITALIZATION

Capital letters give writing clarity. They tell readers when a new sentence starts, and they highlight the names of people, places, and things.

Incorrectly capitalized words can confuse readers. When you don't use capital letters at all, readers have trouble finding where sentences start. When you capitalize every letter, readers have trouble taking in words at a glance, because they rely on variation across the individual letters to decipher them quickly. Experienced emailers know that capitalizing too much text comes across as shouting to readers: WATCH OUT!

Learning when to use capital letters is not difficult except, as usual, for special cases, some of which we will cover in this chapter. There are two general rules to keep in mind. First, always capitalize the first word of a complete sentence. Second, capitalize proper nouns (names of people and places, official titles, brand names), proper adjectives, and all significant words in a title.

When you are uncertain about whether a word should be capitalized, look it up in a good college dictionary.

Complete Sentences

- **After a colon, capitalize or do not capitalize a sentence, as you choose; do not capitalize a phrase.**

Hammurabi's Code seems harsh today: **It** [or **it**] called, quite literally, for "an eye for an eye."

The material after the colon has a subject, *It,* and a verb, *called,* but no subordinating word; it is an independent clause. Compare the clause with the material after the colon in this sentence, which has no subject or verb:

My department manager has one major concern: **overspending** in my department.

- **After a colon, capitalize a question.**

Darius III came to his throne by way of a string of murders: **Didn't** his own later murder mark the end of the Persian Empire?

- **In free-standing parentheses, capitalize.**

Most full-time jobs offer some form of health insurance. (**If** health insurance costs keep rising at this rate, only employers from the largest corporations will be able to offer any kind of insurance.)

- **In parentheses within another sentence, do not capitalize.**

Helen wished that she could afford to buy a new car (**this** car, she thought, is a real wreck!), but she knew she was lucky to own even her old Ford Escort.

- **Between dashes within another sentence, do not capitalize.**

Cellular bonding—the process has been a common laboratory procedure for generations—is normally taught in the second semester.

Intentional Sentence Fragments

Hey, you!
Whatever.
Honest?
Yikes!

The first word of a sentence always begins with a capital letter:

> **H**ammurabi was the king of Babylonia.
> **H**e is known for his far-reaching code of laws.
> **H**ave you heard of it?

If you write a complete sentence *after* a colon, you can choose either to capitalize the first word of that sentence or to use a lowercase letter. Both options are correct, but you should choose the style you prefer and use it consistently in a document. When the information after a colon is not a complete sentence, use a lowercase letter to begin the phrase.

If a question follows a colon, capitalize the first word of the question.

When you write a complete sentence in parentheses, capitalize the first word and end the sentence with the period, question mark, or exclamation mark inside the parentheses. However, if the parenthetical comment is *within* another sentence, do not capitalize the first word or use an end period in the parentheses, although you can use an exclamation point or question mark if necessary.

It is customary *not* to capitalize the first word of a sentence enclosed by dashes.

Capitalize the first word of intentional sentence fragments.

Proper nouns are used to designate specific people, places, and things. They are capitalized except in rare cases in which a person has managed to establish (legally or otherwise) unconventional usage. Sometimes a phrase with a proper noun includes a common noun that is capitalized as part of the phrase—the word *mountains* in *Rocky Mountains,* for example.

Proper adjectives are adjectives formed from proper nouns: *Marxist* is formed from *Karl Marx*. They are always capitalized. If you use a hyphen to combine a proper noun with another word in order to form an adjective, capitalize only the proper noun: ***French**-speaking.* Don't capitalize prefixes used with proper adjectives—for example, ***pre**-Columbian*—except when they appear in titles or begin a sentence.

Proper Nouns and Adjectives

	Capitalize	But don't capitalize
Names of people and characters and adjectives formed from their names	Emma Goldman; Charles Darwin, Darwinian; Mother Jones; Mom, Mother, Dad [emphasizes the named individual]. Some people, such as writer *bell hooks* and poet *e. e. cummings,* do not capitalize their names. Follow their lead, but use capitalization if the name begins the sentence (e.g., E. E. Cummings). Aunt Helen Grandpa Joe Harry Potter	 my mom, my mother, my dad [emphasizes relationship]. Some names include elements such as *van, ten, de,* and *der,* which should not be capitalized unless the individual traditionally does so. your aunt Robert's grandfather Joe
Titles	Senator Rick Santorum President Clinton, the President of the United States Condoleezza Rice, National Security Advisor the Vice President for Academic Affairs	the senator the president, a president, a former president a new national security advisor the vice president
Academic degrees	Harold K. Oates, PhD Dr. Atkins	a doctor of philosophy the doctor
National, political, and ethnic groups	South African, Mexican; Republican, Democrat, Maoist; Latina, Hispanic, African American, Black, White Note that the words *black* and *white* used to refer to race can be either capitalized or spelled lowercase, depending on your preference. Whichever you choose, be consistent throughout your text.	upper middle class [a socioeconomic group], black, white

	Capitalize	But don't capitalize
Names for God, religious leaders, religious groups, and sacred books	God, Allah, Zeus, Diana; the Buddha, the Dalai Lama, the Pope; Baptists, Islam, Islamic, Jews, Jewish; the Qur'an, Koranic, the Bible, the Torah, Scripture	gods and goddesses; a priest, rabbi, or pastor; a religion; religious people or group; a holy book, biblical times; scriptural interpretation
Languages	French, Kiswahili, Arabic	
Organizations, companies, clubs	National Organization for Women, Bard College, Halliburton, Fox Network, WiFi Communications, Lions Club	the company, the club
Trademarked products and brand names	Rice-a-Roni, Big Mac, Subaru Legacy, BCBG Max Azria	
Place names and geographic regions and features	Las Vegas, Nevada; the Northeast, the Badlands [regions]; the Snake River; the Pyrenees Mountains	to the north, south of Baghdad, east of Eden [directions]
Buildings, monuments, and bridges	Empire State Building, the Washington Monument, the Golden Gate Bridge	
Academic courses	English 103, Psychology of Women, Introduction to Chemistry	introductory chemistry course
Specific time periods, historical events, and significant historical documents	Mesozoic Era, the Ming Dynasty, the Renaissance; the Civil Rights Movement, World War Two, the American Revolution; the Declaration of Independence, the Magna Carta	medieval, renaissance, a declaration of independence
Literary, artistic, and cultural movements	Formalism, Dadaism, the Beat Generation	
Days, months, holidays	Sunday, New Year's Day, February, St. Patrick's Day, Hanukkah	spring, summer, fall, winter
Scientific and technical terms	Mars, Jupiter, Earth [when discussed as a planet]; Milky Way	
Acronyms and initialisms	DNA, OPEC, UN, NATO	

57c Using Capital Letters in Titles

In MLA style, all significant words in the titles of books, articles in journals and magazines, movies, television shows, plays, newspaper stories, and works of art are capitalized.

In APA reference lists, capitalize the first word of a title, proper nouns and proper adjectives, and the first word after a colon: *Blink: The power of thinking without thinking*. However, capitalize all important words in journal names: *Journal of Family Psychology*.

In CMS style, capitalize every major word of the title and the first and last words of both title and subtitle. Use lowercase for articles *a*, *an*, and *the;* conjunctions *and*, *but*, *for*, *or*, and *nor;* the words *to* and *as;* and most prepositions, except when they are emphasized: *The Devil in the White City: Murder, Magic, and Madness at the Fair That Changed America*.

Capitalization in Titles, MLA Style

Book	*The Mind at Night: The New Science of How and Why We Dream*
	Harry Potter and the Half-Blood Prince
Essay	"Eight Simple Rules for Dating My Daughter"
Movie	*Star Wars: Revenge of the Sith*
Painting	*Water Lilies*

In MLA style, capitalize

- the first and last word of the title
- the first and last word of a subtitle that follows a colon
- all other major words, including those that follow hyphens

Certain words are not capitalized, unless they appear at the beginning or end of the title or subtitle:

- prepositions (such as *on, in, at*)
- coordinating conjunctions (*and, but, or, nor, for, so, yet*)
- articles (*a, an, the*)
- the word *to* in infinitives

57d Using Capital Letters When Quoting Prose

Whether you capitalize the first word in a quotation depends on the material you are quoting and where you place it in your sentence. If you are quoting a complete sentence or starting a sentence with a quotation, capitalize the first word. However, if you are quoting directly from another work using a verb such as *said* or *stated,* capitalize the first word of the quoted material only if it is capitalized in the original work.

Capitalization When Quoting Prose

Capitalize the first word of a quotation . . .

- **when quoting a complete sentence:**

  George told me, "Don't recycle that kind of plastic anymore."

  Walker writes, "Womanism is the fullest expression of life." [Capital letter used in original work]

  Gladwell said Levi's had found that "baby boomer men felt that the chief thing missing from their lives was male friendship." [No capital letter in original]

- **when beginning your sentence with a quotation:**

  "Of the many ways to fail on a dating website, not posting a photo of yourself is perhaps the most certain," claim Levitt and Dubner (82).

Do not capitalize the first word of a quotation . . .

- **if the quotation is not a complete sentence:**

  Walker describes a "system wherein slave labor is turned into capital."

  The best way to investigate a story is "to follow the money."

- **if the quotation follows an interruption created by your own words:**

  "When my sister eats popcorn," he explained, "she loves to watch a movie."

57d Do not capitalize a quotation if it is not a complete sentence.

When you interrupt a quoted sentence with your own words, don't capitalize the first word after your interruption.

Using Capital Letters When Quoting Poetry 57e

Capitalization When Quoting Poetry

- **First word of line capitalized in original:**

  When Donne wrote "That thou may'st know me" (42), he was admitting that full disclosure was critical to salvation. . . .

- **First word of line not capitalized in original:**

  In "anyone lived in a pretty how town," e. e. cummings writes, "she laughed his joy she cried his grief" (14).

Capitalize the first word in each line of quoted poetry if the poet has done so. If the poet has not used capitals, neither should you.

Capitalizing the Pronoun *I* and the Interjection *O* 57f

Example 1 *I* and *O*

Look at the new grow light I bought for my tomatoes.

O, Brother Where Art Thou? [A movie title]

Always capitalize the pronoun *I*, no matter where it appears in a sentence. Similarly, most people always capitalize the interjection *O*. This convention does not apply to the interjection *oh*, which should not be capitalized unless it begins a sentence or is capitalized in the original.

Using Capital Letters in the Parts of a Letter 57g

Capitalization in Letters

Greetings	**Closings**
To Whom It May Concern:	Sincerely yours,
Dear Sir:	Best regards,
Dearest Friend,	All my love,

Capitalize all the words in a greeting (called the salutation) at the beginning of a letter. However, when you write the closing, capitalize only the first word.

57h Using Capitals with Abstractions

Although words for abstract concepts like *liberty, happiness,* or *freedom* normally start with a lowercase letter, they can be capitalized when you are discussing the concepts as topics or want to emphasize them. This style of capitalization is somewhat unusual in contemporary writing.

Example 2 Capitalizing abstractions

Frenchman Maximilien Robespierre claimed he beheaded reactionaries in the name of Liberty, Equality, and Fraternity.

I think that Freedom is worth dying for.

57i Using Capital Letters in Lists

When the list items are complete sentences, you should generally use a capital letter to start off each item in the following kinds of lists:

- lists within a paragraph (called run-in lists)
- lists displayed vertically
- formal outlines
- series of questions

When the list items are not complete sentences but are arranged vertically or are in the form of questions, you may capitalize or not as you choose, but be consistent throughout a writing project. When the list items in a run-in list are not complete sentences or questions, do not capitalize the first word of each item.

Example 3 Capitalization in run-in lists

LIST ITEMS ARE COMPLETE SENTENCES (QUESTIONS, IN THIS CASE):

A job candidate may be asked a number of painful questions in a job interview: (1) What is your most obvious character weakness? (2) What would your current co-workers say they like least about you? (3) How well would you say you handle stressful situations?

LIST ITEMS ARE NOT COMPLETE SENTENCES:

Teach children that before they cross the street, they need to (1) stop, (2) look, and (3) listen.

Example 4 Capitalization in formal outlines

START EACH LINE WITH A CAPITAL LETTER AND END FULL SENTENCES WITH A PERIOD:

I. Communicating-to-Learn Activities
  a. Follow the principles in informal writing.
    i. Put the principles into practice daily.
    ii. Focus on elaborating content, not on correctness.
  b. Use the principles for in-class focused communication.
    i. Review course material.
    ii. Organize your discussions.
  c. Use the principles outside of class.

Example 5 Capitalization in a series of questions

QUESTIONS AFTER THE FIRST ONE MAY START WITH CAPITAL LETTERS:

What time did you find it? When? Where?

OR THEY MAY START WITH LOWERCASE LETTERS:

What time did you find it? when? where?

Using Capital Letters in Email Addresses and URLs 57j

Although most of what you encounter on the Internet is not case sensitive, all parts of a URL that appear after the domain name are case sensitive. So when tracking down a website, listing a URL in your citations or text, or sending someone a URL, make sure that you don't deviate from the capitalization used in the original URL. Email addresses are not case sensitive, so it doesn't matter whether you capitalize them or not.

Example 6 Capitalization in URLs and email addresses

THESE TWO URLS ARE THE SAME:

http://www.POWELLS.com http://www.powells.com

THESE TWO ARE *NOT* THE SAME:

http://www.virtualparlor.org/Rhetoric http://www.virtualparlor.org/rhetoric

THESE TWO EMAIL ADDRESSES ARE THE SAME:

joe.schmoe@google.com Joe.Schmoe@google.com

Activity 57-1: Editing for Capitalization

Read the paragraph below and capitalize all the words that incorrectly start with lowercase letters.

why i love *the matrix*

there are several aspects of *the matrix* that intrigue and interest me. i really enjoy the action sequences, especially the ones with agent smith and neo. apparently the main reason that these two characters fight so often and so intensely is because agent smith has been changed by his encounter with neo. when zion is threatened and neo must visit a god-like man—who reminds me of dad—in a room full of what look like sony television monitors, viewers have a chance to understand the main motivation for neo's change to a person who can control the matrix. i enjoy sci-fi because this genre challenges me to think about what life is like here on earth and what it might be like in a parallel universe. *star trek: the next generation* was one of my favorite shows when i was a kid. i suppose that tv shows like that helped me understand the world as i grew up in small-town rural america.

58

SPELLING AND HYPHENS

Attention to spelling and hyphenation in your writing communicates your respect for readers and your commitment to your ideas. Readers are more likely to give your writing serious consideration and to have confidence in what you have to say if they think you care about what you wrote. Sloppy spelling or hyphenation can indicate sloppy thinking, sloppy work habits, or just plain old do-the-least-you-can-to-get-by-ism. If you struggle with spelling, don't throw up your hands—dig in. Mastering these kinds of details takes patience and persistence.

58a Developing Good Spelling Habits

Like most things worth doing, spelling correctly takes time and practice. The guidelines that follow suggest ways to incorporate better spelling habits into your overall writing process.

The most important skill a good speller has isn't a good memory—it's knowing when to reach for the dictionary. A good speller reaches for the dictionary whenever in doubt. For most of us, that doubt arises frequently. Choose a dictionary and use it.

Some writers check their spelling as they write. Others find it important to separate the writing from the editing and proofreading stages. Otherwise, it's easy to get tangled up in details when you need to focus on substance. Even if you check spelling as you go, you'll want to review your completed writing project word by word for spelling errors and typos.

A Practical Proofreading Strategy

frenzy antibeef an promted States United the in disease mad-cow of case single a after 2004 early in point this made Jersey, New Princeton, in consultant" comunications "risk self-discribed a Sandman, Peter assesors. Risk terrible parent, Molly's like are, us of most But

From Steven D. Levitt and Stephen J. Dubner, *Freakonomics* (New York: William Morrow, 2005), 150. Reordered, with spelling and punctuation mistakes added.

Project Checklist

Developing Good Spelling Habits

- ❑ Reach for the dictionary whenever in doubt.
- ❑ Check words as you go for spelling, meaning, and usage—or save that step for after you've completed a draft. See which approach or combination of approaches works best for you. If you like to write first and think about spelling later, you can still flag words you're not sure about as you go. Simply write *(sp?)* after a word you're unsure about. Now you've flagged it for the editing and proofreading stage without slowing down the more difficult phase of composition.
- ❑ Once your draft is complete, run the spell checker and find as many errors as you can. Then print out your document, grab a pen and your dictionary, sit down in a quiet place, and check your spelling.
- ❑ When all revisions are complete, repeat the previous step and then proofread one last time. When proofreading, look for typographical errors rather than reading for substance.

Try Proofreading Backward

One proofreading strategy is to start with the last word in a document and read backward. To show you the effectiveness of this strategy, the words to the left have been arranged from last to first. Notice how your eye lingers on each word when you can't make sense of surrounding word groups, as you would naturally do when reading. What spelling errors do you find? Which words would you need to look up in a dictionary to see if they were spelled correctly?

Use a Spell Checker, but Beware!

The spell check feature in most word-processing programs can be a big help, but beware: your computer will never be as smart as you are. Spell check won't recognize when you use *it's* incorrectly for *its, who's* for *whose,* and a host of other spelling errors that depend on context as well as on the word itself.

58b Checking for Commonly Misspelled Words

Use this list of commonly misspelled words as a starting point.

225 Commonly Misspelled Words, Spelled Correctly					
absence	changeable	encouragement	inevitable	permissible	restaurant
accidentally	choose	encouraging	inoculate	perseverance	rhyme
accommodate	chose	environment	intellectual	personal	rhythm
accumulate	commission	equipped	intelligence	personnel	ridiculous
achievement	committee	especially	interesting	perspiration	roommate
acquaintance	comparative	exaggerate	irresistible	physical	sacrifice
acquire	compelled	excellence	knowledge	picnicking	sacrilegious
acquitted	complexion	exhilarate	laboratory	possession	schedule
advice	conceivable	existence	laid	possibility	seize
advise	conceive	existent	led	possible	separate
affidavit	conferred	experience	lightning	practically	separation
amateur	conscience	explanation	loneliness	precede	sergeant
analysis	conscientious	familiar	lose	precedence	severely
analyze	conscious	fascinate	maintenance	preference	siege
apparatus	controversial	February	maneuver	preferred	similar
apparent	controversy	fiery	manufacture	prejudice	sincerely
appearance	criticize	fitting	marriage	preparation	sophomore
arctic	deferred	foreign	maybe	prevalent	specifically
arguing	definitely	formerly	miniature	principal	specimen
argument	definition	forty	mischievous	principle	succeed
arithmetic	describe	fourth	misspell	privilege	succession
ascend	description	frantically	mysterious	probably	supersede
athletic	desperate	generally	necessary	procedure	surprise
attendance	dictionary	government	noticeable	proceed	technique
balance	dining	grammar	occasionally	profession	temperamental
battalion	diphtheria	grandeur	occurred	professor	tendency
beautiful	disappearance	grievous	occurrence	prominent	tragedy
beginning	disappoint	harass	omitted	pronunciation	transferring
belief	disastrous	height	opinion	pursue	truly
believe	discipline	heroes	opportunity	quantity	tyranny
beneficial	dissatisfied	hindrance	optimistic	quizzes	unanimous
benefited	dormitory	humorous	paid	recede	undoubtedly
boundaries	effect	hypocrisy	parallel	receive	unnecessary
business	eighth	hypocrite	paralysis	receiving	villain
calendar	eligible	immediately	paralyze	recommend	weather
candidate	eliminate	incidentally	particular	reference	weird
category	embarrass	incredible	pastime	referring	
cemetery	eminent	independence	performance	repetition	

Watching for Homonyms and Other Commonly Confused Words 58c

Homonyms are words that sound alike but have different meanings: *pair / pear; bare / bear; to / too / two.* Homonyms and near-homonyms, such as *accept / except, affect / effect,* and *conscience / conscious,* are a common source of misspellings. Three of the most frequently misused homonym pairs are *it's / its, you're / your,* and *who's / whose. It's* is a contraction of *it is,* whereas *its* is the possessive form of *it; you're* is a contraction of *you are,* whereas *your* is the possessive form of *you; who's* is a contraction of *who is,* whereas *whose* is the possessive form of *who.*

Watching out for homonyms and other commonly confused and misused words will improve your spelling and your writing. You will find many of these words in the Glossary of Usage that begins on page G-13 at the end of the book.

Example 1 Using *it's/its, you're/your,* and *who's/whose*

It's a wonder that our cat left **its** food untouched.

You're so possessive about **your** cat that no one else can pet her.

Who's going to drive **whose** car when we shuttle back from our bike trip?

Example 2 Using the Glossary of Usage

To find out whether *adverse* or *averse* is the appropriate word in a particular context, consult the entry in the Glossary of Usage:

> **adverse, averse** *Adverse* (adjective) means "harmful" or "unfavorable"; *averse* (adjective) means "having strong feelings of dislike or distaste for."
>
> I am **averse** to driving in **adverse** conditions.

Following Spelling Rules 58d

Knowing and following a handful of simple spelling rules can increase your spelling power considerably.

Forming Plurals

The plurals of most nouns are formed by adding *s* to the end of the word.

Nouns ending in *-s, -sh ,-ch,* or *-x* require the addition of *es* to form the plural.

Examples of Making Nouns Plural

elephant + *s* = elephants

muffin, muffin**s**

prize, prize**s**

table, table**s**

process + *es* = processes

dish, dish**es**

church, church**es**

fox, fox**es**

Nouns ending in *-o* require *s* or *es*, depending on whether the *o* is preceded by a vowel or a consonant.

Vowel: patio + *s* = patios
radio, radio**s**
taboo, taboo**s**
zoo, zoo**s**

Consonant: potato + *es* = potato*es*
tomato, tomato**es**
veto, veto**es**
Exceptions:
memo, memo**s**
solo, solo**s**
piano, piano**s**
zero, zero**s** (or zero**es**)

For nouns ending in *-y*, change *y* to *i* and add *es*.

party ⟶ part*i* + *es* = part*ies*
responsibilit**y**, responsibilit***ies***
fort**y**, fort***ies***

Nouns ending in *-f* or *-fe* vary. Some form plurals by adding *s*. For others, change *f* to *v*, and add *es* or *s*.

belief + *s* = beliefs
fife, fife**s**

cal*f* ⟶ cal*v* + *es* = cal*ves*
half, hal**ves**
leaf, lea**ves**
thief, thie**ves**
life, li**ves**
wife, wi**ves**

Closed compound nouns (compounds written as one word) take *s* or *es* at the end of the last word.

Closed Compounds

breakthrough**s**
superhero**es**
cupful**s**
teaspoonful**s**
handful**s**
toolbar**s**

For hyphenated and open compounds (that is, compounds that are two separate words), add *s* or *es* to the more significant word, usually the noun that can be counted.

Hyphenated Compounds

city-state**s**
hanger**s**-on
sister**s**-in-law

Open Compounds

child wi**ves**
civil right**s**
history major**s**

Some words form plurals irregularly.

Irregular Plurals

child, children
foot, feet
man, men
mouse, mice
ox, oxen
tooth, teeth
woman, women
deer, deer
elk, elk
fish, fish
moose, moose
series, series
sheep, sheep
species, species

Plurals from the Original Language

bacterium, bacteria
criterion, criteria
datum, data
medium, media
phenomenon, phenomena

analysis, analyses
basis, bases
crisis, crises
hypothesis, hypotheses
thesis, theses

alumnus, alumni
locus, loci
nucleus, nuclei
syllabus, syllabi

alga, algae
vertebra, vertebrae

beau, beaux
chateau, chateaux

Other Foreign-Derived Plurals in Transition

curriculum, curricul**a** *or* curricul**ums**
index, indi**ces** *or* inde**xes**

Numbers and Abbreviations

in 1980	in the 1980**s**
She scored a perfect 100.	Her SAT scores were in the 700**s**.
URL	URL**s**
CD	CD**s**

Example 3 Changes in word forms governed by spelling rules

CHANGING TO A COMPARATIVE OR SUPERLATIVE:

fat, fatter — happy, happiest

CHANGING FROM ONE PART OF SPEECH TO ANOTHER:

deputy, deputize — occur, occurrence
cry, crying — floor, floored
depend, dependable

CHANGING VERB FORMS:

worry, worries — shop, shopped

Some words borrowed from other languages form the plural according to the original language.

Note that *criteria* and *media* are plural words, although they have become such a part of the English language that they are often used with a singular meaning. Other foreign-derived words are now acceptably made plural according to rules of English spelling; *agenda,* formerly the plural of *agendum,* is now itself made plural by adding *s: agendas.*

In general, the basic *-s* or *-es* rule also applies to numerals and abbreviations.

Other Changes in Word Form

Along with the formation of plurals, spelling rules govern other changes in word form. Luckily, these rules apply to particular letters and letter groupings and remain consistent regardless of the grammatical change being made.

58d

Doubling Consonants to Retain Short Vowel Sounds

In changing word forms, the general rule is to use double consonants to retain a short vowel sound. Compare the groups of words presented here; in each case, the first group requires double consonants, and the second does not.

In words of more than one syllable in which the stress in pronunciation shifts from one syllable to another when the word changes form, do not double the consonant.

Exceptions to the doubling rules are words like *travel* and *cancel,* which can acceptably become *traveled, traveling, travels, traveler* or *travelled, travelling, travels, traveller* and *canceled, canceling* or *cancelled, cancelling,* respectively. The single *l* is the preferred spelling in American English, the double *l* in British English. Both spellings can be found in American usage dictionaries. (But make sure that you use only one spelling in your paper!)

Short Vowel Sound and Long Vowel Sound Pairs

hop, hopped, hopping
hope, hoped, hoping

slop, sloppy, sloppier, sloppiest
slope, sloping

Rule: Double the consonant when a one-syllable stem ends in one vowel and one consonant

sla***p***, sla***pp***ed, sla***pp***ing
dro***p***, dro***pp***ed, dro***pp***ing
bi***g***, bi***gg***er, bi***gg***est
slo***p***, slo***pp***y, slo***pp***ier, slo***pp***iest
sho***p***, sho***pp***ed, sho***pp***ing, sho***pp***er

Rule: Double the consonant when a stem of more than one syllable ends in one vowel and one consonant and the stress remains on that syllable

Stress remains on the short-vowel syllable—consonant doubles

infer´, inferred´, infer´ring, infer´rer
refer´, referred´, refer´ring, refer´ral
prefer´, preferred´, prefer´ring, prefer´rer

Stress shifts to another place— consonant does not double

in´ference, inferen´tial, inferen´tially
ref´erence, ref´erent, referee´, referen´tial
pref´erence, preferen´tial

Rule: Keep the final silent *e* with a suffix beginning with a consonant; drop the final silent *e* with a suffix beginning with a vowel

+ consonant: state, state*ment* + vowel: state, stat*ing*	+ consonant: force, force*ful* + vowel: force, forc*ible*
+ consonant: like, like*ly* + vowel: like, lik*ing*	+ consonant: require, require*ment* + vowel: require, requir*ing*

Exceptions:

dye, dyeing
shoe, shoeing
courage, courageous
outrage, outrageous
change, changeable
embrace, embraceable
manage, manageable
notice, noticeable
marriage, marriageable
argue, argument
due, duly
true, truly

Vowel + *y*—keep the *y*

cloy, cloying
joy, joyous
play, playful

Exceptions:

day, daily
gay, gaily

Consonant + *y*—omit the *y*

city, cities
deputy, deputize
lively, livelier

Exceptions:

dry, drying, dryly
try, trying
reply, replying

i before *e* except after *c*

achieve, retrieve, sieve, aerie, friend, pier, town crier, pliers, diet, hierarchy; ceiling, receive, inconceivable

or when pronounced "ay" as in *neighbor* or *weigh*

lei, sleigh, weight, freight, beige, dreidel, eight, rein, veil, vein

Exceptions:

-ei: weird, seize, caffeine, protein, either, neither, deity
-ie: fallacies, frequencies, species, science, society

Keeping or Dropping the Final e

Suffixes are word endings such as *-ed, -ing, -er, -est, -ance, -ment,* and *-or.* Keep a word's final silent *e* when adding a suffix that begins with a consonant. Drop a word's final silent *e* when adding a suffix that begins with a vowel.

Note that with the suffix *-ment,* the word *judge* can become either *judgment* or *judgement* (but not both in the same paper). The preferred American spelling is *judgment;* the preferred British spelling is *judgement.*

Keeping or Dropping the Final y

When adding a suffix to a word ending in *-y,* keep the final *y* when the *y* is preceded by a vowel. Change the word's final *y* to *i* when the *y* is preceded by a consonant, unless the suffix itself also begins with an *i.*

With some proper nouns, you retain the *y* (*Kennedy, Kennedyesque*); with others, you do not (*Kentucky, Kentuckian*). Check a dictionary.

The *ie* Rule

Remembering the familiar rhyme will help you use *-ie* and *-ei* properly.

i before *e* except after *c*
or when pronounced "ay"
as in *neighbor* or *weigh*

58e Using Hyphens in Compound Words

Compound words—that is, words made up of two or more words—can be open, closed, or hyphenated: *water ski, waterskiing,* and *water-skier*. Because our language is in flux, hyphens come into play as new words are coined. Some words start out open, then become hyphenated, and finally enter the dictionary as closed compounds: *on line* becomes *on-line* becomes *online*. When in doubt, use your dictionary.

Contrasting Examples

Open	Closed	Hyphenated
water ski	waterskiing	water-skier
water buffalo	waterfowl	water-resistant
water hole	waterfall	water-repellent

58f Using Hyphens with Prefixes and Suffixes

Prefixes are word parts added to the beginning of words to form new words; some examples are *re-, de-, anti-, mini-,* and *in-*. Suffixes are word parts added to the ends of words—for example *-ism, -ian, -er, -ent,* and *-ion*. Words formed with prefixes and suffixes—*cyberspace, interfaith, minivan, postmodern, socioeconomic, underemployed*—are almost always closed. But there are some exceptions.

In general, use a hyphen . . .

- **to form words with the prefix *all-, ex-* (used to mean "former"), or *self-***

  all-purpose, all-star   ex-president, ex-husband, ex-marine   self-expression

- **to form words with the suffix *-elect* or *-odd***

  president-elect, mayor-elect   hundred-odd, 350-odd

- **to join a prefix to a capitalized word**

  anti-Semitism   non-Euclidian   sub-Saharan
  pre-Columbian   post-Victorian   un-American
  mid-Atlantic   post-Vietnam

- **to join a capitalized initial to a word**

  T-shirt   I-beam   X-ray

- **to join a prefix to a number**

  pre-1950   post-2004

- **to clarify potentially ambiguous meaning**

  re-creation vs. recreation   re-dress (dress again) vs. redress (set right)
  re-ally vs. really   re-sort vs. resort

- **to enhance readability**

  anti-intellectual   wall-less
  de-ice   sub-subentry

Using Hyphens to Eliminate Ambiguity 58g

When two words modify a third, meaning can become ambiguous. Is a *camel hair brush* a hairbrush for camels or an artist's brush made out of camel hair? How about a *camel-hair brush?* The general rule is to use a hyphen to avoid ambiguity when two modifiers come before a noun. The hyphen explains how the words relate to each other, which in turn reveals what the phrase means. By this same principle, when the compound modifier follows the noun, you don't need the hyphen. *The brush made out of camel hair* is clear enough on its own.

Example 4 Using hyphens to eliminate ambiguity

an over-the-counter drug

Example 5 Exceptions: no hyphens with *-ly* adjectives, comparatives and superlatives, and proper nouns that are not themselves hyphenated

highly contagious disease
most frequent response
Civil War veterans
Bronze Age tools
French Canadian music [Music from French-speaking Canada]
But French-Canadian trade agreement [A trade agreement between Canada and France]

Using Hyphens with Numbers 58h

Numbers *twenty-one* through *ninety-nine* are hyphenated when spelled out, as are simple fractions: *one-half, three-quarters, five-eighths,* and so on. All other numbers are open.

Example 6 Using hyphens with 21–99 and with simple fractions

two-thirds, three-fifths, one and five-eighths
one hundred one, three hundred twenty-four

Numbers in compound modifiers follow the same rules as all other words: hyphenate before the noun, don't hyphenate after it.

Example 7 Using hyphens with compound modifiers that precede a noun

I wouldn't touch that with a ten-foot pole.

The ceilings soared up to ten feet.

The 165-million-year-old stegosaurus was at last on display.

One hundred sixty-five million years ago, the stegosaurus roamed the Earth.

The stegosaurus roamed the Earth more than 165 million years ago.

But percentages are always open.

Example 8 No hyphens with percentages

All employees received a 6 percent raise.

A suspended series, in which each of the words in the series connects with the last modifier to form a compound modifier, takes a hyphen.

Example 9 Using a hyphen with a suspended series

Pa Barker's general store carries ten-, twenty-, and fifty-pound bags of flour.

The 350- and 500-mile marathons put the bikers to the test.

Both over- and underfed pets suffer from nutrition problems.

But underfed and underpaid workers (*not* underfed and -paid workers)

When one element of a compound modifier is itself two words, use an en dash instead of a hyphen between the two elements. An en dash is a special character that tells the reader that the two words preceding or following it form a unit. The en dash can be found in the special characters or symbols menu of most word-processing programs; some programs allow the user to create en dashes using keystrokes.

Example 10 Using an en dash when one or both parts of a compound modifier consist of more than one word

post–Vietnam War era
a Civil War–era sword
a Los Angeles–New York flight
red-state–blue-state divide

Activity 58-1: Editing for Spelling

Edit the following paragraph for mistakes in spelling and usage.

Altho meny scientistes refoosed to except the pots provenance, carbun datting prooved that the tappestry wuz a precolumbian artefact, but the debbate over who's responsible for creatteing it continus. The peepul who mad the tapestry were acceptional at dying the many diffrent colours of yarn. The processis of createing the tapestry have yett to be documentted. Arkeolojists are hoppeing to travell to the ruines for furthur eggsploration.

Activity 58-2: Editing for Spelling and Hyphenation in Your Own Writing

Choose a piece of writing that you are working on. Underline every word in it that you are not sure is spelled correctly. Use all the tools you have—spell checker, dictionary, spelling rules, and so on—to find the correct spellings. If you have any hyphens in your writing, examine each one to be sure you have used it correctly. Make any necessary edits. Print another copy of your edited work and examine it for spelling and hyphens. Did you catch all the errors? What steps can you take to ensure that every piece of your writing is edited for spelling and hyphens?

PART 11

Grammar for Multilingual Writers

New Contexts for Writing Wikipedia

Wikipedia (http://www.wikipedia.org) is the world's largest encyclopedia, with more free content about more topics than any other encyclopedia ever published. It has grown so large so fast because it has become a new context for writing, a place on the Internet where anyone with an Internet connection and a Web browser can create, revise, and improve the sum of human knowledge, at least as that knowledge is represented at Wikipedia.

A **wiki** (pronounced "wick-ee") is software that enables authors to collaborate on a common text on the Internet using only a Web browser (such as Internet Explorer or Firefox). People also use the term to refer to websites built by this method of collaborative authorship. Wikis allow users to add, delete, move, and revise the content on a website. A **version tracking system** keeps a record of these changes and previous drafts so that—when mistakes are made, for example—site administrators can use the wiki's **rollback** feature to restore a previous version.

WIKIPEDIA

English
The Free Encyclopedia
1 006 000+ articles

Deutsch
Die freie Enzyklopädie
365 000+ Artikel

Français
L'encyclopédie libre
250 000+ articles

Polski
Wolna Encyklopedia
218 000+ haseł

日本語
フリー百科事典
188 000+ 記事

Nederlands
De vrije encyclopedie
145 000+ artikelen

Italiano
L'enciclopedia libera
142 000+ articoli

Svenska
Den fria encyklopedin
141 000+ artiklar

Português
A enciclopédia livre
119 000+ artigos

Español
La enciclopedia libre
99 000+ artículos

search • suche • rechercher • szukaj • 検索 • zoeken • ricerca • sök • busca • buscar

English >

What Should You Use an Encyclopedia to Do?

Good encyclopedias sum up general knowledge about a wide range of subjects. Ideally, encyclopedic information should be **reliable, accurate, timely, accessible,** and **comprehensive.** Even the best encyclopedias, however, are not meant to be the final word on a subject. Think of encyclopedias as starting points for further research, the touchstones that can stimulate your deeper consideration of complex subjects.

For Internet researchers, Wikipedia is a good place to begin research because it offers rich linking to other sources on the Internet (and within Wikipedia itself), it is free and easily accessible, and it covers a huge range of topics.

Make the World a Better Place Right Now . . .

- Read Wikipedia's "Policies and Guidelines" so that you understand how (and why) a publicly authored encyclopedia works: **http://en.wikipedia.org/wiki/Wikipedia:Policies_and_guidelines**
- Click on the "History" tab at a Wikipedia article to see how it has changed over time.
- The next time you come across a Wikipedia article that contains inaccurate or incomplete information, click on the [edit] link next to each section. You'll find good directions for contributing.

59

WRITING IN ENGLISH FOR ACADEMIC PURPOSES

Expectations for academic writing vary not only from one type of writing task to another within a given language but also across languages and cultures. What is considered good writing in one language or culture may be considered ineffective writing in another. A fundamental requirement for good writing, then, is knowledge of your audience and their expectations for specific types of writing.

If English is not your native language, you may be less familiar with the expectations for academic writing in English than your peers whose first language is English. In addition, you probably have less experience using English grammar and vocabulary to convey your ideas, and thus you may have more difficulty doing so in your writing. The four chapters in this section are designed to help you with these issues—specifically, to help you meet the rhetorical and linguistic expectations for English academic writing.

This introductory chapter presents some general rhetorical preferences of English-speaking readers of academic texts, as well as guidelines for using feedback to revise and edit your writing. Chapters 60, 61, and 62 address specific grammatical structures that are troublesome for multilingual writers, with the goal of helping you learn to edit your own writing for these errors.

Although expectations about the organization of texts vary across disciplines and genres, readers of academic English share some general preferences. Broadly speaking, readers of English expect the main idea of an academic text, referred to as its thesis, to be explicitly stated early on (usually somewhere in the first few paragraphs) and then developed throughout the remainder of the paper. This preference is not a hard-and-fast rule, but it is common among readers of academic discourse, particularly writing for college courses. Delaying your main point until the end of an academic paper or leaving your thesis unstated (expecting readers to infer it) will generally be seen as ineffective.

Readers also expect writers to remain closely focused on their main point (thesis) throughout the body of a paper and to avoid digressing into topics that are not strictly related to the thesis, regardless of how interesting these topics may be.

A common way for writers to show that they are remaining on topic is by beginning each paragraph in the body of a paper with an explicit statement of its main point. These paragraph introductory sentences are referred to as *topic sentences,* and they generally announce the subtopics or subpoints that a writer is going to discuss to support the thesis.

Typical Organizational Pattern of the Academic Essay in English

INTRODUCTORY PARAGRAPH	■ Grab readers' attention ■ Introduce topic and place it in context ■ Present main idea of entire essay (the thesis)
BODY PARAGRAPH 1 First idea in support of thesis	■ State main idea of paragraph 1 (topic sentence 1) ■ Explain main idea 1 ■ Provide facts, quotations, statistics, and so on, to support main idea 1
BODY PARAGRAPH 2 Second idea in support of thesis	■ State main idea of paragraph 2 (topic sentence 2) ■ Explain main idea 2 ■ Provide facts, quotations, statistics, and so on, to support main idea 2
THIRD AND SUBSEQUENT PARAGRAPHS Third and subsequent body ideas in support of thesis	■ State main idea of each paragraph (topic sentences) ■ Explain main idea ■ Provide facts, quotations, statistics, and so on, to support main idea
CONCLUDING PARAGRAPH	■ Present concluding ideas ■ Sometimes restate main point of paper (thesis)

Following the general pattern shown here can help you organize your writing for English-speaking audiences, but keep in mind that readers have different expectations for the organization of different types of writing, so it is always a good idea to inquire about the organizational requirements of the writing task you are being asked to complete. Your instructors and writing tutors are good sources of guidance. There are also a variety of print and online resources that offer help to multilingual writers; refer to the list on page 1015.

The best way to learn to meet the expectations for academic writing in English is to write a first draft, get feedback from readers on that draft, and then revise in response to their feedback. Feedback from your teachers can not only help you identify your strengths and weaknesses in a given piece of writing but also provide direction concerning areas you should work on in future writing.

To get an idea of how you can make use of teacher feedback, consider this sample student draft. The assignment required students, working in pairs, to conduct a survey on a topic of interest to them and then write a report presenting their findings.

1

Youjin Song and MeeSook Wang

Survey Report, First Draft

English 101: Cross Cultural Composition

American and International Students' Perceptions of Studying Abroad

This survey was done to find out what students think about studying abroad. As we all may realize, studying abroad means having to make several changes in our lifestyles. People living in different parts of the world have different cultures. We decided to pursue this topic because we [verb tense] would like to know if students ever [verb tense] considered to further their studies in a different place. There are many possible reasons that could affect their decisions to either study or not study abroad. The reason that we are most interested in is the cultural differences. We [verb tense] would like to find out how far the cultural differences affect their decisions. Do students find cultural differences as a positive or negative factor in deciding to study abroad?

We developed a questionnaire to gather information from the students in the campus. The first segment of the questionnaire asked questions regarding to the respondents' demographic factors such as sex, age, and nationality. The second segment of the questionnaire [verb tense] asks eight questions that are directly related to our topic. We distributed 20 questionnaires to the students on campus. The students were surveyed at different places that included dorms, classes, apartments, library, and sidewalks. This was done to ensure that we gathered information from a variety of students. We surveyed the students at convenient times such as during our breaks in between classes. All of the students were cooperative and did not hesitate to fill out the questionnaire. They seemed comfortable with the questions asked on the questionnaire and that made our tasks run smoothly.

Don't Edit Yet

While it may be tempting to go through your first draft, correcting all of the errors marked in the margins, and then deal with the suggestions in the end comment, this would not be the best strategy to adopt. In fact, there are a number of good reasons for postponing editing until after you have had a chance to make meaningful revisions. For one thing, this approach allows you to focus your attention on the larger and usually more complex task of revising your writing for content and organization issues. For another, it is more efficient: as you revise, you may end up correcting some of your errors and/or deleting portions of text that contain errors, so there is really no point in attending to these errors before revising. The teacher's feedback on the sample draft (shown on pages 1012 and 1013) explicitly advises the writers to delay editing until after they have revised for focus and development.

Not needed; repeats info from previous ¶. Topic sentence of this ¶ should reflect its focus, which = who your participants included.

2

20 questionnaires were distributed to the students on campus in order to get the relevant information for our topic. We surveyed 12 American students that consisted of six females and six males, and eight international students that consisted of five females and three males. The students consisted of 11 freshmen, three sophomores, and six juniors. We did not get any senior or graduate student respondents, although we were hoping to get respondents from all categories of students. Out of the 20 students, 12 were from the School of Management while the rest were from other schools such as Engineering, Mathematics, and Computer Science. All of the American students that filled out the questionnaire have never studied abroad. Amazingly, 92% of them have considered to study. However, only 42% of them actually have plans to study abroad in the future. Most of the students who are thinking of studying abroad in the future would want to start their education in the foreign country in the junior year for a duration of two to three years. In our opinion, most of the students chose the junior as the starting point of their studies abroad because a majority of them are freshmen. They might not get any information about the opportunities of studying abroad until they have entered college. Therefore, they could only make plans after their freshmen year.

verb tense

After analyzing the questionnaires, we found that the three major reasons that affected the American students' decisions to study abroad are to gain more knowledge about the world, to escape from the usual environment, and to learn new culture. These findings showed that cultural differences affected their decisions in a positive way. They would want to go to another country knowing that it is a perfect opportunity for them to learn about other people's culture.

When all of the members of a group have not done something, make the quantity word negative rather than the verb: "None of the American students have studied abroad."

3

On the other hand, financial difficulties, no application to majors, and language differences are the three major reasons that are stopping them from studying abroad. Language differences might be the main reasons why students chose countries such as England and Australia where English is used widely. We think that students are concerned about the differences in *noun number* language spoken in a country because it could cause some communication problems.

As for the international students who are currently studying in the United States, their reasons to *verb form* study abroad are exactly the same as the American students. However, compared to the American students, the international students planned to stay longer in the foreign country, which is four to five years. This might be due to the fact that they are starting their education in the foreign country from the freshman year.

As we had expected, cultural differences as well as language differences have a great effect on students' decisions to study abroad. Most of the students that were surveyed listed the opportunity to learn a new culture as one of the strongest reasons that affected them to study abroad. They are willing to live in another country with different lifestyles. However, the American students are more interested to *verb form* go to countries that are similar to their own country. This might be because they *verb tense* have to learn many aspects of life that may not be common in the Western countries. On the other hand, language differences *verb form* affected them not to study abroad. They are more inclined to go to English-speaking countries to avoid any problems in communication. However, most of the students see the point of studying abroad is to know more about the world as a whole.

Verb form: when the object of the verb affect is human, it can be either (1) a noun/pronoun that refers to the humans (x affected them) or (2) a noun referring to the humans' thoughts or actions plus an infinitive complement (x affected their decision to study . . .).

Revise for Content and Organization

A better strategy for responding to your teacher's feedback, then, is to start by addressing comments related to issues of content and organization. Notice that three-fourths of the teacher's comments at the end of the sample draft (pages 1012 and 1013) focus on content and organization. These comments not only give the writers insight into how well their current draft meets the rhetorical expectations for survey reports but also provide direction for revision. If you need help understanding your teacher's suggestions for revision, you should speak to the teacher and/or consult a writing center tutor, who can help you put revision strategies into action.

Learn a Few Things at a Time

As the sample draft illustrates, teacher feedback is generally selective. Rather than addressing everything at once, it focuses on specific aspects of writing that your teacher thinks you should work on at a given point. This is because our capacity to learn complex processes like writing is limited—we can learn only a few things at one time. With this fact in mind, the teacher who responded to the sample draft limited her comments to three major (related) content issues.

The language issues the teacher chose to mark in Youjin and MeeSook's draft paper include two types of errors (verb tense and verb form errors). These errors form a pattern in the draft, are considered serious by English-speaking readers, and are governed by rules that can be fairly readily taught and learned. The teacher's goal in marking these errors is to help the writers learn to edit for these errors themselves.

Youjin and MeeSook:

All of the hard work you put into designing your questionnaire clearly paid off. Your report is interesting and includes good information about the administration of the survey and the demographics of your participants. I can see that you have worked on developing generalizations based on your findings, which is very good. The main weakness in the current draft is the lack of a comprehensive thesis statement (stating your overall finding) and insufficient support for the generalizations/main points you make. Below, I offer suggestions for improving these aspects of your report.

(1) <u>Focus/Thesis Statement</u>: Overall, what did you learn about international and American students' attitudes toward study abroad? Your answer to this question will be your thesis statement. One of the main goals of the survey report assignment is to help you learn to develop and support a thesis statement, so you will want to work on this first. Keep in mind that your thesis should be included early in the report (a good place would be at the end of your introduction). Review what you've written in the conclusion of your report, as this may help you develop your thesis. You can refer to section 4b in your handbook if you need help.

(2) <u>Content</u>: When reporting research, it is crucial that your generalizations (the thesis and main points of individual paragraphs) accurately reflect your findings. In the current draft, you say that one of the top three reasons American students gave for wanting to study abroad is to learn new cultures, but you also found that they would prefer to study in English-speaking countries that are similar

to the US. What can you conclude from the conflicting data? What do these two findings (together) show about American students' attitudes toward cultural differences? You may need to revise your thesis and the main points of specific paragraphs to reflect this contrast. You can refer to section 6c in your handbook if you need help with this.

(3) Development: The generalizations you make (based on your analysis of participants' responses) need to be supported with evidence from the data to convince readers of the credibility of your report. When you report that "most" American students would prefer to study abroad in their junior year, you need to follow up with a sentence reporting the details. How many Americans chose junior year? How many chose other years? Similarly, after you report Americans' major reasons for studying abroad, you need to report the specifics. What reasons were given and by how many students? Look through your draft to be sure that you support main points with details from the results. You can refer to section 11h in your handbook for help with this.

(4) Editing for Grammar: After you have revised your draft for focus and development, you can edit for errors. I have selected two patterns of errors to mark in this draft: verb tense and verb form errors. I recommend editing for all verb tense errors first, then editing for all verb form errors. Sections 44e and 44a in your handbook can help you with these issues.

Learning a second language is a complex and gradual process, and errors are a natural—and unavoidable—part of this process. Generally speaking, grammatical errors will disappear on their own as your skill in using a second language develops. But the process takes time—and both the rate at which your accuracy improves and the skill level you ultimately attain will depend on a number of factors, including your motivation to learn the language, your need to write in the language, and the amount of reading and writing you do in the language, to name a few. Unfortunately, second language writers rarely find themselves in situations where grammatical accuracy is not important. Usually, readers expect academic writing to conform to standard rules for English grammar, regardless of the amount of time students have had to develop their English proficiency. Thus, multilingual students generally cannot wait for their grammar to improve slowly.

Understand Teachers' Comments

Teachers' comments generally fall into two broad categories: comments on *content and organization issues* and comments on *language issues.*

Decoding Your Teachers' Comments

Your teachers may comment on the following aspects of your writing.

Content and organization issues

Content: the ideas and information in a paper. Comments on content may refer to the accuracy of ideas; the appropriateness and relevance of the topic to the assignment; and/or specific ideas, facts, arguments, and other evidence used to support your thesis.

Focus: the extent to which your writing establishes a main point (thesis) and sticks to it

Development: the extent to which your main points are supported with relevant facts, data, ideas, research, statistics, experiences, and the like

Organization: the order in which your ideas are presented and linked together in the paper and in individual paragraphs. The organization is expected to reflect typical preferred patterns for writing in English. (If it does not, some readers will deem the writing illogical—though logic, of course, is culture-specific.)

Audience awareness: the extent to which your writing takes into account your readers' knowledge of and attitudes toward your topic

Language issues

Sentence structure: the extent to which your sentences meet accepted standards for construction (word order, punctuation) and readers' expectations for complexity

Grammar: the extent to which your writing follows grammatical rules regarding verb tense, verb form, modals, noun number, subject/verb agreement, and the like

Vocabulary (or style): the extent to which the words you use accurately express your intended meaning and are appropriate to the rhetorical situation

Convention use (or mechanics): the extent to which your writing follows rules regarding punctuation, spelling, capitalization, style for citing sources, margin size, spacing, pagination, and the like

Helpful Resources for Multilingual Writers

Purdue University's Online Writing Lab (OWL): **http://owl.english.purdue.edu/handouts/esl/**. This site contains resource pages, handouts, and interactive grammar exercises for multilingual writers; in addition, you can email questions about your writing to an online tutor, who will email a response within 48 hours.

Dave's ESL Cafe: **http://www.eslcafe.com**. This site contains an ESL Help Center, where you can post questions and receive answers from teachers around the world 24 hours a day, 7 days a week.

OneLook Dictionary Search: **http://www.onelook.com**. This site allows you to search more than 900 online dictionaries for the translation and meaning of any word or phrase, including idioms and slang terms.

Heinle's Newbury House Dictionary of American English with Integrated Thesaurus, 4th edition. Ed. Philip M. Rideout. Boston: Thomson Heinle, 2004. This dictionary has a thesaurus integrated right into it, as well as activities to help you build your vocabulary, and a CD-ROM to help you learn to pronounce new words.

Writing Clearly: An Editing Guide, 2nd edition. Janet Lane and Ellen Lange. Boston: Thomson Heinle, 1999. This book covers fifteen of the language problems multilingual students most commonly encounter in their writing, providing instruction and practice activities to help you learn to edit your own work for these errors.

Consider Hiring an Editor in Certain Rhetorical Situations

Some rhetorical situations require a high degree of grammatical accuracy—for example, job application letters, materials intended for publication, and undergraduate- or graduate-level theses. When you are preparing such materials, it might be wise to employ someone else to edit your writing. However, it is generally not considered acceptable to have someone else edit the writing you are required to do *for* university courses, so you need to carefully consider your context when making decisions of this nature.

Resources for Learning to Edit

Although you cannot become proficient in a second language overnight, what you *can* do is learn to edit for error, which involves learning how to find errors in your own writing and how to correct them. Your teacher's comments can help you learn to edit for error, primarily by identifying the patterns of error in a draft and the location of each instance. To obtain further assistance with editing, you can consult tutors at your institution's writing center and a number of online resources. But learning to edit is still a time-consuming and daunting task. The next three chapters in this handbook (Chapters 60–62) are designed to help you with the process by teaching you about specific grammatical constructions that are problematic for multilingual writers and providing you with strategies for finding these types of errors in your own writing.

60

NOUNS AND ARTICLES

Nouns refer to the things we talk and write about, so they abound in our speech and writing. Nouns can occur in sentences as subjects, objects, objects of prepositions, or clausal complements. Although the rules for forming plural nouns are fairly straightforward, there are several distinctions made among noun types in English that can make noun formation difficult for multilingual writers. Most noun form errors result from problems in distinguishing between countable and uncountable nouns. Compounding the difficulty, English speakers frequently use determiners *(the, this, some)* before nouns, and the rules for their use are complicated. Articles are among the last features of English that second language learners master. In fact, many highly educated and proficient multilingual writers—professors and CEOs, for example—continue to have minor problems using articles in their writing. So, if you have difficulty with article use, rest assured that you're not alone.

The good thing is that errors in article use generally do not affect meaning, so they rarely confuse readers. Nonetheless, many academic audiences find such errors annoying; thus, article use is an aspect of grammar that you will likely need to work on. This chapter is designed to help you learn the rules for using different types of nouns with and without different types of determiners. It focuses on specific aspects of noun formation and determiner use that have proven to be difficult for multilingual writers.

Example 1 Capitalization of proper nouns

TITLES ARE CAPITALIZED WHEN THEY APPEAR WITH PROPER NOUNS:

President Clinton visited **Prime Minister Blair** in May.

Example 2 Capitalization of common nouns

COMMON NOUNS ARE NOT CAPITALIZED:

No My **Aunt** encouraged me to major in **Chemistry** in college.

Yes My **aunt** encouraged me to major in **chemistry** in college.

A NOUN THAT IDENTIFIES AN ACADEMIC SUBJECT IS CAPITALIZED WHEN A SPECIFIC COURSE IS NAMED:

I want to be an **accountant,** so I am taking **Accounting 101** this semester.

Four Categories of Common Nouns

	Singular	Plural
Uncountable	advice	—
	information	—
Countable	day	days
	jury	juries [if preceded by consonant, *y* → *ie* before *s*]
	foot	feet
	child	children

English speakers differentiate among nouns in three ways. Every noun is either

- proper or common
- countable or uncountable
- singular or plural

Nouns Are Either Proper or Common

Proper nouns name specific people, places, time periods, events, groups, or things. They must be capitalized. They usually do not take determiners.

Common nouns name people, places, things, processes, and the like that are *not* specific or unique. They are not capitalized.

Nouns that refer to academic disciplines and relatives (*uncle, aunt,* etc.) are not capitalized when they are used in a general sense or when they do not immediately precede the name of a specific course or person. When such nouns identify a specific course or person, they are capitalized.

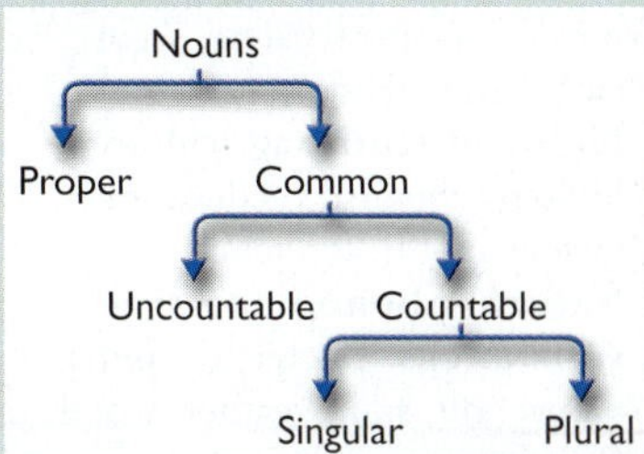

Common Nouns Can Be Uncountable or Countable

Uncountable nouns name things that cannot be counted because they are abstractions or substances or processes that cannot be divided into individual parts. Uncountable nouns often have a collective or mass meaning. They do not have a plural form.

Uncountable nouns require singular verbs. They are not typically used with numbers or the indefinite article (*a/an*).

Common Uncountable Nouns
Masses: advice, art, clothing, environment, equipment, experience, fuel, furniture, glue, hair, homework, information, knowledge, labor, luggage, medicine, money, news, paint, plastic, progress, research, technology, time, trade, traffic, training, water, wealth, work
Abstract concepts: existence, failure, faith, freedom, independence, intelligence, justice, mercy, patience, peace, poverty, respect, safety, security, status, trust
Fields of study: agriculture, biology, chemistry, education, history, political science
Natural phenomena and substances: electricity, metal, nature, oil, soil, weather, wood
Food: milk, spaghetti

Uncountable Nouns

Example 3 Uncountable nouns are always singular (never add plural marker -s)

No I have increased my **knowledges** of the topic through **researches.**

Yes I have increased my **knowledge** of the topic through **research.**

Example 4 An uncountable noun takes a singular verb

The **homework** *is* due tomorrow.

Example 5 An indefinite article is never used with an uncountable noun

No She gave me *an* **advice** about buying a used car.

Yes She gave me **advice** about buying a used car.

If the noun is . . .	Choose one of these quantity terms:		
uncountable	a great deal of a large/small amount of a little a piece/pair/liter of one or more pieces/pairs/cups of less little much		a lot of all all of the any enough more most no
plural and countable	a few few many	both fewer several	not any other some
singular and countable	another either	each every	

Example 6 Some nouns can be either uncountable or countable

AUDIENCE IS REFERRED TO AS A MASS, SO THE NOUN IS UNCOUNTABLE:

The magician searched *the* **audience** for a volunteer.

DIFFERENT TYPES OF *AUDIENCES* ARE REFERRED TO, SO THE NOUN IS COUNTABLE (AND PLURAL):

Television shows have to appeal to the tastes of different **audiences.**

Example 7 Indicating quantity with uncountable nouns

AN APPROPRIATE QUANTITY TERM IS USED TO INDICATE THE QUANTITY OF AN UNCOUNTABLE NOUN:

No *Every* **furniture** was delivered today.

Yes *All of the* **furniture** was delivered today.

THE VERB AGREES IN NUMBER WITH THE QUANTITY TERM, NOT THE UNCOUNTABLE NOUN:

A piece of **luggage** *was* lost by the airline.

Two pieces of **luggage** *were* lost by the airline.

A number of uncountable nouns are tricky because they end in *-s,* which makes them look like plural countable nouns. Keep in mind that these are uncountable nouns and should be treated as singular.

Nouns Ending in* s *That Are Uncountable

Diseases: arthritis, bronchitis, diabetes, herpes, multiple sclerosis, rabies

Fields of study: aeronautics, classics, economics, genetics, linguistics, mathematics, physics, politics, statistics

Games: billiards, cards, checkers, chess, darts, dominoes, tennis

Nouns with Both Uncountable and Countable Forms

Some nouns may be uncountable *or* countable, depending on their meaning and the context in which they are used. They are uncountable when they refer to something in general or as a mass and countable when they refer to a specific instance of something or different types of something.

Nouns That Are Both Uncountable and Countable

audience, cast, committee, conflict, family, light, opposition, victory, work

Indicating Quantity with Uncountable Nouns

To refer to a quantity of an uncountable noun, you need to use an appropriate quantity term. Refer to the chart on page 1018 for a selection of quantity terms that may be used with uncountable nouns.

Countable nouns name things that can be counted. You can put numbers (*one, two,* etc.) in front of them.

Countable Nouns
accident, chapter, college, effect, group, hour, job, library, method, model, product, project, thought

Countable Nouns Have Singular and Plural Forms

Singular countable nouns take singular verbs. They require determiners (section 60b).

The plural form of a regular countable noun is created by adding *s* or *es* to the singular form. However, there are some irregular plurals that do not follow this rule (for example, *woman/women*). These plurals must be memorized. Nouns must be marked for plurality *even when a number is used with them.* Plural nouns take plural verbs. Adjectives that modify nouns are *never* made plural in English.

Special Plurals

Some nouns refer to tools and clothing composed of two identical parts. The nouns that refer to such items are always plural.

Countable Nouns

Example 8 Verb agreement with countable nouns

A SINGULAR VERB FORM IS USED WHEN A COUNTABLE NOUN IS SINGULAR:

My **friend** *loves* to go hiking.

A PLURAL VERB FORM IS USED WHEN A COUNTABLE NOUN IS PLURAL:

My **friends** *love* to travel.

Example 9 Nouns modified by numbers

WHEN A SPECIFIC QUANTITY (OTHER THAN ONE) IS INDICATED, A COUNTABLE NOUN IS MADE PLURAL:

Three **cats** live in that house.

Example 10 Adjective form with plural nouns

AN ADJECTIVE THAT MODIFIES A PLURAL NOUN IS NOT MADE PLURAL:

No Discount stores sell *inexpensives* **products.**

Yes Discount stores sell *inexpensive* **products.**

Special Plurals

Special plurals for things people wear:

glasses (spectacles)	gloves	jeans
	overalls	pajamas
pants	shorts	slacks

Special plurals for tools:

binoculars	pliers	scissors
shears	skis	tongs

To refer to one of these items, use *a pair of* before the noun. To refer to a quantity (more than one) of these items, use a quantity term with *pairs of:*

I packed *two pairs of* **pajamas** for my trip.

To refer to an unspecified number or to make a generalization about a special plural, use the noun alone (without a determiner):

The children used **scissors** to cut out paper snowflakes.

Example 11 Definite articles are not used with most proper nouns

No We celebrated *the* **Halloween** by dressing in costumes.

Yes We celebrated **Halloween** by dressing in costumes.

Example 12 Using the definite article with proper nouns

THE DEFINITE ARTICLE IS NOT CAPITALIZED WITH PROPER NOUNS:

No We studied *The* Great Lakes in environmental science.

Yes English has changed a great deal since *the* Middle Ages.

AN ARTICLE IS CAPITALIZED WHEN IT IS PART OF A TITLE:

I read *The Catcher in the Rye* last week.

Most proper nouns do not take definite articles. However, certain categories of proper nouns require the definite article:

- *Specific bodies of land and water:* deserts, oceans, lakes, rivers, regions of a country
- *Specific physical structures:* museums, monuments, buildings, bridges
- *Specific time periods and events:* historical eras, wars

***Proper Nouns That Take* the**
the Sahara Desert, the Atlantic Ocean, the Grand Canyon, the West, the Museum of Modern Art, the Washington Monument, the Golden Gate Bridge, the Middle Ages, the Renaissance

When used with a proper noun, the definite article is not capitalized *unless* it is part of the title of a publication or performance.

Determiners indicate whether the things being referred to are general or specific. There are three questions you need to answer in order to decide whether a common noun needs a determiner and, if it does, what kind.

1. **General or specific?** Does the noun *make a generalization* about something or refer to something *general,* something *of a particular type,* or something *that has not yet been mentioned or is not known to readers?* Or does the noun refer to something *specific* or something *already mentioned to or known by readers?*
2. **Uncountable or countable?** Is the noun uncountable or countable?
3. **Singular or plural?** If the noun is countable, is it singular or plural?

If your answer to question 1 is *general* and the noun is *uncountable* or *countable* and plural, use the noun without a determiner. If your answer to question 1 is *general* and the noun is *countable* and *singular,* use an indefinite article (*a/an*) with the noun.

If your answer to question 1 is *specific,* use a specific determiner (refer to the chart to the right for choices). Note that *this* and *that* are used with uncountable nouns and with singular countable nouns; *these* and *those* are used with plural nouns.

Determiners for Different Types of Common Nouns

	Uncountable	Countable	
		Singular	Plural
General	—	a, an	—
Specific	the, this, that	the, this, that	the, these, those
	my, our, your, his, her, its, their		

Example 13 Using determiners with common nouns that have a general reference

NO DETERMINER IS USED WITH A PLURAL NOUN THAT HAS A GENERAL REFERENCE:

Cats and **dogs** are the most common house pets.

AN INDEFINITE ARTICLE IS USED WITH A SINGULAR NOUN THAT HAS A GENERAL REFERENCE:

We went to the humane society today to adopt *a* **cat.**

Example 14 Using determiners with common nouns that have a specific reference

A DEFINITE ARTICLE IS USED WHEN THE COMMON NOUN HAS ALREADY BEEN REFERRED TO:

The deans will make *a* **recommendation** to the board. The board can accept or reject *the* **recommendation.**

ALTERNATIVELY, A POSSESSIVE DETERMINER COULD BE USED:

The board can accept or reject *their* **recommendation.**

Example 15 Using the definite article to refer back to known information

AN INDEFINITE ARTICLE IS USED TO INTRODUCE A GENERAL COUNTABLE NOUN; A DEFINITE ARTICLE IS USED TO REFER BACK TO THE NOUN:

My doctor gave me *a* **prescription** for antibiotics. *The* **prescription** seemed illegible to me, but the pharmacist was able to read it.

Example 16 Using the definite article with uncountable nouns that are qualified

THE DEFINITE ARTICLE IS USED WHEN THE UNCOUNTABLE NOUN IS QUALIFIED IN A PREPOSITIONAL PHRASE:

No Social workers are concerned about **welfare** of foster children.

Yes Social workers are concerned about *the* **welfare** of foster children.

Example 17 Using the definite article with superlative or sequential adjectives

THE DEFINITE ARTICLE IS REQUIRED BEFORE NOUNS MODIFIED BY ADJECTIVES:

No I had **best** ice cream **last** time we ate at this restaurant.

Yes I had *the* **best** ice cream *the* **last** time we ate at this restaurant.

Example 18 Using the definite article to refer to an entire group or human body part

The fastest animal on land is *the* **cheetah.**

The **Andersons** have a big family reunion each August.

Excessive consumption of alcohol can severely damage *the* **liver.**

The definite article *the* is the most common specific determiner. It is used in a number of ways:

- with a noun that refers to a unique thing that everyone knows (shared knowledge): *the Web, the Moon*
- with common time expressions: *in the past, in the evening*
- with a noun that refers back to something that has already been mentioned or that is clear from the context or from what you have already written
- with an uncountable noun that is followed by a qualifier that relates it to a particular group or makes it specific: *The kindergarten teacher has the* ***patience*** *of a saint.*
- before a superlative or sequential adjective (*best, fastest, next*)
- to make a comment about all members of a group or species or about a human body part

61

VERBS AND VERBALS

This chapter is designed to help you learn the rules for using different types of verbs and verb phrases in your writing. It focuses on specific aspects of verb use that have proven to be difficult for multilingual writers, including phrasal verbs, *-ing* versus infinitive versus plain form verbs, modal auxiliaries, and the use of present participle (*-ing*) and past participle (*-ed*) verbs as adjectives.

Common Separable Phrasal Verbs

The phrases with asterisks (*) can be used transitively and intransitively.

add up	hold on*	point out	tell apart
bring up	keep up*	push over	tell off
buy out	kick out	put off	think over
clean up*	knock out*	put on	think through
draw up	lay down	rip off	tie down
drop off	lay off*	scale down*	tip off
fill in	let down*	seal off	tire out
filter out	let up*	seek out	try on
find out*	look up	set aside	try out
finish up*	make up	set off	turn in
follow up*	mess up	settle down	turn up*
give away	pay back	settle in*	use up
give up*	phase out	show off	waste away*
hand down	pin down	start out*	wrap up
hand out	plug in	take off*	

Example 1 The separable phrasal verb *call off* (meaning "to cancel")

THE DIRECT OBJECT CAN FOLLOW THE PARTICLE OR BE INSERTED BETWEEN VERB AND PARTICLE:

Yes The couple decided to **call off** *the wedding.*

Yes The couple decided to **call** *the wedding* **off.**

IF THE DIRECT OBJECT IS A PRONOUN, IT MUST SEPARATE VERB AND PARTICLE:

No The couple decided to **call off** *it.*

Yes The couple decided to **call** *it* **off.**

IF THE DIRECT OBJECT IS A LONG PHRASE, IT SHOULD FOLLOW THE PARTICLE (*NOT* SEPARATE THE PHRASAL VERB):

No The couple decided to **call** *the wedding they had been planning for the last two years* **off.**

Yes The couple decided to **call off** *the wedding they had been planning for the last two years.*

A phrasal verb consists of a verb followed by one or more words (particles) that help specify the verb's meaning. The verb and particle(s) function together as a single verb whose meaning is rarely the same as the meaning of its component parts. Most phrasal verbs are idiomatic.

Like other verbs, when used in clauses, phrasal verbs must be inflected for tense, person, and number. Some phrasal verbs can be used both transitively (with a direct object) and intransitively (without a direct object); others are exclusively transitive (they require a direct object). Be aware of the three types of phrasal verbs.

Separable Phrasal Verbs

Separable phrasal verbs allow a direct object to be inserted between the verb and the particle. If the direct object is a pronoun, separation is *required.*

Inseparable Phrasal Verbs

Inseparable phrasal verbs do not allow the verb and particle to be separated.

Common Inseparable Phrasal Verbs

The phrases with asterisks (*) can be used transitively and intransitively.

account for	drop by*	look into	reason with
back down	expand on	look like	settle on
back off*	fall apart*	miss out	speak up*
bow out*	fall behind*	move over*	stand back*
chip in*	fall out*	opt out*	stay up*
come across	flare up*	own up	step down*
come out	get ahead*	make for	stop by*
crop up*	get by*	meet with	tamper with
dawn on	get over	pay up*	wait on
die down*	go ahead	pick on	wait up*
double back*	go over	pitch in*	watch out*
draw on	lay into	provide for	

Example 2 The inseparable phrasal verb *reason with* (meaning "to persuade through logic")

THE DIRECT OBJECT CANNOT BE INSERTED BETWEEN VERB AND PARTICLE:

No I tried to **reason** *my opponent* **with,** but she refused to listen.

Yes I tried to **reason with** *my opponent,* but she refused to listen.

Example 3 Agreement in person and number with the phrasal verb *fall behind* (meaning "to be late in doing something")

THIRD PERSON SINGULAR VERB IS REQUIRED TO MATCH SUBJECT IN PERSON AND NUMBER:

No Every year during football season, *Pat* **fall behind** in his studies.

Yes Every year during football season, *Pat* **falls behind** in his studies.

Common Inseparable Three-Word Phrasal Verbs

back away from	cut back on	keep up with	run up against
back down from	cut down on	lay off of	shy away from
be on to	drop in on	live up to	sit in on
bear down on	ease up on	look forward to	stand up for
bow out of	end up with	look in on	stick up for
break out of	get along with	look out for	stock up on
break up with	get away with	look up to	talk down to
brush up on	get back to	make off with	walk away with
catch up with	get by with	make up for	watch out for
check out of	get down to	miss out on	zero in on
check up on	give in to	pick up on	
clean up after	give up on	play along with	
crack down on	go in for	put up with	

Example 4 Forming three-word phrasal verbs with *look down*

ON IS REQUIRED TO CONVEY THE MEANING "VIEW AS INFERIOR":

My boss **looks down on** applicants who have not graduated from high school.

AT CONVEYS A DIFFERENT MEANING—THAT THE DIRECT OBJECT IS PHYSICALLY LOWER THAN THE SUBJECT:

My boss **looks down at** the workers on the floor below.

Example 5 Using an *-ing* form following a three-word phrasal verb

AFTER A THREE-WORD PHRASAL VERB, THE *-ING* FORM OF A VERB (NOT THE PLAIN FORM) IS REQUIRED:

No I **look forward to** *hear* from you soon.
Yes I **look forward to** *hearing* from you soon.

Three-Word Phrasal Verbs

Three-word phrasal verbs must be used with specific prepositions in order to convey the intended meaning. In these cases, the preposition can be considered part of the phrasal verb (verb + particle + preposition). Three-word phrasal verbs are inseparable. It would be a good idea to learn these verbs as units; you will notice that they have their own entries in most dictionaries.

Infinitives (*to* + verb) and *-ing* forms (verb + *ing*) are two of the most troublesome structures in English for multilingual writers to master. These forms share some functions, but they also perform distinct functions and differ in the grammatical structures in which they can be used. The following guidelines can help you determine when to use each form.

When and How Infinitives Are Used

An **infinitive** consists of *to* plus the uninflected (plain) form of a verb: *to dance, to read.* Infinitives perform a variety of functions in English.

1. **Infinitives may be subjects.** Infinitives can be used as subjects when you want to highlight the activity they refer to. They require a third person singular verb: ***To lose*** *ten pounds by summer is Yu's goal.*
2. **Infinitives may be verbal complements.** Infinitives are used following main clause verbs—in complement clauses—to convey activities that are hypothetical, that failed to take place, or that will take place in the future: *The witness swore* ***to tell*** *the truth in the courtroom.* Verbs that take infinitive complements tend to have subjects that are somehow related to or interested in the real or hypothetical occurrence of

Verbs That Take Only Infinitive Complements, Not *-ing* Forms

The phrases with asterisks (*) can take a noun or pronoun before the infinitive complement.

afford	deserve	long	resolve
agree	desire*	manage	seek
aim	endeavor	mean	seem
appear	expect*	need*	survive
arrange	fail	neglect	swear
ask*	fight*	offer*	tend
attempt	grow	opt	threaten*
beg*	happen	pay*	volunteer*
care	have	plan	vote
choose*	help*	pledge	vow
claim	hesitate	prepare*	wait
consent	hope	pretend	want*
dare*	intend*	promise*	wish*
decide	learn	prove	
demand	live	refuse	

Example 6 Using the plain form of the verb in an infinitive verbal complement

THE VERB USED IN AN INFINITIVE IS NEVER MARKED FOR TENSE OR NUMBER:

No Xiao *decided* **to helped** raise money for the school

No Xiao *decided* **to helps** raise money for the school.

Yes Xiao *decided* **to help** raise money for the school.

Example 7 Using the infinitive complement to describe events that have not taken place

ACTIVITY OF PAYING BILLS FAILED TO TAKE PLACE AND SUBJECT *I* IS RELATED TO ITS OCCURRENCE, SO INFINITIVE IS REQUIRED:

No I *neglected* **paying** my bills last month.

Yes I *neglected* **to pay** my bills last month.

ACTIVITY OF FINISHING HOMEWORK HAS NOT YET TAKEN PLACE AND SUBJECT *SHE* HAS AN INTEREST IN ITS COMPLETION, SO INFINITIVE IS REQUIRED:

She *wanted* me **to finish** my homework.

Verbs That Require a Noun or Pronoun before an Infinitive Complement in Active Voice

advise	command	force	lead	recruit	tempt
allow	convince	hire	move	remind	train
appoint	defy	induce	order	require	trust
authorize	enable	inspire	permit	select	urge
buy	encourage	instruct	persuade	teach	use
cause	forbid	invite	program	tell	warn
challenge					

Example 8 A noun or pronoun may appear before the infinitive complement *to leave*

I *asked* **to leave** the room. I *asked* my friend **to leave** the room.

Example 9 A noun or pronoun is required before the infinitive complement *to pursue* in active voice

No A former teacher *convinced* **to pursue** my master's degree.

Yes A former teacher *convinced* me **to pursue** my master's degree.

Example 10 The infinitive *to take* used to express a purpose

BOTH VERSIONS CONVEY THE SAME MEANING; THE REQUIRED DIRECT OBJECT IS THE INSTRUMENT USED TO ACHIEVE THE GOAL EXPRESSED IN THE INFINITIVE CLAUSE:

I *bought* a camera **to take** photographs on our trip.

I *bought* a camera **in order to take** photographs on our trip.

FOR IS NEVER USED BEFORE AN INFINITIVE COMPLEMENT:

No I *bought* a camera for **to take** photographs on our trip.

Example 11 Infinitives are used following certain nouns

AN INFINITIVE IS USED FOLLOWING A NOUN THAT EXPRESSES ABILITY OR CIRCUMSTANCE:

The mayor has the *ability* **to improve** the budget.

The junior executive chose the right *time* **to ask** for a promotion.

AN INFINITIVE IS USED FOLLOWING A NOUN THAT IS THE DIRECT OBJECT OF A CAUSATIVE VERB:

I finally made the *decision* **to fire** my real estate agent.

the event depicted in the infinitive clause.

Some verbs *allow* a noun or a pronoun before an infinitive complement. Verbs that can function either transitively or intransitively take an object (noun or pronoun) before the infinitive complement when used transitively.

Transitive verbs *require* a noun or pronoun before an infinitive complement.

3. **Infinitives may express a purpose.** When an infinitive is used to express a purpose, a noun or pronoun is *required* between the main clause verb and the infinitive. You can replace *to* in the infinitive with *in order to,* and the sentence will still convey the same meaning.
4. **Infinitives follow some nouns.** Infinitives are used following certain nouns that express ability, desirability, possibility, necessity, or circumstance (place or time). These nouns are limited in number, and many of them are used idiomatically. Examples include *ability, choice, decision, desire, duty, job, necessity, need, obligation, option, place, possibility, time.*

5. **Infinitives follow some adjectives.** Infinitives are used following adjectives that function as main clause predicates and that convey either (1) the subject's attitude toward *or* (2) the writer's or a general/conventional evaluation of the event or behavior described in the infinitive complement. The latter often occurs in sentences that have *it* as empty subject: *It is wrong* **to steal**. This type of sentence can be rewritten as a single clause with the infinitive as subject and still convey the same meaning: **To steal** *is wrong.*

Multilingual writers of English often make errors when using adjective + infinitive sequences in sentences. This is because these sequences are used in sentences that look alike but have quite different underlying structures.

Adjectives That Take Infinitive Complements When They Function as Predicates

annoying	delighted	happy	nice
anxious	difficult	hard	safe
boring	eager	important	sorry
challenging	easy	impossible	
dangerous	fun	interesting	

Example 12 Infinitives are used following certain adjectives

AN INFINITIVE (NOT A PLAIN FORM OR *-ING* FORM) IS USED AFTER AN ADJECTIVE THAT IS A PREDICATE:

No I am *eager* **graduate** from school.

Yes I am *eager* **to graduate** from school.

Example 13 Tricky adjective + infinitive combinations

Yes I am *easy* **to please.** [Meaning "It is easy (for anyone in general) to please me."]

Yes I am *delighted* **to meet** you. [Meaning "I am very happy to meet you."]

No I am *easy* **to learn** math. [Meaning "It is easy for me to learn math."]

The reason the third sentence above is *not* grammatical is complicated. To avoid making this type of error, ask yourself the following question: Does the adjective I'm using describe (a) the subject's *attitude toward* or (b) the subject's *ability to perform* the activity in the infinitive? If the answer is (b), you probably *cannot* use the structure subject + *be* verb + adjective + infinitive + object. Instead, use one of these:

- *It* + *be* verb + adjective + *for* + subject of infinitive + infinitive + object

  It is *easy* for me **to learn** math.

- subject + *find[s] it* + adjective + infinitive + object

  I find it *easy* **to learn** math.

Verbs That Take Only *-ing* Form Complements, Not Infinitive Complements

admit	contemplate	dread	go	postpone	risk
appreciate	delay	endure	imagine	practice	sit
avoid	deny	enjoy	keep	recall	stand
celebrate	describe	fancy	mention	report	start out
commence	discontinue	finish	mind	resent	suggest
consider	dislike	give up	miss	resist	

Example 14 The *-ing* form as subject takes a third person singular verb

No **Reading** novels *are* my favorite leisure activity.

Yes **Reading** novels *is* my favorite leisure activity.

Example 15 The *-ing* form is used as the object in certain prepositional phrases

I stay in shape *by* **exercising** three times every week.

Example 16 An *-ing* form must be used as the object of a preposition following a three-word phrasal verb

No How can I **make up <u>for</u>** *forget* your birthday?

Yes How can I **make up <u>for</u>** *forgetting* your birthday?

USE OF *HAVING* + PAST PARTICIPLE, WHICH IS MORE FORMAL AND MORE COMMON IN WRITING THAN IN SPEECH, EMPHASIZES THAT THE ACTION OCCURRED IN THE PAST:

How can I **make up <u>for</u>** *having forgotten* your birthday?

Example 17 The *-ing* form is used as the complement of certain verbs

THE EVENT IN THE COMPLEMENT IS REAL AND ONGOING, SO THE *-ING* FORM IS USED:

No I *enjoy* **to cook** for my friends.

Yes I *enjoy* **cooking** for my friends.

THE EVENT IN THE COMPLEMENT IS REAL AND HAS TAKEN PLACE, SO THE *-ING* FORM IS USED:

The defendant *denied* **shooting** the victim.

When and How *-ing* Forms Are Used

The **-ing form** of a verb has a variety of functions.

1. ***-ing* form as subject:** *-ing* forms frequently function as subjects (see section 40m). They require the third person singular form of the verb in the predicate: ***Sleeping** eight hours a night refreshes most people.*
2. ***-ing* form as object:** *-ing* forms act as objects in prepositional phrases that describe actions instrumental in bringing about the event in the main clause: *I learned to write by* ***writing.***
3. ***-ing* form as verbal complement:** *-ing* forms are used following certain verbs and phrasal verbs—in complement clauses—to add information to sentences that describe activities that are real and ongoing or that have taken place. In such instances, the *-ing* form represents the subject's success in accomplishing some outcome.
4. ***-ing* form as nonfinite participial clause***:* *-ing* forms are used in nonfinite clauses to add information to the main clause: *The defendant walked out of the courtroom* ***crying.***
5. ***-ing* form in progressive tense:** *-ing* forms are used with forms of *be* to form progressive tenses: *I am* ***walking*** *to school tomorrow.*

Some verbs can take both infinitive complements and *-ing* complements. For some of these verbs, it makes no difference which complement type you use. For other verbs, however, the meaning changes when you change the complement type. Be careful when using these verbs to ensure that you convey the meaning you want.

When and How to Use Plain Form Infinitives

Some verbs take **plain form infinitives,** which consist of the verb without the word *to.* These include causative verbs (*have, help, let, make*) and sensory/perception verbs (*feel, hear, notice, perceive, see*). **Causative verbs** depict situations in which the subject of one clause *causes* the subject of the other clause to perform some action.

- The causative verb ***have*** is used when the subject of the main clause causes the infinitive-clause subject to perform an activity based on authority or a business relationship between them.
- The causative verb ***make*** is used when the subject of the main clause uses its power (coercive or otherwise) to cause the infinitive-clause subject to perform an activity: *The devil made me* ***do*** *it.*
- Three causative verbs (*help, let, make*) take *only* plain form infinitive complements.

Verbs That Can Take Infinitive and *-ing* Complements

The asterisk (*) indicates that the meanings of the infinitive and *-ing* forms are different.

begin	hate	prefer	stop*
continue	like	remember*	try
forget*	love	start	

Example 18 Verbs that have the same meaning with infinitive and *-ing* complements

Lassie *began* **to act** when he was just a puppy.

Lassie *began* **acting** when he was just a puppy.

Example 19 Verbs that have different meanings with infinitive and *-ing* complements

I will *forget* **to take** this medicine. [Medicine has not been taken—prediction about future behavior.]

I will *forget* **taking** this medicine. [Medicine is being taken or has just been taken—prediction that in the future I will not remember that I have done so.]

We *stopped* **to eat** lunch at noon. [We ceased some activity in order to eat lunch—lunch has been eaten.]

We *stopped* **eating** lunch at noon. [We no longer eat lunch at noon, as was our ongoing habit.]

Example 20 Verbs that take plain form infinitives

THE CAUSATIVE VERBS *MAKE* AND *LET* REQUIRE PLAIN FORM INFINITIVES (NOT FULL INFINITIVES):

No Their parents *made* them **to wash** the family car every weekend.

Yes Their parents *made* them **wash** the family car every weekend.

Yes The professor *let* us **leave** class early.

But The professor *allowed* us **to leave** class early.

THE SENSORY VERB *HEARD* REQUIRES A PLAIN FORM INFINITIVE (NOT A FULL INFINITIVE):

No The witness said she *heard* a woman **to scream** that night.

Yes The witness said she *heard* a woman **scream** that night.

Verbs That Can Take Both Plain Form and *-ing* Complements

Some verbs allow both plain form and *-ing* complements. These include most sensory/perception verbs and the causative verb *have*. When a verb can take either type of complement, the plain form is used for discrete events whereas the *-ing* form is used for ongoing or repeated events without a specific beginning or ending.

Example 21 Sensory verbs that take both plain form and *-ing* complements

PLAIN FORM IS USED FOR DISCRETE OR COMPLETED EVENTS:

They *saw* Chris **steal** the candy.

-ING FORM IS USED FOR ONGOING EVENTS:

I *smelled* the cookies **baking** in the oven.

Present (*-ing*) and Past (*-ed*) Participles as Adjectives 61d

The *-ing* and *-ed* forms of some transitive verbs can function as adjectives. The two forms have different meanings:

- ***-ing* adjectives** report someone's perceptions of the subject of the sentence: they describe enduring aspects of the subject (not something that changes over time).
- ***-ed* adjectives** report the perceptions of the subject of the sentence: they describe the subject's thoughts or feelings. They refer to living beings almost exclusively. The characteristics that *-ed* adjectives attribute to humans and animals are usually temporary and related to a particular context or circumstance.

Verbs That Can Be Used as *-ing* Adjectives or *-ed* Adjectives, with Different Meanings

alarm	charm	disturb	humiliate	overwhelm	surprise
amaze	confuse	embarrass	inspire	please	thrill
amuse	convince	encourage	interest	satisfy	tire
annoy	depress	excite	intimidate	shock	touch
bore	disappoint	frighten	intrigue		

Example 22 Differences between *-ing* and *-ed* forms of the same adjective

I am **boring.** [I and/or other people find *me* (the subject) to be *dull and uninteresting* in general.]

I am **bored.** [I (subject) feel that *my current situation or activity* is *dull and uninteresting*.]

-ING FORM IS USED TO DESCRIBE SOMEONE ELSE'S PERCEPTIONS OF THE SUBJECT OF THE SENTENCE:

No Mosquitoes are quite **annoyed** in Minnesota in late summer.

Yes Mosquitoes are quite **annoying** in Minnesota in late summer.

-ED FORM IS USED TO REPORT PERCEPTIONS/FEELINGS ABOUT SOMETHING ON THE PART OF THE SUBJECT OF THE SENTENCE:

No I am **exciting** about my trip to the city this weekend.

Yes I am **excited** about my trip to the city this weekend.

Modals are a special type of auxiliary (helping) verb in English. Like other auxiliaries, they are never used alone. Unlike other auxiliaries, however, they are not marked for tense, person, or number, and they do not combine with full infinitives. They directly precede the plain form of the main verb (the verb without *to*).

Modals

can	ought to
could	shall
may	should
might	will
must	would

The modal *ought to* is used in casual speech but rarely in writing; *shall* is used primarily in speech, but infrequently. The remainder of the chapter focuses on modals that are used in academic writing, excluding forms that are primarily or exclusively spoken.

Expressing Present, Future, and Past Time Frames with Modals

Because modals do not indicate the time frame referred to in writing, time is marked in other ways, such as through context and through the addition of an auxiliary + present or past participle structures.

Example 23 Using modal verbs

MODALS ARE NOT USED ALONE IN WRITING; THEY PRECEDE VERBS:

No We have decided against pursuing a lawsuit at this time; however, we **may** later.

Yes We have decided against pursuing a lawsuit at this time; however, we **may** *pursue* one later.

Yes We have decided against pursuing a lawsuit at this time; however, we **may** *do so* later.

MODALS ARE NOT MARKED FOR SUBJECT-VERB AGREEMENT OR TENSE:

No He **musts** *exercise* twice a week.

Yes He **must** *exercise* twice a week.

THE PLAIN FORM OF THE VERB IS REQUIRED FOLLOWING A MODAL (NO SUBJECT-VERB AGREEMENT):

No My flight **should** *departs* at 9:00 a.m.

Yes My flight **should** *depart* at 9:00 a.m.

Example 24 Forming present, future, and past tenses with modals

PRESENT ONGOING IS MODAL + *BE* VERB + *-ING* FORM:

They **could** *be taking* the final now.

PRESENT HABITUAL IS MODAL + PLAIN FORM:

My cat **can** *fetch* toy mice.

FUTURE IS MODAL + PLAIN FORM:

Miss Kitty **might** *play* fetch with you tonight.

PAST IS MODAL + *HAVE* + *-ED/-EN* FORM OF VERB:

We **should** *have washed* the dishes.

PAST ONGOING IS MODAL + *HAVE* + *BEEN* + *-ING* FORM OF VERB:

We **must** *have been working* for hours.

Keep in mind that certain modals cannot be used with certain time frames (*will*, for example, cannot be used for past time), so you need to attend to meaning when selecting modals to insert into these patterns.

True Modal	Phrasal Modal with Similar Meaning
can, could	be able to
may, might	be allowed to, be permitted to, be able to
must	have to
should	be supposed to
will	be going to, be about to
would (to refer to a past habit)	used to

Note that *used to* is already in the past tense and is used only in that form.

Example 25 Using phrasal modals

PHRASAL MODALS ARE MARKED FOR SUBJECT-VERB AGREEMENT AND TENSE:

No She **have to** *exercise* twice a week.

Yes She **has to** *exercise* twice a week.

Yes She **used to** *go* to the gym after work. [Past tense]

Yes She **is able to** *work out* in the morning now that she has retired. [Present tense]

THE FULL INFINITIVE VERB FORM IS USED FOLLOWING A PHRASAL MODAL:

Restaurant servers **are** not **permitted** *to wear* jewelry.

They **are going** *to file* a complaint with the labor union.

Example 26 Marking tense with phrasal modals

PHRASAL MODALS MUST BE MARKED FOR TENSE WHEN NOT PRECEDED BY A TRUE MODAL:

No We **are supposed to** study last night.

Yes We **were supposed to** study last night.

THE PHRASAL MODAL IS NOT MARKED FOR TENSE WHEN IT FOLLOWS A TRUE MODAL:

We **may be able to** *buy* pizza at the fair.

Using Phrasal Modals

In addition to true modals, English speakers regularly make use of phrasal modals. Phrasal modals are multi-word sequences that end with the infinitive marker *to* and carry modal-like meanings. Unlike true modals, phrasal modals *are* marked for tense and subject-verb agreement, and the full infinitive form is required for verbs following them.

Phrasal modals are more casual than true modals, but they also carry an added element of meaning: because they are inflected for tense, they allow writers to indicate aspects of time, duration, and modality. In fact, they developed because true modals—which started out as regular, tensed verbs—lost their tense distinctions over time.

The only time phrasal modals are *not* marked for tense is when they follow a true modal.

Combining Modals in Sentences

Modals and phrasal modals can be combined, but only in specific ways. A clause should contain only one true modal, but it can be combined with a phrasal modal. And phrasal modals can be combined. It is not uncommon to see three phrasal modals in succession.

Forming Negatives and Questions with Modals

To form the negative of a sentence that contains one or more modals, insert a negative word (*not, never*) immediately after the modal or, if the sentence does not include a true modal, after the first word of a phrasal modal. In conversation and informal writing, negatives and modals are often combined in contractions: *cannot* → *can't, should not* → *shouldn't, will not* → *won't*. However, contractions are rarely used in formal academic writing.

To form a question, switch the sentence's subject with the true modal or with the first word of the phrasal modal that immediately follows it. In cases where the phrasal modal does not start with a *be* verb (such as *have to* and *used to*), the appropriately tensed form of *do* must be inserted before the subject to create a question.

Example 27 Combining modals and phrasal modals

TRUE MODAL + TRUE MODAL + VERB IS UNGRAMMATICAL:

No I **should could** *run* five miles without taking a break.

PHRASAL MODAL + TRUE MODAL + VERB IS UNGRAMMATICAL:

No I **used to could** *run* five miles.

TRUE MODAL + PHRASAL MODAL + VERB IS GRAMMATICAL:

Yes I **should be able to** *run* five miles without taking a break.

PHRASAL MODAL + PHRASAL MODAL + VERB IS GRAMMATICAL:

Yes I **am supposed to be allowed to** *swim* in the lake.

Example 28 Forming negatives with modals and phrasal modals

I **will** not *attend* the graduation ceremony.

Inmates **are** not **supposed to be able to** *purchase* drugs inside the prison.

Example 29 Forming questions with modals and phrasal modals

IN PHRASAL MODALS THAT DO NOT START WITH A *BE* VERB, INSERT *DO* BEFORE THE SUBJECT:

I **have to** *serve* on the jury.

No **Have** I **to** *serve* on the jury?

Yes Do I **have to** *serve* on the jury?

He **used to** *smoke* as a teenager.

Did he **used to** *smoke* as a teenager?

IF THE SENTENCE ALREADY CONTAINS A TRUE MODAL, INVERT SUBJECT AND MODAL:

I **can** *go* to the concert.

No Do I **can** *go* to the concert?

Yes **Can** I *go* to the concert?

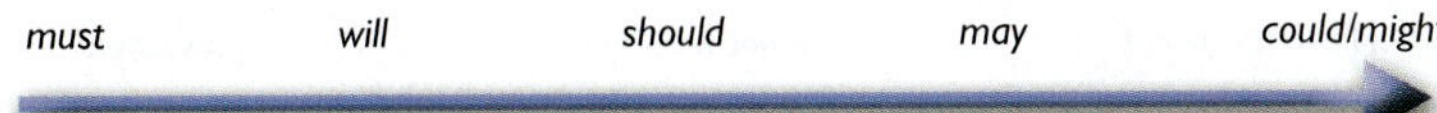

The same scale applies to expressing degrees of certainty about events in the past, but the past participle (*have* + *-ed* or *-en* form of verb) is added to each modal: **should** *have studied.*

Example 30 Using modals to express present inferences

MUST EXPRESSES A HIGH DEGREE OF CERTAINTY:

I have been coughing all day; I **must** *have* a cold.

WILL EXPRESSES A HIGH DEGREE OF CERTAINTY:

We **will** *present* our findings at the conference.

SHOULD EXPRESSES A MODERATE DEGREE OF CERTAINTY:

The article **should** *appear* in this week's news.

MAY EXPRESSES A LOW DEGREE OF CERTAINTY:

The senator **may** *run* for President.

MIGHT EXPRESSES AN EVEN LOWER DEGREE OF CERTAINTY:

She **might** *win* the election.

Example 31 Using modals to express past inferences

HIGH DEGREE OF CERTAINTY:

The cat **must** *have escaped* when you left for work.

MODERATE DEGREE OF CERTAINTY:

You **should** *have received* your acceptance letter by now.

Expressing Perspective with Modals

Consider these sentences:

She *pays* the bills on time.
She **might** *pay* the bills on time.

The first sentence merely reports a fact, whereas the second sentence includes an assessment of probability—by including *might,* the writer implies that the action expressed by the main verb is not very likely.

Modals perform a variety of functions in discourse, including logical ones, such as expressing degrees of certainty, and social ones, such as making requests politely. Almost all modals can perform both logical and social functions; likewise, the same meaning can be expressed by more than one modal. These multiple meanings are the cause of most difficulties writers encounter. To help you detect and avoid these problems, this section discusses how modals are used to perform three logical functions (expressing probability, necessity, and ability) and two social functions (making requests and giving advice).

Modals Expressing Degrees of Probability

Modals are used to express different degrees of probability or certainty regarding the inferences we make.

Modals can also be used to express present inferences in *negative* terms.

might not/may not — *will not/would not* — *cannot/could not*

Low Possibility → Impossible

The modals *should* and *must* are not used to express negative present inferences.

Example 32 Using modals to express negative present inferences

MIGHT NOT/MAY NOT EXPRESSES LOW POSSIBILITY:

I liked the offer, but I **might not** *take* the job.

WILL NOT/WOULD NOT EXPRESSES IMPROBABILITY:

I **will not** *move* for my job.

CANNOT/COULD NOT EXPRESSES IMPOSSIBILITY:

I **cannot** *meet* you before noon today.

Modals Expressing Degrees of Necessity

The modals most commonly used to express necessity or obligation are *must* and *have to.* A primarily spoken form, *have to* is considerably more informal than its true modal counterpart. *Must* and *be required to* are preferred forms in much academic writing.

Example 33 Using modals to express necessity

Students **must** *maintain* a B average in order to qualify for a scholarship.

THE PAST TENSE OF *HAVE TO* IS USED TO EXPRESS PAST NECESSITY; *WERE REQUIRED TO* COULD BE SUBSTITUTED FOR IT HERE:

In the past, international students **had to** *pay* out-of-state tuition.

Modals Expressing Ability

The modals most commonly used to express ability or potentiality are *can, could,* and *be able to. Can* and *cannot* are used to express ability and lack of ability, respectively, whereas *could* and *could not* are used to express past ability and lack of ability, respectively. *Not be able to* carries the same meaning as *cannot,* but *be able to* and *can* are not exactly synonymous. In contrast to other phrasal modals, *be able to* is more formal than its modal counterpart *can* (which is used more frequently in speech), and it is used primarily to indicate that some effort or difficulty is involved. *Be able to* is also used in structures where a true modal (*can*) cannot be used, such as following another true modal, in perfect forms (*have* + *been able to* + *-ed* or *-en* verb), and with *-ing* and infinitive forms (*being able to; to be able to*).

Example 34 Using modals to express ability or lack of ability

CAN EXPRESSES ABILITY IN THE PRESENT:

I **can** *speak* four languages.

COULD EXPRESSES PAST ABILITY:

When she was young, my cat **could** *jump* onto the refrigerator.

THE PAST PERFECT FORM OF *COULD* EXPRESSES THE IDEA THAT THE SUBJECT HAD THE ABILITY TO COMPLETE THE HOMEWORK IN THE PAST, BUT DID *NOT* DO IT:

You **could** *have finished* your homework last night.

BE ABLE TO EXPRESSES EFFORT OR DIFFICULTY:

After hours of searching, we **were** finally **able to** *find* a hotel room.

CAN CANNOT BE USED IN A PRESENT PERFECT CONSTRUCTION DESCRIBING AN ABILITY THAT STARTED AT SOME POINT AND CONTINUES INTO THE PRESENT:

No — She *has* **can** *play* guitar since she was a child.

Yes — She *has* **been able to** *play* guitar since she was a child.

Example 35 Using modals with requests

No **Can** you *write* a letter of recommendation for me?

IN THIS PREFERRED FORM, *WOULD* MAKES IT CLEAR THAT THE PERSON TO WHOM THE QUESTION IS ADDRESSED HAS A CHOICE—THAT THE SPEAKER IS ASKING A FAVOR:

Yes **Would** you *write* a letter of recommendation for me?

COULD INCLUDES A SLIGHT CONNOTATION OF ABILITY, ALLOWING FOR THE POSSIBILITY THAT THE PERSON TO WHOM THE QUESTION IS ADDRESSED MAY BE UNABLE TO PERFORM THE ACTION:

Could you *write* a letter of recommendation for me?

To decide which form to use, consider the facts of the social situation, such as the status of the person to whom you are making a request or responding and the context of the interaction.

might/might not/could *should/should not* *must/must not*

Less Authority/Less Urgent Great Authority/Very Urgent

Should/should not are used most commonly to indicate whether or not something is advisable.

Example 36 Using modals to give advice

You **must not** *plagiarize;* be sure to document all of your outside sources. [Teacher to class]

You **should** *save* ten percent of your earnings each month. [Banker to client]

You **should** *have gone* to the doctor as soon as you started coughing. [Mother to child]

You **should not** *have cheated* on your final exam. [Dean to student]

You **might** *ask* the professor for an extension on the assignment. [Roommate to roommate]

Modals Used to Make Requests

The modals *will/would, can/could,* and *may/might* are used to make and respond to requests. The forms *would, could,* and *might* are preferred for making requests because they are considered more polite and deferential; they allow for the possibility of a negative reply. In contrast, the forms *will, can,* and *may* are preferred for responding to requests because they are more direct and they do not make the reply sound conditional.

Modals Used to Give Advice

Modals that are used to give advice can be organized on a continuum according to the urgency of the advice and/or the writer's degree of authority.

The present perfect form (*should have* + *-ed* or *-en* verb) is used to express an advisable action that did not occur in the past; the present perfect negative (*should not have* + *-ed* or *-en* verb) is used to indicate a past action that occurred but was not advisable. *Must* is used when the message is very urgent or the writer has great authority. In its negative form (*must not*), it expresses a prohibition (that is, that something is highly unadvisable). *Might/might not* and *could* are used when the writer has a low level of authority or is addressing a person of higher status or when the advice is tentative or not very urgent.

62

ENGLISH SENTENCE STRUCTURE

The rules for forming sentences in English are fairly straightforward, but they differ in a number of ways from those used in other languages. These differences are frequently the source of errors in texts by multilingual writers. This chapter focuses on subjects in sentences, the order of direct and indirect objects with specific verbs, the placement of adjectives in sentences, word order in different types of questions, and the structure of sentences containing direct versus indirect discourse.

You may also find sections 40j through 40o of this handbook particularly useful as you consider how to structure English sentences. For help with editing and proofreading strategies, refer to sections 6i and 6j. Finally, each of the chapters in Part 8 (Chapters 40–46) offers information about composing, revising, and editing sentences.

Subjects 62a

The subject should be mentioned only once per clause in a sentence. Do not repeat it within a clause, not even by substituting a pronoun.

Example 1 Subject is named only once per clause in a sentence

No The **kitty she** is very playful.
Yes The **kitty** is very playful.

No **Ramon,** after **he** graduated from high school, **he** came to the United States.
Yes After **Ramon** graduated from high school, **he** came to the United States.

Order of Direct and Indirect Objects Following Different Verbs 62b

Some verbs allow or require both a direct and an indirect object. A **direct object** denotes the person or thing that is acted upon in a sentence. An **indirect object** denotes the person or thing that receives or benefits from the action expressed by the verb. The order in which direct and indirect objects occur in a sentence is determined by the main verb. Different verbs allow different orders. There are two basic orders you should remember.

Order 1: Verb + Direct Object + *to* or *for* + Indirect Object

Some verbs are never immediately followed by an indirect object; they can take an indirect object only *after* a direct object—and the indirect object must be preceded by a preposition (*to* or *for*). The preposition used to introduce the indirect object is determined

Verbs That Are Never Followed by an Indirect Object (Order 1)

Introduce indirect object with *to:*	Introduce indirect object with *for:*	Introduce indirect object with either *to* or *for:*
announce	answer	introduce
confess	cash	recommend
donate	close	suggest
explain	narrate	transmit
mention	open	
reveal	repair	

Example 2 Some verbs require order 1

THE INDIRECT OBJECT CANNOT IMMEDIATELY FOLLOW THE VERB:

No Dr. Rodriguez carefully explained **us** *the surgery.*

THE INDIRECT OBJECT FOLLOWS THE DIRECT OBJECT:

Yes Dr. Rodriguez carefully explained *the surgery* (DO) **to us.** (IO)

by the verb. Some verbs introduce indirect objects with *to;* other verbs introduce indirect objects with *for.* Still other verbs introduce them with either *to* or *for,* and the preposition that is chosen affects the meaning of the sentence. *To* is used to introduce indirect objects that receive something (concrete or abstract), whereas *for* is used to introduce indirect objects that benefit from the action of the verb.

Order 1 is also commonly used with indirect objects that are lengthy, to aid readability.

Order 2: Verb + Indirect Object + Direct Object

Some verbs are almost always followed by indirect objects; they take indirect objects *before* direct objects. In these cases, no preposition (*to* or *for*) is used before the indirect object. This order is commonly used when the direct object is a pronoun. Because the end of a clause receives emphasis in English, this position is generally reserved for new information. Pronouns, by definition, refer back to things that have already been introduced—old information—so when a pronoun is a direct object it is generally placed in the middle of a clause, where it will not receive emphasis. This allows the indirect object to be emphasized.

Example 3 Preposition use varies with indirect objects that follow direct objects

FOR IS USED TO INTRODUCE INDIRECT OBJECTS OF THE VERB *ANSWER:*

No The explanation answered *many questions* **to both of us.**

Yes The explanation answered *many questions* **for both of us.**

TO IS USED TO INTRODUCE INDIRECT OBJECTS OF THE VERB *ANNOUNCE:*

No Who will announce *the merger* **for the public**?

Yes Who will announce *the merger* **to the public**?

Example 4 Order 1 is used with lengthy indirect objects

The game show offers *a recording contract* **to the singer who receives the most votes.**

Verbs That Are Almost Always Followed by Indirect Objects (Order 2)

allow	cause	deny	promise
ask	charge	envy	refuse
bet	cost	forgive	teach
bill			

Example 5 Some verbs require order 2

No Juan promised *a new bicycle* (DO) **to/for his daughter.** (IO)

Yes Juan promised **his daughter** (IO) *a new bicycle.* (DO)

Example 6 With order 2, no prepositions are used with indirect objects that follow verbs

No The trainer asked **to new clients** *many questions about their general health.*

Yes The trainer asked **new clients** *many questions about their general health.*

Verbs That Allow Either Order

Many verbs can take objects in either order—order 1 *or* order 2. With these verbs, you can switch the order of the objects without altering the meaning of the sentence. The order of the objects determines only what is emphasized in the sentence. The object that is placed second receives emphasis because it is at the end of the clause.

Verbs That Allow Objects in Either Order (Order 1 or Order 2)

When using Order 2, introduce indirect object with *to:*	When using Order 2, introduce indirect object with *for:*	When using Order 2, introduce indirect object with either *to* or *for:*
advance	book	bring
award	build	fax
deal	buy	get
forward	cook	leave
give	design	mail
grant	find	pay
hand	guarantee	read
lease	make	send
lend	mix	sing
offer	order	take
owe	paint	write
pass	play	
rent	pour	
sell	prepare	
serve	reserve	
show	save	
tell	secure	
throw	set	
	spare	
	win	

Example 7 When the indirect object is a pronoun, it precedes the direct object

My boss offered **me** *a big raise* to stay with the company.

Example 8 Sentence meaning changes when different prepositions introduce indirect objects

Administrative assistants sometimes *write* letters *for* **their managers.** [Managers do not write letters themselves; assistants write letters on their behalf.]

Administrative assistants sometimes *write* letters *to* **their managers.** [Assistants write letters addressed to their managers.]

Adjectives are used in two primary ways in English: (1) to add information about nouns (**attributive adjectives**) and (2) to complement *be* and linking verbs (**predicative adjectives**). When used attributively, adjectives are placed immediately before the noun they modify and after any determiners (*a, the, her*): *the* **stunning** *cathedral.* Used predicatively, adjectives are placed after the linking verb.

A third way in which adjectives are used is to modify nouns that function as direct objects of certain transitive verbs, including verbs of causation and verbs indicating a person's opinion of or preference for something. Adjectives used in this way are called **object complements,** and they are placed *after* the noun (direct object) they modify.

Adjective Form

Adjectives have one form; they remain the same regardless of whether the noun they modify is singular or plural or acts as subject or object. Note that many adjectives end in *ing* (most of which are related to the present participles of verbs) or *ed* (most of which are related to the past participles of verbs). Refer to Chapter 61 for more information on the meaning and use of *-ing* and *-ed* adjectives.

Example 9 Placement of attributive adjectives

ATTRIBUTIVE ADJECTIVES PRECEDE THE NOUN THEY MODIFY:

No The *tree* **old** was struck by lightning.

Yes The **old** *tree* was struck by lightning.

Example 10 Placement of predicative adjectives

The attorney's closing argument *was* **convincing.**

Verbs That Take Adjectives as Object Complements

believe	hold	pick	think
consider	keep	prefer	want
drive	leave	render	wipe
eat	like	send	
find	make	serve	
get	paint	show	

Example 11 Placement of object complements

(OBJ = *italic*; OBJ COMP = **bold**)

They keep *their lawn* **immaculate.**

The cab ride made *me* **dizzy.**

I like *my water* **chilled.**

Example 12 Adjectives are never inflected for number or person

No Lee's **musicals** *performances* are **impressives.**

Yes Lee's **musical** *performances* are **impressive.**

Order of Adjectives

NUMBER	EVALUATION	PHYSICAL DESCRIPTION (SIZE, SHAPE, AGE, COLOR)	NATIONALITY	RELIGION	CLASSIFYING ADJECTIVES

The **two, handsome, tall, thin, young, tanned, Greek Orthodox male** *models* smiled at us.

Example 13 Order of adjectives in sequence

EVALUATIVE ADJECTIVES PRECEDE COLOR ADJECTIVES, WHICH PRECEDE CLASSIFYING ADJECTIVES:

No My **leather red beautiful** *briefcase* is from Florence.

Yes My **beautiful red leather** *briefcase* is from Florence.

Yes/No Questions

Example 14 Inverting *were* and subject when main verb is *be*

They **were** happy.

No *Do* they **were** happy?

Yes **Were** they happy?

Example 15 Inverting modal and subject

Corinna **should** adopt a cat.

Should Corinna adopt a cat?

Example 16 Inserting *do* before subject and using plain form of main verb

The virus **affects** your immune system.

No *Does* the virus **affects** your immune system?

Yes *Does* the virus **affect** your immune system?

62c

Order of Adjectives

When a sequence of adjectives is used to modify the same noun, the order of adjectives within that sequence is not completely arbitrary; rules govern the order of certain types of adjectives. In general, qualitative or evaluative adjectives come first, followed by color adjectives, followed by classifying adjectives.

Forming Questions 62d

There are two types of questions in English: *yes/no* questions and *wh-* information questions. Both types end with a question mark. ***Yes/no* questions** can be answered with a simple *yes* or *no* (in practice, answers often include more information and may not contain the word *yes* or *no*).

To form yes/no questions from sentences

- If the predicate is a single *be* verb, reverse the order of the subject and the *be* verb.
- If the predicate contains one or more modals, reverse the order of the subject and the first modal.
- If the predicate is a single main verb (with no modals), insert *do* or *did* before the subject.

Note: *Do* must be marked for tense and must match the subject in person and number. Use the plain form of the main verb.

***Wh-* information questions** begin with a question word (*who, what, when, where, why, how*) and cannot be answered with a simple *yes* or *no*. They are used to request specific information and can refer to any component of a proposition (its subject, objects, verb, etc.).

S DO IO
Who *gave* what to whom?

To form wh- information questions from sentences

Step 1. Express the question you wish to ask in statement form, including the appropriate *wh-* word in place of the information (answer) you seek.

Step 2. Move the *wh-* word to the beginning of the sentence. If the *wh-* word introduces a noun or noun phrase (i.e., *which* + noun), move both the *wh-* word and the noun to the front.

Step 3. Follow the rules for *yes/no* question formation that apply to the predicate of the sentence:

- With a *be* verb, reverse the subject and the *be* verb:

  wh- word + *be* verb + subject + . . . ?

- With a modal, reverse the subject and the first modal:

  wh- word + modal + subject + main verb + . . . ?

- With a main verb, insert *do/did* before the subject:

  wh- word + *do/did* + subject + plain form verb + . . . ?

Choosing the Appropriate *Wh-* Word for Your Question

To ask about . . .	**Use this *wh-* word:**
a person or group of people	*who*
an object or activity	*what* or *which/whose* + noun
time of action	*when*
location	*where*
reason for or cause of action	*why*
manner in which action is performed	*how*

Example 17 Forming *wh-* information questions

STATE QUESTION — MOVE *WH-* TO FRONT — APPLY Y/N QUESTION RULE

Your office *is* **where?** → **Where** your office *is?* → **Where** *is* your office?

Example 18 Word order with *wh-* questions

WITH MODAL, INVERT SUBJECT AND MODAL:

Why *the candidate* **should** resign? → Why **should** *the candidate* resign?

WITH SINGLE MAIN VERB, USE STANDARD WORD ORDER (SVO):

How did **escape** *the inmates* from prison? → How did *the inmates* **escape** from prison?

WHEN *WH-* WORD IS SUBJECT, USE STANDARD ORDER:

Who **wrote** this book?

Example 19 Verb form with *wh-* questions containing single main verb

DO TAKES ON TENSE OF MAIN VERB, SO MAIN VERB CONVERTS TO PLAIN FORM:

Chris supported **who**? → **Who** Chris supported? → **Who** *did* Chris support?

DO IS MARKED FOR THIRD-PERSON SINGULAR, SO *S* IS REMOVED FROM MAIN VERB, LEAVING PLAIN FORM:

Li enjoys **what**? → **What** Li enjoys? → **What** *does* Li enjoy?

DO MATCHES SUBJECT, NOT OBJECT, IN PERSON AND NUMBER:

Jo prefers **which** ones? → **Which** ones Jo prefers? → **Which** ones *does* Jo prefer?

In academic writing, you will frequently need to report what other people have said or written about a topic. You can do this by quoting the exact words of the original source (direct quotation), by reporting the content of the original source using indirect quotation (indirect reported speech), or by rewriting the ideas of the original source entirely in your own words (paraphrase). This section focuses on the second of these three methods. Refer to Chapter 17 for a detailed treatment of direct quotation and paraphrase.

Indirect reported speech, which is used to convey the ideas of a source but not the source's exact words, is far more common in academic writing and everyday conversation than direct quotation. Reporting speech indirectly involves (1) creating a **reporting clause** containing a **reporting verb** and (2) attaching the clause to a **complement clause** containing the information being reported. The type of complement clause you use depends on the type of structure you are reporting (a statement or a question) and the reporting verb you use (different verbs allow different complements).

Example 20 Components of indirect quotation

REPORTING CLAUSE — COMPLEMENT CLAUSE

The author contends **that** the planet is shrinking.

Reporting Verbs That Take Ordinary (Tensed) *that* Clauses as Complements

acknowledge	complain	find	mention	report
admit	conclude	forget	note	reveal
agree	decide	guarantee	observe	say
allege	determine	guess	predict	show
answer	discover	hear	promise	state
argue	doubt	imply	prove	suggest
assume	estimate	know	read	think
believe	expect	learn	realize	understand
claim	explain	maintain	remember	write
comment				

Reporting Verbs That Take an Indirect Object + *that* Clause

assure convince inform persuade remind tell

Reporting Verbs That Take Subjunctive (Uninflected) *that* Clauses as Complements

advise	insist	propose	require
ask	order	recommend	suggest
demand	prefer	request	urge

Example 21 Verb form in *that* complements of reporting verbs

THINK REQUIRES INFLECTED VERB IN *THAT* COMPLEMENT:

I think **that** she *is* treasurer of the organization.

REQUEST REQUIRES PLAIN FORM VERB IN *THAT* COMPLEMENT:

The teacher requested **that** she *arrive* on time for her piano lesson.

Reporting Statements and Thoughts

Using that complements

The most common way to report statements and thoughts is to use a complement clause beginning with *that*. Many reporting verbs take *that*-clause complements, which consist of *that* plus a clause containing a verb that may or may not need to be inflected for tense, person, and number. Some of these verbs require an indirect object; in these cases, the indirect object precedes the *that* clause.

Omitting that

You may have noticed that *that* is sometimes absent from reporting clauses. The decision to omit *that* is based on several factors. In formal contexts and academic writing, *that* is generally included. *That* can be omitted when (1) the subject of the *that* complement is a pronoun (*it, she*), (2) the reporting clause and the *that* clause have the same subject, and/or (3) the writing context is informal.

Infinitive and -ing complements

Some reporting verbs can take infinitive complement clauses (starting with *to* + verb) or *-ing* complement clauses (starting with the *-ing* form).

Example 22 Reporting verbs *say* and *tell*

SAY DOES NOT TAKE AN INDIRECT OBJECT:

The flight attendant said **that** the seat cushions function as flotation devices.

TELL REQUIRES AN INDIRECT OBJECT:

The flight attendant told passengers **that** the seat cushions function as flotation devices.

Example 23 Omitting *that* in complements of reporting verbs

THAT IS FREQUENTLY OMITTED WHEN THE SUBJECT OF THE COMPLEMENT CLAUSE IS A PRONOUN:

The surgeons said (*that*) **he** was doing better.

THAT IS USUALLY OMITTED WHEN THE REPORTING CLAUSE AND COMPLEMENT CLAUSE HAVE THE SAME SUBJECT:

The pilot said (*that*) **she** enjoyed flying.

THAT IS USUALLY RETAINED IN MORE FORMAL AND ACADEMIC TEXTS:

Scientists discovered *that* extensive exposure to ultraviolet light correlates with skin cancer.

Reporting Verbs That Can Take Infinitive Complements

An asterisk (*) indicates that the verb requires an indirect object before the complement.

advise*	instruct*	plan	tell*
ask	intend	promise	urge*
beg	invite*	refuse	want
decide	order*	remind*	warn*
forbid*	persuade*	teach*	

Reporting Verbs That Can Take *-ing* Form Complements

advise	predict	recommend	suggest

Example 24 Infinitive and *-ing* complements of reporting verbs

The test supervisor *instructed* us **to use** a number two pencil to write answers.

Lifeguards *recommend* **waiting** thirty minutes after a meal to swim.

Reporting Verbs That Take *if* and *whether* Clauses as Complements

ask	inquire	remember	see
discover	know	say	wonder

Example 25 Complement clauses with indirect *yes/no* questions

COMPLEMENT CLAUSES IN REPORTED QUESTIONS MUST START WITH *IF* OR *WHETHER*:

No The prosecuting attorney asked me *did I witness* the crime.

Yes The prosecuting attorney asked me **if/whether** *I witnessed* the crime.

INFINITIVE COMPLEMENTS MUST BEGIN WITH *WHETHER; OR NOT* MAY BE INCLUDED BUT IS OPTIONAL:

No I wondered **if** *to bring* an umbrella on my trip.

Yes I wondered **whether (or not)** *to bring* an umbrella on my trip.

TENSED COMPLEMENTS MAY BEGIN WITH *WHETHER* OR *IF*:

I wondered **if/whether** *I should bring* an umbrella on my trip.

Example 26 Word order with indirect *yes/no* questions

REPORTED QUESTIONS FOLLOW STATEMENT ORDER, NOT QUESTION ORDER:

No An accountant would know **whether** *is* the company financially sound.

Yes An accountant would know **whether** the company *is* financially sound.

Reporting Verbs That Take *wh-* Question Complements

ask	forget	realize	suggest
decide	guess	remember	teach
describe	imagine	reveal	tell
discover	inquire	say	think
discuss	know	see	understand
explain	learn	show	wonder
find out			

Example 27 Form of complement clauses with indirect *wh-* questions

REPORTED *WH-* QUESTIONS CAN HAVE TENSED OR INFINITIVE CLAUSES AS COMPLEMENTS:

He explained **where** we *should go* in the event of a tornado. [*wh* word + tensed clause]

He explained **where** *to go* in the event of a tornado. [*wh* word + infinitive clause]

Reporting Questions

In addition to reporting statements in your writing, you may wish to report questions that people ask. These are referred to as **indirect questions,** since you are reporting—not actually asking—the questions.

Indirect yes/no questions

The complement clause of an indirect *yes/no* question consists of *whether* or *if* followed by a tensed or infinitive clause. If the complement clause contains a modal or tensed verb (that is, if it is a tensed clause), it may begin with *whether* or *if.* If the complement contains an infinitive, it must begin with *whether.* Unlike direct questions, indirect questions follow standard statement word order (SVO)—subjects are not inverted with verbs, *do* is not inserted, and question marks are not used.

Indirect* wh- *questions

Indirect *wh-* information questions contain complement clauses that consist of a *wh-* word followed by a tensed or infinitive clause in standard statement word order (SVO). Do not invert subjects and verbs, insert *do,* or use a question mark as end punctuation with indirect questions.

Tense Shifts in Indirect Quotations

Verb tense is one of the most confusing aspects of indirect reporting for multilingual writers of English. Usually when you use indirect speech, you are reporting something that another person said, thought, wrote, or asked in the past. Thus, the reporting verb and the verb in the complement clause are often in past tense. However, if you are reporting something that is still (currently) true or something that is said frequently, you may use either a present tense or a past tense verb in the reporting clause. When you are reporting published statements, it is common to use present tense reporting verbs because what the author wrote remains the same eternally.

Whatever the tense of the verb in the reporting clause, you should put the verb in the complement clause in the tense that is appropriate at the time you are writing (or speaking). See Chapter 44 for more detail on verb tense.

Example 28 Word order with indirect *wh-* questions

REPORTED QUESTIONS FOLLOW STATEMENT ORDER, NOT QUESTION ORDER:

No The researcher asked participants **how** *did* they *exercise* each week.

Yes The researcher asked participants **how** they *exercised* each week.

Example 29 Punctuating indirect questions

USE A PERIOD, NOT A QUESTION MARK, AT THE END OF A REPORTED QUESTION:

No The officers wondered **what** we were doing**?**

Yes The officers wondered **what** we were doing.

INCLUDE A QUESTION MARK WHEN A QUESTION IS REPORTED IN A DIRECT QUOTATION:

The officers asked, "**What** are you doing**?**"

Example 30 Verb tense with indirect quotations

SENTENCES DESCRIBING SITUATIONS THAT ARE STILL TRUE CAN TAKE A PAST OR PRESENT TENSE VERB IN THE COMPLEMENT:

Mary *said* (that) she *was* an associate professor of history.

Mary *said* (that) she *is* an associate professor of history.

TO SHOW THAT A SITUATION IS NO LONGER TRUE, A PHRASAL VERB IS OFTEN USED IN THE COMPLEMENT:

Mary *said* (that) she *used to be* an associate professor of history.

FREQUENTLY REPORTED OR PUBLISHED STATEMENTS CAN TAKE PRESENT TENSE REPORTING VERBS:

Doctors *say* (that) drinking a glass of wine each day *can reduce* the risk of heart disease.

Example 31 Pronoun and verb changes required in indirect speech

DIRECT QUOTATION:

Steve agreed: "You should take the trip alone."

IN INDIRECT REPORTING, SECOND PERSON (*YOU*) CHANGES TO FIRST PERSON OBJECT CASE (*ME*); TENSED VERB CHANGES TO INFINITIVE BECAUSE *ADVISE* TAKES INDIRECT OBJECT + INFINITIVE COMPLEMENT:

No Steve advised **I** *should* take the trip alone.

Yes Steve advised **me** *to take* the trip alone.

Example 32 Modal changes required in indirect speech

DIRECT QUOTATION:

"I will observe the class for one year," said Jane Doe.

IN INDIRECT REPORTING, MODAL *WILL* (PRESENT) CHANGES TO *WOULD* (PAST):

No Doe reported that she **will** observe the class for one year.

Yes Doe reported that she **would** observe the class for one year.

Example 33 Choosing reporting verbs that convey your interpretation of reported information

The researchers _______ that their discovery represents a significant advance in science.

say	neutral
suggest	implies doubt or tentativeness on the part of the researchers
claim	implies that the researchers' statement is nonobvious or unproven
argue	implies that the researchers are making a claim and can support it with reasons
assume	implies that the researchers believe the statement but do not offer reasons for their belief

Other Changes with Indirect Quotations

In addition to modifying the tense of the verb in the reporting clause and/or the complement clause, converting direct to indirect speech may require you to change other expressions, including pronouns, modals, and words for time and place.

Common Changes in Pronouns

I	→	*she* or *he*
we	→	*they*
me	→	*her* or *him*
my	→	*her* or *his*
you	→	*me*

Common Changes in Modals

can	→	*could*
may	→	*might*
will	→	*would*
must	→	*had to*

Common Changes in Expressions of Time and Place

this	→	*that*
these	→	*those*
here	→	*there*

Varying Reporting Verbs

When reporting information in your writing, try to vary the reporting verbs and, where appropriate, incorporate verbs that convey your attitude toward the information you are reporting. Avoid overusing *say, report,* and *state.*

A

absolute link A link to a complete URL, with the protocol (http://) and domain name.

access Availability of computing technology or entry to a website.

accessibility A Web authoring standard designed to ensure that people with disabilities can perceive, understand, navigate, and interact with the World Wide Web and that they can contribute to its growth and refinement.

analog signal An electronic signal, transmitted from one medium to another, that is directly representative of the source. For example, an analog telephone transmits a signal whose form mimics the sound of a voice and allows that sound to be re-created on the receiving end. In contrast, digital signals use numbers (not direct representations) to define and re-create source content across media.

anchor tag An internal, relative link on a Web page from one point to another, always beginning with the # sign.

annotation A note attached electronically to a document.

application Any program designed to perform a specific function directly for the user or the operating system.

ASCII American standard code for information interchange; a code that assigns numbers to a character set of 128 letters, numbers, and symbols (or glyphs).

asynchronous Describes events, including communication via email, blogging, and forum posts, that are not coordinated in time and may take place over extended periods.

authoring program A computer application designed to help people create documents for the Web or print.

B

backup A copy of a file or set of files created to protect a user in case of unexpected loss of data.

bandwidth A measure of the capacity of a communication channel, such as an Internet connection. The higher the bandwidth, the more information the channel can carry.

binary code A symbol system consisting of two states, On (1) and Off (0), that turn circuits in a computer on and off.

bit Binary digit; a single instance (symbol) of binary code. Every message or action on a computer is translated into a collection of bits.

blog, blogging See **weblog.**

Bluetooth A communication standard that helps different types of electronic equipment (such as cell phones, PDAs, laptops, keyboards, and mice) communicate wirelessly.

bookmarks Website addresses stored on a user's machine and available in the browser. Sometimes bookmarks are called favorites.

boot, boot up To start (or restart) a computer.

bps Bits per second; a measure of the amount of data sent through a connection.

broadband A form of data transmission that carries signals in different frequencies at the same time, such as Internet, telephone, and television signals.

browser A program used to view and interact with various types of resources available on the World Wide Web.

byte A series of 8 bits (1s and 0s) that represent a single character.

C

cable modem A device that enables a broadband connection to the Internet over cable TV lines.

cache An area of computer data storage where files can be stored for rapid access. Browsers use cached files to speed up the loading of Web pages.

CD-ROM Compact disk read-only memory; a disk used to store digital data files for reading by optical readers, such as CD-ROM drives.

chat Real-time, text-based communication between two or more people via the Internet.

click To position the pointer on an object or text on the screen and then press and quickly release the mouse button.

client A program used to request information or services from another computer, such as a server. Email programs are clients that request information from mail servers.

code Instructions to a computer in a programming language. HTML code, for example, consists of tags and other commands that tell browsers how to display text and images on a Web page.

compression A process of reducing the number of bytes in a file to make the file smaller in size and easier to transmit across a network.

content management system (CMS) Server software used to organize and facilitate collaborative creation and sharing of documents and other content on the Internet or an intranet or network.

cookie A file, stored on a browser, that may contain information about the user (such as the contents of a shopping cart) and may be transmitted back to the server each time the user visits the site.

copyleft A stipulation that software or any other content may be copied freely and redistributed provided the user adheres to or passes along the copyleft agreement.

copyright The legal right of an author, artist, or publisher to retain ownership of his or her work and to grant others the rights to reprint or distribute it.

courseware A prepackaged set of software tools for delivering course content on the Internet or CD-ROM, often used for distance learning and self-paced courses.

Creative Commons A nonprofit organization that offers flexible copyright options to facilitate free distribution of audio, images, text, video, and educational material.

CSS Cascading style sheet; a set of commands that specifies how a browser should display content and that allows Web designers to treat design and layout separately from content. One CSS file can be used to control all the pages on a website, creating a consistent and easily updated design.

D

database A structured collection of information sources broken into discrete units that can be accessed and reassembled quickly by browsers and clients.

default A setting or value automatically assigned to a computer program or device by its creators.

desktop publishing A method of producing high-quality printable documents using only a personal computer, layout and graphic design software, and a good printer.

dial-up A connection to the Internet via a phone modem.

digital A type of signal based on bits (binary code), which can be transmitted and then reassembled on the fly. Because digital content can be reconstructed, reshaped, and modified without a loss of quality, analog signals (such as sound and images) are often transformed into digital ones.

digital divide Differences in access to and use of Internet and computing technologies across class, race, gender, and socioeconomic boundaries.

disk A storage device for computer data, such as a floppy disk, a CD, or a DVD.

distance learning, distance education Courses and other learning that take place via the Internet or other communication technologies, such as video and audio, allowing teachers and students to interact from remote locations.

DMCA Digital Millennium Copyright Act; a US law passed in 1998 that attempts to outlaw technologies that help people violate traditional copyrights through such means as file-sharing and copying of DVDs and other digital content.

domain name A unique website address, like a vanity license plate, that allows Web servers to use text names rather than numbers to identify themselves on a network.

dot-com A company involved in Internet business.

double-click To position the pointer on an object or text on the screen and then press and quickly release the mouse button twice.

dpi Dots per inch; a measure of the resolution of a device such as a printer or monitor. The higher the number, the sharper the type and images will appear when printed or viewed.

DSL Digital subscriber line; a broadband connection to the Internet via phone lines.

DVD Digital video disk or digital versatile disk. Although the same size as a CD, a DVD holds six to twenty-five times as much data.

E

ecommerce Business conducted electronically.

email Electronic mail; the exchange of digital messages between two or more people across a network. The messages can include attached files, computer code, or any other kind of data, including viruses.

execute To run a program by giving commands via the keyboard or mouse.

extension See **file extension.**

F

FAQs Frequently asked questions; a format used by website authors to provide readers with information that will help them access and interact with the site or learn about its content.

favorites Another term for bookmarks, which are stored website addresses.

file A collection of data (bits) grouped into one unit on a disk.

file extension The three or four letters following the period at the end of a file name that identify the file's format, used by the OS to determine which program created or can open it.

file sharing A method of sharing files across a computer network with various levels of access privileges.

firewall A software or hardware security system that protects a computer or a network from unauthorized access by computers outside the network.

FireWire® A version of the IEEE 1394 communication standard, developed by Apple Computer, that enables a high-speed cable used to transfer video, audio, and other digital content between a computer and a peripheral, such as a digital camera.

floppy disk A flexible magnetic disk (a 3.5" disk or the older 5.25" disk) inside a plastic sleeve, used for storing computer files (usually 1.44 MB) and read only by floppy drives.

folder A directory on the computer's hard drive where files are stored. Folders, and sometimes multiple subfolders, are used to manage and categorize files for easier retrieval.

font A complete set of characters in a particular size and typeface.

frames A system for displaying multiple HTML files on screen simultaneously so that a given Web page can be composed of multiple pages divided into sections.

freeware Software that is available free of charge for personal use.

ftp File transfer protocol; a standard for transferring files between computers on a network.

G

GB See **gigabyte.**

GIF Graphic interchange format; an image file format with built-in compression, useful for graphics containing text and simple design elements and few variations in color.

gigabyte (GB) 1,000 MB, or 1 billion bytes.

glyphs All the letters, numbers, and symbols associated with a particular font.

GUI Graphical user interface; a computer interface that incorporates graphics rather than text only; pronounced GOO-ee.

H

hacker A person who explores the capabilities of a computer system, network, or software; often used as a slang term for someone who breaks into computer networks with malicious intent.

hardware The physical equipment used in computing, including the computer itself and all of the peripherals, such as a printer, monitor, keyboard, and mouse, that connect to it.

home page The default or front page of a website.

HTML Hypertext markup language; the programming code read by browsers to create Web pages. It consists of tags that tell a browser how to display information and images.

HTTP Hypertext transfer protocol; the standard servers use to transfer and display information on the World Wide Web.

hyperlink A link in a document, such as a Web page, that cross-references or points to another file on a server or to another location within the same document.

hypertext A form for presenting text or information that allows readers to select a nonsequential or nonlinear reading path.

I

image editor A graphics editing and authoring program.

image map A graphic, used on a Web page, that includes HTML code for hotspots that function as hyperlinks.

interface A boundary or connection between two objects, such as computers, or between a user and information. An interface, for example, controls how users see, hear, and interact with information on a computer screen.

Internet A communication network with millions of access points, connecting computers around the world and allowing rapid transfer of data.

intranet A local communication network, used within an organization, that restricts outside access but connects computers and information within a predefined space.

IP Internet protocol; a standardized method of transferring information in packets across a network.

ISP Internet service provider; a company that provides users with access to the Internet via phone line, cable modem, or DSL.

J

JPG, JPEG Joint Photographic Experts Group; an image file format that allows the user to optimize the file for the Web by compression (usually to 80 percent of its original size) without much loss of quality; pronounced JAY-pehg. The JPG format is useful for images with fine detail, such as photographs.

K

KB See **kilobyte.**

keyboard An input device used with computers to transfer text, symbols, and commands.

kilobyte (KB) 1,000 bytes.

L

LAN Local area network; a network of computers, found in a local space such as an office, home, or college, that allows users to share information and applications easily.

learning management system (LMS) A software application or Web-based technology used to plan, implement, and assess a specific learning process.

license A prewritten agreement, attached to software or other content, that protects the copyright and outlines the ways in which people may use or distribute the content.

link Short for **hyperlink.**

listserv A program that distributes email to the members of a group who have subscribed to the service.

login The process of entering unique user information to gain access to a website or server.

Luddite A person who fears or loathes technology, especially new forms of technology that threaten existing methods of communication or jobs.

M

machinima Machine cinema or machine animation; a process of using existing virtual gaming environments to create customized movies.

MB See **megabyte.**

megabyte (MB) 1,004 kilobytes; more precisely, 1,048,576 bytes.

menu A list of commands in a software program, usually broken into categories such as File, Edit, View, Tools, and Help.

menu bar A horizontal list of menu categories, normally found at the top of a software program's window.

monitor A device for displaying text, images, and video sent from a computer.

MOO Multi-user object-oriented; a derivative of MUD; an online space in which multiple users can interact and share documents synchronously and notes, conversations, and actions are recorded.

mouse An input device that allows users to interact with objects, menus, windows, or other elements on the screen by clicking, double-clicking, or clicking and holding.

MP3 Moving Picture Expert Group layer 3; a method of compressing audio files, such as music. Such files are playable on a wide range of devices, including computers, digital music players, PDAs, and cell phones.

MUD Multi-user dungeon; a text-based online environment that allows synchronous communication and records conversation in an archive.

multimedia composing Integrating different media (sometimes called multiple media), often including text, graphics, audio, video, and animation, to create rich content for display on computer monitors, TVs, or projection devices.

N

navigation A system or map that guides users to important content and categories on a website.

netiquette A set of community-defined practices for communicating effectively via email or on the Web.

network A system of connections for networking.

networking The process of making connections with other people or computers across space and time using the Internet.

newsgroup An electronic discussion group, focused on a topic of common interest to the group's members, that allows users to read, post, and reply to messages.

node A connection point in a network or, commonly, an individual page on a website.

O

OCR Optical character recognition; a process used by some software for converting images of letters into text that can then be edited on a computer.

offline Not connected to the Internet.

online Connected to the Internet.

open access Describes resources that are openly available to users on the Internet with no requirements for authentication or payment by the user. Costs are covered by sponsoring agencies, copyright owners, or authors.

open source A method of sharing a program's code among users in a community who contribute to its refinement and development. Open source also describes the collaborative, developmental model itself, which involves committed users contributing their time and expertise to improve a product so that everyone can benefit.

operating system See **OS.**

optimize To make something as well suited as it can be to the medium for which it is intended—for example, to prepare a file for Web viewing by compressing it or ensuring that it uses Web-safe colors.

OS Operating system; the software that controls a user's access to programs and files on a computer. The three most popular operating systems are the Mac OS®, Windows®, and LINUX®.

OWL Online writing lab; a website where people can find information about writing or receive help with writing.

P

password A series of characters that enables someone to access a protected network or system.

PC Personal computer; the designation for a computer that uses the Windows®, UNIX®, or LINUX® operating system.

PDA Personal digital assistant; a handheld, mobile device that provides basic computing programs, including email, calculator, note-taking, and audio playback, in addition to functioning as a personal organizer, ebook reader, and file storage device.

PDF Portable document format; a file format that preserves page layout regardless of the software or computer system used to view it. Adobe® Reader® is used to view PDF files and Adobe® Acrobat® to create them.

peer-to-peer networking (P2P) A method of sharing designated files with others on the Internet using the same software.

pixel The smallest unit of light displayed on a monitor.

plug-in A program that adds additional capabilities or features to software such as a browser.

PNG Portable network graphic; an image file format with automatic compression. It functions like GIF, but the absence of any restrictions on its use by software companies in their products makes it more universal. PNG files can have transparent colors, which let background colors through, and differing levels of opacity.

podcasting The production and distribution, via RSS feeds or other means, of audio files for a digital media player.

POP Post office protocol; a method for transferring email from a server to the user's computer.

portal A website that collects a variety of information, resources, and links tailored to a user's preferences.

printer Hardware for producing printed documents and images, using inkjet or laser technology and a variety of paper types and sizes.

program Software that manages a collection of related processes on a computer, such as word processing, image editing, or Web browsing.

R

RAM Random access memory; a type of data storage on a computer that allows data to be accessed quickly and in any order for routine computing tasks.

refresh A common command for a browser, usually executed using the F5 key on a PC, that works under certain circumstances to force the computer to reload the information displayed on the screen.

relative link A partial URL that links to a file within the local website. The path in the URL is relative to the file where the link appears.

reload See **refresh.**

resolution The number of pixels (points of color) displayed on a monitor, expressed in terms of the numbers of pixels on the horizontal and vertical axes.

RSS Rich site summary or really simple syndication; a method of spreading, via automatic processes, the content of weblogs, news sites, and podcasts, as well as other frequently updated information. RSS feeds automatically send to subscribing websites and individual users the hyperlinks and summary information they need to keep up to date on subjects of interest.

RTF Rich-text format; a file format and extension that preserves basic formatting, such as italics, font styles, boldface, and page layout, and can be read by a wide variety of word processing programs.

S

scannable resume An electronic resume in plain text (ASCII) or HTML format, often submitted with an employment application, that uses keywords to provide an employer with information regarding a job candidate's experience and qualifications.

scanner A hardware device used to capture high-resolution images of printed material. These images can then be edited with an image editor or converted into text characters through OCR (optical character recognition).

screen capture, screenshot An image of something that appears on screen, captured for later viewing or editing. Pointer movements and other motion and events can be captured as an animated movie.

SCSI Small computer system interface; a standard connection allowing computers to communicate with peripherals; pronounced SKUH-zee.

search engine A Web-based program that allows users to search the World Wide Web for text and images, often providing organized directories of information and other tools to assist with information retrieval and management.

server A computer (or a program running on it) that provides services, files, and information to other computers through a network. Servers deliver Web page content, files, and other data in response to user requests and also run software for weblogs, discussion boards, courseware, and content management systems.

shareware Software that can be downloaded online, generally for free, although payment may be required for long-term use or a fully functional version.

site Short for **website.**

SMTP Simple mail transfer protocol; a protocol used to define how email is sent.

social networking software Web-based software that facilitates the formation of online communities, using weblogs, forums, and file sharing, by people who share an interest, hobby, or goal.

software The programs and instructions that run a computer or perform certain tasks.

source code See **code.**

spam Unsolicited and unwanted email.

spyware Software, installed on a user's computer, that covertly gathers information about the user and his or her activity and sends it back to some other entity.

standards See **Web standards.**

synchronous Describes events that are coordinated in time or that take place at the same time or in real time (one after the other), not over an extended period. Chat is synchronous; email is asynchronous.

T

table A feature of HTML code used to control the layout of a Web page, to place images in proper relation to text, and to present information in grid format. Tables are made up of rows and columns.

tablet computer A laptop or portable computer whose screen can rotate and fold flat, allowing for pen-based and touch-screen input.

tag A label for identifying the nature or structure of content. Tags are used in markup languages such as HTML. Each tag name is enclosed within angled brackets; an end slash before the tag name indicates a closing tag. In HTML, tags also tell the browser how to display text. For example, in a browser, <em> italic text </em> would display as *italic text.*

telework, telecommuting Conducting work entirely over communication networks, including the Internet, phone, fax, or video.

toolbar A collection of frequently used tools or commands in a software program, which can often be undocked from a fixed menu and moved anywhere on the screen.

track changes A method of making visible any changes to a document, including additions, deletions, reformatting, comments, and other annotations.

troll A person who invades an online community by posting nasty messages meant to incite angry responses. Trolls normally post their messages and then leave without waiting for replies, simply for the purpose of disrupting communication.

typeface A set of fonts that have a single design. The typeface Helvetica, for example, comes in a variety of sizes and styles, including roman, italic, and bold.

U

UNIX A computer operating system that can perform multiple tasks for multiple users simultaneously.

upgrade A new version of software with improved functionality, fixes, or new features.

URL Uniform resource locator; a Web address pointing to a specific file on a server. URLs can be absolute links, relative links, or anchor tags.

usability A measure of the efficiency and ease with which a user can interact or perform tasks with hardware, software, or a document.

usability testing A systematic method of testing how users interact with a product such as a website or piece of hardware, with a focus on ease of use.

USB Universal serial bus; a protocol, used for connecting hardware to a computer, that allows the device to be used immediately and characterized as "plug and play."

USB drive, USB flash drive A small, portable data storage device that can be used to transport and share files between computers. USB drives come in a wide variety of capacities, from 16 MB to 6 GB or more.

username A name used by a server to identify a person who seeks to gain access to features of a system or a website.

V

validation A method of testing to determine whether HTML or CSS code meets W3C standards for accessibility and composition.

virtual reality (VR) A computer-simulated, three-dimensional world that one has the illusion of being immersed in and that one can interact with using gloves, glasses, and other input devices.

virus Programming code that replicates itself automatically, causing a program such as an email client to spread it further without the user's knowledge. A virus may corrupt or erase data on a computer.

VR See **virtual reality.**

W

W3C World Wide Web Consortium; an organization of companies that creates international standards, guidelines, and specifications for the Web, including standards for accessibility and HTML, XHTML, and CSS code.

Web A shorter and more informal way of referring to the World Wide Web (WWW).

weblog A type of website often used for comment, critique, and discussion. In many cases, weblogs are linked across a network through syndication (RSS).

webmaster The person responsible for creating, maintaining, and/or updating a website.

website A collection of connected Web pages and files, located on a server at a particular URL and usually consisting of a home page, nodes, files, and navigation.

Web standards A set of recommendations endorsed by the W3C for designing accessible and functional websites.

WiFi The standard for wireless fidelity, used to determine whether a wireless network conforms to a common standard for transmitting data wirelessly between computers, PDAs, cell phones, and other hardware. The standard for the slower speed is IEEE 802.11b and for the higher speed is 802.11g.

wiki An application that allows multiple users to author and edit a document on the Web through a browser, often with unrestricted access; it provides for regression to previous versions if deemed necessary by editors or other users; pronounced WICK-ee.

wireless network A network that allows computers and other hardware to communicate over radio waves. To connect to the network, users are often required to provide identifying information and to use a client.

WWW World Wide Web; a system or network of computers (servers) that allows access to remote files and sharing of information across the Internet.

WYSIWYG What you see is what you get; a term used to describe any authoring program, such as a word processor or Web authoring software, that displays content as it will be rendered through another interface, such as in print or in a Web browser.

X

XML Extensible markup language; a standard for coding data and information that allows authors to create their own tags to structure documents. XML allows the design of a document to be distinguished from its content, making it possible to repurpose information (for the Web or print, for example) without redesigning its presentation.

Z

ZIP® disk A disk similar to a floppy disk, but readable in ZIP drives and capable of holding 100 to 1,000 times as much data.

A

absolute phrase A phrase, composed of a noun or pronoun and a participle, that functions as an adverb for an entire clause. An absolute phrase is set off from the clause it modifies by a comma: ***The horse cared for,*** *the veterinarian left.* See 40m.

abstract noun A noun that names something that cannot be known through the five senses, but only sensed internally as a feeling or thought: *poverty, triumph, spirituality.* See also **concrete noun.**

action verb A verb that expresses action by an agent: *The circus performer* ***leaped.*** The agent needn't be present in the sentence, however; in passive sentences (see 44g), action verbs are accompanied by auxiliary verbs (*am, are, is, was, were*): *The old playground equipment* ***was bulldozed.***

active voice The form of a sentence in which the action described by the verb is performed by the subject of the sentence: *The baseball commission* ***instituted*** *a tough new drug policy for players.* See also **passive voice.** See 44g.

adjective A word that describes, limits, or specifies a noun or pronoun by showing its quantity, location, ownership, or other qualities: *tall, green, four.* See 40e and Chapter 46.

adjective clause A dependent clause, introduced by a relative pronoun such as *who, which,* or *that* (or occasionally *when, where,* or *why*), that answers the question "Which one?" or "What kind of?" about the noun or pronoun it follows. See 40n, esp. p. 816.

adverb A word that modifies a verb, adjective, other adverb, or whole clause. An adverb answers the question "When?" "Where?" "How?" or "To what degree or extent?": *ran* ***yesterday, deceptively*** *simple,* ***very*** *loudly.* See 40f and Chapter 46.

adverb clause A dependent clause, introduced by a subordinating conjunction, that modifies a verb, adjective, other adverb, or entire clause. An adverb clause answers the question "How?" "When?" "Where?" "Why?" "In what manner?" "Under what conditions?" "With what result?" or "To what degree?" See 40n, esp. p. 816.

agreement Match in number and person between a subject and its verb: *The* ***plumber fixes*** *the pipes* (see Chapter 45); match in number, person, and sometimes gender between a pronoun and its antecedent: *The* ***woman*** *loves* ***her*** *job* (see 43i–m); and match in number between a demonstrative adjective and its noun: ***These shoes*** *are tight.*

antecedent The noun or pronoun that a pronoun refers to or replaces: *The* ***nurses*** *taught first aid to* ***their*** *students.* See 43n–r.

appositive A word or phrase that functions as a noun equivalent. It restates, renames, or otherwise more fully defines the noun immediately preceding it: *Candace,* ***an avid golfer,*** *started playing at 7 a.m.* See 40m, esp. p. 814, and 43e.

article The word *a, an,* or *the.* Articles are used with nouns: *a crisis, an ordeal, the solution.* See Chapter 60.

auxiliary verb Also known as a *helping verb,* a verb that works with other verbs to indicate mood, voice, and tense: *Her son* ***did*** *graduate; he* ***will be*** *working soon.* See 44c and 61e.

C

case The form of a noun or pronoun that indicates whether it is acting as subject (***I*** *enjoyed his quick wit*), object (*He laughed with* ***me***), or possessive (***His*** *face glowed*). See 43b–h.

clause A word group that contains both a subject and a verb. An independent clause—as the name implies—can function independently as a simple sentence: *Americans typically have less vacation time than Europeans.* (See 40j–l.) A dependent clause (also called a *subordinate clause*) cannot stand alone as a sentence: *although top managers often have four-week vacation packages.* (See 40n.)

collective noun A noun that names a collection or group: *police, faculty, team, family, army, class.* See 40b, 43k, and 45g.

comma splice The error caused by joining two independent clauses with a comma but no coordinating conjunction. See Chapter 42.

common noun A noun that names a generic member of a group: *school, woman, river.* See also **proper noun.** See 40b and Chapter 60.

complement A word or word group that completes (renames, identifies, or describes) the subject, verb, or object. See sentence patterns 4 and 5 in 40l.

complete predicate See **predicate.**

complete subject See **subject.**

complex sentence A sentence that consists of one independent clause and at least one dependent clause. See 35d–e and 40o.

compound sentence A sentence that consists of at least two independent clauses, joined by a comma and a coordinating conjunction (*and, but, or, nor, for, so, yet*) or by a semicolon. See 35 a–c and 40o.

compound-complex sentence A sentence that consists of two or more independent clauses and at least one dependent clause. See 40o.

concrete noun A noun that names things that can be sensed—seen, heard, tasted, smelled, touched, or experienced in the world: *computer, woodlands, pockets.* See 40b.

conjunction A word that connects two or more clauses, phrases, or words. See also **coordinating conjunction, subordinating conjunction, correlative conjunction.**

coordinating conjunction A conjunction that joins two or more elements (words, phrases, clauses) of equal grammatical rank: *and, but, so, yet, for, or, nor.* See 35a–c and 40h.

coordination The joining of two or more grammatical elements of equal weight, typically with a coordinating conjunction—for example, adjectives (*stormy **and** dark*) and clauses (*Brian was accepted into the Marines, **but** Justin was rejected*). See 35a–c.

correlative conjunction A conjunction that works in a pair (*both . . . and, either . . . or, neither . . . nor, not only . . . but also*) to express a relationship of contrast or similarity between different elements. See 34b and 40h.

countable noun A noun that names something that can be counted: *voter, tree, shoe, byte.* See 40b and Chapter 60.

D

dangling modifier A modifier that refers to a word or phrase that is either not obviously connected to it or not in the sentence at all. See 46n.

demonstrative adjective An adjective that limits or emphasizes a noun: ***this** pencil, **that** night, **these** ideas, **those** people.*

demonstrative pronoun A pronoun that points to the antecedent: ***This** is the case, **These** are the ones.*

dependent clause Also known as a *subordinate clause,* a clause that begins with a subordinating word and cannot function independently as a sentence. Dependent clauses function as a single part of speech: they can be nouns, adjectives, or adverbs. See 40n.

determiner An adjective that precedes and limits a noun: a definite article *(the),* indefinite article *(a, an),* quantifier (such as *a little, many, every*), possessive pronoun (such as *her*), or demonstrative pronoun (*this, that, these, those).* See Chapter 60.

direct object A word or word group that receives the action of a transitive verb: *He mailed **the letter**.* See sentence patterns 2–4 in 40l.

E

expletive A sentence that begins with *it* or *there* and a form of the verb *to be* instead of the subject: ***There were** horses in the pasture.* See 36e and 45e.

F

finite verb A verb that is used as the main verb of a sentence and thus is marked for tense, voice, mood, person, and number: *She **insisted** on it.*

fragment See **sentence fragment.**

G

gerund An *-ing* form of a verb (present participle) acting as a noun: ***Crying** helps.* See 43h.

gerund phrase A gerund and its modifiers and objects acting as the subject or object: ***Going home** is comforting.* See 40m, esp. p. 813.

I

imperative mood A command, with *you* as the understood subject: *Don't walk on the grass.* See 40p and 44f.

indefinite pronoun A pronoun, such as *all, anyone, each, everybody,* or *some,* that refers to an unnamed or indefinite antecedent. See 40c, 43l, and 45f.

independent clause A group of words with a subject and a verb that can stand alone as a sentence. See 40j–l.

indicative mood The mood of sentences that make statements or ask questions: *That dog is barking.* See 44f.

indirect object A noun, pronoun, or word group that indicates to whom, to what, for whom, or for what an action is performed: *He mailed the letter to **Sheila.*** See sentence pattern 3 in 40l.

infinitive A verbal made of the plain form of a verb and often the word *to: to dance.* See 43f, 43g, and 44e.

infinitive phrase An infinitive and its modifiers and object functioning as a noun, adjective, or adverb. See 40m, esp. p. 813, 61b–c, and 61e.

intensive pronoun A pronoun that ends in *-self* or *-selves* and emphasizes the antecedent: *Shelley **herself** said it was fine.*

interjection A word, standing alone as a sentence or interrupting a sentence, that expresses strong or sudden emotion: ***Hey! Oh, no,** that guy hit my car!* See 40i.

interrogative pronoun A pronoun, such as *who, whom, which, what, whoever, whomever, whichever,* or *whatever,* that introduces a question: ***What** happened?* For *who* versus *whom,* see 43g.

intransitive verb A verb that does not take a direct object: *The child **panicked**.* See sentence pattern 1 in 40l and 44d.

irregular verb A verb that forms its past tense and past participle in some way other than by adding *d* or *ed.* See 44b.

M

main verb The verb in a sentence that expresses the main meaning: *She may have been **walking** to the store.*

misplaced modifier A descriptive word or phrase that is located too far away from the word it modifies, creating confusion about the intended meaning. See 46i.

modal auxiliary verb A helping verb (*can, could, may, might, must, shall, should,* or *will*) that adds shades of meaning to another verb. See 44c and 61e.

modifier A word or word group that limits the meaning of another word or phrase. A modifier functions as an adjective or adverb. See Chapter 46.

mood The attitude that is expressed by a writer or speaker in a sentence. See also **indicative mood, imperative mood, subjunctive mood.** See 44f.

N

noncountable noun See **uncountable noun.**

nonfinite verb See **verbal.**

nonrestrictive (nonessential) element A word or word group that does not provide information essential to understanding the meaning of the element it modifies (and typically follows) and thus is set off from the sentence with punctuation, usually a pair of commas: *Her only brother,* ***Lee,*** *lives in Michigan.* See 48f.

noun A word that names a person, place, thing, quality, or concept. Anything that can be discretely isolated or referred to—pointed to or singled out—can be named with a noun. A noun can function as a subject, object, or complement. See 40b.

noun clause A dependent clause that functions as a subject, object, or complement. See 40o.

noun phrase A noun and its modifiers functioning as a subject, object, or complement. See 40n.

number The form of a word that indicates whether it refers to one (singular number) or more than one (plural): *toy / toys, I / we, swims / swim, this / these.*

O

object A noun, pronoun, or group of words functioning as a noun that receives the action of a verb (direct object), tells to or for whom an action is done (indirect object), or follows a preposition (object of a preposition). See also **direct object, indirect object, prepositional phrase.** See sentence patterns 2–4 in 40l.

object complement A noun or adjective that describes or renames a direct object that follows a verb such as *call, elect, make,* or *name: They named him **chief**. I'll make you **sorry**.* See sentence pattern 4 in 40l.

objective case The case of a noun or pronoun functioning as the object of a verb, verbal, or preposition: *He loves **me**. I care about **him**.* See 43b.

P

parallelism The use of repeated grammatical elements in coordinated sentence structures: *an acute attack or a lingering disease.* See Chapter 34.

participial phrase A phrase that consists of a present or past participle and any objects or modifiers. A participial phrase functions as an adjective. See 40m, esp. p. 813, and 61d.

participle See **present participle, past participle.**

parts of speech The eight categories into which words in a sentence are placed based on function, meaning, form, and placement. See also **noun, pronoun, adjective, verb, adverb, interjection, conjunction, preposition.** See 40a–i.

passive voice The form of a sentence in which the subject receives (rather than performs) the action of a transitive verb: *The train **was wrecked**.* See also **active voice.** See 44g.

past participle A verbal formed by adding *d* or *ed* to a regular verb (*liked, wanted*) or by transforming an irregular verb (*been, hidden, rode;* see 44b). The past participle functions as an adjective (see 61d) or part of a verb phrase (44a): ***Delighted,*** *I winked. We had **been** playing for hours.* See also 43h.

personal pronoun A pronoun that refers to particular people or things: *I, you, he, she, it, we, they.* See 40c and Chapter 43.

phrasal verb A verb followed by one or more words (particles) that help specify its meaning. Together, the verb and particle(s) function as a single verb whose meaning is rarely the same as the meaning of its component parts: *add up, phase out, get ahead.* See 61a.

phrase A word group that does not contain a subject, a predicate, or both. Phrases function as a single part of speech: as a noun, verb, adjective, or adverb. See also **absolute phrase, noun phrase, prepositional phrase, verb phrase, verbal phrase.** See 40m.

possessive case The case of a noun and pronoun showing ownership or possession. See 43b.

predicate The part of a sentence that expresses the subject's action or state of being: *Alternative energies* ***should be explored more carefully.*** The complete predicate includes the verb and any modifiers or objects. The simple predicate includes only the main verb and any auxiliary verbs: *should be explored.* See 40k.

preposition A word, such as *in, on, above, below, beside,* or *between,* that indicates a certain relationship between the nouns or pronouns that follow it and the other words in a sentence: *The patient rested* ***in*** *bed.* See 40g.

prepositional phrase A phrase that consists of a preposition followed by a noun, pronoun, or noun phrase known as the *object of the preposition.* The prepositional phrase also includes any modifiers of the object of the preposition: *among the tall yellowed grasses of autumn.* See 40m, esp. p. 813.

present participle A verbal formed by adding *ing* to the plain form of a verb: *caring.* The present participle functions as an adjective (*The couple exchanged a* ***knowing*** *look;* see 61d) or as part of a verb phrase (*The company is* ***dumping*** *chemicals into the river;* see 44a). See also 43h.

pronoun A word used in place of a noun. See **personal pronoun, indefinite pronoun, relative pronoun, interrogative pronoun, demonstrative pronoun, reflexive pronoun, intensive pronoun, reciprocal pronoun.** See 40c and Chapter 43.

proper adjective An adjective formed from a proper noun: *the* ***British*** *empire.* See 57b.

proper noun A noun that names a specific person, place, or thing. The first letter of a proper noun is capitalized: *The* ***Vatican*** *is the administrative headquarters of the* ***Roman Catholic Church.*** See 57b.

R

reciprocal pronoun The pronoun *each other* or *one another.* A reciprocal pronoun acts as a direct object to a verb describing an action that members of a plural antecedent perform mutually: *The board members trust* ***one another***.

reflexive pronoun The pronoun *myself, yourself, himself, herself, itself, ourselves, yourselves,* or *themselves.* A reflexive pronoun refers back to a noun or personal pronoun when the subject of an action and the object of that action are the same: *She had only* ***herself*** *to blame.*

regular verb A verb that forms its past tense and past participle by adding *d* or *ed* to the plain form: *typed, slipped, regarded.* See 44a.

relative pronoun A pronoun, such as *who, whom, whose, that, which,* or *whoever,* that introduces a subordinate (dependent) clause: *The hurricane,* ***which*** *hit land on August 29, devastated New Orleans.* See 43r; for *who* versus *whom,* see 43g.

restrictive (essential) element A word or word group that provides information essential to understanding the meaning of the sentence: *I'm going to buy the car* ***that I saw advertised in the Sunday paper***. No commas set off a restrictive element. See 48f.

run-on sentence A group of words that is grammatically incorrect because it does not include the punctuation necessary between independent clauses in a sentence. See Chapter 42.

S

sentence A string of words that obeys the grammatical rules of a language. Sentences are the basic units of language for expressing ideas. See 33a and 40j.

sentence fragment A part of a sentence incorrectly punctuated as a complete sentence. Either a subject or a verb may be missing, or if both are present, they appear in a subordinate clause that must be attached to another complete sentence. See Chapter 41.

simple predicate The verb that relays the subject's action or state of being. See **predicate.** See 40k.

simple sentence A sentence that consists of a single independent clause. See 40l.

simple subject The noun or pronoun in the subject; whoever or whatever the sentence is about: *His fuzzy* ***earmuffs*** *covered more of his head than his Mohawk.* See also **subject.** See 40k.

split infinitive A phrase in which a word or words are placed between the two parts of an infinitive (*to* + plain form of verb): *to* ***boldly*** *go.*

squinting modifier A modifier placed in a sentence in such a way that it could modify two different words, causing confusion. See 46k.

subject The word or phrase that names the topic of the sentence, including any modifiers: ***His fuzzy earmuffs*** *covered more of his head than his Mohawk.* See also **simple subject.** See 40k.

subject complement A noun, pronoun, or adjective that follows a linking verb and renames or describes the subject: *Their pourable yogurt is* ***a drink***. See sentence pattern 5 in 40l.

subjective case The case of a noun or pronoun that functions as a subject or subject complement (***She*** *loves chocolate; It is* ***I***). See 43b.

subjunctive mood The mood of a verb that indicates speculation, a condition contrary to fact, a request, a demand, or a suggestion. See 44f.

subordinate clause See **dependent clause.**

subordinating conjunction A word or words that express a logical or temporal relationship among elements in a sentence or between ideas across sentence boundaries. When a subordinate clause precedes an independent clause to which it is attached, it is followed by a comma. See 35d–e and 41d.

subordination De-emphasizing one grammatical element by making it dependent on another independent element (for example, beginning it with a subordinating conjunction): ***Although*** *the fan was working, the air felt heavy and inert.* See also **coordination.** See 35a and 35d–e.

T

tense The form of a verb that expresses the time of its action (past, present, or future) and the relationships among events: *He* ***had left*** *before Chloe* ***arrived***. Changes in verb form and endings show tense (*came, come, coming*), and so do combinations of auxiliary verbs and main verbs (*will come, was coming, has come*). See 44e.

transitive verb A verb that requires a direct object to complete the thought. See 44d.

U

uncountable noun Also called a *noncountable* or *noncount noun,* a noun that names something that can't be counted: *mud, confusion, water.* See 40b and Chapter 60.

V

verb A word that indicates the action or state of being of a subject. Verbs can change form and be combined with auxiliary verbs to indicate tense (time of action), voice (whether the subject performs the action or receives it), mood (attitude), number (singular or plural), and sometimes person (the *-s* ending with a subject like *she, he,* or *it eats*). See 40d and Chapters 44 and 61.

verbal Also known as a *nonfinite verb,* a verb form that functions as a noun, adjective, or adverb and so cannot be the complete verb of a sentence. The three types of verbals are infinitives (***To love*** *is divine*), gerunds (***Saluting*** *the flag is a form of respect*), and participles (*The dog* ***burying*** *its bone didn't respond to a whistle*). See 40m and 61b.

verbal phrase A phrase that consists of a verbal and its accompanying modifiers, objects, or complements. See 40m.

verb phrase A verb that consists of a main verb and any accompanying auxiliaries, including *be, do, have, can, could, may, might, must, shall, should, will,* and *would,* in all their forms: *We* ***could have danced*** *all night.* See Chapters 44 and 61.

voice A quality of transitive verbs that indicates whether the subject is acting (active voice: *I* ***lost*** *my homework*) or being acted upon (passive voice: *My homework* ***was lost***) by the verb. See 44g.

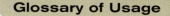

This glossary is a guide to common misuses of words: nonstandard, informal, and regional usages not suitable for formal written prose; commonly confused pairs of words; tricky points of grammar that are difficult to remember; and common mistakes in spelling. As in a dictionary listing, *nonstandard* refers to usages that are not accepted as standard spoken or written English; *informal* refers to usages that are common in conversation but not suitable for formal prose; *regionalism* refers to those informal usages typical of a particular part of the country. The glossary does not cover all usages; consult a dictionary as needed.

A

a, an The article *a* is used before consonant sounds (*a piano, a ukulele, a harmonica, a one-man band*); the article *an* is used before vowel sounds (*an apple, an umpire, an hourglass, an ox*).

accept, except The verb *accept* means "to receive"; the verb *except* means "to exclude." The preposition *except* means "other than."

> She **accepted** all his love tokens **except** the live boa constrictor.

> **Excepting** rum raisin, I love all flavors of ice cream.

adverse, averse *Adverse* (adjective) means "harmful" or "unfavorable"; *averse* (adjective) means "having strong feelings of dislike or distaste for."

> I am **averse** to driving in **adverse** conditions.

advice, advise Related concepts but different parts of speech. *Advice* is a noun that means "counsel," "recommendation," or "opinion"; to *advise* is to give advice.

> Professor Jones **advised** him to read *The Odyssey* out loud.

> Sometime past midnight, he remembered Professor Jones's **advice:** to read *The Odyssey* out loud.

affect, effect The verb *affect* means "to influence"; the verb *effect* means "to accomplish" or "to bring about." An *effect* (noun) is a result or outcome.

> Her binge drinking began to **affect** her health.

> The drastic new policy sought to **effect** campus-wide sobriety.

> Slurred speech is a common **effect** of heavy drinking.

agree on, agree to, agree with Each idiomatic pair conveys a different shade of meaning. *Agree on* implies a process of negotiation, arriving at a consensus, reaching an understanding, or coming to terms.

> After much negotiation, the president and the committee **agreed on** the campus guidelines for ethical behavior.

Agree to implies giving one's assent to a proposition made by someone else.

> Having been threatened with expulsion for her disruptive actions, Sarah finally **agreed to** the campus guidelines for ethical behavior.

Agree with implies that both parties are already of like mind or are already in harmony.

> An upstanding and proper young woman, Sarah wholeheartedly **agreed with** the campus guidelines for ethical behavior.

ain't Nonstandard; do not use. Use *am not, are not, is not,* or the appropriate contraction.

all, all of In general, use *all,* not *all of.*

> The case was such that **all** the witnesses received 24-hour police protection.

However, use *all of* before personal pronouns, proper nouns, and possessive nouns.

> The case was such that **all of** them received 24-hour police protection.

all ready, already In the phrase *all ready,* meaning "completely prepared," the adverb *all* modifies the adjective *ready.*

> By Tuesday the care packages were **all ready** for distribution.

Already is an adverb that means "before," "prior to a specified time," or "so soon."

By the time we arrived at the station, he had **already** departed.

Are you leaving **already**?

all together, altogether The phrase *all together* is used to mean that all the members of a group perform or receive an action together.

As the lightning crashed, the cowboys worked desperately to herd the cows **all together.**

In all such sentences, you can reword to separate *all* and *together.*

As the lightning crashed, the cowboys worked desperately to herd **all** the cows **together.**

Altogether is an adverb that means "wholly," "utterly," "with all counted," or "all things considered."

After the storm, the cowboys were **altogether** exhausted.

After the storm, there were **altogether** 36 cows missing.

Altogether, the cowboys performed bravely during the storm.

allude, elude, refer Both *allude* and *refer* involve making reference to something. But *allude* means "to refer to indirectly" or "to suggest or imply without saying explicitly"; *refer* is more direct. *Elude* means "to avoid" or "to escape."

Clark **alluded** to pressure from higher-ups within the organization but would not give specific names, titles, or departments.

As usual, Professor Chang ended the class on literature of the Civil War by **alluding** to Mitchell's *Gone with the Wind:* "Don't forget, class, 'tomorrow is another day,' and all final papers will be due."

Professor Chang reminded her students of the bylaws against plagiarism and **referred** them to article 16 of the campus charter.

In *The Prisoner of Azkaban,* the dangerous criminal Sirius Black **eludes** capture.

allusion, illusion An *allusion* is an indirect reference; an *illusion* is a false or misleading impression. See also **allude, elude, refer.**

almost, most *Almost* is an adverb that means "not quite" or "nearly." *Most* is both an adjective and an adverb and means "to the greatest degree or extent."

Almost all dogs like bones.

Most dogs like bones.

The center fielder **almost** caught the ball that scored the winning run.

The player with the **most** runs is automatically nominated for the prize.

a lot of Informal for *many, much, a great deal of.* Do not misspell as *alot.*

alright Nonstandard; use *all right.*

a.m., p.m. *a.m.* stands for *ante meridiem* (the period between midnight and noon), and *p.m.* stands for *post meridiem* (the period from noon to midnight). Both are always lowercase, with each letter followed by a period.

among, between *Between* denotes a one-on-one relationship of individuals; *among* denotes an unspecified relationship of a group or collective entities. The notion that *between* is always used for two items and *among* for three or more items is unfounded. While only *between* can be used for two items, which to use when describing a relationship between or among three or more items depends on your intended meaning. For example, describing a bull as charging madly *between* festival goers suggests that no one is being gored, trampled, or otherwise injured. However, describing a bull as charging madly *among* festival goers suggests that someone is likely to get injured any minute.

amoral, immoral *Amoral* means "outside or beyond the moral order"; *immoral* means "not in accordance with accepted moral principles."

Many hold that pure science is by its very nature **amoral.**

The protestors called the war **immoral.**

amount, number See **number, amount.**

an, a See **a, an.**

and etc. See **etc.**

and/or Although suitable in some legal and business communications, avoid in formal prose as awkward and imprecise.

ante-, anti- The prefix *ante-* means "before"; the prefix *anti-* means "against."

The **antislavery** movement thrived in the **antebellum** northern states.

anxious, eager Although both denote a state of urgent desire, *anxious* implies fear, worry, or distress, while *eager* implies keen interest or happy anticipation.

anybody, any body; anyone, any one *Anybody* and *anyone* are both singular indefinite pronouns that mean "any person." In *any body* and *any one, any* acts as an adjective modifying the nouns *body* and *one,* respectively.

Anyone can play chess.

Any one of the chess players could have won the match.

anymore, now, nowadays In formal prose use *anymore* in negative constructions and questions only; in positive constructions use *now* or *nowadays.*

Most people do not travel by horse and buggy **anymore.**

Nowadays we travel by car.

Do they travel by horse and buggy **anymore**?

anyways Nonstandard; do not use. Use *anyway.*

anywhere, any place Use *anywhere* when referring to a general or indefinite location; use *any place* only when referring to a single or specific location. Do not use *anyplace.*

My coat could be **anywhere.**

I couldn't find **any place** to hang up my coat.

anywheres, everywheres, nowheres, somewheres Nonstandard; do not use. Use *anywhere, everywhere, nowhere,* or *somewhere.*

apt to, liable to, likely to Although all three adjectives refer to probability, each has a different shade of meaning. *Apt* connotes a natural talent or tendency (as in *aptitude*); *liable* is most often used with undesirable outcomes (as in *liability*); *likely* conveys a more general sense of probability.

My three-year-old is **apt** to cry when she falls off the jungle gym.

If she doesn't stop jumping on the jungle gym, that child is **liable to** fall.

Most children are **likely to** prefer chocolate ice cream to pistachio.

as, like Accepted practice in formal prose is to use the conjunction *as* before subordinate clauses and the preposition *like* before nouns or pronouns only.

He swims **as** though he might drown.

He swims **like** a duck.

No one knows her **as** I do.

Nobody knows **like** me.

Note, however, that many dictionaries condone the use of *like* as a conjunction and give evidence that it has been used as such since at least the fourteenth century.

assure, ensure, insure See **ensure, insure, assure.**

as to Stuffy; use *about.*

as to whether Redundant; use *whether.*

at the present time, at this point in time, at this time, at present Wordy and pretentious; use *now, nowadays, today,* or *currently.*

averse, adverse See **adverse, averse.**

awful, awfully Do not use for *very* in formal prose.

B

backup, back up *Backup* is a noun or adjective; *back up* is a verb.

bad, badly *Bad* is an adjective; *badly* is an adverb.

Sparky is a **bad** dog.

I feel **bad** about her injury.

She limps **badly.**

being as, being that Nonstandard; do not use in formal prose. Use *because.*

beside, besides Use *beside* to mean "by the side of"; use *besides* to mean "in addition to" or "except for."

My cat likes to sit **beside** me.

Besides my cat, I have three parrots and a gerbil.

best, had best; better, had better The idioms *had best* and *had better* are often shortened in everyday speech to *best* and *better,* respectively (*You best stay. We better go*). In formal prose, use *had best* or *had better.*

between, among See **among, between.**

bias, biased *Bias* is generally a noun (the adjective *bias* refers to cloth or clothing only); *biased* is an adjective.

bring, take In general, *bring* means "to convey *toward* you" (or toward the governing point of view of the statement); *take* means "to convey *away from* you" (or away from the governing point of view of the statement).

The senator vowed to **bring** home our troops.

Don't **take** jobs out of the country.

bunch Appropriate in conversation when used to refer to a lot or a group (as in *a bunch of papers* or *a bunch of students*); do not use in formal prose.

bust *Bust* (noun, verb) is considered slang in many instances. Consult a dictionary when using.

but however, but yet Wordy; do not use. *But, however,* and *yet* all stand alone.

He wanted to watch the sentencing, **yet** he could not bring himself to see her face to face.

He wanted to watch the sentencing, **but** he could not bring himself to see her face to face.

He wanted to watch the sentencing; **however,** he could not bring himself to see her face to face.

but that, but what Colloquial redundancies; often used after *doubt* or *help.* Do not use in formal prose.

I don't doubt ~~but~~ that you are right.

C

calculate, figure, reckon Colloquial when used to mean "consider," "predict," or "suppose"; do not use in formal prose.

can, could *Can* expresses ability; *could* is used to make a conditional statement.

He **can** run fast.

He **could** run faster if he would work out more often.

can, may *Can* refers to ability; *may* refers to permission or possibility.

Having passed the test, you've proven that you **can** drive safely.

You **may** take the car if you bring it back by midnight.

You **may** need to adjust the rearview mirror.

can't hardly, couldn't hardly; can't scarcely, couldn't scarcely Double negatives; do not use.

The room was so crowded we **could scarcely** move.

can't help but Double negative; do not use in formal prose. Instead of *I can't help but ask why,* use *I cannot help asking why,* or *I can but ask why.*

capital, capitol A *capital* is a city that serves as the seat of government to a state, nation, or other political entity; a *capitol* is the specific building in which a government's legislature meets.

censor, censure *Censor* means "to remove or suppress material deemed unsuitable"; *censure* means "to strongly criticize or reprimand."

center about, center around Use *center on;* do not use *center about* or *center around.*

chair, chairperson, chairman, chairwoman When referring to a specific chairperson, be gender specific. See also p. 788.

cite, sight, site Similar sounding words with unrelated meanings. *Cite* is a verb meaning "to refer to or quote as an authority or example"; *sight* is the sense of seeing or a specific image; a *site* is a specific place.

Once again, our director **cited** Hamlet's advice to the players, and we all groaned.

The fever affected his hearing but not his **sight.**

We beheld a terrible **sight.**

The archeological **site** was damaged in the bombing.

climactic, climatic *Climactic* means "of or relating to the climax"; *climatic* means "of or relating to climate."

cloth, clothe *Cloth* (noun) is material made from fibers; *clothe* (verb) means "to dress."

coarse, course Similar sounding words with unrelated meanings. *Coarse* (adjective) means "uncouth" or "rough in texture"; *course* (noun) means, among other things, "a class or series of classes," "a route," or "progress."

compare to, compare with Use *compare to* when describing similarities between unlike things; use *compare with* when evaluating similarities and differences between like things.

"Shall I **compare** thee **to** a summer's day?" (Shakespeare, sonnet 18)

The committee is **comparing** the House's bill **with** the Senate's.

complement, compliment A *complement* is something that completes or makes perfect; a *compliment* is a remark of praise or admiration. Similarly, *complement* (verb) is to complete or enhance; *compliment* (verb) is to offer a remark of praise or admiration.

comprise, compose Use with care. *Comprise* means "to contain" or "to be made up of"; *compose* means "to form the substance of." Do not use *comprised of;* use *is composed of* or *consists of* instead.

The whole **comprises** the parts.

The parts **compose** the whole.

The wrestling league **comprises** ten counties throughout the state.

The wrestling league **is composed of [consists of, is made up of]** ten counties throughout the state.

conscience, conscious *Conscience* (noun) is one's inner moral compass; *conscious* (adjective) refers to the state of being awake and aware. The adjective form of *conscience* is *conscientious;* the noun form of *conscious* is *consciousness.*

consensus of opinion, general consensus of opinion Redundant; do not use. *Consensus* itself means "an opinion reached by a group."

contact Traditionally considered too colloquial for use in formal prose, the verb *contact* is now deemed standard English usage by most dictionaries.

continual, continually; continuous, continuously Related but distinct meanings. *Continuous* refers to something that is constantly ongoing or never stops; *continual* means "recurring regularly or frequently."

The **continuous** roar of traffic outside my window drove me mad.

Every day I make my **continual** round from home to office and back again.

convince, persuade Traditionally, *convince* has to do with beliefs and understandings; *persuade* has to do with actions.

She **convinced** him that spinach was both healthy and tasty.

She **persuaded** him to eat his spinach.

could care less Illogical and nonstandard; use *couldn't care less.*

could of, should of, would of; may of, might of, must of Nonstandard; do not use. Use *could have, should have, may have, might have, must have;* or the contraction, if appropriate to your rhetorical situation.

council, counsel; councilor, counselor Similar sounding words with related but not interchangeable meanings. A *council* is a governing body. *Counsel* (noun) is advice or guidance; *counsel* (verb) is to give advice. A *councilor* is someone who is part of a council. A *counselor* is someone who gives advice.

couple of Colloquial; do not use in formal prose to mean "a few" or "several."

credible, credulous, creditable; incredible, incredulous *Credible* means "believable" or "plausible" (a credible person is trustworthy). *Credulous* means "willing to believe on slight evidence" (a credulous person is gullible). *Creditable* means "of some merit" (a creditable job is a job done well enough).

The defense presented a **credible** case for the defendant's innocence.

He lost all his hair after he was **credulous** enough to buy a tonic off the Internet.

This paper is **creditable;** but I think you can do better.

Incredible means "not credible." *Incredulous* means "not credulous."

criterion, criteria At all levels of usage, use *criterion* as singular and *criteria* as plural. See also **datum, data** and **medium, media.**

D

datum, data Although *data* entered English from Latin and traditional usage calls for *datum* to be used as singular and *data* as plural, most dictionaries now consider *data* a collective noun that can take a singular or plural verb depending on one's meaning. See also **criterion, criteria** and **medium, media.**

device, devise Similar sounding words with different meanings. A *device* (noun) is a machine, tool, or invention; *devise* (verb) is to design.

Glenda **devised** a plan to market her new **device.**

different from, different than In general, use *different from* when the object of comparison is a noun or noun phrase. Use *different than* when the object of comparison is a clause.

Although we look alike, my twin sister is **different from** me in interests and abilities.

He remembered the incident **differently than** did his siblings.

differ from, differ on, differ with *Differ from* is to be different; *differ on* or *differ with* is to disagree.

The wild cat **differs from** the domestic cat in many ways.

My mother and I **differ on** many issues.

She often **differed with** her constituents on environmental issues.

discreet, discrete Distinguish carefully between these homonyms. *Discreet* (adjective) means "marked by prudence or self-restraint" or "unobtrusive"; *discrete* (adjective) means "separate" or "distinct."

disinterested, uninterested Use *disinterested* to mean "impartial"; use *uninterested* to mean "bored" or "not interested in."

due to the fact that Wordy; use *because.*

E

each and every Wordy and clichéd; do not use.

eager, anxious See **anxious, eager.**

effect See **affect, effect.**

e.g. Abbreviation of *exemplia gratia,* which means "for instance." Avoid in formal prose; instead use *for example* or *for instance.*

elicit, illicit Similar sounding words with different meanings. The verb *elicit* means "to bring forth" or "to draw out"; the adjective *illicit* means "unlawful" or "immoral."

elude See **allude, elude, refer.**

emigrate, immigrate, migrate *To emigrate* is to leave one's home country to settle elsewhere; to *immigrate* is to enter a new country to settle.

After much thought, Igor decided to **immigrate** to Canada rather than to France or to the United States.

> Her grandmother **emigrated** from Romania in the early 1920s and came to Canada.

To *migrate* is to move from one place to another, especially in a way that is seasonal or periodic.

eminent, imminent, immanent Similar sounding adjectives with entirely different meanings. *Eminent* means "prominent" or "outstanding"; *imminent* means "about to occur"; *immanent* means "within" or "inherent."

ensure, insure, assure While all three verbs share a general meaning of "to make sure or certain," each has a different shade of meaning. *Ensure* is the most general of the three. *Assure* refers specifically to setting someone's mind at rest, and *insure* refers specifically to taking out insurance.

> The agent **assured** us that we were **insured** against floods but suggested we build a dam to **ensure** that our home remained safe.

enthuse In formal prose, do not use as a verb (*to enthuse*) or adjectivally as a past participle (I was *enthused* about my new classes). For the adjective form, use *enthusiastic.*

especially, specially *Especially* means "particularly" and is used as an intensifier; *specially* means "in a special manner" or "for a special purpose."

> Some dogs are **specially** trained to sniff out bombs.

> These dogs must train **especially** hard to meet the program's rigorous requirements.

et al. Abbreviation for *et alii,* which means "and others" and is used in reference to people only. Note the period after *al.* Used in source citations.

etc. Abbreviation for *et cetera,* which means "and other things." Avoid in formal prose, as it is often an indication of sloppy writing or thinking. Do not use the redundant *and etc.* Do not use *etc.* in a list introduced by *for example.*

everybody, every body; everyone, every one *Everybody* and *everyone* are both singular indefinite pronouns that mean "every person." In *every body* and *every one, every* acts as an adjective modifying the nouns *body* and *one,* respectively. *Every one* is used as an emphatic way of saying *each.*

> **Everyone** wants to play chess.

> **Every one** of the chess pieces had to be picked up.

See also **anybody, any body; anyone, any one.**

everyday, every day *Everyday* (adjective) means "ordinary"; *every day* is an adjective-noun pair meaning "each day in a series or succession."

everywheres See **anywheres, everywheres, nowheres, somewheres.**

except See **accept, except.**

except for the fact that Wordy; do not use.

explicit, implicit *Explicit* means "fully and clearly spelled out"; *implicit* means "implied."

F

farther, further Although the traditional distinction is that *farther* is used for literal distances and *further* is used for metaphorical distances, many dictionaries note that the terms have long been used interchangeably. However, only *further* is used to mean "additional" or "moreover."

> We couldn't go any **farther** until we consulted a map.

> **Further** discussion is clearly needed.

> **Further,** before we can decide on this issue, more discussion is clearly needed.

fewer, less Use *fewer* with nouns that can be counted (*fewer students, fewer complaints*); use *less* with nouns that cannot be counted (*less learning, less creativity*).

figure See **calculate, figure, reckon.**

firstly (secondly, thirdly, and so on) Do not use the *-ly* form; use *first* (*second, third,* and so on) or some other transitional expression.

fixing to Regionalism; do not use in formal prose.

flaunt, flout Similar sounding words with different meanings. To *flaunt* is "to show off ostentatiously"; to *flout* is "to defy" or "to show scorn or contempt for."

> He **flaunted** his new wealth by buying ten gold Cadillacs.

> He **flouted** authority by breaking all the rules and then laughing about it.

flunk Informal; do not use in formal prose. Use *fail.*

former, latter Traditionally in formal prose, *former* and *latter* are used only in referring to pairs; the first item is referred to as *the former* and the second item as *the latter.*

fun Traditionalists hold that in formal prose *fun* should be used as a noun only—not as an adjective.

further See **farther, further.**

G

get In formal prose avoid such colloquial usages as *I have got to leave now, We got snubbed, Trudy got upset, His snoring really gets to me, He got back at his detractors by becoming the queen's closest adviser,* or *Let's get started.* If unsure whether a usage is standard or colloquial, consult a dictionary.

good, well *Good* is an adjective; *well* is an adverb.

> She has a **good** voice. She sings **well.**

H

had better See **best, had best; better, had better.**

had ought to; hadn't ought to Nonstandard; do not use in formal prose.

> He ~~had ought to~~ ought to apologize.

> He ~~hadn't ought to~~ should not apologize.

half Use *half a* or *a half;* do not use *a half a.*

> We bought **half a** gallon of milk.

> We bought **a half** gallon of milk.

hanged, hung Both are past tenses of the verb *to hang.* Use *hanged* as the past tense and past participle for the meaning "to execute by hanging from the neck"; use *hung* as the past tense and past participle for all other meanings.

> Jud was **hanged** at sunrise.

> I **hung** my coat in the closet.

hardly, scarcely Both are negatives. Do not use as part of a double negative, as in *couldn't hardly move* or *without scarcely a sound.* When used to mean "no sooner," *hardly* is accompanied by *when.*

> I could **hardly** speak.

> One can **scarcely** believe that this is true.

> I had **hardly** boarded the bus **when** it zoomed back into traffic.

he, he/she, s/he, his/her Avoid using the masculine pronoun to refer to someone whose gender remains unspecified; also avoid such awkward construction as *he/she, s/he,* or *his/her.* For alternative strategies, see pp. 785–786.

himself, herself See **myself, ourselves, yourself, yourselves, himself, herself, itself, themselves.**

hisself Regionalism; do not use in formal prose.

hopefully Standard when used to mean "in a hopeful manner," as in *We waited hopefully for signs of spring.* Controversial when used as a sentence adverb, as in *Hopefully, the bill will pass.* Avoid the latter usage in formal prose.

hung See **hanged, hung.**

I

i.e. Abbreviation for *id est,* which means "that is." Avoid in formal prose. Instead, use *that is* or a similar English equivalent.

if, whether Although in informal prose *if* and *whether* are often used interchangeably, formal prose requires greater clarity and precision. For example, the statement *We'll tell you* ***if*** *you pass the test* could mean either *We'll tell you* ***whether*** *you pass the test* (i.e., we'll let you know **whether** you've passed or failed) or ***If*** *you pass the test, we'll tell you* (which implies that **if** you don't pass the test, we won't). In formal prose, use *if* to mean "in the event that" or "on the condition that"; use *whether* to express alternatives.

> **If** we exit now, I'm not sure **whether** we'll be going north or south.

illicit See **elicit, illicit.**

illusion See **allusion, illusion.**

immigrate See **emigrate, immigrate, migrate.**

immoral See **amoral, immoral.**

impact In formal prose, do not use as a verb to mean "to affect or influence."

implicit See **explicit, implicit.**

imply, infer To *imply* is to suggest without stating outright; to *infer* is to deduce or figure out.

incredible, incredulous See **credible, credulous, creditable; incredible, incredulous.**

individual, party, person In formal prose, avoid using *individual* or *party* as a general substitute for *person.* Use *individual* to contrast a single person to a group or to emphasize a person's specialness or distinction. *Party* is often used in legal contexts; *party* can also be used to mean a "participant in or accessory to an enterprise."

> Each **individual** must make his or her own choice.

> The ~~individual~~ person indicted in the cover-up pleaded not guilty.

> The school board will hold a hearing for ~~all individuals~~ anyone wanting to respond to the proposed changes.

Stanwich refused to be a **party** to the governor's scheme.

infer See **imply, infer.**

in regards to See **regard, regarding, regards.**

inside of, outside of When *outside* or *inside* is used as a preposition referring to location, *of* is awkward and unnecessary. In formal prose, do not use *outside of* to mean "except for."

insure See **ensure, insure, assure.**

inter-, intra- The prefix *inter-* means "between or among"; the prefix *intra-* means "within." *Interstate traffic* is traffic between states; *intrastate traffic* is traffic within a single state.

irregardless Nonstandard; use *regardless.*

is when, is where, reason . . . is because Avoid in formal prose as illogical and ungrammatical. The verb *is* can be followed by a noun or adjective that renames the subject, but not by an adverbial clause.

> Plagiarism is ~~when you copy~~ copying someone else's work without proper acknowledgment.
>
> Totalitarianism is ~~where~~ the centralization of all power ~~is centralized~~ under a single authority.
>
> ~~The reason we~~ We are changing the menu ~~is~~ because so many students are now vegetarian.

its, it's *Its* (no apostrophe) is the possessive of *it*. *It's* is the contraction of *it is* or *it has.* Never use *its'*.

> **It's** a shame that the airline has canceled all **its** flights for today.

itself See **myself, ourselves, yourself, yourselves, himself, herself, itself, themselves.**

-ize Do not use this suffix to coin new words. When in doubt, consult a dictionary.

K

kind of, sort of, type of Synonyms for a group or category sharing characteristics. Do not use *kind of* or *sort of* to mean "somewhat" or "rather." Use only as necessary to your meaning, as these phrases can contribute to wordiness. Do not use *kind of a, sort of a, type of a.* Do not use without *of,* as in *This type argument is unacceptable.*

> That **type of** person is dangerous. [*type* necessary to emphasize the category itself]
>
> I enjoy eating in family~~-type~~ restaurants. [*type* unnecessary to meaning]
>
> That **kind of** ~~a~~ book is fun to read.

The plural forms are *kinds of, sorts of, types of.*

L

later, latter *Later* refers to time; *latter* is the second of two items.

> She got stuck in traffic and had to take a **later** ferry.
>
> Between the Lynx and Interislander ferries, I recommend the **latter** for first-time visitors.

latter See **former, latter** and **later, latter.**

lay, lie To *lay* is to put something down; to *lie* is to be in a lying position. The past tense of *lay* is *laid;* the past participle is *laid.* The past tense of *lie* is *lay;* the past participle is *lain.*

> Whenever I **lay** my glasses down, I lose them.
>
> Yesterday I **laid** my glasses on the table, but today I cannot find them.
>
> My great-grandmother had **laid** her hand-crocheted bedspreads in the trunk.
>
> My glasses now **lie** on my desk.
>
> Yesterday my glasses **lay** on the table, but today I cannot find them.
>
> The hand-crocheted bedspreads had **lain** in the trunk for decades before I found them.

learn, teach To *learn* is to acquire knowledge; to *teach* is to impart knowledge.

> After I **taught** my little brother how to tie his shoes, he then **learned** how to dress himself completely.

less, fewer See **fewer, less.**

let, leave Not interchangeable. To *let* is to allow; to *leave* is to depart or to go away from. An exception is the phrase *leave me alone* or *let me alone.* Some experts accept only the former in formal prose, others accept either one.

liable to See **apt to, liable to, likely to.**

lie See **lay, lie.**

like See **as, like.**

likely to See **apt to, liable to, likely to.**

literally *Literally* means "in a literal manner"; do not use to mean "really" or "actually" (*Some people are **literally** incapable of washing their own clothes*), as an intensifier before a figurative statement (*Her hair was **literally** standing on end*), or as a general intensifier (*When pressed by reporters, he **literally** said nothing*).

loose, loosen, lose To *loose* is to let loose, release, or detach; to *loosen* is to make looser; to *lose* is to misplace or be deprived of something.

lots, lots of, a lot of Informal; do not use in formal prose.

M

man, mankind When referring to people of both genders, avoid using terms that imply that everyone is male. Try using *humanity, humankind,* or *people.*

may, can See **can, may.**

may be, maybe Related meanings but different parts of speech. The verb phrase *may be* means "might possibly be" (*The river **may be** flooding soon*). The adverb *maybe* means "perhaps" or "possibly" (***Maybe** the river will flood*).

may of See **could of, should of, would of; may of, might of, must of.**

medium, media Although *media* entered English from Latin and traditional usage calls for *medium* to be used as singular and *media* as plural, some dictionaries now consider *media* a collective noun that can take a singular or plural verb depending on one's meaning. However, in scientific and some other contexts (consult current practice in your field), *medium* is still used as the singular and *media* as the plural. See also **datum, data** and **criterion, criteria.**

might of See **could of, should of, would of; may of, might of, must of.**

migrate See **emigrate, immigrate, migrate.**

moral, morale As an adjective, *moral* means "ethical" or "in accord with accepted notions of right and wrong"; as a noun, a *moral* is a lesson or ethical understanding. *Morale* is one's enthusiasm for the job at hand.

> What **moral** can we draw from this example?
>
> When the union failed to win health benefits, **morale** plummeted.

most See **almost, most.**

must of See **could of, should of, would of; may of, might of, must of.**

myself, ourselves, yourself, yourselves, himself, herself, itself, themselves Do use correctly as reflexive or intensive pronouns; see 40c.

> Bruce cut **himself** while shaving.
>
> The president **herself** will address this fiasco.

Do not use in place of personal pronouns as either subjects or objects.

> Bonnie and ~~myself~~ I will lead the discussion.
>
> The discussion will be led by Bonnie and ~~myself~~ me.
>
> She gave the keys to Jorge and ~~myself~~ me.
>
> She was an avid chess player like ~~myself~~ me.
>
> The notices were posted entirely by ~~myself~~ me.

N

nor, or In general, use *nor* in comparisons following *neither;* otherwise, use *or.*

> This movie is **neither** engaging **nor** funny.
>
> The hero is either cowardly **or** confused, but it is difficult to tell which.

nothing like, nowhere near Avoid in formal prose; use *not nearly.*

nowheres See **anywheres, everywheres, nowheres, somewheres.**

number, amount Use *number* with nouns that can be counted (*a **number** of teaspoons, the **number** of attempts, the **number** of books*); use *amount* with nouns that cannot be counted (*a small **amount** of sugar, the **amount** of effort, the **amount** of information*).

O

off of Do not use; use *off.*

OK, okay Informal; do not use in formal prose.

on, upon Use *on; upon* is considered stilted in most usages.

on account of, owing to the fact that Wordy; use *because.*

on the one hand, on the other hand When using one of these transitional expressions, you should use the other. However, it's often more succinct to use *but, however, yet,* or *in contrast* instead.

or See **nor, or.**

ourselves See **myself, himself, herself, itself, ourselves, yourself, yourselves.**

outside of See **inside of, outside of.**

owing to the fact that See **on account of, owing to the fact that.**

P

party, individual, person See **individual, party, person.**

passed, past Different parts of speech from the same root. *Passed* is the past tense and past participle of *to pass* (*Yesterday, I **passed** him on the street; The opportunity had **passed***). *Past* can be an adjective (*Helen's neighbors speculate about **past** events in her life*), noun (*Gilbert learns the secret of Helen's **past***), adverb (*The queen waved as her car drove **past***), or preposition (*We drove **past** our exit and had to turn around*).

people, person See **person, people.**

per Latin word meaning "for each." Avoid in formal prose except technical documents.

percent, percentage *Percent* is used with numbers; *percentage* is used with qualifying adjectives or when the word stands alone.

> Today, 70 **percent** of American homes boast computers.
>
> Only a small **percentage** own typewriters.

person, individual, party See **individual, party, person.**

person, people *People* is the plural of *person. Persons* is used in some idioms as the plural, such as in *missing persons.*

phenomenon, phenomena *Phenomenon* is singular; *phenomena* is plural. See also **datum, data; criterion, criteria; medium, media.**

plenty Do not use as an adverb meaning "very" (*It's plenty hot*).

plus Standard when used as a conjunction to mean "added to" or "along with" (*Strength* ***plus*** *agility makes for a talented gymnast*). Do not use as a synonym for *and;* do not use to introduce an independent clause; do not use the phrase *plus which.*

p.m. See **a.m., p.m.**

practicable, practical *Practicable* and *practical* come from a common root and overlap in meaning. The distinction is that *practicable* connotes feasible or capable of being done, whereas *practical* connotes useful.

> While it's **practicable** to build a monorail around campus, it's not **practical.**

precede, proceed To *precede* is to go or come before; to *proceed* is to continue or go forward, either literally or figuratively. (A helpful mnemonic device is to remember that *precede* shares root meanings with *precedent* while *proceed* shares root meanings with *procession.*)

> John's interview **preceded** Mary's.
>
> We will **proceed** with these hearings tomorrow.

prejudice, prejudiced *Prejudice* is a noun; *prejudiced* an adjective.

pretty Traditionally considered colloquial when used as an adverb meaning "fairly" or "somewhat" (*pretty difficult*). While this usage is now listed as standard in some dictionaries, be aware that such qualifications as *very, pretty,* or *nearly* tend to weaken your prose.

previous to, prior to Awkward and wordy; use *before.*

principal, principle Similar sounding words that have no meanings in common. *Principal* as both a noun and an adjective is related to *main* (*Brazil's* ***principal*** *exports are its most important exports; the* ***principal*** *is the leading authority in a school*). *Principle* is a noun only and means "an underlying rule or law" (*He couldn't eat meat without violating his* ***principles***). A helpful, if clichéd, mnemonic device is "The principal is your pal."

proceed See **precede, proceed.**

provided, providing Traditionally only *provided* was acceptable to mean "on the condition" (*I will go,* ***provided*** *you go too*). Do not use *provided that* or *providing that.* Both *provided* and *providing* can often be more succinctly restated as *if.*

Q

question of whether, question as to whether Wordy; use *whether.*

quote, quotation Use *quote* as a verb and *quotation* as a noun.

> I **quoted** the author three times.
>
> I used three **quotations** in my essay.

R

raise, rise *Raise* is a transitive verb (a verb that takes an object) meaning "to lift." *Rise* is an intransitive verb (a verb that does not take an object) meaning "to move upward."

> Every spring, the melting snow **raises** the water level in the creek.
>
> The creek **rises** every spring when the snow thaws.

rarely ever Do not use in formal prose; use *rarely.*

real, really *Real* is an adjective; *really* is an adverb. Do not use *real* to mean "very."

reason . . . is because See **is when, is where, reason . . . is because.**

reason why Use with care. While often criticized as redundant, it is considered acceptable by many dictionaries.

reckon See **calculate, figure, reckon.**

regard, regarding, regards Correct usage in formal prose is as follows: *in regard to, with regard to, regarding, as regards.* Do not use *in regards to* or *with regards to.*

reoccur No such word. The correct word is *recur.*

respectful, respective *Respectful* means "full of respect"; *respective* means "particular" or "in the order given."

rise See **raise, rise.**

S

scarcely See **hardly, scarcely.**

secondly See **firstly (secondly, thirdly, and so on).**

sensual, sensuous Both mean "of the senses," but *sensual* implies physical and sexual gratification and *sensuous* implies the sensory appeal of the arts, especially.

set, sit In most usages, *set* is a transitive verb (a verb that takes an object) meaning "to put down" and *sit* is an intransitive verb (a verb that does not take an object) meaning "to be in a sitting position." Some exceptions include the intransitive use of *set* as in *The sun* ***sets*** and the transitive use of *sit* in *This lecture hall* ***sits*** *2,000 students.*

shall, will *Shall* is rarely used in American English, except in legal contexts and in phrasing polite questions such as *"Shall I bring you a menu?"* or *"Shall we go?"*

should of See **could of, should of, would of; may of, might of, must of.**

since *Since* can relate to time (*I've been waiting since noon*) or causation (*Since you want the truth, I'll tell you*). *Since* is considered less emphatic than *because.* Do not use *since* in contexts in which it can be construed to have both meanings.

sit, set See **set, sit.**

site See **cite, sight, site.**

so Do not use as an intensifier unless it is part of an overall phrase such as a *so . . . that* phrase (*She was so drunk that she couldn't walk*).

some Do not use in formal prose as a synonym for *remarkable* (*She was some athlete*).

somebody, some body; someone, some one *Somebody* and *someone* are both singular indefinite pronouns that mean "some person." In *some body* and *some one, some* acts as an adjective modifying the nouns *body* and *one,* respectively. See also **anybody, any body; anyone, any one** and **everybody, every body; everyone, every one.**

someplace Informal; do not use in formal prose. Instead use *somewhere.*

sometime, sometimes, some time *Sometime* is an adverb meaning "at an indefinite time"; *sometimes* is an adverb meaning "now and then." In the phrase *some time, some* is an adjective modifying the noun *time.*

> I'll see you **sometime** tomorrow.
>
> She **sometimes** walked in the park.
>
> It will be **some time** before he fully recovers.

somewheres See **anywheres, everywheres, nowheres, somewheres.**

sort of, kind of, type of See **kind of, sort of, type of.**

specially See **especially, specially.**

stationary, stationery *Stationary* is an adjective meaning "not moving"; *stationery* is a noun meaning "writing paper."

such *Such* has standard usages as an adjective, adverb, and pronoun. In formal prose, use the phrase *such that* to mean "of a nature that" (*Her performances were* ***such that*** *people happily stood in the rain to buy tickets*), but do not use *such that* to mean "in such a way that" or "so that" (*She plays* ***such that*** *the audience loses itself in the music*).

suppose to, supposed to Do not drop the final consonant; use *supposed to.*

sure, surely *Sure* is an adjective; *surely* is an adverb. Do not use *sure* as an adverb meaning "surely" or "certainly."

T

take, bring See **bring, take.**

than, then *Than* is a conjunction used to make comparisons; *then* is an adverb that expresses time.

that, which, who See **who, which, that.**

their, there, they're Similar sounding words with different meanings. *Their* is a possessive pronoun; *there* is an adverb meaning "in that place"; *they're* is a contraction of *they are.*

> They lost **their** house in the storm.
>
> If it's not **there,** look elsewhere.
>
> **They're** excited to be moving.

theirself, theirselves, themself Nonstandard; use *themselves.*

themselves See **myself, ourselves, yourself, yourselves, himself, herself, itself, themselves.**

then, than See **than, then.**

thirdly See **firstly (secondly, thirdly, and so on).**

thru No such word; use *through.*

thusly Do not use for *thus.*

till, until Generally interchangeable, but better to use *until* to begin sentences. Do not use *'til.*

time period Redundant; use *time* or *period.*

to, too, two Similar sounding words with no meanings in common. *To* is a preposition (*I go to the store*); *too* is an adverb meaning "also" or "excessively"; *two* is a number. Do not overuse *too.*

toward, towards American usage is *toward;* British usage is *towards.*

try and Nonstandard; use *try to.*

TV Abbreviation for *television;* use *television* in formal prose

type of See **kind of, sort of, type of.**

U

uninterested See **disinterested, uninterested.**

unique *Unique* means "one of a kind," so something that is *unique* cannot be *more unique, less unique, very unique,* or *quite unique.*

until See **till, until.**

upon See **on, upon.**

use, usage, utilize Use *use* unless your context requires one of the specific, more technically precise meanings of *usage,* such as "the way in which words are written and spoken in a language community." Note that *usage* has a connotation of habit. *Use* has a multiplicity of meanings, including a connotation of practice or employment. Avoid *utilize* when *use* will do. Similarly, try *use* (noun) for *utilization.*

use to, used to Do not drop the final consonant; use *used to.*

utilize See **use, usage, utilize.**

V

very Do not overuse.

W

wait for, wait on To *wait for* someone is to be in expectation of that person's arrival; to *wait on* someone is to serve that person.

ways In formal prose, use *way,* not *ways,* in such contexts as *We're a long way from home.*

weather, whether Similar sounding words with entirely unrelated meanings. *Weather* (noun) is what makes you bring your umbrella or slather on suntan oil; *whether* is a conjunction used to introduce alternatives (*She didn't know* ***whether*** *to order chocolate or vanilla ice cream*).

well See **good, well.**

were, we're *Were* is a past tense form of *to be; we're* is the contraction of *we are.*

where Do not use for *that,* as in *I read in the newspaper where he had been voted out of office.*

where . . . from, where . . . to, where . . . at Correct usage is to include the preposition *from* in *where* expressions of the type *Where are you coming from?* or *from where I sit.* However, the prepositions *to* and *at* are considered superfluous in *where* expressions:

Where are you going ~~to~~?

Where is the library ~~at~~ on this campus?

whether, if See **if, whether.**

whether or not In general, the *or not* is considered to be superfluous in formal prose. Better to use *whether* unless your meaning is "regardless of whether" (*We'll play soccer this Saturday* ***whether or not*** *it snows*). However, many writers defend the redundancy of *or not* as a legitimate means of creating emphasis.

who, which, that Use *who* for people and named animals; use *which* or *that* for objects, unnamed animals, and abstract concepts. See 43r. Use *that* for restrictive clauses; use *which* for nonrestrictive clauses.

Books **that** bore me don't get read. [I only read books that I like.]

Books, **which** bore me, don't get read. [I find all books boring and don't read any of them.]

who, whom Use *who* as a subject; use *whom* as an object. Case is governed by the word's grammatical function within its clause, not by that clause's grammatical function in the sentence as a whole. See 43g.

I was delighted to interview a man **who** had entertained so many.

I was eager to interview a man **whom** so many had vilified.

whose, who's Similar sounding words with different meanings. *Whose* is a possessive pronoun (***Whose*** *dog is this?); who's* is a contraction of *who is* (*my aunt,* ***who's*** *living in Boston now*). *Whose* may be used to refer to things as well as people.

will, shall See **shall, will.**

-wise Suffix meaning "in the manner of" or "in the direction of" (as in *clockwise*). In formal prose, avoid using jargon coined by using *-wise* as a suffix meaning "in regard to" or "concerning" (*marriagewise, performancewise, dancewise*).

with regards to See **regard, regarding, regards.**

would of See **could of, should of, would of; may of, might of, must of.**

Y

your, you're *Your* is a possessive pronoun (*Your dog is biting my leg*); *you're* is a contraction of *you are.*

yourself, yourselves See **myself, ourselves, yourself, yourselves, himself, herself, itself, themselves.**

These pages constitute an extension of the copyright page. We have made every effort to trace the ownership of all copyrighted material and to secure permission from copyright holders. In the event of any question arising as to the use of any material, we will be pleased to make the necessary corrections in future printings. Thanks are due to the following authors, publishers, and agents for permission to use the material indicated.

Text Credits

Chapter 4. **52:** Hunter Williams, "Prof Potpourri." *The Independent Florida Alligator Online,* 2/18/04. Copyright © 2004 Independent Florida Alligator. Used with permission; Felipe Camacho, "The Market-Driven University." Used with permission. **53:** Jammy Inton, "*Initial D*'s Myth." Used with permission; Nichole Eastman, "Rocket Challenge." Used with permission. **64:** Angela Garrison, "From Over There to Over Here: War Blogs Get Up Close, Personal, and Profitable." Used with permission.

Chapter 5. **72:** From Malcolm Gladwell, THE TIPPING POINT. Copyright © 2000 by Malcolm Gladwell. Used by permission of Little, Brown and Co. Inc. **82:** © The New Yorker Collection 1993 Peter Steiner from cartoonbank.com. All rights reserved.

Chapter 6. **92:** Wyatt Roth, "Competition at Its Best." Used with permission. **114:** Gina Wolf, "Still Guarding the Fort." Used with permission.

Chapter 7. **129:** "Three Models of Déjà Vu" by Chronicle Reporting, *The Chronicle of Higher Education,* July 23, 2004. Copyright © 2004, The Chronicle of Higher Education. Used with permission.

Chapter 8. **133:** Excerpt from Malcolm Gladwell, THE TIPPING POINT. Copyright © 2000 by Malcolm Gladwell. Used by permission of Little, Brown and Co. Inc. **135:** Excerpt from Steven Johnson, "Tool for Thought" *New York Times,* January 30, 2005. Copyright © 2005 New York Times Co. Inc. Used with permission. **137:** Jay Chiat, "Illusions are Forever" *Forbes,* 10/20/2000. Copyright © 2000 Forbes Inc. Reprinted by permission of FORBES ASAP Magazine. **147:** L. Franklin Jewell, "Things We Carry: A Multicultural Awakening." Used with permission.

Chapter 9. **163:** Anne Sexton, "The Starry Night" from ALL MY PRETTY ONES. Copyright © 1962 by Anne Sexton, renewed 1990 by Linda G. Sexton. Reprinted by permission of Houghton Mifflin Company and Sll/Sterling Lord Literistic, Inc. All rights reserved. **166:** William Carlos Williams, from "The Red Wheelbarrow" from COLLECTED POEMS: 1909-1939, VOLUME I. Copyright 1938 by New Directions Publishing Corp. Reprinted by permission of New Directions Publishing Corp. **169:** Kim Caliandro, "Who's that bell tolling for?: The Vanity of Freedom at Any Cost in 'The Story of an Hour.'" Used with permission.

Chapter 10. **184:** "Let America Be America Again" from THE COLLECTED POEMS OF LANGSTON HUGHES by Langston Hughes. Copyright © 1994 by the Estate of Langston Hughes. Used by permission of Alfred A. Knopf, a division of Random House, Inc. and Harold Ober Associates. **185:** Ambigram copyright © 1985 by John Langdon. www.johnlangdon.net. Used by permission; Logo designed by Michael Buchmiller in consultation with Guillermo Nericcio Garcia. Used with permission of Hyberbole Books. **189:** Kathy Kane, "*The Migration of the Negro*'s Place in the Harlem Renaissance." Used with permission.

Chapter 11. **211:** Jacob Warrington, "Postmodernism and the IKEA Nesting Instinct: Consumerism and Commodification in David Fincher's *Fight Club.*" Used with permission.

Chapter 12. **226:** Eugene Rhee, Resume. Used with permission.

Chapter 14. **277:** Excerpt from Kellie Bartlett, "A Glance at the February 5 Issue of *Neuron:* Seeing but not believing—or not noticing" *The Chronicle of Higher Education,* 2/10/04. Copyright © 2004 The Chronicle of Higher Education. Reprinted with permission. **279:** Lambert, Hogan, and Barton, "Collegiate Academic Dishonesty Revisited" from www.sociology.org, September 2004. **283:** "Ethics and Discussion" overview from www.savingsandclone.com. Copyright © 2005 Genetic Savings & Clone. Used with permission. **285:** Excerpt from Kamil Skawinski, "IT & SETI: The Role of Computer Technology in the Search for Extraterrestrial Intelligence" *California Computer News,* July 2, 2002. Copyright © 2002 by Kamil Z. Skawinski. Used with permission.

Chapter 17. 341: Tim Berners-Lee, et al. "The Semantic Web" *Scientific American,* May 2001. Copyright © 2001. Used with permission. **342:** Hazel Muir, "Beagle 2's Demise Remains a Mystery, *New Scientist,* August 24, 2004. Copyright © 2004 New Scientist. Reprinted by permission. **345:** Kyle Wingfield, "Study: Misdiagnosis Led to Birds' Death." Copyright © 2004 Associated Press. Used with permission. **351:** Jean Nash Johnson, "Blogging May Make Teens Better Writers" *Sun Herald.* Copyright © Knight Ridder/Tribune. Used with permission.

Chapter 18. 370: Pamela LiCalzi O'Connell, "Blog Bog and an E-mail Pony Express" 10/23/03. Copyright © 2003 New York Times Co. Inc. Used with permission. **372:** Sarah Boxer, "McLuhan's Messages, Echoing in Iraq Coverage" 4/3/03. Copyright © 2003 New York Times Co. Inc. Used with permission.

Chapter 19. 432: Molly McClure, "Get a Life! Misconceptions about the Tolkien Fan Fiction Culture." Used with permission.

Chapter 20. 456: James Andrew Laspina, "The Visual Turn and the Transformation of the Textbook," p. 17, Fig. 1.1, © 1998. Reprinted by permission of Lawrence Erlbaum & Associates. **478:** Jenny Chow, Mira Zaharopoulos, Nancy Huynh, and Xin Xin Wu, "Constellations of Parental Risk Factors Associated with Child Maltreatment." Used with permission.

Chapter 21. 516: Michael Vogel, "War on the Budget Plan: The Elizabethan War with Spain." Used with permission.

Chapter 24. 565: "When We Leave for Work" by Shannon Reilly and Gia Kereselidze, *USA Today.* Copyright © *USA Today.* Used with permission.

Chapter 26: 597: "10 Tips for Public Speaking" Reprinted with permission by Toastmasters International.

Chapter 28: 630: "Ten Tips for a Better Weblog" © 2005 Rebecca Blood. Used with permission. **640:** © David Pescovitz. Used with permission.

Chapter 29. 648: Core techniques for Web Content Acessiblity Guidelines 1.0. Copyright © 2000 World Wide Web Consortium (Massachusetts Institute of Technology, European Research Consortium for Informatics and Mathematics, Keio University). All Rights Reserved. **650:** "Galileo" entry from *The Internet Encyclopedia of Philosophy,* 2001. Copyright © 2001. Used with permission. **656:** "Diverse Contexts for Visiting a Website" from www.w3.org/TR/WAI-WEBCONTENT Copyright © 2000 World Wide Web Consortium (Massachusetts Institute of Technology, European Research Consortium for Informatics and Mathematics, Keio University). All Rights Reserved. **657:** "W3C Priority 1 Principles of Accessibility" Copyright © 2000 World Wide Web Consortium (Massachusetts Institute of Technology, European Research Consortium for Informatics and Mathematics, Keio University). All Rights Reserved.

Chapter 37. 760: "Salon Women" by Emily Bilski and Emily Braun, 3/31/05, *Chronicle of Higher Education.* Copyright © 2005 Emily Bilski and Emily Braun. Used with permission. **767:** Cary Tennis, "Since you asked . . ." 4/14/05, *Salon.com.* Copyright © 2005 Salon, Inc. Used with permission.

Chapter 38. 775: Definition of "easy" from *The American Heritage Dictionary of the English Language,* Fourth Edition. Copyright © 2000 by Houghton Mifflin Company. Reproduced with permission. **776:** Judith Cofer, excerpt from *The Latin Deli: Prose and Poetry.* Copyright © 1993 Judith Cofer. Reprinted by permission of the University of Georgia Press.

Chapter 53. 967: Excerpt from "Mending Wall" from *The Poetry of Robert Frost,* edited by Edward Connery Lathem. Copyright 1930, 1939, © 1969 by Henry Holt and Company. Copyright © 1958 by Robert Frost. Copyright © 1987 by Lesley Frost Ballantine. Reprinted by permission of Henry Holt and Company, LLC.

Image Credits

Chapter 1. 4: © Images.com/CORBIS **5:** © Matthias Kulka/CORBIS **6:** top left, © Jose Luis Pelaez, Inc./CORBIS; top right, © Paul Edmondson/CORBIS; center left, © Ariel Skelley/CORBIS; center right, Lucky Look/Danita Delimont; bottom left, David Young-Wolff/PhotoEdit; bottom right, © Tom Stewart/CORBIS **9:** bottom center, right, © Anthony Redpath/CORBIS; top and bottom left, © BettmannCORBIS; top right, © CORBIS **11:** Copyleft, Wikipedia.org. **14:** Photo by Gina Wolf, used with permission.

Chapter 2. 28: Photo by Gina Wolf, used with permission.

Chapter 3. 32: David Parker/Photo Researchers, Inc. **33:** Photo by Gina Wolf, used with permission. **41:** top, Copyright © 2005 War of the Worlds - Official Site; bottom, www.war-of-the-worlds.org.

Chapter 5. 76: © Seth Joel/CORBIS **77:** © Gallo Images/CORBIS **78:** bottom center, © Hulton-Deutsch Collection/CORBIS; bottom right, © Araldo de Luca/CORBIS **79:** Carraher, R. G.; Thurston, J. B. (1996). *Optical Illusions and the Visual Arts.* New York: Reinholt, p. 18. Permission for use granted from the photographer, Ronald C. James, who originally published the image in *Life* magazine (Life, February 19, 1965 Vol. 58, No. 7). **80:** Nimatallah/Art Resource, NY **81:** © Patrick Johns/CORBIS **83:** © CORBIS **84:** ©Royalty-Free/Corbis **85:** center, Courtesy Nikon, Inc.; center left, Getty Images Publicity Business Wire; center right, © Reuters/CORBIS; far right, ©Yuriko Nakao/Reuters/CORBIS.

Chapter 6. 89: bottom left, Bonnie Kamin/PhotoEdit **97, 104, 105, 106, 110, 111, 112, 113:** Microsoft product screen shot(s) reprinted with permission from Microsoft Corporation.

Chapter 7. 122: © Copyright 2006 Digital Universe.

Chapter 8. 133: Courtesy Time Warner Book Group UK **136:** © Willie Hill, Jr./The Image Works **143:** Michael Newman/PhotoEdit, Inc.

Chapter 9. 163: Gogh, Vincent van (1853-1890). *The Starry Night.* 1889. Oil on canvas, 29 x 36 1/4". Acquired through the Lillie P. Bliss Bequest. (472.1941) The Museum of Modern Art, New York, NY, U.S.A. Digital Image The Museum of Modern Art/Licensed by SCALA/Art Resource, NY **165:** center left, © 2006 London Features International (USA) Ltd.; bottom center, Paramount/The Kobal Collection.

Chapter 10. 177: bottom, Photofest, Inc.; top, © Barbara Davidson/Dallas Morning News/CORBIS **178:** bottom, Excerpt from *Pantone Guide to Communicating with Color,* by Ms Leatrice Eiseman, published by Design Books International, Distributed by F&W Publications, Cincinnati, OH. To order, call 1-800 289 0963; center, Hans Namuth; top, National Gallery of Australia, Canberra. © 2005 The Pollock-Krasner Foundation/Artists Rights Society (ARS), New York **179:** top, © Barbara Davidson/Dallas Morning News/CORBIS; bottom, Photograph by Ansel Adams. Collection Center for Creative Photography, University of Arizona. © Trustees of the Ansel Adams Publishing Rights Trust **180:** © 1993 Universal City Studios, Inc. and Amblin Entertainment, Inc **181:** AP Photo/Alan Diaz **182:** top left, R.G. Ojeda. Réunion des Musées Nationaux/Art Resource, NY; top right, © B.S.P.I/CORBIS; bottom, © Robert Holmes/CORBIS **183:** top, © Layne Kennedy/CORBIS; bottom, © Shamil Zhumatov/Reuters/CORBIS **184:** Web design by Hello Design; © 2003 whiteground Ltd. Site owned by Eyestorm Britart; Courtesy of the National Museum of American History; from "Separate Is Not Equal: Brown v. Board of Education," National Museum of American History **185:** United States Holocaust Memorial Museum **189:** Digital Image © The Museum of Modern Art/Licensed by SCALA/Art Resource, NY. © 2005 The Jacob and Gwendolyn Lawrence Foundation, Seattle/Artists Rights Society (ARS), New York.

Chapter 11. 193: Gary Conner/PhotoEdit, Inc. **197:** top and center, Bill Aron/PhotoEdit, Inc.; bottom, Colin Young-Wolff/PhotoEdit, Inc.

Chapter 12. 219: © David Pollack/CORBIS **220:** top, © Chuck Savage/CORBIS; bottom and center left, © Dennis MacDonald/PhotoEdit, Inc.; center right, © Michael A. Keller/zefa/CORBIS **230, 231:** Microsoft product screen shot(s) reprinted with permission from Microsoft Corporation.

Chapter 14. 246: del.icio.us and del.icio.us logo are trademarks of Yahoo! Inc. Reproduced with permission of Yahoo! Inc. **248:** bottom, © Jeff Greenberg/PhotoEdit, Inc.; center, © Nancy Richmond/The Image Works **249:** top, bottom, © David Young-Wolff/PhotoEdit, Inc.; center, © Jeff Greenberg/PhotoEdit, Inc. **254:** © Skjold/The Image Works **257:** © Jeff Greenberg/PhotoEdit, Inc. **258:** By permission. From Merriam-Webster On-Line © 2005 by Merriam-Webster, Incorporated (www.Merriam-Webster.com) **268:** top, © Michael St. Maur Sheil/CORBIS; center, akg-images; center, William Faulkner Collection, Special Collections, University of Virginia Library; bottom, © Deborah Davis/PhotoEdit, Inc. **270:** top, © 1958 Universal City Studios, Inc. for Samuel Taylor and Patricia Hitchcock O'Connell as trustees. Courtesy of Universal Studios Licensing LLLP; center, © Bettmann/CORBIS; center right, © CORBIS SYGMA; bottom, © Lightscapes Photography, Inc./CORBIS **272:** top, © Bettmann/CORBIS; center left, © Ruth Orkin/Getty Images; center right, Courtesy of the Albert Einstein Archives, Jewish National & University Library, Hebrew University of Jerusalem, Israel; bottom, © Gerrit Greve/CORBIS **273:** © Getty Images Entertainment/Getty Images **274:** top, © Philip Gould/CORBIS; center left, © Images.com/CORBIS; center, © Images.com/CORBIS; center right, © Royalty-Free/CORBIS; bottom, © Michael Keller/CORBIS **276:** top, © Images.com/CORBIS; center, © LWA-Stephen Walstead/CORBIS; center right, © Royalty-Free/CORBIS; bottom, © CORBIS **277:** Reprinted from *Neuron,* Vol. 41, No. 3, 2004, 'The Neural Fate of Consciously Perceived and Missed

Events in the Attentional Blink,' page 467, with permission from Elsevier. **278:** top, © Images.com/CORBIS; center left, © Ed Bock/CORBIS; center right, © 2005 Pew Internet & American Life Project; U. S. Census Bureau; bottom, © Royalty-Free/CORBIS **280:** top, © Museum of the City of New York/CORBIS; © Seth Joel/CORBIS; center left, © LWA-Stephen Westead/CORBIS; center right, © Roger Ressmeyer/CORBIS; ©Andrew Brookes/CORBIS; bottom left, © Bettmann/CORBIS; bottom right, Courtesy Camino Books, Inc. **282:** top, Courtesy NHGRI; center left, © David Pollack/CORBIS; center right, © Charles Gupton/CORBIS; bottom, Courtesy of Oak Ridge National Laboratory, managed for DOE by UT-Battelle, LLC; bottom right, © Andrew Brookes/CORBIS **283:** © Kim Kulish/CORBIS **284:** top, NASA; center left, © Thom Lang/CORBIS; center right, © NASA/Roger Ressmeyer/CORBIS; bottom, NASA/HST/ASU/J.Hester et al; bottom right, © Roger Ressmeyer/CORBIS **285:** Courtesy SETI@home.

Chapter 15. **290:** Reproduced with permission of Yahoo! Inc. © 2005 by Yahoo! Inc. **301:** © Amazon.com, Inc. All Rights Reserved. **308:** http://www.martinlutherking.org/ **309:** © 2004 - The King Center - Atlanta, GA.

Chapter 16. **317:** By permission, University of Massachusetts Amherst **319:** By permission, Seattle Central Community College **323, 324:** Copyright © 2005, Endeavor Information Systems Incorporated. All rights reserved. Screen shot of Endeavor's Voyager Product. **325:** Library of Congress **326:** Courtesy Arizona State University Libraries. **327:** © Amazon.com, Inc. All Rights Reserved.

Chapter 18. **360:** top, NASA/Comstock RF; bottom, © BananaStock RF **361:** top: Linear/Peter Arnold, Inc; bottom, © Dennis di Cicco/CORBIS **362:** © The Corcoran Gallery of Art/CORBIS.

Chapter 19. **376:** © Copyright 2006 Podcast Networks (TM). All Microsoft product screen shot(s) reprinted with permission from Microsoft Corporation.

Chapter 24. **558:** © Chuck Savage/CORBIS **560:** top, © 2005 C. Herscovici, Brussels/Artists Rights Society (ARS), New York. Photo Credit: Banque d'Images, ADAGP/Art Resource, NY; bottom, © 2005 C. Herscovici, Brussels/Artists Rights Society (ARS), New York. Photo Credit: Banque d'Images, ADAGP/Art Resource, NY **563:** © 1958 Universal City Studios, Inc. for Samuel Taylor and Patricia Hitchcock O'Connell as trustees. Courtesy of Universal Studios Licensing LLLP **566:** Microsoft product screen shot(s) reprinted with permission **568:** The Broad Art Foundation, Santa Monica. Courtesy Mary Boone Gallery, New York.

Chapter 25. **573:** © 1958 Universal City Studios, Inc. for Samuel Taylor and Patricia Hitchcock O'Connell as trustees. Courtesy of Universal Studios Licensing LLLP **574:** top, Courtesy of Jennifer Sterling; bottom, Courtesy of EMI **575:** left, Image reproduced with permission of copyright owner, Temple University. All rights reserved. **579:** © Association of Research Libraries, Washington, DC **580:** top, istockphoto.com; center, © Frans Lanting/CORBIS; bottom, © Mark Bolton/CORBIS.

Chapter 26. **593:** © Royalty-Free/CORBIS **598:** top, North Wind Picture Archives bottom, Declaration of Independence, John Dunlap, printer, 1776, (Ab1776-25), The Historical Society of Pennsylvania **600:** Microsoft product screen shot(s) reprinted with permission from Microsoft Corporation.

Chapter 27. **602:** www.musicforamerica.org **604:** © Nation Wong/CORBIS **610, 615:** Microsoft product screen shot(s) reprinted with permission from Microsoft Corporation. **612:** Finder screenshot reprinted by permission from Apple Computer, Inc. **612, 613:** Mail screenshot reprinted by permission from Apple Computer, Inc.

Chapter 28. **622:** © 2005 by America Online, Inc. Netscape content © 2005 Netscape. Used with permission. **623:** Copyright © 1990-2006 by the EServer. All rights reserved. **625:** Cynthia Haynes **628:** Michael Montoure, http://seattle.blogmob.org/ **637:** MOO provided by the author. enCore Copyright © Sindre Sarensen and Jan Rune Holmevik. **638:** Copyleft, Drupal.org.

Chapter 29. **642:** Dynamic Graphics Group/Creatas/Alamy **643:** Justin Pumfrey/Getty Images **646:** from Marshall Deutelbaum, "The Role of Set Design" in "Constructing Cinemascope Composition" from Linda Lewis, ed. *Filmbuilding: Selected Papers and Presentations.* Volume 1 (2001) **647:** Adrian Miles, "Hypertext Syntagmas: Cinematic Narration with Links" Journal of Digital Information 1.7 (20 December 2000). http://jodi.tamu.edu/Articles/v01/i07/Miles/ **649:** By permission, Michael Angeles, http://urlgreyhot.com/ **650:** Text, design, and layout by Megan Wilde for the Electronic Text Center. This biography is based upon information culled from The Galileo Project website. **653:** Creative Commons Attribution 2.5 License http://creativecommons.org/

licenses/by/2.5/ **655:** The Writing Instructor, Sept 2001 www .writinginstructor.com/columns/ absolutwriting/index.html.

Chapter 30. 661: © David Raymer/CORBIS **663, 670:** Microsoft product screen shot(s) reprinted with permission from Microsoft Corporation. **672:** Amy Kimme-Hea, Gertrude's Pet Shop http://pw.english.edu/ resources/gertrude/gert.html **674:** Library of Congress **677:** David Blakesley and Dawn Forma, The Writing Instructor: http://www .writinginstructor.com.

Chapter 31. 686, 687: © UltraStar Entertainment **688:** top, http://cw.english.purdue.edu/speakers.html; bottom, By permission: Funny Monkey—Tools for Teachers **689:** The four-column design concept of Arts & Letters Daily, with teasers and click-through links, was originated in 1998 by Denis Dutton of the University of Canterbury, New Zealand, based on an 18th-century broadsheet. Web realization was by Peter Fitzpatrick of Christchurch, New Zealand. **690:** http://www.refdesk.com **691:** By permission, Michael Angeles, http:// urlgreyhot.com/; © UltraStar Entertainment **692:** By permission, Jack Hamilton, Doodlelab.com **694:** top, Library of Congress **702:** Colormixers © 2004 Twyst **704:** © Zoological Society of San Diego.

Chapter 32. 706: © Lightscapes Photography, Inc./CORBIS **719:** By permission, Michael Angeles, http://urlgreyhot.com/

Chapter 33. 722: © 826 Valencia **724:** Big Cheese Photo LLC/Alamy **725:** center left, NASA/Comstock RF **726:** © Mustafa Ozer/REUTERS/CORBIS.

Chapter 40. 797: © Bob Rowan; Progressive Image/CORBIS.

Chapter 42. 834: Microsoft product screen shot(s) reprinted with permission from Microsoft Corporation.

Chapter 47. 912: © Lionhead Studios Limited.

Chapter 54. 970: Halo 2 (TM) copyright Bungie Studios, a division of Microsoft Corporation. This Spartan Life copyright Damian Lacedaemion.

Chapter 59. 1006: Copyleft, Wikipedia.org.

Trademarks

Product names may be trademarks of their respective owners and they are used for identification purposes only. All other trademarks contained herein are the property of their respective owners.

A9 is a trademark of A9.com, Inc. or its affiliates in the United States and other countries.

Adaptec Toast and ZIP are registered trademarks of Iomega Corporation.

Adobe Acrobat, Adobe Garamond, GoLive, InDesign, Illustrator, Photoshop, Photoshop Elements, Premiere, Reader, and SoundEdit are registered trademarks or trademarks of Adobe Systems Incorporated in the United States and/or other countries.

Amazon, Amazon.com, and the Amazon.com logo are registered trademarks of Amazon.com, Inc. or its affiliates.

AOL and AIM are registered trademarks of America Online, Inc. The AIM Instant Message design and "look and feel" © 2005 by America Online, Inc. The America Online content, name, icons and trademarks are used with permission.

Apple Mac, Final Cut Pro, iMovie, iTunes, QuickTime, and Safari are registered trademarks of Apple Computer, Inc. Apple Garage Band, iSight, Keynote, Finder, Spotlight, and Geneva are trademarks of Apple Computer, Inc.

Arial, Century Gothic and Times New Roman are trademarks of The Monotype Corporation registered in the US Patent and Trademark Office and elsewhere.

The Ask logo and other Ask logos and product and service names are service marks or trademarks of IAC Search & Media.

Avery Design Pro Limited is a trademark of Avery Dennison Corporation.

Blackboard is a trademark or registered trademark of Blackboard Inc. in the United States and/or other countries.

Boing Boing is a trademark of Happy Mutants LLC in the United States [and other countries].

The Clusty mark belongs to Vivísimo, Inc., and is protected by trademark laws.

Corel WordPerfect and CorelDRAW are registered trademarks of Corel Corporation and/or its subsidiaries in Canada, the United States and/or other countries.

Dogpile is a registered trademark of InfoSpace, Inc.

EarthLink is a registered trademark of EarthLink, Inc.

Eudora is a registered trademark of QUALCOMM Incorporated.

ExpressionEngine is a registered trademark of pMachine, Inc.

Final Draft is a registered trademark of Final Draft, Inc.

FirstClass is a registered trademark of Open Text Corporation.

FrameForge 3D Studio is a registered trademark of FrameForge 3D Studio.

Friendster is a service mark of Friendster, Inc.

Google Desktop Search, Google Directory, Google Glossary, Google Groups, Google Images, Gmail, Google News, Google Print, Google Scholar, Google Toolbar, Google Zeitgeist, Blogger and Orkut online community are trademarks of Google, Inc.

Groupee and the Groupee logo are trademarks of Groupee Systems Incorporated.

Helvetica, Palatino, and Times are registered trademarks of Linotype Corporation.

HyperSnap is a trademark of Hyperionics, Inc

ICQ is a registered trademark of ICQ, Inc. and America Online, Inc.

ITC Garamond and ITC Zapf Dingbats are registered trademarks of International Typeface Corporation.

The registered trademark Linux® is used pursuant to a license from Linus Torvalds, owner of the mark in the U.S. and other countries.

LISTSERV is a registered trademark licensed to L-Soft International, Inc.

LiveJournal is a trademark of LiveJournal in the United States.

Macromedia, Breeze, Dreamweaver, Fireworks, Flash, and SoundEdit are trademarks or registered trademarks of Macromedia, Inc. in the United States and/or other countries.

Mamma is a registered trademark of Mamma.com, Inc.

Microsoft, Windows, Entourage, Front Page, Hotmail, Internet Explorer, MSN Chat, NetMeeting, Outlook, PowerPoint, MSN Search, and Word are registered trademarks of Microsoft Corporation in the United States and/or other countries.

Georgia and Verdana are trademarks of Microsoft Corporation registered in the U.S. Patent & Trademark Office and may be registered in other jurisdictions.

The name Moodle is a trademark and/or registered trademark of The Moodle Trust in the U.S. and other countries.

Moveable Type and TypePad are registered trademarks of Six Apart in the United States.

Movie Magic is a registered trademark of Screenplay Systems, Inc.

Mozilla, Firefox, Thunderbird, Mozilla Mail are trademarks or registered trademarks of the Mozilla Foundation.

Nero is a registered trademark of Nero AG.

Netscape, Netscape Navigator, Netscape Composer, the Netscape N and Ship's Wheel logos are registered trademarks of Netscape Communications Corporation in the United States and other countries.

Nvu is a trademark of Linspire, Inc.

Palm OS and Palm Powered are trademarks or registered trademarks of PalmSource, Inc. or its affiliates, or its licensor, Palm Trademark Holding Company, in the United States, France, Germany, Japan, the United Kingdom, and other countries. All rights reserved.

Pinnacle Studio is a trademark of Pinnacle Systems, Inc. in the United States and/or other countries.

Roxio is a trademark of Roxio, a division of Sonic Solutions which may be registered in some jurisdictions.

SecureFX is a registered trademark of VanDyke Software, Inc.

Skype is a trademark of Skype Technologies SA

UNIX is a registered trademark of the Open Group.

USB is a trademark of Universal Serial Buss Implementers Forum, Inc.

ViaVideo is a trademark of Polycom, Inc. in the US and various countries.

WebCT is a registered trademark in the U.S. Patent and Trademark Office and in the European Union of WebCT, Inc. in the United States and other jurisdictions.

Wikipedia is a registered trademark of the Wikimedia Foundation, Inc.

WriteNote is a registered trademark of Cengage Learning.

XANGA is a registered trademark of Xanga.com, Inc.

YAHOO!, del.icio.us, and the YAHOO! logo are trademarks of Yahoo! Inc.

URLs

Every effort has been made to verify the authenticity and sources of the URLs listed in this book. All URLs were correctly linked to their websites at the time of publication. Due to the quickly evolving nature of the Internet, it is possible that a link may break or a URL may change or become obsolete. Should you discover any inconsistencies, please contact **academic .cengage.com/support/** and a correction will be made for the next printing.

Section numbers are printed in blue. They correspond to the tabs on the outside top of each page of the handbook. Black numbers are page numbers, which you will find at the bottom of each page. Topics of interest to multilingual writers are followed by the designation (ESL).

A

C

D

D

E

F

G

H

J

K

M

N

O

P

Q

R

T

U

V

W

X

Y

Z